Tenth Book of Junior Authors and Illustrators

EDITED BY

CONNIE C. ROCKMAN

The H.W. Wilson Company
New York • Dublin
2008

Biographical Reference Books and Databases
from The H. W. Wilson Company

Junior Authors Electronic Edition
The Junior Book of Authors
More Junior Authors
Third Book of Junior Authors
Fourth Book of Junior Authors and Illustrators
Fifth Book of Junior Authors and Illustrators
Sixth Book of Junior Authors and Illustrators
Seventh Book of Junior Authors and Illustrators
Eighth Book of Junior Authors and Illustrators
Ninth Book of Junior Authors and Illustrators

Wilson Biographies Plus Illustrated

American Reformers

Greek and Latin Authors 800 B.C.–A.D. 1000
European Authors 1000–1900
British Authors Before 1800
British Authors of the Nineteenth Century
American Authors 1600–1900
World Authors 1900–1950
World Authors 1950–1970
World Authors 1970–1975
World Authors 1975–1980
World Authors 1980–1985
World Authors 1985–1990
World Authors 1990–1995
World Authors 1995–2000
World Authors 2000–2005
Spanish American Authors of the Twentieth Century

Old Worlds to New

Great Composers: 1300–1900
Composers Since 1900
Composers Since 1900: First Supplement
Musicians Since 1900
American Songwriters
World Musicians

Nobel Prize Winners
Nobel Prize Winners: Supplements I, II, & III
World Artists 1950–1980
World Artists 1980–1990

Leaders of the Information Age

World Film Directors: Volumes I & II

For Michael

Library of Congress Cataloging-in-Publication Data

Tenth book of junior authors and illustrators / edited by Connie C. Rockman.
      p. cm.
  Includes bibliographical references and index.

  ISBN 978-0-8242-1066-3 (alk. paper)

  1. Children's literature—Bio-bibliography—Dictionaries. 2. Children's literature—Illustrations—Bio-bibliography—Dictionaries. 3. Children— Books and reading—Dictionaries. I. Rockman, Connie.

  PN1009.A1T46 2008
  809'.8928203—dc22
  [B]   2008043312

Printed in the United States of America

Visit H. W. Wilson's Web site: www.hwwilson.com

Contents

List of Authors and Illustrators

(Updated Profiles from earlier volumes are preceded by an asterisk.)

Preface

The year 2009 marks the 75th anniversary of the publication of *The Junior Book of Authors*, the first volume of its kind to celebrate the people who create books for young people. Many changes in writing style, artistic interpretation, publishing techniques, and marketing venues have occurred since that time, but one thing has remained constant. Children and teenagers respond with passionate devotion to the writers and illustrators who fire their imaginations and feed their thirst for knowledge. The present volume includes examples of exciting new authors and artists of recent years as well as updated profiles on those whose careers have grown far beyond their original profiles in this series. A new addition is the geographical index, listing the states and countries where the authors and illustrators profiled in this volume were born, where they have spent significant portions of their lives, and/or where they currently reside.

Since 1934, the ten volumes of the Junior Authors and Illustrators series have provided information about the finest creators of books for children and young adults. They contain short, often autobiographical, sketches of writers and artists written in a conversational style, accompanied by editorial comments about each person's work, awards and prizes received, representative bibliographies, and suggested lists of books and articles for further research. In recent years, volumes have been added to the series with increasing frequency, reflecting the growth in the field and the constant influx of new authors and artists. Updated profiles in this current volume include a few of the 20th century's most popular figures in children's literature, such as Roald Dahl, Astrid Lindgren, and Dr. Seuss, as well as those who continue to astound us with their prolific and creative work—Avi, Leo and Diane Dillon, Patricia Reilly Giff, Rosemary Wells, and more.

Within these pages you will meet authors and illustrators of picture books, novels, poetry, and informational books. These writers and artists come from a variety of ethnic and cultural backgrounds; they may live in the United States or in other countries around the world. But they all have one thing in common. Through their artistry, they share deeply-held beliefs and dreams with young readers. As you read through these profiles, you will meet people who are dedicated to passing on what they have learned about joy and sadness, courage and compassion, humor and hope through the magic of books.

The Junior Authors and Illustrators series provides a unique approach to biographical information. Every attempt is made to obtain a statement in the author's or artist's own words, so that readers can feel they are getting to know each one in a personal, informal way. The editorial piece in every profile points out information about the life and work that was not mentioned in the autobiography. The bibliographies are meant to give a representative sampling of each person's work. They include books that are out of print as well as current titles.

A list of suggested reading accompanies most of the sketches. This volume, used in conjunction with earlier books in the series or with the Junior Authors Electronic Edition, offers an excellent point of entry for young readers who are learning about their favorite writers and illustrators. It also provides insight for adult researchers, teachers, librarians, and parents.

This volume, like the others in the series, is the work of many minds. First, the editor compiles a voting list of names gleaned from award winners, annual lists of Best Books, and core lists developed by booksellers and librarians. The list is sent to experts in the children's literature field, chosen to represent various geographical areas of the country, asking them to vote for the subjects they feel are most prominent today and to add others that should be included. These experts also vote on the profiles from earlier volumes that will be updated. Members of the advisory committee for the *Tenth Book of Junior Authors and Illustrators* were: Ellen Fader, youth services coordinator, Multnomah County Library, Oregon; Ginny Moore Kruse, former director, Cooperative Children's Book Center, University of Wisconsin-Madison; Martha V. Parravano, executive editor, *The Horn Book* magazine, Boston, Massachusetts; Grace Ruth, children's materials selection specialist, San Francisco Public Library, California; and Pat Scales, formerly at the South Carolina Governor's School for the Arts, Greenville, South Carolina. The expertise of this advisory committee and their collective years of dedicated work in the field ensured the best possible selection of subjects for this volume.

After the votes are tallied, the authors and illustrators on the final list are contacted through their most recent publisher and asked to contribute an autobiographical sketch. The paragraphs after each autobiography were written either by the editor or a freelance writer. Contributing editors for this volume in the early stages were Tess Beck, Sara Miller, and various members of the H. W. Wilson Company *Current Biography* staff. Susan Sinnott contributed several profiles, including the updates on Aiken, Dahl, and Seuss. Julie Cummins, a featured author in the *Ninth Book of Junior Authors and Illustrators*, wrote a number of articles, including the updates on Danziger, the Dillons, Giff, Lionni, and O'Dell. Martha Parravano, who also served on the advisory committee, wrote the retrospective articles on Lindgren and Pearce. Catherine Balkin served as my right-hand helper throughout the final months of compiling profiles. She wrote editorial comments for eighty of the entries and contributed updates on Avi, Jeffers, Kerr, Kuskin, and Yolen. The editor wrote updated entries on Aliki, Crossley-Holland, and Wells, in addition to the editorial comments for sixty other profiles. I am deeply grateful for the dedication shown by all these writers as they tracked down information, verified facts, and searched out award information, as well as crafting enlightening articles to accompany each author's or illustrator's words. The completed articles were sent to each of the subjects for a final verification of facts.

No work of this magnitude exists without the support and encouragement of many people behind the scenes. Special thanks to Lynn Messina, former editor in the General Reference department, and to Paul McCaffrey, who took on this project in midstream, for their guidance and direction; to Rich Stein for his technical expertise with photographs and signatures; to Norris Smith, whose line-editing is exacting in the best way; and to Joseph Miller, who inherited this project half-way through, and whose support and understanding helped move it to a satisfying conclusion. To Michelle Bayuk of the Children's Book Council, much appreciation for her help and for the CBC's excellent electronic resource file, Awards and Prizes. Thanks to all the members of my New York–based book discussion group for their continued friendship, support, and stimulation. And to my family—for their patience and their constant encouragement—I am eternally grateful. My grandson Michael's arrival in the midst of this project reminded us all of the innocent joys of childhood and the enormous importance of literature for children.

I can never adequately express my gratitude for the help and support that I received from the marketing and editorial departments of the various publishing houses, too numerous to mention here. They contacted authors, provided bibliographic information and biographical pamphlets, answered dozens of questions, and rounded up book jacket images to illustrate the articles. Those who edit, publish, and market children's books are a community of spirited, dedicated professionals; their friendship and support over the years I have worked on this series have made this work deeply rewarding. Finally, I want to thank all of the authors and illustrators who appear in the *Tenth Book of Junior Authors and Illustrators* and who took time away from their own lives and work to write the wonderful autobiographical statements you can enjoy in this volume. They made this book as vibrant and accurate as it could possibly be. Their work may be summed up by this statement from Lori Marie Carlson's profile: " . . . all writers, I believe, share several goals; one is to empower their readers and another is to transport them, to take them on a journey of self-discovery and discovery of the world."

Connie C. Rockman
Stratford, Connecticut
November 2008

Joan Delano Aiken was born in Rye, Sussex, England, to a family of readers and writers. Just a few years before she was born, her father, the Pulitzer Prize-winning American poet Conrad Aiken, and her mother, the Canadian author Jessie McDonald Aiken, moved from the United States to a remote English village. Even though the Aikens were both from North America, they forgot to register Joan's birth at either the U.S. or Canadian embassy, and so she automatically became a British citizen.

Aiken's father left the family when she was still very young and she spent long hours alone while her older brother and sister were in school. Aiken's mother taught her to read at an early age and allowed her to read at will from works in the family library. When Aiken wasn't reading, she loved to take long walks by herself on the country lanes near their rural village.

In 1929 Aiken's mother married the English novelist and poet Martin Armstrong. After a short while, Aiken's solitude was broken by the arrival of a baby brother. Once he was old enough to follow along on her walks, Aiken made up fanciful stories to entertain him along the way. Many of her best-known characters—among them Dido Twite, the indomitable heroine of the Wolves Chronicles—were invented during these strolls.

Reading aloud was a part of every family gathering. Joan's mother would pile books into baskets to take on Sunday picnics, and the children would carry them to their favorite spots in the surrounding Surrey countryside. Mrs. Aiken mother would begin by reading from novels, the works of Charles Dickens or Sir Walter Scott, for example, or poems by John Masefield (among others) and then pass the books to the children so they could have their turns. Sixty or more years later, Joan could still find the exact places, beneath leafy trees or in open meadows, where her favorite books and characters first came to vivid life.

Courtesy of Random House, Inc.

Joan Aiken

September 4, 1924–
January 4, 2004

When Aiken was seventeen she wrote down many of the fantasy stories she'd first told her younger brother and sent them to the British Broadcasting Corporation (BBC), which featured them on a radio program called "The Children's Hour." However, the United Kingdom, in the midst of World War II, was fighting for its very survival, and a teenager's literary debut did not attract much notice. After completing boarding school, Joan worked briefly at the BBC and later at the London office of the newly formed United Nations (UN).

In 1945 Joan married journalist Ronald Brown and within a few years was the mother of two children, John and Elizabeth. Despite her busy family life, Aiken found time to devote to her writing, and in 1952 she published her first collection of short stories, *All You've Ever Wanted*. She followed this with a second collection entitled *More Than You Bargained For*. She then commenced work on a children's novel, *The Kingdom and the Cave*, which was published in both Great Britain and the United States in 1960.

> *Reading aloud was a part of every family gathering. Joan's mother would pile books into baskets to take on Sunday picnics, and the children would carry them to their favorite spots in the surrounding Surrey countryside.*

Finally an established writer, Aiken settled down to begin the children's novel she'd envisioned since her solitary country walks with her brother. She already knew what its title would be: *The Wolves of Willoughby Chase*. She was forced to set the story aside, however, when her husband was diagnosed with lung cancer. Brown died in 1955, and his young widow returned to full-time employment to support her two children. While writing jingles for the London office of J. Walter Thompson, an American advertising company, Aiken still managed to compose her own stories in the evening and on weekends.

Aiken finally published *The Wolves of Willoughby Chase* in 1962. The story is set during a period of alternative history—in an 1830s that didn't actually exist but could have. In faraway America, which was once invaded by the Romans, Latin is still spoken, and England is no longer strictly an island nation but is joined to France by a tunnel under the English Channel. (A 31-mile-long English Channel Tunnel actually did open in 1994, 32 years later). In this strange British landscape, where the dark woods are thick with wolves, two orphaned cousins, Bonnie and Sylvia, have been left in the care of a tyrannical governess. The cousins manage to escape and travel to London, where they plot to reclaim their ancestral home, Willoughby Chase.

The Wolves of Willoughby Chase became an immediate success in both Great Britain and the United States, where it was cited as a Lewis Carroll Shelf Award title. With this success, Aiken was at last able to give up her advertising job and devote herself to writing the second and third books in what became the Wolves Chronicles. *Black Hearts in Battersea* appeared in 1964 and introduced readers to Dido Twite. *Nightbirds on Nantucket* followed in 1966. Forty years after the publication of *The Wolves of Willoughby Chase*, Aiken was still adding installments to the Wolves Chronicles, publishing *Midwinter Nightingale* in 2003; *The Witch of Clatteringshaws* appeared posthumously, in 2005.

In the course of her long career, Aiken wrote more than 100 fantasy, mystery, horror, and Gothic romance novels and short stories, both for children and for adults. She also published plays, poetry, and even a guidebook for authors called *The Way to Write for Children*. She won several prestigious awards, including the *Guardian* Children's Book Award in 1969 for *The Whispering Mountain* and an Edgar Allan Poe Award for the best juvenile mystery for *Night Fall* in 1972. In 1999 Queen Elizabeth II made Aiken a Member of the Order of the British Empire (MBE) for her contributions to children's literature.

Aiken was often asked how she was able to write so easily for both adults and children. She replied that it helped to have a foot firmly planted in each camp. Her own literary voice, she believed, was neither young nor old but somewhere in the middle—just where it needed to be.

Among her later books were popular tales of a young girl named Arabel Jones, whose life is quite normal until her father brings home an injured raven that he has found on a busy roadway. As the bird recuperates, it begins eating everything in sight, from cakes to clocks, and flying about the house screeching "Nevermore!" Mr. and Mrs. Jones are horrified, but Arabel is completely smitten with her new pet, naming him Mortimer. Appealing to a younger audience, the tales of Arabel and Mortimer—all illustrated by Quentin Blake—are decidedly sillier and more lighthearted than Aiken's famous fantasy and mystery stories. The BBC ultimately adapted them into a popular children's television series.

In 1976 Aiken married Julius Goldstein, an American painter, and began to divide her time between England and New York City. Upon Goldstein's death in 2002, she retired to her beloved English countryside, where she painted, gardened, and wrote stories, typing them on an old, noisy typewriter. The windows in her study looked out on the same landscape that had inspired her imagination since she was a little girl. Aiken died in January 2004 in Petworth, West Sussex, at the age of 79. She is survived by her children, John S. Brown and Elizabeth D. Charlaff, and two grandchildren.

> *Finally an established writer, Aiken settled down to begin the children's novel she'd envisioned since her solitary country walks with her brother.*

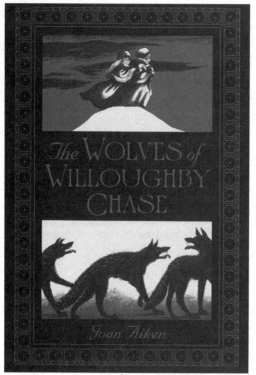

Courtesy of HarperCollins Publishers

SELECTED WORKS FOR YOUNG READERS: *All You've Ever Wanted and Other Stories*, 1953; *More Than You Bargained For*, 1957; *The Kingdom and the Cave*, 1960 [first U.S. edition, 1974]; *The Wolves of Willoughby Chase*, 1962; *Black Hearts in Battersea*, 1964; *Nightbirds on Nantucket*, 1966; *A Necklace of Raindrops: and Other Stories*, illus. by Jan Pienkowski, 1968 [new edition with illus. by Kevin Hawkes, 2001]; *The Whispering Mountain*, 1969; *The Cuckoo Tree*, 1971; *Night Fall*, 1971; *The Green Flash: And Other Tales of Horror, Suspense, and Fantasy*, 1971; *Winterthing: A Play for Children*, 1972; *Arabel's Raven*, illus. by Quentin Blake, 1972; *The Mooncusser's Daughter: A Play for Children*, 1973; *Not What You Expected: A Collection of Short Stories*, 1974; *Midnight Is a Place*, 1974; *The Skin Spinners: Poems*, illus. by Ken Rinciari, 1976; *The Far Forests: Tales of Romance, Fantasy, and Suspense*, 1977; *Go Saddle the Sea*, 1977; *The Faithless Lollybird*, illus. by Eros Keith, 1978; *Arabel and Mortimer*, illus. by Quentin Blake, 1981; *The Stolen Lake*, 1981; *Mortimer Says Nothing*, illus. by Quentin Blake, 1985 [first U.S. edition, 1987]; *Up the Chimney Down and Other Stories*, 1985; *The Last Slice of Rainbow and Other Stories*, 1985 [first U.S. edition, illus. by Alix Berenzy, 1988]; *Past Eight O'Clock: Goodnight Stories*, illus. by Jan Pienkowski, 1987; *The Moon's Revenge*, illus. by Alan Lee, 1988; *Give Yourself a Fright: Thirteen Tales of the Supernatural*, 1989; *Return to Harken House*, 1990; *The Shoemaker's Boy*, illus. by Alan Marks, 1991; *A Foot in the Grave*, illus. by Jan Pienkowski, 1991; *Is Underground*, 1993; *Cold Shoulder Road*, 1996; *Dangerous Games*, 1999; *Shadows and Moonshine: Stories by Joan Aiken*, illus. by Pamela Johnson, 2001; *Midwinter Nightingale*, 2003; *The Witch of Clatteringshaws*, 2005.

SELECTED WORKS FOR ADULTS: *The Embroidered Sunset*, 1970; *Died on a Rainy Sunday*, 1972; *Voices in an Empty House*, 1975; *The Weeping Ash*, 1980; *The Girl from Paris*, 1982; *The Way to Write for Children*, 1982; *Mansfield Revisited*, 1985; *Jane Fairfax: Jane Austen's Emma Through Another's Eyes*, 1991; *Deception*, 1987; *The Teeth of the Gale*, 1988; *Blackground*, 1989; *A Fit *of Shivers: Tales for Late at Night*, 1992; *Morningquest*, 1993; *Eliza's Daughter*, 1994; *Emma Watson: The Watsons Completed*, 1996; *The Youngest Miss Ward*, 1998; *Lady Catherine's Necklace*, 2000.

SUGGESTED READING: Clere, S. V., *Dictionary of Literary Biography: British Children's Writers since 1960*, vol. 161, 1996; Drew, Bernard A., *The 100 Most Popular Young Adult Authors*, 1997; Egoff, Sheila A., *Thursday's Child: Trends and Patterns in Contemporary Children's Literature*, 1981; Silvey, Anita, ed., *Children's Books and Their Creators*, 1995; *Something about the Author*, vol. 152, 2005; *Something About the Author: Autobiography Series*, vol. 1, 1986. Periodicals—David Rees, "The Virtues of Improbability: Joan Aiken," *Children's Literature in Education 19*, Spring 1988; *New York Times*, Jan. 9 2004 (obituary). Online—Interview by Gavin Grant for Book Sense, Oct. 16, 2001 at www.booksense.com/people/archive/aikenjoan.jsp

An earlier profile of Joan Aiken appeared in *Third Book of Junior Authors*, 1972.

"I was almost born in Philadelphia where I grew up, but I appeared unexpectedly on my family's seashore vacation in Wildwood Crest, New Jersey. I guess I couldn't wait.

"My parents, who were born in Greece, raised their four children in all the Greek traditions. We were surrounded by our musical extended family—a self-contained world of warmth, love, food, and Sunday gatherings—where everyone, young and old, played an instrument, sang, danced, and displayed their talent.

"I started to draw when I first held a pencil. Drawing was so natural, it was like my twin. In Kindergarten, where I learned to speak English (later described in *Marianthe's Story*) I painted two family portraits: my own, with three girls and a boy named Peter, and Peter Rabbit's. My teacher told my parents I would be an artist someday. Then and there, Miss Hollingshead gave me my star to follow, and I've never forgotten her for it. An

Photo by Mary Bloom

Aliki

September 3, 1929–

artist is all I ever wanted to be. It's a lucky child who finds her path in Kindergarten.

"In third grade we moved to Yeadon, a small suburb of Philadelphia. Our school was an example of perfection—for me at least. Besides the core subjects, which I loved—science, history, geography, poetry, reading, handwriting—there was an abundance of art and music, and two brilliant teachers who taught them. There were after-school art clubs and before-school rehearsals for choir, chorus, band, and orchestra. All through school, I was encouraged by my teachers and my family alike. I was called 'the artist' and given all the art jobs—murals, posters, decorations—which gave me a feeling of worth.

"Education was my parents' priority. They taught us by example: work hard, do your best, give back. Their silent motto was Keep Them Busy—with art classes, piano lessons, Greek school, and helping in my father's grocery store, which gave us our respect for food and my love of cooking it.

"After high school, I spent four blissful years at the Philadelphia College of Art—now the University of the Arts—learning to draw, paint, and especially to SEE. At lunchtime, the auditorium doubled as a darkened 'music room' where we'd listen to classical records. Hearing one of them now brings it all back.

"I started to draw when I first held a pencil. Drawing was so natural it was like my twin."

"After graduation and my only job—a year creating displays at J. C. Penney's design department in New York—I gravitated to all phases of advertising. That is what I was doing when I met my husband, Franz Brandenberg. I continued advertising design while we lived in Switzerland, but one day I saw a delightful children's book, *How St. Francis Tamed the Wolf*, illustrated by Gerald Rose. I thought, I can do that, and as we were living in William Tell country I researched, wrote and illustrated *The Story of William Tell*, first published by Faber and Faber in London. As far as I was concerned, that was that.

"But, a year later, the published book was in my portfolio when we moved to book-booming New York. I was soon inundated with work—not only advertising, but books to illustrate, including a script for a new series of children's books, called the Let's Read and Find Out series. While working on it, I was hit by an idea of my own: *My Five Senses*. I wrote it, made the dummy, and a week later the book was accepted by the formidable editor Elizabeth Riley. That book changed my life and my direction. This is where I wanted to be: alone in my studio, free of art directors, drawing pictures for books, in control of my fate.

"I never thought I would be a writer, but my interests became ideas, and I had to try. I leaned on my love of words and my long-held habit, started in third grade, of writing down my feelings. Hurt, joy and anger were expressed in poems, diaries and letters. Writing clarified my thoughts. But this was different. Writing a book can be torture. Writing is rewriting, finding the words to express emotion or information clearly. Once I have the thread, words flow, but mostly it is carving out one paragraph at a time until thoughts are defined and all unnecessary words have been edited out, to give the pictures their space. The illustrations themselves are another story, and twice as hard.

"One book followed another—my own and those I illustrated for other authors, including my husband Franz. When our children, Jason and Alexa, were born, they were an inspiration to us both. I wrote stories they sparked (*At Mary Bloom's*; *Keep Your Mouth Closed, Dear*), 'feeling books' (*The Two of Them*; *Feelings*) and 'research books' (biographies of George Washington Carver, William Penn, Benjamin Franklin, and science books about dinosaurs, fossils, woolly mammoths, growing corn, etc.). I call doing them 'hard fun.'

"We spent summers traveling to our roots (Greece and Switzerland), and throughout Europe. In the British Museum one day I saw a mummified cat that sparked one of my many 'three year' books (*Mummies Made in Egypt*). More would follow (*William Shakespeare and the Globe*; *Ah, Music!*). In the late 1970s we moved to London, but most everyone I love lives far away, including my precious grandchildren—Willa, Lucas and Kosmas—so traveling is a fixture in my life.

"And what of the importance and value of books in all our lives? To that end, I have spent many gratifying years visiting schools throughout the U.S., Africa, Europe, India and China. It isn't easy for a recluse who spends 18 hours a day working on a book (presently the 57th of my own) but children need to meet an author for the books they read to come alive. I am always touched and amazed when I see the bright eyes of those who have read my books. I recognize them instantly. They feel they know me. I tell them that's because they know my soul."

"I never thought I would be a writer, but my interests became ideas, and I had to try. I leaned on my love of words and my long-held habit, started in third grade, of writing down my feelings."

CB   CB   CB

Aliki Brandenberg's prolific and successful career in children's books has created a significant body of work in both fictional picture book stories and a variety of informational books for young readers. Using only her first name on her books, Aliki has developed a distinctive style of art, one that is bright, colorful, and child-centered. In her picture book stories, the illustrations carry the story and provide plenty of background detail. Her informational books range from paleontology to mythology, from biography to agriculture. She exudes an enthusiasm in both her writing and her pictures for every subject or story that she tackles.

After graduating from art school in 1951 and spending a year in New York in the display department of the J. C. Penney Company, Aliki returned to Philadelphia to work as a freelance advertising and display artist. In 1956 she journeyed to Greece to visit her family's roots; traveling in Europe that year she met her future husband, Franz Brandenberg, a native of Switzerland. As Franz described the meeting in his autobiographical sketch in the *Fifth Book of Junior Authors and Illustrators*, he was working in a bookstore in Florence, Italy, when an American girl named Aliki Liacouras came in looking for a guide to Florence. He offered to guide her around the city himself. They were married in 1957 in Berne, Switzerland. In 1960 the couple settled in New York, where Franz started a literary agency, representing European authors, and Aliki began writing and illustrating children's books. Jason, their son, was born in 1964 and their daughter, Alexa, in 1966. Both soon became inspirations for the stories their parents would create together.

Aliki's informational books are notable for their child-friendly look. Her illustrations—executed in pen and ink, watercolor, and crayon—exhibit a simplicity of line and freshness of style that delight young learners and make each subject accessible and enticing. Her first entry in the Let's-Read-and-Find-Out series, illustrating Paul Showers' *The Listening Walk*, set the tone for her later work and created a standard for nonfiction directed toward preschoolers and the primary grades. Her own *My Five Senses* is a classic concept book for young children. *Corn Is Maize* tells the story of the importance of this grain throughout the ages and was recognized as an award-winning title by the New York Academy of Sciences. Her books on prehistoric life have been used for many years to answer children's perennial questions about dinosaurs and woolly mammoths and how we've come to know about them. *Dinosaur Bones* was cited by the John Burroughs list of Nature Books for Young Readers as an outstanding title when it was published in 1988. *Digging Up Dinosaurs, Dinosaurs Are Different* and *My Visit to the Dinosaurs* have been featured on the *Reading Rainbow* program on educational television. Aliki's aim is always to research a subject thoroughly and to turn complicated facts into simple, easily understood books for young readers.

Aliki has also received critical acclaim for her historical studies on such subjects as medieval feasts, Shakespeare's theater, and life in Ancient Egypt. Her *Mummies Made in Egypt* won the Garden State Award in New Jersey for grades 2–5 as well as the Dutch Children's Book Council Silver Slate Pencil Award. *My Visit to the Aquarium* also won the Garden State Children's Book Award and was named an Outstanding Science Trade Book. One of her most successful nonfiction titles, *William Shakespeare and the Globe*, recounts the history of the Globe Theater in London. The book itself is arranged as a play, with "acts" one through five, rather than chapters, and quotes from the plays on each page spread. Sidebars highlight significant people in the Bard's life, and a section on Sam Wanamaker, the man who dreamed of reopening the Globe Theatre in the 20th century, brings the subject up to date. This remarkable book was named a nonfiction honor book for the *Boston Globe–Horn Book* Award and received an honorable mention for the Bologna Ragazzi Award. It was cited as a *School Library Journal* Best Book, a Notable Social Studies Trade Book, and an ALA Notable Children's Book, as many of her titles have been over the years.

Courtesy of HarperCollins Publishers

Aliki's Greek heritage has been featured in several of her books: *The Gods and Goddesses of Olympus* and picture book retellings of Greek folk tales—*The Eggs*, *Three Gold Pieces*, and *The Twelve Months*. One of her most touching and honored fictional works, *Marianthe's Story*, which received a Jane Addams Book Award and was cited as a Notable Social Studies Trade Book, recalls her own experience as a child learning English for the first time in school, having been raised in a Greek-speaking household. Many of her fictional stories were inspired by her home life and the experiences of her own children, with texts written by both herself and her husband, Franz Brandenberg. In 1984 Aliki created a nonfiction title that discusses in words and pictures the emotions that are felt by all children. Titled *Feelings*, the book won the Prix du Livre pour Enfants in Geneva in 1987.

Aliki's most recent book combines many themes of her work over the years. *The Play's the Thing*, named a *School Library Journal* Best Book, recounts in comic book style panels and dialogue boxes a teacher solving a student behavior problem through the use of theater arts. The importance of the arts in education, teaching manners to unruly children, and telling a story in an everyday setting that children are familiar with—all are causes that have become hallmarks of Aliki's body of work. Her art is included in the Kerlan Collection at the University of Minnesota, the de Grummond Collection at the University of Southern Mississippi, the Mazza Collection at the University of Findlay in Ohio, and the Arne Nixon Center at California State University in Fresno. In 1991 she won both the Pennsylvania School Librarian Association Award and the Drexel University/Free Library of Philadelphia Citation. Today she lives and works in London.

Written and Illustrated by *Aliki*

Courtesy of HarperCollins Publishers

SELECTED WORKS WRITTEN AND ILLUSTRATED: *The Story of William Tell*, 1960; *My Five Senses*, 1962; *My Hands*, 1962 (rev. ed., 1990); *The Story of Johnny Appleseed*, 1963; *The Story of William Penn*, 1964; *A Weed Is a Flower: The Life of George Washington Carver*, 1965; *Keep Your Mouth Closed, Dear*, 1966; *Three Gold Pieces*, 1967; *Hush Little Baby: A Folk Lullaby*, 1968; *The Eggs: A Greek Folk Tale*, 1969; *Diogenes: The Story of the Greek Philosopher*, 1969; *My Visit to the Dinosaurs*, 1969; *June 7!*, 1972; *Fossils Tell of Long Ago*, 1972; *The Long Lost Coelacanth and Other Living Fossils*, 1973; *Green Grass and White Milk*, 1974; *Go Tell Aunt Rhody*, 1974; *Corn Is Maize: The Gift of the Indians*, 1976; *At Mary Bloom's*, 1976; *Wild and Woolly Mammoths*, 1977 (rev. ed. 1998); *The Many Lives of Benjamin Franklin*, 1977; *The Twelve Months: A Greek Folktale*, 1978; *Mummies Made in Egypt*, 1979; *The Two of Them*, 1979; *Digging up Dinosaurs*, 1981; *We Are Best Friends*, 1982; *Use Your Head, Dear*, 1983; *A Medieval Feast*, 1983; *Feelings*, 1984; *Dinosaurs Are Different*, 1985; *How a Book Is Made*, 1986; *Jack and Jake*, 1986; *Welcome Little Baby*, 1987; *Overnight at Mary Bloom's*, 1987; *Dinosaur Bones*, 1988; *The King's Day: Louis XIV of France*, 1989; *Manners*, 1990; *My Feet*, 1990; *Christmas Tree Memories*, 1991; *I'm Growing!*, 1992; *Milk: From Cow to Carton*, 1992; *My Visit to the Aquarium*, 1993; *Communication*, 1993; *The Gods and Goddesses of Olympus*, 1994; *Best Friends Together Again*, 1995; *Tabby: A Story in Pictures*, 1995; *My Visit to the Zoo*, 1997; *Those Summers*, 1996; *Marianthe's Story: Painted Words and Spoken Memories*, 1998; *William Shakespeare & the Globe*, 1999; *All by Myself*, 2000; *One Little Spoonful*, 2000; *Ah! Music*, 2003; *The Play's the Thing*, 2005.

SELECTED WORKS ILLUSTRATED: *Cathy Is Company*, by Joan M. Lexau, 1961; *The Listening Walk*, by Paul Showers, 1961; *What's for Lunch, Charley?*, by Margaret Hodges, 1961; *This Is the House Where Jack Lives*, by Joan M. Heilbroner, 1962; *That's Good, That's Bad*, by Joan M. Lexau, 1963; *Bees and Beelines*, by Judy Hawes, 1964; *One Day It Rained Cats and Dogs*, by Bernice Kohn, 1965; *Five Dolls in a House*, by Helen Clare, 1965; *Mother's Day*, by Mary K. Phelan, 1965; *I Want to Read!*, by Betty Ren Wright, 1965; *Everything Has a Shape and Everything Has a Size*, by Bernice Kohn, 1966; *Oh, Lord, I Wish I Was a Buzzard*, by Polly Greenberg, 1968; *Five Dolls and Their Friends*, by Helen Clare, 1968; *At Home: A Visit in Four Languages*, by Esther R. Hautzig, 1968; *Birds at Night*, by Roma Gans, 1968; *Evolution*, by Joanna Cole, 1987; *Mommy's Briefcase*, by Alice Low, 1995. Written by Franz Brandenberg—*I Once Knew a Man*, 1970; *Fresh Cider and Pie*, 1973; *No School Today!*, 1975; *A Robber! A Robber!*, 1976; *I Wish I Was Sick, Too!*, 1976; *What Can You Make of It?*, 1977; *Nice New Neighbors*, 1977; *A Picnic, Hurrah!*, 1978; *It's Not My Fault*, 1980; *Leo and Emily*, 1981; *Leo and Emily's Big Idea*, 1982; *Aunt Nina and Her Nephews and Nieces*, 1983; *Aunt Nina's Visit*, 1984; *Leo and Emily and the Dragon*, 1984; *The Hit of the Party*, 1985; *Cock-a-Doodle-Doo*, 1986; *What's Wrong with a Van?*, 1987; *Aunt Nina, Good Night!*, 1989.

SUGGESTED READING: *Something About the Author*, vol. 157, 2005; Pendergast, Tom and Sara, *St. James Guide to Children's Writers*, 5th ed., 1999; Silvey, Anita, *Children's Books and Their Creators*, 1995; *Children's Literature Review*, vol. 9, 1985.

An earlier profile of Aliki appeared in *Third Book of Junior Authors* (1972).

Photo by Keith Pattison

David Almond

May 15, 1951–

"I was born in Newcastle in the north of England and I grew up in a Catholic family in an old coal-mining town, Felling-on-Tyne. My dad had been in Burma during World War II. He came home determined that his children would never have to go to war, that they would be educated, that they would help to build a better world. He and my mum married in the late 1940s. Dad became an office manager in an engineering factory. Mum was a shorthand typist until she had the children. There were five of us: three girls, two boys. We were happy and much-loved, but there was pain as well: we lost our sister Barbara when she was just one year old; Mum was always poorly with arthritis; and Dad died much too young at the age of 43.

"The people, events and places of my childhood have given me many of my stories. It was an 'ordinary' town, but like all ordinary places it was suffused with the extraordinary, and it contained everything necessary to the imagination. I loved the landscape: the tangled streets of the little town; its parks and squares; the abandoned coalmines; the distant horizons of moorland and sea. The river at the foot of the town was lined with warehouses and shipyards. At the summit of the town was a wild area we called the Heather Hills. I loved playing soccer in the fields, camping out with my friends, messing about with my grandfather in his allotment. I loved the voices of the people, the rhythms of their voices, their northern dialect, their toughness and tenderness. I was an altar boy, and I still know snatches of the Latin mass by heart. I loved our local library, and dreamed of seeing my books on its shelves one day. I didn't have a literary background, but I always wanted to be a writer. My Uncle Amos had a small printing works. Mum said that she used to take me there as a baby and I used to laugh and point at the printed pages coming off the rollers—so I began to fall in love with print when I was just a few months old. Amos also wrote poetry and stories. None of them was ever published, but the knowledge that I had an uncle who loved to write was an inspiration to me.

"I enjoyed primary school, hated secondary, but I was bright enough and I went on to the University of East Anglia and did a degree in English and American Literature. I kept on writing, writing, experimenting with lots of different forms. I supported myself with work as a hotel porter, a postman, a labourer. I became a teacher, and wrote in the evenings, at weekends, during holidays. My short stories began to be published in obscure little magazines. I gave up teaching and went to live in a commune for a year until my tiny pot of money ran out. I wrote a novel that was rejected by every single UK publisher. I sighed, spat, cursed, and kept on writing. I went back to teaching—part-time, three days a week, which was just perfect. I ran a little literary magazine, *Panurge*. I had two tiny collections of stories published by a tiny press.

"I began another novel, abandoned it, and suddenly a new story, *Skellig*, came out of the blue, as if it had been waiting a long time to be told. It almost seemed to write itself, and I saw with some astonishment—and a good deal of excitement—that it was a children's book. Since then, there have been many more novels, stories, plays, picture books, and more are on the way. My work's been published and produced all around the world and has won a string of major prizes. The product of dedication and hard work, yes, but also of a little ordinary town, an ordinary family, and their ordinary aspirations, pains and joys.

"Now, I live with my family (Sara Jane and our daughter, Freya) in Northumberland. We live just beyond the Roman Wall, which for centuries marked the place where civilization ended and the wastelands began."

த த த

David Almond's novels have been widely praised from his first published book for young readers. *Skellig* received the Whitbread Award and the Carnegie Medal, as well as the Lancashire award and the Stockton award for Children's Book of the Year, in the author's native England. The following year, when the book appeared in the United States, it received an honor book citation for the Michael L. Printz award and was named an ALA Notable Children's Book and Best Book for Young Adults, as well as a *School Library Journal* Best Book and a *Horn Book* Fanfare title. An auspicious beginning that heralded a unique and compelling voice in books for youth, *Skellig* seemed to defy genre categories and led some critics to use the term "magical realism" to describe it. Though the plot is rooted in the reality of a boy's new neighborhood, his distracted parents, and a baby sister who is seriously ill, Almond introduces a mystery, a creature lurking in

"The people, events and places of my childhood have given me many of my stories. It was an 'ordinary' town, but like all ordinary places it was suffused with the extraordinary, and it contained everything necessary to the imagination."

the garage of the new home. Skellig may be a homeless person, an otherworldly presence, an angel—but the interpretation is left up to the reader. Michael and his new friend—the precocious, home-schooled Mina—try to communicate with Skellig and are profoundly affected by their interaction with him.

Almond's second novel, *Kit's Wilderness*, is suffused with details of the coal-mining town where it is set and a brooding history of mining disasters. Kit's family moves to the area to care for his grandfather, and Kit finds himself drawn to John Askew, a boy who introduces the symbolic game of "Death" to the local children. This is another tale that blurs the edges of reality and myth, present-day situations and historic happenings, all the while providing compelling plot development. *Kit's Wilderness* won the Smarties Silver Award and the British Arts Council Award for outstanding literature for children in the U.K. It went on to win the Michael L. Printz Award in the U.S., as well as being named an ALA Notable Children's Book, a Best Book for Young Adults and a *School Library Journal* Best Book.

Each of David Almond's books has found its own appreciative readers on both sides of the Atlantic. *Heaven Eyes* again explores the gray area between reality and dream, myth and history as three orphans embark on a liberating journey by raft—only to become stuck in the oily mud of a place called The Black Middens. Beguiled by a strange child living there, called Heaven Eyes, the runaways must come to terms with what they are searching for in their break for freedom. This title was named an ALA Notable Children's Book, a *Booklist* Editors' Choice, and a *Publishers Weekly* Best Book. *Secret Heart* features another child living on the fringes of society in a town perched on the edge of a wilderness. Joe Maloney's only advocate is his loving mother until the circus comes to town. Joe is attracted to the carnival folk and their wandering ways, while they encourage him to find his own true nature.

The Fire-Eaters takes place during the tense days of the Cuban Missile Crisis in 1962, as 12-year-old Bobby becomes aware that the difficult situations that loom large in his young life—his father's mysterious illness, shifting friendships, a new school, and a cruel teacher—are being played out in a world that could be on the brink of annihilation. The strange character McNulty, veteran of an earlier war and a one-man sideshow (based on a performer Almond remembers from his own childhood) is always on the edge of Bobby's consciousness as he struggles to accept the fragile nature of life itself. *The Fire-Eaters* received the Whitbread Children's Book Award and the Nestlé Smarties Gold

> "I began another novel, abandoned it, and suddenly a new story, Skellig, came out of the blue, as if it had been waiting a long time to be told. It almost seemed to write itself, and I saw with some astonishment—and a good deal of excitement—that it was a children's book."

Prize in the U.K., as well as being shortlisted for the Carnegie Medal. In the U.S. it won the *Boston Globe/Horn Book* Award for fiction and was named an ALA Notable Children's Book and a Best Book for Young Adults. It was also cited as a *Bulletin of the Center for Children's Books* Blue Ribbon title, and was included on the *Horn Book* Fanfare list, as was Almond's next title, *Clay*. With overtones of the Golem legend of ancient times, this novel relates the story of a bully, his victims, and a troubled new boy in town who appears to possess strange powers. Can his sculpted clay figures actually come to life? Once again, Almond writes of an ordinary northern English town in which the extraordinary lurks around the corner and in the shadows of the mind. *Clay* was shortlisted for the Carnegie Medal in the U.K. and named a Best Book for Young Adults in the U.S.

Courtesy of Random House, Inc.

In all of David Almond's novels for older children, his characters learn and grow, struggling to understand the world around them and the spirit within. He does occasionally write in a lighter vein. His picture book, *Kate, the Cat, and the Moon*, has a lyrical text accompanied by Stephen Lambert's dreamlike illustrations to show Kate's joy in her cat-like abilities one magical night. Almond's latest novel tells the story of Lizzie who carefully watches over her father in *My Dad's a Birdman*. There are dark undertones in this tale of a child who acts more like an adult to curb her father's seemingly irresponsible behavior, but the light preposterous humor along with Polly Dunbar's cheerful illustrations make this book reminiscent of the writing of his countryman, Roald Dahl. In 2007 Almond contributed to *Click*, a collection of interlocking short stories written by prominent authors of literature for young people. Each story connects with the others to express the inter-relatedness of all people, and all royalties for this volume will be donated to Amnesty International.

David Almond does much of his writing in a little log cabin behind his house in the Tyne River Valley in the north of England, but he also enjoys traveling and has visited schools and libraries in a variety of countries, including Germany, the U.S., China, and Thailand. Almond's books have been translated into many languages, and although he writes about a very specific area in northeast England, his stories speak directly to the hearts of readers everywhere. He has created stage adaptations of several of his novels and written the libretto for an opera of *Skellig* with music by the American composer Tod Machover. Premiering in November 2008, the opera opened at The Sage Gateshead, a live music venue on the River Tyne. Film versions of several of Almond's books are on the horizon.

SELECTED WORKS (Dates are for British publication, U.S. dates, if different, are in parentheses): *Skellig*, 1998 (1999); *Kit's Wilderness*, 1999 (2000); *Heaven Eyes*, 2000 (2001); *Counting Stars*, 2000 (2002); *Secret Heart*, 2001 (2002); *Wild Girl, Wild Boy: A Play*, 2002; *The Fire-Eaters*, 2003 (2004); *Kate, the Cat, and the Moon*, illus. by Stephen Lambert, 2004 (2005); *Two Plays: Skellig and Wild Girl, Wild Boy*, 2005; *Clay*, 2005 (2006); *My Dad's a Birdman*, illus. by Polly Dunbar, 2007 (2008); *Click*, as contributor, 2007; *The Savage*, illus. by Dave McKean, 2008.

SELECTED WORKS FOR ADULTS: *Sleepless Nights*, 1984; *A Kind of Heaven*, 1997.

SUGGESTED READING: Latham, Don, *David Almond: Memory and Magic* (Scarecrow Studies in Young Adult Literature), 2006; *Something About the Author*, vol. 158, 2005. Periodicals— "Boston Globe–Horn Book Awards Acceptance Speech," *The Horn Book*, Jan-Feb 2005.

WEB SITES: www.randomhouse.com/features/davidalmond; www.davidalmond.com

Laurie Halse Anderson

(Laurie Haltz *Anderson)*
October 23, 1961–

The daughter of a Methodist minister, Laurie Halse Anderson was born Laurie Beth Halse (rhymes with "waltz") and grew up in Potsdam, a town near the Canadian border in northern New York State. Throughout her childhood, she loved to read: when she was in elementary school, she loved historical fiction, but during her high school years, science fiction and fantasy were her favorites. For 13 months, overlapping her senior year in high school, she lived on a pig farm in Denmark as an exchange student.

Anderson obtained an associate's degree from Onondaga County Community College while working part-time on a dairy farm and earned a bachelor's degree in languages and linguistics from Georgetown University, in Washington, D.C., in 1984. In 1983 she married Gregory H. Anderson, and by 1987 they had two daughters, Stephanie and Meredith.

Interested in a career as an author, Anderson worked as a freelance reporter to gain experience and hone her skills. Her first published book, a picture book for young children entitled *Ndito Runs*, came out in 1995 and was named an American Booksellers "Pick of the Lists." Inspired by a National Public Radio (NPR) story about Kenyan Olympic marathon runners who spent their youth jogging several miles back and forth to school, *Ndito Runs* is a lyrical tale about a young Kenyan girl who identifies with the various animals she sees as she's running to and from school.

Anderson's own daughter Meredith and her bout with chicken pox provided the impetus for her next picture book, *Turkey Pox*, a humorous story about a young girl suffering from chicken pox on Thanksgiving. The girl's grandmother steps in to save the day when she dresses the turkey with cherries, making the bird look like it too has chicken pox. While these picture books were well received, Anderson is best known for her novels for young adults.

In *Speak* Anderson tells the story of a silent loner's first year of high school. Told in the strong, pained, cynical voice of Melinda, a freshman who is ostracized by her former friends after a life-changing event, the implications of which are only gradually revealed to the reader, *Speak* is a taut drama with some unsettling moments.

Photo by Joyce Tenneson

A breakthrough novel, *Speak* had a huge impact on the field of young adult literature. It was a Michael L. Printz Honor book in 2000, the first year the award was given. It was also a National Book Award finalist, a Golden Kite fiction award winner, and an Edgar Allen Poe Award finalist. Highly praised by reviewers, the book was a *Booklist* Editors' Choice, a *School Library Journal* Best Book of the Year, a *Horn Book* Fanfare title, and among the Top Ten of ALA's Best Books for Young Adults. A *New York Times* bestseller and a Carolyn W. Field Award recipient, *Speak* also won state awards in Washington, New Jersey, South Carolina, Kentucky, Oklahoma, and Tennessee. Several years after its publication, the story was adapted into a television movie that first aired on the Lifetime and Showtime networks in 2005. Anderson herself played a minor role in the film, portraying a lunch lady in the school cafeteria.

Following *Speak*, Anderson returned to an earlier manuscript about the 1793 yellow fever epidemic in Philadelphia, Pennsylvania, which was then the U.S. capital. Carefully researched, *Fever 1793* presents a richly detailed and vivid account of the period. Named an ALA Best Book for Young Adults, *Fever 1793* was also a Junior Library Guild selection, a New York Public Library Best Book for the Teen Age, and an ALA Popular Paperback for Young Adults. It won both the Illinois Rebecca Caudill Young Readers' Book Award and the Michigan Great Lakes Great Book Award.

In contrast to the darker subject matter found in *Speak* and *Fever 1793*, *Prom* is an upbeat modern-day fairytale about a girl who is always in detention and has no desire to go to the prom. She ends up not only planning her prom, but proving, to herself and others, that she is a more capable person than anyone expects. Full of laughter, warmth, and snappy teenage dialogue, *Prom* is a light, quick read that became a *New York Times* bestseller.

Set in the same high school as *Speak* and with cameo appearances by some of the characters from the earlier novel, *Catalyst* is a character study of two girls in conflict—one a straight-A student bent on getting into the Massachusetts Institute of Technology (M.I.T.), the other a bully—both of whom are battling internal demons. Cited among ALA's Top Ten Best Books for Young Adults, *Catalyst* features a protagonist who, like Anderson herself, is the daughter of a minister.

In *Twisted* Anderson speaks through the voice of a male main character, Tyler Miller, whose high school career and family interactions are skewed and twisted by circumstances often beyond his control. Anderson's ability to keep her finger on the pulse of teen experience and convey the vulnerability that all teens feel is especially evident when Tyler's sense of isolation drives him toward a desperate course of action. *Twisted* was named a 2008 ALA Best Book for Young Adults.

Laurie Halse Anderson is a versatile writer with a wide range of interests. Her wry picture book about one woman's struggle to establish Thanksgiving as a major holiday, *Thank You Sarah: The Woman Who Saved Thanksgiving*, was named an IRA Teachers Choice. The little-known historical facts about Sarah Hale's 38-year letter-writing campaign in the 19th century come to life in Anderson's telling. She has also written the Wild at Heart series, reissued in 2007 as Vet Volunteers. Set in a veterinarian's office,

> *Told in the strong, pained, cynical voice of Melinda, a freshman who is ostracized by her former friends after a life-changing event, the implications of which are only gradually revealed to the reader,* Speak *is a taut drama with some unsettling moments.*

these books feature fictional stories that provide information about a variety of animals and birds. *Fight for Life*, a fast-paced story about a young girl determined to save abused puppies, won the ASPCA Henry Bergh Children's Book Award.

Anderson lives with her second husband, Scot Larrabee, in Mexico, New York, where they enjoy cold winters and warm fireplaces. She keeps up with her readers on her chatty web site, www.writerlady.com.

SELECTED WORKS: *Ndito Runs*, illus. by Anita Van der Merwe, 1995; *Turkey Pox*, illus. by Dorothy Donohue, 1996; "Passport" in *Dirty Laundry: Stories about Family Secrets*, ed. by Lisa Fraustino, 1998; *No Time for Mother's Day*, illus. by Dorothy Donohue, 1999; *Speak*, 1999; *Fever 1793*, 2000; *Saudi Arabia*, 2000; *Shy Child: Helping Children Triumph over Shyness*, with Ward K. Swallow, 2000; "Snake" in *Love and Sex: Ten Stories of Truth*, ed. by Michael Cart, 2001; *Thank You Sarah: The Woman Who Saved Thanksgiving*, illus. by Matt Faulkner, 2002; *The Big Cheese of Third Street*, illus. by David Gordon, 2002; *Catalyst*, 2002; *Prom*, 2005; *Twisted*, 2007; *Chains*, 2008.

SELECTED WORKS IN SERIES: Vet Volunteers series (originally Wild at Heart)—*Fight for Life*, 2000; *Homeless*, 2000; *Trickster*, 2000; *Manatee Blues*, 2000; *Storm Rescue*, 2001; *Teacher's Pet*, 2001; *Say Good-bye*, 2001; *Fear of Falling*, 2001; *Trapped*, 2001; *Masks*, 2002; *Time to Fly*, 2002; *End of the Race*, 2003.

Courtesy of Farrar, Straus, and Giroux

SUGGESTED READING: Kaywell, Joan, ed., *Dear Author: Letters of Hope: Top Young Adult Authors Respond to Kids' Toughest Issues*, 2007; *Something About the Author*, vol. 132, 2002. Periodicals—Jackett, Mark, "Something to Speak About: Addressing Sensitive Issues through Literature," *English Journal*, March 2007; Blasingame, James, "Interview with Laurie Halse Anderson, *Journal of Adolescent and Adult Literacy*, Sept. 2005; Anderson, Laurie H., "The Writing of *Fever 1793*," *School Library Journal*, May 2001; Hill, Christine M., "Laurie Halse Anderson Speaks: An Interview," *Voice of Youth Advocates*, December 2000.

Courtesy of Random House, Inc.

**Amelia
Atwater-Rhodes**

April 16, 1984–

Amelia Atwater-Rhodes started her first science fiction "novel" in first grade, handwriting it in a pink diary. In second grade, she wrote another "novel" with her best friend, a story they called "The Hope to Get Out." In fifth grade, she wrote her first complete novel, called "Red Moon," in which she introduced the world of Nyeusigrube; this would become the springboard for her future published works. She had already begun dreaming about getting published one day when she wrote *In the Forests of the Night* to entertain herself over the course of a dull thirteenth summer. Then, on her fourteenth birthday, as she was opening presents, she learned that her manuscript had been accepted by a publisher.

Atwater-Rhodes was a student in the Concord-Carlisle school district in Concord, Massachusetts, from kindergarten until her high school graduation in 2001, and it was a teacher in this district who helped make her dream of publication come true. He was a high school teacher who also worked as a literary agent and he offered to read her work and then to represent it.

About an ancient feud between two vampires, *In the Forests of the Night* grew out of a seventh grade English assignment. Everyone had to memorize and recite a poem in class and, while listening to her best friend, Jessica, recite "The Tiger," Atwater-Rhodes had the image in her mind of a tiger pacing in a cage. The sophisticated structure of the book began to develop from that image. This atmospheric tale was followed by a fast-moving sequel, *Demon in My View*, a book whose working title started out as "Bitter Life," borrowed from a poem written by her friend Jessica. The story features a young writer named Jessica who discovers her characters are actually real and that vampire hunters have learned of their location because of the book's publication. *Demon* was cited as New York Public Library Book for the Teen Age

Inspired by Sarah MacLachlan's *Surfacing* CD, particularly the song "Adia," *Shattered Mirror*, the third book in the series, is about a vampire-hunting witch who is forced to consider whether good and evil are really as absolute as she has always believed after she befriends some vampires who have infiltrated her school. *Midnight Predator* is the conclusion of the series, in which a young mercenary hired to hunt a very cruel vampire is forced to come to terms with her own tragic past and decide what she wants to do with her life. All four of these titles were cited by the American Library Association as Quick Picks for Young Adult Readers.

Atwater-Rhodes's second series is collectively called Kiesha'ra and features two warring, shape-shifting cultures. In the first title, *Hawksong*, the heir to the avian throne decides to wed the leader of the serpiente race in an effort to bring about peace between their peoples. *Hawksong* was named a *School Library Journal* Best Book of the Year, a *Voice of Youth Advocates* Best Science Fiction, Fantasy, and Horror Selection, and nominated for several state awards. Subsequent titles in the series build on the fragile alliance between the shape-shifting snakes and birds, and in the fifth and final title, *Wyvernhail*, a half-breed who is not quite accepted by either race must find a way to protect and save her world and the children in it.

Atwater-Rhodes has made several television appearances on programs such as the *Rosie O'Donnell Show* and *CBS This Morning* and was named one of the 20 Teens Who Will Change the World by *Teen People* magazine as well as a Teen-of-the-Month by *Parenting* magazine.

Courtesy of Delacorte Books for Young Readers

The author has two sisters and a male cousin who is as close to her as a brother. She graduated from the University of Massachusetts in 2008 with an English/psychology major, and is currently working on a master's degree in teaching, hoping to become an English teacher or a Special Ed teacher. She lives with her family, two Labrador retrievers, two Siamese cats, a Berber skink, a cockatiel, and several marine and fresh-water fish, and tends to write with her bird on her shoulder. She has a number of hobbies, including playing the piano, debating, and cooking. With a number of story ideas saved on her computer, she will no doubt continue to write novels as well.

SELECTED WORKS: *In the Forests of the Night*, 1999; *Demon in My View*, 2000; *Shattered Mirror*, 2001; *Midnight Predator*, 2002; *Hawksong* (Kiesha'ra #1), 2003; *Snakecharm* (Kiesha'ra #2), 2004; *Falcondance* (Kiesha'ra #3), 2005; *Wolfcry* (Kiesha'ra #4), 2006; *Wyvernhail* (Kiesha'ra #5), 2007; "Empire of Dirt" in *666—The Number of the Beast*, 2007.

SUGGESTED READING: *Something About the Author*, vol. 170, 2007.

WEB SITES: www.nyeusigrube.com; www.randomhouse.com/features/atwaterrhodes/index.htm

Photo by Gary Isaacs

Avi

(AH-vee)
December 23,
1937–

"When I was born, I had company— my twin sister, Emily. She was the robust one, not I. Some thought I wouldn't live. But I did. As my sister learned to talk she gave me the name Avi. No one knows why. There was no logic or reason for it. It was merely a sound. But the name stuck and eventually became a family name.

"My father was a psychiatrist. After my sister and I were born my mother remained at home to take care of us, as well as my brother Henry, two years older. But soon she went back to college, and would continue her occupation as a social worker.

"Two great-grandfathers were writers. A grandmother was a writer. My mother's sister was a writer. My father's brother had been a journalist. Both my parents wanted to be writers. It's hardly a wonder then that there were many books in my home.

"My mother read to us every night and took us to the local library every Friday. No birthday or Christmas passed without the gift of a book. One of my earliest memories is of my father giving me a picture book, *Otto the Giant Dog*. I can recall with great clarity many pictures books I had as a child. From picture books, I progressed to chapter books, my particular favorite being the writer Thornton W. Burgess, whose animal stories were serialized in the *New York Herald Tribune*. These stories, also available in book form, were the first books I purchased with my own money. I soon progressed to boys' series books (The Hardy Boys, Tom Swift) and Westerns.

"I loved kids' radio stories, like *Superman*, *Jack Armstrong-The All-American Boy*, *Sky King*, and my favorite, *The Lone Ranger*. My novel "*Who Was That Masked Man, Anyway?*" was my attempt to show the impact of radio drama on me, and how I used it to tell my first stories. Although immersed in book culture, I was not a good student. I was bored by school, really. A notion of what I was like may be found in my fourth grade classmate Betty Bao Lord's book, *In the Year of the Boar and Jackie Robinson*. In the story, I'm the character Irvie.

"There was something else. I had—and still have—what's come to be known as symptoms of dyslexia, sometimes called disgraphia. It didn't interfere with my voracious reading, but writing was another matter. I had dreadful spelling, handwriting, and punctuation. The point is I often didn't (and still don't) see these mis-writings. At some point my parents discovered my problems. Embarrassed, I suppose, they didn't tell anyone: not my teachers, or even me. I would discover this explanation for my academic frustrations only as an adult.

"As a kid, I was greatly interested in mechanical things—engines, airplanes, trains—and thought about becoming an engineer. Looking back, I think what I was interested in was 'Tom Swift' mechanics, engineering that belongs more in the realm of science fiction than science fact.

"In high school I did so poorly—flunking all courses—that my parents enrolled me in a small private school. This school put enormous emphasis on literature and writing. Half my class wanted to be writers. I was much happier there, but still not a very good student. The English teacher referred to me as the worst student he ever had. A tutor was required. This tutor, a teacher friend of my parents, was the one who really got me engaged in writing. Somehow she convinced me that I was 'an interesting person,' and that if I wrote better, 'people would know it.' Those words made me want to become a writer. I began by writing plays, and would do so—quite unsuccessfully—for a number of years. Only when I began to have my own children did I switch to writing books for kids. The first one was *Things That Sometimes Happen*, which was published in 1970. Having a family, I wasn't prepared to risk all as a writer. Instead, I worked for some 25 years in libraries as a clerk, intern, and librarian, writing whenever I could find the time. It wasn't until 1986 that I dared to devote myself to writing full time.

"That said, since 1970, I've published over sixty books."

"The English teacher referred to me as the worst student he ever had. A tutor was required. This tutor, a teacher friend of my parents, was the one who really got me engaged in writing."

ભ   ભ   ભ

Avi Wortis was born in Manhattan and raised in Brooklyn. He attended Antioch College and the University of Wisconsin at Madison. As a college student, he took playwriting classes and, winning a playwriting contest, had a play published in a magazine in 1960. After receiving his master's degree, he worked at a variety of jobs, including one in the Theater Collection at the New York Public Library, where he developed an interest in becoming a librarian. He obtained his M.L.S. at Columbia University's library school.

From 1962 to 1970, Avi worked as a librarian at the Performing Arts Research Center, although in 1968, he spent some time at the Lambeth Public Library in London in a librarian exchange program. From 1970 to 1986, he was an assistant professor and humanities librarian at Trenton State College in New Jersey. He also taught various children's literature courses at Trenton State, Simmons College, and UCLA extension.

A 1991 NEWBERY HONOR BOOK

Courtesy of Orchard Books, Scholastic, Inc.

Avi has written novels for many different age levels and in a wide variety of genres, including mystery, humor, adventure, historical fiction, coming-of-age stories, and fantasy. Because some of his early works are set in colonial America, including the 1981 Christopher Award winner *Encounter at Easton* and the 1985 Scott O'Dell Award winner, *The Fighting Ground*, his early reputation was as an historical novelist. *The Fighting Ground*, which takes readers into the world of the American Revolution, is about a teenager who, in a single day, goes from wanting to be a soldier to understanding the true horror of war.

In a marked twist on conventional historical novels, *The True Confessions of Charlotte Doyle*, which was named a Newbery Honor Book, a *Boston Globe–Horn Book* Award winner, and a Golden Kite Award winner, has more than a hint of feminism. The story features a heroine who sets out on a long sea voyage in 1832 as a very proper, well-bred young lady. In the course of her journey, Charlotte is transformed: she rebels with the ship's crew against a tyrannical captain, becomes a skilled and rugged sailor, and comes home profoundly alienated from the social conventions of her time. This book was also a Judy Lopez Memorial Award winner.

Not limiting himself to historical fiction, Avi finds it energizing to explore innovative styles and techniques and find new ways to structure his stories. *Nothing but the Truth*—which was a Newbery Honor Book, a *Boston Globe–Horn Book* Award winner, and an ALA Best Book for Young Adults—is a story told via school memos, diary entries, letters, dialogues, newspaper articles, and radio talk-show scripts. These different points of view allow the reader to see objectively how a simple act of defiance by an adolescent becomes the center of a political correctness debate in the media and the school system. It is a book that sheds an allegorical light on the U.S. school system of the 1990s. The idea for the structure of this novel came from a form of theater of the 1930s, called "Living Newspapers," which dramatized various issues through a hodge-podge of document readings.

"*Who Was That Masked Man, Anyway?*" pays homage to Avi's childhood days of listening to stories on the radio. He introduces a character who is an avid fan of radio dramas and tries to make himself as much of a hero in real life as those imaginary heroes he admires on the airwaves. The story, written entirely in dialogue, including the title, reads very much like a radio script in book form, giving today's readers a taste of that era of entertainment. Avi has also written fast-paced mysteries, and three of these were named Edgar Allan Poe Award runners-up by the Mystery Writers of America: *No More Magic, Emily Upham's Revenge*, and *Shadrach's Crossing*. His books have also won numerous state awards.

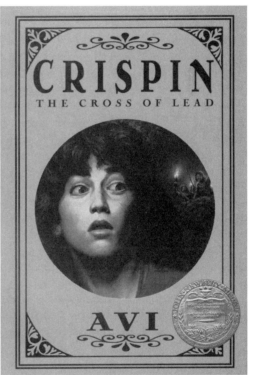

Courtesy of Hyperion Books for Children

Crispin: The Cross of Lead, which won the 2003 Newbery Award, combines mystery, adventure, and historical fiction in a coming-of-age tale. Set in 14th century medieval England on the eve of the Peasants' Revolt, *Crispin* is about an orphaned outcast who must escape his village or be killed. His relationship with a wandering minstrel named Bear, who treats him first like a servant and then like a son, is at the heart of Crispin's story as he journeys toward self-reliance and self-respect. Filled with suspense, the book also offers readers compelling and accurate details about medieval England. Avi has been praised for his command of historical detail and for not glossing over the harshness of medieval life. He continued Crispin's adventures in *Crispin: At the Edge of the World*, an ALA Notable Children's Book for 2008, with a third volume planned to complete the trilogy.

Equally at home with fantasy as with realistic stories, Avi created *Poppy*, which won the *Boston Globe–Horn Book* Award for fiction. In this fast-paced, allegorical animal story, a timid but determined mouse finds the courage to challenge the authority of the tyrannical owl who rules the forest. This story proved so popular that Avi has written several sequels, known collectively as the Poppy Books. Illustrated by Brian Floca, these suspenseful animal tales have captivated readers of all ages.

Keep Your Eye on Amanda was the book that launched Avi's "Breakfast Serials," a business he established to publish serial stories in newspapers across the country and abroad. The venture began with the *Colorado Springs Gazette Tribune* publishing the first chapter of *Keep Your Eye on Amanda* on October 3, 1996 and continuing installments of the story for 21 weeks. Then the *Denver Post* took it up, and soon after, 60 other papers joined in. Eventually, Avi's wife, Linda Wright, took over the business and radically expanded it, so that it now publishes in 365 newspapers.

Avi frequently travels around the country, visiting schools and talking to young readers about his work. He has recently added dramatic readings to his presentations. Avi has two grown children, Shaun and Kevin, and three stepchildren: Katie, Robert, and Jack. He and his wife, make their home in Denver, Colorado.

SELECTED WORKS: *Things That Sometimes Happen*, illus. by Jodi Robbin, 1970 (reissued 2002, illus. by Marjorie Priceman); *Snail Tale: The Adventures of a Rather Small Snail*, illus. by Tom Kindron, 1972; *No More Magic*, 1975; *Captain Grey*, illus. by Charles Mikolaycak, 1977; *Emily Upham's Revenge; or, How Deadwood Dick Saved the Banker's Niece: A Massachusetts Adventure*, illus. by Paul O. Zelinsky, 1978; *Night Journeys*, 1979; *Encounter at Easton*, 1980; *Man from the Sky*, illus. by David Weisner, 1980; *The History of Helpless Harry: To Which Is Added a Variety of Amusing and Entertaining Adventures*, illus. by Paul O. Zelinsky, 1980; *A Place Called Ugly*, 1981; *Who Stole the Wizard of Oz?*, illus. by Derek James, 1981; *Sometimes I Think I Hear My Name*, 1982; *Shadrach's Crossing*, 1983 (reprinted as *Smuggler's Island*, 1994); *S.O.R. Losers*, 1984; *Devil's Race*, 1984; *The Fighting Ground*, 1984; *Bright Shadow*, 1985; *Wolf Rider: A Tale of*

Terror, 1986; *Romeo & Juliet—Together (& Alive) at Last*, 1987; *Something Upstairs: A Tale of Ghosts*, 1988; *The Man Who Was Poe*, 1989; *The True Confessions of Charlotte Doyle*, 1990; *Windcatcher*, 1991; *Nothing but the Truth*, 1991; *Blue Heron*, 1992; *"Who Was That Masked Man, Anyway?"* 1992; *Punch with Judy*, illus. by Emily Lisker, 1993; *City of Light/City of Dark: A Comic Book Novel*, illus. by Brian Floca, 1993; *The Bird, the Frog, and the Light: A Fable*, illus. by Matthew Henry, 1994; *The Barn*, 1994; *Tom, Babette, & Simon: Three Tales of Transformation*, illus. by Alexi Natchev, 1995; *Poppy*, illus. by Brian Floca, 1995; *Beyond the Western Sea, Book One: The Escape from Home*, 1996; *Beyond the Western Sea, Book Two: Lord Kirkle's Money*, 1996; *What Do Fish Have to Do with Anything? And Other Stories*, illus. by Tracy Mitchell, 1997; *Finding Providence: The Story of Roger Williams*, illus. by James Watling, 1997; *Poppy and Rye*, illus. by Brian Floca, 1998; *Perloo the Bold*, illus. by Marcie Reed, 1998; *Abigail Takes the Wheel*, illus. by Don Bolognese, 1999; *Ragweed*, illus. by Brian Floca, 1999; *Midnight Magic*, 1999; *Amanda Joins the Circus*, illus. by David Wisniewski, 1999; *Keep Your Eye on Amanda!*, illus. by David Wisniewski, 1999; *"Oswin's Millenium,"* in *Second Sight: Stories for a New Millenium*, 1999; *Ereth's Birthday*, illus. by Brian Floca, 2000; *The Christmas Rat*, illus. by Leonid Gore, 2000; *Prairie School*, illus. by Bill Farnsworth, 2001; *The Secret School*, 2001; *Don't You Know There's a War On?* 2001; *The Good Dog*, 2001; *Crispin: The Cross of Lead*, 2002; *Silent Movie*, illus. by C.B. Mordan, 2002; *The Mayor of Central Park*, illus. by Brian Floca, 2003; *The End of the Beginning: Being the Adventures of a Small Snail (and an Even Smaller Ant)*, illus. by Tricia Tusa, 2004; *Never Mind! A Twin Novel*, with Rachel Vail, 2004; *Poppy's Return*, illus. by Brian Floca, 2005; *The Book Without Words: A Fable of Medieval Magic*, 2005; *Strange Happenings: Five Tales of Transformation*, 2006; *Crispin: At the Edge of the World*, 2006; *The Traitors' Gate*, 2007; *Iron Thunder: The Battle Between the Monitor and the Merimac* (I Witness series), 2007; *The Seer of Shadows*, 2008; *A Beginning, a Muddle, and an End: The Right Way to Write Writing*, illus. by Tricia Tusa, 2008.

SUGGESTED READING: Speaker-Yuan, Margaret, *Avi*, 2005; Sommers, Michael A., *Avi*; Silvey, Anita, ed., *The Essential Guide to Children's Books & Their Creators*, 2003; *Contemporary Authors*, Gale Database, 2003; *Children's Literature Review*, vol. 68, 2001; *Something About the Author*, vol. 108, 2000; Markham, Lois, *Avi*; Bloom, Susan and Cathy Mercier, *Presenting Avi*, 1997;

The 100 Most Popular Young Adult Authors, 1997; Avi, "Scout's Honor," in *When I Was Your Age*, ed. by Amy Ehrlich, 1996. Periodicals—"Newbery Award Acceptance Speech," *The Horn Book*, July/Aug 2003. DVD/Video—Podell, Tim, *All About the Book: A Kid's Video Guide to Crispin: The Cross of Lead*, Video or DVD, 2005; Podell, Tim, *Good Conversation!: A Talk with Avi*, Video or DVD, 2004.

WEB SITE: www.avi-writer.com

An earlier profile of Avi appeared in *Fifth Book of Junior Authors and Illustrators*, 1983.

Photo by Bill Klein

Blue Balliett

(Bal-E-ett)
May 12, 1955–

Born Elizabeth Balliett, Blue Balliett acquired the nickname "Blue" from her mother, who named her for the color of the sky. Unlike many children with unusual names, she wasn't teased about it in school, and always felt lucky to have such a unique name. Her father was a journalist and lover of jazz who wrote for the *New Yorker*, and Balliett herself wanted to be a writer from the time she was eight years old. As a child she loved books written by E. L. Konigsburg, E. B. White, and Roald Dahl. Growing up in New York City, she would sometimes wander through the Metropolitan Museum of Art or the Frick Museum on her way home from school when she was a teenager. She explains that this was a way to spend some private time with friends, as city apartments were small. It was in both of those museums that she first encountered the compelling art of Johannes Vermeer.

Balliett majored in art history at Brown University in Providence, Rhode Island. When she graduated from Brown, she moved to Nantucket, Massachusetts, where she held a variety of jobs—grill cook, waitress, researcher of old houses, art gallery curator—while she wrote. It was on Nantucket that she met and married her husband and started a family. When their children began reaching school age, the family moved to Chicago. From 1991 to 2002 Balliett taught at the University of Chicago Laboratory School. Starting out as a writing resource teacher, she worked with grades three through six, and eventually became a classroom teacher. During these years she began writing for children, and the Hyde Park neighborhood of the school became the setting for her novels for young readers.

Blue Balliett won the 2005 Edgar Allan Poe Best Juvenile Novel Award for her first children's book, *Chasing Vermeer*, a mystery featuring two sixth-graders who solve the puzzle of a stolen Vermeer painting and its connection to their teacher, Ms. Hussey, and their neighbor, Ms. Sharpe. Balliett, who was inspired as much by her students as she was by her love of fine art and riddles, spent five years writing the novel. Full of codes, math patterns, word play, and the well-developed characters of Calder and Petra, this fast-paced book won the *Chicago Tribune* Young Adult Fiction Prize and the first-ever Midwest Booksellers' Children's Literature Choice Award. It was also a *New York Times* Notable Book, a *Booklist* Editors' Choice, a Parents' Choice Foundation Honor Book, and a *Child* magazine Honor Book, and was chosen for Al Roker's children's book club on NBC's *Today Show*. Warner Brothers Studios is planning a film adaptation to be produced by Brad Pitt.

Chasing Vermeer was heralded by many reviewers as a book that makes children think and interact with the unfolding plot, hearkening back to such classic novels of the 1960s as E. L. Konigburg's *From the Mixed-Up Files of Mrs. Basil E. Frankweiler* and Ellen Raskin's *The Westing Game*. Illustrator Brett Helquist provides additional puzzles in his illustrations, including a hidden secret message for readers to decode. As an interesting sidelight Balliett tells how she wrote the end of *Chasing Vermeer* on a piece of cardboard from a pair of boxer shorts she had purchased for her son. It was written one winter night when she suddenly had the idea for how the story should end, but she couldn't find paper in the darkened bedroom. Not wanting to waken her husband by turning on a light, she pulled the cardboard from the trash and jotted down the ending. Balliett still has the cardboard and shows it to students when she visits their classrooms.

The same young sleuths from *Chasing Vermeer* reappear in Balliett's second novel, *The Wright 3*, with the addition of Tommy, Calder's friend who has just moved back to Chicago. Initially there is some tension in the three-way friendship, but the young detectives soon find themselves working together to solve the mystery of unexplained accidents and ghostly happenings in Frank Lloyd Wright's 1910 Robie House, which is slated for demolition. Although she didn't plan on writing a sequel to *Chasing Vermeer*, Calder and Petra's voices were still in the author's head, so she gave them a new adventure about a Chicago landmark structure that intrigued her. Her book, in

> *Although she didn't plan on writing a sequel to* Chasing Vermeer, *Calder and Petra's voices were still in the author's head, so she gave them a new adventure about a Chicago landmark structure that intrigued her.*

fact, has helped in the preservation of the Robie House as an architectural treasure. *The Wright 3* spent many weeks on the *New York Times* bestseller list, was a *USA Today* bestseller, a *Child Magazine* Best Children's Book Award winner, and the first children's book to win the Chicago Public Library Foundation's 21st Century Award. Brett Helquist added further mystery to this book as well by including hidden images in his eerie illustrations.

Balliett's third children's book, *The Calder Game*, takes the young protagonists far away from their Chicago neighborhood.

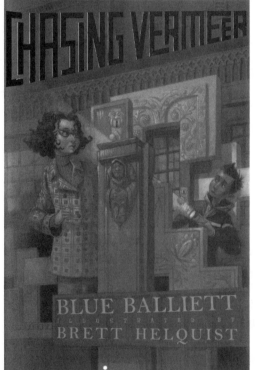

Courtesy of Scholastic, Inc.

Inspired by a book tour Balliett and her husband made in England, Ireland, and Scotland, this novel opens with Calder traveling to England with his father, where he is drawn to an oddly familiar piece of sculpture in the town square in the tiny village of Woodstock. When both the boy and the sculpture disappear, Calder's Chicago friends come to look for him and to help solve the mystery.

Balliett is also the author of *Nantucket Ghosts: 44 True Accounts*, a collection of short stories for adults, all of which were inspired by the time she lived on Nantucket Island and include many tales about the local ghosts, some friendly, some antagonistic.

Blue Balliett has done much of her children's book writing in her laundry room, first on a spare bed and then later at a table, accompanied by the huge and bossy family cat, Pummy. This much-loved pet died at age 19 just as the author was finishing *The Calder Game*, but he is immortalized as a character in the book. Balliett has three grown children and lives in Chicago, in the same world in which her children's books are set, along with her husband, Bill Klein. So far, her work has been translated into 34 languages.

SELECTED WORKS FOR YOUNG READERS: *Chasing Vermeer*, illus. by Brett Helquist, 2004; *The Wright 3*, illus., by Brett Helquist, 2006; *The Calder Game*, illus. by Brett Helquist, 2008.

SELECTED WORKS FOR ADULTS: *The Ghosts of Nantucket: 23 True Accounts*, illus. by George Murphy, 1984; *Nantucket Hauntings*,

1990; *Nantucket Ghosts: 44 True Hauntings*, illus. with photos by Lucy Bixby, 2006.

SUGGESTED READING: *Something About the Author*, vol. 156, 2005. Online—*Contemporary Authors Online*, June 15, 2005. Periodicals—Springen, Karen, "The Kid 'Code,'" *Newsweek*, May 17, 2004; "Going Mobile with Blue Balliett," *Newsweek*, April 11, 2008; Collison, Cathy, "Another Blue Has Clues for You, Too," *Detroit Free Press*, July 11, 2006; "Doing What's Wright," *Washington Post*, April 11, 2006.

WEB SITE: www.scholastic.com/blueballiett/

"Looking back, it's not surprising that I became a children's author or that I write books about American history. I grew up the daughter of a college history professor in a town that was packed with history—Lexington, Virginia. I loved writing and reading as much when I was a kid as I do today. Even so, during my childhood I considered many careers in addition to that of an author—everything from school teacher to flight attendant to librarian to veterinarian to politician to playwright. It took years of adulthood and several career choices for me to find my way back to that earliest childhood ambition of becoming a children's author.

Photo by Ann Bausum

Ann Bausum

November 12, 1957–

"Lexington's history revolves around the Civil War and its two colleges with rich ties to the past: Virginia Military Institute and Washington and Lee University. During my childhood, history surrounded all my ordinary experiences: walks to and from school, games with friends, and independent prowls. I roller-skated past the chapel where Robert E. Lee lay buried. My friends and I collected buckeyes on the campus where George C. Marshall had trained for his military career. I visited the museum that displayed the stuffed remains of Stonewall Jackson's horse. (Truly!) Every breath carried a trace of history. Ties to the past seeped into my pores. Without realizing it, I grew to love history and to expect it around every corner. Later on, I was shocked to learn that not all cities came so packed with historic connections! How lucky for me to have grown up in one that did.

"My schooling included several years of segregated instruction, then, beginning in fourth grade, a switch to integrated classrooms. Those experiences helped inspire me to write about segregation years later in my book *Freedom Riders*. My favorite childhood hobbies included stamp collecting, gardening, and reading—everything from the Little House books, to Nancy Drew, to the fantasies of J.R.R. Tolkien, to lots of biographies. I still enjoy these pastimes today. My family traveled a lot, too, with plenty of stops at historic places. I even met one historic figure during these years, Alice Paul, whom I would write about many years later in *With Courage and Cloth*.

"During high school I spent three years at an all-girls boarding school, the Madeira School. We made regular trips from our secluded campus into nearby Washington, D.C., and my love of U.S. history and government took hold as a result. Books like *Our Country's Presidents* and *Our Country's First Ladies* connect to these early experiences in our nation's capital. When it came time for college, I sought the chance to explore a new part of the country and enrolled at Beloit College in Wisconsin. I loved the winters I found there, plus great new friends, wonderful professors, the chance to study abroad, and lots of writing opportunities.

"After I graduated from Beloit, I moved to New York City and wrote marketing copy for publishing companies. I helped read the slush pile, too—that mountain of submissions from writers trying to break into the publishing business. Seeing all those unpublished manuscripts made me even more wary of trying to write my own books.

"Personal ties to a friend from college led me back to Wisconsin and married life on an old farmstead. I kept writing, but this time I wrote public relations pieces at my alma mater, Beloit College. One of these writing assignments introduced me to Beloit alumnus Roy Chapman Andrews and led to my book about him a decade later, *Dragon Bones and Dinosaur Eggs*.

"When I was about 30 years old, I stopped working altogether to stay home and raise a family. That decision changed my life. Those years as a stay-at-home mom gave me the freedom and confidence to face the challenge of breaking through the slush pile of unpublished manuscripts. I thank my sons, Sam and Jake (who reintroduced me to children's literature), and my husband Dan (who paid the bills while encouraging me to write) for

> *"During my childhood, history surrounded all my ordinary experiences: walks to and from school, games with friends, and independent prowls."*

bringing me back full circle to my earliest career choice: being a children's book author.

"I love to write nonfiction because I love to do research. Each new book leads to new discoveries, fresh adventures, and the rewards of sharing my love of history with young readers."

Cજ Cજ Cજ

Born in Tennessee, but raised in the history-filled town of Lexington, Virginia, Ann Bausum grew up surrounded by America's past. Her father taught history at a local college, and their home was always filled with books and newspapers and the talk was often of current events. Since she attended local schools during the 1960s when racial integration was not just in the news but taking place in her own elementary school, family discussions were crucial to Ann's understanding of the world around her.

Ann's commitment to exploring social and political issues was enhanced by her high school years spent near Washington, D.C., with frequent visits to the historic institutions there. After graduating in 1979 from Beloit College in Wisconsin, then moving briefly to New York City, Ann returned to Wisconsin to marry and raise a family. Her first book, *Dragon Bones and Dinosaur Eggs: A Photobiography of Explorer Roy Chapman Andrews*, grew out of an article she wrote for the Beloit College alumni magazine. Andrews had led scientific expeditions to Mongolia's Gobi Desert during the 1920s where he discovered new species of dinosaurs and the first nests of dinosaur eggs. Telling his story was a labor of love that took the author nearly five years to complete. During that period she drew inspiration from a photo and a quote, both of which she kept near her computer. The quote described some of the near-death adventures Andrews had, including once being nearly eaten by wild dogs.

Dragon Bones and Dinosaur Eggs was an auspicious debut for a new writer. Named a Blue Ribbon title by the Bulletin of the Center for Children's Books, it was included on New York Public Library's Books for the Teen Age list and on CCBC Choices, received a Gold Award from the National Parenting Publications, and was honored as one of ten children's books named "Outstanding books by Wisconsin Authors and Illustrators for 2001." Her second book, *Our Country's Presidents*, was designated a Notable Social Studies Trade Book. It profiles each of the Presidents, providing clear, concise biographical information as well as illuminating anecdotes.

"My family traveled a lot, too, with plenty of stops at historic places. I even met one historic figure during these years, Alice Paul, whom I would write about many years later in With Courage and Cloth."

Courtesy of the National Geographic Society

Choosing another subject dear to her heart, Bausum next returned to the lessons about social justice she had learned during her childhood. In her book *With Courage and Cloth: Winning the Fight for a Woman's Right to Vote*, she recounted the story of Alice Paul, a woman she once met during a family vacation. Alice Paul had been a suffragist who literally went into battle for women's right to vote, often facing angry mobs armed only with the cloth banners she herself had designed. *With Courage and Cloth* was named an ALA Notable Children's Book and a Best Book for Young Adults, as well as a *School Library Journal* Best Book of the Year. It received the Jane Addams Children's Book Award for older readers, sponsored by the Jane Addams Peace Association and the Women's International League for Peace and Freedom. Named to both the children's and teen lists of best books of the year by the New York Public Library, as well as the recommended list for the Orbis Pictus award, *With Courage and Cloth* firmly established Bausum as a major writer of informational books for young readers.

For *Freedom Riders: John Lewis and Jim Zwerg on the Front Lines of the Civil Rights Movement*, Bausum again used personal history as the starting point for her research. Remembering the tense years of school desegregation while she was in elementary school in Virginia, she was attracted to the story of two civil rights activists. She interviewed Jim Zwerg, a Wisconsin native and alumnus of Beloit College, for a magazine article. Recounting how he grew up without knowing any black people at all, the book shows how, as a young man, he was drawn into the fight for integration. In May 1961, Zwerg and John Lewis, a black man, boarded a bus bound for Montgomery, Alabama, to join the movement led by Martin Luther King, Jr. During their rides, they were taunted and beaten, and Zwerg nearly died from his injuries. When the 43rd anniversary of the Freedom Rides occurred, a nonfiction research work-in-progress grant (the Anna Cross Giblin Grant) helped to fund Bausum's two-week, 4,000-mile journey to Washington, D.C. and then along the trail of the Rides in order to tell the story with authenticity. *Freedom Riders* was named the Top of the List: *Booklist* 2006 Editors' Choice for Youth Nonfiction, a Sibert Award Honor Book, an ALA Notable

Children's Book, an ALA Best Book for Young Adults, and a Recommended title for the Orbis Pictus Award.

As a writer drawn to real life stories of social justice and activism, Ann Bausum retells inspirational stories of America's past for today's young readers. In *Muckrakers: How Ida Tarbell, Upton Sinclair, and Lincoln Steffens Helped Expose Scandal, Inspire Reform, and Invent Investigative Journalism*, she tells the story of reporters who used their newspaper columns to campaign for political and social reforms in the early 20th century. This vital book was named an ALA Notable Children's Book, won a Golden Kite award, and received an honor book citation for the Orbis Pictus Award.

Ann Bausum lives in Wisconsin with her husband, Dan, and her teenage sons, Jake and Sam.

SELECTED WORKS: *Dragon Bones and Dinosaur Eggs: A Photobiography of Explorer Roy Chapman Andrews*, 2000; *Our Country's Presidents*, 2001; *With Courage and Cloth: Winning the Fight for a Woman's Right to Vote*, 2004; *Freedom Riders: John Lewis and Jim Zwerg on the Front Lines of the Civil Rights Movement*, 2006; *Our Country's First Ladies*, 2007; *Muckrakers: How Ida Tarbell, Upton Sinclair, and Lincoln Steffens Helped Expose Scandal, Inspire Reform, and Invent Investigative Journalism*, 2007.

SUGGESTED READING: Mattson, Jennifer, "The Booklist Interview," *Booklist*, Jan. 1 & 15, 2007; Bausum, Ann, "From the Pages of a Wisconsin Author: Looking at the past with an eye on the future," September, 2005, Wisconsin Women's Council at www.womenscouncil.wi.gov.

WEB SITE: www.annbausum.com

"I was born in Chico, California, the youngest of six children. At some point, long before I was born, my family had purchased a set of books, ten volumes entitled 'Classics of Children's Literature.' They are almost the only novels I remember in our house. When I was about five years old, perhaps feeling it was time they got their money's worth, my mother started reading those books out loud to me after dinner. My brothers and sisters were all busy with their own activities, their own big-kid lives. It was just my mother and me and Black Beauty and Heidi and Alice and Long John Silver. I loved lying

Margaret Bechard

(BAY-shard)
August 3, 1953–

on the couch next to her, listening. I loved those books.

"By the time I was ready to start school, we had moved across the continent to Pembroke, Ontario. When I was about seven, I went over to my best friend's house one Saturday afternoon. She couldn't play with me that day because they were going to go to the library. 'Go where now?' I asked. It turned out there was a big building, full of books, and they let people just walk right in and take those books home. I made my father take me there that afternoon, and I got my first library card. I would walk to the library—when the snow wasn't too deep—every two weeks and check out another stack of books. In the summer, I took my cat along—he would wait in the garden behind the building. On the way home, we'd stop at Dairy Queen and share an ice cream cone.

Courtesy of Margaret Bechard

"I read all of the Nancy Drew and Hardy Boys books as well as Trixie Belden and Cherry Ames, Student Nurse. My friends and I used the Black Stallion books as the basis for our own elaborate make-believe games; we spent hours making up identities for ourselves and our imaginary horses and spent even more hours arguing over whose horse was the fastest, the smartest, the most beautiful. I read all of the adventure books of Enid Blyton. I longed to be captured by spies, to spend my summer holidays on a mysterious island or in a haunted castle, and to have a talking parrot for a pet.

"And, secretly, I longed to be a writer. But, although I always loved to read, I did not do much writing in school or on my own. When I was twelve, we moved to Toronto, Ontario, and when I was sixteen, we moved back to Chico, California. I finished high school there and eventually studied English literature at Reed College in Portland, Oregon. I read and discussed many wonderful pieces of literature, but I didn't take any writing courses in high school or college. I was never on a school newspaper or the yearbook staff. For a very long time, I was afraid to write. I didn't dare to write. I wanted to be a writer so badly, I was afraid to find out that I couldn't do it.

"It wasn't until I had three sons of my own, and I was reading out loud every day to them, that I started to think about writing children's books. And it took me several more years to finally start writing, to finally risk losing my dream by trying to make it actually come true.

"I love to write contemporary, humorous stories; I think a sense of humor is the greatest gift we can offer our children. As a long-time fan of *Star Trek*, I also love to write science fiction. I love imagining what the future might be like, the problems and possibilities humankind might face. But all of my stories, whether they are set in the 21st century or in the 25th, start with a character, a person I want to get to know better. The characters who call to me tend to be young adolescents, people who are, I think, more open to change and to discovery; people at that terrifying moment in life when dreams seem so real and yet so unobtainable."

CB CB CB

Margaret Bechard is known for her ability to bring likeable, realistic characters to life, placing them in difficult situations that force them to change and grow past their own prejudices. Her books sparkle with humor and a deep sympathy for her characters' dilemmas. Born the youngest of six children to Earl J. Bechard, a businessman, and Catherine Hanson Bechard, a homemaker, Margaret claims she was the quiet one, always behind the couch, reading. But she also loved creating and acting out stories with her friends, especially if they involved horses. And on Sundays, because she wanted time with her father, she developed an avid interest in football games on TV, which continues to this day.

Bechard attended California State University in Chico from 1971 to 1973, then transferred to Reed College in Oregon, where she received her B.A. in English literature in 1976. That same year she married Lee Boekelheide, a software design engineer. They have three sons—Alex, Nicholas, and Peter—and live in Tigard, Oregon.

In terms of her writing, Bechard says she's been helped immensely by the workshop to which she's belonged for over 20 years—"Not just for their keen critical eyes that have made my manuscripts so much better, but especially for their help and support and encouragement. Sharing the tears and the laughter. Or the rejections and the rewards." She has also had a long-term relationship with an editor "who has been willing to help me through my successes and my failures—something that is becoming increasingly rare today." Twenty-five years of membership in the Society of Children's Book Writers & Illustrators (Bechard was a regional advisor for the Oregon chapter from 1990 to 1992) has also enriched her work. Now, she says, she gains a deeper understanding of writing from her

"I love to write contemporary, humorous stories; I think a sense of humor is the greatest gift we can offer our children. As a long-time fan of Star Trek, *I also love to write science fiction."*

HANGING ON TO MAX by MARGARET BECHARD

Courtesy of Roaring Brook Press

experiences as a faculty member in the Vermont College MFA program in Writing for Children and Young Adults. Bechard adds, "Of course I have the one thing every writer needs—a supportive, patient family who have always understood when, after gazing off into space for fifteen or twenty minutes, I have suddenly announced, 'I have to write this down.'"

Bechard's first novel, *My Sister, My Science Report*, is a well-paced, light-hearted story of middle-schooler Tess and her changing relationship with her sister and with the "geek" who is her partner in science class. Her second book, *Tory and Me and the Spirit of True Love*, which combines humor with a poignant look at the protagonist's uncle's grief for his lost wife, was an American Booksellers Association Pick of the Lists and a finalist for the 1993 Oregon Book Awards. *Really No Big Deal*, involving Jonah Truman's parents' divorce and his adjustment to the fact that the new man in his mother's life is his middle school principal, was on the Bank Street College of Education's Best Children's Books of the Year list and chosen as a Junior Library Guild Selection. Shifting to science fiction, *Star Hatchling* explores themes of belonging and being the outsider when an earthling, Hanna, lands on a planet where residents look distinctly non-human. Told from the points of view of Hanna and her new alien acquaintances, *Star Hatchling* was a Bank Street Children's Book of the Year, a Junior Literary Guild Selection, and winner of the Golden Duck Award, given by the DukCon Science Fiction Convention for best middle grade science fiction book of the year. In *If It Doesn't Kill You*, Bechard takes on a more controversial subject as a high school freshman struggles with his feelings after learning that his father is gay; now he wonders about his own desire to be accepted by his fellow football players and about his blossoming friendship with a girl who isn't one of the in-crowd. *Hanging on to Max* portrays 17-year-old Sam trying to care for his illegitimate son, Max. An honest, sensitive story, it was chosen as a *School Library Journal* Best Book of the Year, an ALA Best Book for Young Adults, and an ALA Quick Pick for Reluctant Readers. *Spacer and Rat*, a fast-paced science fiction adventure, was named an ALA Best Book for Young Adults.

SELECTED WORKS: *My Sister, My Science Report*, 1990; *Tory and Me and the Spirit of True Love*, 1992; *Really No Big Deal*, 1994; *Star Hatchling*, 1995; *My Mom Married the Principal*, 1998; *If It Doesn't Kill You*, 1999; *Hanging on to Max*, 2002; *Spacer and Rat*, 2005.

SUGGESTED READING: *Contemporary Authors*, vol. 151, 1996 (updated in *Contemporary Authors Online*, 2005); *Something About the Author*, vol. 85, 1996.

Photo by West Edell

Hilari Bell

February 2, 1958–

"**T**here are writers who didn't read much when they were kids—I'm not one of them. I like movies and TV, but books are my favorite storytelling medium. The first full-length novel I ever read, I was in first grade. Every day or so I'd go to the school library and check out a stack of picture books as long as my arms could hold, with my chin tucked on top to steady them. (Of course, my arms were a lot shorter then.) One day the librarian handed me *The Book of Three* by Lloyd Alexander and said I should try it.

"'I don't know,' I said. 'It's awfully thick.' (Having been a librarian, I know now that this is what every kid in the world says when you hand them their first novel. Alien kids on other planets probably say it.)

"'Just start it,' said the librarian. 'See if you like it.'

"I spent the next two years living in the world Lloyd Alexander created. My body might have been attending school, eating dinner, doing homework, but my mind and heart were helping Taran and Eilonwy fight the Cauldron-Born, rescue gwythaints, and generally save the world by swinging a sword and outwitting the bad guys.

"Now, as a writer, I make my living doing the same thing.

"Some writers write for their readers, and are very aware of them, but I have to confess I really don't. I tell the tales I'd like to read myself, with characters whose struggles I want to share. I'm glad when other people enjoy my writing—I know how much other writers' creations delight me—but my readers don't come first. For me, it's about the story.

"Even if you only do it on paper, there are worse ways to make a living than swinging a sword, outwitting bad guys, and saving the world."

☙ ☙ ☙

Born in Denver, Colorado, Hilari Bell had a childhood ambition to be a stewardess or a spy until eventually settling on the idea of becoming a writer. Her early experience with the imaginative and heroic novels of Lloyd Alexander surely led to her affinity for writing in the fantasy genre. She didn't begin writing with publication in mind, however, until after she finished college. Bell worked as a part-time reference librarian until 2005, when she left that job to become a full-time writer.

Bell, who writes for both adults and youth, clearly lives within her books. She is a pacifist, and this philosophy is at the heart of her books, where there are no clear-cut heroes or obvious villains. She had already written a number of novels before her first book was accepted for publication. *Songs of Power*, the first novel that Bell sold, was actually the fifth that she had written. Set in a research station at the bottom of the ocean and combining technology, magic and a futuristic ecology, this book relates the suspenseful struggle for survival of two very different species.

In her second book for youth, the imaginative *A Matter of Profit*, a warlike species meets a peaceful race whose philosophy is to simply make a "profit." The wisdom of this philosophy is lost on the young warrior who is the book's main character, until one of the antlike T'Chin characters helps him understand the full meaning of the word 'profit.' Designated an ALA Best Book for Young Adults, *A Matter of Profit* was also named a *Booklist* Editors' Choice, and Bell's career was well established.

In *The Goblin Wood*, a young hedgewitch allies herself with goblins to fight the Hierarch's forces who, in trying to stop an invasion, are bent on wiping out all magical creatures. A knight, sent to eliminate the hedgewitch, instead falls in love with her, and together they work to make the world safe for all species. Inspired by the losses experienced on both sides of the Gulf War, Bell created a captivating tale with strong characters. In 2006, *The Goblin Wood* was nominated for the Connecticut Nutmeg Book Award, the South Carolina Book Award, and the Georgia Children's Book Award. *The Goblin Wood* was also cited as an

> "Some writers write for their readers, and are very aware of them, but I have to confess I really don't. I tell the tales I'd like to read myself, with characters whose struggles I want to share."

ALA Best Book for Young Adults and one of the New York Public Library's Books for the Teen Age.

The Farsala series, Bell's first trilogy, began with a volume titled *The Book of Sorahb: Fame*. Repackaged the following year and renamed *Fall of a Kingdom*, this title was a *VOYA* Best Science Fiction, Fantasy and Horror selection, and a *Booklist* Top Fantasy Book. Told from the perspective of three different young people who are drawn into the conflict between the mighty country of Farsala and its invaders, *Fall of a Kingdom* explores class issues on both sides as well as the personal struggles of the three main characters. With themes of honor, danger, and magic, the Farsala series is a sweeping fantasy saga with an intricate political plot. The story continues in *Rise of a Hero* and concludes in *Forging the Sword*, wrapping up the trilogy with riveting and action-packed scenes that nevertheless reveal the many shades of gray inherent in warfare.

Bell creates a plausible alternative society in very few words in *The Wizard Test*, about a 14-year-old boy who wants to be a soldier but has been proved to be a wizard in a city where people don't trust wizards. The boy comes to learn that appearances can be deceiving and enemies are not always as threatening as they seem. In *The Prophecy*, a young prince, scorned as a pathetic bookworm, seeks through the use of his books and the help of magic, to slay the dragon threatening his father's kingdom.

Bell's own favorites among her books are the fast-paced medieval "Knight and Rogue" series, because she enjoys writing about the characters: a young idealistic hero and his sarcastic, cynical sidekick. In the first title, *The Last Knight*, full of tongue-in-cheek humor, the duo rescue a woman who turns out to be a suspected criminal, whom they now must try to apprehend. Told in the alternating voices of the 18-year-old Sir Michael and his reluctant 17-year-old squire, this rollicking tale emphasizes the themes of friendship, courage, and self-discovery. Their adventures continue in *Rogue's Home*. The Shield, Sword, and Crown series, which began in 2007 with *Shield of Stars*, features the offbeat character Weasel, a former pickpocket. Rescued from

Courtesy of HarperCollins Publishers

his life on the streets, Weasel realizes how much he cares for his mentor when Justice Holis is arrested for treason and Weasel may be the only one who can save him from the gallows.

An aficionado of board gaming and fantasy gaming, both tabletop and live action, Hilari Bell also enjoys camping, and she claims camping is the only time she gets to read a lot. She and her mother have a no-frills pop-up trailer and spend time hiking and reading. She lives with her family in her hometown of Denver, Colorado.

SELECTED WORKS FOR YOUNG ADULTS: *Songs of Power*, 2000; *A Matter of Profit*, 2001; *The Goblin Wood*, 2003; *The Book of Sorahb: Flame*, 2003: renamed *Fall of a Kingdom* (Farsala, Book 1), 2004; *The Wizard Test*, 2005; *Rise of a Hero* (Farsala, Book 2), 2005; *Forging the Sword* (Farsala, Book 3), 2006; *The Prophecy*, 2006; *The Last Knight* (A Knight and Rogue novel), 2007; *Shield of Stars* (The Shield, Sword, and Crown #1), 2007; *Rogue's Home* (A Knight and Rogue Novel), 2008.

SELECTED WORKS WRITTEN FOR ADULTS: *Navohar*, 2000.

SUGGESTED READING: *Something About the Author*, vol. 151, 2004. Online—*Contemporary Authors Online* (6/13/07).

WEB SITE: www.sfwa.org/members/bell

Carmen T. Bernier-Grand

November 22, 1947–

"When I was in first grade, my sister Lisette and I walked between a DO NOT ENTER sign and an abandoned mansion in Isabel Street in Ponce, Puerto Rico. I told her that the sign warned people not to enter the house because it belonged to a witch. Lisette, who was older than me, gave me the look. 'A witch? You're a liar!'

"In second grade I wrote a story about my teacher chewing gum in school. The next day my teacher read the story to the class. I freaked out! I was sure she would send me to the office where the principal would call my parents to tell them that I couldn't stay in school because I was a liar. I could already hear Lisette chanting, 'I told you!' I was about to cry when my teacher said, 'I love this story, and I'll publish it in the school's newspaper.'

"When Lisette saw that my teacher had written 'Great imagination!' on my paper, she said, 'That means you're a liar.'

"That was my first published story, but instead of believing I was a writer, I believed I was a liar. I stopped writing.

"In eighth grade I went to a private school where all the courses except for Spanish were taught in English. Almost every student in that school had been learning English since kindergarten. When I read aloud to the class, the word 'lawn' came out as 'loan,' Everybody laughed. The teacher asked if I understood what I was reading. I said no, and everybody laughed again.

"At night Mamita sat by me so I could read to her in English and practice. Her hands were still warm after washing a tall pile of dishes. She never corrected my reading. It wasn't until many years later that I discovered that Mamita didn't know English. But it is to her I owe my published books.

"What do I owe Papito?

"'I want to be a mathematician,' I announced one evening.

"'A mathematician!' Lisette said. 'You can't be a mathematician. Math is for boys!'

"Lisette was partly right. But Papito was right, too. 'As long as it is good for you, you can be whatever you want to be,' he said. When I entered the master's degree program at the University of Puerto Rico in Mayagüez, I was one of only two women. But I became a mathematician. When the University of Puerto Rico granted me a scholarship to study more math, I chose to go to the University of Connecticut. In spite of her teasing, I missed Lisette. I also missed her challenges.

"At first I regretted my decision. For a year, I didn't dare open my mouth to speak English. When I had a question, I asked it in the professor's office—never in class. I made friends only with Spanish speakers. How stupid of me! This was my opportunity to learn to speak English. And make more friends!

Photo by Bob Byrd

Carmen T. Bernier-Grand

"The following fall, I went to a math department party. I sat in a corner, as nervous as a puppy on the Fourth of July. A new math student entered the room and sat by me. He was cute!

"'Do you know Spanish?' I asked.

"He made a zero with his fingers.

"He was Jeremy Grand from Portland, Oregon.

"'Living in Oregon,' I said, 'must be like heaven.'

"He didn't laugh at my accent.

"The following spring we got married, and soon we were living in Portland. I gave birth to my son Guillermo and, thirteen months later, to my daughter Juliana. They kept me busy at home, but I needed a challenge. Why not challenge Lisette?

"I wrote a lie in English, sent it to the Kay Snow Willamette Writers contest, and I won! The contest judge was children's book author Eric Kimmel. I asked how I could start publishing, and he told me to begin by writing stories I heard when I was growing up. What were those stories? They were the stories of Juan Bobo, a Puerto Rican noodle-head that we love. I wrote them in an easy-to-read format, and I became an author!

"Today my sister Lisette is very proud of me—my math and my books. She claims she called me a liar all those years ago because she didn't know the word 'fiction.' That is a lie."

℃ ℃ ℃

> "The contest judge was children's book author Eric Kimmel. I asked how I could start publishing, and he told me to begin by writing stories I heard when I was growing up."

Carmen T. Bernier-Grand was born and grew up in Puerto Rico as Carmen T. Bernier Rodriguez, according to the Spanish custom of using both her father's last name and her mother's maiden name, which was Rodriguez. She likes to joke that when she took her husband's last name, Grand, it was a misnomer since she is less than five feet tall.

Carmen's first book, *Juan Bobo: Four Folktales from Puerto Rico*, is a joyful retelling of some of the humorous stories she heard when she was growing up, stories about the bumbling Juan Bobo, who never seems to get anything right. His foolish misconceptions create the humor that stories about fools evoke in many cultures around the world. *Juan Bobo* received a Blue Ribbon citation from the *Bulletin of the Center for Children's Books* and a commendation from the Américas Award. For her second book, the author chose a more serious topic—a biography of Luis Muñoz Marín, the poet-politician who was largely responsible for Puerto Rico becoming a Commonwealth of the United States. Inspired by an adult book written by her own uncle about Muñoz Marín, she wanted to share this inspiring story with young people. *Poet and Politician of Puerto Rico* was named a Book of the Year by *El Nuevo Día*, the most widely read newspaper in Puerto Rico.

Drawing on memories of her own childhood, Carmen next wrote a middle-grade fiction story, *In the Shade of the Níspero Tree*, which was a finalist for the Oregon Book Award as well as being named a Capitol Choice and a *Smithsonian* Notable Book. With vivid characterization and the richly realized setting of Puerto Rico in the 1960s, the story is a thoughtful depiction of the protagonist's slow awakening to the bigotry in her society and how it affects friendships. Carmen first conceived the book to remember a childhood friend, but she found the characters taking on a life and a story of their own. The island culture is brought vividly to life, but the theme of the story is universal.

Another book for younger children, *Shake It, Morena: Folklore from Puerto Rico*, is a collection of songs, games, and stories from the island, arranged to accompany a little girl through her day from waking up, through school and play, and finally to bedtime. Illustrated by Lulu Delacre, another Puerto Rican native, it is a joyous celebration of a child's interaction with her oral heritage.

Turning from her native country, Carmen expanded her range of interest to research the pioneering farm worker–activist, César Chávez. Her free verse poems in *César: ¡Sí, Se Puede! Yes, We Can!*, highlight aspects of the life and beliefs of Chávez as he struggled to make the world aware of the plight of migrant farm workers. Illustrated in David Diaz's stylized art, this book won Pura Belpré Honor Awards for both author and artist. It was also named an ALA Notable Children's Book, a Notable Social Studies Trade Book, and a Notable Book for a Global Society. A similar volume—*Frida: ¡Viva la Vida! Long Live Life!*—explores in verse the life of Mexican artist Frida Kahlo. Illustrated with reproductions of Kahlo's paintings, this remarkably evocative book introduces young readers to an artistic spirit and a vibrant culture. *Frida* was named a Pura Belpré Honor Award and was cited as an ALA Notable Children's Book.

Courtesy of Orchard Books, Scholastic, Inc.

Carmen T. Bernier-Grand's children are now grown—Guillermo is an engineer and Juliana teaches first grade. Carmen lives today with her husband, Jeremy Grand, in Portland, Oregon. In addition to writing, she visits schools and conferences to tell stories, discuss the creative process, and share her own cultural roots.

SELECTED WORKS: *Juan Bobo: Four Folktales from Puerto Rico*, illus. by Ernesto Ramos Nieves, 1994; *Poet and Politician of Puerto Rico: Don Luis Muñoz Marín*, 1995; *In the Shade of the Níspero Tree*, 1999; *Shake It, Morena: Folklore from Puerto Rico*, illus. by Lulu Delacre, 2002; "Indian Summer," in *Once Upon a Cuento*, ed. by Lyn Miller-Lachman, 2003; "You Are a Señorita," in *Period Pieces: Stories for Girls*, sel. by Erzi Deak and Kristin Embry Litchman, 2003; *César: ¡Sí, Se Puede! Yes, We Can!*, illus. by David Diaz, 2004; *Frida: ¡Viva la Vida! Long Live Life!*, 2007.

SUGGESTED READING: Online—Interview with Cynthia Leitich-Smith, April, 2001, at www.cynthialeitichsmith.com/lit_resources/authors/interviews/CarmenTBernierGrand.html

WEB SITE: www.hevanet.com/grand/

Photo by Nic Bishop

Nic Bishop

Nic Bishop

August 26, 1955–

"When I was a child our family moved a lot. We traveled from England to Bangladesh when I was three, where my father worked as a biology teacher for the British Council. We moved to Sudan when I was nine, and I lived in the highlands of Papua New Guinea during most of my teenage years. In between overseas postings our family lived in England where my father wrote science textbooks and my mother pursued a medical research career.

"It was my New Guinea years that particularly instilled a love of adventure and nature. I was a home-school student and just about the only white teenager in our small town for most of the year. At weekends I'd hike into the mountains to accompany village elders on hunting trips for birds of paradise. They were intent on shooting them with their bows and arrows, while I was hopeful of photographing them with an old camera. When I was sixteen and seventeen, I did some very long trips by foot and dugout canoe over mountain ranges and into unmapped regions. I carried both a camera and a tape recorder to record the customs, music and folklore of the people I visited. Most had never seen a tape recorder before, so were amazed and amused to hear their voices being replayed. I traveled with local guides on these trips and was entirely dependent on the generosity of the people, who were always kind to me and let me stay in their villages, the old women clucking with dismay that I wasn't safe at home with my parents. I'd eventually turn up back home with assorted fleas and sometimes strange diseases that would have my mother worried and doctors shrugging their shoulders.

"After completing a B.Sc. in Plant Science at Nottingham University in England, I traveled overland across Europe and Asia, then through Australia to New Zealand where I settled for sixteen years. I took several different jobs and then pursued a Ph.D. in Plant Science, while investing most of my energy hiking and mountaineering in the Southern Alps. Then at age 31, after completing my Ph.D., I decided I should make a career choice. My passion had long been observing and photographing nature. I had carried a camera on all my adventures since I was nine and had become reasonably proficient at taking good images. So becoming a natural history author and photographer seemed an obvious option. But in other ways it wasn't. I read relatively little as I grew up, and wrote even less.

"At first I took tentative steps freelancing travel and nature stories for magazines, and I was happy they were accepted. Then I started writing and photographing books on New Zealand natural history. These books were for adults. I never considered doing children's books. But it was evident that young readers liked some of my photographs, especially those of animals like frogs, insects and spiders. As a scientist I had long held a fascination for some of the small creatures of our planet, which in biological terms are the most numerous, interesting and important. After publishing several books for adults I had a call from a children's educational publisher. They wanted to develop a series of nonfiction books for emergent readers and asked if I would be interested. They explained how some children do not respond well to fictional books and their interest in reading can languish as a result. I realized, on looking back to my early school years, that I was one of those children who didn't take to fiction. Reading never piqued my interest until much later when I discovered books that were about the real world of science and natural history.

"Switching from adult to children's books was quite easy. As a writer one might have to work with a smaller palette in terms of vocabulary and sentence construction. But as a photographer, very little change is needed. Even young children can interpret sophisticated images of nature. I invest all the same skills and efforts in photographing for children that I do for adults.

"In 1994 I moved to the United States to accompany my wife when she took a position as a research microbiologist at Harvard

"I realized, on looking back to my early school years, that I was one of those children who didn't take to fiction. Reading never piqued my interest until much later when I discovered books that were about the real world of science and natural history."

Medical School. Since then I have worked exclusively on children's books and not looked back. Because they are usually shorter, I have found children's books more fun to produce than adult books. A children's book is never the protracted and sometimes stressful Odyssey that an adult book can become. One can work on several titles at once, and each is an exciting adventure. A book I recently illustrated about tree kangaroos even took me back to New Guinea—for the first time in thirty-two years."

೮೮ ೮೮ ೮೮

Nic Bishop's singular experiences as a child and teenager laid the groundwork for his present career as an award-winning writer and photographer of wildlife and nature. Born in Kimbolton, England, he lived in a variety of exotic locales, where his father took the family. Certainly Bishop's botanist/teacher father and chemist/researcher mother influenced his own work habits by their example of a freelance approach to careers. Both parents helped with his home schooling, and Bishop's mother also taught him techniques of black-and-white photographic printing, which she used in her own research on human chromosomes.

Bishop received his B. Sc. degree in 1976 from the University of Nottingham, in England. While working toward his Ph.D. at Canterbury University, in New Zealand, he met his wife. They were married in 1989, the same year he completed his doctorate. Bishop's wife later received a Ph.D. at the University of Otago, in New Zealand, and the couple subsequently moved to the United States. At present she is a professor of microbiology at a liberal arts college in the Midwest.

Bishop's interest in photography started at the age of nine, when he borrowed his sister's Instamatic camera to take pictures in Sudan. He began his publishing career with magazine articles and photographic volumes on New Zealand for adults. His *Natural History of New Zealand* received the 1993 Wattie Book Award and was named one of the Ten Best Books of 1992 by the magazines *Metro* and *North and South*. His early books for young readers were published exclusively for the school market, but Bishop soon broadened his focus with books for the general public.

The Secrets of Animal Flight, cited as a *School Library Journal* Best Book and a *Bulletin of the Center for Children's Books* Blue Ribbon title, explained the aerodynamics of birds, insects, and butterflies. Using stop-action photography to create clear images of the smallest creatures and to delineate actions such as the

Courtesy of the Houghton Mifflin Company

flight of a bird, Bishop conveyed hard-to-understand concepts in visual terms.

For *Digging for Bird-Dinosaurs*, Bishop followed a group of paleontologists to Madagascar, where they discovered fossils of previously unknown prehistoric creatures. The title was named an ALA Notable Children's Book, a *Smithsonian* Notable Book for Children, and an Outstanding Science Trade Book for Students, recognized for Bishop's text as well as his photographs. His *Backyard Detective*, which earned an Oppenheim Toy Portfolio Gold Award and was named a Notable Children's Book in the Language Arts, introduced younger children to a wealth of creatures they might encounter close to home. Using high-speed photography, Bishop captured a variety of wildlife while his text provided information about each species as well as guidelines for projects, such as creating a butterfly garden.

Bishop's stunning photographs for Joy Cowley's *Red-Eyed Tree Frog* helped earn the title the *Boston Globe–Horn Book* Award for picture books, a prize that is seldom presented to a volume with photographic illustration. Named an ALA Notable Children's Book and Blue Ribbon title by the *Bulletin of the Center for Children's Books*, it was also cited by *Booklist* Magazine as a Top of the List winner for youth nonfiction and was a finalist for the New Zealand *Post* Children's Book Awards. *Chameleon, Chameleon*—a second collaboration between Bishop and Cowley, who lives and writes in New Zealand—was named a *Bulletin* Blue Ribbon book and a Gryphon Award Honor Book, the latter prize celebrating especially books that help children bridge the gap between beginning reader and independent reader.

In another highly successful collaboration, Bishop teamed with writer Sy Montgomery. Their first title for the acclaimed Scientists in the Field series—*The Snake Scientist*—focused on the work of Bob Mason as he studied the lives of red garter snakes in Manitoba, Canada. Bishop's exceptional photographs and Montgomery's lively text helped garner a number of awards for this fascinating study: it was named both a *Bulletin of the Center for Children's Books* Blue Ribbon title and a *Booklist* Editors' Choice, as well as winning an Orbis Pictus Honor Book Award. Their second collaboration—*The Tarantula Scientist*—featured the work of Sam Marshall, a real-life "spider man," both in his lab and in the field in French Guiana. Named a Robert F. Sibert Honor Book, *The Tarantula Scientist* was also designated an ALA Notable Children's Book and one of *School Library Journal*'s Best Books of the Year. For their third entry in the Scientists in the Field series, *Quest for the Tree Kangaroo*, Bishop and Montgomery conducted research in the cloud forest of Papua New Guinea. Among other honors, the work captured the Orbis Pictus Award and was named a Robert F. Sibert Honor Book.

Bishop's third Robert F. Sibert Honor book citation was awarded in 2008 for his solo work, *Nic Bishop Spiders*, which was also named an ALA Notable Children's Book. In all of Nic Bishop's books, his enthusiasm and fascination for each subject is contagious and compelling. Both as a writer and as a skilled photographer, he has had a great impact on creative nonfiction publishing for children and teens.

SELECTED WORKS WRITTEN AND ILLUSTRATED FOR ADULTS: *Untouched Horizons: Photographs from the South Island Wilderness*, 1989; *Natural History of New Zealand*, 1992; *Wildflowers of New Zealand*, with Owen Neville Bishop, 1993; *From the Mountains to the Sea: The Secret Life of New Zealand's Rivers and Wetlands*, 1994; *New Zealand Wild: The Greenest Place on Earth*, 1995.

SELECTED WORKS WRITTEN AND ILLUSTRATED FOR YOUNG READERS: *The Secrets of Animal Flight*, 1997; *Strange Plants*, 1997; *Katydids*, 1998; *This Gecko*, 1999; *Digging for Bird-Dinosaurs: An*

Expedition to Madagascar, 2000; *Backyard Detective: Critters Up Close*, 2002; *Forest Explorer: A Life-Sized Field Guide*, 2004; *The Fantastic Flying Squirrel*, 2005; *Look Out, Butterfly!*, 2005; *Real Monsters*, 2006; *The Rainforest at Night*, 2006; *Nic Bishop Spiders*, 2007; *Nic Bishop Frogs*, 2008.

SELECTED WORKS ILLUSTRATED FOR YOUNG READERS: *The Red-Eyed Tree Frog*, by Joy Cowley, 1999; *The Snake Scientist*, by Sy Montgomery, 1999; *Looking for Life in the Universe: The Search for Extraterrestrial Intelligence*, by Ellen Jackson, 2002; *The Tarantula Scientist*, by Sy Montgomery, 2004; *Chameleon, Chameleon*, by Joy Cowley, 2005; *Quest for the Tree Kangaroo*, by Sy Montgomery, 2006; *The Mysterious Universe: Supernovae, Dark Energy, and Black Holes*, by Ellen Jackson, 2008.

SUGGESTED READING: Bishop, Nic, "Boston Globe–Horn Book Award Acceptance Speech", *The Horn Book*, Jan/Feb 2000; Stevenson, Deborah, "Rising Star," *Bulletin of the Center for Children's Books*, April, 2000.

"My love of books was either instilled in me very early on by my parents, or else carried over from a previous life. While I was still young enough to be sleeping in a crib, I struck a deal with my mother: I'd give up sucking my thumb if she bought me a series of Gene Autry comics I'd seen advertised on the back of a cereal box. From those comics I learned to read crucial words such as 'Bang!' and 'Whee-hee-hee-ugh!' (the sound reputedly made by cowboys' horses).

"My first three years of school were spent in one of the last surviving one-room schoolhouses in the state. Though our library consisted of a single set of bookshelves, it did contain a full set of *Dr. Doolittle* books. I had a competition going with one of my classmates to see who could read the entire series first. I don't recall who won, but it was probably me; I've always been the sort to pursue things relentlessly and single-mindedly. It's a good thing, or I probably would never have realized my dream of becoming a published writer.

"Our family didn't have a telephone or TV. Although I had a few favorite radio shows—*Gunsmoke, Suspense, Johnny Dollar*—my entertainment came mainly from books and comics. But I was no stereotypical bookworm; I loved the outdoors, too, and spent as much time roaming our neighbors' fields and woods as I did reading. Often I combined the two interests by walking the three

Gary Blackwood

October 23, 1945–

miles into town, buying several comics, and reading them as I walked home. My favorites were the Classics Illustrated Comics, even though at 25 cents they made a large dent in my allowance. I especially relished the adventure stories like *The Prince and the Pauper*, *The Prisoner of Zenda*, *Ivanhoe*, and *Under Two Flags*.

"I'm not sure at what point I started creating stories of my own. According to my mother, even before I started writing them down I was making them up and telling them aloud. By the time I was thirteen or so, I was submitting handwritten stories to magazines. (Note to aspiring writers: handwritten manuscripts are a no-no.) At sixteen, I got my first real boost—an encouraging letter from the writer Frederik Pohl, who was editing a science fiction magazine at the time. Three years later, I sold my first story, to a now defunct magazine for young readers, *Twelve/ Fifteen*.

Courtesy of Gary L. Blackwood

"If I'd been smart, I would have done more writing for magazines, but I had grown up thinking that a *real* author wrote novels. I proceeded to write nine of them—some for adults, some for kids—over a period of sixteen years before I finally managed to publish a novel for middle-grade readers, *Wild Timothy*. Since it got good reviews and sold a reasonable number of copies, I didn't mess with success; I went on writing for that age level.

"And I'm glad I did. Young readers are into such a wide range of things, they're not as likely as adults to limit themselves to just one type of book; they're willing to try anything as long as it's good. That gives me the freedom to explore a variety of genres and styles. I also like the fact that I get to travel to schools regularly and meet my readers. They're so interested and enthusiastic that it encourages me to keep writing—and believe me, writers need all the encouragement they can get."

☙ ☙ ☙

Gary L. Blackwood was born in Meadville, Pennsylvania, and raised outside the hamlet of nearby Cochranton. After completing high school, he matriculated at Grove City College, a liberal arts institution in Grove City, Pennsylvania, from which he received his B.A. degree in 1967. After graduating, Blackwood was drafted into the U.S. Army and served from 1968 to 1970; he was discharged with the rank of sergeant. Over the years, he has taught writing and playwriting courses at Missouri Southern State College. After submitting many books to publishers, he had his first success with *Wild Timothy* in 1987, a story of wilderness survival that set him on a course of writing for young readers. Blackwood's childhood love of adventure and science fiction is apparent in *The Dying Sun*, a futuristic story for which he received the Best Young Adult Novel award from the Friends of American Writers. Several more science fiction novels for young readers followed, as well as a biography, *Rough Riding Reformer: Theodore Roosevelt*.

It was the publication of *The Shakespeare Stealer* in 1998, however, that marked Gary Blackwood's emergence as an important voice in young adult literature. Set in Elizabethan London, *The Shakespeare Stealer* follows an orphaned country boy named Widge as he adjusts to life in the city and discovers the world of the theater. Widge is sent by his employer, a mysterious traveling man, to Shakespeare's Globe Theatre to copy down in shorthand a play being produced in order to steal it before it is published. Befriended by the players of the Globe, Widge learns much about himself and his own values as his conscience is awakened. Praised for its characterization and depiction of the historic era, *The Shakespeare Stealer* was named an ALA Notable Children's Book, an ALA Best Book for Young Adults, a *School Library Journal* Best Book, and a Notable Social Studies Trade Book.

"But I was no stereotypical bookworm; I loved the outdoors, too, and spent as much time roaming our neighbors' fields and woods as I did reading."

Since the success of *The Shakespeare Stealer*, Blackwood has written two sequels, *Shakespeare's Scribe* and *Shakespeare's Spy*, also named a Notable Social Studies Trade Book. The series has continued to receive fine reviews and delight readers as it delves further into the complicated world of Shakespeare's era. The author's stage adaptation of *The Shakespeare Stealer* has been produced at the Kennedy Center and the Seattle Children's Theatre, among other venues. He has also received recognition for historical novels set at different stages of American history. *Moonshine*, a coming-of-age story that takes place in the Ozark Mountains during the Great Depression, was designated a Notable Book by *Smithsonian* magazine, and *The Year of the Hangman*, set during the American Revolutionary War, was named a Best Book of the Year by *School Library Journal*.

Blackwood has written vibrant nonfiction as well as novels. His books in The Way People Live series chronicle details of life in a medieval castle and along the Oregon Trail. In the Bad Guys series, he has written about pirates, gangsters, highwaymen, swindlers, and outlaws. His interest in science fiction and the paranormal is evident in volumes written for a series entitled Secrets of the Unexplained, while his delight in mystery, intrigue, and the past has led him to contribute to a series called Unsolved History. He has also written plays, both for child and adult audiences, which have been produced at college and regional theatres.

Courtesy of Dutton Children's Books, Penguin Putnam Inc.

After living many years in Missouri, Blackwood currently resides in Nova Scotia, Canada, with his wife, Jean, to whom he has been married since 1977. They have three children: Gareth, Giles, and Tegan.

SELECTED WORKS: *Wild Timothy*, 1987; *The Dying Sun*, 1989; *Attack of the Mushroom People*, 1990; *Beyond the Door*, 1991; *The Masters*, 1995; *Rough Riding Reformer: Theodore Roosevelt*, 1997; *The Shakespeare Stealer*, 1998; *Moonshine*, 1999; *Life on the Oregon Trail*, 1999; *Life in a Medieval Castle*, 1999; *Alien Astronauts*, 1999; *Extraordinary Events and Oddball Occurrences*, 1999; *Fateful Forebodings*, 1999; *Long-Ago Lives*, 1999; *Paranormal Powers*, 1999; *Spooky Spectres*, 2000; *Shakespeare's Scribe*, 2000; *Gangsters*, 2002; *Highwaymen*, 2002; *Outlaws*, 2002; *Pirates*, 2002; *Swindlers*, 2002; *The Year of the Hangman*, 2002; *Shakespeare's Spy*, 2003; *Alien Creatures*, 2004; *Second Sight*, 2005; *Legends or Lies?*, 2005; *Debatable Deaths*, 2006; *Enigmatic Events*, 2006; *The Just-so Woman*, illus. by Jane Manning, 2006; *The Amazing Round-the-World Auto Race of 1908*, 2008.

SUGGESTED READING: *Something About the Author*, vol. 169, 2006; *Authors and Artists for Young Adults*, vol. 40, 2001.

WEB SITE: www.writers.ns.ca/Writers/gblackwood.html

"I wasn't supposed to be an artist or a writer. Not in my family. I was supposed to be something, anything else. But for some reason the gene pool took a sudden turn and there I was, left-handed with a vengeance.

"I was born in Springfield, New Jersey in 1953. My first memory was of thinking that the world seemed to be an interesting place. I was one of those kids who covered his crib with crayon drawings. One day I also covered an entire hallway with drawings while my mother was taking a nap. I drew everywhere and on everything until my second grade teacher gave me a sketchbook and said, 'Draw in here.' I am now on my 115th sketchbook.

Courtesy of Robert J. Blake

Robert J. Blake

May 6, 1953–

"We had a lot of pets. We had ant farms and fish, turtles and snakes, lizards and birds, gerbils, guinea pigs, some odd little squigglers called Sea Monkeys, a horse, mice, hamsters, two flying squirrels, a tarantula and always a dog.

"My grandfather bought a whole lake in 1929 before he lost his money during the Depression. Somehow over the years our family managed to hold onto the lake. When I was growing up, my aunts and cousins and our pets would stay there all summer without electricity or running water. The men worked all week and came down on the weekends. Every day my cousins and I would swim and play and make up adventures. At night everyone, adults and children alike, told stories by the light of a kerosene lamp. I used to draw, nose close to the paper, as I listened.

"So as I grew up, my world was full of stories. Even if the place or event I was at was dull, I learned to find something interesting in it that made for a story. I believe that the person we are today is the person we were when we were children. I know I am. I still create the same way—I go to a place that seems like it might be interesting. Then I start talking to people and while listening to stories I write and draw in my sketchbook. The story itself evolves. It takes on a life of its own. I cannot say if this approach is good or bad. It takes a lot of time and a lot of listening. But it certainly makes for an interesting life.

"As for the development of my career, I attended the Ringling School of Art, then graduated from the Paier College of Art. I also attended the Art Students League in New York. After art school I worked making art for filmstrips. That's how I learned to paint quickly. I also drew for newspapers. That's how I learned how to work with patterns of dark and light. I created illustrations for phonics sheets and learned about characters. Making pictures for textbooks taught me how to make art for odd shaped-spaces. Painting jackets for young adult book covers taught me about rendering.

"I also made a lot of fine art paintings and continued to study art. I believe the most important part of my education has come from keeping sketchbooks. I draw and write in a sketchbook every day. In 1979 I made my first picture book and immediately knew that picture books were the most creative form of art being made. The marriage of art and words fascinates me. And, of course, I get to travel all over the world, to hear stories, to write stories and meet lots of interesting people."

ೞ ೞ ೞ

"I go to a place that seems like it might be interesting. Then I start talking to people and while listening to stories I write and draw in my sketchbook. The story itself evolves."

Robert J. Blake's illustrations in picture books celebrate the natural world that has been important to him throughout his life. The courage of a sled dog who refuses to leave the race; the resilience of a stray cat who makes a special home in a deserted amusement pavilion; the endurance of a dog that races to deliver life-saving serum to people during an epidemic—these are the subjects of Blake's most enduring work. He celebrates the beauty and harshness of nature as a backdrop for heroic tales of everyday people and the animals that are an integral part of their lives.

Blake won early acclaim for his evocative paintings in *Riptide*, by Frances Ward Weller. Based on a true story, Riptide is a dog that most people felt was a pest on the beach of Cape Cod. He is rambunctious and lively, a nuisance to everyone except his owner; but when a young girl nearly drowns, caught in an actual riptide in the ocean, the dog is the one who saves her. Blake's lively rendering of the dog and the sweeping panoramic views of beach and ocean brought the story vibrantly to life and helped it to win both the Nebraska Golden Sower Award and the New Jersey M. Jerry Weiss Award in the K–3 category.

One of Blake's best-loved characters is Akiak, a sled dog who competes in the punishing Iditarod, the 1,151-mile endurance race from Nome to Anchorage, Alaska. In the course of the race, Akiak is lamed by ice jammed in her paw and taken off her team. The dog breaks free before she can be shipped home and finds her team again. She cannot be re-harnessed with her team, according to the rules, but she runs alongside them and saves them from taking a wrong turn. A story of loyalty, trust, and endurance, *Akiak* was named a *School Library Journal* Best Book and a Notable Social Studies Trade Book. It received the Irma S. and James H. Black Award from Bank Street College and won children's choice awards in Washington, Vermont, Virginia, and Indiana.

In *Togo*, another tale of endurance and loyalty, Blake relates the true story of a dog who carried life-saving serum to Nome, Alaska during a diphtheria epidemic in 1925. Smaller than many sled dogs, Togo had to prove to his master that he had the heart to be part of a team, making him a true hero to his child readers. *Togo* was named an ALA Notable Children's Book and a Notable Social Studies Trade Book. It won the Texas Bluebonnet Award as well as children's choice awards in Washington, Michigan, Nebraska, North Carolina, and New Mexico. In a very different setting, the story of *Yudonsi* takes place in the American

Courtesy of Philomel Books, Penguin Putnam Inc.

Southwest. Yusi, a boy in a native tribe, must learn how to respect the country and landscape of his birth. Rendered in the earth tones of the canyon country, the rugged illustrations beautifully depict the desert landscape and earned Blake the Southwest Book Award.

Blake can also capture the small moments of shared experience between family members, as he does in *The Perfect Spot*, named an Outstanding Science Trade Book. An artist father and his son tramp in the woods looking for the perfect place for the father to paint and the boy to search for insects. Blake's watercolors evoke the play of light and shadow and the deep silence of the wooded terrain. The same woodland setting is captured again in Ann Turner's *Rainflowers*, with double-page panoramic spreads of animals during a thunderstorm. Every child's dream of flying is at the heart of *Fledgling*, Blake's story of a young kestrel taking her first frightening plunge into a dizzying cityscape.

Lauded by readers and critics alike, Robert J. Blake continues to create books with strong visual representations of human and animal characters and richly realized settings. Whether it is the soft colors of a beach scene and a boardwalk amusement center, the majestic reddish brown desert country, or the harsh, cold landscape of ice and snow in the north, his evocative art becomes a vigorous component of each story he tells and illustrates.

After years of living in New Jersey, Blake moved to Long Beach, California. Recently he has spent a year in Australia, working on a book about marsupials. He lives with his wife, Lynn, and has one grown son.

SELECTED WORKS ILLUSTRATED: *The Spider's Dance*, by Joanne Ryder, 1981; *The Care Bears and the New Baby*, by Peggy Kahn, 1983; *The Velveteen Rabbit*, by Margery Williams, 1985; *Bobby the Circus Bear*, by Barbara Mariconda, 1986; *The Baby Unicorn*, by Jean and Claudio Marzollo, 1987; *Riptide*, by Frances Ward Weller, 1990; *Finding Foxes*, by Alison Blyler, 1991; *Rainflowers*, by Ann Turner, 1992; *Maggie and Silky and Joe*, by Amy Ehrlich, 1994; *Mississippi Mud*, by Ann Turner, 1997; *The Angel of Mill Street*, by Frances Ward Weller, 1998; *Santa Paws*, by Ellen Emerson White, 2003.

SELECTED WORKS WRITTEN AND ILLUSTRATED: *All Around the Town*, 1987; *The Perfect Spot*, 1992; *Dog*, 1994; *Spray*, 1996; *Akiak: A Tale from the Iditarod*, 1997; *Yudonsi: A Tale from the Canyons*, 1999; *Fledgling*, 2000; *Togo*, 2002; *Carousel Cat*, 2005; *Swift*, 2007.

SUGGESTED READING: *Something About the Author*, vol. 160, 2005.

WEB SITE: www.robertblake.com

Tonya Bolden

March 1, 1959–

"My autobiographical sketch is still a work in progress, as am I. When I finally nail it, I'm sure the following will be among the scenes.

"*Memory #1:* Loving books as a child, down to the sight and feel of them. There were times when my parents said 'No' to more money for bubblegum, Twin Pops, or rides at Coney Island, but whenever I came home from school with a long list of books I wanted to buy at the book fair they never denied me. Both were readers. In fact, there is a lost picture of a very young me sitting up in my parents' bed with Mommy's glasses askew across my face and a book in my hands, upside down. Books were revered in our home.

"*Memory #2:* Daddy helping me with my homework at the kitchen table in our East Harlem apartment. Mostly I see him helping me with sentences. If I had to use, say, the words 'ball' and 'boy' in a sentence, I thought something like 'The boy has a ball' was good enough. My father did not, prodding me to expand—to do more than the minimum. In time, writing became, like reading, a favorite pastime. When it was too dark or stormy to be outside playing handball, freeze tag, or zooming around on roller skates or when the weather *was* fine but I was on punishment, I was often in the bedroom I shared with my sister writing short stories—if not reading. (Later, as a teen, I wrote scads of poetry.)

"*Memory #3:* Wanting to be a teacher. After my parents, teachers were my favorite grownups.

"*Memory #4:* Being fascinated with languages, the rhythms of different tongues: the bits of Yiddish I heard when visiting my father's workplace; the Italian and Puerto Rican Spanish in the airwaves of my neighborhood; the Southern drawls of kin along with the Southernisms that spiced my parents' speech.

"*Memory #5:* Being entranced by Robert Frost's poem 'Two Tramps in Mud Time.' One of the few books that I have kept from my secondary school days is a collection of Frost poems, a small, now yellowed, fragile paperback that cost $.95 back in the 1970s. I think I've held onto this book because of that one poem, 'Two Tramps,' with the lines: 'My object in living is to unite / My avocation and my vocation/ As my two eyes make one in sight.'

Photo by Hayden R. Celestin

'He enjoys his work' . . . 'Everything is in harmony' . . . 'When you love what you do, you do it better' . . . 'Your hobby should = your work'—These are some of the notes I scribbled in the margins of that poem.

"*Memory #6:* Feeling betwixt and between about career as a young adult, now thinking schoolteacher, now thinking college professor, and even for a time, actor, all the while wondering if wanting to be a writer was an impossible dream.

"*Memory #7:* Connie Green, a friend from college who was an editor at *Black Enterprise* magazine, asking me in the early 1980s if I'd be interested in doing some book reviews for her. She said that she remembered that I wrote well and was disciplined. That opportunity was the springboard to my following my bliss and working toward making my avocation and my vocation unite as my brown eyes make one in sight."

୪   ୪   ୪

The daughter of a garment-center shipping manager and a homemaker, Tonya Bolden grew up in New York City and graduated from the Chapin School in 1976. She received her bachelor of arts degree in Slavic languages and literatures with a concentration in Russian from Princeton University in 1981, graduating magna cum laude. She received the Nicholas Bachko Jr. Scholarship Prize and was University Scholar. She later studied Russian at Columbia University, from which she received a master's degree in the subject. She earned a Harriman Institute's certificate for the advanced study of the Soviet Union and, drawn to a career in teaching, took some courses at Teacher's College.

Bolden taught English at Malcolm–King College from 1988 to 1989 and at the College of New Rochelle, School of New Resources, from 1989 to 1990 and from 1996 to 2000. In addition to teaching, she has worked in the bookkeeping and sales departments of a dress manufacturer (the same company for which her father worked); as an administrative assistant for the writer James Goldman; as an editorial consultant for New York's MTA Arts for Transit office and for Harlem River Press/ Writers & Readers Publishing Inc. (composing study guides for the Carter G. Woodson Foundation's Artists-in-the-Schools program); and as an editor for *HARKline* (1989–1990), the quarterly newsletter of a Harlem homeless shelter, and for the *Quarterly Black Review of Books* (1994–1995). Along the way, Bolden wrote for numerous national magazines and newspapers, including *Black Enterprise*, *Essence*, and the *New York Times Book Review*.

Early in her writing career, Bolden wrote for adult audiences. Her first book, *The Family Heirloom Cookbook*, was published in 1990. Later she created business books such as *Starting a Business from Your Home* and *Mail-Order and Direct Response*. However, her best-known books are those she has written for young readers.

History is Tonya Bolden's passion, and it shows in her books. *Wake Up Our Souls: A Celebration of Black American Artists* presents a history of African American art from the late 18th to the 20th century and features more than thirty influential artists. Chronological entries on each artist flow seamlessly into the next, highlighting how each artist's work served as a building

> *"There were times when my parents said 'No' to more money for bubblegum, Twin Pops, or rides at Coney Island, but whenever I came home from school with a long list of books I wanted to buy at the book fair they never denied me."*

block for those who followed. Published in conjunction with the Smithsonian American Art Museum, this lyrically informative book won a National Parenting Publications Award and was on *VOYA*'s Nonfiction Honor list.

Maritcha: A Nineteenth-Century American Girl, based on the unpublished memoir of a black girl born into freedom in 1848 in Manhattan, was named a Coretta Scott King Honor Book, won the James Madison Book Award, and was cited as an ALA Notable Children's Book and a *School Library Journal* Best Book. Descriptions of Maritcha's struggle to attend a whites-only high school and her experiences during the New York City Draft Riots of 1863 are vividly portrayed in this vibrant story of a real-life heroine.

Poetic writing underscores *The Champ*, Bolden's picture book chronicling the life of Muhammad Ali. With evocative illustrations by R. Gregory Christie, this book was named a *Booklist* Top 10 Youth Sports Book. Bolden doesn't merely describe Ali's boxing achievements, but presents the whole man, including his religious conversion to Islam, his opposition to the Vietnam War, and his struggle to overcome the physical disabilities brought on by his boxing career.

In the insightful *Strong Men Keep Coming: The Book of African-American Men*, a Black Expressions Book Club Selection, Bolden presents over 100 biographies of such individuals as W.E.B. DuBois, Dred Scott, and Jesse Jackson, as well as lesser-known figures like

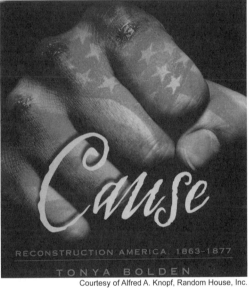

Courtesy of Alfred A. Knopf, Random House, Inc.

Dave Dinwiddie, a pioneer quietly determined to make a good life for himself and his family. Published as an adult title, this book was listed among the New York Public Library's Books for the Teen Age. (Three other books by Bolden have been named Books for the Teen Age—*Mama, I Want to Sing*; *And Not Afraid To Dare: The Stories of Ten African-American Women*; and *Cause: Reconstruction America, 1863–1877*.)

In *Tell All the Children Our Story*, Bolden explores all aspects of African-American history, beginning with the first black child born in the Jamestown colony, through the expansion of slavery across the country, to the civil rights movement and the struggle for equality in the 20th century. Cited as a *School Library Journal*

Best Book, it shows Bolden's ability to research a topic thoroughly and to turn her research into a cohesive and creative volume.

Three of her titles were named ALA Best Books for Young Adults—33 *Things Every Girl Should Know*; *Wake Up Our Souls: A Celebration of Black American Artists*; and *Maritcha: A Nineteenth Century American Girl*. The semi-autobiographical *Just Family* was a Junior Library Guild selection, and *Rites of Passage: Stories About Growing Up by Black Writers from Around the World* was a Mother-Daughter Book Club pick. In 2008 Bolden won the prestigious Orbis Pictus Award for nonfiction with her insightful and moving biography, *M.L.K.: Journey of a King*.

Tonya Bolden lives in her native New York City.

SELECTED WORKS: *Mama, I Want to Sing* (with Vy Higginsen), 1992; *Rites of Passage: Stories about Growing Up by Black Writers from Around the World* (as editor), 1994; *Just Family*, 1996; *Through Loona's Door: A Tammy and Owen Adventure with Carter G. Woodson*, illus. by Luther Knox, 1997; *And Not Afraid to Dare: The Stories of Ten African-American Women*, 1998; 33 *Things Every Girl Should Know: Stories, Songs, Poems, and Smart Talk by 33 Extraordinary Women* (as editor), 1998; *Rock of Ages: A Tribute to the Black Church*, illus. by R. Gregory Christie, 2001; *Tell All the Children Our Story: Memories and Mementos of Being Young and Black in America*, 2001; 33 *Things Every Girl Should Know about Women's History: From Suffragettes to Skirt Lengths to the E.R.A.* (as editor), 2002; *American Patriots: The Story of Blacks in the Military from the Revolution to Desert Storm*, by Gail Buckley (adapted for young people by Tonya Bolden), 2002; *Portraits of African-American Heroes*, illus. by Ansel Pitcairn, 2003; *Wake Up Our Souls: A Celebration of Black American Artists*, 2003; *Maritcha: A Nineteenth-Century American Girl*, 2004; *The Champ: The Story of Muhammad Ali*, illus. by R. Gregory Christie, 2004; *Cause: Reconstruction America, 1863–1877*, 2005; *Take-Off: American All-Girl Bands During WWII*, 2007; *M.L.K.: Journey of a King*, 2007; *George Washington Carver* (in association with The Field Museum of Chicago), 2008.

SELECTED WORKS WRITTEN FOR ADULTS: *The Family Heirloom Cookbook*, 1990; *Starting a Business from Your Home*, 1993; *Getting into the Mail-Order Business*, 1994; *Mail Order and Direct Response*, 1994; *The Book of African-American Women: 150 Crusaders, Creators, and Uplifters*, 1995; *Forgive or Forget: Never*

Underestimate the Power of Forgiveness (with Mother Love), 1999; *Strong Men Keep Coming: The Book of African-American Men*, 1999; *Rejuvenate! It's Never Too Late* (with Eartha Kitt), 2001; *Chaka! Through the Fire* (with Chaka Khan), 2003; *Half the Mother, Twice the Love: My Journey to Better Health with Diabetes*, 2006; *Weddings: Valentine Style: Rich Inspiration for Every Woman's Dream Day* (with Diann Valentine), 2006.

SELECTED WORKS CONTRIBUTED TO: *African-American History*, 1990; *Notable Black American Women*, 1992; *Black Arts Annual*, ed. by Donald Bogle, 1990, 1992; *Go Girl! The Black Woman's Book of Travel and Adventure*, ed. by Elaine Lee, 1997; *Hands On! 33 More Things Every Girl Should Know*, ed. by Suzanne Harper, 2001; *I Speak of the City: Poems of New York*, ed. by Stephen Wolf, 2007.

SUGGESTED READING: *Something About the Author*, vol. 138, 2003; *Contemporary Authors Online*, 6/12/07.

WEB SITE: www.tonyaboldenbooks.com

Colin Bootman

December 23, 1965–

"I believe that life is the culmination of one altering experience after another. These experiences come together like a puzzle and give shape to our purpose.

"When I look back to my first seven years of existence, the formative years, I realize just how lucky I was. I was born in Trinidad, an island surrounded by sunshine and natural beauty. I loved being in the outdoors and I loved observing things and people, especially in animated situations. I truly believe that in those years I was inadvertently given lessons on aesthetics.

"Just after my seventh birthday my family moved to the United States. It was January in New York. I hated it! At the time I felt as though I had left behind everything that meant anything to me. Don't get me wrong—at first I was excited. Couldn't wait to leave for the U.S. I thought life in America would be just like being in the Caribbean. I was so wrong!

"In America, I couldn't see the ocean from my window as I did at Grandma's house in Grenada. I no longer witnessed the rise and fall of the sun behind the ocean. I no longer went fishing up in the mountains with my cousins as I did in Trinidad. There were no familiar faces, no morning greetings, smells and tastes were different, and the sun seemed dull and colors drab and faded.

"Starting elementary school in the Bronx was equally unpleasant. I was tanned, had no friends, and spoke with an accent. In short, I was target practice. I can't remember all of the names kids used to call me, but there were many. I do, however, recall 'Jamaican coconut.' In those days I hated school, too!

"One day on my way home from school I found a comic book. It was *Spider-Man*. I can't remember the number, but the story was a good one. He was fighting the Rhino. I fell in love! I always liked a good story. I think this was because of my Pentecostal upbringing. I enjoyed going to Sunday school because of the stories told to me about biblical heroes and heroines. I especially liked the way by which they were delivered—with passion and reverence.

Photo by Sharon Jackson

"Comic books did two things for me. They provided me with great stories and spectacular art. When I found that Spider-Man comic book, I did my first complete drawing and hung it on my bedroom wall. It was an action drawing of Spider-Man. I was complimented and encouraged by my family to do more. I did! Almost every day! My family, especially my father, was very proud of me. A watercolorist, he came to the U.S. in part to pursue a career in art. When he saw my early interest in drawing he allowed me to blossom. His drawings did much to inspire me.

"I became a comic book collector. I drew and read from them as often as I could. I even made a few of my own, as well as a 10-year-old could, anyway. Drawing became my passion. I had no idea then that I would someday be doing it for a living. All I knew was that I liked drawing superheroes and I enjoyed reading their stories.

"High school was a good experience. I graduated from LaGuardia High School of the Arts. There I met other artists doing great work. Of course, we were all still budding artists, but we felt like we were seasoned. One of the many things attending LaGuardia did for me was to help develop an appreciation for the other disciplines of art, such as dance, theater, music, and literature.

"By the time I became a senior and was accepted to The School of Visual Arts, I had been drawn to other influences. But

I will always revere comic books in that they essentially were the springboard to some of my favorite artists and periods in art.

"When I graduated college I thought I wanted to paint book covers and record jackets. Maybe even do some editorials. In truth I was confused and didn't really know what I wanted to do. All I knew was that I wanted to create art and receive payment for it. To further complicate things, I was a Marine Corps reservist, and we were at war in the Middle East. Operation Desert Storm, they called it. I openly protested by declaring conscientious objector status. I was denied! However, I was granted a jail sentence. Between the time that I spent battling the U.C.M.J. (Uniform Code of Military Justice) and in prison, a year of my life was gone. But, I had developed a better sense of tolerance and perseverance.

"When I was released from military prison I worked on my portfolio. I then started showing my work to other artists for feedback. Brian Pinkney, a renowned illustrator, liked what I showed him and directed me to an agent, Kirchoff/Wohlberg. They also liked my art and we decided to work together. My first year with them I did lots of textbook work. By the second year I landed my first picture book, *Young Frederick Douglass*. Even at this point it didn't quite register that I was actually living my dream. I think it sunk in after my third book.

"It took me a long time to feel comfortable saying to others that I am an artist. However, the more I have embraced this concept, the more expansive my creativity has become.

"I have now broadened my palette to include writing. I figured after illustrating so many books and being exposed to so many stories, the next and natural step would be to write. My first written and illustrated book, *Fish for the Grand Lady*, debuted in the fall of 2006, and I am now working on my third written and illustrated book. I am also involved in gallery work, portraiture, and teaching. I am an artist."

"One day on my way home from school I found a comic book. It was Spider-Man. I can't remember the number, but the story was a good one. He was fighting the Rhino. I fell in love!"

଄ଷ   ଄ଷ   ଄ଷ

Colin Bootman graduated in 1990 from The School of Visual Arts in New York City, and his career in illustration took off soon afterward. Joanne Hyppolite's 1995 *Seth and Samona*, which he illustrated, was an American Booksellers Pick of the Lists. A few years later, *The Music in Derrick's Heart*, written by Gwendolyn Battle-Lavert, was named a Parents' Choice Recommended title and a *Reading Rainbow* review book. Bootman's art for books about African-American leaders, notably Frederick Douglass and Dr. Martin Luther King Jr., showed great sensitivity to African American heritage. He also illustrated a picture book about Harriet Beecher Stowe, the author of *Uncle Tom's Cabin*, which emphasized how her famous book inflamed abolitionist sympathies in the years leading up to the Civil War.

Bootman's work has a lighter side that can be seen in his illustrations for Katrin Tchana's *Oh, No, Toto!*, the story of a toddler creating havoc at a marketplace in Cameroon. In this book his palette is considerably lighter than in Vaunda Nelson's *Almost to Freedom*, a very different type of story that chronicles a family's nighttime escape from slavery in the American South. Told from the point of view of a doll belonging to the young girl in the family, this affecting tale was illustrated by Bootman in the blue and purple hues of night and won a Coretta Scott King Honor Award for illustration. He effectively portrayed a later period of African American history in *Papa's Mark*, a story by Gwendolyn Battle-Lavert on the struggle for voting rights. It was cited as an honor book by the Society of School Librarians International. And in *Grandmama's Pride*, which won a Golden Kite award in picture book writing for author Becky Birtha, Bootman effectively expressed the quiet dignity of Southern blacks living under Jim Crow laws in the 1950s.

Courtesy of Holiday House, Inc.

Myron Uhlberg's affecting story—*Dad, Jackie, and Me*—provided Colin Bootman another very special venue for his art. In lighthearted watercolors and with meticulous accuracy to the era, he illustrated the story of Uhlberg's experience attending a 1940s Brooklyn Dodgers game with his hearing-impaired father at the start of Jackie Robinson's career. *Dad, Jackie, and Me* won the Schneider Family Book Award for its sensitive portrayal of disabilities; it was also named a Notable Social Studies Trade Book for Children, an NCTE Notable Book in the Language Arts, and an IRA Teacher's Choice, among other honors.

Bootman has recently added writing to his talents and created the text as well as the illustrations for *Fish for the Grand Lady*, named a Best of the Year by the Children's Book Committee at Bank Street College of Education. In the dialect of his native Trinidad, enhanced by rich-hued oil paintings, he created a sensual experience of island culture in this story of two brothers who catch fish for their grandmother.

Colin Bootman lives and works today in Brooklyn, New York, but makes frequent trips to visit his roots in Trinidad. In 2006 he received the Ashley Bryan Medal at the Children's Literature Conference sponsored by the Atlanta-Fulton Public Library System for a notable body of work in African American literature for children.

SELECTED WORKS ILLUSTRATED: *Young Frederick Douglass: The Slave Who Learned to Read*, by Linda Walvoord Girard, 1994; *Seth and Samona*, by Joanne Hyppolite, 1995; *Louise's Gift: or What Did She Give Me That For?*, by Irene Smalls, 1996; *Follow the Leader*, by Vicki Winslow, 1997; *Oh, No, Toto!*, by Katrin Hyman Tchana and Louise Tchana Pami, 1997; *In My Momma's Kitchen*, by Jerdine Nolen, 1999; *The Music in Derrick's Heart*, by Gwendolyn Battle-Lavert, 2000; *Dr. Martin Luther King, Jr.*, by David A. Adler, 2001; *A Picture Book of Harriet Beecher Stowe*, by David A. Adler, 2003; *Don't Say Ain't*, by Irene Smalls, 2003; *Papa's Mark*, by Gwendolyn Battle-Lavert, 2003; *Almost to Freedom*, by Vaunda Micheaux Nelson, 2003; *Grandmama's Pride*, by Becky Birtha, 2005; *Dad, Jackie, and Me*, by Myron Uhlberg, 2005; *The Broken Bike Boy and the Queen of 33rd Street*, by Sharon Flake, 2007.

SELECTED WORKS WRITTEN AND ILLUSTRATED: *Fish for the Grand Lady*, 2006.

SUGGESTED READING: *Something About the Author*, vol. 159, 2005.

WEB SITE: www.colinbootman.net

"As a child I was always drawing. My ambition at age six was to paint the world's most beautiful picture of a sunset. By the time I was ten, that ambition was tamed. That was also the year we moved north from Milwaukee to New London, Wisconsin, population 4,000. I immediately fell in love with the 'country' one block away. And all through junior high and high school I carried the label of 'class artist,' drawing for the school newspaper and yearbook.

"At the University of Wisconsin, I discovered poetry and took a writing class. The professor noted that I had 'unusual promise,

Ruth Lercher Bornstein

April 28, 1927–

a pleasing humanity.' I didn't give it a thought. I was going to be a painter.

"In New York after college, every afternoon I conducted art classes for children at a Settlement house and every morning painted at the Art Students League. After an unforgettable year and a half in Israel and Paris, I married, and my husband Harry and I attended Cranbrook Academy of Art in Michigan. Soon after, my daughter Noa was born. After more moves, we settled near Los Angeles where my three sons were born.

"I discovered children's books with my children, never tired of reading to them, but never dreamed I'd ever write books myself. I thought that painting what I needed to say was enough for one lifetime. But then in 1970 I found myself drawing little green elephants talking to flowers, rabbits peeking out of the ground, creating funny little drawings instead of big serious paintings. I was having fun so I just let it happen. In 1971, I grew my first vegetable garden. I spent more time holding hands with the cucumber vine than working in my studio. And finally—by some mysterious organic process, as the plants began to die and sink into the ground, and feeling that I had witnessed the whole cycle of life and death in one summer, I began to write. Simple words like 'Green,' 'Grow,' 'Flower,' became as real and solid to me as paint. I filled up

Courtesy of Ruth Lecher Bornstein

sketchbook after sketchbook with words and pictures of everything I imagined and loved. My first picture book was published in 1973 and—interspersed with periods of painting—I haven't stopped writing since.

"*Indian Bunny* (now *Brave Bunny*) was inspired by my feelings of connection with the natural world. Then, because I've always loved gorillas, it was natural for me to make the hero of my story of love (and don't we all need love?) a little gorilla. There are only one hundred and thirty-three words in *Little Gorilla* but it took me two years to uncover what it was that I really wanted to say. *The Dancing Man* evolved over a period of seven years and is the story of a creative life from beginning to end—and beyond. I chose dance as the medium because I love to dance, have folk-danced for many years, and believe in the power of dance to bring people together. The illustrations for the book are set in my parents' Eastern Europe and have a *shtetl* flavor.

"*That's How It Is When We Draw*, poems and art inspired by my dig-down-past-the-adult-judgmental kind of drawing, is dedicated to 'every growing and surprising thing.' And my novel, *Butterflies and Lizards, Beryl and Me*, has given me a second chance to grow up, and has given my character Charley a chance to say at the end, 'at least for this minute, the space inside of me is big enough, and wide enough, to hold us all.' This story is now being developed as a musical theatre production.

"When I wake before dawn and think about the terrible events in the world, or slip into sadness about my own fears, Joseph Campbell's words, 'joyful participation in the sorrows of the world,' help bring me back to the only thing I can do—which is to live in the 'Now.' I'm lucky that some days I can retreat and at other times can reach out. Lucky that I've had the time to slowly develop and keep on 'beginning.' Lucky that my children have grown to be resourceful and creative adults. I'm lucky that I've had other people's art and poetry in my life. I'm lucky that children's books found me."

> "*I'm lucky that I've had other people's art and poetry in my life. I'm lucky that children's books found me.*"

03   03   03

The author and illustrator of picture books that celebrate creativity, nature, and special relationships in children's lives, Ruth Lercher spent her early childhood in the city of Milwaukee and later moved to the small town of New London, Wisconsin. Majoring in art education at the University of Wisconsin, Madison, she graduated with a B.S. in 1948 and went on to a year of graduate studies at the Art Students League in New York City before traveling abroad. Married to Harry Bornstein in 1951, she studied along with her husband at Cranbrook Academy of Art in Bloomfield Hills, Michigan. The Bornsteins have four children: Noa, Jonah, Adam, and Jesse. Ruth's art has been featured in many juried exhibitions over the last 50 years, and she has had 10 solo shows. Ruth taught a course in "Creating the Picture Book" at the University of California, Los Angeles (UCLA), from 1980 to 1987, and at ISOMATA, a summer art program at the University of Southern California (USC), from 1981 to 1982.

Ruth's illustrations for Edith McHale's *Son of Thunder* and her own *Little Gorilla* received awards from the Southern California Council on Literature for Children and Young People in 1974 and 1977, respectively. *Little Gorilla* has been transformed into a board book, packaged with audiocassettes, anthologized, and

published in several countries. *The Dancing Man* was a *Reading Rainbow* selection and adapted into a musical by a professional children's theater in Madison, Wisconsin. In the 20th anniversary edition, Ruth re-illustrated *The Dancing Man* using oil pastels rather than the original pencil drawings, further enriching her tale of a poor orphan who is inspired by a gift of silver shoes to do what he has always wanted to do—dance and bring joy to others. The Spence School of Dance in Riverton, Utah, and the University of Utah Children's Dance Theatre performed *The Dancing Man* as part of its 20th anniversary celebration.

Full-color illustrations grace *The Seedling Child* in which birds drop a seed that is later planted by a little girl. The seed blossoms into a flower with a tiny seedling child that resembles the little girl for one magical day. Like most of Bornstein's books, the text is poetic, suggestive, and tuned to the inner life of children. *A Beautiful Seashell* depicts a great-grandmother recounting her experiences as a child in another country and her voyage across the sea to her young great-granddaughter, with pastel paintings softly evoking her memories of a ship on the ocean, gulls flying against the sun, and other images. Like *The Dancing Man* and his silver shoes, *A Beautiful Seashell* uses an object to symbolize larger themes; in this case a seashell represents the passing on of love and family history. Turning from prose to poetry in *I'll Draw a Meadow* and *That's How It Is When We Draw*, Bornstein explores the nature of drawing and how it can transform the experience of the artist.

In 2002 Bornstein published her first novel for middle-grade children, *Butterflies and Lizards, Beryl and Me*. Set during the Great Depression, it tells the story of 11-year-old Charlotte, nicknamed Charley, who leaves the tenements of the city for a town where her mother can work seven days a week in a cannery, leaving Charley on her own. Filled with images of soup kitchens and unemployment lines, the story centers on Charley's growing friendship with an old woman named Beryl. Beryl is odd but wise, with a hobo for a boyfriend, and introduces Charley to the world of animals and gardening while helping the girl find a sense of herself.

As one might expect from the themes of her books, Ruth Lercher Bornstein loves folk dancing, singing, walking, traveling, growing vegetables, and, of course, painting and writing. She lives in Santa Monica, California.

SELECTED WORKS WRITTEN AND ILLUSTRATED: *Indian Bunny*, 1973; *Little Gorilla*, 1976; *The Dream of the Little Elephant*, 1977; *Jim*, 1978; *The Dancing Man*, 1978; *Annabelle*, 1978; *I'll Draw a Meadow*, 1979; *Of Course a Goat*, 1980; *The Seedling Child*, 1987; *A Beautiful Seashell*, 1990; *Rabbit's Good News*, 1995; *That's How It Is When We Draw*, 1997; *The Dancing Man* (20th Anniversary ed. with new illustrations), 1998; *Butterflies and Lizards, Beryl and Me*, 2002; *Brave Bunny* (30th Anniversary ed. of *Indian Bunny*), 2003.

SELECTED WORKS ILLUSTRATED: *Son of Thunder*, by Edith McHalee, 1974; *Your Owl Friend*, by Crescent Dragonwagon, 1977; *Flocks of Birds*, by Charlotte Zolotow, 1981; *Mama One, Mama Two*, by Patricia MacLachlan, 1982; *Summer Is*, by Charlotte Zolotow, 1983; *Mommy, Daddy, Me*, by Lyn Hoopes, 1988.

SUGGESTED READING: *Contemporary Authors Online*, 2001.

Photo by Peter Freed

Ann Brashares

March 19, 1967–

Born and raised in Chevy Chase, Maryland, with her three brothers, Ann Brashares attended Sidwell Friends School, a Quaker school with campuses in Bethesda, Maryland, and Washington, DC. As a child, she used to pretend to travel and wrote letters from these imaginary trips, keeping them in a scrapbook, little knowing how these "pretend" travels would inform her best-selling books when she became a writer. She studied philosophy at Barnard College, where, in her freshman year, she met her future husband.

After graduating from Barnard, Brashares planned to take a year off to work and save money to further her education. She took a job with a publishing company and found her editorial work so fulfilling that she began building a career in children's book publishing. While working on ideas for children's book projects, Brashares decided to write several volumes in a nonfiction series on the lives of "Techies." These were her first two books: *Steve Jobs: Thinks Different* and *Linus Torvalds: Software Rebel*.

The Sisterhood of the Traveling Pants, Brashares' first novel, took off from a conversation with a colleague and friend who told her about a summer when she had shared a pair of pants with a group of girlfriends until the pants were lost in Borneo. The concept for the book was also related to Brashares's experiences with her wedding dress, a dress that she had imagined in detail and then found in a catalog. Serendipitously, a woman whose engagement had been broken off gave Brashares that very dress. Brashares in turn shared it with all three of her brothers' wives and her own best friend, thus creating her own ongoing "sisterhood."

The Sisterhood of the Traveling Pants follows four teenage girlfriends, all of different body types, who share a pair of pants that magically fits each of them during a summer when they are separated. Before going their separate ways to California, South Carolina, and Greece, while one remains in Maryland, the girls make up ten rules to the pants; one rule is that each friend will wear the pants for one week only, and then forward them by mail to the next. When they reunite at the end of the summer, the girls symbolically record their experiences on the pants themselves. The book is a tribute to female friendship, self-image, personal challenge, and the abilities and strengths that each girl ultimately exhibits as she becomes her own person. Each character has her own story, one of which Brashares says she based on the Greek myth of Artemis and another on the movie *It's a Wonderful Life*. The other two girls, the author has stated, say things she herself could never say and do things that she would never do.

The Sisterhood of the Traveling Pants was named an ALA Best Book for Young Adults and won many state teen book awards, including those in Rhode Island, Maryland, Indiana, Washington, New Jersey, Missouri, Iowa, Oklahoma, and Tennessee. It received a Pacific Northwest Young Reader's Choice Award for grades 10-12, was cited as a *Publishers Weekly* Flying Start and was a *New York Times* Best Seller.

Courtesy of Random House, Inc.

The sequel, *The Second Summer of the Sisterhood*, takes place during the following summer and has a similar format. Separated from each other, the girls share once more the thrift-store jeans via the U.S. Post Office even as they face new challenges, learn old lessons more deeply, deal with their personal demons, and negotiate life's ongoing journey. The relationship of each girl with her mother plays a stronger role in this sequel, which won Delaware's Blue Hen Teen Book Award.

A third title in the series, *Girl in Pants: The Third Summer of the Sisterhood*, won the Quill Award for Young Adult/Teen Literature. Now the friends, ready to go off to colleges in four different cities, deal with bittersweet issues related to what they must leave behind—parents, siblings, boyfriends—and what they are moving towards—new relationships, new educational settings, and new ways of being in the world.

Four more intertwining stories connect *Forever in Blue*, which finds the girls leading ever more separate lives at the end of their freshman year in college. The loss of the pants brings the friends together again in an exciting climax. Brashares's first adult book, *The Last Summer (of You and Me)*, a page-turner about a love triangle, shares the themes of friendship, family, love, and loss that made her books for teen readers so enormously popular. A feature length film of *The Sisterhood of the Traveling*

Pants, with screenplay by Delia Ephron, was released in 2005. A sequel, *Sisterhood of the Traveling Pants 2*, is in production at this writing, scheduled for release in 2008.

With her husband, the artist Jacob Collins, Ann Brashares has three children, Sam, Nate, and Susannah, and a dog named Phineas. They live in New York City and spend their summers on Fire Island, New York. The author's own favorite pair of pants is a bright red pair of slightly flared summer pants that make her feel every bit as loved as the protagonists in her Sisterhood books.

SELECTED WORKS FOR YOUNG READERS: *Steve Jobs: Thinks Different*, 2001; *Linus Torvalds: Software Rebel*, 2001; *The Sisterhood of the Traveling Pants*, 2001; *The Second Summer of the Sisterhood*, 2003; *Girl in Pants: The Third Summer of the Sisterhood*, 2005; *Keep in Touch: Letters, Notes, and More from The Sisterhood of the Traveling Pants*, 2005; *The Sisterhood of the Traveling Pants: The Official Scrapbook*, 2005; *Forever in Blue: The Fourth Summer of the Sisterhood*, 2007.

SELECTED WORKS FOR ADULTS: *The Last Summer (of You and Me)*, 2007.

SUGGESTED READING: *Something About the Author*, vol. 145, 2004; *Authors and Artists for Young Adults*, vol. 52, 2003. Periodicals— *Scholastic Scope*, vol. 54, issue 8, December 12, 2005. Online— *Contemporary Authors Online*, August 22, 2006.

WEB SITES: www.annbrashares.net
www.randomhouse.com/teens/sisterhoodcentral/home.html

Kevin Brooks

March 30, 1959–

"When I was five years old, my father made me a writing desk for Christmas. He was an amateur carpenter, and he always took great pride in his work, and the desk he made for me was a beauty. It had a sloping lid of shiny black wood, lots of little drawers and compartments, an inkwell, a beautifully carved groove for my pencils and pens. It had everything. Best of all, though, was the secret compartment inside. A little niche, hidden away in the bottom of the desk, accessed by a disguised wooden latch underneath . . . perfect for hiding away all my secret things.

"The only trouble was . . . I was five years old. I didn't *have* any secret things. No cigarettes, no drugs, no naughty pictures (these things didn't come into my life until I was at *least* seven or eight). And also, I eventually realized—what good is a secret compartment made by your dad? Even if I *did* have any secrets to hide, which I didn't, the only person to hide them from was . . . my dad.

"My mother assures me that I spent the whole of that Christmas Day sitting at my brand new writing desk, happily writing stories. I have no conscious recollection of this—but who am I to argue with an author's proud mother?

"When I was older, my mum and dad would take me to the library once a week. We'd jump in the car, drive into town, and spend an hour or two browsing the library shelves. Mum and Dad would disappear into the adult section, leaving me to wander around the children's section on my own. I loved it. The peace and quiet, the library smell, the shelves full of books . . . thousands of books . . . and all for free! I don't remember much about the books that I borrowed, but I know that my favorite authors were always American. And they still are.

My English teacher was one of those English teachers who encourage their students to read books that they don't *have* to read. Every now and then he'd just give me a book and say, 'Try that, see what you think of it.' And I'd try it. And maybe I'd like it, and maybe I wouldn't. But it didn't matter. He'd just nod his head and give me another one. *The Catcher in the Rye*. *Last Exit to Brooklyn*. *On the Road*. Of course, this English teacher was also quite mad, and at times his behavior was somewhat questionable, to say the least. He once hit

Photo by Susan Williams

me in the head with a metal chair as punishment for some minor indiscretion. But . . . at least he got me reading good books.

"I always wanted to be a writer, and somewhere deep inside me, I always knew that I would be. I was *me* when I wrote. The real me. Poetry, thoughts, diaries, short stories, plays, weird little things . . . I wrote and wrote and wrote. But I also loved music. And from the age of fifteen until I was twenty-five, I devoted myself to music. Writing songs, recording, producing, performing. It was a love affair that took me to lots of strange places and introduced me to lots of strange people, and eventually I decided it was all *too* strange for me. So I stopped. I didn't stop writing songs, but I stopped trying to make a living out of it. I made my living however I could: unemployment benefits, university grants, loans, overdrafts, jobs. I sold hot dogs. I sieved human ashes. I worked for the Post Office, the Civil Service, a railway company. And I hated every minute of it.

"So I wrote stories, getting closer all the time to what I really wanted to do, but I still didn't have the patience/discipline/commitment/courage to do it. For five years or so, I was a painter. I painted big colorful paintings, and small dark paintings. I thought they were pretty good. But no one else did. In all my time as a painter, I only managed to sell one picture (and a very poor one at that). But—as I never tire of reminding myself—that's one more painting than Vincent Van Gogh ever sold.

> *"My English teacher was one of those English teachers who encourage their students to read books that they don't have to read. Every now and then he'd just give me a book and say, 'Try that, see what you think of it.'"*

"So it gets to the stage when I'm suddenly nearly forty (how did *that* happen?), and I say to myself: 'Look, if you *really* want to be a writer, if you really want to be a *novelist*, then you'd better start doing it now.' So that's what I do. I sit down, take a deep breath, and start writing novels. At first it's really hard. I know how to use words, because I've been writing all my life, but novels are more than just words. They're more than anything I've ever done before, and they take absolutely ages to write. But I like doing it, and I keep doing it, and eventually I finish one. It's not very good, but I'm proud of myself for simply finishing it. So I start writing another one. And then another one. And another, and another . . . until, finally, I write one called *Martyn Pig* that makes me think: 'Hmm . . . this isn't bad, you know. This actually reads like a real book . . . the kind of book that a writer might write.' So I send it off to a publisher. And it gets rejected. So I send it off again. And it gets rejected again. And again, and again, and again . . . until there's no one left to send it to. I've used up all the publishers in the entire United Kingdom (and most of the agents too).

"But I don't mind. I've been rejected by record companies and art galleries for years . . . it's no big deal. You just keep trying. Do something else. Something better. So that's what I do. I keep trying. Then one day I get a telephone call, and when I answer it, a kindly-voiced man says, 'You know that story you sent me, *Martyn Pig*?' And I say, 'Yes.' And he says, 'Well, I'd like to publish it. . . .' And now I'm five years old again, sitting at my writing desk, as happy as a boy on Christmas Day."

CR CR CR

Born in Exeter, England, Kevin Brooks attended Aston University in 1980 and completed his B.A. at North East

London Polytechnic in 1983. Brooks realized his dream of writing professionally only after working a variety of jobs. A poet, lyricist, and always an inveterate reader, he brings a wealth of experience and dedication to his current life as a writer of young adult novels.

Brooks's books combine elements of mystery and suspense, at very high tension, and feature teenaged characters caught up in desperate, violent worlds. In *Martyn Pig* his hero accidentally kills his abusive father and needs to dispose of the corpse. Dark, funny, poetic, and tightly-plotted, *Martyn Pig* was an instant success on both sides of the Atlantic, receiving the Bradford Boase Award for a first novel of distinction in the United Kingdom and shortlisted for the Carnegie Medal. In the United States it was designated a *School Library Journal* Best Book of the Year.

His second novel, *Lucas*, is about two kinds of outsiders: Caitlin, who finds herself ostracized by old friends when she takes up with the mysterious Lucas; and Lucas himself, who is met with prejudice and misunderstanding in the conservative island community where their love story unfolds. Nominated for the *Guardian* Children's Book Prize and the Book Trust Teenage Prize in the United Kingdom, *Lucas* became the first Barnes & Noble Teen Discover title in the United States and was named an ALA Best Book for Young Adults.

Kissing the Rain, which appeared on *Booklist*'s 2004 "Top 10 Youth Mysteries," involves an overweight, harried youth called Moo, who witnesses a road-rage

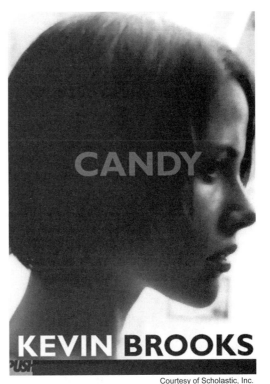

Courtesy of Scholastic, Inc.

incident that soon catapults him and his working class father into danger. *Candy* tells the story of a suburban fifteen-year-old band member's sudden and passionate love for a girl who, in spite of first impressions, turns out to be a prostitute with a heroin addiction and a thoroughly nasty pimp.

In *Road of the Dead*, fourteen-year-old Ruben has second sight, or extra-sensory perception (ESP), and feels/knows that his older sister has been killed and that his brother, Cole, is headed for trouble when he decides to find the men responsible. Brutal and haunting, *Road of the Dead* is a tale in which the dark setting is as fully realized a character as the two brothers.

With these disturbing, deeply felt books, Kevin Brooks has established himself as an uncompromising new voice in literature for young adults. He and his wife, Susan, live and work in their home in Manningtree, Essex, a coastal farming community.

SELECTED WORKS: *Martyn Pig*, 2002; *Lucas*, 2003; *Kissing the Rain*, 2004; *Candy*, 2005; *Road of the Dead*, 2006; *Being*, 2007; *Black Rabbit Summer*, 2008.

SUGGESTED READING: *Something About the Author*, vol. 150, 2004. Periodical—Eccleshare, Julia, "Apprenticeship and Arrival," *Publisher's Weekly*, Feb. 16, 2004. Online—"An Interview with Kevin Brooks." *Push*, at www.thisispush.com, June 3, 2004.

Courtesy of Tor Books

Orson Scott Card

August 24, 1951–

The first writer to receive both the Hugo and Nebula awards for science fiction two years in a row, Orson Scott Card is a prolific author of international best-sellers whose work is often described as multifaceted. Many of Card's most thought-provoking books weave realism with fantasy and sharpen suspense with ethical dilemmas. In addition to the science fiction and fantasy novels for which he's become well known, Card has also written short stories, nonfiction, biblical novels, poetry, illustrated novels and comic books, video games, audio and stage plays, contemporary fiction, and a screenplay of his classic novel, *Ender's Game.*

A descendant of the Mormon pioneer leader Brigham Young, Card was born in the state of Washington and grew up in California, Arizona, and Utah. He served as a missionary for the Church of the Latter Day Saints in Brazil from 1971 to 1973. From 1974 to 1975, he operated a repertory theater in Provo, Utah and served as an editor for the Brigham Young University Press from 1974 to 1976. He later worked for such periodicals as *Ensign Magazine* (in Salt Lake City from 1976 to 1978) and *Compute! Books* (in Greensboro, North Carolina in 1983).

As a college theater student on a presidential scholarship, Card developed his ability to create believable characters and page-turning plots by listening to young actors perform his work and by observing audience reactions. His early work often had religious and biblical themes. He received his B.A. from Brigham Young University in 1975. Even before completing his master's degree at the University of Utah in 1981, Card was gaining recognition for his writing.

His first published short story, "Gert Fram," appeared in the July 1977 issue of *Ensign*, the official magazine of the Church of Jesus Christ of Latter-day Saints; that same year he won the John W. Campbell Award for best new writer. He received Hugo Award nominations for his short stories, which appeared in *Omni* and other magazines, in 1978, 1979, and 1980; the stories were also nominated for Nebula Awards in 1979 and 1980. (One of his early short stories, "Ender's Game," served as the basis of his breakthrough novel of the same title.) Card also won the 1980 Utah State Institute of Fine Arts Prize for his epic poem, "Prentice Alvin and the No-Good Plow," which set the stage for the later Alvin Maker series.

At least two of Card's novelettes received widespread recognition in the 1980s. *Hatrack River* was nominated for a Hugo Award in 1986 and captured the 1987 World Fantasy Award. In 1988 *Eye for an Eye* received the Hugo Award and a Locus Award nomination.

In 1985 Card published *Ender's Game*, a novel that depicted the military apprenticeship of a six-year-old genius named Andrew "Ender" Wiggin who is expected to save Earth from alien invaders. Recognized in both science fiction circles and the young adult field, *Ender's Game* won the Nebula Award and the Hugo Award and was included in the *Locus* Best SF Novels Before 1990. It was also named to ALA's 100 Best Books for Teens and ALA's Page Turners–Adult Novels for Teens.

The sequel, *Speaker for the Dead*, which won the Nebula Award, the Hugo Award, and the Locus Award, delves into questions pertaining to the peaceful coexistence between species and the need for empathy between cultures. Once again Ender is at the center of these conflicts. The Ender books continue with the Shadow series, of which *Ender's Shadow* is the first title. Named to ALA's Top Ten Best Books for Young Adults as well as VOYA's Outstanding Books of the Year, it was also chosen as a *Booklist* Editors' Choice. *Ender's Shadow* features a superhuman child hero who learns not only how to become a skilled soldier but also what it means to be human.

Before finishing the Ender series, Card began working on the Tales of Alvin Maker series, in which he mixes history, fantasy, and philosophy as a way to reinvent the American frontier.

Ender's Shadow *features a superhuman child hero who learns not only how to become a skilled soldier but also what it means to be human.*

Courtesy of Tor Books

Historic figures interact with fictional ones in an alternative American landscape inhabited by witches and other beings with magical powers. *Seventh Son*, the first title in the series, won the Locus Award, the Mythopoeic Fantasy Award, and Washington State's Evergreen Young Adult Book Award. The book features Alvin Maker, who, with the help of a young girl endowed with second sight, learns to use and control his ability to manipulate reality. *Red Prophet*, the second title in the series and a Locus Award winner, looks at the conflict between Native Americans and white settlers though a fantasy lens in an attempt to discover why different races cannot seem to get along. Another title in the series, *Heartfire*, which won the Grand Prix de L'Imaginaire, examines legal ambiguities and the depth of human tolerance by exploring witch-burning in an alternative New England and the plight of slaves in a Camelot version of the southern colonies.

Continuing his fascination with history, Card's *Pastwatch* won the Israeli Society's first Geffen Award for best translated science fiction in 1999. A powerful portrait of Christopher Columbus, this novel focuses on a group of time travelers from a ruined future who return to the past to try to repair the damage caused by Columbus's arrival in America. As with his other books, Card's grasp of science and history is evident and impressive.

Four of Card's titles have been named ALA Best Books for Young Adults: *Ender's Game* in 1986, *Pastwatch* in 1997, *Ender's Shadow* in 2000, and *Shadow of the Hegemon* in 2002. Three of his titles were named ALA Popular Paperbacks for Young Adults: *Ender's Game* in 2000, *Ender's Shadow* in 2004, and *Enchantment* in 2005.

In his Homecoming series, Card mixes philosophy, moral issues, and futuristic technology. On the planet Harmony, a powerful computer called Oversoul rules the populace. When the machine falls into disrepair, the inhabitants must learn to regulate their own affairs and understand their own natures. Card has also turned his hand to examining the roots of Western religion by writing about historical religious figures; books in the Women of Genesis series include *Sarah*, *Rebekah*, and *Rachel and Leah*, and Moses is a principle character in *Stone Tables*. Joseph Smith, the founder of the Mormon religion, makes an appearance in *Saints*, a fictional tale about one of Smith's wives.

In addition to writing books and stories, Card continues to work in a variety of media. In the mid-1980s, he wrote screenplays for animated children's videos based on the New Testament and the Book of Mormon. He also offers commentaries on subjects ranging from literature and film to restaurants and consumer products in a column called "Uncle Orson Reviews Everything," which is published by the *Rhinoceros Times* in Greensboro, North Carolina. His writings on culture, politics, and world affairs are among the new blog journalism featured online at "The Ornery Americans." Card has shared his ideas on the writing process and how it relates to the science fiction and fantasy genres, in his 1991 Hugo Award-winning book, *How to Write Science Fiction and Fantasy*. In addition to teaching various writers' workshops, Card became a professor of writing and literature at Southern Virginia University in 2005.

Since 1977 Orson Scott Card has been married to Kristine Allen Card with whom he has five children: Michael Geoffrey, Emily Janice, Charles Benjamin, Zina Margaret, and Erin Louisa. (Each child was given at least one name to honor a writer their parents admire: Geoffrey Chaucer, Emily Brontë and Emily Dickinson, Charles Dickens, Margaret Mitchell, and Louisa May Alcott.) Although they travel widely, Card and his wife make their home in Greensboro, NC, where they have lived since 1983. In 2008 Orson Scott Card received ALA's Margaret Edwards Award for lifetime achievement in writing for young adults.

SELECTED WORKS: *Hot Sleep: The Worthing Chronicle*, 1979; *Songmaster*, 1980; *Saintspeak: The Mormon Dictionary*, illus. by Calvin Grondahl, 1981; *The Worthing Chronicle*, 1983; *A Woman of Destiny*, 1984; *Wyrms*, 1987; *Characters & Viewpoint*, 1988; *Hart's Hope*, 1988; *Treason*, 1988 (originally published as *A Planet Called Treason*, 1979); *Saints*, 1988 (originally published as *A Woman of Destiny*, 1984); *Folk on the Fringe*, 1989; *How to Write Science Fiction and Fantasy*, 1990; *Maps in a Mirror*, 1990; *Eye for Eye and the Tunesmith*, with Lloyd Biggle Jr., 1990; *The Worthing Saga*, 1990; *Lost Boys*, 1992; *Flux: Tales of Human Futures*, 1992; *Cruel Miracles*, 1992; *The Changed Man*, 1992; *Monkey Sonatas*, 1993; *Lovelock*, with Kathryn H. Kidd, 1994; *Pastwatch: The Redemption of Christopher Columbus*, 1996; *Treasure Box*, 1996; *Stone Tables*, 1997; *Homebody*, 1998; *Enchantment*, 1999; *Magic Mirror*, illus. by Nathan Pinnock, 1999; *Robota*, illus. by Doug Chiang, 2003; *An Open Book*, 2004; *Magic Street*, 2005; *Posing as People: Three Stories, Three Plays*, with play adaptations by Scott Brick, Emily Janice Card and Aaron Johnston, 2005; *Empire*, 2006; *Ultimate Iron Man*, Vol. 1, 2006; *Space Boy*, 2007; *Invasive Procedures*, with Aaron Johnston, 2007; *Keeper of Dreams*, 2008.

SELECTED WORKS IN SERIES: Ender series—*Ender's Game*, 1985; *Speaker for the Dead*, 1986; *Xenocide*, 1991; *Children of the Mind*, 1996. Shadow series—*Ender's Shadow*, 1999; *Shadow of the Hegemon*, 2000; *Shadow Puppets*, 2002; *First Meetings in Ender's Universe*, 2002; *Shadow of the Giant*, 2005; *A War of Gifts*, 2007. Alvin Maker series—*Seventh Son*, 1987; *Red Prophet*, vol. 1, 1987; *Prentice Alvin*, 1989; *Alvin Journeyman*, 1995; *Heartfire*, 1998; *The Crystal City*, 2003; *Red Prophet*, vol. 2, 2007. Homecoming series—*The Memory of Earth*, 1992; *The Call of the Earth*, 1992; *The Ships of Earth*, 1994; *Earthfall*, 1995; *Earthborn*, 1995; Women of Genesis series—*Sarah*, 2000; *Rebekah*, 2001; *Rachel and Leah*, 2004.

SELECTED WORKS AS EDITOR: *Dragons of Light*, 1980; *Dragons of Darkness*, 1981; *The Best Horror Stories of the Year, 1989*, with Martin H. Greenberg, 1989; *The Best Science Fiction Stories of the Year, 1989*, with Martin H. Greenberg, 1989; *Future on Fire*, 1991; *Future on Ice*, 1998; *Masterpieces: The Best Science Fiction of the Twentieth Century*, 2001; *Empire of Dreams and Miracles: The Phobos Science Fiction Anthology*, with Keith Olexa, 2002; *Hitting the Skids in Pixeltown: The Phobos Science Fiction Anthology 2*, with Keith Olexa, 2003.

SUGGESTED READING: *Orson Scott Card: Architect of Alternate Worlds*, by Edward Willett, 2006; *Orson Scott Card*, by Edith S. Tyson, 2003; *Something About the Author*, vol. 127, 2002; *Storyteller: The Official Orson Scott Card Bibliography and Guide 2001*, by Michael R. Collings, 2001; *The Work of Orson Scott Card: An Annotated Bibliography and Guide*, by Michael R. Collings, 1998; *In the Image of God: Theme, Characterization, and Landscape in the Fiction of Orson Scott Card*, by Michael R. Collings, 1990. Periodicals—Oatman, Eric, "The Ornery American," *School Library Journal*, June 2008.

WEB SITE: www.hatrack.com

"One day in 1981, when I was in my second year of graduate school, a professor asked me a puzzling question: 'So, when are you going to write your novel?'

"'What novel?' I answered. 'I don't think I can write a novel.'

"'Sure you can,' he said. 'And what's more, you are going to write many books.'

"That professor, Dr. Jose Miguel Oviedo, and my mother—who had been telling me ever since I could remember that I was born to be a writer—so believed in my abilities that I could not let them down.

"That same year I received my master's degree in Hispanic Literature and traveled to New York City to begin my professional life. Within days I was given my first job, an ideal position for someone like myself: working as an editor and translator on a literary magazine that published in English

Photo by Marion Etlinger

Lori Marie Carlson

June 21, 1957–

translation the works of the best Latin American authors in the world. Among the hundreds of novelists and poets with whom I collaborated were Mario Vargas Llosa (Peruvian), Reinaldo Arenas (Cuban), and Carlos Fuentes (Mexican). It was at this job that I would also meet my future husband, the novelist Oscar Hijuelos. As part of my duties, I worked directly with these authors by presenting them at readings and receptions in a beautiful building on Park Avenue called the Americas Society.

"My job was quite glamorous. Not only did I work in elegant surroundings with fascinating people but I was also meeting and befriending diplomats and the best editors in New York. I realized then just how important, even essential, it was to be a dreamer. Ever since I was 13, I had wanted to live in New York City. I had followed my love of Spanish all the way from my hometown to the Big Apple.

"It was in the mid-1980s that I began to think about the impact of a robust Latin American immigration on North American culture. Working as I did with the Spanish-speaking population, it occurred to me that bilingual books were needed in the marketplace. I also started to investigate the matter of children's books. I needed to find out if there was good material relating to Latin American traditions and values. I soon discovered that there was very little available, either in public libraries or bookstores.

"Then, one day, I had lunch with an editor from HarperCollins (then called Harper and Row) at the Museum of Modern Art. The editor, Marc Aronson, wondered aloud if I was writing anything he might want to see. I answered by telling him that I was working on a book of Latin American stories for children. I had asked some of the excellent writers I knew to write tales that would illuminate their cultural backgrounds for American kids. Lo and behold, Marc decided to publish them.

"Since then most of my work has sought to highlight Latin American and Latino culture for American readers. It is my passion and mission to support and encourage Latino youth in particular. Today, as I travel the country, I am often asked how and why I became a writer of books pertaining to Latino life. For many people it is hard to understand why I, the daughter of a Swedish-American man and an Italian-American woman, would so appreciate Spanish and its many related cultures and histories. But for me the answer is simple. It all started with a love of books and music. As a child, I was an avid reader. In fact, my parents had to take me to the public library at least three times a week because I loved books so much. In addition, I was taught Spanish in my elementary school library. Spanish sounded like music to my ears. I added it to piano, voice and violin lessons. But it was Spanish I liked best.

"It can happen. People can fall in love with a culture that is not their own by birth."

"Now when I meet a group of Latino high school students and see the look of surprise on their faces when they see I'm a blue-eyed blonde who speaks *español*, I simply smile and say, 'It can happen. People can fall in love with a culture that is not their own by birth.' Writers, all writers I believe, share several goals; one is to empower their readers and another is to transport them, to take them on a journey of self-discovery and discovery of the world. Knowing that there are so many children in our country who need extended community to grow up strong, I hope that—through my books—I am helping in some small way."

෬ ෬ ෬

Born into the charming but decidedly homogeneous community of Jamestown, New York, Lori Marie Carlson loved to write, even as a child. She wrote poetry in elementary school and short stories in junior high. Her parents, Marie and Robert Vernon Carlson, supported her love of reading and literature. She has one sister, Leigh Ann Brattain. Earning her B.A. in Spanish Literature and Linguistics from the College of Wooster, in Ohio, Carlson spent her junior year in Madrid and graduated with honors in 1979. She completed a master's degree in Hispanic Literature from Indiana University, in 1981, where she taught Spanish. She has also taught at Columbia University and conducted a seminar in literary translation at New York University.

Serving as the Director of Latin American Literature at the Americas Society for eight years, Carlson edited *Review*, a Latin American literature and arts magazine, and worked with over 400 Latino writers and artists. In 1989–90 she was the editor-in-chief of *Círculo de Lectores*, the first Spanish-language book club in the U.S. She has also been a volunteer teacher for poetry workshops in Spanish/English at P.S. 199 in New York City.

An editor, translator, and novelist, Carlson has described herself as a person who tries to bridge divides. Whether the chasm is between races, ethnic groups, languages, genders, or generations, her aim has been to offer encouragement and hope

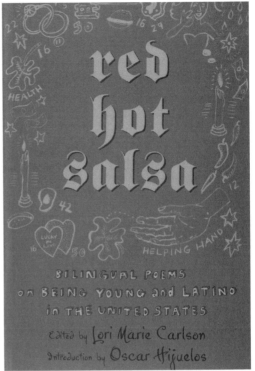
Courtesy of Henry Holt and Company

to her readers. The first collection of stories she edited, *Where Angels Glide at Dawn*, brought little-known Latino writers to the attention of young readers. (Two later titles—*American Eyes* and *Moccasin Thunder*—featured stories from Asian-American and Native American authors.)

Cool Salsa, Carlson's groundbreaking anthology, arose from a desire to provide teenagers with an appealing collection of Latino poetry, a genre traditionally celebrated in Hispanic countries. *Cool Salsa* was named an ALA Best Book for Young Adults, an ALA Quick Pick for Young Adults, a *Bulletin of the Center for Children's Books* Blue Ribbon title, a *School Library Journal* Best Book of the Year, and a *Horn Book* Fanfare title.

A companion volume to *Cool Salsa*, *Red Hot Salsa* was published ten years later. Carlson has said that editing a collection of bilingual poetry is about sensibility. The challenge in translating poetry is that it requires precision of thought as well as faithfulness to one's own interpretive writing skills. She often has worked on nine or ten versions of one poem before settling on the final translation. *Red Hot Salsa* was an ALA Quick Pick for Reluctant Young Adult Readers and an Américas Award Commended Title.

Cool Salsa, Hurray for Three Kings' Day!, and *Sol a Sol* have all been named Notable Social Studies Trade Books for Young People. A collection of bilingual poetry for children, *Sol a Sol*, an IRA/CBC Children's Choice, celebrates a day of family activities. *Moccasin Thunder* was cited as a New York Public Library's list, Book for the Teen Age.

Lori Marie Carlson lives in New York City with her husband, the novelist Oscar Hijuelos. She is a consulting editor for Atheneum Books, a division of Simon and Schuster, and a frequent speaker on issues involving Latino literature for youth.

SELECTED WORKS FOR YOUNG READERS: *Where Angels Glide at Dawn: New Stories From Latin America* (as editor with Cynthia L. Ventura), illus. by José Ortega, 1990; *American Eyes: New Asian-American Short Stories for Young Adults* (as editor), 1994; *Cool Salsa: Bilingual Poems on Growing Up Latino in the United States* (as editor), 1994; *Barrio Streets, Carnival Dreams: Three Generations of Latino Artistry* (as editor), 1996; *Sol a Sol: Bilingual Poems*, written and selected by Lori Marie Carlson, illus. by Emily Lisker, 1998; *Hurray for Three Kings' Day!*, illus. by Ed Martinez, 1999 (Spanish edition: *Vivan Los Reyes Magos!*, 2000); *You're On! Seven Plays in English and Spanish* (as editor), 1999; *Moccasin Thunder: American Indian Stories for Today* (as editor), 2005; *Red Hot Salsa: Bilingual Poems on Being Young and Latino in the United States* (as editor), 2005.

SELECTED WORKS FOR ADULTS: *The Sunday Tertulia*, 2000; *The Flamboyant: A Novel*, 2002; *Burnt Sugar: Caña Quemada: Contemporary Cuban Poetry in English and Spanish*, (edited with Oscar Hijuelos), 2006.

SUGGESTED READING: Carlson, Lori Marie, "Translation: A Struggle with Words," *School Library Journal*, June 1995. Online—Article written for the Children's Book Council, at www.cbcbooks.org/cbcmagazine/meet/carlson_lorimarie.html; Interview by Cynthia Leitich Smith at cynthialeitichsmith.blogspot.com/2005/09/author-interview-lori-m-carlson-on-red.html.

Daniella Carmi

September 1, 1941–

"Growing up in Tel-Aviv, the daughter of parents who emigrated from France (though they were born in Poland), my 'mother-tongue' was French. I learned Hebrew in street-games and later at school. Having learned to read and write, I immediately started writing short stories and was encouraged by my teachers. As for reading, it has been my favorite occupation all through the years. I can say that my whole education was formed by reading.

"We were rather lucky as Israeli kids in the 1940s and 1950s because, side by side with the recent rebirth of the Hebrew language and the relative lack of a developed Hebrew literature for youth, a lot of the very best foreign children's books were translated into Hebrew by local authors and poets. I used to 'swallow' these translations, and having read mostly about children in various countries and cultures, I grew up with the feeling of being a 'citizen of the world.'

"Though I always planned to write in the future, I did not dare to actually do it for a long time. Rather bored by university studies, I tried to amuse myself by translating French poetry—Prevert, Michaux—and some Saroyan short stories. Only at the age of 38 did I first try to write a scenario, which turned into a television drama. Then I gladly abandoned all prospects of an academic career.

Courtesy of Scholastic, Inc.

"My first book was written for adults in 1984, called *Nitzan in the Snows*. Since then I write for children and youth as well as for adults. I have also written some plays and screenplays. My first book for children and youth (*Explosion on Ahalan Street*) was about racism in Israel. It was rather a success among children, maybe because it was written as a suspense story and told by Natasha, daughter of a Jewish mother and an Arabic father who were Israeli citizens. When the book was adapted to theater, and schoolchildren were the main audience, the minister of education banned the play, in a very sensational press conference. It was only a few years later that some teachers started a campaign for the inclusion of the book in school curriculum, and they finally succeeded.

"Another of my youth books, *Samir and Yonatan*, was rather ignored by the Israeli educational system. This did not disturb the Thai educational ministry, however; they selected the book for translation and inclusion in the school program in Thailand. I have been very encouraged by prizes and awards abroad (from UNESCO especially) and the translation of this book into many languages. On a tour that I was invited to make in Germany a few years ago, I discovered a library in East Berlin where a school class can sleep overnight. Then the children wake up in the morning in the special boarding room and adapt their dreams into stories. I was happy to be told that they had worked on *Samir and Yonatan* last winter and adapted the book into a play. Then they talked about their impressions of the characters, and gladly played to me some scenes from the play in German.

"I am sometimes asked by children why my characters tend to be 'different' or rebellious. Indeed, I have always been aware of living in a country at war for so many years, where conformity with the Israeli government's political position has for a long time been the rule. I think that my main motive for writing—it's practically a need and an urge—has been to try to spread some feeling of freedom, of breaking rules; the same kind of 'blessed anarchy' that I have cherished in the writings of Mark Twain, George Sand, Albert Camus, Yanoush Korchak, Astrid Lindgren, and others."

"I think that my main motive for writing—it's practically a need and an urge—has been to try to spread some feeling of freedom, of breaking rules."

Daniella Carmi was born in Tel Aviv in 1941, seven years before the state of Israel was established. She studied philosophy and communication at the Hebrew University of Jerusalem, but her first love was always literature. Her books, for both children and adults, demonstrate her sensitivity toward the outcasts of society and her deep understanding of all sides of an issue. She is particularly sensitive to concerns on both sides of the Israeli-Palestinian conflict, which forms the backdrop of her children's book *Samir and Yonatan*. Winner of the American Library Association's Mildred Batchelder Award for translation, the book tells of Samir, a Palestinian boy who is wounded in street fighting and sent to an Israeli hospital for treatment. Though many of the children there ignore or tease him, he is befriended by an Israeli boy named Yonatan, and this friendship makes it possible for Samir to enjoy simple childhood pleasures with the others. Translated by Israeli writer and journalist Yael Lotan, this book is, to date, the only one of Carmi's books to be published in English.

Samir and Yonatan earned an Honorable Mention in the 1997 UNESCO Prize for Children's and Young People's Literature in the Service of Tolerance as well as the Adei-Wizo Prize in Italy in 2003. It was also cited by the Middle East Outreach Council as one of three recipients of the 2001 Middle East Book Award, established to recognize books for children and young adults that are judged to be outstanding for literary quality and appeal for the intended audience as well as for the authenticity of their portrayal of Middle Eastern subject matter. *Samir and Yonatan* has been adapted twice for theatrical productions in Israel: as a monodrama for adults in the Habima National Theater in 1998, and as a children's play in the Haifa Festival for Children's Drama in 2004. When newly published, it received the Award of the Jury from the Israeli Union of Publishers and the Ministry of Education in 1994.

Carmi's first children's book, *Explosion on Ahalan Street*, was adapted for the Youth Theater founded by the Ministry of Education of Israel in 1987 but was later banned after some teachers protested. Another group of teachers then advocated including the book in the recommended list of readings of the educational system in Israel and won. The story was later adapted for television by the Israeli Public Channel. *A Lady Hippopotamus on the Roof* was among five books nominated for the Hadassa Children's Book Award in Israel in 2003. Carmi's books have been translated into 15 different languages around the world.

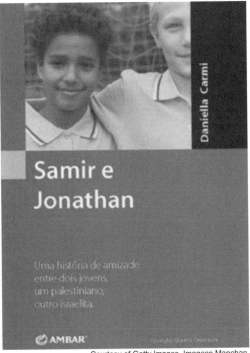

Courtesy of Getty Images, Imageon Manchan

SELECTED WORKS FOR CHILDREN: *Explosion on Ahalan Street*, 1986; *Samir and Yonatan*, 1994 (American edition, translated from the Hebrew by Yael Lotan, 2000); *To Be the Daughter of a Gipsy*, 1997; *A Lady Hippopotamus on the Roof*, 1999; *Bianka the Ghost*, 2001; *Journey on a Scooter*, 2003.

SELECTED WORKS FOR ADULTS: *Nitszan in the Snows*, 1984; *All the Time in the World for Picking Plums*, 1987; *Cleo's Night Life*, 1991; *To Free an Elephant*, 2001; *Summer Honey*, 2003.

" As a child I was always drawing. I found it much easier to express myself with art than with writing. Like so many little girls I was brought up on fairy tales and predictably became obsessed with princesses and ballerinas. My parents even told me I was a real princess of Denmark (where we lived briefly) but that they were taking care of me until I was 'trained.'

Nancy Carpenter

July 30, 1964–

"In elementary school, my mother was the art teacher in my school. Because she didn't want other students or teachers to think she was playing favorites, she always gave me an 'Average' grade. I tried for years to earn an 'Outstanding' on my report card but to no avail. Many years later my mother admitted that I was always one of the best artists in her class.

"I was a less than gifted gymnast in middle school, though I did manage to get on a competitive team. However, I loved to make flip-books of my balance beam routine (or what my ideal routine would look like). Those flip-books were instrumental in developing my eye for the human figure and its proportion. Plus, it made me interested in movement within a drawing.

"I took a 30-minute commuter train to and from central Philadelphia to attend the Creative and Performing Arts High School. We spent our days copying the techniques of the Renaissance masters, especially Caravaggio and his use of contrast. In college I majored in illustration. In my four years at Parsons School of Design I didn't take a single children's book illustration class. At Parsons I learned more about creative thinking than technique, which was invaluable. I imagined I would pursue editorial illustration for magazines and newspapers when I graduated.

Photo by Kevin Hogan

"After college I got my first job as a 'graphic reporter' for the Associated Press. At AP I learned to work on tight deadlines doing maps, charts, logos and the occasional illustration for the opening of football season or baseball Spring training. On Fridays I had to wake up super-early to pick up the weather forecast from 30 Rockefeller Plaza and bring it over to the AP office to create the weather map for the whole country. I overslept once and there was no weather map for the country that day. I'll never know why I wasn't fired on the spot.

"I happened into children's books by chance and, perhaps, dumb luck. Several years after graduating college, I was working sporadically as an editorial cartoonist/illustrator and was commissioned to draw just the background for a book cover. After I handed it in, the art department ruined the piece by spraying it with old fixative. I redid the painting (I'm always happy to be given more time to try to perfect a piece) and handed it in the next day. The editor was so pleased she offered me a children's book manuscript very shortly after. The book was *At Taylor's Place* by Sharon Phillips Denslow, and I've been busy illustrating books ever since.

"I've been lucky to get all my children's book training while on the job. My first book was an attempt to emulate Chris Van Allsburg. At that time, I didn't even know what a book dummy was and had to be told to break up the text into 32 pages. Since that first book, my work has changed and evolved enormously. Upon reflection, I realize I've been trying to unlearn my photorealistic training and capture a more intuitive style, in the way that children themselves approach art. I still love Chris Van Allsburg's work, but I know better than to attempt to draw like him. I gravitate toward manuscripts that allow me to try something new. Some of my influences now are Shel Silverstein, Roz Chast and Quentin Blake for their wonderful humor and Barbara Cooney for her elegant painting.

"Having children has changed the way I approach illustrating books, too. I read so many books to my daughter (my son is not yet old enough to voice opinions) and I not only see books through her eyes but I see the importance of keeping the adult reader interested. I am far more focused on the continuity of a book and the character than on technique or style. I want the reader to return to the story many times without getting tired. Plus, I know now how much children want to find hidden treasures within the picture and I try to incorporate that as often as possible.

"Once I was reading Barbara Cooney's *Hattie and the Wild Waves* to my daughter. She asked, 'Mommy, did you illustrate this book?' 'No,' I replied. And she said, 'But I can tell people you did, okay?' Works for me."

"Those flip-books were instrumental in developing my eye for the human figure and its proportion. Plus, it made me interested in movement within a drawing."

CS CS CS

Born in Harrisburg, Pennsylvania, Nancy Carpenter spent two years of her childhood traveling all over Europe. Her father had a teaching fellowship in Denmark and the family traveled extensively during that time, so Nancy was exposed to Renaissance art at an early age. Her career in illustrating children's books has echoed the influence of art throughout her life, as well as an interest in history and global issues.

Several of her books have been named *School Library Journal* Best Books, including *Sitti's Secrets*. For this story by Naomi Shihab Nye, Carpenter created mixed-media paintings that reflect the color and light of the desert as a young Arab-

American girl journeys halfway around the world to visit her Palestinian grandmother. Winner of a Jane Addams Children's Book Award, this title was also a Notable Social Studies Trade Book, as was *Washing the Willow Tree Loon*, Jacqueline Briggs Martin's story about the care given to damaged birds after an oil spill. Carpenter's illustrations for this environmentally themed book show just enough detail for readers to understand the process of reclaiming the birds while feeling a part of the larger bayside community.

In *Apples to Oregon: Being the (Slightly) True Narrative of How a Brave Pioneer Father Brought Apples, Peaches, Pears, Plums, Grapes, and Cherries (and Children) Across the Plains*, Deborah Hopkinson's upbeat, tongue-in-cheek narrative is perfectly matched by Carpenter's exuberant pictures, tracing a long, challenging journey of pioneers in the 19th century and loosely based on a factual account. Named an ALA Notable Children's Book, *Apples to Oregon* was also a *School Library Journal* Best Book and won a Golden Kite Award for picture book text and well as a Western Writers of America Spur Award. Carpenter had earlier paired with writer Deborah Hopkinson for a humorous picture book story about Fannie Farmer, the domestic artist of cookbook fame in *Fannie in the Kitchen*, a *Parenting* Magazine Best of the Year. To create her evocative period illustrations for this title, the artist combined 19th century etchings and engravings with her own pen-and-ink and watercolor illustrations, blending them into an effective representation of Farmer's world.

Illustrating Linda Arms White's chronicle of the women's suffrage advocate Esther Morris in *I Could Do That!*, Carpenter again enlivened a larger-than-life character with her vibrant illustrations. Morris was instrumental in obtaining the right to vote for women in Wyoming, the first state to pass such a law, and became the first woman in the country to hold public office. Paying attention to period details as well as the strength of Morris's character, Carpenter does not neglect humorous touches that are in keeping with the text. *I Could Do That!* won a Christopher Award in the category for ages 6–8, an award that had also been won by Carpenter's earlier book, *Little Bear's Little Boat* with text by Eve Bunting. Her illustrations are spare and sweet for this gentle story of a childlike bear letting go of something he has outgrown.

Carpenter's humor and historically vibrant folk art work equally well with tall tales. *Loud Emily*, a rollicking story by Alexis O'Neill, is set in a whaling village. Emily refuses all

Courtesy of Atheneum Books for Young Readers

attempts to stifle her boisterous voice, and the child ends up calling orders to the sailors on a whaling ship. With endpapers that depict sea chanteys and scrimshaw and interior backdrops of embroidery cloth behind the illustrations, Carpenter's art enhances this outlandish story that was named a *School Library Journal* Best of the Year. She is just as adept at illustrating quiet contemporary stories of growth in character and overcoming fear, as she exhibited in Karen Hesse's *Lester's Dog*, a *School Library Journal* Best Book and a Notable Social Studies Trade Book.

Though she has used a wide variety of styles in the body of her work, Carpenter's signature style seems to be high-spirited mixed-media illustrations, incorporating photographic objects into her painting, as she does in such recent titles as *17 Things I'm Not Allowed To Do Anymore*, by Jenny Offill, and *M is for Mischief: An A to Z of Naughty Children*, with text by Linda Ashman.

Nancy Carpenter lives with her husband, Kevin, and their two children in Brooklyn, New York.

SELECTED WORKS ILLUSTRATED: *At Taylor's Place*, by Sharon Phillips Denslow, 1990; *Riding with Aunt Lucy*, by Sharon Phillips Denslow, 1991; *Treasure in the Stream: The Story of a Gold Rush Girl*, by Dorothy and Thomas Hoobler and Carey-Greengerg

Associates, 1991; *Our Mountain: As Told by Jimmy and Corey Allder*, by Ellen Harvey Showell, 1991; *Masai and I*, by Virginia Kroll, 1992; *Bus Riders*, by Sharon Phillips Denslow, 1993; *Lester's Dog*, by Karen Hesse, 1993; *Sitti's Secrets*, by Naomi Shihab Nye, 1994; *Washing the Willow Tree Loon*, by Jacqueline Briggs Martin, 1995; *Sing Noel: Christmas Carols*, edited by Jane Yolen, 1996; *Only a Star*, by Margery Facklam, 1996; *A Sister's Wish*, by Kate Jacobs, 1996; *Can You Dance, Dalila?*, by Virginia Kroll, 1996; *The Tree That Came to Stay*, by Anna Quindlen, 1997; *Twinnies*, by Eve Bunting, 1997; *Loud Emily*, by Alexis O'Neill, 1998; *Someone's Coming to Our House*, by Kathi Appelt, 1999; *Twister*, by Darleen Bailey Beard, 1999; *A Picnic in October*, by Eve Bunting, 1999; *Brooklyn, Bugsy, and Me*, by Lynea Bowdish, 2000; *If You Ever Get Lost: The Adventures of Julia and Evan*, by Barbara Ann Porte, 2000; *Fannie in the Kitchen: The Whole Story from Soup to Nuts of How Fannie Farmer Invented Recipes with Precise Measurements*, by Deborah Hopkinson, 2001; *A Far-Fetched Story*, by Karin Cates, 2002; *Little Bear's Little Boat*, by Eve Bunting, 2003; *Abe Lincoln: The Boy Who Loved Books*, by Kay Winters, 2003; *Baby Radar*, by Naomi Shihab Nye, 2003; *Apples to Oregon: Being the (Slightly) True Narrative of How a Brave Pioneer Father Brought Apples, Peaches, Pears, Plums, Grapes, and Cherries (and Children) Across the Plains*, by Deborah Hopkinson, 2004; *The Secret Garden*, by Frances Hodgson Burnett, adapted by James Howe, 2005; *I Could Do That!: Esther Morris Gets Women the Vote*, by Linda Arms White, 2005; *17 Things I'm Not Allowed To Do Anymore*, by Jenny Offill, 2006; *M is for Mischief: An A to Z of Naughty Children*, by Linda Ashman, 2008.

SUGGESTED READING: Online—Bean, Joy, "Children's Bookshelf Talks with Nancy Carpenter," November 11, 2006, at www.publishersweekly.com/article/CA6391923.html

---

Mary Casanova

February 2, 1957–

"I grew up in a family of benevolent neglect. As one of ten children, my childhood bustled with the activity and chatter of two sisters and seven brothers, and we raised pets of every kind, from goats to guinea pigs. In the outskirts of St. Paul, Minnesota, my backyard was Lake Johanna, where I sailed, water-skied and played tag off the pontoon in the summers; and in the winters, I skated over new ice as sunfish darted beneath my blades, and played hockey with my brothers on our homemade ice rink. Growing up, animals and the outdoors called to me more loudly than books: I rode my appaloosa, Keema, and explored fields and woods miles from home. I breathed in the pine-scented air at our cabin in northern Minnesota and felt the loon's haunting song in my bones. My mother taught me to pay attention to life's simple gifts, from the elegant interior of a tulip to the miracle of witnessing a beetle climb from the lake to the dock, only to crawl from its nymph form as a dragonfly, wet wings slowly unfurling in the sun and eventually taking flight. My father was an incredible storyteller, filling his jokes and tales with specific details, emotion, and drama, always entertaining his audiences, whether within the family or in the business world. My parents loved people and always sought to bring out the best in anyone they met.

"Though I enjoyed school and was a good student, I struggled to finish many of the books I eagerly brought home from the library. My mind wandered easily; I had trouble sitting still and concentrating on the words. All too often I found myself back outside—where I could always find adventure—without finishing a book. When that happened, I felt I harbored a shameful secret, since many of my friends could finish every book they picked up. That's why I am now passionate about writing books that kids can't put down. I don't want kids to feel like a failure when they pick up one of

Photo by Nagurski Studio

my stories. Whether they're a strong reader or a struggling reader, I hope to hook their interest in the first pages and pull them in like a fish on a line, all the way through to the last page. I'm honored if anyone picks up one of my books; it's my responsibility to earn their interest, page by page. When one reader tells me that they love one of my books, that's the highest honor and award I could ever hope for.

"That said, I write first for myself. I cannot write a story without believing that it's something worth exploring. I write to better understand things that trouble me, whether it's a girl's need to find a voice (*Stealing Thunder*) or struggling to understand mob behavior (*Riot* and, in part, *Curse of a Winter Moon*). When I've taken on books for American Girl (*Cecile: Gates of Gold* and *Jess: Girl of the Year*), I must travel to the places I write about and experience the setting through my senses before I write about it. Even in books that I write seemingly just for fun (*One-Dog Canoe*), there's always something I'm exploring at a deeper level, like the need to set boundaries in life.

"Ever since I discovered the power and magic of words in high school, I've wanted to be an author. Now that I am, I find it to be the greatest adventure possible. Ideas come from a limitless well of creativity, and there's something of the Divine in drawing from that source and sharing what comes with others. Writing is hard work, as is being on the road and speaking at schools and conferences, but I wouldn't trade it for anything. I love what I do. I'm blessed to live out my dream and eager to write the next story that calls my name."

03   03   03

Mary Casanova is a versatile author whose stories range from picture books to historical novels. Many of her books stem from her life on the Minnesota-Canadian border; yet some have taken her as far away as France and Norway for research. Whatever the setting for her books, Casanova strives to write stories that are compelling to read.

Born Mary Gazelka in Duluth, Minnesota, she grew up in a bustling camp-like atmosphere and found that writing became her voice in a large, boisterous family life where it was often hard to be heard. She graduated from the University of Minnesota in 1981. Married to Charles Casanova, she has two grown children, Kate and Eric, who were her first critics when she began to publish for children.

Her first novel, *Moose Tracks*, in which a boy tries to save a young moose from poachers, was a Children's Book-of-the-Month Club selection and has appeared on many state award master lists. *Riot*, a Junior Library Guild Selection and an ALA Quick Pick for Young Adult Reluctant Readers, depicts the tensions that develop when a non-union company displaces union workers in a small town. The events in *Riot* were based on an actual situation in the author's hometown in northern Minnesota. Casanova's concern for animals and memories of riding her own horse as a young girl combined to create a compelling story in *Stealing Thunder*, about a girl's love for a horse and her efforts to save him from an abusive owner.

In 2001 Casanova was a two-time winner of the Minnesota Book Award. In the category for older readers, the winner was *Curse of a Winter Moon*—a riveting story of danger and intrigue in 16th century France. *The Hunter*, a picture book story, won in the category for younger readers. Casanova was intrigued by the Chinese folk tale of Hai Li Bu, the hunter, when she first heard it from a Chinese exchange student who stayed with her family. Her retelling of the tale, with illustrations by Ed Young, was also named an ALA Notable Children's Book, won a Parent's Choice Gold Award, and received an Aesop Accolade from the Children's Folklore Section of the American Folklore Society. Another of her historical novels, *Cécile: Gates of Gold*, chronicles the life of a 17th century girl who serves at the opulent court of Louis XIV at Versailles. It won a National Parenting Publications Honor Award.

Mary Casanova makes her home in a 100-year-old house on Rainy Lake, in Minnesota, with her husband, Charles, and their two "above average" dogs.

Courtesy of Atheneum/Simon & Schuster

SELECTED WORKS: *Moose Tracks*, 1995; *Riot*, 1996; *Wolf Shadows*, 1997; *Stealing Thunder*, 1998; *The Hunter*, illus. by Ed Young, 2000; *Curse of a Winter Moon*, 2000; *One-Dog Canoe*, illus. by Ard Hoyt, 2002; *Cécile: Gates of Gold* (Girls of Many Lands series), 2002; *When Eagles Fall*, 2003; *Trouble in Pembrook* (Dog Watch series), illus. by Omar Rayyan, 2006; *Dog-napped!* (Dog Watch series), illus. by Omar Rayyan, 2006; *Danger at Snow Hill* (Dog Watch series), illus. by Omar Rayyan, 2006; *Some Dog!*, illus. by Ard Hoyt, 2007; *The Klipfish Code*, 2007.

SUGGESTED READING: *Something About the Author*, vol. 136, 2003; Casanova, Mary, *Mary Casanova and YOU*, 2006.

WEB SITE: www.marycasanova.com

"As long as I can remember, watching someone create a drawing or a doodle was a magical experience for me. My first inspiration to becoming an artist was my mother. I used to sit next to her as she did funny drawings of men with pompadour hairdos. As a five your old, I truly felt she was the best artist in the world. I eventually realized that she wasn't very artistically talented, but watching her do those drawings truly amazed and inspired me.

Robert Casilla

April 16, 1959–

"As the new kid in my second grade class, I remember doing a drawing of two birds with colored chalk on construction paper during art. As my teacher walked by she noticed my drawing, then told the whole class: 'We have an artist in the class!'

"I lived in Puerto Rico for a few months when I was in fourth grade. I really loved living in Puerto Rico where I could go out and play all day. But we had to move back to New Jersey because I was not doing well in school. I didn't speak much Spanish and the teacher told my mother that they were going to demote me to 3rd grade. So we ended back in Jersey City where the neighborhood was not very safe. Since I couldn't go out to play I would stay home and draw all the time.

"In sixth grade I had a teacher named Ms. Ping (yes, her name was really Ms. Ping). Ms. Ping was an aspiring artist. One day she told me that when I grew up I was going to be an artist. She gave me a box of Rembrandt pastels and told me to keep drawing at home. I put those pastels to good use. I'd bring in one or two drawings every week to show her. Thanks to Ms. Ping and all of my teachers I realized that I was pretty good at art.

"As a teenager in high school I would spend half of my school day in the art department. I would take my art class and then come back during lunch and study hall periods. Ms. Hughes, my high school art teacher, asked me during my junior year about my plans after graduation. I told her that I had spoken to a recruiter and that I was considering joining the Air Force. Ms. Hughes then told me that I should really go

Photo by Robert Casilla, Jr.

to college to major in art. Teachers throughout elementary school and high school had always steered me towards an art career.

"After high school I attended Kean College in Elizabeth, New Jersey where I majored in art. One day I met a graduate of the School of Visual Arts; he was working as a graphic artist where a friend of mine worked. I showed him my work and he suggested that I transfer to the School of Visual Arts. He made a call to the school and had them mail me a catalog and an application. I continued to work on improving my portfolio, because I heard it was very difficult to get accepted into SVA. On the day of my interview at SVA I was very nervous, but when the person viewing my portfolio told me that I was really going to like SVA, my nerves felt more at ease.

"Going to SVA was a great experience. I couldn't believe how talented most of the students were. I was always the best artist in my class growing up, but SVA was a different world and very challenging. I ended up graduating in 1982 near the top of my class, and then I got married. After graduation I worked for a year at Garan Inc. where I designed tee-shirt graphics licensed for Major League Baseball, the NFL, the NBA, and others. Then I went on to work as a graphic artist for Avon and numerous other catalog companies. In 1984 with the support of my wife, I went on to pursue a full-time career as an illustrator. I had a big heavy portfolio that I would carry around to show to art directors for magazines, book publishers and newspapers.

"My first illustration job was with *Scholastic Scope* magazine. Other magazines that I worked with were *Black Enterprise* and *Video Review*; I also did illustrations for the *New York Times* and *New York Daily News*. My first job in book publishing was a cover illustration for a book titled *One Way to Ansonia* for a small publisher called Bradbury Press. That was my foot in the door of book publishing. As a young illustrator I took my portfolio to every place I could find that needed illustrations, but I had never targeted a career as a children's book illustrator.

"Somehow I simultaneously caught the attention of two publishers, Holiday House and Bradbury Press, who offered me my first books. My first book with Holiday House, *Martin Luther King, Jr.: Free at Last*, written by David Adler, kicked off my career with a starred review from *Booklist*. *The Train Trip to Lu Lu's*, by Elizabeth F. Howard, which was published by Bradbury Press, ended up as a *Reading Rainbow* book.

"Getting the first two book assignments was a great learning experience. Regardless of the subject matter, a lot of things go into illustrating a children's book. I make many preliminary thumbnail sketches and do a lot of planning. Research is a very important part of illustrating children's books. When I'm illustrating a biography, I read as much as I can find about that person. I like to view as many photographs of the person as possible, which help me in capturing the likeness and also help me feel closer to the person who I'm illustrating.

"In fiction books there is more freedom to be creative. I can rely sometimes on my own experiences when coming up with the images for a story. My wife Carmen, my son Rob Jr., and my daughter Emily and their friends often work as models, and

> "As a teenager in high school I would spend half of my school day in the art department. I would take my art class and then come back during lunch and study hall periods."

sometimes *I* even model for my illustrations. You can see me as old Hoonch, the mean school bus driver in *First Day in Grapes*, written by L. King Pérez. I'm also the train conductor in *The Train to Lulu's* by Elizabeth Fitzgerald Howard and I appear in *The Little Painter of Sabana Grande* by Patricia Markun.

"I work at home in my studio in New Fairfield, Connecticut. I spend a lot of time there because illustrating a children's book can take 4 to 6 months. I'm often working on several jobs at the same time. I visit many schools in the New York area and in other states. I also teach art once a week to gifted young inner city artists from the Bronx. The children I teach range from sixth grade to twelfth grade. I work with Neil Waldman, a renowned illustrator, in sponsorship for the Children's Aid Society. Our goal is for each student to attain art skills and financial assistance to attend college or art schools to pursue an art career. It's really rewarding for me to teach aspiring young artists."

CB CB CB

Robert Casilla was born in Jersey City, New Jersey, the son of parents from Puerto Rico. Although he grew up in New Jersey, he spent part of his fourth grade year in Puerto Rico where he experienced his cultural heritage firsthand. Since becoming a full-time illustrator, he has created art for over 25 children's books of many kinds, both fiction and nonfiction, and received many awards for his work. He has also designed postage stamps for nations such as Grenada, Micronesia, and Sierra Leone.

Casilla has created well-researched and evocative illustrations for many of David A. Adler's *Picture Book of . . .* series of biographies for primary grade readers, including books on such diverse subjects as Jesse Owens, Rosa Parks, John F. Kennedy, and Simón Bolívar. The books he illustrated in that series about Eleanor Roosevelt and Martin Luther King, Jr. were named Notable Trade Books in the Field of Social Studies. These short profiles are often the first encounter young children have with the lives of famous people, and Casilla's art helps them to visualize the subjects and their backgrounds.

A theme that runs through many of Casilla's books is overcoming obstacles to follow a dream. *The Little Painter of Sabana Grande*, by Patricia M. Markun, is based on a true story of a boy in Panama who wants to create art. He makes his paints from natural materials, but he has no paper on which to draw, so he paints murals on the white walls of his house. This book was a *Reading Rainbow* selection and a commended title for the

Américas Award. It also won the Washington Irving Award in Westchester County, New York. *The Dream on Blanca's Wall/El Sueño Pegado en la Pared de Blanca*, by Jane Medina, features a young girl who longs to become a teacher, even as she struggles with the hardships of life in her barrio. This book was also commended for the Américas Award.

Another theme that is prevalent in Casilla's illustration work is the importance of family. In *Daddy Poems*, selected by John Micklos, Jr., Casilla's art finds just the right way to show the many ways that children relate to their fathers and to express the joy in the father-child bond. This Children's Choice title echoes the subject of an earlier book illustrated by Casilla, Myra Cohn Livingston's *Poems for Fathers*. In *The Legend of Mexicatl*, by Jo Harper, it is the legendary character's mother who gives him the key to learning the humility and compassion necessary to be a great leader of his people, the original Aztecs of Mexico. Cited as a Notable Social Studies Trade Book, *Jalapeño Bagels*, written by Natasha Wing, is a contemporary story about a boy named Pablo who brings a treat to his school's International Day that represents both his parents' cultures.

Courtesy of Lee & Low Books

In 2004 Casilla won a Pura Belpré Illustrator Honor award for his work in L. King Pérez's story, *First Day in Grapes*, about a migrant family. Chico must use his math skills in a face-off with bullies while adjusting to life in a new school. This insightful look at the plight of migrant kids, and any children who have had to move frequently and encounter new situations, was cited as a Notable Book by *Smithsonian* Magazine and named to CCBC's Choices list. Casilla's watercolor, pastel, and colored pencil illustrations perfectly convey Chico's emotions and the background of southern California.

Many of Robert Casilla's books have been issued in Spanish editions and several are bilingual. He lives in New Fairfield, Connecticut, with his wife and two children, three cats, and a feisty little shih tzu dog.

SELECTED WORKS ILLUSTRATED: *Martin Luther King, Jr.: Free at Last*, by David A. Adler, 1986; *The Train to Lulu's*, by Elizabeth

Fitzgerald Howard, 1988; *A Picture Book of Martin Luther King, Jr.*, by David A. Adler, 1989; *Jackie Robinson: He Was First*, by David A. Adler, 1989; *Poems for Fathers*, by Myra Cohn Livingston, 1989; *A Picture Book of John F. Kennedy*, by David A. Adler, 1991; *A Picture Book of Jesse Owens*, by David A. Adler, 1992; *A Picture Book of Simón Bolívar*, by David A. Adler, 1992; *The Little Painter of Sabana Grande*, by Patricia M. Markun, 1993; *The Pool Party*, by Gary Soto, 1993; *A Picture Book of Rosa Parks*, by David A. Adler, 1993; *A Picture Book of Jackie Robinson*, by David A. Adler, 1994; *Rodeo Day*, by Jonelle Toriseva, 1994; *Con Mi Hermano: With My Brother*, by Eileen Roe, 1994; *Boys at Work*, by Gary Soto, 1995; *Jalapeño Bagels*, by Natasha Wing, 1996; *The Good Samaritan*, by Jane Q. Saxton, 1996; *A Picture Book of Thurgood Marshall*, by David A. Adler, 1997; *A Picture Book of Eleanor Roosevelt*, by David A. Adler, 1997; *The Legend of Mexicatl*, by Jo Harper, 1998; *Daddy Poems*, sel. by John Micklos, Jr., 2000; *First Day in Grapes*, by L. King Pérez, 2002; *Mama Had to Work on Christmas*, by Carolyn Marsden, 2003; *The Dream on Blanca's Wall/El Sueño Pegado en la Pared de Blanca: Poems in English and Spanish/Poemas en Ingles y Español*, by Jane Medina, 2004; *Midnight Forests: A Story of Gifford Pinchot and Our National Forests*, by Gary Hines, 2005.

SUGGESTED READING: *Something About the Author*, vol. 146, 2004.

WEB SITE: www.robertcasilla.com

Lauren Child

November 29, 1967–

The daughter of two teachers, Lauren Child spent some time in the school where her father taught art and she attributes some of her inspiration to his teaching talents. She grew up in Marlborough, Wiltshire, the middle child of three sisters, and studied at Manchester Polytechnic and The City and Guilds (now called London College of Art), but she left school early to work in a variety of jobs.

Although she wanted to illustrate for children, she was unsure how to go about it, so Child and an actor friend started their own company called Chandeliers for the People. They designed and produced exotic lampshades. But a business manager suggested she write a children's picture book, and the result was *Clarice Bean, That's Me!* The exuberant and witty heroine is a middle child who describes the relationships within her large family, situations that were partly inspired by Child's own family. It took five years to be published, but the results were worth the wait when *Clarice Bean, That's Me!* won the Nestlé Prize Bronze Award and the Norfolk Children's Book Award, and was named a Highly Commended Title for the Kate Greenaway Medal. Child's career in children's books was launched. Eventually a few of the lampshades from her first business found their way into the background of her later books.

Drawing on family life in the 21st century and her lifelong love of cartoons, Child uses a computer for much of her work, combining bold black lines, flat colors, and bits and pieces of the world around her—including photographs and magazine clippings, scraps of wallpaper and linoleum—to create kaleidoscopic collages upon which she superimposes her pencil-drawn figures. She then finishes the work with traditional watercolors. Each of the Clarice Bean characters has a unique typeface to further distinguish individual voices. Child's imaginative artwork combined with very funny stories proved to be a hit with British and American children alike.

Courtesy of Hyperion Books

Child's first novel about Clarice had her picture-book heroine solving a school mystery in *Utterly Me, Clarice Bean*, which won the Literacy Association's WOW Award. From this success, a whole series of chapter books was born. The second title, *Clarice Bean Spells Trouble*, about trying to be a good friend to a troubled friend, was shortlisted for the W.H. Smith Book Award, the British Children's Book Award, the Hounslow Book Award, the Hillingdon Primary Book Award, and the Red House Children's Book Award. Clarice finds herself embroiled in an environmental protest that she doesn't fully understand in the wacky *What Planet Are You From, Clarice Bean?*—a title that won the Nestlé Prize Bronze Award and the Nestlé Kids' Club Network Special Award.

Beware of the Storybook Wolves also won the Nestlé Prize Bronze Award and was shortlisted for the Kate Greenaway Medal. And in 2000, Child won the Greenaway Medal with *I Will Not Ever Never Eat a Tomato*. A story about an imaginative brother who gets his little sister to eat foods she doesn't want to taste, the book was re-titled in the U. S. as *I Will Never Not Ever Eat a Tomato* and won the California Young Reader's Medal. The characters of Charlie and Lola, who made their first appearance in this book, went on to star in two animated television series for the British Broadcasting Corporation (BBC) that later aired on the Disney Channel in the U.S. and also on Canadian television. A fussy eater herself, Child identifies with the picky Lola. She continues to use her signature collage style and in the "Charlie and Lola" books, Lola wears pajamas made from the fabric of a baby nightdress Child's mother once made for her. The patient Charlie and irrepressible Lola are featured in *I Am Not Sleepy and I Will Not Go to Bed*, which was shortlisted for the Children's British Book Award, and *I Am Too Absolutely Small for School*, which was shortlisted for the Stockport Book Award, among other honors.

Because of their popularity, Charlie and Lola can now be found on birthday cards and lunch boxes, and in spin-off books based on television scripts written by others (although the book adaptations bear Child's name as the characters' creator). Child has produced books in many formats, from picture books to chapter books to pop-up books to board books to lift-the-flap and sticker activity books.

> *Child freely admits to eavesdropping on conversations to help set the tone for the hilarious dialogue that is a trademark of her books.*

That Pesky Rat was inspired when, for several months, Child was without her own place to live and spent her time house-sitting and making long visits to friends. Both funny and touching, this story features a street rat seeking a loving owner and a permanent home. This book won the Nestlé Children's Book Gold Award and Nestlé Kids Club Network Award and was named a Kate Greenaway Medal Highly Commended Title. Two of Child's other titles were shortlisted for the Kate Greenaway Medal: *Who's Afraid of the Big Bad Book?* and *Hubert Horatio Bartle Bobton-Trent*. The former was also included on the 2004 Honor List of the International Board on Books for Young People (IBBY).

Child freely admits to eavesdropping on conversations to help set the tone for the hilarious dialogue that is a trademark of her books. A great fan of children's television, Child also loves dollhouses, which inspired her retelling of Hans Christian Andersen's classic story, *The Princess and the Pea*. She enjoys collecting Barbie dolls and *Star Wars* memorabilia. Living in North London, she has the butterfly motif from her books on her doorbell.

SELECTED WORKS ILLUSTRATED: *Addy the Baddy*, by Margaret Joy, 1993; *The Complete Poetical Works of Phoebe Flood*, 1997; *Dan's Angel: A Detective's Guide to the Language of Painting*, by Alexander Sturgis, 2002; *You Must Be Joking, Jimmy*, by Jenny Oldfield, 2002; *Dream On, Daisy!*, by Jenny Oldfield, 2003; *Just You Wait, Winona*, by Jenny Oldfield, 2003; *Not Now, Nathan*, by Jenny Oldfield, 2003; *What's the Matter, Maya?*, by Jenny Oldfield, 2003; *You're a Disgrace, Daisy*, by Jenny Oldfield, 2003; *I'd Like a Little Word, Leonie!*, by Jenny Oldfield, 2003; *Pippi Longstocking*, by Astrid Lindgren, 2007.

SELECTED WORKS WRITTEN AND ILLUSTRATED: *Clarice Bean, That's Me!*, 1999; *I Want a Pet!*, 1999; *I Will Not Ever Never Eat a Tomato*, 2000 (U.S. ed.: *I Will Never Not Ever Eat a Tomato*, 2000); *My Uncle Is a Hunkle, Says Clarice Bean*, 2000; *Beware of the Storybook Wolves*, 2000; *I Am Not Sleepy and I Will Not Go to Bed*, 2001; *Clarice Bean, Guess Who's Babysitting*, 2001; *My Dream Bed*, 2001; *What Planet Are You From, Clarice Bean?*, 2001; *That Pesky Rat*, 2002; *Utterly Me, Clarice Bean*, 2002; *Who's Afraid of the Big Bad Book?*, 2002; *I Am Too Absolutely Small for School*, 2003; *Hubert Horatio Bartle Bobton-Trent*, 2005; *Clarice Bean Spells Trouble*, 2005; *But, Excuse Me, That Is My Book*, 2006; *I Absolutely Must Do Colouring-in Now or Drawing or Sticking*, 2006 (U.S. ed.: *I Absolutely Must Do Coloring Now or Painting or Drawing*, 2006); *My Wobbly Tooth Must Not Ever Never Fall Out*, 2006; *Whoops! But It Wasn't Me*, 2006; *We Honestly Can Look After Your Dog*, 2005; *I've Won, No I've Won, No I've Won*, 2006; *Snow Is My Favorite and My Best*, 2006; *The Princess and the Pea*, adapt. from Hans Christian Andersen, 2006; *Cla-*

Courtesy of Candlewick Press

rice Bean, Don't Look Now, 2007; *Boo! Made You Jump!* 2007; *Charlie and Lola's Numbers*, 2007; *Charlie and Lola: Say Cheese!* 2007; *I'm Really Ever So Not Well*, 2007; *My Very Busy Sticker Stories*, 2007; *This Is Actually My Party*, 2007; *Charlie and Lola's Opposites*, 2007; *My Picnic Sticker Stories*, 2007; *Sizzles Is Completely Not There*, 2007; *You Can Be My Friend*, 2007; *I Completely Must Do Drawing Now and Painting and Coloring*, 2007; *Clarice Bean, Don't Look Now*, 2007.

SUGGESTED READING: *Something About the Author*, vol. 183, 2008. Online—"The World of Lauren Child, Children's Author,"

Telegraph.co.uk, at www.telegraph.co.uk/arts/main.jhtml?xml=/arts/2007/10/27/sm_laurenchild.xml; The Magic Pencil exhibit, at www.magicpencil.britishcouncil.org/artists/child

WEB SITES: www.milkmonitor.com
www.charlieandlola.com

Photo by Tom Collicott

**Margaret
Chodos-Irvine**

October 7, 1961–

"When I was a child, if anyone asked me 'Who taught you how to draw so well?' I always gave the credit to my babysitter. She was the one who first pointed out that people don't really have sticks for arms—two lines represent an arm much more accurately, one line for each side. That is my first recollection of learning to draw.

"Besides having an insightful babysitter, I was lucky that my parents were both involved in the arts. My mother loved to draw and paint, and began to study art seriously after I was in school and my brother was in college. My mother and I would have drawing sessions together; we'd draw a still life, or my father, or our dog, or each other. She gave me tips for improving my drawing technique. I still hear her instructive voice when I shade pencil with my fingertip.

"My father taught ceramics at a community college. At the end of each school year he would clean out the student lockers and come home with a big box of *real* art supplies: oil pastels, paints, brilliant bottles of colored inks, all sorts of treasures that the art students had left behind. They were all for me. I didn't know how to use many of them, but I had fun experimenting, and often made a big mess. The only supply I ever ran out of was paper.

"My father had summers off, so we traveled abroad almost every year. This was a wonderful and enlightening part of my young life, but it also meant I spent long stretches of time without my friends or my dog to play with, and no TV (at least not in English). So along with doing untidy art projects, I read a lot—and dreamed about how I would illustrate my favorite stories.

"It wasn't until college that I figured out that I really was an illustrator. I started with anthropology as my major, but soon added art as a second major. I discovered printmaking then and felt I'd found my heart's medium; printmaking offers plenty of room for experimenting, and it is satisfyingly messy. I made prints representing mythological characters, personal histories, and anthropological theories. It soon became obvious to me that I liked communicating stories and ideas through my work—that I was an illustrator.

"My first professional illustration job was for Ursula K. Le Guin's book *Always Coming Home*, which I completed while I was still in college. I went on to pursue commercial art as a career, my images adorning everything from book covers to water bottles. Now I have children, and illustrating children's books is what I enjoy most. I have been fortunate to illustrate works by many wonderful authors. I also like to illustrate my own writing. Observing my daughters and their friends has provided the inspiration for my stories.

"I continue to use printmaking to illustrate my children's books. My methods evolved from a desire to maximize color, texture, and shape, and to explore what I already knew about printmaking. I use an etching press to transfer images from inked surfaces onto paper. Anything I can ink up and run through my press becomes a candidate for an element in one of my images. My art supplies are collected from all sorts of odd places: rummage sales, fabric shops, hardware stores, my mother-in-law's basement. I am happiest when I have something new to play with.

"So here I am, once again playing with art supplies, learning new techniques, and dreaming up how to illustrate my favorite stories. And I still make a big mess."

"I discovered printmaking then and felt I'd found my heart's medium; printmaking offers plenty of room for experimenting, and it is satisfyingly messy."

ଔ   ଔ   ଔ

Margaret Chodos-Irvine was born in Whittier, California, and raised on the West Coast. She attended the University of Oregon in Eugene, graduating with a B.A. in both anthropology and art in 1986. She stayed on in Eugene after college, working in the restaurant business and then as an assistant to a graphic designer. For years she was employed as a commercial artist before entering the field of children's books.

Chodos-Irvine uses a unique style of relief printing from mixed media to illustrate her picture books. The process involves a combination of methods borrowed from various printmaking techniques, including relief printing, chine colle, collography, and monotyping. Cutting shapes out of various flat materials such as poster board, vinyl, plastic lace, and textured wallpaper, she colors them up with relief inks, and then, using a press, transfers the inks to printmaking paper. Each print runs through the press many times to build up layers of colors and textures, producing a multi-dimensional page that conveys movement and feeling.

In an inventive approach for her first book—*Buzz*—Chodos-Irvine created an image of a bee for the cover. The bee leads the reader's eye from the front jacket into the book and through to the end of Janet Wong's tale about a small boy's delight in a busy morning and the noises involved in getting up and starting his day. Named a *School Library Journal* Best Book of the Year, *Buzz* became the first of several collaborations with author Janet S. Wong. It was followed by *Apple Pie Fourth of July*, in which a first generation Chinese-American girl fears that her parents won't understand that Americans do not eat Chinese food on such a quintessentially American holiday. For this work, which won an Asian/Pacific American award for Literature and was named a *Booklist* Editors' Choice, the artist left a white edge around many images, highlighting each item as well as each character's significance in a satisfying story about blending cultures.

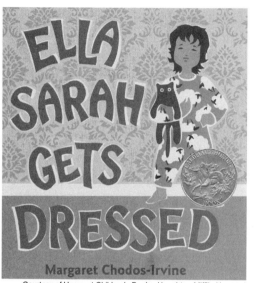

Courtesy of Harcourt Children's Books, Houghton Mifflin Harcourt

Hide & Seek grew out of a conversation between Wong and Chodos-Irvine. The illustrator mentioned that she wanted to do a concept book and the author started thinking about activities that naturally involved children in counting. In the finished book, Chodos-Irvine's large, bright shapes, interestingly askew, carry and extend the tale with an additional game of item and color matching that young readers enjoy solving.

For *Hello, Arctic!* by Theodore Taylor, which won an Oppenheim Toy Portfolio Gold Award, Chodos-Irvine produced a sparkling landscape of blues and whites with lively textured animals. She used a lighter, more open composition to illustrate *My House Is Singing*, a book of poetry for young children by Betsy Rosenthal.

Chodos-Irvine's first foray into both writing and illustrating, *Ella Sarah Gets Dressed*, won a Caldecott Honor Medal and was an ALA Notable Children's Book. Based on the author's experience with her older daughter, this book presents an independent toddler who insists on wearing exactly what she wants in spite of her family's suggestions. A joyful combination of yellows, oranges, greens, pinks, blues, and purples evoke Ella Sarah's outlandish outfits, which are topped off with a red hat, and how right they are for her.

In *Best Best Friends*, which was named an ALA Notable Children's Book, Chodos-Irvine produced a warm, realistic tale of pre-school friendship, conflict, and reconciliation, depicting her characters' emotions through color and body language as well as simple, straightforward text. Always in tune with the inner world of the child, Chodos-Irvine employed color, form, line, and texture to convey a wealth of feeling.

Married with two daughters, Chodos-Irvine lives in Seattle, Washington. For her own enjoyment, she is usually involved in some kind of craft activity—sewing, knitting, hammering tin, making brass and copper jewelry, to name a few. She occasionally teaches classes and workshops in printmaking.

SELECTED WORK WRITTEN AND ILLUSTRATED: *Ella Sarah Gets Dressed*, 2003; *Best Best Friends*, 2006.

SELECTED WORK ILLUSTRATED: *Buzz*, by Janet S. Wong, 2000; *Apple Pie Fourth of July*, by Janet S. Wong, 2002; *Hello Arctic!* By Theodore Taylor, 2002; *My House Is Singing*, by Betsy R. Rosenthal, 2004; *Hide & Seek*, by Janet S. Wong, 2005.

SUGGESTED READING: Online—Interviews with Janet S. Wong and Margaret Chodos-Irvine, at www.harcourtbooks.com/AuthorInterviews/bookinterview_Wong.asp

WEB SITE: www.chodos-irvine.com

Gennifer Choldenko

October 20, 1957–

"When I was a kid, I lived in an isolated spot on a mountain next to a canyon full of yucca and rattlesnakes. Though I came from a large family, my three siblings were all quite a bit older than I was. The sister closest to me in age had severe autism, and though I occasionally tried to play with her, I quickly grew frustrated because I was not able to engage her. Left to my own devices, I developed a rich and detailed fantasy life.

"At the bottom of the canyon next to our house was a rock the size of a small room, which had cracked and split apart with just space between the cracks for a child to slip through. We called this enormous cracked stone Eagle Rock because it resembled a great bird hunkered down in our canyon. Oh, how I loved to fight my way through the brush and the rattlesnakes to the bottom of the canyon, scramble up to the top of that enormous rock and sing crazy made-up songs to the world.

"My own peculiar made-up humor made a debut one evening when our family went to visit some friends of my parents. During dinner at the kids' table I was faced with the challenge of holding my own in a large group of older kids, some of whom I had never met before. That night a peculiar slaphappy feeling hit me and I began to make up jokes and stories, which made no sense whatsoever, yet were strangely funny. Since that time, my family has referred to this kind of quirky nonsensical humor as Gennifer Jokes.

Photo by Michael Fahey

"Along with the Gennifer Jokes and the Eagle Rock Songs, I spent a great deal of time making up my own words and stories. When I was seven, I created an elaborate dictionary of made-up words, which I defined and illustrated. I also had a large stuffed animal collection, which I played with endlessly creating complicated soap operas about each of the animal's lives. My first book, 'The Adventures of Genny Rice,' about the journey of a grain of rice down the garbage disposal, was written in second grade.

"It seems funny now, but my dad was inordinately proud of 'The Adventures of Genny Rice.' Both of my parents clearly encouraged creativity. My mother was a physical therapist who worked with little kids by day and in the evening she was a sculptor, patiently shaping and polishing large pieces of stone. My father left for work in the morning wearing a starched white shirt and shiny black wing tip shoes. But when he got home, he slid his feet into blue canvas slip-ons, donned a loud plaid shirt that buttoned easily over his belly and sat behind an enormous Underwood typewriter. Writing was the treat he had been waiting for all day.

"Although my father secretly wished to be a writer, his day job was extremely exciting and brought all manner of enchantment to our household. My father worked for Walt Disney. He began as a messenger at the studio and worked his way up to President of the Walt Disney Music Company. My father worked closely with Walt and Roy Disney as well as a whole host of extraordinary musicians, singers and songwriters. Every day my dad brought the infectious spirit of the studio home to us. I grew up believing that anything was possible.

"When I sit down at my computer in the morning, I feel as if anything is possible again. I am so very lucky to get to write books for children. It is the world's best profession."

ᘓ ᘓ ᘓ

Gennifer (Johnson) Choldenko was born and raised in Southern California. She received a B.A. in 1979 from Brandeis University, where she graduated Cum Laude with Honors in English, and a B.F.A. in Illustration in 1992 from Rhode Island School of Design. When she married Jacob Brown, she became Gennifer Choldenko, taking a name from Brown's extended family.

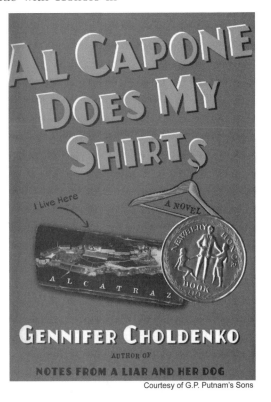
Courtesy of G.P. Putnam's Sons

Gennifer's first book was a picture book, illustrated by Paul Yalowitz, entitled *Moonstruck: The True Story of the Cow Who Jumped over the Moon*. A humorous look at an old nursery rhyme, it received a National Parenting Award. Her first novel, *Notes from a Liar and Her Dog*, was named a *School Library Journal* Best Book of the Year and received a California Book Award Silver Medal. It was also chosen as a Junior Library Guild selection and an IRA/CBC Children's Choice. Depicting a middle child who feels overshadowed by her talented sisters, the novel captures many of the poignant feelings of a preteen struggling to find her own way.

The unique setting of Choldenko's second novel, *Al Capone Does My Shirts*, immediately caught the attention of readers and critics alike. Twelve-year-old Moose Flanagan moves to Alcatraz Island in 1935 when his father accepts a job working at the prison while his mother looks for a special school in San Francisco for his autistic sister. Moose's adjustment problems are exacerbated by the island prison setting and the prison warden's attractive and troublesome daughter. *Al Capone Does My Shirts* was named a *School Library Journal* Best Book and captured both the Beatty award for historical fiction and the Sid Fleischman Humor

Award. Named a Newbery Honor Book, the novel was on the *New York Times* Bestseller list for more than six months.

Gennifer Choldenko lives in the San Francisco Bay area with her husband, her son Ian, her daughter Kai, and a white German shepherd named Sophie.

SELECTED WORKS: *Moonstruck: The True Story of the Cow Who Jumped Over the Moon*, illus. by Paul Yalowitz, 1997; *Notes from a Liar and Her Dog*, 2001; *Al Capone Does My Shirts*, 2004; *How to Make Friends with a Giant*, illus. by Amy Walrod, 2006; *If a Tree Falls at Lunch Period*, 2007; *Louder, Lili*, illus. by S. D. Schindler, 2007.

SUGGESTED READING: *Something About the Author*, vol. 135, 2003.

WEB SITE: www.choldenko.com

Photo by Don Landwehrle

Bonnie Christensen

January 23, 1951–

"My family moved frequently when I was a child. Since my father was a professor and forest economist we often lived in or near rural areas and spent many summers in a national forest where he taught. Some of my happiest childhood memories involve simple moments in the forest or countryside and it's been suggested that many of my illustrations reflect a strong sense of place.

"My father encouraged drawing and painting and was a stern teacher when it came to writing. He kept binders of all the drawing I made from the time I was five to seven years old. All my life he was convinced, and tried to convince me, that I should study and practice visual art. After college I worked in the theater and film industry, but I continued to draw for enjoyment and took printmaking classes as well.

"My mother, for her part, was enthusiastic about all the arts and, though we had little money, made sure my sister and I took music and dance lessons as well as some art classes. She exposed us to history, architecture, theater, music, the opera and the visual arts.

"I attended nine schools in twelve grades but only had the opportunity to take one art class, in third grade. I remember my teacher and the artwork we created very, very well. In fact I still have a 'hot pad' I painted, as a gift for my mother, in that class. I have tried many times to find my teacher, Mrs. Fertig, to thank her for her enthusiasm, encouragement, and for being such a downright warm and kindhearted person.

"During college I was an 'activist' 'hippie' 'flower child,' and though writing those words makes me smile a bit ruefully and feel a bit 'dated,' I am genuinely proud to have been and remain a part of that culture of activism and open-mindedness. Illustrating books about social upheaval or writing and/or illustrating biographies of social activists is certainly a job I relish.

"During my theater career I lived in New York City for 13 years and took many classes in both writing and visual arts. At the same time I was longing for the green hills and countryside of Vermont, where I'd attended college. I returned to Vermont, married, had a child, and began illustrating local magazines and catalogues. I also worked in an old printing shop at the Shelburne Museum, hand-setting type, printing, and giving visitors a bit of printing history. There I also printed a book of verse written for my daughter and illustrated with my wood engraving.

"Friends suggested I approach publishers to have the book printed and distributed on a large scale. Though no publisher was interested in that first book it opened doors for me. I was lucky enough to meet a very enthusiastic and creative editor, Ann Petracek, who published my first book, *An Edible Alphabet*. Since then I've been very fortunate and have continued to write and illustrate. I have used many printmaking techniques in illustrating books but always try to find a technique that reflects the story well. For Mary Pope Osborne's *Pompeii: Lost & Found*, I used true fresco, the same process and pigments that a painter in Pompeii would have employed 2000 years ago. For Nikola-Lisa's *Magic in the Margins: A Medieval Tale of Bookmaking*, I used pen and ink with egg tempera just as the medieval monks did.

"I teach in the art department at St. Michael's college in Vermont and spend as much time as possible working at large-scale fine art printmaking in Venice, Italy. I feel very fortunate to work in the world of children's books where the artist and writer can sometimes be the very same person, creating an entire world with words and pictures."

"Illustrating books about social upheaval or writing and/or illustrating biographies of social activists is certainly a job I relish."

03 03 03

Born in Saranac Lake, New York, Bonnie Christensen received a B.A. degree from the University of Vermont in Theater Arts and Communication in 1973. After college her artistic talent helped her land a job in the theater world, and she spent a number of years in New York City, working in Joseph Papp's Public Theater and the New York Shakespeare Festival, and even wrote several plays that were produced off-off Broadway. She also wrote screenplays and worked for the Screen Actor's Guild (SAG) and Paramount Pictures. All through her New York years, Christensen took courses in wood engraving, printmaking, and letterpress printing at Parsons School of Design and the Center for Book Arts.

After moving to Vermont in the 1980s, Christensen eventually found her way to book illustration. Her first book, *An Edible Alphabet*, was designated a *Smithsonian* Notable Book. Introducing a variety of cultures and habitats, as well as unusual foods ("ulu"—the Hawaiian name for breadfruit) the book includes a glossary describing each plant and how it is used. An artist's note explains the specific method of woodcutting that was developed in the 17th century, while watercolor highlights create vibrant hues on each page. For Stephen Krensky's *Breaking Into Print*, about the history of bookmaking, she employed wood engravings that evoke the early years of print. This title was named a Notable Social Studies Trade Book for Young People and an ABA Pick of the Lists.

Always interested in the plight of the downtrodden, Christensen created illustrations for a new edition of John Steinbeck's *Grapes of Wrath* published by the Folio Society of London in 1998. She always listens to music appropriate to the project while she is illustrating, and the music for that book was the "Dust Bowl Ballads" of Woody Guthrie. That led her to learn more about Guthrie's life and work, and the result was her own fine picture book biography of the protest singer, songwriter, and activist, illustrated in woodcut-like mixed media evocative of the Great Depression era. *Woody Guthrie: Poet of the People* was named a *Boston Globe–Horn Book* Honor Book, an ALA Notable Children's Book, a *New York Times* Notable Book and was cited as a Notable Social Studies Trade Book. In *The Daring Nellie Bly: America's Star Reporter*, Christensen celebrated the pioneering newspaper journalist who broke many conventions for women of her time. For this picture book biography, she created illustrations that echo the look of a 19th century newspaper. *The Daring Nellie Bly* received numerous accolades, including an Oppenheim Toy Portfolio Gold Award. It was cited as an Orbis

Pictus recommended title, a Junior Library Guild selection, and a Notable Social Studies Trade Book.

Though she is generally considered an artist first, Christensen is also a fine writer, creating the text for her most praised titles—*Woody Guthrie* and *The Daring Nellie Bly*. She spearheaded a book to gather memoirs from other children's book writers and wrote one of the stories herself. *In My Grandmother's House*, compiled and illustrated by Christensen with dry point pictures that were inspired by photographs received from each contributor, is a collection of stories about grandmothers. Ranging from gentle memories to difficult family issues, the book celebrates a wide range of family experiences and personalities and includes stories by Pat Cummings, Beverly Cleary, Jean Craighead George, and Alma Flor Ada, among others. It was recommended in the New York Public Library's Books for the Teen Age.

Courtesy of Alfred A. Knopf, Random House, Inc.

Bonnie Christensen has shown her prints in solo exhibits at the Vermont State Craft Center and the Scuola Internazionale di Grafica in Venice, Italy, where she has been a guest lecturer and artist-in-residence. Her work has appeared as part of group exhibits in various galleries in Vermont, at the Society of Illustrators in New York, the International Youth Library in Munich, Germany, and the Line Gallery in Linlithgow, Scotland, among other venues. The artist lives with her daughter, Emily in Essex Junction, Vermont. Discerning readers who look very carefully will find the artist's daughter's name hidden in the dust jacket art on nearly every book she has illustrated.

SELECTED WORKS WRITTEN AND ILLUSTRATED: *An Edible Alphabet*, 1994; *Rebus Riot*, 1997; *Woody Guthrie: Poet of the People*, 2001; *In My Grandmother's House: Award-winning Authors Tell Stories about Their Grandmothers*, (as editor) 2003; *The Daring Nellie Bly: America's Star Reporter*, 2003.

SELECTED WORKS ILLUSTRATED: *Green Mountain Ghosts, Ghouls & Unsolved Mysteries*, by Joseph Citro, 1994; *Putting the World to Sleep*, by Shelley Moore Thomas, 1995; *Breaking Into Print: Before and After the Invention of the Printing Press*, by Stephen

Krensky, 1996; *Moon over Tennessee: A Boy's Civil War Journal*, by Craig Crist-Evans, 1999; *I, Dred Scott: A Fictional Slave Narrative Based on the Life and Legal Precedent of Dred Scott*, by Shelia P. Moses, 2005; *Pompeii: Lost & Found*, by Mary Pope Osborne, 2006; *Magic in the Margins: A Medieval Tale of Bookmaking*, by W. Nikola-Lisa, 2007; *Ida B. Wells: Let the Truth Be Told*, by Walter Dean Myers, 2008.

SUGGESTED READING: *Something About the Author*, vol. 157, 2005

WEB SITE: www.bonniechristensen.com

Courtesy of David Christiana

David Christiana

April 18, 1960–

"Sometimes, when I'm lucky, I forget what I'm doing. I'll be drawing along, trying to convince the lines at the end of my pencil to turn into fairies or trolls or a mouse, when all of the sudden there's another striped wiggly thing with whacked out mismatched eyes, fingers like slugs and teeth fit to be played like a xylophone, staring up from my paper. It's always a surprise when it happens, even after all these years. Naturally, I try to befriend these slithering things, shaping them this way and that, coaxing out their finer points, erasing their flaws. I lie to myself that if only I can get them just so, they'll eventually breath on their own, maybe speak even. Who am I kidding? Drawings don't breath.

"But still, a worm that I drew only yesterday told me that all serious slitherers know at least this one thing—being lost now and then is required to make finding one's way worthwhile. I didn't understand what he was talking about, but it didn't much matter. I erased that worm and drew another less wizened one, then a plump one popped out, one with a cowlick who spoke with a lisp."

ଔ ଔ ଔ

David Christiana and his four sisters grew up in Huntington, Long Island and New York City; Bloomfield Hills and Monroe, Michigan; and eastern Pennsylvania. His mother was stricken with polio before David's birth, but despite physical limitations she won a Businesswoman of the Year award in 1973. His father was a school superintendent.

An imaginative child, Christiana had a panther as an imaginary friend and pretended that he himself was a cheetah. Although he liked drawing, he thought being an artist wouldn't be a good way to make a living, so he planned to be a professional football player to support his art. His first book, written while he was a child, was about a fish with a long tail—the word "long" having so many o's that it took up most of the book.

In 1982 Christiana received his bachelor's degree in fine arts from Tyler School of Art in Elkins Park, Pennsylvania. In 1986 he started teaching illustration at Northern Arizona University as a visiting lecturer. Discovering that he enjoyed teaching, he decided to stick with it and enrolled in the Independent Study Degree Program at Syracuse University, where he obtained a master's degree in fine arts in 1989.

In *I Am the Mummy Heb-Nefert*, Christiana's striking and realistic illustrations lent a haunting aura to Eve Bunting's story of a museum mummy remembering her life as the beautiful wife of the Pharaoh's brother. This unusual volume was cited as a Notable Children's Trade Book in the Field of Social Studies and an *American Bookseller*'s Pick of the Lists.

Christiana's watercolor illustrations are brooding and mysterious for Jane Yolen's story, *Good Griselle*, in which the stone angels and gargoyles of a French cathedral test a woman's goodness by sending her an ugly child to love. This mysterious tale, which takes place on Christmas Eve, is enhanced by Christiana's impressionistic watercolors dominated by tones of gray and brown. Another thoughtful and poignant story set during the holiday season, by Susan Campbell Bartoletti, *The Christmas Promise*, features Christiana's intense, expressionistic illustrations. Named a Notable Social Studies Trade Book for Young People, it tells of a train-hopping hobo who leaves his daughter in a foster home until he can find a job, a promise he keeps just in time for Christmas. The double-page illustrations on oversized pages are deeply evocative of the Great Depression.

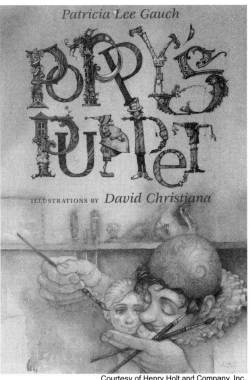

Courtesy of Henry Holt and Company, Inc.

The Magical, Mystical, Marvelous Coat, by Catherine Ann Cullen, which won a National Parenting Publications Award, is about a girl with a coat whose magical buttons come to the aid of an assortment of characters she meets. Christiana adds visually to the story with a mouse-like creature that appears to have special knowledge about the buttons. The whimsical watercolors include backgrounds that are dark and shadowy.

By contrast, words like "lavish," "sumptuous," and "gorgeous" describe Christiana's illustrations for Gail Carson Levine's *Fairy Dust and the Quest for the Egg*, a *New York Times* best seller and a *Publishers Weekly* best seller. This Peter Pan–inspired novel is about a fairy who doesn't know her talent but nevertheless participates in an exciting adventure to save her fairy world and its leader. Its sequel, *Fairy Haven and the Quest for the Wand*, a *New York Times* bestseller, involves the threat of a flood, a perilous quest, and a magic wand with a mind of its own.

David Christiana has written several of the books he's illustrated. *Drawer in a Drawer*, a surreal poem with a rap rhythm about an artist who lives in a drawer, came to him while he was doodling on an airplane and hearing rap music through another passenger's headphones. Inspired by a store he once saw that was full of butterfly wings, *White Nineteens* is about a fairy missing a pair of wings. *A Tooth Fairy's Tale*, born from the idea that the Tooth Fairy and the Sandman could be related, is a quirky fantasy about a tooth fairy trying to save her mother from a human who turned her into stone. Because he missed snow after moving south, Christiana wrote *First Snow*, about Mother Nature as a young girl and Winter who tries to make her accept the coldest season. Each of Christiana's texts provides an excellent venue for his signature evocative artwork.

Christiana currently teaches illustration at the University of Arizona in Tucson, where he and his wife, Kristie Atwood, a photographer and writer, have lived since they married in 1992. Christiana describes his teaching at the University of Arizona as an evolving program that views illustration as an art form that tells *visual* stories, with drawing, particularly figure drawing, as a fundamental tool. While his coursework includes classes in technology, design, and commercial applications, visual art and storytelling are the basics. His own work for children's books exemplifies his belief that telling a story is the most important aspect of illustration.

SELECTED WORKS ILLUSTRATED: *Fat Man in a Fur Coat*, by Alvin Schwartz, 1984; *Tales of Trickery from the Land of Spoof*, by Alvin Schwartz, 1985; *Run for Your Sweet Life*, by Rex Benedict, 1986; *The Revenge of Jeremiah Plum*, by Elizabeth Muskopf, 1987; *Gold and Silver, Silver and Gold: Tales of Hidden Treasure*, by Alvin Schwartz, 1993; *Good Griselle*, by Jane Yolen, 1994; *The Mouse Bride*, by Joy Cowley, 1995; *I Am the Mummy Heb-Nefert*, by Eve Bunting; 1997; *Silver Morning*, by Susan Pearson, 1998; *Poppy's Puppet*, by Patricia Lee Gauch, 1999; *The Tale I Told Sasha*, by Nancy Willard, 1999; *The Magical, Mystical, Marvelous Coat*, by Catherine Ann Cullen, 2001; *The Christmas Promise*, by Susan Campbell Bartoletti, 2001; *O Come, All Ye Faithful*, 2003; *Fairy Dust and the Quest for the Egg*, by Gail Carson Levine, 2005; *Fairy Haven and the Quest for the Wand*, by Gail Carson Levine, 2007.

SELECTED WORKS WRITTEN AND ILLUSTRATED: *Drawer in a Drawer*, 1990; *White Nineteens*, 1992; *A Tooth Fairy's Tale*, 1996; *The First Snow*, 2001.

SUGGESTED READING: *Book Links*, August/September 2001.

WEB SITE: www.davidchristiana.com

Perhaps Esmé Raji Codell was destined to be an author from birth since her parents named her after a character in a short story by J. D. Salinger, "For Esmé, with Love and Squalor." Another book figured prominently in her life when she was looking for a college. Remembering the idyllic Vermont countryside described in *Soup and Me*, by Robert Newton Peck, a book she read when she was about 10 years old, Codell decided on her choice of college based almost solely on the dream of exchanging a small apartment in a rough Chicago neighborhood for the setting of that children's novel. Though she dropped out of school her first year in Vermont, she did meet the man who would eventually become her husband. When they returned together to Chicago, she took a job in the bookstore where she first purchased *Soup and Me*, a move that started her career in children's literature.

Codell soon returned to college and received her bachelor of arts degree from Northeastern Illinois University in 1992,

Courtesy of Hyperion Books for Children

Esmé Raji Codell

October 5, 1968–

graduating *summa cum laude*. After graduation, she began teaching in Chicago's public school system and documented her year of teaching inner-city fifth graders in her inspirational memoir, *Educating Esmé*. In the school where she worked, Codell encountered opposition to her teaching methods, which included using a time machine made out of a refrigerator box to teach history. She connected with her students in unusual ways; once she exchanged places for the day with a rambunctious student to show him what it was like to try to teach with a disruptive child in the room. She made school life interesting for her students and made (often dull) subjects intriguing in creative ways, earning her the respect of colleagues who were impressed with the progress her students made. *Educating Esmé*, which received a 2000 ALA Alex Award as an Outstanding Adult Book for Young Adults and won *ForeWord* Magazine's memoir of the year award, chronicles Codell's methods and the difficulties she had with the educational establishment. It also includes a myriad of fascinating teaching methods.

> *Perhaps Esmé Raji Codell was destined to be an author from birth since her parents named her after a character in a short story. . . .*

Although she was named the region's best new reading teacher, Codell only taught for one year before going on to become a school librarian. Using her seven years' experience as a children's bookseller, she currently makes children's literature recommendations to the educational community and offers author studies and other programs via her popular website.

In 2003 Codell published her first novel for young readers. Recalling a young friendless student in one of her classes who was shy but a very good reader and writer, Codell wrote *Sahara Special*. The book features a special-needs student who writes letters to an absent father and a fifth-grade teacher whose unconventional teaching methods help encourage the girl to use journal writing as a way to reach self-understanding. The relationship Codell developed with her own shy student forms the basis for *Sahara Special*, which received an IRA Children's Book Award in Intermediate Fiction, and was included in the Chicago Public Library's Best of the Best list.

Three years and three books later, Codell wrote a companion to *Sahara Special* called *Vive La Paris!*. In that story, a young African-American student tries to understand her place in a world where such things as music, love, and laughter exist side-by-side with bullying, racism, and loss. The book provides an interesting history lesson as well, featuring a piano teacher who has a concentration camp tattoo and once served as a spy during World War II. This book was a Sydney Taylor Honor Award winner for older readers in 2007.

Sing a Song of Tuna Fish developed as a result of a trip Codell made to her former school, where the students asked her to tell them a personal story from her youth. Unable to immediately recall one, she later thought of several stories and put them in a book to help show children that they don't have to make things up to write something interesting. *Sing a Song of Tuna Fish* has since been used in many schools to teach children the skill of journal writing.

Codell is also adept at writing picture books for younger children. Disappointed in the things Cinderella wished for in the traditional folk tale, she wrote *Diary of a Fairy Godmother*, about a student studying "wishcraft" (rather than witchcraft) to learn the art of creative wish-making. In *Hanukkah, Shmanukkah!* Codell combines a retelling of the classic Charles Dickens novella, *A Christmas Carol*, with actual historical facts about Jewish immigration to New York City in the early years of the 20th century.

Courtesy of Hyperion Books for Children

Codell shares her "Three I" theory of reading motivation—interest, integration, and invention—in *How to Get Your Child to Love Reading*, which was written for parents and all those who want to instill in children a love of reading. Her work has been featured in numerous periodicals, including *Five Owls*, *Instructor*, and *Reader's Digest*. She has appeared on *CBS This Morning* and CNN, and her public radio reading, "Call Me Madame," produced for the Life Stories series earned her first place for National Education Reporting from the Education Writer's Association. She also won the 2005 Patterson Pageturner Award for promoting children's books in an effective and original way.

Codell has been married to artist Jim Pollock since 1995; their son Russell is named after another favorite author, Russell Hoban. Although she travels around the country to give talks on teacher empowerment and literacy, she enjoys life in Chicago with her family, where she spends her leisure time singing gospel songs, dancing, listening to jazz and show tunes, and cooking. She also studies the Chinese zodiac and palmistry and collects autographs of her favorite children's book authors and artists.

Codell's web site, PlanetEsme.com, has become a standard source for information about new and exciting books for young readers.

SELECTED WORKS: *Educating Esmé: Diary of a Teacher's First Year*, 1999; *How to Get Your Child to Love Reading: For Ravenous and Reluctant Readers Alike*, 2003; *Sahara Special*, 2003; *Sing a Song of Tuna Fish: Hard-to-Swallow Stories from Fifth Grade*, illus. by Leuyen Pham, 2004; *Diary of a Fairy Godmother*, illus. by Drazen Kozjan, 2005; *Hannukah, Shmanukkah!*, illus. by Leuyen Pham, 2005; *Vive La Paris!*, 2006.

SUGGESTED READING: *Something About the Author*, vol. 160, 2005; *Contemporary Authors Online*, 7/26/07.

WEB SITE: www.PlanetEsme.com

Photo by Peter Frey

Judith Ortiz Cofer

February 24, 1952–

Born in Hormigueros, Puerto Rico, Judith Ortiz Cofer traveled between the United States and Puerto Rico in her early years because her father, Jesus Lugo Ortiz, was in the U.S. Navy. When her father was home, she lived with her family in Paterson, New Jersey. When he went to sea, she and her mother lived in Puerto Rico. Spanish was her home language and English became her literary language and the one in which she had more experience. As a child, she became the translator for her mother, who spoke only Spanish.

Growing up, Cofer felt pressured by her father to learn American customs and by her mother to remember her heritage. She deeply felt the differences between the urban high-rise city life in New Jersey and the balmy weather and rural village life of Puerto Rico. Different from the other children in both places, she sought refuge in books when she was in Paterson and oral tales from her grandparents when she was in Puerto Rico. Thus, she absorbed both spoken and written narratives, yet discovered that finding her place in two cultures proved challenging, a fact that was to have a tremendous influence on her writing.

When Judith was 16 the Ortiz family moved to Augusta, Georgia. When she was 19 she married John Cofer, a fellow student, then finished her undergraduate degree from Augusta College. She went on to obtain her master of arts degree from Florida Atlantic University in 1977. A bilingual teacher in the Florida public schools and an adjunct professor and lecturer at the University of Miami during her postgraduate years, Judith moved with her husband to Louisville, Georgia in 1984. She has also taught English at the University of Georgia, the Georgia Center for Continuing Education, Macon College, and Mercer University. Since 1992 she has been an English and creative writing professor at the University of Georgia.

Cofer's first published writing was poetry. She received a 1989 National Endowment for the Arts fellowship in poetry and has subsequently received over 30 fellowships and grants, as well as an honorary doctorate degree from Lehman University in 2007. Her first adult novel, *The Line of the Sun*, was a 1990 Pulitzer Prize nominee and a New York Public Library Outstanding Book of the Year. Cofer wove her own roots into this novel, which is told in two parts and includes the magical but stifling world of Puerto Rican village life and the gritty, contemporary world of Paterson, New Jersey. The lyrical story tells of a wild young Puerto Rican who runs away and eventually meets his Americanized niece in New Jersey; it continues with the niece's struggles to balance her American and Puerto Rican selves. *Silent Dancing*—part autobiography, part fiction, and part social commentary—is a sweeping memoir written in prose and poetry that received a PEN/Martha Albrand Special Citation and was included in the New York Public Library's Outstanding Books of the Year.

Published directly for the teen audience, *An Island Like You: Stories of the Barrio* consists of 12 moving stories set in a Paterson neighborhood and populated by memorable teenagers caught between childhood and adulthood and between their parents' culture and their American way of life. Although each story focuses on a different teenager and can stand alone, the characters are linked to each other, and their stories gain strength from appearing together in one book. This title won the first Pura Belpré Award in 1996, was cited as an ALA Best Book for Young Adults, and received an honorable mention for the Américas award.

Set in the barrio tenement where Cofer grew up, *The Latin Deli* features stories, essays, and poetry dealing with young Puerto Ricans trying to cope with prejudice and issues of faith and maturation. It won the Anisfield-Wolf Book Award in Race Relations. One story from the collection, "Nada," about a woman driven to suicide by the deaths of her husband and son, won the 1994 O. Henry Award.

The Meaning of Consuelo takes place in San Juan in the 1950s and features a teenager struggling with her family's expectations, the disintegration of her parents' marriage, and the problems generated by a schizophrenic sister. Grim but humorous, this title was among the New York Public Library's Books for the Teen Age and won the Américas Award for Children's and Young Adult Literature. Also cited as an Américas award honorable mention, was Cofer's novel for younger readers, *Call Me María*. The title character struggles to come to terms with her new life in America, her parents' divorce, and the dignity of her own Latina heritage. *The Year of Our Revolution*, a collection of stories and poems about being caught between Hispanic and mainstream American lifestyles while growing up in New Jersey during the 1960s, won the Paterson Prize for Books for Young People.

Many of Cofer's short stories, essays, and poems have been anthologized in high school literature textbooks. She uses her art as a bridge between her two cultures—a bridge appreciated by Americans of all ethnicities searching for self-discovery and reconciliation. In addition to her creative writing, Cofer has published many articles and essays in academic journals and travels widely to speak about her work and her life. In her current position as Regents' and Franklin Professor of English and Creative Writing at the University of Georgia, she teaches a variety of courses featuring multicultural literature, women's literature, and creative writing as well as traditional American literature. Cofer and her husband, a high school mathematics teacher, live in Louisville, Georgia and visit Puerto Rico frequently. They have a grown daughter, Tanya, who is a research mathematician.

She uses her art as a bridge between her two cultures— a bridge appreciated by Americans of all ethnicities searching for self-discovery and reconciliation.

SELECTED WORKS: *Peregrina*, 1985; *Terms of Survival*, 1987; *The Line of the Sun*, 1989; *Silent Dancing: A Partial Remembrance of a Puerto Rican Childhood*, 1990; *The Latin Deli: Prose and Poetry*, 1993; *An Island Like You: Stories of the Barrio*, 1995; *Reaching for the Mainland and Selected New Poems*, 1995; *The Year of Our Revolution: New and Selected Stories and Poems*, 1998; *Sleeping with One Eye Open: Women Writers and the Art of Survival*, 1999; *Woman in Front of the Sun: On Becoming a Writer*, 2000; *Riding Low on the Streets of Gold: Latino Literature for Young Adults* (as editor), 2003; *The Meaning of Consuelo*, 2003; *Call Me María*, 2004; *A Love Story Beginning in Spanish: Poems*, 2005; *The Hunger of Birds*, 2005.

SELECTED WORKS CONTRIBUTED TO: *Triple Crown: Chicano, Puerto Rican and Cuban American Poetry*, by Roberto Durán and Gustavo Pérez Firmat (trilogy containing *Reaching for the Mainland*), 1987; *Pushcart Prize XV Anthology*, ed. by Bill Henderson, 1990.

SUGGESTED READING: Martinez Wood, Jamie, *Latino Writers and Journalists*, 2007; *Something About the Author*, vol. 164, 2006; Henderson, Ashyia N., *Contemporary Hispanic Biography*, 2002; Pendergast, Tom, ed., *St. James Guide to Young Adult Writers*, 2nd ed., 1998; *Authors and Artists for Young Adults*, vol. 30, 1999; Palmisano, Joseph, ed., *Notable Hispanic American Women*, Book 2, 1998; Tardiff, Joseph, ed., *Dictionary of Hispanic Biography*, 1995. Periodicals—"Writers Who Make a Difference, *The Writer*, Jan. 2003; Ford, Wayne, "For UGA English Professor Judith Ortiz Cofer, Writing is Art," *Athens Banner-Herald*, Dec. 14, 2003.

WEB SITE: www.english.uga.edu/~jcofer/vita.html

Courtesy of Scholastic, Inc.

"**I** was born with a pen in my hand. Which is unusual. I immediately dropped the pen and sent my chubby fingers out searching for some food instead.

"Okay. Not strictly true. What kind of parent gives a potentially dangerous ballpoint to an infant? There was no pen. But it does seem to me, when I look back on my early years, that pens and crayons were never far away. Our house was a hive of creativity. Again there was no actual *hive*, but by now you will realise that I am prone to hackneyed imagery.

"My Dad is a teacher, writer, artist, and scuba diver. And my Mom is an actress, writer, and drama teacher. My goodness, if you couldn't pick up a bit of writing talent in that house, you were either in a coma or living in the tree house. Even traveling salesmen went away with blockbuster ideas. I remember one guy selling life insurance who went down the driveway scribbling notes about a possessed car. I wonder what ever happened to him.

Eoin Colfer

(OH-wen)

May 14, 1965–

"So my four brothers and I were submersed (hackneyed imagery) in art and writing materials from a very early age. We had chalkboards and paint pots, staplers and blunted craft knives. Anything the inquisitive and creative mind could want. And once I worked out that you could not, in fact, drink the water used for washing paintbrushes, I got on with being creative.

"Cartoons, I thought. That is where my future lies. So I spent years inventing superheroes and cobbling together magazines for five pence, but unfortunately the art materials cost about two pounds, so I quickly went out of business.

Photo by Susan Greenhill

"Several years later, I realised that my stories were better without the pictures, simply because my pictures were what is technically known as *junk*. And so I began to write down the crazy ideas that bounced around in my head. It would be several years before I learned from a man in a darkened office with comfortable chairs and comforting artwork, that not everybody had crazy ideas bouncing around in their heads and not everybody argued with their voices. Luckily, when you write for a living, these things are definite advantages.

"It would be several years before any of my ideas were coherent or long enough to form a book. My stories were short and sharp. I needed inspiration to draw the words out. I found this in Africa. I was married and thirty, and my wife and I were working in Tunisia with an Idaho tough guy, mountain man and poet. We hung around the industrial city of Sfax together, and one day I realised that the entire country was walking, talking, breathing inspiration.

"I began to write my first proper book, *Benny and Omar*, a rite-of-passage tale about a pampered Irish boy who befriends a homeless Tunisian orphan. And somehow, I managed to keep it going for 100,000 words. Of course, my editor later chopped out 30,000 words to make the story less, as she put it, boring as hell.

"And so a year later I had an actual published book in my hand. This had happened to me thousands of times before, but this time I had actually *written* the published book. I have to say, in a rare moment of sincerity, that there cannot be many feelings in life finer than reading your own book to your own child.

"Thirteen books later and I am still at it—borrowing the lives of friends and family and stuffing them into fantasy books. My brothers are goblins, my boss is a troll, and two of my friends are flatulent dwarfs. It is a wonderful way to live, taking what's inside your head and dragging it outside. If you start doing that in any other profession, they give you early retirement, but in children's book writing they give you a contract, if you're lucky.

"My ambition now is to keep writing for as long as I can, until I have scooped my brain clean, like a snail sucked out of its shell (hackneyed imagery, remember?). It would be nice to have an entire wall covered with my books and translations. I'm 40 now. Two books a year for the next twenty years should do it.

"So what am I doing here talking to you? I should get writing."

                 CR CR CR

Growing up as part of a creative, literary family in Wexford on the southeast coast of Ireland, Eoin Colfer was never at a loss for activity. He was the second of five brothers. His father taught at the local elementary school and his mother was a drama teacher. On weekends and school holidays, the family would travel to the picturesque fishing village of Slade, where Colfer's father had grown up and where there were plenty of cousins to visit. A favorite activity when Eoin was in secondary school was attending céilis, traditional Irish dances, with local girls' schools, and it was at one such evening that he met his future wife, Jackie. In 1986 he graduated from a teacher training course in Dublin and returned to Wexford to teach primary school, spending his spare time writing and working with an amateur theatre group and the Wexford Light Opera Society.

A year after marrying in 1991, Colfer and his wife left Ireland to teach abroad, serving stints in Saudi Arabia, Tunisia, and Italy. Though some of these experiences inspired Colfer's later writing, he and his wife opted, after four years overseas, to settle back home in Wexford. In 1997 their first son, Finn, was born. A year later, Colfer published his first book, *Benny and Omar*, based on his experiences in Tunisia. This fast-paced narrative about the friendship between an Irish boy and a street-smart Tunisian child combines humor with a poignant depiction of poverty. It became a bestseller in Ireland and was on the Honor List of the International Board on Books for Young People. A sequel, *Benny and Babe*, was shortlisted for the Bisto Children's Book of the

> *"My brothers are goblins, my boss is a troll, and two of my friends are flatulent dwarfs. It is a wonderful way to live, taking what's inside your head and dragging it outside."*

Year award sponsored by Children's Books Ireland; Colfer's next published book, *The Wish List*, received a Bisto Merit Award.

Fascinated since childhood by the rich folklore of his native Ireland, Colfer decided to put a 20th century twist on the old legends. As a teenager he had read widely and especially enjoyed the thrillers of such writers as Robert Ludlum and Jack Higgins; he also liked watching the American police series *Hill Street Blues* on television. All of these influences came together in his most enduring and original creation, the young criminal mastermind Artemis Fowl. Published in 2001, the first book in the series, *Artemis Fowl*, pits twelve-year-old Artemis and his bodyguard Butler against the advanced technology of "the people," the fairies that live underground. These creatures bear little resemblance to "the folk" of ancient legend, except in their quirky personalities and contempt for humans. With a masterful blend of humor, intrigue, and techno-talk, Colfer generated a startling new vision of the fairy world in the 21st century.

Courtesy of Hyperion Books for Children

Artemis Fowl was named the British Book Awards Children's Book of the Year, received a Bisto Merit Award, and became an international bestseller. In America, it was named to the *Bulletin of the Center for Children's Books* Blue Ribbon List and won the Delaware, Massachusetts, New Jersey, and Pacific Northwest young readers' choice awards.

Colfer soon followed up *Artemis Fowl* with several sequels. The third book in the series, *Artemis Fowl: The Eternity Code*, was named a Best Children's Book of the Year by both the Bank Street College of Education and the Cooperative Children's Book Center, and received an Oppenheim Toy Portfolio award. *Artemis Fowl: The Arctic Incident* and *Artemis Fowl: The Opal Deception* were both shortlisted for the Bisto Award in the U.K.

Colfer has also written three books in the O'Brien's Flyers series for young children and several adventure stories for middle grade readers. In 2005 he contributed a story to *Higher Ground*, an anthology of short pieces about the real-life experiences of tsunami victims.

The great success of the Artemis Fowl series—12 million copies sold in 42 countries to date—has allowed Colfer to resign his teaching post and devote more time to his writing and to his family, which now includes a second son, Seán.

SELECTED WORKS (dates are original U.K. publication, U.S. dates, if different, are in parenthesis): *Benny and Omar*, 1998 (2001); *Benny and Babe*, 1999 (2001); *Going Potty*, illus. by Woody, 1999; *Ed's Funny Feet*, illus. by Woody, 2000; *The Wish List*, 2000 (2003); *Ed's Bed*, illus. by Woody, 2001; *Artemis Fowl*, 2001; *Artemis Fowl: The Arctic Incident*, 2002; *Artemis Fowl: The Eternity Code*, 2003; *Artemis Fowl Files*, 2004; *Legend of Spud Murphy*, illus. by Glenn McCoy, 2004; *The Supernaturalist*, 2004; *Legend of Captain Crow's Teeth*, illus. by Glenn McCoy, 2005; *Artemis Fowl: The Opal Deception*, 2005; *Half Moon Investigations*, 2006; *Legend of the Worst Boy in the World*, illus. by Glenn McCoy, 2007; *Artemis Fowl: The Graphic Novel*, adapt. by Eoin Colfer and Andrew Donkin, illus by Giovanni Rigano, color by Paolo Lamanna, 2007; *Airman*, 2008; *Artemis Fowl: The Time Paradox*, 2008.

SUGGESTED READING: *Something About the Author*, vol. 148, 2004. Periodicals—McGavin, Harvey, "Eoin Colfer: My Best Teacher," *Times Educational Supplement*, May 28, 2004.

WEB SITES: www.eoincolfer.com
www.artemisfowl.com

Sneed B. Collard III

November 7, 1959–

"In 1975, when I was fifteen years old, I traveled overseas for the first time. My stepfather happens to be one of the world's foremost authorities on fireflies, and during this period in his career he regularly traveled to Southeast Asia to conduct research. In the summer after I finished tenth grade, he arranged for my mother and me to join him.

"For five weeks we toured Hong Kong, Malaysia, Singapore, Thailand, and Indonesia. My mind was blown forever. Not only did I dive into 'un-American' cultures for the first time, I visited my first tropical rainforest, learned to use chopsticks, and experienced many other wondrous things our planet has to offer. In at least two important ways, that trip would have an enormous impact on my writing career.

"The first thing the trip did for me was to give me a lifelong travel bug. Ever since experiencing other cultures for the first time, I've had an insatiable appetite to explore and learn about all parts of the world. Perhaps of even greater import, however, that trip compelled me to keep my very first journal. Every day of the trip, I religiously recorded what I'd seen, heard, smelled, and tasted. It was a habit that I continue to this day, and turned out to be the beginning of my writing career, although I didn't know that at the time. When I entered the University of California at Berkeley, my most immediate passion was marine biology. After graduating, however, I realized that my interests were too broad for me to become a professional biologist. One night, lying in my sleeping bag, I decided that I should become a writer.

"Many people think that's a radical switch, to go from biology to writing, but it wasn't as big a leap as it seems. Even though I

Photo by Wendy Norgaard

Sneed B. Collard III

never grew up wanting to become a writer, I was an avid reader. I devoured books of all kinds, books often recommended to me by my father (also a biologist) who was equally rabid about books. My journal-writing had also ingrained a writing habit in me, and when I began my writing career, I already had a vague idea I wanted to become a novelist. I discovered, though, that I had a knack for writing children's books. I began writing children's magazine stories, but quickly moved to writing science articles and, after seven or eight years, science books.

I wasn't content to write books composed of library research. I had—and still have—a strong taste for adventure. In 1994, I decided to go out on a limb and travel to Costa Rica to interview scientists who worked in an ecosystem called a tropical cloud forest. That trip resulted in a number of books for me including *Monteverde—Science and Scientists in a Costa Rican Cloud Forest* and the picture book *The Forest in the Clouds*. I thought it would be my last big research adventure. Fortunately, I was very wrong!

"Since that first research trip to Costa Rica, I've traveled to Australia, Hawaii, the Caribbean, and many other places to interview people and see firsthand the subjects for my books. One of my most exciting adventures happened weeks after September 11th, when I had the opportunity to dive in a deep-sea submarine to the ocean floor. These trips have inspired dozens of books, from more in-depth science books such as *A Whale*

Biologist at Work and *The Prairie Builders* to popular picture books such as *Beaks!*, *Leaving Home*, *The Deep-Sea Floor*, and *One Night in the Coral Sea*.

"But I've always felt that there's no point being a writer if I can't continue to grow and take risks. All the time I was writing science books, my dream of being a novelist never left me. Over the years I wrote 5 or 6 novels that fell short of getting published. In 1999, though, I adopted a beautiful Border collie from the local Humane Society. I quickly learned that Mattie was incredibly smart as well as being a great companion. With the help my ten year-old neighbor, I taught Mattie to catch a Frisbee. And that gave me an idea for a new novel—one about a boy who moves to Montana against his will, but gets a Border collie that he enters in Frisbee contests.

"That book turned into my breakthrough first novel, *Dog Sense*, published in 2005. And while I continue to write science books, I am now embarking on a brand new career. My second novel, *Fire Birds*, was published in 2006, and I know that others will follow. I don't feel that this evolution is unique to writers. All of us are growing, changing human beings. I simply feel grateful to have found a career that allows me the flexibility and freedom to become myself. I wish the same good fortune for all of my readers."

ଔ   ଔ   ଔ

A freelance writer since 1984, Sneed B. Collard III was born in Phoenix, Arizona. His father was a professor of biology and his mother was a high-school biology teacher. His parents divorced when he was eight years old. His stepfather made possible the trip he describes in his autobiographical statement. After finishing high school Collard traveled widely—working as a cook at Mt. Rushmore, spending four months on a kibbutz in Israel, taking a ferry to hitchhike in Greece. He attended the University of California at Davis and studied at the Friday Harbor Marine Laboratories of the University of Washington. He graduated from the University of California at Berkeley with a degree in marine biology in 1983. In 1986 he earned a M.S. degree in scientific instrumentation from the University of California at Santa Barbara.

After graduate school Collard worked for six years at the University of Santa Barbara as a manager of a computer lab, spending his off-hours writing. He contributed many articles and stories to periodicals such as *Highlights*, *Cricket*, and *Children's*

> *"I've always felt that there's no point being a writer if I can't continue to grow and take risks. All the time I was writing science books, my dream of being a novelist never left me."*

Digest as well as the *Christian Science Monitor* and *Earth Steward Journal*. In 1992 he decided to write full time, with a strong desire to influence readers to take better care of the natural world. His science-oriented informational books have been directed to many age groups and have received wide praise. Six have been named Outstanding Science Trade Books: *Butterfly Count*; *Forest in the Clouds*; *Our Wet World*; *A Playtpus, Probably*; *The Prairie Builders*; and *One Night in the Coral Sea*. Several of his titles for older readers have been named ALA Best Books for Young Adults, including *Alien Invaders*, *Monteverde*, *Acting for Nature*, and *Lizard Island*. Whether intended for primary-grade children, for middle grades, or for teenagers, Collard's research is meticulous, often involving trips to exotic locations and interviews with scientists in the field.

Courtesy of Peachtree Publishers

One of his most acclaimed books, *The Prairie Builders: Reconstructing America's Lost Grasslands*, describes through expressive writing and stunning photography the work of scientists and volunteers in reestablishing the prairie at the Neal Smith National Wildlife Refuge in Iowa. Beautifully designed, the book follows the efforts of conservationists to return a stretch of Iowa farmland to its original ecosystem, and includes the history of the area as well as a description of plants and wildlife. Named a best book of the year by *School Library Journal*, *Booklist*, and *Book Links*, this title also won the Middle Grades award of the AAAS/Subaru *Science Books & Films* Prize for Excellence in Science Books.

Several of Collard's books for younger readers have been illustrated by award-winning artist Steve Jenkins, and one of those—*Animal Dads*—was named to the Recommended List by the Orbis Pictus committee of the NCTE. *One Night in the Coral Sea*, with illustrations by Robin Brickman, won the John Burroughs Award for Nature Writing. Several Collard titles have been named Junior Library Guild selections, and in 2006, he received the *Washington Post*/Children's Book Guild Nonfiction Writer of the Year Award for his body of work.

Collard's fiction is also beginning to be recognized for its excellence. His novel for middle grades, *Dog Sense*, won the Henry Bergh Award given by the ASPCA. *Dog Sense* is a fast-moving story about Guy Martinez, whose move to a small town in Montana is softened by acquiring a Border collie. He trains the dog to compete in a Frisbee-catching contest in which he is pitted against the dog of the school bully.

Sneed B. Collard III lives in Montana where he enjoys playing Frisbee with his own Border collie, Mattie. He conducts teacher workshops and visits schools to speak to students about his work.

SELECTED WORKS: *Sea Snakes*, illus. by John Rice, 1993; *Tough Terminators: Twelve of the Earth's Most Fascinating Predators*, 1994; *Green Giants*, 1994; *Smart Survivors: Twelve of the Earth's Most Remarkable Living Things*, 1994; *Alien Invaders: The Continuing Threat of Exotic Species*, 1996; *Our Natural Homes: Exploring Terrestrial Biomes of North and South America*, illus. by James M. Needham, 1996; *Creepy Creatures*, illus. by Kristin Kest, 1997; *Animal Dads*, illus. by Steve Jenkins, 1997; *Monteverde: Science and Scientists in a Costa Rican Cloud Forest*, 1997; *Our Wet World: Exploring Earth's Aquatic Ecosystems*, illus. by James M. Needham, 1998; *Animal Dazzlers: The Role of Brilliant Colors in Nature*, 1998; *1,000 Years Ago on Planet Earth*, illus. by Jonathan Hunt, 1999; *Birds of Prey: A Look at Daytime Raptors*, 1999; *Making Animal Babies*, illus. by Steve Jenkins, 2000; *Forest in the Clouds*, illus. by Michael Rothman, 2000; *A Whale Biologist at Work*, 2000; *Lizard Island: Science and Scientists on Australia's Great Barrier Reef*, 2000; *Amazing Animals: Nature's Most Incredible Creatures*, 2000; *Acting for Nature: What Young People around the World Have Done to Protect the Environment* (with Action for Nature); illus. by Carl Dennis Buell, 2000; *A Firefly Biologist at Work*, 2001; *Butterfly Count*, illus. by Paul Kratter, 2002; *Leaving Home*, illus. by Joan Dunning, 2002; *Beaks!*, illus. by Robin Brickman, 2002; *The Deep-Sea Floor*, illus. by Gregory Wenzel, 2003; *B is for Big Sky Country: A Montana Alphabet*, illus. by Joanna Yardley, 2003; *Animals Asleep*, illus. by Anik McGrory, 2004; *One Night in the Coral Sea*, illus. by Robin Brickman, 2005; *The Prairie Builders: Reconstructing America's Lost Grasslands*, 2005; *A Platypus, Probably*, illus. by Andrew Plant, 2005; *In the Deep Sea*, 2005; *In the Rain Forest Canopy*, 2005; *On the Coral Reefs*, 2005; *In the Wild*, 2005; *Dog Sense: A Novel*, 2005; *David Crockett: The Man from Tennessee*, 2006. *Sacagawea: Brave Shoshone Girl*, 2006; *Shep: Our Most Loyal Dog*, illus. by Joanna Yardley, 2006; *Benjamin Franklin: The Man Who Could Do Just about Anything*, 2006; *John Adams: Our Second President*, 2006; *Flash Point*, 2006; *Pocket Ba-*

bies *And Other Amazing Marsupials*, 2007; *Teeth*, illus. by Phyllis V. Saroff, 2008; *Wings*, illus. by Robin Brickman, 2008.

SUGGESTED READING: *Something About the Author*, vol. 184, 2008; Periodicals—Collard, Sneed B., III, "Using Science Books to Teach Literacy," *The Reading Teacher*, Nov. 2003.

WEB SITE: www.author-illustr-source.com/sneedbcollard.htm

Courtesy of Henry Holt and Company

Bryan Collier

January 31, 1967–

"Making art really became important to me when I turned 15 years old. I loved sports—football, basketball—but art took me to a place where the element of time and circumstance disappeared and dreams replaced it. It was like art chose me. I couldn't shake art from my spirit if I wanted to. I didn't want to, and I still don't. Responses from family and friends gave me encouragement. I received a scholarship to Pratt Institute in Brooklyn, New York, which put me in an environment around other young artists like me with the endless possibilities of New York City and new energy radiating in all directions.

"At this point, recalling only three children's books from my childhood that had African American boys in them (*A Snowy Day*, *Whistle for Willie*, and *Harold and the Purple Crayon*), it became important to me to do more books like that. Not knowing how to get a book deal, I just started going from publishing house to publishing house. After seven years of knocking on doors, I got my first offer with Henry Holt and Company. Three years later *Uptown* was published."

○ ○ ○

Bryan Collier grew up in Pocomoke, Maryland, on the lower Eastern Shore of the state, the youngest of six children. His interest in art began when, as a teenager, he started to paint the world around him—the bay, ducks, water, and marshland. He gradually developed a unique style of painting that incorporated both watercolors and collage. He has said, "Collage is more than just an art style. Collage is all about bringing different elements together. Once you form a sensibility about connection, how different elements relate to each other, you deepen your understanding of yourself and others."

As he neared the end of high school, football recruiters were pursuing him to attend college on a sports scholarship, but Collier's interest in art had always been encouraged both at home and at school. At the last minute, he chose art over football. In 1985 he won first place in a Congressional Competition, and his art was displayed in the Capitol Building in Washington D.C. Later that year he was awarded a scholarship to Pratt Institute in New York City through the school's national talent competition, and in 1989 he graduated with honors and bachelor's degree in fine arts.

While attending college in New York, Collier began to volunteer at the Harlem Horizon Studio and Harlem Hospital Center in a program that provides working space and materials for self-taught artists in the community. He went on to become the Program Director, a position he held for twelve years. He still works with the program in Harlem as a consultant, finding that the community feeling between school, students, and parents helps the children to build a sense of self esteem and connectedness, as well as an appreciation for the arts. As part of that program, he helped young artists create murals in city parks and playgrounds that were featured as backdrops in the motion picture *Above the Rim* and on a *Sesame Street* episode on television.

Bryan Collier's path to publication was the result of his own self-determination and persistence, as he took samples of his work to publishers for seven years before landing a contract. His first published book, *These Hands*, with text by Hope Lynne Price, introduced the artist's distinctive collage style. In *Uptown*, which Collier both wrote and illustrated, his groundbreaking technique was even more vibrant, and the book won both the Ezra Jack Keats New Illustrator Award and the Coretta Scott King Award for illustration. Named a *Parenting* Magazine Best of the Year and a Notable Social Studies Trade Book for Young People, *Uptown* expresses a young boy's delight in his Harlem neighborhood and all its special attributes—chicken and waffles, barber shop talk, the Apollo theater, and the brownstone townhouses that remind him of chocolate.

The richly textured collage of paint, photographs, pieces of fabric and cut paper that has become Collier's signature style was inspired by his childhood love of the books of Ezra Jack Keats and his fascination with the quilts his grandmother stitched. Watching her piece together the many shapes, textures, and

> *The richly textured collage of paint, photographs, pieces of fabric and cut paper that has become Collier's signature style was inspired by his childhood love of the books of Ezra Jack Keats and his fascination with the quilts his grandmother stitched.*

patterns of those quilts led to Collier's insight that we all piece our lives together from many experiences to make ourselves whole. It is that concept he tries to convey in his work.

Bryan Collier won a Coretta Scott King Honor Award for his illustrations in *Freedom River*, Doreen Rappaport's historical account of the daring activities of John Parker in Ripley, Ohio, in the years before the Civil War. Parker was a freed black man with a successful business who risked his life many times to help slaves cross the river from Kentucky into freedom. With overtones of blue and violet to represent the nighttime escape, Collier's intricate collage work expresses the harrowing experience of a slave family during one of Parker's rescues. *Freedom River* was named an ALA Notable Children's Book as well as a Notable Social Studies Trade Book and established Bryan Collier as a powerful visual force in children's book illustration.

The next collaboration between Rappaport and Collier was an oversized, larger-than-life portrayal of the iconic Civil Rights leader and Nobel Peace Prize winner—*Martin's Big Words: The Life of Dr. Martin Luther King, Jr.* The front cover of the book boldly shows only the smiling face of King, so familiar that no identifying title is needed. The title appears on the back cover in large print to echo the importance of King's "big" words. Collier traveled to the places where King lived, preached, and marched to research his illustrations and, once again, his collage technique expresses the underlying depth and feeling behind his subject's actions and words. Named a *New York Times* Best Illustrated Book of the Year, *Martin's Big Words* won a Caldecott Honor Award as well as a Coretta Scott King Honor Award and a Jane Addams Children's Book Award.

In 2005 Bryan Collier received his second Coretta Scott King Award and his second Caldecott honor award for *Rosa*, a book written by Nikki Giovanni about the life of Rosa Parks. Spending four days in Montgomery, Alabama, Collier met with a close friend of Parks to gain insight into her character. Though she is often portrayed as shy and soft-spoken, he learned that she was a strong and determined woman whose act of civil disobedience did not surprise those who knew her. Conveying the intense heat of the southern city through his use of tone and color, Collier also expressed the character of Rosa Parks with his layered technique of collage and watercolor, bathing her in light to reflect the radiance of her personality and the effect that her actions had on others.

In addition to creating picture books about well-known personalities—he has also illustrated books about John Lennon,

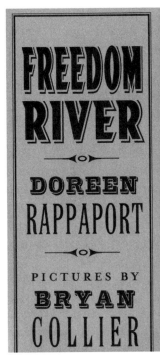

Courtesy of Hyperion Books for Children

Muhammad Ali, and Barack Obama—Collier enjoys illustrating the everyday delights of childhood and parenthood. Revisiting the Harlem setting of *Uptown*, he depicts a father taking his daughter to visit the home of poet Langston Hughes in Willie Perdomo's book, *Visiting Langston*. Celebrating the centennial of the poet's birth and seen through the eyes of the young girl, an aspiring writer, this Coretta Scott King Honor Book conveys the quiet excitement of a child honoring her literary hero. Another contemporary story, *Cherish Today: A Celebration of Life's Moments*, written by Collier's wife, poet and teacher Kristina Evans, channels all the joys of the everyday world through a child's eyes, in school, at play, and with her family.

Bryan Collier especially enjoys visiting classrooms to talk with teachers, librarians, and students about books and art. He likes to engage students in the process of creative thinking, finding ways to express what is inside them, and drawing them out to tell about their own dreams. He lives with his wife and their daughter Haley in upstate New York.

SELECTED WORKS WRITTEN AND ILLUSTRATED: *Uptown*, 2000.

SELECTED WORKS ILLUSTRATED: *These Hands*, by Hope Lynne Price, 1999; *Freedom River*, by Doreen Rappaport, 2000; *Martin's Big Words: The Life of Dr. Martin Luther King, Jr.*, by Doreen Rappaport, 2001; *I'm Your Child, God*, by Marian Wright Edelman, 2002; *John's Secret Dreams: The Life of John Lennon*, by Doreen Rappaport, 2004; *What's the Hurry, Fox?: And Other Animal Stories*, by Zora Neale Hurston, adapted by Joyce Carol Thomas, 2004; *Visiting Langston*, by Willie Perdomo, 2005; *Cherish Today: A Celebration of Life's Moments*, by Kristina Evans, 2007; *Twelve Rounds to Glory: The Story of Muhammad Ali*, by Charles R. Smith, Jr., 2007; *Rosa*, by Nikki Giovanni, 2007; *Lift Every Voice and Sing*, by James Weldon Johnson, 2007; *Doo-Wop Pop*, by Roni Schotter, 2008; *Lincoln and Douglass: An American Friendship*, by Nikki Giovanni, 2008; *Barack Obama: Son of Promise, Child of Hope*, by Nikki Grimes, 2008.

SUGGESTED READING: *Something About the Author*, vol. 174, 2007; Smith, Henrietta, *The Coretta Scott King Awards 1970-2004*, 2004. Periodicals—"Interview with Bryan Collier," *School Library Journal*, May, 2001.

WEB SITE: www.bryancollier.com

Photo by Cap Pryor

Suzanne Collins

Suzanne Collins

August 10, 1962–

"The first book I remember reading on my own was *Snow* by Roy McKie and P. D. Eastman. I was alone in a bedroom of a small apartment in Indianapolis that we were renting for just one year. 'Snow! Snow! Come out in the snow!' *Snow* conjures up two emotions in me. The magical sense of power you feel when you learn to transform letters to words to stories. And the sadness I felt because my dad had just left for Viet Nam and I was not going to see him for an entire year. When you are little, the concept of a year is impossible to wrap your mind around. Past your birthday, Halloween, Thanksgiving, Christmas, Easter and you'll be out of school again, entirely through first grade before that time is up. I read the book over and over. Did they have snow in Viet Nam? I didn't think so. My dad said it was a hot place with bright sunlight and jungles. Maybe, like the children in the book, I could put some snow in the freezer in winter and keep it for another day, a day when my dad would be home again.

"Being a military brat defined much of my childhood and, by extension, the topics I write about for children now. When I graduated high school, I'd had ten addresses in the vicinity of places like West Point, the Pentagon, and NATO. I had visited more battlefields, fortresses, and monuments than most people see in a lifetime. And then there were the many hours of historical discussion that my dad, a doctor of political science and specialist in international relations, wanted so badly for all his children to understand. Perhaps he wanted to make it their passion as well.

"Instead, I went into acting, enrolling in performing arts schools in my last years of high school and college. But at the age of twenty, after appearing in some forty odd plays with varying degrees of success, (I've accepted now that I might never have developed the acting chops to play the lead in Edward Albee's *Tiny Alice* and certainly didn't have them at the time), I discovered writing. This was the creative equivalent of falling madly in love. For many years, I concentrated solely on plays, probably peaking with my master's thesis in the Dramatic Writing Program at NYU, a full-length work based on St. Augustine's *Confessions*. It still awaits production.

"Fortunately, more pragmatic minds at NYU directed me towards television, and in 1991 I got my first job writing for Nickelodeon. One show led to another and I realized how much I enjoyed writing for children. If I had to pick a project I worked on that will outlive me, I'd bet on *Little Bear*, a Nick Jr. series based on the classic book by Else Minarik.

"But children's television has clear content limitations. And the memories of my own childhood, the deployed father, the bases locked down for war games, the cadets drilling on the field, were not likely to find a place there. In 1999 I worked with James Proimos, the very talented children's author and illustrator, on a television project, and he talked me into trying my hand at books. After a few attempts at picture books, I woke up one morning with the idea for 'The Underland Chronicles,' and I knew I had a place to channel my thoughts and feelings about war and violence and loss to the audience I care most about.

"I was about three-fourths of the way through the first book, *Gregor the Overlander*, on September 11, 2001. As a resident of Manhattan, I had the experience of having both my country and my city under attack. And there were my children, Isabel, just two and unaware, but Charlie, seven, who I thought was unaware until I went to his second grade conference and the walls were covered by crayon pictures of planes flying into burning buildings.

> "*I woke up one morning with the idea for 'The Underland Chronicles,' and I knew I had a place to channel my thoughts and feelings about war and violence and loss to the audience I care most about.*"

That's when I realized war would be a part of his childhood, too, and sadly, it becomes more present every day.

"What I hope for is that my books, both 'The Underland Chronicles' and my new trilogy, 'The Hunger Games,' will give young readers a context in which to begin to understand the conflicts in our world."

CR CR CR

Suzanne Collins has been attracted to the creative arts since high school. After graduating from the Alabama School of Fine Arts in 1980, she attended the North Carolina School of the Arts from 1981 to 1983. She then transferred to Indiana University, from which she received her B.A. degree in theater and telecommunications in 1985. In 1989 she earned her M.F.A. from the Dramatic Writing Program at New York University.

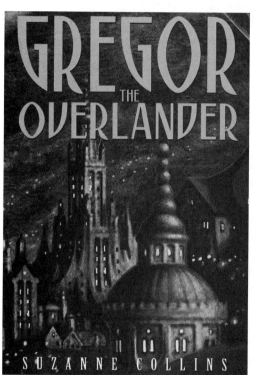
Courtesy of Scholastic, Inc.

After traveling around the world as a child with her father, mother, two sisters, and brother during her father's Air Force career, Collins settled in New York City in 1987 and lived there until 2003. She began writing for children's television in 1991 after taking a job with the Nickelodeon network, and she wrote scripts for various television shows, including *Clarissa Explains It All*, *The Mystery Files of Shelby Wood*, *Little Bear*, and *Oswald the Octopus*. She was also the co-author of *Santa Baby*, a critically acclaimed Christmas special produced by Rankin/Bass and, in more recent years, was the head writer for *Clifford's Puppy Days*, from Scholastic Entertainment.

Having grown up in so many different places as a child, Collins understood the idea of being a "stranger in a strange land" and that became the theme she embraced when she began writing children's books. Mulling over the idea of the classic story *Alice's Adventures in Wonderland*, she wondered how today's urban children would react to that setting. City children would be more likely to imagine falling down a manhole than a rabbit hole, and what sort of unknown world might they find lurking beneath the streets? From this premise, she developed the plot for her first book, *Gregor the Overlander*, which describes the adventures of a young boy from New York

City and his sister Boots, who fall down a laundry chute and into a world filled with giant talking bats, cockroaches, rats, and spiders. Even more remarkably, the inhabitants of Underland seem to be expecting Gregor and hail him as a mighty warrior. Warmly reviewed upon publication, the book received numerous citations, including a *Kirkus Reviews* Editor's Choice. It was named a New Atlantic Independent Booksellers Association Book of the Year and one of the best science fiction, fantasy, and horror books of 2003 by the *Voice of Youth Advocates*.

Gregor and Boots return to Underland in *Gregor and the Prophesy of Bane*. In this installment, Gregor must find his sister, who has been kidnapped by giant roaches, while at the same time uncovering the mystery of the Prophesy of Bane, which predicts the coming of a dangerous white rat. This second volume of the series was a finalist for the Connecticut Book Award. The third book, *Gregor and the Curse of the Warmbloods*, has Gregor and Boots again climbing below the city streets at the request of several friends from Underland in order to find a cure for a deadly plague. The adventure is particularly harrowing for Gregor, who must race against time to cure not only his friends, but also a member of his own family who has caught the disease. *Gregor and the Curse of the Warmbloods* won an Oppenheim Toy Portfolio Gold Award. In the fourth volume, *Gregor and the Marks of Secret*, the intrepid young hero arrives in Underland to help solve a mystery surrounding the Underland mice, but discovers a frightening secret, one that is not fully revealed until the final book, *Gregor and the Code of Claw*. The first volume in her new series, *The Hunger Games*, was published to much acclaim in 2008.

In addition to her series, Collins is also the author of a rhyming picture book, *When Charlie McButton Lost Power*, which was illustrated by Mike Lester. Having moved from New York City in 2003, Collins now lives in Sandy Hook, Connecticut, with her family and a pair of kittens rescued from their backyard.

SELECTED WORKS: *Gregor the Overlander*, 2003; *Gregor and the Prophecy of Bane*, 2004; *Gregor and the Curse of the Warm-bloods*, 2005; *When Charlie McButton Lost Power*, illus. by Mike Lester, 2005; *Gregor and the Marks of Secret*, 2006; *Gregor and the Code of Claw*, 2007; *The Hunger Games*, 2008.

WEB SITE: www.suzannecollinsbooks.com

Photo by Steve Colman

Penny Colman

September 2, 1944–

"When I was eight years old, my mother got a job as a photojournalist at a newspaper in Warren, Pennsylvania, a small town tucked between two rivers at the edge of the Allegheny Mountains in the northwest corner of the state. Occasionally, I got to go with her as she pursued real-life stories, and that is how I learned that there are adventures in writing nonfiction—adventures that ranged from interviewing Chris Pepkey, the saddlemaker, to covering the annual field day and watermelon-eating contest at a state mental hospital, to checking out the rumor that a group of gypsies were camping in a nearby state park.

"At the same time my father, who was a psychiatrist, was writing a newspaper column, 'Everyday Psychology,' and articles for medical journals. Then there were close friends of our family, such as Eda LeShan, a widely published nonfiction writer, and Marian Potter who wrote the children's book *The Little Red Caboose*. When I was in 10th grade I had a teacher—Meredith Coe—who loved grammar and delighted in good writing.

"With all those role models (who not only wrote, but also *read* all the time), no wonder I became a writer, although I did not start my full-time writing career until shortly after my 43rd birthday—proof that it's never too late to find your career-passion!

"I began my writing career as a journalist and wrote articles and essays for magazines and newspapers. Within a few years, I started writing fiction and nonfiction for young readers. In 1992, I published my first two biographies for young readers—*Breaking the Chains: The Crusade of Dorothea Lynde Dix* and *Spies!: Women in The Civil War*. Since then, I've written other biographies and social histories, including *Corpses, Coffins, and Crypts: A History of Burial* (look for the photograph of the grave with two parking meters and the grave with the epitaph 'I Told You I Was Sick'), a book that was named a Best of the Best for the Twenty-first Century by the American Library Association, and *Rosie the Riveter: Women Working on the Home Front in World War II* (check it out and you'll find a photograph of Marilyn Monroe when she was a war worker) that was named an Orbis Pictus Honor Book. My most recent book is *Adventurous Women:*

Eight True Stories about Women Who Made a Difference (you'll 'meet' amazing women, from an Arctic explorer to a woman who started a school with $1.50!) that was named a Notable Social Studies Trade Book.

"All my books require what journalists call 'shoe-leather research,' or going places, talking to people, and searching far and wide for facts and details and true stories. I also spend innumerable hours reading. For *Adventurous Women*, I read rolls of microfilm that contained photographic reproductions of old newspaper and magazine articles. I read scientific reports, books, speeches, and letters. I studied numerous photographs and maps. I also do the picture research for my books, a time-consuming but essential endeavor that involves locating vivid, unusual, and interesting images; ordering prints and getting permission to publish the image; cuing the images into the text and dealing with design issues; and writing captions. I also take the photographs that appear in many of my books.

"To date, I have written many stories, essays, articles, books, and a one-act play. I also blog. In 2001 I began teaching pre-service and in-service teachers (currently I'm a Distinguished Lecturer at Queens College, the City University of New York). I speak in a variety of venues from conferences to classrooms. My favorite topics are women's history and nonfiction writing and reading. I have appeared on television and radio including a segment with Linda Ellerbee on Nickelodeon's 'Nick News'; interviews with Tom Bodett on the 'Looseleaf Book Company' and with Linda Wertheimer on Morning Edition on National Public Radio; and a school visit featuring *Where the Action Was: Women War Correspondents in World War II* on 'Book TV,' C-Span2.

"Take a look at my website for photographs, classroom connections, and lots of other material, including poems written by students who read my book, *Rosie the Riveter*, and pictures by students who read *Toilets, Bathtubs, Sinks, and Sewers: A History of the Bathroom*."

"With all those role models (who not only wrote, but also read all the time), no wonder I became a writer, although I did not start my full-time writing career until shortly after my 43rd birthday— proof that it's never too late to find your career-passion!"

CB CB CB

Born in Denver, Colorado, Penny Colman lived in Oregon, Washington, and Kentucky before her family settled in Pennsylvania in 1949. There she and her three brothers lived with their parents on the grounds of the state mental hospital in North Warren where her father worked as a psychiatrist. When she was eleven, a writer wrote an article about the family for

Redbook called "The Strangest Place to Find a Happy Family." Colman was herself inspired by her experiences there to later write *Breaking the Chains*, a biography of Dorothea Dix, the 19th century crusader for humane treatment of people with mental illness. The year Colman graduated from high school, her parents had a fifth child, Catherine Ann, known as Cam, whose picture Colman later included in *Girls: A History of Growing Up Female in America*.

Colman received her bachelor of arts degree from the University of Michigan, but interrupted her college years by taking time off to hitchhike through Europe, traveling by truck, motorcycle, train, ferry, ship, and even in the cab of a Caterpillar Road Scraper. Returning to the United States she finished college, married, attended graduate school and had three children—Jonathan and the twins David and Stephen. After obtaining her master's degree in teaching from Johns Hopkins University, and while raising her sons, Colman worked as a teacher, a director of an antipoverty agency, an art gallery owner, and an occasional writer. In 1987 she decided to become a full-time writer. Although she has published some fiction, her true passion is the writing of creative, exciting nonfiction.

Courtesy of Crown Publishers, Random House, Inc.

Her first nonfiction titles were stirring biographies of women who became agents of social change in American history. Two of them—*A Woman Unafraid: The Achievements of Frances Perkins* and *Mother Jones and the March of the Mill Children*—were cited as Notable Trade Books in the Field of Social Studies, as was *Strike!: The Bitter Struggle of American Workers from Colonial Times to the Present*, which explored 200 years of labor struggles. With the publication of *Rosie the Riveter* in 1995, Colman became widely recognized as one of the top nonfiction writers for young people. Emphasizing the many changes in women's lives as they took on male-dominated jobs during World War II, *Rosie the Riveter* was named an Orbis Pictus Honor Book, an ALA Best Book for Young Adults, an ALA Notable Children's Book, an IRA Teachers' Choice, an IRA Young Adult Choice, and a *School Library Journal* Best Book of the Year.

In *Girls: A History of Growing Up Female in America*, which won a Parents' Choice Award, Colman highlighted the experiences of American girls from the pre-Colonial era to present times. Her approach to history, through the lives of ordinary girls and how they lived, provides a fascinating perspective for today's readers. In *Where the Action Was: Women War Correspondents in World War II*, an ALA Notable Children's Book and a Notable Social Studies Trade Book, Colman wrote about 18 groundbreaking female journalists and photographers who found ways to overcome discrimination and intimidation and break some of the biggest stories during the war.

While she has focused on women's history and social issues in most of her books, Colman has explored other themes as well. In *Corpses, Coffins, and Crypts*, she answered questions people are often reluctant to ask about burial procedures through the ages. She wrote the book at a time when death was a subject generally avoided in books for middle graders. This groundbreaking title became a Society of School Librarians International Honor Book, a Bank Street College of Education Best Children's Book of the Year, an ALA Best Book for Young Adults, and a *Publishers Weekly* Best Book of the year. *Toilets, Bathtubs, Sinks, and Sewers* examined the history and rites of cleanliness and offered details to pique the interest of young readers—like the fact that Queen Isabella of Spain took only two baths in her lifetime. This title was named an ALA Recommended Book for Reluctant Readers as well as a Children's Book of the Year by the Bank Street College of Education.

Penny Colman lives in Englewood, New Jersey. A frequent speaker at schools and conferences, she has become a well-known advocate for the importance of nonfiction reading and writing for people of all ages.

SELECTED WORKS: *Dare to Seek* (a play), 1976; *I Never Do Anything Bad*, illus. by Pamela T. Keating, 1988; *Dark Closets and Noises in the Night*, illus. by Pamela T. Keating, 1991; *Breaking the Chains: The Crusade of Dorothea Lynde Dix*, 1992; *Spies!: Women in the Civil War*, 1992; *Fannie Lou Hamer and the Fight for the Vote*, 1993; *A Woman Unafraid: The Achievements of Frances Perkins*, 1993; *101 Ways to Do Better in School*, 1993; *Madam C. J. Walker: Building a Business Empire*, 1994; *Mother Jones and the March of the Mill Children*, 1994; *Toilets, Bathtubs, Sinks, and Sewers: A History of the Bathroom*, 1994; *Women in Society: United States of America*, 1994; *Rosie the Riveter: Women Working on the Home Front in World War II*, 1995;

Strike!: The Bitter Struggle of American Workers from Colonial Times to the Present, 1995; *Corpses, Coffins, and Crypts: A History of Burial*, 1997; *Girls: A History of Growing Up Female in America*, 2000; *Where the Action Was: Women War Correspondents in World War II*, 2002; *Adventurous Women: Eight True Stories about Women Who Made a Difference*, 2006; *Thanksgiving: The True Story*, 2008.

SUGGESTED READING: *Something About the Author*, vol. 160, 2005; *Contemporary Authors*, vol. 145, 1995. Periodicals—Colman, Penny, "Adventures in Nonfiction," *Journal of Children's Literature*, Fall, 2002; Colman, Penny, "A New Way to Look at Literature: A Visual Model for Analyzing Fiction and Nonfiction Texts," *Language Arts*, Jan. 2007.

WEB SITE: www.pennycolman.com

Photo by Shauna B. Peet

Elisha Cooper

(el-EYE-sha)
February 22, 1971–

"**D**on't believe what you are about to read. Anyone asked to write an autobiographical essay can't be trusted, not really. Especially someone who writes and draws, someone who uses words and pictures to impose order where none may exist at all. But, if you accept that making art requires making certain choices, and accept that what I say may or may not be true, read on.

"Believe me when I say that I was born in 1971. Trust me when I say that I grew up on a farm . . . a farm in Connecticut with an apple orchard, a view of Long Island Sound, and lots of goats. I took care of the goats. I did!

"I also drew the cows on the farm, who wandered around the fields swishing their tails and chewing their cuds. Then I ripped the drawings up. It made me angry that I couldn't make my cows turn out the way I wanted them to.

"I also drew football players. Those drawings came out better. When I was eight I sent Lynn Swann, the great and graceful Pittsburgh Steelers wide receiver, a drawing I'd done of him. He sent me a signed photo. I loved that photo, and loved Swann, until last year when he ran for governor of Pennsylvania as a conservative Republican and it became clear that he was an idiot. There's a lesson here: it's okay to look up to people, but not too much, because from that perspective all you see is the person's feet.

"In high school, I loved writing and art. I loved sports even more (at some deep level, I still do). In college I played football. If I were a better football player I'd still be playing football. I drew caricatures of my coaches and professors and taped them to the locker and classroom walls. I wasn't the best student. After college I was a messenger at *New Yorker* magazine. I carried manuscripts and art around the city, along with a sketchbook which I'd pull out to draw commuters on the subway, a Soho street, a Yankees game. I wasn't the best messenger, but that sketchbook of my year in New York became my first book.

"My books are nonfiction. I'm interested in how things work: the construction of a building, the production of ice cream, the life of a ballpark. I like following a process, how a place changes over time, how a day unfolds. I like to look as carefully as I can at something, then write about it.

"I'm interested in how things work: the construction of a building, the production of ice cream, the life of a ballpark."

"For a book about the beach, I spent a summer sitting in the sand along Lake Michigan, watching bathers and listening to the gulls overhead and trying to describe it. For a book of essays about becoming a father, I tried to do the same thing, though this process involved looking at myself. For an upcoming book about high school, I spent a year interviewing eight students in a Chicago high school, sketching and recording their experiences.

"Most children's books have talking cats or talking bunnies. That's not my style. I write about what I see. You don't need imagination if your eyes are open. At least, that's how I look at it.

"Okay, that's all for now—an essay on my life so far. I live in Chicago, near the lake. We're about to move to New York. I spend my days writing and drawing and thinking about books, and taking care of my daughters, and wishing I were a wide receiver for the Chicago Bears. What you just read is true, or at least I like to think it is.

"It's all fragments, though. I could have chosen other fragments, like how I feel when I watch a ball spiral through the air, how I like to dance to The Shins when I paint, how the rain is pounding on the pavement outside my café window at this very instant. And these details are as much me as anything else about my life. Believe me."

☙ ☙ ☙

The son of a lawyer and writer who were also farmers, Elisha Cooper grew up near New Haven, Connecticut. He had a lawn-mowing business with a friend when he was young in order to save money so that he could travel. On his travels he took along a tin of watercolors his mother had given him, which he still uses today. As a college student he wrote for the *New Journal*, producing articles about things that he had done on various road trips, including working in a factory bottling beer. The summer before his senior year at Yale University, he worked for the Forest Service in Idaho.

In 1993, when Cooper graduated from Yale, he went to New York and in 1995, his first book, *A Year in New York*, was published, inspired by the sights and sounds he experienced working in the city. Shortly thereafter, he quit his job and traveled around the country, sleeping in his car, bathing in rivers, and creating his second book for adults, *Off the Road: An American Sketchbook*.

For his first two children's books, *Country Fair* and *Ballpark*, Cooper did his research by spending time at New England country fairs and various ballparks, like Fenway Park, Camden Yards, Shea Stadium, and Yankee Stadium. A compact-sized book about the sights, sounds, and scents of that quintessential fall event, *Country Fair* was written with a flair for precise and quirky language and was named a Charlotte Zolotow Highly Commended book for its text. *Ballpark*, which looks at the community within the ballpark, including such behind-the-scenes personnel as the groundskeepers and trainers, was included in the *New York Times* Ten Best Children's Books and became a Parents' Choice Recommended Book.

Like his texts, Cooper's art is spare but specific. With just a few words or a few lines, he evokes for the reader the sensory experience related in each book. *Dance*, which was one of the *New York Times* Best Illustrated Books of 2001, a *Bulletin of the Center for Children's Books* Blue Ribbon book, and a National Parenting Publications Award winner, invites repeated browsing and close inspection. Cooper, who once took a ballet class in college to improve his football skills, drew sketches for *Dance* by watching a class at the Alvin Ailey School in New York and seeing dancers rehearse for an actual production.

For *Beach*, which won the 2006 Society of Illustrators Gold Medal at the Original Art show, Cooper studied beaches in Illinois and Connecticut and combined them with the Fire Island and Cape Hatteras beaches of his memory to come up

Courtesy of Orchard Books

with the impressionistic diminutive figures and scenes he created for the book. While working on *Building*, Cooper spent a month sketching at downtown construction sites in Oakland, California and also worked a few days at an Oakland Habitat for Humanity to get a feel for the physical work of construction. These experiences and his watercolor and pencil drawings bring a true-to-life quality to *Building*, which received a Bologna Ragazzi Award Honorable Mention and was included in the *New York Times* Ten Best Children's Books.

Inspired by the evening walks he used to take with his infant daughter in the Berkeley hills around his home to lull her to sleep, *A Good Night Walk*, a Great Lakes Booksellers Association Book of the Year, is an evocative and poetic look at the small changes in a neighborhood as dusk falls. Cooper's luminous watercolors and gentle text highlight each small, familiar event as day fades into night. *Ice Cream*, on the other hand, returned Cooper to his youthful challenge of trying to draw cows, which he masterfully accomplishes in this book. He explored San Francisco dairies and observed ice cream–making at Dreyer's ice cream factory, with the result being a delicious tale of how ice cream comes into being. *Ice Cream* was honored by *San Francisco Magazine*, which named it a Best of the Bay Area Illustrated Children's Book.

Married to Elise Cappella, a psychologist who teaches at New York University, Elisha Cooper is the father of Zoe, age 5, and

Mia, age 3. He lives with his family in the Greenwich Village section of New York City.

SELECTED WORKS FOR ADULTS: *A Year in New York*, 1995; *Off the Road: An American Sketchbook*, 1996; *A Day at Yale*, 1998; *California, a Sketchbook*, 2000; *Crawling: A Father's First Year*, 2006; *ridiculous/hilarious/terrible/cool; a year in an american high school*, 2008.

SELECTED WORKS FOR CHILDREN: *Country Fair*, 1997; *Ballpark*, 1998; *Building*, 1999; *Henry: A Dog's Life*, 1999; *Dance*, 2001; *Ice Cream*, 2002; *Magic Thinks Big*, 2004; *A Good Night Walk*, 2005; *Beach*, 2006; *Bear Dreams*, 2006.

SUGGESTED READING: *Something About the Author*, vol. 99, 1999. Periodicals—Hulick, Jeannette, "Rising Star: Elisha Cooper," *Bulletin of the Center for Children's Books*, October 2001.

WEB SITE: www.elishacooper.com

Kevin Crossley-Holland

February 7, 1941–

"The motto of my public school was *et nova et vetera*: both new and old. This fairly describes my own life too. Decade after decade I have known and relished change (new people, new places, new experiences, new ideas) and yet have remained faithful to many of the interests and values of my boyhood.

"My father introduced me to the story of Britain's change and continuity. Sitting high above our little cottage on the escarpment of the Chiltern Hills, he invited me to remove elements of the landscape at my feet (a new council house estate, cement works, the railway line) until it became ancient again. With his Welsh harp he said-and-sang folk-tales—old, yet always as young as their most recent retelling. He told my younger sister Sally and me how King Arthur and his warriors lay sleeping under a hill, and I was convinced it must be our hill. And in our garden shed, where once I painted our bull terrier Bruce with bright green spots, my father helped me to set up my 'museum' of potsherds, coins, fossils, and stamps.

"So history and traditional tale were both early interests, and I've never lost them. For all this, I was not at all a keen reader as a boy, much more interested in sport and competition of all kinds and, in time, pretty girls. My first ambition was to be a radio commentator (I used to drive my parents crackers on long car journeys, commentating from the back seat on anything and everything); my second was to be an archaeologist; and my third, throughout my teens, a Church of England priest.

"As a student at Oxford, where I read English, I had to learn the Anglo-Saxon language. Although I'm utterly in love with language, and the music of meaning, I'm not a good linguist, and first time round I failed my Anglo-Saxon exams. But then the passionate, mournful poems of the Anglo-Saxons got into my bloodstream. I began to translate them, including the epic *Beowulf*, and in this I was encouraged by J.R.R. Tolkien.

"I wrote poems in my teens, as many of us do, trying to come to terms with our rampant emotions and with knots in the grain of things. Fifty years on, it's plain that my main preoccupation as a poet has been warmly to record relationships— with my parents, and the women I have loved, my two sons and two daughters; and, secondly, to respond to the harsh, beautiful coastline of North Norfolk where I so often stayed with my grandparents, and where my Minnesotan wife and I now live in an old converted barn.

Courtesy of Kevin Crossley-Holland

"It wasn't until I was in my fifties that I was able to make a living from my writing. Before that, I worked for fifteen years in publishing (with Macmillan and then as editorial director with Victor Gollancz), and for a short term as a BBC talks producer, and I taught in universities in Bavaria and Minnesota, as well as making visits for the British Council to India, Yugoslavia, Iceland, Malawi and elsewhere. When I was a boy, my indefatigable mother (a well-known potter) led the family on annual sorties to the Alps, and I think those trips imbued me with a great love of abroad. As author, professor and publisher, I've had very many opportunities to travel, and I edited *The Oxford Book of Travel Verse*.

"As befits the son of a composer-father and potter-mother, I've always welcomed the chance to collaborate with artists in other disciplines—especially composers and painters. Crossing-places are often potent and in ferment, and the making of an opera, involving so many artistic elements, is perhaps the most hazardous and exciting of all.

"I work hard. In fact, I suppose I'm driven. I'm eager and an enthusiast. And I'm committed to enabling as well as achieving. But I get anxious, and occasionally depressed. I'm a hypochondriac. A romantic. A doer and a dreamer . . .

"That hill. And that king. For many years, I kept thinking about how to add my voice to his never-ending story. And in finding how, I also found myself as a historical novelist. The writing of the *Arthur* trilogy and *Gatty's Tale* involved sustained historical research; I loved that, and I loved shaping the 'intricate dance' of a full-length novel. I loved having room to explore ideas, emotions, relationships, the meeting-place of Christians and Muslims; and I loved drafting and redrafting (seven times). I knew myself to be at full stretch, and therefore fulfilled.

"Not long ago, a boy asked me whether, now I was 65, I would (or even could) write another book! What else should I do? How could I ever stop? I'll go on being an amateur juggler, a man of letters, call it what you will, for as long as I have my wits about me. *Et nova et vetera.*"

"I wrote poems in my teens, as many of us do, trying to come to terms with our rampant emotions and with knots in the grain of things."

୪ ୪ ୪

Steeped in the folklore and history of his native England from earliest childhood, Kevin Crossley-Holland has spent his adult life interpreting that history and lore for audiences of all ages. As an editor, poet, translator, and reteller of old tales, he has celebrated the English language from its earliest Anglo-Saxon roots to the present day. Most recently, he has enjoyed great acclaim as a novelist, combining his historical perspective, gift for research, lyrical writing style, and knowledge of the legends of King Arthur to create a series of highly successful books that combine all these elements.

Born in Mursley in North Buckinghamshire, Crossley-Holland grew up in the village of Whiteleaf among the Chiltern Hills northwest of London. After graduating from Oxford University with honors in 1962, he worked as a fiction and poetry editor for Macmillan publishers until 1969. During those years he published his early children's books and several volumes of poetry for adults and began lecturing for the Tufts-in-London program. His career continued to intertwine periods of editing, teaching, and writing in the following decades. Throughout the 1960s he immersed himself in translating Anglo-Saxon poems, starting with short playful riddles, and eventually, in 1968, publishing his own translation of *Beowulf*, the epic poem that he has called "so entire a world in itself."

Crossley-Holland's first two children's books were spirited retellings of medieval romances, *Havelok the Dane* and *King Horn*, stories that originated with anonymous 13th century bards. In 1968 he collaborated with Jill Paton Walsh in *Wordhoard*, a collection of Anglo-Saxon tales for children. His trilogy of short fictional stories about an Anglo-Saxon boy, beginning with *The Sea Stranger*, appeared in the 1970s, while he was also producing picture book retellings of English folk tales, such as *The Pedlar of Swaffham*. In 1985 the author blended fiction and legend in *Storm*, his short novel about a girl, a ghost, and the courage to face one's fears, which won the Carnegie Medal that year. In 2007 *Storm* was named one of the top ten Carnegie Medal winners in the 70-year history of the award.

During the 1980s Crossley-Holland published some of his finest collections of folktale retellings. After visiting Iceland, he became fascinated by what he has called the "glorious, racy, ice-bright myths" of northern lands. His collection of *The Norse Myths* appeared in the United States to great acclaim in 1980. Returning to the lore of his homeland in *British Folk Tales: New Versions*, he retold 55 heroic legends, homespun tales, and stories of enchantment that included many standards, such as "Jack and the Beanstalk" and "Dick Whittington" as well as lesser-known stories of ghosts, wee folk, and magical transformations. This definitive volume was named an ALA Notable Children's Book and reissued 20 years later in a new edition entitled *The Magic Lands: Folk Tales of Britain and Ireland*.

All his study of legend and language, and the development of his lively writing style, provided rich background for the triumphal and groundbreaking novels of Crossley-Holland's *Arthur* trilogy and its companion volume, *Gatty's Tale*. *The Seeing Stone*, the first volume of the *Arthur* trilogy, was published to great acclaim in 2000 in the United Kingdom. It won the *Guardian* Award for children's fiction, the Nestlé Smarties Prize bronze medal, and the Welsh Books Council's Tir na n-Og Award. Featuring a medieval boy named Arthur in the early years of the 13th century, the books interweave historical fiction with the legends of King Arthur, vividly demonstrating how folklore can inform the development of character and growth of self-knowledge. Published in 2001 in the U.S., *The Seeing Stone* was named an ALA Notable Children's Book, a *Bulletin of the Center for Children's Books* Blue Ribbon title, and a Notable Social Studies Trade Book for Young People, among other accolades.

Arthur de Caldicot grows from an adolescent boy to a young man in the course of the trilogy; and all the while his life-changes

"That hill. And that king. For many years, I kept thinking about how to add my voice to his never-ending story. And in finding how, I also found myself as a historical novelist."

are anticipated, reflected, and illuminated by the stories he sees unfolding in his "seeing stone," a polished piece of obsidian that he carries like a talisman. As the Arthur of legend in the stone grows to manhood, so does Arthur de Caldicot, learning to be a squire and eventually accompanying his knight and mentor on the ill-fated Fourth Crusade, mirrored in the stone by the fall of Camelot. The sweeping breadth of this saga—from the Welsh Marches to the Mediterranean—is matched by its psychological depth as the young protagonist struggles with family ties, friendships, love interests, idealism, and disillusionment before heading home to take up his rightful place in his own manor.

One of the best-loved characters in the Arthur series, Gatty, daughter of an overseer and Arthur's childhood companion,

Courtesy of Arthur A. Levine Books, Scholastic Press

embarks on a harrowing journey of her own in *Gatty's Tale*, when she joins a group of pilgrims heading to Jerusalem in the year 1203. Based on extensive research, *Gatty's Tale* features one of the most fully realized, and least likely, heroines in all of literature as she follows her own pathway to maturation. *Gatty's Tale*, which was retitled *Crossing to Paradise* in its U.S. edition, was shortlisted for the Carnegie Medal in 2008. The Arthur saga has been embraced by readers around the world, translated into more than 20 languages, and has sold over a million copies.

Praised for his memorable characters, vivid writing style, and poetry for all ages, Crossley-Holland has found creative ways to combine his works with other art forms. He has written libretti for operas of two of the East Anglian folk tales he retold. *The Green Children* has been staged in England, Ireland, and Minnesota; *The Wildman* debuted in 1996. Other collaborations with musicians have involved his poetry and translation of *Beowulf* and his retellings of Norse myth. He has written and presented many BBC radio programs and is a frequent speaker at schools and libraries. As a university professor he has held posts at the University of Leeds, St. Olaf College in Minnesota as a Fulbright Scholar, and the University of St. Thomas, also in Minnesota, as Endowed Chair in the Humanities and Fine Arts in the early 1990s. Today he lives on the north Norfolk coast in East

Anglia, England, with his American wife Linda. He has two sons and two daughters from previous marriages. He is an Honorary Fellow of St. Edmund Hall, Oxford, a patron of the Society of Storytelling, and a Fellow of the Royal Society of Literature.

SELECTED WORKS FOR YOUNG READERS (Dates are for British publication; U.S. dates, if different, are in parentheses): *Havelok the Dane*, illus. by Brian Wildsmith, 1964 (1965); *King Horn*, illus. by Charles Keeping, 1965 (1966); *The Green Children*, illus. by Margaret Gordon, 1966 (1968) rev. ed. illus. by Alan Marks, 1994; *The Callow Pit Coffer*, illus. by Margaret Gordon, 1968 (1969); *Wordhoard: Anglo-Saxon Stories*, with Jill Paton Walsh, 1969; *Storm and Other Old English Riddles*, illus. by Miles Thistlethwaite, 1970; *The Pedlar of Swaffham*, illus. by Margaret Gordon, 1971 (1972); *The Sea Stranger* (Vol. 1 of the "Wulf" series), illus. by Joanna Troughton, 1973 (1974); *The Fire-Brother* (Vol. 2 of the "Wulf" series), illus. by Joanna Troughton, 1975; *Green Blades Rising: The Anglo-Saxons*, 1975 (1976); *The Earth-Father* (Vol. 3 of the "Wulf" series), illus. by Joanna Troughton, 1976 (all three volumes combined as *Wulf*, 1988); *The Wildman*, illus. by Charles Keeping, 1976; *The Penguin Book of Norse Myths: Gods of the Vikings*, 1980 (published in the U.S. as *The Norse Myths*, 1980); *The Dead Moon and Other Tales from East Anglia and the Fen Country*, illus. by Shirley Felts, 1982; *Beowulf*, illus. by Charles Keeping, 1982; *Tales from the Mabinogion*, with Gwyn Thomas, illus. by Margaret Jones, 1984 (1985); *Axe-Age, Wolf-Age: A Selection from the Norse Myths*, illus. by Hannah Firmin, 1985; *Storm*, illus. by Alan Marks, 1985 (1989); *The Fox and the Cat: Animal Tales from Grimm*, illus. by Susan Varley, 1985 (1986); *Northern Lights: Legends, Sagas, and Folk Tales*, illus. by Alan Howard, 1987; *British Folk Tales: New Versions*, (1987) illus. by Peter Melnyczuk (reissued as *The Magic Lands: Folk Tales of Britain and Ireland*, 2006); *The Quest for Olwen*, with Gwyn Thomas, illus. by Margaret Jones, 1988; *Under the Sun and Over the Moon: Poetry*, illus. by Ian Penney, 1989; *Sleeping Nanna*, illus. by Peter Melnyczuk, 1989 (1990); *Sea Tongue*, illus. by Clare

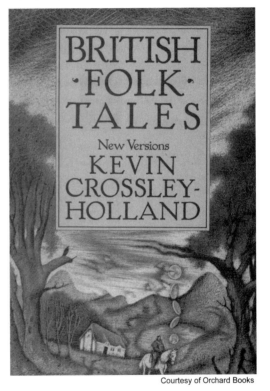

Courtesy of Orchard Books

Challice, 1991; *Tales from Europe*, illus. by Lesley Buckingham, Phyllis Mahon and Emma Whiting, 1991; *Long Tom and the Dead Hand*, illus. by Shirley Felts, 1992; *The Tale of Taliesin*, with Gwyn Thomas, illus. by Margaret Jones, 1992; *The Labours of Herakles*, illus. by Peter Utton, 1993; *The Old Stories: Tales from East Anglia and the Fen Country*, illus. by John Lawrence, 1997; *Short! A Book of Very Short Stories*, 1998; *The King Who Was and Will Be*, illus. by Peter Malone, 1998 (retitled in the U.S.: *The World of King Arthur and His Court: People, Places, Legend, and Lore*, 1999; reissued as *King Arthur's World*, illus. by Hamesh Alles, 2004); *The Young Oxford Book of Fairy Tales*, 1998 (1999); *Enchantment: Fairy Tales, Ghost Stories, and Tales of Wonder*, illus. by Emma Chichester Clark, 2000; *Arthur: The Seeing Stone*, 2000 (2001); *The Ugly Duckling*, illus. by Meilo So, 2001; *Arthur: At the Crossing Places*, 2001 (2002); *Viking! Myths of Gods and Monsters*, 2002 (2003); *Arthur: King of the Middle March*, 2003 (2004); *How Many Miles to Bethlehem?*, illus. by Peter Malone, 2004 (2004); *Outsiders*, 2005; *Gatty's Tale*, 2006 (U.S. title: *Crossing to Paradise*, 2008).

SELECTED WORK FOR ADULTS: *On Approval*, 1961; *My Son*, 1966; *Beowulf*, 1968; *Norfolk Poems*, 1970; *The Rain Giver*, 1972; *The Dream-House*, 1976; *The Exeter Book of Riddles*, 1979; *Time's Oriel: Poems*, 1983; *The Oxford Book of Travel Verse*, ed., 1986; *Waterslain and Other Poems*, 1986; *East Anglian Poems*, 1988; *Oenone in January*, 1988; *The Painting Room*, 1988; *New and Selected Poems, 1965-1990*, 1990; *Eleanor's Advent*, 1992; *The Language of Yes*, 1996; *Poems from East Anglia*, 1997; *The New Exeter Book of Riddles*, ed. with Lawrence Sail, 1999; *Selected Poems*, 2001; *Light Unlocked: Christmas Card Poems*, ed. with Lawrence Sail, 2006.

SUGGESTED READING: *Something About the Author*, vol. 165, 2006; *Children's Literature Review*, vol. 47, 1998; *Dictionary of Literary Biography*, vol. 161, 1996; *Poets of Great Britain and Ireland since 1960*, 1985. Periodicals—Zvirin, Stephanie, "The *Booklist* Interview: Kevin Crossley-Holland," *Booklist*, April 15, 2002. Online—"Arthur Trilogy Discussion Guide," at www.scholastic. com

WEB SITE: www.kevincrossley-holland.com

"The summer after sixth grade, my goal was to read *The Complete Works of Sir Arthur Conan Doyle*. It was over 1000 pages long, but I was so fascinated by the stories about Sherlock Holmes and his faithful sidekick, Watson, that I didn't care how long it took me to finish. A few months later, I discovered Edgar Rice Burroughs, H. G. Wells, and Jules Verne and spent many hours in the portable extension of the Dublin (California) Public Library reading their fascinating tales of the imagination.

"It was during my Doyle/Burroughs/Wells/Verne phase that I decided to become a writer. Using the hunt-and-peck two-fingered typing method on our ancient Underwood typewriter, I banged out several attempts at a novel—none ever longer than ten pages—and each bore an amazing resemblance to *War of the Worlds*.

"When it became clear that I would never become a novelist if all my books were just one-chapter rip-offs of *War of the Worlds*, I shelved my dream of becoming a writer and allowed sports to occupy most of my time.

Photo by Elizabeth Crowe

Chris Crowe

May 28, 1954–

"After seventh grade, we moved from California to Tempe, Arizona, and my sports career revved up. At McClintock High School, I played football, basketball, and track and limited my writing to weird and rambling parodies of short stories or poems I'd read or weird and rambling (and funny, I thought) notes to my best friend in the margins of his American history book, which I borrowed every day because I'd lost my book.

"Although I still read lots of fiction, sports continued to dominate my life. By my junior year, football and track were my best sports, and I started thinking that maybe I had a future in at least one of them. A football injury made my senior track season too mediocre to interest any colleges, but I was good enough in football that a couple of Division I schools offered scholarships, and I decided to leave Arizona to play football for Brigham Young University in Utah.

"Being an athlete made high school life fun and earned me a college scholarship, but it also overshadowed my dream of becoming a writer because, as far as I knew, it was impossible for anyone to be a writer *and* a football player. In high school and college, I read a lot, got decent grades, wrote when I was required to but never had the guts to write what I really wanted to write.

"Things changed when I got married. My wife, Elizabeth, came from a family of artists and writers, a family about as opposite mine as it could possibly be. Elizabeth and her family valued the fine arts with the same passion that my family valued sports, and it was her influence that finally got me started on writing.

"By the time I was 24 and was teaching high school English full-time at McClintock High (my alma mater!), I started working seriously at writing, spending many nights, weekends, and holidays pounding out stories and articles on my new Smith Corona electric typewriter; that year, I had my first article published. When I was 25, I landed a summer job as a writer for *The Arizona Golfer*, and the next summer, I started writing a humor column for *The Latter Day Sentinel*. The following year, while still writing the column, I sold a few freelance magazine articles but also received more than 100 rejections.

"With each acceptance and even each rejection, I learned something new about writing, and I kept at it, have kept at it all these years. Since then, I've published hundreds of articles, a handful of short stories, a few poems, and eight books. And I now have several more books in the works.

"Unfortunately, I have outgrown being an athlete, but I suppose I have never quite outgrown adolescence. I loved high school and all the goofiness and angst and growing up it involved, and that's probably why I spent ten years as a high school English teacher and why I still read and write stories about teenagers. I hope to keep it up long after my own teenagers have grown up and started raising teenagers of their own."

> *"Being an athlete made high school life fun and earned me a college scholarship, but it also overshadowed my dream of becoming a writer because, as far as I knew, it was impossible for anyone to be a writer and a football player."*

 C3　C3　C3

Born in Danville, Illinois, Chris Crowe moved to California when he was in sixth grade and spent his teenage years in Tempe, Arizona. He attended Brigham Young University (BYU), in Provo, Utah, on a football scholarship, playing all four years and competing in the 1974 Fiesta Bowl, the university's first-ever bowl-game appearance. Though he originally planned to major in history and become a high school history teacher and coach, after taking a history course, he changed his mind and decided to return to his first love—reading and writing. He graduated in 1976 with a B.A. in English. Crowe's early interest in history would later resurface when he began to write for young adults.

Following graduation, Crowe returned to Arizona to teach high school English. After earning a master's degree in education from Arizona State University, in Tempe, in 1980, Crowe taught night classes at Mesa Community College and found that, although he enjoyed teaching high school, he also liked working with older students. He received his Ph.D. in education in 1986, also from Arizona State.

As part of a teacher-exchange program, Crowe spent the 1983–84 school year in Japan, with his wife, Elizabeth, whom he had married in 1973, and their two young children, Christy and Jonathan. Later, after Crowe finished graduate school, he accepted an English professorship at a new university in Himeji, Japan. By this time two more children, Carrie and Joanne, had joined the family. The Crowes lived in Japan for the next three years. They loved the excitement and challenge of living in another culture, but they missed the United States, so moved back in stages—first to the island of Oahu, where Crowe taught at BYU-Hawaii. After four years there, he accepted a job in the English department at the main campus of BYU in Provo, Utah. One of his areas of expertise has been young adult literature, and he has been active in the Assembly on Literature for Adolescents (ALAN) of the National Council of Teachers of English.

Crowe's first books were published by the Church of Jesus Christ of Latter-day Saints and dealt with issues of religious life.

Courtesy of Phyllis Fogelman Books, Penguin Putnam, Inc.

He then wrote a biography of the African American author Mildred Taylor. While researching Taylor's life story, Crowe came across a reference to a crime that occurred in the 1950s, an event that helped spark the civil rights movement. Puzzled as to why he had never heard the name Emmett Till before, Crowe started researching the case and felt compelled to tell the story.

Crowe first approached the story of Emmett Till—a young African American from Chicago who was brutally murdered in Mississippi—from a fictional perspective. In *Mississippi Trial, 1955*, he told the story from the viewpoint of a 16-year-old who is visiting with his grandfather at the time of the murder. The book met with great critical success, winning an International Reading Association Young Adults' Choices Award. It was named an ALA Best Book for Young Adults, a Notable Book for a Global Society, and a Notable Social Studies Trade Book for Young People. It also earned the Jefferson Cup Award in Virginia and the Nebraska Golden Sower Award.

Having gathered a wealth of background material for the novel, and concerned that his readers know the facts, Crow decided to write an informational book on the same subject. *Getting Away with Murder: The True Story of the Emmett Till Case* was named a Best Children's Book of the Year by Bank Street College of Education, a Capitol Choice, and a Cooperative Children's Book Center (CBC) Choice. It was also cited as an ALA Best Book for Young Adults, a Jane Addams Honor Book, and an Orbis Pictus Award Recommended Title.

The role of sports in the life of teens has interested Crowe since his own adolescence. In *More Than a Game*, he authored a book to help teachers, librarians, and teens realize the importance of sports themes in contemporary writing for young adults.

In his free moments, Crowe enjoys spending time with his family, especially his granddaughter, Ella Ruth Hughes. He and his wife enjoy long walks in Rock Canyon, near their Utah home. They also love to travel.

SELECTED WORKS FOR YOUNG READERS: *Two Roads*, 1994; *For the Strength of You*, 1997; *From the Outside Looking In: Short Stories for LDS Teenagers*, as editor, 1998; *Presenting Mildred D. Taylor*, 1999; *Mississippi Trial, 1955*, 2002; *Getting Away with Murder: The True Story of the Emmett Till Case*, 2003; *More Than a Game: Sports Literature for Young Adults*, 2004; *Up Close: Thurgood Marshall*, 2008.

SELECTED WORKS FOR ADULTS: *Fatherhood, Football, and Turning Forty: Confessions of a Middle-aged Mormon Male*, 1995; *Teaching the Selected Works of Mildred D. Taylor*, 2007.

SUGGESTED READING: Crowe, Chris, "Rescuing Reluctant Readers," *English Journal*, May 1999; Crowe, Chris, "Young Adult Literature," *English Journal*, March 2003; Lesesne, Teri, "History as Story: An Interview with Chris Crowe," *Teacher Librarian*, April 2004; Crowe, Chris, "Going Deep: A Fan Applauds a Growing Genre of YA Sports Novels," *School Library Journal*, March 2005.

WEB SITE: www.chriscrowe.com

The events of Roald Dahl's childhood—full of both sadness and whimsy—could have come right out of one of his novels. Roald's father, Harald, was a wealthy ship's broker who had immigrated to the British Isles from Norway near the turn of the 20th century. He returned to his homeland in 1911 to marry his second wife, Sophie Hesselberg. Roald, born in 1916 in Llandaff, Wales and the third of five children, was three when his seven-year-old sister, Astri, died of appendicitis. Grief-stricken at the loss of his daughter, Harald Dahl contracted pneumonia and died two months later.

Sophie remained in Wales because her husband had wanted his children to attend British schools. When Roald was nine and a student at the Llandaff Cathedral School he was beaten so severely by the headmaster that Sophie decided to send him to Repton, a highly regarded boarding school. The young boy had found the experience terrifying, and cane-wielding headmasters became a staple feature in many of the books he wrote as an adult. Roald managed to survive in the rough-and-tumble atmosphere of boarding school because he was good at sports. He was also enthralled by one particular school activity that took place with happy regularity. Each month a representative from the Cadbury chocolate company would come to the school and present every boy with a plain gray cardboard box. Inside the box were eleven chocolate bars, including new varieties that Cadbury wanted the lucky Repton boys to taste test. The experience planted the seeds in Roald's mind for his most famous story, *Charlie and the Chocolate Factory*.

Summers were a wonderful escape from the discipline and dreariness of boarding school life. Each June, Sophie Dahl took her children to an island in Norway—"Magic Island," the Dahl children called it. There, surrounded by a doting extended family, Roald heard stories about witches and trolls. The Dahl children, who spoke Norwegian with Sophie at home, were taught to take pride in their Norse heritage.

When Roald Dahl left the Repton School in 1934, he didn't choose to attend Oxford or Cambridge, as Sophie wished, but went to work in British East Africa (which included the present-day countries of Kenya, Tanzania, and Uganda) with the Shell

Courtesy of Library of Congress, Prints & Photographs Division, Carl Van Vechten Collection

Roald Dahl

September 13, 1916–
November 23, 1990

Oil Company. There he learned to speak Swahili. During World War II Dahl joined the Royal Air Force as a fighter pilot and flew many missions over the Mediterranean. In 1940, on one of his first flights, his plane crashed in the Sahara desert and he sustained multiple head injuries, needing repeated surgeries to repair his nose and facial bones. He completed his wartime service in Washington, DC, as a British embassy attaché.

Dahl's writing career began while he was living in Washington. A writer for the *Saturday Evening Post* interviewed him about his wartime experiences. Dahl ended up taking more notes than the reporter, and what he had written down became a story called "Piece of Cake," which the *Post* published. This story was later included in a collection, *Over to You: Ten Stories of Fliers and Flying*. Before long his stories began appearing in other national magazines. As part of his job with the British Embassy, Dahl met political and artistic celebrities, including Walt Disney, who loved Roald's first story for children, "The Gremlins." Disney purchased the rights to the story and planned to turn it into an animated feature. The story was based on an RAF myth about gnome-like creatures that caused planes to crash. The animated feature was never made, but Disney did produce a picture book called *Walt Disney: The Gremlins (A Royal Air Force Story by Flight Lieutenant Roald Dahl.)* The story was a favorite of Eleanor Roosevelt, wife of President Franklin Roosevelt, who read the book to her children. (An unrelated movie called *Gremlins* was produced by Warner Brothers in 1984. Though the story was completely different, director Joe Dante claimed that Dahl's book had some influence on the film.)

> *Each month a representative from the Cadbury chocolate company would come to the school and present every boy with a plain gray cardboard box.*

Throughout the 1940s and early 1950s, Roald Dahl wrote short stories for adults, most of them set during World War II. Though today Dahl is best known as a writer of children's books, he won the Edgar Allan Poe Award from the Mystery Writers of America in 1954, 1959, and 1980 for his adult writing, and was praised as a "master of the macabre." One criticism often made about his adult work, however, was that he didn't show much compassion for his main characters.

In 1945 Dahl had moved back home to England to be near his mother, but in the early 1950s he applied for a permanent American visa and went to live in New York, where he met the American actress Patricia Neal. Dahl and Neal were married in 1953 and bought a house near his mother's home in Buckinghamshire, England. The Dahls had seven children, but tragically, one of their daughters died at age seven of complications from the measles, a strange echo of the sister Roald had lost when he was a child. Later their infant son, Theo, was severely injured when his baby carriage was struck by a car while his nanny pushed him across a New York City street. Theo developed hydrocephalus, or fluid build-up in the brain. As a result Dahl helped develop a device, the Wade-Dahl-Till valve, which was designed to relieve the condition. A few years later, in 1965, Patricia Neal suffered a debilitating stroke at the age of 39.

During the 1960s, as Roald Dahl endured these personal tragedies, he created many of his most memorable works of children's fiction, inspired by his own children. These books contain both the cynical bite and the madcap whimsy that became Dahl's trademark. In *James and the Giant Peach*, Aunt Sponge and Aunt Spiker, who have made James's life a misery following the death of his parents, are crushed by the runaway peach. Charlie Bucket of *Charlie and the Chocolate Factory* finds a dollar on the street and—despite his family's poverty—uses it to buy a Whipple-Scrumptious Fudgemallow Delight. Inside this chocolate treat Charlie finds a coveted Golden Ticket, which permits him to join four other children for a private tour of Willy Wonka's chocolate factory. The other four are spoiled, greedy, unpleasant children and during the factory tour, Roald Dahl, through his main character, Willy Wonka, takes pleasure in treating them harshly.

Courtesy of Alfred A. Knopf, Random House, Inc.

Throughout the 1960s and 1970s, Dahl wrote movie screenplays as well as plays, poetry, works of nonfiction, and novels and stories for both children and adults. Two of his scripts—the James Bond film *You Only Live Twice* and *Chitty Chitty Bang Bang*—were adaptations of novels by Ian Fleming. He also adapted *Charlie and the Chocolate Factory* for the Walt Disney film *Willy Wonka and the Chocolate Factory* in 1971. During this time adult critics often saw Dahl's work as too acidic and his characters randomly subjected to cruelty. Young readers, on the other hand, usually found Dahl a comforting advocate for their own sense of powerlessness in the world. His depiction of parents, guardians, and other adults may reflect the strict discipline common during his own childhood, when children were often punished harshly for what today seem like minor misdeeds. In the 1980s he told about those early days in his autobiography

Boy: Tales of Childhood. A second autobiographical book, *Going Solo*, recounts his war experiences.

Roald Dahl's marriage to Patricia Neal ended in divorce in 1983 and shortly afterwards he married Felicity Crosland. He began to approach his fiction with more compassion than before. During this time he created *The Witches*, *The BFG*, and *Matilda*, all of which feature an unusually close bond between the main child character and an adult. In *The Witches*, a young boy learns the terrible truth about witches from his Norwegian grandmother, who vows to help him defeat them. In *The BFG*, Sophie, a lonely orphan, befriends the one giant who refuses to eat humans. And in *Matilda*, a young girl with magical powers and nasty parents bonds with a kind teacher, Jennifer Honey, to thwart her school's evil headmistress. The essential Dahl protagonist—like James, Charlie, or Matilda—is often a shy, insecure child who learns to trust him- or herself and stand up to evil. Dahl never forgot how it felt to be treated unfairly by adults, and that is undoubtedly one of the reasons his stories are so popular with children.

Over the course of his career, Roald Dahl won numerous children's choice awards in America and Australia as well as his native Britain. In 1983 he was presented a World Fantasy Convention Lifetime Achievement Award, and in 1989 was named the Children's Author of the Year by the British Book Awards. *The Witches* won the Whitbread Children's Book of the Year award in 1983, and *Esio Trot* captured the Nestlé Smarties Prize in the ages 6–8 category in 1990.

Roald Dahl continued writing until just before his death from leukemia in 1990. Every day he walked the two hundred yards from his home to a little brick hut in an apple orchard where he would write for at least two hours. After his death his widow, Felicity Dahl, opened the one-room hut to the public on selected days during the year. Adults would often exclaim about the dingy, untidy room while children would delight at the sight of a huge ball made up of foil candy wrappers, which the author added to each day after finishing his daily chocolate bar. In 2005 the Roald Dahl Museum and Story Centre opened in Great Missenden, Buckinghamshire, England, where visitors can now see a replica of the writing hut as well as many fascinating exhibits related to the author. The Roald Dahl Children's Gallery in Aylesbury uses scenes from Dahl's stories as interactive exhibits and is visited by school classes as well as individuals. The Roald Dahl Foundation, established to continue the charitable support the author provided when he was alive, gives grants in three areas: neurology, hematology, and literacy. On September 13, 2006, which would have been the author's 90th birthday, Roald Dahl Day was celebrated all over England with activities related to his books.

SELECTED WORKS WRITTEN FOR CHILDREN: *The Gremlins: A Royal Air Force Story*, 1943; *James and the Giant Peach*, illus. by Nancy Ekholm Burkert, 1961 (illus. by Lane Smith, 1996; illus. by Quentin Blake, 2001); *Charlie and the Chocolate Factory*, illus. by Joseph Schindelman, 1964 (illus. by Quentin Blake, 1998); *The Magic* Finger, illus. by William Pène du Bois, 1966 (illus. by Quentin Blake, 1995); *Fantastic Mr. Fox*, illus. by Donald Chaffin, 1970 (illus. by Quentin Blake, 2002); *Charlie and the Great Glass Elevator*, illus. by Joseph Schindelman, 1972 (illus. by Quentin Blake, 2001); *Danny the Champion of the World*, illus. by Jill Bennett, 1975 (illus. by Quentin Blake, 1998); *The Wonderful Story of Henry Sugar and Six More*, 1977; The *Enormous Crocodile*, illus. by Quentin Blake, 1978; *The Twits,* illus. by Quentin Blake, 1980; *George's Marvelous* Medicine, illus. by Quentin Blake, 1981; *The BFG*, illus. by Quentin Blake, 1982; *Revolting Rhymes*, illus. by Quentin Blake, 1982; *Dirty Beasts*, illus. by Rosemary Fawcett, 1983 (illus. by Quentin Blake, 1984); *The Witches*, illus. by Quentin Blake,1983; *Boy: Tales of Childhood*, 1984; *The Giraffe and the Pelly and Me*, illus. by Quentin Blake, 1985; *Going Solo: The Thrilling Sequel to Boy*, 1986; *Matilda*, illus. by Quentin Blake, 1988; *Esio Trot*, illus. by Quentin Blake, 1990; *The Minpins*, illus. by Patrick Benson, 1991.

SELECTED WORKS WRITTEN FOR ADULTS: *Over to You*, 1946; *Sometime Never: A Fable for Supermen*, 1948; *Someone Like You*, 1953; *My Uncle Oswald*, 1980; *The Collected Short Stories*, 1991.

SUGGESTED READING: Farrell, Barry, *Roald and Pat*, 1969; Treglown, Jeremy, *Roald Dahl: A Biography*, 1994; Shavick, Andrea, *Roald Dahl: The Champion Storyteller*, 1998; Woog, Adam, *Roald Dahl* (Inventors and Creators series), 2004; Houle, Michelle H., *Roald Dahl: Author of Charlie and the Chocolate Factory*, 2006. Periodicals—*New York Times* Obituary, Nov. 24, 1990; Talbot, Margaret, "The Candy Man," *The New Yorker*, July 11 and 18, 2005.

WEB SITES: www.roalddahl.com
www.roalddahlmuseum.org

An earlier profile of Roald Dahl appeared in *Third Book of Junior Authors* (1972).

Courtesy of Penguin Young Readers Group

Paula Danziger

August 18, 1944–
July 8, 2004

Funny, flamboyant, fascinating, fun loving, friendly, and felicitous were all facets of Paula Danziger's irrepressible personality, imbuing her books from the first to the last. She was always outgoing, energetic, bubbling over with enthusiasm, and displaying a riotous sense of humor; she had a passion for travel and for meeting new friends.

Born in Washington, DC and raised in New York, Paula knew from the time she was in second grade that she wanted to be a writer. In an interview for Teenreads.com, she said, "When my father would yell at me, I told myself someday I'd use it in a book." However, that day would take almost thirty years to arrive.

A strong influence on her life was the work of poet John Ciardi, whom she met while she was studying to be a teacher at Montclair State College in New Jersey. She landed a job babysitting for Ciardi's family and accompanied them to several summer writers' conferences. It was Ciardi who instilled in her an appreciation for poetry and writing and encouraged her own efforts. After graduating from college in 1967 with a degree in English, Paula taught at the junior high, senior high, and college levels, as well as counseling students. Those first-hand experiences with adolescent issues laid the groundwork for her young adult fiction, in which she tackled family relationships, teenage obesity, social interactions, and personal development.

Her first book was a result of two bizarre back-to-back car accidents during the time she was working on a master's degree in reading. The first mishap resulted in whiplash, but the second one was much more serious. Just days after the first incident Paula was riding in a car that was hit head-on by a drunken driver and she struck the windshield. She suffered temporary brain damage that brought on dyslexia, leaving her unable to read and haunted by nightmares.

The shock of the accidents was a wake-up call; if she wanted to pursue a career in writing, she'd better do it before she was "hit by a truck." She confronted her trauma by beginning a novel about a girl who confronts the feeling of powerlessness; *The Cat Ate My Gymsuit* is a story of survival and being able to celebrate one's uniqueness. Published in 1974, its fresh and humorous approach grabbed teenagers' attention immediately; it is a funny/sad story about an unglamorous but plucky girl beset by self-doubt who leads a protest over a teacher's firing. Danziger's therapeutic novel was at the forefront of realistic books for teenagers that tackled painful adolescent issues with a sense of humor and created an audience that clamored for more.

Her second book, *The Pistachio Prescription*, featured another insecure teenage girl who overcomes health problems and conflicts with her feuding parents. Danziger's spirited and resilient style had taken root. One year later, in 1979, *Can You Sue Your Parents for Malpractice?* was published, followed in 1980 by *There's a Bat in Bunk Five.* Danziger was now an established author for young adults, and her popularity was soaring. From the interest-piquing titles to the first-person narrative voices to the humor and breezy dialogue, she had tapped into the "teen scene" with brio and gusto.

When asked if she consciously wrote about serious issues, Danziger answered, "Yes . . . [because] life is both serious and funny. Ciardi told me, 'If you underline the funny lines in red and the serious lines in blue, by the end of the poem it'll be purple.' That's what I try to do—blur the lines."

In 1996 she turned her intuitive connection with teens toward younger readers by writing the first in a chapter-book series about a feisty young girl who would become her most popular character. *Amber Brown Is Not a Crayon* was the beginning of over a dozen stories starring likeable Amber as she deals with typical grade school crises. Danziger's fast-paced and breezy text addresses such familiar contemporary traumas as divorce and blended families with empathy and humor. A second series of books for younger readers features the irrepressible Amber at a younger age.

The saying "opposites attract" could easily be applied not only to Danziger and Ann M. Martin, famed author of the Baby Sitters Club books, but also to the main characters in the two books that they wrote together. Introduced by a fan of both writers, the candid, effervescent Danziger and the quiet, serious Martin were an unlikely author team, but it was the differences in their personalities that made their two collaborations so successful. In *P.S. Longer Letter Later* and *Snail Mail No More*, two junior high school best friends are suddenly separated when one moves to a new community. They sustain their friendship through an exchange of letters, with each author giving voice to one of the girls. As the title of the sequel indicates, e-mail later became the two friends' preferred mode of communication.

> *When asked if she consciously wrote about serious issues, Danziger answered, "Yes . . . [because] life is both serious and funny."*

Given her adeptness with words, Danziger surprised fans by both writing and illustrating *United Tates of America* with her own 32 pages of scrapbook art. When Sarah Kate Tate's great uncle dies and leaves the Tate family a large sum of money to travel and expand their horizons, Sarah creates a scrapbook with photos of their journeys and adventures. Danziger enjoyed surprises ,and in a wry twist her final book was another first for her, a picture book that was published posthumously in 2004, *Barfburger Baby, I Was Here First.*

The degree to which Danziger connected with kids' inner feelings, worries, fears, insecurities, and emotions was evident in the numerous awards she received, including several Children's Choice awards, the Parents' Choice Award for Literature, Children's Books of the Year citations from the Child Study Association of America, IRA-CBC Children's Choice Awards, a nomination for the British Book Award, and multiple state awards for young readers.

Courtesy of Penguin Young Readers Group

Her untimely death at age 59 sent a wave of sadness through the children's book community. Her uproarious personality and "tell-it-like-it-is" directness made her one of the most beloved children's authors of modern times. To honor her zeal for bringing children and books together, the Society of Children's Book Writers and Illustrators created the Amber Brown Grant, named for her most popular character, which provides funding for schools to bring authors and illustrators into the classrooms Nothing would have pleased Danziger more. This comedienne of children's books left behind a bevy of characters, a legion of fans, and her distinct "Danziger" mark in children's literature; Zorro-style, she brandished her pen with a "D" for dynamic, daring, and down-to-earth.

SELECTED WORKS: *The Cat Ate My Gymsuit*, 1974; *The Pistachio Prescription*, 1978; *Can You Sue Your Parents for Malpractice?*, 1979; *There's a Bat in Bunk Five*, 1980; *The Divorce Express*, 1982; *It's an Aardvark-Eat-Turtle World*, 1985; *This Place Has No Atmosphere*, 1986; *Remember Me to Harold Square*, 1987; *Everyone Else's Parents Said Yes*, 1989; *Make Like a Tree and*

Leave, 1990; *Earth to Matthew*, 1991; *Not for a Billion, Gazillion Dollars*, 1992; *Thames Doesn't Rhyme with James*, 1994; *P.S. Longer Letter Later* (with Ann M. Martin), 1998; *Snail Mail No More* (with Ann M. Martin), 2000; *United Tates of America*, 2002; *Barfburger Baby, I Was Here First!*, illus. by G. Brian Karas, 2004.

SELECTED WORKS IN SERIES: Amber Brown series (all illus. by Tony Ross): *Amber Brown Is Not a Crayon*, 1994; *You Can't Eat Your Chicken Pox, Amber Brown*, 1995; *Amber Brown Goes Fourth*, 1995; *Amber Brown Wants Extra Credit*, 1996; *Forever Amber Brown*, 1996; *Amber Brown Sees Red*, 1997; *Amber Brown Is Feeling Blue*, 1998; *I, Amber Brown*, 1999; *What a Trip, Amber Brown*, 2001; *It's Justin Time, Amber Brown*, 2001; *Get Ready for Second Grade, Amber Brown*, 2002; *It's a Fair Day, Amber Brown*, 2002; *Amber Brown Is Green with Envy*, 2003; *Second Grade Rules, Amber Brown*, 2004; *Orange You Glad It's Halloween, Amber Brown*, 2005.

Courtesy of Penguin Young Readers Group

SUGGESTED READING: *Something about the Author*, vol. 155, 2005; *Something about the Author*, vol. 149, 2004; Silvey, Anita, *The Essential Guide to Children's Books and Their Creators*, 2002; Cullinan, Bernice and Diane Person, *The Continuum Encyclopedia of Children's Literature*, 2001; Drew, Bernard A., *The One Hundred Most Popular Young Adult Authors*, 1996; Krull, Kathleen, *Presenting Paula Danziger*, 1995; Feitlowitz, Marguerite, *Authors and Artists for Young Adults*, vol. 4, 1990. Periodicals— *The New York Times*. Obituary, July 10, 2004; *Washington Post*, Obituary, July 13, 2004; Elliot, Ian, "Paula Danziger: A Zest for Living," *Teaching PreK–8*, November/December 1995.

WEB SITE: www.teenreads.com/authors/au-danziger-paula.asp

An earlier profile of Paula Danziger appeared in the *Fifth Book of Junior Authors and Illustrators* (1983)

Courtesy of Kate Denslow

Sharon Phillips Denslow

Sharon Phillips Denslow

August 25, 1947–

"I was born in Murray, a small town in western Kentucky. When I was five, we moved to Marshall County where both sets of my grandparents lived. I visited my grandparents on their farms every chance I got and loved listening to them tell stories, including their own version of 'The Three Billy Goats Gruff Upstairs in the Attic.'

Out in the country I had to learn to entertain myself. I put together a crystal radio, glued and assembled and painted a plastic tiger head model (complete with fangs and whiskers), attempted dozens of paint-by-number kits, wrote to five pen pals, made my own mock-up of a magazine, joined the Natural Wildlife club for kids and pasted animal and insect stickers dutifully next to the appropriate description, carved peach-seed baskets, made sculptures out of wadded-up aluminum foil and pearls from a broken necklace and different colors of nail polish, rode ponies, explored the countryside from Soldier Creek to Slick Back, ran through fields avoiding hateful turkey gobblers and bulls with long horns who chased me up pear trees, and read everything I could find, starting with Golden Books and moving up to comics and Nancy Drew.

"Our public library was one room in a building next to the fire department uptown in Benton. Sometimes when they parked the fire truck outside you had to squeeze by to get to the library door. That little city library was where I first saw beautiful picture books with thick pages and shiny covers . . . an entire bookcase of them! I was amazed that grown-up people had a job doing something so wonderful. I wanted to write books like those too. I wanted to be a part of that writing, drawing, storytelling world.

"But I had no clue how to become an author. And I had no idea I even had any talent for writing until I met Miss Newton. When we walked into our eleventh grade English class we didn't know what to expect, and we were scared. Rumor had it Miss Newton was tough. Rumor had it Miss Newton took no prisoners.

"Miss Hazel Newton might have been about five feet tall. She wore stiletto heels with pointy toes and big cat's eye glasses. When she smiled you didn't know if she was amused or merely getting ready to pounce. Behind her glasses one of her eyes roamed just short of center, so you never knew exactly which of us she was watching.

"After the first week she decided we were lazy as sloths. She shook her head, put her hands on her hips, and set us to work. She handed out small, square writing notebooks. She smiled at us in pouncing amusement.

"'Essays,' she said. 'You are going to write three-page essays every day.'

"When someone groaned at the idea of three whole pages a day, she assured us that if we could write an introduction, three supporting points, and a conclusion in one page that made sense, that was all right with her (knowing full well that the shorter and tighter you write, the harder it is).

"We read short stories from the mounds of jacketless old books on her desk and wrote essays.

"We wrote essays about the topics she put on the blackboard.

"We wrote essays about the day's current events.

"We wrote essays about our feelings.

"The rumors about Miss Newton had been right. She was tough. Nobody dared act up in class. Who wanted to have her stand in front of you, her hands on her hips, glaring?

"When the first graded essays came back, she announced to the class that there was only one essay worthy of an A and it was actually an A-minus-minus. She handed all the other papers out, said 'Miss Phillips,' plopped the A-minus-minus paper on my desk, and smiled a real smile.

"I never doubted that I was a writer after that.

"Miss Newton was the first person to tell me I could write.

"My grandfather was the first person to pay me for writing. At the time, since I spent a lot of afternoons in his yard drawing and painting, he thought he was paying me for art. Only my Granddad Riley could see art in a 'For Sale by Owner' sign.

"'Just remember, years from now,' he said as he handed me a ten-dollar bill, 'that I was the first one to buy something from you.'"

> *"But I had no clue how to become an author. And I had no idea I even had any talent for writing until I met Miss Newton."*

ଔ   ଔ   ଔ

Sharon Phillips Denslow attended elementary school and high school in Benton, Kentucky, but moved back to the town of her birth to obtain a degree in Journalism and English at Murray State University. She married an Ohioan and settled in Westlake, Ohio where she became a children's librarian at the local library. That job provided much opportunity for her creative talents—making life-size mummies and papier-mâché chairs to look like Frankenstein's monster, writing puppet plays, dramas, and comedies for kids to act out. When her youngest daughter was two years old, she decided to work at her writing to fulfill a longstanding dream of publishing a children's book.

Denslow's family life, pets, and experiences often find their way into her books for children. Her own high school librarian was the namesake for Miss Pace in *On the Trail with Miss Pace*. Her dogs have provided the basis for dog characters in *Night Owls* and *Big Wolf and Little Wolf*. Countless incidents from her

own childhood roaming in the hills and fields of Kentucky have found their way into her stories. Her first book, *Night Owls*, won a Friends of American Writers' Merit Award. Several of her titles have appeared on the *Smithsonian* magazine's Notable Books list. *Big Wolf and Little Wolf*, a playful and warm-hearted family bedtime story, won an Oppenheim Toy Portfolio Gold Award.

Perhaps her most successful title, *Georgie Lee*, proves the theory that authors write best when they rely on their own experience. The story, exuberantly illustrated by Lynne Rae Perkins, tells of a young boy, J. D., spending time on his grandparents' farm, just as Denslow did when she was young. The title character is a cow of uncanny cleverness. *Georgie Lee* was cited as an ALA Notable Children's Book and appeared on Bank Street College's Best Books of the Year list. *All Their Names Were Courage*, a book for older children, is based on Denslow's great-grandmother Sallie and tells of a girl who compiles a book about horses that were used in the Civil War and the soldiers who honored and cared for them. Both *Georgie Lee* and *All Their Names Were Courage* appeared on New York Public Library's list, 100 Books for Reading and Sharing.

In 2000 Sharon Phillips Denslow retired from library work to write full time. Her husband, Tony, a retired journalist, runs a charter fishing boat on Lake Erie. They live in Elyria, Ohio, with a very independent black cat named Archie Graham. Their older daughter, Erin, is an education specialist, and their younger daughter, Kate, is majoring in art at Kent State University.

Courtesy of Greenwillow Books

SELECTED WORKS: *Night Owls*, illus. by Jill Kastner, 1990; *At Taylor's Place*, illus. by Nancy Carpenter, 1990; *Riding with Aunt Lucy*, illus. by Nancy Carpenter, 1991; *Hazel's Circle*, illus. by Sharon McGinley-Nally, 1992; *Bus Riders*, illus. by Nancy Carpenter, 1993; *Woollybear Good-bye*, illus. by Nancy Cote, 1994; *Radio Boy*, illus by Alec Gillman, 1995; *On the Trail with Miss Pace*, illus. by G. Brian Karas, 1995; *Big Wolf and Little Wolf*, illus. by Cathie Felstead, 2000; *Georgie Lee*, illus. by Lynne Rae Perkins, 2002; *All Their Names Were Courage: A Novel of the Civil War*, 2003; *In the Snow*, illus. by Nancy Tafuri, 2005.

SUGGESTED READING: *Something About the Author*, vol. 142, 2004.

The daughter of two educators who loved to read, Sarah Dessen was born in Evanston, Illinois but grew up in Chapel Hill, North Carolina, where her parents were both professors at the University of North Carolina. She has one brother who is now a musician living in California. Like her parents, Dessen loved reading. As a middle-grade student, she received an old manual typewriter from her parents, upon which she composed her earliest stories. All her stuffed animals and dolls had elaborate histories, and when she studied history in fifth grade, she wrote a series of stories on the American Revolution. Dessen was shy as a child and low on self-esteem, characteristics shared by some of the characters in her novels.

Courtesy of Penguin Young Readers Group

Sarah Dessen

June 6, 1970–

In 1993 Dessen received her B.A. in English from the University of North Carolina at Chapel Hill. She decided to continue writing while working as a waitress at the Flying Burrito Restaurant, where she sometimes researched her stories by eavesdropping on customers' conversations and also enjoyed free Mexican food. She was still working as a waitress when her first book was published. *That Summer*, a perceptive and comic story about an awkward teenager who must adjust to her sister's impending marriage, her mother's makeover after a divorce, her father's remarriage, and changes in her own body and social world, was named an ALA Best Book for Young Adults. Like many of her novels, *That Summer* was inspired by an event in Dessen's own life and incorporated feelings she experienced when a very close cousin was married.

Her next book, *Someone Like You*, was also inspired by a real-life incident, the motorcycle accident and death of a popular high school boy when Dessen was in ninth grade. *Someone Like You* explores the dynamics of friendship and family, sexual responsibilities, and the adolescent need for independence, as two teenagers, one pregnant by a boyfriend killed in an accident and one trying to decide about having her first sexual encounter, struggle to make the right choices. The winner of the Maryland Black-Eyed Susan Award and the South Carolina Young Adult Book Award, the book was also cited as an ALA Quick Pick for Reluctant Young Adult Readers.

Courtesy of Viking Books, Penguin USA

The success of Dessen's first two novels resulted in the stories being combined into a movie starring Mandy Moore, which was released in theatres in 2003 as *How to Deal*. The two novels were also published together under the film's title. By that time, Dessen had published three more novels.

Keeping the Moon, which was an ALA Quick Pick for Reluctant Young Adult Readers and an IRA Young Adult Choice, explores the idea of both external and internal transformation. The title character, after losing 45 pounds, still feels rejected, isolated, and angry until the summer she spends with her eccentric aunt. A makeover directed by two waitresses at the Last Chance Diner where she works gives her a new view of herself and the world.

Dreamland, about a teenager trying to negotiate the boundaries between romantic love and physical abuse, and her defensive withdrawal into a dream-like state of being, won the Indiana Eliot Rosewater High School Book Award and was included in ALA Popular Paperbacks for Young Adults. A modern-day love story, *This Lullaby* features a witty teenager who, after living with four former stepfathers, is cynical about romantic relationships. She falls in love in spite of herself. Wickedly funny, the story nevertheless has its serious side as the cynic comes to understand that some risks are worth taking. This book became a finalist for the *Los Angeles Times* Book Prize.

Nearly every one of Dessen's titles has been named an ALA Best Book for Young Adults. Two of her books were also named Best Books of the Year by *School Library Journal*—*Someone Like You* and *Keeping the Moon*. *Dreamland*, *Keeping the Moon*, and *The Truth About Forever* were all among the New York Public Library's Books for the Teen Age. *Just Listen*, about a teenager whose family avoids confrontations, was on the *New York Times'* bestseller list for a number of weeks.

Currently a writing teacher at the University of North Carolina, Sarah Dessen lives with her husband in the country, along with some lizards, two dogs, and their daughter, Sasha, born in September 2007.

SELECTED WORKS: *That Summer*, 1996; *Someone Like You*, 1998; *Keeping the Moon*, 1999; *Dreamland*, 2000; "Umbrella" in *This Is Where We Live: Short Stories by 25 Contemporary North Carolina Writers*, ed. by Michael McFee, 2000; *This Lullaby*, 2002; "Someone Bold" in *One Hot Second: Stories about Desire*, ed. by Cathy Young, 2002; *How to Deal* (combines *That Summer* and *Someone Like You*), 2003; *The Truth About Forever*, 2004; "Infinity" in *Sixteen: Stories About That Sweet and Bitter Birthday*, ed. by Megan McCafferty, 2004; *Just Listen*, 2006; "Sha-la-la" in *Twice Told: Original Stories Inspired by Original Artwork*, by Scott Hunt, 2006; *Lock and Key*, 2008.

SUGGESTED READING: *Something About the Author*, vol. 172, 2007; *Sarah Dessen: From Burritos to Box Office*, by Wendy J. Glenn, 2005; *Authors and Artists for Young Adults*, 2001. Online—*Contemporary Authors Online*, 01/23/07.

WEB SITE: www.saradessen.com

Baba Wagué Diakité

(ba-ba wah-GAY DJAH-kee-tay)
September 14, 1961–

Baba Wagué Diakité was named after his maternal grandfather, Wagué, a name that means "a man of trust." Born in Bamako, Mali, in West Africa, he spent his early years in the care of his grandparents in the village of Kassaro. There he lived among a large extended family, tended his uncles' sheep, and worked in his family's rice and peanut fields. He played with the other children in the bush, catching lizards and protecting the fields from marauding monkeys.

To attend formal school, Diakité moved to Bamako, where he lived with his mother. He remembers in great detail the stories told to him by his mother and grandparents in his early years—stories about the animals and the First People. These are the tales he would draw on later in life to share with children as a storyteller and to use as inspiration for his award-winning books, illustrations, and artwork.

From his earliest years Diakité enjoyed drawing. After meeting the American artist Ronna Neuenschwander, who later became his wife, he developed an interest in working in clay and has created internationally acclaimed painted pottery. After moving to Portland, Oregon, in 1985, he had his first exhibition in 1988, and has since presented his art in both group and solo shows throughout the United States. His exhibition at the Pulliam Deffenbaugh Gallery, in Portland, in November 2006, featured large ceramic sculptures drawn from the culture and traditions

Photo by Leo Arfer

of his homeland. His earlier work consisted mostly of smaller pieces—highly decorated bowls, plates, and teapots with distinctly Malian design. The artist has taught in many Oregon public school systems through the Art-in-Education program since 1989 and has made presentations at many schools and museums, including Washington State University, the Los Angeles County Museum of Art, and the Smithsonian African Art Museum. He has created posters for a number of citywide festivals in Portland and designed the artwork for recipients of the 1990 Governor's Arts Awards in Oregon. In 2001 Diakité created an 84-foot-long mural, among other artworks, for the Walt Disney Company's Animal Kingdom Lodge in Orlando, Florida.

His first picture book for children, *The Hunterman and the Crocodile*, tells a traditional tale from Mali. In an author's note, Diakité explains how stories were used in his culture to educate children, to teach good morals, and to stress the importance of people's relationship to the natural world. His illustrations in this book are images on glazed ceramic tiles, bordered in black-and-white traditional designs. *The Hunterman and the Crocodile* was named a Coretta Scott King Award Honor Book, an ALA Notable Children's Book, and a Notable Trade Book in the Field of Social Studies, among other honors.

Another story remembered from his childhood, "BaMusa and the Monkeys," became Diakité's second published book, *The*

Hatseller and the Monkeys, and earned him an Aesop Accolade from the American Folklore Society. One of the strengths of Diakité's folktale picture books is the author's note at the end that connects each story to his cultural background and lists variations of the tale in other cultures around the world; in this case he cites Esphyr Slobodkina's *Caps for Sale*, from that author's European roots, as well as Indian and other African versions of the story. Named an ALA Notable Children's Book and an IRA Teacher's Choice, *The Hatseller and the Monkeys* is vibrantly illustrated with paintings made on ceramic tile; the black-and-white borders in this book show the monkeys in a variety of humorous poses.

For a collection of African Ananse stories, *The Pot of Wisdom*, retold by Ghanian storyteller Adwoa Badoe, Diakité created one of his painted-tile illustrations for each of the tales in the book. His border pictures and endpapers show the trickster spider man in many poses. *The Magic Gourd*, another of Diakité's Malian folktales, won a 2004 Aesop Prize as well as an award from Parents' Guide to Children's Media. It was also named an NCTE Notable Book in the Language Arts. The hero of this tale is a familiar creature in the stories of the author's childhood—Zozani, the rabbit. Rabbit is given a magic gourd by his friend Chameleon and uses it to teach a lesson to a greedy king. The story includes a "praise song," a traditional Malian custom to keep alive the spirit of good deeds, respect, and appreciation for others. The illustrated borders and endpapers incorporate mud cloth designs, a unique textile technique of the Bamana people of Mali that Wagué had learned from his mother.

Baba Wagué Diakité lives today in Portland, Oregon, with his wife, Ronna, and their two daughters, Penda and Amina. The family makes frequent visits to Mali, and one of those visits is the subject of the picture book, *I Lost My Tooth in Africa*, written by Penda Diakité and illustrated by her father. Named a Notable Children's Book by both the American Library Association (ALA) and the National Council of Teachers of English, the story relates Amina's universal childhood experience of losing her tooth while the girls are visiting their relatives in Bamako, Mali. Leaving her tooth under a gourd in the courtyard, Amina discovers a chicken, which she then cares for throughout their stay. Her sister Penda wrote the story, which expresses the love and enjoyment of a large extended family and a close-knit community.

Baba Wagué Diakité loves to share the culture of his homeland with his adopted country. He has been instrumental in building the Toguna Cultural Center in the capitol city of Bamako, which

Baba Wagué Diakité loves to share the culture of his homeland with his adopted country.

Courtesy of Scholastic Press

brings people from the West directly into contact with traditional Malian art and culture.

SELECTED WORKS WRITTEN AND ILLUSTRATED: *The Hunterman and the Crocodile*, 1997; *The Hatseller and the Monkeys*, 1999; *The Magic Gourd*, 2003; *Mee-An and the Magic Serpent*, 2007.

SELECTED WORKS ILLUSTRATED: *The Pot of Wisdom: Ananse Stories*, by Adwoa Badoe, 2001; *Jamari's Drum*, by Eboni Bynum and Roland Jackson, 2004; *I Lost My Tooth in Africa*, by Penda Diakité, 2006.

SUGGESTED READING: *Something About the Author*, vol. 174, 2007. Periodicals—Rovine, Victoria, "Baba Wagué Diakité: Respect Yourself as Well as Your Tradition," *African Arts*, Summer 2001.

"We believe in magic. To sit down with a blank piece of paper and see scenes and characters take form . . . it is magic. There's a voice inside guiding, saying 'no, that's not right . . . change that line . . . add a bit here . . . take away there. . . .'

"Children accept these things. As adults, we lose the faith. The best things come when we let go and accept the guidance from that voice. Maybe that's why we love doing children's books . . . knowing that they (the children) will understand the zany logic and eagerly accept the impossible.

"We came to children's books after many years of adult book jackets, album covers, and advertising art, and found a freedom we didn't know before. When doing a book or record cover, everything must be summed up in one picture. In a children's book there are pages and pages to build an idea—to add nuances and visual comments.

"There are many levels of recognition and understanding. A book can be read again and again with new discoveries: expressions and details that were missed the first time will be discovered the second or third or fourth time.

"It has been a form of magic that in working together as one artist, we created a third artist. What takes form on paper is a surprise to both of us and something neither of us would have come up with individually.

"We met at the Parsons School of Design and competed with each other until we joined forces. It didn't come easy, this working together. Two egos and one piece of paper are a dangerous combination!

"Now, when we sit down and talk about what we're going to do, we let the ideas fly until one triggers excitement in both of us. From that point on, it's an adventure.

"One of the greatest gifts, we think, is to love what you are doing. And we do. We don't work for children; we work for the child in each of us. Children are little people, as complicated and mysterious as any adult. Unfortunately, too many adults feel that things must be simplified for children. We try not to fall into that trap. We must please ourselves first, and if we've been honest

Photo by Lee Dillon

Leo and Diane Dillon

Leo Dillon
March 2, 1933–

Diane Dillon
March 13, 1933–

with ourselves and have worked with love, the reader—child or adult—will know that.

"Our reward is the respect of our peers, the joy of children, and the freedom we take in listening to our own drummer."

Ⓖ Ⓖ Ⓖ

Leo and Diane Dillon were born 11 days apart on opposite coasts: he—Lionel John Dillon, Jr.—in Brooklyn, New York, the son of immigrant parents from Trinidad; and she—Diane Claire Sorber—in Glendale, California, the daughter of a schoolteacher father and concert pianist mother. Art and drawing played significant roles in each of their lives as they grew up. Both of them, as children, were encouraged by their parents to pursue their artistic talent, but the forces that influenced them were as diverse as their backgrounds.

> *"It has been a form of magic that in working together as one artist, we created a third artist. What takes form on paper is a surprise to both of us and something neither of us would have come up with individually."*

For Leo, it was an artist friend of his father's who became a mentor. Ralph Volman took him to Greenwich Village, gave him a drawing board, and used his own pen-and-ink drawings as models. Leo studied illustrated books for style, and *The Arabian Nights* changed his life. He was captivated by the excellent drawings; that led him to the Old Masters, and he couldn't get enough of them.

Diane was influenced by fashion illustrations, especially those of the famous designer Dorothy Hood. Not only was she attracted to the designer's lines, which had a different look from others, she was also inspired by the fact that the wonderful figures were drawn by a woman.

Diane and Leo met as students at Parsons School of Design in New York City in 1954, where they discovered a mutual admiration for each other's work. Each one thinking the other one was a superior artist led to a competitive relationship, one that eventually turned into romance. Despite the prejudice often felt by interracial couples during the racially separate culture of the mid-20th century, they married in 1957. Leo went to work as an art director for West Park Publications in New York, while Diane tried to be the model housewife, which didn't include painting. It wasn't long, though, before Leo began bringing work home and encouraged Diane to work on the designs with him. That was the beginning of the two of them working together as one artist.

In the late 1950s and early 1960s they worked under the name of Studio 2 to give the impression that there was a studio full of artists, which enabled them to work in a variety of styles. Those years were filled with drawing illustrations for textbooks, book jackets, and album covers that established them in the fields of jazz, African-American experience, Scandinavian epics, African folktales, and especially science fiction. A big break came when they met Harlan Ellison, a Chicago magazine editor (and later a noted science fiction author), who signed them on to design cover art. He became their connection to science fiction and fantasy art, which earned them a 1971 Hugo Award presented by the Science Fiction Association.

Inevitably, their creativity found a road to illustrating children's books. At first, their art graced fiction and folklore collections with occasional pictorial rendering. *Claymore and Kilt*, a collection of Scottish folktales and legends published in 1967, and a picture book, *The Ring in the Prairie* published in 1970, set the tone for many later works in which they illustrated stories from the oral history of various indigenous peoples. In 1975 the Dillons collaborated with folklorist Verna Aardema to create the now-classic picture book, *Why Mosquitoes Buzz in People's Ears: A West African Tale*, for which they won the prestigious Caldecott Medal in 1976. The following year they were awarded a second Caldecott Medal for *Ashanti to Zulu: African Traditions*, written by Margaret W. Musgrove. The consecutive wins set three records: back-to-back Caldecott Medals for illustration, the first couple to win the award, and Leo as the first African American to receive the Medal.

"Our reward is the respect of our peers, the joy of children, and the freedom we take in listening to our own drummer."

As to their unique collaboration, Leo and Diane explained it more fully in an interview in *Locus* magazine. Leo said, "I'm constantly surprised at how our work is melding more and more as the years go on. In the beginning it was a conceived plan for us to work in a particular style that we both could master. So in reality we were both working for 'someone else'—the style. Forty years ago there were techniques neither one of us would attempt, and somewhere along the line, one picked it up and the other followed, and back and forth."

"At this point we hit the 'Third Artist' concept," Diane added, "it helped us a lot, because we could look at ourselves as one artist rather than two individuals, and that third artist was doing something neither one of us would do—the same as writers who talk about how their characters take over their work."

Beginning in 1985 the Dillons combined their talent with the evocative writing of eminent children's author Virginia Hamilton in several volumes of African American folktales and true stories. The first was *The People Could Fly: American Black Folktales*, which collected many of the stories that were shared during slavery days and later. A companion book published in 1993, *Many Thousand Gone: African Americans from Slavery to Freedom*, recounted the devastating real-life experience of "the middle passage" and hair-raising escapes from bondage by Frederick Douglass, Harriet Tubman, and many other courageous individuals. The third compilation, *Her Stories: African American Folktales, Fairy Tales, and True Tales*, was published in 1995 and brought full circle an homage to African American culture and spirit, powerfully told and movingly depicted. Both *The People Could Fly* and *Her Stories* received a Coretta Scott King Award for text and an honor book award for illustration.

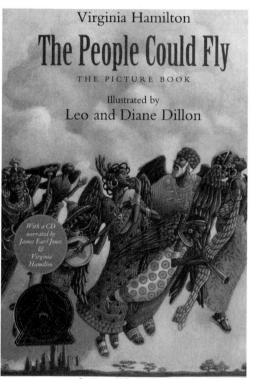

Courtesy of Alfred A. Knopf, Random House, Inc.

The Dillons' artistic style is never static. They tackle each book with a fresh eye and experiment with a look that will reflect the book's subject matter; but their style is unmistakably recognizable, consistently characterized with clean, precise lines, painstaking attention to thoroughly researched details, compelling page design, and a rich color palette or—in the case of the first two Hamilton titles—beautifully nuanced black and white drawings. The title story from Virginia Hamilton's folk tale collection, *The People Could Fly*, originally rendered in black and white, was re-illustrated in full color and reissued in a single picture-book edition in 2004 and earned many accolades for the Dillons, including a Coretta Scott King Honor Award.

Recent collaborations have taken on a new dimension, as this prize-winning artistic duo has started to write the texts as well as to illustrate. In *Rap a Tap Tap: Here's Bojangles—Think of That!*, they pay tribute to legendary tap dancer, Bill "Bojangles" Robinson, with a rhythmic text and illustrations in flat shapes and subtle hues on a white background. The page composition of this Coretta Scott King Illustrator Honor Award–winner suggests a syncopated rhythm and the motion of the dancer's fast-flying feet; it is strikingly effective. For a younger audience, their *Mother Goose: Numbers on the Loose*—named an ALA Notable Children's Book in 2008—animates counting rhymes with playful, energetic, and mischievous portrayals. In sharp contrast and as thrilling as unexpected riffs in music, the strong shapes, shadows, and darkly intense colors of *Jazz on a Saturday Night* backlight the audience, spotlight the musicians, and evoke the feelings of a magical evening of jazz. Once again, exceptional artistry meshes illustration with story in this title, which was named a 2008 Coretta Scott King Honor book for illustration.

Married for more than 50 years, with over 50 illustrated books to their credit, the Dillons have garnered a cornucopia of awards. They have received four *New York Times* Best Illustrated Awards for *Ashanti to Zulu*, *The People Could Fly*, *The Tale of the Mandarin Ducks*, and *The Girl Who Dreamed Only Geese*. Seven books have been honored with Coretta Scott King Awards or Honor citations. Other coveted awards include four *Boston Globe–Horn Book* Awards, a highly commended citation from the Hans Christian Andersen Committee in 1978, and a Society of Illustrators Gold Medal for *Northern Lullaby*. Their son Lee (Lionel John Dillon III), born in 1965, grew up to be an artist and sculptor in his own right, and in 1991, collaborated with his parents on Nancy Willard's book, *Pish, Posh, Said Hieronymus Bosch*, creating an elaborate framing structure for their detailed illustrations.

Courtesy of The Blue Sky Press, Scholastic, Inc.

The Dillons have received the Knickerbocker Award, the Empire State Award, and the Virginia Hamilton Award for lifetime achievement. They have been inducted into the Society of Illustrators Hall of Fame and received honorary doctorates from the Parsons School of Design and the Montserrat School of Art. Throughout their career, Leo and Diane Dillon have worked to convey two essential truths: that the human experience is universal to all races and cultures, and that art, in its many forms, is an inspiring and transforming experience.

SELECTED WORKS ILLUSTRATED: *Hakon of Rogen's Saga*, by Erik Christian Haugaard, 1963; *A Slave's Tale*, by Erik Christian Haugaard, 1965; *Claymore and Kilt: Tales of Scottish Kings and Castles*, by Sorche Nic Leodhas, 1967; *Dark Venture*, by Audrey

White Beyer, 1968; *The Rider and His Horse*, by Erik Christian Haugaard, 1968; *Why Heimdall Blew His Horn: Tales of the Norse Gods*, by Frederick Laing, 1969; *The Ring in the Prairie: A Shawnee Legend*, by John Bierhorst, 1970; *The Untold Tale*, by Erik Christian Haugaard, 1971; *Gassire's Lute: A West African Epic*, by Alta Jablow, 1971; *Behind the Back of the Mountain: Black Folktales from Southern Africa*, by Verna Aardema, 1973; *The Third Gift*, by Jan Carew, 1974; *Whirlwind Is a Ghost Dancing*, by Natalia Belting, 1974; *Burning Star*, by Eth Clifford, 1974; *The Hundred Penny Box*, by Sharon Bell Mathis, 1975; *Song of the Boat*, by Lorenz Graham, 1975; *Why Mosquitoes Buzz in People's Ears*, by Verna Aardema, 1975; *Ashanti to Zulu: African Traditions*, by Margaret W. Musgrove, 1976; *Who's in Rabbit's House?: A Masai Tale*, by Verna Aardema, 1977; *Honey, I Love: And Other Love Poems*, by Eloise Greenfield, 1978; *Tales from Scandinavia*, by Frederick Laing, 1979; *Children of the Sun*, by Jan Carew, 1980; *The People Could Fly*, by Virginia Hamilton, 1985; *Brother to the Wind*, by Mildred Pitts Walter, 1985; *The Porcelain Cat*, by Michael Patrick Hearn, 1987; *The Color Wizard*, by Barbara Brenner, 1989; *Moses' Ark: Stories from the Bible*, by Alice Bach and J. Cheryl Exum, 1989; *Aïda*, edited by Leontyne Price, 1990; *The Tale of the Mandarin Ducks*, by Katherine Paterson, 1990; *The Race of the Golden Apples*, by Claire Martin, 1991; *Pish, Posh, Said Hieronymus Bosch*, by Nancy Willard, with Lee Dillon, 1991; *Northern Lullaby*, by Nancy White Carlstrom, 1992; *The Sorcerer's Apprentice*, by Nancy Willard, 1993; *Many Thousand Gone: African Americans from Slavery to Freedom*, by Virginia Hamilton, 1993; *What Am I? Looking Through Shapes at Apples and Grapes*, by N. N. Charles, 1994; *Her Stories: African American Folktales, Fairy Tales and True Tales*, by Virginia Hamilton, 1995; *The Girl Who Dreamed Only Geese, and Other Tales of the Far North*, by Howard Norman, 1997; *To Every Thing There Is a Season: Verses from Ecclesiastes*, 1998; *Wind Child*, by Shirley Rousseau Murphy, 1999; *The Girl Who Spun Gold*, by Virginia Hamilton, 2000; *Mansa Musa: The Lion of Mali*, by Khephra Burns, 2001; *Two Little Trains*, by Margaret Wise Brown, 2001; *One Winter's Night*, by John Herman, 2003; *Between Heaven and Earth: Bird Tales from around the World*, by Howard Norman, 2004; *The People Could Fly: The Picture Book*, by Virginia Hamilton, 2004; *Where Have You Been?*, by Margaret Wise Brown, 2004; *Earth Mother*, by Ellen Jackson, 2005.

SELECTED WORKS WRITTEN AND ILLUSTRATED: *Rap a Tap Tap: Here's Bojangles—Think of That!*, 2002; *Mother Goose: Numbers on the Loose*, 2007; *Jazz on a Saturday Night*, 2007.

SUGGESTED READING: Marcus, Leonard, *Side by Side: Five Favorite Picture Book Teams Go to Work*, 2001; *Something about the Author*, vol. 106, 1999; Cummins, Julie, ed., *Children's Book Illustration and Design*, vol. II, 1998; Silvey, Anita, *Children's Books and Their Creators*, 1995; Collier, Laurie and Nakamura, eds., *Major Authors and Illustrators for Children and Young Adults*, 1993; Cummings, Pat, *Talking with Artists*, 1992; Roginski, Jim, compiler, *Newbery and Caldecott Medalists and Honor Book Winners*, 1982; Preiss, Byron, ed., *The Art of Leo and Diane Dillon*, 1981. Periodicals—Dillon, Diane, "Leo Dillon," *The Horn Book*, August 1977; Dillon, Leo, "Diane Dillon," *The Horn Book*, August 1977; Dillon, Leo and Diane, "Caldecott Acceptance Speech," *The Horn Book*, August 1977; Fogelman, Phyllis, "Leo and Diane Dillon," *The Horn Book*, August 1976; Dillon, Leo and Diane, "Caldecott Acceptance Speech," *The Horn Book*, August 1976. Online—"Leo and Diane Dillon: The Third Artist Rules," *Locus*, April, 2000, at www.locusmag.com/2000/Issues/04/Dillons.html

An earlier profile of Leo and Diane Dillon appeared in *Fifth Book of Junior Authors and Illustrators*, 1983.

Jennifer Donnelly

1963–

"I love spending time in the company of old dead people. In fact, I often prefer it to talking with living ones. That's why I write historical fiction.

"When I was a kid, I never wanted to go to Disneyland. Mickey and Minnie held no allure for me. 'Please, please, please can we go to Colonial Williamsburg this summer?' I would beg my parents.

"What could be more fascinating, more exciting, than riding through the night with Paul Revere? Donning armor with a young Joan of Arc? Or dancing at the court of the Sun King?

"I caught the history bug in third grade when my mother took me to see the movie *Mary, Queen of Scots* starring Vanessa Redgrave and Glenda Jackson. I loved the drama and the intrigue, to say nothing of the dresses and the jewelry. In the movie Mary and Elizabeth meet, though in fact they never did—but who cares? Every student of Tudor history wishes they had. It was such a great moment—the two rulers and adversaries sitting down to talk. I loved their power and strength. I loved that they were 'mere' women and yet they ruled entire countries.

"The only problem with this passion of mine was that it was all-consuming. I wanted to ride with Marco Polo into China, not study my multiplication tables. I wanted to wear silk gowns embroidered with pearls and rubies, edged with lace that had taken twenty convent girls half a decade to make, not tee shirts and Levi's. I still find it hard to leave the past for the real world. It's tough to do the dishes or walk the dog when you've just been at the Battle of Agincourt or the trial of Marie Antoinette. History ruins you for real life.

"My ideas for books all come from the past. Something clutches at me and catches me. It's usually a dark thing. I hear or see or read about someone or something, and it grabs hold of me and won't let go of me—or maybe it's that I can't let go of it—and so to resolve my obsession, I do what writers do, which is make up a story. At first it's all ideas and imagination, which is exciting and wonderful, but then the ideas have to be converted into a book. I outline neurotically, blocking out each and every scene, fitting them together, taking them apart, smoothing and finessing, until I'm satisfied that there is indeed a story there and that it has a beginning, middle, and end.

Photo by Jerry Bauer

"I also do a ton of research. There is nothing I like better than poking about in dusty old archives, reading yellowed diaries, notebooks, and letters to hear the voices of another century. A point eventually comes when I feel I have enough control of the facts to start writing, but I always *have* to stop researching before I *want* to stop. I like a certain level of richness in what I write and read. I don't enjoy skinny books. I want to create believable human beings and believable stories; to do that one needs layers, complexity, and verisimilitude. There are duties and responsibilities peculiar to historical fiction, and I take them very seriously. It's my job to create a seamless and compelling past. If I don't, I won't earn my readers' trust.

"I don't remember making a conscious decision to become a writer. It's something that was always there. Words have always been a part of my life. I was always read to as a child, always told stories. My parents and many members of my extended family were storytellers, and so it seemed perfectly natural to me to go from hearing stories to telling them myself.

"I can't imagine I'll ever write a novel set in the present, because it bores me . . . or the future, because it terrifies me. I'm pretty sure I'll stick to the past and hopefully use the glory, idiocy, majesty, madness, beauty and sorrow to be found there to inspire a love of history in a new generation of readers."

෴ ෴ ෴

Born in Port Chester, New York, Jennifer Donnelly spent significant parts of her childhood in Port Leyden, a small town on the western edge of the Adirondack Mountains. It is the place where her Irish ancestors settled when they came to this country to escape the Potato Famine of the 1840s. The Adirondack landscape plays a significant role in Donnelly's award-winning novel, *A Northern Light*, which is based, in part, on the true story of the murder of Grace Brown in 1906. Touched by Grace's plight—the same story that inspired Theodore Dreiser's 1925 classic novel, *An American Tragedy*—Donnelly created a fictional girl who would eventually have more choices in her life than the unfortunate Grace. Her own grandmother, like her heroine Mattie Gokey, worked as a waitress at a large resort hotel on Big Moose Lake, where the real-life Grace Brown died.

In *A Northern Light* Donnelly conveys the resilience and power of women in all eras to overcome poverty and prejudice. Though Mattie loves her family, she longs for a life of independence, study, and learning. *A Northern Light* garnered the *Los Angeles Times* Book Award for Young Adults and was named an honor book for ALA's Michael L. Printz Award. Equally honored in the United Kingdom, the book received the prestigious Carnegie Medal, with Donnelly being only the second American writer to be so honored. In the British edition, the title became *A Gathering Light*. Translated into Dutch, the book earned a Gouden Zoen (Golden Kiss) Honor award in books for teenagers in The Netherlands.

A versatile writer, Donnelly has also published for younger children and for adults. Her picture book, *Humble Pie*, was illustrated by Stephen Gammell and inspired by her childhood reading of Grimm's fairy tales. Her historical novel for adults, *The Tea Rose*, is set in late 19th century London and New York, and was named a Top Pick by the Romantic Times Book Club. Copious research gives Donnelly's novels a wealth of detail and

> *"My ideas for books all come from the past. Something clutches at me and catches me. It's usually a dark thing."*

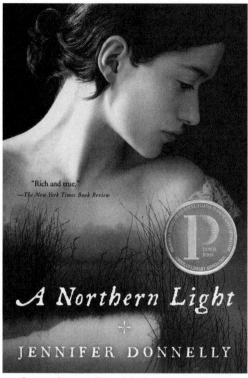

"Rich and true."
—*The New York Times Book Review*

A Northern Light

JENNIFER DONNELLY

Courtesy of Harcourt Children's Books, Houghton Mifflin Harcourt

information about the period. She studies newspapers, diaries, photos, courthouse records, menus—anything that will add substance and historical accuracy to her stories.

Jennifer Donnelly received her bachelor's degree in 1986 from the University of Rochester, in New York, where she majored in English literature and European history. Always an avid reader, she has worked as an antiques dealer, a journalist, and a copywriter. Today she divides her time between Brooklyn and the town of Callicoon in Sullivan County, New York, with her husband, their young daughter, and two rescued greyhounds.

SELECTED WORKS: *The Tea Rose: A Novel*, 2002; *Humble Pie*, illus. by Stephen Gammell, 2002; *A Northern Light*, 2003 (British edition title: *A Gathering Light*, 2003); *The Winter Rose*, 2007.

SUGGESTED READING: *Something About the Author*, vol. 154, 2005. Periodicals—Donnelly, Jennifer, "Who says children's books are for children only?" *The Guardian*, July 10, 2004; Mattson, Jennifer, "The story behind the story: Donnelly's *A Northern Light*, *Booklist*, May 15, 2004; Maughan, Shannon, "Donnelly's light shines: talks with Jennifer Donnelly," *Publishers Weekly*, May 12, 2003.

WEB SITE: www.jenniferdonnelly.com

Rebecca Kai Dotlich

July 10, 1951–

"I was born Rebecca Thompson, the middle child of John and Charlotte Thompson, a banker and a homemaker. My brother Curt was almost two years older, and my sister Beth Ann came along five years later. We lived in a small ranch house, in a suburban neighborhood called Eagledale, in Indianapolis. Our backyard fence divided our yard and one of the blacktop entrances to the Indianapolis 500 Race Track. We sold lemonade and cookies to fans waiting in line, reaching over the fence to hand them our wares. Once or twice, my dad and uncles hauled lawn chairs up to the roof so we had front row seats, so to speak. All during the month of May, the roar of car engines echoed through the neighborhood. For years, it was an exciting, yet familiar and comforting background noise for riding bikes, exploring creeks, skating, playing jacks and jumping rope.

"We only watched television during the day if we stayed home sick from school or on Saturday mornings, when my mom went to the grocery store. Then my brother and I turned on cartoons like *Mighty Mouse*, and programs like *Sky King*. We were almost always outside, partly because our mother shooed us there, and partly because we never considered doing anything else. We built tents out of sheets that were stretched from fence to ground, knotted and secured on the twist of barbed wire, then draped down and held in place by bricks or rocks on the ground. Then we went about our business of fixing the inside, creating spaces or rooms from rugs, bringing out Kool-Aid and cakes, books and comic books, paper and pencils for creating maps of the neighborhood and anonymous notes to neighbors.

Photo by Karen Young

"We didn't have a library close by, so every two weeks we walked down to the bookmobile. I carried home armloads of books, including *Pippi Longstocking* and Nancy Drew mysteries. In our house, we had books of fairy tales, which I knew by heart, and Golden Books like *Peter Pan*, *The Three Little Pigs*, *The Gingerbread Man*, and *Cinderella*. *The Three Billy Goats Gruff* was one of my all time favorites. Deliciously scary! I couldn't wait to repeat the words, 'Who's that walking on my bridge?' My brother, whom I adored, was an even bigger reader, so I came to the conclusion that reading must be pretty exciting. I settled into the world of books quite easily.

"During this time, I never imagined being a writer. I knew I loved stories and nursery rhymes, memorized and made up jump-rope chants, but I didn't write stories or dream about being a writer. I honestly thought about being a nurse (just like in the Golden Book, *Nurse Nancy*). Or maybe a teacher, because I adored Mrs. Rapp, my kindergarten teacher.

"In high school, Mrs. Doris Bradford, my 10th grade teacher, told me I had a way with words and that she was sure I'd be a poet one day. She showed some of my themes and poems to the class, and by this time, I started to have this wonderful little nagging feeling of maybe . . . I had also just gotten my driver's license. I was cautious and careful, but still something happened that was unforeseen and horrific. A little girl ran out between parked cars, right in front of me, and I couldn't avoid hitting her. Later I learned her older brother had thrown her barrette into the street, and she darted out to pick it up. This was horribly reminiscent of my friend Dana being run over by a car in front of me when we were five. Dana had spent a year in traction and wore a football helmet to protect her brain. This little girl, Kimberly (who was later to become my young friend), sustained internal injuries and deep scrapes to her face. I was devastated, praying and sobbing, and this affected the way I later parented. If my children even went close to the side of the road, I pulled out all the stops. I was not a spanker, but for this, they got a solid whop on the bottom, quick and swift.

"Speaking of children, I knew, as soon as I had them, that I wanted to write for them. Poetry is where my heart took me. I devoured poetry books and biographies of poets. I spent hours reading in the library. I began to write and send my poems to magazines and book publishers. But I had a long way to go. There were years of rejections, and years of learning the craft on my grandfather's old manual typewriter.

> *"They say it takes a village to raise a child, and so too it takes a village to raise a writer. The villagers just don't know they're doing it!"*

"They say it takes a village to raise a child, and so too it takes a village to raise a writer. The villagers just don't know they're doing it! The parent, the brother, the sister, the teacher, the bookmobile lady, the librarian, they all play a part. The story ends as it begins. I was born Rebecca Thompson, the middle child of John and Charlotte Thompson. I am that same lucky little girl who grew up to be a writer."

ଔ ଔ ଔ

Rebecca Kai Dotlich graduated from Northwest High School in Indianapolis in 1969 and attended Indiana University in Bloomington. The girl who wrote rhymes on the cardboards that came inside her father's newly laundered shirts became the teenager who wrote for the school newspaper and composed poems for the prom invitations. In college she wrote a newsletter for her dorm.

Dotlich's middle name started out as Kay, which she changed to Kai when she was ten, in honor of a favorite uncle who had lived in places like Japan, Denmark, and Germany. She felt the name change connected her to him and sounded as exotic as the places he lived. He died as a solidier during the Vietnam War, as did her brother, Curt; her father died shortly thereafter. To ease her grief, she turned to writing poetry.

Before concentrating on being a poet, Dotlich held a variety of jobs unrelated to writing. She worked in a real estate company and a clothing store, and as an envelope stuffer for a congressman. In 1973 she married Steven E. Dotlich, her high school sweetheart. Her husband started his own construction business and the couple settled into their life together. They had two children, Chad Curtis, born in 1976, and Lara Rebecca, born in 1979. Dotlich's writing life truly began once she had children. She had a busy schedule but squeezed in her writing between typing up invoices for her husband's business and taking care of her children.

In 1995 Dotlich sold her first manuscript. There is a snug feeling to the poetry in *Sweet Dreams of the Wild*, featuring imaginary conversations between a child and various animals and insects talking about where they sleep. Shortly after its publication, the poet and anthologist Lee Bennett Hopkins invited Dotlich to write for some of his poetry anthologies. This sparked a friendship and professional relationship that still exists today. Besides many of Hopkins's collections (*My America*, *Behind the Museum Door*, and others), her poems have been included in such anthologies as Paul Janeczko's *A Kick in the Head*, Dilys Evans's *Fairies, Trolls & Goblins Galore*, and Jack Prelutsky's *20th-Century Children's Poetry*.

Courtesy of Boyds Mills Press

Dotlich's own volumes of poems offer a wide array of sensory experiences and startling imagery for all ages. *Lemonade Sun and Other Summer Poems* presents readers with a roster of that season's creatures, celebrations, and feelings. Named an IRA/CBC Children's Choice and an American Booksellers Pick of the Lists, it was also included in the Indiana Read-Aloud Books Too Good to Miss.

A rhyming text offers very young children a lively introduction to various modes of transportation in *Away We Go!*, which won an Oppenheim Toy Portfolio Gold Award. Aided by clever word clues and illustrations, readers must guess what each poem is about in *When Riddles Come Rumbling*, a Junior Library Guild

Selection. *What Is Science?* is a rhyming concept book that begins and ends with the line, "What is science?/So many things." Included on Bank Street College's Best Children's Books of the Year in the Science category and a finalist for the 2006 AAAS/ Subaru Science Books & Films Prize, this poem, which touches on various areas of science such as botany and meteorology, initially appeared in a different version in Lee Bennett Hopkins's *Spectacular Science*.

Dotlich's books appeal to a broad age-range. Written with J. Patrick Lewis, *Castles: Old Stone Poems* was selected for the Pennsylvania School Librarians Association's annual Young Adult Top Forty list; the poems recount legends surrounding historic castles. For much younger children, Dotlich used short playful verse and focused on familiar items in concept books such as *What Is Round?* and *What Is Square?* Aimed at emerging readers, *Peanut and Pearl's Picnic Adventure* is an easy reader that stars two forgetful friends.

Dotlich's work has been featured on *Reading Rainbow* and has appeared in anthologies, textbooks, and magazines such as *Ladybug* and *Highlights*. She has been a poetry advisor and contributing columnist for *Creative Classroom* and *Teaching K–8*. She frequently gives poetry workshops at national and local conferences. A former writer-in-residence in the DeKalb County School District in northern Indiana, she has taught poetry at the Buffalo Writing Conference and the Kentucky Bluegrass Writing Project. Dotlich and her husband now live in Carmel, Indiana. Their children are grown, and they now have a grandson, Ian, and a granddaughter, Mia.

SELECTED WORKS: *Sweet Dreams of the Wild: Poems for Bedtime*, illus. by Katharine Dodge, 1996; *Lemonade Sun: And Other Summer Poems*, illus. by Jan Spivey Gilchrist, 1998; *What Is Square?*, illus. by Maria Ferrari, 1999; *What Is Round?*, illus. by Maria Ferrari, 1999; *What Is a Triangle?*, illus. by Maria Ferrari, 2000; *Away We Go!*, illus. by Dan Yaccarino, 2000; *When Riddles Come Rumbling: Poems to Ponder*, illus. by Karen Dugan, 2001; *A Family Like Yours*, illus. by Tammie Speer Lyon, 2002; *In the Spin of Things: Poetry of Motion*, illus. by Karen Dugan, 2003; *Mama Loves*, illus. by Kathryn Brown, 2004; *Over in the Pink House: New Jump-Rope Rhymes*, illus. by Melanie W. Hall, 2004; *Grandpa Loves*, illus. by Kathryn Brown, 2004; *What Is Science?*, illus. by Sachiko Yoshikawa, 2006; *Castles: Old Stone Poems*, with J. Patrick Lewis, illus. by Dan Burr, 2006; *Peanut and Pearl's Picnic Adventure*, illus. by R.W. Alley, 2007.

SUGGESTED READING: Online—Interview, at www.embracingth-echild.org/Bookspecialdotlich.htm

WEB STE: www.rebeccakaidotlich.com

"When I was young I loved to read and I loved to draw. Some of my earliest memories involve the words and pictures in books. My mother read aloud to my brothers and me every night and I remember lying in bed and listening to the adventures of Alice and the white rabbit from *Alice in Wonderland*, or imagining a picnic from *The Wind in the Willows*. I loved stories about animals because I was allergic to everything except goldfish. I spent lots of time drawing imaginary pets and reading animal stories. I developed a great affection for books, but never knew real people were responsible for the words and pictures in the book.

Photo by Katherine Tillotson

Julie Downing

January 2, 1956–

"Although I loved to draw, I never set out to be an artist. My three brothers collected Hardy Boys books, and written on the back of each book was 'These books are perfect for BOYS from 8–14.' I was angry that girls weren't supposed to read them, so I did. At eight I decided to be a detective too. I invented fantastic cases, set up a chemistry lab in my basement and tested evidence. One summer, in a particularly difficult case, I pretended my neighbors' pool was poisoned and I had to neutralize the water in order to save them. So, I filled a bucket with every liquid I could find: ketchup, dishwashing detergent, salad dressing, and lots of food coloring. Climbing over the fence, I emptied the bucket into the pool, just as my neighbor came out for a swim. I got in a lot of trouble and my career as a detective ended.

"I also thought about becoming an actress, singer, or famous figure skater. Despite many career changes, I never lost the magic feeling that comes from drawing and painting. I was never the *best* artist in class, but I drew all the time. When I was a senior in high school, I met someone who had gone to the Rhode Island School of Design. She told me it was a wonderful place where you could learn about all different kinds of art. It sounded so exciting! I finally realized I could be an artist.

"Being around so many artists was both exciting and scary. I studied painting, sculpture, stained glass, and printmaking. During my second year I took a class about illustrating children's books and immediately felt at home. I'd found a way to combine everything I love to do. Illustrating a book is like acting. I get to pretend to be the different characters in the story. I am the director, deciding what happens on each page. I design costumes and scenery. I even use my detective skills to find out what kind of clothes a shepherd might wear, or what a medieval king eats for breakfast. I snoop through libraries, museums, antique stores, and even the post office to find the perfect chair or a pattern for a castle floor. Of course, I get to draw too!

"Currently, I live in a hundred-year-old Victorian house in San Francisco, with my husband and two children. My studio is a short walk from my house, and overlooks Golden Gate Park. If I lean my head out the window I can see the fog come over the Golden Gate Bridge. Every day is different. Some days I spend the whole day at my drawing board, and other days I might do research at the library, take pictures of models or run to the art supply store. I love the variety that comes with my job.

"Each book is a challenge and seems to take longer than the last one. I love writing, researching and illustrating. It is hard work, often frustrating, and at times a little scary, but never dull. Sometimes I am still surprised that I became an artist, but I feel lucky to have a job I love."

"Illustrating a book is like acting. I get to pretend to be the different characters in the story. I am the director, deciding what happens on each page. I design costumes and scenery."

ଔ ଔ ଔ

Julie Downing's love of animals as a young girl growing up in Denver, Colorado, became a significant influence in her career as an illustrator. Because she was allergic to so many actual animals, she drew lots of imaginary pets and read animal stories. After high school, her interest in drawing and painting lured her to the Rhode Island School of Design. Her soft, appealing artwork was a natural for preschool children's books about animals, families, lullabies, and everyday feelings.

Following graduation from art school, a variety of jobs broadened her experience and paved the way toward a career in children's books. She was an exhibit technician at the Smithsonian Institution in Washington, DC, and a graphic designer for Macy's department store in New York City. She also worked for a while at the Denver Museum of Natural History in Colorado. In 1981 she became a freelance illustrator and set out to create children's books.

The first two books that she illustrated were *Clues in the Desert* and *Hannah's Alaska*, both published in 1983. After illustrating four books written by other authors, Downing ventured into writing a story herself and illustrating it. *White Snow, Blue Feather* came from her memories of growing up in Colorado and her fascination with the way familiar things changed after a snowfall.

A Christmas visit to Vienna, Austria, inspired the second book that she both wrote and illustrated. Downing discovered many tributes and plaques to Mozart on that trip. Already in love with the city and Mozart's music, she became intrigued with the composer's difficult life and wrote a biography titled *Mozart Tonight*. She underscored the challenges Mozart faced, to convey the idea that "even great people feel frustrated and worried."

Despite the number of books she has created, Downing often thinks about ideas for years before she writes anything. Often those ideas come after she's made hundreds of sketches. In an interview she compared the design process to "an onion, with very thin layers, and with each sketch, I peel away a layer and get closer to what I want." Her evocative watercolor paintings tenderly infuse the text with comfort and reassurance. To be as accurate as possible in her illustrations, Downing often spends hours doing research. *The Firekeeper's Son*, a story by Linda Sue Park that takes place in 18th century Korea, required that historic details be as accurate as possible. Her diligence was rewarded when her illustrations won the Asian/Pacific American Award for Literature in 2006. The book was also named an Honor Book for the Irma S. and James H. Black Award for Excellence in Children's Literature. From depicting Shakespearean England to imagining how a goldfish feels, Downing explores the worlds of her informed imagination to present stories respectful of children and reflective of their world.

Her diligence in making each book distinctive is exhibited in the tender scenes in *Little Kisses*, the mouse-eye perspectives in *Tom Mouse*, and the fog-enshrouded images in *How Do You Know?* Whether illustrating a realistic story, like the intergenerational bond between a boy and his great-grandfather in *The Chicken Salad Club*—a Notable Social Studies Trade Book—or a fantasy like Ursula K. LeGuin's *A Ride on the Red Mare's Back*, this artist evokes character, liveliness, and emotion. Soft-edged and realistic, her artwork establishes a sense of time and place for each story.

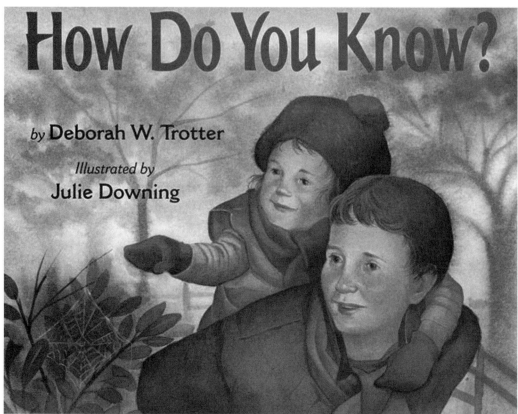

by **Deborah W. Trotter**

Illustrated by
Julie Downing

Courtesy of Clarion Books

SELECTED WORKS WRITTEN AND ILLUSTRATED: *White Snow, Blue Feather*, 1989; *Mozart Tonight*, 1991; *Lullaby and Good Night: Songs for Sweet Dreams*, 1999; *Where Is My Mommy?*, 2003; *No Hugs Till Saturday*, 2008.

SELECTED WORKS ILLUSTRATED: *Clues in the Desert*, by Emmett Davis, 1983; *Hannah's Alaska*, by Joanne Reiser, 1983; *Oh, No! Miss Dent Is Coming to Dinner: A Story of Manners*, by Raymond and Dorothy Moore, 1985; *Quit? Not Me!: A Story of Dependability*, by Raymond and Dorothy Moore, 1985; *Sonia Begonia*, by Joanne Rocklin, 1986; *Prince Boghole*, by Erik Christian Haugaard, 1987; *Margaret's Moves*, by Berniece Rabe, 1987; *Daniel's Gift*, by M.C. Helldorfer, 1987; *Mr. Griggs' Work*, by Cynthia Rylant, 1989; *A Ride on the Red Mare's Back*, by Ursula K. LeGuin, 1992; *The Night Before Christmas*, by Clement Clarke Moore, 1994; *Water Voices*, by Toby Speed, 1998; *Cabbage Rose*, by M.C. Helldorfer, 1993; *Soon Annala*, by Riki Levinson, 1993; *The Magpies' Nest*, by Joanna Foster, 1995; *The Chicken Salad Club*, by Marsha Diane Arnold, 1998; *Tom Mouse*, by Ursula K. LeGuin, 1998; *A First Bible Story Book*, retold by Mary Hoffman, 1999; *A First Book of Fairy Tales*, retold by Mary Hoffman, 2001; *The Firekeeper's Son*, by Linda Sue Park, 2003; *Papa Panov's Special Day*, by Rueben Saillens, 2005; *Little Kisses*, by Jolie Jones, 2005; *How Do You Know?*, by Deborah Trotter, 2006.

SUGGESTED READING: McElmeel, Sharron, *Authors in the Kitchen: Recipes, Stories, and More*, 2005; *Something about the Author*, vol. 148, 2004; Cummings, Pat, *Talking with Artists*, vol. 2, 1995.

WEB SITE: www.juliedowning.com

"I was born in California and have lived in the San Francisco Bay Area almost my whole life. From early childhood, I was an avid reader. My mother encouraged me; she was a reader herself and also a talented writer and painter. My father, an executive with the U.S. Steel Corporation, sang opera in his spare time and also was an ingenious woodworker. He made jigsaw puzzles, kites, and darts for my two sisters and me. From my mother, who read over my school papers and made sure they were clear and correct, I learned to work hard at my writing and take great satisfaction in doing it well; from my father, I learned a love of puzzles and humor and the natural world.

"I read a great deal as a child, and when I wasn't reading, I liked to be in motion— roller skating, ice skating, bike riding, tree climbing, diving, collecting caterpillars and birds' eggs, and making whistles out of grass blades (another thing my father taught me). I graduated from high school in 1962 and went to Scripps College, where I majored in English literature and received my B.A. in 1966. At that time, English majors usually went into teaching, so that is what I did. I went to the University of California at Berkeley for my teaching credential and taught in junior high and high school for a few years. It wasn't until much later, however, when I taught writing to adults, that I really enjoyed being a teacher.

Photo by Ruth Carranza

Jeanne DuPrau

(du-PRO)
June 9, 1944–

"All my jobs have had something to do with reading and writing. After I left teaching, I became an editor and worked for various publishing companies for about ten years. Then came the personal computer revolution, which fascinated me; I worked as a writer for Apple Computer for another ten years or so. During these periods, I was also writing on my own and beginning to be published. Over the years, I've published magazine articles (in both children's and adults' periodicals), essays, and book reviews. I wrote several nonfiction books for publishers of supplemental classroom materials, and in 1991 I wrote a memoir called *The Earth House* about my experience with Zen meditation, homebuilding, and my partner's death from cancer.

"Almost all my writing was nonfiction until I was in my late forties. Then the idea for *The City of Ember* occurred to me and I began trying to write a novel. It was a long process. My first version was unsatisfactory, I knew; I put it away and rewrote the whole thing a few years later, and to my astonishment it was not only bought by Random House at auction but has gone on to be very successful. I have written a sequel (*The People of Sparks*) and a prequel (*The Prophet of Yonwood*) and am currently working on the fourth and last of the series.

"I am not married and don't have children. I live in a suburban house with a Cairn terrier named Ethan, and when I am not writing or doing writing-related business, I am likely to be reading, working in my garden, cooking for friends, or, now and then, playing the piano."

> *"From my mother, who read over my school papers and made sure they were clear and correct, I learned to work hard at my writing and take great satisfaction in doing it well; from my father, I learned a love of puzzles and humor and the natural world."*

☙ ☙ ☙

Jeanne DuPrau grew up in California during the 1950s, an era overshadowed by the Cold War and the vague threat of nuclear destruction, with people building bomb shelters in their backyards. She was an avid reader and many of her favorite books included elements of fantasy and underground worlds: *Alice in Wonderland*, the Narnia books, and the cave scene in *Tom Sawyer*. These influences from her childhood would eventually find their way into her stories of Ember, about an underground post-apocalyptic society.

In 1966 DuPrau received her B.A. in English literature from Scripps College, in Claremont, California. She went on to obtain her teaching certificate from the University of California, Berkeley, and taught junior high and high school English for several years. She left teaching to work as an editor in various San Francisco–based publishing companies. In 1980 she became a staff writer for a pioneering local company called Apple Computer.

Even while DuPrau spent her days as a teacher, editor, or writer of computer manuals, she still found time for her own creative work. She published articles in both adult and children's magazines and wrote essays and book reviews. After editing and writing nonfiction articles and books for nearly her entire adult life, she decided to attempt a work of fiction. She had an idea for a young adult novel: the story of a city, completely surrounded by darkness, whose only light comes from the yellow glow of flood lamps that stay on for half of each twenty-four hour period. Her main characters, 12-year-old Doon and Lina, find mysterious instructions, hard to decipher, which seem to indicate that the people of Ember must leave their city if they are going to survive. When Ember's street lamps begin to flicker, Doon and Lina realize they have no time to lose and find the key to escape from their underground world.

The PROPHET of YONWOOD
the third BOOK OF EMBER

New York Times Bestselling Author
JEANNE DuPRAU

Courtesy of Random House Books for Young Readers

The City of Ember was very successful, becoming both a *New York Times* bestseller and an ALA Notable Children's Book. It was named a *Kirkus* Editor's Choice, appeared on the year's best books lists of *Child* magazine and the New York Public Library, and has won children's choice awards in many states, including California, Vermont, Connecticut, Florida, Utah, Kansas, Nevada, and Indiana.

The popularity of *City of Ember* prompted DuPrau to write both a sequel, *The People of Sparks,* and a prequel, *The Prophet of Yonwood*. When *The People of Sparks* begins, Lina and Doon have led the residents of Ember to the safety of a new city. The citizens of Sparks, however, are also survivors of disaster and they doubt that living in harmony with these newcomers is in their best interest. *The Prophet of Yonwood* tells the story of 11-year-old Nickie, who visits the town of Yonwood with her aunt and finds herself in the midst of a society that is gripped by an end-of-the-world frenzy. The series concluded with *The Diamond of Darkhold*, published in 2008, the same year in which the film version of *The City of Ember* appeared.

In a departure from her science fiction stories about Ember, DuPrau has also written a realistic humorous novel for teens, *Car Trouble*, a story populated with interesting characters on a cross-country road trip. The author lives in Menlo Park, California.

SELECTED WORKS FOR YOUNG READERS: *Adoption: The Facts, Feelings, and Issues of a Double Heritage*, 1981, rev. ed., 1990; *Cloning*, 1999; *The American Colonies*, 2001; *Cells*, 2002; *The City of Ember*, 2003; *The People of Sparks*, 2004; *Car Trouble*, 2005; *The Prophet of Yonwood*, 2006; *The Diamond of Darkhold*, 2008.

SELECTED WORKS WRITTEN FOR ADULTS: *The Earth House*, 1993.

SUGGESTED READING: Brown, Jennifer M., "Flying Starts: Six First-time Children's Authors and Illustrators Talk about Their Road to Publication," *Publishers Weekly*, June 30, 2003.

WEB SITE: www.jeanneduprau.com

Photo by David Rodgers

Julie Andrews Edwards

October 1, 1935–

" As a child performer growing up in England, my education was limited, since I was never in one place long enough to attend a regular school. With so many hours spent in the theatre or traveling, I became a passionate reader. It didn't matter if it was a 'Peg's Own' paper (a periodical from my childhood), an Enid Blyton adventure, or a book by Jane Austen or Sir Walter Scott . . . . I read anything and everything I could get my hands on. The books I loved best reflected on fundamental values—the gifts of nature, the miracles of life that were under our noses every day. There was no greater joy for me than to be curled up with a good book. The power of language inspired and delighted my imagination. Books transported me into the realm of other worlds and ideas and instilled in me a powerful sense of wonder.

"Eventually a tutor was hired to travel with me, and I have to thank that good woman for encouraging my early enthusiastic but clumsy attempts to write. She knew that I loved to create stories and would hold out the promise of allowing me to scribble all I wanted, provided I dealt with math and history and geography first.

"My first published book came about as a sort of happy accident. I was playing a game with my children that required a forfeit—and I was the first to lose. I asked my stepdaughter what my forfeit should be, and she said, 'Write me a story.' Because she was a stepdaughter (and a fairly new one at that), I didn't want to just toss something off, so I tried to write something that would help us bond. I got carried away, and the story turned into a children's novel, entitled *Mandy*, which recently celebrated its 35th anniversary. I enjoyed the process so much that I have been writing ever since.

"Ten years ago, my daughter Emma (who is an educator and theater producer) and I began collaborating as authors. To date we have written sixteen books together for children of all ages, and have created our own publishing program, The Julie Andrews Collection.

"It is an awesome responsibility to write for young people, for I am always aware that they face more challenges today and have to make more choices and difficult decisions than I have ever known. In today's media- and electronically-driven world, I worry that we are spoon-feeding our young people such a steady diet of 'manufactured' slices of life, that they run the risk of becoming very isolated. All they have to do is to receive rather than participate in any way. The joy of reading is that it asks us to engage, to use our imaginations, and to play an active role in our experience. I can think of no better way to discover our passions, our values, our world and our own place in it than through the portal of a wonderful book.

"To quote the legendary actress Helen Hayes, 'From your parents you learn love and laughter and how to put one foot in front of the other. But when books are opened you discover you have wings.'"

"My first published book came about as a sort of happy accident. I was playing a game with my children that required a forfeit—and I was the first to lose."

ऒ ऒ ऒ

Julie Andrews has been one of the most recognized figures in the entertainment industry since the 1960s. Her legendary career encompasses the Broadway and London stages, blockbuster Hollywood films, award-winning television shows, multiple album releases, and concert tours, as well as children's book publishing.

Born Julia Elizabeth Wells on October 1, 1935, in Walton-on-Thames, Surrey, England, Julie was a child star of the British vaudeville circuit. Her mother, Barbara Wells, was a concert pianist, and her stepfather, Ted Andrews, was a tenor; together they had a popular double act that toured the country. Julie made her stage debut in their act, and at the age of 12 began to perform on her own in variety shows, music hall performances, holiday pantomimes, and on British radio and television. Her schoolteacher father, Ted Wells, fostered Julie's love of reading and writing from an early age—gifts that served her well during her touring years, when her academic education was curtailed by her professional commitments.

At the age of 19 Julie was chosen to star as Polly Browne in Sandy Wilson's play *The Boyfriend* on Broadway. She subsequently received critical acclaim for her stunning stage performances as Eliza Doolittle (opposite Rex Harrison) in *My Fair Lady* and as Queen Guenevere (opposite Richard Burton) in *Camelot*. She made her Oscar-winning film debut in Walt Disney's *Mary Poppins*. Her extensive film career includes such screen classics as *The Sound of Music, Thoroughly Modern Millie, 10*, and *Victor/Victoria* (for her reprisal of the title role on Broadway a decade later, she earned a Tony nomination for best actress). Most recently she has been seen portraying Mia's grandmother in *The Princess Diaries* and heard as the voice of Fiona's mother, the Queen, in the second and third Shrek animated films.

> *"It is an awesome responsibility to write for young people, for I am always aware that they face more challenges today and have to make more choices and difficult decisions than I have ever known."*

Throughout her career she has also been a vivid presence on television. Her weekly variety series *The Julie Andrews Hour* won multiple Emmy Awards during its run in the 1970s. Other notable TV appearances include the televised version of Rodgers and Hammerstein's *Cinderella*, several award-winning variety specials (including three with Carol Burnett), *Eloise at the Plaza* for Disney and ABC, and CBS's special live theater presentation of *On Golden Pond*, co-starring Christopher Plummer.

Julie Andrews began writing books for young readers when her own children were growing up. Her first two novels, *Mandy* and *The Last of the Really Great Whangdoodles*, were published under her married name, Julie Andrews Edwards, and have remained in print and in high demand since they first appeared in the 1970s. *Mandy*, the story of an intrepid orphan girl who creates a place of her own outside the walls of the orphanage, was written to pay off a bet she lost to her stepdaughter. It has been compared to such classics as *The Secret Garden* and *A Little Princess. The Last of the Really Great Whangdoodles* can be enjoyed both as a read-aloud and a read-alone adventure story set in a fantasy kingdom, as well as for its witty style and wordplay.

In 1999 Julie returned to children's books with *Little Bo*, the captivating story of a tiny kitten who grows into the grand name her father gives her, Boadicea, and becomes attached to a young seaman, Billy Bates. *Little Bo* received a California children's book award; a few years later, the adventures of the pair were continued in the sequel, *Little Bo in France*. Both stories are accompanied by evocative full-page watercolor illustrations by Henry Cole.

Teaming up with her daughter, Emma Walton Hamilton, Julie has created a best-selling series of picture books that started with *Dumpy the Dump Truck* in 2000. Brightly illustrated by Emma's dad and Julie's first husband, Tony Walton, these stories have been embraced by young children and parents alike. Each adventure of the anthropomorphic automotive characters emphasizes the values of cooperation, community awareness, and self-esteem. *Dumpy and the Big Storm*, in which Dumpy and his pals provide backup power for the lighthouse to save ships at sea during a storm, won an Oppenheim Toy Portfolio Award.

Courtesy of The Julie Andrews Collection

In 2001 the mother and daughter team founded the Julie Andrews Collection imprint for HarperCollins Publishers, with Emma taking on the role of editorial director. The Collection's mission "encompasses quality books for young readers of all ages that nurture the imagination and celebrate a sense of wonder while embracing themes of integrity, creativity, and the gifts of nature and the arts." It includes new works by established and emerging authors in addition to books written by Emma and Julie. In 2008 the Julie Andrews Collection moved to Little, Brown Books for Young Readers to continue its ongoing celebration of "Words, Wisdom, and Wonder."

Julie Andrews has also collaborated with her daughter on an original fable called *Simeon's Gift*, which was lavishly illustrated by Gennady Spirin. This story was actually their earliest joint effort, when Emma was just six years old. Newly divorced from Emma's father, and living on opposite coasts, Julie created the story project as a symbol of their continuing relationship; mother and daughter wrote the story together and Tony added the illustrations. Years later, while developing their new imprint, they revisited the story, added some further development to the plot, and the published book became one of *Child* magazine's Best Books of the Year. *Dragon: Hound of Honor*, based on

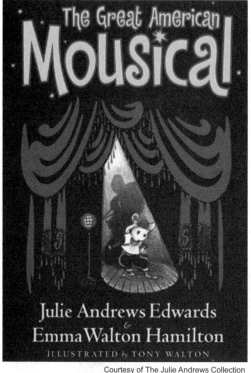

Julie Andrews Edwards
&
Emma Walton Hamilton

ILLUSTRATED by TONY WALTON

Courtesy of The Julie Andrews Collection

the medieval French legend of the Dog of Montargis, required extensive research by the writing pair. Period details, lyrical prose, and a tense mystery combine to make this historical novel a memorable one.

Most recently Julie and Emma have worked together to create two very different titles, *The Great American Mousical* and *Thanks to You: Wisdom from Mother and Child*, which was a #1 *New York Times* bestseller. *Thanks to You*, with a spare rhythmic text accompanied by photographs from the authors' extended family collection, is an affirmation of the universal joys that children bring to mothers and the delight that mothers convey to children about the world around them. *The Great American Mousical* echoes the theatrical background of both authors; a group of thespian mice stage their own performance under the floorboards of a Broadway theater in this chapter book for elementary school children. Both *Simeon's Gift* and *The Great American Mousical* have been adapted for stage performances.

Julie Andrews's considerable charity work has been consistent throughout her career. In 2000 the title of Dame Julie Andrews was bestowed upon her by Queen Elizabeth II to recognize her lifetime achievements in the arts and humanities. Her many other honors include being named one of the 100 Greatest Britons by the British Broadcasting Corporation, serving as Goodwill Ambassador for the United Nations Development Fund for Women (UNIFEM), a Lifetime Achievement Award from the British Academy of Film and Television Arts and a prestigious Kennedy Center honor in the fall of 2001. In 2008 she served as the National Library Week (April 13–19) honorary chairperson for the American Library Association and appeared in public service announcements to spread the word about the importance of reading for every age.

Julie Andrews is married to film director Blake Edwards. In addition to her daughter Emma, she has two stepchildren, Jennifer and Geoffrey. She and Blake Edwards are the adoptive parents of Joanna Lynn and Amy Leigh, who were born in Vietnam. They also have seven grandchildren and two great-grandchildren.

SELECTED WORKS FOR YOUNG READERS: *Mandy*, illus. by Judith Gwyn Brown, 1971 (reissued, illus. by Johanna Westerman, 2006); *The Last of the Really Great Whangdoodles*, 1974; *Little Bo: The Story of Bonnie Boadicea*, illus. by Henry Cole, 1999; *Little Bo in France*, illus. by Henry Cole, 2002; *Simeon's Gift*, with Emma Walton Hamilton, illus. by Gennady Spirin, 2003; *Dragon: Hound of Honor*, with Emma Walton Hamilton, 2004; *Thanks to You: Wisdom from Mother & Child*, with Emma Walton Hamilton, 2007; *The Great American Mousical*, with Emma Walton Hamilton, illus. by Tony Walton, 2007.

SELECTED WORKS IN SERIES (all with Emma Walton Hamilton; all illus. by Tony Walton): *Dumpy the Dump Truck*, 2000; *Dumpy at School*, 2000; *Dumpy and His Pals*, 2001; *Dumpy's Friends on the Farm*, 2001; *Dumpy Saves Christmas*, 2001; *Dumpy and the Big Storm*, 2002; *Dumpy and the Firefighters*, 2003; *Dumpy to the Rescue!*, 2004; *Dumpy's Apple Shop*, 2004; *Dumpy's Happy Holiday*, 2005; *Dumpy's Valentine*, 2006; *Dumpy's Extra Busy Day*, 2006.

SUGGESTED READING: Andrews, Julie, *Home: A Memoir of My Early Years*, 2008; *Something About the Author*, vol. 153, 2005. Periodicals—*Current Biography*, 1994, 1956.

WEB STE: www.julieandrewscollection.com

A profile of Emma Walton Hamilton also appears in this volume.

Deborah Ellis
August 7, 1960–

"I grew up in the small town of Paris, in Southern Ontario. As a socially awkward kid, I didn't know how to make friends. Reading and writing kept me company, and made me feel that I was not constrained by the boundaries of my town and my life. Writing—and wanting to write—made me believe that I might, one day, join the mysterious and exalted world of authors.

"Books justified me, especially books about children who were not perfect, or who were on the outside of things. I drank in the glory of Louise Fitzhugh's *Harriet the Spy*, James Lincoln Collier's *The Teddy Bear Habit*, and Betty Smith's *A Tree Grows in Brooklyn*. I carried a notebook with me everywhere, scribbling down conversations with myself. A notebook, a pen, and a book to read made me feel safe. They still do, no matter where I am.

"I got involved with the anti-war movement when I was seventeen. Someone came to my high school to talk about a campaign for nuclear disarmament. This was in 1977, a time in our human history when we were moving closer and closer to atomic Armageddon. Disarmament made complete sense to me—take the weapons away from the idiots who run the world and they won't be able to kill people. I was immediately hooked. Political activism, on issues of war, women's rights, the environment, and economic justice helps me to feel powerful and connected to the world. Instead of going to university, I took a series of bottom-of-the-barrel jobs to pay the rent while I wrote and did political work.

"I kept writing, producing many horrible books that no one would publish, and reams of bad poetry and putrid stories. I had a long apprenticeship. I always hoped that the next book would be a little less horrible than the last one. Finally, in 1998, I sold a book called *Looking for X*, which was published the year after.

Photo by Deborah Ellis

Deborah Ellis

"A couple of years before that, Afghanistan, a small country in Central Asia, was taken over by a backward and brutal group called the Taliban. They threw girls out of school, women out of their jobs, burned books, banned music, and committed all manner of other crimes upon the people there. The Taliban grew out of the chaos of the previous twenty years of superpower battles in their country. Horror begat horror.

"I became involved with supporting women and kids in Afghanistan, and decided to travel there to learn first hand what their lives were like. With incredible graciousness and generosity, Afghans invited me into their hovels and tents, sharing with me their stories of pain and survival.

"That was my first such experience. Out of it grew four books on Afghanistan, one for adults and three for younger readers. Since then, I have traveled to Israel and Palestine to meet with children of that war; to two countries in Africa to learn from children affected by HIV/AIDS, and to Bolivia to hear from kids involved in the drug trade.

"Reading and writing continue to open up new worlds for me. The courage of ordinary people gives me hope, especially when those in power, who should know better, continue to act like criminals."

⊗ ⊗ ⊗

A writer of novels and nonfiction books that speak specifically to the needs of children and women surviving in war-torn or disease-ridden countries, Deborah Ellis is determined to make changes—and she's willing to use her own resources, time, and energy to do so. Focusing in her books on those suffering from poverty and injustice, she writes to tell their stories and to help the more fortunate to understand why we all must care about their plights.

Born in Cochrane, Ontario, Deborah Ellis moved with her parents and her older sister Carolyn to Paris, Ontario, two years later and lived there until she completed her high school education. She submitted poems, plays, and stories to magazines and contests—early training in the craft of writing.

After high school Ellis worked various jobs while putting her energies into political activism and writing. In 1988 she began working as a mental health counselor at the Margaret Frazer House, a psychiatric group home for women. In the 1990s, deeply moved by the plight of Afghan women under the Taliban, she helped found the organization Canadian Women for Women in Afghanistan. In 1997 she visited Afghan refugee camps in Pakistan and, upon her return, organized funding for schools to educate refugee children. That was the first of several trips; in 1998 she also went to Moscow where she researched the 1979 Soviet invasion of Afghanistan and interviewed hundreds of Russian and Afghan women about the war. The result of these journeys was a book for adults entitled *Women of the Afghan War*.

Deborah Ellis's first real writing break came through Groundwood Publishers Twentieth Anniversary First Novel for Children Contest. She had never written for children but she developed a contemporary novel, *Looking for X*, which features an independent and fiercely devoted child named Kyber, her single mother (a former stripper), and her two autistic younger brothers. The book was a runner-up for the contest but went on to win the Governor General's Literary Award for Juvenile English Fiction, as well as being short-listed for both the Canadian Library Association's Children's Book of the Year and the Silver Birch Reading Award.

> "With incredible graciousness and generosity, Afghans invited me into their hovels and tents, sharing with me their stories of pain and survival."

Ellis's next novel for children made use of a conversation she had with an Afghan woman in Pakistan. The woman spoke of a daughter who had cut her hair and disguised herself as a boy in order to find work to support her family. Girls were not allowed to study or to work at that time, and she would have been severely punished if discovered—yet quite a few girls did the same thing to keep themselves and their families from starving. Fascinated by these courageous young women, Ellis wrote *The Breadwinner*, a young adult story about 11-year-old Parvana who first undertakes work as a letter-writer in the marketplace and then learns to dig up graves to sell bones for chicken feed and soap. Published in 2001, the book became particularly important after the September 11th attacks on the United States, when so many were trying to understand what was happening in Afghanistan. It has since been translated into many languages. The sequel, *Parvana's Journey*, received the Ruth Schwartz Children's Book Award in the young adult/middle reader category and the Jane Addams Children's Book Award. It was also named an ALA Best Book for Young Adults. Both *The Breadwinner* and the third book in the series, *Mud City*, won Canada's Red Cedar Award.

At first glance *A Company of Fools*, Ellis's only work of historical fiction so far, seems an unusual departure. But once again she has found a way to center on young people caught up in desperate circumstances, exploring the lives of a group of young entertainers who perform in the shadow of the bubonic plague in 1348. It received a Mr. Christie's Silver Seal Book Award for 8–11 year olds. For her next book she traveled to Israel and the Gaza Strip in 2002 and interviewed children on how their lives had been impacted by war. *Three Wishes: Palestinian and Israeli Children Speak*, a nonfiction oral history, consists of interviews with twenty young people ranging in age from 8 to 18 and lists the names and ages of the 429 children killed in the Arab-Israeli war between September 2000 and March 2003.

The following year Ellis traveled to sub-Saharan Africa to conduct interviews for an oral history of children impacted by AIDS. Millions died of the bubonic plague in the 14th century;

millions are dying of AIDS in our time, and Ellis feels strongly that many die unnecessarily. From this research, she wrote both the nonfiction *Our Stories, Our Songs: African Children Talk About AIDS*—which was named a *School Library Journal* Best of the Year as well as an ALA Notable Children's Book—and a middle-grade novel, *The Heaven Shop*. A Jane Addams Honor Book, *The Heaven Shop*'s royalties are donated to UNICEF.

Deborah Ellis makes her home in Simcoe, Ontario.

SELECTED WORKS FOR YOUNG READERS: *Looking for X*, 1999; *The Breadwinner*, 2000; *Parvana's Journey*, 2002; *A Company of Fools*, 2002; *Mud City*, 2003; *Three Wishes: Palestinian and Israeli Children Speak*, 2004; *The Heaven Shop*, 2004; *Our Stories, Our Songs: African Children Talk About AIDS*, 2005; *I Am a Taxi*, 2006; *Bifocal*, with Eric Walters, 2007; *Jakeman*, 2007.

SELECTED WORKS FOR ADULTS: *Women of the Afghan War*, 2000.

SUGGESTED READING: *Authors and Artists for Young Adults*, vol. 48, 2003; *Contemporary Authors*, 2003; *Major Authors and Illustrators for Children and Young Adults*, 2nd ed, 2002. Periodicals—Huron, Debra, "Transcending Borders," in *Herizons*, Summer, 2001; Jenkinson, Dave, "Deborah Ellis, Profile," in *CM: Canadian Review of Materials*, 2003.

Louise Erdrich

UR-drick
June 7, 1954–

The eldest of seven children, Louise Erdrich was born in Little Falls, Minnesota, to Ralph Louis Erdrich and the former Rita Joanne Gourneau. Erdrich's mother hailed from the Turtle Mountain Ojibwe, or Chippewa, tribe while her father was of German descent. Erdrich grew up in Wahpeton, North Dakota, where her parents worked as teachers at a school run by the Bureau of Indian Affairs. As a child, thanks in part to the efforts of her maternal grandfather, who was once tribal chairman of the Turtle Mountain Reservation, Erdrich absorbed the traditions of her Chippewa ancestry and developed a passion for storytelling. As a young writer she received considerable support from her parents, her father paying her a nickel for every story she penned and her mother making book covers for her works out of construction paper.

A gifted student, Erdrich attended mostly public schools in Wahpeton before matriculating at Dartmouth College, in New Hampshire, in 1972, a member of the school's first coeducational class. While at Dartmouth, Erdrich met her future husband, the anthropologist Michael Dorris, who was then chairman of the school's nascent Native-American Studies department. In 1978, two years after graduating from Dartmouth, Erdrich entered a master's program in creative writing at John Hopkins University in Baltimore, Maryland, where she honed her talent as an author, completing her degree in 1979. Before returning to Dartmouth in 1980 as a writer-in-residence, Erdrich began a collaborative relationship with Dorris, exchanging detailed notes and suggestions with him on various writing projects. With Erdrich back in New Hampshire, this partnership soon blossomed into romance and the two were married in 1981.

After their wedding Dorris and Erdrich expanded on their unique creative relationship, sending drafts back and forth between them and reading work aloud to each other until they both more or less agreed on every word. They published a number of books together, including romantic short stories that they wrote under the pseudonym, Milou North. Milou was a combination of their first names and North represented their home in New Hampshire. The one book for which they were listed as joint authors is *The Crown of Columbus*, a novel published just before the Columbus quincentenniel in 1992.

Photo by Persia Erdrich

Since publishing her first novel, *Love Medicine*, in 1984, Erdrich has proven a prolific author, writing a number of works for adult audiences, including ten more novels, several volumes of poetry, numerous short stories, and works of nonfiction. Drawing heavily on her Ojibwe heritage, Erdrich is perhaps best known for her Machimanito series, a collection of novels charting the lives of the residents of Argus, a fictional reservation town in the Red River Valley, on the Minnesota-North Dakota border. For her first book, *Love Medicine*, she received the National Book Critics Circle Award, the first time a debut novelist was so honored. Later books in that series—*The Beet Queen*, *Tracks*, and *The Bingo Palace* followed three generations of Ojibwe in the 20th century. Another novel, *The Antelope Wife*, captured a World Fantasy Award in 1999, and *The Last Report on the Miracles at Little No Horse* was a finalist for the National Book Award. For her short fiction, she has been honored with an O. Henry Award for "Fleur." She is also a recipient of a Guggenheim Fellowship, a Pushcart Prize in Poetry, and a Western Literacy Association Award.

Erdrich made her debut as a children's author with the picture book *Grandmother's Pigeon*. Featuring illustrations by Jim LaMarche, *Grandmother's Pigeon* is the story of a family whose unique grandmother has set off for Greenland on the back of a porpoise, leaving behind her two grandchildren and a room full of strange objects, including a stuffed pigeon and a bird's nest with three unhatched eggs. Another picture book, *The Range Eternal*, illustrated with paintings by Steve Johnson and Lou Fancher, focuses on a young mother as she recalls the enamel stove that kept her warm and cooked her food when she was a child.

Erdrich's groundbreaking novel for older children, *The Birchbark House*, was published in 1999. Featuring pencil drawings by the author, *The Birchbark House* chronicles four seasons, over the course of a year, in the life of a young Ojibwe girl named Omakayas, or Little Frog. Living on an island in Lake Superior at the time white settlers are first beginning to appear, Omakayas finds that the traditional way of life for her tribe is in danger of disappearing, threatened by disease as well as the encroaching pioneers. Praised by critics and embraced by young readers, *The Birchbark House* was a finalist for the National Book Award for Young People's Literature in 1999. It was also named an ALA Notable Children's Book, received a Parents' Choice Gold Award, and was cited as a Notable Trade Book in the Field of Social Studies. Erdrich continued Omakayas's saga in a sequel, *The Game of Silence*, which takes place over four seasons in 1850, three years after the events in *The Birchbark House*. This book was named an ALA Notable Children's Book and also received the Scott O'Dell Award for Historical Fiction. In the third title, *The Porcupine Years*, the young heroine, now twelve years old, suffers the pain of displacement from her childhood home.

Erdrich's husband, Michael Dorris, died tragically in 1997. Today she owns and operates BirchBark Books and Native Arts, a store in Minneapolis, Minnesota, where she makes her home. In 2002 she received the Minnesota Humanities Prize for Literature for the body of her work.

> The Birchbark House *chronicles four seasons, over the course of a year, in the life of a young Ojibwe girl named Omakayas, or Little Frog.*

SELECTED WORKS WRITTEN FOR YOUNG READERS: *Grandmother's Pigeon*, illus. by Jim LaMarche, 1996; *The Birchbark House*, 1999; *The Range Eternal*, illus. by Steve Johnson and Lou Fancher, 2002; *The Game of Silence*, 2005; *The Porcupine Year*, 2008.

SELECTED WORKS WRITTEN FOR ADULTS: *Jacklight: Poems*, 1984; *Love Medicine*, 1984; *The Beet Queen*, 1986; *Tracks*, 1988; *Bap-*

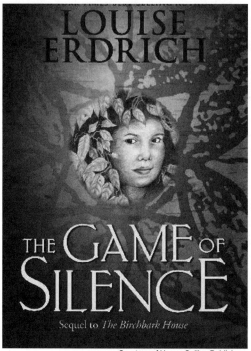

Courtesy of HarperCollins Publishers

tism of Desire: Poems, 1989; The Crown of Columbus, with Michael Dorris, 1991; The Bingo Palace, 1994; The Blue Jay's Dance: A Birth Year, 1995; Tales of Burning Love, 1996; The Antelope Wife, 1998; The Last Report on the Miracles at Little No Horse, 2001; Books and Islands in Ojibwe Country: Traveling in the Lands of My Ancestors, 2003; The Master Butcher's Singing Club, 2003; Original Fire: Selected and New Poems, 2003; Four Souls: A Novel, 2004; The Painted Drum, 2005; The Plague of Doves, 2008.

SUGGESTED READING: Something About the Author, vol. 141, 2003; Contemporary Authors, New Revision Series, vol. 62, 1998; Authors and Artists for Young Adults, vol. 10, 1993; Chavkin, Allan and Nancy Feyl Chavkin, Conversations with Louise Erdrich and Michael Dorris, 1994; Stookey, Lorena, Louise Erdrich: A Critical Companion, 1999.

WEB SITE: www.birchbarkbooks.com

Timothy Basil Ering

June 13, 1965–

"I moved away from my birthplace of Rochester, Michigan before I was old enough to remember much about it. Clear and fond memories of childhood began for me around 1969 when my family moved to Cape Cod, Massachusetts. My two brothers, two sisters and I, along with our pet goat and dog, would run barefoot across our crabgrass lawn, hop the split-rail fence, and scurry across the shell driveway. Half a minute from there, we were chasing each other down the sandy beach road that meandered through the trees and then through the beach grass, and finally to the fishing docks of Rock Harbor. We knew all the names of the boats there. We would leap off the docks into the water, sometimes by swinging from the rope that was left tied to the great wood beam from which giant bluefin tuna were hoisted and hung high by their broad forked tails. We caught flounder and tomcod by the dozens with our hand lines from those docks and we were proud to be referred to as harbor bums. We lived in a little town called Orleans. Our house was just a hop, skip and a wild blackberry patch away from Cape Cod Bay.

"In 1976, we moved to a historical little town on the bay called Brewster, just three miles west of Orleans. Our house was built in the late 1700s, and it required all five of us kids to adhere to a very large chore chart. Though we had fun being so close to the beach, chores were a bummer, especially if the chores had to be done when the fish were biting! But those chores I did when I was growing up prepared me to have a strong work ethic as an artist now. And it's true that I scrape paint and apply paint on my artwork in a way very similar to how I scraped paint and applied paint on our old house. I used to hate that chore, but today one of my favorite things to do is to experiment with paint and art mediums by layering them and scraping them.

"I was surrounded by exciting visuals like breaching whales, fantastical fish, colorful boats, pounding surf, mighty storms, towering sand dunes and marvelous sunsets over the ocean. All these sights would eventually be a tremendous influence on my art.

Photo by Jennifer A. B. Ering

"I thank my mother and father for nurturing the artist in me before I even knew what art was. I remember being so impressed when I saw for the first time some of the oil paintings my mother had created before I was born. It was probably then that I was first enlightened by the concept of talent. She became a sort of celebrity in my eyes. I also remember quite vividly being wide-eyed with awe when she showed me for the first time how to draw a person's face with line and shading, in a simple oval shape. I was very young and it made quite an impact on me.

"My mom sacrificed her beautiful piano playing and art-making when she devoted all of her time to us five children. I didn't grow up watching my mom oil-paint and play piano every day. But I did grow up surrounded every day by her creativity, talent, and sensitivity to beautiful detail, right down to the way she set the dinner table. She has always been tremendously encouraging, and God bless all the precious times that I was smart enough to pay close attention to her wonderful advice and artful touch.

"Equally inspiring to me at a young age, though in a much different way, was my father. My dad opened my mind to the infinite wonders of nature by introducing me to the great outdoors. And he, by example, showed me that hard work creates time to play hard. And that we did! We had a plethora of adventures from spending countless hours in boats out on the ocean to exploring miles and miles of beaches on Cape Cod.

"I remember drifting offshore in the frigid Atlantic, jigging in the deep water for codfish, our noses dripping, our fingers numb. I remember when my dad would cheer about how alive he felt when a thin sliver of sunshine would peek through the gray winter clouds and warm us for just a second before it vanished. I would learn later that these experiences in nature are imperative for me to have, because to me, they go hand in hand with making art.

"From elementary school through high school I liked to practice my drawing skills. I learned a lot by copying things like fish, boats, animals, and faces. I remember being excited that I could re-draw things from memory. I also enjoyed manipulating clay, and I looked forward to the times that we were encouraged to embellish our school projects with drawing or art. Though I enjoyed art very much, I don't recall having making plans to become an artist. And, I must admit that I never dreamed of becoming an author.

"I was surrounded by exciting visuals like breaching whales, fantastical fish, colorful boats, pounding surf, mighty storms, towering sand dunes and marvelous sunsets over the ocean."

"I was craving travel and adventure after graduating from high school in 1983. I joined the United States Navy after a semester of general education and drawing classes at the local community college on Cape Cod. In February of 1984, I left home to start boot camp in San Diego, CA. I loved boot camp and I was so proud to be the one chosen to create and paint our company flag! Then I had amazing adventures on board an aircraft carrier, the USS *Kitty Hawk*.

"In 1989, overlapping the tail end of my six-year sailing voyage in the Pacific, I began taking art courses at Grossmont Junior College in San Diego. I was excited about ancient art history, and thrilled to be involved with drawing classes again. I devoured all the art courses available: ceramics, figure drawing, composition. But best of all was experiencing Harry Lum. Mr. Lum is a masterful and memorable art instructor who (at the beginning), ironically, knocked the fun out of drawing! He constantly had us answer the question 'why?' to everything we drew. And, 'What does it all mean?' But I hung in there, taking class after class with him when others found it torture. I learned invaluable lessons from him that I still use today. I'll always remember when Mr. Lum, ribbing me about my love of drawing fish, asked me if I had ever seen a Winslow Homer fish. I immediately searched my books for fish painted by Winslow Homer (and any other famous artists that I could find), and I think my art became more interesting overnight.

"I thank my lucky stars that I attended a presentation one day given by a recruiter from a prestigious art school in Pasadena, CA. The Art Center College of Design enamored me! I worked hard on my portfolio. I was adamant about my next goal; to be accepted to this school! I graduated from Grossmont with my Associate's degree, and started at the Art Center in 1990. The Art Center was a melting pot of incredible talent from around the world. I studied illustration with a minor in fine art under the masterful instruction of David Mocarski, Vern Wilson, Gary Meyers, Burne Hogarth, Harry Carmean, Steve Houston, Lori Madden, Dwight Harmon, Phillip Hayes, George Hampft, and Lawrence Carol. All of them amazing, and I have no words that could describe my gratitude for everything they did for me.

"I would learn later that these experiences in nature are imperative for me to have, because to me, they go hand in hand with making art."

"Burne Hogarth was still teaching at 83 years old and with more energy than most people sixty years younger. He was the artist who did the original Tarzan drawings years before. I was lucky enough to enroll in his famous dynamic anatomy class. I loved to watch him move through our class holding a piece of charcoal or chalk in his fingers as he lectured us. We were all quietly drawing from a young model one day while Burne worked his way around the room, scrutinizing everyone's drawing. You could always feel Burne's presence if he was behind you, and you could smell his cologne. That day, Burne stopped behind me and said loudly (with a tone of disappointment) for all to hear, that I was drawing the model's beautiful smooth knees to look like raisins! And he was right. Because of my bad drawing, our class benefited from an impromptu lesson about the anatomy of a knee. I loved it!

"I graduated from the Art Center in 1994 with invaluable skills and knowledge needed to start a professional career as an artist. I had grown to love aspects of life such as persistence, patience, sharing, taking chances, risk, noticing, paying attention to detail, self-exploration, and striving to reach one's potential. These, for me, are the key ingredients to achieving deep inner happiness. I try to write stories and make art that will encourage children to be open-minded about the aspects of life that I have found to enrich my own life so much.

"I currently live in Somerville, Massachusetts with my wife Jen and our son Phineas. My art is inspired by our adventures and my daily exposure to the omnipresent aura of the whaling history around New England. And the interesting characters that I meet, like fisherman, clam diggers and lobstermen, definitely influence my love of being a storyteller."

CG CG CG

Timothy Basil Ering's illustrative style was instantly and widely recognized with the publication of Kate DiCamillo's fanciful novel, *The Tale of Desperaux*. Both a critical and a popular success, *Desperaux* won the Newbery Medal as well as a large number of state awards from Wyoming to Maine. An ALA Notable Book, a *Booklist* Editors' Choice, and a NCTE Notable Children's Book in the Language Arts, the book was widely praised for its imaginative text and Ering's whimsical illustrations, which perfectly matched the story. His soft pencil drawings, with shadings from dark to light and meticulous renderings of both animal and human characters, created just the right backdrop for DiCamillo's old-fashioned fable of heroism, romance, and adventure.

Courtesy of Candlewick Press

The first picture book that Ering both wrote and illustrated, *The Story of Frog Belly Rat Bone*, was a finalist for the Borders Original Voices Award in 2003. A combination of hand-lettered text and expressive art, this book (which celebrates creativity and hope) was born in an urban garden created by schoolchildren in Pasadena, where Ering found himself sketching a scarecrow and remembering a string of silly words he had put together once to amuse himself. In the story a boy looking for treasure in the ugly world of Cementland spots a box that contains colorful packets of gray specks with the directions, "Put my wondrous riches in the earth and enjoy." When the "treasures" are mysteriously dug up, the boy creates a guardian out of junk, named Frog Belly Rat Bone, who helps him to plant some more mysteriously wait patiently for the results. The ending is joyous, as the seeds bring colorful flowers and fruit to the gray world and the "thieves" repent to help reap the harvest. The surreal swirls and smears of the background and the squiggly, expressive characters are perfectly matched to a child's imagination and helped this book capture notice at both the New England Book Show and the New York Book Show, where it was the winner in the children's category; it was also cited as a *Nick Jr. Family Magazine* Best Book of the Year. In 2007 the Rogue Artists Ensemble, based in Long Beach, California, developed a theatrical version of the story using puppetry, music, video projections, and innovative prop design.

Ering's charming ink and acrylic illustrations for Nancy Wood's picture book, *Mr. and Mrs. God in the Creation Kitchen*, set the mood for the humor of this offbeat look at the creation story. The artist's energetic line and playful approach in depicting the chaotic kitchen and its heavenly inhabitants make the story spring to life. His colors range in tone from muted to exuberant, reflecting the ethereal scene. The Cooperative Children's Book Center chose *Mr. and Mrs. God in the Creation Kitchen* as one of their Choices titles in 2007.

Reflecting his own lifelong love for the seashore, Ering next created a fully realized world of expressive undersea creatures in *Necks Out for Adventure!* The "wiggleskins" hero is young Edwin, who not only sticks his neck out for adventure and flows with the current but also rescues his entire clan from the terrible prospect of turning into clam chowder at the hands of the monstrous clam digger. Against a backdrop of landscapes evocative of both the undersea world and the sweeping shoreline, Ering's creatures act out their miniature drama while his swirling lines and colors reflect every nuance of the story's plot.

Timothy Basil Ering's art has appeared in exhibitions at the Society of Illustrators in New York and the Provincetown Art Association, as well as in a solo show at the Provincetown Group Gallery in Massachusetts. As a creator of original picture books and an illustrator of longer novels, he has brought a unique voice and vision to the children's book field.

SELECTED WORKS ILLUSTRATED: *The Diary of Victor Frankenstein*, by Stephen R. Cooper, 1997; *Sad Doggy*, by Jennifer B. Lawrence, 2001; *The Tale of Desperaux*, by Kate DiCamillo, 2003; *Don't Let the Peas Touch!: and Other Stories*, by Deborah Blumenthal, 2004; *Mr. and Mrs. God in the Creation Kitchen*, by Nancy Wood, 2006.

SELECTED WORKS WRITTEN AND ILLUSTRATED: *The Story of Frog Belly Rat Bone*, 2003; *Necks Out for Adventure: The True Story of Edwin Wiggleskin*, 2007.

SELECTED WORKS ILLUSTRATED FOR ADULTS AND TEENS: *Heaven Help Us: The Worrier's Guide to the Patron Saints*, by Alice and Clare LaPlante, 1999; *Dear Saint Anne, Send Me a Man: And Other Time-Honored Prayers for Love*, by Alice and Clare LaPlante, 2002; *33 Snowfish*, by Adam Rapp, 2003.

SUGGESTED READING: *Something About the Author*, vol. 176, 2007.

WEB SITE: www.timothybasilering.com

Lou Fancher and Steve Johnson

The youngest of three children, Steve Johnson grew up in a suburb of St. Paul, Minnesota. As a child, he enjoyed reading the books of Dr. Seuss. He also drew all the time, even in church and during school hours. In first grade, he drew Santa with reindeer and from then on became known as "the kid who could draw." The only time he wasn't drawing was when he was playing whatever sport was in season. Although he possessed an aptitude in science and chemistry like the rest of his family, by 10th grade, Johnson knew he wanted to be an artist. He studied illustration and painting at the School of Associated Arts in St. Paul and received his B.F.A. in 1982. After graduating he worked as a freelance illustrator.

Lou Fancher grew up in Ann Arbor, Michigan. She always had plenty of energy and played basketball, climbed trees, swam, acted things out, built sculptures, and, when she couldn't sleep, practiced dance steps. She also made weekly trips to the local library with her mother and was always amazed that she could take a treasure of books home in her large canvas bag.

Photo by Steve Johnson

Lou Fancher
September 1960–

Although she doesn't remember consciously deciding to become an artist, it seems Fancher was born with a heart destined to become one. Her artistic life took two courses. She studied art history while earning her B.F.A. in dance at the University of Cincinnati. After graduation she pursued a successful career in dance as a ballet dancer, choreographer, coach and instructor to dance companies throughout the United States. In 2002 Fancher received the Minnesota State Arts Board's artist fellowship for choreography. She has been a ballet mistress for the Alberta Ballet, the James Sewell Ballet in Minneapolis, and the associate artistic director for New Dance Ensemble. She is currently the ballet mistress for Company C Contemporary Ballet in Walnut Creek, California. In addition to her dance career, she is a highly successful designer, illustrator, and writer of children's books.

Johnson and Fancher have been working together for many years and approach their work collaboratively by conceiving, drawing, and designing each painting together. Occasionally, they use family, friends, children of friends, and strangers as models; other times, they simply make their characters up. The results of their efforts have been very successful.

Fancher and Johnson's first children's book, *No Star Nights*, by Anna Egan Smucker, about a girl growing up in a 1950s steel-mill town, was illustrated with vibrant images and subtle shadings and received a Children's Book Award from the International Reading Association. Their illustrations for Jon Scieszka's *The Frog Prince, Continued*, an ALA Notable Children's Book, enhanced a whimsical and humorous take-off on the traditional fairy tale. They created textured oil paintings that lent a quiet, nostalgic atmosphere to Marsha Wilson Chall's story of a young girl's vacation experiences in *Up North at the Cabin*, which received the 1993 Society of Illustrators Gold Medal.

Photo by Steve Johnson

Steve Johnson
June 1960–

With lush, overflowing pictures, Fancher and Johnson transformed a child's bedroom into a deep green forest as a boy tries to create a home for a salamander in the 1992 Minnesota Book Award winner, *The Salamander Room*, written by Anne Mazer. Several of their books have been Minnesota Book Award finalists over the years: *Up North at the Cabin*; *Cat, You Better Come Home*; *My Many Colored Days*; *The Lost and Found House*; *Coppélia*; *The Day Ocean Came to Visit*; and *Silver Seeds: A Book of Nature Poems*.

The estate of Theodore Seuss Geisel (better known to the world as Dr. Seuss) chose Fancher and Johnson to illustrate *My Many Colored Days*, an unpublished manuscript that Dr. Seuss

Courtesy of HarperCollins Publishers

wrote but never illustrated. This story is about a child comparing his many feelings to various colors was nominated for the 1997 American Booksellers Book of the Year (ABBY). Fancher and Johnson illustrated the book in an expressionistic, child-friendly style. In 2004, the centenary year of Dr. Seuss's birth, the pair continued their tribute to the legendary author/illustrator by illustrating Kathleen Krull's biography, *The Boy on Fairfield Street: How Ted Geisel Grew Up to Become Dr. Seuss*.

Besides working on children's books, Fancher and Johnson produces illustrations for annual reports, brochures, posters, advertisements, book covers, movies, and magazines. They have also provided pre-production set and character design for such animated films as *Toy Story* and *A Bug's Life*. Fancher wrote *The Quest for the One Big Thing*, a counting book based on *A Bug's Life*. Illustrated by the Fancher/Johnson team, this title also celebrates teamwork, as a group of insects work together to move a large particle of food to their colony for harvesting.

In Lois Duncan's picture book *I Walk at Night*, a *New York Times* Best Illustrated Children's Book about the nocturnal world as seen through the eyes of a prowling cat, the illustrators produced an interesting textured surface using string and oil painting, an unusual and highly successful medium. In Mary Pope Osborne's *New York's Bravest*, which came out soon after September 11, 2001, they emphasize the strength of a legendary 19th-century volunteer firefighter with oil paintings that evoke a somber mood when the hero is lost in a fire.

Shortlisted for the Nestlé Children's Book Prize, the Irish Children's Book of the Year, and the Highland Book Award, *The Dancing Tiger*, with text by Malachy Doyle, features luminous double-page pastel paintings that perfectly capture the mystical landscape where a mysterious tiger and a young girl dance on a quiet, moonlit night. Accompanied by delicate but vivid paintings, Fancher's first original text for a picture book, *Star Climbing*, is about a child's fantasy journey to various constellations before she drifts off to sleep.

In 2005 Fancher and Johnson moved with their son to Moraga, California, where Fancher started working as ballet mistress for Company C Contemporary Ballet in Walnut Creek, California. Fancher and Johnson continue to create children's books and other artwork while enjoying life in Moraga.

SELECTED WORKS ILLUSTRATED BY FANCHER AND JOHNSON: *No Star Nights*, by Anna Smucker, 1989; *The Frog Prince Continued*, by Jon Scieszka, 1991; *The Salamander Room*, by Anne Mazer, 1991; *Penelope's Pendant*, by Douglas Hill, 1991; *Up North at the Cabin*, by Marsha Wilson Chall, 1992; *The First Night*, by B. G. Hennessy, 1993; *Peach and Blue*, by Sarah S. Kilborne, 1994; *Cat, You Better Come Home*, by Garrison Keillor, 1995; *My Many Colored Days*, by Dr. Seuss, 1996; *The Lost and Found House*, by Michael Cadnum, 1997; *Coppélia*, by Margot Fonteyn, 1998; *The Lost Boy and the Monster*, by Craig Kee Strete, 1999; *Bambi*, by Felix Salten, adapted by Janet Schulman, 1999; *I Walk at Night*, by Lois Duncan, 2000; *Horsefly*, by Alice Hoffman, 2000; *Silver Seeds: A Book of Nature Poems*, by Paul Paolilli and Dan Brewer, 2001; *The Day Ocean Came to Visit*, by Diane Wolkstein, 2001; *Robin's Room*, by Margaret Wise Brown, 2002; *The Range Eternal*, by Louise Erdrich, 2002; *New York's Bravest*, by Mary Pope Osborne, 2002; *You're a Bear*, by Marvis Jukes, 2003; *The Boy on Fairfield Street: How Ted Geisel Grew Up to Become Dr. Seuss*, by Kathleen Krull, 2004; *Momma, Will You?*, by Dori Chaconas, 2004; *Bebop Express*, by H. L. Panahi, 2005; *The Dancing Tiger*, by Malachy Doyle, 2005; *All God's Creatures*, by Karen Hill, 2005; *We're All God's Creatures*, by Karen Hill, 2006; *Casey Back at Bat*, by Dan Gutman, 2007; *The Cheese*, by Margie Palatini, 2007; *The Ugly Duckling*, by Hans Christian Andersen, retold by Stephen Mitchell, 2007; *Bugtown Boogie*, by Warren Hanson, 2008; *Amazing Peace*, by Maya Angelou, 2008.

SELECTED WORKS WRITTEN BY FANCHER AND ILLUSTRATED BY FANCHER AND JOHNSON: *The Quest for the One Big Thing* (based on the film *A Bug's Life*), 1998; *Margery Williams's The Velveteen Rabbit* (adapted by Lou Fancher), 2002; *Star Climbing*, 2006.

SUGGESTED READING: *Something About the Author*, vol. 177, 2007.

WEB SITE: www.johnsonandfancher.com

Photo by Meredith French

Jean Ferris

January 24, 1939–

"I wrote my first book when I was seven. I drew the illustrations for it, too. My mother still has it. I never drew any more illustrations, but I kept writing all through my childhood . . . and I'm still doing it.

"Although I didn't like it at the time, I now think that all the moving around I had to do as a child (my father was an Army doctor) gave me all the tools I needed to be a writer. Because I was often the 'new kid' at school and in the neighborhood, I spent a lot of time alone—and I spent a lot of that alone-time reading. Once we even lived right across the street from the library—very convenient!

"Books were my refuge and my comfort, my education and my entertainment. I got to live many other lives through the lives of the characters in books—which was especially appealing when my own life seemed so uninteresting.

"Three other things I did in each new place: I eavesdropped on other people's conversations in an attempt to find clues to the local ways. For the same reason, I liked looking into the lighted windows of other people's houses at dusk as my father drove down the new streets. And I kept a diary, writing down what I did, and how I felt, and what I was thinking. These three things turned out to be the basis of every story I've ever written: what I've heard, seen, and felt.

"We didn't have a TV in our home until I was thirteen, and there were no such things as computers, iPods, video games, or cell phones. These are all good things in their proper places, but they all can also be black holes of time consumption. I didn't have to worry about that. I had plenty of free time—for thinking, dreaming, reading, and writing. When I wasn't out on my bike with my dog, or sitting in a big leather chair at the library reading my way through the children's section, I was writing.

"You'd think with this kind of a start I'd have published something long before I was forty, which is when I sold my first book—but trying to get published never even occurred to me. Writing was just something I did in my spare time, the way other people played golf or knit sweaters. It wasn't until my husband suggested that I do something about that overflowing box of stories under the bed that publication entered my mind—and it was still five years of submissions and rejections before I made my first sale. That was *Amen, Moses Gardenia*, based on a friend of my daughters' who had attempted suicide in junior high. I wanted to understand how she, at fourteen, could decide that there would never ever again be anything worth living for.

"Writing that book taught me that my best work comes from writing about something I feel passionately about. And I'm such a slow writer—a book takes me about a year—that I need a subject that will hold my interest for that long.

"I tried to write other things—a screenplay, an adult mystery, picture books—but they haven't worked. I most love writing for and about teens. Adolescence is a time of great change—every day there are changes in body, spirit, ideas, friendships—and change is such an interesting thing to write about, although often not to live through.

"I've had other jobs, so I know how bad a bad job can be. That's why I feel so lucky to do every day something I love as much as I love writing for young people."

෮ ෮ ෮

Though she now writes in other genres, Jean Ferris gained her reputation as an author of realistic novels about adolescents caught in difficult life situations without simple solutions. She doesn't pretend that life is easy for her teenaged characters or for the readers who will be drawn to her books. But she *does* believe in the redemptive power of love—love of a friend, a counselor, a cook, a co-worker as well as a traditional romantic love interest. Ferris insists that someone in her books care enough about her protagonists to give them a reason to hope, to see past the present into a possible future. She thinks of herself as a writer friend, hoping to reassure her readers that life is worth the living.

Born Jean Schwartz in Fort Leavenworth, Kansas, she received her B.A. in speech pathology and audiology from Stanford University in 1961. She earned an M.A. in that discipline in 1962, the same year she married Alfred G. Ferris, an attorney.

Starting her career as a clinical audiologist, first at the Veterans Administration Hospital in San Francisco and then at the San Diego, California, Speech and Hearing Association, Ferris worked in the field from 1962 to 1965 and again in 1975–1976. Later, while writing in her spare time, she worked as a secretary and office assistant in San Diego from 1979 to 1984.

> *"Although I didn't like it at the time, I now think that all the moving around I had to do as a child (my father was an Army doctor) gave me all the tools I needed to be a writer."*

Following the publication of her first novel *Amen, Moses Gardenia*, Ferris received a 1984 grant from the Society of Children's Book Writers and Illustrators to work on her next book, *Invincible Summer*. An ALA Best Book for Young Adults, a *School Library Journal* Best Book of the Year, and a *Booklist* Young Adult Editors' Choice, *Invincible Summer* introduces two high school students diagnosed with leukemia, who meet in the hospital and find love in the midst of uncertainty. *Looking for Home*, which was named an IRA Young Adult Choice, features Daphne, who leaves an abusive father and a boyfriend she doesn't want to make a life for herself and her unborn child. Will, a character in *Across the Grain*—an ALA Best Book for Young Adults—develops a sense of self-worth when a middle-aged man teaches him to carve wood and build houses. Another male protagonist, Brian, in *All That Glitters*, finds the way at last to heal his relationship with his father.

After writing a trilogy of historical romances about swashbuckling adventures on the high seas in the early 1800s, Ferris returned to the problem novel with the much-praised *Bad*, about 16-year-old Dallas, who is caught with a weapon during an armed robbery and remanded to a correctional facility for teens. Winner of a California Young Reader Medal and listed as an ALA Quick Pick for Reluctant Young Readers, *Bad* was also an ALA Best Book for Young Adults. The sensitive portrayal of a burgeoning homosexual relationship in *Eight Seconds* earned that book, among other honors, a place on the list of Notable Social Studies Trade Books for Young People. The author's determination to tackle life issues continued in *Of Sound Mind*, in which a high school senior bears much responsibility as the only hearing member of his family.

Ferris's writing is not all problem-oriented: *Love Among the Walnuts* is a comic melodrama and in *Once Upon a Marigold* she produced a light-hearted fantasy for a younger audience. *Love Among the Walnuts*, an ALA Quick Pick for Reluctant Young Adult Readers and a nominee for the 1998 National Book Award, and *Once Upon a Marigold*, a Junior Library Guild Selection and

JEAN FERRIS

Underground

Courtesy of Farrar, Straus, and Giroux

ALA Notable Children's Book, were both also named ALA Best Books for Young Adults.

The author has been married to her husband, Alfred, since 1962. They have two grown daughters, Kerry Ordway and Gillian Anne, who are both teachers. Ferris and her husband currently live in San Diego.

SELECTED WORKS: *Amen, Moses Gardenia*, 1983; *The Stainless Steel Rule*, 1986; *Invincible Summer*, 1987; *Looking for Home*, 1988; *Across the Grain*, 1990; *Relative Strangers*, 1993; *Signs of Life*, 1995; *Into the Wind* (American Dreams, Part One), 1996; *Song of the Sea* (American Dreams, Part Two), 1996; *Weather the Storm* (American Dreams, Part Three), 1996; *All That Glitters*, 1996; *Love Among the Walnuts: or How I Saved My Family from Being Poisoned*, 1998; *Bad*, 1998; *Eight Seconds*, 2000; *Of Sound Mind, 2001; Once Upon a Marigold*, 2002; *Much Ado About Grubstake*, 2006; *Underground*, 2007; *Twice Upon a Marigold*, 2008.

SUGGESTED READING: *Something About the Author*, vol. 149, 2004; *Authors and Artists for Young Adults*, vol. 38, 2001; *St. James Guide to Young Adult Writers*, 2nd ed., 1999.

WEB SITE: www.jeanferris.com

Barbara Firth

September 20, 1928–

"I was born in Hyde, Cheshire, in Northwest England. "'You're going to be an artist,' said my school-mates as we gathered in the playground. 'I want to be a nurse,' I said, because my best friend wanted to be a nurse. I was eight years old at the time and had been drawing animals, plants and people's 'portraits' ever since I could hold a pencil. I just liked drawing. My father, who knew about horses—Granddad was a Yorkshire farmer—would look at my drawings of horses and suggest kindly how they could be improved anatomically.

"When I was ten, Dad enrolled me in a Saturday morning class at the Art School over the Public Library. I was the only pupil in the vast, dusty room, where I was left alone to draw from enormous plaster models of classical ears, noses and feet. That was the end of Art School for a while, but below was the Children's Library, where I spent half my time reading. I especially liked the many Andrew Lang 'Color' Fairy Books; they opened up a world of imagination for me.

"After Grammar School, when I was 17, my family moved to London where I had a junior's job in a display studio, mixing paint, cleaning pots, drawing show-cards. Sometimes I helped paint stage scenery, which introduced me to a love of the theatre backstage.

"I was mad about fashion, and in the evenings studied fashion drawing and pattern cutting, hoping to become a couturier. Eventually I took a job in the production department of a fashion magazine, drawing step-by-step diagrams of hands doing crochet or knitting and dressmaking diagrams. The people I worked with moved on to new jobs and remembered my work, so I freelanced on the craft part-works diagrams. It was hard work, work that had to be produced exactly on time.

Courtesy of Candlewick Press

Barbara Firth

"Then one day I met Sebastian Walker, who had once worked on the part-works and who had started his own publishing house for children's books—Walker Books. He gave me work illustrating natural history books—plants, animals, geology. Finding reference was wonderful: visits to the London Zoo to draw huge Mexican orange-kneed spiders (they took away my coat as I entered, in case I went away with the stock!). For another book, I sketched round the Cotswold herb gardens of a great plantswoman and writer, Rosemary Verey.

"Then I was given my first stories. They all involved animal characters, with the emotions of people perhaps, but reflecting life's experiences which often fit animals as well as humans. Jack the dog, Barnabas the guinea pig (borrowed from my friend's children), a tadpole, a mouse—all written by many wonderful writers.

"Then came a story from Martin Waddell called *Can't You Sleep, Little Bear?* It was the story of a loving relationship between Big Bear and Little Bear, written by someone who really understands children's feelings about the world. Back I went to the zoo, where I sketched brown bears as they wrestled over my one small sandwich and disappeared growling into the woods. The first thing I thought about them was that they had such mean little eyes, but of course I had to get rid of that thought immediately as it would frighten the children!"

CB CB CB

When she was only three years old, Barbara Firth began drawing plants and animals. When she was eleven her family moved to the country, which afforded her more time to spend in the natural world, where she could record what she saw in her drawing. As she grew older, she studied pattern cutting at the London College of Fashion and worked at *Vogue* books, producing illustrations for knitting, crocheting, and dressmaking patterns.

But when she discovered illustrating children's books, she found the work that was most satisfying to her. Sebastian Walker, the founder of Walker Books in England, gave her illustration work that allowed her to return to the joy she had always discovered in the natural world of her childhood. Later, in a brilliant pairing of author and illustrator, she found herself drawing pages and pages of bears for the books by Martin Waddell. Firth's gentle illustrations for the books about Big Bear and Little Bear reflect the long hours she spent at the zoo, carefully watching and recording the movements and habits of bears. These books have become modern classics. Firth and Waddell won the Nestlé Smarties Children's Book Prize for age 0–5, as well as the overall prize for all categories, for *Can't You Sleep, Little Bear?*, a tranquil bedtime story in which Big Bear helps Little Bear overcome a fear of the dark. For the serene watercolor and soft pencil illustrations she did for this book, Firth also captured the Kate Greenaway Medal for Illustration. The Little Bear books, over 7 million copies of which have been sold worldwide, feature themes as gentle as the illustrations. For example, Little Bear shows off by climbing and hopping in *Well Done, Little Bear*, until he falls and Big Bear comes to the rescue. And in *Let's Go Home, Little Bear*, Big Bear comforts Little Bear when the trip home through the woods seems scary.

Barbara Firth teamed up again with Martin Waddell to illustrate *Tom Rabbit*, the tale of little Tom experiencing the anxiety of being forgotten as well as the relief of being found again. In 2003 the pair collaborated on the whimsical *Hi Harry! The Moving Story of How One Slow Tortoise Slowly Made a Friend*. For inspiration, the illustrator turned to her own pet tortoise, Waldo, who has lived with her for 25 years. Firth's watercolor and ink illustrations add a touch of charm to the comforting message that there is a friend out there for everyone. *Hi Harry!* became a Parents' Choice Silver Honor Book and a *Horn Book* Fanfare title.

Another book she worked on with Martin Waddell, *The Park in the Dark*, won the 1989 Kurt Maschler Award. Discontinued in

> "'You're going to be an artist,' said my school-mates as we gathered in the playground. 'I want to be a nurse,' I said, because my best friend wanted to be a nurse."

Courtesy of Candlewick Press

1999, this award was for "a work of imagination in the children's field in which text and illustration are of excellence and so presented that each enhances yet balances the other." Administered by the Book Trust in Great Britain, it was established by the founder of Atrium Press in Zurich, which published banned German writers in the 1930s and honored Erich Kästner's *Emil und die Detektive*. *The Park in the Dark* is a picture book about three stuffed animals (a rag monkey, a knitted elephant, and a cuddly dog) who, discovering that the friendly park seems different and rather frightening at night, make their way home again. Firth's watercolor illustrations ably communicate the friendship of the animals during their nighttime escapade.

Barbara Firth now lives in Middlesex, England, with her pets, Waldo the tortoise, who is nearly 100 years old, another tortoise, Little Feller, who is about 30, her dog, Tess, and lots of birds.

SELECTED WORKS: *Exciting Things to Do with Nature Materials*, by Judy Allen, 1977; *Herb Growing Book*, by Rosemary Verey, 1981; *Special Days Cookbook*, by Sue John, illus. with Charles Raymond, 1982; *Amazing Air*, by Henry Smith, illus. with Elizabeth Falconer and Rosalinda Knightley, 1983; *The Spider*, by Margaret Lane, 1983; *Quack! Said the Billy-Goat*, by Charles Causley, 1986; *The Munro's New House*, by Jonathan Gathorne-

Hardy, 1987; *Barnabas Walks*, by William Mayne, 1987; *At the Edge of the Forest*, by Jonathan London, 1988; *The Park in the Dark*, by Martin Waddell, 1989; *We Love Them*, by Martin Waddell, 1990; *The Grumpalump*, by Sarah Hayes, 1991; *Can't You Sleep, Little Bear?*, by Martin Waddell, 1992; *Sam Vole and His Brothers*, by Martin Waddell, 1992; *Let's Go Home, Little Bear*, by Martin Waddell, 1993; *Wag Wag Wag*, by Peter Hansard, 1994; *Bears in the Forest*, by Karen Wallace, 1994; *A Song for Little Toad*, by Vivian French, 1995; *You and Me, Little Bear*, by Martin Waddell, 1996; *Well Done, Little Bear*, by Martin Waddell, 1999; *Good Job, Little Bear*, by Martin Waddell, 1999; *Tom Rabbit*, by Martin Waddell, 2001; *Hi Harry! The Moving Story of How One Slow Tortoise Slowly Made a Friend*, by Martin Waddell, 2003; *Sleep Tight, Little Bear*, by Martin Waddell, 2005; *Bee Frog*, by Martin Waddell, 2007.

WEB SITE: www.walkerbooks.co.uk/Barbara-Firth

Photo by Richard Bosworth

"Until I was five, I lived on the third floor of an old building. The ground floor was a shop—my grandfather's shop—a dark dusty place that sold paint and wallpaper. It had a secret passage behind the shelves and a back workshop, dangerous with jagged glass and solvents. Upstairs the rooms were big and old, draughty and strange at night.

"Just around the corner was the public library. It was a small building in a street where the weather always seemed to be wet, and it was there that I would go most Wednesday evenings after school to change my three books. The junior library was a ceiling-high bookshelf in one corner, and if you could manage to ignore the drunken old men who fumbled over the newspapers, you could stand on tip-toe and reach up as far as H or stand on the rickety steps and reach A.

"The idea of free books seems astounding even now, but then I think I just accepted it. Certainly I was rarely able to buy books, although they were very cheap then. There was no need, because the library had more than I could read.

Catherine Fisher

1957–

"I read all the 'William' books, the astounding *Treasure Island* and *Kidnapped*, endless books about exploring children and hidden treasure. One shelf was totally lined—or 'so it seemed then—with books of fairytales, from Russia and Japan and Ireland and Germany, as well as Wales. They were thick, heavy hardback books, with cream paper and black-and-white engravings of mermaids, emperors, dragons, princesses. I think I must have read all of them.

"I learned a few things—that 'fairytale' is a word that encompasses a lot of what I now would call folktale, legend, ghost story, fantasy. I learned about the structure of story, about the forbidden taboo, the door not to be opened, the apple not to be eaten, the ring not to be worn. I learned that a man's soul could be held in an egg, that six brothers could be swans, that a beast might change into a prince, that there are countries at the bottom of the well.

"These were stories of strict morality, where the evil witch was always ugly, and always received her punishment, and where the good were also beautiful and lived happily ever after. Even then I didn't quite believe that, but the pattern was immensely satisfying—the way the events were always in threes, that magic number.

> *"I learned about the structure of story, about the forbidden taboo, the door not to be opened, the apple not to be eaten, the ring not to be worn."*

"There are no real characters in fairytales, only stereotypes, but the stories have very webbed corners, and above all, they have their own landscapes, those worlds of dark forests and grim castles that underlie all of Western fantasy.

"I discovered them again in the tales of King Arthur, whose knights ride forever through perilous woods. I particularly liked the Grail myth, and the way the Quest was fulfilled and yet it destroyed the very men who achieved it. The sense of doom and sadness that overlies most legends appealed to me. I loved the Norse myths because of that moody gloom, the knowledge that Odin and the gods themselves cannot escape their fate.

"This was the source material. After reading it, I was ready for Tolkien and Garner and LeGuin and T. H. White and all those who have followed the trail into those forests before me, who have learned to introduce real people into those places.

"And if I left the library and went out of the town where I lived, there was the countryside of South Wales, still marked with the names of its legends. Just up the road was Caerleon, where Arthur's court had been, and on the ridge was Wentwood, the great royal hunting forest where the King of the Nightingales is said to sing eternally. It was as if the land of the stories was all around, and I was a character in it, and all the people I knew and the school I went to and even the sea-wall and its wet marshes and factories were places where magic still happened, oddly, out of the corner of your eye.

"People often ask authors questions, as if we know any answers. One is, 'Why do you like to write fantasy?' I usually just shrug and say, 'I just like it.'

"But the real answer is in the library and the land."

 CB CB CB

Born in Newport in the region of Gwent in Wales, Catherine Fisher attended St. Joseph's School and Gwent College of Higher Education, where she received a B.A. in English literature.

She wrote her first poem when she was 11 and started to write stories in college. Before beginning her writing career, however, she worked as a broadcaster, a lab technician, and a primary school teacher. Over one 18-month period, she took part in an archeological dig at Caerleon, thought to be a possible spot for King Arthur's court. She also has taught children's writing at the University of Glamorgan in Wales.

Fisher's first book, *The Conjuror's Game*, a fantasy adventure about a boy who accidently unleashes dark forces upon the world, was short-listed for the 1990 Smarties Award and heralded her arrival as an exciting newcomer among British fantasy writers. Soon her popularity had reached other parts of Europe and the United States as the publication of her books expanded into those countries. First among these was *The Oracle*, published in the U.S. as *The Oracle Betrayed*. Short-listed for the Whitbread Children's Book Award in Great Britain, in the U.S. it was named an ALA Best Book for Young Adults, included in the New York Public Library's Best Books for the Teen Age, and nominated for the Bram Stoker Award for Young Readers. With a mixture of Ancient Greek and Egyptian influences, the *Oracle* series is rich with intrigue, mystical elements, fast-paced action and well-drawn characters. Fisher also used many Italian settings for the *Oracle* and has said that the warm climate she experienced traveling in Italy inspired the idea for the story.

A collection of mysterious legends from medieval Welsh manuscripts, the *Mabinogion*, is the inspiration for Fisher's Snow-Walker trilogy. These ancient stories are based partly on early historical events, possibly harkening as far back as the Iron Age, and a rich sense of history suffuses these books. As in the *Mabinogion*, strong women populate Fisher's books. The Snow-Walker series is told mainly from the point of view of a

Catherine Fisher

THE
SPHERE
OF SECRETS

The Oracle Prophecies

Courtesy of Greenwillow Books

nobleman's daughter trying to resist the ice-witch's cruelty. The first title, *The Snow-Walker's Son*, was short-listed for the W. H. Smith Mind Boggling Award in England. All three titles in the series were published in one volume in the U.S. and listed among the New York Public Library's 2005 Books for the Teen Age.

The Candle Man, which won the 1995 Tir-Na-n'Og Award (the highest award for a book set in Wales), is about a boy helping a strange fiddler avoid a curse; the setting for the story is in the Gwent Levels region of South Wales where Fisher was born.

A modern retelling of the Grail legend, *Corbenic*, which was short-listed for the Tir-Na-n'Og Award, is among the books of which Fisher is most proud. Set on the border country between Wales and England in the contemporary town of Chepstow, the story involves a modern-day teenager who is transported back to the world of King Arthur in a journey of self-discovery and redemption. In 2007 *Corbenic* won the Mythopoeic Fantasy Award for Children's Literature, presented by the Mythopoeic Society in the U.S.

Fisher's love of richly nuanced language and imagery are firmly rooted in the Celtic tradition. In addition to her novels, she has published several books of poetry and short stories. Early in her career, in 1989, she won both the Welsh Arts Council Young Writers' Prize and the Cardiff International Poetry Competition with her very first published book, *Immrama*.

Collaborating with her sister, artist Maggie Davies, Fisher has also tried her hand at writing a picture book. *The Weather Dress*, a sophisticated fairy tale about a magical encounter involving an unusual dress, evokes an eerie sense of foreboding reminiscent of her novels.

Living today in the Gwent Levels of Wales, Fisher draws her inspiration from environs she has described as watery and spooky. She enjoys fencing, gardening, drawing, and exploring old British castles and is a self-proclaimed chocolate lover. She owns no computer. She writes first in longhand, which she then transcribes into a word processor. With background music playing, she writes her stories in a book-lined study frequented by her two cats.

SELECTED WORKS [Dates are for U.K. publication, U.S. dates, if different, appear in parentheses]: *Immrama*, 1988; *The Conjuror's Game*, published in *Three in One* in the U.K., 1990; *Fintan's Tower*, 1991; *Saint Tarvel's Bell*, 1992; *The Snow-Walker's Son* (Snow-Walker sequence, Book 1), 1993; *The Candle Man*, 1994; *The Hare and Other Stories*, 1994; *The Unexplored Ocean*, 1994; *The Empty Hand* (Snow-Walker sequence, Book 2), 1995; *The Soul Thieves* (Snow-Walker sequence, Book 3), 1996; *Scared Stiff: Stories*, 1997; *Belin's Hill*, 1998; *The Relic Master* (Book of the Crow, Vol. 1), 1998; *The Interrex* (Book of the Crow, Vol. 2), 1999; *Altered States*, 1999 (2000); *Magical Mystery Stories*, 1999; *The Lammas Field*, 1999; *Flain's Coronet* (Book of the Crow, Vol. 3), 2000; *Darkwater Hall*, 2000; *The Margrave* (Book of the Crow, Vol. 4), 2001; *Old Enough and Other Stories*, 2002; *Corbenic*, 2002 (2005); *The Oracle* (Oracle Prophecies, Book 1), 2003 (renamed *The Oracle Betrayed* in the U.S., 2004); *Snow-Walker Trilogy* (includes *The Snow-Walker's Son*, *The Empty Hand*, and *The Soul Thieves*), 2003 (renamed *Snow-Walker* in the U. S., 2004); *The Glass Tower: Three Doors to the Other World* (includes *The Conjurer's Game*, *Fintan's Tower*, and *The Candle Man*), (2004); *The Archon* (Oracle Prophecies, Book 2), 2004 (renamed *The Sphere of Secrets* in the U.S., 2005); *The Weather Dress*, illus. by Maggie Davies, 2005; *The Scarab* (Oracle Prophecies, Book 3), 2005 (renamed *Day of the Scarab* in the U.S., 2006); *Darkhenge*, 2005 (2006); *Incarceron*, 2007; *Sapphique*, 2008.

SUGGESTED READING: *Something About the Author*, vol. 155, 2005.

WEB SITE: www.geocities.com/catherinefisheruk

Candace Fleming

May 24, 1962–

"The summer I turned ten, my mother instituted a new house rule—no reading at the dinner table. Without this rule, my father would have forked up salad and scanned the day's baseball scores, my teenaged sister would have flipped through her latest issue of *Seventeen* magazine, and I would have devoured another Nancy Drew mystery along with my pork chop. But my mother—no slouch of a reader herself—wanted to hear more than pages turning.

"'Let's talk,' she said.

"'Talk?' I replied. 'About what?' From my place at the kitchen table I could see *The Secret in the Old Attic* sitting on the counter where I'd left it. I didn't want to talk. I wanted to read. So did my father and sister.

"My mother thought for a moment. Then she smiled and asked, 'Read any good books lately?'

"Had we ever! We answered with a flood of titles and an avalanche of plot summaries. It was forty-five minutes before we got up from the table.

"If you haven't guessed it by now, my family was book-crazy. They were everywhere—in the bedrooms, in the kitchen, even in the bathrooms. Books filled our home and our lives. They excited us. They informed us. They tickled and transported us. If we weren't reading, we weren't happy.

Photo by Scott Fleming

"I remember one Saturday afternoon, my father suddenly leaped to his feet, flung on his jacket and grabbed up his car keys. 'Where are you going?' my mother asked. 'To the library,' he said. 'I need something to read. I need a book.'

"Funny how such a small incident can reveal such a big truth. My family, I realized, didn't just *like* books. We *needed* them—the way we needed air, water, chocolate cake. Basically, we couldn't live without them. You would think this passion for books would logically have led to a career as a writer, but as a kid I never thought about writing my own books. I thought about becoming a spy, because I loved eavesdropping. And for a while I wanted to be an actress, because I loved to pretend. But a writer? No way! Writers, I thought, were much deeper than I.

"I knew this because the boy my sister briefly dated in high school was a writer. He made up poems in which she either appeared as a cat or a wisp of smoke. Dressing all in black, he spent their three weeks together clutching his hair and listening to Mahler. He made writing seem so serious and painful.

"I, on the other hand, just wanted to tell a good story. And I told them all the time. Even before I could write my name, I could tell a good tale. As a preschooler, I told my neighbors all about my three-legged cat named Spot. In kindergarten, I told my classmates about the ghost that lived in my attic. And in first grade I told my teacher, Miss Harbart, all about my family's trip to Paris, France.

"None of these stories was true, of course. I simply enjoyed telling a good story . . . and seeing my listener's reaction. Luckily, my parents encouraged this fun. Instead of calling my stories 'fibs,' they called them 'imaginative.' They encouraged me to put them down on paper, and I did. Amazingly, once I began writing, I couldn't stop. I filled notebook after notebook with stories, poems, plays. I still have a few of those notebooks. They're precious to me because they're a record of my writing life from elementary school on.

"In second grade, I discovered a passion for language. I can still remember the day my teacher, Miss Johnson, held up a horn-shaped basket filled with papier-mâché pumpkins and asked the class to repeat the word 'cornucopia.' The word sounded so good I said it again and again and again. I tasted it on my tongue. I tested it on my ears. I skipped home from school that day chanting, 'Cornucopia! Cornucopia!' From then on I really began listening to words—to the sounds they made, the way they were used, and how they made me feel. I longed to put them together in ways that were beautiful and yet told a story.

"As I grew, I continued to write stories. But I still didn't think about becoming a writer. Instead I went to college where I discovered yet another passion—history. I didn't realize it then, but studying history was really just an extension of my love of stories. Some of the best stories are true ones—tales of heroism and villainy made more incredible by the fact they really happened.

"My family, I realized, didn't just like books. We needed them—the way we needed air, water, chocolate cake. Basically, we couldn't live without them."

"After graduation, I got married and had children. I read to them all the time, and that's when I discovered the joy and music of children's books. With my two sons in tow, I made endless trips to the library. I read stacks of books. And I found myself begging, 'Just one more, pleeeese!' while my boys begged for lights-out and sleep. Then it struck me. Why not write children's books? It seemed the perfect way to combine all the things I loved—history, stories, musical language, and reading. I couldn't wait to get started.

"But writing children's books is harder than it looks. For three years I wrote story after story. I sent them to publisher after publisher. And I received rejection letter after rejection letter. Still, I didn't give up. I kept trying until finally one of my stories was pulled from the slush pile and turned into a book. My career as a children's book author had begun.

"Today I live in a house much like the one I grew up in. It too is filled with books—some of them even written by me. And that's just about the best thing that can happen to a girl who grew up loving books, stories, and the magic of words."

ଔ   ଔ   ଔ

Growing up in the small town of Charleston, Illinois, Candace Groth Fleming was surrounded by cornfields, cows, and books. Whether reading or making up her own, she thrived on stories. After graduating in 1985 with a degree in history from Eastern Illinois University, in Charleston, she married and had two sons, Scott and Michael. Reading to her sons on a daily basis soon inspired her to combine her love of literature with her love of history in writing books for children.

It took three years of rejection slips before her first book was released in 1994. Published under the name Candace Groth-Fleming, *Professor Fergus Fahrenheit and His Wonderful Weather Machine* is about a Texas rainmaker who offers to save a drought-ridden town.

Two years later Fleming wrote *Women of the Lights*, which chronicled the lives of a dozen of the approximately 300 female American lighthouse keepers. Drawing upon extensive primary documents and other sources, Fleming thoroughly researched her subjects to create a compelling and historically accurate account of their individual stories.

In her third book, *Madame LaGrande and Her So High, to the Sky, Uproarious Pompadour*, Fleming appealed to her readers' sense of humor. The title sets the absurd scene as a woman's effort to be stylish in 19th century Paris takes a laughable turn when her ridiculously high hair-do acquires a menagerie of objects.

For *Gabriella's Song*, Fleming traveled to Venice, Italy, to absorb the sights, sounds, and smells of that vibrant city. Her story is a tribute to the power of everyday sounds—the calls of street merchants, the rhythm of the gondolas, the ringing of bells—to inspire musical composition. A critical success, *Gabriella's Song* earned Fleming her first ALA Notable Children's Book citation.

While Fleming"s childhood ambition to become a spy never led to a career in espionage, it resurfaced in her keen researching skill, which enabled her to uncover fascinating and largely forgotten tidbits of history. In *The Hatmaker's Sign: A Story by Benjamin Franklin* (1998), she tells how Franklin, hoping to ease Thomas Jefferson's anxiety about writing the Declaration of Independence, recounts the tale of a hatmaker who asked a variety of people what his new sign should say. Each person gave a different answer, and the hatmaker ended up with a blank sign. Fleming's clever retelling of the story won an Aesop Prize from the Children's Folklore Section of the American Folklore Society and was a Storytelling World honor book.

In *A Big Cheese for the White House: The True Tale of a Tremendous Cheddar*, Fleming transformed another historical footnote into a compelling narrative. Based on an actual newspaper headline from 1801 in Cheshire, MA, the picture book recounts how a 1,235-pound wheel of cheddar cheese was taken to Washington, DC, as a gift for President Thomas Jefferson.

Fleming's fascination with the stories and celebrities of America's early years can be traced back to her childhood reading of Robert Lawson's *Ben and Me*, a fictional and humorous account of Benjamin Franklin. Years later, herself an established author, Fleming was looking for a new approach to the inventor, author, and statesman, and created a unique biography in the form of a scrapbook. In *Ben Franklin's Almanac: Being a True Account of the Good Gentleman's Life*, Fleming gathered memorabilia from the many facets of Franklin's life to construct a captivating and visually stimulating biography. Praised as a fine introduction to Franklin for readers of all ages, *Ben Franklin's Almanac* was cited as an ALA Notable Children's Book, an ALA Best Book for Young Adults, a Parents' Choice Gold winner, and a Notable Social Studies Trade Book for Young People.

Courtesy of Atheneum Books for Young Readers, Simon & Schuster

Fleming used the scrapbook technique again for *Our Eleanor: A Scrapbook Look at Eleanor Roosevelt's Remarkable Life*, which was awarded a Gold Medal by both Parents' Choice and the Oppenheim Toy Portfolio. It was also named an ALA Notable Children's Book and an ALA Best Book for Young Adults.

Fleming's picture books for young children include *Muncha! Muncha! Muncha!*, which grew out of her own gardening experiences. This hilarious romp about three bunnies who raid a vegetable garden employs repetitive words and phrases to create a memorable experience for readers. *Muncha! Muncha!*

Muncha! was named an ALA Notable Children's Book and a *School Library Journal* Best Book of the Year.

Boxes for Katje was inspired by Fleming's mother's efforts to aid the people of the Netherlands during the difficult aftermath of World War II. A Junior Library Guild selection, *Boxes for Katje* was also named an IRA Teachers' Choice and a Notable Social Studies Trade Book for Young People, among other citations.

Three passions rule Candice Fleming's life: storytelling, history, and children's books. She says, "Overall, I want to tell a 'good story' with the magic and music of words." This infectious enthusiasm for story has been passed on to her sons: Scott is a college student majoring in art, telling stories with paint and canvas, while Michael, a high school student, currently has a fervor for filmmaking.

SELECTED WORKS WRITTEN: *Professor Fergus Fahrenheit and His Wonderful Weather Machine* (as Candace Groth-Fleming), illus. by Don Weller, 1994; *Women of the Lights*, illus. by James Watling, 1996; *Madame LaGrande and Her So High, to the Sky, Uproarious Pompadour*, illus. by S.D. Schindler, 1996; *Gabriella's Song*, illus. by Giselle Potter, 1997; *The Hatmaker's Sign: A Story*, illus. by Robert Andrew Parker, 1998; *Westward Ho, Carlotta!*, illus. by David Catrow, 1998; *A Big Cheese for the White House: The True Tale of a Tremendous Cheddar*, illus. by S.D. Schindler, 1999; *When Agnes Caws*, illus. by Giselle Potter, 1999; *Who Invited You?*, illus. by George Booth, 2001; *Muncha! Muncha! Muncha!*, illus. by G. Brian Karas, 2002; *Boxes for Katje*, illus. by Stacey Dressen-McQueen, 2003; *Ben Franklin's Almanac: Being a True Account of the Good Gentleman's Life*, 2003; *Gator Gumbo: A Spicy-Hot Tale*, illus. by Sally Ann Lambert, 2004; *Smile, Lily!*, illus. by Yumi Heo, 2004; *This Is the Baby*, illus. by Maggie Smith, 2004; *Sunny Boy! The Life and Times of a Tortoise*, illus. by Anne Wilsdorf, 2005; *Lowji Discovers America*, 2005; *Our Eleanor: A Scrapbook Look at Eleanor Roosevelt's Remarkable Life*, 2005; *The Fabled Fourth Graders of Aesop Elementary School*, 2007; *Tippy-Tippy-Tippy, Hide!*, illus. by G. Brian Karas, 2007; *The Lincolns: A Scrapbook Look at Abraham and Mary*, 2008.

SUGGESTED READING: *Something about the Author*, vol. 143, 2004. Periodicals—Fleming, Candace, "Ben . . . and Me," *Booklist*, June 1, 2004. OnLine—Children'slit.com, "Meet Authors and Illustrators, " at www.childrenslit.com/f_flemingcandace.html;

WEB SITES: www.candacefleming.com

"**M**y childhood was spent afloat on a sea of words.

"This was a fortunate thing for a future writer, though of course I didn't know it at the time. I thought every family was like mine, with parents who sang to their children, and a father who read aloud every night after supper and organized weekly trips to the library. My father's love of books came naturally—his father had owned a bookshop as a young man—and many of his read-aloud choices still shine brightly in memory, including *Old Mother West Wind*, *Charlotte's Web*, and *James and the Giant Peach*.

"If the Vogels were a family of bookworms, the MacDougalls—my mother's side of the family—were what we called 'Big Talkers,' especially my grandmother. Nana Mac could spin words into stories like nobody's business. She worked as a housekeeper for a wealthy family in a nearby town, and as a treat I was allowed to spend the night with her once a month or so. I didn't care about the palatial house—to me, her tiny apartment over the garage was infinitely more appealing. We'd retreat to this snuggery after her workday was done, climbing the narrow staircase off the kitchen armed with popcorn, ginger ale, and a box of her favorite chocolates. We'd watch TV for a while, and later, before sleep, Nana Mac would tell me about her childhood in rural Nova Scotia—growing up on a farm, getting into mischief with her five brothers and sisters, attending school in a one-room schoolhouse. She had an endless supply of stories, and I begged to hear the best ones over and over again.

"I was born in Peterborough, New Hampshire, a town so tiny that although I arrived on January 3rd, I still qualified as the New Year's baby. Later, we moved to Lexington and then neighboring Concord, Massachusetts, towns steeped in history. Our Concord house was a short bike ride away from Walden Pond, the Old North Bridge, Sleepy Hollow Cemetery, and Orchard House, which had been Louisa May Alcott's home. Fertile soil for growing a writer, though again, I didn't know it at the time. I did know I loved to read, however, and the library was my second home. It was there that I discovered *Half Magic*, *The Borrowers*,

Photo by Steve Frederick

Heather Vogel Frederick

Heather Vogel Frederick

January 3, 1958–

The Book of Three, and *The Wolves of Willoughby Chase,* to name just a few of my childhood favorites.

"When I was eleven my family moved to England for a while, where we lived in a 300-year-old stone cottage with a roof made of thatch. Down the street were castle ruins where I played with my sisters, and I rode a red double-decker bus to school. All very exotic for an American girl from the suburbs! Most days after school I helped out on a local farm with some of the village children, milking cows by hand, gathering eggs, and occasionally being chased by Elizabeth the pig. It was a magical place and time, and I loved every minute of our stay there.

"The summer I turned twelve, my parents sent me to camp in Maine. I was shy and homesick and the only thing I liked about camp was rest hour. I lived for that solitary stretch of quiet when I could lie in my bunk and read or dream up stories. I wrote my first novel that summer, and although it wasn't very good, I was enormously proud of it. Plus, writing it was pure joy, and from that time on I knew that I wanted to create books of my own someday.

"Before that 'someday' arrived, however, I grew up, married my college sweetheart, and became a journalist. The busy newsroom of the *Christian Science Monitor* was an exciting place to work, and a splendid training ground for a writer. I was assigned to the features department, where I learned how to research and interview, how to shape words into articles that would interest readers, and how to write on deadline.

"After our two sons arrived, I launched a freelance career and eventually started noodling around with stories of my own. People always ask me where I get the ideas for my books, and I tell them that story ideas are like stray cats—you never know when one is going to show up on your doorstep . . . or in your mailbox, as the case may be. That's where the idea for *The Voyage of Patience Goodspeed* arrived, in the form of a receipt for whaling gear for my great-great-grandfather. It was mailed to me by a relative while I was doing some genealogical research—I can trace my ancestry back to Nantucket's original settlers—and before I knew it I was off and running with my first novel. The idea for *Spy Mice* was sparked by my love of the 'spy-fi' TV shows I grew up watching—shows like *Get Smart* and *The Avengers* and *Mission: Impossible.* The idea for another book came to me out of the blue during a PTA budget meeting. I still have the agenda, on the back of which I scribbled the opening line and a rough plot for the story! No matter where my ideas come from, whether I'm writing picture books or fantasy, contemporary realism or

"People always ask me where I get the ideas for my books, and I tell them that story ideas are like stray cats—you never know when one is going to show up on your doorstep . . . or in your mailbox, as the case may be."

historical fiction, my goal is to create the kinds of stories that I loved best when I was young—the ones that sweep readers out of their ordinary lives and off into a vividly imagined world.

"Today I write full-time from my home in Portland, Oregon, where I live with my husband, our two sons, our beloved Shetland sheepdog, and three fun-loving chickens."

ငဒ ငဒ ငဒ

If Heather Vogel Frederick's passion for reading stems from her book-filled childhood in New England, then her inspiration to become a children's book writer came while she was an undergraduate at Principia College, from which she graduated with a bachelor of arts degree in English literature and German in 1979. In her senior year she decided to take a children's literature course taught by Marjorie Hamlin, a former children's librarian. With Hamlin's guidance, Frederick gained new insight into the classic books that she had read as a child. She also realized that children's literature had the potential to be as inventive, creative and well written as its adult counterpart. Upon completing the class she was convinced that her destiny lay in becoming a children's author.

After spending the 1979–1980 school year at the University of Cologne, in Germany, as a Fulbright Scholar, Frederick came home to write her first novel. Though she received an encouraging rejection letter from one publisher, Frederick nevertheless turned to journalism for her career. She honed her writing skills in the features department of the *Christian Science Monitor* and served as the paper's children's book editor. Later she worked as a freelance writer for such periodicals as the *New York Times*, *Family Life*, and *Child*, and most notably as a book reviewer for *Publishers Weekly*. She has described book reviewing as both her "graduate school" and an extension of her childhood love affair with reading. Not only did it enable her to earn a steady freelance living while working from home after the birth of her first son, but it also allowed her to peruse a wide variety of books and interview authors about their work. That experience helped her better understand the creative process, and learn what works and what doesn't in a narrative.

When her younger son went to first grade, Frederick found time for her own writing as well as her freelance work. Her first book, *The Voyage of Patience Goodspeed*, which takes place in 1835, features a 13-year-old mathematics genius who is whisked away from her studies in Nantucket to accompany

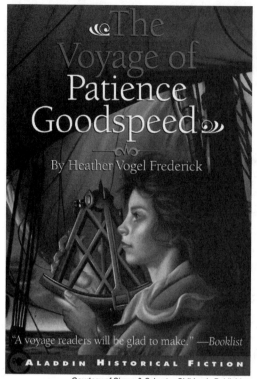

"A voyage readers will be glad to make." —*Booklist*

ALADDIN HISTORICAL FICTION

Courtesy of Simon & Schuster Children's Publishing

her father, Captain Isaiah Goodspeed, on a whaling voyage. During the course of the novel Patience, who would rather learn to navigate than serve as the ship's cook's assistant, is confronted by a band of mutinous sailors who strand her father and much of the crew on a deserted island, leaving her to rescue them before it's too late. This debut novel appeared on several notable lists, including the *St. Louis Post-Dispatch* Best Books for Young Readers, the New York Public Library's Books for the Teen Age, and the ALA Amelia Bloomer Project. It won the 2003 Oregon Book Award for Young Adult Literature and was a finalist for a number of other state book awards. In a sequel, *The Education of Patience Goodspeed*, which was also cited by the ALA Amelia Bloomer Project, the young heroine earns the right to serve as assistant navigator of her father's whaling ship.

Frederick's love of the spy-themed television shows of the 1960s, as well as her early fascination with the James Bond series by Ian Fleming, inspired her Spy Mice stories. After a visit to the International Spy Museum in Washington, DC, rekindled her interest, she decided to write a series for children about mice in the museum who are also skilled at espionage. The first book—*Spy Mice: The Black Paw*—was shortlisted for Ottakar's Children's Book Prize in the United Kingdom, a distinction for newly published authors sponsored by Ottakar's Bookstores. The sequel, *Spy Mice: For Your Paws Only*, was listed among the New York Public Library's 100 Titles for Reading and Sharing.

SELECTED WORKS: *The Voyage of Patience Goodspeed*, 2002; *The Education of Patience Goodspeed*, 2004; *Spy Mice: The Black Paw*, illus. by Sally Wern Comport, 2005; *Spy Mice: For Your Paws Only*, illus. by Sally Wern Comport, 2005; *The Mother-Daughter Book Club*, 2007; *Spy Mice: Goldwhiskers*, illus. by Sally Wern Comport, 2007; *Much Ado about Anne*, 2008.

WEB SITE: www.heathervogelfrederick.com

"I was born in 1958 on the day before Halloween and grew up in the suburbs of New York. On my eighth birthday, I received my first (and long anticipated) pocketknife, which I used that very day to carve my first pumpkin. Unfortunately, I cut myself so much that the gift was confiscated for six months. Years later, I would carve most of the characters in *Play With Your Food* with that knife (there is even a photograph of the knife in the book!), and my parents were proud of me for not cutting myself once.

"As a child I loved to draw, preferring paper and pencils to pumpkins. I loved to climb trees, wear unusual hats and costumes, and make people laugh. I spent summers on the shore of Massachusetts with my brother and sister and my many wonderful cousins and uncles and aunts. I also loved spending time at my grandfather's farm in the hills of New Hampshire. As I turned ten, my family moved to England for two years, where I had my first taste of independence and life in a city. London in the late sixties was a memorable place, and moving back to the American suburbs was difficult for me. I spent practically all of the next six years drawing, reading, and playing the guitar.

"I graduated from Williams College in 1980, majoring in philosophy and art. My parents were very supportive, suggesting I could always become a philosopher if my plan to become an artist did not succeed. In 1981, I moved to New York City and spent the rest of the decade painting and drawing, reading and writing, and doing a lot of artwork that combined images with text, including some handmade books. I lived and worked in a narrow sixth-floor walk-up apartment with the bathtub under the kitchen counter. I did all sorts of extremely odd jobs, including book illustration, model-making for film and TV special effects, being an artist's assistant, working in construction, playing and teaching guitar, casting paper sculpture, and drawing storyboards for films. I even spent a day dancing in front of a building on 34th Street in a ten-foot tall Carnivale costume.

"In 1990, I married Mia Galison, moved to the Upper West Side, continued to paint, did some commercial artwork, and exhibited my paintings in a number of galleries in New York City

Courtesy of Saxton Freymann

Saxton Freymann

October 30, 1958–

and elsewhere. In 1994, I helped Mia start eeBoo Corporation, which makes products that feature the art of children's book illustrators (Lizzy Rockwell, Melissa Sweet, Dan Yaccarino). Almost immediately thereafter, we created three children of our own as well: Eyck in 1994, and Finn and Elodie in 1996. This trio became eeBoo's distinguished Research and Development team.

"In 1996, Mia learned through a mutual friend that the innovative publisher Joost Elffers was looking for people to carve food in interesting ways for a book he wanted to produce. It sounded like a delightful idea, so I made some vegetable characters and sent him some snapshots. He called and said, 'Let's start right away.' Over the next year I went armed with groceries to a photographer's studio for about six sets of two- to three-day sessions. The result was *Play With Your Food*, quickly followed by *Play With Your Pumpkins*.

> "On my eighth birthday, I received my first (and long anticipated) pocketknife, which I used that very day to carve my first pumpkin."

"These led to a series of children's books with Arthur A. Levine Books at Scholastic. For many years, calendars, cards, and posters featuring my work have been produced by Graphique de France. In 2003 the Katonah Art Museum arranged an exhibit of my food pictures. Since 2002 I have done all my own photography, using a Hasselblad camera with a digital back, which I love. I am currently developing other book projects, including photographs of inedible subjects, as well as a return to drawing. In the meantime, there are always things to be done for eeBoo, where I am fortunate to be able to work with my brilliant wife. We have recently acquired a dog named Augie, because our children are just too well behaved."

C03   C03   C03

Saxton Freymann is a New York artist who paints, draws, and creates emotional animals and other designs completely out of produce. His fruit and vegetable books came about after he met Joost Elffers, a creative entrepreneur, who is, among other things, a publisher and book packager. A native of Holland, Elffers wanted to produce a book about food carving or presentation for the American market similar to one he had created in Europe. He conceived the project as a community effort, but Freymann proved to have a unique talent for crafting characters and stories out of produce. Freymann and Elffers subsequently became partners, with Elffers funding and handling the business side of projects while Freymann concentrated on the writing and artwork.

In his books Freymann captures the universal childhood instinct to make playthings out of ordinary objects. His works are filled with the kind of silliness that young children find irresistible. By using an Exacto knife, he turns bananas into octopi and pears into bears. He uses peppercorns or black-eyed peas for eyes, and beet juice or kernel corn for teeth. His oranges express a variety of moods. Inspired by the produce aisle of the grocery store, he claims each vegetable or fruit already has its own personality, he just helps it along a bit. Even his background scenery—skies, forests, flora, and fauna—is created from produce. In *How Are You Peeling? Foods With Moods*, the food sculptures embody a range of human emotions. Designed to start conversations between adults and children about feelings, the book is written in an easy-going conversational style that is both reassuring and upbeat. A *New York Times* Best Illustrated Children's Book of the Year, *How Are You Peeling?* was also an Oppenheim Toy Portfolio Platinum Award winner, a recipient of the Gradiva Award from the National Association for the Advancement of Psychoanalysis, and a NAPPA (National Parenting Publications) Gold Award winner in the preschool category.

Courtesy of Arthur A. Levine Books, Scholastic, Inc.

Food for Thought received an Oppenheim Toy Portfolio Platinum Award, was among the New York Public Library's 100 Titles for Reading and Sharing, and was a CCBC Choice. It plays with fruits and vegetables to introduce children to five major concepts—shapes, colors, numbers, letters, and opposites. *Dog Food*, which features clever puns and funny canine scenes, including pepper puppies and banana beagles, was a *New York Times* Best Illustrated Book of the Year and received an Oppenheim Toy Portfolio Gold Award. *One Lonely Seahorse*, an underwater counting adventure, was likewise an Oppenheim Toy Portfolio Gold Award winner and an IRA/CBC Children's Choice. A garlic kitten and an orange piglet reside in a clever petting zoo in *Baby Food*, which received an Oppenheim Toy

Portfolio Gold Award and was named a Best Children's Book of the Year by *Child* magazine.

Currently at work on a collection of food pictures for a 300-page book, Freymann intends to do more drawing and photographic work in the future. While he has no plans to turn his attention to other food items, he enjoys "assisting found objects" with his photography, and his fans can only wait to see what he comes up with next.

SELECTED WORKS (all created with Joost Elffers): *Play With Your Food*, 1997; *Play With Your Pumpkins*, with text by Johannes van Damm, 1998; *How Are You Peeling? Foods With Moods*, 1999; *One Lonely Seahorse*, 2000; *Dr. Pompo's Nose*, 2000; *Gus and Button*, 2001; *Dog Food*, 2002; *Baby Food*, 2003; *Food for Thought: The Complete Book of Concepts for Growing Minds*, 2005; *Fast Food*, 2006.

SUGGESTED READING: Periodicals—Homes, Marian Smith, "Please Eat the Art," *Smithsonian*, Feb. 2001.

Photo by Jim Burger

Garret Freymann-Weyr

June 9, 1966–

"I grew up in a house full of books and good china. There were, of course, things like beds, lamps, and shelves, but it was the miles of books and the china we used for dinner parties that grabbed my attention. I was expected to read the books. My parents were very clear about this. Here's what I was clear about: I would read what I wanted. This did not always include the books in our house. Worse, I would read the books I wanted as many times as I wanted.

"My mother might take *Harriet the Spy* away from me, and my father might stare disapprovingly at my ancient copy of *Jane Eyre*, but I would keep reading them. Or re-reading. Or, as my parents whispered to each other in the dead of night, 'Wasting her mind. All that tuition money. This is our child?'

"Looking back on this, I have to wonder if my parents (usually very bright people with good memories) had forgotten about my dyslexia. The dyslexia that made me invert not just letters, but entire syllables. The dyslexia that allowed me to read to myself, but froze my brain when I was forced to read aloud. The dyslexia that forced them to pay, in addition to New York City private school tuition, for a private tutor named Miss Brooke. My love affair with books had begun as a form of torture. But with time (and plenty of re-reading) I became one of those readers who has the misfortune to believe that books are a religion and writers are the priests.

"Of course, not every reader becomes a writer. It would be much easier and far less embarrassing to say that I became a writer because nothing else worked out. But the truth is that I became a writer on the night my mother used the good china to teach us how to eat a banana with a knife and fork. It's pretty easy actually, if fairly useless. She explained to us that now if we were at a dinner party and the fruit bowl was passed, there would be nothing in it that we could not manage.

"Yes, the best way to manage, when confronted with a bowl of fruit, a glass plate, a knife and a fork is to say, 'Thank you, no.' I thought of that right away. But her solution was, I believed, the one to keep alive.

"I should back up a bit and explain.

"My mother's father was a diplomat, stationed in different cities across several continents. Her mother was famous for being beautiful and exceedingly well dressed. My grandmother never arrived in any city without being written up in the papers for either her elegance or her parties. I understood that in many ways, my mother was raising us to fit into a world that no longer existed.

"At his or her best, a writer shows us what is lost as we move forward."

"My father and his parents were, by contrast, refugees who left Austria eight months after the Nazis came. It's fair to say that my father raised us to live in a world where one should always keep a bag packed. Just in case. The world of his suitcase and her fruit bowl was gone. I would find it only in their books, in their stories and in their china.

"At his or her best, a writer shows us what is lost as we move forward. Sitting at the table that night, surrounded by both good china and books, I thought it was possible that I could become one of those people who kept an eye on what slowly vanishes. Vanishes so slowly, that by the time we think to miss it, it is no longer needed by anyone but a writer."

ᏟᎶ   ᏟᎶ   ᏟᎶ

Garret Freymann-Weyr, born Rhoda Garret Michaela Weyr, grew up in New York City with three sisters. Her parents divorced in the mid-1980s, and when they both remarried, she acquired a larger family of mostly adult step-siblings. Freymann-Weyr has said it seemed more like she belonged to "a loose gang of distant cousins who liked each other a lot."

She received a B.A. in history from the University of North Carolina in Chapel Hill and a master's degree in fine arts in film from New York University. During her sophomore year at the University of North Carolina, she wrote her first novel, *Pretty Girls*. Writing about what she knew, Freymann-Weyr set her book at the University of North Carolina and built the story around three college girls. Dealing with the demands of loyalty and friendship and developing a sense of their own worth, her characters struggle with bulimia, fear of sex, unplanned pregnancy, and the death of loved ones.

Courtesy of the Houghton Mifflin Company

A dozen or so years passed, during which time Freymann-Weyr worked in children's book publishing. In 1995 she worked in the subsidiary rights department of HarperCollins Children's Books. She also spent time in the 1990s doing freelance work at the Anita Diamont Agency and the Book-of-the-Month Club as well as a stint as an artist's model. Like the main characters in *Pretty Girls*, Freymann-Weyr never thought she would get married, but on March 15, 1997, she married Jeffrey Freymann, a freelance musician who composed music for advertising, film, and dance projects. Shortly after their marriage the couple moved from Brooklyn to Baltimore. Her second book, *When I Was Older*, about one girl's attempt to understand the death of her brother, the breakdown of her parents' marriage, and a confusing friendship/romance with a boy who has also encountered death, was consciously directed at a young adult audience.

Her next book was *My Heartbeat*, the sensitive portrayal of a love triangle between a girl, her beloved brother, and his close friend. The idea for this book, which won a Michael L. Printz Honor Award, came after an argument with her sister (who unlike the brother in the book, is neither gay nor a math genius); however, the argument sparked Freymann-Weyr's imagination with regard to the nature of conflict within important relationships. *My Heartbeat* was also named an ALA Best Book for Young Adults, an ALA Notable Children's Book, a *Booklist*

Editors' Choice "Top of the List" for Youth Fiction, a *School Library Journal* Best Book of the Year, and a *Publisher's Weekly* Best Children's Book.

Freymann-Weyr builds on her own early ballet-class experiences in *The Kings Are Already Here*. Two accomplished teenagers—one a ballet dancer, the other a chess prodigy—re-evaluate the purpose and cost of pursuing their obsessions and search for the lives they really want, in a novel which was cited on New York Public Library's Books for the Teen Age list. Recalling a couple of older boyfriends she had dated when she was a young adult, Freymann-Weyr then wrote *Stay With Me*, the story of a 17-year-old girl who considers a relationship with an older man after her half-sister commits suicide and her family's world is turned upside down.

Garret Freymann-Weyr's husband currently works for National Public Radio in Washington, DC, and they live in the Maryland suburbs.

SELECTED WORKS: *Pretty Girls*, as Garret Weyr, 1988; *When I Was Older*, 2000; *My Heartbeat*, 2002; *The Kings Are Already Here*, 2003; *Stay With Me*, 2006.

SUGGESTED READING: *Something About the Author*, vol. 145, 2004; *The New York Times*, March 23, 1997.

WEB SITE: www.freymann-weyr.com

Cornelia Funke

(FOON-kah)
December 10, 1958–

Cornelia Funke was born in Dorsten, Westphalia, in the central region of Germany. At age 18 she left home to attend the University of Hamburg to study educational theory. After graduating she became a social worker. Three years later she decided to hone her drawing talent by taking a post-graduate course in book illustration at the Hamburg State College of Design. Funke then started designing board games and illustrating children's books. She soon realized, however, that she was bored with many of the stories she illustrated. As a child she had preferred exciting stories of dragons and adventure, so she tried her hand at writing a tale herself. At first she wrote for a young audience, children of about eight years old, and her books were immediately successful.

Funke's first book for older readers, published in 1997, was *Drachenreiter* (later published in English as *Dragon Rider*). In 2000 her novel *Herr der Diebe* was a tremendous success with German children. That same year Barry Cunningham, a longtime publisher who had a talent for finding new authors, established The Chicken House, his own publishing firm in England. When he received a letter from a young bilingual girl asking why her favorite German author wasn't published in English, Cunningham discovered that Funke was second only to J. K. Rowling in popularity with German children. He soon had *Herr der Diebe* published in Great Britain and the United States (through his connection with Scholastic Press) as *The Thief Lord*, with the English translation by Oliver Latsch, Funke's cousin.

The Thief Lord is a spellbinding adventure of two runaway brothers. Fleeing from a dreadful relative who wants to separate them after they are orphaned, the boys go to Venice where they join a band of street urchins who live in an abandoned theater. Controlled by the oldest boy, who calls himself the "thief lord" and disguises himself with a carnival mask, the gang becomes involved in a mystery featuring a missing piece from an old carousel. When the book was published in the U.S., it won the Mildred L. Batchelder Award for best-translated children's book and became instantly popular with both children and critics. Named an ALA Notable Children's Book and a *New York Times* Notable Book of the Year, it was also cited as a Best of the Year by *School Library Journal* and *Parenting*. *The Thief Lord* enjoyed many weeks on the *New York Times* bestseller list and won children's choice state awards in Arizona, Massachusetts, Michigan, and New Jersey. In the U.K. it won the Askews Torchlight Children's Book Award. In its original German publication, it had received the Zurich Children's Book Award as well as an award from the Vienna House of Literature. In 2006 the book was made into a motion picture featuring veteran actress Vanessa Redgrave.

Courtesy of Scholastic, Inc.

Many of Cornelia Funke's most popular books have been described as "magical realism"—stories that are firmly rooted in a real-world setting despite their magical elements. Funke herself believes reality is often more understandable when it is disguised in fantasy. She finds that she can touch on subjects she wouldn't otherwise be able to bring up in realistic stories. To help her write about the characters she creates, Funke returns to her talent for drawing and creates sketches of them in pen and ink; many of her novels are enhanced by her own illustrations.

Funke's most ambitious novel to date, *Inkheart*, was named an ALA Notable Children's Book, an ALA Popular Paperback for Young Adults and an American Booksellers Association Children's Book of the Year, and became a *New York Times* bestseller as well. *Inkheart* tells the story of a girl named Meggie whose bookbinder father, Mo, by reading aloud from books, can draw characters and objects out into the real world. The price he must pay is that, in turn, a person from his life will disappear into the book; unhappily, this happened to Meggie's mother, so Mo now refuses to read aloud. But the evil character he has released into the real world lures Meggie and her father to his hideout. An intricately plotted and thrilling adventure, with many twists and turns, *Inkheart* won the Askews Torchlight Children's Book Award in England as well as awards in Germany and Austria. Before writing it, Funke, who chose Italy as the setting because of her love for that country, researched booksellers, book collectors, book thieves, and even book murderers to make the magic as real as possible. While writing *Inkheart*, Funke created the character of Mo with the actor Brendan Fraser in mind, and he was, indeed, cast to play the role in the film.

The sequel, *Inkspell*, an ALA Notable Children's Book and a *New York Times* bestseller, is another page-turner. Meggie and her father move from the real world into the actual book, where a war is brewing and Mo is threatened with execution. The cliffhanger ending heralded the arrival of *Inkdeath*, the exciting conclusion of the trilogy published in 2008.

Dragon Rider, Funke's first published novel for middle-grade readers, was translated into English in 2004. This charming story—which became a *Child Magazine* Best Children's Book, a *New York Times* bestseller, and won awards in Germany, Switzerland, and Japan—features a brave young dragon, a human orphan who becomes a dragon rider, and a quest to find a legendary mountain haven where the remaining dragons can be safe from the humans who are encroaching on their territory. Brendan Fraser lent his voice to the audio version of the tale and it has also been optioned for film.

Funke's picture books for young children have also met with great success in translation. Both *The Princess Knight* and *Princess Pigsty* were featured on ALA's Annual Amelia Bloomer List of books for young readers that feature strong feminist themes. Funke is also the author of the Ghosthunters series of light and humorous ghost stories, enhanced by her own illustrations.

Cornelia Funke moved with her family from Hamburg to Los Angeles, California, in the spring of 2005, a move that allowed the

> She soon realized, however, that she was bored with many of the stories she illustrated. As a child she had preferred exciting stories of dragons and adventure, so she tried her hand at writing a tale herself.

Courtesy of The Chicken House, Scholastic, Inc.

author greater involvement in the making of the *Inkheart* movie. That same year she was featured as one of *Time* magazine's 100 Most Influential Men and Women. In 2006 her husband of 26 years, Rolf, died of cancer.

Funke lives in Los Angeles with Anna and Ben, her two teenaged children, Luna, their dog, and two Iceland ponies, Snegla and Jarpur. Deeply concerned about issues of fairness and humane treatment, she is a member of Amnesty International and the Green Party in Germany. Her books have been published in more than 30 countries around the world.

SELECTED WORKS (Dates are all for U.S. publication): *The Thief Lord*, 2002; *Mick and Mo in the Wild West*, 2002; *Inkheart*, 2003; *The Dark Hills Divide*, 2003; *Dragon Rider*, 2004; *The Princess Knight*, illus. by Kerstin Meyer, 2004; *Inkspell*, 2005; *Pirate Girl*, illus. by Kerstin Meyer, 2005; *Ghosthunters and the Incredibly Revolting Ghost!*, 2005; *When Santa Fell to Earth*, 2006; *The Wildest Brother*, illus. by Kerstin Meyer, 2006; *Ghosthunters and the Gruesome Invincible Lightning Ghost!*, 2006; *Shrek: Classic Shrek Halloween*, with Marcie Aboff, 2006; *Ghosthunters and the Bloodthirsty Baroness!*, 2007; *Igraine the Brave*, illus. by the author, 2007; *Ghosthunters and the Muddy Monster of Doom!*, 2007; *Ghosthunters and the Totally Moldy Baroness!*, 2007: *Ghosthunters and the Mud-Dripping Monster!*, 2007; *Dragon Slippers*, 2007; *Princess Pigsty*, illus. by Kerstin Meyer, 2007; *Inkdeath*, 2008; *A Princess, a Pirate, and One Wild Brother*, 2008.

SUGGESTED READING: *Something About the Author*, vol. 174, 2007; *Biography Today*, vol. 14, issue 3, September 2005; Tomljanovic, Tatiana, *Cornelia Funke: My Favorite Writer*, 2006. Online— Contemporary Authors Online, December 16, 2007.

WEB SITES: www.corneliafunkefans.com

www.corneliafunke.de/en

Photo by Elias Barkey

Susan Gaber

June 23, 1956–

"For a number of years while I was little, my mother had an appreciation for beautiful children's books. When my sister and I were young, she not only read to us but highlighted illustrations she particularly enjoyed. My mother had been interested in fashion illustration but studied to be an art educator. Her interest in art and fashion was inescapable. At some point, maybe when I was seven, I remember admiring and copying the illustrations from picture books that I preferred. I'm sure this must have pleased her. I can recall one particular children's book I kept for years because I liked the elaborate paintings done by a European illustrator. The book was left to mold in our garage after a bottle of children's play cologne spilled all over it. I very reluctantly let it go years later when the scent was still a problem.

"I'm sure if my father had not been sick, creating art would not have been the refuge that it was for me. My father battled depression and an illness that began when I was five. His mental and physical health, as well as our relationship, slowly deteriorated over the years. Like many people facing challenges beyond our capabilities, we all chose simple therapies that consoled us. My sister chose music. I chose art. By the time I reached adolescence, I was drawing every day. A sketchpad was where I could question, be angry or happy, and dream. As I grew even older, I discovered the library and I fell in love with the world of fine arts through art books.

"Upon graduating with a degree in Fine Arts, I created samples for an illustration portfolio and pushed myself to make appointments for interviews in New York City. I had hoped I would gain entrance to the picture book market, but despite my efforts, initially assignments came primarily from magazines and cookbook publishers. In reality, I was grateful for any work. After about a year, I landed a freelance job that became a steady source of income, illustrating a weekly garden column for a prominent newspaper where I lived. It was a two-part assignment. The opening illustration could be a fanciful imaginative piece, the second one was more instructional.

"Shortly after this event, I was introduced to a woman who was a professional storyteller. Her name was Heather Forest.

Years later, after our friendship deepened, Heather proposed collaborating on a book, a folktale she retold, acted, and sang in a performance called 'The Baker's Dozen.' She played the story/song on her guitar for me and made a tape that I later transcribed. Over the next year, I worked to develop the characters and design of the book in between my various paying assignments. It being my first picture book, I fumbled my way through the research, design and dummy. I began to bring the work to some publishers, but there was no interest.

"During this time, I met another woman who became a close and influential friend, Helena Clare Pittman. An artist and writer, she too was interested in breaking into the picture book market. We inspired and emotionally supported one another through the rejections and trials of publishing. Helena found an independent study class that Ed Young was giving in his home. Together we traveled to see him about four times. He shared his book-making process with the handful of students of which we were a part, and he offered valued guidance on the work we brought to him. Helena went on to both write and illustrate her own picture books.

"By the time I reached adolescence, I was drawing every day. A sketchpad was where I could question, be angry or happy, and dream."

"Many months later, while illustrating the end papers of a young adult book for Harcourt Brace and Jovanovich, I mentioned to the art director that I had a proposal for a children's book called *The Baker's Dozen* about a greedy baker who learns about generosity. I wondered if she would be interested in seeing it. She asked me to send it to her in California. A week later I received a call from Elinor Williams, editor at Gulliver books, a division within HBJ, who was willing to bring the story to publication. It is amazing to me now that this was over twenty books ago."

ⅭⅫ ⅭⅫ ⅭⅫ

Born in Brooklyn, New York, Susan Gaber grew up in Wantagh, Long Island. She received her B.F.A. from Long Island University, graduating with honors in 1978. As a freelance illustrator she has worked for *Newsday* and a variety of magazines, including *Child, House Beautiful, Fifty Plus, Spider*, and *Home*. She has also designed greeting cards for Ellen Anderson Productions and created a logo for the nonprofit Reaching for the Stars, an organization that is raising funds to build schools and improve literacy in Pakistan.

Gaber's first children's book was published in 1988, the same year she married Richard Barkey, a police officer. *The Baker's Dozen* received an American Institute for Graphic Arts Award.

Courtesy of Candlewick Press

A year later her son Elias was born. At their editor's suggestion, Susan Gaber and Heather Forest teamed up again in 1990 to create *The Woman Who Flummoxed the Fairies*, a tale about a clever baker woman who figures out a way to prevent the fairies who have kidnapped her from keeping her forever as their cook. This title was selected as an American Booksellers Pick of the Lists.

Gaber has teamed with a number of excellent picture book authors, including Erica Silverman, who wrote *Raisel's Riddle*, a Jewish Cinderella story featuring a heroine for whom knowledge is as essential to happiness as love. With her bright appealing paintings, Gaber underscored the text's emphasis on the character's inner resources. Besides winning an Oppenheim Toy Portfolio Gold Award, *Raisel's Riddle* was an NCTE Notable Children's Book in the Language Arts, a Sydney Taylor Book Awards Notable Honor Book for Younger Readers, an IRA Notable Book for a Global Society, an American Booksellers Pick of the Lists, and a Parents' Choice Recommended title for children 4–9 years old. A book she illustrated for Jacqueline Briggs Martin—*The Finest Horse in Town*—was named a Blue Ribbon title by the *Bulletin of the Center for Children's Books*. Gaber has also illustrated picture books for poet Lee Bennett

Hopkins, storyteller Steve Sanfield, and award-winning writers Nancy Van Laan and Jennifer Armstrong.

In *The Brave Little Parrot* by Rafe Martin, Gaber heightens the drama of this traditional Indian tale about a small gray parrot's battle against a forest fire by alternating between aerial and ground-level perspectives. Besides winning Michigan's Great Lakes Great Books Award for grades K–2, this title was one of the Bank Street College Best Children's Books of the Year. *The Language of Birds*, also written by Rafe Martin, is a retelling of a Russian fairytale about a merchant's son who uses his gift and can understand the language of the birds to save his brother; it won a Parent's Guide to Children's Media Award.

The publication of *Stone Soup* came about when Heather Forest asked Gaber to work with her on a book for August House publishers. Gaber's bold and brightly colored acrylic paintings were an excellent match for the retelling of this traditional tale about two hungry travelers who trick mountain villagers into helping them make "stone soup" by slyly asking them for a few additional ingredients. This collaboration resulted in a Parents' Choice Recommended Title and a Bank Street College Best Book of the Year. The illustrations for *When Winter Came*, which was a Highly Commended book among the 2001 Charlotte Zolotow Awards, were also done in acrylics, while those for *The Princess and the Lord of Night*, a Children's Book nominee for the Mythopoeic Fantasy Award, were done in watercolor and colored pencil.

Susan Gaber and her husband, who is now studying to become a librarian, live with their teenage son in Huntington, New York. For several years, she has worked with the literacy organization in her community and volunteers weekly to tutor English in her local library.

SELECTED WORKS: *The Baker's Dozen*, by Heather Forest, 1988; *The Woman Who Flummoxed the Fairies*, by Heather Forest, 1990; *The Finest Horse in Town*, by Jacqueline Briggs Martin, 1992; *Good Times on Grandfather Mountain*, by Jacqueline Briggs Martin, 1992; *Zeee*, by Elizabeth Enright, 1993; *The Princess and the Lord of Night*, by Emma Bull, 1994; *Small Talk: A Book of Short Poems*, by Lee Bennett Hopkins, 1995; *Bit by Bit*, by Steve Sanfield, 1995; *Jordi's Star*, by Alma Flor Ada, 1996; *Eli and Uncle Dawn*, by Liz Rosenberg, 1997; *The Brave Little Parrot*, by Rafe Martin, 1998; *Stone Soup*, by Heather Forest, 1998; *Raisel's Riddle*, by Erica Silverman, 1999; *The Stable Where Jesus Was Born*, by Rhonda Growler Greene, 1999; *Pierre's Dream*, by

Jennifer Armstrong, 1999; *The Language of Birds*, by Rafe Martin, 2000; *When Winter Came*, by Nancy Van Laan, 2000; *The Very First Thanksgiving*, by Rhonda Growler Greene, 2002; *Ten Sleepy Sheep*, by Phyllis Root, 2004; *Angel Coming*, by Heather Henson, 2005; *Mama Outside, Mama Inside*, by Dianna Hutts Aston, 2006; *The Little Red Hen*, by Heather Forest, 2006.

SUGGESTED READING: *Something About the Author*, vol. 115, 2000.

WEB SITE: www.susangaber.com.

"Looking back, I'm no longer certain what the important bits were. All I know is that I didn't know they were important when they were happening. For example, during my school holidays, when I was a boy in Sussex, I would get my parents to drop me off at the local library on their way to work. I read through the children's area of the library, assisted by the card-file index, which helped me find books about myth and magic, giants and witches, aliens and dimensions, until I had read everything they had, and then I started on the adult books, working my way through the alphabet. I thought this was something that was happening *between* the important bits, but I think I was wrong.

"Or age twelve, on the train to visit my cousins in North London each weekend for the bar mitzvah lessons I couldn't get in Sussex, I read the paperback works of Moorcock, Delany, Zelazny, often getting so engrossed I would miss my underground stop or the place I was meant to change trains, so I would have to phone my aunt begging to be picked up from somewhere in London I wasn't meant to be in the first place. (Much of my growing up was spent like that. I would be late for school, which I traveled to by train, because, reading, I had forgotten to get off the train. Stories were more interesting to me than anything else, so I read a lot of books and comics, but also spent most of my school years in a vague sort of

Photo by Sophia Quach

Neil Gaiman

(Neel Gaym'n)
November 10,
1960–

fog, always puzzled how other boys had no trouble at all knowing which rooms they were meant to be in and when.)

"I am fairly certain that the most important bit of school once I turned fourteen was, in the late afternoon, getting to wander through the back streets of Croydon, going from dusty newsagent to shadowy second-hand magazine shop, hunting mostly for the American comics I had secretly decided I wanted to write when I grew up. I had not realised how irrational or unlikely a career choice this was.

"One day they sent in an outside careers adviser. We had spent the previous day doing tests to find what kind of professions we would be best suited for. We waited in a line to go in to a small room and meet the careers adviser. When it was my turn, I went inside. 'And what would you like to be, young man?' he asked.

"'I want to write American comics.' He was the first person I had ever admitted this to. I was nearly sixteen, and I'd been looking forward to this day for a very long time.

"He did not look pleased. He said, 'Ah. How do you go about doing that, then?'

"I could feel the disappointment starting to creep in. 'I don't know,' I said. 'I was hoping you would be able to tell me.'

"He didn't say anything for a long while. Then he asked if I had ever thought about accountancy. I had never thought about accountancy, and I admitted this, and then we sat and stared at each other until I offered to send the next boy in, and I left that meeting having concluded that there was no way that I could get there from here. Fifteen-year-old boys in Croydon, I understood, didn't grow up to write American comics, and that was just how it was.

"When I started out working, I was a journalist. It's a good sort of job for a writer—you can learn a lot about how the world works, about economies, about deadlines, and there's nothing quite like seeing your sentences in print for giving you a feeling for how they could have been better. I also realised that you *could* do whatever you wanted. You just had to do it, that's all.

"I was a journalist for about five years, until I began to write American comics, which I did for a decade and still do from time to time; and I write books for adults and for children, funny ones and scary ones and ones that make them dream, and radio plays, and movies, and even short stories and poems. I cannot imagine anything I would rather do, even if I didn't keep track of the important bits along the way."

> *"Looking back, I'm no longer certain what the important bits were. All I know is that I didn't know they were important when they were happening."*

৪ ৪ ৪

Neil Gaiman has had the good fortune to grow up and live the life he envisioned for himself when he was 15, and with enormous success. Critics have credited him with playing an influential role in making the comic book—and its more recent incarnation, the graphic novel—a respected and acclaimed form of literature. Born in Portchester, England, Gaiman developed an early interest in the literature of the surreal. He recalls reading *Alice's Adventures in Wonderland* at about age five, and rereading it in subsequent years. In an interview for *Booklist* he stated, "There are things Lewis Carroll did in *Alice* that are etched onto my circuitry." That influence is apparent to readers of his books for both children and adults with their recurring theme of dreams and alternate realities.

Gaiman wasn't aware of American comic books and superheroes until a friend of his father's gave him a box of old DC and Marvel comic books; he was immediately captivated by them. He later said, "[In England], American comics were like postcards from Oz. They had fire hydrants, pizza parlors and skyscrapers in them. For us fire hydrants and skyscrapers were every bit as strange as superheroes flying through the air. For us that world remained strange."

While working as a journalist in his early twenties, Gaiman published his first book, a biography of the pop group Duran Duran. He eventually began contributing scripts for comic books to DC Comics. In 1987 the editors at DC offered to let Gaiman choose one of their defunct characters and bring him back for a new series of comics. Gaiman picked a character called the Sandman, who in the 1940s used a sleeping-gas gun to fight crime. Gaiman kept the name Sandman but changed everything else. The character morphed into a mythic immortal entity known as Dream, whose siblings, called The Endless, included Death, Desire, Despair, Delirium, Destruction, and Destiny. *The Sandman* series, filled with references to literature and mythology, became one of the first modern series of comic books to get wide attention from critics and won nine Will Eisner Comic Industry Awards. In 1991, issue #19 of *The Sandman*, "A Midsummer Night's Dream," became the first comic book to win a World Fantasy Award in the short story category. The 75 issues of *The Sandman* comics were collected and published in 10 volumes, the first of which was titled *The Sandman: Preludes and Nocturnes*. Like *The Sandman*, Gaiman's imaginative novels for adults have all encompassed plots that involve the world of faerie, myth, folklore, and magic.

A second career to Neil Gaiman's highly successful comic books and adult novels surfaced when he began writing children's books. He describes the genesis of his first picture book in an afterword to the 2004 edition. Angry with his father one night, Gaiman's son Michael shouted, "I wish I didn't have a dad! I wish I had . . . goldfish!" before he stomped off to bed. The idea was stored in Gaiman's computer for several years before it surfaced and he wrote the rest of the story. Named one of *Newseek* magazine's best children's books of the year in 1997, *The Day I Swapped My Dad for Two Goldfish* is a cumulative tale of a boy's frustration

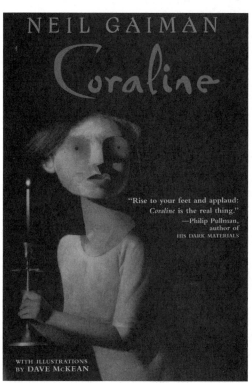

NEIL GAIMAN

Coraline

"Rise to your feet and applaud:
Coraline is the real thing."
—Philip Pullman,
author of
HIS DARK MATERIALS

WITH ILLUSTRATIONS
BY DAVE McKEAN

Courtesy of HarperCollins Publishers

with his newspaper-reading parent and his quest to retrieve him after a series of swaps sends the dad farther and farther from their home. Illustrated in surreal mixed media by Dave McKean, the book exhibited a fresh approach to picture book art and theme.

In *Coraline*, Gaiman and McKean collaborated again, this time on a novel for older children. The surrealism in this book is more frightening, but the heroine of the title learns at last she is in charge of her destiny. Discovering an alternative reality on the other side of a locked door, Coraline steps into a world that mirrors her own, but provides more of the excitement and attention that she has been craving. This nether world, where her parents have black buttons for eyes, soon turns dark and creepy; however, returning to her real home the girl finds her true parents missing, so her ultimate quest is to put things right again. A *New York Times* bestseller, *Coraline* was also cited as a *School Library Journal* Best Book, a *Bulletin of the Center for Children's Books* Blue Ribbon title, and an ALA Notable Children's Book. Gaiman won the Elizabeth Burr Award for this book, presented annually to a Wisconsin author or illustrator for a book of distinguished achievement. *Coraline* will soon be an animated feature film.

A second picture book by Gaiman and McKean, *The Wolves in the Walls*, continued the pair's interest in the surreal, as a little girl warns her parents that there are wolves in the walls of their home. Eventually the family must hide in the walls after the wolves take over the house, but the wolves are frightened away when people emerge from the walls. McKean's mixed-media paintings earned a *New York Times* Best Illustrated Book award for this title. A children's edition of *Mirrormask*, adapted from a film written by Gaiman and illustrated by McKean, was shortlisted for the Kate Greenaway Medal in England.

Neil Gaiman's novels for adults have won many awards and spent many weeks on bestseller lists. His novel *Stardust*, a richly imagined fantasy tale, was named an ALA Alex Award title as one of the top adult novels for young adults in the year 2000 and became a major motion picture in 2007. Equally adept at performing, Gaiman has been the narrator for the audio production of *Stardust* and for several of his children's books. Though born in England, Gaiman has lived for many years near Minneapolis, Minnesota, with his American wife and their three children.

SELECTED WORKS FOR ADULTS: *Duran Duran: The First Four Years of the Fab Five*, 1984; *Violent Cases*, illus. by Dave McKean, 1987; *Good Omens*, with Terry Pratchett, 1990; *Black Orchid*, illus. by Dave McKean, 1991; *Signal to Noise*, with Dave McKean, 1992; *Angels & Visitations: A Miscellany*, 1993; *Neverwhere: A Novel*, 1997; *Stardust: Being a Romance within the Realms of Faerie*, illus. by Charles Vess, 1998; *Smoke and Mirrors: Short Fictions and Illusions*, 1998; *American Gods*, 2001; *Anansi Boys*, 2005; *The Alchemy of Mirrormask*, with David McKean; *Fragile Things: Short Fictions and Wonders*, 2006; *Eternals*, illus. by John Romita, Jr., 2007; *The Facts in the Case of the Departure of Miss Finch*, illus. by Michael Zulli, 2007; *Signal to Noise*, (new and expanded ed.) *with Dave McKean, 2007.* The Sandman Library—*Preludes and Nocturnes*, Vol. 1, illus. by Sam Kieth, and others, 1991; *The Doll's House*, Vol. 2, illus. by Michael Zulli, and others, 1991; *Dream Country*, Vol. 3, illus. by Kelley Jones, and others, 1991; *Season of Mists*, Vol. 4, illus. by Mike Dringenberg, and others, 1992; *A Game of You*, Vol. 5, illus. by Colleen Doran, and others, 1993; *Fables and Reflections*, Vol. 6, illus. by Bryan Talbot, and others, 1994; *Brief Lives*, Vol. 7, illus. by Jill Thompson, and others, 1994; *World's End*, Vol. 8, illus. by Michael Allred, and others, 1994; *The Kindly Ones*, Vol. 9, illus. by Marc Hempel, and others, 1996; *The Wake*, Vol. 10 illus. by Charles Vess, and others, 1997; *The Dream Hunters*, illus. by Yoshitaka Amano, 1999; *Endless Nights*, illus. by P. Craig Russell, and others, 2004.

SELECTED WORKS FOR YOUNG READERS: *The Day I Swapped My Dad for Two Goldfish*, illus. by Dave McKean, 1997; *Coraline*, illus. by Dave McKean, 2002; *The Wolves in the Walls*, illus. by Dave McKean, 2003; *Mirrormask* (children's ed.), illus. by Dave McKean, 2005; *M Is for Magic*, 2007; *The Dangerous Alphabet*, illus. by Gris Grimly, 2008; *The Graveyard Book*, illus. by Dave McKean, 2008.

SUGGESTED READING: McCabe, Joseph, *Hanging Out with the Dream King*, 2004; Kwitney, Alisa, *The Sandman: King of Dreams*, 2003; *Authors and Artists for Young Adults*, vol. 42, 2002; *Dictionary of Literary Biography*, vol. 261, 2002; Bender, Hy, *The Sandman Companion*, 1999; *St. James Guide to Horror, Ghost, and Gothic Writers*, 1998; Gaiman, Neil and Edward E. Kramer, eds., *The Sandman: Book of Dreams*, 1996. Periodicals—Olson, Ray, "Interview: Neil Gaiman," *Booklist*, August 2002; Lodge, Sally, "Crossing Over: Authors of adult fiction seek a younger audience," *Publishers Weekly*, Sept. 2, 2002. Online—*World Authors Electronic*, 2001.

WEB SITE: www.neilgaiman.com

Rita Golden Gelman

July 2, 1937–

"I have to admit that I never did think much about becoming a writer when I was a kid. Actually, I didn't think much about becoming anything. During my growing-up years, I was far more interested in climbing trees, catching frogs, collecting lightning bugs in jars, playing in the street (there weren't that many cars) and playing in the park at the end of my block. Jumping into piles of leaves, sledding, and rolling down hills won over sitting at home reading books or writing. Doing just about anything with the neighborhood kids always won out over doing things by myself.

"When I was fourteen, I worked behind the soda fountain in my father's pharmacy. The store was in a part of Bridgeport, Connecticut, where there were a lot of immigrant families. I scooped ice cream, dribbled hot fudge, squirted whipped cream, and whirred milk, ice cream, and syrup in the milkshake machine. I loved the job, partly because it was a lot like playing with food, and partly because I got to meet and talk to all the people who sat at my soda fountain. I felt lucky to be able to connect to so many different kinds of people from all over the world. Being with people was always what I loved most to do.

"I also had fun working on school newspapers in eighth grade and in high school. I was writing; but when I think back on it, it was the teamwork I loved, that wonderful sense of being part of a group working toward a goal. And the goal was so tangible: a newspaper that went out to the whole school.

"When I graduated from Brandeis University, I went to New York City to seek my fortune. That's when I realized I had no career goals or skills. Well, I can always write, I thought, remembering all those school papers I had helped to create. But I was 21 years old and couldn't imagine myself writing for adults. So how about kids? Yeah. That I could do.

"I went off to find a job as a writer on a children's magazine; but the only available job on a kids' magazine was as 'file clerk.' At the time I didn't realize that my organizational skills were seriously deficient, so I interviewed and got the job. I was in charge of the files for the whole magazine. It took about six months before we all realized that I was a lousy file clerk; I had messed up the files so badly that they made me a writer. And that was the beginning of my career as a writer for children.

"I wrote my first book ten years later. By then I had two children who were in school in Greenwich Village, New York City. My first book, *Dumb Joey*, is about a group of kids who live in a big city where there are no parks or car-less streets. They have nowhere to play except the school playground, which isn't available after school. So they figure out a way to get there, and then get locked in. The pesky little brother, Joey, gets them out.

Photo by Carolyn Herter

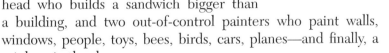

"Since then, I've written more than seventy books. Silly rhyming books about characters who can't stop talking, a cat who won't wear a hat, a man with a pot on his head who builds a sandwich bigger than a building, and two out-of-control painters who paint walls, windows, people, toys, bees, birds, cars, planes—and finally, a rainbow in the sky.

"Over the years I've also written many nonfiction books, including books about monkeys and apes, the Galapagos Islands, rice, pandas, koalas, and famous sports stars. Writing nonfiction is like taking a course. You have to find out everything there is to know about the subject. It's a wonderful excuse for indulging my curiosity about a subject. I can curl up with a pile of books and read. These days I love reading; I'm making up for all those years when I thought books were boring.

"One of the best parts of being a writer is that I can do it wherever I am. About twenty years ago, I decided to do it all over the world. I got rid of everything I owned (house, car, clothes, books, furniture), put a couple things into a backpack, and took off. I have been homeless, free, and adventurous ever since. I love it. I have learned how to be by myself and enjoy it. I have lived and written in Mexico, Guatemala, Indonesia, Thailand, New Zealand, Suriname, Nicaragua, Israel, and many other countries.

"I still love being with people. Wherever I travel, I try to stay with families and live their lives. I go to their ceremonies, eat their food, and play their games. I try to learn their languages and crafts and songs. And I often dress in their style of clothes. I have learned that wherever they live, whatever their language or color or customs, people are people. They laugh, cry, love, learn, and play all over the world. I turned seventy in July 2007, and I still get my greatest pleasure when I am connecting with other people, working with them on projects, cooking with them, singing with them, sharing their lives. I never tell people how to live. Instead I learn from them. I have written one adult book about my life these last years; it is called *Tales of a Female Nomad*."

> *"One of the best parts of being a writer is that I can do it wherever I am. About twenty years ago, I decided to do it all over the world."*

ఐ   ఐ   ఐ

After growing up in Bridgeport, Connecticut, where she attended local public schools, Rita Golden received her B.A. in English and American literature from Brandeis University in 1958. From 1958 to 1960 she worked at a magazine called *For Young New Yorkers*, which later became known as *Young Americans*. She was also an editor at the Crowell-Collier and Macmillan publishing companies and a juvenile consultant for Book-of-the-Month Club. In 1960 she married writer/editor Steve Gelman and they had two children: Mitchell in 1962 and Jan in 1963. The family moved to Los Angeles in 1976, and Rita received a master's degree in anthropology from the University of California, Los Angeles, in 1984. Divorced in 1987, and with her children grown, Rita Golden Gelman began the itinerant life described in her adult memoir, *Tales of a Female Nomad*.

Many of Gelman's books are a result of her love of travel, her love of animals, or both. For a time, she lived in Nicaragua, where she learned what it was like to live in a country under siege and discovered first-hand how the Nicaraguans felt about the Sandinista-Contra conflict. Their feelings were compellingly expressed in Gelman's *Inside Nicaragua*, which was named an ALA Best Book for Young Adults and a CCBC Choice. She spent time in the Galapagos Islands, residing on a boat and exploring islands inhabited by iguanas, frigate birds, sea lions, and other animals. In *Dawn to Dusk in the Galapagos*, which received a John Burroughs Association commendation as an Outstanding Nature Book for Children, Gelman explores one day in the life of Galapagos Island creatures while explaining how such creatures developed.

Gelman's books cover a wide age range of readers. They include riddle books, how-to's, fiction, and nonfiction. *More Spaghetti, I Say!*, features Gelman's favorite monkey character, Minnie, who loves spaghetti so much, she can't stop eating it. *Splash! All About Baths* (written with Susan Buxbaum), which joyfully explains such bath time experiences as why things float, why a mirror fogs up, and what creates bubbles, was an American Institute of Physics Best Science Book for Children and received a Science-Writing Award. *Queen Esther Saves Her People*, a stirring retelling of the Purim legend, won a Sydney Taylor Honor Award. Written in a direct, lively manner, the story is full of details about the Persian court life. A more recent title, *Doodler Doodling*, was named an ALA Notable Children's Book; it presents a playful 21-word homage to the creative process that inspires the hands of young doodlers everywhere. Gelman has stated that her own favorite of all her books is *Why Can't I Fly?*; the idea came from her own childhood when she watched birds and dreamed of flying herself.

"I have learned that wherever they live, whatever their language or color or customs, people are people. They laugh, cry, love, learn, and play all over the world."

Although Gelman sometimes wonders how a gregarious person like herself chose the solitary profession of writing, she does note that many of her books are collaborations, which allow her to work with people on stories that neither might have written alone. One such collaboration was with Nancy Lamb Austin, with whom she created the Which Way and Secret Door series under the pseudonym R. G. Austin. Both series allow readers to choose how the adventure develops by giving them the opportunity to make choices at the end of each page. While the Which Way books were geared towards fourth and fifth graders, the less scary Secret Door books appealed to second and third graders. Her collaborations with Susan Buxbaum explored various science topics.

At present Rita Gelman's life centers around the people that she encounters in her travels. More than a mere tourist, Gelman

becomes emotionally invested in the lives of those she meets, and this investment shows in her writing, as she continues to roam the globe.

SELECTED WORKS: *Dumb Joey*, illus. by Cheryl Pelavin, 1973; *The Can*, illus. by John Trotta, 1975; *Comits: A Book of Comic Skits*, illus. by Robert Dennis, 1975; *The Me I Am*, photos by Michael Heron, 1975; *Fun City*, illus. by Tom Herbert, 1975; *Great Quarterbacks of Pro Football*, written with Steve Gelman, 1975 (new edition 1978); *Why Can't I Fly?* illus. by Jack Kent, 1976; *Hey, Kid!*, illus. by Carol Nicklaus, 1977; *More Spaghetti, I Say!* illus. by Jack Kent, 1977 (new edition illus. by Mort Gerberg, 1992); *OUCH!: All about Cuts and Other Hurts*, with Susan Kovacs Buxbaum, illus. by Jan Pyk, 1977; *Professor Coconut and the Thief*, with Joan Richter, illus. by Emily Arnold McCully, 1977; *America's Favorite Sports Stars*, with Steve Gelman, 1978; *Cats and Mice*, illus. by Eric Gurney, 1978; *UFO Encounters*, with Marcia Seligson, 1978; *Uncle Hugh: A Fishing Story*, with Warner

Friedman, illus. by Eros Keith, 1978; *Hello Cat, You Need a Hat*, illus. by Eric Gurney, 1979 (new edition illus. by Dana Regan, 1998); *The Biggest Sandwich Ever*, illus. by Mort Gerberg, 1980; *The Incredible Dinosaurs*, illus. by Christopher Santoro, 1980; *Favorite Riddles, Knock Knocks, and Nonsense*, illus. by Mort Gerberg, 1980; *Great Moments in Sports*, 1980; *Benji at Work*, 1980; *Boats That Float*, with Susan Kovacs Buxbaum, illus. by Marilyn MacGregor, 1981; *Fabulous Animal Facts That Hardly Anybody Knows*, illus. by Margaret Hartelius, 1981; *Mount St. Helens: The Big Blast*, 1981; *ESP and Other Strange Happenings*, 1981; *Mortimer K Saves the Day*, illus. by Bernie Gruver, 1982; *Benji Takes a Dive at Marineland*, 1982; *Body Noises*, with Susan Kovacs Buxbaum, illus. by Angie Lloyd, 1983; *Wet Cats*, illus. by Eric Gurney, 1985; *Listen and Look: A Safety Book*, illus. by Cathy Beylon, 1986; *Care and Share: A Book about Manners*, illus. by Cathy Beylon, 1986; *A Koala Grows Up*, illus. by Gioia Fiammenghi, 1986; *Pets for Sale*, illus. by Fredrick Winkowski, 1986; *Splash! All About Baths*, with Susan Kovacs Buxbaum, illus. by Maryann Cocca-Leffler, 1987; *Leave It to Minnie*, illus. by Mort Gerberg, 1987; *Inside Nicaragua: Young People's Dreams and Fears*, 1988; *Stop Those Painters*, illus. by Mort Gerberg, 1989; *Monkeys and Apes of the World*, 1990; *Monsters of the Sea*, illus. by Jean Day Zallinger, 1990; *Dawn to Dusk in the Galapagos: Flightless Birds, Swimming Lizards, and Other Fascinating Creatures*, photos by Tui De Roy, 1991; *A Monkey Grows Up*, illus. by Gioia Fiammenghi, 1991; *What Are Scientists? What Do They Do? Let's Find Out*, with Susan Kovacs Buxbaum, illus. by Mark Teague, 1991; *Vampires and Other Creatures of the Night*, with Nancy Lamb, illus. by C. B. Mordan, 1991; *Body Battles*, illus. by Elroy Freem, 1992; *I Went to the Zoo*, illus. by Maryann Kovalski, 1993; *A Panda Grows Up*, illus. by Mary Morgan, 1993; *Body Detectives: A Book about the Five Senses*, illus. by Elroy Freem, 1994; *Queen Esther Saves Her People*, illus. by Frané Lessac, 1998; *Pizza Pat*, illus. by Will Terry, 1999; *Rice Is Life*, illus. by Yangsook Choi, 2000; *Mole in a Hole*, illus. by Holly Hannon, 2000; *Doodler Doodling*, illus. by Paul O. Zelinsky, 2004.

SELECTED WORKS WRITTEN AS R. G. AUSTIN: "Which Way?" Series written with Nancy Austin—*The Castle of No Return*, illus. by Mike Eagle, 1982; *Vampires, Spies, and Alien Beings*, illus. by Anthony Kramer, 1982; *The Spell of the Black Raven*, illus. by Anthony Kramer, 1982; *Famous and Rich*, illus. by Mike Eagle, 1982; *Lost in a Strange Land*, illus. by Lorna Tomei, 1982; *Curse of the Sunken Treasure*, illus. by Lorna Tomei, 1982; *Cosmic*

Encounters, illus. by Doug Jamieson, 1982; *Creatures of the Dark*, illus. by Gordon Tomei, 1982; *Invasion of the Black Slime*, illus. by Joseph A. Smith, 1983; *Trapped in the Black Box*, illus. by Doug Jamieson, 1983; *Poltergeists, Ghosts, and Psychic Encounters*, illus. by Joseph A. Smith, 1984; *Islands of Terror*, illus. by Gordon Tomei, 1984. Secret Door Series with Nancy Austin—*Wow! You Can Fly!* illus. by Joseph A. Smith, 1983; *Giants, Elves and Scary Monsters*, illus. by Ed Parker; 1983; *The Haunted Castle*, illus. by Winslow Pels, 1983; *The Secret Life of Toys*, illus. by Sal Murdocca, 1983; *The Visitors from Outer Space*, illus. by Blanche Sims, 1983; *The Inch-High Kid*, illus. by Dennis Hockerman, 1983; *The Magic Carpet*, illus. by Winslow Pels, 1983; *Happy Birthday to You*, illus. by Joseph A. Smith, 1983; *The Monster Family*, illus. by Blanche Sims, 1984; *Brontosaurus Moves In*, illus. by Joseph A. Smith, 1984; *The Enchanted Forest*, illus. by Winslow Pels, 1984; *Crazy Computers*, illus. by Joseph A. Smith, 1984.

SELECTED WORKS FOR ADULTS: *Tales of a Female Nomad: Living at Large in the World*, 2001.

SUGGESTED READING: *Something About the Author*, vol. 131, 2002. Online—McMahon, Mark, "Rita Golden Gelman: Female Nomad Crosses the Globe Solo!" August 2005, at www.escapeartist.com/efam/73/Nomad_Adventure.html

WEB SITE: www.ritagoldengelman.com

Lindsay Barrett George

July 22, 1952–

"I was born on an island where parrots, crabs, starfish and whales lived outside my bedroom window. I drew them. I now live in the country, where deer, otter, bear and heron inhabit my backyard. I draw them. Some things, thankfully, never change.

"My sense of wonder and belief in the power of books goes way back, to my encounter with my parents' volume of the *Wonder Book of Knowledge*. On page 469, there was a photo of a sea monster caught off the coast of Florida. Books have power. At the age of two, I believed that the sea monster was alive in the book, and I would avoid walking close to the *Wonder Book*, so as not to be eaten by the sea creature.

"My artwork has always been about my environment. When I lived in New York City, I worked in children's publishing. But in my free time, I made many wordless books about the city—city dogs, city foods, and city stories. I fell in love with the book as a storytelling object.

"The words and pictures that children see and read can affect how they experience their world. The nature books my husband Bill and I made came directly out of our five years living with our children in a log cabin in the wilds of northeastern Pennsylvania. We spent much time walking, canoeing, swimming, fishing, and most importantly, listening in the woods.

"Children are fascinated with how animals live, and we believed it was important for young readers to understand how everything in nature is connected, and that this understanding would ultimately lead children to make choices to help preserve and protect the animals and their habitats. Our 'Long Pond' books depict people living respectfully with animals, but the books really tell us that we are not alone. Ever.

"I love mysteries. As I start out to create each of my books, I feel as though I have a mystery to solve. Writing the story and designing the book is my way of finding the solution. There is magic for me in creating children's books. I also love the 'aha!' moments, when ideas come together and pop. That often happens while I'm driving the car, walking my dogs, or in the moments just before waking, in the very early morning. I often look for happy accidents, or patterns.

Photo by Mickey Kaufman

"My art has always been about the familiar things in my life. For example, *Inside Mouse, Outside Mouse* came out of a personal challenge. I wanted to see what I could do with my daughter's third-grade homework assignment—writing about a mouse in one's house. I had always liked mice and had several pictures of them on my studio wall. The concept of an outside mouse meeting an inside mouse was intriguing, and using the middle of the book, or the gutter, as the place where the two mice meet, felt right. At the end of the book, the mice do not say 'goodbye,' but 'hello.' The fact that it took six years to complete is still a bit of a shock.

"*The Secret* evolved, thankfully, in a much shorter time. The idea of a line running through every page, combined with the game of Telephone—that was all easy. But the secret, what could it be? Then came the timely playing on my car radio of the Beatles' song "Do You Want to Know a Secret?" That was the gift, the happy accident. The story fell into place, and the look of the book, combining painted images with natural objects, was something new for me, extremely satisfying, and a lot of fun to do.

"For my next book, we have to go back to the beginning, or at least my beginning. Remember the sea monster in the *Wonder Book of Knowledge* and the idea of a picture coming to life inside a book? Watch for it, and think *aardvark*.

"For a little girl whose passion was drawing birds, fish, flowers and trees, to end up being an artist whose passion is drawing birds, fish, flowers and trees . . . well, it doesn't get any better. I'm proud to say that I make children's books."

ଓ ଓ ଓ

"As I start out to create each of my books, I feel as though I have a mystery to solve. Writing the story and designing the book is my way of finding the solution."

The daughter of a brew master and a homemaker, Lindsay Barrett George was born in the Dominican Republic. As a little girl, she received a set of paints and brushes from her grandfather and has remained a devoted artist ever since. Spanish was her first language, but when she was eight years old, she moved from the West Indies to the United States. Growing up in New Jersey, she found that drawing pictures of the country of her birth helped her to make friends in her new home. Today she is still doing that—making friends with children by drawing pictures in her books.

After attending the Boston Museum School of Fine Arts from 1972 to 1973, George went on to earn a B.F.A. degree from Manhattanville College in 1974 and an M.A and M.F.A. from the University of Wisconsin–Madison, where she majored in drawing and printmaking. Returning to the East Coast, she worked for fine art printers in Englewood, NJ, and New York City. In 1981, she took a job in publishing, working as a designer in a children's book department. That job ultimately led to her becoming a writer and illustrator. In 1984 she married William T. George, and in 1987, after moving to Pennsylvania, she published her first book, *William and Boomer*, a quiet tale about a boy who befriends a gosling and learns to swim with him.

George's gouache paintings are notable for their realism, controlled composition, and detailed, scientific qualities. In 1990, she received the Carolyn W. Field Award of the Pennsylvania Library Association for her illustrations in *Box Turtle at Long Pond*. Praised for their accuracy, accessibility to children, and usefullness in teaching about nature, George's books include the Long Pond series, many of which were written by her husband. Three Long Pond titles—*Beaver at Long Pond*, *Box Turtle at Long Pond*, and *Fishing at Long Pond*—were named Outstanding Science Trade Books for Children. *Box Turtle at Long Pond*, which chronicles a day in the life of a box turtle, was also chosen by the Library of Congress as a Children's Book of the Year and named to the John Burroughs List of Nature Books for Young Readers. *Fishing at Long Pond*, in which a girl and her grandfather observe such pond visitors as a deer, an osprey, and a goose while they fish for bass, was an American Booksellers Association Pick of the Lists.

In 2004 *Inside Mouse, Outside Mouse* was selected by the Pennsylvania Center for the Book as one of its Baker's Dozen Best Books for Family Literacy. In 2006, it was chosen by the Pennsylvania One Book, Every Young Child program to launch an initiative for connecting early book experiences with the development of reading skills. For that campaign, George led drawing sessions and gave talks about the book to audiences of children and adults all across Pennsylvania. The Pennsylvania Center for the Book also developed a "Family Fun Night" session as well as resources to support the use of *Inside Mouse, Outside Mouse* in families, in libraries, and in early childhood education programs.

Courtesy of Greenwillow Books

Today, Lindsay Barrett George lives in White Mills, a town in northeastern Pennsylvania, with her two children, a quail, three dogs, two cats, a tortoise, and a rabbit. Her husband and writing partner, William Trimpi George, whom she married in 1984, died in 1999. Her latest book, *In the Garden*, is another in the popular Who's Been Here? series. In this title, two children embark on a scientific journey as they set out to discover who's been destroying the plants in their vegetable garden.

SELECTED WORKS WRITTEN AND ILLUSTRATED: *William and Boomer*, 1987; *Beaver at Long Pond*, with William T. George, 1988; *In the Snow: Who's Been Here?* 1995; *In the Woods: Who's Been Here?* 1995; *Around the Pond: Who's Been Here?* 1996; *Around the*

World: Who's Been Here? 1999; *My Bunny and Me*, 2001; *Inside Mouse, Outside Mouse*, 2004; *The Secret*, 2005; *In the Garden: Who's Been Here?* 2006; *Alfred Digs*, 2008.

SELECTED WORKS ILLUSTRATED: *Box Turtle at Long Pond*, by William T. George, 1989; *Fishing at Long Pond*, by William T. George, 1991; *Christmas at Long Pond*, by William T. George, 1992; *Secret Places: Poems*, selected by Charlotte Huck, 1993; *Pick, Pull, Snap! Where Once a Flower Bloomed*, by Lola M. Schaefer, 2003.

SUGGESTED READING: *Something About the Author*, vol. 155, 2005; *Contemporary Authors*, Gale Literary Database: May 23, 2001.

Courtesy of Random House, Inc.

Patricia Reilly Giff

April 26, 1935–

"While the rest of the kids were playing hide-and-seek, I sat under the cherry tree, reading. On winter evenings, I shared an armchair with my father while he read *Hiawatha* and *Evangeline* to me. I read the stories of my mother's childhood, and every book in our little library in St. Albans.

"I wanted to write. Always.

"But the people who wrote were dead . . . or important, far away and inaccessible. And who was I to dream about writing something like *Little Women* or *The Secret Garden*, or *Jane Eyre?*

"In college, I studied Keats, and Poe, and Pope, and Dryden and, overcome by their genius, switched from English to business, and then to history, where I listened to a marvelous man named Mullee spin tales about the past. I fell into teaching because my beloved dean, who had no idea that I wanted to write, saw that it was a good place for me.

"I taught for almost twenty years before I wrote a story. I was married and had three children. I had a Master's Degree in history, a Professional Diploma in reading. I had started doctoral studies.

"Then suddenly I was forty. I hadn't written a story; I hadn't even tried. By this time I'd taught hundreds of children and many of them had hard lives. I wanted to say things that would make a difference to them. I wanted to tell them that they were unique because they were themselves. That we all are. Maybe I didn't have to be a Milton or a Longfellow to do that.

"I began. Early on dark cold mornings, fortified by innumerable cups of hot tea, I worked at it. It was hard. It was really so hard. But then I began to feel the joy of it, learning as I wrote.

"So that's what I've been doing all these years. I have grandchildren now, seven of them, and I have things to tell them, as well as all of today's children. I want children to know about our American heritage—that all of us are here because someone had the courage to come to this country, either today or in the past.

"I want children to read about some of the stories I've heard from my parents about the Great Hunger of Ireland, or my great-grandparents' lives as immigrants. I want to tell them about what it was like to grow up during the Second World War, or to wonder about the people who struggled to build the beautiful Brooklyn Bridge. Most of all, I want children to see themselves in these stories, to know that they have the courage, and the ability, to do what all these storybook characters have done."

ଔ   ଔ   ଔ

Patricia Reilly Giff's childhood was spent in St. Albans, a middle-class neighborhood in the Queens borough of New York City. After high school she attended Marymount Manhattan College, graduating in 1956. She went on to receive a master's degree from St. John's University in 1958 and a diploma in reading from Hofstra University on Long Island In 1975.

An elementary school teacher from 1964 to 1971 and a reading consultant from 1971 to 1984, Giff later found that her classroom experiences provided the raw material for many books. In 1979 she published her first book and her new career began to develop. She would soon become a very prolific fulltime writer.

Drawing on her familiarity with the drama of real childhood situations and humorous school episodes, Giff's first book, *Fourth Grade Celebrity*, precisely hit the target audience of middle grade readers and quickly developed into a series. The author's fingers were, and still are, definitely on the pulse of children—their emotions, worries, funnybones, and sensibilities.

The great success of Giff's Polk Street School series proved her ability to connect with younger readers, those who are just beginning to move beyond easy readers and toward chapter books. After she had written 15 titles in the first Polk Street

"It was hard. It was really so hard. But then I began to feel the joy of it, learning as I wrote."

School series, several of Giff's characters seemed to insist on having their own series; and so she has produced additional series, including New Kids at the Polk Street School, Polka Dot, Private Eye, Lincoln Lions Band, Polk Street Special, Ballet Slippers, and Friends and Amigos.

Another aspect of Giff's commitment to literacy is the children's bookstore in Fairfield, Connecticut—The Dinosaur's Paw—that she and her family opened in 1990. School classes visit the store where Giff talks to them about her books. She also teaches writing classes for adults who want to create books for children. These classes, offered three times a year, have produced many successfully published manuscripts and helped many new writers get started.

In the late 1990s, having written over 60 contemporary school stories, Giff turned her writer's eye to history—her own family history and memories of growing up. *Lily's Crossing* is a poignant, coming-of-age story that takes place during the summer of 1944 when World War II was raging across Europe. Fifteen-year-old Lily is sent to stay with her grandmother when her widowed father joins the army to fight in the war. The emotional level of this tender story was drawn from Giff's own remembrances of those war years. The book was a critical success, receiving a Newbery Honor citation and a *Boston Globe–Horn Book* Honor Award. The applause for *Lily's Crossing* encouraged Giff to pursue writing historical fiction, and *Nory Ryan's Song* followed in 2000, based on research into Giff's family ancestry. Twelve-year-old Nory and her Irish family struggle to survive the Potato Famine in 1845. The urgency of their plight and that of their neighbors is fully portrayed through Giff's atmospheric writing and emotional connection to her characters. *Maggie's Door*, published in 2002, continues Nory's saga, relating her harrowing voyage from Ireland to a new life in America. Some years later Giff wrote *Water Street*, set in Brooklyn in 1875, in which she narrates a wonderful friendship story told in alternating chapters by Bird Mallon (the daughter of Nory Ryan) and Thomas Neary. In the background is the excitement of the building of the Brooklyn Bridge and the pride of the workers who contributed to its completion. The connection of these characters to those of the earlier novels gives readers a sense of family history across generations.

In *All the Way Home*, Giff brought together two unusual but appealing characters: a boy who is sent to stay with a friend in Brooklyn when fire destroys the apple crop on his family's upstate farm in 1941 and a girl he meets whose life has changed by polio.

"Most of all, I want children to see themselves in these stories, to know that they have the courage, and the ability, to do what all these storybook characters have done."

In *Pictures of Hollis Woods*, Giff tackled a contemporary situation for a foster child. She had encountered many foster children in her teaching days and wanted to express their difficulties through a fictional character. Troubled 12-year-old Hollis Woods, after many foster homes, is sent to live with a retired art teacher. As the woman slowly develops dementia, Hollis tries to protect her and, in doing so, she learns to accept and embrace the family that truly wants her. This moving story about the meaning of family won Giff her second Newbery Honor citation and became a Hallmark Hall of Fame TV movie that aired in December 2007.

Calling on another branch of her own family history, Giff based *A House of Tailors* on her great-grandmother's experiences. The title refers to a cramped Brooklyn tenement where 13-year-old Dina is sent after being accused of acting as a spy during the Franco-Prussian War. Giff has stitched together believable characters with historically accurate realism in a rich tapestry of story. The theme of family again plays a major role in *Willow Run*. Maggie, a character first introduced in *Lily's Crossing*, begins to understand what courage means when her father moves the family from Queens, New York to Willow Run, Michigan, so he can help in the war effort by working in a factory building airplanes. With her brother overseas and her German grandfather back home, Maggie learns the importance of friends and family support both in battle and on the home front.

Courtesy of Delacorte Press, Random House, Inc.

Patricia Reilly Giff is that rare writer who can channel children's inner feelings and weave characters, plots, and settings into a textured fabric. Whether she is writing humorous school stories for emerging readers, crafting contemporary fiction for middle school children, or recounting the struggles of young people from the past, at the core of each of her books are the themes of belonging and self-disocvery. In recognition of her contributions to children's literature and to education, she has received Doctorates of Humane Letters from Hofstra University in New York and from Sacred Heart University in Connecticut. Giff lives with her husband, Jim, in Trumbull, Connecticut.

SELECTED WORKS: *Fourth-Grade Celebrity*, illus. by Leslie Morrill, 1979; *The Girl Who Knew It All*, illus. by Leslie Morrill, 1979; *Today Was a Terrible Day*, illus. by Susanna Natti, 1980; *Next Year I'll Be Special*, illus. by Marylin Hafner, 1980; *Left-Handed Shortstop: A Novel*, illus. by Leslie Morrill, 1980; *Have You Seen Hyacinth Macaw? A Mystery*, illus. by Anthony Kramer, 1981; *The Winter Worm Business: A Novel*, illus. by Leslie Morrill, 1981; *The Gift of the Pirate Queen*, illus. by Jenny Rutherford, 1982; *Loretta P. Sweeny, Where Are You? A Mystery*, illus. by Anthony Kramer, 1983; *The Almost Awful Play*, illus. by Susanna Natti, 1984; *Rat Teeth*, illus. by Leslie Morrill, 1984; *Love, from the Fifth Grade Celebrity*, 1986; *Tootsie Tanner Why Don't You Talk? An Abby Jones Junior Detective Mystery*, illus. by Anthony Kramer, 1987; *Poopsie Pomerantz, Pick Up Your Feet*, illus. by Leslie Morrill, 1989; *Matthew Jackson Meets the Wall*, illus. by Blanche Sims, 1990; *The War Began at Supper: Letters to Miss Loria*, 1991; *Shark in School*, illus. by Blanche Sims, 1994; *Lily's Crossing*, 1997; *Katie Cobb Two*, 1999; *Nory Ryan's Song*, 2000; *All the Way Home*, 2001; *Pictures of Hollis Woods*, 2002; *Maggie's Door*, 2002; *A House of Tailors*, 2004; *Willow Run*, 2005; *Water Street*, 2006; *Eleven*, 2008.

Courtesy of Yearling Books, Random House, Inc.

SELECTED WORKS IN SERIES: Kids of Polk Street School series (all illus. by Blanche Sims)—*The Beast in Ms. Rooney's Room*, 1984; *The Candy Corn Contest*, 1984; *December Secrets*, 1984; *Lazy Lions, Lucky Lambs*, 1985; *Say "Cheese"*, 1985; *Purple Climbing Days*, 1985; *In the Dinosaur's Paw*, 1985; *Snaggle Doodles*, 1985; *The Valentine Star*, 1985; *Sunny-Side Up*, 1986; *Fish Face*, 1986; *Pickle Puss*, 1986; *Emily Arrow Promises to Do Better This Year*, 1990; *Beast and the Halloween Horror*, 1990; *Monster Rabbit Runs Amuck!*, 1991; *Wake Up Emily, It's Mother*, 1991. Ronald Morgan series (all illus. by Susanna Natti)—*Watch Out, Ronald Morgan*, 1985; *Happy Birthday, Ronald Morgan*, 1986; *Ronald Morgan Goes to Bat*, 1988; *Ronald Morgan Goes to Camp*, 1995; *Good Luck, Ronald Morgan*, 1996. New Kids of Polk Street School series (all illus. by Blanche Sims)—*Watch Out! Man-Eating Snake*, 1988; *Fancy Feet*, 1988; *All about Sta-*

cy, 1988; *B-E-S-T Friends*, 1988; *Spectacular Stone Soup*, 1988; *Stacy Says Good-Bye*, 1989. Polk Street Special series (all illus. by Blanche Sims)—*Write up a Storm with the Polk Street School*, 1993; *Turkey Trouble*, 1994; *Count Your Money with the Polk Street School*, 1994; *Postcard Pest*, 1994; *Look Out, Washington, D.C.!*, 1995; *Pet Parade*, 1996; *Green Thumbs, Everyone*, 1996; *Oh Boy, Boston!*, 1997; *Next Stop, New York City! The Polk Street Kids on Tour*, 1997; *Let's Go, Philadelphia!*, 1998. Polka Dot, Private Eye series (all illus. by Blanche Sims)—*The Mystery of the Blue Ring*, 1987; *The Powder Puff Puzzle*, 1987; *The Riddle of the Red Purse*, 1987; *The Secret at the Polk Street School*, 1987; *The Case of the Cool-Rich Kid*, 1989; *Garbage Juice for Breakfast*, 1989; *The Clue at the Zoo*, 1990; *The Trail of the Screaming Teenager*, 1990. Lincoln Lions Band series (all illus. by Emily Arnold McCully)—*Meet the Lincoln Lions Band*, 1992; *Yankee Doodle Drumsticks*, 1992; *The Jingle Bells Jam*, 1992; *The Rootin' Tootin' Bugle Boy*, 1992; *The Red, White and Blue Valentine*, 1993; *The Great Shamrock Disaster*, 1993. Ballet Slipper series (all illus. by Julie Durrell)—*Dance with Rosie*, 1996; *Rosie's Nutcracker Dreams*, 1996; *Starring Rosie*, 1997; *Not-So-Perfect Rosie*, 1997; *A Glass Slipper for Rosie*, 1997; *Rosie's Big City Ballet*, 1998. Friends and Amigos series (all illus. by DyAnne DiSalvo-Ryan)—*Good Dog, Bonita*, 1998; *Adios, Anna*, 1998; *Happy Birthday, Anna, Sorpresa!*, 1998; *Ho, Ho, Benjamin, Feliz Navidad*, 1998; *It's a Fiesta, Benjamin*, 1998; *Say Hola, Sarah*, 1998.

SUGGESTED READING: *Something about the Author*, vol. 160, 2005; Collier, Laurie and Nakamura, eds. *Major Authors and Illustrators for Children and Young Adults*, vol. 3, 1993. Periodicals— "Standing on Water Street," *Teaching PreK-8*, May 2007; Lodge, Sally A., "Tracing Her Roots," *Publishers Weekly*, March 7, 2005; Lodge, Sally A., "The Author as Bookseller: P. R. Giff Opens the Dinosaur's Paw, Fairfield, Conn.," *Publishers Weekly*, April 18, 1994. Online—Giff, Patricia Reilly, "Why I Write for Children":

WEB SITE: www.cbcbooks.org/cbcmagazine/meet/patricia_reilly_giff; www.randomhouse.com/features/patriciareillygiff/

An earlier profile of Patricia Reilly Giff appeared in *Fifth Book of Junior Authors and Illustrators*, 1983.

Courtesy of K. L. Going

K. L. Going

August 21, 1973–

"I was born in Rhinebeck, NY and grew up in a small town in the Hudson Valley region of New York State. My family rented half of a building on the old Borden Estate in Wallkill, NY. The building had once been Mr. Borden's dance hall, and the estate, though no longer in use, included an overgrown greenhouse, a long barn full of theater props, a waterfall in the woods and a mansion on a hill that I always day-dreamed about. It was the perfect place for a writer to grow up.

"I spent all of my elementary years there, and then we moved a short distance away for my middle school and high school years. After graduation, I attended college in St. Davids, Pennsylvania. I was a sociology major, and even though that isn't the most practical degree, I absolutely loved it. Sociology fits my personality because it's the study of people and trends and I'm always interested in the world around me. That interest has led me in many different, often surprising directions.

"One unexpected twist was traveling to New Orleans, Louisiana to do two and a half years of volunteer service with an organization called Mennonite Central Committee. One of the last things people expect from someone who has written a book featuring punk rock is to hear that they spent more than two years working with the Mennonites, who are often best known for the roots they share with the Amish. My years of volunteer service stem directly from an experience I had in sixth grade when I read the book *Christy*. I decided right then that I wanted to do volunteer service and I held onto that dream my whole life. I thought I would work with the Peace Corps, but as the time got closer and I began to look into different organizations, I found I was attracted to what Mennonite Central Committee stands for and the way they build partnerships with the communities they work with. I went to Louisiana and worked as an adult literacy tutor with the YMCA. It was one of the most rewarding experiences of my life.

"When I came home I did lots of odd jobs, mostly related to the travel industry. I worked as a front desk clerk and an airline ticket agent, bailed wells for my Dad who does environmental testing . . . but I was always writing, just for fun, along with whatever else I was doing. The idea for my first book—*Fat Kid*

Rules the World—came to me one morning when I was living in Brooklyn. I rode the subway every day, and the first line of the book just popped into my head and stuck there. 'I'm a sweating fat kid standing just over the yellow line. . . .' I was reading a lot of rock biographies, listening to Nirvana, and exploring vintage punk music at the time, so those ideas gradually intertwined themselves with the book through the character of Curt.

"My second book, *The Liberation of Gabriel King*, draws on my experience of living in the South during my New Orleans years, and growing up in New York in the 1970s. I tried to capture both the flavor of the humid southern summer and the feelings I had as a child—all the joys and fears, and the way my imagination was always working. There is a particular scene where Gabe sits outside with his parents on a hot summer night watching fireflies that reminds me of my own childhood. This is what I love about writing books. You take all the puzzle pieces of your life and rearrange them into new characters, settings, and events, but the emotions remain the same."

ℭ ℭ ℭ

As a child in upstate New York, living with her parents and her older sister April, Kelly L. Going had little intention of becoming a writer, though she did find the act of writing pleasurable. She completed her first book—a fantasy novel—while attending Wallkill High School, and she continued to write throughout her undergraduate years at Eastern College, in Pennsylvania, where she majored in sociology and minored in Biblical studies. She graduated in 1995, and didn't give serious consideration to writing professionally until some years later, while she was working in the publishing industry. She held jobs the manager of an independent bookstore, Merritt Books in Cold Spring, New York, and as an assistant in a literary agency in New York City.

Writing for Going is an exploration of extreme emotions, often pertaining to feelings of alienation. Troy, the main character of her first novel, *Fat Kid Rules the World*, weighs nearly 300 pounds and is an outsider in his high school. As the novel opens, he is contemplating throwing himself onto a subway track in New York City, but at that very moment he meets Curt MacCrae, a homeless teen and aspiring punk-rock musician, who sees in Troy what he cannot see in himself—potential. After a shared meal, Curt offers Troy a chance to play drums in his band, and the two outsiders go on to forge an unbreakable bond. *Fat Kid Rules the World* was named a *School Library Journal* Best Book and to the

"This is what I love about writing books. You take all the puzzle pieces of your life and rearrange them into new characters, settings, and events, but the emotions remain the same."

Courtesy of G.P. Putnam's Sons

Booklist Editor's Choice List as well as the *Bulletin of the Center for Children's Books* Blue Ribbon List. It also received a Michael L. Printz Honor Book designation from the Young Adult Library Services Association of the ALA and was named an ALA Best Book for Young Adults.

For *The Liberation of Gabriel King*, Going chose to depict life in the southern U.S. in the 1970s during a particularly tumultuous summer in the lives of a pair of friends—one black, the other white—as they seek to conquer their respective fears. For Gabriel King this will be no easy task. In addition to being terrified of everything from cows to corpses, he's convinced that fifth grade will bring even more horrors into his life and wants to do all he can to stay in the fourth grade. However, Gabe's best friend, Frita Wilson, a spunky African American girl who seems not to be intimidated by anything, is determined to use her summer vacation to help Gabe overcome his fears. The threat of racial violence, compounded by the presence of the Ku Klux Klan in town, gives the two friends a real and mutual fear that they must surmount together. *The Liberation of Gabriel King* was named a notable book by the International Reading Association.

In *Saint Iggy*, Going examines the directionless life of Iggy Corso, who has just been kicked out of high school. Though this would be a huge problem for most teenagers, Iggy is no stranger to adversity. His mother deserted the family long ago, while his father does little but sit in their public housing apartment and get high, and their social worker has not been heard from since the phone was disconnected. Iggy doesn't get much help from his best friend Mo, who dropped out of law school and spends most of his time smoking pot and thinking about joining the Hare Krishnas. In the week before Christmas, Iggy travels around the city contemplating his life with a wisdom and an insight remarkable for his age.

All three of Going's novels have been released in audio editions. For leisure, in addition to listening to a broad range of music, Going enjoys reading, traveling, working out at the gym, and taking classes on interesting subjects. Now living in

Glen Spey, New York, she writes full-time in her spare bedroom, whenever her two cats, Merry and Pippin, aren't distracting her.

SELECTED WORKS: *Fat Kid Rules the World*, 2003; *The Liberation of Gabriel King*, 2005; "Samuel," in *Rush Hour: Faces*, Vol. III, ed. by Michael Cart, 2005; *Saint Iggy*, 2006; "Poker for the Complete Idiot," in *Full House: Ten Stories about Poker*, ed. by Pete Hautman; *The Garden of Eve*, 2007; *Writing and Selling the YA Novel*, 2008.

SUGGESTED READING: *Something About the Author*, vol. 156, 2005. Online—Interview at, www.teensreadtoo.com/InterviewGoing. html

WEB SITE: www.klgoing.com

"I grew up in the Mojave Desert of Southern California in the 1960s and '70s in a town called Lancaster. I felt like I was out in the middle of nowhere. The world was all sky and desert. My father was a lineman and my mother was a homemaker. My father is Mexican American and my mother is white. I have a younger brother close to my age named David.

"My favorite thing about the desert was the sunset. In general, there wasn't a lot of vibrant color. Things were very beige and muted. But nearly every evening, the sky at the end of our street looked like smeared fuchsias—all reds, pinks, purples and oranges. I became fixated on what I used to call Hot Pink. It was my personal color. The sky presented it to me every night in a passionate way that I took very personally.

"My love of Hot Pink followed my love of drawing. I tell this story often to grown-ups and kids when I speak about my work. As a little kid, my favorite parts of coloring books, or any book for that matter, were the very first and very last pages—the empty ones. I would draw in my big round Chicana face every time. I believe in some way I knew that I belonged in those books, that my face should be reflected back at me from those pages. Growing up, while I did come in contact with a great many books,

Courtesy of Maya Gonzalez

Maya Christina Gonzalez

January 24, 1964–

I never saw myself in any of them. Not only did I not see myself, I was never struck by the art or the characters in them, the way I was struck by the sunset. The books felt valuable because I loved learning, but they felt far away.

"I longed for reflections like the sunset. I looked for myself, for my face, out there in the world around me. When I grew up, I retained a feeling that the literature and media that a child reads and looks at should be a real reflection of her life, inside and outside. This provides a sense of being embedded in reality, a sense of belonging.

"I believe that belonging is one of the subtexts that can be found in all of my books in some way. It's in the way that I paint, the way I develop the characters, the environments I create, even the intention with which I paint. At each step in the process, I hold my own heart as a child in my awareness, as I hold the collective heart of the children I paint for. I focus on a sense of belonging, of being reflected, on the reality of being a child in this world. I imagine my father at five years old as he entered a school where only English was spoken. He spoke only Spanish. Although half of my family spoke primarily Spanish at family events, I was not taught Spanish growing up. The lesson of my father and much of our culture at that time was of assimilation. On one level, I am painting these books for the little boy my father used to be and hoping that our world is changing, expanding its perceptions.

> "I focus on a sense of belonging, of being reflected, on the reality of being a child in this world."

"I have come to understand that I am primarily an emotional and spiritual painter. I do not consider myself an illustrator and have been lucky enough to work under circumstances and with publishers who are interested in that about me. When I paint a book, I'm constantly thinking of a child in the classroom or library grazing the book spines with her fingers, her eyes searching for something that catches them like sunsets caught mine.

"Painting books also provides me with a way to spread some of my personal propaganda, which can be summed up in my three rules:

1. Everyone is an artist.
2. There is never a right or wrong way to make art, and
3. Art is always an act of courage.

"When I work with kids, I believe it's important to empower them with a form of expression we are fast losing in our culture. Art. Sometimes there are not words to say what we are experiencing. Art is the powerful tool we need."

CB CB CB

Maya Christina Gonzalez never intended to be an artist. She was working on a program in writing at the University of Oregon when she decided to take an art history class. After that, art took over her life and has led her to a stellar career as a painter and an illustrator of children's books with her own unique vision.

When Gonzalez and her family moved from California to Oregon, the move proved to be a culture shock. Living in a rural area where the neighbors thought of her as "exotic," Gonzalez was inspired to express herself first as a writer, and later as an artist. From 1988 to 1994, she owned her own jewelry business, and in 1989, she taught a program called "Fearless Art" at the University of Oregon and "Fearless Art for Kids" at the Maude Kernes Art Center in Eugene, Oregon.

After moving back to California, she taught in the Children's Book Press Outreach Program in the San Francisco Bay area and Los Angeles schools from 1996 to 2003. She participated in the WritersCorp teacher-training program in San Francisco from 1996 to 2001, and has been named an honoree of the "Hispanic Americans Profiles of Excellence" by the San Francisco Board of Supervisors. She has been featured on the cover of *Contemporary Chicana and Chicano Art*, a highly respected two-volume reference source used in universities and museums.

Her entry into the world of children's books began with *Prietita and the Ghost Woman / Prietita y la Llorona*, a bilingual story by Gloria E. Anzaldúa, which appeared on the Commended list for the Américas Award. Gonzalez next collaborated with Francisco X. Alarcón on a bilingual series of poetry books about the four seasons. In *Laughing Tomatoes*, which was a *Riverbank Review* Children's Book of Distinction finalist and won a Pura Belpré Honor Award, the poems celebrate the spring season. In the pictures Gonzalez invites readers to experience spring with a lively cast of characters including a spirited grandmother, vivacious children, and teasing, playful pets. Her lighthearted illustrations perfectly capture the nature of a Mexican summer in *From the Bellybutton of the Moon*, which was a Cooperative Children's Book Center Choice title. Her animated images bring the fall season and the people of Los Angeles to life in *Angels Ride Bikes*, which was named a Notable Book for a Global Society and a Parent's Choice Recommended Picture Book. *Iguanas in the Snow*, the final volume in the series, features a city where people are bridges to each other as they frolic through colorful pages. This title was a 2002 Pura Belpré Honor Book.

Four of Gonzalez's books have appeared on the Américas Award Commended lists: *Prietita and the Ghost Woman, From*

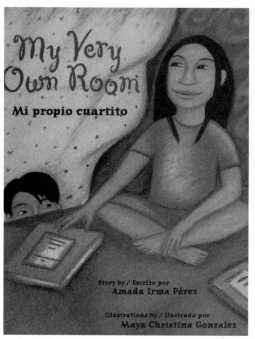

Story by / Escrito por
Amada Irma Pérez

Illustrations by / Ilustrado por
Maya Christina Gonzalez

Courtesy of Children's Book Press

the *Bellybutton of the Moon*, *Angels Ride Bikes*, and *My Diary from Here to There*. *My Very Own Room* received an Américas Award Honorable Mention.

Gonzalez's bright and lively acrylic paintings are always strong, vigorous, and colorful. In *Fiesta Femenina*, she illustrated a sophisticated collection of folklore stories about Mexican women, and the book won an Aesop Prize as well as being named a *Booklist* Editors' Choice, a Notable Social Studies Trade Book, and a Parents' Choice Recommended title. *Laughing Tomatoes* and *Angels Ride Bikes* have both won the National Parenting Publications Gold Medal Award. *From the Bellybutton of the Moon* was a Skipping Stones Honor Book, and *My Very Own Room* won the Skipping Stones Book Award. *My Very Own Room* also won the Tomás Rivera Children's Book Award.

From 2003 to 2005 Gonzalez suffered health problems related to lead poisoning, but she has since recovered and continues participating in shows and exhibits of her art as well as working on her books. In 2008 the first book she has both written and illustrated—*My Colors, My World / Mis colores, mi mundo*—was presented a Pura Belpré Honor Award. Gonzalez has called painting her healer, her teacher, and her guide. She is now teaching again, working primarily with educators. She lives in San Francisco with her young daughter, Zai Velvet.

SELECTED WORKS ILLUSTRATED: *Prietita and the Ghost Woman/ Prietita Y la Llorona*, by Gloria E. Anzaldúa, 1996; *Laughing Tomatoes and Other Spring Poems / Jitomates Risueños y otros poemas de primavera*, by Francisco X. Alarcón, 1997; *The Crying Mountain: A Mexican Legend*, by Patricia Almada, 1997; *Face to the Sky*, by Alba Ambert, 1999; *From the Bellybutton of the Moon and other Summer Poems / Del Ombligo de la Luna y otros poemas de verano*, by Francisco X. Alarcón, 1999; *Angels Ride Bikes and Other Fall Poems / Los Ángeles Andan en Bicicleta y otros poemas de otoño*, by Francisco X. Alarcón, 1999; *My Very Own Room / Mi Propio Cuartito*, by Amada Irma Pérez, 2000; *Fiesta Femenina: Celebrating Women in Mexican Folktales*, retold by Mary-Joan Gerson, 2001; *Iguanas in the Snow and other Winter Poems / Iguanas en la Nieve y otros poemas de invierno*, by Francisco X. Alarcón, 2001; *My Diary from Here to There / Mi diario de aquí hasta allá*, by Amada Irma Pérez, 2002; *Nana's Big Surprise / Nana, Que Sorpresa!*, by Amada Irma Pérez, 2007.

SELECTED WORKS WRITTEN AND ILLUSTRATED: *My Colors, My World / Mis colores, mi mundo*, 2007.

SUGGESTED READING: Keller, Gary D., *Contemporary Chicana and Chicano Art: Artists, Work, Culture, and Education*, 2002; *Something About the Author*, vol. 115, 2000; Rohmer, Harriet, ed., *Honoring Our Ancestors: Stories and Portraits by 14 Artists*, 1999; Rohmer, Harriet, ed., *Just Like Me: Stories and Self Portraits by 14 Artists*, 1997.

WEB SITE: www.mayagonzalez.com

Throughout her childhood and adolescence Mary GrandPré progressed from drawing Disney characters to Salvador Dalí-like paintings to black-and-white drawings she copied from encyclopedias. Born in South Dakota, she moved to Minnesota when she was less than a year old. Though she had displayed artistic tendencies since age five, she did she consider attending art school until she was in her twenties. A graduate of the Minneapolis College of Art and Design, GrandPré has worked on greeting cards, advertisements, editorial illustrations, book covers, fine-art paintings, and children's books. Over time she has developed an evocative and distinctive style she calls "soft geometry," encompassing a light, whimsical approach with pastels. She does a wide range of work for advertising agencies, magazines, corporate clients, and publishers, but in the late 1990s she found herself caught up in a publishing phenomenon as the American illustrator for the remarkably successful Harry Potter books by J. K. Rowling.

GrandPré was drawn to the field of children's books for the free range they gave her imagination. The first picture book she illustrated was *Chin Yu Min and the Ginger Cat*, a heartwarming story written by Jennifer Armstrong. Set in China, the tale describes the ways in which a widow learns happiness and humility

Courtesy of Scholastic, Inc.

Mary GrandPré

(GRAN-pray)
February 13,
1954–

from a cat she befriends after her husband dies. The paintings in this ALA Notable Children's Book resemble silk material and have a surreal, expressionistic quality. The story was later made into a play, commissioned by the Arts in Education Institute of Western New York for its 2005–2006 season. It now seems almost prophetic that this was the illustrator's first children's picture book since, over a decade after its publication, GrandPré and her husband adopted a baby girl from China. By that time she had illustrated four of the *Harry Potter* titles. Wanting to do something special for Chinese children, she donated four of her original working sketches from the *Harry Potter* books to an auction benefiting a Chinese orphanage.

GrandPré's flair for unusual perspectives is apparent in another of her early books, Christopher L. King's *The Vegetables Go to Bed*, which features purplish blue skies and amusingly anthropomorphic vegetables in a wry twist on goodnight stories for young children. In Dominick Vittorini's *The Thread of Life*, a collection of classic Italian fairy tales, her expressive, angular style vividly evokes the Italian setting and captures the adventure, humor, and romance in each of the tales. An original contemporary creation story by Marguerite W. Davol, *Batwings and the Curtain of Night*, is enhanced by GrandPré's lush pastel illustrations that hold the reader's attention with their interesting shifts of light and strikingly unusual colors.

After demonstrating her skill in these early picture books, GrandPré was approached to create the jacket art and provide spot illustrations for each chapter heading in the American edition of a new British fantasy series about a boy wizard. Arthur A. Levine, the U.S. publisher and editor of the *Harry Potter* series, and David Saylor, art director at Scholastic Press, looked through many samples of artists' work to find the right illustrator for the first volume of this now familiar and enormously popular series. Coming upon Mary GrandPré's work, they both decided on the spot that she had just the right magical quality they were looking for in an artist.

GrandPré found that she could create the cover art and black-and-white chapter headings in the *Harry Potter* volumes by carefully reading each manuscript. The strong characterizations and vivid descriptions in J. K. Rowling's writing provided the artist with rich material from which to fashion her visual interpretations. When she received the manuscripts (before anyone else), she was bound to secrecy and could never divulge any plot details, not even to her family. She brought her own special interpretation to the books, always grounded by Rowling's descriptive writing.

Coming upon Mary Grand-Pré's work, they both decided on the spot that she had just the right magical quality they were looking for in an artist.

TONI BUZZEO ❖ *illustrated by* MARY GRANDPRÉ

Courtesy of Dial Books for Young Readers, Penguin Group USA

When she created Harry Potter's first portrait, there was no time to find a model, so she sketched from a mirror and transformed her own features into young Harry's. Hagrid's look was inspired by her dog, Chopper, who is part Saint Bernard and very protective of her. Choosing just the right way to illustrate each chapter heading, rendered in charcoal, was a challenge for the artist, always trying to find an image that would provide interest without giving anything away.

Mary GrandPré has continued to illustrate picture books as well, with great success. Deborah Blumenthal's *Aunt Claire's Yellow Beehive Hair* is about a girl and her grandmother gathering memorabilia. For Toni Buzzeo's *The Sea Chest*, about a baby in a chest washed up on shore and raised with the daughter of a lighthouse family, GrandPré's oil paintings draw the reader deeply into the story, and her close-up portrait of the child when she is first found is especially poignant. With a muted sunrise on the endpapers and a sunset on the back cover, *The Sea Chest* is an enchanting book that was cited as a Bank Street College Best Children's Book of the Year, and also won the Children's Crown

Gallery Award winner and a Lupine Award Honor Book in the author's home state of Maine.

In Jennifer Armstrong's allegorical *Pockets,* a broken-hearted seamstress creates clothes for people who want only plain clothes. When she embroiders the insides of the pockets with colorful scenes of faraway places, she gives the villagers a new lease on life, as well as healing her own heart. GrandPré's undulating, expressionistic artwork balances the somber tones of the villagers' lives with the brilliant colors they are inspired to imagine. In *The House of Wisdom* by Florence Parry Heide and Judith Heide Gilliland, about a boy in ninth-century Baghdad who is transformed into a scholar, GrandPré's dreamy pastels in Islamic patterns and radiant colors provide an authentic context. This title was cited as a Notable Social Studies Trade Book for Young People.

With her husband, Tom Casmer, GrandPré wrote and illustrated *Henry and Pawl and the Round Yellow Ball,* about a young artist who retrieves his dog's lost ball with the help of his new artistic skills. And for a new edition of poems by Barbara Juster Esbensen, *Swing Around the Sun,* GrandPré joined with three other distinguished artists to illustrate the poet's rhymes about the four seasons. GrandPré's artistic endeavors have also included work in the film industry; she developed scenery for Dreamworks studio's animated movie *Antz* and for Disney's *Ice Age.* Her work can be found in the permanent collection of the Society for Illustrators as part of the "Women Illustrators, Past and Present" exhibit.

After many years residing in Minnesota, the artist currently lives in Sarasota, Florida, with her husband, three stepchildren, and their adopted daughter.

SELECTED WORKS ILLUSTRATED: *Chin Yu Min and the Ginger Cat,* by Jennifer Armstrong, 1993; *The Vegetables Go to Bed,* by Christopher L. King, 1994; *A Creepy Company,* by Joan Aiken, 1995; *Give Yourself a Fright,* by Joan Aiken, 1995; *The Thread of Life: Twelve Old Italian Tales,* by Dominick Vittorini, 1995; *Batwings and the Curtain of Night,* by Marguerite W. Davol, 1997; *Pockets,* by Jennifer Armstrong, 1998; *The House of Wisdom,* by Florence Parry Heide and Judith Heide Gilliland, 1999; *The Purple Snerd,* by Rozanne Lanczak Williams, 2000; *Aunt Claire's Yellow Beehive Hair,* by Deborah Blumenthal, 2001; *Sea Chest,* by Toni Buzzeo, 2002; *Plum,* by Tony Mitton, 2003; *Swing Around the Sun,* by Barbara Juster Esbensen, as contributor, 2003; *Henry and Pawl and the Round Yellow Ball,* written and illus. with Tom

Casmer, 2005; *Sweep Dreams*, by Nancy Willard, 2005; *Lucia and the Light*, by Phyllis Root, 2006. Harry Potter series, all by J. K. Rowling—*Harry Potter and the Sorcerer's Stone*, 1998; *Harry Potter and the Chamber of Secrets*, 1999; *Harry Potter and the Prisoner of Azkaban*, 1999; *Harry Potter and the Goblet of Fire*, 2000; *Harry Potter and the Order of the Phoenix*, 2003; *Harry Potter and the Half-Blood Prince*, 2005; *Harry Potter and the Deathly Hallows*, 2007.

SUGGESTED READING: *Biography for Beginners*, vol. 2, Fall 2003. Periodicals—Heller, Steven, "Mary GrandPré, Harry Potter Illustrator," *Print Magazine*, November/December 2000; "Who's That Girl?" *American Girl*, July/August 2000; Jarvis, John, "Mary GrandPré," *Communication Arts*, January/February 2000. Online—Kurowski, Trish Higgins, "From Fine Arts to Finger Paints: A Chinese Child Casts a Spell on Harry Potter Illustrator," *The Red Thread Connection*, October/November 2006, at www.chinesechildren.org/Branches/Doc/FLNL1006.pdf; Morreale, Marie, "Meet the Illustrator of Harry Potter," Scholastic web site, at www.content.scholastic.com/browse/article.jsp?id=5825

WEB SITE: www.marygrandpre.com

Dan Gutman

October 19, 1955–

"I was born in New York City but my family moved to Newark, New Jersey when I was about a year old and that's were my sister Lucy and I grew up. Lucy is now a librarian in Medford, Oregon. My father worked in advertising but he and my mother split up when I was twelve. He dropped me off at my Little League game one Saturday, and I didn't see him again for 10 years. He abandoned my family. Some people might notice in a number of my books the father is absent or magically reappears in the last chapter, and I think that probably has something to do with my own background. I know a lot of kids out there come from families whose parents are divorced. It's not the end of the world. You can overcome obstacles like that.

"I went to Rutgers University and got a degree in psychology, but after spending a few unhappy years in graduate school, I decided that psychology wasn't for me either. I decided what I really wanted to do was write humor, like Art Buchwald and Erma Bombeck. So in 1980, I did what I thought writers were supposed to do—I moved to New York City.

"My writing career started with me cranking out 'humorous essays,' some of which got published in the *Advance*, a Staten

Island newspaper. I still have the first check I ever received for my writing. It was for $15, and now it's on the wall over my desk. I also tried writing magazine articles and a few screenplays, but like a lot of writers just starting out, I received a lot of rejection letters. It was frustrating, but I was determined and persistent. I felt I had some ability as a writer. I just didn't know where to direct it.

"In the early 1980s, I fell into the computer magazine business. I became the co-editor of *Electronic Fun* magazine; then in 1982, during the Pac-Man craze, I started a video games magazine called *Video Games Player*. The magazine sold pretty well, and two years later it was renamed *Computer Games*.

"Surprisingly, I became known as a 'computer expert.' This was remarkable to me, because I didn't feel I knew very much about computers. But somewhere along the way, I must have managed to pick up some computer knowledge because not only did my articles on the subject get published, I began writing a syndicated newspaper column that appeared in papers like the *Philadelphia Inquirer* and the *Miami Herald*.

"When *Computer Games* went out of business in 1985, I became a full-time freelance writer. Eventually, my writing

Photo by Carol Van Hook

appeared in *Esquire*, *Newsweek*, *Science Digest*, *Writer's Digest*, *Success*, *Psychology Today*, *New Woman*, *USA Today*, and the *Village Voice*. I was gaining confidence, but I still hadn't found the type of writing I really wanted to do. In 1987, I decided to try writing about something I always loved— sports. I sold an article to *Discover* magazine, which led to my first adult baseball book, *It Ain't Cheatin' If You Don't Get Caught*. It sold pretty well, and I wrote several more adult baseball books. None of them were huge sellers, but it was fun writing them.

"Then in 1990, my son, Sam, was born and I started reading a lot of children's books for the first time since I was a kid, and I decided to try writing for children myself. I wrote a few nonfiction sports books; then in 1994, I decided to try fiction. Surprisingly, I sold the first novel I wrote, and kids loved it. Finally, after fifteen years, I figured out what my career should be—writing fiction for kids. For the first time, I felt I was doing something that I was really good at, something that was fun, creatively rewarding, and appreciated by an audience. I love when kids tell me my books make them laugh, because writing humor was what I wanted to do when I got started back in 1980! It just took awhile to find an audience who had the same kind of sense of humor that I do."

C3 C3 C3

Dan Gutman is a man of contradictions. Although known for writing humorous middle-grade novels, he hated to read until he was in fourth grade, and then he only read because he loved sports and wanted to find out more about the subject. As a child, he was a right fielder for a Little League baseball team in Newark, New Jersey, but he was never very good at sports. He received his B.A. in 1977 and his M.A. in 1979 and became a writer, but he never took a writing class.

What Gutman likes about writing is not having a boss and working in his backyard, where he can take his laptop on nice days. He works fast and hard, usually only taking a month for research and plotting and then another couple of months for writing and revision. Gutman's books have received numerous state awards and been nominated for children's choice awards all over the United States, including Florida, Georgia, Illinois, Indiana, Iowa, Maryland, Massachusetts, Minnesota, Nebraska, Nevada, North Carolina, Oklahoma, Pennsylvania, South Carolina, Tennessee, Texas, Virginia and Washington.

After writing several nonfiction books on baseball, gymnastics, and ice-skating, Gutman found himself speculating about politics. When Bob Dole ran for president in 1996 and people considered he might be too old for the job, Gutman wondered who would be considered too young. He wrote two books on the subject and named the hero after his eye doctor. *The Kid Who Ran for President*, which was a Junior Library Guild selection, is now used in some elementary schools, along with *The Kid Who Became President*, to teach about government.

Baseball, time travel, and magic converged in Gutman's concept for *Honus & Me*, in which a boy discovers a baseball card can transport him back to 1909. There he meets Honus Wagner, the famous baseball player who helps him with his swing and a tough moral dilemma. Rejected by ten publishers before it sold, *Honus & Me* went on to become a New York Public Library Book for the Teen Age, an IRA Teacher's Choice, an ALA

"I love when kids tell me my books make them laugh, because writing humor was what I wanted to do when I got started back in 1980! It just took awhile to find an audience who had the same kind of sense of humor that I do."

Courtesy of Hyperion Books for Children

Popular Paperback for Young Adults, and the winner of the California Young Reader Medal. It was made into a movie called *The Winning Season*.

Finding the themes in *Honus & Me* a winning combination, Gutman has created more volumes in what is now known as the Baseball Card Adventure series. He is able to convey facts about social history in *Jackie & Me*, which won Pennsylvania's Keystone to Reading Award, the Massachusetts Children's Book Award, and Maryland's Black-Eyed Susan Book Award. In this book, the hero goes back to 1947 to meet a young Jackie Robinson and is himself transformed into an African American, introducing some interesting perspectives on race in the mid-20th century. *Babe & Me*, which transports the hero back to the 1932 World Series, won the Arizona Young Readers' Award and the Nutmeg Award in Connecticut.

The Million Dollar Shot, winner of children's choice awards in six states, is about a boy who wins the chance to take a foul shot in the middle of the NBA finals and possibly win a million dollars. Obviously another popular theme, the book has led to others in the series, such as *The Million Dollar Kick* and *The Million Dollar Putt*. Two of Gutman's titles were Nevada Young Readers' Award winners—*Virtually Perfect*, about a computer-simulated twelve-year old, and another time travel tale, *Back in Time: The Edison Mystery*. *The Homework Machine*, about four fifth graders using an invention that does their homework for them, was a *Booklist* Editors' Choice, a *Book Links* Lasting Connection, and among the New York Public Library's 100 Titles for Reading and Sharing.

Combining a fictional approach to an historic event and celebrating the 100th anniversary of the Wright Brothers' flight, Gutman created one of the more vibrant stories to commemorate that milestone in *Race for the Sky: The Kitty Hawk Diaries of Johnny Moore*. Johnny's rustic voice captures the view of local residents of Kitty Hawk, first deriding and slowly coming to appreciate the pioneers of flight. *Race for the Sky* was named a Notable Social Studies Trade Book.

In each of his books, Gutman finds a way to include the name of Herb Dunn, an old college friend of his; for *Jackie Robinson: Young Sports Trailblazer*, one of his nonfiction titles, he even adopted the name as a pseudonym. Whether writing fiction, informational books, or biographies, Gutman is able to engage his readers and keep their interest. A member of the Society for American Baseball Research, Gutman lives in New Jersey with his wife, Nina, a graphic designer, their two children, Sam, born in 1990, and Emma, born in 1995, and their cat, Scrumpy.

SELECTED WORKS WRITTEN AS DAN GUTMAN: *Baseball's Biggest Bloopers: The Games That Got Away*, 1993; *Baseball's Greatest Games*, 1994; *World Series Classics*, 1994; *They Came from Center Field*, 1995; *Taking Flight*, with Vicki Van Meter, 1995; *Ice Skating: From Axels to Zambonis*, 1995 (rev. as *Ice Skating: An Inside Look at the Stars, the Sport, and the Spectacle*, 1998); *Gymnastics*, 1996; *The Kid Who Ran for President*, 1996; *Honus & Me*, 1997; *The Pitcher Who Went Out of His Mind*, 1997; *The Catcher Who Shocked the World*, 1997; *The Green Monster in Left Field*, 1997; *The Shortstop Who Knew Too Much*, 1997; *The Million Dollar Shot*, 1997; *Katy's Gift: An Amish Story*, written with Keith Bowen, 1998; *Virtually Perfect*, 1998; *Joe DiMaggio*, 1999; *Cal Ripken, Jr.: My Story*, adapt. by Dan Gutman, 1999; *Jackie & Me*, 1999; *Funny Boy Meets the Airsick Alien from Andromeda*, illus. by John S. Dykes, 1999; *The Kid Who Became President*, 1999; *Babe & Me*, 2000; *Funny Boy Versus the Bubble-Brained Barbers from the Big Bang*, 2000; *Funny Boy Meets the Chit-Chatting Cheese from Chattanooga*, 2000; *Landslide! A Kid's Guide to the U.S. Elections*, 2000; *Johnny Hangtime*, 2000; *The Million Dollar Kick*, 2001; *The Secret Life of Dr. Demented*, 2001; *Qwerty Stephens, Back in Time: The Edison Mystery*, 2001; *Qwerty Stephens, Stuck in Time with Benjamin Franklin*, 2002 (paperback ed. retitled *Back in Time with Benjamin Franklin*); *Shoeless Joe & Me*, 2002; *Mickey & Me*, 2003; *The Million Dollar Goal*, 2003; *Race for the Sky: The Kitty Hawk Diaries of Johnny Moore*, 2003; *The Million Dollar Strike*, 2004; *The Get*

"Laugh-out-loud."
—*Kirkus Reviews*

Courtesy of Simon & Schuster

Rich Quick Club, 2004; *Babe Ruth and the Ice Cream Mess*, illus. by Elaine Garvin, 2004; *Jackie Robinson and the Big Game*, illus. by Elaine Garvin, 2006; *Satch & Me*, 2006; *The Homework Machine*, 2006; *The Million Dollar Putt*, 2006; My Weird School series (all illustrated by Jim Paillot)— *Miss Daizy Is Crazy!*, 2004; *Ms. Hannah Is Bananas!*, 2004; *Mr. Klutz Is Nuts!*, 2004; *Mrs. Roopy Is Loopy!*, 2004; *Abner & Me*, 2005; *Ms. LaGrange Is Strange!*, 2005; *Mrs. Cooney Is Looney!*, 2005; *Miss Small Is Off The Wall!*, 2005; *Mr. Hynde Is Out Of His Mind!*, 2005; *Miss Lazar Is Bizarre!*, 2005; *Miss Holly Is Too Jolly!*, 2006; *Mrs. Patty Is Batty!*, 2006; *Mr. Docker Is Off His Rocker!*, 2006; *Ms. Todd Is Odd!*, 2006; *Mrs. Kormel Is Not Normal!*, 2006; *Mr. Macky Is Wacky!*, 2006; *Ms. Coco Is Loco!*, 2007; *Miss Suki Is Kooky!*, 2007; *Casey Back at Bat*, illus. by Steve Johnson and Lou Fancher, 2007.

SELECTED WORKS WRITTEN AS HERB DUNN: *Jackie Robinson: Young Sports Trailblazer*, illus. by Meryl Henderson, 1999

SELECTED WORKS WRITTEN FOR ADULTS: *The Greatest Games*, 1985; *I Didn't Know You Could Do That with a Computer!* 1986; *It Ain't Cheatin' If You Don't Get Caught*, 1990; *Baseball Babylon: From the Black Sox to Pete Rose: The Real Stories Behind the Scandals That Rocked the Game*, 1992; *Banana Bats and Ding-Dong Balls: A Century of Unique Baseball Inventions*, 1995; *The Way Baseball Works*, 1996.

SUGGESTED READING: *Something About the Author*, vol. 139, 2003; *My Favorite Writer: Dan Gutman*, by Gillian Richardson, 2005.

WEB SITE: www.dangutman.com

Georg Hallensleben

1958–

"I have always loved to draw and paint. When I was 17, I wrote to the Austrian artist Paul Flora whose work I admired, sending him photocopies of some of my drawings and a letter asking him for technical advice. By way of response, he sent me a charming letter along with a box of pen nibs—the steel part you attach to a pen holder for making ink drawings—and, as a sample of how the pens work, he included in the package one of his own original drawings. He even invited me, shortly afterwards, to live with him, his wife and his daughter in his beautiful house in Innsbruck for a month—and he did this without ever having met me. (I did send him a photo so he would recognize me at the railroad station.)

"The walls of his house were filled with an incredible collection of drawings and paintings. Above the table where we dined was a large and beautiful Steinberg drawing—one of his variations on airmail envelopes—and in the living room there were drawings by Klimt, Kubin, Gustav Thoeny, and some very lovely works of Kurt Moldovan, Markus Vallazza, Sempé, and Ronald Searle. I was amazed at the way Flora and his family lived so naturally amidst all these beautiful works of art. In later years, each time I passed through Innsbruck to see him he would choose some of my own drawings to buy.

"In Paul Flora I had found the most charming patron imaginable. He showed my drawings to Daniel Keel, his Swiss editor, who also ran an art gallery in Zurich. This was Flora's main gallery in Switzerland, and it was Keel who organized my first show, in this gallery in 1977. I was 18 years old. The gallery exhibited drawings of Flora, Sempé, and Tomi Ungerer—all artists I admired a great deal. I was even more impressed that Ungerer himself came to see my show.

"At the time, I was working on drawings and watercolors. Later I moved on to paint with oil on wood or paper, the same technique that I still use today for my illustrations. Then, I was mostly involved with painting interiors and landscapes, as well as many roads. Paul Flora introduced me to the incredible art lover that was Hans van der Grinten. Nobody looked at the piles of drawings and paintings that I had brought along with me with more patience and interest. Subsequently, he organized an exhibition for me in the small museum of Kranenburg where he was curator, and I was very impressed with the intelligence of his choices and the arrangements of the paintings, drawings, and sketches on the walls and showcases.

Courtesy of Georg Hallensleben

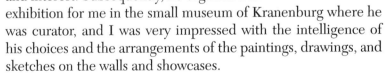

"When I wanted to try creating illustrations for children's books I found an old story I had written and illustrated while at school and made new drawings for it. Then I submitted a 'dummy'—a mock-up of the book—at the International Book Fair in Bologna. Many editors found it a bit too painterly in style, but it did interest Pierre Marchand from Gallimard, the French publishing house; and that turned out well, as it was Gallimard's booth where the books themselves and the spirit behind them had impressed me the most. On the same occasion I met Annebeth Suter, who tried for some time to find me an editor in the U.S. and who introduced me to the German editor Gertraud Middelhauve. Middelhauve gave me excellent advice and even came to see me in Rome, where Leo Lionni, whom she knew well, was showing his paintings in a local gallery.

"Not long afterwards I met the author Kate Banks. Kate had already published several children's books in the U.S. She told me about one story she had put away in a drawer—a story about a little monkey, Baboon, who was discovering the jungle. Well, my own story took place in the jungle too. I showed her my 'dummy' book and the following year we found ourselves together in Bologna at the Gallimard booth, this time with Kate's text for *Baboon* along with some photocopies of my attempts to illustrate the story. I was happy that Anne de Bouchoy and Christine Baker, who were working at Gallimard, remembered me. We left them our project, and when I phoned Gallimard in Paris a little later on with the minimal amount of French I spoke at the time, they told me that they would like to publish the book. That's how my career in children's books began.

"Kate had editing experience, having worked at the publishing house of Farrar, Straus & Giroux in New York, as assistant to the editor Frances Foster. She knew, for example, the appropriate length for a picture book. Even so, we made a mistake that can still be seen in the published book—there was one double page spread missing inside, and *Baboon* starts very slowly with endpapers, a pre-title page and then the title page. Kate had a little Macintosh computer that would be considered pretty basic today, but it still permitted us to print out the text and cut it into pieces to lay over my illustrations and see if it would fit.

"Kate lived at the time with her husband and oldest son in a lovely apartment in Rome. We worked there or in the park of the Villa Ada, where she often went with her son, and where I showed her my sketches and my many variations for each illustration. After *Baboon*, we did other works together, for Gallimard in France and also with Farrar, Straus & Giroux in New York.

"In 1996, Pierre Marchand asked me to illustrate a little series of books on music, after which he ordered text and pictures from Kate and me for another series of little books. These were folded in a particular way, an inventive device that pleased him. At that time, I was coming from Rome, where I was living, and making the long trip to Paris in my white truck, which I had rigged up as a kind of rolling studio. Inside, I had outfitted it with some

> *"Kate lived at the time with her husband and oldest son in a lovely apartment in Rome. We worked there or in the park of the Villa Ada, where she often went with her son, and where I showed her my sketches and my many variations for each illustration."*

homemade furniture, including a folding shower. This greatly impressed Anne Gutman, who was working at Gallimard then and who became my wife and the mother of our two daughters.

"We began working together on the books with Anne doing the layout. People were beginning to abandon working with photocopies, cutting and pasting, and to use a computer, and people saw how much we enjoyed working together. We were very flattered when Pierre Marchand invited us to join him at Hachette, where he had just been hired. We showed him a series of books Anne had written and I had illustrated which would be called 'Gaspard and Lisa.' Thanks in large part to Pierre's involvement, the series was published in many countries. Sadly, Pierre Marchand passed away, much too early, and after his death we went back to Gallimard where his beloved friend Hedwige Pasquet was continuing on in his memory. With her, we began what was to be the adventure of the Penelope series. I continue too, to do books with Kate and Frances Foster and have just returned to painting as well."

ଔ   ଔ   ଔ

Georg Hallensleben was born in Wuppertal, an industrial city on the River Wupper, and grew up in Bonn, the capital of what was then West Germany. An artist from an early age, he found school boring and much preferred roaming the countryside on his bicycle and drawing landscapes and sketches. Soon after finishing school, he moved to Rome and it was there he met Kate Banks, an American writer who had married an Italian. Their first collaboration, *Baboon*, which was also Hallensleben's first children's book, met with great success and was named a Fanfare title by the *Horn Book* in 1998. The following year *And If the Moon Could Talk* was also cited as a *Horn Book* Fanfare title as well as winning the *Boston Globe–Horn Book* Award for picture books. This charming goodnight story, with Banks's lilting text and Hallensleben's softly saturated colors and child-friendly shapes, was also named an ALA Notable Children's Book. The same honor was bestowed on *The Night Worker*, which effectively conveys the excitement of a young boy going to work with his father at a construction site.

Picture books for which Kate Banks writes the text have continued to inspire Hallensleben's work with *The Cat Who Walked Across France*, *Close Your Eyes*, and *Fox*, among others. Seasonal changes, everyday objects, and familiar emotions inform both text and illustration in all of these collaborations.

Courtesy of Farrar, Straus, and Giroux

Their appeal for children and adults alike is strongly rooted in their intuitive understanding of the feelings and objects that are most prevalent in the life of young children.

The books that Hallensleben has created with his wife, Anne Gutman, are equally successful and touch on many aspects of the life of preschoolers. In the series known as The Misadventures of Lisa and Gaspard, the title characters are two little dogs, one white and one black, who act out scenarios familiar to the very young—jealousy of a new sibling, rainy day blues, feelings of inadequacy, making a gift for a teacher, visiting a new city, getting lost. Gutman's minimal texts along with Hallensleben's saturated colors and child-friendly characters are right on target for the audience, appealing to children and parents alike. Georg Hallensleben lives today in Paris with his wife and two young daughters.

SELECTED WORKS ILLUSTRATED: *Baboon*, by Kate Banks, 1997; *Spider, Spider*, by Kate Banks, 1997; *And If the Moon Could Talk*, by Kate Banks, 1998; *The Night Worker*, by Kate Banks, 2000; *Isabelle and the Angel*, by Thierry Magnier, 2000; *A Gift from the Sea*, by Kate Banks, 2001; *Gaspard and Lisa at the Museum*, by Anne Gutman, 2001; *Gaspard in the Hospital*, by Anne Gutman, 2001; *Gaspard on Vacation*, by Anne Gutman, 2001; *Lisa's Air-*

plane Trip, by Anne Gutman, 2001; *Gaspard at the Seashore*, by Anne Gutman, 2002; *Gaspard and Lisa's Christmas Surprise*, by Anne Gutman, 2002; *Close Your Eyes*, by Kate Banks, 2002; *Lisa in New York*, by Anne Gutman, 2002; *Daddy Kisses*, by Anne Gutman, 2003; *Mommy Hugs*, by Anne Gutman, 2003; *Gaspard and Lisa, Friends Forever*, by Anne Gutman, 2003; *Lisa in the Jungle*, by Anne Gutman, 2003; *Gaspard and Lisa's Rainy Day*, by Anne Gutman, 2003; *Lisa's Baby Sister*, by Anne Gutman, 2003; *The Cat Who Walked Across France*, by Kate Banks, 2004; *Gaspard and Lisa's Ready for School Words*, by Anne Gutman, 2004; *Penelope at School*, by Anne Gutman, 2004; *Penelope at the Farm*, by Anne Gutman, 2005; *Penelope in the Winter*, by Anne Gutman, 2005; *The Great Blue House*, by Kate Banks, 2005; *Daddy Cuddles*, by Anne Gutman, 2005; *Penelope Says Good Night*, by Anne Gutman, 2006; *Fox*, by Kate Banks, 2007.

SELECTED WORKS WRITTEN AND ILLUSTRATED: *Pauline*, 1999.

SUGGESTED READING: *Something About the Author*, vol. 173, 2007. Periodicals—"Boston Globe–Horn Book Award Acceptance Speech," *The Horn Book*, January/February 1999.

Emma Walton Hamilton

November 27, 1962–

"I've been a book lover all my life, and as such I've always looked up to writers with a kind of reverence and awe. When I was little, I wrote a lot of short stories, which gave me the chance to live and participate in worlds and lives different from my own. In my stories I could be anyone I wanted to be and direct the results according to my dreams. I lived out a lot of girlhood fantasies that way.

"My mother and I wrote our first story together when I was just six, and my father illustrated it. Mom and Dad were newly divorced and living on opposite coasts. The book was intended as a way for me to feel a continued family connection, and Mom had it bound and kept for me—a gift I cherish to this day. Many years later, after she and I began collaborating professionally as authors, we adapted that story into a picture book called *Simeon's Gift*, so I always tell kids to hold onto their stories. You never know!

"As I moved into adulthood, I became involved with theater and drifted away from writing for a while, but I continued to read a great deal. Maybe because I left college mid-stream to pursue a career in the theater, I tried to make up for my lack of formal education by learning everything I could about the world from books—and that is a practice I still engage in today. I turn to books over and over again for pleasure, for knowledge, for empowerment. My particular fondness for nonfiction—biographies, historical books, motivational or informational—has taught me how to be a better parent, wife, producer, writer, teacher, traveler, homemaker, gardener, organizer . . . I could go on and on.

"Ten years ago, Mom's publisher asked if she would consider writing something for very young children. My son was a year old at the time and, fishing for ideas, Mom asked me what he loved reading about best. Without hesitation I said, 'Trucks!' He was crazy about them—but I was having trouble finding books that were more than just 'the bulldozer goes CRUNCH!'

"'Well, why don't we try to write one?' Mom said. So DUMPY THE DUMP TRUCK, the picture-book series that started our professional collaboration, was born. Since then we've written sixteen books together for children of all ages.

"Writing with my Mom is pretty wonderful. We were initially concerned that it might not work—we can both be fairly opinionated and bossy! But happily, we couldn't be more compatible in our writing. We finish each other's sentences,

Photo by David Rodgers

and somehow know just when to defer to each other. It's a joy to spend creative time together, playing in our make-believe worlds and thinking about all the ways in which we hope to reach out to young readers and make them think, feel or smile.

"Now, whenever I fill out a form that asks for my job information, I put down 'writer'—and just about burst with pride and amazement."

ଓ   ଓ   ଓ

Born in London, England, Emma Walton Hamilton soon moved with her parents—singer, actress, and author Julie Andrews and stage and film designer Tony Walton—to the United States, which has been her primary residence ever since. Because of her parents' busy careers, Emma attended schools in

California, London, Switzerland, and New York before going to college at Brown University.

As an actress and director, Emma worked in theater, film, and television for about a decade before turning her attention towards production, education, and writing. She served as a faculty member at the Ensemble Studio Theatre Institute in New York City, co-teaching acting classes with her husband, Stephen Hamilton. The pair also headed the Ensemble's annual summer conference in Tannersville, New York.

In 1991, in partnership with Sybil Christopher, Emma and Steve co-founded the Bay Street Theatre in Sag Harbor, New York, which was called "one of the pre-eminent regional theatres in the country" by the CBS *Sunday Morning* show. Emma served as Bay Street Theatre's Co-Artistic Director for 13 years before she chose to focus her energies on creating and managing the Theatre's educational and young audience programs. In her role as Director of Education and Programming for Young Audiences for the Bay Street Theatre, she helps bring theatrical performances to young people on Long Island and in New York City. In addition to managing the Young Playwrights Program (the flagship of Bay Street's educational outreach), Emma administers Bay Street's internship program for serious students of technical theater and their Continuing Classes courses for adults and children in acting, singing, and playwriting. She is also responsible for creating, booking, and managing Kidstreet, the Theatre's highly acclaimed, year-round variety performance series for young audiences.

In 2000 Emma and her mother co-authored their first children's book, *Dumpy the Dump Truck*, which was illustrated by Emma's father. Emma and her mother have subsequently co-written many children's books, including more Dumpy picture books, board books, and early readers, an original fable called *Simeon's Gift*, the medieval novel *Dragon: Hound of Honor*, and two bestsellers: *The Great American Mousical* and *Thanks to You: Wisdom from Mother and Child*, which topped the *New York Times* bestseller list.

In 2001 Emma took on the additional role of editorial director for the newly founded Julie Andrews Collection imprint of HarperCollins Publishers. The Collection's mission states that it "encompasses quality books for young readers of all ages that nurture the imagination and celebrate a sense of wonder while embracing themes of integrity, creativity, and the gifts of nature and the arts." In addition to books written by Emma and Julie, it includes new works by established and emerging authors; as of

"I turn to books over and over again for pleasure, for knowledge, for empowerment."

this writing, the imprint has published over two-dozen children's books, a number of which have achieved bestseller status. In early 2008 the Julie Andrews Collection moved to Little, Brown Books for Young Readers.

Emma has co-written lyrics for several songs, including "The Show Must Go On" recorded by Julie Andrews for *The Great American Mousical* webgame, and "On My Way," a celebration of growing up, co-written and recorded by the acclaimed family band, Laughing Pizza. Recently, Emma and her mother completed a stage adaptation of *Simeon's Gift*, which is being developed for a national symphonic tour. They are also working with Goodspeed Musicals in East Haddam, Connecticut, on a theatrical adaptation of *The Great American Mousical*, as well as developing a television program based on the Dumpy series.

Julie Andrews Edwards and Emma Walton Hamilton
Illustrated by Gennady Spirin
Courtesy of the Julie Andrews Collection

Emma is a member of the Author's Guild, the Dramatists' Guild, the Society of Children's Book Writers and Illustrators, the International Reading Association, SAG, AEA, AFTRA, and ASCAP. She has served on the theater panel for the New York State Council on the Arts, and as a trustee for the Morriss Center School in Bridgehampton, New York. Though she no longer performs on stage, Emma enjoys doing voiceover work, and has provided voicing for radio and television spots, industrial pieces, and various elements at Bay Street Theatre. When time permits, she also works as a freelance editor and writer. An ongoing interest of hers is creating partnerships between literacy and the arts and encouraging children's reading and creativity. Her book for parents, *Raising Bookworms*, is directed to all the adults who have asked her how to encourage reading in their own children. Emma Walton Hamilton lives in Sag Harbor, New York, with her husband, producer and actor Steve Hamilton, and their two children, Sam and Hope.

SELECTED WORKS FOR YOUNG READERS (all co-authored with Julie Andrews Edwards): *Dumpy the Dump Truck*, illus. by Tony Walton, 2000; *Dumpy at School*, illus. by Tony Walton, 2000; *Dumpy's Friends on the Farm*, illus. by Tony Walton, 2001; *Dumpy Saves Christmas*, illus. by Tony Walton, 2001; *Dumpy and the Big Storm*, illus. by Tony Walton, 2002; *Simeon's Gift*, illus. by Gennady Spirin, 2003; *Dumpy and the Firefighters*, illus. by Tony Walton, 2003; *Dumpy to the Rescue!*, illus. by Tony Walton, 2004; *Dumpy's Apple Shop*, illus. by Tony Walton, 2004; *Dumpy's Happy Holiday*, illus. by Tony Walton, 2005; *Dumpy's Extra-Busy Day*, illus. by Tony Walton, 2006; *Dumpy's Valentine*, illus. by Tony Walton, 2006; *Thanks to You: Wisdom from Mother & Child*, 2007; *The Great American Mousical*, illus. by Tony Walton, 2007.

SELECTED WORKS FOR ADULTS: *Raising Bookworms: Getting Kids Reading for Pleasure and Empowerment*, 2008.

SUGGESTED READING: *Something About the Author*, vol. 177, 2007.

WEB SITES: www.emmawaltonhamilton.com
www.julieandrewscollection.com

A profile of Julie Andrews Edwards also appears in this volume.

Born in Melbourne, Australia, Sonya Hartnett grew up in the suburb of Box Hill and was educated at the Royal Melbourne Institute of Technology. The second oldest in a family of six children, she has described herself as being "shy and fairly withdrawn" as a child. Watching and listening to the world around her helped develop her powers of observation. As a teenager she read books by S. E. Hinton, Paul Zindel, and Robert Cormier. She has often referred to Cormier's *After the First Death* as a book that showed her that writing for teens could be challenging and daring for both writer and reader. Writing was her outlet, and by the time she received her B.A. degree in 1988, she had already published two novels. *Trouble All the Way*, her first, came out when she was 15, and *Sparkle and Nightflower* appeared two years later.

Courtesy of Candlewick Press

Sonya Hartnett

March 23, 1968–

While her books are generally considered to be for a teenage audience, Hartnett writes with great psychological depth and complexity, so that her novels blur the lines between adult and young adult fiction. Each of her books is unique in form and content. Her narrative voice is adapted to suit the subject matter and characterization for every new story. Not an author who avoids hardship, traumatic experience, anger, and tragedy in the lives of her characters, she writes with an uncompromising intensity and integrity.

Hartnett's novels have won many awards in her native country. She received a 1992 Writer's Fellowship for *Wilful Blue*, a poignant story of two young artists who react very differently to new circumstances. The pain and guilt of those who survive a friend's suicide is deftly explored, and this book received the Ena Noël Award from the Australian section of the International Board on Books for Young People (IBBY), an award specified for a new and promising Australian writer or illustrator. *Sleeping Dogs,* her next novel, dealt with the difficult subject of incest in a reclusive family living in a remote area of the Australian outback. It won the inaugural Kathleen Mitchell Award in 1996, a prize intended to encourage young Australian writers under the age of 30, and the Victorian Premier's Literary Award, among other honors. For the brooding inevitability of the plot and the dysfunctional family dynamics, many critics compared *Sleeping Dogs* to the works of William Faulkner and Tennessee Williams.

Courtesy of Candlewick Press

Thursday's Child is an intriguing story set during the era of the 1930s. Winner of the Aurealis Award for best novel in the young adult division, the story shimmers on the edge of the science fiction, fantasy, and horror genre that the award honors, though a comparison to the type of "magical realism" written by David Almond may be more accurate. Harper Flute's younger brother appears to be living underneath the family's house in a series of dugouts and tunnels, eventually becoming a feral boy completely outside the social context of the world around him. Told from Harper's perspective, the story focuses on her struggle to endure and make meaning of her own life in spite of the tragedy of her brother's withdrawal and the indifference of her family. When it was published in England, *Thursday's Child* won the Guardian Children's Fiction prize.

An avowed animal lover, Hartnett wrote *Forest* from the point of view of a house cat who is dumped in the wilderness with two kittens and struggles to find his way home. Threatened by feral cats that fiercely guard their territory, Kian is challenged constantly in his unswerving determination. Hartnett's ability to communicate the cat's sensations and her evocative rendering of the landscape earned *Forest* the Children's Book Council of Australia's Book of the Year award in the older readers category. *Stripes of the Sidestep Wolf*, chosen as an ALA Best Book for Young Adults in 2006, features a young man faced with a moral dilemma. Tied to his roots in a depressed rural town, but desperate to establish his independence, Satchel spots a strange wolf-like creature that may be an animal considered extinct. He agonizes over leaving the animal in peace with its cub or exploiting its existence for the benefit of his family, his town, and himself.

Sonya Hartnett's themes of individual growth, power and dependence, grace under pressure, and the interrelationships between people offer insights to the reader of each of her novels. She is fascinated by strange stories that appear in newspapers. One of these was a real case of missing children in 1960s Australia. In *Of a Boy*, which won the Commonwealth Writers Prize, three children disappear on their way to an ice cream shop, and a lonely, fearful boy speculates on their fate. Published in the United States under the title *What the Birds See*, this haunting story explores the dark depths of fear and loneliness. Another stark psychological drama that features a lonely, damaged child, *Surrender*, won a Michael L. Printz honor book award when it was published in the United States.

Though her work has been called "dark," Sonya Hartnett prefers to think of it as "simply clear-eyed."

Writing for a younger audience in *The Silver Donkey*, Hartnett chose the setting of western France during World War I. Two girls aid a traumatized soldier who has deserted his regiment; in turn he tells them stories about the silver donkey charm he carries in his pocket. The plot was inspired by a little silver donkey statue the author found in a country antique store and kept on her desk while she was writing the story. *The Silver Donkey* won the Australian Children's Book of the Year award for younger readers.

Sonya Hartnett's novels have been translated into a number of languages, including Danish, German, Swedish, Italian, and Chinese. In 2008 she received the Astrid Lindgren Memorial Award, one of the most prestigious international children's book awards. In making the announcement, the Swedish Arts Council stated: "Astrid Lindgren's works are permeated by an empathy with children living under difficult circumstances. Hartnett's original and provocative writings take this subject matter into a new era."

Though her work has been called "dark," Sonya Hartnett prefers to think of it as "simply clear-eyed." Like Robert Cormier before her, Sonya Hartnett leads a fairly ordinary life even though she writes about extraordinarily difficult subjects. She has described herself as cheery and loving animals, gardening, and wild weather. She lives in Melbourne, Australia.

SELECTED WORKS (Dates are for first Australian publication; U.S. dates are in parentheses): *Trouble All the Way*, 1984; *Sparkle and Nightflower*, 1986; *The Glass House*, 1990; *Wilful Blue*, 1994; *Sleeping Dogs*, 1995; *The Devil Latch*, 1996; *Black Foxes*, 1996; *Princes*, 1997 (1998); *All My Dangerous Friends*, 1998; *There Must Be Lions: Stories about Mental Illness*, with Nick Earls and Heide Seaman, 1998; *Stripes of the Sidestep Wolf*, 1999 (2005); *Thursday's Child*, 2000 (2002); *Forest*, 2001 (2001); *Of a Boy*, 2002 (U.S. title: *What the Birds See*, 2003); *The Silver Donkey*, illus. by Anne Spudvilas, 2004 (U.S. ed. illus. by Don Powers, 2006); *Surrender*, 2005 (2006); *The Ghost's Child*, 2008 (2008).

SUGGESTED READING: *Something About the Author*, vol. 176, 2007. Online—Interview with Julie Danielson, "Seven Impossible Things Before Breakfast #31: A Blog About Books," June 19, 2007, at www.blaine.org/sevenimpossiblethings/?p=701

WEB SITE: www.candlewick.com/authill/asp

Pete Hautman

September 29, 1952–

"Back in 1995 I was about as interested in writing for teens as I was in learning to play the accordion. I had a successful career as an adult novelist and I had little interest in revisiting my adolescence. But things change.

"For some years I had been toying with an idea based on a recurring childhood dream in which I discovered a small door at the back of a closet in my grandparents' home. The door would lead to forgotten rooms and spaces. I might find myself in a dusty, dead, forgotten world. Once in a while I would encounter old friends, lost toys, or dead pets come back to life. Often the dreams were pleasant, but sometimes I would wake up with my heart hammering.

"I began work on a story about a man who passes through this dream door and finds himself in another reality. But for some reason, my story wasn't working. I kept returning to the dream, trying to recapture some of its magic. Finally, it hit me that the magic I was seeking was magic seen through adolescent eyes. So I changed my protagonist from a 30-year-old man to a 15-year-old boy.

"The story, *Mr. Was*, was about a boy who is thrust into quasi-adulthood by the sudden and brutal death of his mother. It was completely unlike anything I had ever written. *Mr. Was* was not written for children. Or for teenagers. Or for adults. It was written for the kid I once was: a boy caught between the *Hardy Boys* and *The Brothers Karamazov*. I had no plans to write another YA book. But shortly after *Mr. Was* was published, I began work on the story of a poker player consumed by his own passion—a realistic, gritty inside look at a man who could not save himself from his addiction because his habit produced a positive cash flow.

"After writing and discarding several drafts, it occurred to me to make my protagonist about thirty years younger. Once again, the strategy worked. I soon found myself the author of a second YA novel, *No Limit*. Then I found myself thinking a lot about teen books. How does one define the YA novel? *Mr. Was* and *No Limit*, on the surface, seemed about as similar as King Kong and asparagus. *Mr. Was* is a science fiction/mystery/romance/adventure that spans six decades of its protagonist's life. *No Limit* is a straightforward, contemporary account of one summer in the life of a 15-year-old gambling addict.

"But those books did have something in common—a quality shared both with great books such as *Huckleberry Finn* and with lesser works such as the Hardy Boys mysteries: They were stories about adolescents suddenly thrust into adult roles. Most 'teen books' are simple, straightforward thrill rides—adventures, mysteries, horror stories, and so forth. They promise an exciting reading experience, and most of them deliver. But the truly memorable stories tell us about a young person crossing a bridge from one set of challenges to another even more difficult set of problems. Teen books address the greatest mystery of our teenage years, and that is simply, 'What does it mean to be an adult?'

Photo by Pete Hautman

"I won't say that any YA novel can answer that question. Books certainly didn't answer all of *my* adolescent questions. But when I think back on the books that really affected me, books that I still remember vividly, most of them were books I read as a teenager. Hardly a month went by that I didn't discover some new book that just *had* to be the greatest book ever written.

"Ages 12 through 16 were my personal Golden Age of reading. Every book was a new adventure to be entered fully and completely without the self-conscious, hypercritical and jaded attitudes of the typical adult reader. I loved the idea of writing for such an audience. I still do.

"So I wrote another YA novel. And another. And I'll probably keep writing them for as long as I can remember what it was like to stay up all night long reading the greatest book ever written."

СЗ СЗ СЗ

> *"Teen books address the greatest mystery of our teenage years, and that is simply, 'What does it mean to be an adult?'"*

Pete Hautman is a prolific and versatile author of adult novels, young adult fiction, and nonfiction titles for children. His work ranges from mystery and science-fiction adventure to coming-of-age novels to science books for elementary school students. His young adult work has garnered particular critical attention, including a National Book Award for Young People's Literature for *Godless* in 2004.

Born in Berkeley, California, Hautman moved to St. Louis Park, Minnesota at the age of five and attended elementary and high school there. He attended the Minneapolis College of Art and Design and later the University of Minnesota, without receiving a degree, and worked a variety of jobs in marketing and graphic arts for nearly twenty years. Luckily for his readers, Hautman decided to become a freelance writer at that point.

Under the name of Peter Murray, Hautman began writing children's science books for the publisher Child's World. His titles ranged from *Beavers* to *Silly Science Tricks* to *The World's Greatest Chocolate Chip Cookies*. While working on these short, clearly written, and often humorous introductions to a number of subjects, he also began his first novel. *Drawing Dead*, a thriller for adults, came out in 1993.

In 1996 *Mr. Was*, with Pete Hautman's first adolescent protagonist, was named an ALA Notable Book and a Best Book for Young Adults as well as receiving a Mystery Writers of America Edgar Allan Poe Award nomination. The novel involves alcoholism, a parent's death, time travel, and a surprising number of plot twists and unexpected turns. Next came *Stone Cold*, an

ALA Quick Pick for Reluctant Readers, with narrator Denn describing his growing addiction to gambling and consequent withdrawal from family, girlfriend, and business. The title of this book was later changed to *No Limit*. Moving into the future in *The Hole in the Sky*, Hautman portrays a world devastated first by a deadly influenza and then threatened by a cult group believing that they are "the chosen." Switching to horror with *Sweetblood*, he introduces an insulin-using diabetic named Lucy who thinks she has found a link between vampires and diabetic ketoacidosis and decides to risk her life testing her theory. *Sweetblood* won the Minnesota Book Award for teen fiction.

In *Godless* the teen hero Jason, an agnostic rebelling against his Catholic father, decides to create his own god and a religion to go with it. The results are funny, poignant, and provocative as even this thoroughly improbable religion develops many of the traits that seem to bedevil actual faiths. Jason watches as his small congregation founders on the all-too-familiar rocks of zealotry, misuse of power, and doubt. An ALA Best Book for Young Adults as well as winner of the National Book Award, *Godless* is a thoughtful, thought-provoking book. *Invisible*, also named an ALA Best Book for Young Adults, balances between being a thriller and a psychological study. Its narrator Dougie tells a taut, increasingly compelling tale about a friendship between two very different boys that is disintegrating, along with the narrator's tenuous hold on sanity. A writer who enjoys looking at a culture's assumptions and their consequences, Hautman creates a taut study of aggression in the novel *Rash*. Set in the future, *Rash* places its protagonist in a penal colony because of his unmanageable anger and then introduces the illegal sport of football.

Pete Hautman is currently co-authoring a series of middle-grade mysteries with the poet and mystery writer Mary Logue. They met when he was a student in a class she taught on suspense writing and began dating after the class was over. At present Hautman and Logue divide their time between Golden Valley, Minnesota and a farm in Stockholm, Wisconsin.

PETE HAUTMAN

Author of GODLESS, the National Book Award winner

Invisible

Courtesy of Simon & Schuster Children's Publishing

SELECTED WORKS FOR YOUNG ADULTS: *Mr. Was*, 1996; *Stone Cold*, 1998 (reissued as *No Limit*, 2005); *Hole in the Sky*, 2001; *Sweetblood*, 2003; *Godless*, 2004; *Invisible*, 2005; *Rash*, 2006; *Snatched*, with Mary Logue, 2006; *All-in*, 2007; *Skullduggery*, with Mary Logue, 2007; *Full House: Ten Stories about Poker*, as editor, 2007; *Doppelganger*, with Mary Logue, 2008.

SELECTED WORKS FOR ADULTS: *Drawing Dead*, 1993; *Short Money*, 1995; *The Mortal Nuts*, 1996; *Ring Game*, 1997; *Mrs. Million*, 1999; *The Rag Man*, 2001; *Doohicky*, 2002; *The Prop*, 2006.

SELECTED WORKS FOR YOUNG READERS (as Peter Murray): *Beavers*, 1992; *Black Widows*, 1992; *Dogs*, 1992; *Planet Earth*, 1992; *The Planets*, illus. by Anastasia Mitchell, 1992; *Rhinos*, 1992; *Silly Science Tricks*, 1992; *Snakes*, 1992; *Spiders*, 1992; *The World's Greatest Chocolate Chip Cookies*, illus. by Anastasia Mitchell, 1992; *The World's Greatest Paper Airplanes*, illus. by Anastasia Mitchell, 1992; *You Can Juggle*, illus. by Anastasia Mitchell; *Your Bones: An Inside Look at Skeletons*, illus. by Viki Woodworth, 1992; *The Amazon*, 1993; *Beetles*, 1993; *Chameleons*, 1993; *The Everglades*, 1993; *Frogs*, 1993; *Gorillas*, 1993; *Parrots*, 1993; *Porcupines*, 1993; *The Sahara*, 1993; *Saturn*, 1993; *Sea Otters*, 1993; *The Space Shuttle*, 1993; *Tarantulas*, 1993; *Silly Science Tricks: with Professor Solomon Snickerdoodle*, illus. by an Anastasia Mitchell, 1993; *Dirt, Wonderful Dirt!*, illus. by Penny Dann, 1994; *Make a Kite!*, illus by Penny Dann, 1995; *The Perfect Pizza*, illus. by Penny Dann, 1995; *Professor Solomon Snickerdoodle's Air Science Tricks*, 1995; *Sitting Bull: A Story of Bravery*, 1996; *Cactus*, 1996; *Orchids*, 1996; *Roses*, 1996; *Earthquakes*, 1996; *Mushrooms*, 1996; *Hurricanes*, 1996; *Tornadoes*, 1996; *Volcanoes*, 1996; *Deserts*, 1996; *Lightning*, 1997; *Mountains*, 1997; *Rainforests*, 1997; *Redwoods*, 1997; *Prairies*, 1997; *Floods*, 1997; *Scorpions*, 1997; *Pigs*, 1998; *Snails*, 1998; *Sheep*, 1998; *Curiosity: the Story of Marie Curie*, illus. by Leon Baxter, 1998; *Perseverance: the Story of Thomas Alva Edison*, illus. by Robin Lawrie, 1998; *Dreams: The Story of Martin Luther King, Jr.*, illus. by Robin Lawrie, 1999; *A Sense of Humor: The Story of Mark Twain*, 1999; *Copper*, 2001; *Silver*, 2001; *Oil*, 2001; *Diamonds*, 2001; *Gold*, 2001; *Iron*, 2001; *Apatosaurus*, 2001; *Stegosaurus*, 2001; *Pterodactyls*, 2001; *Tyrannosaurus Rex*, 2001; *Triceratops*, 2001; *Velociraptor*, 2001; *Beetles*, 2003; *Black Widows*, 2003; *Amphibians*, 2004; *Birds*, 2004; *Fish*, 2004; *Insects*, 2004; *Mammals*, 2004; *Mollusks and Crustaceans*, 2004; *Reptiles*, 2004; *Spiders and Scorpions*, 2004; *Worms*, 2004; *Kan-*

garoos, 2005; *Rhinos*, 2005; *Squirrels*, 2005; *Tigers*, 2005; *Frogs*, 2006; *Snails*, 2006.

SUGGESTED READING: *Something About the Author*, vol. 128, 2002.

WEB SITE: www.petehautman.com

"I was a somewhat solitary single child of older parents, so it would be tempting to say that I found companionship in books at an early age and thus an ambition to write and illustrate was seeded from that time. That would be an untruth.

"I was born at the beginning of the Second World War in Gourock, a small seaside town on the west coast of Scotland. There were few books for children in the 1940s and certainly not in our house. Tomes by my Victorian missionary grandfather chronicling his achievements in Central Africa sat beside John Bunyan's *Pilgrim's Progress*, Robert Burns's *The Collected Poems*, and later an entire set of Winston Churchill's *The Second World War*. There were a lot of Bibles and volumes of architectural reference. My father was an architect.

"Had I been born in England, Beatrix Potter, A. A. Milne, Lewis Carroll, and Arthur Ransome would have been part of my childhood reading (and cultural formation). But I would not have become what I am today—a writer of books for children and adults whose subjects and visuals are based on my years of living in the Highlands and Islands of Scotland. I have traveled extensively, but always come home to where the landscapes and seascapes are without compare.

"My lifelong love affair with this part of my country came to joyous fruition after leaving Edinburgh College of Art and Teacher Training in the 1960s and heading for a small island in the Hebrides where we brought up our family in a very remote house without running water or electricity—or disposable nappies. I churned out drawings and sketches for the holiday-

Photo by D. C-K.

Mairi Hedderwick

May 2, 1939–

makers in the summer. One of the visitors happened to be an editor from the London publishers, Macmillan—a lucky break that, in truth, I had not been looking for. I preferred to feed the geese and the goat.

"After several years of illustrating for other authors I was asked to think about creating my own character specifically for picture storybook format. By now we were living on the mainland and our children were teenagers. Inevitably, my chosen source material was from that idyllic time on the island, and thus *Katie Morag* was born. I sometimes call her my third child. She is now 25 years old and shows no sign of leaving home. Her real-life siblings are now parents themselves, so source material is still readily available—especially on the island, where one set of grandchildren lives, as do I.

"I believe that most children's writers have had unresolved childhoods. Certainly that was true in my case. All my work is subjective; each *Katie Morag* story has a subtext that I, and only I, know the truth behind. Maybe that is why she has lasted so long—that there is something to poke at between the lines? Whatever, I make a point of including the adult reader in the jokes and double entendres, especially in the illustrations. If the adult is enjoying the bedtime story as well as the child, then the shared experience is doubly, or trebly, enjoyed. I do try to break away from the tyranny of *Katie Morag* but have to admit, self-indulgently, to the fatal attraction of her therapeutic powers.

> *"All my work is subjective; each Katie Morag story has a subtext that I, and only I, know the truth behind."*

"There *have* been other characters and stories—most recently *A Walk with Grannie* and *The Utterly Otterleys*. *A Walk* is about a child's discovery of the world beyond her home and the surprise awaiting her return. The characters and location are based on my Highland grandchildren and their surroundings. Now isn't that surprising? But the *Otterlys* is about a family of *otters*, believe it or not. Maybe I am at last moving on to anthropomorphized fiction? However, I know exactly where they live on the island . . .

"Interspersed between the children's books have been my adult books, which are all personal travel journeys through the Highlands and Islands of Scotland—always illustrated, for why shouldn't grownups have pictures in their books too? I learned to read the illustrations in *Pilgrim's Progress* long before I ever read the words."

 CsquaredB CsquaredB CsquaredB

Katie Morag's home on the Isle of Struay provides a wonderful antidote for today's hurried children in other parts of the world. It is Mairi Hedderwick's great gift that she is able to transport her readers so completely to this island world in the Hebrides and immerse them in Katie's homespun adventures. Her characterizations are especially sharp and realistic. Katie runs interference between her two grandmothers—Grannie Island and Granma Mainland—with their very different ways of life. Her big boy cousins have a knack for getting into trouble and bringing Katie with them. Katie's unhappy reaction to a new baby in the family is realistically explored in *Katie Morag and the Tiresome Ted*. Each story about the irrepressible Katie touches on the true emotions, joys, and longings of childhood.

At the age of 17 Mairi Hedderwick went to work as a mother's helper to a family living on Coll, an island off the coast of Scotland. That experience began her lifelong love of the island culture. It was there she returned in 1962, after attending the Edinburgh College of Art, to raise her own family, and it was Coll that would eventually serve as a model for the imaginary island of Struay, the home of Katie Morag.

In addition to her children's books, Mairi Hedderwick has written travel books for adults about her beloved Scotland that are profusely illustrated with her characteristic evocative water colors. Exploring the country by both land and sea, Hedderwick takes her readers along on a personal trek, sketching as she goes, with a sure eye for the rough beauty of the mountains and seacoasts of her homeland.

SELECTED WORKS ILLUSTRATED: *The Old Woman Who Lived in a Vinegar Bottle*, by Rumer Godden, 1972; *Brave Janet Reachfar*, by Jane Duncan, 1975; *Janet Reachfar and the Kelpie*, by Jane Duncan, 1976; *Janet Reachfar and Chickabird*, by Jane Duncan, 1978; *The Spell Singer, and Other Stories*, ed. by Beverley Mathias, 1989; *Venus Peter Saves the Whale*, by Christopher Rush, 1992; *Callum's Big Day*, by Tom Pow, 2001.

SELECTED WORKS WRITTEN AND ILLUSTRATED: *Katie Morag Delivers the Mail*, 1984; *Katie Morag and the Two Grandmothers*, 1985; *Katie Morag and the Tiresome Ted*, 1986; *Katie Morag and the Big Boy Cousins*, 1987; *P. D. Peebles' Summer or Winter Book*, 1989; *Katie Morag's Island Stories*, 1995; *The Big Katie Morag Storybook*, 1996; *Katie Morag and the Wedding*, 1997; *Katie Morag and the Grand Concert*, 1997; *Katie Morag's Rainy Day Book*, 1999; *The Second Katie Morag Storybook*, 1999; *More Katie Morag Island Stories*, 2004; *A Walk with Grannie*, 2004; *Katie*

KATIE MORAG and the TWO GRANDMOTHERS

Mairi Hedderwick

Courtesy of Random House Group Ltd., U.K.

Morag and the Birthdays: A Story, Activity & Birthday Book, 2005; *The Utterly Otterleys,* 2006.

SELECTED WORKS FOR ADULTS: *An Eye on the Hebrides: An Illustrated Journey,* 1991; *Highland Journey: A Sketching Tour of Scotland, Retracing the Footsteps of Victorian Artist John T. Reid,* 1992; *Sea Change: The Summer Voyage from East to West Scotland of the* Anassa, 1999.

SUGGESTED READING: *Something About the Author,* vol. 145, 2004. Periodicals—Hedderwick, Mairi, "The Artist at Work: A Sense of Place," *The Horn Book,* March/April 1990.

WEB SITE: www.randomhouse.co.uk/childrens/katiemorag/struay.htm

Brett Helquist

Born in Ganado, Arizona, Brett Helquist grew up in Orem, Utah with six sisters. His favorite subject in school was science. Though his love of art came primarily from comic books, he also counts the classic 20th century illustrator N. C. Wyeth among his early influences.

Although he started to pursue an engineering major at Brigham Young University, Helquist soon realized this was not the right choice for him. He took some time off and went to Taiwan, where he found a job illustrating English textbooks. After a year in Taiwan, he returned to B.Y.U. to study illustration and received his B.F.A. degree in 1993. Shortly after graduating,

Helquist moved to New York City with his wife, Mary Callister, where he worked making type corrections at advertising agencies. Eventually, his art began appearing in publications such as *Cricket* magazine, the *New York Times*, and *Time for Kids*. After illustrating in *Cricket* for several years, he decided to try his hand at book illustration.

Brett Helquist's debut in the children's book field was an auspicious one—he was chosen to illustrate what became the enormously popular chronicle of woe, A Series of Unfortunate Events, written by the elusive author Lemony Snicket. These mock Gothic novels, which eventually grew to a series of 13 titles, tell the unhappy story of the Baudelaire orphans and the villainous Count Olaf, who is bent on getting his hands on their family fortune. Helquist's exquisitely detailed drawings with their hint of mischief perfectly capture the atmosphere of these dark but droll tales. With illustrations reminiscent of the work of Edward Gorey, Helquist created a style for these elegantly designed books that helped to catapult them to bestseller status.

Photo by Mary Jane Callister

In the first book of the series, *The Bad Beginning*—winner of children's choice state awards in Colorado, Hawaii, and Nevada—the three Baudelaire children lose their parents in a fire and fall into the hands of the wicked Count. In *The Ersatz Elevator* melodrama meets slapstick as the ill-fated siblings find themselves adopted by a wealthy couple, climbing countless stairs, and trying to rescue friends that Count Olaf has abducted and is holding at the bottom of an elevator shaft.

Branded eventually as murderers, the unlucky children hide among a group of oddly happy hospital workers in *The Hostile Hospital*, where Count Olaf attempts to perform a lethal operation on one of them. This title was on the Children's Book Council's 2002 "Not Just for Children Anymore!" Reading List and was named an IRA/CBC Children's Choice, as were both *The Wide Window* and *The Vile Village*. The children find themselves on a submarine as they continue investigating their parents' deaths in *The Grim Grotto*, nominated for a 2005 Quill Award.

In *The Penultimate Peril*, the winner of a 2006 Quill Award and a Nickelodeon Kids' Choice Award, the children act as concierges in the Hotel Denouement, which not only holds many secrets, but is organized according to the Dewey Decimal System. In *The End*, the 13th and final book in the series, the children discover missing pieces of their family's story and the Count meets his demise, but there is no neat ending with all questions completely answered. Marketed as books that should be diligently avoided by sensible children (but priced to be accessible to them), the series was made popular, at least in part, by young fans' word-of-mouth enthusiasm for the books. A film adaptation of the first three books released as *Lemony Snicket's A Series of Unfortunate Events* in 2004 further heightened their success.

The first picture book illustrated by Helquist was *Milly and the Macy's Parade*, which received an Oppenheim Toy Portfolio Gold Award. Written by Shana Corey, it tells the story of how the first Macy's Thanksgiving Day Parade in 1924 came about, and most of Helquist's research material came from the department store's archives, which helped him replicate many details from the first parade. Helquist also created evocative cover art for books by authors Peter W. Hassinger and Louise Arnold and interior art as well as cover designs for novels by Blue Balliett and Tor Seidler.

No stranger to illustrating mysterious tales, Helquist placed coded messages for the reader in his illustrations for Blue Balliett's *Chasing Vermeer*, a novel about two sixth-graders trying to solve the question of a stolen Vermeer painting. Winner of a Great Lakes Book Award and a *Chicago Tribune* Young Adult Fiction Prize, as well as being named the first-ever Midwest Booksellers' Children's Literature Choice Award, *Chasing Vermeer* was also a *Booklist* Editors' Choice, a Parents' Choice Foundation Honor Book, and a *Child Magazine* Honor Book. The same sixth-grade sleuths reappear in Blue Balliett's Lamplighter Award winner *The Wright 3*, which tells about unexplainable accidents and ghostly happenings at Frank Lloyd Wright's 1910 Robie House when it is slated for demolition. Again, Helquist adds mystery to the tale by including hidden images in his intriguingly eerie illustrations.

Helquist wrote his own text for *Roger the Jolly Pirate*, a picture book featuring a bumbling pirate, who saves the day for his crew when he bakes a cake that explodes, frightening off the enemy. This offbeat story provides a fictional, tongue-in-cheek account of the origins of the pirates' "Jolly Roger" flag. Nominated for the North Carolina Children's Book Award, the humorous verse and hilariously exaggerated illustrations of this picture book have made it a children's favorite. Helquist has also produced haunting new cover art for new editions of the classic Green Knowe books by Lucy M. Boston, as well as fully illustrating James Howe's lighthearted Tales from the House of Bunnicula series about the literary dog, Howie.

Brett Helquist lives and works in Brooklyn, New York.

SELECTED WORKS ILLUSTRATED: *The Revenge of Randal Reese-Rat*, by Tor Seidler, 2001; *Milly and the Macy's Parade*, by Shana Corey, 2002; *Chasing Vermeer*, by Blue Balliett, 2003; *Capt. Hook: The Adventures of a Notorious Youth*, by J. V. Hart, 2005; *The Floating Island*, by Elizabeth Haydon, 2006; *The Wright 3*, by Blue Balliett, 2006; *The Calder Game*, by Blue Ballett, 2008.

SELECTED SERIES ILLUSTRATED: A Series of Unfortunate Events series, all by Lemony Snicket—*The Bad Beginning*, Book 1, 1999; *The Reptile Room*, Book 2, 1999; *The Wide Window*, Book 3, 2000; *The Miserable Mill*, Book 4, 2000; *The Austere Academy*, Book 5, 2000; *The Ersatz Elevator*, Book 6, 2001; *The Vile Village*, Book 7, 2001; *The Hostile Hospital*, Book 8, 2001; *The Carnivorous Carnival*, Book 9, 2002; *Lemony Snicket: The Unauthorized Autobiography*, 2002; *The Slippery Slope*, Book 10, 2003; *The Blank Book*, 2004; *The Grim Grotto*, Book 11, 2004; *The Penultimate Peril*, Book 12, 2005; *The Beatrice Letters*, 2006; *The Notorious Notations: A Blank Journal*, 2006; *The End*, Book 13, 2006. Tales from the House of Bunnicula series by James Howe—*It Came from Beneath the Bed*, 2002; *Invasion of the Mind Swappers from Asteroid 6!*, 2002; *Howie Monroe and the Doghouse of Doom*, 2002; *Screaming Mummies of the Pharaoh's Tomb II*, 2002; *Bud Barkin, Private Eye*, 2003; *The Amazing Odorous Adventures of Stinky Dog*, 2003.

SELECTED WORKS WRITTEN AND ILLUSTRATED: *Roger, the Jolly Pirate*, 2004.

SUGGESTED READING: *Something About the Author*, vol. 146, 2004. Periodicals—Lodge, Sally, "Oh, Sweet Misery!" *Publishers Weekly*, May 29, 2000.

WEB SITES: www.bretthelquist.com
www.lemonysnicket.com/artist.cfm

Photo by Randy Vaughn-Dotta

Juan Felipe Herrera

December 27, 1948–

" A tiny crimson address book from the Elvis 1950s—that is what my mother, Lucha Quintana, left me when she passed away in 1986. I keep it in a small bundle of things that I hold dear. On occasion I scan through its jottings, some addresses and short lists of fruit purchased in small-town California country stores. Just the other day I opened it and noticed that it was not an address book. It was an intimate diary of her life and how she cared for me as a child.

"My mother's makeshift diary book is a lesson of my literary beginnings—*writing is a way to record our lives, from the materials in our lives.* The pages were born of the substance of daily things—like me. Since we were a farmworker *familia*—my father Felipe Emilio, mama Lucha and myself, el Juanito—the bare-boned world of simplicity was our day-to-day landscape. During the summer, the iceman would drop a block of ice into the tin box in the yard. In winter, for ice, mama would place a bowl of water on the steps of our trailer. Our one-room home was hammered out of found wood nailed to a car chassis my father found half-buried in the hills. By the time I was five, my mother bought me my first book at a second-hand store. It was a Spanish reading primer from the late 1800s. This was how I learned to read in Spanish.

"When I entered first grade in Escondido, California, I was ready to show off my linguistic prowess out loud. Only one thing stopped me: everything in school was in English. Slaps and spankings were my rewards for asking questions in another language. At times, I sat in the corner facing the wall. At other instances, I would guess it was lunch hour and dart out into the wide yard with a burrito only to face a little circus singing, 'It's recess, you dummy!'

"By the time I was in third grade I had become a sad, silent boy in a checkered yellow shirt. Then, one day everything changed. My third grade teacher, Mrs. Lucille Sampson, invited me to sing in front of class. 'You have a beautiful voice,' she purred, after I finished 'Three Blind Mice.' By the end of that year, I was hollering gospel solos in front of the entire school assembly. From that moment on, I knew I had a unique shimmery-timbre I could call upon—*my voice*. This calling-out of the voice became my life-project.

"After testing myself in choirs all through middle school and high school, I became more comfortable with my human singing instrument. Yet, nerves would overtake me and a whispery sigh was easier than a deep arpeggio flowing out of my chest. Mr. Harrison-Maxwell, my choir teacher pulled me aside. 'John-John,' he said facing me, 'you do have a beautiful voice, but you are only using one third of it!' Then, boom! Something strange happened to me that would change my life forever; except *this* time, this new force would surround me.

"The year was 1967. People were marching against the Vietnam War, and César Chávez, a farmworker himself, was speaking out about the sufferings of the California migrant workers who only spoke Spanish, like my parents, like me in first grade. African-American poets were standing on the corner jammin' with saxophones and words. I knew then what I had to do—become a poet for the people! In the late 1960s, I began my life as a poet—writing about the lives of those at the margins of our communities. My poetry and writing worked the way a choir works—with music, with theatre, with murals, *with* and *for* groups—out in the open air.

"By the time I was in third grade I had become a sad, silent boy in a checkered yellow shirt. Then, one day everything changed."

"For a short while, during the 1930s, in El Paso, Texas, mama Lucha had been a singer and was about to join a theatre troupe of the day, Los Pirrines. My grandmother Juanita and older uncles forbade her to go to the audition. 'A woman of "good character" would never do this,' they exclaimed. That was the end of her almost–singing career. She retreated and wrote on small pieces of paper. But then, as the years passed, she resolved to encourage me. During high school, at my mother's urgings, I picked up a steel-string Stella guitar for $17.00. And it happened that the folksong movement was also in the air. The working-class songs of Woody Guthrie and Pete Seeger were being reinvigorated by wild-eyed troubadours like Bob Dylan, Phil Ochs, Joan Baez and Mimi Fariña. I practiced, I sang, I wrote my songs and poems, I plucked the chords, I became a poet-singer, a songwriter.

"Then boom-bam! A knock-knock on my own apartment door was about to launch me further into the world—as a Chicano poet and author. By a stroke of whimsy, my father moved us into a bleak apartment building in downtown San Diego. One day, a young Mexican boy with a crew cut and checkered shirt like the ones I used to wear in elementary school tap-tapped on my door. Slowly, I opened it. He asked, 'Do you have a piece paper?' His name was Alberto Urista. In time he would grow to be one of the foremost Chicano poets. And we would become bards on the rad, reading to multitudes across the nation and across Mexico, writing for the people of the world.

"I look at my mother Lucha's tiny red book of sayings and diary accounts. It fits in the center of my palm. It is a seed the color of fire and dawn. This is where I come from. This is my first book. Its pages are of family, love, community and writing from the heart."

ૠ ૠ ૠ

Juan Felipe Herrera was born in Fowler, California and traveled as a child with his farmworker parents through many small towns and cities before settling in San Diego. He received a bachelor of arts degree in social anthropology from UCLA in 1972 and a master's degree in the same field from Stanford University in 1980. While at Stanford he was a teaching fellow in Chicano anthropology. In the 1980s Herrera taught creative writing in the Poetry in the Schools program, grades K–12, in the San Francisco Bay Area as well as teaching at De Anza Community College and the New College of California. From 1988 to 1990 he was a teaching fellow at the University of Iowa Writer's Workshop, where he earned a second master's degree in Fine Arts and received an Excellence in Teaching Award. He has also taught at the University of Southern Illinois and California State University at Fresno, where he chaired the Chicano and Latin American Studies Department. In 2005 he joined the Creative Writing Department at University of California, Riverside, as the Tomás Rivera Endowed chair. He also serves as director of the Art and Barbara Culver Center for the Arts, a new multimedia space in downtown Riverside.

Herrera's career as a published writer and poet began with the rhythms and colors of his Chicano background in family, work, and community. *Calling the Doves / Canto a las palomas*, Herrera's first book for young readers, is a collection of evocative poems in both English and Spanish recalling his own experiences growing up in California. It won the Ezra Jack Keats Award for new writers in 1997. He had previously published several volumes of poetry and his autobiographical travel book, *Mayan Drifter*, for adults, but *Calling the Doves* was his first book for young readers, and he was hailed as a bright new voice in the field. This first poetry collection was followed by another, *Laughing Out Loud, I Fly*, which won a Pura Belpré Honor award. In 1999 his novel in verse for teenagers, *Crash Boom Love*, was given the Américas Award, presented by the Consortium of Latin American Studies Programs, an award he won again in 2005 for *Cinnamon Girl: Letters Found Inside a Cereal Box*. Both of these novels are powerful depictions of the life of Chicano youth in today's American culture.

For younger readers, Herrera's picture book, *The Upside Down Boy/El niño de cabeza*, provides an inside look at the feelings of a boy who starts school speaking only Spanish. Herrera later adapted the story for the stage as the first Latino musical for young audiences in New York. It premiered in January 2004. He is also an actor who has appeared on film and stage. He recently produced *The Twin Tower Songs*, a San Joaquin Valley performance memorial on the September 11th tragedy and he writes poetry sequences for the PBS television series *American Family*. An accomplished photographer, he has shown his work in community art spaces throughout the United States since 1970.

Courtesy of Children's Book Press

During the last three decades Professor Herrera has received numerous awards and fellowships, including two National Endowment for the Arts Writers' Fellowships, four California Arts Council grants, the UC Berkeley Regent's Fellowship, the Breadloaf Fellowship in Poetry and the Stanford Chicano Fellows Fellowship. He has given lectures, workshops, readings and performances of his work and writing across the nation. He lives in Redlands, California, with his partner, the poet and performance artist, Margarita Luna Robles.

SELECTED WORKS FOR YOUNG READERS *Calling the Doves/Canto a las palomas*, illus. by Elly Simmons, 1995; *Laughing Out Loud, I Fly: Poems in English and Spanish*, illus. by Karen Barbour, 1998; *Crash Boom Love: A Novel in Verse*, 1999; *The Upside Down Boy/El niño de cabeza*, illus. by Elizabeth Gómez, 2000; *Grandma & Me at the Flea/Los Meros Meros Remateros*, illus. by Anita de Lucio-Brock, 2002; *Super Cilantro Girl/La Superniña del Cilantro*, illus. by Honorio Robledo Tapia, 2003; *Coralito's*

Bay/Bahía de Coralito, illus. by Lena Shiffman, 2004; *Feather-less/Desplumando*, illus. by Ernesto Cuevas, 2004; *Downtown Boy*, 2005; *Cinnamon Girl: Letters Found Inside a Cereal Box*, 2005.

SELECTED WORKS FOR ADULTS: *Exiles of Desire*, 1985; *The Roots of a Thousand Embraces: Dialogues*, 1994; *Night Train to Tuxtla: New Stories and Poems*, 1994; *Love After the Riots*, 1996; *Mayan Drifter: Chicano Poet in the Lowlands of America*, 1997; *Border-Crosser with a Lamborghini Dream*, 1999; *Lotería Cards & Fortune Poems: A Book of Lives*, illus. by Artemio Rodriguez, 1999; *Thunderweavers*, 2000; *Giraffe on Fire: Poems*, 2001; *Notebooks of a Chile Verde Smuggler*, 2002.

SUGGESTED READING: *Something About the Author*, vol. 127, 2002; Binder, Wolfgang, ed., *Partial Autobiographies: Interviews with Twenty Chicano Poets*, 1985, pp. 95–108.

Carl Hiaasen

(HI-ah-sen)
March 12, 1953–

Carl Hiaasen was born and raised in Plantation, Florida, a suburb of Fort Lauderdale. From an early age Carl's twin passions were the great outdoors and writing. He requested and received his first typewriter at age six and used it to create a sports page for the kids in his neighborhood. He also enjoyed reading, and he completed the Hardy Boys series when he was in the fourth grade. Ian Fleming, J.D. Salinger, and sports biographies were some of his other early favorites.

From 1970 to 1972 Hiaasen attended Emory University, in Atlanta, Georgia, the only time he has lived outside of Florida. There he wrote articles for the student newspaper, *The Emory Wheel*. He later transferred to the University of Florida, in Gainesville, from which he earned his bachelor's degree in journalism in 1974. After graduating he worked as a reporter for *Cocoa Today*, in Cocoa, Florida. At age 23 he began working at the Miami *Herald*, first as a general assignment reporter and later as a special investigative reporter. Since 1985 he has written a regular column for the *Herald* that has often stirred controversy with its forthright opinions. Hiaasen says, "A columnist is paid to take a stand. If a reader can't figure out how I feel about something, then I don't deserve to take my paycheck home that week, because I copped out. I feel strongly about the advocacy role of the columnist."

For his reporting and commentary, Hiaasen has received numerous awards, including the Silver Gavel Award from the

American Bar Association and the Damon Runyon Award from the Denver Press Club. A selection of Hiaasen's columns has been published in two anthologies, *Kick Ass* and *Paradise Screwed*, both edited by Diane Stevenson. His recent columns can be found at: www.miamiherald.com.

In the early 1980s Hiaasen began co-authoring novels for an adult audience with the late journalist William D. Montalbano. They wrote three mystery thrillers together—*Powder Burn*, *Trap Line*, and *Death in China*—before Hiaasen published his first solo effort, *Tourist Season*, in 1986. Eight other novels followed, one of which was made into a feature film. Altogether, these nine books have been translated into 30 languages. His satirical novels for adults have led critics to compare his work to that of Preston Sturges, Woody Allen, and S. J. Perelman. He also published a witty diatribe against the Walt Disney Company, *Team Rodent: How Disney Devours the World*.

Photo by Fenia Hiaasen

In 2002 *Hoot*, Hiaasen's first book for young readers, was published to rave reviews. On his official Web site, Hiaasen explains why he wanted to start writing books for children: "First, it was something I'd never done before, and it's important for writers to take chances. Secondly, I really wanted to write something that I could give to my nephew, nieces and stepson without worrying about the salty language or adult situations. They've all been asking to read my other novels and I've been trying to stall them, at least until they hit the teenage years . . . The biggest challenge was trying not to subconsciously "write down" for younger readers. As J. K. Rowling and others have proven, kids are sophisticated readers with terrific vocabularies. They're also quite aware when adults are underestimating them."

Set in Coconut Cove, Florida, *Hoot* is an ecological mystery. The protagonist, Roy Eberhardt, is a new kid in town—a familiar situation for him since his family moves around frequently. Struggling yet again to make new friends, Roy meets a homeless runaway, a strange boy who calls himself Mullet Fingers and who has dedicated himself to protecting the small owls that live in burrows underneath a local construction site. At night Mullet

Fingers sabotages the site by pulling up the survey stakes, in the hopes of slowing down the construction and protecting the owls. This plot idea came straight out of Hiaasen's own childhood. He and his friends would pull up or relocate surveyor's stakes in a futile attempt to slow down the massive development that was paving over their bike paths and camping grounds. "We were kids," he says. "We didn't know what else to do. We were little and the bulldozers were big."

Critics praised *Hoot* for its humor and its ecological conscience; it was selected as a Newbery Honor Book, an ALA Notable Children's Book, and an ALA Best Book for Young Adults, as well as winning top awards from the Southeastern Booksellers Association and the Association of Booksellers for Children. Popular with young readers as well as adult critics, *Hoot* has won readers' choice awards in Illinois, Pennsylvania, Connecticut, Minnesota, and Wisconsin. A film version of *Hoot*, starring Luke Wilson, was released in spring 2006. Hiaasen has said in interviews that he has received more fan mail from readers of *Hoot* than for any of his adult novels.

Hiaasen's second book for young readers, *Flush*, is also focused on environmental issues. The dedicated activist in this story, however, is not a child but the father of the young protagonist. At the beginning of the book, Noah Underwood's dad is arrested for having sunk the *Coral Queen*, a casino boat that he claims was illegally dumping raw sewage in the Florida Keys. Noah and his sister, Abbey, try to gather evidence that will vindicate their father, and in the process they cross paths with a cast of quirky characters. Critics were again pleased with Hiaasen's work, and many suggested that parents as well as children would enjoy this comedic mystery.

Carl Hiaasen works from his home on the east coast of Florida. He has two sons, Scott and Quinn, and a stepson, Ryan. He is also the grandfather of twins, the children of his grown son, Scott. On a vacation trip to Montana, Hiaasen had the opportunity to have an effect on another area of books for children and teens when his wife picked up a self-published book in a local bookstore. Ryan, age 11 at the time, devoured the long novel that had been written by a teenager, declaring it one of the best books he had ever read. Back home, Hiaasen called his editor at Knopf and suggested she take a look at the book. When Knopf published the book, *Eragon*, by Montana native Christopher Paolini, it became a bestselling fantasy novel, the first in a highly praised series.

SELECTED WORKS FOR YOUNG READERS: *Hoot*, 2002; *Flush*, 2005.

> *This plot idea came straight out of Hiaasen's own childhood. He and his friends would pull up or relocate surveyor's stakes in a futile attempt to slow down the massive development that was paving over their bike paths and camping grounds.*

SELECTED WORKS FOR ADULTS: *Powder Burn*, with William D. Montalbano, 1981; *Trap Line*, with William D. Montalbano, 1982; *A Death in China*, with William D. Montalbano, 1984; *Tourist Season*, 1986; *Double Whammy*, 1987; *Skin Tight*, 1989; *Native Tongue*, 1991; *Strip Tease*, 1993; *Stormy Weather*, 1995; *Naked Came the Manatee*, 1996; *Lucky You*, 1997; *Team Rodent: How Disney Devours the World*, 1998; *Kick Ass: Selected Columns of Carl Hiaasen*, 1999; *Sick Puppy*, 2000; *Paradise Screwed: Selected Columns of Carl Hiaasen*, 2001; *Basket Case*, 2002; *Skinny Dip*, 2004; *Nature Girl*, 2006.

SUGGESTED READING: *Current Biography*, April 1997. Periodicals—Beauregard, Sue-Ellen, "Carl Hiaasen, Interview," *Booklist*, May 1, 2006; Hiaasen, Carl, "How I Write," *The Writer*, June 2003; Lodge, Sally, "Crossing Over: Authors of adult fiction seek a younger audience," *Publishers Weekly*, September 2, 2002. Online—Weich, Dave, "A Kinder, Gentler Carl Hiaasen," at www.powells.com/authors/hiassen

WEB SITE: www.carlhiassen.com

Courtesy of Random House, Inc.

"When I was a kid, I wanted to be a rock star. I played a red electric guitar, beginning when I was 11, and I thought that it would be great to make a living from six strings. I also entertained fantasies about being a cowgirl or a Roller Derby queen. But then I found something even more fun! Being a writer is magic, because with just 26 letters of the alphabet, one can create a zillion different stories.

"I've always loved to read. My favorite books as a child were *Baby Island* by Carol Ryrie Brink and all the Nancy Drew books. In first grade, I attended a one-room school that did not have a library. By second grade, the brand new Caernarvon Elementary School had been built and it had the most miraculous library. I still dream of being in that library, reaching up for a shiny new book.

Linda Oatman High

April 28, 1958–

"The Bookmobile was a big thing in the 1960s and 1970s. I lived so far out in the country, on Swamp Road near Morgantown, PA, that the Bookmobile didn't visit our area. However, my Aunt Mary would choose armfuls of books for me when the Bookmobile came to her town. I was always so excited to see the books Aunt Mary had chosen.

"Despite my love of reading, I never thought of being a writer until my 11th grade Creative Writing teacher, Mrs. Severs, said to me one day: 'You're very creative. You should think about becoming a writer.' Mrs. Severs planted the seed of an idea, and I'm forever grateful. I always tell kids that they should listen to their teachers, because they can change lives with ten simple words.

Courtesy of Linda Oatman High

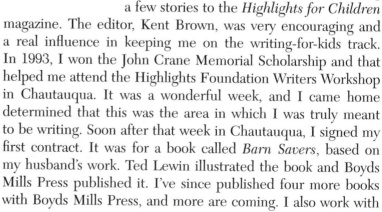

"I took a few detours: getting married at the age of 20 and becoming a mother a few years later, working as a secretary and a lifeguard and an exercise attendant at a place called 'Slender You.' I gave up my dream of writing until my son Justin was born in the early 1980s. It was then, after I quit my office job to stay home with the baby, that I saw an ad for a feature writer in a local newspaper. I applied for it, got the job, and my love of writing was reignited by seeing my byline and my words in print. I wrote lots of newspaper articles, and also fiction for literary and women's magazines. When Justin was a toddler, I became fascinated by the field of children's literature. Kids' books had changed a lot in the past decade, and I was surprised by the beautiful works of art I was reading to my son. I started submitting a few stories to the *Highlights for Children* magazine. The editor, Kent Brown, was very encouraging and a real influence in keeping me on the writing-for-kids track. In 1993, I won the John Crane Memorial Scholarship and that helped me attend the Highlights Foundation Writers Workshop in Chautauqua. It was a wonderful week, and I came home determined that this was the area in which I was truly meant to be writing. Soon after that week in Chautauqua, I signed my first contract. It was for a book called *Barn Savers*, based on my husband's work. Ted Lewin illustrated the book and Boyds Mills Press published it. I've since published four more books with Boyds Mills Press, and more are coming. I also work with

Holiday House, Philomel, Bloomsbury and Walker, Eerdmans, Scholastic, and Penguin Putnam.

"My youngest son, Zach, has a creative side, having published a poem in an anthology of poetry by kids. My older son, Justin, is now a father, and 2-year-old Connor is a joy. I babysit him several days a week when I'm not on the road. I've been inspired to write more picture books since Connor's birth, so my writing really does seem to follow real life.

"In addition to writing, I travel a lot, presenting programs at schools and conferences. I'm on the faculty of Writing by the Seaside, and this year I'll be teaching in Italy! Writing has taken me much further than I ever dreamed, and those magical 26 letters of the alphabet have served me well."

C3   C3   C3

Linda Oatman High's full name is actually Linda Louise Haas Oatman High. Besides writing books for children and teens, she is also a songwriter, journalist, playwright, poet, grandmother, and she has played in a rock band called Tickled Pink. Self-described as a "free spirit," High uses many of her own life experiences in her books. She once, for example, painted her husband's toenails pink, an incident that is echoed in *Hound Heaven*.

Born and raised in Ephrata, Pennsylvania, she grew up not far from where the novelist John Updike was raised, a fact that always impressed her. Her childhood included a variety of pets and one brother, Randy. When she was young, she had an electric Epiphone guitar, which she still owns, but she has also acquired a Fender jazz bass. She teaches classes in lyrics and songwriting as well as facilitating workshops for writers and visiting schools to talk about her books.

A writer who has tackled a variety of subjects and genres, High finds inspiration in many different ways. Her husband, John, was the model for her picture book *Barn Savers*, illustrated by Ted Lewin, and based on John's experience in dismantling old barns and recycling the materials. This title became a Booklist Top of the List Best Picture Book and an NCTE Notable Book in the Language Arts. A resident of the Amish country of Pennsylvania, High chronicled the life of the Amish and Mennonite people of Lancaster County in *A Humble Life: Plain Poems*, which received a Lee Bennett Hopkins Poetry Award Honor citation and a Great Lakes Book Award.

As one who loves the city as much as the country, she wrote a fascinating picture book that celebrates New York City both

> "Writing has taken me much further than I ever dreamed, and those magical 26 letters of the alphabet have served me well."

Courtesy of Walker & Company

above and below ground, focusing on subway musicians and hot dog vendors, among other city phenomena, and offering tidbits of New York history. *Under New York*, illustrated by Robert Rayevsky, was named a *Bulletin* Blue Ribbon book and a PBS Teachers' Source Recommended Book, as well as receiving a *Parenting* magazine Reading Magic Award.

Hound Heaven, a Junior Library Guild selection, is about an orphaned Appalachian girl who pursues her dream of having a dog by working to earn the money for one. In *Beekeepers*, High created a poetically suspenseful story about a girl who is fearful of bees but helps her grandfather harvest honey from his hives. *Sister Slam and the Poetic Motormouth Road*, a coming-of-age story written in verse, features an unconventional overweight teen poet with spiky red hair who wears combat boots. Two of High's titles were named Notable Social Studies Trade Books for Young People: *A Humble Life* and *City of Snow: The Great Blizzard of 1888*. Another two of her books have been nominated for Pennsylvania's Keystone to Reading Book Award: *Barn Savers* and *The Girl on the High-Diving Horse*, a story based on the true-life daredevil girls who once rode horses that dove into water tanks on the Atlantic City boardwalk.

High is currently working on a series of early reader graphic novels, some picture books, and several young adult novels. She has two sons: Zach, a teenager, and Justin, who lives nearby with his wife and child. High also has two stepchildren, J.D. and Kala. A lifelong Pennsylvanian, she lives in Bowmansville with her husband, their son Zach, and two dogs.

SELECTED WORKS: *Maizie*, 1995; *Hound Heaven*, 1995; *The Summer of the Great Divide*, 1996; *A Stone's Throw from Paradise*, 1997; *A Christmas Star*, illus. by Ronald Himler, 1997; *Beekeepers*, illus. by Doug Chayka, 1998; *Barn Savers*, illus. by Ted Lewin, 1999; *Under New York*, illus. by Robert Rayevsky, 2001; *Winter Shoes for Shadow Horse*, illus. by Ted Lewin, 2001; *The Last Chimney of Christmas Eve*, illus. by Kestutis Kasparavicius, 2001; *A Humble Life: Plain Poems*, illus. by Bill Farnsworth, 2001; *Strum a Song of Angels: Poems About Music*, 2002; *The President's Puppy*, illus. by Steve Björkman, 2002; *The Girl on the High-Diving Horse: An Adventure in Atlantic City*, illus. by Ted Lewin, 2003; *Sister Slam and the Poetic Motormouth Road Trip*, 2004; *City of Snow: The Great Blizzard of 1888*, illus. by Laura Francesca Filippucci, 2004; *The Cemetery Keepers of Gettysburg*, illus. by Laura Francesca Filippucci, 2007; *Cool Bopper's Choppers*, illus. by John O'Brien, 2007; *Tenth Avenue Cowboy*, illus. by Bill Farnsworth, 2008.

SUGGESTED READING: *Something About the Author*, vol. 145, 2004. Online—High, Linda Oatman, "Freelance Success Story," *Writer's Weekly*, Sept. 05, 2001, at www.writersweekly.com/success_stories/000932_09052001.html

WEB SITE: www.lindaoatmanhigh.com

Holly Hobbie

October 31, 1942–

"I was the middle child and the only girl born to Stella and Geddes Ulinskas. My childhood has everything to do with who I became as an artist. My mother, always home, made everything. She knit our sweaters and mittens, sewed all my dresses, made the quilts on the beds, and wove and hooked the rugs on the floors. She also collected a wide array of things, like buttons, postage stamps, old crocks, and anything Japanese. Our modest home's vivid jumble of stuff had an inspirational dimension for me. I would retreat to a corner and draw, losing myself in drawing for hours. From the beginning, my finished work was taped to the wall above the living room fireplace. That sort of encouragement and approval from my parents was a crucial boost to my first view of myself as an artist.

"When I was ten my parents purchased a dilapidated farm in rural Connecticut, which represented a whole new world to me. We were encouraged to raise ducks, chickens, geese, and rabbits. We had a dog, of course (Buster), numerous cats, a pig one year, and a beautiful Guernsey cow named Tinkerbell, our source of milk for years. I loved to explore the woods for wildflowers, dogwood, laurel, and the more I traipsed through woods and pastures, the more I fell in love with the landscape. That became the inspiration for my first watercolors and remained the focus of my painting through high school. I had a gift, it seemed; I was always considered the best artist in my class, but I worked very hard at mastering the skills. And I was passionately motivated. There was nothing more thrilling for me than capturing the shadows of trees on a clapboard house, or autumn clouds, or the gleam of a rainy day.

Courtesy of Holly Hobbie

"After high school in Connecticut, I studied at Pratt Institute in Brooklyn, New York. That was a profound change, which proved a hotbed of creative excitement, and I thrived in the city. Then I switched to Boston University of Fine Arts, mostly to be near a romantic interest of mine. In 1964 I married Douglas Hobbie (we're still married). A year later we had our first child, Brett, and life swerved in a whole new direction for me. As I wrote in my illustrated memoir, *The Art of Holly Hobbie*, my children—Brett, Jocelyn, and Nathaniel—became the primary source of my art and the wellspring of my imagination. For fifteen years or so, they inspired a line of cards for American Greetings, which led to licensing and big business and made my name a world-wide brand for some time. There were highs and lows, and eventually I moved on from that career.

"But what was next? Suddenly, life took a turn that overwhelmed every other consideration. Just two years out of college, Brett was diagnosed with Hodgkin's disease. For the next four years, she and the rest of the family endured a roller coaster of hopes and fears. Following each presumably successful course of treatment, the cancer returned, finally culminating in a bone marrow transplant. When that excruciating ordeal failed as well, Brett was facing the end of her life. She died at her home surrounded by loved ones on October 14, 1992. She had been magnificent through the whole unbearable journey, and her death left the rest of us shattered.

"Somehow I gravitated to children's picture books, and found myself creating a world around two inseparable pigs named Toot and Puddle. It was only after I had published the first book of that series that I realized where these two endearing characters had their beginning. To mark hopeful turning points of her treatment in San Francisco, Brett would send us funny and touching postcards featuring joyous pink piglets. That's what had subliminally inspired my Woodcock Pocket duo. *Toot & Puddle* saved me from a dark time, and the characters now seem a final gift from my eldest daughter.

"The series also taps into my Connecticut childhood, especially with the evocation of the landscape, the light in the woods changing with the seasons. I have published eleven Toot & Puddle books now. I have loved creating the books—they're part of me—and I believe they contain my best work. But the time has come to move on again. I don't want my beloved Toot and Puddle to become formulaic or routine. I'm not sure what will be next. As always, that's part of the excitement."

03   03   03

Holly Hobbie has had the unique experience of having her own artistic creation turn into such an iconic figure that people are often astounded to find out that she, herself, is a real person. In 1967 she created a line of cards for American Greetings that incorporated this originally nameless figure—an old-fashioned little girl wearing a large bonnet—who eventually came to be called by her own name. In 1974 Knickerbocker Toys licensed the "Holly Hobbie" character for a line of rag dolls, all wearing the familiar patchwork dress and bonnet, and these became extremely popular, inspiring many spin-off products as well as books and calendars. In 2006 a new line of "Holly Hobbie" products—dolls, plush animals, and animated DVDs—was launched with an updated 21st century girl, but this newest incarnation is completely independent of the original artist.

That her original creation, the "Holly Hobbie" character, took on a life of its own amazed the artist. Along with greeting cards and rag dolls developed around the original character, the Holly Hobbie line grew to include a wide variety of items, from books and dishes to wallpaper and clothing. The popularity extended to adult collectors as well as young girls and continues to this day. Meanwhile the artist employed the same gently nostalgic

"My childhood has everything to do with who I became as an artist."

style to illustrate the classic poem "The Night Before Christmas" by Clement C. Moore, and later went on to describe her work techniques in an autobiographical book, *The Art of Holly Hobbie: Drawing on Affection*, which was published in 1986.

Today Holly Hobbie is best known to a new generation of young readers and children's book enthusiasts as the author/illustrator of the delightful Toot and Puddle series. In the great literary tradition of friends who are very different and yet complement and support each other—such as Rat and Mole, Pooh and Piglet, Frog and Toad—Hobbie's charming pig characters show again and again that they will remain best pals despite their disparate personalities. Toot loves to explore, travel, and have adventures, while Puddle is most happy staying at home, but each appreciates the other's unique nature and sometimes makes concessions to the other's needs. The first title in the series, *Toot & Puddle*, was an American Booksellers Pick of the Lists and an ABBY award winner when it was published in 1997. The piglets have now appeared in nearly a dozen separate titles.

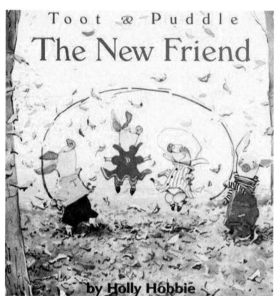

Courtesy of Little, Brown Books for Young Readers

Hobbie's masterful watercolor work in the series depicts the characters' personalities through facial expression and body language as well as the outdoor landscapes and cozy interior backgrounds for each story. Her gentle humor, exhibited in both text and drawings, as well as her great affection for the characters, shines through each individual book and has endeared them to readers and critics alike. *Toot & Puddle: ABC* won a National Parenting Publications Award (NAPPA) in 2000 with its delightfully alliterative text and framing story of how Puddle is trying to teach Otto the turtle to write his name. *The Charming Opal*, which introduces Puddle's visiting cousin Opal and her encounter with the tooth fairy, was named a *New York Times* Best Illustrated Book of the Year in 2003. To celebrate the tenth birthday of the series, Little, Brown Books for Young Readers published a special anniversary edition of *Toot & Puddle* with a 50,000 copy print run.

Holly Hobbie lives today in a country house in Conway, Massachusetts with her writer husband Douglas. She is presently at work on a new series of books, about a girl named Fanny.

SELECTED WORKS WRITTEN AND ILLUSTRATED: *Toot & Puddle*, 1997 (new edition, 2007); *Toot & Puddle: A Present for Toot*, 1998; *Toot & Puddle: You Are My Sunshine*, 1999; *Toot & Puddle: Puddle's ABC*, 2000; *Toot & Puddle: I'll Be Home for Christmas*, 2001; *Toot & Puddle: Welcome to Woodcock Pocket*, (miniature boxed set of Toot & Puddle, *A Present for Toot, and You Are My Sunshine*), 2001; *Toot & Puddle: Top of the World*, 2002; *Toot & Puddle: Travel with Toot & Puddle*, 2003; *Toot & Puddle: The Charming Opal*, 2003; *Toot & Puddle: The New Friend*, 2004; *Toot & Puddle: Wish You Were Here*, 2005; *Toot & Puddle: The One and Only*, 2006; *Toot & Puddle: Let It Snow*, 2007; *Fanny*, 2008.

SELECTED WORKS ILLUSTRATED: *Holly Hobbie's The Night Before Christmas*, by Clement C. Moore, 1976; *Bloodroot*, by W. D. Hobbie, 1991.

SUGGESTED READING: *Something About the Author*, vol. 178, 2007; Hobbie, Holly, *The Art of Holly Hobbie: Drawing on Affection*, 1986. Online—Lodge, Sally, "Toot and Puddle Turn Ten," Children's Bookshelf—*Publishers Weekly*, May 31, 2007, at www.publishersweekly.com/eNewsletter

---

Valerie Hobbs
April 18, 1941–

"When people ask me if I always wanted to be a writer, I'd love to be able to say 'yes!' But that wouldn't be true. I wanted to be a figure skater. For years, until we moved to California, I daydreamed of the day I would step onto the podium in Oslo or Tokyo, and then gracefully bow my head to receive the gold medal. I suppose it's good that we moved. On Badgley's Pond, where my cousin Linda and I spent all our waking winter hours (at least when we weren't in school), I never really got much past loopy figure-eights. Dreaming was the fun part, not the work.

"Then, for a while, I was sure I'd one day be a world-renowned classical pianist. But that too was dreaming. When it came time to practice my Scarlatti, I could find a hundred excuses not to. The piano I had begged for was little more than a dust catcher.

"Moving to California was devastating for me. I was fifteen, a cheerleader and honor student, and had just completed my sophomore year. Sobbing, I handed my brand-new Riddell skates to Linda. We sold the piano. From then on, I vowed to make my parents the most miserable people on earth. Crossing the country in Bess, my father's old Plymouth, I did just that. I whined and sobbed, demanded endless movie magazines, Cokes, and sympathy. I'm sure my parents considered abandoning me at the first gas station that had a clean restroom.

"As Bronwyn Lewis says in *How Far Would You Have Gotten If I Hadn't Called You Back?*, my first novel, California kids were 'different . . . slicker, cleverer. . . .' The only ones that would have anything to do with me raced cars and partied nonstop, even on school nights. Soon I was one of them. The faster my time at the drag strip, the faster my grades went straight downhill.

"As life would have it, I soon met a very different kind of boy, a boy who lived on a ranch and who was mature, thoughtful,

Photo by Jack Hobbs

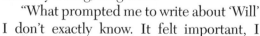

and smart. I began to see my 'town life' and the friends I'd made through different eyes. And I began to find my way back to the girl I'd once been. My grades climbed; I began to plan for college. For the first time since moving to California, I was happy.

"Then one morning I awoke to find my father sitting on the end of my bed. 'There's been an accident,' he said. And my life changed forever. I can say that even now, as an adult, a grandmother. Life can change in an instant, though it can take a lifetime to understand exactly how. The boy I call Will in *How Far . . .* was dead, shot with his own gun. Friends consoled me, my parents held me while, time and again, I sobbed my heart out. There was nothing I could do to feel better, to understand what had happened, or, of course, to 'get over it.' I simply felt very sorry for myself for what seems in memory a long, long time.

"What prompted me to write about 'Will' I don't exactly know. It felt important, I suppose, and maybe a way to honor his memory. I began to write my very first story and, when I'd finished, gave it the perfect title: 'Loved and Lost.' Who knows how many stories have been given that awful hackneyed title? But I loved the story and was quite proud of it.

"Thirty-five years later, when I was a Fellow in the South Coast Writing Project, I wrote that story again. It was better this time; after all, I'd learned a thing or two about writing in the meantime. Some stories stay with us forever, I guess, because

I still wasn't finished with this one. I had it in my mind when I began writing *How Far . . .*, and I still do as I work on a sequel.

"We are all storytellers. Some of us just need to write the stories down. As a Writing Project colleague of mine tells all her students: 'Only you can tell your story.' If you really think about that, as I have, how can you *not* write?"

03 03 03

Born in Metuchen, New Jersey, Valerie Hobbs spent her later teenage years in California. She is an author whose real-life connections to her novels are important to her. Always a reader as a child, she especially enjoyed dog and horse stories and Nancy Drew mysteries. Enrolling in Pasadena City College after high school, she flunked out, married in 1962 and had a daughter, Juliet. Later she returned to school at Ventura Community College, where she developed a love of literature and began reading long 19th century novels with the same delight she had once experienced reading Nancy Drew. She finished her B.A. degree in 1968 at the University of California, Santa Barbara, while her husband, Gary Johnson, worked as an abalone diver. Working as his "tender," she stored up experiences that would later be used in her young adult novel *Tender*. Her brother Allan was drafted during the turbulent years of the Vietnam War, which laid the groundwork for Hobbs's 2002 novel, *Sonny's War.*

"Life can change in an instant, though it can take a lifetime to understand exactly how."

Before creating her young adult novels, Hobbs had various teaching jobs. She taught high school on the Hawaiian island of Oahu from 1971 to 1974. After her first marriage ended in divorce in 1973, she returned to Santa Barbara to teach and complete her master's degree in 1978. That same year, she married Jack Hobbs, a teacher. From 1981 to 2001, Valerie Hobbs was a lecturer in the writing program at the University of California, Santa Barbara, where she is now retained as a professor emeritus.

Her first novel, based on the painful experience of the death of a dear friend in adolescence, *How Far Would You Have Gotten If I Hadn't Called You Back?*, was named an ALA Best Book for Young Adults and praised for its fine portrayal of adolescent emotions and needs. *Get It While It's Hot—or Not*, her second novel, was cited in IRA Teen Choices, and *Carolina Crow Girl* gained a spot on the New York Public Library's list, 100 Titles for Reading and Sharing. In 1999 Hobbs received the PEN Norma Klein Award, a prize that recognized "an emerging voice of literary merit" in the field of children's and young adult fiction.

Though she did not set out to write for the teen audience originally, Valerie Hobbs has made many excellent contributions

Courtesy of Farrar, Straus, and Giroux

to young adult literature. Her novels *Tender* and *Charley's Run* received *Voice of Youth Advocates* Top Shelf Awards, and both *Tender* and *Defiance* were designated as Junior Library Guild selections. *Letting Go of Bobby James, or, How I Found My Self of Steam* was named an ALA Quick Pick for Reluctant Readers. Tackling the difficult issues that face teens in any era—abuse, alcoholism, family tensions, peer pressure, work—Valerie Hobbs has shown that she has a finger on the adolescent pulse. Now a grandmother living in San Diego, she has published a story at the other end of the age spectrum for adults. *Call It a Gift* is the tale of two adventurous older adults trying to get the most out of life while they can. Hobbs continues to produce fine books for youth; in 2003 she was named Young Adult Author of the Year by the Arizona Library Association.

SELECTED WORKS FOR YOUNG ADULTS: *How Far Would You Have Gotten If I Hadn't Called You Back?*, 1995; *Get It While It's Hot—or Not*, 1996; *Carolina Crow Girl*, 1999; *Charley's Run*, 2000; *Tender*, 2001; *Sonny's War*, 2002; *Stefan's Story*, 2003; *Letting Go of Bobby James, or, How I Found My Self of Steam*, 2004; *Defiance*, 2005; *Sheep*, 2006; *Anything But Ordinary*, 2007.

SELECTED WORKS FOR ADULTS: *Call It a Gift*, 2005.

SUGGESTED READING: *Something About the Author*, vol. 145, 2004; *Authors and Artists for Young Adults*, vol. 28, 1999. Periodicals— "Flying Starts,' *Publishers Weekly*, Dec. 18, 1995; Blassingame, James, "Interview with Valerie Hobbs," *Journal of Adolescent & Adult Literacy*, Oct., 2004.

WEB SITE: www.valeriehobbs.com

"Some families go on car trips. Some go to football games. My family painted. Just about every weekend we'd organize our art supplies, then load up the car and find a scene to paint. Dad used oils, Mom, watercolors. My sister and I drew with pen and ink, then borrowed Mother's paints to color in the picture. There would be some instruction, things like 'Arthur, use a bigger brush. Don't be afraid of making a mistake.' Sometimes I got frustrated—drawing from life isn't easy. Still, I decided when I grew up I was going to be an artist.

"I was born in New York City but the first home I remember was in New Jersey— an old white house next to a brook. When I wasn't drawing, that wonderful brook kept me busy. In summer there were frogs and dragonflies and turtles and lots and lots of ducks that waddled to our back porch every morning quacking for breakfast. In winter, the brook froze over and I'd skate past the neighbor's yard, through the woods to a big pond where the whole town seemed to be ice-skating.

"In high school I concentrated on artwork, and I don't think I ever handed in a paper that didn't include some kind of illustration. But in college I decided to try something new, acting, and that's what I focused on for the next twenty years. For six of those years I appeared on a PBS children's television show called *Square One* in which I played all kinds of characters, including Superguy. For those of you who haven't seen him, Superguy had huge muscles, but I have to admit that the muscles came off with the costume. I also played a four-armed Martian named Blotmo. Well, actually I was only half of Blotmo. The front half. There were two of us in the costume.

"I loved performing—even though I had to share a costume now and then—but eventually I made up my mind to return to artwork. What I really wanted to do was illustrate children's books, but first a friend and I collaborated on a collection of cartoons, *The World According to He & She*. It didn't sell very well, but a magazine editor liked the book and bought a few of the cartoons. Then she asked for a few new pieces and before we knew it, 'The World According to He & She' had become a humor column in *Glamour* magazine.

Photo by Beverly Mayeri

Arthur Howard

January 26, 1948–

"While I was still working on the column, I met a children's book editor who happened to be looking for an illustrator for a new easy-reader series called Mr. Putter and Tabby, written by Cynthia Rylant. The editor suggested I try doing a few sketches. 'But don't spend too much time on them,' she warned me. 'I'm not sure you're right for the job.'

"So I didn't spend much time on the pictures—only about ten hours a day for the next six weeks, and that's how my children's book career started.

"One pleasant surprise has been to discover how useful my training as an actor has been in my illustration work. Whether an actor 'gets into character' or an illustrator draws a character, it's pretty much the same process. In both cases you sort through the possibilities trying to make the strongest, most vivid choices to show what the character wants at any given moment. When I draw Tabby I kind of become Tabby . . . in the way that Marlon Brando had to become Stanley Kowalski in *A Streetcar Named Desire*. It's the Stanislavski School of children's book illustration.

"After illustrating a few books written by others, I tried writing one. Turning out a story is a slow process for me—it's a challenge to make the text concise but not too predictable, funny but not forced. The first book I wrote was *When I Was Five*. It's not exactly autobiographical; still, there's one picture of a boy by a brook watching frogs and dragonflies and looking very, very happy."

> *"Some families go on car trips. Some go to football games. My family painted."*

૭ઙ ૭ઙ ૭ઙ

Known principally for his vivid and hilarious artwork in the Mr. Putter and Tabby series by Cynthia Rylant, Arthur Howard has also written and illustrated five picture books of his own: *When I Was Five, Cosmos Zooms, Hoodwinked, Serious Trouble,* and *The Hubbub Above.* He has also collaborated with Kathi Appelt, providing the pictures for her Bubba and Beau titles, and with Margaret Cuyler, on her humorous picture books about the everyday world.

Working primarily in watercolor, Howard creates characters with expressive and eye-catching features. After completing high school in New Jersey he went to Portland, Oregon, to attend Reed College. Upon his graduation in 1970, Howard embarked on his acting career. In addition to PBS's *Square One,* he also appeared in Broadway productions and in television commercials.

In 1994 Howard began his successful partnership with Rylant by illustrating *Mr. Putty and Tabby Pour the Tea.* To date the two have produced over a dozen Mr. Putty and Tabby titles. The series chronicles the adventures of Mr. Putty, a lonely old man, and Tabby, the cat he has adopted from the local pound. Their activities range from the mundane, like stirring soup, to the heart-stopping, like flying a plane, and all of these are evoked in captivating detail by Howard's illustrations. The Mr. Putty and Tabby books have earned Rylant and Howard a number of awards and citations: *Mr. Putter and Tabby Bake the Cake* was designated an ABC Children's Bestsellers Choice, as was *Mr. Putter and Tabby Pick the Pears*, which was also declared an American Booksellers Association Pick of the Lists and an ALA Notable Book. *Mr. Putter and Tabby Toot the Horn* received *Parenting* magazine's Reading Magic Award, while *Mr. Putty and Tabby Paint the Porch* was an ABA Pick of the Lists and the recipient of an Oppenheim Toy Portfolio Platinum Award. Howard earned another Oppenheim Platinum Award for *Mr. Putter and Tabby Write the Book* and an Oppenheim Gold Award for *Mr. Putter and Tabby Stir the Soup*.

Howard first tried his hand as a writer (as well as illustrator) in *When I Was Five*, about a wizened six-year-old boy who looks back on his life as a five-year-old. Among the book's many laurels were an Oppenheim Toy Portfolio Best Book Award, an IRA/CBC Children's Choice Award, and an ABA Pick of the Lists designation.

Cosmos Zooms, which features an insecure miniature schnauzer who discovers a hidden talent for skateboarding, won an IRA/CBC Children's Choice Award and an ABA Pick of the Lists citation, among other

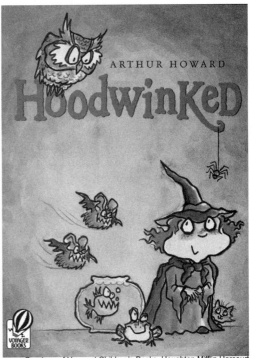

Courtesy of Harcourt Children's Books, Houghton Mifflin Harcourt

honors. In *Hoodwinked*, a witch named Mitzi searches for a pet but can't find one that is sufficiently creepy. However, a kitten takes a shine to Mitzi, who eventually comes to realize that this cat is just what she wanted. A *School Library Journal* Best Book of the Year, *Hoodwinked* also earned an IRA/CBC Children's Choice Award and a Best of the Best citation from the Children's Book Committee at Bank Street College of Education.

Featuring Howard's charcoal and watercolor illustrations, Kathi Appelt's Bubba and Beau series charts the adventures of a baby named Bubba and his dog Beau. Howard has also illustrated

The SOS File, written by Newbery Award–winner Betsy Byars and her daughters, Betsy Duffy and Laurie Myers.

Howard's latest works as author and illustrator are *Serious Trouble* and *The Hubbub Above*. A fanciful tale with straightforward title, *Serious Trouble* is about a prince named Ernest who longs to be a jester but must first convince a dragon not to eat him. In *The Hubbub Above*, young Sydney discovers that her noisy upstairs neighbors are in fact elephants who throw parties for all their wild animal friends.

Adept at finding the whimsy in every story, Arthur Howard delights and entertains with each of his books, and his work has been published abroad in the United Kingdom, France, and Korea. He lives in New York City.

SELECTED WORKS WRITTEN AND ILLUSTRATED: *When I Was Five*, 1996; *Cosmos Zooms*, 1999; *Hoodwinked*, 2001; *Serious Trouble*, 2003; *The Hubbub Above*, 2005.

SELECTED WORKS ILLUSTRATED: *Gooseberry Park*, by Cynthia Rylant, 1995; *Battlefield Ghost*, by Margaret Cuyler, 1999; *100th Day Worries*, by Margaret Cuyler, 2000; *Stop Drop and Roll*, by Margaret Cuyler, 2001; *Bubba and Beau, Best Friends*, by Kathi Appelt, 2002; *Bubba and Beau Go Night-Night*, by Kathi Appelt, 2003; *Bubba and Beau Meet the Relatives*, by Kathi Appelt, 2004; *The SOS File*, by Betsy Byars, Betsy Duffey, and Laurie Myers, 2004; *Hooray for Reading day*, by Margery Cuyler, 2008. Mr. Putter and Tabby Series, all by Cynthia Rylant—*Mr. Putter and Tabby Pour the Tea*, 1994; *Mr. Putter and Tabby Bake the Cake*, 1994; *Mr. Putter and Tabby Walk the Dog*, 1994; *Mr. Putter and Tabby Pick the Pears*, 1995; *Mr. Putter and Tabby Fly the Plane*, 1997; *Mr. Putter and Tabby Row the Boat*, 1997; *Mr. Putter and Tabby Take the Train*, 1998; *Mr. Putter and Tabby Toot the Horn*, 1998; *Mr. Putter and Tabby Paint the Porch*, 2000; *Mr. Putter and Tabby Feed the Fish*, 2001; *Mr. Putter and Tabby Catch the Cold*, 2002; *Mr. Putter and Tabby Stir the Soup*, 2003; *Mr. Putter and Tabby Write the Book*, 2004; *Mr. Putter and Tabby Make a Wish*, 2005; *Mr. Putter and Tabby Spin the Yarn*, 2006; *Mr. Putter and Tabby See the Stars*, 2007.

SUGGESTED READING: *Something About the Author*, vol. 165, 2006

Photo by Lois Lowry

"I was born in Springfield, Massachu-setts, where my father owned a filling station—now we call them gas stations. That filling station and the rock collection inside it play an important role in a picture book I would write many years later, *Rocks in His Head*. On the same property, my father and his father built our home. I'm next to the youngest of seven kids, and having my father working right next door was handy for us all. When I was four, we moved ten miles west to Westfield, a move that is also part of *Rocks in His Head*.

"I was a good student, although not a particularly good writer, so writing was not a career I even considered. I did, however, love to read. I truly thought that the children's librarian in Westfield waited for my arrival every afternoon, and I rarely disappointed her.

"Most of the people in my extended family were avid readers and, even more importantly, they were storytellers. I knew which of them told which kind of stories and I was, apparently, a very good listener. Some of those stories were the 'once-upon-a-time' sort told to entertain the children, but many, many others were real-life stories. They usually began with the word 'remember,' and they were stories the adults in that large extended family told to each other about themselves, their friends and those who had come before. As a child and as a young adult, I was an eavesdropper, but I had no idea how important those stories were.

"The 'once-upon-a-time' stories told to me were wonderful and surely enriched my childhood literacy, but the real-life stories I overheard were more important. They made me feel part of something bigger. They made me feel less alone. They were history in a way that no history book ever can be. Those adults remembered together through the stories they told, stories that sometimes caused them to rock with laughter and other times moved them to tears.

"I went to the local teachers' college, married and moved first to Tennessee, then Ohio, and then Minnesota, where my husband was a professor of psychology. When we divorced, I moved, with my three children, back to Westfield. My youngest child, David, died in infancy. My daughters, Jill and Rebecca, got

Carol Otis Hurst

October 13, 1933–
January 21, 2007

to hear some of those old stories and a good many new ones as I shared the books and stories I was reading and telling to my first, second and third grade classes.

"I then became a school librarian and found more books and stories to share. I told more stories too and became fairly well known for that storytelling. When Jill and Rebecca were grown, I traveled the country telling stories and lecturing about children's books. I wrote a lot of books for teachers and librarians. When people asked if I'd written a children's book, I'd say that that was like asking an opera singer if she'd written any good operas. But those old stories kept whispering in my head.

"When I was 67 years old, I sat down to see if I could write my grandmother's story. I tried it from every direction I could think of, but it didn't work. I put it aside and began thinking about my grandfather's story. I tried writing it down, but it didn't work either. Then one day I cast reality aside, moved them both back in time forty years and placed them as homeless young adults meeting each other on the banks of a failed canal, and it worked. I used many of those stories they told about themselves and about each other all those years ago. I used friends they had spoken of and laughed and cried about.

"I was lucky enough to get my first children's book—*Through the Lock*—accepted by Walter Lorraine, a wonderful editor at Houghton Mifflin. And then I was off. I dug back to more stories. There was all that wonderful stuff about my father's rock collecting and how his passion for those rocks saved us all. There was the family story about my great-great-grandfather, Abner Otis, who went off to find gold in California and supposedly was killed, except that he turned up years later in a different place. That story became *In Plain Sight*. Four other novels followed. Grandpa Otis and Grandpa Clark sat on the porch and reminisced about the awful time they had had during the Blizzard of 1888. *The Terrible Storm*, illustrated by S. D. Schindler, consisted of an almost verbatim conversation between those old men.

"And so I became a writer—my fourth or maybe my sixth career. Who would have thought? Certainly not my teachers, who said my spelling and grammar were good but that there was nothing special about my writing. And there wasn't. Not then. But years later, in Westfield, Massachusetts, there I was, stirring those real bits of story and coming up with new ones. Let me tell you about the night my mother was born and Rooshy Clark set off on horseback to tell all the neighbors, but he stopped for a drink at each house and began to forget who'd been born and where and to whom. And then. . . ."

"The 'once-upon-a-time' stories told to me were wonderful and surely enriched my childhood literacy, but the real-life stories I overheard were more important."

☙ ☙ ☙

Carol Otis Hurst's upbringing was a stimulating one. Surrounded by her six siblings and many relatives who had been displaced by the Great Depression, she was deeply affected by the rich storytelling that occurred around the dinner table. While her father owned and operated a gas station during her youth, his interest in rocks and minerals eventually led to a position as curator of mineralogy at the Springfield Science Museum. He would later be named director of that museum.

After completing her education Hurst embarked on a career in elementary education, teaching in PreK through third grade. Early in her teaching career, Hurst's students recognized her storytelling abilities, remarking upon them to other teachers. After teaching in Columbus, Ohio, and Minneapolis, Minnesota, she spent many years as school librarian at the Juniper School in Westfield, Massachusetts, where her storytelling earned further raves from students. In 1973 she began a long association with *Teaching PreK–8* magazine. Through her columns for the magazine, her ideas on literature in the curriculum reached teachers in the field on a regular basis, and her children's literature web site, www.carolhurst.com, incorporated those columns in an informative on-line resource. She was soon traveling the country conducting workshops for teachers on integrating literature into the classroom. Her reference books for educators outline many of those ideas.

Hurst's first novel for children, *Through the Lock*, was published in 2001. The story takes place in western Massachusetts during the 19th century and revolves around the construction of the Farmington Canal, a waterway that ran through the backyard of Hurst's childhood home. The characters are based on two of Hurst's grandparents—her orphaned grandmother, Etta Clark, and Grandfather Otis. A second novel, *In Plain Sight*, again mined her family history for inspiration, fictionalizing the aftermath of her ancestor Abner Otis's departure for California during the gold rush of 1849. In her retelling, Miles Corbin, like Abner Otis, leaves his wife, Delina, and daughter, Sarah, to seek his fortune. Life for the women left behind is a hard one; Delina must find work in a factory as well as manage the farm, but she manages to hold the family together.

A Killing in Plymouth Colony, co-authored with her daughter, Rebecca Otis, who had worked for a year at the living history museum, Plimoth Plantation, is a story based on an actual historical event. A murder in the original Plymouth settlement involved two of the Otis family's ancestors: the colony's governor, William Bradford, who oversaw the case, and the accused, John Billington. The story is seen through the eyes of Bradford's 11-year-old son, John, who struggles to gain his father's attention and respect. *You Come to Yokum* is set in a hunting lodge on Yokum Pond in the Berkshire hills of western Massachusetts just after World War I. The large family includes a suffragette mother whose advocacy sometimes antagonizes others in the community, a father who struggles to keep up the lodge, and their two boys, as well as eccentric aunts, uncles, and handymen. In *Torchlight*, Hurst explored yet another era amid the ethnic unrest between Irish immigrants and the native-born inhabitants

Courtesy of Greenwillow Books

of western Massachusetts. Set in the 1850s, it is the story of the friendship between two young girls, Charlotte, a descendant of the colony's first settlers, and Maggie, an Irish immigrant.

The same year her first historical novel was published, Hurst wrote a picture book story recalling her father's passion for rock collecting and how his hobby held the family together through difficult economic times. *Rocks in His Head*, featuring artwork by James Stevenson, was named an honor book in the nonfiction category for the *Boston Globe–Horn Book* Award and was also cited as an ALA Notable Children's Book and an Outstanding Science Trade Book. Her picture book text for *The Terrible Storm*, published in 2007, recalls her two grandfathers reminiscing about the Blizzard of 1888 with a humorous look at the difference in their personalities. The split-page design of the illustrations by S. D. Schindler cleverly echoes the two accounts of survival during the epic storm.

Carol Otis Hurst died in her home on January 21, 2007, at the age of 73, just as the first glowing reviews of her new book, *The Terrible Storm*, were being published. She is survived by her two daughters, Rebecca Otis and Jill Hurst, and her grandsons, Jesse and Keith Otis. Her daughter and collaborator, Rebecca Otis, is continuing her children's literature web site.

SELECTED WORKS: *Through the Lock*, 2001; *Rocks in His Head*, illus. by James Stevenson, 2001; *In Plain Sight*, 2002; *A Killing in Plymouth Colony*, with Rebecca Otis, 2003; *The Wrong One*, 2003; *You Come to Yokum*, illus. by Kay Life, 2005; *Torchlight*, 2006; *The Terrible Storm*, illus. by S. D. Schindler, 2007.

SELECTED WORKS WRITTEN FOR ADULTS: *Once Upon a Time: An Encyclopedia for Successfully Using Literature with Young Children*, with Margaret Sullivan Ahearn, et al., 1990; *Long Ago and Far Away: An Encyclopedia for Successfully Using Literature with Intermediate Readers*, with Margaret Sullivan Ahearn, et al., 1991; *Curriculum Connections: Picture Books in Grades 3 and Up*, 1998; *Open Books: Literature in the Curriculum, Kindergarten through Grade Two*, 1999; *Using Literature in the Middle School Curriculum*, with Rebecca Otis, 1999; *Friends and Relations: Using Literature with Social Themes, Grades K–2*, with Rebecca Otis, 1999; *Friends and Relations: Using Literature with Social Themes, Grades 3–5*, with Rebecca Otis, 2000.

SUGGESTED READING: Romano, Katherine, "Carol Otis Hurst: The Stories in Her Head," *Teaching PreK-8*, May 2001; Newman, Patricia M., "Who Wrote That? Featuring Carol Otis Hurst," *California Kids!* February 2003.

WEB SITE: www.carolhurst.com

"I was born in Romford, Essex, on the suburban frayed edge of London, at a time when there were still stinky pigs squealing in the market on Saturdays. By the time I left, the pigs had vanished and Romford had become nationally infamous as the butt of jokes about Essex boys and girls on the make.

"The intervening years gave me an education at the Royal Liberty Grammar School, which apart from a couple of zinging whacks around the ear, I enjoyed hugely. I was one of those lucky kids cut out for school, good at most things, excelling in a few. My Achilles heel was swimming. The school had its own freezing outdoor pool, so for me swimming contrived to be both compulsory and impossible.

"Many people can point to a teacher who inspired them, and an English master called Victor Slade was just such a teacher. He commanded a natural respect without ever having to raise his voice, and had a contagious enthusiasm for English literature, which he dispensed as if his charges were already mature adults. As a consequence we behaved like adults in his classes. Art and English were my favourite subjects. I won the school prizes for

Mick Inkpen

December 22, 1952–

these and came away with a decent crop of exam results, and a place to study English at Cambridge, which I never took up.

"Instead I began a career as a graphic designer under the excellent tutelage of Nick Butterworth, now a children's author and long time friend, who had set up a studio with a couple of old school pals. Although based in the suburbs we thought of ourselves as London designers and we did have some good clients, among them the fashion designer Bill Gibb (who was particularly adventurous) and the Post Office (who were not). But our real area of expertise lay in devising strategies for avoiding work. Office-chair racing was just one of the many skills we developed to a very high standard.

Courtesy of Mick Inkpen

"I learned a great deal during this period from Nick. It constituted a kind of informal apprenticeship in graphic design for which he had a considerable talent. This period also gave me the chance to develop my style as an illustrator, initially producing a string of instantly forgettable cartoons for a journal called *Banker's Magazine*. I would be sent articles on such opaque subjects as the futures markets and the world of insurance, and I would attempt to wring humour out of them. Later on, finding ideas for children's picture books would prove to be child's play by comparison. But it was working on greeting cards that gave me the opportunity to explore and develop confidence an illustrator. It's a route that many picture book authors have taken.

"I didn't start my career in children's books until Debbie and I had our own family: Simon and Chloë were 6 and 4 (they are adults now). Apart from the publication of my first book, I think the biggest buzz came a couple of years later. It was the first time I didn't have to look to find my work in the stores. There they were, luxurious piles of *The Blue Balloon*, stacked prominently. That moment marked the point at which I began to think of myself as a proper children's author. This was also the first time my most well-known character—Kipper—appeared, although it wasn't until he stood up on his back legs a year or so later that he became the eponymous hero of his own series of books.

"Kipper has subsequently appeared in many picture books and in his own animated TV series, for which he won a BAFTA (British Academy of Film and Television Arts) award. The excursion into TV was an enjoyable and happily collaborative one, but series animation requires that large batches of work are completed within exacting deadlines by very big teams of people, and it doesn't afford the creative freedom to play with ideas in quite the same way that picture books do. So although there are another couple of TV projects in the pipeline, I'm very happy to view those as excursions from my real profession.

"I have always divided my time between those characters like Kipper and Wibbly Pig, around whom I can build a series of titles, and one-off projects, which give me the stimulation of an entirely blank canvas. It's that early part of the process, the playing with ideas, that I really enjoy."

ଔ   ଔ   ଔ

After a 16-year career as a graphic designer, Mick Inkpen decided in 1986 to devote himself fulltime to writing and illustrating children's books in 1986. At first he collaborated with Nick Butterworth on both the writing and illustrating of books for young children. These included a series of retellings of the parables of Jesus in an accessible picture-book format with easy-to-read text and bright, colorful illustrations. The individual volumes were later published in one collection titled *Stories Jesus Told*. Another collaboration produced a winsome cat character named Jasper. With large print, cheerful watercolor illustrations, and topics that have enormous appeal for preschool children, the stories that featured Jasper were well received by parents, librarians, and toddlers alike.

By 1990, Inkpen was producing more books on his own, and his work began to be recognized by critics. He received the Children's Book Award, presented by the Federation of Children's Book Groups in England, for *Threadbear*, a gentle story about a patched-up teddy bear who wants to ask Santa Claus to fix the squeaker in his tummy. At the end of the story, children are delighted to find a picture of Threadbear that does, indeed, squeak when they push on it. Two years later, Inkpen received the British Book Award Best Illustrated Children's Book of the Year for *Penguin Small*, in which the title character journeys with a friendly snowman to rejoin his friends at the South Pole. He also received a British Book Award for *Lullabyhullaballoo*, a

"Many people can point to a teacher who inspired them, and an English master called Victor Slade was just such a teacher."

rollicking bedtime story that never grows stale, despite repeated readings.

Perhaps Inkpen's best-known character is Kipper, who made his debut in the United Kingdom in 1991. With a deceptive simplicity in both illustration and text, these stories of an engaging and child-like dog capture the imagination of preschoolers and beginning readers alike. The humor of everyday situations enlivens each tale and brings delight to young readers. In the first book, *Kipper*, the title character looks outdoors for a different place to sleep, returning at last to his familiar basket and blanket. The success of *Kipper*, which was presented the Acorn Award by the Nottinghamshire Libraries in 1992, inspired the creation of the many Kipper stories that followed. In 2001 *Kipper's A to Z* won the Smarties Prize Silver Medal in the U.K. and was named an ALA Notable Children's Book in the United States. *Where, Oh Where, Is Kipper's Bear?* won the Petits Filous/Right Start Magazine Award. The pup has universal appeal, and books about him have sold millions of copies worldwide. A second series, Little Kipper, for even younger children, debuted in 1998. Kipper has also starred in his own animated TV series, which earned a British Academy of Film and Television Arts award in 1998 for best-animated children's film and aired in the United States on the Nick, Jr. channel.

Courtesy of Hodder and Stoughton, LTD. © 1999

Another well-loved character created by Inkpen is Wibbly Pig. The small piglet with the big ears, along with his animal friends, encounters many of the simple pleasures of small children. Building a tent from blankets, playing at the beach, choosing favorite foods, blowing bubbles, and other events that loom large in a small child's life make these books perfect companions for preschoolers and their parents. *Wibbly Pig's Silly Big Bear* won a Smarties Prize Bronze Award, but all of Wibbly Pig's adventures score high with child readers.

One of the top-selling picture book creators in the world, Mick Inkpen has seen his books translated into over 20 languages with combined sales of over five million copies. Many of his books are innovative and interactive, with foldout pages and paper engineering. His well-loved characters have reached many more children through the media of animated film and television. Inkpen lives in Suffolk, England, with his wife, Debbie.

SELECTED WORKS WRITTEN AND ILLUSTRATED: (Dates are for British publication; U.S. publication dates, if different, are in parentheses): With Nick Butterworth—*The Nativity Play*, 1985; *The House on the Rock*, 1986; *The Precious Pearl*, 1986; *The Lost Sheep*, 1986; *The Two Sons*, 1986; *Nice and Nasty: A Book of Opposites*, 1987; *The Sports Day*, 1988; *The Good Stranger*, 1989; *Just Like Jasper!*, 1989; *The Rich Farmer*, 1989; *Ten Silver Coins*, 1989; *The School Trip*, 1990; *Jasper's Beanstalk*, 1992 (1993); *Opposites*, 1997; *Stories Jesus Told*, 2002; *Animal Tales*, 2002.

SELECTED WORKS WRITTEN AND ILLUSTRATED: *One Bear at Bedtime: A Counting Book*, 1987; *If I Had a Sheep*, 1988; *If I Had a Pig*, 1988; *Jojo's Revenge*, 1989; *Gumboot's Chocolatey Day*, 1989 (1991); *The Blue Balloon*, 1989 (1990); *Threadbear*, 1990; *Billy's Beetle*, 1991, (1992), new ed., 2007; *Penguin Small*, 1992 (1993) new ed., 2007; *Lullabyhullaballoo!*, 1993 (1994); *Nothing*, 1995 (1998); *Bear*, 1997; *The Great Pet Sale*, 1999; *The Mick Inkpen Treasury*, 2001; *Baggy Brown*, 2007; *We Are Wearing Out the Naughty Step*, 2008.

SELECTED SERIES WRITTEN AND ILLUSTRATED: Kipper series—*Kipper*, 1991 (1992); *Kipper's Toybox*, 1992; *Kipper's Birthday*, 1993; *Kipper's Book of Counting*, 1994; *Kipper's Book of Colours*, 1994; *Kipper's Book of Opposites*, 1994; *Kipper's Book of Weather*, 1994; *Where, Oh Where, Is Kipper's Bear?*, 1994 (1995); *Kipper's Snowy Day*, 1996; *Kipper Story Collection*, 1998; *Kipper's Christmas Eve*, 1999 (2000); *Kipper's A to Z*, 2000; *Kipper and Roly*, 2001; *Kipper's Monster*, 2002; *Kipper's Balloon*, 2002; *Kipper's Beach Ball*, 2003; *One Year with Kipper*, 2006; *Hide Me, Kipper*, 2008. Little Kipper series—*Honk!*, 1998; *Arnold*, 1998; *Splosh!*, 1998; *Sandcastle*, 1998; *Butterfly*, 1999; *Hissss!*, 1999; *Miaow!*, 2000 (*Meow!*, 2000); *Swing!*, 2000; *Skates*, 2001; *Picnic*, 2001; *Thing!*, 2001; *Rocket*, 2001. *The Little Kipper Collection*, 2000; *The 2nd Little Kipper Collection*, 2002. Wibbly Pig series—*Everyone Hide from Wibbly Pig*, 1997; *In Wibbly's Garden*, 2000; *Wibbly Pig Is Happy!*, 1995; *Wibbly Pig Can Make a Tent*, 1995; *Wibbly Pig Makes Pictures*, 1995; *Wibbly Pig Likes Bananas*, 1995; *Wibbly Pig Can Dance!*, 1995; *Wibbly Pig Opens His Presents*, 1995; *It's Bedtime, Wibbly Pig!*, 2004; *Tickly Christmas, Wibbly Pig*, 2005; *Wibbly Pig's Silly Big Bear*, 2006. Blue Nose Island series—*Ploo and the Terrible Gnobbler*, 2003; *Beachmoles and Bellvine*, 2004; *Bokobikes*, 2005.

SUGGESTED READING: *Something About the Author*, vol. 154, 2005.

WEB SITE: http://authorpages.hoddersystems.com/MickInkpen/

Courtesy of Susan Jeffers

Susan Jeffers

October 7, 1942–

"My mother was a painter. My first painting lessons came from her. They were really lessons in seeing. She would ask me, 'What is the color of that tree shadow? Is it blue? Is it violet?' And 'What is the shape of the highlight on the kettle? Is it round or oval?' She was teaching me to paint what I saw, not what I knew. What I knew would never be enough.

"Her favorite thing to do was to walk outside and see what she could see. She loved ice storms. My older sister Judy and I were taken on walks in winter, spring, summer, and fall. She left us with a lifelong love of the natural world. Like Hiawatha's grandmother, Nokomis, she named all the birds and flowers. I didn't have to go far to find inspiration for the books I would later illustrate: *Hiawatha*; *Brother Eagle, Sister Sky*; *Stopping by Woods on a Snowy Evening.*

"Somewhere in childhood, my passion for horses came alive. This led me to unexpected places. I suppose any desire takes you away with it, and you learn a lot about yourself trying to satisfy it. Horses were too expensive for my parents to give us, so I read avidly and I drew, constantly trying to make these creatures my own. Because of this love, I discovered *Black Beauty* and *National Velvet* and *King of the Wind*. In the originals (not the Hollywood versions), these are stories of compassion, bravery and self-discovery. In them, I found the life-altering power of literature. I wanted to be as kind as Black Beauty and as courageous as he was in the face of stupidity and cruelty. I wanted to be as dauntless as Velvet.

"About sophomore year in high school, I decided I wanted to become an artist. I had no idea what that meant or how to make a living at it. I just wanted to draw. I chose Pratt Institute in Brooklyn for my school. Probably the best thing about the experience at Pratt was the serious atmosphere. Everyone took for granted that what we were doing was of value. We were all

Artists. It was a way of thinking and solving problems that was new to me.

"After graduation in 1964, I worked in publishing, doing entry-level assignments, and moved up to designing book jackets. In three years, I was ready to go out and work on my own. I had found in children's book publishing a combination of my favorite things: fine art and literature.

"It seemed to me that success was closely linked to how clearly you expressed your innermost self. When I illustrated Joseph Jacobs's *The Buried Moon*, it was met with critical success, and I felt secure with my interpretation of the story, but then I had a disaster with *The Three Jovial Huntsmen*. I had completely missed the point of the book, and the artwork was so strained that my publisher and I decided not to publish it. I quit the book world for a year, but was unwilling to give up on my art. When my publisher suggested I try again, I did. Persistence paid off when the book became an award winner.

"I learned a few things in this experience and felt I understood when one day I heard Paul Newman interviewed. Asked to name the most important thing an actor needed to succeed, he didn't mention talent or good looks; instead he said, 'persistence.' I read more about persistence in Norman Rockwell's biography when he wrote about sinking, for a while, in the public estimation of his work. He said the way he came out of his slump was to simply do more of the only thing he knew how to do, or cared about, which was his painting."

೮೪ ೮೪ ೮೪

Born and raised in northern New Jersey, Susan Jeffers has never lived far from her home roots. After graduating from Pratt Institute in New York, Jeffers worked for three different publishing firms in the city and then left to pursue freelance projects. Jeffers has been captivated throughout her career by stories of the imagination, animals, and the natural world. She has illustrated children's novels, poetry books, nursery rhymes, folk tales, retellings of classic children's stories, and picture book stories. Her series of picture books about a West Highland Terrier named McDuff is one of several collaborations with her long-time friend and colleague Rosemary Wells.

Jeffers's first critical success came with her swirling, atmospheric illustrations in a 1969 picture book version of an old English folk tale originally collected by Joseph Jacobs in *More English Fairy Tales* in the late 19th century. In *The Buried*

"Probably the best thing about the experience at Pratt was the serious atmosphere. Everyone took for granted that what we were doing was of value. We were all Artists."

Moon, the moon is caught by evil spirits in a swamp and must be rescued by the common people. Reviewers and readers alike were attracted by the illustrations—fine, detailed pen-and-ink drawings colored in shades of gray and violet.

The Three Jovial Huntsmen, a 1974 Caldecott Honor book, also received the 1975 Golden Apple Award given by the Biennial of Illustrations at Bratislava. It was the first book by an American to receive this international award. The rhyme had once been illustrated by Randolph Caldecott himself, and Jeffers's sly visual humor invites children to linger over her own interpretations of the silly huntsmen and their dog. Jeffers's work is often laced with a hidden humor in the pictures that provides further commentary on the words in the text. This humor is also evident in the harried father's attempts to put his lively son to bed in *Close Your Eyes*, a 1978 ALA Notable Children's Book.

Jeffers works mostly in pen, ink, and wash. Using a crosshatch method, she makes thousands of little lines to detail forms, a process she claims is easier than it looks. She then washes her detailed artwork in color, which intensifies and defines her sketches.

Believing that archetypal stories reflect our innermost being, Jeffers has throughout her career illustrated classic works, such as *Thumbelina* and *Hansel and Gretel*. Both of her versions of these classics, with their oversized pictures and intriguing details, received citations of merit from the Society of Illustrators. Another recurring theme in her work is celebration of the natural world. *A Forest of Dreams*, winner of the SCBWI Golden Kite award, portrays a young girl's excitement at watching winter turn into spring. Delicate but powerful images illustrate *Brother Eagle, Sister Sky*, winner of the American Booksellers Book of the Year (ABBY) Award, the Kentucky Bluegrass Award, and a National Parenting Publications (NAPPA) Award. This title was also on the John Burroughs List of Nature Books for Young Readers and the Growing Good Kids Book Award, Top 40 Books of the Last 100 Years. Including pictures depicting Native Americans living at peace with their natural surroundings, *Brother Eagle, Sister Sky* became one of the few children's books to be included on the *New York Times* general bestseller list.

Reeve Lindbergh's *Midnight Farm*, a 1987 *Redbook* Children's Picture Book Award winner illustrated by Jeffers, is both a counting book and a story in verse. In *Lassie Come-Home*, a Parents' Choice Gold Award winner, Jeffers and Rosemary Wells combined their talents to adapt Eric Knight's classic story for today's young readers. Wells adapted the text and Jeffers provided evocative watercolors to depict the Yorkshire setting of this well-loved dog story. Tackling another classic title of children's literature, the pair produced an adaptation of Rachel Field's Newbery award title, *Hitty, Her First Hundred Years*. Wells's adaptation and Jeffers's full color gouache paintings create a new life for the little doll and her many adventures, highlighting some of the historic events of those 100 years. Jeffers and Wells later collaborated on the popular McDuff series, about the adventures of a lovable West Highland terrier whose feelings are brought to vivid life in Jeffers's pictures. The little terrier fairly leaps off the pages and into the hearts of readers of all ages, reflecting the joy that both author and illustrator had in their own real-life Westies. *McDuff's Wild Romp* won an Oppenheim Toy Portfolio Gold Award.

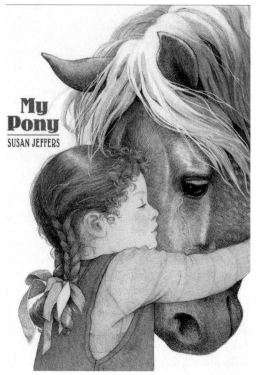

My Pony
SUSAN JEFFERS

Courtesy of Hyperion Books for Children

Known throughout her career for creating books that are easily accessible to young children as well as pleasing to adults, Jeffers was presented the 1990 Rip Van Winkle Award for her outstanding contribution to children's literature. Many of her books have been cited for honors and award lists by organizations such as the American Library Association and the Children's Book Council. The American Institute of Graphic Arts has showcased her illustrations, and her work has been included in shows at the New York Metropolitan Museum of Art, the National Women's Museum of Art, the Brooklyn Museum of Art, and the Norman Rockwell Museum.

My Pony, published in 2003, is a culmination of Jeffers's childhood longing to have her own horse. Today her favorite things still include horses and drawing as she studies landscape and portrait painting with the renowned teacher and painter Kirril Doron and the art of dressage with a horse named Hans. She lives in Westchester County, New York, and has one grown daughter, Ali, and a son-in-law, Chad Phillips.

SELECTED WORKS ILLUSTRATED: *The Buried Moon*, by Joseph Jacobs, 1969; *Why You Look Like You Whereas I Tend to Look Like Me*, by Charlotte Pomerantz, illus. with Rosemary Wells, 1969; *The Spirit of Spring: A Tale of the Greek God Dionysos*, by Penelope Proddow, 1970; *The Circus Detectives*, by Harriette Sheffer Abels, 1971; *The First of the Penguins*, by Mary Q. Steele, 1973; *All the Pretty Horses*, 1974; *The Wild Swans*, by Hans Christian Andersen, retold by Amy Ehrlich, 1976; *Close Your Eyes*, by Jean Marzollo, 1978; *Stopping by Woods on a Snowy Evening*, by Robert Frost, 1978 (reissued with additional illustrations, 2001); *If Wishes Were Horses: Mother Goose Rhymes*, 1979; *Thumbelina*, by Hans Christian Andersen, retold by Amy Ehrlich, 1979 (reissued 2005); *Hansel and Gretel*, by the Brothers Grimm, 1980; *Little People's Book of Baby Animals*, 1980; *Snow White and the Seven Dwarfs*, retold by Freya Littledale, 1981; *The Snow Queen*, by Hans Christian Andersen, retold by Amy Ehrlich, 1982; *Wynken, Blynken, and Nod*, by Eugene Field, 1982; *Hiawatha*, by Henry Wadsworth Longfellow, 1983; *Silent Night*, by Joseph Mohr, 1984; *Cinderella*, by Charles Perrault, retold by Amy Ehrlich, 1985 (reissued 2004); *Black Beauty*, by Anna Sewell, adapted by Robin McKinley, 1986; *The Midnight Farm*, by Reeve Lindbergh, 1987; *Forest of Dreams*, by Rosemary Wells, 1988; *Baby Animals*, by Margaret Wise Brown, 1989; *Benjamin's Barn*, by Reeve Lindbergh, 1990; *Brother Eagle, Sister Sky! The Words of Chief Seattle*, by Chief Seattle, 1991; *Waiting for the Evening Star*, by Rosemary Wells, 1993; *Lassie Come-Home*, Eric Knight's original 1938 classic, adapted by Rosemary Wells, 1995; *McDuff Moves In*, by Rosemary Wells, 1997; *McDuff Comes Home*, by Rosemary Wells, 1997; *McDuff and the Baby*, by Rosemary Wells, 1997; *McDuff's New Friend*, by Rosemary Wells, 1998; *Rachel Field's Hitty: Her First Hundred Years*, new edition by Rosemary Wells, 1999; *The McDuff Stories*, by Rosemary Wells, 2000; *McDuff Goes to School*, by Rosemary Wells, 2001; *McDuff Saves the Day*, by Rosemary Wells, 2001; *Love Songs of the Little Bear*, by Margaret Wise Brown, 2001; *K is for Kitten*, by Niki Leopold, 2002; *McDuff's Favorite Things: Touch and Feel*, by Rosemary Wells, 2004; *McDuff's Hide-and-Seek*, by Rosemary Wells, 2004; *Blueberries for the Queen*, by John and Katherine Paterson, 2004; *McDuff's Wild Romp*, by Rosemary Wells, 2005.

SELECTED WORKS WRITTEN AND ILLUSTRATED: *Three Jovial Huntsmen*, adapted, 1973; *Wild Robin*, retold, 1976; *My Pony*, 2003; *The Nutcracker*, retold, 2007; *My Chincoteague Pony*, 2008.

SUGGESTED READING: *Something About the Author*, vol. 137, 2003; Silvey, Anita, *Children's Books & Their Creators*, 1995; *Children's Literature Review*, vol. 30, 1993; Kauffman, Linda, "The Caldecott Medal and Honor Books: *Three Jovial Huntsmen*," in *Newbery and Caldecott Medal and Honor Books: An Annotated Bibliography*, 1982. Periodicals—*Bookbird*, vol. XV, no. 3, September 15, 1977.

WEB SITE: www.susanjeffers-art.com

An earlier profile of Susan Jeffers appeared in *Fourth Book of Junior Authors and Illustrators*, 1978.

Photo by Heather Weston

Emily Jenkins

September 13, 1967–

"I'm the child of a pre-school teacher (mother) and a playwright (father). I grew up in Cambridge, Massachusetts in the 1970s. I used to visit my mother's classrooms and play or read with the children there. I also used to sit in the back row of theaters, watching rehearsals. My mother read to me every night until I was twelve, and my father gave me books he loved: *Alice's Adventures in Wonderland, Huckleberry Finn, Sherlock Holmes*.

"When I was young, I would read in the bath, at meals, in the car—everywhere. (I still do, and now I also listen to audiobooks, so I can read walking, exercising, and cleaning the house!) When I was eight, I began writing my own stories, which were imitations of books I loved—in particular, *The Wolves of Willoughby Chase* by Joan Aiken and *Pippi Longstocking* by Astrid Lindgren.

"I was determined to share my Pippi story with the world, and my dad was very encouraging. He typed it up on an old electric typewriter and photocopied it fifty times. Then we went to an artist friend's studio and silk-screened 50 copies of a drawing I'd made for the cover. I considered it 'published' and gave it to everyone I knew. It meant a lot to me that my dad took my work so seriously.

"I think my interest in picture books comes, in part, from my background in theater. I am curious about the connections between words and image. An actor changes his tone, an illustrator changes a color scheme or a line, and the meaning of a story is remade.

"When I was in college and graduate school I studied illustrated books from an academic standpoint. My dissertation was on 19th century and early 20th century illustrated novels. But I also spent a lot of my early adult years working with children. I worked in the lab pre-school at Vassar nearly every term, and after graduation I worked as an assistant in Montessori school. So it was natural that when I escaped academia, I would turn to writing for young audiences.

"Now I write full time, in a small office in my Brooklyn apartment. I have been exceptionally lucky in my collaborations with artists. I've done numerous books with Tomek Bogacki, some of which stemmed from my visits to his studio in Queens, NY, where I got ideas from looking at his sketches. I've worked twice with Pierre Pratt, who draws the most wonderful dogs in all of picture books, and have worked and learned so much from Paul O. Zelinsky and Sergio Ruzzier. Upcoming books are with illustrators Alexandra Boiger, Lauren Castillo, and Giselle Potter."

CB CB CB

Emily Jenkins earned her B.A. degree from Vassar College in 1989 and her Ph.D. in English literature from Columbia University in 1998. She has received a variety of fellowships in writing and the arts to support her research and teaching. Her doctoral dissertation focused on a particular phenomenon in British publishing at the turn of the 20th century and was entitled *The Reading Public and the Illustrated Novel in Britain, 1890–1914*. With this strong academic background, Jenkins has taught as an adjunct faculty member at Barnard College and Columbia University. Her courses ranged from Introductory British Literature to Essay Writing, and the authors covered in her classes were as disparate as William Shakespeare, Sigmund Freud, Lewis Carroll, Virginia Woolf, and Joan Didion. As a freelance editor she has worked for *Publishers Weekly*, and she served as a reviewer of children's books from 1996 to 2001. She has also taught courses in the craft of writing picture books and led other writing seminars at New York University.

While she has written articles for a wide variety of print magazines (*Wired*, *Vogue*, *Mademoiselle*, among others), New York area newspapers, and on-line journals (*Salon*, *Underwire*, *Feed*), her first published book was one for children written with Len Jenkin, her playwright father. The two wrote alternating chapters that they sent to each other when Jenkins was living in Chicago and her father was in New York. *The Secret Life of Billie's Uncle Myron*, published in 1996, is a madcap adventure of a young heroine and her brother Bix who, in search of adventure, find themselves lost in a bizarre world known as Borderland.

In 2002 Jenkins published an adult novel, *Mister Posterior and the Genius Child*, with an eight-year-old protagonist, Vanessa, a humorous foil for the narcissistic culture of the 1970s. Barnes & Noble named Jenkins a "Discover Great New Writers" pick and reviewers called the novel funny, touching, and deceptively lighthearted. Using the pseudonym E. Lockhart, she has written a number of well-received novels for teens.

> "I am curious about the connections between words and image. An actor changes his tone, an illustrator changes a color scheme or a line, and the meaning of a story is re-made."

Courtesy of Farrar, Straus, and Giroux

It is in writing picture books, however, that Emily Jenkins has received her greatest accolades to date. *Five Creatures*, illustrated by Tomek Bogacki, was named an ALA Notable Children's Book and an Honor Book for both the *Boston Globe–Horn Book* Award for picture books and the Charlotte Zolotow Award for picture book writing. It has been published in French, Spanish, and Japanese editions. A humorous tale that also teaches the principles of grouping and sorting, *Five Creatures* has been popular with both children and teachers. *Daffodil*, her second picture book with Bogacki, about a child's need to speak up for herself, was a *Parenting* magazine pick, a *Reading Rainbow* choice, an IRA/CBC Children's Choice title, and a Capitol Choices pick.

When Jenkins teamed with illustrator Pierre Pratt for *That New Animal*, she struck a universal chord with parents and children. Two dogs in a family react to the fuss made over a new baby with a series of attention-getting pranks. Named a *School Library Journal* Best of the Year and a Blue Ribbon title by the *Bulletin of the Center for Children's Books*, *That New Animal* was also named a *Boston Globe–Horn Book* Award Honor Book. Jenkins's four board books about Bea and HaHa, illustrated by Tomek Bogacki, pair a large hippo and a small ferret for adventures that delight very young children. *Love You When You Whine*, which was named a Bank Street College Best Children's Book of the Year, tackles a universal situation between toddlers and parents—how to handle bad behavior—and grew directly out of Jenkins's experiences with her own daughter.

Emily Jenkins continued to channel the emotions of young children with her early chapter book, *Toys Go Out*, a collection of short stories about three distinctive toys, their adventures, their fears, and their sometime rivalry for a little girl's affections. The humor and insight in the writing, along with Paul O. Zelinsky's expressive black-and-white drawings, brought this title many honors, including an ALA Notable Book, a Parents' Choice silver award, an Oppenheim Toy Portfolio Platinum award, and a spot on many Best of the Year lists. It was also named *Nick Jr.* magazine's Best Toy Story of the Year.

Whether she is writing about imaginary creatures, toys that come to life, or an everyday neighborhood, Jenkins has an uncanny knack for expressing a child's sensibility. Her picture book illustrated by first-time artist Lauren Castillo, *What Happens on Wednesdays*, was inspired by walking through her Brooklyn neighborhood with her preschool daughter and realizing that children use different landmarks from those adults rely on. The book follows a child from waking in the morning to getting into bed at night with all the ordinary, yet special, events that make up her day. Emily Jenkins lives with her family in Brooklyn, New York.

SELECTED WORKS FOR CHILDREN: *The Secret Life of Billie's Uncle Myron*, with Len Jenkin, 1996; *Five Creatures*, illus. by Tomek Bogacki, 2001; *Daffodil*, illus. by Tomek Bogacki, 2004; *My Favorite Thing (According to Alberta)*, illus. by Anna Laura Cantone, 2004; *That New Animal*, illus. by Pierre Pratt, 2005; *Toys Go Out: Being the Adventures of a Knowledgeable Stingray, a Toughy Little Buffalo and Someone Called Plastic*, illus. by Paul O. Zelinsky, 2006; *Love You When You Whine*, illus. by Sergio Ruzzier, 2006; Bea and HaHa Board Books: *Hug, Hug, Hug!*, *Num, Num, Num!*, *Up, Up, Up!*, *Plonk, Plonk, Plonk!*, all illus. by Tomek Bogacki, 2006; *Daffodil, Crocodile*, illus. by Tomek Bogacki, 2007; *SkunkDog*, illus. by Pierre Pratt, 2007; *What Happens on Wednesdays*, illus. by Lauren Castillo, 2007.

SELECTED WORKS FOR YOUNG ADULTS (as E. Lockhart): *The Boyfriend List*, 2005; *Fly on the Wall: How One Girl Saw Everything*, 2006; *The Boy Book: A Study of Habits and Behaviors, Plus Techniques for Taming Them*, 2006; *Dramarama*, 2007.

SELECTED WORKS FOR ADULTS: *Tongue First: Adventures in Physical Culture*, 1998; *Mister Posterior and the Genius Child*, 2002.

SUGGESTED READING: *Something About the Author*, vol. 174, 2007. Periodicals—Jenkins, Emily, "Peter Pan. I am he. I am not," *The Horn Book*, September/October 2007.

WEB SITE: http://WEB SITE: www.emilyjenkins.com

Cynthia Kadohata

July 2, 1956–

"I was born in Chicago, but my earliest memories are of the South, where my family moved in 1957, and of the highway, since my family moved several times during my childhood. American highways have always seemed strikingly romantic to me, filled simultaneously with the known and the unknown. Years ago I was traveling across country by Greyhound bus. I got off at a rest stop somewhere in Nebraska in the middle of the night. Under the glare of fluorescent lights, I looked around at the unfamiliar surroundings and at the unfamiliar people, and I felt right at home. I had an almost overwhelming feeling of happiness. For many years, I felt addicted to the road, addicted to those moments of feeling at home on the American highway.

"Recently I was interviewing a woman for a book I'm writing about the Japanese American expatriates of World War II—the people who objected so strenuously to being interned that, after the war, they ended up renouncing their American citizenship and were shipped, citizens of no country, to Japan. She talked of the intense emotions some of these people felt even today, and she said she had become addicted to sharing their 'original moments,' by which she meant formative moments, moments that made them who they are. She felt—through others—that she was in another time and another place, feeling what others had felt during some of the most important days of their lives, seeing what others had seen. Memory and place and time and even identity became all mixed up into a breathtaking and epic moment. In many ways, I think what I am searching to create in my stories is these original moments.

Photo by George Miyamoto

"In Georgia my father worked as a chicken sexer, a profession that at the time was almost all Japanese. We lived in a couple of different towns as he changed hatcheries. I believe the only other people of Japanese ancestry in our towns worked in the hatchery business. We moved the next year to Arkansas, near the Ozarks. My parents felt their greatest love and their greatest enmity for each other in the South. My family formed and broke apart in the South. I learned how to talk and how to read in the South. I learned to love animals. I formed a bond that would never be broken with my younger brother and older sister. We spent all our time together. Back then, parents could let you run off and play by yourself all day and nobody thought it was dangerous. I remember spending humid summer days stringing thread through dandelion necklaces, and I remember catching bumblebees in a fancy gold change purse left over from the days when my parents were courting. Where we lived, there were no fences or bushes between homes. You didn't know where one property ended and another began. Dogs ran freely through the fields, and a six-year-old could walk to school by herself. At night we would burn our garbage in the incinerator, or lie outside and stare at the stars. When my parents divorced, my mother, sister, brother, and I moved up north. I think many of my original moments had already occurred by then, and that's why I love to write from the child's perspective."

ଓ ଓ ଓ

Like the heroine of her first book for young readers, Cynthia Kadohata is Japanese-American and grew up in the American South, first in Georgia and then in Arkansas. As a child she spoke with such a heavy Southern accent that when she moved north in her teens, people could hardly understand a word she said. Her teacher threatened to put her in speech therapy if she didn't lose her accent.

Kadohata's father was the son of Japanese immigrants who came to the United States in the early 1920s. During World War II, he and his family were interned at the Poston camp on the Colorado River Indian Reservation in the Sonoran Desert. Eventually he was drafted out of the camp and assigned to the U.S. Army Military Intelligence Service. Three brothers that he'd never met lived in Japan. Two of them were killed during the war, and he met the third when he was stationed in Japan with the U.S. Army after the war. Cynthia Kadohata's mother was born in Southern California and grew up in Hawaii (where people of Japanese ancestry were not interned during the war) before moving to Chicago, the city where Cynthia was born.

Since she was born to a family prone to wanderlust, it is not surprising that Kadohata draws much of her inspiration from her own travels around the country, which, she says, is one of the things that gives her "writing energy." After dropping out of high school for a time and working a number of odd jobs, she received a degree in journalism from the University of Southern California. Later, as a graduate student at the University of Pittsburgh, she became friends with another writing student named Caitlyn Dlouhy, with whom she stayed in touch over the years.

Determined to become a writer, Kadohata submitted stories to a number of magazines. After many rejections, one of her short stories appeared in the *New Yorker*, and the author was on her way to a writing career. In 1989 her first book, *The*

"American highways have always seemed strikingly romantic to me, filled simultaneously with the known and the unknown."

Floating World, appeared to excellent reviews. Published as an adult novel, it nevertheless featured a young protagonist and was cited by Erica Bauermeister and Holly Smith in their volume, *Let's Hear It for the Girls: 375 Great Books for Readers 2–14*. The "floating world" of the title is the world Olivia, a teenage Japanese-American, experiences as her family travels the country in search of work.

A National Endowment for the Arts Fellowship and the Whiting Writers Award, given to "a writer of exceptional promise," came close on the heels of that early success. However, her next two books, which feature futuristic and science fiction themes, did not receive much notice.

In the 1990s, after receiving a Chesterfield Screenwriting Fellowship, Kadohata tried her hand at writing for film but did not find it satisfying. Her old friend Caitlyn Dlouhy had been working as a children's book editor and urged Kadohata to send her ideas for a children's novel. Since the protagonists in her adult books were young people, it seemed natural that she should write for younger readers. With Dlouhy's encouragement, she began work on her first book for children, a story that was based on many of the experiences from her own childhood. *Kira-Kira* appeared in 2004 and was awarded the 2005 Newbery Medal. It was also placed on several awards lists, including ALA's Notable Children's Books, CCBC Choices, *Booklist* Editors' Choices, *Book Links* Lasting Connections, the New York Public Library's Books for the Teen Age, and the Capitol Choices List.

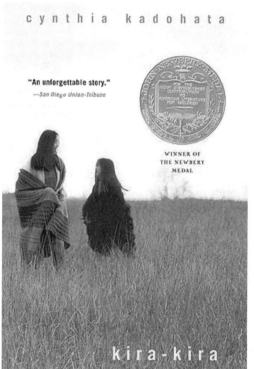

cynthia kadohata

"An unforgettable story."
—*San Diego Union-Tribune*

WINNER OF THE NEWBERY MEDAL

kira-kira

Courtesy of Simon & Schuster Children's Publishing

Following her initial success in the children's book field with a novel about the Japanese internment camps of the 1940s in America, Kadohata had another winner in *Weedflower*. The book was awarded the Jane Addams Children's Book Award, given annually to books that effectively address themes or topics that promote peace, justice, world community, and/or equality of the sexes.

Today Cynthia Kadohata lives in Southern California with her son, Sammy, whom she adopted from Kazakhstan in 2004, and her Doberman, Shika Kojika, which means "deer, little deer" in

Japanese. Her older sister, who lived in Asia for twenty years, now resides in Boston, and her younger brother lives near her in the Los Angeles area.

SELECTED WORKS FOR CHILDREN: *Kira-Kira*, 2004; *Weedflower*, 2006; *Cracker: The Best Dog in Vietnam*, 2007; *Outside Beauty*, 2008.

SELECTED WORKS FOR ADULTS: *The Floating World*, 1989; *In the Heart of the Valley of Love*, 1992; *The Glass Mountains*, 1996.

SUGGESTED READING: Faust, Susan, "The Comeback Kid," *School Library Journal*, May 2005; Dlouhy, Caitlin, "Cynthia Kadohata," *The Horn Book*, July/August 2005; Kadohata, Cynthia, "Newbery Medal Acceptance," *The Horn Book*, July-August, 2005.

WEB SITE: www.kira-kira.us

"Since I founded *The Dorothy Weekly News* with my best friend when I was nine (a useful escape from the five thousand laying hens my family raised), I suppose I've always been writing. I'll never forget the exhilaration of actually being *paid* cash money for my first essays in a local magazine during high school! Off I went to study literature in college—and instantly was diverted by film. This diversion lasted several decades until I finally got movies out of my system. Yes, I was still writing, although it was movie reviews and scholarly articles on the silent cinema. But I was avidly reading, too—until one day I tossed aside a popular novel in disgust, telling my husband, 'I could write a better book than this!' His reply? 'Stop complaining and do it!'

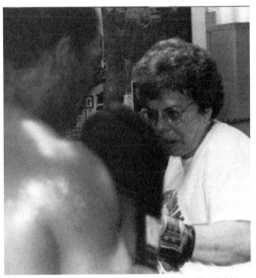

Photo by Daniel Karr

Kathleen Karr

April 21, 1946–

"So I did. I wrote my first novel all the way through. It wasn't good enough to sell, but it taught me that I did possess the words and the patience necessary for the job. Then I wrote my second novel all the way through. Still not good enough, but I was getting the knack of dialogue and description. The third book sold! I wrote another handful for the women's market—part time, while still in the film biz and raising two young children—until my children asked me to write a book for them. So I did. *It Ain't Always Easy* was bought by a prestigious New York publisher. I forgot about adult fiction. Writing for kids was more fun. Along the way I learned that all my years spent with movies weren't wasted time. Subconsciously I'd picked up the moving picture's method of storytelling. My books have a certain cinematic quality: the stories move fast, dialogue pushes along the action, and the descriptions are as visual as I can make them.

"Now I write full time. I love historical fiction—making my own time machine and plunging into the past. I'm particularly comfortable in the 19th and early 20th centuries, but have begun stretching a bit to earlier times, such as the 17th century in *Worlds Apart*. It's a stretch because each period has its own issues, and particularly its own dialogue patterns. It is a challenge to capture these and modify them for contemporary readers. I do this by heavy research: full immersion in period literature, diaries, and journals; trips to capture the lay of the land; 'reality' research such as learning to box before writing *The Boxer*. It's an all-encompassing job that I take on with enthusiasm.

> "By high school my son was doing photo shoots of my favorite boxers (for The Boxer) with the comment, 'You're never boring, Mom.'"

"And how does my family react to all of this? I've been blessed with a proud, supportive husband, and a daughter and son who grew up completely involved with my manuscripts in progress. I dragged them all on summer 'novel fodder' trips. We camped across the Oregon Trail. We panned for gold in California's icy American River, trekked with burros, traveled in Gypsy caravans across Ireland, and descended into countless caves. In the process of these journeys we explored 49 states, nearly every national park, Canada, Mexico, Europe, and beyond. During the school year both kids would arrive home each afternoon demanding to read my latest scene. By high school my son was doing photo shoots of my favorite boxers (for *The Boxer*) with the comment, 'You're never boring, Mom.'

"The kids are grown up, but I'm still writing—and they still critique my latest manuscripts long distance. Now my husband bears the brunt of reading the dailies. It's a satisfying life."

అ అ అ

Born in Allentown, Pennsylvania and raised in Dorothy, New Jersey, on a chicken farm, Kathleen Karr attended the Catholic University of America, where she received an B.A. in English in 1968. That same year she married Lawrence F. Karr, a physicist and computer consultant, and took a job as an English and speech teacher in a Rhode Island high school. Continuing her education at Providence College, she received a M.A. in 1971 and then took courses in visual communications, advertising, and sculpture at Corcoran School of Art. While she was working in the film industry, Karr also taught in colleges, lectured in a variety of settings, and began to write, first articles and then books for adults.

Karr's first children's book, *It Ain't Always Easy*, a thoughtful, heartwarming story of two 19th century orphans, was selected by the New York Public Library as one of its 100 Titles for Reading and Sharing. She followed this success with another late–19th century historical novel, the lighthearted account of how six determined sisters rescue their hapless father and their West Texas homestead from bankruptcy. *Oh Those Harper Girls!* received a Parents Choice Award. *The Great Turkey Walk*—in which 15-year-old Simon tries to make his fortune by herding a thousand turkeys from Missouri to Denver in 1860—was named a Best Book of the Year by both *Publishers Weekly* and *School Library Journal*. Chosen for over 25 state reading lists, it was also cited as a Notable Children's Trade Book in the Field of Social Studies. The struggles of a Hungarian immigrant family in southern New Jersey are chronicled in *Man of the Family*, which was named an ALA Notable Children's Book.

Noted for her boldly drawn characters, action-driven plots, and an ability to identify with the pains of growing up in any era, Karr has often imbued her texts with a sense of humor and a distinctive point of view so that desperate situations do not overwhelm the reader. *The Boxer*—an enticing mixture of sports action and family drama set in the gritty tenement world of New York City's Lower East Side in 1885—won a Golden Kite Award for Fiction and was named an ALA Best Book for Young Adults. In *Gilbert and Sullivan Set Me Free*, Karr weaves a true-life incident—a 1914 performance of *The Pirates of Penzance* in a women's prison—into a novel that is as thought-provoking as it is poignant. It was voted a Best Book of the year by the ALA Amelia Bloomer Project, as was *Mama Went to Jail for the Vote*, a picture-book story about the fight for women's suffrage.

Karr brings history to life in varied and interesting ways. *It Happened in the White House* chronicles tales of ghosts in the bedrooms and dinosaur bones in the East Room. In *Exiled, Memoirs of a Camel*, she tells the story of a little-known mid-19th century experiment to help United States soldiers to function in the desert by importing camels from Egypt. This title was named

KATHLEEN KARR

BORN FOR ADVENTURE

Courtesy of Marshall Cavendish

a Notable Social Studies Trade Book and a *VOYA* Top Shelf Pick.

Kathleen Karr lives with her husband in Washington, DC. The children who inspired her first book for young readers are now grown. Her daughter has been awarded a Ph.D. in art history and her son is working in computer management.

SELECTED WORKS: *It Ain't Always Easy*, 1990; *Oh Those Harper Girls! Or Young and Dangerous*, 1992; *Gideon and the Mummy Professor*, 1993; *The Cave*, 1994; *In the Kaiser's Clutch*, 1995; *Go West, Young Women!*, 1996; *Spy in the Sky*, 1997; *The Great Turkey Walk*, 1998; *The Lighthouse Mermaid*, 1998; *Man of the Family*, 1999; *The Boxer*, 2000; *Skullduggery*, 2000; *It Happened in the White House: Extraordinary Tales from America's Most Famous Home*, illus. by Paul Meisel, 2001; *Playing with Fire*, 2001; *Bone Dry*, 2002; *Gilbert & Sullivan Set Me Free*, 2003; *Dwight D. Eisenhower: Letters from a New Jersey Schoolgirl* (Dear Mr. President series), 2003; *The Seventh Knot*, 2003; *Exiled, Memoirs of a Camel*, 2004; *Worlds Apart*, 2005; *Mama Went to Jail for the Vote*, illus. by Malene Laugesen, 2005; *Born for Adventure*, 2007; *Fortune's Fool*, 2008.

SUGGESTED READING: *Something About the Author*, vol. 127, 2002; *Contemporary Authors*, New Revision Series, vol. 106, 2002. Periodicals—Karr, Kathleen, "Ladies, and I Do Mean Ladies, Put Up Your Dukes," *Washington Post*, March 26, 1998.

WEB SITE: www.childrensbookguild.org/kathleenkarr.html

Barbara Kerley

June 26, 1960–

"The first book I ever fell in love with was *Harriet the Spy*, by Louise Fitzhugh, a novel about a girl who spies on her friends and neighbors and writes down what she sees. My mom gave me a copy in third grade, and I read it over and over again—so many times, in fact, that I had to duct-tape the spine to hold the book together. The characters were so complex and interesting, as were the problems they faced.

"I don't remember wanting to be a writer specifically because of Harriet, but my mom has told me that after I read the book I began to write a lot. (Though, unlike Harriet, I did not sneak into people's houses to spy on them!) What I liked about Harriet was how observant she was and how much value she placed on *paying attention*. I identified with her because I have always found people fascinating. Like Harriet, I often took a step back from whatever was going on and simply watched things unfold—a habit that I still have today.

"All through my childhood I read lots of books. When I wasn't reading (which wasn't often), a friend and I played 'dress-ups.' Our favorite was a game we called 'Pioneers.' We both had long skirts and *real* sunbonnets and went west to our own little house on the prairie. Playing 'dress-ups' soon led to making up and putting on plays for anyone my friends and I could rope into being an audience. I donned a sparkly silver dress to wriggle, snake-like, out of a big basket while a friend played the part of a snake charmer. I rode a squeaky rocking horse as Romeo to a friend's Juliet. (I was taller, so I had to be the boy.) I played 'Bones,' the doctor, in our homemade episode of 'Star Trek.'

Photo by Natasha Wing

"In junior high and high school, I pursued theater more formally (like, with an actual script and a real stage). I loved the rehearsals, the camaraderie of cast and crew, and the excitement of opening night. Theater felt absolutely magical to me— how, starting with words printed on a page, a group of people could create a whole other universe. Theater was also a way to

explore that most fascinating of topics: people. A group of us did improvisational theater, where two or more actors would go onstage without discussion or script and just see what kind of action developed. Improv helped me understand the connection between character and story.

"During this time, I also became quite involved in community theater, sometimes on stage but more often off stage, working the lights or making sets. The great thing about community theater was that most of the other folks were adults. Because I was organized and hard-working, I was a respected member of the crew. But because I was a teenager, the adults sometimes forgot I was there . . . talk about a great opportunity to people-watch! These were no ordinary adults—they were *actors*. I witnessed such drama—envy and ego and love affairs—and that was just between the actors during rehearsals! Like Harriet, I was fascinated. "The other thing my theater years gave me was an awareness of language and how the right choice of words can move the audience. All through my theater years, I continued to write stories and poetry, and by the time I finished college, I decided that I didn't want to be an actor. I wanted to be a writer.

"I'll always be grateful for my years filled with books and plays. They've proved to be a great foundation for my work now as a writer, developing my awareness of character, story, and the power of words. And I've learned that one of the best ways to understand people is to write about them.

"I do believe that Harriet would agree."

ᘓ   ᘓ   ᘓ

"The first book I ever fell in love with was Harriet the Spy. . . . *What I liked about Harriet was how observant she was and how much value she placed on paying attention."*

The youngest of three children, Barbara Kerley was born in Washington, DC and grew up in Reston, Virginia. Immediately after graduating from the University of Chicago in 1981, she joined the Peace Corps and spent two years in Nepal, teaching math, science, and English in a rural secondary school. Her older sister had served in the Peace Corps in Kenya in the 1970s; having grown up in a comfortable suburb of Washington, Kerley wanted to experience another way of life. While in Nepal, she met her future husband, Scott Kelly, and together they moved to Seattle in 1983 where she worked for several years in a bakery. Barbara and Scott were married in 1987. In 1988, after Barbara graduated from the University of Washington with a master's degree in English and a M.A.T. in English as a Second Language, they moved to Guam for two years.

The years in Guam included teaching English and ESL at the University of Guam, learning to scuba dive, and having a daughter, Anna, in 1989. When the family moved back to the United States, they settled in Northern California, living first in Eureka and then in McKinleyville, the small coastal town where they live today. Barbara began writing for adults and published several short stories about her time in Nepal, one in a collection entitled *From the Center of the Earth: Stories out of the Peace Corps*. Her true calling came several years after returning from Guam, when her daughter began to ask questions about the place where she was born and Kerley wrote *Songs of Papa's Island*. In ten short chapters, a mother tells of encounters with nature and wildlife on a Pacific Island just before and after her daughter's birth. Displaying sensitivity to nature and a lively humor, this book was named an ALA Notable Children's Book and was listed as one of New York Public Library's 100 Books for Reading and Sharing.

Her second book, which took five years to research and write, was submitted to publishers seventeen times before it was accepted. Fascinated by a drawing she had seen of a dinner party held inside the life-size model of a dinosaur in the mid-19th century, Kerley looked up information on the man who was responsible for it. After studying the life of Benjamin Waterhouse Hawkins, the first person to create dinosaur models, she brought all her sense of drama to telling the story of this little-known historical figure. The resulting picture book, superbly illustrated by Brian Selznick, earned accolades for both author and artist. Named a Notable Social Studies Trade Book and an Outstanding Science Trade Book, it also won an NCTE Orbis Pictus Honor Award and the Garden State (New Jersey) award for nonfiction. Selznick's illustrations earned a Caldecott Honor award for the artist.

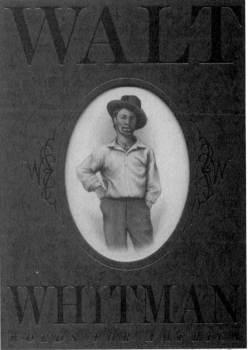

Courtesy of Scholastic Press

Kerley's next book, *A Cool Drink of Water*, reflects her Peace Corps experience in a desire to show the connections among people all over the planet through their common need for water, one of our most precious resources. Highlighting the responsibility we all have for safeguarding limited resources, and illustrated with photographs from the files of the National Geographic Society, it received a Blue Ribbon citation from the *Bulletin of the Center for Children's Books* and a silver medal from the National Parenting Publications Awards. A similar theme informed *You and Me Together: Moms, Dads, and Kids Around the World*, a photographic essay on the way families spend time together all over the world, which was named an ALA Notable Children's Book.

Walt Whitman: Words for America, Kerley's most lauded book to date, tells the remarkable life of this quintessential American poet in a way that is accessible to young readers. A picture book biography that touches on the main aspects of Whitman's life and work, it was named a *School Library Journal* Best Book of the year and an ALA Notable Children's Book; it also won a California Book Award and earned a Sibert Honor Award for nonfiction. Illustrated by Brian Selznick, *Walt Whitman* was also named one of the *New York Times* Best Illustrated Books of the Year and was cited as a Selector's Choice on the Notable Social Studies Trade Books list.

Another biographical picture book, *What to Do About Alice?*, is a rollicking tribute to President Theodore Roosevelt's oldest child, an irrepressible heroine who astounded White House visitors with her unconventional manners and grew to be one of her father's most trusted advisers. For this spirited story about Alice Roosevelt's life, Kerley received an Honor Book citation for the 2008 *Boston Globe-Horn Book* Award for nonfiction.

Barbara Kerley lives with her family in McKinleyville, CA, where her husband runs a small engineering firm. She enjoys hiking, biking, community work, and playing the banjo when she is not writing.

SELECTED WORKS: *Songs of Papa's Island*, illus. by Katherine Tillotson, 1995; *The Dinosaurs of Waterhouse Hawkins: An Illuminating History of Mr. Waterhouse Hawkins, Artist and Lecturer*, illus. by Brian Selznick, 2001; *A Cool Drink of Water*, illus. with photographs, 2002; *Walt Whitman: Words For America*, illus. by Brian Selznick, 2004; *You and Me Together: Moms, Dads, and Kids Around the World*, illus. with photographs, 2005; *Greetings from Planet Earth*, 2007; *What to Do About Alice? How Alice Roosevelt Broke the Rules, Charmed the World, and Drove Her Father Teddy Crazy!*, illus. by Edwin Fotheringham, 2008.

SUGGESTED READING: *Something About the Author*, vol. 138, 2003; Periodicals—Kerley, Barbara, "Josiah, the White House Badger," *Highlights for Children*, April, 2006; Kerley, Barbara, "Waterhouse Hawkins: Dinosaur Artist," *Highlights for Children*, August 2003: On-line—Interview at www.peacecorpswriters.org/pages/2002/0209/209talkkerley.html.

WEB SITE: www.barbarakerley.com

"I can't remember a time when I didn't want to be a writer. Even when I was just a child, I learned to type by hunt-and-peck on a huge standard typewriter my father brought me from his office. This was before computers were invented, and I still type that way, but now I'm as fast as any trained typist.

"I credit my father for encouraging me. I also became a reader because he was a big reader. But it was my mother who taught me about storytelling, for she was the neighborhood gossip, and a world-class pro! I couldn't wait to get home from school to hear her tales.

"'Marijane, you should have seen what Billy Nolan did today! It was about three o'clock this afternoon, just as I was going to take Skipper for a walk. I looked across the street and there he was, sneaking down the driveway toward the garage, looking over his shoulder to see if someone was watching. He had on that blue cap he always wears, the one with a white C on it, for Cornell, I suppose, where his father went to college. He was almost running.'

Photo by Zoé Kamitses

"M. E. Kerr"

May 27, 1927–

"This was her report of 14-year-old Billy Nolan sneaking the family Chevrolet out for a drive while his mother was napping. But my mother would never begin by saying, 'Billy Nolan sneaked the car out for a drive today.' She'd build up to it, offering detail after detail. She knew everyone's business, and she knew never to just blurt the story out. She would make you wait and keep you in suspense.

"I chose a college far away from my hometown of Auburn, New York. I went to the University of Missouri, where writing was stressed, to study journalism. I think getting away from home to attend a big university forces you to make new friends that are unlike the ones you grew up with. Also, most universities where writing is taught have courses in education, advertising, television and other communication skills, and those will help you earn a living while you're trying to do all the things you need to do to become a full-time freelance writer.

"When I landed in New York City with some roommates from college, I couldn't find an agent. Writers really need agents. So I finally had to become my own agent. I had stationery printed, and all of my clients were me. I thought up tough names like Vin Packer when I was writing mystery stories, and soft names like Laura Winston when I was writing for the *Ladies' Home Journal*. My favorite inventions were Edgar and Mamie Stone, a couple from Maine who, I told editors, were too old to travel to Manhattan to meet the people who bought their stories. They specialized in confessions for magazines like *True Confessions* and *Modern Romances*. I (as they) wrote stories that sounded very risqué, with titles like 'I Lost My Baby at a Pot Party.' The reader would be well into the story before realizing it was a party where a saleswoman was selling Teflon pots and during the sales spiel, the baby had crawled out to play in the yard.

"Working as an assistant file clerk at E. P. Dutton Publishing, I would take the subway to midtown Manhattan during my lunch hour and call on magazine editors. I would rave about my writers, always watching the clock so I could be back to the office in an hour. That experience is the main reason I have so many pseudonyms. Even after I began selling my work, I liked having different names. After writing many mystery and suspense stories as Vin Packer, I became M. E. Kerr to tell stories to young adults. That 'disguise' was a take-off on my real last name: Meaker. I also wrote some middle grade books as Mary James, which is a name that echoes my first name: Marijane.

"It was Louise Fitzhugh, the author of *Harriet The Spy*, who encouraged me to try writing for young adults. As Vin Packer, I'd already written several suspense novels told from a teenager's point of view. This fact often came up in our conversations and, eventually, I wrote *Dinky Hocker Shoots Smack*. Since then, I've written over 25 young adult books as M. E. Kerr. So not only do I have my parents to thank for my career, I have Louise to thank for putting me on the road to young adult books."

"I credit my father for encouraging me. I also became a reader because he was a big reader. But it was my mother who taught me about storytelling, for she was the neighborhood gossip, and a world-class pro! I couldn't wait to get home from school to hear her tales."

ରେ ରେ ରେ

The daughter of a mayonnaise manufacturer, Marijane Meaker (M. E. Kerr) was nearly expelled from an Episcopal boarding school for girls, Stuart Hall in Staunton, Virginia. She later attended Vermont Junior College and received a B.A. from the University of Missouri in 1949. That year, Meaker settled in New York City to become a writer. When the editors of the *Ladies' Home Journal* discovered she had posed as her own agent to get a story published in their magazine, they used this information as a publicity ploy. This brought her to the attention of a book editor who invited her to write for a newly launched paperback series. Her subsequent novel, *Spring Fire*, was a success, enabling her to write full-time.

In 1968 Meaker volunteered in a high school program in which authors tried to interest students in writing. In one class, she met an overweight girl whose mother was an ardent community service do-gooder who couldn't see her own daughter's problems. This became the inspiration for *Dinky Hocker Shoots Smack!*, the first book she published under the pseudonym M. E. Kerr. Named an ALA Notable Children's Book and a *School Library Journal* Best Book, this novel launched her career in the new field of young adult literature. After this initial success, she began seeing the humor in her own past, using incidents from her life experience for some of her books. She began to explore such serious topics as mental illness, physical disability, substance abuse, anti-Semitism, prejudice, and class issues. Her parents had had trouble accepting her homosexuality, and that theme found its way into her books as well. Writing for teens under the pseudonym M. E. Kerr, Meaker found material in her own family, in the lives of people in her neighborhood, and in remembered incidents from communities where she had lived.

Her second book for young readers, *If I Love You, Am I Trapped Forever?*, was named a Children's Book of the Year by the Child Study Association and a *New York Times* Outstanding Children's Book. *Is That You, Miss Blue?* was the first of her many books that have been designated as ALA Best Books for Young Adults. By the mid-1970s Kerr had become one of the most respected writers in the fast-growing field of literature for teenage readers. In *Gentlehands*, which won a Christopher Award and was named an ALA Notable Children's Book, she wrote of a lower-middle-class teenage boy who falls for an upper-class teenage girl and gets romantic advice from his sophisticated, cultured grandfather. But eventually the teenagers, like the readers, must find a way to bridge the horrifying gap between the kindly grandfather they know and the cruel Nazi war criminal they learn he once had been. The novel provoked negative comments from some Jewish groups, who found it disturbing that the nicest adult in the book turns out to be a former Nazi. Kerr, never one to shrink from difficult topics, simply pointed out the fact that, though we try to distance ourselves from evil, it can sometimes lurk in our own families. She based the teenagers in the story on a couple she knew in her East Hampton neighborhood, and created a timeless tale that shines light on the paradoxes existing in the human heart, making it as relevant today as it was upon publication.

"Writers really need agents. So I finally had to become my own agent. I had stationery printed, and all of my clients were me."

Little Little, which won a Golden Kite Award and was an ALA Notable Children's Book, is about tolerance, social position and an unusual minority group of people who grow up without growing bigger. It tells the story of Little Little La Belle, a sophisticated "little person" from a wealthy family, and Sydney Cinnamon, a lower-class hunchbacked dwarf who loves her. Because it was so challenging to write about this minority group, this book remains among Kerr's favorites today.

Deliver Us from Evie, narrated by Evie's youngest brother, features a masculine girl who's unable and unwilling to look feminine. Kerr chose a butch stereotype for Evie in order to address the tendency of the majority to accept those members of minority groups who appear most like them. This title was an ALA Recommended Book for Reluctant Young Adult Readers, a *Horn Book* Fanfare title, and among the NCTE's Best Young Adult Novels of the 1990s.

Courtesy of HarperCollins Publishers

In *Night Kites*, which won the California Young Reader Award, among many other accolades, a young man must tell his family he is gay and dying of AIDS. Although Kerr believes that alluding to current pop music will date a book, she allowed herself to do so in this case, assuming AIDS too would become a thing of the past and thus render the book obsolete. However, *Night Kites* remains as relevant today as it did upon publication. It was named an ALA Best Book for Young Adults and a *Booklist* Best of the 1980s, but it continues to be met with censorship and hostility in various parts of the country.

Combining romance, mystery, humor and a slightly surreal quality, the Fell series explores themes of betrayal, class conflict, prejudice, and prep school politics. In the first book, *Fell*, a policeman's son named John Fell is paid to impersonate a rich neighbor's son. As such, he attends an exclusive school where he joins a secret society, only to discover the tyranny hidden in elitism. In *Fell Back*, an Edgar Allan Poe Award finalist, Fell becomes involved in a love affair and murder when he investigates what seems to be the suicide of one of the secret society's members. In *Fell Down*, there are two narrators, one being Fell, who is searching for his girlfriend's missing sister, and the second being a ventriloquist who tells his story through the voice of his dummy.

Many of Kerr's books have been named ALA Best Books for Young Adults, and three of her titles were among ALA's Best of the Best compilation lists: *Night Kites*, *Gentlehands*, and *Dinky Hocker Shoots Smack!* In 1993 the American Library Association presented her with the Margaret A. Edwards Award for her body of work, the highest honor in the field. In 1999 she received the Knickerbocker Lifetime Achievement Award from the New York State Library Association. In 2000 the Assembly on Literature for Adolescents of the National Council of Teachers of English presented her with its Lifetime Achievement Award.

M. E. Kerr lives in East Hampton, New York, where she continues to tackle controversial and challenging topics, such as the complicated issues of a conscientious objector in *Slap Your Sides*. Her primer for young writers, *Blood on the Forehead: What I Know about Writing*, generously shares insights into her profession with advice and examples from her own distinguished career.

SELECTED WORKS FOR YOUNG READERS: As M.E. Kerr—*Dinky Hocker Shoots Smack!*, 1972; *If I Love You, Am I Trapped Forever?*, 1973; *The Son of Someone Famous*, 1974; *Is That You, Miss Blue?*, 1975; *Love Is a Missing Person*, 1975; *I'll Love You When You're More Like Me*, 1977; *Gentlehands*, 1978; *Little, Little*, 1981; *What I Really Think of You*, 1982; *Me, Me, Me, Me, Me: Not a Novel*, 1983; *Him She Loves?*, 1984; *I Stay Near You: One; Story in Three*, 1985; *Night Kites*, 1986; *Fell*, 1987; *Fell Back*, 1989; *Fell Down*, 1991; *Linger*, 1993; *Deliver Us from Evie*, 1994; *"Hello," I Lied*, 1997; *Blood on the Forehead: What I Know About Writing*, 1998; *What Became of Her?*, 2000; *Slap Your Sides*, 2001; *The Books of Fell* (contains *Fell*, *Fell Back*, and *Fell Down*), 2001; *Snakes Don't Miss Their Mothers*, 2003; *Your Eyes in Stars*, 2006, *Someone Like Summer*, 2007.

SELECTED SHORT STORIES FOR YOUNG ADULTS: "Jimmy from Another World" in *Cosmopolitan's Winds of Love*, 1975; "Only the Guilty Run" in *Some Things Weird and Wicked*, ed. by Joan Kahn, 1976; "Do You Want My Opinion?" in *Sixteen: Short Stories by Outstanding Writers for Young Adults*, ed. by Donald R. Gallo, 1984; "The Sweet Perfume of Good-bye" in *Visions*, ed. by Donald R. Gallo, 1984; "Sunny Days and Sunny Nights" in *Connections*, ed. by Donald R. Gallo, 1989; "The Author" in *Funny You Should Ask*, ed. by David Gale, 1992; "We Might as Well All

Be Strangers" in *Am I Blue?* ed. by Marion Dane Bauer, 1993; "The Green Killer" in *Bad Behavior*, ed. by Mary Higgins Clark, 1995; "I've Got Gloria" in *No Easy Answers*, ed. by Donald R. Gallo, 1997; "Guess Who's Back in Town, Dear?" in *Stay True*, ed. Marilyn Singer, 1998; "I Will Not Think of Maine" in *Dirty Laundry: Stories About Family Secrets*, ed. by Lisa Rowe Fraustino, 1998; "Grace" in *I Believe in Water*, ed. by Marilyn Singer, 2000; "Great Expectations" in *On the Fringe*, ed. by Donald R. Gallo, 2001; "I'll See You When This War Is Over" to *Shattered*, ed. by Jennifer Armstrong, 2003; "Hearing Flower" in *Face Relations*, ed. by Marilyn Singer, 2004.

SELECTED WORKS FOR YOUNG READERS: As Mary James—*Shoebag*, 1990; *The Shuteyes*, 1993; *Frankenlouse*, 1994; *Shoebag Returns*, 1996.

SELECTED WORKS FOR ADULTS: As M. J. Meaker—*Sudden Endings*, 1964 (paperback edition as Vin Packer, 1964). As Marijane Meaker—*Hometown*, 1967; *Game of Survival*, 1968; *Shockproof Sydney Skate*, 1972; *Highsmith: A Romance of the 1950's*, 2003. As Vin Packer—*Dark Intruder*, 1952; *Spring Fire*, 1952; *Look Back to Love*, 1953; *Come Destroy Me*, 1954; *Whisper His Sin*, 1954; *The Thrill Kids*, 1955; *Dark Don't Catch Me*, 1956; *The Young and Violent*, 1956; *Three-Day Terror*, 1957; *The Evil Friendship*, 1958; *5:45 to Suburbia*, 1958; *The Twisted Ones*, 1959; *The Damnation of Adam Blessing*, 1961; *The Girl on the Best Seller List*, 1960; *Something in the Shadows*, 1961; *Intimate Victims*, 1962; *Alone at Night*, 1963; *Sudden Endings*, 1964; *The Hare in March*, 1967; *Don't Rely on Gemini*, 1969; *Scot Free: A Book by Marijane Meaker Writing as Vin Packer*, 2007. As Ann Aldrich—*We Walk Alone*, 1955; *We Too Must Love*, 1958; *Carol in a Thousand Cities*, 1960; *We Two Won't Last*, 1963; *Take a Lesbian to Lunch*, 1972.

SUGGESTED READING: Spring, Albert, *M. E. Kerr*, 2005; Silvey, Anita, ed., *The Essential Guide to Children's Books and Their Creators*, 2002; *Something About the Author*, vol. 111, 2000; *Something About the Author*, vol. 61, 1990; *Children's Literature Review*, vol. 29, 1993; Nilsen, Alleen P., *Presenting M. E. Kerr*, 1997.

WEB SITE: www.mekerr.com

An earlier profile of M. E. Kerr appeared in *Fourth Book of Junior Authors and Illustrators*, 1978.

"Writing novels, especially for young adults, is the great creative joy of my life. I started writing in my teens and now, as I near fifty, I still get a thrill out of spinning a tale and making an imaginary world come to life.

"I grew up in a family that loved literature and theater. My mother, Sheila Solomon Klass, is a college English professor who has published eighteen novels, including many for young adults. My father, Morton Klass, was a professor of anthropology at Barnard College. But before my dad took up anthropology, he was a science fiction writer and editor, and even while teaching and raising a family, he found time to play roles in productions of the local theater guild. My older sister, Perri, is a doctor who has written extensively on women in medicine and has won several O. Henry Awards for her short stories. My younger sister, Judy, is a playwright.

"In such a family it's hard not to be a writer, but I almost managed it. I was a reluctant reader. The other members of my family always seemed to be devouring three or four books at a time, but I had other interests. I loved sports and would play until it got dark: baseball, soccer, basketball, tennis, bowling, and golf.

"I remember my parents bringing books home from the library that they thought would interest me. Sometimes they hit it right. I developed an early love of adventure stories. Jack London was a favorite author, as well as Robert Louis Stevenson and Alexandre Dumas. My father would read to us every night from his own favorite books, using his acting ability to make the books dramatic and give each of the characters a funny and distinctive voice.

"I'm very competitive and had a bit of sibling rivalry with my older sister. Every year *Seventeen* magazine runs a short story contest, and Perri won the contest twice. I decided that I would win it too, even though I had never read an issue of the magazine in my life. Sure enough, when I was a senior in high school in 1978, I won first prize in *Seventeen*'s contest. My winning entry, "Ringtoss," was my first published short story.

Photo by Giselle Benatar

David Klass

March 8, 1960–

"At Yale University I was a history major, but I had the good fortune to study writing with a number of brilliant teachers, including John Hersey, Gordon Lish, John Hollander, and Richard Price. In my senior year, I won the Veech Award for Best Imaginative Writing at Yale.

"After Yale I got a wonderful job teaching English in Japan and wrote my first novel, *The Atami Dragons*, about that experience. Many of my books are about teenage boys who play sports, but I try to build the novels around larger social issues and coming-of-age themes. I remember what a reluctant reader I was, and I try to write books that I would have wanted to read during my own teenage years.

"I have another side to my career. I also write action movies for Hollywood. For example, I wrote the screenplay for *Kiss the Girls*, which starred Morgan Freeman and Ashley Judd, and I scripted *Desperate Measures*, starring Michael Keaton and Andy Garcia. Most recently, I wrote the screenplay for the remake of *Walking Tall*, starring The Rock. I feel lucky to be working in Hollywood, but writing novels remains my true passion.

"Even now, at the ripe old age of forty-seven, I still play on a competitive soccer team, but I'm slowing down and may soon have to devote myself to tennis, golf, and reading."

[This autobiographical statement first appeared on the web site of Farrar, Straus, and Giroux publishers: www.fsgkidsbooks.com]

"I remember what a reluctant reader I was, and I try to write books that I would have wanted to read during my own teenage years."

ଔ   ଔ   ଔ

Novelist and screenwriter David Klass was born in Vermont, but spent most of his early years in Leonia, New Jersey, across the Hudson River from New York City. He attended Yale University as a history major and received his B.A. in 1982. He also earned a master's degree from the School of Cinema-Television at the University of Southern California in 1989.

In Atami, Japan, in the mid-1980s, Klass taught in a public high school three days a week and visited other high schools. He also coached the high school baseball and soccer teams. His first two books were set in Atami: *The Atami Dragons*, about a teenage boy who comes to terms with his mother's death during a business trip to Japan with his father, and *Breakaway Run*, which depicts a boy adjusting to both a new culture and the breakup of his parents' marriage.

Klass moved to California after his first book was optioned for film and worked various odd jobs, doing treatments for producers and working as a teacher's assistant. All the while he continued writing novels and working on his master's degree.

Klass's novels for teens are evocative and multi-layered. In *Danger Zone*, the themes of family conflict, personal rivalry, and racism on a sports team are set against the background of a terrorist threat during an international high school basketball tournament. Frank, thoughtful, and fast-paced, this title won the Nebraska Golden Sower Award, the Oklahoma Sequoyah Young Adult Book Award, and the Maryland Black-Eyed Susan Award. It was also cited as an ALA Best Book for Young Adults and an ALA Popular Paperback for Young Adults.

The Children's Literature Council of Southern California named two of Klass's titles—*Danger Zone* and *Wrestling with Honor*—Outstanding Fiction for Young Adults. *Wrestling with Honor*, which explores the controversy that surrounds drug testing in high school sports, was included on ALA's 100 Best of the Best list for teen readers.

California Blue, which focuses on the environmental issues associated with the preservation of a rare butterfly as well as the tensions between a father and son, was an ALA Best Book for Young Adults, a Notable Children's Trade Book in the Field of Social Studies, and a runner-up for Bank Street College's Annual Children's Book Award. It also received the Friends of Children and Literature (FOCAL) Award. Handling complex issues with subtle grace, this absorbing title stirred up controversy by including a romantic attraction between the teenager and his teacher.

Courtesy of Farrar, Straus, and Giroux

Named an ALA Best Book for Young Adults, Klass's *You Don't Know Me* is a vivid and gripping story about 14-year-old John, who is abused by his soon-to-be stepfather. As a coping mechanism, John creates alternate realities in his head.

Turning to the science fiction genre, Klass produced *Firestorm*, an exciting page-turner featuring a teenager from the future who must save the planet from an environmental disaster. The first of The Caretaker trilogy, *Firestorm* was named an ALA Best Book for Young Adults in 2008.

David Klass continues to work on both action screenplays and young adult novels. He lives with his wife, Giselle Benatar, and their two children in New York City.

SELECTED WORKS FOR YOUNG READERS: *The Atami Dragons*, 1984; *Breakaway Run*, 1986; *A Different Season*, 1988; *Wrestling with Honor*, 1989; *California Blue*, 1994; *Danger Zone*, 1995; *Screen Test*, 1997; *You Don't Know Me: A Novel*, 2001; *Home of the Braves*, 2002; *Dark Angel*, 2005; *Firestorm* (The Caretaker Trilogy), 2006; *Whirlwind* (Caretaker Trilogy), 2008.

SELECTED WORKS FOR ADULTS: *Night of the Tyger*, 1990; *Samurai Inc.*, 1992.

SELECTED SCREENPLAYS: *Kiss the Girls*, 1997; *Desperate Measures*, 1998; *Runaway Virus*, 2000; *In the Time of Butterflies* (written with Judy Klass and based on the novel by Julia Alvarez), 2001; *Walking Tall*, 2004.

SUGGESTED READING: *Something About the Author*, vol. 142, 2004; *Authors and Artists for Young Adults*, vol. 26, 1999; *St. James Guide to Young Adult Writers*, 2nd Ed., 1999.

A profile of David Klass's mother, Sheila Solomon Klass, can be found in *Eighth Book of Junior Authors* (2000).

Amy Goldman Koss

January 26, 1954–

"I was born and raised in Detroit, then Southfield, Michigan. My dad was a jukebox man and my mom taught school. Both of them did artsy things in their free time. My dad played violin and painted spooky paintings and did marvelous and fanciful woodwork. He and my uncle built an ornate harpsichord—a genuine Goldman. My mom sang in choruses and acted in community theatre.

"So, I grew up thinking that being grown-up meant doing something dull by day to make a living, and that all the fun and passionate stuff had to be squeezed in on evenings and weekends. I guess I thought the people who did art by day—who sang or acted or painted or danced or sculpted or wrote—were some separate and unknowable species. It didn't really occur to me until I was in my twenties that I too could try to do what I loved to do—write stories—as my day gig.

"My brother who is a mediator (but also a writer and a musician) is two years older than me. I pretty much hated him while we were growing up, but all my girlfriends had crushes on him. He and I are close now, but we disagree about almost all of our childhood memories. For example, I distinctly recall the guilt and thrill of pushing him off the roof of our red garden shed. My fingertips remember the feel of his sweaty T-shirt and the oomph behind my shove. My brother, however, swears that he fell by himself and that never in my life was I anywhere near the shed's roof because I was and still am such a total wuss. It's true that I am terrified of heights, so maybe I've just been writing fiction for longer than I thought!

"My best friend lived two doors down and we spent every possible moment together playing elaborate games of pretend and fighting and making up. Other than the time spent with her, my impression of myself as a kid is as the daydreaming, socially invisible type—but I may have made that up, too. Memory is tricky that way and as I get older it gets trickier and trickier!

Courtesy of Amy Goldman Koss

"I was a mediocre to lousy student and still can't spell or comprehend math or, in fact, do much else besides make up stories. I read a lot as a kid and I still do. I don't have TV in my home, not because I think it's evil but because I know it would suck me in by the eyeballs and I'd never be able to get anything done. When I go to diners with TV, I can barely remember to swallow.

"As a semi-adult I moved here and there—Boston, Massachusetts; Stuart, Florida—working odd jobs, taking random college classes, getting married and divorced and married again. I now live in Southern California with my husband, two (artistic and musical) kids, a dog, a rabbit, two turtles and a goldfish. I have a studio out back where I write in spurts—all day and night sometimes, and not at all other times. I teach a class for UCLA extension in writing the YA novel, although (just between you and me) I'm pretty sure it can't really be taught.

"I've been writing for ages, have a whole ton of books published, and yet it is still a mystery to me where ideas come from and how books go from first idea to full-blown story. The only thing I can say for sure is that when the writing is going well, it's a fabulously wonderful feeling, like no other. And that when it's going badly or isn't going at all, the accompanying feeling is total gloom and despair. That said, there is absolutely nothing I'd rather be doing for a living, and I know I am very lucky!"

ଔ   ଔ   ଔ

The daughter of Max and Harriet Goldman, Amy Goldman Koss attended Wayne State University and took various college courses elsewhere. It wasn't until 1982, when she married news producer Mitchell Koss, who willingly took chances with his career in order to do what he really wanted to do, that Amy decided to take a few chances of her own. Although she met with countless rejections, eventually her drawings, poems, articles, and short stories started getting published in newspapers and literary magazines. When a book publisher finally took an interest in one of her manuscripts, the one that was ultimately published was not the one they were initially interested in. Her first illustrated picture book, *What Luck! A Duck!*, about a frustrated painter who is aided accidentally by a passing duck, was published in 1987.

Koss continued producing picture books until she started having children and it became difficult to paint. However, before she took a few years off to raise her son and daughter, two of her picture books received wide recognition. *Where Fish Go in Winter*, which answers in humorous poems questions kids love to ask but parents can rarely answer, became a Book-of-the-Month selection. *Curious Creatures in Peculiar Places*, which introduces animals from exotic lands around the world, was named to the John Burroughs Award List for Outstanding Nature Books for Children.

When Koss resumed writing, editor Cindy Kane suggested she turn a picture book she had submitted into a chapter book for intermediate grades. In *How I Saved Hanukkah*, which was among Bank Street College's Children's Books of the Year, a fourth-grader embarks on a mission to make the holiday fun for her family and neighborhood. Once Koss discovered writing for middle grade and young adult readers, she felt there was no turning back. Early adolescence is that time in life she most identifies with—a period when life is vivid, wonderful, and terrible all at the same time. Koss became known for her ability to look at the problems and adventures of middle-graders with a humorous, insightful, and realistic eye.

Koss explored peer pressure issues in *The Ashwater Experiment* when the main character, who moves so frequently she starts questioning reality, settles down in a new town and

"I don't have TV in my home, not because I think it's evil but because I know it would suck me in by the eyeballs and I'd never be able to get anything done."

becomes friends with two people at either end of the social spectrum in her new school. This title, inspired by a feeling Koss had as a child that things in her life were unreal, was named a *School Library Journal* Best Book of the Year and a *Bulletin of the Center for Children's Books* Blue Ribbon book.

In *The Girls*, an ALA Best Book for Young Adults and an IRA Young Adult Choice, Koss tackles the cruelty of middle school social status when one of the characters is ostracized from a popular clique. Reflecting the book's appeal for all readers, it was also named to the Top Ten among ALA Quick Picks for Reluctant Readers. *Stolen Words*, which was cited as a Notable Book for Older Readers by the Association of Jewish Libraries, examines emotional recovery after the trauma of a death in the family.

In *Side Effects*, an ALA Best Book for Young Adults that was included on the New York Public Library's Books for the Teen Age, Koss celebrates the life of a girl who survives cancer. Her goal was to tell the story without sentimentality or sensationalism, to show the dark humor as well as the serious side of a battle with cancer.

Amy Goldman Koss and her own family now live in Glendale, California, where she takes classes in crafts, such as making stained glass, and writes books while her children are in school.

Courtesy of Roaring Brook Press

SELECTED WORKS WRITTEN AND ILLUSTRATED: *What Luck! A Duck!*, 1987; *Where Fish Go in Winter, and Answers to Other Great Mysteries*, 1987 (reissued in 2002 as *Where Fish Go in Winter and Other Great Mysteries*, with new illus. by Laura J. Bryant); *Curious Creatures in Peculiar Places*, 1989; *City Critters Around the World*, 1991.

SELECTED WORKS WRITTEN: *How I Saved Hanukkah*, illus. by Diane deGroat, 1998; *The Trouble with Zinny Weston*, 1998; *The Ashwater Experiment*, 1999; *The Girls*, 2000; *Smoke Screen*, 2000; *Strike Two*, 2001; *Stranger in Dadland*, 2001; *Stolen Words*, 2001; *The Cheat*, 2003; *Gossip Times Three*, 2003; *Kailey*, 2003; *Poison Ivy*, 2006; *Side Effects*, 2006.

SUGGESTED READING: *Something About the Author*, vol. 158, 2005. Online—Smith, Cynthia Leitich, "Author Interview: Amy Goldman Koss on Side Effects," August 2006, at www.cynthialeitich-smith.blogspot.com/2006/08/author-interview-amy-goldman-koss-on.html.

WEB SITE: www.amygoldmankoss.net

Courtesy of Random House, Inc.

Trudy Krisher

December 22, 1946–

"I was born in Georgia, raised in Florida, attended college in Virginia, and taught English in elementary schools, high schools, community colleges, and universities. But all you really need to know about me is that I've raised three children—Laura, Kathy, and Mark—whom I love with all my heart, and that I love to write.

"I think that the reason I'm a writer is that I have an insatiable curiosity. I'm curious about the way an historical time and place impacts the people who are living through its important events. In my books, I have dealt with the civil rights movement of the early 1960s, the Jacksonian age of the 1830s, and the Cold War period of the 1950s. Currently I am working on a book set in France in 1572, a period which witnessed great religious turmoil.

"I owe my curiosity about history to my father. He was a classic Southern gentleman and student of the Civil War who never met an historical marker he didn't like. Our family vacations were spent in museums and on battlegrounds, and whenever we traveled my mother kept an old pair of muddy shoes in the car that she affectionately called her 'battlefield shoes.' In our living room hung an authentic flag from a Civil War battlefield ripped by an authentic flying minié ball. Daddy gave a lot of talks. If the Rotary, the Kiwanis, or the local women's club needed a speaker, my father would readily agree, eager to delight them with what he knew of the Civil War, which was considerable. He'd whistle out the door with his satchel of Confederate money and his tape-recorded rendition of 'Dixie' and his Southern charm well in hand, and his daughter knew that his audience was in for a treat.

"My father made the people in history seem real. He loved to quote Stonewall Jackson and Nathan Bedford Forrest, and he taught me to marvel at the courage of heroes I had never even heard of. General George Gordon of Georgia, for instance, was wounded seven times in a single battle, including a vicious head wound. Listening to Daddy, I could picture General Gordon holding his hat out in front of him like a basin, the basin filling up rapidly with his own heroic blood.

"I spent many a rainy Sunday looking through hundreds of Daddy's history books. Somehow my imagination connected the people in those books with the people I saw around me. Those people rode in buggies, not automobiles; they wore hoop skirts and not short skirts, but I recognized the jug-handled ears and the widow's peaks and the clefts in the chins as the same as those I saw every day and knew in my heart. Through the perfume of Daddy's old books, I caught the whiff of an historical truth: those people may have lived in a different time and place, but they were, somehow, intimately connected to me.

"Still, some might wonder why I write about history for the young, those who have barely begun to stick a toe in history's vast waters. I believe that history, like our very lives, is filled with unanswered questions and that young people are some of the world's best questioners. They look at their own personal experiences, for instance, and wonder: Does the religion or politics or lifestyle of my parents fit me? How can I determine my purpose in life? Am I proud of the way I behaved in a certain situation, or do I wish I had behaved differently? When faced with challenges, have I made mostly the right decisions, mostly the wrong decisions, or a little of both?

"History, too, is filled with difficult questions that float up to us on the river of time, and it is those questions that inspire my books. When you write about history, you come to realize that, in human terms, the more things change, the more they remain the same. Awkward human beings that we are, we haven't walked a straight line called progress from the past into the present. Instead, we groped and stumbled our way into this moment, weighed down by a satchel full of unanswered questions. The questions are all connected to the responses made by our fragile humanity. If you write about history for young adults, your job is to open the satchel and lovingly place the old questions in new hands."

> *"I believe that history, like our very lives, is filled with unanswered questions and that young people are some of the world's best questioners."*

 og og og

The daughter of businessman Whitley Herron Butner and Lois Drane Butner, Trudy B. Krisher graduated from the College of William and Mary, in Williamsburg, Virginia, with a B.A. in English in 1968 and received her masters degree from Trenton State College, in Trenton, New Jersey, in 1972.

Inspired by her daughter Kathy's battle with cancer, Krisher wrote her first book, *Kathy's Hats: A Story of Hope*, about a young girl who comes to think of the hats she wears after her hair falls out from chemotherapy treatments as thinking caps which can help her fight the disease. A realistic portrayal of cancer treatment written in a positive tone, *Kathy's Hats* has been integrated into a national hospital program to benefit children with cancer.

Courtesy of Random House, Inc.

Rooted in the Jim Crow South of Krisher's childhood, her next book, *Spite Fences*, features a young woman, Maggie, whose evolving social consciousness causes her to stand up for civil rights in Georgia during the summer of 1960. Krisher developed the character of Maggie in an attempt to answer the question, "Why do people try to wall each other out with fences?" *Spite Fences* earned Krisher a Cuffie mention from *Publishers Weekly* for 1994's most promising new author. The book also was cited as an ALA Best Book for Young Adults and won an International Reading Association Award for Older Readers as well as a Jefferson Cup Honor from the Virginia Library Association. *Spite Fences* was made available to young people in Sarajevo, in November 1999, in an effort to help them discuss the ethnic tensions in their own society.

Krisher revisits the same Georgia town as *Spite Fences* in her novel *Kinship*, which explores family and community relationships through the eyes of Pert, the young girl who was Maggie's friend in *Spite Fences*. Told in Pert's voice as well as that of a Greek chorus of trailer-park residents, the story revolves around efforts to save a trailer-park community from being re-zoned. It also examines the morality involved in an unplanned pregnancy, risky financial dealings, and "kinship" between neighbors as well as family members. *Kinship* was declared an ALA Best Book for Young Adults.

In *Uncommon Faith*, the central character is Faith Common, the daughter of a Methodist minister in the early 1800s, before the Civil War, and Krisher introduces her to the reader through the perspectives of ten other characters. Although proper ladies in polite society were supposed to be submissive and demure, Faith cannot bear the injustices she witnesses and battles for the rights of women and African Americans. *Uncommon Faith* was named an Amelia Bloomer Project Recommended Book, a Capitol Choice, and an ALA Best Book for Young Adults.

In *Fallout*, Krisher wrestles with the question, "Who is my neighbor?" Set in North Carolina during 1954 (one of the most active hurricane seasons on record), *Fallout* examines the impact the Cold War atmosphere of suspicion and rumor has on the relationship between two teens.

In her career as a teacher, Krisher has been an assistant professor and writing center coordinator at the University of Dayton. Currently she is an associate professor at Sinclair Community College, also in Dayton, Ohio, where she makes her home. Between her writing and her work as a teacher, Krisher hopes that in some small way, her work may help heal a troubled world.

SELECTED WORKS: *Kathy's Hats: A Story of Hope*, 1992; *Spite Fences*, 1994; *Kinship*, 1997; *Uncommon Faith*, 2003; *Fallout*, 2006.

SUGGESTED READING: *Something About the Author*, vol. 86, 1996. Periodicals: "McCarthy and More: A Conversation with Trudy Krisher," *The ALAN Review*, Fall 2007; Trites, Roberta Seelinger "Narrative Resolution: Photography in Adolescent Literature," *Children's Literature*, Annual 1999; "Flying Starts," *Publishers Weekly*, December 19, 1994

WEB SITE: www.trudykrisher.com

Karla Kuskin

July 17, 1932–

"My childhood was filled with poetry, books, reading aloud, and art, all of these were encouraged by my parents. One of my earliest poems, written when I was four, was about the hydrangea bushes that grew outside the front door of a fieldstone country house in Connecticut where we lived one year. My mother wrote it down for me because I couldn't write yet. She had been on stage for a time before turning to photography, which she eventually gave up for motherhood.

"Often praised as a child, I was also frequently judged by my mother's sharp eyes, which I inherited. A dry cleaner's daughter, she could always spot imperfections in the material at fifty feet. It's a good characteristic to have, although as a young girl, I found it a bit tiresome for my work to be so continually judged. My father was in advertising but would have preferred journalism, and it is probably from him that I inherited my love of wordplay. To write things down, preserve the moment in words, has always been a necessity to me.

"An only child, I grew up on one of New York City's tree-lined Greenwich Village streets. The sense of being a small child in big places was so much a part of my childhood that I was determined to remember those places and feelings. I went to private schools, where my teachers were very encouraging, but by adolescence, I didn't feel very popular among my peers. Reading and writing, which I had always loved, became my refuge, as did the Hudson Street Library. With the support of my favorite teachers, I spent long hours writing poems and short stories.

Photo by Julia Kuskin

"My books are for children because of a bond I still have with my own childhood. There is an understanding, a way of seeing things that I never completely outgrew. Frustration, pleasure, humor, what I saw as injustices—all were childhood elements I later tried to breathe into my books. Speaking in verse came naturally to me, and although I've never written an autobiography, the closest I ever came to it was probably in *Alexander Soames*, about a boy who only speaks in rhyme.

"Like most people who write, I want to be heard and understood. Poetry is my vehicle. The children who hear my verses or read them will, I hope, recognize a familiar feeling or thought. Or possibly an unfamiliar feeling or thought will intrigue them, and maybe even inspire them to try writing their own poetry.

"I've written a lot of verses that sounded splendid in my mind, but once read aloud, they, like the proverbial beach glass, lost their luster. Because poems are tuneless songs, they almost beg to be read aloud, and sometimes need to be, in order to be revised. But I am a firm believer in reading aloud anyway. Reading and writing encourage each other. Once you want to write, you read more. Once you read something good, it makes you want to write something even better."

ଔ   ଔ   ଔ

Born Karla Seidman, the daughter of Sidney and Mitzi Seidman, Karla Kuskin attended the Little Red School House and Elisabeth Irwin High School in New York. From 1950 to 1953, she attended Antioch College where, through a work-study program, she started writing promotional material for a Chicago department store; this experience sparked her interest in graphic arts. Transferring to Yale University's School of Fine Arts, she graduated from there in 1955. For an undergraduate class project she wrote, illustrated, and printed a book called *Roar and More*, which was published in 1956 by Harper & Brothers. Receiving an award from the American Institute of Graphic Arts for this title, Kuskin earned early recognition as both an author and an illustrator.

After college she worked for a time for the fashion photographer Erwin Blumenfeld. Later she wrote copy and created layouts for a magazine and an advertising agency, but she found these jobs unrewarding. After creating the picture book *James and the Rain*, the story of a young boy investigating the rainy-day habits of animals, she began working on writing and illustrating books full-time for Harper, working under the legendary children's book editor, Ursula Nordstrom.

"The sense of being a small child in big places was so much a part of my childhood that I was determined to remember those places and feelings."

In the 1960s another publisher approached her about some book projects. Since authors at that time did not typically work with more than one publisher, Kuskin accepted those projects using a pseudonym, Nicholas J. Charles, which was created by combining the names of her son, Nicholas, her daughter, Julia, and her first husband, Charles. She was also hired to write some screenplays, but most of her creative energy went into creating children's books.

By the late 1970s Kuskin had created the text, artwork, or both for over 30 children's books. Many of these titles were recognized on lists of distinguished books, such as the ALA Notable Children's Books and the IRA/CBC Children's Choices. In response to many children's inquiries about where she got her ideas and how she wrote her poetry, Kuskin wrote and illustrated two volumes—*Near the Window Tree: Poems and Notes* and *Dogs and Dragons, Trees and Dreams*—both of which offer a collection of some of her best-loved poems along with writing tips and notes about what inspired the work.

THE
PHILHARMONIC
GETS DRESSED

by Karla Kuskin
illustrations by Marc Simont

Courtesy of HarperCollins Publishers

For many years Kuskin assumed she would illustrate everything she wrote. But in the late 1970s, as rapid advances in children's book illustration started to occur and two-color illustrations gave way to full-color productions, she began to consider other artists for her books. She asked the artist Marc Simont to illustrate *A Space Story*, a book that introduces the characteristics of the sun and planets to young children.

The Kuskin/Simont partnership achieved even greater success with *The Philharmonic Gets Dressed*. Kuskin's first husband was an oboist, and her young daughter used to watch him prepare for his performances and say, "Mom, Dad's putting on his tails again." This child's perspective spurred Kuskin to write *The Philharmonic Gets Dressed*, which became a 1983 National Book Award finalist. Describing the bathing, shaving, mustache trimming, powdering, hair drying, dressing, and other pre-performance primping of 105 orchestra members, accompanied by Simont's humorous illustrations, the book became an instant classic. It was so successful that it led to another Kuskin/Simont collaboration, *The Dallas Titans Get Ready for Bed*, in which 45 members of a football team reluctantly get ready to go home after a victorious game. This title received a Parents' Choice Award and was favorably reviewed in *Sports Illustrated*.

For *Jerusalem, Shining Still*, a book Kuskin wrote after an official invitation to visit the city in 1982, she spent considerable time deciding what elements of the city to include, cutting and condensing until she had summarized 3,000 years of history in 27 pages. Praised for making the city's complex history accessible to children, and for the stunning woodcuts by David Frampton, it became a *School Library Journal* Best Book of the Year and won a Parents' Choice Award. Another book with a religious theme, *A Great Miracle Happened There*, tells about a Christian youth spending his first Chanukah with a Jewish family and recounts the questions children ask about religous tradition.

With her reputation for finely honed wordcrafting, Kuskin was urged to try her hand at creating books for early readers by Harper & Row editor Charlotte Zolotow, who had succeeded

Ursula Nordstrom. The results were two books she wrote and illustrated: *Something Sleeping in the Hall*, and a *Parenting* Magazine Reading Magic Award title, *Soap Soup*. A simple book featuring things children often wonder about, *Soap Soup* included explanations for phenomena like why elbows bend.

City Dog, the last book Kuskin both wrote and illustrated, is about a dog's first trip to the country. The story was inspired by a dog she knew on Prince Edward Island in Canada, where she and her family once had a summer home. With childlike watercolor-and-ink drawings to accompany the text, this title was cited on the John Burroughs List of Nature Books for Young Readers. *So, What's It Like to Be a Cat?*, an animal-themed story about the self-centered feline psyche with lively illustrations by Betsy Lewin, was named an IRA/CBC Children's Choice, a Bank Street College Best Book of the Year, a Society of School Librarians International Honor Book, and an ASPCA Henry Bergh Book Award winner.

The Sky Is Always in the Sky brought together a humorous and intelligent collection of 36 of Kuskin's previously published poems, illustrated by French artist Isabelle Dervaux. It was cited as a *Riverbank Review* Children's Book of Distinction. Many of her best poems have been included in anthologies compiled by some of the finest contemporary poets and anthologists, including Lee Bennett Hopkins, Jack Prelutsky, and Myra Cohn Livingston. She has also contributed essays and reviews to books and periodicals over the years, among them an article on book reviewing for a special 1998 issue of *The Horn Book Magazine* that focused on picture books.

Karla Kuskin received the 1979 National Council of Teachers of English Award for Excellence in Poetry for Children for her body of work and was named an Outstanding Brooklyn Author in 1981. In 1998 she delivered the First Annual Charlotte Zolotow Lecture at the University of Wisconsin-Madison, which had been established to honor Zolotow's 38-year career in editing and the 65 books she wrote herself. Kuskin's talk was entitled "The Ins and Outs of Words."

From her marriage to Charles M. Kuskin, which lasted from 1955 to 1987, she had two children, Nicholas, born in 1960, and Julia, born in 1965. Both are now professional photographers. Kuskin also has three grandchildren, Madeleine, Amelia, and Ian. In 1989 she married William L. Bell, who died in 2006. Today she divides her time between her homes in Brooklyn, New York and Bainbridge Island, Washington. Although having recently developed Cortical-Basal Ganglionic Degeneration, a

Moon,
Have You Met
My Mother?

The collected poems of
Karla Kuskin

Illustrations by Sergio Ruzzier

Courtesy of HarperCollins Publishers

progressive neurological disorder, Kuskin continues to create books for children.

SELECTED WORKS WRITTEN AND ILLUSTRATED: *Roar and More*, 1956 (rev. and reissued, 1990); *James and the Rain*, 1957 (reillus. by Reg Cartwright, 1995); *In the Middle of the Trees*, 1958; *The Animals and the Ark*, 1958 (reillus. by Michael Grejniec, 2002); *Just Like Everyone Else*, 1959; *Which Horse Is William?* 1959 (reissued, 1992); *Square as a House*, 1960; *The Bear Who Saw the Spring;* 1961; *All Sizes of Noise*, 1962; *Alexander Soames: His Poems*, 1962; *How Do You Get from Here to There?* (as Nicholas J. Charles), 1962; *ABCDEFGHIJKLM-NOPQRSTUVWXYZ*, 1963; *The Rose on My Cake*, 1964; *Sand and Snow*, 1965; *Jane Anne June Spoon and Her Very Adventurous Search for the Moon* (as Nicholas J. Charles), 1966; *The Walk the Mouse Girls Took;* 1967; *Watson, the Smartest Dog in the U.S.A.*, 1968; *In the Flaky Frosty Morning*, 1969; *Any Me I Want to Be: Poems*, 1972; *What Did You Bring Me?*, 1973; *Near the Window Tree: Poems and Notes*, 1975; *A Boy Had a Mother Who Bought Him a Hat*, 1976; *Herbert Hated Being Small*, 1979; *Dogs & Dragons, Trees & Dreams: A Collection of Poems*, 1980; *Night Again*, 1981; *Something Sleeping in the Hall*, 1985; *Soap Soup and Other Verses*, 1992; *City Dog*, 1994.

SELECTED WORKS ILLUSTRATED: *Xingu*, by Violette and John Viertel, 1959; *Who Woke the Sun*, by Mitzi S. Seidman, 1960; *The Dog That Lost His Family*, by Jean Lee Latham and Bee Lewi, 1961; *Sing for Joy*, by Margaret and Norman Mealy, 1961; *O Ye Jigs and Juleps!*, by Virginia Cary Hudson, 1962 (reissued 1987); *Harrison Loved His Umbrella*, by Rhoda Levine, 1964; *Credos & Quips*, by Virginia Cary Hudson, 1964; *Boris, the Lopsided Bear*, by Gladys Schmitt, 1966; *Look at Me*, by Marguerita Rudolph, 1967; *Big Enough*, by Sherry Kafka, 1970; *What Shall We Do and Allee Galloo! Play Songs and Singing Games for Children*, ed. by Marie Winn, 1970; *Traces*, by Paula Fox, 2008.

SELECTED WORKS WRITTEN: *A Space Story*, illus. by Marc Simont, 1978; *The Philharmonic Gets Dressed*, illus. by Marc Simont,

1982; *The Dallas Titans Get Ready for Bed*, illus. by Marc Simont, 1986; *Jerusalem, Shining Still*, illus. by David Frampton, 1987; *A Great Miracle Happened There: A Chanukah Story*, illus. by Robert Andrew Parker, 1993; *Patchwork Island*, illus. by Petra Mathers, 1994; *Paul*, illus. by Milton Avery, 1994; *City Noise*, illus. by Renée Flower, 1994; *The Sky Is Always in the Sky*, illus. by Isabelle Dervaux, 1998; *The Upstairs Cat*, illus. by Howard Fine, 1997; *I Am Me*, illus. by Dyanna Wolcott, 2000; *Moon Have You Met My Mother?: The Collected Poems of Karla Kuskin*, illus. by Sergio Ruzzier, 2003; *Under My Hood I Have a Hat*, illus. by Fumi Kosaka, 2004; *Toots the Cat*, illus. by Lisze Bechtold, 2005; *So, What's It Like to Be a Cat?*, illus. by Betsy Lewin, 2005; *Ice Cream Dreams*, illus. by Lewis Matheney, 2005; *Green as a Bean*, illus. by Melissa Iwai, 2007.

SUGGESTED READING: *Contemporary Authors*, Gale Literary Database, November 15, 2005; Silvey, Anita, ed., *The Essential Guide to Children's Books & Their Creators*, 2003; Pendergast, Sara and Tom, eds., *St. James Guide to Children's Writers*, 1999; Kuskin, Karla, *Thoughts, Pictures and Words*, photos. by Nicholas Kuskin, 1995; *Something About the Author Autobiography Series*, vol. 3, 1987; *Children's Literature Review*, vol. 4, 1976; Larrick, Nancy, ed., *Somebody Turned on a Tap in Those Kids: Poetry & Young People Today*, 1971. Periodicals—Kuskin, Karla, "To Get a Little More of the Picture: Reviewing Picture Books," *The Horn Book*, Mar/Apr, 1998.

WEB SITE: www.charlottezolotow.com/karla_kuskin.htm

An earlier profile of Karla Kuskin appeared in *Third Book of Junior Authors and Illustrators*, 1972.

Barbara Lavallee

November 6, 1941–

"I was born a month and a day before the bombing of Pearl Harbor. I was the second of four daughters; my father was a minister and my mother a former art teacher. My earliest memories are of making art with my sisters. We grew up before television was invented and spent many hours entertaining ourselves by telling stories and illustrating them on the blackboard in our playroom. We lived in a small town in Iowa during the years just after the Depression when hoboes often ended up at the minister's door, asking to sharpen knives or mow lawns in exchange for a meal. Mom always fed them.

"When I was in the third grade, we moved to Wisconsin, and I rebelled against the perceived image of preachers' kids as 'goodies.' We always felt as if people expected us to behave better than others. I did a lot of detention to prove I could be as naughty as anyone else.

"I took piano lessons, violin lessons, and swimming lessons. I was never very devoted to any of them, but I always loved to make art. Having taught art, Mom had a large assortment of art materials around the house, and we were always doing something artsy. I never considered majoring in anything but art in college.

© 1999 Boyer Photography

Barbara Lavallee [signature]

I loved drawing best, but was exposed to many different media while in school. In 1964, I graduated from Illinois Wesleyan University with a degree in art education. It was no secret that you could never expect to make a living being an artist. You had to have a real job to make a living and do your art on the side. I wasn't ready to be an artist then anyway, because I felt I needed some experience in living.

"That experience came when I moved to Alaska with my husband. We came to Alaska to teach in a boarding school run by the Bureau of Indian Affairs. At that time, native children from rural villages attended high school at boarding schools because there were no high schools in most of the small, remote villages. I was fascinated with the native way of life in Alaska, and intrigued by the rich cultural traditions in each of Alaska's diverse native groups. My experiences with my students changed my life. I was developing a passion—I had found what I wanted to paint. In 1975, I quit teaching to paint full time. Since then, I've painted hundreds—perhaps thousands—of paintings, mostly of people, because that is what I like to paint best. Since my divorce in 1981, I have raised my two sons as a single mom and supported us by making art. I feel like the luckiest person alive to be able to make a living doing something I love.

"In 1986, a chance meeting with author Vicki Cobb led to my first children's book illustrations. Together, Vicki and I traveled around the world researching the Imagine Living Here series for Walker and Co. That led to other book contracts. I love the challenges presented in illustrating books. Each book has its own set of problems to solve. Whether it is a nonfiction piece that requires meticulous research, or an imaginary character that must maintain integrity throughout a story, each is a delicious dilemma to analyze and resolve.

"I've had a life full of adventure and creative accomplishment. Along the way, my life experiences have included recreation, counseling, social work, teaching, owning a restaurant, and being a mom to my two sons. It is those life experiences that I draw upon in the art I create. My current delights include my grandchildren, Justus and Fannie; my cat, Moonie; and a long-time passion for travel."

ଓ ଓ ଓ

One of Barbara Lavallee's earliest jobs was with the U.S. Army Special Services as a Recreation Specialist in an Army Service Club in Lenggries, Germany. It was there that she met her husband. After they married, they moved first to Maine, then to Arizona. When they reached Alaska in 1970, Lavallee found her adoptive home. She had taught art on a Navajo Indian Reservation in Arizona for the Bureau of Indian Affairs, and now she started teaching at Mount Edgecombe Native School in Sitka. She stayed on for 12 years.

Teaching gave Lavallee a rich knowledge of Alaskan native culture, which is reflected in her art. Working predominantly in watercolor, she developed her whimsical stylized characters dressed in vibrant colors by first working with silkscreen prints. She is known for creating happy people—working, playing, and living with smiles on their faces. "I want people to have fun," she once said in an interview with the Art Shop Gallery in Homer, Alaska. "If people look and smile, then I feel the art is a success."

When it came time to illustrate her first book, Lavallee read Uri Shulevitz's *Writing with Pictures* to get an idea of how to go about it. While her initial illustrations were for cookbooks, she soon teamed up with Vicki Cobb to create the Imagine Living Here series. This series satisfied another passion of Lavallee's—travel. She went to exciting locales such as Brazil, Bolivia, Peru, Australia, and Japan to bring back images that were eventually portrayed in the series.

In producing the illustrations for *Mama, Do You Love Me*, by Barbara Joosse, Lavallee found an outlet for her passion for Alaska's indigenous people and cultures. The book, which has sold more than a million copies worldwide and been translated into fifteen

"I was fascinated with the native way of life in Alaska, and intrigued by the rich cultural traditions in each of Alaska's diverse native groups. My experiences with my students changed my life."

Mama,
Do You
Love Me?

by Barbara M. Joosse   illustrated by Barbara Lavallee

Courtesy of Chronicle Books

languages, earned Lavallee a Golden Kite Award for picture book illustration. Reading the manuscript, the artist identified with both characters: the mother and the little girl. It was only after the book had been published that she learned that Joosse had written the book about a mother and a little boy. Lavallee and Joosse teamed up again to work on a companion title—*Papa, Do You Love Me?*—which is set in Africa and features a Masai father and son. Lavallee visited Africa twice to absorb the culture and landscape, and continues to be fascinated by that part of the world.

Lavallee's books have received many awards and honors. In addition to the Golden Kite Award, *Mama, Do You Love Me?* earned an Oppenheim Toy Portfolio Blue Chip Award, an ABC Children's Booksellers Choices Award in the picture book category, and a NAPPA (National Association of Parenting Publications Award). *All You Need for a Snowman* was named to CCBC Choices and was cited as an Outstanding Book by Wisconsin Authors and Illustrators. *This Place Is Wild: East Africa* was one of Bank Street College's Best Children's Books of the Year, and *Uno, Dos, Tres = One, Two, Three* was a 1996 Tomás Rivera Mexican American Children's Book Award Nominee. In recognition of her accomplishments, the YWCA named Lavallee one of its ten Women of Achievement in 2005.

Now living in Anchorage, Alaska, Lavallee is known for her original artwork, reproduction prints, and note cards. A prolific artist, she produces about 150 paintings a year, with many of those reproduced in limited-edition prints and displayed in galleries throughout Alaska and the Pacific Northwest. Her depictions of Alaskan life have made her one of the most celebrated artists in the state.

A single mother, Lavallee credits her two sons, Chip and Mark, with adding immensely to the wealth of experiences and memories from which she derives much of the humor found in her characters. Her family remains a strong influence on her life and work.

SELECTED WORKS ILLUSTRATED: *The Snow Child*, by Freya Littledale, 1989; *This Place Is Cold: Alaska*, by Vicki Cobb, 1989; *This Place Is Dry: Arizona's Sonora Desert*, by Vicki Cobb, 1989; *This Place Is Wet: The Brazilian Rainforest*, by Vicki Cobb, 1990; *This Place Is High: The Andes Mountains of Bolivia*, by Vicki Cobb, 1990; *This Place Is Lonely: The Australian Outback*, by Vicki Cobb, 1991; *Mama, Do You Love Me?* by Barbara Joosse, 1991; *This Place Is Crowded: Japan*, by Vicki Cobb, 1992; *Uno, Dos, Tres = One, Two, Three*, by Pat Mora, 1996; *This Place Is Wild: East Africa*, by Vicki Cobb, 1998; *The Gift*, by Kristine L. Franklin, 1999; *All You Need for a Snowman*, by Alice Schertle, 2002; *All You Need for a Beach*, by Alice Schertle, 2004; *Papa, Do You Love Me?*, by Barbara Joosse, 2005; *Grandma Calls Me Beautiful*, by Barbara Joosse, 2008.

SUGGESTED READING: *Something About the Author*, vol. 74, 1993.

John Lawrence

September 15, 1933–

"I was born in Hastings on the south coast of England in 1933 and have always had a love and attraction for the sea. Sadly, I was sent away inland to boarding school when I was seven because of German bombing raids over the coast at the beginning of the war. The school was run by the Salesians, a Roman Catholic order of priests, and I was with them for ten years.

"I was always drawing, but with little sense of direction until, at eighteen, I went to my local art school in Hastings. It was there that I was introduced to wider horizons and basic skills. I decided after two years to get my National Service over (compulsory then) with a view to applying to one of the London art schools later. I went into the army and had the good luck to be sent to West Africa after my basic training. I found time for drawing and painting and I was greatly influenced by the brilliant light and colour, the depth of shadows, and the whole narrative of a different way of life in a continent that was new to me. It was this work, fifty years ago, that got me into the Central School of Art, now part of London University of the Arts.

"There were no degrees in Art in those days and I took a diploma in Illustration and Printmaking and was particularly caught up with wood engraving, which was taught by Gertrude Hermes, a fine engraver and sculptor. I loved the smoothness of the boxwood blocks, the spikiness of the tools with their odd names (spitstickers, gravers, scorpers, etc.) and the filaments of light that came through the darkness as metal purred through wood, or at least, it did purr if you sharpened the tools properly.

"As a book illustrator, I have not concentrated unduly on engraving, although my first fully engraved children's book, *Rabbit and Pork Rhyming Talk*, was published in 1976. In the last six or seven years, however, I have had more opportunities to use it in my children's picture books. I now do most of my engraving on vinyl, which is a floor covering somewhat similar to linoleum but easier to engrave. It is a cheaper and much more adaptable surface than wood for the larger picture books and provides softer and chunkier images. In *The Sea Horse: The Shyest Fish in the Sea*, written by Christine Butterworth, I used a combination of wood and vinyl—the wood being very suitable for describing the intricacies of the delicate, scaly creatures and the vinyl the colourful coral and plant life on the seabed. One of my favourite recent books is *This Little Chick*.

Photo by Peter Mennim

"My other method of work is using pen and watercolour. Two of the books that have given me the greatest pleasure in this medium are an illustrated edition of *Watership Down* by Richard Adams published in 1976 and *Christmas on Exeter Street* by Diana Hendry published in 1989. In the first one, I enjoyed roaming around Watership Down, a beautiful hillside area in Berkshire, for several weeks drawing the flora and fauna for reference. The latter is a Christmas romp about all sorts of people, old and young, turning up on Christmas Eve seeking beds for the night and poor Mrs. Mistletoe having to find places for them to sleep—on mantelpieces, window sills, kitchen shelves and the bathtub—great fun.

"Another aspect of my work is part-time lecturing at art schools. At the moment, I'm at Cambridge Art School for one day a week teaching an MA course in Children's Books. This I enjoy very much, as it allows me to interact and share work and ideas with a younger generation."

❧ ❧ ❧

John Lawrence attended Hastings School of Art from 1951 to 1953, the Central School of Arts and Crafts from 1955 to 1957, and spent the interval between in military service. It was at the Central School of Arts and Crafts that he met his future wife, Myra Bell. Some of Lawrence's drawings appeared in a leading British short-story magazine while he was still a student, and as a postgraduate, he received a best student of the year award.

When his wife was expecting their first child, Lawrence began working on the Imperial Chemical Industries' house journal, as well as contributing artwork for *Black's Children's Encyclopaedia*, published in 1961. At about the same time, one of his first linocut illustrations appeared in *Musical Instruments*, a children's book by Denys Darlow. Soon after, he started working for a large advertising agency, engraving magazine advertisements. This was a productive time for Lawrence. In the 1960s he worked for nine publishers, illustrating over thirty books for both adults and children, including the first book he wrote himself, *The Giant of Grabbist*.

A member of the Art Workers Guild and the Society of Wood Engravers, Lawrence has, for most of his artistic career, also been a part-time teacher—first at Brighton School of Arts, in the 1960s, and later at Camberwell School of Art, where he taught for about 30 years. Currently he is a visiting professor at the Cambridge School of Art. He has also enjoyed a close association with the Folio Society, which published his first book with wood engravings, Daniel Defoe's *The History and Remarkable Life of the Truly Honourable Colonel Jack*. This work received second prize in the 1972 Francis Williams Book Illustration Awards, the United Kingdom's premier award for book and editorial illustration. When it was published in the United States it appeared on the Metrowest Massachusetts Regional Library System's Books Not To Be Missed list and the Maine Regional Library System's Cream of the Crop list. Other classic authors whose works Lawrence has illustrated include Alphonse Daudet and Thomas Hardy.

Throughout his career, Lawrence has illustrated books for both adults and children. *Rabbit and Pork Rhyming Talk*, which demonstrates the artist's fascination with language as well as his skill at engraving, won a 1977 Francis Williams Book Illustration

"I was always drawing, but with little sense of direction until, at eighteen, I went to my local art school in Hastings. It was there that I was introduced to wider horizons and basic skills."

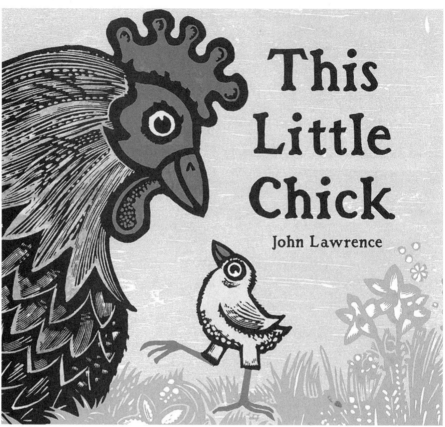

This
Little
Chick

John Lawrence

Courtesy of Candlewick Press

Award and, in the U.S., was included in the Children's Book Council's 1976 Showcase of finely designed books for young readers. Much of Lawrence's illustration work in children's books has been in the realm of fantasy, folklore, and stories of mystery and magic. While his illustrations for young children have gained much recognition, he has also created evocative art in books for older readers. Two haunting Christmas stories written by Paul Theroux—*A Christmas Card* and *London Snow*—are greatly enriched by the artist's atmospheric black and white engravings. The same style, with its old-fashioned, nostalgic feeling, was the perfect choice to illustrate Philip Pullman's follow-up volume to the enormously popular His Dark Materials trilogy. *Lyra's Oxford*, set two years after *The Amber Spyglass*, follows the main character around the city in her alternative universe, and the timeless quality of Lawrence's wood engraving gave that short novel just the right complementary illustrations.

Though he uses old techniques for his engraving work, Lawrence also employs new technology, manipulating his original art with a computer to achieve various effects. In recent years, he has especially enjoyed working on books for young children. In his own story, *This Little Chick*, the title character is a great mimic of the other animals around him, but it is Lawrence's visual representation of the barnyard sounds and his stunning vinyl engravings that draw readers into the story. This title, which was a 2002 *New York Times* Best Illustrated Book of the Year, a *School Library Journal* Best Book of the Year, and a *Child Magazine* and *Parenting* magazine Best Book of the Year, was also named an Oppenheim Toy Portfolio Gold Award Winner and listed on the New York Public Library's 100 Titles for Reading and Sharing, as well as the Chicago Public Library's Best Books for Children and Teens.

Another barnyard story, *Tiny's Big Adventure*, written by Martin Waddell, is about young barn mice exploring the wide world around them. Lawrence's vinyl engravings, watercolor washes, and textured printing enrich this vibrant tale. It was named a *School Library Journal* Best Book of the Year, appeared on the *Horn Book* Fanfare list, and was among the New York Public Library's 100 Titles for Reading and Sharing. For *Sea Horse: The Shyest Fish in the Sea*, a factual work by Chris Butterworth that explains the unusual lifecycle of sea horses, Lawrence provided beautiful and colorful images, enhanced by his own specially created letterforms. *Sea Horse* was named an honor book for the Gryphon Award, presented by the Center for Children's Books at the Graduate School of Library and Information Science at the University of Illinois, Urbana-Champaign. The award is given to titles for children in grades K–4 that best exemplify the qualities that help emerging readers make the transition to independent reading.

John Lawrence's art has been displayed in museums in England, Wales, and the United States. Renowned for using tools and engraving methods from the 18th century, Lawrence has illustrated over 150 books. He has two grown daughters and lives on the south coast in England.

SELECTED WORKS WRITTEN AND ILLUSTRATED (Dates are for British publication; U.S. publication dates, if different, appear in parentheses): *The Giant of Grabbist*, 1968 (1969); *Pope Leo's Elephant*, 1969 (1970); *The King of the Peacocks*, 1970 (1971); *Rabbit and Pork Rhyming Talk*, 1975; *A Pair of Sinners*, 1980; *George: His Elephant and Castle*, 1983; *This Little Chick*, 2002.

SELECTED WORKS ILLUSTRATED FOR YOUNG READERS: *Dragons Come Home! And Other Stories*, by Janet McNeill, 1969; *Stumpf and* the Cornish Witches, by John Onslow, 1969; *The Courage of Sarah Noble*, by Alice Dalgliesh, 1971; *The Boy on the Ox's Back and Other African Legends*, by Forbes Stuart, 1971; *The Magician's Heart*, by Edith Nesbit, 1971; *Maildun the Voyager*, by James Reeves, 1971; *To and Fro the Small Green Bottle*, by J.B. Simpson, 1971; *Jemima and the Welsh Rabbit*, by Gillian Avery, 1972; *The Life and Strange Surprising Adventures of Robinson Crusoe of York*, by Daniel Defoe, 1972; *A Fairy Called Andy Perks*, by Janet McNeill, 1973; *The Mouth of the Night: Gaelic Stories*, adapted by Iris Macfarlane, 1973 (1976); *The Sound of Coaches*, by Leon Garfield, 1974; *Blue Fairy Book*, by Andrew Lang, ed. by Brian Alderson, 1975 (1980); *Dragons and More: Dark Fables with Some Light Patches*, by Mildred Davidson, 1976; *Watership Down* (illus. ed.), by Richard Adams, 1976; *A Christmas Card*, by Paul Theroux, 1978; *London Snow*, by Paul Theroux, 1980; *The Everyman's Book of English Folktales*, by Sybil Marshall, 1981; *Precisely Pig*, by Michael Berthoud, 1982; *The Magic Apple Tree*, by Susan Hill, 1984 (1983); *Mabel's Story*, by Jenny Koraleck, 1984 (1987); *Awful Annie and Perfect Percy*, by J. B. Simpson, 1986; *Awful Annie and Nippy Numbers*, by J. B. Simpson, 1987; *Emily's Own Elephant*, by Philippa Pearce, 1987; *Christmas in Exeter Street*, by Diana Hendry, 1989; *A New Treasury of Poetry*, comp. by Neil Philip, 1990; *Poems for the Young*, comp. by Neil Philip, 1992; *King of Kings*, by Susan Hill, 1993; *Charles Causley's Collected Poems for Children*, by Charles Causley, 1996 (2000); *The Mysteries of Zigomar*, by Allan Ahlberg, 1997; *The Old Stories: Folk Tales from East Anglia and the Fen Country*, by Kevin Crossley Holland, 1997 (1999); *A Treasury of Five-Minute Stories*, by Fiona Waters, 2000; *Lyra's Oxford*, by Philip Pullman, 2003; *Tiny's Big Adventure*, by Martin Waddell, 2004; *Sea Horse: The Shyest Fish in the Sea*, by Chris Butterworth, 2006; *Once Upon a Time in the North*, by Philip Pullman, 2008.

SELECTED WORKS ILLUSTRATED FOR ADULTS: *The Little Store on the Corner*, by Alice P. Miller, 1962 (1961); *The History and Remarkable Life of the Truly Honourable Colonel Jack*, by Daniel Defoe, 1967; *Enjoy Reading!* ed. by Robert E. Rogerson and C. M. Smith, 1968; *Gunpowder Treason*, by Margaret J. Miller, 1968; *Rebel Admiral*, by Frank Knight, 1968; *The Diary of a Nobody*, by George and Weedon Grossmith, 1969 (1989); *The Kitchen Book/The Cook Book*, by Nicolas Freeling, 1970 (1994); *That Rare Captain—Sir Francis Drake*, by F. Knight, 1970; *Tales in School: An Anthology of Boarding School Life*, ed. by Jacynth

Hope-Simpson, 1971; *The Mule of Avignon*, by Alphonse Daudet, trans. by Sybil Brown, 1972 (1973); *No Magic Eden*, by Shirley Guiton, 1972; *Rogues, Vagabonds and Sturdy Beggars*, by Arthur F. Kinney, 1973 (1990); *Our Exploits at West Poley*, by Thomas Hardy, ed. by Richard L. Purdy, 1978; *Too Many Husbands*, by Sheila Lavelle, 1978; *The Autobiography of Luke Hansard*, by Luke Hansard, 1991; *Venice*, by Jonathan Keates, 1994.

SUGGESTED READING: *Something About the Author*, vol. 30, 1983; Peppin, Brigid and Lucy Micklethwait, *Book Illustrators of the Twentieth Century*, 1984. Periodicals: Carey, Joanna, "The Spitsticker Wizard," *The Guardian*, June 21, 2003, at http://books.guardian.co/uk/review/story/0,12084,981409,000.html

WEB SITE: www.walkerbooks.co.uk/John-Lawrence

"I was born in Chicago and raised in New Jersey, just outside of New York City. I grew up in a family of four children. As a young kid, I was allowed to walk to three places off my block: school, my best friend's house, and the library. Part of my early impression of going to the library was feeling a sense of intoxicating independence; not just because I was crossing streets without an adult, but because I felt very free within the library itself. It seemed to me that as long as I was relatively quiet, I was allowed to explore anywhere and look at anything I liked without asking. And I was impressed that a children's section even existed. Looking at the pictures, I'd wonder how I would ever learn to do complicated things like shading, which seemed to be terribly adult and mysterious. . . .

"In kindergarten I had my first memorable art crisis. Our kindly teacher had handed out paper and crayons and drew a stick figure on the blackboard for us all to copy. I loved my teacher, but I couldn't bring myself to draw that figure. I just didn't think that people looked that way. I struggled terribly with the sense that I could be bringing on my own doom, but finally decided I had to draw a person how I thought one looked. When my teacher saw it, she was positively impressed and said that I was quite an artist. Besides my obvious relief, it was the first time I connected my strong interest in drawing with the experience of being called an 'artist.'

"Since I became a compulsive reader as well, the idea of one day becoming an illustrator made perfect sense—but I had never heard of anyone really being something like that, and even

Barbara Lehman

December 14, 1963–

though I saw the names on the books, the existence of real artists and writers seemed mythological and remote to me.

"When I was twelve, we had a presentation about careers at school, and to my surprise I found in the materials a description of something called a 'commercial artist.' I had never heard of such a thing. I devoured the information in astonishment. It all made sense, and suddenly I saw things involving 'commercial art' all around me: books, clothes, games, magazines, stamps, puzzles, cards—even the wallpaper—it was everywhere! I wanted to study commercial art and to become an illustrator. That same year my father died, and as a teen I became focused on how I would one day get myself off to college.

"After much work—studying illustration techniques from a book to help me make a portfolio, receiving invaluable practical help from a high-school guidance counselor and support from friends—I found myself in art school in Brooklyn at the age of seventeen. I was only twenty miles from home, but going to Pratt Institute felt like interplanetary travel. I was living in a seventeen-story high-rise filled with students, taking almost all art classes, and feeling as if I had been miraculously transported to some kind of earthly paradise. Since graduation I have done many different types of work, including animation, graphic design, lettering, decorative painting, fabric design, and window displays, but the work that means the very most to me is my work in books."

Photo by Richmond Johnston

ભ ભ ભ

Barbara Lehman's education at Pratt Institute led her to a varied career in many types of art, but her books for children will surely be her lasting contribution. In 2005 her innovative and startling *The Red Book*, inspired by her interest in maps and fascination for faraway places, was named a Caldecott Honor Book. Creating a story that uses unusual perspectives and flights of imagination, the wordless story connects children across cultures and eras through their sense of adventure. With clear, child-centered paintings in pen and ink, watercolor, and gouache, Lehman made a world that her young readers can enter easily and completely in their own imaginative ways. It is a fanciful journey for those who enjoy "reading" pictures and following visual clues in an eye-catching context. *The Red Book* was also named a *Horn Book* Fanfare title and an ALA Notable Children's Book.

Lehman has long been interested in visual literacy. Her favorite artists are Hergé (the pen name of Georges Prosper Remi, creator of the *Tintin* books); George Herriman, of *Krazy Kat* fame; and the early cartoonist and animator Winsor McCay, whose most famous creation was the cartoon *Little Nemo*. Lehman's work echoes the influences of these graphic artists and the cartoon style that they developed; however, she has created her own unique style. With a deceptive simplicity, her ink, watercolor, and gouache work suggests a world under the surface of reality with great depth and finesse.

Following the success of *The Red Book*, Lehman created another wordless story in *Museum Trip*, which was inspired by the field trips to New York art museums that she took as a young student. Separated from his classmates, a boy finds himself magically entering a piece of the art in *Museum Trip*. The journey might be all in the boy's imagination, but viewers can see that he has brought something away from the maze he wandered through. Her next book, *Rainstorm*, a wordless, magical adventure for a gloomy day, was named a Junior Library Guild selection and an ALA Notable Children's Book.

Earlier in her career, Lehman provided the art for a number of picture books. *Moonfall*, written by Susan Whitcher, is a story about the waning moon that a little girl is sure that she has seen fall into a lilac bush. Lehman's cartoon-like illustrations perfectly complemented the whimsy of the storyline and helped *Moonfall* earn a Parents' Choice award. *Something for Everyone*, also written by Whitcher, celebrates the inventiveness and imagination of the very young and the very old. *Say Boo!*, with text by Lynda Graham-Barber, is a gentle Halloween story for young children, designed not to frighten but to delight. *Abracadabra to Zigzag*, written by Nancy Lecourt, is an alphabet book of unusual words and includes etymological information on many of the phrases illustrated, such as "odds and ends" and "lickety-split."

Barbara Lehman lives in Claverack, New York. She still likes to read *Tintin*, but also enjoys bicycling, knitting, and the martial art Aikido.

"I was only twenty miles from home, but going to Pratt Institute felt like interplanetary travel."

SELECTED WORKS WRITTEN AND ILLUSTRATED: *The Red Book*, 2004; *Museum Book*, 2006; *Rainstorm*, 2007; *Trainstop*, 2008.

Courtesy of the Houghton Mifflin Company

SELECTED WORKS ILLUSTRATED: *Abracadabra to Zigzag: An Alphabet Book*, by Nancy Lecourt, 1991; *Timothy Twinge*, by Florence Parry Heide and Roxanne Heide Pierce, 1993; *Moonfall*, by Susan Whitcher, 1993; *A Chartreuse Leotard in a Magenta Limousine and Other Words after People and Places*, by Lynda Graham-Barber, 1994; *Something for Everyone*, by Susan Whicher, 1995; *Say Boo!*, by Lynda Graham-Barber, 1996; *Christmas Cookies*, by Susan Devins, 2003.

SUGGESTED READING: *Something About the Author*, vol. 170, 2006.

David Levithan

1972–

David Benjamin Levithan was born in Short Hills, New Jersey, where he had a happy childhood and an equally happy adolescence. In high school, he used to carve the names of his favorite writers—Alice Hoffman, Anne Tyler, and Margaret Atwood—on his desks. Since his graduation from Millburn Senior High in Millburn, New Jersey, in 1990, these authors still rank among his favorites.

A 1994 graduate of Brown University, Levithan started his publishing career when he became an intern at Scholastic Press at the age of 19. He has edited over a hundred Star Wars books for Scholastic, including *The Complete Star Wars Trilogy Scrapbook*. In 2002 he founded Scholastic's PUSH imprint, dedicated to seeking out new writers and publishing cutting-edge young adult books. The new imprint was launched with an anthology he edited, *You Are Here, This is Now*, which included stories, poems, essays, photos and paintings by teenagers who had won Scholastic's 1999, 2000, and 2001 art and writing awards. To celebrate PUSH's fifth anniversary in 2007, Levithan edited and published an anthology of stories by PUSH authors in *This Is PUSH: New Stories from the Edge*.

Levithan's first novel, *Boy Meets Boy*, began as a short story written as a Valentine's Day gift. Laced with a good deal of humor, the story is about a utopian high school where all sexual preferences are tolerated and accepted. *Boy Meets Boy* received the 2003 Lambda Literary Award and was named one of the American Library Association's Top Ten Best Books for Young Adults. It also became an ALA Quick Pick for Reluctant Young Adult Readers, a *Bulletin of the Center for Children's Books* Blue Ribbon title, a *Booklist* Editors' Choice, and a Notable Social Studies Trade Book. Levithan has said that his purpose in writing this groundbreaking book was to get away from the gloomy, sad and grim stories often seen in gay literature for teens. As a gay man himself, he wanted to see a manuscript come across his desk that was about a happy homosexual adolescence. Finally, he just wrote it himself.

Courtesy of Random House, Inc.

His second novel, *The Realm of Possibility*, which was shortlisted for the 2004 Lambda Literary Award, also started out as a Valentine's Day gift. Written in verse from the various perspectives and points of view of twenty different students, the book nevertheless forms a cohesive narrative as the students' lives intersect. Noted for the variety of voices and the distinctive style, this title was also cited as one of ALA's Top Ten Best Books for Young Adults. A third novel that also started as a Valentine's Day short story gift, *Are We There Yet?*, became a Best Book for

Young Adults as well. This complex and insightful novel is set in Italy, where a love triangle involves two very dissimilar brothers.

Always searching for new formats, Levithan next penned *Nick and Norah's Infinite Playlist*, a collaborative work in which he wrote in Nick's voice and Rachel Cohn wrote in Norah's. Without ever discussing the book, the two authors sent chapters back and forth between them to put the story together. The result was a popular modern love story set against a backdrop of New York City nightlife, music and bands, heartbreak and romance, wit and spontaneity. Although the authors originally intended to write it for each other, once published, this book became both a Best Book for Young Adults and a Quick Pick for Reluctant Young Adult Readers. In light of that success, Levithan and Cohn teamed up again for *Naomi and Ely's No Kiss List*, another story told from alternating points of view, this one exploring the nature of friendship and love.

A book Levithan edited with Billy Merrell, *Full Spectrum*, was the 2006 Lambda Literary Award winner. It features original poetry, essays and stories by gay, lesbian, bisexual, and straight teenagers and slightly older young adults on a variety of subjects. To find the selections for the books, Levithan and Merrell, in conjunction with the Gay, Lesbian, and Straight Education Network (GLSEN)—which receives a portion of the proceeds from the book—set up a website. They requested writings and received a large number of responses; forty of these made their way into this diverse and compelling collection.

Currently, Levithan works as executive editorial director for Scholastic Fiction, Multimedia Publishing and PUSH. He lives in Hoboken, New Jersey. An amateur photographer, he started in 2001 to take one photograph a day, and he believes that it has helped him to pay more attention to details. As a music lover, he often plays different kinds of music when he is writing. Besides being a writer and an editor, Levithan finds time to teach. Since 2004 he has taught children's and young adult writing at the New School for Social Research in New York City. He also belongs to a book club that reads and discusses teen books. As a member of the organization Authors Support Intellectual Freedom (AS IF), Levithan hopes to not only fight against censorship but to bring about positive changes in the world.

SELECTED WORKS: *In the Eye of the Tornado*, 1998; *In the Heat of the Quake*, 1998; *10 Things I Hate About You* (adapted), 1999; *The Mummy: A Junior Novelization* (adapted with Stephen Sommers), 1999; *The Mummy: The Complete Movie Scrap-*

Levithan's first novel, Boy Meets Boy, *began as a short story written as a Valentine's Day gift.*

book, with Anne Downey, James Preller and Stephen Sommers, 1999; *Journey through the Lost Canyon* (Pokemon Challenge Series), 2000; *My Class Project* (Malcolm in the Middle), 2000; *You Are Here, This Is Now: The Best Young Writers and Artists in America*, as editor, 2002; *101 Ways To Get Away With Anything* (Malcolm in the Middle), 2002; *Malcolm's Really Useful Guide to Getting Away with Anything!* (Malcolm in the Middle), 2002; *101 Ways to Stop Being Bored* (Malcolm in the Middle), 2003; *Boy Meets Boy*, 2003; *Charlie's Angels: Full Throttle* (novelization of John August's screenplay), 2003; *The Perfect Score* (adapted from Jon Zack's screenplay with Marc Hyman), 2003; *Realm of Possibility*, 2004; *Complete Star Wars Trilogy Scrapbook*, as ed., 2004; "The Alumni Interview," in *Sixteen: Stories about that Sweet and Bitter Birthday*, ed. by Megan McCafferty, 2004; "What a Song Can Do," in *What a Song Can Do: 12 Riffs on the Power of Music*, ed. by Jennifer Armstrong, 2004; *Marly's Ghost: A Remix of Charles Dickens' A Christmas Carol*, illus. by Brian Selznick, 2005; "Princes," in *Every Man For Himself* , ed. by Nancy Mercado, 2005; "The Justice League" in *Friends*, ed. by David Levithan and Ann Martin, 2005; *Where We Are, What We See: Poems, Stories, Essays, and Art from the Best Young Writers and Artists in America*, as ed., 2005; *Are We There Yet?*, 2005; *Friends: Stories About New Friends, Old Friends, and Unexpectedly True Friends*, ed. with Ann M. Martin, 2005; *Nick and Norah's Infinite Playlist*, with Rachel Cohn, 2006; "Breaking and Entering," in *Rush Hour: Reckless*, ed. by Michael Cart, 2006; *Full Spectrum: A New Generation of Writing about Gay, Lesbian, Bisexual, Transgender, Questioning, and Other Identities*, ed. with Billy Merrell, 2006; *Wide Awake*, 2006; *Naomi and Ely's No Kiss List*, with Rachel Cohn, 2007; *21 Proms*, ed. with Daniel Ehrenhaft, 2007; *This Is PUSH: New Stories From the Edge*, as ed., 2007; "Lost Sometimes," in *21 Proms*, ed. by David Levithan and Daniel Ehrenhaft, 2007; "The Good Girls," in *Girls Who Like Boys Who Like Boys*, ed. by Tom Dolby and Melissa de la Cruz, 2007; *Up All Night*, with Peter Abrahams, Libby Bray, Sarah Weeks, Gene

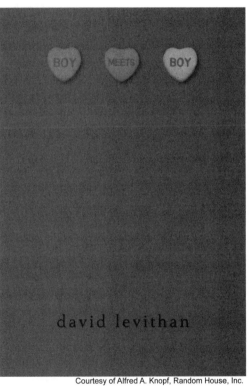

Courtesy of Alfred A. Knopf, Random House, Inc.

Yang, and Patricia McCormick, 2008; *How They Met, and Other Stories*, 2008.

SUGGESTED READING: *Something About the Author*, vol. 166, 2006. Online—Lodge, Sally, "PUSH Celebrates Five Years of Publishing New Voices," *Children's Bookshelf*, February 15, 2007, at www.publishersweekly.com/article/CA6416603.html

WEB SITES: www.davidlevithan.com
www.thisispush.com

Courtesy of Grace Lin

Grace Lin

May 17, 1974–

"I grew up in upstate New York where there were few minorities, especially Asian. My parents wanted us to blend; they wanted us to grow up really 'American' and made the decision to speak to us only in English. So, my sisters and I grew up very Americanized. There were subtle differences, like Chinese food or red envelopes, but most of the time we glossed over them.

"Even the books I read when I was younger ignored my Asian heritage. All the books we read in school—*Little House on the Prairie, B Is for Betsy*—never had any Asian characters. But I still loved them. In fact, I loved all books.

"So when I found out that an author/illustrator was a real job, I knew that was what I wanted to be. I loved making books. Even in elementary school, whenever there was a class assignment I always made a book. No matter what the subject matter—cloud formation, multiplication tables, Vikings—I always stapled my homework pages together, trying to make it look as much like a book as possible.

"Now, I am an author and illustrator and I make 'real books.' And it's great. When kids tell me they love my books or tell me I'm their favorite author, I know I have the best job ever. The only bad thing is that authors and illustrators work at home and not in an office, so sometimes I stay in my pajamas all day long. And then, the mailman will ring and I'll have to answer the door in my pajamas and that's really embarrassing. Especially when I'm wearing my fuzzy slippers.

"A lot of my books, like *The Year of the Dog* or *The Ugly Vegetables*, deal with Asian culture because, in a way, I'm trying to find the culture I lost. When I was younger, I was ashamed or sometimes angry about being Asian. Sometimes I would see myself in the mirror and be surprised to see an Asian girl looking back at me. It's only now, after becoming an adult, that I realize there was something I lost, ignoring these parts of my heritage. There were a lot of things that we did, traditions like eating ginger soup at a baby shower, which I never bothered to learn more about. So now, I research these kinds of things about my heritage. I'm making the books I missed when I was younger. That's why I started doing these kinds of books and why I will keep doing them."

∞ ∞ ∞

Grace Lin's choice of career stems directly from her childhood love of creating "books" and drawing. Her father was a doctor, and her mother spent much of her time gardening and judging flower shows. Grace, whose nickname was Pacy when she was small, was the middle child in the family. While her two sisters grew up to become scientists, Grace attended the Rhode Island School of Design to pursue her interest in art, graduating with a B.F.A. in 1996. On a trip to Italy with the school, Lin was especially impressed with the dark outlines in stained glass windows and the wonderful way they highlighted the bright colors of the glass. Later, dark outlines and jewel-like colors would become a signature aspect of her picture books.

Her first book, *The Ugly Vegetables*, published in 1999, was named an American Booksellers Association Pick of the Lists, a Bank Street College Best Book of the Year, and a Notable Social Studies Trade Book for Young People. About a young Asian-American girl who complains that her mother's garden has no pretty flowers but discovers the joys of Chinese vegetable soup later, when the plants are harvested, *The Ugly Vegetables* also received a Growing Good Kids book award from the Junior Master Gardener program of the American Horticultural Society.

With that initial success, Grace Lin achieved her career goal of being a children's book creator and established her own distinctive voice and style of illustration. Of her picture books that followed, many were related to aspects of Asian-American culture. The saturated colors and bright appeal of each of these stories delighted young readers and critics alike. *Dim Sum for Everyone!* introduced a family of three sisters and their parents

"My parents wanted us to blend; they wanted us to grow up really 'American' and made the decision to speak to us only in English."

enjoying a traditional meal in Chinatown, where they feast on small portions of various dishes. The characters appear again in *Fortune Cookie Fortunes* and *Kite Flying* as Lin continues to explore the warmth of this contemporary family enjoying its cultural roots. In *Lissy's Friends*, Lin shows a girl who is lonely on her first day of school and creates origami figures to keep her company. The gentle magic of the story comes full circle when her origami "friends" help her to become friends with one of her classmates.

Several of Lin's picture books feature animal characters whose exploits sometimes embody subtle messages for their audience. In *Olvina Flies*, a chicken is concerned about attending a bird conference in Hawaii because, being a chicken, she can't fly. Even though she solves the problem by taking a plane, she still has to conquer her fear of flying, and Lin takes every opportunity that this scenario presents for lighthearted humor. *Okie-Dokie, Artichokie!* features a monkey and a giraffe living in an apartment house where it's easy to develop misunderstandings, but in the end they learn to coexist and accommodate each other's lifestyles.

In *Robert's Snow*, a small mouse wanders away from his home during a snowstorm, only to be rescued and returned by a very special person. This story had deeper meaning for the author/artist; she told it to her husband, Robert Mercer, the winter he was diagnosed with bone cancer. Like his namesake in the story, Robert was confined to home, but in his case it was due to weakness from aggressive treatment for the disease. In 2003 Robert was declared cancer-free and the story of *Robert's Snow* was accepted for publication. When the cancer returned in 2004, the couple used the book as inspiration for a fundraiser for cancer research. Grace Lin contacted children's book illustrators across the country, asking them to donate painted wooden snowflakes to be auctioned on eBay with all proceeds going to the Dana-Farber Cancer Institute. Response was overwhelming; the auction raised $100,000. The art is featured in a book, *Robert's Snowflakes*. Sadly, Robert Mercer lost his battle with cancer in August 2007, but artists and illustrators continue to contribute their exquisite work so that the *Robert's Snow* auctions will raise more money for research.

Grace Lin has now branched out from her picture book writing and illustrating to writing novels based on her experiences growing up. *The Year of the Dog* was named an ALA Notable Children's Book in 2008. The story begins on the first day of the Chinese New Year, a year in which the protagonist makes friends with the only other Asian-American girl in her class.

The character of Melody, Grace's friend in the book, is based on the author's childhood friend Alvina Ling, who grew up to be a children's book editor and published both *The Year of the Dog* and its sequel, *The Year of the Rat*. Recently the two friends visited China together, traveling to Beijing and Shanghai and walking the Great Wall.

Grace Lin lives in Somerville, Massachusetts. In addition to illustrating and writing children's books, she has exhibited her work in museums and galleries, including a one-woman show at the Danforth Museum of Art in Framingham, Massachusetts.

SELECTED WORKS WRITTEN AND ILLUSTRATED: *The Ugly Vegetables*, 1999; *Dim Sum for Everyone!*, 2001; *Kite Flying*, 2002; *Olvina Flies*, 2003; *Okie-Dokie, Artichokie!*, 2003; *Robert's Snow*, 2004; *Fortune Cookie Fortunes*, 2004; *Our Seasons*, with Ranida T. Mckneally, 2006; *Olvina Swims*, 2007; *The Red Thread: An Adoption Fairy Tale*, 2007; *Lissy's Friends*, 2007; *The Year of the Dog*, 2007; *Bringing in the New Year*, 2008; *The Year of the Rat*, 2008.

SELECTED WORKS ILLUSTRATED: *Where on Earth Is My Bagel*, by Frances and Ginger Park, 2001; *My Favorite Foods*, by Dana

Meachen Rau, 2001; *Red Is a Dragon: A Book of Colors*, by Roseanne Thong, 2001; *A New Roof*, by Cari Meister, 2002; *The Seven Chinese Sisters*, by Kathy Tucker, 2003; *One for Me, One for You*, by C. C. Cameron, 2003; *Merry Christmas: Let's All Sing*, 2004; *One Is a Drummer: A Book of Numbers*, by Roseanne Thong, 2004; *Christmas Carols: Let's All Sing*, 2005; *One Year in Beijing*, by Xiaohong Wang, 2006; *The Jade Necklace*, by Paul Yee, 2006.

SUGGESTED READING: *Something About the Author*, vol. 162, 2006; Lin, Grace and Robert Mercer, *Robert's Snowflakes*, 2005. Periodicals—Taylor, Denise, "For Little Museumgoers, Picture-book Art," *The Boston Globe*, January 12, 2006. Online—Henneman, Heidi, "Sharing Asian Traditions with Young Readers," *Bookpage*, February 2006, at www.bookpage.com/0602bp/grace_lin.html

WEB SITES: www.gracelin.com
www.robertssnow.com

Courtesy of Penguin Books for Young Readers

Astrid Lindgren

November 14, 1907–
January 28, 2002

Astrid Lindgren, the acclaimed Swedish author and editor of children's books, created one of the best-known characters in all of children's literature. The cheerfully anarchic, larger-than-life Pippi Longstocking burst on the scene in 1945 in a volume by the same name, and was happily followed by the sequels *Pippi Goes on Board* and *Pippi in the South Seas*. Despite a childhood vow never to become an author, Lindgren was a prolific writer of picture books and novels, mysteries and adventure stories, realistic stories and fantasies. Her books have traveled all over the world, with over seventy titles translated into some ninety languages.

Astrid Anna Emilia Ericcson was born in 1907 in the southern province of Småland in Sweden. She and her three siblings grew up on a 500-year-old working farm outside the town of Vimmerby. Her childhood was an extremely happy one, which she described succinctly in an autobiographical sketch in *More Junior Authors* in 1963:

"I was number two among four children and I cannot imagine any children having more fun than we had. In those days there were no automobiles, no radios, no films, no television, no nothing—but there were people, lots of interesting people and there was a lot of room for imagination. I was a very happy child. I loved people, I loved nature, and I loved books."

Lindgren was blessed with the twin gifts of freedom and security throughout her childhood, playing constantly but also doing her share of farm chores, absorbing adult conversation and learning about the complexities of the adult world. She re-created this idyllic childhood in her Noisy Village books, in which six Swedish children living in the countryside "romped through green forests in summer, skated on a frozen lake in winter, and went fishing for crayfish in the fall."

Reading was a vital component of Lindgren's childhood. "All the wonderful books for girls. . . . There were so many girls in the world who were suddenly as close to oneself as ever any beings of flesh and blood!" Her literary friends included Pollyanna, Sara Crewe (of Frances Hodgson Burnett's *A Little Princess*), and especially L. M. Montgomery's Anne Shirley. "How I lived with that girl! A whole summer, my sisters and I played at *Anne of Green Gables* in the big sawdust heap at the sawmill. . . . " In high school, her teachers and classmates predicted that Astrid Lindgren would grow up to become a writer. She stubbornly vowed not to, claiming to be put off by her impression that once authors started writing, they couldn't stop.

In 1926, at age nineteen, Lindgren left Vimmerby under challenging circumstances (she was pregnant and did not wish to marry the child's father) and made her way to Stockholm, where she supported herself and her newborn son Lars as a secretary. She struggled financially, and for a while was forced to place her son with a foster family in Copenhagen. But circumstances improved greatly when, in 1931, she married Sture Lindgren, a man she met while working at the Royal Automobile Club, and settled down to raise her two children, Lars and Karin, born in 1934.

Then, in 1941, seven-year-old Karin, ill with pneumonia, begged her mother for a story about a girl she called Pippi Langstrump. Lindgren began to make up outrageous stories to match the outrageous name her daughter had created, and told them to Karin and her friends for several years, finally writing them down in 1944 as a present for Karin's tenth birthday. Again, her own telling is brief and to the point: "I had two children always pestering me to tell them stories and so I did. One day in March 1944, when snow had fallen in Stockholm, I went for a walk. It was very slippery. I fell, broke my ankle, and had to

"I was number two among four children and I cannot imagine any children having more fun than we had."

Astrid Lindgren
Pippi Longstocking
Illustrated by Lauren Child

Courtesy of Penguin Books for Young Readers

stay in bed for a week with nothing to do but write. Actually I became an author just because it snowed in Stockholm one day in March 1944."

She entered the Pippi manuscript in a children's book contest sponsored by Swedish publisher Rabén & Sjögren and won first prize. *Pippi Langstrump* was published in Sweden in 1945 and translated as *Pippi Longstocking* in 1950 by Viking Press in the United States. The book's huge and immediate success led not only to Lindgren's prolific career as an author but also to her becoming a children's book editor at Rabén & Sjögren, a position of influence in the field of Swedish children's books she held for many years.

Pippi, with her famous carrot-colored hair in jaunty, stick-straight-out braids, is the epitome of a strong, independent heroine—no doubt influenced by her literary forebears (and Lindgren's childhood "friends") Pollyanna, Sara Crewe, and Anne Shirley, strong-minded girls and orphans all. Pippi's superhuman physical strength allows her to easily lift a horse above her head and escort from the premises two interfering policemen, one in each hand; her strength of character and will are a match for any adult. Despite Pippi's claims that her sailor father is living as king of the cannibals in the South Seas, she is the ultimate orphan, completely free of adult control. Living alone at Villa Villekula with her only companions Mr. Nilsson (a monkey) and her horse, she inspires the envy of conventional neighbor children Annika and Peter. Though the book at first generated controversy because of Pippi's defiance of authority and blithe rudeness, the appeal to child readers was obvious and complete from the start. *Pippi Longstocking* has been described as a "safety valve [for children] against the pressure of authority and everyday life."

Lindgren's many other books range from suspenseful mysteries (*Bill Bergson, Master Detective* and *Rasmus and the Vagabond*) to picture books based on Swedish folklore (*The Tomten*) to small-scale realistic stories celebrating the joys of everyday life (*Children of Noisy Village* and *Lotta on Troublemaker Street*). In *Ronia, the Robber's Daughter*, a young girl unites rival robber clans in a Romeo-and-Juliet-like adventure story with a happy ending. The English translation of *Ronia* garnered the American

Library Association's Mildred L. Batchelder Award as the finest translated book in the United States in 1984. Lindgren's darkest book, in which she addresses children's fear of death, is *The Brothers Lionheart*, about a pair of brothers who die young and engage in subsequent heroic adventures in the imaginary land of Nangilyala. But whatever the tone or genre, Lindgren's books are unfailingly true to children's internal lives; they are all written directly to children, with no pretension, and children have taken them all to heart.

"I write to amuse the child within me," Astrid Lindgren once said; but more than that, she found a way to write from inside that child, turning vivid memories of her own childhood into timeless stories. "I still know exactly how it feels to enter a warm cow barn from biting cold and snow. I know how the tongue of a calf feels against a hand and how rabbits smell . . . and how milk sounds when it strikes the bottom of a bucket, and the feel of small chicken feet when one holds a newly hatched chick. Those may not be extraordinary things to remember. The extraordinary thing about it is the intensity of these experiences when we were new here on earth."

Astrid Lindgren's numerous awards in her own country include the Nils Holgersson Plaque in 1950 and the Swedish Academy's Gold Medal in 1971. Her ongoing concern for animal welfare and for humane treatment of animals led her to campaign vigorously for a new law that the Swedish government passed in 1988 to control factory farming, making Sweden one of the most progressive of all countries on that issue. In 1994 she was presented with an Honorary Right Livelihood Award, given to honor those "offering practical and exemplary answers to the most urgent challenges facing us today," and often referred to as the "Alternative Nobel Prize." Lindgren's award recognized "her unique authorship dedicated to the rights of children and respect for their individuality."

As early as 1958 Astrid Lindgren was awarded the prestigious Hans Christian Andersen Medal by the International Board on Books for Young People for her contribution to children's literature. She was the recipient of countless awards and prizes and received honorary degrees from universities at home and abroad. Perhaps the greatest testament to her influence is the annual Astrid Lindgren Memorial Award, which was established by the Swedish government after her death in 2002 and comes with a five million kronor (about $700,000) cash prize, the most lucrative award in the field of children's literature.

Courtesy of Penguin Books for Young Readers

Perhaps the legacy she would enjoy the most is the theme park that has been created near her hometown of Vimmerby, Sweden—Astrid Lindgren's World—where visitors can play in carefully re-created literary settings such as Emil's farm (from *Emil in the Soup Tureen*) and Ronia's fort (from *Ronia, the Robber's Daughter*). Complete with costumed performers playing the roles of the characters and staged shows from the books themselves, Astrid Lindgren's World offers children of all ages a wonderful dream-come-true, the chance to step inside the pages of their favorite books and interact with the characters.

SELECTED WORKS: (Dates are for original U.S. publication): *Pippi Longstocking*, illus. by Louis S. Glanzman, 1950 (reissued 2007, illus. by Lauren Child); *Bill Bergson, Master Detective*, illus. by Louis S. Glanzman 1952; *Bill Bergson Lives Dangerously*, illus. by Don Freeman, 1954; *Mio, My Son*, illus. by Ilon Wikland, 1956 (reissued 2003); *Pippi Goes On Board*, illus. by Louis S. Glanzman, 1957; *Pippi in the South Seas*, illus. by Louis S. Glanzman, 1959; *Rasmus and the Vagabond*, illus. by Eric Palmquist 1960; *The Tomten*, illus. by Harald Wiberg, 1961 (reissued 1997); *The Children of Noisy Village*, illus. by Ilon Wikland, 1962; *Mischievous Meg*, illus. by Janina Domanska, 1962; *Christmas in the*

Stable, illus. by Harald Wiberg, 1962; *Lotta on Troublemaker Street*, illus. by Ilon Wikland, 1963 (reissued 1984, illus. by Julie Brinckloe; reissued 2002, illus. by Robin Preiss Glasser); *Happy Times in Noisy Village*, illus. by Ilon Wikland 1963; *The Children on Troublemaker Street*, illus. by Ilon Wikland, 1964 (reissued 2001, illus. by Robin Preiss Glasser); *Christmas in Noisy Village*, illus. by Ilon Wikland, 1964; *The Tomten and the Fox*, illus. by Harald Wiberg, 1965 (reissued 1997); *Bill Bergson and the White Rose Rescue*, illus. by Don Freeman, 1965; *Springtime in Noisy Village*, illus. by Ilon Wikland, 1966; *Seacrow Island*, illus. by Robert Hales, 1969; *Emil in the Soup Tureen*, illus. by Björn Berg, 1970; *Emil's Pranks*, illus. by Björn Berg, 1971; *Karlsson-on-the-Roof*, illus. by Jan Pyk, 1971; *Of Course Polly Can Ride a Bike*, illus. by Ilon Wikland, 1972; *Emil and Piggy Beast*, illus. by Björn Berg, 1973; *The Brothers Lionheart*, illus. by James Keaton Lambert, 1975 (reissued 2004, illus. by Ilon Wikland); *Of Course Polly Can Do Almost Everything*, illus. by Ilon Wikland, 1978; *Ronia, the Robber's Daughter*, illus. by Trina Schart Hyman, 1983; *The Runaway Sleigh Ride*, illus. by Ilon Wikland, 1984; *My Nightingale Is Singing*, illus. by Svend Otto S., 1986; *The Dragon with Red Eyes*, illus. by Ilon Wikland, 1986; *The Ghost of Skinny Jack*, illus. by Ilon Wikland, 1987; *I Want to Go to School Too*, illus. by Ilon Wikland, 1987; *I Don't Want to Go to Bed*, illus. by Ilon Wikland, 1988; *I Want a Brother or Sister*, illus. by Ilon Wikland, 1988; *Lotta's Bike*, illus. by Ilon Wikland, 1989; *Lotta's Easter Surprise*, illus. by Ilon Wikland, 1991; *Pippi Longstocking's After-Christmas Party*, illus. by Michael Chesworth, 1996; *The Adventures of Pippi Longstocking* (contains *Pippi Longstocking*, *Pippi Goes On Board*, and *Pippi in the South Seas*), illus. by Michael Chesworth, 1997; *Pippi Goes to School*, illus. by Michael Chesworth, 1998; *Pippi Goes to the Circus*, illus. by Michael Chesworth, 1999; *Pippi's Extraordinary Day*, illus. by Michael Chesworth, 1999; *Pippi to the Rescue*, illus. by Michael Chesworth, 2000; *Pippi Longstocking in the Park*, illus. by Ingrid Nyman, 2001; *Most Beloved Sister*, illus. Hans Arnold, 2002.

SUGGESTED READING: Silvey, Anita, ed., *Children's Books and Their Creators*, 1995; Hurwitz, Joanna, *Astrid Lindgren: Storyteller to the World*, illus. by Michael Dooling, 1989; *Something about the Author*, vol. 38, 1985; Cott, Jonathan, *Pipers at the Gates of Dawn: The Wisdom of Children's Literature*, 1982. Periodicals—Swanson, Susan Marie, "Astrid Lindgren's Swedish Legacy," *The Horn Book*, Nov/Dec 2007; Cott, Jonathan, "Profiles: The

Astonishment of Being," *The New Yorker*, February 28, 1983; Lindgren, Astrid, "The Importance of Children's Books," *The Quarterly Journal of the Library of Congress*, summer, 1983; Lindgren, Astrid, "A Short Talk with a Prospective Children's Writer," *The Horn Book*, June 1973; Binding, Paul, "Long Live Pippi Longstocking," *The Independent*, Aug. 26, 2007, at www. independent.co.uk/arts-entertainment/books/features/long-live-pippi-longstocking-the-girl-with-red-plaits-is-back-462744.html

WEB SITES: www.astridlindgrensworld.com www.astridlindgren.se/eng/

Courtesy of Random House, Inc.

Leo Lionni

May 5, 1910–
October 12, 1999

Leo Lionni transformed one of the simplest approaches to art into one of the most creative mediums in children's book illustration. He was the first artist to successfully use collage in children's books, and his technique combined with his sharp eye for design created a new look that not only earned him considerable commercial and critical success, but also inspired other artists in the field.

Lionni's distinguished career began in Amsterdam, Holland, where he was born into an artistic family. His father was a diamond cutter and his mother an opera singer. Lionni knew at an early age that he wanted to be an artist, and the numerous Amsterdam art museums provided inspiration and instruction as he taught himself to draw. He steeped himself in the works of the classical Dutch masters but also, with the help of an uncle who was a passionate collector, became familiar with the early works of such modernists as Marc Chagall, Paul Klee, and Piet Mondrian.

Instead of pursuing a formal artistic education, Lionni earned a doctorate in economics from the University of Genoa, in Italy, in 1935, while working as a freelance designer. As a student he met and married Nora Maffi, the sister of a classmate, who came from a family that thrived on intellectual pursuits and interest in politics. Lionni called Nora the "keeper and light of [my] world." As it turned out, politics would influence many decisions in his life.

In 1939 he left Europe to escape the spreading control of the Nazi party and settled in the United States. After securing a job as art director for the Philadelphia-based advertising agency N. W. Ayer & Sons, he was able to bring his wife and two young sons, Mannie and Paolo, to America before Italy entered World War II. In the United States, Lionni was immediately recognized as a new dynamic talent in commercial design. He commissioned artwork from such celebrated fine artists as Willem de Kooning, Alexander Calder, and Saul Steinberg for the agency's high-profile clients—Ford Motor Company, General Electric, and *Ladies Home Journal*, among others. He also famously became the creator of the well-known "Keep 'em flying" poster designed for the U.S. War Department during World War II. (The Museum of Modern Art in New York now owns the original poster.)

After the war, in 1949, Lionni became the design director for the Olivetti Corporation of America, art director for *Fortune* magazine, chairman of the Graphic Design Department of Parsons School of Design, and coeditor of *Print* magazine. During this period he began exhibiting his paintings and sculpture in one-man shows: the Museum of Modern Art in 1953; the American Institute of Graphic Arts in 1957; and venues in Portland, San Francisco, and Philadelphia in 1959. Rave reviews crowned him as one of the world's most original and artistic designers.

Leo Lionni's use of collage as an innovative, creative form did not emerge until mid-career in 1959 when he was already 50 years old and a grandfather; it came about in a moment of serendipity. He was traveling on a train with his two grandchildren, ages five and three. He pulled a copy of *Life* out of his briefcase, found a page with blue, yellow, and green colors, and improvised a story with the colors as characters to amuse the restless preschoolers. The other passengers were as captivated as the children, and the classic tale of *Little Blue and Little Yellow* was born along with the invention of a new medium and technique in illustration. Having his first book for children chosen as one of the *New York Times* Best Illustrated of the year promptly brought him recognition in the field. In an essay, "My Books for Children," he said, "Among the varied things I have done in my life, few have given me more and greater satisfaction than my children's books."

Lionni knew he wanted his second book to be completely different from his first. He tinkered with and refined his collage technique, using many different textures and colors of paper. The result, the beautifully designed and composed *Inch by Inch*, received a coveted Caldecott Honor citation in 1960. The book was also chosen for the Lewis Carroll Shelf Award, the German

Alexander and the Wind-Up Mouse

by Leo Lionni

Courtesy of Knopf Books for Young Readers, Random House, Inc.

Children's Book Prize, and the *New York Times* Best Illustrated Books list. Lionni had carved a new niche for himself; *Inch by Inch* became the first of many fables about small animals who accomplish great things.

While graphic design always formed the foundation for his illustrations, Lionni played with patterns, textures, and composition to create an appropriate mood for each story. His original style, handsome designs, and charming fables earned three more Caldecott Honors: for *Swimmy*, which relates how a tiny, insignificant fish in the vast ocean ingeniously fends off a large predator by developing teamwork; for *Frederick*, which features a poet mouse who demonstrates that neither mice nor men live by bread alone; and for *Alexander and the Wind-Up Mouse*, which relates a touching story of wish fulfillment and friendship. *Alexander* also garnered a Christopher Award and a *New York Times* Best Illustrated award. Lionni's popularity with children and admiration from adults elicited many more awards, including a gold medal from the American Institute of Graphic Arts in 1984. He was the first American to win the Bratislava Biennale Gold Award for *Swimmy* in 1963.

Leo Lionni's innovative use of collage influenced the work of celebrated illustrators Eric Carle and Ezra Jack Keats, among countless others, with its fresh way of telling stories with pictures. His signature style was a white backdrop that spotlighted crisp shapes and clean blocks of text type; his dramatic compositions and keen esthetic eye became hallmarks of good design. In a career spanning 35 years, he wrote and illustrated more than 40 picture books. His last picture book, *An Extraordinary Egg*, appeared in 1994.

Three years later Lionni published his memoirs, *Between Worlds: The Autobiography of Leo Lionni*. The title refers to the way Lionni saw himself as he looked back on the many facets of his life: born to a gentile mother and Jewish father; growing up speaking Dutch while his grandmother in Brussels taught him French; studying in Switzerland and living in Italy (which added Italian and German to his language repertoire), and finally learning English in America. Like his dual passion for illustration and painting, Lionni loved the two countries in which he lived his adult life. Beginning in the 1960s he and Nora split their time between an apartment in New York City and their Tuscan farmhouse in the Chianti region of Italy. It was the Italian landscape that provided much of the inspiration for his children's books. Living so close to nature, he saw beauty in the plants, pebbles, lizards, mice, and old stone walls—and all of those evolved into story ideas.

The autobiography also describes how the publication of *Little Blue and Little Yellow* became the key to unlocking Lionni's childhood joys and insecurities (which formed the basis of his creativity) and how he meshed his fascination with commercial art with his love of fine art. He described his significant contribution to children's literature this way: "My books, like all fables, are about people. Worms don't measure, torn paper doesn't go to school, little fish don't organize, and . . . pebbles don't make words. My characters are humans in disguise."

In the 1980s Leo Lionni developed Parkinson's disease. By the late 1990s the disease had seriously impaired his mobility. He died at the age of 89 in his beloved Italy. Like Frederick, his much-loved mouse character who gathered colors and words for the other mice to enjoy during the harsh winter, Lionni's legacy is a storehouse of treasured words with evocative and animated art that will enrich the imagination of generations to come.

"My books, like all fables, are about people. . . . My characters are humans in disguise."

SELECTED WORKS WRITTEN AND ILLUSTRATED: *Little Blue and Little Yellow*, 1959; *Inch by Inch*, 1960; *On My Beach There Are Many Pebbles*, 1961; *Swimmy*, 1963; *Tico and the Golden Wings*, 1964; *Frederick*, 1967; *The Alphabet Tree*, 1968; *The Biggest House in the World*, 1968; *Alexander and the Wind-up Mouse*, 1969; *Fish Is Fish*, 1970; *Theodore and the Talking Mushroom*, 1971; *The Greentail Mouse*, 1973; *In the Rabbitgarden*, 1975; *A Color of His Own*, 1976; *Pezzettino*, 1975; *A Flea Story: I Want to Stay Here! I Want to Go There!*, 1977; *Geraldine, The Music Mouse*, 1979; *Let's Make Rabbits: A Fable*, 1982; *Cornelius*, 1983; *Who?*, 1983; *What?*, 1983; *Where?*, 1983; *When?*, 1983; *Frederick's Fables: A Leo Lionni Treasury of Favorite Stories*, 1985; *Colors to Talk About*, 1985; *Letters to Talk About*, 1985; *Numbers to Talk About*, 1985; *Words to Talk About*, 1985; *It's Mine!*, 1986;

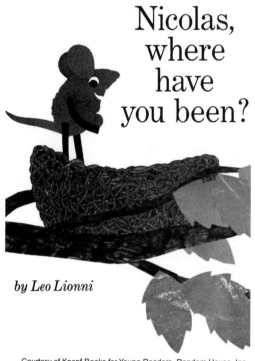

Nicolas, where have you been?

by Leo Lionni

Courtesy of Knopf Books for Young Readers, Random House, Inc.

Nicholas, Where Have You Been?, 1987; *Six Crows*, 1988; *Tillie and the Wall*, 1989; *Frederick and His Friends*, 1989; *Matthew's Dream*, 1991; *A Busy Year*, 1992; *Mr. McMouse*, 1992; *An Extraordinary Egg*, 1994.

SELECTED WORKS ILLUSTRATED: *Mouse Days*, by Hannah Solomon, 1981; *Come with Us*, by Naomi Lewis, 1982.

SUGGESTED READING: Carle, Eric and Frances Foster, *Leo Lionni: A Passion for Creativity*, 2003; *Something About the Author*, Obit: vol. 118, 2001; Lionni, Leo, *Between Worlds: The Autobiography of Leo Lionni*, 1997; Silvey, Anita, *Children's Books and Their Creators*, 1995; Hopkins, Lee Bennett, *Pauses: Autobiographical Reflections of 101 Creators of Children's Books*, 1995; *Something about the Author*, vol. 72, 1993; Cummins, Julie, *Children's Book Illustration and Design*, vol. II, 1992; Bader, Barbara, *American Picture Books from Noah's Ark to the Beast Within*, 1976; Hopkins, Lee Bennett, *Books Are By People*, 1969. Periodicals— Funk, Roger, "Of Beaches and Fans," *Technology and Children*, March 1, 2004; Heller, Steven, "Tribute: Leo Lionni, 1910-1999," *PRINT* May/June 2000; *Los Angeles Times*, Obit: October 18, 1999; *Washington Post*, Obit: October 18, 1999; *New York Times*, Obit: October 17, 1999; McQuade, Molly, "The Year of Leo Lionni," *Book Links*, May 1998; Lionni, Leo, "My Books for Children," *Wilson Library Bulletin*, October 1964.

WEB SITE: www.randomhouse.com/kids/lionni/author.html

An earlier profile of Leo Lionni appeared in Third Book of Junior Authors, 1972.

Loren Long

April 24, 1964–

"**I** wish I could say that for as long as I can remember I wanted to be an artist. I could tell you that drawing pictures has always been like breathing for me and I was destined to be an artist right out of the womb. And what if I could say my father was a classical pianist, and my mother was an accomplished oil painter in her own right? And in my childhood they took me antiquing and to art museums on weekends, when we were not in Europe learning about other cultures. If only I could say these things this author bio might be more interesting. If I could say these things perhaps *I* would sound more interesting.

"Unfortunately, I can't.

"Nope, born in Missouri and raised in Kentucky, I grew up in a very conventional middle American setting where my father was something called a sales rep and my mother was a bunch of things from a retail clerk to a bridal consultant and eventually the secretary for a number of different, very lucky, 'important' people.

"But, then there were the Sunday comics. And there was Charles Schulz and a funny little dog named Snoopy.

"The story goes that my Aunt LaForest (great name!) screamed everyone into the hallway to see me, barely four years old, lying on the floor with the comics drawing Snoopy. I always thought Snoopy was cool and he was easy to draw so I did it a lot. I suppose I did draw fairly often as a kid but in hindsight not often enough. There were too many other things to do, like playing baseball and goofing around. You see, even though I had some natural artistic abilities, it still did not come as easily to me as goofing around. I was a natural at goofing around.

Photo by Paul Schliesser

"This is where my mom came in. My mother was no worldly, sophisticated, artsy person. But she thought I could draw better than I thought I could draw. And she nagged, I mean encouraged, me to not let it go by the wayside. She did not hesitate to point out my lazy streak. But my mom always made me feel special. As I began to take art classes in school she would frame nearly every picture I made and soon our home was filled with my artwork all over the walls.

"When my dad was doing a remodeling project around the house he turned an old door into an art table for me by turning it on its side and putting four legs on it. I remember how excited I was to have such a big drawing table. During my high school years my mother got me gigs at a real estate company (one of her secretary jobs) drawing houses for extra money. I began to be introduced as 'the artist of the family.'

"And there were teachers. . . . I had an influential art teacher who inspired me at every level of my education. In Junior High School I got kind words and a little extra attention from the art teacher, Mr. Pennington, who was also the football coach. I couldn't believe the football coach even knew my name. In High School, Ms. Clifton introduced me to Vincent Van Gogh and Norman Rockwell. I could sit with Ms. Clifton and study those pictures for hours. And in college after majoring in four different areas other than art, I finally had a graphic design teacher, Mr. Foose, who began singling me out as the 'illustrator' of the class.

"After college, as many of my friends were heading off to graduate school to become doctors, lawyers and dentists, I waved the white flag and surrendered. I would become an artist. By then I knew that if I was ever going accomplish something as unconventional as drawing pictures for a living it would be up to nobody in this world but me. I would have to figure that one out all on my own, and it would not happen by goofing around.

"You see, even though I had some natural artistic abilities, it still did not come as easily to me as goofing around. I was a natural at goofing around."

"I went to art school in Chicago for a year and got my first job as an illustrator at a greeting card company. After a few years as a greeting card artist I left the company to do freelance work, and I spent about ten years making pictures for magazines, posters and advertisements. I then started getting calls to do book covers, which lead to my first picture book assignment.

"Children's book publishing changed my career. I love the art of making pictures that tell a story and striking the perfect balance between text and imagery. Suddenly my art seemed to have a deeper, lasting meaning. I had found what I wanted to do for the rest of my life. I feel incredibly blessed and fortunate to be able to make a living creating art and telling stories for children.

"By the way, all those things I wished I could say at the beginning of this bio were just for fun. I wouldn't change a thing about my childhood (although a trip to Europe would have been nice). And my parents are perfect just as they are."

ଔ   ଔ   ଔ

Born in Joplin, Missouri and raised in Lexington, Kentucky, Loren Long graduated from the University of Kentucky with a B.A. degree in 1987. After a year of graduate study at the American Academy of Art in Chicago, he worked for the Gibson greeting card company in Cincinnati, Ohio until 1992, when he became a freelance illustrator. His work has appeared in many magazines and journals, including *Time, Sports Illustrated, Forbes, Reader's Digest,* and the *Atlantic Monthly*. His art hangs in the permanent collections of the Cincinnati Art Museum, the U.S. Golf Association Museum, and the archives of *Sports Illustrated*. He has also been an instructor in illustration at Northern Kentucky University.

Influenced by the WPA muralists of the Great Depression, as well as American regional artists, Long's style has a strong, vigorous quality and narrative strength. He received the Golden Kite award for picture book illustration from the Society of Children's Book Writers and Illustrators for his work in Angela Johnson's *I Dream of Trains*, the fictional story of a young field worker who is inspired by the legendary engineer, Casey Jones. The railroad becomes a metaphor as the boy stops his work to marvel at its power and ability to move quickly to a faraway place. *I Dream of Trains* was also cited as a Notable Social Studies Trade Book.

Long received a Golden Kite Honor Book award and a Parent's Choice Gold Award for *When I Heard the Learn'd Astronomer*, in which his visual storytelling ability is especially strong. The words are a poem by Walt Whitman, but Long creates a parallel narrative in the illustrations of a boy being taken to a lecture by his parents. Bored, the boy slips out of the auditorium to look at the stars himself, joined later by his parents.

Two of Long's books have achieved first place on the *New York Times* list of children's bestsellers. The first was written by the pop star Madonna, who requested that Long illustrate her children's story, *Mr. Peabody's Apples*, a cautionary tale about a boy who learns a life lesson from his teacher. Long's pictures depict a bygone day in small-town America and perfectly fit the story's theme. His second bestseller paid homage to one of the favorite classic stories from his own childhood—*The Little Engine That Could*. In a larger format than the original, but echoing the color palette and child-friendly atmosphere of that edition from the early 20th century, Long captured the essence of this tale with its well-known refrain, "I think I can, I think I can."

Having received two Gold Medals from the Society of Illustrators, Long is well on his way to a strong career in children's books. With the publication, in 2007, of *Barnstormers, Game 1*, he also became an author. Along with co-author Phil Bildner, he indulged his lifelong love of baseball in this story of three children who travel around the country with a ball team and a special baseball that may have magical powers. The first in a series of books for older children, *Barnstormers* takes place in 1899 in the

Courtesy of Philomel Books, Penguin Group USA

early days of the game, providing a great deal of baseball's history in a fast-moving story.

Married to Tracy Maines since 1993, Loren Long is the father of two sons, Griffith and Graham. He lives in West Chester, Ohio, with his family and their dog, Stella, a personable weimaraner.

SELECTED WORKS WRITTEN AND ILLUSTRATED: *Barnstormers, Game 1: Three Kids, a Mystery, and a Magic Baseball*, with Phil Bildner, 2007; *Barnstormers, Game 2*, with Phil Bildner, 2007; *Drummer Boy*, 2008.

SELECTED WORKS ILLUSTRATED: *My Dog, My Hero*, by Betsy Byars, Betsy Duffy and Laurie Myers, 2000; *The Wonders of Donal O'Donnell*, by Gary Schmidt, 2002; *I Dream of Trains*, by Angela Johnson, 2003; *The Day the Animals Came*, by Frances Ward Weller, 2003; *Mr. Peabody's Apples*, by Madonna, 2003; *When I Heard the Learn'd Astronomer*, by Walt Whitman, 2004; *The Little Engine that Could*, by Watty Piper, 2005; *Wind Flyers*, by Angela Johnson, 2007; *Toy Boat*, by Randall DeSeve, 2007.

SUGGESTED READING: *Something About the Author*, vol. 151, 2004; Kreimer, Peggy, "Interview with Loren Long," *Cincinnati Post*, November 8, 2003.

WEB SITE: www.lorenlong.com

" **A**s a child, my two favorite pastimes were making things and making things up. I loved to draw and paint, mold with clay, batik fabric, sew, and create collages. I also loved to invent stories about myself: I was a gold-medal-winning Olympic gymnast or a twin or a Broadway musical dancer. These fantasies would live in my imagination and sometimes make it into stories I wrote. But often I tried to convince others, even my friends, that they were true. (Miraculously, those same kids still wanted to be my friends!) I was mischievous, and I delighted in playing practical jokes— switching pictures around on the walls in our house to see if my parents would notice or deepening my voice on the telephone to trick my brothers' friends into thinking they were talking to one of them. I was fascinated by *Harriet the Spy* and created my own spy club called Rat Fink. I would skulk around the neighborhood, spy on the neighbors, and take copious notes. Maybe it's because I was always the littlest kid in my class, and the youngest of three siblings, that I dreamed big. I loved the enormous sense of possibility inside my imagination.

Photo by Stephen Mack

Tracy Mack

February 3, 1968–

"I grew up in a family of creative people. My father's photographs hung in our kitchen, my mother's paintings in our playroom. My oldest brother made amazing vases and jewelry out of glass, my middle brother played guitar and wrote songs. They were my role models. Watching them, I learned that creative self-expression was important. It was a way to show the world who you were and what you cared about. Inside myself, even at a very young age, I felt those same longings to create. But I was still searching for my medium.

"My mother fed me the best kind of food for my imagination— books! A former third-grade teacher and a voracious reader, she read to me every night before bed, instilling in me her love of story and language. She had studied theater and always read with dramatic flair, becoming Frances and Fudge and Harriet. I loved the sound of my mother's voice reading and this closeness and connection we shared through books. Our evening ritual went on for years, long after I settled into reading on my own.

"In college, I pursued my interest in art, but soon discovered that I wasn't very talented. Although I could see elaborate pictures in my head, I could never transfer them to paper. So I taught myself how to 'paint' with words, using them to describe what I saw in my imagination. By this point, I had begun keeping journals, experimenting with poetry, and writing short stories. Much to my friends' relief, I had stopped trying to convince them of untruths and put those into my stories instead.

"I guess it's not surprising that my books are filled with people doing creative things. Creative people have been close to me, influencing me and inspiring me for as long as I can remember. Through my characters, I experience the sense of possibility that I loved as a child. I become who I am in my fantasies: an accomplished painter, a brilliant filmmaker, a young detective.

"Now that I'm grown up, I've developed new pastimes. But I still love to make things and make things up. I feel so lucky to be an author because writing books allows me to do both."

> *"Through my characters, I experience the sense of possibility that I loved as a child. I become who I am in my fantasies: an accomplished painter, a brilliant filmmaker, a young detective."*

ଔ   ଔ   ଔ

Tracy Mack grew up in a small village near the Hudson River, just north of New York City. She spent most of her childhood climbing trees, riding her bike, hiding out in the woods behind her house, and daydreaming. Her mother instilled in her a love of literature and introduced her to many great books, including such mystery series as the Bobbsey Twins, Nancy Drew, and Encyclopedia Brown. These, along with the classic *Harriet the Spy*, sparked her later interest in writing mysteries herself. Mack received her B.A. from the University of Pennsylvania, where she majored in 20th century American and British literature and minored in art history, and also attended Queen Mary College in London to study British literature and modern drama. She has worked as a camp counselor, a waitress, a tutor, a theater intern, and an English teacher in Spain. She is currently executive editor-at-large at Scholastic Press, where she has worked since 1992. There, she has edited such luminaries as Pam Muñoz Ryan, Brian Selznick, Julius Lester, Christopher Myers, Mark Teague, and Mary Pope Osborne.

Mack's first novel, *Drawing Lessons*, about a gifted 12-year-old artist who is mentored by her artist father and struggling with her feelings about her parents' separation, was published in 2000. The story is infused with Mack's love of art and shows the importance of creative self-expression, a theme she would continue to explore in future books. Warmly received by both critics and readers, *Drawing Lessons* was named a 2002 Charlotte Book Award nominee, a *Teen People* NEXT Award finalist, one of *Booklist*'s Top 10 First Novels for Young Adults, a New York Public Library Book for the Teen Age, a Bank Street College Best Children's Book of the Year, and a CCBC Choices title.

In 2001 Mack married Michael Citrin, a writer, a lawyer, and a long-time Sherlock Holmes enthusiast. The two settled in Brooklyn, New York, in an historic neighborhood brimming with artists and writers, a setting that would prove inspirational for their own writing.

Mack's second novel, *Birdland*, was published to great acclaim. Set in Manhattan's East Village neighborhood shortly after September 11, 2001, the story weaves poetry, music, and filmmaking into a pulsating narrative that explores a young teen's searing sense of loss after his older brother's sudden death. As the city struggles to heal, so does Jed, who finds sadness, solace, and inspiration all around him, much as Mack did while living in New York at that time. *Birdland* was a named a Sydney Taylor Award Honor Book, an ALA Best Book for Young Adults, a *Booklist* Editors' Choice, a *Kirkus* Editors' Choice, a Bank Street College Best Children's Book, and a CCBC Choices title.

Meanwhile, another book was evolving. For years, Mack and Citrin had wanted to collaborate as writers. Since they had both loved mysteries when they were young, that seemed like a good place to start. As they brainstormed Citrin recalled his childhood obsession with the master detective, Sherlock Holmes, and especially one aspect of Sir Arthur Conan Doyle's stories that always bothered him: the Baker Street Irregulars. Holmes refers to this gang of street kids who assist him in his cases as his "eyes and ears on the street," and yet, they are mentioned only four times in all of the 56 short stories and four novels that make of up the Holmes canon. Who were they? And why had Conan Doyle not written more about them? Citrin and Mack agreed that the Irregulars deserved their due and set out to create original mysteries from *their* point of view. Further, they were attracted by the idea of writing traditional mystery stories where the reader, along with the Irregulars, would uncover information bit by bit, analyze clues, and attempt to solve the cases. And

Courtesy of Orchard Books, Scholastic, Inc.

because so little had been written about the Irregulars, Mack and Citrin had the freedom to imagine their characters. They drew their greatest inspiration from a gang of ragtag children they had befriended while traveling together in Oaxaca, Mexico in 1999.

It would take the couple four years to fully flesh out the series and write the first book, *Sherlock Holmes and the Baker Street Irregulars: Casebook No. 1: The Fall of the Amazing Zalindas*, published in 2006. In this inaugural title, Holmes calls upon the Irregulars to help unravel the mysterious deaths of a family of circus tightrope walkers, only to discover a far more treacherous crime involving the royal family and a stolen treasure. The book also contains a section at the back called "Facts and Practicals for the Aspiring Detective," which includes a cockney rhyming slang dictionary, instructions for creating your own rhyming slang, the art of disguise, the science of deduction, and an essay on transportation during the Victorian Era. A secret message is embedded in the text.

Tracy Mack, Michael Citrin, and their two children live in the Berkshire Hills of Western Massachusetts, in a crooked Greek Revival house built in 1847, where they once uncovered a 19th century journal in the attic. They are still trying to deduce the mystery of its owner.

SELECTED WORKS: *Drawing Lessons*, 2000; *Birdland*, 2003; *The Fall of the Amazing Zalindas* (Sherlock Holmes and the Baker Street Irregulars, Casebook No.1), with Michael Citrin, illus. by Greg Ruth, 2006; *The Mystery of the Conjured Man* (Sherlock Holmes and the Baker Street Irregulars, Casebook No. 2), with Michael Citrin, illus. by Greg Ruth, 2008.

SUGGESTED READING: *Something About the Author*, vol. 183, 2008. Online—Interview, *Publishers Weekly Children's Bookshelf*, August 31, 2006, at www.publishersweekly.com/article/CA6367255.html

Simon Mason

1962–

Born in Sheffield, England, the son of a professional soccer player, Simon Mason enjoyed soccer himself but never planned to play it professionally. What he loved was telling stories and, before telling them to other people, he would practice telling them to his dog. He believed he could tell from the dog's reactions if the story was good or not. At fifteen he started writing poetry, which he still enjoys. Mason went to local comprehensive schools—that is, public schools—and has admitted he is rather pleased that he didn't have a privileged early education. He later studied English Literature at the University of Oxford's Lady Margaret Hall and graduated with 'a first' (the British equivalent of an honors degree) in 1984.

Mason's versatility as a writer is evident in the types of books he has written, which include tragicomic novels for adults and a hilarious series of books for children. Before turning his attention to children's books, Mason wrote *The Great English Nude*, winner of Great Britain's Society of Authors' Betty Trask Award, given for first novels by authors under the age of 35. A sarcastically witty and compelling dark comedy, it's the story of a man murdered by a failed poet who deludes himself into believing his wife had an affair with the victim. Only after the crime does the poet come to understand his delusions. Mason's second adult novel was *Death of a Fantasist*, about a man who flees reality. His third adult novel, *Lives of the Dog-Strangler*, is a fractured narrative with a series of funny but tragic stories about British suburbanites.

Mason is best known, however, for his highly popular British children's book series about the eccentric Quigley family: Dad, Mum, Will, and Lucy. Each story is about ordinary family events, yet they become extraordinary in these engaging and comical chapter books. All of the books feature snappy dialogue, and each chapter profiles a different member of the family. The inspiration for the books came from Mason's own family. In fact, all the Quigley stories actually happened to his family, a fact that endears them to his readers. When his own children were aged nine and seven, he used to read them these stories, but he hid them within the pages of another book so they wouldn't know he'd written them; after a few minutes, the children would squeal with excitement and delight because they recognized their own experiences in the tales.

The family stories proved to be winners outside of Mason's family as well. The first title in the series, *The Quigleys*, received a Highly Commended citation from the Branford Boase Award, which celebrates the most promising books for children seven and up that have been written by novice children's book writers. In one chapter of this first title, Dad loses a child he is babysitting while watching soccer on TV; in another, Lucy wears a bumble-bee costume instead of a junior bridesmaid's dress to a wedding. Will campaigns for a pet for Christmas, despite a "no pet" rule in the house, and in the funniest chapter, the children try to make Mum's awful birthday better by dancing ballet and concocting treats for her, including some powerful alcoholic beverages.

The family humor continues in *The Quigleys at Large*, which finds Dad trying to catch the family parrot but only catching

Courtesy of Random House, Inc.

himself instead, Lucy trying to make a new friend while vacationing in France, Will trying to get out of the school he's been accidentally locked in, and the whole family trying to take care of Mum after some dental work. In *The Quigleys: Not for Sale*, Will and Lucy are prominently featured. They fail uproariously to behave themselves at a hotel and end up embarrassing a sauna filled with naked adults, try a series of money-making schemes to help their parents out with a financial problem, experience a memorable hiking trip on Mother's Day, and succeed in preventing their parents from selling their house by pointing out all its flaws to prospective buyers.

In *The Quigleys in a Spin*, there are five related stories wherein Mum gets stuck on a roof with a cat named Fatbrain, Mum takes a wild ride at a fair, Will has to deal with a rude child, Lucy must contend with a very difficult birthday party, and Dad has problems with a bottle of purple nail polish and his big toe.

A former Senior Acquisitions Editor at ABC-CLIO Inc., Simon Mason currently works in the small Oxford office of Greenwood Publishing, a worldwide publisher of reference, academic, and general interest books. He's responsible for a new list of nonfiction titles ranging from history to current affairs to literature. Mason lives in Oxford with his wife, Eluned, a science teacher, and their two children, Gwilym and Eleri, the models for Will and Lucy of the Quigley family.

SELECTED WORKS FOR ADULTS (U.S. publication dates are in parentheses): *The Great British Nude*, 1990 (U.S. title: *Portrait of the Artist with My Wife*, 1991); *Death of a Fantasist*, 1994 (1995); *Lives of the Dog-Stranglers*, 1998.

SELECTED WORKS FOR YOUNG READERS: (all illus. by Helen Stephens) *The Quigleys*, 2002; *The Quigleys at Large*, 2003; *The Quigleys: Not for Sale*, 2004; *The Quigleys in a Spin*, 2006.

SUGGESTED READING: *Something About the Author*, vol. 178, 2007; *Contemporary Authors Online*, August 29, 2007.

"**M**y three-year-old son plays with his head on the floor watching the wheels of whatever vehicle he happens to be pushing. I realized this is the same thought process I have in my books. I have a need to see every pencil grain, shadow or speck of dirt to have its own existence. I don't look for balance; I turn the page around and upside down to make sure any piece of the drawing can shine alone. I have been called intense, freakish, but the most polite description was, ethereal. I hate all those terms. I think it is more like my three-year-old son, just absolutely thorough.

"I am pretty sure all this started when I was left to my own devices to entertain myself. I grew up in the time when children had a bike or friends to play with. Television was not cabled. Games were not electronic. I had books, which my little sister would cut up, and I had scrap paper and a pen. My training as an illustrator started when I could hold a pen. But it really opened worlds when I could cross two lines together and I declared it a "plane." My mother says I was about three years old. When my brothers and I were not fighting each other, we would draw out stories of fighting. If we ran out of paper, we would use my sister's dolls or her arm. Illustrators who are just starting out always have the same question, 'What kind of stories should I write about?' I have to reply, remember what it was like to be bored, scared, angry, curious, or happy when you were three.

Photo by Yunhee Pettibone

Peter McCarty

October 16, 1966–

"Our family had some talented artists, like my grandmother. Even though she was deaf and nearly blind, she created work that was inspiring and some of her paintings scared the living daylights out of us. She is still my greatest influence. When I am in the pits of despair and feel there is nothing in me that can pass as being remotely original, I visit museums and look at paintings by Rembrandt or Redon. Other times I like to eat jujubes and watch movies based on graphic novels. I am researching various mediums for my epic stories and recently sent out tendrils into Hollywood. I would love to see one of my characters become animated in a film.

"Teaching children's book illustration is a different sort of beast but necessary in the creative life span. The first part is a duty to pass down information that was given to me by my previous teachers and share my professional experiences. The second part is to keep the gears moving even when I am tired or when my back hurts. I look forward to discussing the same subjects with fresh new minds, and the students keep me updated on new technology."

"My training as an illustrator started when I could hold a pen. But it really opened worlds when I could cross two lines together and I declared it a 'plane.'"

୧ ୧ ୧

Peter McCarty was born in Westport, Connecticut. Because his father's job with IBM moved the family around the country often, McCarty, his two older brothers, and two younger sisters lived in many places growing up. When Peter graduated high school, they were living in Boulder, Colorado, and he went on to the University of Colorado. At first he thought of becoming a scientist and took math and science classes. But he continued to love drawing and finally he started fresh at the School of Visual Arts in New York City, graduating in 1992.

At art school, he learned to paint and create with other mediums, but his preference was always for drawing and illustration. One of McCarty's illustration teachers, William Low, introduced him to Laura Godwin, a children's book editor at Henry Holt and Company. She gave him his first job, illustrating David Getz's *Frozen Man*, an account for young readers of the 1991 discovery of the 5,000-year-old body known as "The Ice Man." McCarty's hazy drawings enhanced the mystery surrounding the ancient corpse, and the book was named an Outstanding Science Trade Book.

McCarty has described his illustrative style as a yin-yang effect. He begins with shapes like an abstract painting, applies a simple palette of colors, and polishes them for warmth and

Hondo & Fabian

written and illustrated by

Peter McCarty

Courtesy of Henry Holt and Company

atmosphere. In his second book, *Night Driving*, written by John Coy, the black-and-white shaded illustrations simulate the hushed quiet of an evening automobile ride shared by father and son. This book was named a *Horn Book* Fanfare title. For *Mary on Horseback*, an evocative account written by Rosemary Wells about a pioneering nurse in the 1920s Kentucky Hills, McCarty created illustrations based on old photographs that capture the atmosphere of these true-life stories. *Mary on Horseback* was cited as a best of the year by *School Library Journal* and *The Horn Book*, as well as being named a Notable Social Studies Trade Book.

Newly married in 1995, and offered a chance to write his own story as well as illustrate it, McCarty moved back to live in Colorado in search of story ideas. While waiting for inspiration to strike, he took a job driving a truck to deliver doorknobs to new housing developments. His route was through flat country and the beautiful mountains of his dreams seemed far away. It wasn't until he saw a television documentary on the Oregon Trail that *Little Bunny on the Move* began to take shape. The book was published in 1999 and was chosen as one of the *New York Times* Best Illustrated Books of the Year.

McCarty's next book, *Hondo and Fabian*, established his signature style, in which subtly textured graphite illustrations washed with watercolor appear to be seen through hazily filtered light. What seems to be simple is, in fact, a sophisticated technique with immense child appeal. In this simple story about a day's adventures in the lives of a dog and a cat, the illustrations perfectly convey the action and the quiet ending to the day. *Hondo and Fabian* was presented with a Caldecott Honor Book Award and was cited as one of the *New York Times* Best Illustrated Books of the Year. It was also the Please Touch Museum Award winner and an ALA Notable Children's Book.

In *T Is for Terrible*, McCarty zooms in on a subject that continues to fascinate young people—dinosaurs. He takes the viewpoint of Tyrannosaurus Rex, who wonders why others think he is so terrible; after all, he can't help it that he's big, hungry, and not a vegetarian! The Bank Street College of Education selected the book as one of the Best Children's Books of the Year. For *Moon Plane*, McCarty tapped into another childhood favorite—airplanes. The opposite of the setting in his land-bound dinosaur book, this story launches a young boy up to the moon.

The success of *Hondo and Fabian* brought numerous requests for more tales of the dog and cat, and McCarty plans sequels. The two lovable characters have also been optioned for television. Peter McCarty lives in upstate New York with his family and new puppy, Daisy. He is often on the move. As an artist and explorer, he craves new landscapes daily.

SELECTED WORKS WRITTEN AND ILLUSTRATED: *Little Bunny on the Move*, 1999; *Baby Steps*, 2000; *Hondo and Fabian*, 2002; *T Is for Terrible*, 2004; *Moon Plane*, 2006; *Fabian Escapes*, 2007.

SELECTED WORKS ILLUSTRATED: *Frozen Man*, by David Getz, 1994; *Night Driving*, by John Coy, 1996; *Mary on Horseback: Three Mountain Stories*, by Rosemary Wells, 1998; *Frozen Girl*, by David Getz, 1998; *Purple Death: The Mysterious Flu of 1918*, by David Getz, 2000; *Life on Mars*, by David Getz, 2004.

SUGGESTED READING: *Publishers Weekly*, August 3, 2006.

WEB SITE: www.petermccarty.net

"**M**y very first memory is of lying on my stomach on the floor, a crayon in each hand, drawing large, colorful circles. My mother's biggest fear was of running out of paper for me to draw on. I sat in front of the TV and drew through stacks of paper. If paper ran out, she salvaged envelopes and pieces of cardboard for me to draw on. I filled up the margins of church bulletins on Sundays, drew on strips of wallpaper, napkins, and any surface that would not get me in trouble, and, sometimes, ones that did.

"I was born in Clinton, New Jersey, and lived there with my parents, my older sister, and our cat DeeDee. My grandparents lived seven miles from our house and were an important part of my growing up. Our house was modern—white wall-to-wall carpeting, linoleum floors, large picture windows, and the requisite Danish modern furniture. My grandparents lived in an 18th century stone farmhouse with Victorian furniture and odd stuff from their travels: a Mexican Day of the Dead mask, complete with multiple snakes climbing in and out of its colorful nostrils, ears and grinning mouth; old Kabuki masks; African beaded tablecloths; gaucho spurs from Argentina. They also had a library with deep, comfy chairs. My grandmother had her collection of books by women authors. I was drawn to the comfort and charm of my grandparents' home. It caught my imagination and has never let go.

"My parents had a portrait photography studio in Clinton. My father used a large wooden bellows camera to take black and white portraits of his clients. Dad loved to tell jokes; he timed the punch line so that he could snap a picture just as his subject began to laugh or smile. He taught me that the expression and placement of someone's hands in a picture was every bit as important as the expression on their face. He also taught me about color and light. I knew I had really grown up when I was old enough to stay in his darkroom while he developed his pictures. He had all but two chemicals on the shelves in his darkroom to make nitroglycerine, which in my mind made him the most powerful man in Clinton.

"My mother tinted and colored the black and white portraits with oil paints, brushes, and Q-Tips. She was a talented artist in her own right. She drew paper dolls for me, along with dresses

Photo by David A. Johnson

Barbara McClintock

Barbara McClintock

May 6, 1955–

she helped me cut out and attach to the paper dolls with tabs. My mom was a textile and design major in college, and she designed her own patterns, and made clothing for my sister and me. She admonished us to get away from the TV and go outside to invent our own world of play.

"Music was an important part of family life. On Sundays we listened to everything from Wagner's Ring Cycle to Glenn Miller to 'The Monster Mash.' Dad sang along with everything.

"I loved the old children's books and illustrated albums in my parents' and grandparents' homes. I also fell head over heels for the cartoon character Top Cat. I spent so many hours drawing and writing and making comic books that by the time I was in the second grade, I had a prominent callus on my index finger from holding pencils and crayons. I was a daydreamer—much of my school day involved staring out the window of the classroom. Nothing was as interesting as the characters and dramas and images in my mind. By the time I was seven, I knew I would be an artist when I grew up—but what kind of artist? I asked my sister, and she replied, 'Be a children's book illustrator, of course!' My destiny was set.

"When I was nine, my parents divorced, and my mother, sister, and I moved to North Dakota near my Mom's hometown. My adolescent years were spent riding my horse through the fields surrounding Jamestown, N.D., and drawing pictures of horses.

"I attended Jamestown College two blocks from my mom and step-dad's house. I taught myself how to draw and developed my style and technique by checking out library books of drawings by Rembrandt and Albrecht Dürer, and copying every drawing before returning the books and checking out more books by other artists and copying their artwork. I worked my way through the entire art section of 18th and 19th century artists. Just weeks after my 20th birthday, I moved to New York City with a basket of loose drawings to begin my career as an illustrator of children's books.

"Today I live in Windham, CT with my paramour, David Johnson, and our two cats, Pip and Emma. My son attends college in Providence, Rhode Island."

ଔ   ଔ   ଔ

With the same sense of adventure that is often seen in her picture book stories, Barbara McClintock set off at age twenty to become a children's book artist. Encouraged by an art professor, she called the well-known illustrator Maurice Sendak to ask

> *"I spent so many hours drawing and writing and making comic books that by the time I was in the second grade, I had a prominent callus on my index finger from holding pencils and crayons."*

him what to do. Helpful and supportive, Sendak told her how to put together a book dummy and suggested she move to New York. Within several months of that move, she had her first book contract, though she acknowledges that she was very lucky and the first few years in New York were difficult. In the early years she illustrated the Fraggle Rock books based on Jim Henson's Muppets. She spent some time in Paris researching two mystery stories, written by James Duffy, about a character named May Gray, a poodle police officer. That setting would show up many times in her future work, including several award-winning titles.

McClintock's illustrations are meticulous in their detail. They have a pleasing old-fashioned look that reflects her appreciation of 19th century artists such as Grandville, Daumier, Doré, Cruikshank, and Caldecott. With a delicate line and a colorful palette, her settings and characters seem to take on a life of their own. Four of McClintock's books have been cited as *New York Times Best Illustrated Books*: *The Heartaches of a French Cat*, *The Fantastic Drawings of Danielle*, *The Gingerbread Man*, and *Adèle & Simon*. Three of these express her love of the city of Paris, and *Adèle & Simon* even features endpapers with a detailed map of Parisian sites. *The Fantastic Drawings of Danielle* also echoes McClintock's early years as the daughter of a photographer.

Courtesy of Farrar, Straus, and Giroux

A number of McClintock's books are based on folk tales, such as the award-winning *Gingerbread Boy*, which is retold with a wry twist by Jim Aylesworth. McClintock herself adapted the text for her version of *Cinderella*, a Golden Kite award-winner for illustration. *Animal Fables from Aesop* was named an ALA Notable Children's Book and adapted for the stage by the Minneapolis Children's Theater that produced it as a ballet/opera. McClintock has also designed sets and costumes for that same theater's production of *The Twelve Dancing Princesses*.

Dahlia, with its tomboy heroine Charlotte, received a *Boston Globe–Horn Book* Honor Award in the picture book category. Many of McClintock's books have been chosen for Parents' Choice Awards, *School Library Journal*'s Best of the Year lists, and the New York Public Library's 100 Titles for Reading and

Sharing. Several of her books have been translated and published in Germany, France, and South Korea. Her artwork has also appeared in the *New York Times* and the *New Yorker.*

Married in 1982 to Lawrence DiFiori, another illustrator, McClintock was divorced in 1995. Her son, Larson DiFiori, is recently graduated from Brown University.

SELECTED WORKS WRITTEN AND ILLUSTRATED: *The Little Red Hen*, 1979; *The Heartaches of a French Cat*, 1989; *Animal Fables from Aesop*, retold, 1991; *The Battle of Luke and Longnose*, 1994; *The Fantastic Drawings of Danielle*, 1996; *Frances Hodgson Burnett's A Little Princess*, adapted, 2000; *Molly and the Magic Wishbone*, 2001; *Dahlia*, 2002; *Cinderella*, retold from the Charles Perrault version, 2005; *Adèle & Simon*, 2006; *Adèle & Simon in America*, 2008.

SELECTED WORKS ILLUSTRATED: *Potbellied Possums*, by Elizabeth Winthrop, 1977; *What's a Fraggle?*, by Louise Gikow, 1984; *Marooned in Fraggle Rock*, by David Young, 1984; The *Legend of the Doozer Who Didn't*, by Louise Gikow, 1984; *Why Wembley Fraggle Couldn't Sleep*, by H. B. Gilmour, 1985; *Waggleby of Fraggle Rock*, by Stephanie Calmenson, 1985; *The Revolt of the Teddy Bears: A May Gray Mystery*, by James Duffy, 1985; *The Christmas Gang: A May Gray Mystery*, by James Duffy, 1989; *The Gingerbread Man*, retold by Jim Aylesworth, 1998; *When Mindy Saved Hanukkah*, by Eric Kimmel, 1998; *Aunt Pitty Patty's Piggy*, retold by Jim Aylesworth, 1999; *The Prog Frince: A Mixed-up Tale*, by C. Drew Lamm, 1999; *The Tale of Tricky Fox: A New England Trickster Tale*, retold by Jim Aylesworth, 2001; *Goldilocks and the Three Bears*, retold by Jim Aylesworth, 2003; *Rebecca of Sunnybrook Farm*, by Kate Douglas Wiggin, 2003 (100th anniversary edition); *Mary and the Mouse, the Mouse and Mary*, by Beverly Donofrio, 2007; *The Mitten*, retold by Jim Aylesworth, 2008.

SUGGESTED READING: *Something About the Author*, vol. 146, 2004

Colleen O'Shaughnessy McKenna

May 31, 1948–

"I started out as a television scriptwriter. It all began when I was in eighth grade and fell in love with Little Joe of *Bonanza*. All I wanted was for him to notice me. But how do you do that when the love of your life is in Hollywood and you live nowhere near there? Simple. You write for his television show and make yourself the main character. I wrote twenty-seven scripts and I mailed in the best three to *Bonanza*. Alas, Little Joe and I were never destined to fulfill our romantic potential; however, writing those *Bonanza* scripts was a good experience because I learned about the opening, middle, and end of a story.

"When I grew up, I became a teacher and hung out with third and fourth graders. They inspired me to write plays. It wasn't exactly your typical inspiration, though. They didn't try to encourage me to write because they thought my prose was brilliant and witty. Oh no, these plays were written out of necessity—that is, the need to survive a classroom full of elementary students. Keep in mind, there were nearly 40 students in each of my classes. I did it to gain control of my classroom. The kids enjoyed working on the plays, and I'd say things like, 'I guess we can't have rehearsal today because someone is throwing spitballs.' The happy result was that the kids started disciplining each other in order to rehearse!

"After a few years, I traded in a classroom full of kids for a houseful of kids. Within six years, our family grew to include Collette, Jeff, Laura, and Steve—and me and my husband. Once again, I had children to inspire me. It was my oldest daughter, Collette, who once complained that I had too many babies, who became the inspiration for the character of Collette in my first children's book, *Too Many Murphys*. Between my children and their friends, I've had material to last a whole career. Of course, I deliberately exaggerate a bit from time to time, stretching out the awfulness of certain situations, not just to get laughs, but to force the characters to react, which is what attracts readers and helps them identify with the characters.

Courtesy of Colleen O'Shaughnessy McKenna

Colleen O'Shaughnessy McKenna

"And okay, I have to admit I'm a little bit of a ham, too. As an actress, I've been in a number of community productions in the Pittsburgh area. And I often visit schools to talk to kids about the importance of reading and about 'what makes a writer a writer.' Entertainment is a great teaching tool, and not just with kids. Adults can be entertained into learning more about reading and writing too. To show audiences what I used to be like as a kid, I start by acting out scenes from *Bonanza*. Basically, I try to show them that ordinary people choose to be writers and that if I can do it, they can do it. Being ordinary has been my greatest asset. It creates the bond needed for communication.

"And that, Little Joe, is my story."

CS   CS   CS

The daughter of a civil engineer and an office manager, Colleen O'Shaughnessy McKenna received a B.S. from Slippery Rock University and did post graduate work at Carnegie Mellon University and Pitt University. In 1992 she was awarded the Distinguished Alumnae Award from Slippery Rock.

In the early 1970s McKenna taught elementary school in Bethel Park, Pennsylvania; and in 1972, she married attorney J. Frank McKenna III. She stopped teaching once they started their family, but when they discovered that her husband would have to be out of town for 14 weeks to try a case, McKenna decided she needed something besides mothering to do. Since she missed writing, she signed up for a course in children's literature. This became a turning point in her life, for an important piece of information she learned from the writing course was "write about what you know." The part-time writer and full-time mother realized it would be only natural to write about her own children. Her first books—the Murphy chapter books—revolve around the fictional Murphy family whose children attend Sacred Heart Elementary School in East Liberty, where McKenna's own children went to school. The Murphy children even share the McKenna children's first names: Collette, Jeff, Laura, and Stevie. All the things McKenna's family faced—sibling rivalry; birth order dilemmas; family and social responsibilities; learning how to get along with parents, teachers, and classmates; dealing with bullies; navigating ethical issues like lying and stealing— her characters encounter too, with the author's distinctive blend of humor and seriousness. For a long time McKenna wrote whenever she had a moment—around car pool schedules and trips to the neighborhood playground. "Writing is great," she has said. "It's portable." A parishioner of St. Joseph Church in O'Hara Township, McKenna has taught CCD (Catholic education) to elementary students for nearly 17 years and continues to be inspired by young people.

McKenna's books have appeared on numerous approved reading lists of elementary school districts around the country and have been nominated for several state awards, including Florida, Missouri, and New Hampshire. Most recently, *Third Grade*

> *"It was my oldest daughter, Collette, who once complained that I had too many babies, who became the inspiration for the character of Collette in my first children's book,* Too Many Murphys. *"*

Wedding Bells was cited as one of the best books of the year by the Bank Street College of Education.

McKenna's children all survived the trials and tribulations of childhood and are now adults. Collette is a freelance and string writer for such major magazines as *Time* and the *Boys & Girls Club of America* and lives in Atlanta with her husband and two daughters; Jeff is a pilot in the United States Navy, living in Virginia Beach with his wife and son; Laura is a nurse in the critical-care cardio unit at Massachusetts General Hospital and lives in New Hampshire with her husband and two children; and Steve, the youngest, is a sergeant in the U.S. Army Rangers. McKenna and her husband live in Pittsburgh. Active in various community volunteer efforts, she is a past member of the Institute of Children's Literature and has been an adjunct professor for creative writing at Seton Hill University. She is currently completing a young adult novel that is a true account of a Union prison for Confederate officers during the Civil War.

Courtesy of Holiday House, Inc.

SELECTED WORKS: *Too Many Murphys*, 1988; *Fourth Grade Is a Jinx*, 1989; *Fifth Grade: Here Comes Trouble*, 1989; *Eenie, Meanie, Murphy, No*, 1990; *Merry Christmas, Miss McConnell!*, 1990; *Murphy's Island*, 1991; *The Truth about Sixth Grade*, 1991; *Mother Murphy*, 1992; *Camp Murphy*, 1993; *Not Quite Sisters*, 1993; *Stuck in the Middle*, 1993; *Good Grief . . . Third Grade*, 1993; *The Brightest Light*, 1993; *Live from the Fifth Grade*, 1994; *New Friends* (Dr. Quinn, Medicine Woman), 1995; *Queen of May* (Dr. Quinn, Medicine Woman), 1996; *Valentine's Day Can Be Murder*, 1997; *Third Grade Stinks!*, illus. by Stephanie Roth, 2001; *Third Grade Ghouls!*, illus. by Stephanie Roth, 2001; *Doggone . . . Third Grade!*, illus. by Stephanie Roth, 2002; *Third Grade Wedding Bells?*, illus. by Stephanie Roth, 2006.

SUGGESTED READING: *Something About the Author*, vol. 136, 2003.

Photo by Eileen Hurley

Kate and Jim McMullan

Kate McMullan
January 16, 1947–

Jim McMullan
June 14, 1934–

Kate McMullan writes: "Here is how I tell the story of my husband's childhood: Jim was the grandson of British missionaries in China. His father, Jimmy, was a jazz musician who spoke fourteen dialects of Chinese. His mother, Rose, was Canadian, and very beautiful. Jim was born in Tsingtao, China, in 1934. When World War II broke out, Jimmy feared that Rose and Jim might be put into a prison camp, so he took them to Shanghai and put them on a ship called the *President Coolidge*. They sailed for Canada, and Jimmy joined the British Army, serving with the force later depicted in the film *The Bridge on the River Kwai*.

"Rose and Jim arrived in Canada, and at the tender age of seven, Jim was sent off to a boarding school. Two years later, even though the war was raging, Jimmy telegraphed Rose, saying that he'd arranged for her and Jim to join him in India. They traveled to New York and made a perilous trans-Atlantic crossing, their ship in constant danger of being bombed and torpedoed. At last they reached India, where Jim was once again enrolled in boarding school.

"Jim was eleven when the war ended. He believed that he would go back to China and resume life as he knew it. But because Jimmy could speak so many dialects of Chinese, he was asked to fly one last mission to remote parts of China to let villagers know that the war was over. En route, a thick fog enveloped his plane. It crashed into a mountain, killing everyone on board. Rose then took Jim back to Canada and put him in a local school where his British accent made him a target for bullying—even by his teacher. Over the next nine years, Jim attended eight different schools, and at each one, he quickly learned to speak exactly as the other children spoke. To this day, when people try to figure out where he's from by the way he speaks, Jim baffles them.

"It has taken me over 30 years to draw this history from Jim because Jim does not remember many details about his remarkable childhood.

"I grew up in suburban St. Louis in the 1950s. My childhood was uneventful. And I remember it all.

"My father was an obstetrician and our phone was always ringing at odd hours of the night. After a call, I'd often hear the engine of my father's car start up. Off he'd drive to help deliver a baby into the world. My mother had been a teacher, a stewardess and a recreation director for the Red Cross before she married. When my father came home from the war, my mom stopped working outside the home, but she remained a recreation director in our home, throwing wonderful parties. Many a night, I fell asleep listening to clinking glasses and guests talking and laughing.

"I was an only child, which was unusual for the time. My parents seemed to feel sorry that they could not provide me with siblings, so they filled our house with dogs and cats and birds and guinea pigs. I remember wrestling doll clothes onto any of them I could catch—guinea pigs were the easiest—and parading them up and down the street in my doll carriage. (I told you— uneventful.) Years later, when an editor asked me if I could write stories about a guinea pig named Fluffy, I knew I could.

"Jim read constantly when he was young. He says, 'When I lived in China, *Winnie the Pooh* and *Now We Are Six* gave me a picture of what a proper English house, a proper English landscape, and a proper English boy were like. A. A. Milne was a genius, reaching into my fake-British colonial life and straightening out the furniture and the style of behavior. He also gave me my first experience with whimsy, that particularly English way of seeing the world a little off-center. Of course, Ernest Shepard, the book's illustrator, had as powerful an effect on me as did Milne's writing, since it was the wonderfully fluid and efficient realism of the drawings that gave me the quality to which I would one day aspire as an artist.'

"Our house was filled with books and my mother read to me every night. We laughed together over the Heffalump in *Winnie the Pooh*, and the fence-painting antics in *Tom Sawyer*. We wept together over Beth's death in *Little Women*. When my father came home from the office at a decent hour, I'd snuggle up with him while he read me the funnies. My early political education came from *Pogo*. Psychology, I learned from *Peanuts*. I wanted nothing to do with Blondie Bumstead and her foolish husband, Dagwood. I wanted to grow up to be a newspaper reporter like Brenda Starr and fall in love with someone exactly like the elusive Basil St. John.

"After college, I taught fourth and sixth grades. I loved reading to my students every day after lunch. When I'd finish a chapter and close the book, all my students had to do was say, "Oh, please, Miss Hall! One more chapter!" and I'd open the book again and read on—into math period, into science time. After a while, I began to wonder whether I had what it took to write children's books. I tried writing in the evenings, but if you've ever been a teacher, you know that after a day in the classroom, you have not one ounce of energy left. In time, I moved to New York City, where I'd heard that writers lived, and took a job as an assistant editor with a publishing company. I hadn't been there long when a friend introduced me to Jim. He came over to my apartment one night and looked through my bookshelves and pulled out three books with Jim McMullan covers. I married him shortly after. When we moved into our apartment together, and combined our libraries, we had a duplicate of only one book: *Winnie the Pooh*.

"I had hoped that Jim would be eager to illustrate stories that I wrote right away, but this was not the case. The differences in our backgrounds came into play, and Jim told me my stories were 'too happy' for him. I tried writing a few sad stories, but they were so awful, I quickly gave up. It wasn't until our daughter Leigh was born that Jim and I found common ground and the impulse to work together on books for her. Our first title was *The Noisy Giants' Tea Party*, written to calm Leigh when street noises scared her in the night. When Leigh was older and taking ballet classes, we collaborated on *Nutcracker Noel* and *Noel the First*. (Leigh liked to negotiate raises in her allowance in exchange for being our inspiration.)

"After we had a couple of books under our belt, Jim decided to try to write a 'bully book' about being picked on as a boy. I worked with him on the text of what became *Hey, Pipsqueak!* and this remains one of our favorite books. Lately, we've had a fine time giving voice to large vehicles: *I Stink!*, a monologue by a garbage truck; *I'm Mighty!*, the tale of a small but mighty harbor tug; and *I'm Dirty!*, a day in the life of a hard-working backhoe loader. We're now working on our tenth book together: *I'm Bad!*, a Tyrannosaurus Rex tell-all, and if kids laugh half as hard as Jim and I have as we've put the story and pictures together, we'll have created a very funny book."

> *"I tried writing in the evenings, but if you've ever been a teacher, you know that after a day in the class-room, you have not one ounce of energy left."*

CB CB CB

After his father's death in 1945, Jim McMullan and his mother moved to Vancouver Island in Canada, where Jim finished his high school education. When he was seventeen they immigrated to the United States, where he studied at the Cornish School of

Allied Arts in Seattle, Washington. In 1953 he joined the U.S. army and served by illustrating diagrams of where to position propaganda loudspeakers on Sherman tanks. He later attended Pratt Institute in New York City, where he partially supported himself by illustrating book jackets. As the illustrator of Kathy Braun's *Kangaroo & Kangaroo* in 1965, he earned recognition when it became one of the *New York Times* Best Illustrated Children's Books.

In 1966 Jim joined Push Pin Studios, where he sharpened the style of psychologically intense realism that was to become his most expressive mode. During the 1970s he provided journalistic illustrations for many magazines, including some for *New York* magazine that became the visual inspiration for the movie *Saturday Night Fever*. Since then, he has done a wide variety of work, including creating posters for Broadway shows, making a short PBS Christmas film, and teaching at the School of Visual Arts. As the principal artist for Lincoln Center Theater, he has created over 40 posters for a variety of plays, such as *Six Degrees of Separation* and *Carousel*. All of these posters in some way explore the expressive possibilities of the human body.

In the meantime, Katy Hall (Kate McMullan's maiden name) was busy with her own career. Having earned a B.A. from the University of Tulsa in 1969 and an M.A. from Ohio State University in 1972, she taught in public schools in Los Angeles and on an American Air Force base in Hahn, Germany. In the late 1970s and early 1980s, she worked at Harcourt, Brace & Jovanovich publishers in New York and was a consultant for *Let's Find Out* magazine as well an editor of *Early Bird*. Her very first children's book, *Nothing But Soup*, featuring a character—Q. Leonard Faroop—who passionately loved soup, was published in 1976.

In 1979 she married artist Jim McMullan but continued writing under the name Katy Hall. *Magic in the Movies*, a book she wrote with Jane O'Connor about special effects in the film industry, received a Children's Science Book Honor citation from the New York Academy of Sciences. Humor played a large part in her writing from the beginning. For nearly 30 years she has collaborated with Lisa Eisenberg on a variety of joke and riddle books. She has also written several series of her own, including the Dragon Slayers' Academy comic fantasy series; the Fluffy books, early readers about a guinea pig with an attitude; Meg's Prairie Diaries, about the life of a nine-year-old girl in the Kansas Territory in the mid-1800s; the Myth-O-Mania series, retelling Greek myths from the point of view of the god

"When we moved into our apartment together, and combined our libraries, we had a duplicate of only one book: Winnie the Pooh."

Hades; and the Pearl and Wagner books, early readers about the adventures of a rabbit and a mouse. Her Lila Fenwick stories, describing the pitfalls of pre-adolescence, have received much popular recognition. *The Great Ideas of Lila Fenwick* was on the Texas Bluebonnet Award list and Missouri's Mark Twain List of Excellent Books. *Great Advice from Lila Fenwick* was on the West Virginia Master List; and *The Great Eggspectations of Lila Fenwick* won a CRABbery Honor. Two of her books, *Supercat to the Rescue* and *Rock-a-Baby Band*, were *Nick Jr.* Best Books of the Year.

Kate and Jim McMullan have combined their unique talents to produce some fresh and very funny picture books. In *Nutcracker Noel*, an *American Bookseller* Pick of the Lists and a New York Library Association's Intellectual Freedom Award Honorable Mention, Jim's stylized illustrations add humor to the quirky characters in the story of a girl who struggles with jealousy and ambition as she faces performing in the school ballet. In *Hey, Pipsqueak!*, a Parents' Choice Picture Book Award winner and a *Parenting* Magazine Reading Magic Award winner, bright watercolor pictures animate the story of young boy who outwits the giant troll who tries to bully him out of a package on his way to making a delivery.

In *I Stink!*, an enthusiastic garbage truck describes the joys of his daily rounds as he searches for garbage bags left on the curb to satisfy his hearty appetite. Jim's illustrations show the garbage truck having an attitude as gigantic as his appetite, and the text is displayed in graphics that highlight the voice of the truck. Winner of a *Boston Globe–Horn Book* Honor Award and an Irma S. and James H. Black Honor Award, the book was also named an ALA Notable Children's Book, a *New York Times* Best Illustrated Children's Book, a *New York Times* Notable Book, a *Publishers Weekly* Best Book of the Year, a *Horn Book* Fanfare title, and a BCCB Blue Ribbon title. It has also won several young readers' choice awards around the country.

I'm Mighty!, another book in the McMullans' quest to give voice to large city machines, is the story of a tugboat in the New York harbor. Then, returning to the subject of grime and grunge, they created *I'm Dirty!*, with dynamic and energetic color illustrations capturing the character of a sassy backhoe loader that relishes getting dirtier and dirtier as he does his job. A *Booklist* Editors' Choice, *I'm Dirty!* also features text that changes size, shape and orientation to fit the action, and the story works as an unusual counting book. Both *I Stink!* and *I'm Dirty!* were named *Child Magazine* Best Books of the Year.

Courtesy of HarperCollins Publishers

Kate and Jim McMullan now work from their home in Sag Harbor, New York. Their daughter, Leigh, has grown and obtained her law degree, but their dogs and cat keep them busy today.

SELECTED WORKS BY KATE McMULLAN WRITING AS KATY HALL: *Nothing But Soup*, 1976; *Magic in the Movies: The Story of Special Effects*, with Jane O'Connor, 1980; *Garfield: Jokes, Riddles, and Other Silly Stuff*, 1984; *Garfield: The Big Fat Book of Jokes and Riddles*, with Jim Hall, illus. by Katy Fentz, 1985; *Skeletons! Skeletons! All About Bones*, illus. by Paige Billin-Frye, 1991. Paxton Cheerleaders series—*Go for It, Patti!*, 1994; *Three Cheers for You, Cassie!*, 1994; *Winning Isn't Everything, Lauren!*, 1994; *We Did It, Tara!*, 1994; *We're in This Together, Patti!*, 1995; *Nobody's Perfect, Cassie!* 1995. *Really, Really Bad Sports Jokes*, written with and illus. by Rick Stromoski, 1998; *How Do You Know Who to Trust?*, with Devra Newberger Speregen, 1998; *Really, Really, Really Bad Jokes*, written with and illus. by Mike Lester, 1999; *Back-to-School Belly Busters*, illus. by Stephen Carpenter, 2002. Joke books (all written with Lisa Eisenberg)—*Chicken Jokes and Puzzles*, 1978; *A Gallery of Monsters*, illus. by Joe Mathieu, 1981; *Pig Jokes and Puzzles*, 1983; *Fishy Riddles*, illus. by Simms Taback, 1983; *101 Bug Jokes*, illus. by Don Orehek, 1984; *Buggy Riddles*, illus. by Simms Taback, 1986; *101 School Jokes*, illus. by Don Orehek, 1987; *101 Ghost Jokes*, illus. by Don Orehek, 1988; *101 Bossy Cow Jokes*, illus. by Don Orehek, 1989; *101 Cat and Dog Jokes*, illus. by H.L. Schwadron, 1990; *101 Hopelessly Hilarious Jokes*, illus. by Don Orehek, 1990; *Baseball Bloopers*, illus. by Liz Callen, 1991; *Snakey Riddles*, illus. by Simms Taback, 1990; *Quickie Comebacks*, 1992; *Spacey Riddles*, illus. by Simms Taback, 1992; *Batty Riddles*, illus. by Nicole Rubel, 1993; *Three Cheers for You, Cassie*, 1994; *101 Back to School Jokes*, illus. by Don Orehek, 1994; *Go for It, Patti*, 1994; *More Quickie Comebacks*, illus. by John Devore, 1994; *Sheepish Riddles*, illus. by R. W. Alley, 1996; *Grizzly Riddles*, illus. by Nicole Rubel, 1996; *Gobble, Gobble, Giggle: A Book Stuffed with Thanksgiving Riddles*, illus. by R.W. Alley, 1996; *Mummy Riddles*, illus. by Nicole Rubel, 1997; *Bunny Riddles*, illus. by Nicole Rubel, 1997; *Chickie Riddles*, illus. by Thor Wickstrom, 1997; *Easter Yolks: Eggs-Cellent Riddles to Crack You Up*, illus. by R.W. Alley, 1997; *Hearty Har Har: Valentine Riddles You'll Love*, illus. by R.W. Alley, 1997; *Jingle Jokes: Christmas Riddles to Deck the Ha Ha Halls*, illus. by Stephen Carpenter, 1997; *Puppy Riddles*, illus. by Thor Wickstrom, 1998; *Creepy Riddles*, illus. by S.D. Schindler, 2000; *Olive You! And Other Valentine Knock-Knock Jokes You'll A-Door*, illus. by Stephen Carpenter, 2000; *Turkey Ticklers: And Other A-Maize-Ingly Corny Thanksgiving Knock-Knock Jokes*, illus. by Stephen Carpenter, 2000; *Boo Who? And Other Wicked Halloween Knock-Knock Jokes*, illus. by Stephen Carpenter, 2000; *Easter Crack-Ups: Knock-Knock Jokes Funny Side-Up*, illus. by Stephen Carpenter, 2000; *Easter Yolks: Egg-Dyeing Kit*, illus. by R.W. Alley, 2000; *Kitty Riddles*, illus. by R.W. Alley, 2000; *Ribbit Riddles*, illus. by Robert Bender, 2001; *Hanukkah Ha-Has: Knock-Knock Jokes That Are a Latke Fun*, illus. by Stephen Carpenter, 2001; *Ho Ho Ho, Ha Ha Ha: Holly-Arious Christmas Knock-Knock Jokes*, illus. by Stephen Carpenter, 2001; *Summer Camp Crack-Ups: And Lot S'More Knock-Knock Jokes to Write Home About*, illus. by Stephen Carpenter, 2001; *Turkey Riddles*, illus. by Kristin Bora, 2002; *Dino Riddles*, illus. by Nicole Rubel, 2002; *Piggy Riddles*, illus. by Renee Andriani, 2004; *Stinky Riddles*, illus. by Renee Andriani, 2005.

SELECTED WORKS BY KATE MCMULLAN: *The Mystery of the Missing Mummy*, illus. by David Prebenna, 1984; *Dr. Jekyll and Mr. Hyde*, by Robert Louis Stevenson (Stepping Stone Classic), as adapter, illus. by Paul Van Munching, 1984; *Dinosaur Hunt-*

ers, illus. by John Randolph Jones, 1989; *Phantom of the Opera*, by Gaston Leroux (Stepping Stone Classic), as adapter, illus. by Paul Jennis, 1989; *The Story of Harriet Tubman: Conductor of the Underground Railroad*, illus. by Steve James Petruccio, 1990; *Under the Mummy's Spell*, 1992; *The Story of Bill Clinton and Al Gore*, 1992; *The Biggest Mouth in Baseball*, illus. by Anna DiVito, 1993; *Good Night, Stella*, illus. by Emma C. Clark, 1994; *If You Were My Bunny*, illus. by David McPhail, 1996; *The Mummy's Gold*, illus. by Jeff Spackman, 1996; *Supercat*, illus. by Pascal Lemaitre, 2002; *Supercat to the Rescue*, illus. by Pascal Lemaitre, 2003; *Pearl and Wagner: Two Good Friends*, illus. by R. W. Alley; 2003; *Rock-a-Baby Band*, illus. by Janie Bynum, 2003; *Lizzie McGuire: Don't Even Go There! A Little Book of Lizzie-isms*, 2003; *Baby Goose*, illus. by Pascal Lemaitre, 2004; *Pearl and Wagner: Three Secrets*, illus. by R. W. Alley, 2004; *My Travels with Capts. Lewis and Clark by George Shannon*, illus. by Adrienne Yorinks, 2004; *Bathtub Blues*, illus. by Janie Bynum, 2005. Lila Fenwick series (all illus. by Diane deGroat)— *The Great Ideas of Lila Fenwick*, 1986; *Great Advice from Lila Fenwick*, 1988; *The Great Eggspectations of Lila Fenwick*, 1991. Dragon Slayers' Academy series (all illus. by Bill Basso)—*The New Kid at School*, 1997; *Revenge of the Dragon Lady*, 1997; *Class Trip to the Cave of Doom*, 1998; *A Wedding for Wiglaf?*, 1998; *Knight for a Day*, 1999; *Sir Lancelot, Where Are You?*, 1999; *Wheel of Misfortune*, 1999; *Countdown to the Year 1000*, 1999; *97 Ways to Train a Dragon*, 2003; *Help! It's Parents Day at DSA*, 2004; *Danger! Wizard at Work*, 2004; *The Ghost of Sir Herbert Dungeonstone*, 2004; *Beware! It's Friday the 13th*, 2005; *Pig Latin-Not Just for Pigs!*, 2005; *Double Dragon Trouble*, 2005; *World's Oldest Living Dragon*, 2006; *Hail! Hail! Camp Dragononka*, 2006; *Never Trust a Troll*, 2006; *Class Trip to the Cave of Doom*, 2006; *Little Giant–Big Trouble*, 2007. Fluffy the Classroom Guinea Pig series (all illus. by Mavis Smith)—*Fluffy's Silly Summer*, 1998; *Fluffy Goes to School*, 1999; *Fluffy Saves Christmas*, 1999; *Fluffy's Happy Halloween*, 2000; *Fluffy Meets the Dinosaurs*, 2000; *Fluffy's 100th Day of School*, 2000; *Fluffy's Valentine's Day*, 2000; *Fluffy's Thanksgiving*, 2000; *Fluffy's School Bus Adventure*, 2001; *Fluffy and the Firefighters*, 2001; *Fluffy Meets the Groundhog*, 2001; *Fluffy's Funny Field Trip*, 2001; *Fluffy, the Secret Santa*, 2001; *Fluffy Goes Apple Picking*, 2001; *Fluffy's Trick-or-Treat*, 2001; *Fluffy's Spring Vacation*, 2001; *Fluffy Learns to Swim*, 2002; *Fluffy Grows a Garden*, 2002; *Fluffy Meets the Tooth Fairy*, 2002; *Fluffy Goes to Washington*, 2002; *Fluffy's Lucky Day*, 2003; *Fluffy and the Snow Pig*, 2003; *Fluffy's*

School Adventures, 2003; *Fluffy Plants a Jelly Bean*, 2004. Meg's Prairie Diary (My America) series—*As Far as I Can See*, 2001; *For This Land*, 2003; *A Fine Start*, 2003. Myth-O-Mania series (all illus. by David LaFleur)—*Have a Hot Time, Hades!*, 2002; *Phone Home, Persephone!*, 2002; *Say Cheese, Medusa!*, 2002; *Nice Shot, Cupid!*, 2002; *Stop That Bull, Theseus!*, 2003; *Keep a Lid on It, Pandora!*, 2003; *Get to Work, Hercules!*, 2003; *Go for the Gold, Atalanta!*, 2003.

SELECTED WORKS FOR YOUNG READERS ILLUSTRATED BY JIM MCMUL-LAN: *Kangaroo & Kangaroo*, by Kathy Braun, 1965; *The Earth Is Good: A Chant in Praise of Nature*, by Michael DeMunn, 1999.

SELECTED WORKS FOR ADULTS ILLUSTRATED AS JAMES MCMULLAN: *Revealing Illustrations*, 1980; *Drawing from Life: A High-Focus Approach to Drawing the Figure*, 1994; *High-focus Drawing: A Revolutionary Approach to Drawing the Figure*, 1995; *The Theater Posters of James McMullan*, 1998.

SELECTED WORKS BY KATE MCMULLAN ILLUSTRATED BY JIM MCMULLAN: *The Noisy Giants' Tea Party*, 1992; *Nutcracker Noel*, 1993; *Hey, Pipsqueak!*, 1995; *Noel the First*, 1996; *No, No, Jo!*, 1997; *Papa's Song*, 2000; *I Stink!*, 2002; *I'm Mighty!*, 2003; *I'm Dirty!*, 2006; *I'm Bad!*, 2008.

SUGGESTED READING FOR JIM MCMULLAN: *Something About the Author*, vol. 150, 2004. Periodicals—*Los Angeles Times*, August 12, 2001; *New York Times*, October 11, 1998.

SUGGESTED READING FOR KATE MCMULLAN: *Something About the Author*, vol. 132, 2002.

WEB SITE: www.katemcmullan.com
www.jamesmcmullan.com

Diane McWhorter

November 1, 1952–

"If I had to name one school experience that made a writer of me, it would have to be a Baby Boom generation phenomenon known as the 'orange biography.' Orange was the color of the library binding that distinguished this series of biographies for children, which might have been called 'The Lives of Great People When They Were Young and Hadn't Done Anything Yet.' Often it was hard to tell what important stuff the subjects went on to do that made them worthy of books. If anyone can figure out what Jessie Fremont (*Girl of Capitol*

Hill) accomplished, please let me know.

"These biographies were a far cry from art, but they inspired me. I became convinced that one day I would be the subject of an orange biography and began narrating my daily life accordingly. 'Diane tossed her mane of blonde hair as she ran through the backyard to Nancy's house, her faithful dog Bootsie nipping at her heels.' You have to have a certain grandiosity to become a writer, a willingness to inflict your personality on the world, and it was the orange biographies that first motivated me to turn my life into literature, though I use the terms 'life' as well as 'literature' loosely.

"In school, meanwhile, my writing hardly reflected the 'girl of destiny' soundtrack in my head. I used up countless trees filling lined school paper with dead prose for The Book Report, trudging through a rigid outline (Setting, Plot, Character Development. . .). But excruciating as it could be, my school's disregard of creativity in favor of mechanics was not a total waste. The most difficult thing about writing is organizing one's thoughts, the task required simply to begin. The unglamorous work of topic sentences and three-supporting-details serves to demystify the process—and then you are free to experience the mysteries of the art. Once you have practiced—and I mean rehearsed—your craft enough, you can count on professionalism to take over if imagination fails. The process will often bring forth the muse. The process, in fact, *is* the muse.

Photo by G.M. Andrews/Mobile (Ala.) Register

"Ironically, the girl I ended up writing about in my autobiographical histories of the civil rights revolution, *Carry Me Home* and *A Dream of Freedom,* was a me that I wasn't even aware of during my Orange Biography Period. While I was nursing fantasies of being *Girl Olympic Swimmer* or *Girl FBI Agent,* it turned out, one of the biggest turning points in American history was occurring right in my humble hometown. In the spring of 1963, Martin Luther King, Jr. had brought the civil rights movement to Birmingham, Alabama, and fought—won—the epic battle of his career. After black school children who were my age filled our city streets in nonviolent protest against their second-class citizenship, and faced down the police dogs and fire hoses unleashed by our elected officials, segregation in the United States was abolished.

"I was not in favor of those mass marches for freedom at the time, because my father was an active opponent of Dr. King's civil rights movement. And so the story of mine that turned out to be worth telling was that of Girl Segregationist—a witness to American apartheid as a young white supremacist of the Deep South, living on the wrong side of history. Reflecting back on that experience as an adult, I wanted to understand how so many 'decent' people could support a system so egregiously evil. And so I ended up devoting nineteen years to writing about the civil rights struggle, the villains as well as the heroes.

"You, too, may grow up to discover that the reality you now take for granted is in retrospect a haunting milestone in the long march of the human race."

CB   CB   CB

> "Reflecting back on that experience as an adult, I wanted to understand how so many 'decent' people could support a system so egregiously evil."

The experience of growing up in Birmingham, Alabama, during the Civil Rights Movement of the 1960s provided the background for much of Diane McWhorter's writing. The daughter of Elizabeth Gore Biggs and Martin Westgate McWhorter, she traveled north to attend Wellesley College, where she graduated magna cum laude with a degree in comparative literature. Over the years she has written on race, politics, and other topics for many publications, including the *Wall Street Journal*, the *Washington Post*, and *People* magazine. As a journalist she contributes to *USA Today*'s op-ed pages and the *New York Times*.

McWhorter began writing her prize-winning adult book, *Carry Me Home: Birmingham, Alabama: The Climactic Battle of the Civil Rights Revolution*, as a memoir. In order to better understand her own family's part in fighting against integration, she found herself going deeper and deeper into research to understand the events that occurred and the motivations for the actions of the white establishment. When the book was published in 2001, McWhorter's memoir project had become a comprehensive history of the civil rights struggle in her native Birmingham. Designated a *New York Times* Notable Book and one of *Time*'s top ten books of the year, it won the Pulitzer Prize for General Nonfiction and the Southern Book Critics Circle Award, among many other honors.

In *A Dream of Freedom: The Civil Rights Movement from 1954–1968*, McWhorter created a compelling history of the civil

Courtesy of Scholastic Press

rights movement for younger readers. Profusely illustrated with photographs—some of which had been suppressed by her own city's newspaper during that time—the book tells the story in words and pictures of both famous and ordinary people at that extraordinary turning point in history. As McWhorter states in the book's introduction, ". . . the dream of freedom—African Americans' hard passage from slavery to what the Movement song called Freedom Land—is the core struggle between power and justice in our nation." She brings that struggle to life in clear, vigorous prose. Year by year, from 1954 to 1968, the stories that unfold tell of many African Americans' extraordinary courage in the face of entrenched bigotry at such critical junctures as Little Rock, Selma, Montgomery, and McWhorter's own hometown of Birmingham. The book provides a comprehensive picture of institutionalized segregation slowly coming apart. *A Dream of Freedom* won a National Parenting Publications Award and was designated by the *New York Times* as one of its Notable Children's Books of 2004. It appeared in *School Library Journal*'s Best Books list, the *Horn Book*'s Fanfare, and ALA's Notable Children's Books, among others.

Diane McWhorter has two daughters, now teenagers. "I dedicated *A Dream of Freedom* to them," McWhorter says, "In the hope that they might understand why the civil rights movement affected not only African Americans but all of us." The author lives with her family in New York City. She has lectured throughout the United States on the subject of race relations.

SELECTED WORKS FOR YOUNG READERS: *A Dream of Freedom: The Civil Rights Movement from 1954–1968*, 2004.

SELECTED WORKS FOR ADULTS: *Carry Me Home: Birmingham, Alabama: The Climactic Battle of the Civil Rights Revolution*, 2001.

SUGGESTED READING: *Contemporary Authors*, vol. 200, 2002; McWhorter, Diane, "Aftershock (Forty Years after the Birmingham, Alabama, Church Bombing)," *New York Times Magazine*, July 29, 2001.

Courtesy of Paul Meisel

Paul Meisel

(My-zel)
April 14, 1955–

"It always surprises me when I read biographies of other artists and so many of them say that they knew they wanted to be artists for as long as they could remember. I guess not too many of them wanted to pitch for the Mets, as I did! Sure, there were moments when I was young when I drew something that caught the attention of a teacher—like the 'filmstrip' (an illustrated single-serving cereal box with two pencils and a long piece of paper attached) that I did about Abraham Lincoln in the third grade. Or the pencil drawing of a pair of sneakers that I did in the eighth grade which was hung in the school hallway for a month and got lots of compliments.

"My serious interest in art began in high school. I took a class with some of my friends at the home of a local artist and printmaker named Myril Adler. (Milly, as she is known, is now in her eighties and still teaching and making art in her home today.) We learned how to make linoleum cuts and woodcuts and drypoint prints, which are crude etchings that you scratch into a metal plate and then fill the 'holes' with ink and print it on a press. We learned how to paint and draw, and we learned how to think like artists.

"I had a number of artistically talented classmates in high school. There was a creative publication that came out each year that published writing (poetry and fiction) and art. There was a kind of informal competition among us to see which of us could get more pieces published.

"In our basement at home, we had a darkroom. My father and my oldest brother were very interested in photography, as was I. In my senior year of high school, I was the photographer for the yearbook and took and printed most of the photos for the yearbook. I found that seeing the world through the lens of a camera was beneficial to the study of art. I even considered studying photography in college but eventually decided that I preferred drawing and painting and printmaking.

"While all of this artwork was going on, I was also still playing baseball and, later in high school, soccer. In college, I played on the squash team. Sports have always been important to me. I have three sons and they all like sports too. I used to coach them in baseball and soccer when they were young. My oldest son, Peter, is now playing baseball in college. My second son, Alex, is playing soccer in college; and my youngest son, Andrew, plays soccer in high school.

"Although my oldest son enjoys making art and has even helped me paint from time to time, so far none of my kids have really considered art as a career. My hope for them is that they will choose a career in something that they enjoy doing as much as I enjoy being an illustrator.

"Certainly there are better-paying and more stable occupations than being a freelance artist. Even though illustrating isn't something I always wanted to do 'for as long as I can remember,' I'm delighted that I stumbled into it.

"After all, not everyone can pitch for the Mets."

"It always surprises me when I read biographies of other artists and so many of them say that they knew they wanted to be artists for as long as they could remember. I guess not too many of them wanted to pitch for the Mets, as I did!"

CǮ CǮ CǮ

Paul Meisel spent his early childhood with his parents and three brothers in Long Island, New York. When he was about eight years old Meisel moved with his family to Briarcliff in Westchester County, another suburb of New York. At Wesleyan University he majored in fine art and spent his junior year in Rome in the Tyler School of Art program. Following Wesleyan, he went to Yale University, where he received an M.F.A. in graphic design.

After graduating from Yale, Meisel married and moved to New York City where he lived for about a decade in the Tribeca section of the city. One year and two jobs later, his career as a freelance illustrator began to take off. During the 1980s his primary occupation was editorial and advertising work. His work with art directors at the *New York Times* and *New York* magazine led him to freelance jobs with art directors and editors of children's books and magazines, as well as educational publishers.

Meisel has illustrated over 75 children's books. His signature style is child-friendly, upbeat, and bright-colored. Among his many successful titles is Jean Craighead George's *How to Talk to Your Cat*, which was named an IRA/CBC Children's Choice and which features amiable cartoon cats interacting with photographs of the author. He illustrated *Morgan Plays Soccer* by Anne Rockwell, one of the Bank Street College Best Children's Books of the Year as well as a winner of the Oppenheim Toy Portfolio Gold Award. In this title, Meisel makes good use of white space and creates colorful scenes with watercolor and gouache, adding comic touches like a giraffe in a purple soccer uniform and an alligator in bed. The textured gouache-and-acrylic paintings that give *Go To Sleep, Groundhog!* by Judy Cox its visual appeal were featured in the Society of Illustrators Original Art Show in 2004.

Meisel illustrated three of Carol Diggory Shields's books; of these *Lunch Money and Other Poems About School* was an IRA-CBC Children's Choice, and its companion, *Almost Late to School and More School Poems* was a North Carolina Children's Book Award Nominee. *Dear Baby* by Sarah Sullivan, which features clever mixed-media pictures (some designed by Meisel to look as though they'd been drawn by the child in the story), won an Oppenheim Toy Portfolio Gold Award. He was also one of 40 artists who contributed to Reading Is Fundamental's 40th Anniversary publication *The Art of Reading*.

Meisel wrote his own text for *Zara's Hats*, a fictional story inspired by his great-grandfather who ran a hat shop in the early 1900s. Through a seamless combination of watercolor-and-ink illustrations and text, he tells a tale that encompasses not just the story of a daughter who creates decorations for her father's hats when he runs out of feathers, but expands to become a window into a past world.

The most unusual occurrence in his career happened in 2005, when Meisel was asked to appear on the first episode of NBC's *The Apprentice: Martha Stewart*. Chosen by a group of participants to illustrate their version of *Jack and the Beanstalk* in less than 24 hours, he became the project winner and the book appeared in bookstores the day after the show.

Meisel and his wife, Cheryl, live in Connecticut with their three sons.

SELECTED WORKS: *Busy Buzzing Bumblebees and Other Tongue Twisters*, by Alvin Schwartz, 1982; *Weight Training for Cats*, by Anthony Serafini, 1982; *Monkey-Monkey's Trick*, by Patricia McKissack, 1988; *And That's What Happened to Little Lucy: Just Right for 3's and 4's*, by Jill Aspen Davidson, 1989; *The Cow That Got Her Wish*, by Margaret Hillert, 1989; *Mr. Bubble Gum*, by William H. Hooks, 1989; *A Kid's Guide to How to Save the Planet*, by Billy Goodman, 1990; *Mr. Monster*, by William H. Hooks, 1990; *A Kid's Guide to How to Save the Animals*, by Billy Goodman, 1991; *Mr. Baseball*, by William H. Hooks, 1991; *My World & Globe*, by Ira Wolfman, 1991; *What is War? What is Peace? 50 Questions & Answers for Kids*, by Richard Rabinowitz, 1991; *Cousin Markie & Other Disasters*, by Christel Kleitsch, 1992; *Your Insides*, by Joanna Cole, 1992; *All About Magnets*, by Stephen Krensky, 1993; *The Cow Buzzed*, by Andrea Zimmerman and David Clemesha, 1993; *I Am Really a Princess*, by Karen Shields, 1993; *Mr. Dinosaur*, by William H. Hooks, 1993; *1,400 Things for Kids to Be Happy About*, by Barbara Ann Ann Kipfer, 1994; *Max and Maggie in Autumn*, by Janet A. Craig, 1994; *Max and Maggie in Summer*, by Janet A. Craig, 1994; *Max and Maggie in Winter*, by Janet A. Craig, 1994; *Wizard & Wart*, by Janice Lee Smith, 1994; *Games and Giggles Just for Girls* (American Girl Library), 1995; *Lunch Money & Other Poems About School*, by Carol Diggory Shields, 1995; *Max and Maggie in Spring*, by Janet A. Craig, 1995; *Wizard & Wart at Sea*, by Janice Lee Smith, 1995; *My Middle-Aged Baby Book*, by Mary Lou Weisman, 1995; *Howard and the Sitter Surprise*, by Priscilla Paton, 1996; *Kirby Puckett's Baseball Games*, by Kirby Puckett and Andrew Gutelle, 1996; *Mommies at Work*, by Margo Lundell, 1996; *Engine, Engine, Number Nine*, by Stephanie Calmenson, 1997; *Go Away, Dog*, by Joan L. Nødset, 1997; *I Wish My Brother Was a Dog*, by Carol Diggory Shields, 1997; *A Cake All for Me*, by Karen Magnuson Beil, 1998; *More Games and Giggles: Wild about Animals!*, by Jeanette Ryan Wall (American Girl Library), 1998; *The Three Little Pigs*, by Betty Miles, 1998; *The Tortoise and the Hare*, adapted by Betty Miles, 1998; *What Is the World Made Of? All About Solids, Liquids, and Gases*, by Kathleen Weidner Zoehfeld, 1998; *Wizard & Wart in Trouble*, by Janice Lee Smith, 1998; *The Fixits*, by Anne Mazer, 1999; *Morgan Plays Soccer*, by Anne Rockwell, 1999; *On Beyond a Million: An Amazing Math Journey*, by David M. Schwatz, 1999; *The Cool Crazy Crickets*, by David Elliott, 2000; *How to Talk to Your Cat*, by Jean Craighead George, 2000; *It Happened in the White House: Extraordinary Tales from America's Most Famous House*, by Kathleen Karr, 2000; *We All Sing with the Same Voice*, by J. Philip Miller and Sheppard M. Greene, 2000; *Why I Sneeze, Shiver, Hiccup, & Yawn*, by Melvin Berger, 2000; *The Cool Crazy Crickets to the Rescue*, by David Elliott, 2001; *Hooray for St. Patrick's Day!*, by Joan Holub 2002; *Trick or Treat?*, by Bill Martin Jr. and Michael Sampson, 2002; *What's That Noise?*, by Michelle Edwards and Phyllis Root, 2002; *Almost Late to School*, by Carol Diggory Shields, 2003; *Coco and Cavendish: Circus Dogs*, by Judy Sierra, 2003; *Energy Makes Things Happen*, by Kimberly Brubaker Bradley, 2003; *Katie Catz Makes a Splash*, by Anne Rockwell, 2003; *Chip and the Karate Kick*, by Anne Rockwell, 2004; *Go to Sleep, Groundhog*, by Judy Cox, 2004; *Mooove Over!: A Book About Counting by Twos*, by Karen Magnuson Beil, 2004; *Pop Bottle Science*, by Lynn Brunelle, 2004; *What's the Matter in Mr. Whisker's Room?*, by Michael Elsohn Ross, 2004; *Dear Baby: Letters from Your Big Brother*, by Sarah Sullivan, 2005; *Forces Make Things Move*, by Kimberly Brubaker Bradley, 2005; *Jack and the Beanstalk* (Martha Stewart Apprentice Edition) by Primarius Corporation, 2005; *The Three Bears' Christmas*, by Kathy Duval, 2005; *Barnyard Slam*, by Dian Curtis Regan, 2006; *Mr. Ouchy's First Day*, by B. G. Hennessy, 2006; *Take Care, Good Night*, by Shelley Moore Thomas, 2006; *Why Are the Ice Caps Melting? The Dangers of Global Warming*, by Anne Rockwell, 2006; *Take Care, Good Knight*, by Shelley Moore Thomas, 2007; *The Three Bears' Hallowe'en*, by Kathy Duval, 2007; *Stella Unleashed*, by Linda Ashman, 2008.

Courtesy of Holiday House, Inc.

SELECTED WORKS WRITTEN AND ILLUSTRATED: *Zara's Hats*, 2003.

SUGGESTED READING: *Something About the Author*, vol. 184, 2008.

WEB SITE: www.paulmeisel.com

"**I** was sent home my first day of kindergarten. I had bitten another child. My parents were mortified, but I was unrepentant. I had only done what I thought was right. A little boy was tearing the legs off a Daddy Long Legs. When he wouldn't stop, I bit him.

"Today, at age 49, I no longer bite children, but I am still engaged in the same battle: the attempt to persuade other humans to treat our fellow creatures with gentleness and respect.

"It's a splendid way to spend a lifetime. Researching the books, articles, radio commentaries and film scripts that I write about the natural world, I've traveled to some of the planet's most remote and exciting places. I've tracked tigers in India, swum with piranhas and electric eels in the Amazon, and worked in a pit with 18,000 snakes in Canada. In Borneo, I took a bath with an orangutan. In French Guiana, I handled a wild tarantula (she was very gentle). In Costa Rica, I rescued a sloth (he was crossing a road—too slowly).

Photo by Phebe Lewan

Sy Montgomery

February 7, 1958

"Growing up, I was always keenly aware that the planet is host to many kinds of creatures besides humans. (Not that I have anything against humans. I even married one.) But thank God we're not the only species on this sweet green planet. Knowing this makes me feel far more at home here. Turtles, dogs, parrots, dolphins, spiders, snakes, gorillas, bats—these are just a few of the fellow animals who I have found make fascinating companions and excellent teachers.

"When I do slide shows at schools, I often begin my lecture with an homage to my teachers—and the first slide I project is one of an orangutan. Not all teachers come from conventional classrooms: I introduce a bear, a dolphin, an Amazonian shaman, a Bengali fisherman, a tarantula, and a gorilla. All of them have some important truth to tell or show us, I've found. There's an old Buddhist saying: when the student is ready, the teacher will appear. I have been blessed to find teachers all around me.

"Among my most inspiring teachers were wombats. After I graduated college and had been working as a science reporter at a newspaper for a few years, my father gave me the gift of an airplane ticket to a place I had always wanted to visit: Australia. For my big vacation, I wanted to do more than relax. I found out about a group called Earthwatch, which pairs lay volunteers with scientific and environmental projects around the world. They had a project outside Blanchetown, South Australia helping to study and conserve the habitat of the rare southern hairy-nosed wombat, a burrowing relative of the koala. So that's what I did. I spent two weeks camping in the outback, studying the wombats and their scrub-desert habitat. I loved it so much that the head scientist on the project, Dr. Pamela Parker of Chicago's Brookfield Zoo, made me an offer I couldn't refuse. If I wanted to come back and study animals here, she said, she couldn't pay me, nor could she pay my airfare to return—but she would make sure I had food and access to the Flinders University library in Adelaide.

"So I quit my job and moved to a tent in the outback. I ended up spending six months following emus, conducting the first close-range, intimate study of its kind of this four-foot-tall flightless bird. Thanks to the wombats, I have freelanced and traveled ever since.

> *"I was sent home my first day of kindergarten. I had bitten another child. My parents were mortified, but I was unrepentant."*

"People often ask me why I go to places others consider uncomfortable or dangerous. I don't mind the bugs or the shots or the heat; I love the adventure. But more than that, I hope I am doing something that makes a difference: that one day, maybe someone will read my work and not only fall in love with the earth and its creatures, but be moved to change the way they live to protect it. Maybe because of something I write, someone will join a conservation or humane group, or found a new one. . . start recycling . . . buy a smaller car . . . become a vegetarian or buy only organic food . . . or even choose conservation as a career."

ଷ ଷ ଷ

Sy Montgomery's interest in animals began at an early age. Born in Frankfurt, Germany, where her father was stationed with the United States Army, she nearly toddled into the hippo enclosure when her parents took her to the Frankfurt Zoo. The family moved back to the United States before Sy was two years old, where her father was soon promoted to brigadier general, in command of the Brooklyn Army Terminal. An only child, Sy preferred the company of animals to other children until the family moved to Alexandria, Virginia, just before she started junior high school. A backyard neighbor, a girl her own age, showed her a wooded area that the girls happily explored together, giving Sy an inkling of what her future career would involve.

When the family moved again three years later, Sy found the second component of her future career by taking a journalism class in high school. Thanks to a stimulating teacher, she decided to study journalism at Syracuse University. She graduated in 1979 with a triple major in journalism, French language and literature, and psychology. Writing for the college paper during those years, she met Howard Mansfield, the man she would marry in 1987. Immediately after graduation, Sy worked for the *Buffalo Evening News*, but soon took a job for less pay in order to write about biology and the environment for the *Courier-News* in Bridgewater, New Jersey. Five years later she took the trip to Australia that changed her life.

The experience of working on an Earthwatch project with hairy-nosed wombats led Sy to spend six months following a group of emus, recording their movements. Returning home to New Hampshire, she became a freelance science writer, contributing to such magazines as *International Wildlife*, *Ranger Rick*, and *Animals*, as well as writing columns for newspapers such as the *Courier-News* and the *Boston Globe*. Her first book written for adults, *Walking with the Great Apes*, chronicling the work of Jane Goodall, Dian Fossey, and Birute Galdikas, won the New England Writers and Publishers project award for Best New Nonfiction and was a finalist for the *Los Angeles Times* Science Book Award. Her popular nature columns for the *Boston Globe* have been collected into several books: *Nature's Everyday Mysteries*, *Seasons of the Wild*, and *The Curious Naturalist*. She contributes reports and commentaries to National Public Radio's "Living on Earth" programs. An essay on her observations of the emus in South Australia was published in *The Nature of Nature: New Essays by America's Finest Writers on Nature*, a book that was a fundraiser for the anti-poverty organization Share Our Strength.

Sy Montgomery's children's books were a natural outgrowth of her creative approach to reporting animal behavior and a desire to share her excitement with young people. Her first children's book, *The Snake Scientist*, one of the Scientists in the Field series published by Houghton Mifflin, paired her with photographer Nic Bishop; their collaborative work has won numerous accolades. An Orbis Pictus Honor book and winner of the International Reading Association's award for nonfiction, *The Snake Scientist* was also named a Blue Ribbon title by the *Bulletin of the Center for Children's Books* and cited on the John

> *"I've tracked tigers in India, swum with piranhas and electric eels in the Amazon, and worked in a pit with 18,000 snakes in Canada. In Borneo, I took a bath with an orangutan."*

Courtesy of the Houghton Mifflin Company

Burroughs List of Nature Books. In a second collaboration with Nic Bishop, Montgomery wrote about the work of Sam Marshall in *The Tarantula Scientist*. Both in his spider lab at Hiram College in Ohio and hunting tarantulas in the rain forests of French Guiana, Marshall exudes an enthusiasm for his hairy subjects that is contagious and beautifully captured in Montgomery's conversational writing style along with Bishop's astounding photographs. Winner of an Honor Book citation for the Robert F. Sibert Award for nonfiction, *The Tarantula Scientist* was also named an ALA Notable Children's Book, a *Kirkus* Editor's Choice, and a *School Library Journal* Best Book of the Year.

A third collaboration between Montgomery and Bishop, *The Quest for the Tree Kangaroo*, captured the Orbis Pictus Award for nonfiction from the National Council of Teachers of English. Research for this book took the pair to the remote cloud forest of Papua New Guinea with biologist Lisa Dabek and a team of scientists from around the world, tracking the elusive Matschie's tree kangaroo. *The Quest for the Tree Kangaroo* also received an Honor Book citation for the Robert F. Sibert Medal and was named an ALA Notable Children's Book, a *Booklist* Editor's Choice, and a *School Library Journal* Best Book, among other accolades. *The Tarantula Scientist* and *The Quest for the Tree Kangaroo* were each designated a Selectors' Choice in the yearly list of Outstanding Science Trade Books for Children compiled by the National Science Teachers Association and the Children's Book Council.

Several of Montgomery's books are adaptations of work she first published for adults; among them are books that explore the wonders of the Sundarbans tigers of India, the pink dolphins of the Amazon, and the golden moon bear of Southeast Asia. Along the way she has collaborated with some excellent wildlife photographers, including Eleanor Briggs for *The Man-Eating Tigers of Sundarbans* and Dianne Taylor-Snow for *Encantado*. Both of those books received the Nature and Ecology book award created by *Skipping Stones* magazine. *The Man-Eating Tigers* also won an Oppenheim Toy Portfolio Gold Award.

Sy Montgomery lectures widely on conservation topics at zoos, museums, universities, and schools, for both adults and children. Not all of her animal experiences have been in remote areas of the world. Her latest adult book, *The Good, Good Pig*, is a memoir of life at home with her 750-pound pig, Christopher Hogwood; raised from a spotted runt, he lived to the age of 14 and taught Sy, her husband, and their neighbors a great deal about community and compassion. Named a favorite of the year by the *Christian Science Monitor*, *Rocky Mountain News*, and *People* magazine, *The Good, Good Pig* was also a summer reading pick by *O Magazine*.

Sy Montgomery and her husband, Howard Mansfield, live in a 120-year-old farmhouse in New Hampshire with an assortment of animal friends. In May 2004 Keene State College in Keene, NH, awarded her an honorary doctorate of letters.

SELECTED WORKS FOR YOUNG READERS: *The Snake Scientist*, photos by Nic Bishop, 1995; *The Man-Eating Tigers of Sunderbans*, photos by Eleanor Briggs, 2001; *Encantado: Pink Dolphin of the Amazon*, photos by Dianne Taylor-Snow, 2002; *Search for the Golden Moon Bear: Science and Adventure in the Asian Tropics*, 2004; *The Tarantula Scientist*, photos by Nic Bishop, 2004; *Quest for the Tree Kangaroo: An Expedition to the Cloud Forest of New Guinea*, photos by Nic Bishop, 2006.

SELECTED WORKS FOR ADULTS: *Walking with the Great Apes: Jane Goodall, Dian Fossey, Birute Galdikas*, 1991; *Spell of the Tiger: The Man-Eaters of Sundarbans*, 1995; *Nature's Everyday Mysteries*, 1993; *Seasons of the Wild*, 1995; *Journey of the Pink Dolphins*, 2000; *The Curious Naturalist*, 2000; *The Wild Out Your Window*, 2002; *Search for the Golden Moon Bear: Science and*

Adventure in Pursuit of a New Species, 2003; *The Good, Good Pig: The Extraordinary Life of Christopher Hogwood*, 2006.

SUGGESTED READING: *Something about the Author*, vol. 184, 2008. Periodicals—Baxter, Kathleen, "Gorilla of My Dreams: Slithering Snakes, Long-Legged Spiders, and Endangered Apes Entice Readers," *School Library Journal*, December 2005; Montgomery, Sy, "Spider Man," *Ranger Rick*, October 2004; Montgomery, Sy, "Stalking Spiders, *Discover*, February 2004; Montgomery, Sy, "Encounters with Encantados," *Appleseeds*, April 2001; Golden, Frederic, "Captured by the Law of the Jungle," *Los Angeles Times*, April 19, 1995.

WEB SITE: www.authorwire.com

Courtesy of Yuyi Morales

Yuyi Morales

*(JOO-jee
mo-RAH-lace)
November 7, 1968–*

"The eldest of four children, I was born in Mexico while my parents still lived at the house where my father grew up. My father was a student, and my mother took orders from my father's mother. That is why Mama cleaned, did the laundry by hand, prepared the food, and took care of the dozens of caged birds owned by Grandma. At night, to help Papa with the money, Mama made stuffed animals to sell. Some of my first drawings come from those nights when I sat by her side.

"While my mother sewed and stuffed, I drew. I made pictures of myself with long legs and platform shoes. I drew myself wearing a miniskirt and carrying a purse. I drew myself with long hair that curled at the bottom and a little puppy walking at my side. I was two years old. My mother still keeps some of these drawings.

"Then the day came when my dad got us our own house. With very little money to spare, Mama handmade everything we needed. And because I was the oldest daughter, my mother insisted that I learn how to use my hands to create too. When I was five she taught me how to knit, and I made myself a multicolored vest and a hat. Later she showed me how to use her sewing machine to sew clothes for my dolls. Mama could figure how to do anything with her hands. And if *she* could do it, she said, so could I.

"All the while I kept drawing too. I copied my family's portraits from the walls, and sometimes I made my relatives sit still so that I could draw them. Yet most of the time I wanted to draw alone. Going inside a room, I would close the door and sit in front of the mirror to copy my face, again and again. Even now, as an adult, drawing comes to me as an intimate act, one that I prefer to do alone when nobody is watching.

"But as much as I liked to draw, not everybody liked my drawings. Once, in second grade, a teacher made me erase a picture I had made of a woman and a man kissing. I had spent a long time giving them handsome faces and drawing them beautiful bodies, outlining the shadows in the right places. It was my best picture ever, I thought—until the girl sitting next to me glanced at it over my shoulder and called the teacher on me. The teacher wasn't happy; it was not right for me to draw such a thing, she scolded. She made me erase my drawing until there were only gray smudges left.

"Papa, however, loved what I drew. 'Someday,' he would say, 'you are going to be an architect.' I always nodded. After all, what other options were there for a girl who liked to draw? Neither I nor my dad imagined that I could be an artist. How would I even dare to want to be one? In my mind, artists were geniuses, people with exceptional talents whose work went into books and museums. Me? I was only Yuyi.

"In college, I decided architecture was not my thing, and instead I applied to P. E. school. I also studied psychology. During those years, I drew less and less, believing I needed to employ my time in more important ways—like, for example, making a living. It wasn't until some years later, when something marvelous happened in my life, that I returned to drawing: I had become a new mother. With a little baby boy in my arms, I wanted to copy his face—over and over again.

"Something else happened too: my husband, our son, and I came to live in the USA. Life here was very different; it was lonelier too. I spoke almost no English, I had no friends, and I had no job. So while I took care of my son, I drew. I drew him sleeping; I drew him sitting on his chair; I drew him wrapped in his blanket. I also explored other arts and crafts that I learned from library books. I made paper. I made baskets. I even made some puppets that looked like my son.

"Then one day, a friend of my husband asked me what I did. In my broken English I looked for the word housewife. But my

"Even now, as an adult, drawing comes to me as an intimate act, one that I prefer to do alone when nobody is watching."

husband answered for me and said, 'Yuyi is an artist.' Was I? Could I actually dare to be one? The answer was: Yes! Because art is how I wanted to express my life.

"There was still so much to learn. I would have to learn how to use brushes and paint because I had fallen in love with children's books, and I wanted to create picture books of my own. I needed to learn English too, so that I could tell my stories and share them with others. I would learn it all, because I had been raised by my mother who could figure how to do anything with her hands. And so could I."

℃ ℃ ℃

Yuyi Morales was born in the city of flowers, Xalapa, Veracruz, Mexico. She has two sisters: Magaly, who is an artist and Elizabeth, who has a TV/radio show that advocates social service and is running for political office. They also have a brother, Mario Alejandro, nicknamed Chip for his computer expertise, who creates comics. All three of her siblings live in Mexico where Morales spent the first 25 years of her life. She took an early interest in drawing and sports, and as an adolescent, showed promise as a competitive swimmer. Enrolling at the University of Xalapa, she earned her bachelors degree in Physical Education and Psychology.

In 1995 she and her husband, Tim O'Meara, a software engineer, moved with their son to the United States. Speaking no English, she found a universal language in children's picture books at the local library. It was love at first sight and stirred in her the desire to create books herself. But first she had to learn English, which she did with the help of those same picture books and children's television shows. She also began attending writers' and illustrators' conferences, eventually meeting author F. Isabel Campoy, who asked her to illustrate one of her books. This title, *Todas los Bueñas Manos*, became Morales's first book and was published specifically for the school market.

For her next book, Morales used brightly colored acrylics, handmade stamps, and computer-created cutouts to illustrate Kathleen Krull's account of the life of a great Latino leader in *Harvesting Hope: The Story of Cesar Chavez*. This book won a Christopher Award and a Jane Addams Book Award in the picture book category. It was a Pura Belpré Honor Book, an Américas Award Honorable Mention, and an ALA Notable Children's Book, as well as being cited as a Best Book of the Year by *School Library Journal*, *Book Links*, and *Child* magazine. It was also

YUYI MORALES

Courtesy of Roaring Brook Press

named to the Notable Social Studies Trade Book list, and with all this recognition, Morales's career was established.

Morales had started experimenting with puppet-making soon after her move to the United States, and this too was part of her development as a children's book writer and illustrator. Beginning 1997, she hosted a Spanish-language weekly children's storytelling radio program for KPOO of San Francisco. Drawing from myths, legends and stories of Latin America, the show ran for three years. It was this rich background in puppetry and folklore that informed her first book as both author and illustrator.

Just a Minute: A Trickster Tale and Counting Book, is the tale of a grandmother who cheats death using birthday party preparations and a counting game, teaching both Spanish and English words for the numbers. Morales enhanced the story with glowing acrylics and stylized human characterizations reminiscent of Latin American muralists. Her dry-brush technique, which involves a lot of scrubbing with the brush, softens the acrylics and gives them a chalky appearance similar to pastels. This vibrant tale won the Pura Belpré Medal for Illustration, the Américas

Award, and the Tomás Rivera Award. It was also named an ALA Notable Children's Book and received a Golden Kite Honor Book Award for Illustration. Morales's evocative illustrations enhance the spookiness of the holiday in *Los Gatos Black on Halloween*, winner of the 2008 Pura Belpré Illustrator Award and an ALA Notable Children's Book. Her own story, *Little Night*, gives a pleasantly unique twist to bedtime stories as Mother Sky tries to put her child, Little Night, to bed. Sweeping colors, changing perspectives, and a wealth of imagination make this charming goodnight story a sure winner with young readers and earned it an ALA Notable Children's Book citation. *Little Night* also won the Golden Kite award for picture book illustration.

Yuyi Morales and her family live in the San Francisco Bay area. Besides creating children's books, Morales likes dancing, especially Brazilian folk dancing. Her newest passion is gardening, and she loves to grow many kinds of plants. She also enjoys visiting schools, bringing her puppets to show children how she has honed her craft.

SELECTED WORKS ILLUSTRATED: *Harvesting Hope: The Story of Cesar Chavez*, by Kathleen Krull, 2003 (Spanish edition: *Cosechando Esperanza: La Historia de César Chávez*, translated by F. Isabel Campoy and Alma Flor Ada, 2003); *Sand Sister*, by Amanda White, 2004; *Los Gatos Black on Halloween*, by Marisa Montes, 2006.

SELECTED WORKS WRITTEN AND ILLUSTRATED: *Just a Minute: A Trickster Tale and Counting Book*, 2003; *Little Night*, 2007; *Just in Case: A Trickster Tale and Spanish Alphabet Book*, 2008.

SUGGESTED READING: *Something About the Author*, vol. 154, 2005.

WEB SITES: www.yuyimorales.com

Sal Murdocca

April 26, 1943–

"When I was in the eighth grade a teacher gave me a book about different occupations and careers. I looked up occupations for people who loved to draw and paint and that was when I discovered the word 'illustrator.' I fell in love with the word. I thought that there could be nothing better than to be called an illustrator. I decided right there that I was going to do whatever it takes to be one.

"In the ninth grade, I entered a drawing and painting contest about Halloween. After a while, my art teacher told me that, although my painting should have won, the judges decided a boy my age couldn't have done it. I had to write a letter certifying that I was the artist, but the committee did not believe me. I was disappointed, but I kept on drawing and painting because that was what I loved to do.

"When I graduated high school, I became a messenger in an art studio. I went to the Art Students League in the evenings. I continued working hard on my illustrating and began building a portfolio for job interviews. When I was nineteen, I became an illustrator for an art studio. I would stay very late after work, redoing my drawings and paintings until I thought they were right. I also listened to the advice of more experienced artists. Everything a good artist said was important to me. It still is. This was an advertising studio, so I drew all kinds of products and people doing all sorts of things. I knew an illustrator had to know a lot about many subjects, so I also read a lot. I still do and for the same reason.

Photo by Nancy Caravan

"When I was twenty-one, I began freelancing for different companies and continued freelancing until I was drafted. In the army, I kept many sketch and note books and read more than ever. One day I was in a bookstore and started looking at the children's books. I realized then that this was the kind of art I wanted to do. So, while still in the army, I began a new portfolio. This one contained pictures of things like funny animals, knights, and fairytales. Once I was a civilian again, I showed my portfolio to almost every big publisher in New York. Everyone was nice, and very encouraging, but no one gave me any assignments. So I went back to advertising illustration while I continued working on my portfolio.

"One day I got an advertising agency assignment to do an illustration of a bicycle for an airline magazine. I was happy because I love to bicycle. I had a feeling this illustration would be important and put more work into it than usual. Months later an editor from a big publisher called me. He had seen my magazine illustration while he was on an airplane and wanted to see more of my work. I was excited about finally showing my portfolio to someone who wanted to see it. The interview was successful. The editor gave me a story to illustrate. I worked hard on the

Tenth Book of Junior Authors and Illustrators 473

book, and when I delivered it he gave me another! I've been illustrating books ever since. I learned you have to do every job as though it's the most important thing in the world. Since then, I've illustrated all kinds of books and even wrote some myself.

"Although I did this for many years, I still had not illustrated the kind of fantasy stories I dreamed of doing until I was asked to illustrate a new series called 'The Magic Tree House.' These became the most interesting and challenging books I ever illustrated because of the subject, location, time, and ever-changing action of each book. I think I've become a better artist because of these challenges. I was glad I had read so widely, because the Magic Tree House books require lots of research and knowledge on many subjects. I also knew how to research the things I didn't know about. Research is hard but fun and interesting. It's also fun to know I'm among the first people to read a Magic Tree House book. And I'm the one who's going to show the world what the story will look like!

Self-portrait courtesy of Sal Murdocca

"Sometimes my research takes me to places like Venice, where I went to do research for *Carnival at Candlelight*. Among the many pleasing things about this was learning interesting facts about Tiepolo, a favorite artist of mine, and Neptune, the mythological god of the sea. This brought me back to the days when I drew pictures of various Greek gods and soldiers.

"I still keep a sketchbook. I take it with me whenever my wife and I take bicycle trips. Wherever we go, I record the place with a little painting in my sketchbook. I have filled many sketchbooks and they are better than photos for evoking my traveling memories. Sometimes I do larger versions of my sketchbook paintings for art gallery shows. It's always nice when someone likes your painting enough to buy it. Most of the little paintings I do are in color but sometimes, like the old masters, I work in sepia tones. I also still like to read, especially history and poetry. But fairytales and myths remain my favorites."

ભ   ભ   ભ

Born in Brooklyn, New York, Salvatore Murdocca grew up outside the Coney Island amusement park. He attended the High School of Art and Design in New York City, and his last two years there were spent majoring in illustration.

In addition to writing and illustrating children's books, Murdocca has written an operetta for children and made three films: a documentary about his travels through Italy, a fake documentary about a nonexistent artist, and a short film about his travel paintings from 1992 to 2007. *Tuttle's Shell*, a book Murdocca wrote as well as illustrated, was a Junior Literary Guild Selection in 1976. He has illustrated books by such noted authors as Eve Bunting and Bill Martin, Jr., and has worked on several series, including George E. Stanley's fast-paced Ready-for-Chapters: Third Grade Detectives series, in which characters ingeniously solve mysteries using science and secret codes.

Murdocca is best known as the illustrator of the highly popular Magic Tree House series written by Mary Pope Osborne. Noted for the suspenseful adventures of two children named Jack and Annie these stories combine history, mystery, fantasy and magic. They are very popular with young readers and are especially appreciated by teachers as books that appeal to students moving from easy readers to chapter books. Each title features a particular adventure for the children as they travel magically through time and space. Illustrated in black and white, the second book in the series, *The Knight at Dawn*, which was included on the 1994 Massachusetts Children's Book Master List, finds Annie wishing to see a knight, whereupon she and Jack are magically transported back in time to a castle in the Middle Ages. They learn about such things as medieval feasts and armor before being imprisoned in a dungeon and rescued by a knight.

In *High Tide in Hawaii*, a 2007 Ohio Buckeye Children's Book Award nominee, the Magic Tree House takes Annie and Jack to Hawaii, where they learn about Hawaiian culture and history while saving an island community from a tsunami. In *Summer of the Sea Serpent*, a 2008 Colorado Children's Book Award nominee and a *Publishers Weekly* Bestselling Children's Book, the pair must go to a foggy seacoast and secure the future of Camelot by retrieving the Sword of Light from a sea serpent who stands guard over it. Another *PW* Bestselling Children's Book, *Winter of the Ice Wizard*, features a clever introduction to the subject of northern myths and legends when the children must help an ice wizard in order to find their missing friends. Jack and Annie

"I was glad I had read so widely, because the Magic Tree House books require lots of research and knowledge on many subjects."

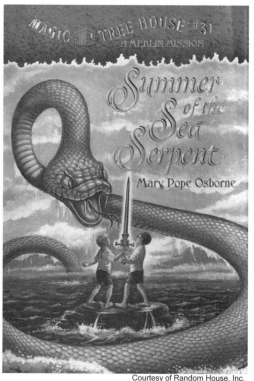

Courtesy of Random House, Inc.

go back in time to Depression-era New York City in *Blizzard of the Blue Moon*, where, in the midst of a snowstorm, they explore Central Park, the subway system, and the Metropolitan Museum's Cloisters, all while trying to save a unicorn. *Blizzard of the Blue Moon* was included on *Publishers Weekly's* Children's Hardcover bestselling titles, as was *Night of the New Magicians*. In the latter title, Annie and Jack are transported to the 1889 World's Fair in Paris to give urgent messages to four magicians before an evil sorcerer gets to them. Biographies of the "magicians"—Alexander Graham Bell, Thomas Edison, Louis Pasteur, and Gustave Eiffel—are included in the tale.

In 2007 a stage adaptation of the books, *Magic Tree House: The Musical*, had its world premiere at the historic Warner Theatre in Torrington, Connecticut. The artist continues to illustrate upcoming titles in the series and to imagine what Jack and Annie's world looks like, even those parts that don't make it to the pages of the books.

Sal Murdocca and his wife, Nancy, who is also an artist, have two grown daughters, Michelle and Jennifer, and three grandchildren who live in California. Michelle is a film producer for Sony Pictures Animation and Jennifer is a psychotherapist. Murdocca and his wife divide their time between their home in New City, New York, and their house in the south of France. After falling in love with the Languedoc region on a bicycle trip in 2000, they later bought a house in the ancient part of a little town called Olonzac, about a mile from the Canal du Midi. Sal's landscapes of the region and some portraits of his wife were included in an exhibit and cultural event there in the summer of 2007.

SELECTED WORKS ILLUSTRATED: *Archimedes Takes a Bath*, by Joan M. Lexau, 1969; *The Wizard*, by Bill Martin, Jr., 1970; *The Maestro Plays*, by Bill Martin, Jr., 1970; *Poor Old Uncle Sam*, by Bill Martin, Jr., 1970; *Have You Seen Wilhelmina Krumpf?*, by Judith Chasek, 1973; *Big Cheese*, by Eve Bunting, 1977; *Strawberry Book of Questions and Answers*, by Anita Malnig, 1977; *Oscar the Grouch's Alphabet of Trash*, by Jeffrey Moss, 1977; *Bean Boy*, by Joan C. Bowden, 1979; *Monday I Was an Alligator*, by Susan Pearson, 1979; *Encyclopedia Brown's Record Book of Weird and Wonderful Facts*, by Donald J. Sobol, 1979; *Big Strawberry Book of Astronomy*, by Jeanne Bendick, 1979; *1000 Monsters*, by Alan Benjamin, 1979; *1000 Space Monsters Have Landed*, by Alan Benjamin, 1980; *1000 Inventions*, by Alan Benjamin, 1980; *First Number Book*, by Shari Robinson, 1981; *Secret Life of Toys*, by Rita G. Austin, 1983; *Everything You Need to Survive: Brothers and Sisters*, by Jane Stine and Jovial Bob Stine, 1983; *Everything You Need to Survive: First Dates*, by Jane Stine and Jovial Bob Stine, 1983; *Everything You Need to Survive: Homework*, by Jane Stine and Jovial Bob Stine, 1983; *Everything You Need to Survive: Money*, by Jane Stine and Jovial Bob Stine, 1983; *Cats to Count*, by Mildred Phillips, 1984; *Tom the TV Cat*, by Joan Heilbroner, 1984; *Encyclopedia Brown's Third Record Book of Weird and Wonderful Facts*, by Donald J. Sobol, 1985; *Worthington Botts and the Steam Engine*, by Betty Baker, 1987; *Pan, Pan, Gran Pan: Big Book*, by Ina Cumpiano, 1990; *Pan, Pan, Gran Pan: Small Book*, by Ina Cumpiano, 1992; *Hallowhat*, by Alan Benjamin, 1992; *Let's Count, Dracula: A Chubby Board Book*, by Alan Benjamin, 1992; *Eureka! It's an Automobile!*, by Jeanne Bendick, 1992; *Eureka! It's a Telephone!*, by Jeanne Bendick, 1993; *Eureka! It's a Television!*, by Jeanne Bendick, 1993; *Freddie the Fly*, by Charles Grodin, 1993; *Eureka! It's an Airplane!*, by Jeanne Bendick, 1994; *Words Around the Year*, by Roy Doty, 1994; *1000 Silly Sandwiches*, by Alan Benjamin, 1995; *Monsters' Test*, by Brian J. Heinz, 1996; *Double Trouble in Walla Walla*, by Andrew Clements, 1997; *The Landry News*, by Andrew Clements, 1999; *A Pig Tale*, by Olivia Newton-John and Brian Seth Hurst, 1999; *Two for Stew*, by Laura Numeroff and Barney Saltzberg, 1999; *Big Numbers and Pictures That Show Just How Big They Are!*, by Edward Packard, 2000; *Little Numbers and Pictures that Show Just How Little They Are*, by Edward Packard, 2001; *Smushy Bus*, by Leslie Helakoski, 2002; *Dancing Granny*, by Elizabeth Winthrop and Maurice Burton, 2003.

SELECTED WORKS WRITTEN AND ILLUSTRATED: *The Boy Who Was a Raccoon*, 1974; *Tuttle's Shell*, 1976 (new ed., 1999); *Take Me to the Moon*, 1976; *Grover's Own Alphabet*, 1978; *The Hero of Hamblett*, 1980; *Sir Hamm and the Golden Sundial*, 1982; *Video Cat*, 1983; *The Visitor*, 1983; *The Nothing*, 1985; *Christmas Bear*, 1987; *Baby Wants the Moon*, 1995; *Lucy Takes a Holiday*, 1998.

SELECTED SERIES ILLUSTRATED: Magic Tree House series, all written by Mary Pope Osborne—*Dinosaurs Before Dark*, 1992; *The Knight at Dawn*, 1993; *Mummies in the Morning*, 1993; *Pirates Past Noon*, 1994; *Night of the Ninjas*, 1995; *Afternoon on the Amazon*, 1995; *Sunset of the Sabertooth*, 1996; *Midnight on the Moon*, 1996; *Dolphins at Daybreak*, 1997; *Ghost Town at Sundown*, 1997; *Lions at Lunchtime*, 1998; *Polar Bears Past Bedtime*, 1998; *Vacation Under the Volcano*, 1998; *Day of the Dragon King*, 1998; *Viking Ships at Sunrise*, 1998; *Hour of the Olympics*, 1998; *Tonight on the Titanic*, 1999; *Buffalo Before Breakfast*, 1999; *Tigers at Twilight*, 1999; *Dingoes at Dinnertime*, 2000; *Civil War on Sunday*, 2000; *Knights and Castles: A Nonfiction Companion to The Knight at Dawn* (with Will Osborne), 2000; *Dinosaurs: A Nonfiction Companion to Dinosaurs Before Dark* (with Will Osborne), 2000; *Revolutionary War on Wednesday*, 2000; *Mummies and Pyramids: A Nonfiction Companion to Mummies in the Morning* (with Will Osborne), 2001; *Twister on Tuesday*, 2001; *Pirates: A Nonfiction Companion to Pirates Past Noon* (with Will Osborne), 2001; *Earthquake in the Early Morning*, 2001; *Rainforests: A Nonfiction Companion to Afternoon on the Amazon*, (with Will Osborne), 2001; *Christmas in Camelot*, 2001; *Stage Fright on a Summer Night*, 2002; *Good Morning, Gorillas*, 2002; *Thanksgiving on Thursday*, 2002; *Space: A Nonfiction Companion to Midnight on the Moon* (with Will Osborne), 2002; *Titanic: A Nonfiction Companion to Tonight on the Titanic* (with Will Osborne), 2002; *Twisters and Other Terrible Storms: A Nonfiction Companion to Twister on Tuesday* (with Will Osborne), 2003; *High Tide in Hawaii*, 2003; *Haunted Castle on Hallow's Eve*, 2003; *Dolphins and Sharks: A Nonfiction Companion to Dolphins at Daybreak*, (with Natalie Pope Boyce), 2003; *Summer of the Sea Serpent*, 2004; *Magic Tree House Research Guide: Ancient Greece and the Olympics* (with Natalie Pope Boyce), 2004; *American Revolution: A Companion to the Revolutionary War on Wednesday* (with Natalie Pope Boyce), 2004; *Winter of the Ice Wizard*, 2004; *Pilgrims: A Nonfiction Companion to Thanksgiving on Thursday* (with Natalie Pope Boyce), 2005; *Sabertooths and the Ice Age: A Nonfiction Companion to The Sabertooth*, (with Natalie Pope Boyce), 2005; *Carnival at Candlelight*, 2005; *Season of the Sandstorms*, 2005; *Night of the New Magicians*, 2006; *Blizzard of the Blue Moon*, 2006; *Dragon of the Red Dawn*, 2007; *Monday with a Mad Genius*, 2007; *Polar Bears and the Arctic: A Nonfiction Companion to Polar Bears Past Midnight* (with Natalie Pope Boyce), 2007; *Tsunamis and Other Natural Disasters* (with Natalie Pope Boyce), 2007; *Dark Day in the*

Deep Sea, 2008; *Sea Monsters: A Nonfiction Companion to Dark Day in the Deep Sea* (with Natalie Pope Boyce), 2008; *Eve of the Emperor Penguin*, 2008. "Third Grade Detectives" series, all written by George E. Stanley—*Bugs for Breakfast*, 1996; *Mrs. O'Dell's Third Grade Class Is Shrinking*, 1996; *The Day the Ants Got Really Mad*, 1996; *There's a Shark in the Swimming Pool!*, 1996; *A Werewolf Followed Me Home*, 1997; *Who Invited Aliens to My Slumber Party?*, 1997; *Vampire Kittens of Count Dracula*, 1997; *The New Kid in School is a Vampire Bat*, 1997; *The Clue of the Left-Handed Envelope*, 2000; *The Puzzle of the Pretty Pink Handkerchief*, 2000; *The Cobweb Confession*, 2001; *The Mystery of the Hairy Tomatoes*, 2001; *The Case of the Dirty Clue*, 2003; *The Secret of the Green Skin*, 2003; *The Riddle of the Stolen Sand*, 2003; *The Mystery of the Stolen Statue*, 2004; *The Secret of the Wooden Witness*, 2004.

Vaunda Micheaux Nelson

October 10, 1953–

"I'm a writer and a librarian. Everything I do seems to find its way back to books and language. Because I am in the world of children's books, some people may think I live in a fantasyland of wishes granted and happy endings. Perhaps I do. I only know that I find more truth in children's literature than anywhere else.

"My parents brought books into my life on the day I was born; my mother found my name in a novel she was reading. I grew up, the youngest of five, in Elizabeth, Pennsylvania, a small town near Pittsburgh. I'm one of those lucky people who can say they had a happy childhood. My parents read to us daily, they were there when we needed them, and there was never a time when I didn't feel their affection.

"My love of books began with bedtime, which was story time for us. Mommy read favorites like *Uncle Wiggily*, *Tom Sawyer* and *The Bobbsey Twins*. Daddy recited story poems from memory like Whitman's 'O Captain! My Captain!' and 'Paul Revere's Ride' by Longfellow. He read from Langston Hughes and other poets, too. And he shared poetry he'd written himself, though he didn't tell us it was his until much later.

"One of my favorite poems then was 'Little Orphant Annie' by James Whitcomb Riley. Dad—in his deepest baritone (which was very deep)—would scare us to death when he'd say, 'An' the gobble-uns'll gitcha . . . Ef ya don't watch out!' Then he'd say, 'Now, go to sleep,' and we'd beg him to tell us a funny one to wash away the fear.

"I loved these magic times—loved what the stories made me imagine and feel. I found myself wanting to be able to do that, to create stories for *other* people to love.

"Mom got us library cards and twice a month took us to the bookmobile. (Our small town had no library.) Thankfully our parents kept reading to us long after we could read on our own. I am lucky that they loved literature and made it an important part of our lives. *They* planted the seeds for my writing life. They taught me the power of language, power that I carry with me everywhere. I started writing poetry and short stories when I was 11 or 12. A serious Beatles fan, I also wrote song lyrics and learned to play the guitar. I was never a great musician, but I believe these efforts added an important dimension to my artistic life.

Courtesy of Drew Nelson

"I studied journalism and English in college, and though I spent some years as a newspaper reporter, I ultimately found my passion in literature. Eventually, that passion carried me to library school.

"Now I find that my reading life and my writing life cannot be separated. I rely on both to keep me centered. As a writer and a librarian, I hope to provide readers with some of what my parents gave me—the opportunity to grow through story. Readers sometimes ask if my stories are true. Much of my writing grows from personal experience. But it's not so much a matter of relating something that happened to me; it's more about facing the questions I *still* have and trying to find answers. What are, I wonder, the possibilities of the human heart?

"I write for children, but I write for *myself* first. Writing is my way of sorting things out. It helps me to see how I fit into the big picture of life. My view of the world is largely determined by language, the language I use to define my experiences—not just on paper. It is language that empowers me to find answers and, hopefully, to grow. I believe that's part of the reason we're here—to keep rewriting the scene again and again, revising, until we get it right. What's great about the writing process is I don't have to figure things out all by myself; my characters help.

"Through reading and writing, I believe we can discover what we know and believe in. We can find ways of coping with difficulties in private, non-threatening ways. We can make connections that help us to understand ourselves and others. We can become better people."

ଔ   ଔ   ଔ

Growing up in an environment surrounded by books, Vaunda Micheaux, Nelson seemed destined to spend her life reading and writing. She received a B.A. degree in English from Point Park College (now Point Park University) in Pittsburgh, Pennsylvania in 1975, having spent one semester of study in Lugano, Switzerland. After obtaining a teaching certificate from Clarion State College (now Clarion University of Pennsylvania) in 1977, Nelson taught writing courses at the University of Pittsburgh and Chatham College, and spent a short time as a high school English teacher. During that time she earned a master's degree in 1980 from the Bread Loaf School of English at Middlebury College, which included two semesters of study at Oxford University in England. She then tried her hand at journalism as a staff reporter for the McKeesport, Pennsylvania, *Daily News* for three years. In 1983 she married Drew Nelson, a writer.

A lifelong interest in literature for children led Vaunda Nelson to work in Pinocchio, a children's bookstore in Pittsburgh. While employed at the store, from 1984 to 1987, she edited a monthly newsletter and worked in all aspects of bookselling, including planning book fairs and aiding school librarians in their selections. This work persuaded her to pursue a master's degree in library science at the University of Pittsburgh, which she received in 1988. After a year working in the children's room of the Carnegie Library of Pittsburgh, Nelson moved on to become school librarian at Shadyside Academy, where she shared her love of literature and research with students in grades K–5 and started a newsletter of student writing.

In 1994 Nelson and her husband moved to Rio Rancho, New Mexico, where she has worked as a youth services librarian in the public library and has taken an active part in training sessions and conferences for the New Mexico Library Association. In 2006 she received the Sagebrush Award from the Young Adult Library Services Association of the American Library Association for an innovative young adult summer reading program.

Nelson's writing career took off the same year she became a librarian. Her picture book, *Always Gramma,* was named a

"I loved these magic times— loved what the stories made me imagine and feel. I found myself wanting to be able to do that, to create stories for other people to love."

Notable Children's Trade Book in the Field of Social Studies. The story, which depicts a little girl's gentle love for her grandmother whose failing memory has made it necessary for her to move into a nursing home, shows how family bonds can be reinforced in difficult circumstances. Nelson's first novel, *Mayfield Crossing*, about racial tensions in an elementary school in 1960, won the Georgia Children's Book Award and was also cited as a Notable Trade Book in the Field of Social Studies. *Beyond Mayfield*, which received a Parents' Choice Gold Award, enlarges on the events of the Civil Rights Movement by describing how one of the citizens of the small Pennsylvania town goes south to help register black voters and dies under suspicious circumstances.

Courtesy of Carolrhoda/Lerner Books

Reaching farther back into African American history, Nelson wrote a powerfully evocative picture book story of the Underground Railroad, *Almost to Freedom*. Told from the point of view of a child's beloved rag doll, left behind inadvertently when the family must flee their hiding place in the middle of the night, the story is enhanced by atmospheric paintings by Colin Bootman. The illustrator won a Coretta Scott King Honor award for this book. By telling the story from the perspective of the doll (who later comforts another girl escaping from slavery), Nelson poignantly emphasizes the stark losses and painful fears of that dark era of American history.

Turning to the lighter side of life, *Ready? Set. Raymond!* is a book for beginning readers about a little boy who likes to do everything *fast*. Co-authored with her husband, Drew, Nelson wrote another book for emerging readers entitled *Juneteenth*, about the holiday that celebrates June 19, 1865, the day that the news of Emancipation finally reached Texas.

Vaunda Nelson has been honored with a Distinguished Alumnus Award from Point Park College in 2001, was named one of the New Mexico Women Who Have Changed America in 2005, and received an Honorary Doctorate of Humane Letters from Point Park University in 2006. Active in the American Library Association, she has twice served on the Newbery committee. Currently the author is youth services librarian at the public library in Rio Rancho, New Mexico, where she lives with her husband, Drew, a freelance writer, and their two cats, Charlie and Punk.

SELECTED WORKS: *Always Gramma*, illus. by Kimanne Uhler 1988; *Mayfield Crossing*, 1993; *Possibles*, 1995; *Beyond Mayfield*, 1999; *Ready? Set. Raymond!*, illus. by Derek Anderson, 2002; *Almost to Freedom*, illus. by Colin Bootman, 2003; *Juneteenth*, with Drew Nelson, illus. by Mark Schroder, 2006; *Bad News for Outlaws: The Remarkable Life of Bass Reeves, Deputy U.S. Marshal*, illus. by Tyrone Geter, 2008.

"**W**hen I was little my father was mostly away from home. He was a doctor who specialised in tropical diseases, and his main work was with lepers in Nigeria. So it was my mother who filled my world. She loved books more than anything, and she read stories to my sister and me every evening. So of course I grew up loving books and believing that writers were the most admired beings of all. I was an unusually pushy little boy, nicknamed 'Me-First' because that was my constant cry, and naturally I aspired to win the biggest prizes. That meant, in our home, being a writer. I don't think I had any natural talent for writing, but I had ambition and determination. All through my childhood I wrote and wrote. My mother rewarded me with lavish praise, but I don't think I was any better than my classmates. I just had this engine in me that wouldn't stop.

Photo by John Timbers

William Nicholson

January 12, 1948–

"One day it struck me like a thunderbolt that my mother might be wrong. Perhaps her praise came from her love for me, not from my talent. Perhaps I wasn't a born writer after all. This was a devastating thought. If I wasn't a writer, what was I? I'd gone too far to stop now. At this point one of my teachers called me out in front of the class to read out a short piece I had written. I'd taken a big risk with this piece and written it from the point of view of a man watching his own execution. My teacher told the class my work was original, and that originality was rare and precious. That praise was crucial to me. It gave me the courage to believe in my own creative powers. All writers face a daily struggle with self-doubt. You hunger for a very particular kind of praise: not that you're clever, or that you've done what you were asked to do, but that the strange secret visions you find inside yourself make sense to other people, and have some value to someone outside yourself.

"So on I plodded, writing, writing. I wrote whole books, which no one wanted. I went to university, wrote for the college newspaper, attracted the attention of a literary agent, wrote more books; and still I got nowhere. I had to make a living somehow, so I went into television journalism, but every morning I got up early and wrote my books. Eight of them, over fifteen years: all rejected, and rightly so. I was trying too hard, and I wasn't good enough at plots and characters, and I just didn't know enough. But I was learning. Why did I go on? I think I'd got the habit by then, and couldn't stop. Also I love writing. It's about more than writing, somehow. It's the way I get to know myself and what I feel and what matters to me. It's my pursuit of wisdom. It's an unending journey, and I don't want it to stop.

> *"It's about more than writing, somehow. It's the way I get to know myself and what I feel and what matters to me. It's my pursuit of wisdom. It's an unending journey, and I don't want it to stop."*

"Anyway, after so many years of failure I took a sidetrack into writing plays for television, where I was working, and to my great surprise my work was accepted. It was produced—and praised. Suddenly I was a screenwriter. When I look back I think all those failed novels weren't wasted. I was learning craft, and humility, and discipline. But now I was launched into the world of television; and from there I went on to stage plays, then movies. I was earning enough by my writing to quit the day job at the age of 39—twenty years later than planned. My film work was hard but successful. I had reason to be proud, but secretly I knew I wouldn't be a real writer until I wrote books. So as soon as I could steal the time from screen work I crept away and wrote a book. By now I was older, wiser, more skilled at the craft, and the book came out well. That was *The Wind Singer*.

"Now I write books more than movies, and that's the way I like it. Books are so much more powerful, and personal, and special. Also I can stay home with my wife and children, who I love more than myself; so maybe at last I'm growing out of being 'Me-First.' As for my mother, she's now almost ninety, and lives round the corner in a tiny cottage packed with books. She thinks I haven't done my best work yet, and I agree."

ოჳ ოჳ ოჳ

William Nicholson grew up straddling worlds. Raised primarily in Sussex and Gloucestershire in England, he spent much of his early years in Nigeria where his father, a doctor who specialized in tropical medicine, worked to eradicate leprosy. Both his father, the son of a Methodist minister, and his mother, a South African Jew, converted to Roman Catholicism when William was seven years old. He was baptized into his parents' new faith at a leper colony when he was eight. Nicholson's Christian faith would shape much of his interior life and morality in the years to come, especially during his time living in the town of Seaford, on the south coast of England, studying under the Dominicans. At 13 he attended Downside School, where he continued his education with the order of the Benedictines. He studied under these religious orders during an era of intellectual and spiritual renewal for the Catholic Church, following in the wake of the Second Vatican Council, which modernized many of the church's traditional practices.

Before attending Christ's College at Cambridge University, Nicholson spent a year as a Volunteer Service Overseas teacher in British Honduras (now the independent nation of Belize) in Central America. Between the time he started his undergraduate degree and the year he received his diploma, he lost his faith in the church, but his love of literature only increased through his studies. While at Cambridge he wrote his first novels with the hope of selling them someday. However, upon graduation in 1970, he received a job offer from the BBC as a General Trainee—a means by which he could make a living while pursuing his literary passions.

During his years at the BBC he woke at six in the morning and wrote for two hours before heading to work. While none of these books was ever published, he did begin to receive some favorable praise: a story was published in *Encounter* magazine, a play was accepted and broadcast on BBC Radio 4, and he won first prize in a writing competition for the *Spectator*. Throughout those years he wrote for television documentaries, which took him on travels to various parts of the world. In 1979 he published his first adult novel, *The Seventh Level*, which while not a commercial hit, helped to boost his confidence after years of rejection. More importantly, it led him into scriptwriting and a first true commercial success. His second television script, *Shadowlands*, based on the relationship between C. S. Lewis and Joy Gresham, was a major award winner in 1985 and was later turned into a successful stage play and film. The play received the *Evening Standard* Best Play award in 1990; and the film version earned Nicholson an Oscar nomination for Best Adapted Screenplay in 1993. After the success of *Shadowlands*, Nicholson spent some years working on film scripts for Hollywood; notable among these screenplays are *Nell*, which starred Jodie Foster; *First Knight*, with Sean Connery; and *Gladiator*, which won the Oscar for Best Picture and earned Nicholson a nomination for Best Screenplay. He both wrote and directed the film *Firelight* in 1997.

Though screenwriting proved to be lucrative, Nicholson returned to his first love, writing novels. Having mastered storytelling techniques and dialogue in his work in Hollywood, he decided that he would write a children's book. The result was a remarkable fantasy novel, *The Wind Singer*. Kestrel and her twin brother Bowman are rebelling against the rigid examinations that control every citizen's life inside the walled city of Aramanth, in this story of innocence overcoming the abuse of power. Their flight from that repressive life became the first adventure in the Wind on Fire trilogy, a story that continued with *Slaves of the Mastery* and *Firesong*. These books have proven immensely successful, selling well in many parts of the world. *The Wind Singer* won the Smarties Gold Award in the ages 9–11 category and the Blue Peter Book of the Year Award in England. Both *The Wind Singer* and *Slaves of the Mastery* were named Notable Children's Books by the American Library Association.

Courtesy of Hyperion Books for Children

Nicholson's The Noble Warriors trilogy began in 2005 with *Seeker*, which takes place on the rocky island of Anacrea where three young heroes, Seeker, Morning Star, and the Wildman, meet on their quest to be chosen to enter the Nom, the castle-monastery where warrior-monks live with the All and Only, the god who made their world. Their adventures continue in *Jango*, where, having been allowed entrance into the Nom, the three friends learn that life there is not what they expected. Nicholson considers the third volume of this trilogy, *Noman*, his most important work to date.

In addition to his children's books, Nicholson has also published two adult novels: *The Society of Others* and *The Trial of True Love*. He lives with his wife and three children in Sussex, England.

SELECTED WORKS FOR YOUNG READERS: Wind on Fire series—*The Wind Singer*, 2000; *Slaves of the Mastery*, 2001; Firesong, 2002. The Noble Warriors series—*Seeker*, 2005 (U.S. 2006); *Jango*, 2005 (U.S. 2007); *Noman*, 2007 (U.S. 2008).

SELECTED WORKS FOR ADULTS: *The Seventh Level*, 1979; *The Society of Others*, 2004; *The Trial of True Love*, 2005.

SUGGESTED READING: Interview, at www.bbc.co.uk/wales/mid/ sites/hay/pages/bp_williamnicolson.shtml

WEB SITE: www.williamnicholson.co.uk

"There are two important influences in my writing life. The most obvious is my early childhood experience. I grew up in Texas as a young child, between the ages of five and twelve years old. We lived in a very small ranching community in south Texas called Falfurrias. Instead of spending my childhood with my head in a book, I spent it outdoors, roaming the countryside, hunting, fishing, riding horses, and the like. It is no wonder then that a good handful of my books focus on nature (*Night Is Coming*, *Storm*, *Till Year's Good End*, *Summer Sun Risin'*).

"The other important set of experiences in my life came at a later date: out of college, I became a teacher and taught primary grades for seven years. It was here that I really began to take notice of books. I had to; my students always wanted me to read to them, and, of course, I would oblige. Not only did I read books to my students, but I also used them as the central focus for our theme-based studies.

"At the end of the seven years, I knew that I wanted to continue to teach, but I also wanted more time to write. So I went back to college, obtained a doctorate in reading and language arts, and set off into the world to find a faculty position in education. I landed a job with National-Louis University in 1986 and have remained there ever since. I love the Chicago area, and I really enjoy working with graduate students. I work in an off-campus

Photo by Barbara Cooper

W. Nikola-Lisa

W. Nikola-Lisa

June 15, 1951–

cohort program, which means that I stay with the same group of teachers, usually 15–18 students, for close to two years as we study the current best practices in education.

"In the two decades I've been at National, I've continued to write, publishing works both for young readers and for professionals in the field of education. But my real love lies in storytelling. I have only recently realized that the most gratifying experiences I have don't involve publishing or writing, but rather sharing stories with an audience. I thrive on the live-performance nature of my appearances in schools and libraries. Over the years, I've developed a repertoire of stories, based on my own writing and that of other authors. For instance, I tell Charles Shaw's *It Looked Like Spilt Milk* using a scarf that I throw into the air for each named object. I sing Bill Martin's *Brown Bear, Brown Bear, What Do You See?* using a blues harmonica for accompaniment, and I tell Leo Lionni's *Inch By Inch* using a lime green glove to signify the main character of the story, a tiny inchworm.

"When I combine all of these aspects of my life together—teaching, writing, and storytelling—it is a very full and rich life. What I realize is that each of these three areas taps a strength in my intellectual and creative life: the ability to think on my feet and improvise, using a story—either made-up or borrowed—as the main form of communication with the intent of both informing and entertaining those around me."

> *"Instead of spending my childhood with my head in a book, I spent it outdoors, roaming the countryside, hunting, fishing, riding horses, and the like."*

○3　○3　○3

W. Nikola-Lisa earned a B.A. in comparative religion in 1974 and his master's degree in education in 1976 from the University of Florida. His career in the field of education began in Bozeman, Montana, where he taught at the World Family School from 1976 to 1978, and then at Irving Elementary School from 1978 to 1982. He received his doctorate in education from Montana State University in 1986.

Nikola-Lisa's first picture book was published in 1991. Inspired by his own Texas childhood, *Night Is Coming* describes the approach of nightfall on a family farm. Another of his early picture books joyfully highlights in lilting language the similarities between all people, no matter how different they may appear to be. *Bein' with You This Way* was named a Jane Addams Honor Book and chosen for the Anti-Defamation League's "Close the Book on Hate" Reading List. A Parents' Choice and a *Parenting* magazine Reading Magic Award book, it was among *Child* magazine's Best Books, American Booksellers "Pick of the Lists," and featured on *Good Morning America*. Both *Bein' with You This Way* and a book that offers a historical look at the Middle Ages, *Till Year's Good End: A Calendar of Medieval Labors*, were selected as CCBC Choices.

The source of many themes in Nikola-Lisa's books is his memory of uncomfortable scenes during his Southern childhood in the mid–20th century, a time when derogatory words and actions and negative stereotypes were commonplace. Facing these experiences from the past has led this author to develop ways to counteract prejudice in the books he writes. *How We Are Smart*, which won a Christopher Award, is a thought-provoking poetic exploration of how men and women of various ethnic and racial backgrounds make smart choices in their lives. From his educational background, the author adapted Howard Gardener's theory of multiple intelligences to apply to the subjects in his book.

Summer Sun Risin', about an African American boy who works on the family farm from sunrise to sunset, is another title that springs from Nikola-Lisa's Southern roots. It was among the Bank Street College Best Children's Books of the Year and the National Christian School Association's Children's Crown Gallery Award nominees. Reflecting the author's interest in the arts, *The Year With Grandma Moses* lyrically introduces children to that remarkable painter's work and was also named a Children's Crown Gallery Award nominee.

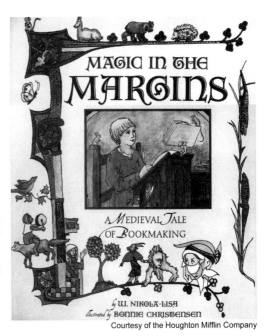

Courtesy of the Houghton Mifflin Company

In a departure from his multicultural books, *Shake Dem Halloween Bones*, winner of the Wisconsin Golden Archer Award, is an imaginative and fanciful rhyming story about fairytale characters hip-hopping at a Halloween Ball. Reflecting his interest in medieval studies, Nikola-Lisa's book *Magic in the Margins* is about an orphan boy learning both the art of bookmaking and patience as he tries to earn a place in a monastery's scriptorium. With evocative illustrations by Bonnie Christensen, this book represents the struggle all children face to find their place in the world.

As an educator and advocate for children's literature, Nikola-Lisa has written articles for periodicals such as the *Horn Book*, *Language Arts*, and the *New Advocate*. Married to sculptor

Barbara Cooper, he lives in Chicago. He has two children, Ylla and Larissa.

SELECTED WORKS: *Night Is Coming*, illus. by Jamichael Henterly, 1991; *1, 2, 3 Thanksgiving!*, illus. by Robin Kramer, 1991; *Storm*, illus. by Michael Hays, 1993; *Bein' with You This Way*, illus. by Michael Bryant, 1994; *Wheels Go Round*, illus. by Jane Conteh-Morgan, 1994; *No Babies Asleep*, illus. by Peter W. Palagonia, 1995; *One Hole in the Road*, illus. by Dan Yaccarino, 1996; *Tangletalk*, illus. by Jessica Clark, 1997; *Till Year's Good End: A Calendar of Medieval Labors*, illus. by Christopher Manson, 1997; *America: My Land, Your Land, Our Land*, 1997; *The Year with Grandma Moses*, 2000; *Shake Dem Halloween Bones*, illus. by Mike Reed, 2000; *Can You Top That?*, illus. by Hector Viveros Lee, 2000; *Hallelujah!: A Christmas Celebration*, illus. by Synthia Saint James, 2000; *America: A Book of Opposites / Un Libro de Contrarios*, 2001; *Summer Sun Risin'*, illus. by Don Tate, 2002; *To Hear the Angels Sing: A Christmas Poem*, illus. by Jill Weber, 2002; *Setting the Turkeys Free*, illus. by Ken Wilson-Max, 2004; *My Teacher Can Teach—Anyone!*, illus. by Felipe Galindo, 2004; *How We Are Smart*, illus. by Sean Qualls, 2006; *Magic in the Margins: A Medieval Tale of Bookmaking*, illus. by Bonnie Christensen, 2007.

SUGGESTED READING: *Something About the Author*, vol. 71, 1993. Periodicals—"'Around My Table' Is Not Always Enough: A Response to Jacqueline Woodson," *Horn Book*, May-June 1998; Online—"Someone You Should Know," *Prairie Wind*: Newsletter of the SCBWI Illinois Chapter, Autumn 2007, at www.intelligentlight.com/PrairieWind/?p=191#more-191

WEB SITE: www.nikolabooks.com

Garth Nix

1963–

Garth Nix was born in Melbourne, Australia to a scientist father and a mother who was an artist. Perhaps he was destined to become a fantasy writer, for Nix's mother was reading Tolkien's the Lord of the Rings trilogy when she was pregnant with him, and Nix has suggested he may have absorbed this masterwork of fantasy *in utero*. Along with one older and one younger brother, Nix went to school in Canberra. A self-described bookworm, he grew up surrounded by books and remembers reading Ursula K. Le Guin, Robert A. Heinlein, Isaac Asimov and Madeleine L'Engle at a young age. He did well in school, and left Australia at age 19 to drive around Great Britain with a load of books and a typewriter. Back home, he obtained a B.A. in professional writing from the University of Canberra in 1986.

Nix's first published story, "Sam, Cars and the Cuckoo," convinced him he could eventually become a professional writer. His self-published parodies of easy readers, the Very Clever Baby books, started as presents for expectant friends. His first fantasy novel, *The Ragwitch*, was started while he was working on his degree and brought his earliest literary recognition, when it was named a Notable Children's Book by Australia's Children's Book Council.

During this time Nix spent six months working in a bookshop, then turned to a career in publishing, working first in sales, then publicity, and finally as a senior editor in 1991. He also served in the Australian Army Reserve one weekend a month for four years. From 1994 to 1997 he worked as a public relations and marketing consultant. During a year of working exclusively as a professional writer in 1998, Nix did some traveling in Eastern Europe, the Middle East, and Asia. In 1999 he joined Curtis Brown Australia as a part-time literary agent. He has been a full-time author since January 2002.

Courtesy of Scholastic, Inc.

The novel that launched Nix's reputation as one of today's top fantasy writers, *Sabriel*, received the Australian Aurealis Award for Excellence in Australian Speculative Fiction in 1995 and became the first book in the Old Kingdom/Abhorsen series. Creating a world populated by both the living and the dead, Nix explores how good triumphs over evil in this series. The plot follows first Sabriel and then Lirael on their respective journeys to bind evil spirits and save the Old Kingdom from a horror that could end all life. The imaginative details, fully realized characters, and heart-stopping action in this series have earned these volumes many devoted readers and much critical acclaim.

Sabriel was the first of Nix's novels to receive notice in the United States. Besides being named an ALA Notable Children's Book, it was listed among the New York Public Library's Books for the Teen Age and *VOYA's* Books in the Middle: Outstanding Titles. The second book in the series, *Lirael*, was shortlisted for the Aurealis Award and received the Adelaide Festival Award for Children's Literature, one of Australia's most competitive literary awards. It won the South Australian Festival National Award for Literature in the Children's Section as well as the West Australian Young Reader's Book Award. *Sabriel* and *Lirael* were both named ALA Best Books for Young Adults. *Abhorsen* completed the trilogy, and all three books are in the process of being adapted as full-color graphic novels; Nix himself is writing the texts.

Shade's Children, also named an ALA Best Book for Young Adults, is set in a future time when evil aliens have destroyed everyone over the age of fourteen. This title, which was among VOYA's Books in the Middle: Outstanding Titles, was also shortlisted for the Aurealis Award in Australia. In The Seventh Tower series, Nix creates a world that is totally dark (literally), and follows a boy's quest for the Sunstones, which he must find to save his family and his own future. Popular with middle graders and older readers alike, this series was on the *Publishers Weekly* children's bestseller lists in 2001.

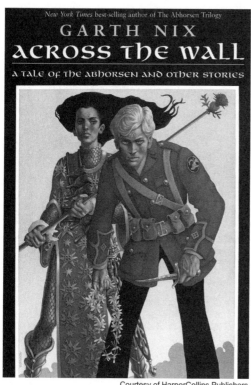

New York Times best-selling author of The Abhorsen Trilogy

GARTH NIX

ACROSS THE WALL

A TALE OF THE ABHORSEN AND OTHER STORIES

Courtesy of HarperCollins Publishers

A mysterious house leads to an even more mysterious world in Nix's Keys to the Kingdom series. In the first volume Arthur Penhaligon suffers a near-fatal asthma attack, and a key, shaped like the minute hand of a clock, saves his life. Each title in this series of seven books contains the name of a day of the week. *Mister Monday*, won the Aurealis Award in the Children's Book category and was named a Children's Book of the Year Honor Book by the Children's Book Council of Australia; *Mister Monday* and *Grim Tuesday* both won Book Design Awards from the Australian Book Publishers Association.

In 1999 Garth Nix received a special Golden Duck Award for Australian Contribution to Children's Science Fiction, presented at the World Science Fiction Convention held in Melbourne. Nix continues to create ever more intricate worlds and intriguing characters for readers of a wide age range. He lives with his wife, Anna, a book editor, and their two sons in Coogee Beach in Sydney, Australia.

SELECTED WORKS: *Very Clever Baby's First Reader: A Simple Reader for Your Child Featuring Freddy the Fish and Easy Words*, 1988; *Very Clever Baby's Ben Hur: Starring Freddy the Fish as Charlton Heston*, 1988; *The Ragwitch*, 1990; *Very Clever Baby's Guide to the Greenhouse Effect*, 1992; *Sabriel*, 1995; *Shade's Children*, 1997; *The Calusari*, 1997; *Very Clever Baby's First Christmas*, 1998; *Bill the Inventor*, illus. by Nan Bodsworth, 1998; *Blackbread the Pirate*, 1999; *The Fall: The Seventh Tower, Book 1*, 2000; *Castle: The Seventh Tower, Book 2*, 2000; *Lirael: Daughter of the Clayr*, 2001; *Aenir: The Seventh Tower, Book 3*, 2001; *Above the Veil: The Seventh Tower, Book 4*, 2001; *Into Battle: The Seventh Tower, Book 5*, 2001; *The Violet Keystone: The Seventh Tower, Book 6*, 2001; *Serena and the Sea Serpent*, illus. by Stephen Michael King, 2001; *Abhorsen*, 2002; *Mister Monday*, 2003; *Across the Wall: A Tale of the Abhorsen and Other Stories*, 2005; *Grim Tuesday*, 2005; *Drowned Wednesday*, 2005; *Sir Thursday*, 2006; *Lady Friday*, 2007; *Superior Saturday*, 2008.

SUGGESTED READING: *Something About the Author*, vol. 143, 2004; *Children's Literature Review*, 2001; *Authors and Artists for Young Adults*, vol. 27, 1999.

WEB SITE: www.garthnix.co.uk

"I was born and raised in Greenville, South Carolina. I grew up to write books for children that draw on my Southern experiences.

"I love the South. The people down there talk real slow and eat pickled okra and biscuits. In the summer, the air is thick and damp and the road gets so hot that the tar sticks to the bottom of your feet. There are towns with names like Six Mile and Pumpkintown. Along the roadside, kudzu vines grow so fast they cover up signs and telephone poles and even whole barns.

"As a child, I loved dogs, salamanders, and tap dancing. I loved the woods and creeks near my house and spent many happy hours collecting rocks and leaves and frogs and crawfish. I didn't spend much time in the house, but when I did, I loved my bedroom. I had white and gold furniture. My ruffled bedspread was silky and cool and felt great to lie down on during those hot Southern summer nights. Beside my bed was a shelf with a collection of china horses.

Barbara O'Connor

November 9, 1950–

"My father entertained the neighborhood children by eating amazing amounts of hot peppers, my mother made doll cradles from oatmeal boxes, and my sister would play paper dolls with me whenever I asked her.

"My grandfather grew peanuts in his garden and my grandmother always kept a big pot of them boiling on the stove. If you've never eaten a boiled peanut, I advise you to try it at least once in your life. You may not like it, but at least you can say you ate it!

"On Sundays, my family often drove to the Smoky Mountains. The higher we got, the more the road twisted around and around. Sometimes we stopped the car and gazed out at the view below. I remember one spot where you could see five states (although I could never remember which states they were.)

Photo by Grady O'Connor

"My favorite day of the week was the day the bookmobile came to my neighborhood. The books were never very good but it was fun to be inside a library with wheels. You had to crawl around on the floor to find the children's books. I remember finding *The Pink Motel* by Carol Ryrie Brink. It held the position of 'My Favorite Book' until I discovered the Trixie Belden mysteries. My second favorite book was *Babar* because that's the only children's book my grandmother had. Luckily, she also had a chicken coop that was filled with sand where my sister and cousins and I played house all day.

"When it was time for me to go to college, it never occurred to me to leave the South. After graduating from the University of South Carolina with a degree in English, I decided it was time to see the rest of the country. I headed west to California, then to New England. I currently live in Duxbury, Massachusetts, a historic seaside village not far from Plymouth Rock. I have one husband, one son, one cat and two dogs.

"When I first started writing books for children, I tried setting my stories in places I didn't know very well. Then one day I sat down and started writing about a boy who lived in a town called Six Mile. In the summer, that boy walked on roads so hot the tar stuck to the bottom of his feet. He ate pickled okra and boiled peanuts. The barns near his home were covered with kudzu.

"I had found my writing voice—and it grew from the memories of my childhood in the South that I love. I went on to write books about children who play in creeks and lie on silky bedspreads and collect china horses and take trips up to the beautiful Smoky Mountains. My stories have pieces of me in them, all mixed in with the made-up parts. That's what writers do—mix in the real stuff with the made-up stuff. And they can wear their pajamas all day long if they want to. What could be better than that?"

03　03　03

Barbara O'Connor was born Barbara Lawrence, in Greenville, South Carolina. A writer at heart, she wrote poems and stories and even a whole book as a child before receiving her B.A. in English from the University of South Carolina in 1972.

After graduating O'Connor felt the urge to experience another part of the country and headed to Southern California. In 1984 she met and married William O'Connor, a risk manager, and bought a home in Venice Beach. About the same time, O'Connor took a class on writing for children at UCLA. She had found her calling: combining her love of writing and her love of children. She started by writing short stories for magazines; her first story was published in *Children's Digest* in 1989. She then moved on to writing biographies and novels and has been writing for children ever since.

O'Connor writes both fiction and nonfiction for middle-grade readers. She loves to follow her imagination in her novels, but she is equally adept at writing biographies. Her books for the Trailblazers and the Creative Minds series have been called compelling and accessible, lauded both for their design and their rich historical details. O'Connor enjoys writing biographies because she likes reading about other people's lives herself. She relishes the research involved and the process of turning the facts about someone's life into a story about that life.

In her fiction O'Connor is drawn to the troubled child. Her first novel, *Beethoven in Paradise*, is about a young Southern boy who overcomes his emotionally abusive father's objections to his desire to become a musician. In this title, which was named an ALA Popular Paperback for Young Adults, a *Family Fun* magazine Best Book and included in the Children's Book Council Summer Reading Showcase, O'Connor exhibits a remarkable ability to capture the rhythms of Southern speech, an ability that is apparent in all her subsequent novels.

Abandonment issues are explored in the Massachusetts Book Award winner *Moonpie and Ivy*. The story of a young girl in rural Georgia struggling with her feelings for a mother who has temporarily abandoned her and an aunt she can't accept as a replacement, this book was also a *Child* magazine Best Children's Book, a *Chicago Parent* magazine Best Book, and a Maine Regional Library System's "Cream of the Crop."

When a sixth grader wants to win a spelling bee to gain fame in her small town as well as a trip to Walt Disney World in *Fame and Glory in Freedom, Georgia*, her plans are thwarted by her spelling bee partner, a social outcast in the community. Enhanced by the narrator's charming and spunky voice and a satisfying resolution, this title was a Chicago Public Library Best of the Best, a Baltimore County Libraries' Great Book for Kids, a Children's Literature Choice Award winner, a Capitol Choice title, and nominated for nearly 20 state awards, including the Texas Bluebonnet.

Courtesy of Farrar, Straus, and Giroux

Racism is the subject of *Me and Rupert Goody*, an ALA Notable Children's Book, a *School Library Journal* Best Book, and Kansas City Public Library Best Book. It is the story of a young girl who resents the long-lost African American son of the white man she considers her surrogate uncle, but who ends up defending the boy against the racism in her community.

Two of O'Connor's titles have won Parents' Choice Gold Awards: *Moonpie and Ivy* and *Fame and Glory in Freedom, Georgia*; *Taking Care of Moses* received a Parents' Choice Recommended Award.

Four of her titles were named Best Books of the Year by the Bank Street College of Education: *Me and Rupert Goody*; *Moonpie and Ivy*; *Fame and Glory in Freedom, Georgia*;and *Taking Care of Moses*.

When their son was born in 1987, Barbara O'Connor and her husband left Southern California in search of a smaller, quieter place to raise him. They found the perfect spot in a quiet New England coastal town near Boston. Although O'Connor and her family currently live in Massachusetts, her heart still lives in the South, and readers can find the South alive in her books.

SELECTED WORKS: *Mammolina: A Story about Maria Montessori*, illus. by Sara Campitelli, 1992; *Barefoot Dancer: The Story of Isadora Duncan*, 1994; *The Soldiers' Voice: The Story of Ernie Pyle*, 1996; *The World at His Fingertips: A Story about Louis Braille*, illus. by Rochelle Draper, 1997; *Beethoven in Paradise*, 1997; *Me and Rupert Goody*, 1999; *Katherine Dunham: Pioneer of Black Dance*, 2000; *Moonpie and Ivy*, 2001; *Leonardo Da Vinci: Renaissance Genius*, 2003; *Fame and Glory in Freedom, Georgia*, 2003; *Taking Care of Moses*, 2004; *How to Steal a Dog*, 2007; *Greetings from Nowhere*, 2008.

SUGGESTED READING: *Something About the Author*, vol. 153, 2005. Periodicals—O'Connor, Barbara, "How to Steal a Dog and Other Lessons in Life," *Journal of Children's Literature*, Spring 2007.

WEB SITE: www.barboconnor.com

Scott O'Dell was a prolific writer, and his novels have had a powerful and resonating influence on their readers. As a long-lasting homage to the importance of historical fiction in children's lives, O'Dell himself established the Scott O'Dell Award for Historical Fiction in 1981. The award is today's standard-bearer for excellence in the writing of historical fiction.

Ironically, the name for which he is so well known is not his given name. He was born Odell Gabriel Scott, but a typesetter's mistake on the byline for an article he wrote early in his career transposed his names and he liked his new moniker and decided to keep it. His family had strong literary ties; one of his ancestors was a cousin to the novelist Sir Walter Scott.

O'Dell grew up in the California countryside in several locales outside of Los Angeles when it was still a frontier town. The wildlife and sound of the sea made a lasting impression on him that can be traced through all his writing. After high school graduation, O'Dell attended Occidental College in 1919, the University of Wisconsin in 1920, Stanford University in 1920–1921, and the University of Rome in 1925, but he didn't receive a degree from any of these institutions.

Courtesy of the Houghton Mifflin Company

Scott O'Dell

May 23, 1898– October 15, 1989

His work experiences were as checkered as his academic pursuits, and all of them contributed to his late-stage career as a writer for children. After Stanford, O'Dell headed to Hollywood where he worked at a variety of jobs in the motion picture industry. He taught a mail-order course in photoplay writing, worked as a technical director for Paramount, and then served as a Technicolor cameraman for Metro-Goldwyn-Mayer on the filming of the original *Ben Hur* in Rome. It was while he was in Italy that he attended Rome University and wrote his first novel, a book that was never published.

Scott O'Dell

Courtesy of the Houghton Mifflin Company

Returning to the United States, he next ventured into work as a newspaperman and book reviewer, serving as book editor for the *Los Angeles Daily News*. He was also on the staff of a number of local California magazines, none of which proved very successful. Throughout that period, he wrote both fiction and nonfiction for adults. The springboard that launched him into children's books occurred while he was researching California history for a guidebook, *Country of the Sun: Southern California, an Informal History and Guide*. He was fascinated by a story about a young Indian girl who spent 18 years alone on the island of San Nicolas off the California coast. The article tantalized him into further research that eventually led to his writing *Island of the Blue Dolphins*, a riveting, fictionalized first-person account of Karana's survival. It was his friend Maud Lovelace, author of the *Betsy-Tacy* books, who told him that what he had written was a children's book.

Seldom does an author's first novel for young readers reap instant acclaim, but *Island of the Blue Dolphins*—which won the Newbery Award in 1961—was just such a book. It has become a modern classic, named by the Children's Literature Association in 1976 as one of the Eleven Best American Children's Books of the Past 200 Years and cited by *School Library Journal* in 2000 as one of the Books That Shaped the Century. The critical success and enduring popularity of *Island of the Blue Dolphins* persuaded O'Dell to write a sequel, *Zia*, published in 1976.

O'Dell was over sixty years old when *Island* was published—late to be starting a new career as a children's author, but O'Dell was just beginning. He subsequently wrote and published more than 25 critically acclaimed books and received numerous awards and citations. His second children's book, *The King's Fifth*, was chosen as a Newbery Honor book in 1967. *The Black Pearl* and *Sing Down the Moon* also received Newbery Honors in 1968 and 1971, respectively. He was awarded both the University of Southern Mississippi Medallion and the Regina Medal for his body of work. His books have been as popular abroad as in the U.S., and he twice won the Deutscher Jugendbuchpreis in Germany—for *Island of the Blue Dolphins* in 1963 and *The King's Fifth* in 1969. In 1972 he became the second American to receive the Hans Christian Andersen Medal for lifetime achievement, assuring his stature in the international world of children's literature.

Scott O'Dell married twice, and both his wives took an active role in his writing. His first wife, Jane Rattenbury, typed his manuscripts and occasionally offered editorial advice. In 1966 he married Elizabeth Hall, also a writer. They met while Hall was working in a public library and helping a school librarian set up a book fair. O'Dell was a visiting author at the fair, and romance bloomed. Hall worked nine years as an editor at *Psychology Today* and served as a sounding board for her husband's work. O'Dell was still writing at the time of his death from cancer at age 91. *My Name Is Not Angelica* was published the year he died, and Elizabeth Hall completed two more manuscripts that he had started: *Thunder Rolling in the Mountains*, which appeared in 1992, and *Venus Among the Fishes*, published in 1995.

In 1981 O'Dell created the Scott O'Dell Award for Historical Fiction with a $5,000 prize to encourage authors to write in this genre for children. In 1987 his own book, *Streams to the River, River to the Sea: A Novel of Sacagawea*, was designated the winner. It recounts the thrilling adventure tale of Sacagawea's contribution to the Lewis and Clark expedition. The O'Dell Award has been won over the years by both established writers and newcomers to the field and is a coveted prize for those who write historical fiction.

Several of O'Dell's books have been adapted for film: *Island of Blue Dolphins* by Universal Films in 1964 and *The Black Pearl* in 1976. *The King's Fifth* was animated for television in 1982 under the title *Mysterious Cities of Gold*. In an interview for *Language Arts* in 1984, O'Dell said: "Many of my books are set in the past but the problems of isolation, moral decisions, greed, need for

> *"Many of my books are set in the past but the problems of isolation, moral decisions, greed, need for love and affection are problems of today as well."*

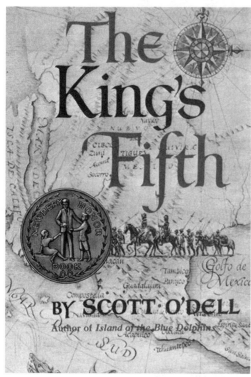

Courtesy of the Houghton Mifflin Company

love and affection are problems of today as well. I want to provide a moral backdrop for readers to make their own decisions. History has a direct bearing on children's lives. I want to make them aware of man's inhumanity but also of the possibilities for endurance, resourcefulness, and moral courage."

With his journalistic curiosity, his distinctive and compelling narrative voice, and skilled, insightful writing, O'Dell mined the rich stores of history for nuggets he could transform into tales that breathed life into the past. His work has become a touchstone by which all historical fiction for young readers can be measured.

SELECTED WORKS: *Island of the Blue Dolphins*, 1960; *The King's Fifth*, 1966; *The Black Pearl*, 1967; *The Dark Canoe*, 1968; *Journey to Jericho*, 1969; *Sing Down the Moon*, 1970; *The Treasure of Topo-el-Bampo*, illus. by Lynd Ward, 1972; *The Cruise of the Arctic Star*, illus. by Samuel Bryant, 1973; *Child of Fire*, 1974; *The Hawk That Dare Not Hunt by Day*, 1975; *Zia*, illus. by Ted Lewin, 1976; *The 290*, 1976; *Carlota*, 1977; *Kathleen, Please Come Home*, 1978; *The Captive: Volume I of the Seven Serpents Trilogy*, 1979; *Sarah Bishop*, 1980; *The Feathered Serpent: Volume II of the Seven Serpents Trilogy*, 1981; *The Spanish Smile*, 1982; *The Amethyst Ring: Volume III of the Seven Serpents Trilogy*, 1983; *The Castle in the Sea*, 1983; *Alexandra*, 1984; *The Road to Damietta*, 1985; *Streams to the River, River to the Sea: A Novel of Sacagawea*, 1986; *The Serpent Never Sleeps: A Novel of Jamestown and Pocahontas*, illus. by Ted Lewin, 1987; *Black Star, Bright Dawn*, 1988; *My Name Is Not Angelica*, 1989; *Thunder Rolling in the Mountains*, with Elizabeth Hall, 1991; *Venus Among the Fishes*, with Elizabeth Hall, 1995.

SUGGESTED READING: *Something About the Author*, vol. 134, 2003; Silvey, Anita, *The Essential Guide to Children's Books and Their Creators*, 2002; *Authors & Artists for Young Adults*, vol. 44, 2002; Russell, David, *Scott O'Dell: Twayne's United States Authors series*, 1999; Hopkins, Lee Bennett, ed., *Pauses: Autobiographical Reflections of 101 Creators of Children's Books*, 1995; "Scott

O'Dell," in *Speaking for Ourselves: Autobiographical Sketches by Notable Authors of Books for Young Adults*, ed. by Donald R. Gallo, 1990; *Children's Literature Review*, vol. 16, 1989; *Dictionary of Literary Biography*, vol.52, 1986; *Contemporary Literary Criticism*, vol. 30, 1984; Townsend, John Rowe. *A Sense of Story: Essays on Contemporary Writing for Children*, 1971; Townsend, John Rowe, *Written for Children: An Outline of English Language Children's Literature*, 1965. Periodicals—"Newbery Acceptance," *Horn Book Magazine*, August 1961; "Hans Christian Andersen Award Acceptance Speech," *Horn Book Magazine*, October 1972; McCormick, Edith, "Scott O'Dell: Immortal Writer," *American Libraries* June 1973; "Acceptance Speech, Regina Medal Award," *Catholic Library World*, July/August, 1978; Roop, Peter, "Profile: Scott O'Dell," *Language Arts*, November 1984; *Los Angeles Times*, Obit: October 17, 1989; *New York Times*. Obit: October 17, 1989; *Washington Post*, Obit: October 18, 1989.

WEB SITE: www.scottodell.com

An earlier profile of Scott O'Dell appeared in *More Junior Authors*, 1963

Photo by Peter Riddihough

"I loved typing when I was a kid. We had an old manual typewriter, and I loved the feeling of hammering on the keys and seeing words fill the page. I'd type pages and pages out of my Dad's old economics textbooks; I took it very seriously. I also liked making up stories of my own, and around twelve I decided I wanted to be a writer (this came after deciding I wanted to be a scientist, and then an architect). I started out writing sci-fi epics (my Star Wars phase), then went on to swords and sorcery tales (my Dungeons and Dragons phase), and then, during the summer holiday when I was fourteen, started on a humorous story about a boy addicted to video games (written, of course, during my video game phase).

"It turned out to be quite a long story, really a short novel, and I rewrote it the next summer. We had a family friend who

Kenneth Oppel

August 31, 1967–

knew Roald Dahl—one of my favorite authors—and this friend offered to show Dahl my story. I was paralyzed with excitement. I never heard back from Roald Dahl directly, but he read my story and liked it enough to pass it on to his own literary agent. I got a letter from them, saying they wanted to take me on and try to sell my story. And they did. *Colin's Fantastic Video Adventure* was published in 1985 just as I was graduating from high school. It was easily the most exciting thing that had ever happened to me—and it gave me the confidence to think I could make writing my career.

"I did my B.A. at the University of Toronto (a double major in cinema studies and English) and wrote my second children's novel, *The Live-Forever Machine*, in my final year for a creative writing course. I married the year after graduation and spent the next three years in Oxford, where my wife obtained a Ph.D. in Renaissance Drama. Money was tight in those years, and I wrote numerous short chapter books, a picture book, a novel, and a screenplay, which was optioned by a Hollywood producer for more money than the advances for all my books combined!

"My wife was offered her first teaching job at Memorial University, so we moved to Corner Brook, Newfoundland. In my two years there, I concentrated on writing screenplays and was fairly successful selling them to producers in Los Angeles. Frustrated that none of my scripts were getting made into movies, I decided to write *Silverwing*, an idea I'd had for a couple of years. I finished the book in 1995 just after we'd moved back to Toronto, where my wife was teaching part-time at the University of Toronto and our first daughter was born.

"My publisher at that time was less than thrilled with *Silverwing*, and didn't want to publish it, so I put it away in a drawer, discouraged. My wife urged me to send it to another publisher and eventually I did. HarperCollins Canada enthusiastically bought it, and it has since gone on to become my most popular book, selling hundreds of thousands of copies all around the world, in many different languages. *Silverwing*, published in 1997, changed my life; it made it possible for me to write full-time without worrying about money. It also helped me realize that writing books was much more creatively satisfying for me than writing screenplays. And, with the exception of one medical thriller for adults (*The Devil's Cure*, 2000) I've focused exclusively on writing books for young readers. I've been typing away happily ever since."

> *"I loved typing when I was a kid. . . . I also liked making up stories of my own, and around twelve I decided I wanted to be a writer (this came after deciding I wanted to be a scientist, and then an architect)."*

C3 C3 C3

Kenneth Oppel was born in Port Alberni, a small mill town in British Columbia, Canada. When Kenneth was a child, his father moved the family first to Victoria, then to Nova Scotia on the opposite coast while he pursued a law degree. Eventually they returned to Victoria, where Kenneth attended high school. Wherever they lived, books were a constant resource. Deciding early in his adolescence that he wanted to be a writer, Oppel achieved his goal of being published at age of 17 with *Colin's Fantastic Video Adventure*.

The Live-Forever Machine, his second book, about the secret of immortality, was named a Canadian Library Association Notable Book. Influenced by his college studies, the story featured cinematic techniques and themes that became Oppel trademarks in later works. *Dead Water Zone* and *Follow That Star* were also named CLA Notable Books and the author was on his way to a satisfying writing career. By 1995, he had earned the Canadian Authors Association's Air Canada Award for promise demonstrated by a young Canadian writer under the age of 30.

Kenneth Oppel has certainly lived up to this promise. In a series of fast-moving action stories—early chapter books featuring three intrepid young ghost-busters—he created the kinds of stories emerging readers can truly enjoy. The team of Giles, Kevin, and Tina take on ghosts, robots, dinosaurs, vampires, and other scourges, neatly figuring out how to vanquish their foes in each volume. Several easy readers and picture books followed before the phenomenal success of Oppel's longer novels.

In the Silverwing trilogy, talking bats abound. Based on actual scientific knowledge of the bat world, an epic journey begins in the first volume when a small bat's curiosity triggers the wrath of the owls and causes trouble for his colony. *Silverwing* won the Ontario Library Association's Silver Birch Award, the IBBY South America Banco del Libro Award, and the Blue Heron Award, as well as being named the Canadian Library Association's Book of the Year. In the United States, it won Minnesota's Maud Hart Lovelace Award and was named an ALA Quick Pick for Reluctant Readers. The young bat's dangerous adventures continue when he and his friends become trapped in an apparent paradise in *Sunwing*, a sequel that captured the province of Alberta's Rocky Mountain Book Award and the Ruth Schwartz Award for Excellence. In the third volume, *Firewing*, the son of the hero of the first two titles must go on a frightening journey into the Underworld. Named a Red Maple Honor Book in Canada, it was also an IRA/CBC Children's Choice in the U.S. This trilogy proved so popular, it inspired a 13-episode animated television series. In 2005 playwright and director Kim Selody adapted the story of *Silverwing* for the stage and it has played successfully in both Winnipeg and Vancouver.

In 2005 *Airborn*, a combination Victorian era fantasy and swashbuckling adventure reminiscent of Jules Verne and Robert Louis Stevenson, won awards in Great Britain and the U.S. as well as Oppel's native Canada. The story follows a young teenage couple as they battle pirates and search for mysterious flying creatures that aren't supposed to exist. Shortlisted for the Carnegie Medal in England, *Airborn* was presented a Michael L. Printz Honor Award by the American Library Association. In Canada it won the Governor General's Literary Award as well as the Ontario Library Association's Red Maple Award, and was named a CLA Young Adult Honor Book. In the U.S. it was among the top ten of ALA's Best Books for Young Adults, an ALA Quick Pick for Reluctant Readers, and an ALA Notable Children's Book. Both *School Library Journal* and the *Bulletin of the Center for Children's Books* named it to their Best Books lists for the year. In *Skybreaker*, the action-packed sequel, the same characters race pirates to reach a ghost ship that holds treasures and secrets. Nominated for the U.K. Carnegie Medal, *Skybreaker* won the Red Maple Award and the Ruth and Sylvia Schwartz Children's Book Award in Canada. In the U.S. it was named an ALA Best Book for Young Adults and a *Kirkus* Editors' Choice.

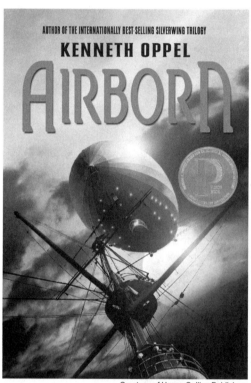

Courtesy of HarperCollins Publishers

In 2006 Kenneth Oppel received the Vicky Metcalf Award presented by the Writers Trust of Canada for a "body of work in children's literature that, in the opinion of the judges, demonstrates the highest literary standards." That same year Oppel received the Libris Award from the Canadian Booksellers Association, as the "author who demonstrates a strong connection and appeal to his or her intended reading audience." This award-winning author, who continues to astonish his readers, lives in Toronto with his wife, Philippa, and their three children.

SELECTED WORKS FOR YOUNG READERS: *Colin's Fantastic Video Adventure*, illus. by Kathleen C. Howell, 1985; *The Live-Forever*

Machine, 1990; *Cosimo Cat*, illus. by Regolo Ricci, 1990; *Dead Water Zone*, 1992; *A Bad Case of Ghosts*, illus. by Peter Utton, 1993; *A Bad Case of Magic*, illus. by Peter Utton, 1993 (Canada: *A Strange Case of Magic*, illus. by Sam Sisco, 2000); *Cosmic Snapshots*, illus. by Guy Parker-Reese, 1993; *Galactic Snapshots*, illus. by Guy Parker-Reese, 1993; *A Bad Case of Robots*, illus. by Peter Utton, 1994 (Canada: *A Crazy Case of Robots*, illus. by Sam Sisco, 2001); *A Bad Case of Dinosaurs*, illus. by Peter Utton, 1994 (Canada: *An Incredible Case of Dinosaurs*, 2001); *Follow That Star*, illus. by Kim LaFave, 1994; *Emma's Emu*, illus. by Carolyn Crossland, 1995 (Canada: 1999); *A Bad Case of Super-Goo*, illus. by Peter Utton, 1996 (Canada: *A Weird Case of Super-Goo*, illus. by Sam Sisco, 2002); *Silverwing*, 1997; *Sunwing*, 1999; *Peg and the Whale*, illus. by Terry Widener, 2000; *A Creepy Case of Vampires*, 2002; *Firewing*, 2002; *Peg and the Yeti*, illus. by Barbara Reid, 2004; *Airborn*, 2004; *Skybreaker*, 2005; *Darkwing*, 2007.

SELECTED WORKS WRITTEN FOR ADULTS: *The Devil's Cure*, 2000.

SUGGESTED READING: *Something About the Author*, vol. 153, 2005. Periodicals—"Rising Star," *Bulletin of the Center for Children's Books*, October 2004.

WEB SITES: www.kennethoppel.ca; www.silverwing.ca; www.air-born.ca

---

Nancy Osa

September 5, 1961–

"'I am the Oddball.' This note on my computer reminds me that I was born a writer. I was born in 1961, in Chicago, Illinois, a place where one can be part of a crowd—or get lost in it. I lived in a Cuban American household, whose circumstances left me just short of understanding the Spanish language or the Cuban mindset. I have danced between shyness and popularity, solitude and group-itude, all my life. Although it pained me in grade school and still haunts me as an adult, I see things uniquely because I am so often on the outside.

"I learned to read music when I was four and grasped the English alphabet and phonics soon afterward. The first thing that I remember writing was a set of directions to my house for a kindergarten friend—complete with a detailed map. Which would have been fine, except that my little friend would have had to walk her little legs across Route 6, a busy highway, to reach my address. So that was also the first thing I got in trouble for writing.

"After that, I composed classroom skits, songs, plays, puppet shows, and radio programs. I created board games and wrote scores of letters to pen pals, friends, and relatives. In high school, I poured myself into journals, poetry, comedy speeches, and satire. I wrote my first novel as my thesis at Reed College, and went on to work as a freelance writer and editor and, eventually, a published novelist.

"I grew up in a suburb of Chicago, and my family often visited country relatives in Missouri. To them, I was the city girl; in downtown Chicago, I felt like a hick. At home, I was somewhere in the middle. Over the years, I grew comfortable with each of these milieus, until I felt like I belonged, no matter where I was. I've lived at the beach in Southern California, in a small town in Alabama, among the concrete and steel of Chicago, and in the woods of the Pacific Northwest. I am able to place my characters in many different settings, call them up, and go visit them. Part of being a writer, for me, is knowing a place, or a person, or an activity—and being able to step outside of it for a larger look.

Photo by Anita Lacy

"A writer also has to be able to look inside. When people marvel over my skill with the teen voice, I think of my sixty-six cheat sheets-my personal journals. I started writing my thoughts in these little spiral-bound notebooks when I was fourteen. Every so often, I'll go back and read them all, the story of my life, to see how I've changed. And you know what? Many of my current journal entries are scarily similar to those early ones! I've grown older, yes; but I'm the same person I was when I was a teenager.

"Although I didn't call myself a writer, I was one all along, zigzagging across social boundaries, wondering about them, and turning those thoughts into stories. A combination of emotion, environment, and inquisitiveness has always made me the oddball. I see now how valuable being the outsider is. If I could, I'd tell every young reader in the world that it's okay to be different. The note on my computer—and the books with my name on them-remind me of that every day."

CB CB CB

Nancy Osa has always found inspiration in humor and history—passions that arose in part due to her Cuban heritage. As she has stated, many immigrants use humor as a tool for coping with their loss, and many of their children develop an interest in the history of their parents' homelands. Osa's father was a Cuban doctor who came to America in the early 1950s. After the Cuban Revolution occurred in 1959, his contact with his home country was cut off by travel restrictions and family relations soon after Nancy, his second daughter, was born. U.S.-Cuba relations were not discussed at home, and visits were no longer an option. While she was growing up, Cuba was as abstract to Osa as Great Britain, where her mother's ancestors originated. Osa spent her early years learning to ride horseback and play the piano, as well as reading voraciously.

After graduating high school, Osa traveled the country for several years, experimenting with various careers that would all provide detail for her writing. During this period, she lived in Long Beach, California, and Selma, Alabama, and then returned to Chicago. Ready to focus on earning her degree, she decided to apply to Reed College, in Portland, Oregon, which purported to teach its students to learn how to learn—and to appreciate the absurd.

"I see now how valuable being the outsider is. If I could, I'd tell every young reader in the world that it's okay to be different."

Both elements served her well. At Reed College, Osa majored in English and completed her first humorous novel for her senior thesis, which remains unpublished. Upon graduating in 1988, she started an editorial consulting business, assisting writers, publishers, and educational institutions in editing books, short stories, and promotional literature. She also worked on her fiction. Searching for story ideas in 1993, she learned of the destruction wrought by Hurricane Andrew's passage through Cuba, which awakened her interest in her Cuban identity. This marked the beginning of the thinking and research that would eventually become her first published novel, *Cuba 15*. The book is about Violet Paz, a Cuban-Polish girl, who has grown up, like Osa, knowing very little about her Cuban background. Unlike Osa, however, Violet is introduced to her heritage as she approaches her 15th birthday, because her grandmother wants her to experience a *quinceañero*, a traditional Latino celebration. Osa herself knew nothing about this tradition before she began researching it for Violet's story, which became a finely developed—and funny—coming-of-age tale as the protagonist learns to accept her Cuban roots.

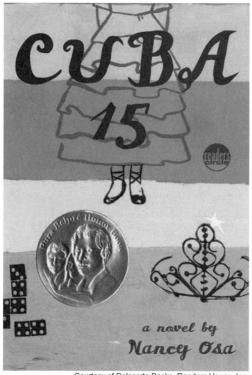

Courtesy of Delacorte Books, Random House, Inc.

Cuba 15 was awarded the Delacorte Press Prize for a First Young Adult Novel and offered a publishing contract by Random House. It became a Pura Belpré Honor Book award winner, an ALA Notable Children's Book and an ALA Best Book for Young Adults. *Cuba 15* was also named a *Booklist* Editor's Choice and a Notable Social Studies Trade Book, and received an Américas Award Honorable Mention. Osa has received grants and fellowships from Literary Arts, Inc., Hedgebrook Foundation, and Centrum Center for the Creative Arts.

Nancy Osa lives near Portland, Oregon. In addition to writing, she enjoys spending time with her Arabian horse and her Irish setters.

SELECTED WORKS: *Cuba 15*, 2003.

SUGGESTED READING: Nix, Nelle, "Coming of Age and Coming to Terms with Cuban Roots," *The Oregonian*, September 18, 2003; Davila, Vianna, "Teen Narrator Takes Spunky, Insightful Walk to Womanhood," San Antonio (Texas) *Express-News*, August 3, 2003. Online—"Spotlight on Nancy Osa," http://www.random-house.com/author/results.pperl?authorid=37094&view=full_sptlght

WEB SITE: www.nancyosa.com

June Otani

July 7, 1934–

June Otani, an illustrator, printmaker, and painter, was born in Santa Paula, California. Her father, a Japanese citizen, met and married her mother, who was born in Hawaii, and they settled in Oxnard, California. In 1942, like many Americans of Japanese decent, the Otani family was taken to an assembly center in Tulare, California and then to the Gila River Relocation Center in Arizona, where they were interned until the end of World War II. After the war the family settled in Pasadena, California.

Otani has always been interested in illustration. Even before entering elementary school she remembers drawing on a large blackboard her father had installed in the kitchen. In high school she developed her passion for drawing and began to pursue formal training, studying advertising design at the Art Center School, which was later called the Art Center College of Design, in Pasadena. After graduating with honors, she decided to start her career in New York.

Otani's first job in New York was as an assistant art director for Grey Advertising. She later became a fashion artist and illustrator. Her work has included editorial illustrations for the *Ladies' Home Journal*, *Parents Magazine*, *Seventeen*, and other periodicals. During that time she began to study printmaking and oil painting, first at the New School and then at Pratt Graphics Institute. Her etchings and paintings have been exhibited in galleries and museums in Westchester County, New York, and across the country as part of several graphics shows run by the National Association of Woman Artists. She has also exhibited in Bologna, Italy, and her works are in private and corporate collections. She has won many awards, including the New York Illustrators Club Award, Mamaroneck Artist Guild Award for sculpture, and the Dr. and Mrs. Gaynor Award from the National Association of Women Artists.

Photo by Robert Baensch

Filled with warmth and humor, Otani's paintings enhance each of the children's books she has illustrated. A number of the books she has worked on explore science themes for young children. For *What Makes a Shadow?*, by Clyde Robert Bulla, her illustrations illuminate each point about the topic as children learn the properties of many types of shadow. This book was named an Outstanding Science Trade Book for Children.

Peach Boy, written by William H. Hooks, tells what is perhaps the most famous of Japanese folktales, the story of Momotaro, a boy who grew from a peach seed to save the people of his village from evil goblins called the *oni*. Otani's pictures are equally effective in depicting the gentle countryside scenes and the wicked supernatural creatures. *Sim Chung and the River Dragon*, a Korean story retold by Ellen Schecter, recounts the tale of a brave girl of legend, while *Chibi: A True Story from Japan* tells a real-life fable about a family of ducklings nesting in busy downtown Tokyo. Otani's ink and watercolor paintings

Little Dog and Duncan

Poems by Kristine O'Connell George
Illustrated by June Otani

Courtesy of Clarion Books

authentically portray city scenes of present-day Tokyo and its people.

Reviewers have praised June Otani's illustrations for two volumes of poetry by Kristine O'Connell George as expressive, charming, and winsome. These short, playful poems are enhanced by her delightful watercolors in a perfect match of text and illustration. *Little Dog Poems* was a *School Library Journal* Best Book and an ALA Notable Children's Book, while *Little Dog and Duncan* received the Claudia Lewis Award for poetry. Both of these titles were recognized by the New York Public Library as selections for their One Hundred Titles for Reading and Sharing list.

June Otani is a resident of Hastings-on-Hudson, New York and the mother of two grown children. Her son, Hiroshi, lives with his family in New Jersey, and her daughter, Miyoko, lives with her husband in California. Currently, Otani is most interested in drawing from life, which is confirmed by her continued enrollment in life drawing and painting courses at the Westchester Art Workshop.

SELECTED WORKS: *The Poodle Who Barked at the Wind*, by Charlotte Zolotow, 1987; *Ten Potatoes in a Pot and Other Counting Rhymes*, by Michael Jay Katz, 1990; *Oh Snow!*, by Monica Mayper, 1991; *Discovering More Science Secrets*, by Sandra Markle, 1992; *Peach Boy*, by William H. Hooks, 1992; *If You Lived in Colonial Times*, by Ann McGovern, 1992; *Sim Chung and the River Dragon: A Folktale from Korea*, ret. by Ellen Schecter, 1993; *What Makes a Shadow?*, by Clyde Robert Bulla, 1994; *Science in a Bottle*, by Sandra Markle, 1995; *Science—Just Add Salt*, by Sandra Markle, 1995; *Science Surprises*, by Sandra Markle, 1996; *Chibi: A True Story from Japan*, by Barbara Brenner and Julia Takaya, 1996; *Breath of the Dragon*, by Gail Giles, 1997; *Little Dog Poems*, by Kristine O'Connell George, 1999; *Little Dog and Duncan*, by Kristine O'Connell George, 2002.

WEB SITE: www.juneotani.com

Though born in Southern California, Christopher Paolini has lived most of his life in Paradise Valley, Montana, with his parents and younger sister, Angela. The tall, jagged Beartooth Mountains rise on one side of Paradise Valley. Snowcapped most of the year, they inspired the fantastic scenery in Christopher's best-selling first novel, *Eragon*.

Christopher was home-schooled by his parents. As a child, he often wrote short stories and poems, made frequent trips to the library, and read widely. Some of his favorite books were Bruce Coville's *Jeremy Thatcher, Dragon Hatcher*, Frank Herbert's *Dune*, and Raymond E. Feist's *Magician*, as well as books by Anne McCaffrey, Jane

Photo by Perry Hagopain

Christopher Paolini

November 17, 1983–

Yolen, Brian Jacques, E. R. Eddison, David Eddings, and Ursula K. Le Guin.

The idea for *Eragon* began in the daydreams of a teenager whose love for the magic of stories led him to craft a novel that he himself would enjoy reading. The project began as a hobby, a personal challenge, without any thought of publication. All the characters in *Eragon* are drawn from Christopher's imagination except Angela the herbalist, who is loosely based on his sister.

Christopher was fifteen when he wrote the first draft of *Eragon*. He took a second year to revise the book and then gave it to his parents to read. The family decided to self-publish the book and spent a third year preparing the manuscript for publication: copyediting, proofreading, designing a cover, typesetting the manuscript, and creating marketing materials. During this time Christopher drew the map for *Eragon*, as well as the dragon eye for the book's cover (an image that now appears inside the Knopf hardcover edition). The manuscript was sent to press and the first books arrived in November 2001. The Paolini family spent the next year promoting the book at libraries, bookstores, and schools in 2002 and early 2003.

In summer 2002, the author Carl Hiaasen, whose stepson had read a copy of the self-published book while on vacation in Montana, brought *Eragon* to the attention of his publisher, Alfred A. Knopf, which is part of Random House. Michelle Frey, executive editor at Knopf Books for Young Readers, contacted Christopher and his family to ask if they would be interested in having Knopf publish *Eragon*. The answer was yes, and after

Christopher Paolini
Courtesy of Alfred A. Knopf, Random House, Inc.

another round of editing, Knopf published *Eragon* in August 2003. Ultimately a tale of the struggle between forces of good and evil, *Eragon* is set in the complex world of Alegaësia, where the title character discovers a fascinating blue stone that turns out to be a dragon's egg. When the dragon hatches, Eragon quickly bonds with the creature and learns that they have a telepathic link.

An immediate success, *Eragon* remained on the *New York Times* bestseller list for well over a year; it was among *Booklist*'s Top Ten Fantasy Books for Youth in 2004 and won state awards in Colorado, Rhode Island, Wyoming, Wisconsin, Arizona, Hawaii, Illinois, Tennessee, and Ohio. It also won the Wisconsin Educational Media Association's Golden Archer Award.

After an extensive United States and United Kingdom book tour for *Eragon*, Christopher returned to writing his second book, *Eldest*, which continues the adventures of *Eragon* and the dragon Saphira. *Eldest* features parallel storylines; in one, Eragon continues training as a Dragon Rider, while in the other his cousin Roran undertakes a quest of his own. *Eldest* was published in August 2005, and was followed by Christopher's book tour throughout the United States, Canada, the United Kingdom, Spain, Germany, France, and Italy, as the books had become an international sensation. *Eldest* won the WAYRBA (West Australian Young Readers Book) Award as well as a Quill Award and a number of state awards. Together, *Eragon* and *Eldest* have sold 12.5 million copies worldwide to date. A movie adaptation of *Eragon* premiered in December 2006 in theaters around the world. Produced by Fox 2000, the film featured veteran actors Jeremy Irons and John Malkovich along with 18-year-old Ed Speleers in the title role.

While Christopher's original intent was to create a trilogy, early in 2007 he realized that the plot and characters demanded more space than could fit in one more volume and that a fourth book would be necessary to give each story element the attention it deserved. What began as the Inheritance trilogy has now become the Inheritance cycle. *Brisingr* appeared in the fall of 2008, and a fourth book will complete the story that Christopher envisioned years ago when he first outlined the adventure.

Christopher is especially heartened to hear that his books have inspired young people to read and to write stories of their own. Once the Inheritance cycle is finished, the young author plans to take a long vacation and ponder which of his many story ideas he will develop next.

{A version of this profile first appeared on the web site of Random House publishers and is used with their permission.}

SELECTED WORKS: *Eragon*, 2003; *Eldest*, 2005; *Brisingr*, 2008.

SUGGESTED READING: Vaz, Marc Cotta, *Mythic Vision: The Making of Eragon*, 2006; Wheeler, Jill C., Christopher Paolini (Children's Authors series), 2006; Paolini, Christopher, "It All Began with Books," in *Guys Write for Guys Read*, ed. by Jon Scieszka, 2005; *Something About the Author*, vol. 157, 2005; *Authors and Artists for Young Adults*, vol. 71, 2006. Periodicals—Schwartz, Heather E., "Behind the Scenes of the New Movie *Eragon*," *National Geographic Kids*, December 2006/January 2007; Smith, Danita, "Finding a Middle Earth in Montana," *New York Times*, October 7, 2003. Online—MacDonald, Jay, "Fantastic Voyage," Book Page Interview, at www.bookpage.com/0509bp/christopher_paolini.html

WEB SITES: www.Alagaesia.com
www.shurtugal.com

Susan Patron

(pa-TRONE)
March 18, 1948–

"I was born in Southern California and have lived here my whole life, in old red-tile-roofed houses complete with antique plumbing. My original intention was to move to France—to Paris or to a small village—and become a novelist; instead I married a Frenchman who helped me discover California's mysteries and wonders. But I knew I needed a back-up plan in case the writing career didn't pan out.

"We didn't have too many books in our house during my early childhood. I do remember a tale by the Brothers Grimm about three sisters: 'Little One Eye, Little Two Eyes, and Little Three Eyes.' As the middle of three sisters myself, I marveled at how this story nailed a universal truth: only the middle sister, Little Two Eyes (me), was normal. Much later I wrote a chapter book, *Maybe Yes, Maybe No, Maybe Maybe*, about PK, a middle sister. My two sisters were and remain my best friends, to this day.

"Other than folktales and the comics section of the *Los Angeles Times*, I didn't read much as a young child. The books at school were tedious and seemed to have nothing to do with my life. I took it as a given that all books were boring as I'd never encountered a really exciting one.

"In fourth grade, a lot of wasted years later, a librarian from the Los Angeles Public Library came to visit our classroom. She told us about Newbery books and honor books. She explained what the award meant and said we could borrow copies from the library. Stroking the books, running her fingers over the interior pages, hugging them to her chest, the librarian showed us *My Father's Dragon*, *The Witch of Blackbird Pond*, *Rabbit Hill*, *Old Yeller*. No one in my experience had ever interacted with books in such a sensual way, as if she actually loved them. I was mesmerized and went to the library for the first time that day. Those Newberys and Newbery honor books turned me into an avid reader; *Charlotte's Web*, the book she left for our teacher to read aloud, made me decide to become a writer, and the librarian herself provided the model for my back-up plan (a 35-year career in Children's Services at the Los Angeles Public Library).

Photo by Ben Chun

SUSAN PATRON

"As a children's librarian, I discovered folklore and storytelling, which led to my first book, *Burgoo Stew*, a contemporary retelling of the 'Stone Soup' tale. This was followed by two other picture books featuring Billy Que and the Dustdobbins who live under his bed, and by *Dark Cloud Strong Breeze*, a rhythmic cumulative story.

"Many children want to know what inspired *The Higher Power of Lucky*. Geography was the tool I found that let me write my way into the heart of the story of Lucky Trimble— geography transcended by the human need to be loved and cherished and cared for. The story's setting, the tiny fictional town of Hard Pan in Inyo County, California, was the first 'character' in the book. Inyo County is roughly the size of Belgium. But where the population density in Belgium is 900 people per square mile, in Inyo County it's two people per square mile. I was fascinated by the people who chose to live in this spacious, beautiful, and often harsh land of many extremes.

"In the 1980s we bought a dilapidated cabin surrounded by shacks and outbuildings in a former mining town in the area. My husband, René, restored one of the shacks, a single room measuring 8 by 10 feet. It is beautiful and plain, with a window in each of the four walls, so that wind blows through from any direction. There is a ceiling fan and an ancient pencil sharpener attached to the wall. On the hottest, driest days of summer, a small black bird nesting nearby makes the exact sound of a little gurgling brook, the sound of water flowing over pebbles. I wrote *The Higher Power of Lucky* in this shack, in longhand on lined paper, during weekends and vacations while employed as a librarian. It took me ten years.

"And fifty years after Newbery award books and honor books turned me into a reader and a writer, the phone rang early one January morning. It was a librarian calling to tell me that I had won the 2007 Newbery Award for *The Higher Power of Lucky*.

"Now that I've retired from the Los Angeles Public Library and have become a full-time writer, I'm working on another story about Lucky. After that, there will be more novels and picture books. And someday, not me, but one of my protagonists may fulfill my old dream by living in Paris or in a little village in France."

Ω Ω Ω

Born Susan Hall, the daughter of George and Rubye Hall, Susan Patron received early encouragement from her father, as well as sound advice: when she told him she wanted to be a writer, he suggested she learn how to type.

While enrolled at Pitzer College, from which she received her B.A. degree in 1969, she spent one year in independent study at Trinity College in Dublin. Her professional training was completed at Immaculate Heart College, School of Library Science, where she received a M.L.S. degree in 1972.

Upon graduation, Patron joined the staff of the Los Angeles Public Library as a children's librarian, where over the years she exerted considerable influence on the reading habits of individual children and their parents. Later in her career she trained hundreds of new children's librarians, and, as children's materials specialist, evaluated children's books for the entire library system. She was involved in many special projects, among them a National Endowment for the Arts grant for teaching storytelling techniques to older adults. An active member of the American Library Association, she served on the Caldecott Award committee in 1988 and later on the Laura Ingalls Wilder Medal committee. She has served on advisory boards for KCET public television's *Storytime* program and *L.A. Parent* magazine.

> *"No one in my experience had ever interacted with books in such a sensual way, as if she actually loved them. I was mesmerized and went to the library for the first time that day."*

She has also contributed to an anthology for blind children called *Expectations*, published in Braille, and has reviewed children's books for journals such as *School Library Journal* and *The Five Owls*. Recently she was appointed to the Board of Advisors of the Society of Children's Book Writers and Illustrators.

Patron's own books have been well received by children and critics alike. *Maybe Yes, Maybe No, Maybe Maybe*, an endearing chapter book about an imaginative eight-year-old struggling to come to terms with a move to a new apartment, was named a *School Library Journal* Best Book, won a Parents' Choice Award, and was designated an ALA Notable Children's Book. The amusing cast of characters featured in her early picture books, many of whom return in subsequent titles, have delighted children since they first appeared. The cunning but well-meaning Billy Que from *Burgoo Stew*, the stubborn but kind bad boys and magical but sensitive Dustbobbin from *Five Bad Boys, Billy Que, and the Dustdobbin*, and the shy but brave Dustbobbin in *Bobbin Dustdobbin*, are imaginative and enduring creations.

> "I wrote The Higher Power of Lucky *in this shack, in long-hand on lined paper, during weekends and vacations while employed as a librarian. It took me ten years."*

Patron's next novel, *The Higher Power of Lucky*, took her a decade to write, but certainly proved to be worth the time and effort when it won the 2007 Newbery Award. *The Higher Power of Lucky* is the heartfelt story of a girl who lives in a tiny desert town, wonders about finding a 'higher power' after eavesdropping on 12-step meetings, and worries about being abandoned until she realizes how much her guardian Brigitte truly loves her. The book's distinctive setting and quirky characters have endeared it to many readers. It was also chosen as an ALA Notable Children's book, a *Kirkus* Editor's Choice, a PEN USA Literary Award finalist, and received the annual FOCAL (Friends of Children and Literature) award for a book with California content.

The Higher Power of Lucky turned a spotlight on children's literature when controversy arose over the use of the word "scrotum" on the first page. Lucky overhears a character talk about the time his dog was bitten by a snake on that tender spot of his anatomy. Some school librarians chose not to include the title in their collections because of that word, and the controversy received wide media coverage. Used to working in a library that provides a large selection of books for a diverse community, Patron was taken aback by the challenge. Ironically, her use of the word "uterus" in *Maybe Yes, Maybe No, Maybe Maybe*, an earlier book meant for even younger children, never received any objections. And in fact, there were no complaints about *The Higher Power of Lucky* before it won the Newbery. Patron appeared on National Public Radio's *Talk of the Nation* to defend her book, and her publisher, Simon and Schuster, posted a video discussion of the book on its website. The vast majority of her fellow librarians as well as the American Library Association Office of Intellectual Freedom were eloquent in defense of the book and of freedom of speech in general. A companion volume, to be published in 2009, features Lucky's friend Lincoln, whose passion is tying knots. While doing research for this book, Patron made friends in the knot-tying community and attended their national convention. She also corresponded with many people who adopt wild burros.

Retired as a librarian since March 2007, Patron lives with her husband of nearly 40 years, René Albert Patron, a rare-book restorer. They divide their time between their home in the Hollywood Hills and a small cabin in the high desert of the Eastern Sierras, away from the distractions of city life, where she does much of her writing. In 2007 the Children's Literature Council of Southern California presented Susan Patron with the Dorothy C. McKenzie Award for a distinguished contribution to the field of children's literature.

Courtesy of Simon & Schuster Children's Publishing

SELECTED WORKS: *Burgoo Stew*, illus. by Mike Shenon, 1991; *Five Bad Boys, Billy Que, and the Dustdobbin*, illus. by Mike Shenon, 1992; *Bobbin Dustdobbin*, illus. by Mike Shenon, 1993; *Maybe Yes, Maybe No, Maybe Maybe*, illus. by Dorothy Donahue, 1993; *Dark Cloud Strong Breeze*, illus. by Peter Catalanotto, 1994; *The Higher Power of Lucky*, illus. by Matt Phelan, 2006.

SUGGESTED READING: *Something About the Author*, vol. 76, 1994; Periodicals—Patron, Susan, "Newbery Medal Acceptance," *The Horn Book*, July/August 2007; Walter, Virginia, "Susan Patron," *The Horn Book*, July/August 2007; Jackson, Richard, "Ten," *The Horn Book*, July/August 2007; Oleck, Joan, "The Higher Power of Patron," *School Library Journal*, May 2007; Patron, Susan, "'Scrotum' as a Children's Literary Tool," *Los Angeles Times*, February 27, 2007. Online—*Publishers Weekly: Children's Bookshelf*, February 15, 2007; *Contemporary Authors Online*, February 22, 2007.

Photo by Charles Emery

Edith Pattou

July 12, 1953–

"I was a timid, only child, raised in Chicago and its suburb, Winnetka, which was immortalized in the jazz standard tune 'Big Noise from Winnetka.' Growing up in Winnetka, I was far from being a Big Noise. In fact, I was barely audible, and from the moment I learned to read I fell in love with books. In a lonely, silent house, books were my companions. I was no longer lonely when stepping into Oz with Dorothy, or comparing spy notebooks with Harriet, or having tea with Mr. Tumnus.

"A love of reading was something I inherited from both my parents. My mother always had her nose buried in a book, favoring thick novels by Russian authors, and my father would read to me every night at bedtime. *Babar* and *Harold and the Purple Crayon* were favorites, but even better were his own stories about a series of bear characters, including Bruce the Bear and James Bear (a debonair spy). I learned later that for his bear stories my father 'borrowed' from such diverse sources as S. J. Perelman, Jack London, Rudyard Kipling and Ian Fleming. (The first time I saw the film *Dr. No* I experienced a strong sense of déjà vu!)

"When I was nine my parents divorced and I retreated into my world of books, reading and rereading the Narnia books more times than I can count. To this day, I credit C. S. Lewis with helping me navigate that very painful period in my life.

"I wrote, too—journals, song lyrics, poems, fairy tales. Throughout my school years I was always trying to substitute a story for an essay, a poem for a report. My senior thesis in high school was a fairy tale about a Prince named Peter. In college I received an award for the short novel I wrote for my senior thesis entitled 'Meet Me in Tetuan' about the unraveling of a girl as she increasingly blurs the line between fantasy and reality. And for my master's thesis in graduate school (a library degree from UCLA), I wrote and illustrated a collection of fairy tales about castles.

"Through the years I rambled through a wide assortment of jobs, working for a trendy dress shop, the Playboy Foundation, an advertising agency, several bookstores, a medical association journal, a public television station. Of course what I really wanted to do was write stories, but the rent had to be paid so I got a degree in library science and became a children's librarian.

"Then my own Prince came along, named Charles not Peter, and he whisked me from California to Colorado and then to Durham, North Carolina, where there were no job openings for a children's librarian. So I finally did what I had wanted to do since I was nine: I wrote a novel in which I created an entire world, a world like Narnia. Inspired by Irish mythology, which I had been enchanted by ever since I had spent a summer in Ireland as a teenager, I called my world 'Eirren.'

"The publication of my first novel, *Hero's Song*, and the birth of my first (and only) child happened in the same 12-month period and a tremendous juggling act ensued, leaving me exhausted but thrilled to be both a mother and a writer. Between carpooling and making cupcakes, I kept writing, and in addition to my usual journals, poems, song lyrics and fairy tales, I wrote three novels, as well as a picture book, which I wrote as a birthday present to my daughter's kindergarten teacher.

"My current project is a semi-autobiographical story that harkens back to that lonely book-loving girl growing up in the Midwest, making me realize that some things never change. I love books as much as I did as a child and although my book companions have changed somewhat—Julian Carax, Briony Tallis, Hercule Poirot, Elizabeth Bennett—I confess that from time to time I still enjoy a cup of tea with Mr. Tumnus."

"So I finally did what I had wanted to do since I was nine: I wrote a novel in which I created an entire world, a world like Narnia."

ଔ   ଔ   ଔ

Edith Pattou's haunting fantasy novels are clearly inspired by her early reading of C. S. Lewis's Chronicles of Narnia series, but she has put her own creative imprint on the age-old themes of folk tale and myth to write books that are all her own. *Hero's Song*, the first in her Songs of Eirren series, tells of a peaceful herbalist and gardener, Collun, who must leave the safety of his home to seek his missing sister Nessa. The mythic land of Eirren is similar to the British Isles of ages past, and Collun's personal quest becomes intricately interwoven with the fate of his kingdom. Joined by traveling companions who prove great friends, Collun is able to defeat the evil queen of a neighboring country when her hunger for power threatens to overwhelm his land. *Hero's Song* was cited as an International Reading Association Young Adult Choice book in 1992.

In *Fire Arrow*, the second Eirren adventure, the character of Brie, the archer who accompanied Collun's quest in the first novel, takes center stage. Seeking to avenge her father's murder, this intrepid heroine is determined to find his killers. In the course of this action-packed adventure, she not only finds clues to her own past but manages to save the kingdom from a tyrant who seeks to rule by force. Ultimately, she comes to realize that revenge is not sweet, and though it may be necessary, she has to heal from the emotional toll it takes on her soul. *Booklist* included *Fire Arrow* on its 1998 list of Top Ten Fantasy Novels of the year.

Choosing a different source of inspiration, Pattou wrote *East*, which was named one of the Top Ten of ALA's Best Books for Young Adults and was chosen an ALA Notable Children's Book and a *School Library Journal* Best of the Year. It was also made a Junior Library Guild selection and won the Ohioana Book Award, as well as earning the author a second IRA Young Adult Choice award. In the United Kingdom, retitled *North Child*, it was shortlisted for the Ottakar's Children's Book Prize (now known as the Waterstone's Children's Book Prize) and nominated for the Swansea, Wales Bay Book Award.

EDITH PATTOU

Author of HERO'S SONG and FIRE ARROW

Courtesy of Harcourt Children's Books, Houghton Mifflin Harcourt

East is an elaborate and creative novel based on the Scandinavian folktale "East of the Sun, West of the Moon" with elements of the customs and beliefs of ancient Nordic lands. The vivid setting of snowy expanses and ice palaces and the compelling narative, unfolding through a variety of voices, combine to create an epic tale with a strong, fully developed female protagonist at its center. Rose learns as she comes of age that she must live out a destiny her mother tried to hide from her. Following the great white bear that comes to her family's door, she ventures on a quest that can only end when she proves her own courage and loyalty against overwhelming odds. The changing voices of the narrative weave a tapestry of viewpoints that keep readers enthralled in this romantic adventure tale for all ages.

Edith Pattou's picture book, *Mrs. Spitzer's Garden*, written for her daughter's kindergarten teacher, is a clever metaphor for the influence of a teacher in the lives of her young students. As the teacher tends the seeds she is given early in the school year, the sprouts grow in different ways, some eagerly and quickly while others unfold more slowly. Tricia Tusa's ink and watercolor illustrations emphasize the different personalities of each "plant" in the teacher's classroom.

A 1975 graduate of Scripps College in Claremont, California, Pattou received an M.A. in English literature from the Claremont Graduate School in 1978 and a master's degree in library science from the University of California, Los Angeles in 1983. She worked as librarian in an advertising agency in Los Angeles, then shifted to a job in the children's department of the Glendale Public Library in Glendale, California. After moving to Denver following her marriage to Charles Emery in 1985, Pattou was a children's librarian at the Denver Public Library while her husband completed an internship in psychology at the University of Colorado Medical Center. In 1986 they moved to North Carolina where her husband did post-doctoral studies at Duke University. With no library jobs available, Pattou worked in a bookstore and found time to begin writing in earnest for publication. Their daughter, Vita, was born in 1990. Today the family lives in Columbus, Ohio, where Charles is a professor of psychology at Ohio State University and Edith continues to write.

SELECTED WORKS: *Hero's Song: The First Song of Eirren*, 1991; *Fire Arrow: The Second Song of Eirren*, 1998; *Mrs. Spitzer's Garden*, illus. by Tricia Tusa, 2000; *East*, 2003 (U.K. ed. entitled North Child).

SUGGESTED READING: *Something About the Author*, vol. 164, 2006.

Philippa Pearce

January 23, 1920–
December 21, 2006

The following Autobiographical sketch by Ann Philippa Pearce Christie was written for the *Third Book of Junior Authors* in 1972.

"The only place I remember living in, until I was quite grown up, was the mill-house in the village of Great Shelford, five miles south of Cambridge. The only reason I wasn't born in the mill-house was that my grandfather was living there at the time: he was the miller, and my father, who lived with his family in another house in the village, worked under him in the mill. My grandfather died when I was about two, my grandmother moved out of the mill-house, and our family—my parents, my sister, my two brothers, and myself—moved in.

"We had a wonderful place to grow up in, to love. Our house stood next to my father's mill, which was partly water-powered.

The river ran beside our garden, and we had a canoe on it. The river and the canoe are really those of my first published book, *The Minnow Leads to Treasure*. We fished—with worms—and bathed; and, in a hard winter, we skated on the flooded water-meadows. None of us ever skated from Cambridge to Ely, but my father did, when he was a young man; and I put some of his experience into my second book, *Tom's Midnight Garden*. Anyone can see what the outside of our house looked like, from Susan Einzig's illustrations for that book; but you must take away the extra story—that was put in only to accommodate Mrs. Bartholomew. The garden of our house was almost exactly the Midnight Garden—or, at least, the garden as my father described it from his boyhood. He had been born in the mill-house.

Photo copyright © Helen Craig

"I went to school in Cambridge, and then to Cambridge University. Then I moved to London to earn a living. Almost my first job was as a scriptwriter and producer in the School Broadcasting Department of the BBC. This was sound radio, of course. I worked there for thirteen years, enjoyed it a great deal, and learnt a great deal. Above all, I learnt to write for speaking, or at least for reading aloud. This is an all-important part of writing, especially in the writing of stories.

"My first book was published while I was still in the BBC; and perhaps I got the idea of publishing rather on the brain. For in 1958 I left for a job as editor in a publishing house. From about that time onwards I have earned my living with a mixture of editing, radio scriptwriting and production, reviewing, lecturing, and so on—all in the field of children's literature. At first I was sure that, as a free lance, my writing would dry up and I would starve; but I wrote *A Dog So Small* and after that several short stories. One of them, *Mrs. Cockle's Cat*, was made into a picture book.

"I have written less since my marriage, and especially since the birth of my daughter. On the other hand, I have done more story-telling—to begin with, stories about teddy bears and pussy-cats; later, fairy stories. For me, story-telling has turned out to be interestingly different from story-writing. Yet probably one kind of story-making helps with the other kind."

 C3 C3 C3

Philippa Pearce is perhaps best remembered for her masterpiece, *Tom's Midnight Garden*, long considered a classic of British children's fantasy. Yet all her work—a select but varied output of novels, short stories, fairy tale retellings, and picture books—reflects her unique strengths. She was a writer of rare insight into the human condition with an unusual understanding of children's interior lives. She had an ability to evoke sensory experience with an almost visceral vividness. In Pearce's work wisdom is always mixed with humor, briskness laced with empathy, and intense emotion presented in a way that speaks directly to children. In an article written for *The Horn Book* magazine in 1962, she said: "Writing about and for children, one should have a view almost from the inside, to re-create not what childhood looks like now, but what it felt like then. What did it feel like, for instance, to be physically little? What did it feel like to be a child among children?"

Ann Philippa Pearce was born in Great Shelford, England, a miller's daughter whose childhood was spent in the freedom of meadow and river and garden—settings that would later inform many of her children's books. Pearce won a scholarship to Girton College at Cambridge University and graduated with honors in 1942. She worked for thirteen years as a scriptwriter and producer for BBC Radio, where, concentrating on the spoken word, she learned to write prose of exceptional clarity and simplicity. Next she entered the publishing world, with positions as a children's book editor at Oxford University Press (1958–1960) and André Deutsch (1960–1967). She married Martin Christie, a fruit grower, in 1963; he died in 1965, having never completely recovered from his experiences in a Japanese POW camp during World War II. With her daughter, Sally, Pearce eventually left London and settled in a cottage near her childhood home, where she continued to write books for children.

Her work has been recognized with many prestigious awards, including the 1959 Carnegie Medal for *Tom's Midnight Garden*. She received Carnegie Commendations for *Minnow on the Say* (the original title of *Minnow Leads to Treasure*), her short-story collection *The Shadow Cage and Other Tales of the Supernatural*, and *The Battle of Bubble and Squeak*, which also won the Whitbread Award. Her picture book *Mrs. Cockle's Cat*, with illustrations by Anthony Maitland, was awarded the Kate Greenaway Medal in 1962. And in 1997 she was presented with the Order of the British Empire for her services to children's literature.

> *None of us ever skated from Cambridge to Ely, but my father did, when he was a young man; and I put some of his experience into my second book,* Tom's Midnight Garden.*"*

The idea for her first novel, *Minnow Leads to Treasure*, came to Pearce when she was recuperating from tuberculosis during a particularly nice summer. "Imprisoned" in the hospital, unable to be at home on the river, she went there in her imagination. Though in some ways a conventional adventure/mystery, her story of two boys searching for a long-lost treasure exemplifies her ability to transport readers into a setting and to sustain an extended re-creation of the sensuous physical world.

Tom's Midnight Garden, a brilliant time-blend fantasy, is the story of two lonely children who become friends across time. Tom

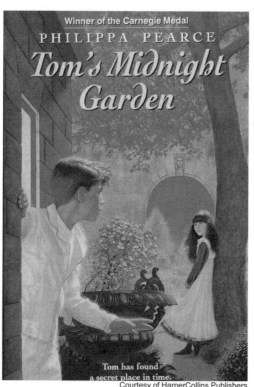

Winner of the Carnegie Medal
PHILIPPA PEARCE
Tom's Midnight Garden

Tom has found a secret place in time.
Courtesy of HarperCollins Publishers

is a modern child spending a dull holiday with his aunt and uncle in their soulless suburban apartment converted from a formerly grand old house. When Tom hears the grandfather clock in the foyer striking thirteen one night, he gains entrance into an enticing walled garden, where he climbs trees, hunts for frogs, and meets Hatty, an unhappy orphan in old-fashioned clothes living in the elegant country house adjacent to the night-time garden. As the story progresses, Pearce explores the power of friendship; the inexorability of change, especially of growing up; and the concept of Time itself. The revelation at the end, which reunites Tom and Hatty in real time, is completely satisfying—emotionally, philosophically, and structurally. Critic John Rowe Townsend, writing in the decade after its publication, called *Tom's Midnight Garden* the "single masterpiece of English children's literature since the Second World War."

After this triumph, Pearce's output slowed: there would be only four more full-length novels in the next half-century. In *A Dog So Small*, Ben wants a dog so badly that he wills into life a picture of a Chihuahua—a dog so small he can see it only with his eyes shut—and becomes absorbed in a "waking dream." The intensity of Ben's feelings finds counterbalance in the wisdom of the resolution, in which Ben "saw clearly that you couldn't have impossible things, however much you wanted them. He saw that if you didn't have the possible things, then you had nothing."

The Battle of Bubble and Squeak is a domestic comedy/drama, the story of a household thrown into turmoil when the oldest boy brings home two gerbils, disobeying his mother's ban on pets. Here the skill with which Pearce formerly evoked landscape or emotion is brought to bear on family dynamics, but there is a great deal of light-heartedness as well, even some slapstick, with scenes of gerbil mischief and falling furniture. *The Way to Sattin Shore* is arguably her darkest novel, a psychological drama in which young Kate Tranter discovers that everything she has been told about her family's past is a lie. Characters and setting are vivid; the sense of the past overlaying the present is palpable.

In 2004, Pearce's first novel for over two decades, *The Little Gentleman*, was published to great acclaim. In this gentle fantasy a little girl must help her friend, a mole, remove the magic spell that has bestowed reluctant immortality on him, even though it means losing his friendship. Pearce's fine sense of the natural world and the nature of friendship are at the center of this charming story, which turned out to be her final novel.

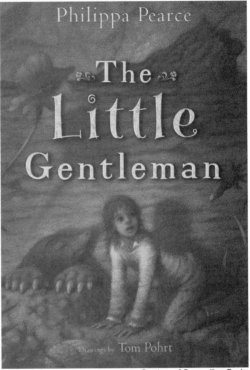

Courtesy of Greenwillow Books

Philippa Pearce was also a consummate writer of short stories. Some are realistic, some deal with the supernatural, but most often in her short stories the line between the ordinary and the eerie is unsettlingly, shiveringly, blurred. Several anthologies were published through the years: *What the Neighbors Did*, *The Shadow Cage*, and *Who's Afraid?*. In 2002 the stories were collected in the omnibus volume, *Familiar and Haunting*, which was published to general acclaim.

For over forty years, Pearce lived happily in her cottage, overlooking a large garden, near her childhood home. Her daughter Sally, when she grew up, lived next door with her own two children. Philippa Pearce often spoke at conferences and was still making appearances, talking about the importance of books and reading for children, until just before her death at the end of 2006. She suffered a stroke and died on December 21, at the age of 86.

For a special issue of *The Horn Book* magazine published at the end of 2000, prominent authors were asked which books they would like to see become "future classics." Newbery medalist Susan Cooper's choice was *Tom's Midnight Garden*, and she wrote about the denouement: "Now there's a gift: the discovery that something most precious, stolen by time, has not been lost after all." Future readers will always retain the gift of Philippa Pearce's legacy—her vivid, insightful, and compassionate children's books.

SELECTED WORKS: *Minnow on the* Say, illus. by Edward Ardizzone, 1955 (U.S. edition, The *Minnow Leads to Treasure*, 1958); *Tom's Midnight Garden*, illus. by Susan Einzig, 1959; *Mrs. Cockle's Cat*, illustrated by Anthony Maitland, 1963; *A Dog So Small*, illus. by Anthony Maitland, 1963; *The Children of the House*, with Brian Fairfax-Lucy, illus. by John Sergeant, 1968; *The Elm Street Lot*, 1969; *What the Neighbors Did and Other Stories*, illus. by Faith Jaques, 1973; *The Squirrel Wife*, illus. by Derek Collard, 1972; *The Shadow Cage and Other Tales of the Supernatural*, illus. by Janet Archer, 1977; *The Battle of Bubble and Squeak*, illus. by Alan Baker, 1978; *The Way to Sattin Shore*, illus. by Charlotte Voake, 1983; *Lion at School and Other Stories*, illus. by Caroline Sharpe, 1985; *Who's Afraid?: And Other Strange Stories*, 1987; Fresh, illus. by Berta Zimdars, 1988; *Emily's Own Elephant*, illus. by John Lawrence, 1988; *Familiar and Haunting: Collected Stories*, 2002; *The Little Gentleman*, illus. by Tom Pohrt, 2004.

SUGGESTED READING: *Something About the Author*, vol. 129, 2002; Silvey, Anita, ed., *Children's Books and Their Creators*, 1995; *Children's Literature Review*, vol. 9, 1985; Rees, David, *The Marble in the Water: Essays on Contemporary Writers for Children and Young Adults*, 1980; Blishen, Edward, ed., *The Thorny Paradise: Writers on Writing for Children*, 1975; Townsend, John Rowe, *A Sense of Story: Essays on Contemporary Writers for Children*, 1971; Cameron, Eleanor, *The Green and Burning Tree: On the Writing and Enjoyment of Children's Books*, 1969; Crouch, Marcus, *Treasure Seekers and Borrowers: Children's Books in Britain, 1900–1960*, 1962; Periodicals—Ellis, Sarah. "Missing from the Meadow: Philippa Pearce 1920–2006," *The Horn Book Magazine*, May 2007; Cooper, Susan, "Future Classics," *The Horn Book Magazine*, Nov. 2000; Natov, Roni and Geraldine DeLuca, "An Interview with Philippa Pearce," *The Lion and the Unicorn*, vol. 9, 1985; Pearce, Philippa, "The Writer's View of Childhood," *The Horn Book Magazine*, Feb. 1962.

"I grew up in a small town not far from Pittsburgh, Pennsylvania. We lived on the raw frontier of a new subdivision, where eighteen small ranch houses sat bravely on eighteen lots with tiny sticks of trees and unpaved driveways. To a child, it was a paradise of uninterrupted backyards with unlimited playmates and extra mothers and fathers available, if you should happen to need one. Not to mention woods and a creek right nearby.

"I thought we must be the luckiest people on earth. I remember even liking my age and feeling a little sorry for anyone born in a year other than 1956.

"My sister Cathie taught me to read when I was four years old and she was six. I remember being able to read about the lifestyle of the hopping bunnies while my fellow kindergartners could only look at pictures of them. Also in kindergarten, we made butter by passing around a jar of heavy cream and shaking it, and we learned to sing 'Dites-moi' from *South Pacific*, which is why I love to cook and why I speak such good French.

"Okay, I don't speak French. Yet. But reading became part of me right away. I can picture myself at every age with my head buried in a book, immersed in the worlds of the Bobbsey Twins, then Sarah Crewe, then David Copperfield, then Kilgore Trout. I was absorbed both by the stories and the pictures that illustrated them. I remember studying intently a drawing of Nan Bobbsey holding her skirt just so to climb up into a sleigh, and later, portrait-style paintings of the Little Women. The *Peanuts* comic strip was a daily source of inspiration.

"I've always loved drawing, and I've always been a reader. I studied art in college at Penn State University and in graduate school at the University of Wisconsin-Milwaukee. In both places, I met wonderful teachers and friends. New worlds were opened to me. I learned to see beauty in unlikely places. My parents thought I was nuts. I was considered a promising student. My parents wondered how I was going to earn a living. So did I.

"Afterwards, I worked at all sorts of jobs while I waited for my real job, my 'me,' to pop up. I worked as a picture-framer, a waitress, a drawing instructor, and at a natural foods grocery

Photo by Kate Fairman

Lynne Rae Perkins

July 31, 1956–

store. I moved to Boston and worked as a graphic designer. All the while, I was reading, drawing, and sometimes writing.

"While in Boston, I met a fellow from Michigan whose ideas about life were as impractical as my own. We fell in love, drove to Michigan, and lived in a cabin on a hillside, which eventually grew larger and more house-like. We have since moved to a little town nearby so that we can walk more and drive less. We have two children, a cat, and a dog.

"While we were still living on the hillside, I had the opportunity to show my artwork to the art director of Greenwillow Books. I had often thought that I would like to draw illustrations for books. To my surprise, while I was showing her my portfolio, the art director asked me if I was also a writer. Thinking suddenly that maybe I was, I went home, wrote down a story I had been mulling over, and sent it to her. This story, *Home Lovely*, became my first picture book. It sounds quick and easy and out-of-nowhere, but I wrote my first story after being a reader for many years. I think that reading a lot, and just living life, gave me some inadvertent training.

"I like that I get to both write and draw. Sometimes words seem like the right way to say something; sometimes pictures do."

"I like that I get to both write and draw. Sometimes words seem like the right way to say something; sometimes pictures do. In *Criss Cross*, I also got to write songs, build models, and take photographs. My daughter told me I was having too much fun.

"My books are peopled by those I have known and loved, and also by those I meet briefly and whose lives I have to imagine. I think reading and writing books is a way of having conversations with people. I was on the reader's side for the first part of my life, and still am. When my first book was reviewed and I realized that a few people besides my mother were actually reading it, I felt lucky to think that I could be on this end of the conversation, too. I still do."

ॐ   ॐ   ॐ

Newbery Award–winning author Lynne Rae Perkins spent her early adolescence being baffled by questions like why football players didn't like smart girls and how she could choose one career and work at it for the rest of her working life. She earned her bachelor's degree in fine arts at Penn State University in 1978 and her M.A. at the University of Wisconsin–Milwaukee in 1981. Since she was good at math and art, her high school guidance counselor had once suggested a career in architecture, but Perkins worked at a wide variety of jobs before she found her way into the children's book field. It wasn't until she met her husband, Bill, who introduced her to the idea of self-employment, that her true career path began to take shape.

In Perkins's first picture book, *Home Lovely*, a lonely little girl plants a garden near the family's trailer home, aided by a friendly mailman. With sunny pen-and-ink and watercolor illustrations, appealing characters, and imaginative details, this warm, nurturing book received a *Boston Globe-Horn Book* Picture Book Honor award as well as a National Parenting Publications (NAPPA) Picture Book Award, and was cited as a *Bulletin of the Center for Children's Books* Blue Ribbon title and a *Horn Book* Fanfare book.

Turning to writing for older children, Perkins continued to include illustrations, finding ways to enhance a longer novel with pictures. *All Alone in the Universe*, an introspective story about two 13-year-old friends who grow apart with the arrival of a third, is accompanied by wry pen-and-ink drawings attributed to the main character. This title explores the nature of friendship, the pain that follows the loss of a friend, and the ways that change can bring about the development of new friendships. Gentle and humorous as well as sad and poignant, this title was named an ALA Notable Children's Book, a *Booklist* Editors' Choice, one of the *Booklist* Top 10 First Novels, and a *Bulletin* Blue Ribbon title.

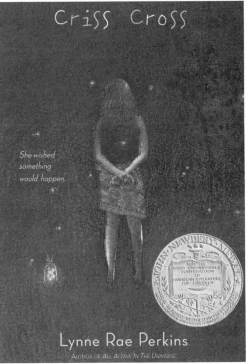

Courtesy of Greenwillow Books

Perkins's illustrations for *Georgie Lee*, an early chapter book by Sharon Phillips Denslow, help to tell the gentle and funny story of a nine-year-old boy and his adventures on his grandmother's farm. The delicate and cozy black-and-white line drawings emphasize the companionable relationships between animals and humans. *Georgie Lee* was cited as an ALA Notable Children's Book and named one of Bank Street College's Best Books of the Year.

Snow Music, a picture book that Perkins wrote and illustrated, was presented with a *Boston Globe–Horn Book* Picture Book Honor award. In this melodious, poetic title, Perkins' whimsical ink and watercolor illustrations—including endpapers covered in snowflake notes—highlight the soft, wintry, orchestral tale of aa lost dog, a boy searching for him, a girl, a deer, a rabbit and a squirrel.

The main character from *All Alone in the Universe* returns in the novel, *Criss Cross*, which won the 2006 Newbery Medal and was named an ALA Notable Children's Book as well as an ALA Best Book for Young Adults. This existential tale is told in a series of 38 short vignettes written as questions-and-answers, poetry, haiku, and prose, as three friends wonder how they fit into the universe, experience romantic yearnings and unrequited loves, and crisscross paths as they move towards adulthood. Like Perkins's earlier novel, *Criss Cross* is illustrated with humorous drawings. The idea of her characters having completely different experiences as they all go down the same road provided the spark that prompted Perkins to write this inventive book.

Pictures from Our Vacation, Perkins's latest picture book, describes a family trip and points out that such excursions are not always light and happy. The two children in the book use their new cameras to record some of the boring parts, but when relatives gather and bonds are forged, they are too busy enjoying themselves to take photos. This quirky look at family dynamics was named a *Horn Book* Fanfare title, a *Bulletin of the Center for Children's Books* Blue Ribbon, and an ALA Notable Children's Book.

Lynne Rae Perkins and her husband have two children, Lucy and Frank. They live in northern Michigan.

SELECTED WORKS WRITTEN AND ILLUSTRATED: *Home Lovely*, 1995; *Clouds for Dinner*, 1997; *All Alone in the Universe*, 1999; *The Broken Cat*, 2002; *Snow Music*, 2003; *Criss Cross*, 2005; *Pictures from Our Vacation*, 2007; *The Cardboard Piano*, 2008.

SELECTED WORKS ILLUSTRATED: *Georgie Lee*, by Sharon Phillips Denslow, 2002.

SUGGESTED READING: *Something About the Author*, vol. 172, 2007. Periodicals—Stevenson, Deborah, "Rising Star: Lynne Rae Perkins," *Bulletin of the Center for Children's Books*, February 1, 2000.

WEB SITE: www.lynneraeperkins.com

Julie Anne Peters

January 16, 1952–

"In my baby book my mother wrote, 'Julie slept from 6:30 P.M. to 6:30 A.M.' This was March 10, 1952, and I was not quite two months old. It was remarkable enough to my mother to note. It's remarkable to me because that was the first—and last—time I ever slept through the night. I'm a terrible insomniac. Even as a child, I had a hard time falling asleep. To quiet my mind, I used to make up stories in my head. My stories weren't about fairy princesses in castles or magic carpet rides. They were epics about terrified children running from enemies with guns, or earthquakes swallowing people whole. I'd drift off to fears about getting shot or buried alive. Am I weird?

"My stories didn't originate in books because I wasn't a reader as a child. I hated to read. I *could* read, and I certainly had the capacity to transport myself via my own imagination, but I didn't discover the joy of reading until I was in seventh grade.

"In seventh grade I had an English teacher who used to require all her classes to check out books from the library each week. I dreaded those days. Libraries were dungeons to me. They were cold, drafty, dreary places where mostly dust and dead bugs collected. I don't think my elementary school even had a library, and public libraries were foreboding institutions. They were places where people weren't allowed to talk, or laugh, or eat. I mostly hid out in the back of the fiction section and wrote notes to my friends. One day the bell rang and I hadn't found a book to check out. We weren't allowed to leave the library without a book, so I grabbed the nearest one. It was *Beany Malone* by Lenora Mattingly Weber.

Photo by Memories by Treva

"I can't imagine why I'd even open the cover of this book and read one page. I must've been grounded or barred from using the telephone. I did read page one, and then page two. Page three . . . four. This book was like, *good*. Beany Malone was a person I could relate to. She was a real girl who lived in real times. She had a brother, like me, and a father she adored. She had ordinary, everyday troubles. I fell in love with Beany Malone, and I fell in love with reading.

"My childhood was both ordinary and extraordinary. I grew up in Jamestown, New York, and we moved to Colorado when I was five. My father worked for Montgomery Ward (a large department store chain, now defunct), and my mother was a smart, creative, ambitious, resourceful housewife. In Colorado my father quit his retail job and bought a Gulf gas station. The gas station was the coolest place in the world for a kid to hang out. I remember the strong smells of gasoline and oil, the noisy whir of traffic, and the bottles of Coke we used to get for free because my dad was boss.

"My mother wrote in my baby book, under *Advice to My Child*: 'Always remember, your mother and father are your best friends.' I came out to my mom as a lesbian when I was twenty-one. Back then gay people didn't come out. We kept our identities secret and our relationships hidden. When you're in love, though, you want to shout it to the world. Even though I was scared to tell my mom I loved a girl, she was there for me. My mother said, 'I'm glad you told me. Don't ever tell anyone else.' Parents want to protect their children, of course, but this made my love for another human being feel somehow 'unspeakable.' It sent me into the closet for twenty years.

"When I was in high school, my parents divorced. This was at a time in history when parents didn't get divorced, especially in Catholic families. A family's dissolution is always traumatic, and I can still conjure up the fear, shame, alienation, and the profound sense of separation and loss. These emotions and themes crop up consistently in my books for young readers.

> "*My young-adult novels about lesbian, gay, and transgender people have been the most rewarding and satisfying books for me to write.*"

"My young-adult novels about lesbian, gay, and transgender people have been the most rewarding and satisfying books for me to write. They incorporate all the strongest themes in my own life. I feel they give my work a higher calling and greater purpose. Readers who write to thank me for reflecting and validating them as a person grant me courage, strength and confidence.

"But it still amazes me that my stories do anything more than engage my own mind. My brother asked me once, 'Should I know your characters from our childhood?' I said, 'Of course, John. They're all me.' Bits and pieces of me, the puzzle of me, snapshots from my babyhood, little parts of my childhood, fragments from my youth."

☙ ☙ ☙

In addition to her older brother, Julie Anne Peters has two younger sisters, Jeanne and Susan. She received a B.A. in elementary education from Colorado Women's College in 1974 and taught fifth grade for one year. Then, after earning a B.S. in computer and management science from the Metropolitan State College of Denver, she worked as a research analyst, computer programmer, and systems engineer for Tracom Corporation and Electronic Data Systems in Denver. When she had earned an M.B.A. in business and computer science from the University of

Colorado in Denver in 1989, she realized that business was not the career for her. However, she did discover she had an aptitude for technical writing. She also began writing short stories and nonfiction articles that she sold to various periodicals, including *Wee Wisdom*, *Hopscotch*, *Purple Cow*, *Lollipops*, and *Wilson Library Bulletin*.

Julie Peters's books are written for a variety of age ranges, but in all the stories her characters typically face the challenges of being 'different' while remaining true to themselves. Her first book, *The Stinky Sneakers Contest*, which was inspired by the memory of her own beat-up sneakers when she was a child, won the KC3 Reading Award, presented by the Greater Kansas City Association of School Librarians. Her middle-grade books include a series about a group of sixth-grade losers who band together to get even with the popular girls—the "Snob Squad"—who torment them.

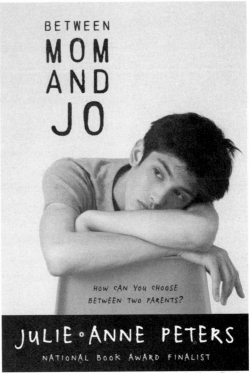

Courtesy of Little, Brown Books for Young Readers

While Peter's books for middle-grade readers have been applauded for their humor and depth, it is her young-adult books that have received the greatest praise. Themes of tolerance and friendship can be found in *Define "Normal,"* in which two middle-school girls, who are complete opposites in personality, style, and social status, learn that judging people by appearances can often be misleading. Although the book is not about special-needs children, the story grew out of the author's experiences working with such children in the 1970s. She began to examine the concept of "normal" and how it is used to label people, particularly teens. (She also claims she has a personal connection to this book in that she always harbored a secret desire to dye her hair pink.) In addition to winning the California Young Reader Medal, the Maryland Black-Eyed Susan Book Award, and the Oklahoma Sequoyah Young Adult Book Award, *Define "Normal,"* was named an ALA Best Book for Young Adults and an ALA Quick Pick for Reluctant Readers.

Peters not only raises important points about the ramifications of a gay teenager's coming out in *Keeping You a Secret*, but also transcends barriers, allowing readers of all persuasions to focus on universal truths about self-knowledge, acceptance, pride, and the hardships of wrestling with the perceptions of others. This book was an ALA Amelia Bloomer title in Recommended Feminist Books for Youth. It was also among the New York Public Library's Books for the Teen Age 75th Anniversary Edition and a Lambda Literary Award finalist.

Luna: A Novel, a groundbreaking book about the relationship between two siblings as a girl's transgender brother struggles for self-identity and acceptance, was a National Book Award Finalist in Young People's Literature. This touching portrayal of the sister's concern for her brother's secret and her own need for a normal life presented a sympathetic look at a problem that is seldom raised in young adult literature. It was named an ALA GLBTQ Stonewall Honor Book, an ALA Best Books for Young Adults, and one of New York Public Library's Books for the Teen Age. It also won the Colorado Book Award for Young Adult Literature.

Peters says writing books for young people takes her back to a time in her life when the decisions she made and the paths she chose determined the kind of person she has become. Remembering that crucial time when she was trying to figure out her place in the world, she hopes to ease the way for teens today. Julie Anne Peters lives in Colorado with the partner she met in college. Together, they share a view of the snow-capped mountains along the Continental Divide.

SELECTED WORKS: *The Stinky Sneakers Contest*. 1992; *Risky Friends*, 1993; *B.J.'s Billion-Dollar Bet*, 1994; *How Do You Spell G-E-E-K?* 1996; *Revenge of the Snob Squad*, 1998; *Romance of the Snob Squad*, 1999; *Love Me, Love My Broccoli*, 1999; *Define "Normal,"* 2000; *A Snitch in the Snob Squad*, 2001; *Keeping You a Secret*, 2003; *Luna: A Novel*, 2004; *Far from Xanadu*, 2005; *Between Mom and Jo*, 2006; *Grl2grl: Short Fictions*, 2007.

SUGGESTED READING: *Something About the Author*, vol. 128, 2002. Periodicals—Peters, Julie Anne, "When You Write Humor for Children," *The Writer*, January 1998.

WEB SITE: www.julieannepeters.com

Myles C. and Sandra L. Pinkney

Sandra Pinkney writes: "I am a native New Yorker and come from a large family of four brothers and six sisters. I was number eight in the group. I spent most of my childhood in Ossining, New York. At the age of three, I became very ill and almost died. I had contracted lead poisoning that left me with a learning disability. This not only caused me difficulty educationally, but also caused social problems.

"In first grade, I was bussed to a special school, separated from my brothers and sisters, so I could receive special services. However, the principal of the school decided to try something new and mainstream me in a regular class (a process known as inclusion today). I walked into the classroom and noticed I was the only person of color. Later, walking out to the playground, I realized I was the only person in the whole first grade that was black. I had problems making friends because of the color of my skin. This situation is the basis of my first published book, *Shades of Black*. I realized I didn't want any children to feel bad about the skin they live in.

"*Shades of Black: A Celebration of Our Children* was written in the genre of poetry. I didn't know I could write poetry until I tried. It wasn't as hard as I thought. I was able to relay my feelings with very few words. I enjoy writing poetry, but you might just see a fictional book from me in the near future.

"I get asked quite often 'What made you become a children's book author?' The answer is simple: I love children, and I love seeing the smiles on their faces when they see themselves inside of a book, or travel to a different place though a story.

"I remember the very first story I wrote, called 'The Year There Was Almost No Santa Claus.' The story was about Santa Claus getting sick and not being able to deliver the Christmas presents. Luckily, they found a substitute Santa Claus who saved the day. I couldn't believe it, but I received an 'A' for my story and a little notation at the end from my fifth grade teacher. It said, 'Sandi, what a great story. I'm so glad the children didn't miss Christmas. You are a great storyteller.' Right then I knew I had a gift, a gift for telling stories.

"People ask me how I met my husband Myles. I met Myles in tenth grade. He walked into the gymnasium with a leather coat,

Courtesy of Myles C. Pinkney

Sandra L. Pinkney
August 9, 1965–

wool cap, and a camera around his neck. I said then I would marry him and later I did. Myles and I married in August of 1984. We now have three children—Myles 'Leon', Charnelle-Rene, and Rashad.

"Myles and I enjoy working together. We have collaborated on all of my published works. My favorite time to write is early in the morning before the birds get up. This is when I feel that God inspires me the most. I believe that with God anything is possible. My future is wide open."

Myles Pinkney writes: "I learned early on the impact that a photograph could have on its viewer. Any emotion that a person can have can be evoked from a single image. A good

Courtesy of Myles C. Pinkney

photograph will capture the essence of a person. I hope the viewer will sense the personality, the emotion, and the uniqueness that each individual possesses.

"Creating children's books is especially rewarding for me for several reasons. I believe that children are a gift from God. I also see that there are so many negative images that they are exposed to every day. I want for them to be able to see positive images of themselves. I hope that our books are able to build them up and let them feel good about themselves. I always hope to not just photograph children, but to capture that quality in every child that makes them special."

CB   CB   CB

Myles C. Pinkney
December 1, 1963–

The award-winning partnership of Myles and Sandra Pinkney began as a high school romance and continues today in their marriage and parenting, and in the vibrant books they have produced together.

Myles Carter Pinkney was born in Massachusetts and grew up in Croton-on-Hudson, New York, in a family of artists. His father is the acclaimed illustrator Jerry Pinkney; his mother, Gloria Jean Pinkney, is the author of several children's books in addition to being a designer of clothes, hats, and jewelry. His brother Brian is also a well-known illustrator, his brother Scott is a painter, and his sister Troy is an art therapist.

Myles first became interested in photography at the age of 12, when he received a camera as a birthday gift from his father. He learned how to develop black-and-white pictures as part of his middle school photography club and was involved in his high school yearbook and college newspaper. In 1993 Myles graduated from Marist College with a B.A. degree in communications. He opened his own photography business, Myles Studio, in Poughkeepsie, New York, and continues to develop his skills through the Professional Photographers Society of New York and the Professional Photographers of America.

Myles Pinkney has a distinct style in his photography, creating natural images to capture the personality of each subject. At the studio he works as a portrait and wedding photographer as well as designing images for commercial clients such as album producers, musicians, business professionals, magazine publishers, and newspapers. In 1997 he published two children's books that demonstrated the creative power of photography as illustration. Pinkney's photographs for *Can You Imagine?*, an autobiographical account of children's author Patricia McKissack, followed the well-known writer through her daily routine, capturing every aspect of her career and life. Nikki Grimes's collection of poetry, *It's Raining Laughter*, gave free range to Pinkney's photographs of children engaging in a variety of childhood pleasures from boisterous play to quiet reading.

> *"This situation is the basis of my first published book, Shades of Black. I realized I didn't want any children to feel bad about the skin they live in."*

It is the books that Myles Pinkney has created with his wife, however, that have brought both of them the most attention. Sandra Pinkney received an associate's degree in early childhood education from Dutchess Community College in Poughkeepsie, New York and a B.S. in management from Nyack College in Nyack, New York. She has been actively involved in organizations that help in the development and enrichment of young children. In 1995 Sandra opened her own business, Li'l Praisers Christian Daycare.

Sandra's poetic language and Myles's photographs proved to be a winning combination in their first collaboration, *Shades of Black*, published in 2000. Sandra used vivid writing to describe the many skin tones, hair textures, and eye colors of African Americans, while Myles's dynamic photography expressed and celebrated this rich diversity. Earning the NAACP Image Award for Children's Literature, this book was also recognized by numerous organizations. It was named a NCTE Notable Book for a Global Society, a *Skipping Stones* honor book, a Parent's Guide to Children's Media winner, and a Highly Commended citation for the Charlotte Zolotow Award for picture book writing.

READ AND RISE

by Sandra L. Pinkney ✳ Photographs by Myles C. Pinkney

Foreword by
Maya Angelou

Courtesy of Cartwheel Books, Scholastic, Inc.

The Pinkneys followed their early success with *A Rainbow All Around Me*, which was nominated for the 2003 NAACP Image Award. Expanding on the concept of teaching about color, they explored the many colors in flags, clothing, and skin tones among a diverse range of children. The award-winning Pinkney team next produced a book for children entitled *Read and Rise*. Part of a collaborative effort launched by Scholastic publishers and the National Urban League, the book was designed to give primary grade children a clear message—reading is the path to achievement. The Read and Rise initiative has distributed literacy guides through Urban League affiliate organizations, schools, libraries, and government agencies, and has also produced a free magazine for parents and children to help improve literacy skills in the African American community. *Read and Rise*, the book, features a foreword by poet Maya Angelou and a compelling text by Sandra Pinkney aimed at convincing young children that reading can lead directly to fulfilling their dreams. The photographs by Myles expand this message visually by showing children interacting with books in a wide variety of situations.

The couple's fourth collaboration celebrates the Latino community in the same way that *Shades of Black* celebrates African Americans. The title, *I Am Latino: The Beauty in*

Me, describes the upbeat message perfectly. Once again, the Pinkneys' winning combination of rhythmic writing and vibrant photography has created a book that all children can embrace and enjoy.

SELECTED WORKS (Illustrated by Myles Pinkney): *Can You Imagine?*, by Patricia McKissack, 1997; *It's Raining Laughter*, by Nikki Grimes, 1997; *Sitting Pretty: A Celebration of Black Dolls*, by Dinah Johnson, 2000; *Meet Shel Silverstein*, by S. Ward, 2001; *Learning How to Appreciate Differences*, by Susan Kent, 2001; *Learning How to Feel Good about Yourself*, by Susan Kent, 2001; *Let's Talk about Feeling Worried*, by Melanie Ann Apel, 2001; *Let's Talk about Feeling Confused*, by Melanie Apel, 2001; *In the Forest of Your Remembrance*, by Gloria Jean Pinkney, illus. with Jerry Pinkney and Brian Pinkney, 2002; *Music from Our Lord's Holy Heaven*, comp. by Gloria Jean Pinkney, illus. with Jerry Pinkney and Brian Pinkney, 2005.

SELECTED WORKS: (Written by Sandra Pinkney and illustrated by Myles Pinkney): *Shades of Black*, 2000; *A Rainbow All Around Me*, 2002; *Read and Rise*, 2006; *I Am Latino: The Beauty in Me*, 2007.

SUGGESTED READING: *Something About the Author*, vol. 128, 2002.

WEB SITE: www.MylesStudio.com

Tom Pohrt

June 18, 1953–

"When we were growing up, my brother and I had two large framed prints by the Mexican muralist and book illustrator Miguel Covorrubias hung on the wall over our beds. My father had bought these on his return from the Second World War in a shop in San Francisco as a gift for my mother. The prints were of maps showing the United States, Asia and the Pacific islands, one illustrating the peoples of these regions and the other showing their traditional art forms. The images were colorful and detailed. These prints encompassed for me my love of narrative art, travel and adventure; I would endlessly study them both for the information they conveyed as well for Covorrubias's fine painting. I still have one and my brother has the other.

"It was not until half way through my undergraduate college years that I seriously took up drawing and painting. Bored and uncertain of my future in school I spent increasing hours in libraries reading about the history and techniques of 19th century British watercolor painting. At first this was simply an extension of a keen interest I'd had in the arts since childhood. I taught myself to draw and paint with watercolors to understand better what I was looking at in books and on the walls of museums. I drew and painted for myself with little idea of someday having work published, much less being paid for it.

"While my two older brothers and I were growing up, my father held a white-collar job at General Motors and my mother was a substitute teacher for grade school in Flint, Michigan. My parents were avid book readers and read to my brothers and myself continuously throughout our childhood until we were reading on our own. I recall the Little Golden Books and the animal stories of Thornton W. Burgess and later the classics illustrated by N. C. Wyeth. The Babar books by Jean De Brunhoff were favorites. My father enjoyed reading aloud Mark Twain's *Adventures of Huckleberry Finn* and *The Adventures of Tom Sawyer*. The illustrations in all of these works captivated me as much as the stories themselves.

Photo by Carmen Pohrt

Tom Pohrt

"We spent summer vacations traveling west into the Dakotas and Montana, following my parent's passion for Native American Indians—their history, religion and art. My father had spent two summers during the Depression years of the 1930s in the Civil Conservation Corp in north central Montana, where he lived, worked and shared in the lives of the Gros Ventre Indian community. It turned out to be a lifelong and meaningful friendship. The stories he told to my brothers and myself of those times in his life seemed as adventurous as anything in the books he read to us.

"My mother still has a photo album from the late 1930s of a Caribbean cruise she took with a girlfriend, the two of them fresh out of college. I pored over these black-and-white snapshots as a child and later, when I was writing and illustrating a picture book I titled *Having a Wonderful Time*. Looking back on my childhood I realize how much my parents gave us, how those stories of their lives are now a part of me, and how much they influence my work."

ରେ   ରେ   ରେ

A self-taught artist, Tom Pohrt has incorporated many interests developed during his growing years into his illustration work. A delight in the world around him, the joy he found in nature and animals, his parents' fascination with Native American lore, as well as the imaginative stories they read to him—all led to the development of his own creative skills. He attended the University of Michigan and worked in automobile factories and in small-press publishing before devoting himself full-time to the pursuit of art and illustration. In addition to children's books, he creates editorial and general illustrations for such clients as the *Wall Street Journal* and *Orion* magazine.

Pohrt's illustrations for *Crow and Weasel*, a coming-of-age fable by the noted environmental writer Barry Lopez, gained early recognition for his talent when the book became a *New York Times* bestseller. His ability to convey the wisdom of Native American folklore and its connection to the animal world helped the book achieve wide acclaim. He paired again with Lopez for *Lessons from the Wolverine*, another story about the wisdom humans can gain from animals. In *Coyote Goes Walking* the artist turned author to retell four Native American trickster tales that he also illustrated. His earthy watercolors proved a perfect match for the gently humorous stories of that classic American Indian character, Coyote, who can act as both creator and cunning trickster. Set against the warm hues of the natural environment, Pohrt's animals come to life in both his descriptions and his drawings, while the stories' lessons emerge with subtle strength— respect all life, listen carefully, and pay attention. A similar tone is found in Howard Norman's collection of Algonquin stories, *Trickster and the Fainting Birds*, which Pohrt illustrated with his usual attention to detail, subtle humor, and earth tones. In these stories the trickster character is a man, though he does have the ability to take on animal form in some of the tales. Once again the message of each story points toward kindness, truthfulness, and being helpful to those in need.

The same theme of the importance of the natural world pervades the novels that Pohrt has illustrated. Jim Harrison's *The Boy Who Ran to the Woods* is a story of redemption. Wild and unruly, the protagonist Jimmy gets into trouble in and out of school, and it is only after spending a summer in the woods that he comes to terms with himself. Pohrt's illustrations capture the story's setting and provide a perfect complement to Harrison's cautionary tale. *The Little Gentleman*, by award-winning British

"I taught myself to draw and paint with watercolors to understand better what I was looking at in books and on the walls of museums."

THE
WISHING
BONE

AND

OTHER POEMS

STEPHEN MITCHELL ILLUSTRATED BY TOM POHRT

Courtesy of Candlewick Press

author Philippa Pearce, chronicles the friendship between a country girl, young Bet, and a magical mole, one who has mysteriously acquired the gift of speech and long life. Pohrt's illustrations again provide the perfect complement to the narrative, helping readers to connect with this gentle tale of magical realism. The book was named an ALA Notable Children's Book and one of *School Library Journal's* Best of the Year.

In *The Wishing Bone and Other Poems*, written by Stephen Mitchell, Pohrt's drawings capture the humor and delight of the poem's fanciful themes, which detail a young girl's wishes to know more about the world. Whimsy and lightheartedness abound in these child-centered rhymes; they include a blend of sense and nonsense, with the wordplay reflected in Pohrt's pen-and-ink drawings that seem to dance across the page. Always at ease with the world of fancy, Pohrt and Mitchell have most recently paired to produce *Genies, Meanies, and Magic Rings*. Retelling three tales from *The Arabian Nights*, the classic collection from the Middle East, Mitchell appeals to children's love of adventure and the exotic. Pohrt's imagination is given new range to depict the sights, characters, and landscape of the world of Aladdin, Ali Baba, and Abu Keer.

Tom Pohrt met his wife, Carmen, while he was engaged in humanitarian work in Cuba. They were married in September 2002 in her hometown of Ciego de Avila. Their daughter, Isabel Pilar, was born in 2006 in Ann Arbor, Michigan, where the family lives today.

SELECTED WORKS ILLUSTRATED: *Who Met the Ice Lynx*, by Howard Norman, 1978; *The Man Who Kept Cigars in His Cap*, by Jim Henen, 1978; *Crow and Weasel*, by Barry Lopez, 1992; *Miko, Little Hunter of the North*, by Bruce Donehower, 1990; *A Child's Anthology of Poetry*, ed. by Elizabeth Hauge Sword and Victoria Flournoy McCarthy, 1995; *Lessons from the Wolverine*, by Barry Lopez, 1997; *An Old Shell: Poems of the Galapagos*, by Tony Johnston, 1999; *Trickster and the Fainting Birds*, by Howard Norman, 1999; *The Tomb of the Boy King: A True Story in Verse*, by John Frank, 2000; *The Boy Who Ran to the Woods*, by

Jim Harrison, 2000; *The Wishing Bone and Other Poems*, by Stephen Mitchell, 2003; *The Little Gentleman*, by Philippa Pearce, 2004; *Genies, Meanies, and Magic Rings: Three Tales from The Arabian Nights*, retold by Stephen Mitchell, 2007.

SELECTED WORKS WRITTEN AND ILLUSTRATED: *Coyote Goes Walking*, as reteller, 1995; *Having a Wonderful Time*, 1999.

Ｏne of the most popular and widely read novelists in England today, Terence David John Pratchett grew up in Beaconsfield, Buckinghamshire, England. He attended High Wycombe Technical High School, preferring woodworking to Latin. An avid reader, he always enjoyed fantasy, myths, and ancient history. He published his first story, "The Hades Business," at age 13 in his school magazine. Denounced as immoral by the headmaster but popular with the students, it was published commercially two years later in *Science Fantasy* magazine. With the earnings of £14, Pratchett bought a typewriter.

Photo copyright © by Robin Mathews

Terry Pratchett

April 28, 1948–

At age 17 he left school to accept a job in journalism at the Bucks Free Press in 1965. Taking the two-year National Council for the Training of Journalists proficiency course while working there, he scored top in the country in the exams. In 1968 he married and two years later took a position with the *Western Daily Press*, moving with his wife Lyn to a cottage in Somerset where their daughter, Rhianna, was born.

At the age of 23 Pratchett published his first novel, *The Carpet People*, a children's fantasy about the adventures of a universe of miniscule people living in a carpet. (Originally written when he was 17, *The Carpet People* was rewritten when Pratchett was 43 to reflect his more mature viewpoint and better developed storytelling skills.) The original 1971 publication was launched at a party in the carpet section of Heal's department store. After it was published, Pratchett continued writing in his spare time and working as a journalist until 1980, when he became a press officer for the Central Electricity Generating Board, where his responsibilities included handling three nuclear power plants.

Pratchett's first conception of the enormously popular Discworld premiered in his adult novel *Strata*, but it is in *The Color of Magic* that readers meet signature characters Rincewind, Twoflower, and the Luggage and get a full tour of Discworld. Like *The Carpet People*, the Discworld series is set in a flat world, but this one sits on the shoulders of four giant elephants, which in turn rest on the back of a giant turtle swimming in space. *Mort*, the Discworld story of how Death takes on a young apprentice, became Pratchett's first bestseller and winner of the Dracula Society's Best Gothic Novel of the Year, enabling the author to write full-time. Since that initial success, Pratchett's books have consistently appeared on bestseller lists.

From time to time, Pratchett has taken breaks from his Discworld series to explore other fantasy realms. In 1989 he published the first of the Bromeliad trilogy: *Truckers*, in which he introduced readers to the hilarious adventures of four-inch high people from another planet who have crashed to earth. The aliens go from living under a department store floor in *Truckers* to a not quite abandoned quarry in *Diggers* to trying to communicate with their mother ship via satellite in *Wings*.

Continuing with the Discworld books, Pratchett published *Pyramids* in 1989. Winner of the British Fantasy Association's Best Novel Award, *Pyramids* spoofs the world of Ancient Egypt by introducing a teenager who is studying to become an assassin until the death of a relative makes him a pharaoh.

In the first volume of the Johnny Maxwell trilogy, *Only You Can Save Mankind*, which was shortlisted for the *Guardian* Children's Fiction Award, Pratchett turned a satirical eye on the 1991 Persian Gulf War. The book's main character enters a computer game and tries to help the aliens from being destroyed by other human computer game-players. In *Johnny and the Dead*, buried dead people take offense at having their final resting places sold to make way for a new housing development. Part commentary on the need for living people to respect the past, this title won the Writers' Guild of Great Britain's Best Children's Book Award, was shortlisted for the Carnegie Medal, and included in the New York Public Library's Books for the Teen Age. Johnny travels back in time to his own town during World War II in *Johnny and the Bomb*, which received the Smarties Book Prize Silver Medal and was shortlisted for the Carnegie Medal. The Johnny Maxwell trilogy became a 1995 British television miniseries. Discworld also came to television when *Hogfather*, a droll Santa Claus satire, was made into an award-winning miniseries.

Set in the Discworld universe, but specifically geared to younger readers, *The Amazing Maurice and His Educated Rodents* won the Carnegie Medal in 2001. A takeoff on the Pied Piper legend, this humorous fantasy and morality tale features Maurice, a streetwise alley cat and master schemer who works with a gang of rats and a piper with a stupid-looking grin to infest various towns with rats so the townsfolk will pay to get rid of them. This scheme is lucrative until they reach a town inhabited by conniving rat-catchers and something evil lurking in the town's cellars. Ideas for this book grew out of a visit Pratchett made to the Palace Hotel in San Francisco, where he saw a Pied Piper mural that included a boy with a stupid grin, the prototype for Pratchett's pied piper. Critically acclaimed in the U.S. as well as England, *The Amazing Maurice and His Educated Rodents* was among ALA's Top 10 Best Books for Young Adults and the New York Public Library's Books for the Teen Age, as well as its 100 Books for Reading and Sharing. It was also a named a Bank Street College Children's Book of Outstanding Merit.

A budding witch named Tiffany Aching teams up with a pack of little blue men to rescue her brother and stop an invasion in the fanciful farce, *The Wee Free Men*, which was a *School Library Journal* Best Book, a *Bulletin of the Center for Children's Books* Blue Ribbon title, and *Horn Book* Fanfare selection in the U.S. In Great Britain it was the winner of the Teen Choice W. H. Smith Book Award. Tiffany returns to hone her witch skills and battle a disembodied monster with the help of the little blue men

Courtesy of HarperCollins Publishers

in the suspense-filled comedy *A Hat Full of Sky*, which won the Mythopoeic Fantasy Award for Children's Literature, the Pacific Northwest Library Association's Young Reader's Choice Award, and the Locus Award. It was also named *Horn Book* Fanfare title.

In *Wintersmith*, which was shortlisted for the British Book Awards Children's Book of the Year, Tiffany deals with a lovesick boy-season named Wintersmith as she and the little blue men work to rescue Summer and set the seasons right. *Wintersmith* and *The Wee Free Men* were both cited as ALA Best Books for

Young Adults, and all three titles in the trilogy were named ALA Notable Children's Books and New York Public Library Books for the Teen Age. The strong, forthright character of Tiffany also earned each title in this trilogy a place on the ALA Amelia Bloomer list of feminist titles.

Pratchett has become known for his humor, creative wordplay, and frequent social commentary. Named the Fantasy and Science Fiction Author of 1993 at the British Book Awards, he went on to be presented the Order of the British Empire for services to literature, an honor conferred by the Prince of Wales at Buckingham Palace. With an education he claims he mostly acquired in the Beaconsfield Public Library, Pratchett nevertheless has received four honorary doctorates: in 1999 from the University of Warwick, in 2001 from the University of Portsmouth, in 2003 from the University of Bath, and in 2004 from Bristol University. He is one of Britain's best-selling living novelists, and his books have been translated into more than 35 languages. Like J.R.R. Tolkien's the Lord of the Rings and Douglas Adams's Hitchhiker's Guide to the Galaxy, Pratchett's Discworld books have inspired obsessive loyalty among his readers. His novels have given rise to annual Discworld Conventions, stage adaptations, role-playing games, hundreds of websites and chat rooms, a Discworld encyclopedia, and merchandise items such as quiz books, calendars, computer games, puzzles, t-shirts, and figurines.

Residing near the city of Salisbury in Wiltshire, England, Terry Pratchett continues to astound his readers with his limitless imagination and a capacity for interpreting his world with keen observation and satirical humor. During his acceptance speech for his Carnegie Medal, he stated: "Fantasy [is] about seeing the world from new directions. And one joke in the right place can make a point that a whole serious chapter can't quite achieve."

> *"Fantasy [is] about seeing the world from new directions. And one joke in the right place can make a point that a whole serious chapter can't quite achieve."*

SELECTED WORKS FOR YOUNG READERS (Dates are for British publication; U.S. dates, if different, are in parentheses): *The Carpet People*, 1971 (rev. and reissued, 1992); *Truckers* (The Bromeliad Trilogy), 1989 (1990); *Diggers* (The Bromeliad Trilogy), 1990 (1991); *Wings* (The Bromeliad Trilogy), 1990 (1991); *Only You Can Save Mankind* (Johnny Maxwell Trilogy), 1992 (2005); *Johnny and the Dead* (Johnny Maxwell Trilogy), 1993 (2006); *Johnny and the Bomb* (Johnny Maxwell Trilogy), 1996 (2007); *The Amazing Maurice and His Educated Rodents*, 2001; *The Wee Free Men* (Tiffany Aching Adventures), 2003; *A Hat Full of Sky* (Tiffany Aching Adventures), 2004 (2005); *Wintersmith* (Tiffany Aching Adventures), 2006.

SELECTED WORKS FOR ADULTS (Dates are for British publication; U.S. dates, if different, are in parentheses): *The Dark Side of the Sun*, 1976; *Strata*, 1981; *The Colour of Magic*, 1983 (U.S. edition, *The Color of Magic*); *The Light Fantastic*, 1986 (1987); *Equal Rites*, 1987 (1988); *Mort*, 1987 (1989); *Sourcery*, 1988 (1989); *Wyrd Sisters*, 1988 (1990); *Pyramids*, 1989; *Guards! Guards!*, 1989 (1990); *The Unadulterated Cat*, illus. by Gray Jolliffe, 1989; *Good Omens*, with Neil Gaiman, 1990; *Eric*, 1990 (1995); *Moving Pictures*, 1990 (1992); *Reaper Man*, 1991 (1992); *Witches Abroad*, 1991 (1993); *Small Gods*, 1992 (1994); *Terry Pratchett's The Colour of Magic: The Graphic Novel*, illus. by Steven Ross, 1992; *Lords and Ladies*, 1992 (1995); *The Streets of Ankh Morpork*, with Stephen Briggs, 1993; *Terry Pratchett's The Light Fantastic: The Graphic Novel*, illus. by Steven Ross and Joe Bennet, 1993; *Men at Arms*, 1993 (1996); *Mort: A Discworld Big Comic*, illus. by Graham Higgins, 1994; *The Discworld Companion*, with Stephen Briggs, 1994 (1997); *Soul Music*, 1994 (1995); *Interesting Times*, 1994 (1997); *The Discworld Mapp*, with Stephen Briggs, 1995 (2002); *Maskerade*, 1995 (1997); *Feet of Clay*, 1996; *The Pratchett Portfolio*, illus. by Paul Kidby, 1996; *Hogfather*, 1996 (1998); *Jingo*, 1997 (1998); *The Last Continent*, 1998 (1999); *Carpe Jugulum*, 1998 (1999); *A Tourist Guide to Lancre: A Discworld Mapp*, with Stephen Briggs, illus. by Paul Kidby, 1998; *GURPS: Discworld*, with Phil Masters, illus. by Paul Kidby, 1998; *The Science of Discworld*, with Ian Stewart and Jack Cohen, 1999; *Nanny Ogg's Cookbook*, with Tina Hannan and Stephen Briggs, illus. by Paul Kidby, 1999 (2001); *Death's Domain: A Discworld Mapp*, illus. by Paul Kidby, 1999 (2002); *Guards! Guards! A Discworld Big Comic*, illus. by Graham Higgins, 2000; *The Fifth Elephant*, 1999 (2000); *The Truth*, 2000; *Thief of Time*, 2001; *The Last Hero: A Discworld Fable*, illus. by Paul Kidby, 2001; *The Wyrdest Link: A Terry Pratchett Discworld Quizbook*, with David Langford, 2002 (2007); *The Science of Discworld II: The Globe*, with Ian Stewart and Jack Cohen, 2002 (2003); *Night Watch*, 2002; *The New Discworld Companion*, with Stephen Briggs, 2003 (2004); *Monstrous Regiment*, 2003; *Going Postal*, 2004; *The Art of Discworld*, illus. by Paul Kidby, 2004; *Darwin's Watch: The Science of Discworld III*, with Ian Stewart and Jack Cohen, 2005 (2006); *Thud!*, 2005; *Where's My Cow?*, illus. by Melvyn Grant, 2005; *Making Money*, 2007;

The Wit and Wisdom of Discworld, comp. by Stephen Briggs, 2007.

SUGGESTED READING: Parker, Vic, *Writers Uncovered: Terry Pratchett*, 2006; Butler, Andrew M., et. al., eds., *Terry Pratchett: Guilty of Literature*, 2000 (rev. ed., 2004); *Something About the Author*, vol. 139, 2003; Butler, Andrew, *The Pocket Essential: Terry Pratchett*, 2001; *Children's Literature Review*, vol. 64, 2000; MacRae, Cathi Dunn, *Presenting Young Adult Fantasy Fiction*, 1998; *Authors and Artists for Young Adults*, vol. 19, 1996; *St. James Guide to Fantasy Writers*, 1996. Periodicals—Barsanti, C., "Terry Pratchett's Flat-Out Success," *Book*, November/December 2002. Online—Web site of Colin Smythe, Limited, at http://www.colin-smythe.com/terrypages/tpindex.html

WEB SITE: www.terrypratchettbooks.com

Courtesy of Sean Qualls

Sean Qualls

1969–

"I was born in Cocoa Beach, Florida. At the time, my father was working for NASA. That probably accounts for my love of things to do with outer space. Shortly after my birth, I moved to a little town in New Jersey called Bordentown with my mom, sister and grandmother.

"I spent my early years scribbling on walls, watching television, listening to Kiss and Stevie Wonder records, playing in the woods and going for long walks on the abandoned railroad tracks. I don't remember when I first decided I would become an artist but I do remember watching friends in amazement as they magically created two-dimensional worlds with pencil and paper. One kid in particular was really amazing to watch. It seemed like he could draw anything while talking at the same time.

"My first ambition was to play guitar in a band like Ace Frehley did in Kiss, but I soon learned pencils and paper were more affordable than an electric guitar. So maybe it was by default that I decided to become an artist and not a musician. In the sixth grade, I created my first picture book with a couple of friends. By the time I was in a senior in high school, I knew I would be an artist; this was cemented by several trips to New York City and New Jersey teen arts festivals with my art class. Artists always seemed like the only group I belonged to.

"I went to art school at Pratt Institute in Brooklyn. However, after a year and a half I found myself broke and dropped out. Still determined to become a professional artist, I got a job working at the Brooklyn Museum, all the while filling up sketchbooks trying to teach myself what I didn't learn in art school. I've taken a few night courses but consider myself to be mostly self-educated. Eventually I put together an illustration portfolio that I began showing to magazine and book publishers. I got work but not right away. My earliest jobs were for magazines. I illustrated a lot of stories about people with depression and illustrated other stories for psychology/health publications.

"In 2002, my work was first noticed by children's book publishers when I sent out two different postcards. The first was an image of a little boy with his head bent over looking sad. That's kind of become my trademark. And the second image was a portrait of the rapper/singer Lauryn Hill. The first postcard landed me an interview with Arthur Levine at Scholastic and then a contract with Farrar, Straus and Giroux to illustrate *The Baby on the Way*. The second postcard got me the contract to illustrate *Powerful Words*. Arthur Levine, whom I had met earlier, saw the work for *Powerful Words* and asked me to illustrate *Dizzy*. Around the same time, Reka Simenson from Henry Holt called and asked if I would like to illustrate *The Poet Slave of Cuba*. While I was working on *Dizzy*, my editor at Holt asked me to illustrate *Before John Was a Jazz Giant*. This all happened in a span of just two years.

"Out of the seven books that I've illustrated so far, six have been biographical and two of those have been about famous musicians. I've always loved music (I listen to a lot of music while I work), so I feel very fortunate to be asked to illustrate books about musicians and other people I care about. One of my goals is to illustrate a story that I also write. I don't know if I'm a good writer but hopefully sometime soon people will pick up one of my books from a bookstore or library and judge for themselves. In the meantime, I hope people will enjoy the pictures I paint and draw."

"I've always loved music (I listen to a lot of music while I work), so I feel very fortunate to be asked to illustrate books about musicians and other people I care about."

CB CB CB

Sean Qualls is a freelance illustrator and artist whose work has appeared in such publications as the *Wall Street Journal*, the

Pennsylvania Gazette, *Ladies' Home Journal*, and the *Harvard Business Review*. He has designed album covers, created artwork for advertisements, and exhibited in galleries across the United States. His children's books have been critically acclaimed.

The first book he worked on, Karen English's *The Baby on the Way*, was actually his second book published, because it took two years to complete. In this *New York Times* Notable Book, a grandmother tells her grandson about her own birth in a poor farming family; Qualls's elegant spreads evoke a strong sense of place in both the past and the present. His second picture book, Wade Hudson's *Powerful Words*, took six months to complete and became his first published book. A Parents' Choice Award winner, it offers writing excerpts from such notable African Americans as Dred Scott, Langston Hughes, and Toni Morrison, along with Qualls's visually striking blue-toned black-and-white illustrations.

Courtesy of Arthur A. Levine Books, Scholastic, Inc.

The artist's expressionistic half-tone illustrations complement Margarita Engle's *The Poet Slave of Cuba*, a biography in verse that pays tribute to a little-known 19th century Cuban slave whose life was torturous but whose poetry inspired hope. Because no photos of Juan Francisco Manzano existed, Qualls worked to make the artwork suggestive and poetic, a technique that proved successful in this title, which won the Américas Award for Illustration. This book also won the ALA Pura Belpré author Award and was named an ALA Notable Children's Book, an ALA Best Book for Young Adults, and a *Bulletin of the Center for Children's Books* Blue Ribbon title.

In Jonah Winter's *Dizzy*, a poetic picture book biography about Dizzy Gillespie's rise from an abused boy to swing band sideman to the creator of a new sound in jazz, Qualls brings the musician to life with his energetic acrylic-and-collage images in muted pinks, blues, and beiges. An ALA Notable Children's Book as well as a *Bulletin* Blue Ribbon title, and named a Best of the Year by *Kirkus* Reviews, *School Library Journal*, *Booklist*, and *The Horn Book*, *Dizzy* brought Qualls a great deal of notice. It was also on *Booklist's* Top 10 Arts Books for Youth and the Chicago Public Library's list of Children's Books for Year-Round Gift Giving.

Exploring the theory of multiple intelligences, W. Nikola-Lisa's *How We Are Smart* examines the lives of twelve high achievers, such as the artist Georgia O'Keeffe and the physicist Luis Alvarez, showing the various ways they have used their gifts. Each subject in this book, which won a Christopher Award for Ages 6–8, is compellingly portrayed by Qualls in muted colors and set against a background of rough sketches clarifying each person's work. This title was also named a Myers Outstanding Book Award Honorable Mention by the Gustavus Myers Center for the Study of Bigotry and Human Rights in North America.

Qualls next illustrated *Phillis's Big Test*, a story written by Catherine Clinton. This title is about Phillis Wheatley, the first African American poet ever published in America. Because of her youth and her position as a slave at the time, she was required to take a test in 1772 to verify that she was actually capable of creating her poetry. Qualls was drawn to the story because most of it takes place while Wheatley is on the way to her exam and it reminded him of his own youth, when he had to walk long distances back and forth to school. Returning to the theme of music and musicians for his next book, Qualls created evocative illustrations for Carole Boston Weatherford's *Before John Was a Jazz Giant*, which focuses on the family life of John Coltrane.

When he's not working, Qualls visits libraries and bookstores and takes long walks in the Park Slope neighborhood of Brooklyn, where he lives with his wife, Selina Alko, who is also a children's book illustrator, and their two children, Isaiah and Ginger.

SELECTED WORKS: *Powerful Words: More Than 200 Years of Extraordinary Writing by African Americans*, edited by Wade Hudson, 2003; *The Baby on the Way*, by Karen English, 2005; *The Poet Slave of Cuba: A Biography in Poems of Juan Francisco Manzano*, by Margarita Engle, 2006; *How We Are Smart*, by W. Nikola-Lisa, 2006; *Dizzy*, by Jonah Winter, 2006; *Phillis's Big Test*, by Catherine Clinton, 2008; *Before John Was a Jazz Giant: A Song of John Coltrane*, by Carole Boston Weatherford, 2008.

SUGGESTED READING: *Something About the Author*, vol. 177, 2007. Online—Interview, The Brown Bookshelf, February 5, 2007, at www.thebrownbookshelf.com/2008/02/05/sean-qualls-illustrator

WEB SITE: www.seanqualls.com

Photo by John Reef

Catherine Reef

Catherine Reef

April 28, 1951–

"When I was a child, my mother teasingly said that she'd like to find me a book called *Ten Thousand Questions to Write Answers To, and Ten Thousand Answers to Write Questions To*. Recalling my mother's joke today, I see that her hardworking little girl has not changed much. Then, as now, I loved to learn, and I loved to write.

"Some of my early learning took place in school, of course, but much of my formal education bored me. I preferred independent projects that let me delve into knowledge on my own and let me write about anything from ancient Egypt or amphibians to Argentina or Helen Keller. My best friend from those years (who is still my friend today) remembers me with a determined face and arms full of library books, eager to get to work. Once or twice a week, the music and art teachers visited our classroom to bring creativity and beauty into our lives, and I valued their visits as well. At home there were bookshelves. I browsed through encyclopedias, dictionaries, glossy volumes on art, and fiction and nonfiction for all ages. There was music, too, in the form of long-playing records of operas, symphonic works, and Harry Belafonte.

"Several times a year, an hour's journey from our Long Island home connected us to a much richer resource: New York City with its museums, theaters, and concert halls. On school and family trips, I marveled equally at dinosaur skeletons, Picasso's *Guernica, Fiddler on the Roof*, and *Gianni Schicchi*. Learning gave rise to writing, and I wrote not only reports for my teachers, but also poems, stories, and plays that I acted out with my brother, friends, and classmates. I founded very short-lived periodicals, and I wrote textbooks for the dolls and stuffed animals that were my pupils. What I wanted to be when I grew up was not a writer, but a teacher.

"As an adolescent, I recognized the strong interest in the arts that no doubt I always had, and I knew I would work in a creative field. But whether I would write or draw or take pictures or act on stage was an open question; more than one path beckoned. It wasn't until I was in college that I knew for sure that I would write. At least for me, no other creative field offered the opportunity for perpetual learning that writing did. Putting words on paper, I better understood my own thoughts and feelings. Seeing ideas spread out before me, I made connections and drew conclusions that might have evaded me otherwise. Even today I am always learning how better to use my chosen medium, the English language.

"I attended college as a married woman with a small son, so I spent my days taking care of him, attending classes, cooking, tidying, and doing homework. No wonder I fell asleep each night before my head hit the pillow! I loved what I was doing, though, and didn't mind the hard work.

"My writing career took several turns before I became a children's book writer. Writing nonfiction for young readers happened almost by chance. I had the idea for a children's book about the Vietnam Veterans Memorial on the National Mall after visiting it with our son, who was then in elementary school. That book was never written, but the editor who read my proposal offered me the chance to write my first published book, *Washington, D.C.*

"More than thirty-five books later, writing nonfiction continues to challenge me, and fascinating topics always beckon: children in orphanages, America's poor, Sigmund Freud, African Americans in service to their country. I go on learning about our history and culture, and I share what I have learned through my books. I like to think about the many young people I've never met who will gain knowledge and pleasure from my books."

03   03   03

"It wasn't until I was in college that I knew for sure that I would write. At least for me, no other creative field offered the opportunity for perpetual learning that writing did."

The daughter of an advertising executive and a teacher, Catherine Reef grew up in Commack, New York, a sprawling Long Island town filled with split-level and ranch houses on treeless streets. Her own home, however, had a yard full of trees that beckoned her and her friends to imaginative play. Dr. Seuss, A. A. Milne, and L. Frank Baum were among her early favorite writers.

By the time she reached college, she had so many interests, she couldn't decide what to do—and so she did nothing. Bored with college, she took a job as a secretary and soon got married. Then, nearly a decade later, at the age of 28, she decided to return to college. At Washington State University she also began her writing career, creating brochures for the College of Pharmacy and developing a research magazine for the graduate school. After relocating to the East Coast, she wrote and edited a healthcare newsletter for adults called *Taking Care*. Eventually she found that writing children's books was something that enabled her to continue learning new things herself. One of the best parts of writing, she discovered, was doing the necessary research. The writing helped her organize and evaluate the facts she gathered, which provided her with insights into human nature and her own beliefs.

Catherine Reef's books both inform and entertain young readers. She has written on a wide variety of subjects, from biography and social history to health and fitness to the stories behind monuments and historical places. Each of the subjects she explores is of keen interest to her, and that excitement is conveyed to her readers. She has written biographies about people as diverse as John Steinbeck, Walt Whitman, George Gershwin, Albert Einstein, Sigmund Freud, Rachel Carson, Jacques Cousteau, Colin Powell, and Paul Laurence Dunbar. She has presented such historical places as Thomas Jefferson's Monticello estate, George Washington's Mount Vernon plantation, Ellis Island, Arlington National Cemetery, and the Lincoln Memorial. Her histories span eras from the Civil War to the Gulf War.

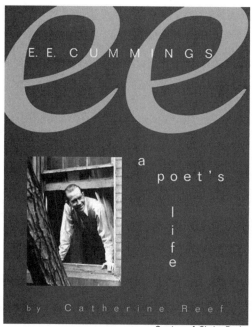

Courtesy of Clarion Books

Sigmund Freud: Pioneer of the Mind won the Sydney Taylor Award, was a National Jewish Book Award Finalist and a Capitol Choice title, and appeared on the *Voice of Youth Advocates* Nonfiction Honor List. *This Our Dark Country: The American Settlers of Liberia* was also on the *VOYA* Nonfiction Honor List. *Walt Whitman* received the Joan G. Sugarman Children's Book Award and was included in Notable Children's Trade Books in the Field of Social Studies, as was *Paul Laurence Dunbar: Portrait of a Poet*. *John Steinbeck* was an ALA Notable Children's Book. Six of her books have appeared on the New York Public Library's Books for the Teen Age: *Walt Whitman*, *John Steinbeck*, *Black Explorers*, *Africans in America*, *Sigmund Freud*, and *This Our Dark Country*. Her latest book, *e.e. cummings: a poet's life*, was named an ALA Best Book for Young Adults.

Catherine Reef lives near Washington, DC, with her husband, John, who is a fine-art photographer, and their Italian greyhound.

Their son, John Stephen, plays piano and is a graduate student in musicology at the University of North Carolina at Chapel Hill.

SELECTED WORKS: *Washington, DC*, 1990; *Baltimore*, 1990; *Albert Einstein: Scientist of the Twentieth Century*, 1991; *Arlington National Cemetery*, 1991; *Monticello*, 1991; *Ellis Island*, 1991; *Rachel Carson: The Wonder of Nature*, 1992; *Henry David Thoreau: A Neighbor to Nature*, 1992; *Jacques Cousteau: Champion of the Sea*, 1992; *Gettysburg*, 1992; *Mount Vernon*, 1992; *Benjamin Davis, Jr.*, 1992; *Colin Powell*, 1992; *Buffalo Soldiers*, 1993; *Civil War Soldiers*, 1993; *Eat the Right Stuff: Food Facts*, 1993; *Stay Fit: Build a Strong Body*, 1993; *Think Positive: Cope With Stress*, 1993; *Black Fighting Men: A Proud History*, 1994; *The Lincoln Memorial*, 1994; *Ralph David Abernathy*, 1995; *The Supreme Court*, 1995; *Walt Whitman*, 1995; *John Steinbeck*, 1996; *Black Explorers*, 1996; *Africans in America: The Spread of People and Culture*, 1999; *Working in America: An Eyewitness History*, 2000; *George Gershwin: American Composer*, 2000; *Paul Laurence Dunbar: Portrait of a Poet*, 2000; *A. Philip Randolph: Union Leader and Civil Rights Crusader*, 2001; *Sigmund Freud: Pioneer of the Mind*, 2001; *Childhood in America: An Eyewitness History*, 2002; *This Our Dark Country: The American Settlers of Liberia*, 2002; *William Grant Still: African-American Composer*, 2003; *African Americans in the Military*, 2004; *Alone in the World: Orphans and Orphanages in America*, 2005; *e.e. cummings: a poet's life*, 2006; *Poverty in America*, 2007.

SUGGESTED READING: *Something About the Author*, vol. 128, 2002. Periodicals—Reef, Catherine, "Traveling with Geniuses," *The Horn Book*, Nov/Dec 2002.

WEB SITE: www.childrensbookguild.org/reef.htm

"I was that kind of kid who was always reading or drawing. Since I was drawing well before I started school, I always considered art to have seniority over the likes of long division and medieval history. This attitude got me into difficulties more than once. My favorite subjects were horses, cartoons, wildlife, and contraptions that rolled, floated, tooted, or flew. My heroes of the day were illustrators like Bill Peet, Robert Lawson, and Kurt Weiss. They provided me with a screenful of imagery that I'll never forget.

Frank Remkiewicz

April 14, 1939–

"Winter in kindergarten found us all painting Santa at our tables. Mine came out so good that I was to do it over again on a huge piece of brown paper that covered the chalkboard. Santa would be bigger than me. I was excused from the regular stuff, given bigger brushes, more paint and sure enough, here came Santa. This was only the beginning. Other teachers, seeing the mural sized figure, 'borrowed' me to do the same for first and second grade classrooms. Flattered but somewhat embarrassed, I took heart since these gigs were getting me out of a lot of tedious activities like nap time, scissors, yarn, and flash cards. 'All I Ever Needed To Know, I Learned In Kindergarten' may be true. Twenty years later I found myself on Madison Avenue at Norcross Greeting Cards, yes, drawing Santa Claus.

"I've always been drawn to the field of humor. Since I'm writing and illustrating my own stories now, I try to make them funny in an outrageous or off-the-wall way. During classroom presentations, again, I find myself by the chalkboard in front of the kids. Now we are seeking ways to write and draw those ideas that squeeze their way through the everyday chores of our minds. It's a thrill to watch my own book being read by a group of children, and I like it when they smile. But I love it when they laugh."

Photo by Angelica Carpenter

FRANK REMKIEWICZ

The son of tool designer Frank Remkiewicz and the former Clara Hyjek, Frank Remkiewicz was born in Rockville, Connecticut, and grew up in nearby Hartford. He graduated with honors from the Art Center College of Design in Los Angeles, California in 1965. After receiving his degree he served in the United States Navy and then worked for the Norcross Greeting Cards Company in New York City from 1968 to 1973.

Between 1973 and 1992 Remkiewicz was a freelance commercial artist and also contributed single-panel cartoons for newspapers in Northern California. As a freelance artist he illustrated greeting cards featuring Curious George, the beloved picture book character originated by H. A. Rey, worked on reprints of *The Pokey Little Puppy*, and created the cover illustration for

Dick King-Smith's book *Babe the Gallant Pig*. Perhaps his most widely known work was a redesign of the Animal Crackers box for Nabisco. His design was used for almost thirty years.

Since the mid-1980s Remkiewicz has concentrated largely on children's book illustration. Beginning with school textbooks and mass-market children's books, he eventually worked into trade book publishing. While attending a professional conference that featured Maurice Sendak, the noted children's book author and illustrator, he met some of the editors at Viking Children's Books who encouraged him to submit his work to them. One of his earliest illustrated efforts, *Horrible Harry in Room 2-B*, written by Suzy Kline and published in 1988, would become the first volume in a very popular series of books for emerging readers. A lovable prankster, Harry finds himself in many humorous situations throughout the series, including a thrilling visit to an amusement park, a mystery surrounding missing pieces to Halloween costumes, a misadventure with leeches, and a riverboat ride. Harry also develops a crush on his classmate Song Lee, for whom Kline eventually created books devoted to her own adventures.

A beloved picture book series, with text written by Jonathan London, depicts the adventures of the irrepressible Froggy. Beginning in 1992 with *Froggy Gets Dressed*, Remkiewicz has created illustrations that bring the title character to life. Though Froggy means well, he often gets into trouble. A typical Froggy plot occurs in *Froggy Plays Soccer*, where the anthropomorphic amphibian makes a mess out of his soccer game, missing important plays and getting knocked about by soccer balls (though in the end he manages to score the winning goal). Froggy has his worst trouble with his favorite girl, Frogilina. He can never seem to do anything right when she is around.

Remkiewicz has also authored a number of books himself, most notably *The Last Time I Saw Harris* and *There's Only One Harris*, about the adventures of Edmund and his best friend Harris the parrot. He is also the author and illustrator of *Fiona Wraps It Up*, about a pink flamingo who talks in rhyme; *Greedyanna*, about a demanding girl who gets whatever she wants from her parents; and *The Bone Stranger*, which tells the adventures of a dog in the Old West who puts on a mask and fights crime like the Lone Ranger.

Often appearing at seminars, schools, and libraries, Remkiewicz gives his audiences the nuts-and-bolts information on how an idea becomes a book. For emerging illustrators, he will discuss pagination, or the breaking of manuscripts into

"Since I was drawing well before I started school, I always considered art to have seniority over the likes of long division and medieval history. This attitude got me into difficulties more than once."

the required number of pages for each genre, even before any artwork can begin. He then shows storyboards, sketches, and original illustrations in various mediums.

Remkiewicz works on all the illustrations for a book at the same time, putting in all the skies, floors, walls, fleshtones etc. When all the elements common to certain colors are done, the pages are then individually finished.

Remkiewicz has received numerous awards for his work, including the *New York Times* Ten Best Books Citation for *The Last Time I Saw Harris*. *I Hate Camping* was named by Bank Street College as a Children's Book of the Year in 1992, the same year it received an IRA/CBC Children's Choice Award. His books have been named Children's Book of the Month Club Selections and selected for the Junior Library Guild and the Oppenheim Toy Portfolio Best Book Awards. His books have been translated into other languages, including Spanish, French, Japanese, and Korean, and a number of his *Froggy* and *Horrible Harry* books have been adapted as sound recordings.

Frank Remkiewicz lives in Sarasota, Florida. He enjoys offshore fishing, cooking, and reading other people's books.

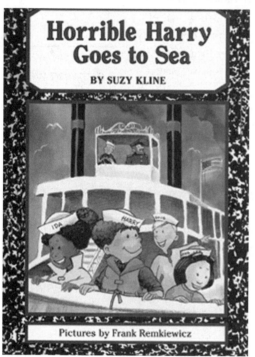

Courtesy of Viking Press, Penguin USA

SELECTED WORKS ILLUSTRATED (All written by Suzy Kline): *Horrible Harry in Room 2B*, 1988; *Horrible Harry and the Ant Invasion*, 1989; *Horrible Harry and the Green Slime*, 1989; *Horrible Harry's Secret*, 1990; *Horrible Harry and the Christmas Surprise*, 1991; *Horrible Harry and the Kickball Wedding*, 1992; *Horrible Harry and the Dungeon*, 1996; *Horrible Harry and the Purple People*, 1997; *Song Lee and Leech Man*, 1997; *Horrible Harry and the Drop of Doom*, 1998; *Song Lee and the "I hate you" Notes*, 1999; *Horrible Harry at Halloween*, 2000; *Horrible Harry Goes to the Moon*, 2000; *Song Lee and the Hamster Hunt*, 2000; *Horrible Harry Goes to Sea*, 2001; *Horrible Harry Moves up to Third Grade*, 2001; *Horrible Harry and the Dragon War*, 2002; *Horrible Harry and the Holidaze*, 2003; *Horrible Harry and the Mud Gremlins*, 2003; *Horrible Harry and the Locked Closet*, 2005; *Horrible Harry and the Goog*, 2006; *Horrible Harry and the Triple Revenge*, 2006; *Horrible Harry Takes the Cake*, 2006.

SELECTED WORKS ILLUSTRATED (all written by Jonathan London): *Froggy Gets Dressed*, 1992; *Let's Go, Froggy*, 1994; *Froggy Learns to Swim*, 1995; *Froggy Se Viste*, 1997; *Froggy Goes to School*, 1998; *Froggy's First Kiss*, 1999; *Froggy's Halloween*, 1999; *Froggy Goes to Bed*, 2000; *Froggy's Best Christmas*, 2000; *Froggy Bakes a Cake*, 2000; *Froggy's Playtime Activity Book*, 2000; *Froggy Plays Soccer*, 2001; *Froggy Eats Out*, 2001; *Hellooo Froggy*, 2001; *Froggy Goes to the Doctor*, 2002; *Froggy Plays in the Band*, 2002; *Froggy's Baby Sister*, 2003; *Froggy's Day with Dad*, 2004; *Froggy's Sleepover*, 2005; *Froggy Rides a Bike*, 2006; *Froggy Plays T-Ball*, 2007.

SELECTED WORKS WRITTEN AND ILLUSTRATED: *The Last Time I Saw Harris*, 1991; *Greedyanna*, 1992; *There's Only One Harris*, 1993; *Bone Stranger*, 1994; *Fiona Raps It Up*, 1995.

SELECTED WORKS ILLUSTRATED: *I Hate Camping*, by P. J. Petersen, 1991; *Just One Seed*, by Shirleyann Costigan, 1992; *Final Exit for Cats*, by Michael Viner, 1992; *The Great Mosquito, Bull and Coffin Caper*, by Nancy Lamb, 1994; *The Joy Boys*, by Betsy Byars, 1996; *Just Enough Carrots*, by Stuart J. Murphy, 1997; *The Magic Squad and the Dog of Great Potential*, by Mary Quattlebaum, 1997; *Elevator Magic*, by Stuart J. Murphy, 1997; *Fact Finding Skills*, by Sally Bell & Jane Sovndal, 1997; *Hiccup*, by Taylor Jordan, 1998; *Rabbit's Pajama Party*, by Stuart J. Murphy, 1999; *Quiet Wyatt!*, by Bill Maynard, 1999; *Incredible Ned*, by Bill Maynard, 1999; *Seaweed Soup*, by Stuart J. Murphy, 2001; *Piggy and Dad*, by David Martin, 2001; *Piggy and Dad Play*, by David Martin, 2002; *Arithme-Tickle: An Even Number of Odd Riddle-Rhymes*, by J. Patrick Lewis, 2002; *Less Than Zero*, by Stuart J. Murphy, 2003; *Scien-Trickery: Riddles in Science*, by J. Patrick Lewis, 2004; *Piggy and Dad Go Fishing*, by David Martin, 2005.

SUGGESTED READING: *Something About the Author*, vol. 152, 2005.

Photo by Becky Riordan

Rick Riordan

(RYER-dan)
June 5, 1964–

A native of San Antonio, Texas, Rick Riordan grew up with parents who were both teachers interested in the arts. His mother was a musician and artist, while his father worked in ceramics. Riordan was well on his way to a writing career while he was a student at Alamo Heights High School. As editor of his school newspaper, he won a statewide third place prize for feature writing. The sense of humor he would later display in the Percy Jackson series was also apparent at that time; he published an underground newspaper that made fun of certain aspects of the school. The losing football team did not appreciate his dark humor and retaliated by 'egging' his car. He wrote some short stories during his high school years and submitted a few for publication, but without success. He was, at the same time, very selective in his reading. The book he enjoyed most in middle school was J.R.R. Tolkien's Lord of the Rings trilogy, but most of the required reading in high school did not appeal to him.

Riordan started college at North Texas State as a music major (he wanted to be a guitar player at the time), but eventually graduated from the University of Texas at Austin with a double major in English and history. He received his teaching certification from the University of Texas at San Antonio. For three summers during his college years Riordan worked as the music director at a summer camp, Camp Capers. That experience provided much of the background for Camp Half-Blood, so familiar today to the many fans of the Percy Jackson series.

As a middle school teacher Riordan enjoyed sharing with his students the stories he himself had loved when he was growing up, especially tales from Greek and Norse mythology. His first teaching job was in New Braunfels, Texas. He and his wife, Becky, then moved to San Francisco, California, where he taught at Presidio Hill School from 1990 to 1998. After the birth of their two sons, Haley and Patrick, the Riordans moved back home to San Antonio, where Rick taught middle school English and social studies at Saint Mary's Hall for six years. Since 2004 he has been a fulltime writer and spends much of his time visiting schools and libraries and speaking at educational conferences.

While Riordan was living in San Francisco he felt nostalgic for his hometown and decided to try his hand at writing a mystery novel for adults set in San Antonio. Featuring detective Tres (pronounced Trace) Navarre, who has a Ph.D. in English and is a tai chi master, *Big Red Tequila* was published in 1997. A reviewer in *Publishers Weekly* stated, "The dialogue is terse and the long first person descriptions show an unbeatable flair for detail." *Big Red Tequila* won the Anthony Award, for best original paperback mystery, and the Shamus Award, for the best first novel about a private investigator. Subsequent books in the series have been equally successful. *Widower's Two-Step* won the Edgar Award for best paperback original, and *Southtown* was a *Publishers Weekly* Editor's Pick. So far there have been seven Tres Navarre mysteries. One stand-alone title—*Cold Springs*—was named one of ALA's Top Ten Crime Novels of the Year. Riordan has also written short stories for *Ellery Queen's Mystery Magazine* and *Mary Higgins Clark Mystery Magazine*.

Publishing award-winning adult books presented a problem for the middle school teacher, however. He could not recommend his own books to his students because of the adult content, and they kept asking why he wasn't writing for kids. A bedtime story created for his older son eventually gave Riordan an answer to that question. Haley, while in second grade, had been diagnosed with Attention Deficit Hyperactivity Disorder (ADHD) and dyslexia. School was challenging for him, but he did enjoy the stories his father told from Greek mythology. Percy Jackson's adventures, as a modern day demigod, son of the god Poseidon and a human mother, began in those bedtime stories and were further enhanced by suggestions from some of the author's middle school students at the time. Riordan has said that he gave Percy the attributes of ADHD and dyslexia as his way of "honoring the potential of all the kids I've known who have those conditions." In the first Percy Jackson adventure, *The Lightning Thief*, Percy discovers that his difficulties in school stem from the fact that he is a demigod; as the son of a Greek god he is hardwired to think in ancient Greek rather than English. He finds, once he arrives at Camp Half-Blood, those who will help him develop his powers as well as those who will try to hurt him. In this way he mirrors many children with learning difficulties who need encouragement to reach their full potential.

The Lightning Thief achieved enormous success almost immediately. Named both an ALA Notable Children's Book and an ALA Best Book for Young Adults, it was popular with a wide age range of readers, from elementary through high school.

> *"For three summers during his college years Riordan worked as the music director at a summer camp, Camp Capers. That experience provided much of the background for Camp Half-Blood. . . ."*

Courtesy of Hyperion Books for Children

Appearing on the Best of the Year lists for *School Library Journal*, *Voice of Youth Advocates*, *Child Magazine*, and the *New York Times*, among others, it quickly became a bestseller. *The Lightning Thief* was chosen for Al Roker's Book Club for Kids on NBC's *Today Show*, and Riordan's appearance on morning television brought even wider recognition. In subsequent titles—*The Sea of Monsters*, *The Titan's Curse*, and *The Battle of the Labyrinth*—the author has continued the adventures of his 21st century teenagers caught up in an ages-old battle with ancient gods and monsters, a battle that has raged, so far, across the landscape of the United States and the mysterious waters of the Bermuda Triangle. Percy and his allies travel by any means possible on their seemingly impossible quests, always staying one step ahead of the forces that threaten to annihilate them. With fast-paced plots, humor, mystery, suspense, and characters that today's readers can relate to, the books have created a wave of new interest in the traditional mythology of ancient Greece.

Rick Riordan lives today with his family in San Antonio, Texas. His interactive Web site, with an ongoing blog, keeps his fans updated on his visits to schools across the country and the students he occasionally taps to be named "demigods of the week." His books have been equally popular abroad, and he has visited schools in England and Scotland, as well as the U.S. In 2006 *The Lightning Thief* captured the Red House Children's Book award as overall winner as well as winning in the Books for Older Readers category. The award, organized by the Federation of Children's Book Groups, is decided by votes from over 100,000 young readers across the United Kingdom.

SELECTED WORKS FOR YOUNG READERS: Percy Jackson and the Olympians series—*The Lightning Thief*, 2005; *The Sea of Monsters*, 2006; *The Titan's Curse*, 2007; *The Battle of the Labyrinth*, 2008.

SELECTED WORKS FOR ADULTS: *Big Red Tequila*, 1997; *The Widower's Two-Step*, 1998; *The Last King of Texas*, 2000; *The Devil*

Went Down to Austin, 2001; *Cold Springs*, 2003; *Southtown*, 2004; *Mission Road*, 2005; *Rebel Island*, 2007.

SUGGESTED READING: *Something About the Author*, vol. 174, 2007. Periodicals—Nawotka, Edward, "Son of Poseidon Gaining Strength," *Publishers Weekly*, April 23, 2007. Online—Interview on the web site of Jen Robinson, November 9, 2007, at www.jkrbooks.typepad.com/blog/2007/11/wbbt-rick-riord.html

WEB SITE: www.rickriordan.com

"Although I was born in a hospital in Brooklyn, New York, my parents were living at the time in suburban Essex County, New Jersey, and that's where I grew up—in West Orange, to be specific. My father, Joe Robbins, was a builder of houses. He died when I was just eleven and, although I remember him very clearly, I never got to know very much about his life. My mother had been a housewife, but when my dad died she became an art dealer and sometimes a gallery owner. She raised me alone until I went off to college. The artists who came and went at her gallery made a big impression on me, I guess; although, at the time, I never dreamed that I'd be an artist myself.

Courtesy of Ken Robbins

Ken Robbins

September 18, 1945–

"At college, among other subjects, I studied English, psychology and philosophy. Also, for three years, I was the editor of the campus humor magazine, *The Cornell Widow*, an experience that gave me my first taste of writing and of laying out text and pictures together.

"After I graduated, I moved to New York City, and began working at Doubleday & Company, first as an assistant to the editor-in-chief, later as an editor. I edited all kinds of books at first, but I gradually realized that I had a special interest in photography books, and I was involved in publishing many of them. In the process, I got to know and like many famous photographers, so when I left that job, it seemed natural to try photography myself. I bought a camera, set up a darkroom in my apartment, and discovered that I had found something I loved to do.

"Right around that time, I married a Doubleday children's book editor, Maria Polushkin, and before long, we moved out of the city and settled in East Hampton, New York, a beautiful town by the sea, out at the end of Long Island. We ran a movie theater for a while—a special one that showed only wonderful, old movies—but we didn't make very much money at that. What we were really doing was starting freelance careers. Maria wrote children's books and later cookbooks, and I started doing commercial photography—record albums, magazine covers, and the like. Then one day, an old friend and colleague of Maria's came over to visit us, and when she saw my photographs, she suggested that I try writing and illustrating a children's book. That resulted in my first book, *Trucks of Every Sort*.

"The book about trucks was in black and white, but back then, I was experimenting with hand-coloring my photographs. That gave them a distinctive look and allowed me to express myself a bit more, because the images were then halfway between photographs and paintings.

Since then, I've written and/or illustrated twenty-five children's books, all in color. I also work as an artist, making photographs just for myself or to sell at my gallery. I still find the place I live extremely beautiful, and many (but not all) of my pictures are landscapes. I also still hand-color my photographs, but these days, I use a digital camera and I do the hand-coloring on a computer."

> *"The artists who came and went at her gallery made a big impression on me, I guess; although, at the time, I never dreamed that I'd be an artist myself."*

ભ   ભ   ભ

Ken Robbins, a fine-art photographer, commercial artist, and writer/illustrator of highly acclaimed children's books, graduated in 1967 from Cornell University with a degree in English. After five years as a book editor in New York City, he and his wife moved to Long Island, where they commenced and continue their freelance careers today.

For his first children's book, Robbins chose a subject that had fascinated him since childhood—trucks. Spending several months traveling throughout New York and New Jersey, he observed trucks in operation and photographed, among others, a moving van, a dump truck, an ice-cream truck, and a fire truck. All of them went into *Trucks of Every Sort*, which was published in 1981, and he has been averaging about a book a year since then.

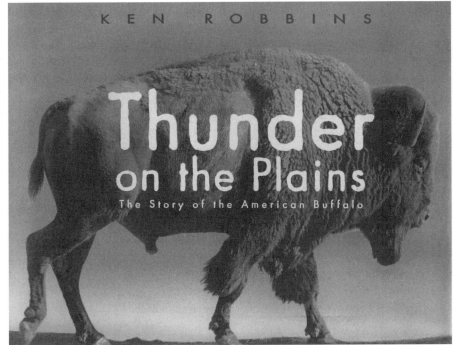

Tools, his second book, was inspired by Robbins's small nephew who enjoyed pointing at various tools in a workshop and then learning their names. This title, lauded for its simplicity and tasteful layout, was named a 1983 *New York Times* Best Illustrated Children's Book and was included in the 1984 American Institute of Graphic Arts Book Show.

For three years Robbins worked on a book series focusing on the four classical elements—earth, air, fire, and water. Robbins spent over six months traveling around the United States and Canada, photographing many varied landscapes, and this diversity in geographical place gave the books a powerful panoramic vision. In *Water*, for example, scenes range from stark desert to lush rain forest. In *Air*, Robbins depicted hurricanes and tornadoes, kites and parachutes. A *Parenting* Best Book of the Year, *Earth* includes such disparate images as headlands and rock erosion along the Oregon coast, a vast open-pit copper mine, and a Native American burial mound. *Fire*, the final book in the series, explored all facets of this transforming element, from the "Big Bang" theory to recreational fireworks. These handsomely designed books feature Robbins's trademark black-and-white photographs painstakingly hand-tinted to impart an elusive quality that is somewhere between illustrative artwork and the artistic technology of photography. The photos are accompanied by brief, eloquently written vignettes that are conversational in tone and appealing to young readers.

Robbins returned to his childhood fascination with trucks in *Trucks: Giants of the Highway*, which was named a Blue Ribbon title by the *Bulletin of the Center for Children's Books*. But in this book, the hand-colored photos add a sometimes retro, sometimes otherworldly look to the varied highways and the big skies overhead. In *Autumn Leaves*, which was named an Outstanding Science Trade Book, Robbins departed from his signature hand-tinted photography to present sharp, striking close-ups in an album of colorful, life-size autumn leaves. In *Seeds*, Robbins used simple language and large readable text to explain basic facts about a variety of seeds and the conditions under which they become plants. The color photographs in *Seeds* are remarkable for their ability to convey clear information as well as the esthetic quality of the seeds, and the book was named to the 2006 Ohio Farm Bureau Federation's Children's Literature Award Honors List.

Ken Robbins and his wife, Maria Polushkin Robbins, live in East Hampton, New York, with their standard poodle Misha. In addition to his children's books, Robbins has published several volumes of photographs of the Long Island seashore area where he lives, while his wife writes cookbooks with mouth-watering titles like *Chocolates for Christmas*.

SELECTED WORKS WRITTEN AND ILLUSTRATED: *Trucks of Every Sort*, 1981; *Building a House*, 1982; *Tools*, 1983; *City/Country: A Car Trip in Photographs*, 1985; *Beach Days*, 1987; *At the Ballpark*, 1988; *Boats*, 1989; *A Flower Grows*, 1990; *Bridges*, 1991; *Make Me a Peanut Butter Sandwich and a Glass of Milk*, 1992; *Power Machines*, 1993; *Water*, 1994; *Earth*, 1995; *Air*, 1995; *Fire*, 1996; *Rodeo*, 1996; *Autumn Leaves*, 1996; *Trucks: Giants of the Highway*, 1999; *Thunder on the Plains: The Story of the American Buffalo*, 2001; *Apples*, 2002; *Seeds*, 2005; *Pumpkins*, 2006.

SELECTED WORKS ILLUSTRATED: *A Horse Named Paris*, by Lynn Sonberg, 1986; *Fireflies at Midnight*, by Marilyn Singer, 2003; *Keepers: Treasure Hunt Poems*, by John Frank, 2008.

SELECTED WORKS FOR ADULTS: *Hamptons: America's East End*, 1983; *A Place of Your Own Making: How to Build a One-Room Cabin, Studio, Shack, or Shed*, with Stephen Taylor, 1988; *The Hampton's Suite*, 2000; *100 Views of the Hamptons*, 2006.

SUGGESTED READING: *Something About the Author*, vol. 147, 2004.

WEB SITES: www.krobbinsphoto.com

"Children often ask me why I 'decided' to become a writer, but it wasn't something I decided at all. Reading was my passion from the age of four, and reading led to writing for me as naturally as a love of music leads others to play an instrument.

"I grew up in Sydney, Australia, with two younger brothers. From babyhood my life was full of stories—stories in books, in songs, in films and in the endless family anecdotes told by my grandmothers and many great-aunts.

"Home was warm and secure, but beyond it was adventure because in our neighbourhood the houses lay on the fringe of miles of natural bushland. My friends and I spent all our free time in the bush—following the creek, making forts and cubby houses, having pretend battles and just sitting around talking, small but capable beings in a vast wilderness. Parents didn't fuss, as long as we were 'home by dark.'

"At home I wrote, and I read. My father was the general manager of a TV station, and TV wasn't restricted in our house, but still I devoured several books a week. At eight my favourite books were Enid Blyton adventure stories and school stories. At ten I adored L. M. Montgomery's Anne of Green Gables series and *The Wind in the Willows* by Kenneth Grahame. At eleven I started on my parents' bookshelf, plunging into *Jane Eyre*, *Wuthering Heights*, Agatha Christie mysteries, historical romances, James Thurber, and anything else that looked interesting. My parents didn't try to restrict my reading. Either they thought it was a hopeless cause or they trusted my judgment.

"Of course I planned to be a writer 'when I grew up.' But ironically, as I grew older and read more, my very love of books and respect for great writers made me give up the idea. At sixteen I came to the conclusion that thinking that I could be a writer was like my little brother thinking he was going to be an astronaut.

Photo by Michael Small

"Emily Rodda"

April 2, 1948–

"So I stopped writing—stopped completely. It was like an amputation, but I thought it was necessary. After school I did a Bachelor of Arts degree majoring in English Literature. Then I went to work as a book editor for a Sydney publishing company. I married in 1969, and the year after that went back to university to do my Master's degree. Later I returned to publishing, this time at Angus & Robertson Publishers.

"And still I didn't write. Then, one night, when I was thirty-five, with two children aged seven and two, Kate—the seven-year-old—asked me to tell her a bedtime story instead of reading one. I made up some little stories for her, and one of them stayed in my mind afterwards. I thought about it, developed it a bit, and then wrote it down. I still remember sitting at the dining table doing this. It was like rediscovering a lost part of myself.

"I sent the manuscript to Angus & Robertson under a false name. I was tentative, and wanted my colleagues' honest opinions of the story. When they recommended publication, I had to tell the publisher my secret. He suggested we publish telling no one that I was the author, to avoid any hint of special treatment. So in 1984 *Something Special* was published under the name 'Emily Rodda,' which was my grandmother's maiden name and my great-grandmother's name too. The following year the book won the Australian Children's Book Council's Book of the Year Award. I took this as permission to write a second book, and *Pigs Might Fly* (which was re-titled *The Pigs Are Flying* in the U.S.) was published in 1986. When it, too, won the Book of the Year Award I began to feel that maybe I could be a writer after all.

"In 1988 I left A & R to become editor of a great Australian institution, the *Australian Women's Weekly*. With a demanding job and four children (twin boys had made a surprise appearance in 1986), my writing time was restricted to a few hours a week after the children had gone to bed. But in 1992, with seven books in print and selling overseas as well as in Australia, I took the plunge into full-time writing.

"Then the floodgates opened. I have now written over sixty children's books. I have also written seven mysteries for adults and a mystery series for television under my real name, Jennifer Rowe. My books now sell in over 30 countries, and have been translated into 25 languages. The fantasy series—Rowan of Rin, Fairy Realm and notably Deltora Quest (which has sold over 10 million copies worldwide)—have been especially popular. With Deltora Quest, I achieved the great ambition of my life in appealing to non-readers as well as to readers, particularly boys.

"My friends and I spent all our free time in the bush—following the creek, making forts and cubby houses, having pretend battles and just sitting around talking, small but capable beings in a vast wilderness."

"I live in the Blue Mountains west of Sydney with my second husband Bob Ryan and our dog, Sunny. The children, grown up now, still come and go, so the house is rarely quiet. We are surrounded by bush very similar to the bush of my childhood. And my life is still filled with stories."

❧ ❧ ❧

One of the most prolific and versatile Australian writers, Jennifer Rowe has written books as Emily Rodda and Mary-Anne Dickinson, as well as under her own name, but most of her children's books are published as Emily Rodda. Her body of work extends from picture books for young children to adult novels and television scripts, but she is best known for her fantasy books in the Rowan of Rin and Deltora Quest series.

Rodda has received many awards in her native Australia. *Something Special*, about a child dreaming of the owner of secondhand clothes, and *Finders Keepers*, about a boy on a game show in a parallel dimension, are just two of Rodda's titles that have won a Children's Book Council of Australia's Children's Book of the Year Award. Other winners include *Pigs Might Fly*, *The Best-Kept Secret*, *Rowan of Rin*, *Green Fingers*, and *Game Plan*. *Finders Keepers* also won a Young Australians Best Book Award (YABBA), and its sequel, *Timekeeper*, was shortlisted for a YABBA Award. *Bob the Builder and the Elves*, a Children's Yearly Best Ever Reads (CYBER), was featured on Canberra's Own Outstanding List (COOL). This tale tells about a supremely messy house and an infestation of tidy elves.

The internationally successful Rowan books combine a classic quest storyline, a tightly woven fantasy rich with political intrigue, and a variety of mysteries. In *Rowan of Rin*, a timid boy joins a dangerous mission to restore the flow of the river that supports his town. Ultimately, he becomes the only one capable of doing the job. In the U.S., this book was an American Booksellers Pick of the Lists. In Australia, it was an Ipswich Festival of Children's Literature's BILBY (Books I Love Best Yearly Award) winner, an International Board on Books for Young People (IBBY) Honor book, and a YABBA winner. *Rowan and the Travelers*, shortlisted for a YABBA Award, involves another dangerous journey, as Rowan searches for the cure to a sleeping sickness overtaking his town. In *Rowan and the Keeper of the Crystal*, an Australian Children's Book Council Honor Book of the Year, Rowan must save his poisoned mother and select the next Keeper of the Crystal so his town will remain safe from the Zebak forces. In

> *"With Deltora Quest, I achieved the great ambition of my life in appealing to non-readers as well as to readers, particularly boys."*

Courtesy of Greenwillow Books

Rowan and the Zebak, Rowan journeys to Zebak to save his kidnapped sister.

The first volume of the Deltora Quest series, *The Forests of Silence*, won a Kids Own Australian Literature Award (KOALA) and a West Australian Young Readers' Book Award (WAYRBA). In this exciting story, two teenagers must retrieve their kingdom's seven gems from an evil Shadow Lord bent on conquering Deltora. In the first title, the golden topaz is found. In the second, *The Lake of Tears*, a third companion joins the boys on a treacherous journey to retrieve the great ruby. In *City of Rats* the three companions venture into a dangerous town seeking the third stone. When all seven stones were retrieved, this series concluded, but readers clamored for more.

In the second Deltora Quest series, the heroic friends seek a powerful weapon to fight the Shadow Lord's magic so they can free the Deltorans enslaved in his lands. The first volume, *Cavern of the Fear*, follows their search for the mysterious Pirran Pipe, which their enemy fears above all. In the third Deltora series, the Shadow Lord has been banished, but has created new enemies who must be overcome. Volumes in this series won a YABBA Award, a KOALA Award, and a YARA (Young Australian Readers' Award).

A companion book providing an illustrated history of the kingdom, *The Deltora Book of Monsters*, was the winner of an Aurealis Award for Australian Speculative Fiction. Translated into 25 languages, the Deltora books have been popular throughout the world. They were turned into an anime television series that premiered in Japan in January 2006. Spin-offs from the Japanese adaptation include a range of Manga comics and graphic novels. All eight books of the first series were combined into a single volume, *Deltora Quest: The Complete Series*, in 2008.

Rodda's other series include the Raven Hill Mysteries and the Fairy Realm books. Meanwhile, under her own name Jennifer Rowe, the author has published cookbooks and adult mysteries, as well as creating and writing most of the episodes for the Australian detective drama television series *Murder Call*, which originally aired from 1997–2000.

Writing as Emily Rodda, Jennifer Rowe has proven her remarkable storytelling ability, which has made her children's books—with their well-drawn characters, finely-crafted plots, and fast-moving action—popular throughout her native Australia and around the world. In 1995, she received the Courtney Oldmeadow Children's Literature Foundation's Dromkeen Medal for her contributions to Australian children's literature.

SELECTED WORKS FOR YOUNG READERS (as Emily Rodda. Dates are for Australian publication; U.S. dates, if different, are in parentheses): *Something Special*, illus. by Noela Young, 1984 (1989); *Pigs Might Fly*, illus. by Noela Young, 1986 (U.S. title: *The Pigs Are Flying!*, 1988); *The Best-Kept Secret*, illus. by Noela Young, 1988 (1990); *Finders, Keepers*, illus. by Noela Young, 1990 (1991); *Crumbs!* illus. by Kerry Argent, 1990; *The Timekeeper*, illus. by Noela Young, 1992 (1993); *Power and Glory*, illus. by Geoff Kelly, 1994 (1996); *Yay!* illus. by Craig Smith, 1996 (1997); *Game Plan*, illus. by Craig Smith, 1998; *Green Fingers*, illus. by Craig Smith, 1998; *Where Do You Hide Two Elephants?* illus. by Andrew McLean, 1998 (2001); *Fuzz, the Famous Fly*, illus. by Tom Jellett, 1999; *The Julia Tapes*, 1999; *Bob the Builder and the Elves*, illus. by Craig Smith, 2000; *Gobbleguts*, 2000; *Dog Tales*, 2001; *The Long Way Home*, illus. by Danny Snell, 2002; *The Key to Rondo*, 2007 (2008).

SELECTED SERIES FOR YOUNG READERS (as Emily Rodda): Rowan of Rin—*Rowan of Rin*, 1993 (2001); *Rowan and the Travellers*, 1994 (U.S. title: *Rowan and the Travelers*, 2001); *Rowan and the Keeper of the Crystal*, 1996 (2002); *Rowan and the Zebak*, 1999 (2002); *Rowan of the Buckshah*, 2003 (U.S. title: *Rowan and the Ice Creepers*, 2003). Deltora Quest—*The Forests of Silence*, 2000 (2001); *The Lake of Tears*, 2000 (2001); *City of the Rats*, 2000 (2001); *The Shifting Sands*, 2000 (2001); *Dread Mountain*, 2000 (2001); *The Maze of the Beast*, 2000 (2001); *The Valley of the Lost*, 2000 (2001); *Return to Del*, 2000 (2001); *Deltora Quest: The Complete Series*, (2008). Deltora Shadowlands—*Cavern of the Fear*, 2002; *The Isle of Illusion*, 2002; *The Shadowlands*, 2002. Dragons of Deltora—*Dragon's Nest*, 2003; *Shadowgate*, 2004; *Isle of the Dead*, 2004; *The Sister of the South*, 2004 (2005). Other Deltora titles—*Deltora Quest Journal*, 2000; *The Deltora Book of Monsters: by Josef, Palace Librarian in the Reign of King Alton*, illus. by Marc McBride, 2001 (2002); *How to Draw Deltora Monsters*, illus. by Marc McBride, 2005 (2005); *Tales of Deltora*, illus. by Marc McBride, 2005 (2006). Raven Hill Mysteries—*The Ghost of Raven Hill*, 1994; *The Sorcerer's Apprentice*, 1994 (U.S. publication: *Emily Rodda's Raven Hill Mysteries #1 and #2*, 2005); *The Disappearing TV Star*, 1994; *Cry of the Cat*, 1994; *Beware of the Gingerbread House*, 1994 (2005); *Green for Danger*, 1994. Fairy Realm (originally published as Mary-Anne Dickinson under the series name Storytelling Charms)—*The Charm Bracelet*, 1994 (2003); *The Flower Fairies*, 1994 (2003); *The Third Wish*, 1995 (2003); *The Last Fairy-Apple Tree*, 1995 (2003); *The Magic Key*, 1995 (2004); *The Unicorn*, 1996 (2004); *The Star Cloak*, 2005, *The Water Sprites*, 2005, *The Peskie Spell*, 2006; *The Rainbow Wand*, 2006.

SELECTED WORKS FOR ADULTS (as Jennifer Rowe): *The Commonsense International Cookery Book*, 1978; *Eating Well in Later Life*, 1982; *Grim Pickings*, 1988 (1991); *Murder by the Book*, 1989 (1991); *Death in Store*, 1991 (1992); *The Makeover Murders*, 1992 (1993); *Stranglehold*, 1993 (1995); *Love Lies Bleeding: A Crimes for a Summer Christmas Anthology*, as editor, 1994 (1995); *Lamb to the Slaughter*, 1996; *Deadline*, 1997 (U.S. title: *Suspect*, 1999); *Something Wicked*, 1999; *Angela's Mandrake and Other Feisty Fables*, 2000 (U.S. title: *Fairy Tales for Grown-Ups*, 2002).

SUGGESTED READING: *Something About the Author*, vol. 146, 2004; *Children's Literature Review*, vol. 32, 1994. Online—Contemporary Authors Online, May 19, 2004.

WEB SITES: www.emilyrodda.com
www.scholastic.com/deltoraquest

Michael Rosen

May 7, 1946–

Named the United Kingdom's Children's Laureate in 2007, Michael Rosen was well prepared for this role as an outspoken advocate for young people's reading. A poet, storyteller, and spirited public speaker as well as a longtime BBC broadcaster, this prolific children's book author derives immense enjoyment from bringing his humorous verse to life in front of an audience, either in a classroom setting where he can introduce young audiences to the poetry of the ages or in his entertaining radio broadcasts.

Introduced to the pleasures of language at an early age by his parents, who were both distinguished educators in London, Rosen started writing poetry when he was still a teenager. His mother was involved in a British radio program that featured poetry, providing fine inspiration for her son. However, he did not take a direct route to his present career. As a young man growing up in northwest London, Rosen first considered acting as a career but later decided to study medicine at Middlesex Hospital Medical School. After transferring to Wadham College at the University of Oxford, he continued for a while with his medical studies, then switched his major to English language and literature. At Oxford he spent considerable time writing, acting, and directing student theatrical productions, and also taking part in the student rebellions of 1968.

After receiving his bachelor of arts from Oxford, Rosen worked at the British Broadcasting Corporation (BBC) from 1969 to 1972, doing radio drama, children's programming, and Schools Television. He then attended the National Film School for three years, all the while continuing to write poetry and acting in various little theatre groups. His writing mostly focused on his childhood and growing years, though he didn't have a child audience in mind; he was simply interested in exploring his own roots. It was a publisher who suggested that the best audience for his writing would be children.

Rosen's first poetry collection, *Mind Your Own Business,* was published in 1974, exuberantly illustrated by the prolific British artist Quentin Blake. It was well received and his fame continued to grow with each new volume. He has produced over 140 books, including poetry collections and anthologies, picture books, and works of nonfiction. He

Courtesy of Candlewick Press

won the *Signal* poetry award in 1982 for *You Can't Catch Me.* His rendition of the children's rhythmic game, *We're Going on a Bear Hunt,* vibrantly illustrated by Helen Oxenbury, won the Nestlé Smarties Grand Prize in England, a *Boston Globe–Horn Book* Picture Book Honor Award in the United States, and a prize in Japan for the most outstanding picture book from abroad in 1990. A perennial favorite in the U.S. since its publication, *We're Going on a Bear Hunt* was also named a *School Library Journal* Best Book and a *Horn Book* Fanfare title; in 2007 a commemorative pop-up edition was published to celebrate the book's popularity.

Michael Rosen is especially known for writing poetry in the language of children's everyday speech, creating verse that is not only accomplished and witty but also extremely popular with its primary audience. In an interview on the BBC web site, he answered a student's question about the importance of poetry by stating: "Poetry is a way of handling anything that you feel, think, say, see, touch . . . and once you get into the poetry habit, you can turn to it whenever it suits you. It helps you understand who you are and how you fit in with people and things in the world."

In addition to writing his own poetry, Rosen is a gifted anthologist with a sure sense for choosing pieces by both familiar and lesser-known writers. He finds just the right mix and arrangement in each volume of poetry that he edits. *Walking the Bridge of Your Nose*, a compilation of verse, wordplay, puns, and tongue twisters, was named "best poetry anthology or collection for children" in the 1992 *Publishers Weekly* Cuffies Awards. *Poems for the Very Young*, skillfully and brightly illustrated by Bob Graham, gathers together some of the finest nursery verse ever collected in a mixture which reviewers called "effervescent" and "refreshing." This title received a National Association of Parenting Publications Best Book Award in 1993. Since Rosen spends a great deal of time visiting schools and sharing his work with children, he has developed a feeling for what children like and what they appreciate. He also has the ability to offer insights into classic poetry by showing his readers the connection between the writing and the context of a poet's life. His respect for children's sensibilities and intelligence is seen especially in his anthology *Classic Poetry: An Illustrated Collection*, which includes selections from William Shakespeare, William Blake, the great Romantic poets, and present-day contributors. Selected as an International Reading Association Teachers' Choices Award Winner, *Classic Poetry* works as a reference volume for classrooms as well as a browsing anthology for individual readers.

While most of Rosen's own writing has focused on the humorous and joyful side of childhood, his life experiences have led him to explore other emotions as well. After the sudden death of his 18-year-old son from meningitis, he turned once again to writing as a way of expressing emotion; this time it was the depth of his sadness and grief that he shared with readers both young and old. Rosen's first collection of poetry for adults, *Carrying the Elephant*, focuses on this devastating event in his life. Writing about grief is an especially difficult topic in children's literature, but in *Michael Rosen's Sad Book*, the author approached the subject with the same respect and honesty that permeates all of his books for children. Perfectly paired with Quentin Blake's evocative ink-and-watercolor illustrations in tones of pastel and

> "Poetry is a way of handling anything that you feel, think, say, see, touch . . . and once you get into the poetry habit, you can turn to it whenever it suits you. It helps you understand who you are and how you fit in with people and things in the world."

gray, the spare text speaks directly to the heart of the experience for anyone who has known unbearable loss. Rosen takes the reader through many stages of grief—anger, loneliness, and despair—with touches of humor and glimmers of hope for a future beyond the sadness. Named a best book of the year by many of the American reviewing journals, *Sad Book* was chosen as a nonfiction honor book for the *Boston Globe–Horn Book Award* in 2005.

Returning to his formal studies later in life, Rosen obtained a master's degree with distinction in the field of children's literature from the University of Reading in 1993 and a Ph.D. from the University of North London in 1997. He has found many ways to be an educator for young readers through his writing, but always with a flair and style that make learning highly enjoyable.

When he was a child his parents took him to see a number of Shakespearean productions—experiences he found immensely enjoyable. With his characteristic wit and straightforward style, Rosen now helps young readers understand the works of this remarkable playwright through the context of the era in which he lived. *Shakespeare: His Work and His World* is an engaging look at the life of the Bard as if he himself were a character in a play. With richly evocative paintings by Robert Ingpen, this volume was named a *School Library Journal* Best Book of the Year as well as a Notable Social Studies Trade Book. Rosen also published a retelling of *Romeo and Juliet*, illustrated by Jane Ray, to make the play more accessible to readers of all ages. In 2005 he completed a similar volume about the Victorian novelist Charles Dickens. *Dickens: His Work and His World*, again with Ingpen's amazingly detailed illustrations, was also chosen as a *School Library Journal* Best Book. Fortunate listeners in Britain were enlightened for over 30 years by Rosen's radio shows, which highlighted groundbreaking titles in children's literature and background information on authors from the Brothers Grimm to Dr. Seuss.

In 1997 Michael Rosen won the Eleanor Farjeon Award for distinguished services to children's literature in his country. As the fifth Children's Laureate of the United Kingdom, for the years 2007–2009, Rosen follows the illustrator of many of his books, Quentin Blake, and authors Anne Fine, Michael Morpurgo, and Jacqueline Wilson in this prestigious position. He has declared it his mission as Laureate to make poetry as accessible and enjoyable as possible, spreading excitement for poetry through his spirited public appearances, interviews, and presentations. With his many years of experience in writing,

We're Going on a Bear Hunt

Michael Rosen   *Helen Oxenbury*

Courtesy of Walker Books, LTD

performing, teaching, and appearing on radio and television for the BBC, he has just the right background to make that goal a reality. Michael Rosen makes his home in London.

SELECTED WORKS FOR YOUNG READERS (Dates are all for original British publication): *Mind Your Own Business*, illus. by Quentin Blake, 1974; *Wouldn't You Like To Know*, illus. by Quentin Blake, 1977 (rev. ed. with some new poems, 1981); *You Tell Me*, with Roger McGough, illus. by Sara Midda, 1979; *You Can't Catch Me*, illus. by Quentin Blake, 1981; *Quick Let's Get Out of Here*, illus. by Quentin Blake, 1983; *Don't Put Mustard in the Custard*, illus. by Quentin Blake, 1985; *Hairy Tales and Nursery Crimes*, illus. by Alan Baker, 1985; *Smelly Jelly Smelly Fish*, illus. by Quentin Blake, 1986; *Under the Bed*, illus. by Quentin Blake, 1986; *You're Thinking About Doughnuts*, illus. by Tony Pinchuck, 1987; *Spollyollydiddlytiddlyitis*, illus. by Quentin Blake, 1987; *Hard-Boiled Legs*, illus. by Quentin Blake, 1987; *The Hypno-*

tiser, illus. by Andrew Tiffen, 1988; *Silly Stories*, illus. by Mik Brown, 1988 (rev. and reissued as *Michael Rosen's Horribly Silly Stories*, 1994); *We're Going on a Bear Hunt*, illus. by Helen Oxenbury, 1989; *The Wicked Tricks of Till Owlyglass*, illus. by Fritz Wegner, 1989; *The Golem of Old Prague*, illus. by Val Biro, 1990 (reissued, illus. by Brian Simons, 1997); *Little Rabbit Foo Foo*, illus. by Arthur Robins, 1990; *Clever Cakes*, illus. by Caroline Holden, 1991; *Burping Bertha*, illus. by Tony Ross, 1993; *The Man With No Shadow*, illus. by Reg Cartwright, 1994; *The Zoo At Night*, illus. by Bee Willey, 1995; *You Wait Till I'm Older Than You*, illus. by Shoo Rayner, 1996; *This Is Our House*, illus. by Bob Graham, 1996; *Tea in The Sugar Bowl, Potato in My Shoe*, illus. by Quentin Blake, 1997; *Michael Rosen's Book of Nonsense*, illus. by Clare Mackie, 1997; *Snore!*, illus. by Jonathan Langley, 1998; *Mission Ziffoid*, illus. by Arthur Robins, 1999; *Rover*, illus. by Neal Layton, 1999; *Lunch Boxes Don't Fly*, illus. by Korky Paul, 1999; *Centrally Heated Knickers*, illus. by Harry Horse, 1999; *Even More Nonsense*, illus. by Clare Mackie, 2000; *Uncle Billy Being Silly*, illus. by Korky Paul, 2001; *Shakespeare: His Work and His World*, illus. by Robert Ingpen, 2001; *Lovely Old Roly*, illus. by Priscilla Lamont, 2002; *No Breathing in Class*, illus. by Korky Paul, 2003; *Oww!*, illus. by Jonathan Langley, 2003; *Howler*, illus. by Neal Layton, 2004; *Michael Rosen's Sad Book*, illus. by Quentin Blake, 2004; *Alphabet Poem*, illus. by Herve Tullet, 2004; *William Shakespeare's Romeo and Juliet*, illus. by Jane Ray, 2004; *You're Thinking About Tomatoes*, illus. by Quentin Blake, 2005; *Dickens: His Work and His World*, illus. by Robert Ingpen, 2005; *Totally Wonderful Miss Plumberry*, illus. by Chinlun Lee, 2006; *Mustard, Custard, Grumble Belly and Gravy*, illus. by Quentin Blake, 2006; *We're Going on a Bear Hunt: A Celebratory Pop-Up Edition*, illus. by Helen Oxenbury, 2007.

SELECTED WORKS EDITED (material selected/edited but mostly not written by Michael Rosen): *The Kingfisher Book of Children's Poetry*, illus. by Alice Englander, 1985; *A Spider Bought a Bicycle*, illus. by Inga Moore, 1987; *The Kingfisher Book of Funny Stories*, illus. by Tony Blundell, 1988; *A World of Poetry*, illus. by various artists, 1991; *Sonsense Nongs*, illus. by Shoo Rayner, 1992 (re-edited selection, *Pilly Soems: Michael Rosen's Book of Very Silly Poems*, 1994; *Poems for the Very Young*, illus. by Bob Graham, 1993; *A Different Story: Poems from the Past*, 1994; *Walking the Bridge of Your Nose*, illus. by Chloe Cheese, 1995; *Classic Poetry: An Illustrated Collection*, illus. by Paul Howard,

1998; *Night-Night, Knight, and Other Poems*, illus. by Sue Heap, 1998.

SELECTED WORKS FOR ADULTS: *Did I Hear You Write?*, 1989; *Goodies and Daddies, An A–Z Guide to Fatherhood*, illus. by Caroline Holden, 1991; *The Chatto Book of Dissent*, co-edited with David Widgery, 1991 (reissued as *The Vintage Book of Dissent*, 1996); *The Penguin Book of Childhood*, as ed., 1994; *A Year with Poetry—Teachers Write about Teaching Poetry*, with Myra Barrs, 1997; *Carrying the Elephant*, 2002; *William Shakespeare in His Times, for Our Times*, 2004; *This Is Not My Nose*, 2004; *In The Colonie*, 2005.

SUGGESTED READING: *Something About the Author*, vol. 181, 2008; *Children's Literature Review*, vol. 45, 1997; Powling, Chris, *What It's Like To Be Michael Rosen*, 1990. Periodicals—Lockwood, Michael, "Michael Rosen and Contemporary British Poetry for Children," *The Lion and the Unicorn*, January 1999. Online—Interview on BBC Onion Street (January 2002), at www.bbc.co.uk/schools/communities/onionstreet/liveguests/interviews/michaelrosen.shtml

WEB SITE: www.michaelrosen.co.uk

Liz Rosenberg

February 3, 1958–

"**I** never stopped reading children's books, so it makes sense that sooner or later I would start writing them. I still have many favorite books from childhood—*Little Women, Anne of Green Gables, Daddy Long-Legs, Heidi, Black Beauty* (which I would re-read every summer, in my parent's air-conditioned bedroom), Robert Frost's *You Come Too, The Wind in the Willows*. I have a boxed set of fairy tales—Andersen in red and Grimm in green—though I find those stories too frightening to re-read unless I absolutely have to. I have *The Bat Poet* by Randall Jarrell and *Harriet the Spy*. My father read some of these books out loud—he especially favored the two Alice books and the books about Winnie the Pooh.

"Both my parents were great readers. So was my big sister Ellen, who taught me how to read when I was two. I thought this very impressive till I realized that she was my reading *teacher* and she was only six.

"Before I had graduated from college I luckily fell into the job of reviewing children's books for the Dallas, Houston and Austin newspapers, in a book supplement called 'The Lone Star Review.' From there, I began reviewing for other newspapers, and magazines, and eventually for my own children's book column. Our house has always been full of children's books, yet the story of how I came to write my own first children's story is still strange and mysterious, even to me. It proves that the world is a marvelous place, magical and unpredictable.

"It was a December afternoon. I had driven far out into the country, to plant some flower bulbs by a lake. The dirt road around the lake was deserted and sprinkled with snow. My car ended up halfway in a ditch, and a rural mailman had to pull me out using a rope and an axe—but that is another story. That night I had a strangely vivid dream: A girl was rearing back in fright from her own shadow; and her shadow, in turn, was rearing back from her.

Photo by Geoff Gould

I awoke laughing, and in less than an hour I had written the first draft of a book called 'Grandmother and the Runaway Shadow.'

"As it turned out, I was two weeks pregnant with my first child, our son Eli. All of my first children's books were for Eli. I wrote two of them when I was pregnant. As he grew older, my books seemed to grow older, too, written for older children.

"Poetry was my first love, and remains crucial to this day. I wrote my first terrible, rhyming poem at age 10 or 11, around the time I received the birthday gift of a beautiful Robert Frost book, *You Come Too*. That book was my first lesson that great poetry can and does speak to children. Because of this I've edited several anthologies of poetry for young readers. I believe that children deserve great poetry.

"I have always felt that my writing for young people comes from my relationship to children—to my own, but also to everyone else's. Children refresh and inspire. Young people are so brave, so strong, kind, eager to love. Children's books are about essentials, things that matter: family, friendship, courage, loyalty, good and evil. There is no need to speak down to a child. E. B. White once said, 'The writer who tries gearing down to write for children will surely wind up stripping some gears.' I feel honored to write for the best readers in the world."

℃ ℃ ℃

Liz Rosenberg received her B.A. in literature from Bennington College in 1976, her M.A. from Johns Hopkins University in 1978, and her Ph.D. in comparative literature from the State University of New York at Binghamton in 1987. She has been teaching creative writing courses, including a course in writing for children, at SUNY Binghamton since 1980. For the 1983–84 school year, she earned a university award for excellence in teaching. The novelist John Gardner was Rosenberg's first husband; they were divorced in 1982. In 1983 she married David Bosnick, a writer who also owns the Bookbridge bookstore in Vestal, New York, and who has taught at SUNY at Binghamton.

A poet and novelist, Rosenberg has written for both adults and young people. She has been a book columnist for *Parents Magazine* and currently writes a monthly book column in the *Boston Globe* newspaper. Her poetry has been published in the *New Yorker*, the *American Poetry Review*, *Harper's Magazine*, the *Nation*, the *New Republic*, and the *Paris Review*. Her first full-length poetry collection for adults, *The Fire Music*, was nominated for the Pulitzer Prize and won the 1985 Agnew Starret Poetry Prize. Written in a relaxed conversational style, *The Fire Music* is about love, mortality, and the grief attending the loss of a loved one. *Children of Paradise* was named a Paterson Prize Honor Book for Poetry. She also has received the Kellogg's National Fellowship and the Pennsylvania Council for the Arts Poetry grant.

> *"Children's books are about essentials, things that matter: family, friendship, courage, loyalty, good and evil."*

Rosenberg's books for children and young adults include picture books and poetry anthologies. As an anthologist she often chooses poetry written for adults, believing that children can understand poetry on that level. In *The Invisible Ladder*, which was the 1997 winner of the Claudia Lewis Award for Poetry given by the Bank Street College of Education, readers are introduced to a wide range of poems that were written for adults but accessible to young adults. Poets such as Galway Kinnell, Robert Bly, Allen Ginsberg, Nikki Giovanni, Alice Walker, and others preface their poems with commentary and photos. *Earth-Shattering Poems* is a collection that captures intense emotions and experiences of love, joy, rage, grief, and wonder. The poets in this collection range from the very famous to lesser-known authors and include writers from around the world. A companion to *Earth-Shattering Poems*, *Light-Gathering Poems*, which won the Lee Bennett Hopkins Poetry Award, features poems by authors from ancient to contemporary times. The collection brings readers messages of light and hope through images such as lighthouses and summer that suggest beauty and eternity.

Among the many poets included in this collection are Elizabeth Barrett Browning, Allen Ginsberg, Robert Frost, Jane Kenyon, and Christina Rossetti. Biographical notes on the poets are included in both titles.

Among Rosenberg's picture books for younger readers, *Monster Mama*, illustrated by Stephen Gammell, is a funny and suspenseful tale about a loving mother who is literally a monster and her sweet-tempered son, who learns to find the monster in himself when he has to deal with three bullies. *Monster Mama* was named an IRA Children's Choice book. *The Scrap Doll, Adelaide and the Night Train*, and *The Carousel* were all named Best Books by *Parents* magazine. *The Carousel* is a magical and poetic story of the adventure of two girls and an abandoned carousel, illustrated with luminous art by Jim LaMarche. It was chosen as a *Reading Rainbow* Feature Selection on PBS television.

Three of Rosenberg's titles have won the Paterson Prize for Books for Young People: *Grandmother and the Runaway Shadow, The Silence in the Mountains*, and *Light-Gathering Poems. The Invisible Ladder* and *Earth-Shattering Poems* were both listed by the New York Public Library as Books for the Teen Age. *Earth-Shattering Poems* was a Bank Street Best Book, a *Riverbank Review* Book of Distinction, and one of ALA's Best Books for the College-Bound.

Liz Rosenberg lives with her husband, their son Eli, and their daughter Lily, in Binghamton, New York.

Courtesy of Henry Holt and Company

SELECTED WORKS FOR YOUNG READERS: *Adelaide and the Night Train*, illus. by Lisa Desimini, 1989; *The Scrap Doll*, illus. by Robin Ballard, 1991; *Window, Mirror, Moon*, illus. by Ruth Richardson, 1992; *Monster Mama*, illus. by Stephen Gammell, 1993; *Mama Goose: A New Mother Goose*, illus. by Janet Street, 1994; *The Carousel*, illus. by Jim LaMarche, 1995; *Grandmother and the Runaway Shadow*, illus. by Beth Peck, 1996; *Heart and Soul*, 1996; *Moonbathing*, illus. by Stephen Lambert, 1996; *A Big and Little Alphabet*, illus. by Vera Rosenberg, 1997; *Eli and Uncle Dawn*, illus. by Susan Gaber, 1997; *I Did It Anyway*, illus. by Stephen Gammell, 1998; *The*

Silence in the Mountains, illus. by Chris K. Soentpiet, 1998; *Eli's Night-Light*, illus. by Joanna Yardley, 2001; *Seventeen, A Novel in Prose Poems*, 2002; *We Wanted You*, illus. by Peter Catalanotto, 2002.

SELECTED ANTHOLOGIES, as editor: *The Invisible Ladder: An Anthology of Contemporary American Poems for Young Readers*, 1996; *Earth-Shattering Poems*, 1998; *Light-Gathering Poems*, 2000; *Roots & Flowers: Poets and Poems on Family*, 2001; *I Just Hope It's Lethal: Poems of Sadness, Madness & Joy*, with Deena November, 2005.

SELECTED WORKS FOR ADULTS: *The Fire Music*, 1986; *Children of Paradise* (Pitt Poetry Series), 1993; *These Happy Eyes*, 2000.

SUGGESTED READING: *Something About the Author*, vol. 129, 2002. Periodicals—Rosenberg, Liz, "Reviewing Poetry," *The Horn Book*, May–June 2005.

Meg Rosoff

October 16, 1956–

"I grew up in Boston, the second of four sisters, in an academic family in the leafy suburbs. We had a dog and a station wagon and a sandbox in the back yard. My sisters and I spent happy summers on Cape Cod. My parents encouraged an early talent to write. I had wonderful English teachers at school, and later, I studied English and Fine Arts at Harvard.

"Not exactly the kind of deranged, twisted background you want as a writer.

"In 1977, twenty years old, I moved to London to study steel sculpture and fell in love with London. Returning (reluctantly) to Boston, I wrote an article about the London music scene and sent it off to *Glamour*. It was rejected with a form letter.

"So much for my career as a writer, I thought, and moved to New York City, settled in a roach-infested apartment and got a terrible job in publishing in a miserable downtown office. It paid so badly, I ate the same sandwich every day for eight months because it only cost 85 cents. From there I went on to work at *People* magazine (as a secretary), the *New York Times*, and finally in advertising because I thought it might be a little more fun and slightly better paid. I also played bass guitar (badly) in a band.

"In 1989, I quit my job and flew to London—for three months, I said. But I met my husband the next day at a party, got a job in advertising, bought an apartment, wrote a guidebook to London, had a baby, and never looked back.

"Despite hating advertising and managing to get fired about every eighteen months, I paid the bills, and before I knew what had happened I'd been at it for fifteen years. I desperately wanted to do something else, but I couldn't tell a joke much less develop a plot, and had to depend on Maurice Sendak for bedtime stories for my daughter.

"In 2001, a mere forty years after my parents had suggested I'd make a good writer, I wrote a picture book called *Meet Wild Boars* with illustrator Sophie Blackall. I stole the plot from my (then) four-year-old, and Sophie took it to her publishers in New York. With the boars and a 'practice novel,' I managed to find an agent, who suggested I try a second book (I assumed she meant 'a better one this time' though she didn't say so). Desperate to impress her, I wrote *How I Live Now*, in the evenings while working full time. The idea of a city cousin coming to live with country cousins was based loosely on one of my favourite books as a child, *The Good Master*. My greatest revelation (at age 45) was that you don't have to be brilliant at plot to write a decent novel.

Photo by Francesco Guidicini / The Sunday Times

"*How I Live Now* went on to sell into 28 languages and allowed me to quit advertising. It was one of the best moments in my life, although I've come to the reluctant realization that advertising was an excellent apprenticeship (which doesn't mean I recommend it). I've gone on to write two more picture books and two more novels, including *Just In Case*, and now have the amazing luxury of staying at home all day to write. We've recently acquired two lurcher puppies who make sure I get out of the house every morning to chase them around the park, and they also stave off boredom by eating the furniture and my husband's shoes and the mail and the laundry and the rugs. They also think un-stuffing pillows is funny.

"So after all this time, I've finally figured out what I want to be when I grow up. Though I think I knew all along."

ভ ভ ভ

Meg Rosoff's vibrant characterizations and unique vision in her first novel, *How I Live Now*, catapulted the book to award-winning status when it was published in 2004. In England, where she lives, it won the Guardian Fiction Prize and the Branford Boase award and was short-listed for the Whitbread Award. In the United States, where she was born, it captured the American Library Association's Michael L. Printz Award for young adult books. This story of a troubled American teen coming of age when she visits a family of eccentric cousins in England takes place just prior to, during, and after a hypothetical war, set in the near future. Daisy, visiting from New York, and escaping a home life that she is intensely unhappy about, finds herself in a very different family situation. She enjoys her newfound freedom with her cousins at first, but the young people are soon thrust into situations beyond their control as a military occupation takes hold while Daisy's aunt is out of the country.

> "In 2001, a mere forty years after my parents had suggested I'd make a good writer, I wrote a picture book. . . ."

The story of how the book got published is almost as fantastic as the book's plot. Rosoff had asked for compassionate leave from her job in advertising after her youngest sister, Debbie, died of cancer in 2001. She used the time to write a novel about a girl and a horse, the type of book she would have loved to read herself as a young girl, as well as a picture book, *Meet Wild Boars*, inspired by her own young daughter. Her agent, Catherine Clarke, urged her to write another novel, the book that became *How I Live Now*. Writing during the onset of the Iraq War, Rosoff found herself affected by current events and wondering how they could affect lives in the future. Once she found Daisy's voice, the book came very quickly and was edited simultaneously by British and American editors—Rebecca McNally at Puffin in England and Wendy Lamb at Random House in New York. Both editors worked hard to make sure the book would sound natural to readers in their respective countries. Narrated in Daisy's compelling voice, the story shows the remarkable resilience of adolescence and the way that deep personal connections can heal physical and emotional trauma.

Meg Rosoff has credited her years of working in the advertising industry with teaching her to edit her prose "ruthlessly," as she stated in her acceptance speech for the Printz award. Her second novel, *Just in Case*, cited by ALA as a Best Book for Young Adults, is as spare and poetic in its style as her first. Exploring the themes of life and death, cause and effect, fate and free will, the book begins with a cataclysmic event. Teenager David Case saves his toddler brother Charlie from toppling out of a window, just in the nick of time, an act that catapults him into re-examining—and attempting to reinvent—his life. Fate itself becomes a voice in the book—watching David (who has changed his name to Justin), commenting on the small events of his life, and toying with his future. *Just in Case* won the 2007 Carnegie Medal in England.

Now a full-time writer, Meg Rosoff lives in Highbury, North London with her British husband, who is a painter, and their daughter Gloria.

SELECTED WORKS FOR CHILDREN AND YOUNG ADULTS: *How I Live Now*, 2004; *Meet Wild Boars*, illus. by Sophie Blackall, 2005; *Just in Case*, 2006; "Resigned," in *Shining On: 11 star authors' illuminating stories*, 2007; *What I Was*, 2008.

SELECTED WORKS FOR ADULTS: *London Guide: Be a Traveler, Not a Tourist*, with Caren Acker, 1995.

Courtesy of Wendy Lamb Books, Random House, Inc.

SUGGESTED READING: Rosoff, Meg, "Michael L. Printz Award Speech," *Young Adult Library Services*, Fall 2005; McCaffrey, Meg, "Answering the Call," *School Library Journal*, March 2005; Rosoff, Meg, "My Unbrilliant Career (or how I wrote my first novel in just 26 years)," *Kliatt*, March 1, 2005; Cooper, Ilene, "Interview with Meg Rosoff," *Booklist*, March 15, 2005; Corbett, Sue, "Flying Starts," *Publishers Weekly*, Dec. 20, 2004; Craig, Amanda, "Suffering? It's How I Live Now," *Sunday Times* (London, England), Nov. 14, 2004.

WEB SITE: www.megrosoff.co.uk

Susan Goldman Rubin

March 14, 1939–

"As a child, I loved to draw and dreamed of becoming an illustrator of children's books. I had it all figured out: I'd have five children, stay at home with them, and illustrate. Of course, it didn't work out that way.

"When I was ten years old, my parents allowed me to take the subway to Manhattan by myself to attend Saturday classes at the Art Students League. One week we would draw a still life, the next a nude model. Fortunately, my parents never looked at my sketchpad, so they had no idea what I was doing. Then I applied to the High School of Music & Art and was accepted. Although I certainly wasn't the best artist, I adored the classes and made friendships that have lasted over the years. At Oberlin College in Ohio, I majored in English but continued taking studio art on the side.

"Upon graduating, I got married and returned to New York. When my husband and I moved to Southern California, I wound up in a miserable suburb far away from the world of publishing. I still hoped to illustrate children's books but with three young children and no money for a babysitter or plane fare, I couldn't go to New York to make the rounds and show what I considered a portfolio. So I started writing stories to give myself something to illustrate and send out.

Photo by Susan Goldman Rubin

"My first picture book, *Grandma Is Somebody Special*, took five years to develop into a text, dummy and sample drawings worthy of attention. The story was based on my children's experience of sleeping over at my mother's apartment—one at a time. Albert Whitman & Company published it with my illustrations and the book stayed in print for 20 years. Two more picture books followed.

"Meanwhile, I had gotten divorced, remarried, acquired two stepsons and had another baby of my own. Now I had a grand total of six children! My second husband and I produced some filmstrips about children with disabilities. I felt inspired to try to write a novel with a heroine who is developmentally disabled and therefore more vulnerable than other teenagers her age. The result was *Emily Good as Gold*, published by Browndeer/Harcourt. Linda Zuckerman, my editor, encouraged me to write a companion book, *Emily in Love*. It has been enormously gratifying to receive letters from so-called 'special' children who see themselves in Emily.

"I still loved art and wanted to share my pleasure and enthusiasm with young readers. So turning to nonfiction, I wrote a biography on Frank Lloyd Wright, published by my favorite art book publisher, Abrams. Next came biographies of photojournalist Margaret Bourke-White and filmmaker Steven Spielberg as well as books done in conjunction with museum exhibitions.

"In recent years, I have turned to another passionate interest—the Holocaust. I stumbled upon a story that I felt compelled to tell: the story of an unsung heroine, Friedl Dicker-Brandeis. An artist and teacher, Friedl worked with children who were her fellow prisoners at Terezin, a ghetto/concentration camp during World War II, and helped them to endure suffering and sustain hope through art. Researching and writing *Fireflies in the Dark* resulted in meeting remarkable survivors who had their own stories to tell. One book led to another, and another.

"When my husband asks me when and if I'll retire, I always say, 'Never.' I love this work too much. I feel privileged to be a children's book writer."

 беспокойство   CR   CR

Susan Goldman Rubin grew up in the New York City borough of the Bronx. Her first marriage, to Dr. Hubert Goldman, ended in divorce in 1976. In 1978 she married Michael B. Rubin. The author of more than 20 books for children and young adults, as well as numerous articles for design magazines and scripts for educational films and filmstrips, she had never expected to be a writer, but thought of herself mainly as an artist. After receiving a number of rejection letters from publishers for her picture books that made suggestions for revising her manuscripts, Rubin began taking writing classes at UCLA Extension to learn the craft. Her first published story appeared in the magazine *Highlights for Children*.

As Rubin has followed her interests from the world of art to the history of the Holocaust, she has found threads that connect her books. She has written about buildings and architecture, including a biography of Frank Lloyd Wright; her interest in Jewish history led her to another architect, Simon Wiesenthal, whose four years in the Mauthausen concentration camp are featured in Rubin's *The Flag with Fifty-Six Stars: A Gift from the Survivors of Mauthausen*. Wiesenthal is the founder of the Simon Wiesenthal Center/Museum of Tolerance in Los Angeles, where Rubin first came across the story of the artist and teacher Friedl Dicker-Brandeis, whose pioneering work in art therapy helped inspire hope in the children imprisoned in Terezin. *Fireflies in the Dark* recounts Friedl's life as a prisoner and teacher in the camp; it also incorporates general Holocaust history. The children's paintings and poems used in this book came from a variety of sources, including the Jewish Museum in Prague and the Holocaust Museum in Washington, D.C.

> *"Researching and writing* Fireflies in the Dark *resulted in meeting remarkable survivors who had their own stories to tell. One book led to another, and another."*

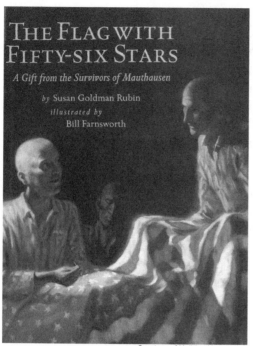

THE FLAG WITH
FIFTY-SIX STARS

A Gift from the Survivors of Mauthausen

by Susan Goldman Rubin

illustrated by
Bill Farnsworth

Courtesy of Holiday House, Inc.

To further explore the idea that art in many forms can provide comfort and joy in times of duress, Rubin wrote *Art Against the Odds*, a book about various forms of art created by people living in extreme poverty, in prisons, and in mental institutions. At the Simon Wiesenthal Center, Rubin viewed videos of Ela Weissberger performing in *Brundibar*, an opera originally written in 1938 to help give Jewish orphans hope in the face of an uncertain future. This opera was first performed in the Terezin camp. One of the few children to survive that camp, Ela sang the role of the Cat in *Brundibar* while she was a prisoner. After the war Ela went to Israel and finally settled in the United States where she became a frequent public speaker on the Holocaust. Susan Rubin, also a well-known speaker on Holocaust studies, collaborated with her on the book *The Cat with the Yellow Star: Coming of Age in Terezin*, which was named an ALA Notable Children's Book, an Orbis Pictus Recommended Book, and a Sydney Taylor Notable Book of Jewish Content for Older Readers.

Rubin has received numerous awards for her work. In 1993 she was given a research grant by the National Endowment for the Humanities for her work on *Frank Lloyd Wright*. *Fireflies in the Dark* won a Golden Kite Honor Book Award in Nonfiction and a Sydney Taylor Honor Book award for Older Readers; it was also named a Notable Book for a Global Society and a Notable Social Studies Trade Book. *Searching for Anne Frank* won an Oppenheim Toy Portfolio Gold Award. *Margaret Bourke-White* was named an ALA Best Book for Young Adults, and *Degas and the Dance* was cited as an ALA Notable Children's Book. *Emily Good as Gold* was named an IRA Young Adults Choice. *There Goes the Neighborhood* was named a Notable Social Studies Trade Book for Young People. *There Goes the Neighborhood*, *The Yellow House*, and *Fireflies in the Dark* have all been included in CCBC Choices. Cited by the New York Public Library's Books for the Teen Age were *Frank Lloyd Wright*, *Margaret Bourke-White*, *Steven Spielberg: Crazy for Movies*, and *There Goes the Neighborhood*. Twice she has received the Children's Literature Council of Southern California Award: for *Margaret Bourke-White* and *Fireflies in the Dark*. *The Flag with Fifty-Six Stars* was cited as a Notable Children's Book of Jewish Content by the Association of Jewish Libraries.

Although she visits New York often, Rubin has remained in California. She and her husband live in Malibu, and her six grown children all reside in California. Besides writing, she teaches in the UCLA Extension Writers' Program and the Haystack summer program sponsored by Portland State University.

SELECTED WORKS: *Emily Good as Gold*, 1993; *Frank Lloyd Wright* (First Impressions series), 1994; *Emily in Love*, 1996; *Margaret Bourke-White* (First Impressions series), 1996; *The Whiz Kids Plugged In*, illus. by Doug Cushman, 1997; *The Whiz Kids Take Off!*, illus. by Doug Cushman, 1997; *Toilets, Toasters, and Telephones: The How and Why of Everyday Objects*, illus. by Elsa Warnick, 1998; *Margaret Bourke-White: Her Pictures Were Her Life*, photos by Margaret Bourke-White, 1999; *Fireflies in the Dark: The Story of Friedl Dicker-Brandeis and the Children of Terezin*, 2000; *The Yellow House: Vincent Van Gogh and Paul Gauguin Side by Side*, illus. by Jos. A. Smith, 2001; *There Goes the Neighborhood: Ten Buildings People Loved to Hate*, 2001; *Steven Spielberg: Crazy for Movies*, 2001; *Degas and the Dance: The Painter and the Petits Rats, Perfecting Their Art*, 2002; *Searching for Anne Frank: Letters from Amsterdam to Iowa*, 2003; *L'Chaim! To Jewish Life in America! Celebrating from 1654 until Today*, 2004; *Art Against the Odds: From Slave Quilts to Prison Paintings*, 2004; *The Flag with Fifty-Six Stars: A Gift from the Survivors of Mauthausen*, illus. by Bill Farnsworth, 2005; *The Cat with the Yellow Star: Coming of Age in Terezin*, with Ela Weissberger, 2006; *Andy Warhol: Pop Art Painter*, 2006; *Delicious: The Life and Art of Wayne Thiebaud*, 2007; *Andy Warhol's Colors*, 2007; *Haym Salomon: American Patriot*, illus. by David Slonim, 2007; *Edward Hopper: Painter of Light and Shadow*, 2007; *Wham! The Art and Life of Roy Lichtenstein*, 2008; *Matisse: Dance for Joy*, 2008.

SELECTED WORKS WRITTEN AND ILLUSTRATED: *Grandma Is Somebody Special*, 1976; *Cousins Are Special*, 1978; *Grandpa and Me Together*, 1980.

SUGGESTED READING: *Something About the Author*, vol. 132, 2002. Periodicals—Rubin, Susan Goldman, "How to Research and Write Nonfiction for Children," *The Writer*, August 2000.

WEB SITE: www.susangoldmanrubin.com

Photo by Gorsefield Photography

Angie Sage

June 20, 1952–

"I have always loved reading. I remember even before I could read being fascinated with the shapes of letters and the idea that they had sounds attached to them. And when I learnt to read it was like being given the key to a whole new world—or lots of worlds. I loved to be around books. My father worked in publishing and used to bring back what he called dummy books—beautifully bound hardback books with blank pages. Sometimes they were so beautiful that I hardly dared write in them, as nothing I wrote ever seemed good enough—or neat enough! But I always had the feeling as a child that there were empty books just waiting for me to fill. The biggest treat was going to Foyles bookshop in London on a Saturday and choosing a book of my own. Of course I read it so fast that I was back to the library in a few days, but seeing all those new books all in one place made a big impression on me.

"Eventually when I left school—after a few false starts—I went to art school and studied illustration with the aim of illustrating children's books. When I graduated I found an agent and began illustrating baby and toddler books, which suited my illustration style—simple flat colour enclosed by a thick, wobbly black line. After a few years doing this—and having also had two daughters—I began to want to do more and dared to think that I might be able to write too.

"The first story I ever got published was a little toddler book called *Monkeys in the Jungle*. It was a simple idea—rhyming couplets about where animals lived. It was a real thrill to see not only my pictures but also my words in print. I actually hand-wrote the words too—so they really *were* my words.

"After that I just kept on going until I was writing chapter books for early readers. It was, in a way, a long apprenticeship during which I discovered that I wrote best by having the stories led by a strong character.

"At this time I was writing and also earning my living as an illustrator. This meant that I did not really have the time I wanted to pay attention to an idea I had for a longer novel, something that I felt was really *me* and would be my own world—a place that I felt I already knew. I knew the story would start off with a baby being found in the snow and it would be a kind of family saga with some magic thrown in, but somehow there was never enough time to actually start writing it. So I thought about it a lot and collected ideas.

"By this time I was living in Cornwall in the far southwest of England, somewhere I had wanted to live for a long time. It's a place where I felt there was space to write and think, and it was here that I began to write about Septimus Heap. As soon as I started the book, I realised that I had found the place in my head that I had wanted to find for a long time. And when I woke up one morning with the name Marcia Overstrand buzzing around and demanding to be written about, I just *knew* that it was going to work out.

"Since then Septimus Heap has become so much part of my life that I can hardly believe that there was a time when he, his family, and his world did not exist—or maybe he always did and I just had to find him."

ଓଃ   ଓଃ   ଓଃ

Born in London, Angie Sage grew up in the Thames Valley, London, and Kent in England. As a child she was fond of history, myths, and legends and enjoyed reading books by E. Nesbit and Elizabeth Goudge. She briefly trained to become a radiographer and was planning to study medicine at the Royal Free Hospital but changed her mind and instead received a degree in graphic design and illustration at Leicester University.

A writer and illustrator of children's books since 1989, Sage has spent many years creating children's picture books and has published over a hundred well-loved titles in the United Kingdom and the United States. Her versatile style with art and words appeals to children of all ages, and she has a fine ability to communicate concepts and ideas for the very young reader in her picture books for toddlers and preschoolers. In recent years her writing for older children has achieved international recognition with the Septimus Heap books.

This highly popular middle-grade fantasy series features a warm and affectionate family unit, well-developed characters who are appealingly quirky, and laugh-out-loud humor. In the first book, *Magyk*, the main character, Septimus Heap, appears to be killed off in the first paragraph while a young Heap daughter turns out to be a princess who must flee her home to avoid the Dark Wizard, DomDaniel. A fast-paced thriller featuring a large and diverse cast of characters, *Magyk* is set in a place not

> ". . . I was living in Cornwall in the far south-west of England, somewhere I had wanted to live for a long time. It's a place where I felt there was space to write and think, and it was here that I began to write about Septimus Heap."

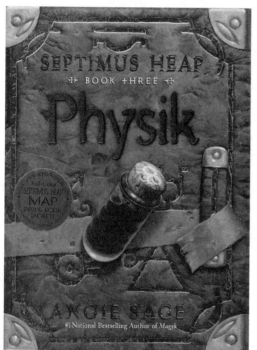

Courtesy of Katherine Tegen Books, HarperCollins Publishers

unlike Sage's beloved Cornwall, with forests, castles, ports, and marshes. *Magyk* achieved instant popularity when it was published in the U.S. and was named an IRA/CBC Children's Choice, a *Kirkus* Editors' Choice, a Parents' Choice Recommended title, a *Child Magazine* Best Book, and one of Bank Street College's Best Children's Books of the Year. *Flyte*, the second book in the series, was among the New York Public Library's Books for the Teen Age. It involves, among other plot elements, a baby dragon that imprints on the Apprentice, Septimus Heap. Sage's imaginative magical world continues to unfold as the series progresses with *Physik* and *Queste*. Three more titles are planned.

Sage is also the author of the humorous Araminta Spookie series, a succession of stories that appeal to a slightly younger audience. Set in a sprawling old house filled with trapdoors, secret passageways, cobwebs, and family ghosts, these books are populated by a cast of lovably eccentric characters, including Uncle Drac who likes to knit, the cranky Aunt Tabby, the Wizzard family, a haunted suit of armour named Sir Horace, and a troupe of acrobatic frogs. In the first book, *My Haunted House*, the Wizzard family moves in with the Spookies when Araminta tries to scare away potential house-buyers. In *The Sword in the Grotto*, the second title, Araminta and Wanda get trapped in a grotto as they try to capture an ancient sword to present to the depressed Sir Horace for his 500th birthday. The acrobatic frogs are kidnapped in *Frognapped*, and Araminta must capture a werewolf in *Vampire Brat*.

No longer working as an illustrator, Sage now devotes her time to writing novels for children. She has two grown children, Laurie and Lois. She and her husband, Rhodri Powell, recently moved from Cornwall to Somerset, in the west of England. They live in a house dating from 1485 that possibly has a secret passage, but no ghosts as far as they know.

SELECTED WORKS WRITTEN AND ILLUSTRATED: *Monkeys in the Jungle*, 1989; *Yellow Ice*, 1998; *The Little Green Book of the Last Lost Dinosaur*, 1995; *In My Home*, 1996; *On the Move*, 1997; *Yellow Lolly*, 1998; *Green Mug*, 1998; *Blue Hat*, 1998; *Red Ball*,

1998; *Beep! Beep! First Picture Word Book*, 1999; *The Little Pink Book of the Woolly Mammoth*, 1999; *Stack-a-Car: Read the Books! Make the Toy!*, 2000; *Where Is My Lamb?* 2000; *Hello Ducks*, 2001; *Molly and the Birthday Party*, 2001; *Molly at the Dentist*, 2001; *Mouse*, 2001; *My Big Busy Bus*, 2002; *No Banana*, 2002; *Inside: Baby's Picture Word Book*, 2004.

SELECTED WORKS ILLUSTRATED: *Who's in the Coop?*, by Richard Powell, 1998; *Who Eats Bananas?*, by Richard Powell, 1998; *Sunday Bunny*, by Lynn Moore, 2000; *Bella's Bedspread*, by Mandy Ross, illus. with Leonie Shearing and Carla Daly, 2000; *Baby Says Love You*, by Opal Dunn, 2003; *Baby Says Hello*, by Opal Dunn, 2003; *Baby Says Hooray*, by Opal Dunn, 2003; *Baby Says Bye-Bye*, by Opal Dunn, 2003; *Say Hello: To Children All Over the World*, by Sue Unstead, 2005.

SELECTED WORKS WRITTEN: *Give a Little Love: Stories of Love and Friendship*, illus. by Valeria Petrone, 2000; *The Lonely Puppy*, illus. by Edward Eaves, 2003; *Magyk* (Septimus Heap, Book 1), illus. by Mark Zug, 2005; *Flyte* (Septimus Heap, Book 2), illus. by Mark Zug, 2006; *My Haunted House* (Araminta Spookie, Book 1), illus. by Jimmy Pickering, 2006; *The Sword in the Grotto* (Araminta Spookie, Book 2), illus. by Jimmy Pickering, 2006; *Frognapped* (Araminta Spookie, Book 3), illus. by Jimmy Pickering, 2007; *Vampire Brat* (Araminta Spookie, Book 4), illus. by Jimmy Pickering, 2007; *Physik* (Septimus Heap, Book 3), illus. by Mark Zug, 2007; *Queste* (Septimus Heap, Book 4), illus. by Mark Zug, 2008.

SUGGESTED READING: Contemporary Authors Online, May 2006.

WEB SITE: www.septimusheap.com

Alex Sanchez

April 24, 1957–

" As a boy, I was a constant daydreamer. When I dreamed about my future life, my heart yearned to some day make a difference in the world. Originally I'm from Mexico. My family immigrated to the U.S. when I was five. I began school speaking only Spanish. For the first time, I experienced prejudice and name-calling for being different. Fortunately, my teachers never made me feel inadequate or inferior. With their help, I worked hard to learn English. My school librarian especially inspired me by reading aloud to us. And though none of my schoolbooks portrayed Mexican people like me, I developed a love of stories.

"In order to fit in, I stopped speaking Spanish and learned to pass as white, hoping others would like and accept me. By the time I reached junior high, I had buried a core part of myself: my Mexican heritage. I was no longer different. Or so I thought. Then came the biggest challenge of my life.

"I was thirteen (in eighth grade) when I read an article in our local newspaper about being gay. Immediately, I knew that's what I was. Going through puberty, I'd kissed girls and also boys. I liked both but knew which my heart yearned for. And I hated myself for it. I had learned to believe that being gay was the worst

Photo by Bill Hitz

thing in the world a boy could be. One boy at my school, who was obviously different in his appearance and mannerisms, was labeled 'queer' and consequently got beat up every day. I stood by, silently watching, wishing I had the courage to stand up for him. But I feared if I did say anything, people might suspect I was gay too.

"After school, alone in my room, I would tell myself, 'I'm not going to feel this way. I refuse to let this happen to me.' And just as I'd learned to hide I was Mexican, I learned to hide I was gay. One of the places I 'escaped' was our school library, which I estimate had several thousand volumes. How many of those books portrayed teens like me, struggling with identity and experiencing prejudice? Not a single one.

"I raced through school, lonely and afraid, and went on to college. Eventually I became a youth and family counselor, working to help discriminated populations of Latino, Black, and Asian youth, street kids, delinquents, troubled families. They reminded me of my own painful growing up. I began to reclaim my Latino heritage and regained my fluency in Spanish.

"And at night, alone, I began to write—about identity, ethnicity, sexuality, differences, and prejudice—the issues I'd struggled with. I wrote about friendship, love, and family—those relationships that had defined me. Writing was a way to heal, to find my voice, to put on paper the story I wished I'd had when I was younger—a book that would have told me: 'It's okay to be who you are.' Eight years later, my first novel, *Rainbow Boys*, was published.

"Immediately, I became deluged with what soon became thousands of e-mails from teens all across America. Many told me the protagonists had become their role models. Many more expressed gratitude: 'It's nice to know I'm not alone.' 'Your book became the peace-saver at my school.' 'Thanks for helping me accept myself.' 'After reading what gay and lesbian teens go through, I've decided to start a Gay-Straight Alliance at my school.' 'I told my mom to read your book so she could understand me.' Until reading these letters, I'd never imagined my writing could help anyone but me. Now I recalled the boy I watched get beat up for being different, and how I didn't have the courage to stand up for him then. I'm speaking up for him now and for thousands of other girls and boys like him.

"I have found my voice. And I have discovered a function of my writing I never foresaw: as an agent of social change, able to inspire, empower, and change lives. I've come to accept myself as a writer who not only tells stories, but who does so in a way that helps promote social justice. The fact that my books do this ceaselessly amazes me. It has given a purpose and meaning to my life that I never imagined—a way to satisfy my young heart's desire to make a difference in the world.

"Looking back, I understand that I saw myself in the boy I watched get beat up. I now write and speak in schools about boys and girls who are somehow different, because they portray all of us. We are all in some way different and very much the same: wanting to fit in, while struggling to be true to who we are."

> *"By the time I reached junior high, I had buried a core part of myself: my Mexican heritage. I was no longer different. Or so I thought. Then came the biggest challenge of my life."*

CB   CB   CB

Born in Mexico City, Alex Sanchez moved to Virginia when he was five years old. His parents were of Cuban and German descent. From his mother, a watercolor artist, he learned to express his creativity, and from his father he learned a strong work ethic. He received his B.A. degree from Virginia Tech University, where he took courses in English, philosophy, and architecture, graduating with honors in 1978. After graduation he went to Hollywood and worked a variety of jobs—usher, projectionist, studio tour guide, and script reader—hoping for a career in the film industry. It was the experience of reading many bad scripts that gave him the feeling he could do better.

For about ten years Sanchez worked as a counselor for youth and families. He completed graduate work at Old Dominion University in education, guidance and counseling, with an emphasis in cross-cultural relations, earning an M.S. in 1985.

Sanchez's work as a counselor for troubled teens reawakened some of the painful issues of his own growing years, and his first language of Spanish came back to him as he worked with many Latino youth. After leaving counseling, Sanchez worked in Washington, D.C. for a trade association in human resources. It was the year after he left counseling that he began writing his breakthrough novel.

Sanchez began writing as way to express his own inner feelings and memories. He took a course at the Writer's Center in Bethesda, Maryland and attended one-week seminars at the Fine Arts Work Center in Provincetown, Massachusetts, where

"Sanchez [is] breaking the silence."
—The Advocate

Courtesy of Simon & Schuster Children's Publishing

he studied with authors such as Michael Cunningham, Richard McCann, and Jacqueline Woodson, who were exploring themes that he was learning to express himself. In 2003 he was a resident fellow in creative writing at the Virginia Center for Creative Arts.

Sanchez's first book, *Rainbow Boys*, is unlike many young adult books that often feature a solitary gay teen struggling in the shadows of high school life. This story is told from the perspective of three high school seniors, who are at various stages of coming to terms with their homosexuality. Nelson is openly gay and has a crush on his best friend Kyle, who is shy and feels he could never let his parents find out about his sexual preferences. Kyle struggles with his feelings for Jason, a star athlete who has a girlfriend. In the course of the story all three young men come out of their respective closets. Designated by *Publishers Weekly* as a "Flying Start" title, *Rainbow Boys* was named an ALA Best Book for Young Adults, an IRA Young Adult Choice, a New York Public Library Book for the Teen Age, and a Lambda Literary Award finalist.

After publishing *Rainbow Boys*, Alex Sanchez immediately began to hear from teens across America who told him the fictional protagonists had become their role models and expressed their gratitude for the story. His second book, *Rainbow High*, was named a Notable Social Studies Trade Book in addition to many of the accolades received by *Rainbow Boys*. The character of Nelson faces a further challenge in this book as he waits to learn if he has contracted the HIV virus. In the third title in the series, *Rainbow Road*, Jason, Kyle, and Nelson take a road trip the summer after their senior year and continue to struggle with the tricky combination of finding love and following their dreams.

In *So Hard to Say*, which won the Lambda Literary Award and was named a New York Public Library Book for the Teen Age, 13-year-old Xio, a bubbly Southern California Latina, decides that the new transfer student from Wisconsin will be her first real boyfriend. Xio, however, hadn't reckoned with the fact the attractive blond boy might be gay. *So Hard to Say* was also a nominee for the Quill Award. In *Getting It*, 15-year-old Carlos Amoroso thinks he's madly in love with vivacious Roxy Rodriguez. When he befriends a gay teen named Sal, he worries that all the other students will question his sexuality. As the friendship between Carlos and Sal deepens, Carlos himself begins to wonder.

Today Alex Sanchez is a full-time writer. He often speaks in schools, colleges, youth groups, and conferences about his writing and about being true to one's own conscience. He lives in Florida where he enjoys hanging out with friends, going to the movies, and biking.

SELECTED WORKS: *Rainbow Boys*, 2001; *Rainbow High*, 2003; "If You Kiss a Boy" in *13: Thirteen Stories About the Agony and Ecstasy of Being Thirteen*, ed. by James Howe, 2003; *So Hard to Say*, 2004; *Rainbow Road*, 2005; *Getting It*, 2006; *The God Box*, 2007.

SUGGESTED READING: *Authors and Artists for Young Adults*, vol. 51, 2003; Emert, Toby, "An Interview with Alex Sanchez," *ALAN Review*, Fall 2002; Murphy, Mekado, "Alex Sanchez Interview: My So-gay Life," *Dallas Voice*, Feb. 15, 2002; Pavao, Kate, "Flying Starts," *Publishers Weekly*, Dec. 24, 2001.

WEB SITE: www.AlexSanchez.com

Ruth Sanderson

November 24, 1951–

"When I was growing up my two favorite places were the woods and the local library. One of my most treasured possessions was a battered copy of Grimm's Fairy Tales given to me by my grandmother, Ruth. She was a librarian for over 40 years and read to me a great deal when I was small. My sister, brother and I spent hours in the library with her in the town next to ours. When I was older I walked to the library near our house and wrestled Black Stallion books out of the hands of my best friend (*sometimes* she won). Later we would gallop through the woods on our imaginary stallions.

"One of the most magical places in the woods near my friend's house was an abandoned Theme Park. I remember singing songs from *The Wizard of Oz* . . . "Lions and Tigers and Bears, Oh my!" . . . as we walked down the long, tree-lined dirt road at the end of which a pink castle loomed. Of course it was locked, but it was easy to get into the old park through the woods. Inside were many buildings in miniature: Santa's workshop, a little church, a miniature railroad. My favorite was a fieldstone cottage—

Photo by Morgan Robison

Ruth Sanderson

probably intended as a fairy-tale house—perhaps the home of the Seven Dwarfs. The place also included a Frontier Land—a main street with a boardwalk, saloon and hotel, and covered wagons left abandoned to rot in a field. I don't believe the place ever opened to the public. (The story was they ran out of money to finish it.) But my imagination was opened there. The combination of my love of fairy tales and actually getting to play in a magical fairy-tale play land, overgrown and mysterious, without a doubt had a profound effect on the direction of my life.

"My love for horses fed into another passion—drawing. I spent hours drawing the object of my dreams. And after years of begging and cajoling, my parents bought me a horse. The happiest times in my teenage years were spent trail riding with my friends. Sadly, when I was a senior in high school, a drunken hunter shot and killed my beloved horse. I found solace in drawing and painting.

"I have always enjoyed a challenge and decided to teach myself oil painting. For my senior Art History project I copied a Manet painting, *The Bar at the Folies-Bergères*, in its original size—almost five feet wide. I decided I wanted to make a career out of art, and after spending a year in a liberal arts college I transferred to an art school so I could take a combination of traditional drawing and painting courses and commercial courses as well. The artists whom I admired the most were the illustrators Howard Pyle, N. C. Wyeth, and Norman Rockwell. The English Pre-Raphaelites and the Hudson River School were also strong influences on my style and still are today. Happily, the children's book market is so diverse that there is room for a vast array of illustration styles, from the very simple to styles with intricate detail.

"I loved fairy tales as a child and still love the depth and imagery in these stories, both visual and symbolic. As a reteller, I find it most rewarding to read many versions of a story and then weave together the parts that appeal to me and that feel satisfying and 'right.' My goal is always to make sure the story has a heart and rings true. Then the pictures can't help following suit.

"My most recent fairy tale, *The Snow Princess*, was inspired by the Russian opera *The Snow Maiden*. In the opera the Snow Maiden is warned by her parents, Father Frost and Mother Spring, not to fall in love or she will die. Of course, she falls in love and eventually perishes by melting in beautiful operatic style. In my version there is a surprise ending, when the character realizes that she is in love and wonders why she has not died. Her mother, Spring, appears as the snow is melting and explains that she will indeed die, for now she is mortal, and like all human beings she too will grow old and die. So, everyone lives happily ever after in fairy tale fashion. This is a coming-of-age story where the character must make a sacrifice and go through an ordeal (a rite of passage) in order to become independent from her parents and make her own way in life.

"For three years I worked on a 64-page *Mother Goose*. I added a little whimsy and fantasy in my version, with fairies and elves in many scenes. I am also developing a humorous cat story. It is important for me as an artist to try different types of stories and styles, to stay excited about my work. That is why whenever I am asked which book is my favorite, the answer is usually, 'The one I'm working on now.'"

"The combination of my love of fairy tales and actually getting to play in a magical fairy-tale play land, overgrown and mysterious, without a doubt had a profound effect on the direction of my life."

Cʒ   Cʒ   Cʒ

When she was a child growing up in the small town of Monson, Massachusetts, Ruth Sanderson's parents recognized her interest in art and provided her with paper and drawing supplies. Ruth's mother—who loved to create by quilting fabric, arranging flowers, and making wreaths of pinecones—gave her a book on how to draw horses, and Ruth, in turn, taught her friends in grade school. At Paier School of Art in Hamden, Connecticut, from which she graduated in 1974, Sanderson studied anatomy, figure drawing, and painting. She decided to major in illustration, because she liked the challenge of figuring out how to express another person's words visually. Sanderson's talent was recognized immediately, and she began illustrating as soon as she left art school, creating book jackets, which she found she could juggle by working on five or six at the same time.

Initially, with tight deadlines, Sanderson needed to use quick-drying mediums, pencil, or watercolors. She illustrated a variety of books, fiction and nonfiction, contemporary works and classics, novels and picture books. Her work captures light and shadow with great skill. Her soft pencil drawings suggest the depth of feeling in the characters of illustrated "problem" novels, such as *Don't Hurt Laurie!* by Willo Davis Roberts, which deals with child abuse, and *The Season of Silence* by Mary Francis Shura, which treats the theme of chronic illness. Sanderson portrays the inner emotional state of a child very effectively in these books and in others with lighter themes, such as *Samantha on Stage* by Susan Clement Farrar. A versatile artist, Sanderson has received notice for her nonfiction books: *Five Nests*, written by Caroline Arnold and illustrated by Sanderson, received an Outstanding Science Book Award, and *A Different Kind of Gold*, with text by Cecily Stern, was selected as a Notable Children's Trade Book in the Field of Social Studies.

> *"I loved fairy tales as a child and still love the depth and imagery in these stories, both visual and symbolic."*

Today, Sanderson is best known for her own retellings of folk and fairy tales illustrated with her sumptuous oil paintings. *Papa Gatto: An Italian Fairy Tale* combines several stories and contains elements of "Cinderella" and "Puss in Boots" with a modern twist at the end. It was named an ABA Children's Booksellers' Choice and one of the *Boston Globe's* twelve best books of 1995. Sanderson's early love of horses is evident in *The Golden Mare, the Firebird and the Magic Ring*, a fine composite retelling of traditional Russian fairy tales, which won the 2003 Texas Bluebonnet Award. Her own original fairy story, *The Enchanted Wood*, which grew out of her childhood memories of playing among woods and trees, received the Irma S. and James H. Black Award from Bank Street College of Education and the Young Hoosier Award in the State of Indiana.

Sanderson is capable of adjusting her style to fit the needs of the text. In *The Little Engine That Could*, she used pencil and watercolor to stay true to the original art of that classic story. Her oil paintings for other stories are lush and impressive, with each detail carefully researched. In William Shakespeare's *The Tempest*, retold by Bruce Coville, the landscapes are reminiscent of scenery for a fine stage production and the characters have the look of costumed players.

Ruth Sanderson enjoys reading, bicycling, and horseback riding. She also likes spending time with her daughters and encouraging their artistic efforts. She lives with her family in Easthampton, Massachusetts.

SELECTED WORKS WRITTEN AND ILLUSTRATED: *The Twelve Dancing Princesses*, 1990; *The Enchanted Wood*, 1991; *The Nativity: From the Gospels of Matthew and Luke*, 1993; *Pappa Gatto: An Italian Fairy Tale*, 1995; *Rose Red and Snow White: A Grimm's Fairy Tale*, 1996; *Tapestries: Stories of Women in the Bible*, 1998; *The Crystal Mountain*, 1999; *The Golden Mare, the Firebird and the Magic Ring*, 2001; *Cinderella*, 2002; *Saints: Lives and Illuminations*, 2003; *The Snow Princess*, 2004.

SELECTED WORKS ILLUSTRATED: *Grandma's Beach Surprise*, by Ilka List, 1975; *Buck, Wild*, by Glenn Balch, 1976; *The Little Engine That Could*, by Watty Piper, 1976; *The Beast of Lor*, by Clyde Robert Bulla, 1977; *Don't Hurt Laurie!*, by Willo Davis Roberts, 1977; *A Child's Garden of Verses*, by Robert Louis Stevenson, 1977; *Walt Disney*, by Gretta Walker, 1977; *The Mystery of Pony Hollow*, by Lynn Hall, 1978; *The Poetry of Horses*, by William Cole, compiler, 1979; *Samantha on Stage*, by Susan Clement Farrar, 1979; *Into the Dream*, by William Sleator, 1979; *Five Nests*, by Caroline Arnold, 1980; *The Mystery of the Missing Pony*, by Margaret Chittenden, 1980; *Good Dog Poems*, by William Cole, comp., 1981; *The Mystery of the Caramel Cat*, by Lynn Hall, 1981; *The Animal, the Vegetable and John D. Jones*, by Betsy Byars, 1982; *When You Were a Baby*,

Courtesy of Little, Brown Books for Young Readers

by Linda Hayward, 1982; *The Owl and the Pussycat*, by Edward Lear, 1982; *One of the Family*, by Peggy Archer, 1983; *Caught in the Turtle*, by Judith Gorog, 1983; *The Store-bought Doll*, by Lois Meyer, 1983; *Heidi*, by Johanna Spyri, 1984; *Five Little Bunnies*, by Linda Hayward, 1984; *The Sleeping Beauty*, by Jane Yolen, 1986; *The Secret Garden*, by Frances Hodgson Burnett, 1988; *Puppies and Kittens*, by Fran Manushkin, 1989; *Beauty and the Beast*, by Samantha Easton, 1992; *William Shakespeare's "The Tempest,"* by Bruce Coville, 1994; *A Treasury of Princesses: Prin-*

cess Tales from around the World, by Shirley Climo, 1996; Cats: A Pop-Up Book, 1997; The Night Before Christmas, by Clement Clarke Moore, 1997; Where Have the Unicorns Gone?, by Jane Yolen, 2000; Mother Goose and Friends, 2008.

SUGGESTED READING: Kingman, Lee, Illustrators of Children's Books: 1967–1976, 1978; Something About the Author, vol. 109, 2000.

WEB SITE: www.ruthsanderson.com

Courtesy of Charles Santore

Charles Santore

(San-TOR-ee
March 16, 1935–

"I started drawing at the age of four. Soon my family began to notice, and my aunt Angela encouraged me further by buying me some paints and brushes. I seem to remember trying to copy pictures from books around the house.

"When I started kindergarten, it wasn't long before my teacher, Mrs. McClosky, had me drawing and painting at every opportunity. Mrs. Degnan, my first grade teacher, loved to spend her summers in Mexico, so I was continually decorating the classroom with murals of Mexico. She would supply me with all the research necessary— pictures, books, and artifacts, brought back from her many trips. That seemed to be the way it continued all through my elementary school years. Every teacher I came into contact with encouraged me to continue drawing and painting.

"My mother recently told me she remembered being invited to a parents' day when I was in second grade. Entering the school, she noticed a picture prominently displayed in the hallway and thought it was really good, especially for a child. On closer inspection she was shocked to see my name on it. She said she had no idea I could do something like that. From then on she became even more supportive of my interest in art.

"As the years passed, junior high, then high school, it was the same story. It finally culminated in my being offered a four-year scholarship to the Philadelphia Museum School of Art (now called the University of the Arts). At first I refused it (don't ask me why). Soon word spread among the faculty about my refusing to accept the scholarship. My English teacher at the time asked me to stay behind after class was dismissed. I had no idea what I had done to be kept after class. When we were alone, she asked if it was true about my refusing such an honor. When I said yes, she asked me to reconsider. She said, 'If you refuse this opportunity now it will never be offered to you again. If you accept, and find after a time you are not happy at art school, you can always leave.'

"Of course she was right, and I accepted the scholarship. I didn't realize it at the time, but it was the best and most timely advice I ever received. Unfortunately, though, as often as I think of that moment in that empty classroom that probably changed my life, I cannot remember the teacher's name. I owe a great deal to the teachers of the Philadelphia Public School System, and especially my senior high school English teacher."

C3 C3 C3

Charles Santore can be described as an illustrator who combines a solid base of traditional fundamentals in painting with contemporary perspectives. When creating illustrations for books, the story is most important to Santore. "I read the text as carefully as I can and then respond pictorially," he has said. His contributions to children's books came after a long career in both commercial and fine art.

After graduating from art school in 1956 and completing his military service, Santore established a small studio in Philadelphia, Pennsylvania. He soon received assignments from the N. W. Ayer Agency, at that time the second largest advertising agency in the world. Throughout the 1960s he honed his skills, producing advertising art, portraiture, book and record jackets, and fine art. By the 1970s he had become one of the most sought-after magazine illustrators, with his work gracing the covers and pages of *Redbook*, *Ladies' Home Journal*, *Esquire*, *Cosmopolitan*, *Time*, *Life*, the *Saturday Evening Post*, and *National Geographic*. Perhaps his best-known work was the celebrity portraits he created for more than 40 covers of *TV Guide*.

In addition to his commercial work, Santore has created fine art that is part of the permanent collections of the Museum of Modern Art in New York, the Brandywine River Museum in Pennsylvania, and the Free Library of Philadelphia, among other venues. Early influences on his style were the works of N. C. Wyeth and Howard Pyle. In 1992 he mounted a one-man exhibit

> *"I didn't realize it at the time, but it was the best and most timely advice I ever received."*

at the Brandywine River Museum, well known for its permanent collections of those earlier artists.

In 1986 Santore added children's book illustration to his broad body of work by invigorating new editions of children's classics with fresh, stylish portrayals. He first created new illustrations for five of Beatrix Potter's classic stories of Peter Rabbit, published in one volume. He later illustrated *Aesop's Fables*, *The Wizard of Oz*, and *The Little Mermaid: The Original Story*. His illustrations for *Aesop's Fables* were the inspiration for a series of Merrill Lynch TV commercials that aired during the 1994 Winter Olympics. His illustrations for *The Wizard of Oz* were used as scenic backdrops for a television production of the story in 1995.

Eventually Santore began writing his own text for picture books. Santore In 1998 *Storytelling* magazine named *William the Curious, Knight of the Water Lilies* a Storytelling World Honor Title. In 2000 *A Stowaway on Noah's Ark* won the Gold Medal at the Society of Illustrators Original Art Show. In 2003 he captured the Silver Medal at the Original Art Show for his detailed and atmospheric illustrations in *Paul Revere's Ride: The Landlord's Tale*. Santore's version of Longfellow's poem was also named a Poetry Book of the Year by the Bank Street College.

Santore is a meticulous draftsman. He fills his watercolor paintings with tightly rendered details of textures, fabrics, flora, and fauna that emerge from his rigorous research. He is often inspired by the early American folk paintings that fill the walls in his home. In 2006 Santore's illustrations for *The Wizard of Oz* were included in an Oz exhibit at the Eric Carle Museum of Picture Book Art in Amherst, Massachusetts. His additional honors include the prestigious Hamilton King Award from the New York Society of Illustrators and a gold medal from the New York Society of Publication Designs.

SELECTED WORKS ILLUSTRATED: *The Complete Tales of Peter Rabbit and Other Favorite Stories*, by Beatrix Potter, 1986; *Aesop's Fables*, 1988, 1995; *The Wizard of Oz*, by L. Frank Baum, condensed from the original, 1991, 2000; *The Little Mermaid: The Original Story*, by Hans Christian Andersen, 1993; *Snow White: A Tale from the Brothers Grimm*, 1996; *The Fox and the Rooster: A Tale from Aesop*, 1998; *Paul Revere's Ride: The Landlord's Tale*, by Henry Wadsworth Longfellow, 2003; *The Camel's Lament: A Poem*, by Charles Edward Carryl, 2004.

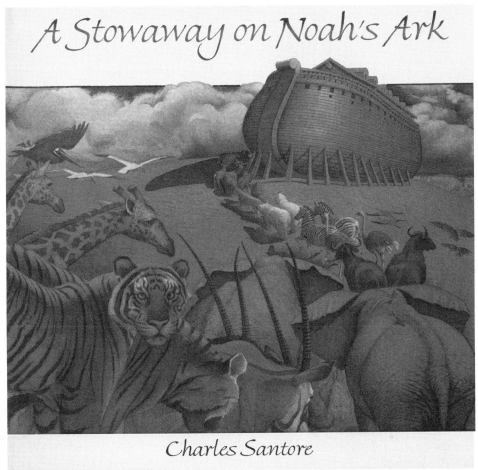

A Stowaway on Noah's Ark

Charles Santore

Courtesy of Random House Children's Books

SELECTED WORKS WRITTEN AND ILLUSTRATED: *William the Curious: Knight of the Water Lilies*, 1997; *A Stowaway on Noah's Ark*, 2000; *Three Hungry Pigs and the Wolf Who Came to Dinner*, 2005; *The Silk Princess*, 2007.

SUGGESTED READING: Meyers, Tiffany, "Charles Santore," *Communication Arts*, 2004.

"Long before becoming a writer, I was a listener, a talker and a reader. My mother liked to say that I talked from the day I was born. My dad said that wasn't quite true. However, he did remember that, after watching and listening to him repeat the names of the animals we could see outside the window, I, at ten months old, clearly said back, 'buhd, buhd' and 'tiny quirrel.'

"My grandpa, whose parents were from Germany, told that once, pre–age one, I was waving my hands and making a baby

Carole Lexa Schaefer

February 23, 1938–

garble speech when he joined me with, 'Und dunder vetter!' 'And then,' Grandpa loved to relate, 'you swung a little fist and repeated exactly, "Und dunder vetter!"' This grandpa, my mom's dad, taught me how to whistle before I turned age two.

"On my dad's side of the family, there were seven aunties and uncles who, along with my dad, spoke Czech, the language of their immigrant parents who died before I was born. Our frequent family gatherings were full of conversation, laughter, singing in Czech, and storytelling, mostly in English. Often, these hilarious stories, peppered with characters from 'the old neighborhood,' were ones the aunties and uncles told about each other from the days when they were growing up.

Photo by Stefan Schaefer

"There were plenty of made-up stories, too. My Aunt Mamie created a thrilling ongoing saga about The Seven-Tailed Rat. Sometimes at the most exciting part of a tale, she'd stop and say, 'Och, I need to eat another piece of cake now.' When my brother, sister, cousins and I begged her to go on, wise Aunt Mamie would say, 'Next Saturday you'll all be over to my house—I'll finish then.' During the week that ensued, we children, especially my cousin Judy and I, would try to figure how Seven-Tail's unfinished episode would end. In the process, we hatched stories of our own.

"I don't remember learning to read. It was before I started school and, according to my mom, 'Just sort of happened.' When I did start school, I brought along a rich tradition of oral language, an early love of reading, and a passion for imaginative play. But, for me, school was definitely the place where the mechanics of writing formally began. Over the years at school, writing was added to my list of big loves. In high school, my dream was to become a fabulous journalist, in college, to become a fine poet. Teachers Irmgard Koch and David Rhode at Lutheran High School in St. Louis, and later Merle Radke at Concordia University in Chicago, encouraged me to 'keep writing.'

"What I became after graduating from college was an enthusiastic teacher who, in places as far-flung as Switzerland, Taiwan and Micronesia, worked at listening to, talking with, and encouraging young people, of middle grade to junior high ages, to use their talents and develop their coping skills.

"When I became a parent, my son Stefan's lively imagination inspired a treasure of silly songs, made-up games, imaginary friends and endless adventures. He caused me to focus on the young child's incredible creative capacities, and led me to decide on Early Childhood Education as the field for my master's degree study.

"It was, at age 43, while finishing work for this degree at the University of Washington in Seattle, that I made a life-changing discovery for my writing. As my final thesis project, I chose to put together a photo-essay picture book for young children. Research for this project required that I read vast numbers of children's picture books—more than I ever had as a teacher or parent. In what I considered the best of these books, I found that the texts contained the energy and succinctness of fabulous journalism, as well as the rhythm and lyricism of fine poetry. Best of all, when read aloud, these stories tapped into what I call 'the music in my ears,' put there during my childhood experience with language and story. Thus I discovered that these word songs were what and how I wanted to write. I've been creating picture book stories for children ever since, and reading them to all who will listen—including the many children at the preschool I founded more than 20 years ago."

℘   ℘   ℘

"Our frequent family gatherings were full of conversation, laughter, singing in Czech, and storytelling, mostly in English."

Born in St. Louis, Missouri, Carole Lexa Schaefer is the oldest of three children. She has a brother, David, who is a retired Army Corps engineer and musician, and a sister, Mary, the director of a theater production company in San Francisco. Schaefer received her B.S. degree from Concordia University in River Forest, Illinois, in 1960.

When Schaefer married her husband, Waldo, the couple found teaching jobs in Switzerland and later joined the Peace Corps. On Tol Island, in the Truk District in Micronesia, they helped found a school; Schaefer taught and helped to develop a curriculum while her husband worked on erecting buildings for what became the Faichuk Post-Elementary School.

Schaefer obtained a master's degree in early childhood education from the University of Washington in Seattle in 1980, the same year she founded the Little Friends Preschool, a venture with which she remains associated today.

Courtesy of Candlewick Press

Schaefer's books are known for their joyful celebration of the imagination of young children, and her writing has met with critical success. *The Squiggle*, a charming story about a group of preschoolers inspired to imaginative flights of fancy by a swirling red ribbon, was named an ALA Notable Children's Book and a *Booklist* Editors' Choice. Schaefer explores the meaning of heritage in *The Copper Tin Cup*, a Notable Social Studies Trade Book, as each child in four generations of one family feels a sense of personal ownership of an heirloom cup. *Down in the Woods at Sleepytime*, a soothing, atmospheric tale about restless baby animals settling down to listen to an owl's bedtime story, won the Washington State Book Award, sponsored by the Washington Center for the Book.

The preschooler stars of *The Squiggle* reappear in *Someone Says*. Using an imaginative variation on the Simon Says game, they transform everyday activities into magical creativity. A rhythmic tribute to imaginative play, *Someone Says* was an American Booksellers Pick of the Lists and was among the 2004 Children's Literature Choices. In *The Biggest Soap*, when a boy sent to buy a large piece of soap for his mother to use for the laundry returns with just a small sliver, he embellishes the story of what happened to the soap on his way back to the washing pool.

A tribute to the Truk islanders Schaefer met in her travels, this title was a Charlotte Zolotow Book Award "Highly Commended" title and a Peace Corps Writers Best Book for Children in 2005.

A 2006 finalist for the Washington Center for the Book Award, *The Bora-Bora Dress* is about the inexplicable magic of a new party dress when a parrot painted on the front of the dress transforms a tomboy into an elegant young lady. *Cool Time Song* is a lyrical, ecological love song promoting peace and describing the sundown movements of African animals. Pierr Morgan's illustrations for this title won an Honor prize from the Society for the Prevention of Cruelty to Animals. In the Charlotte Zolotow Award Honor Book, *Dragon Dancing*, preschoolers learn about dragons in Chinese culture and reinforce their new knowledge with imaginative play as they create dragon decorations for a fellow pupil's birthday celebration.

Two of Schaefer's titles have won Oppenheim Toy Portfolio Awards; *Down in the Woods at Sleepytime* won a Platinum award in 2001, and *Beeper's Friends* won a Gold award in 2003. *The Squiggle*, *Two Scarlet Songbirds*, and *Someone Says* have all been Junior Library Guild selections.

Married 45 years, Schaefer and her husband have one son, Stefan, who now has his own company, INCUS Webworks, which designs websites. Carole Lexa Schaefer's passion for picture books and easy readers—both writing and reading them—remains unabated as she continues to draw on her teaching and life experiences for her vibrant picture book stories. Her books have been translated into over a dozen languages and earned her readers in many parts of the world.

SELECTED WORKS: *Under the Midsummer Sky*, illus. by Pat Geddes, 1994; *In the Children's Garden*, illus. by Lynn Pauley, 1994; *The Squiggle*, illus. by Pierr Morgan, 1996; *Sometimes Moon*, illus. by Pierr Morgan, 1999; *The Copper Tin Cup*, illus. by Stan Fellows, 2000; *Down in the Woods at Sleepytime*, illus. by Vanessa Cabban, 2000; *Snow Pumpkin*, illus. by Pierr Morgan, 2000; *Two Scarlet Songbirds: A Story of Anton Dvorak*, illus. by Elizabeth Rosen, 2001; *Beep, Beep! It's Beeper!: Brand New Readers*, illus. by Julie Lacome, 2001; *Beeper's Friends: Brand New Readers*, illus. by Julie Lacome, 2002; *The Little French Whistle*, illus. by Emilie Chollat, 2002; *One Wheel Wobbles: A Homespun Counting Book*, illus. by Pierr Morgan, 2003; *Full Moon Barnyard Dance*, illus. by Christine Davenier, 2003; *Someone Says*, illus. by Pierr Morgan, 2003; *The Biggest Soap*, illus. by Stacey Dressen-McQueen, 2004; *Cool Time Song*, illus. by Pierr

Morgan, 2005; *The Bora-Bora Dress*, illus. by Catherine Stock, 2005; *Dragon Dancing*, illus. by Pierr Morgan, 2007; *Big Little Monkey*, illus. by Pierre Pratt, 2008; *Kids Like Us*, illus. by Pierr Morgan, 2008.

SUGGESTED READING: *Something About the Author*, vol. 173, 2007.

WEB SITE: www.clschaefer.com

Photo by Janice Rubin

Rosalyn Schanzer

November 26, 1942–

"How did this happen?

"My work is never boring because it's actually eight different jobs rolled into one big lump. I get to be an artist, a writer, an historian, a detective, an adventurer, a comedian, an actress, and maybe even a star-maker.

"How did this happen? The artist part was easy. I must have been born with a Crayola in my fist because I have been coloring ever since day one. But sometimes my art got me into trouble. As a three-year-old, I made beautiful designs all over some furniture by poking curly rows of holes into the paint with a pin. I was absolutely amazed that my mom got mad. My first-grade classmates all wanted me to draw their portraits. This made the teacher furious because she had been trying to teach everyone how to count and nobody was paying any attention.

When I grew up, I drew the pictures for hundreds of books, magazines, posters, games, and other things too numerous and sundry to mention. Then in the early 1990s, my job description began to change.

"And how did this happen? I got bored illustrating things that other people had written, so one day I decided to write some books of my own. Amazingly, I ended up writing lots of books about history.

"What? How did this happen?? I *hated* history when I was a kid!!!! The people we had to study about in school seemed a lot like that famous portrait of George Washington on the $1 bill; to me, they were all old and green and wrinkled and dead.

"So what happened next? I wanted my book to be a funny adventure set in the Wild West, so I wrote a rhyming story about a little kid named Ezra who wakes up one night to see three villains robbing a bank. Way back in the 1960s, I had invented something I called picture mazes where you have to find your way through 3-D scenery while avoiding a bunch of scary dead ends. Kids had always loved these mazes, so I made Ezra chase the robbers all the way from Colorado into Mexico by navigating a ridiculously difficult maze that wove through colorful scenery running from page to page to page. While I was doing the book, I started having fun making everything look the way it had back in 1874. I did tons of research, so the towns, railroads, stagecoach, gold mines, pueblos, Indians, animals, rainforests, and everything else I drew were 100% accurate. At the end of the book, I added some great facts about the places I'd drawn on each spread. History was a blast! I was hooked. By the time I finished another Ezra maze book set in medieval times, I had begun to become an historian. Before long, I had become a detective too.

"How did this happen? History books can be fun and full of adventure, but they must also be correct in every detail. However, so much research material is corrupted by mistakes and propaganda that it often takes a real detective to ferret out the truth. Examples: My next book was *How We Crossed the West: The Adventures of Lewis and Clark.* It took pure detective work to reveal that Sacagawea was a very young teenager and was never the journey's guide, as so many books imply. I recently wrote a book called *George vs. George: The American Revolution As Seen from Both Sides,* and as it turns out, King George III of England wasn't nearly the dim-witted tyrant we thought he was. And remember old green and wrinkled George Washington? Well, he was an incredible athlete and the greatest horseman of his day! He was so tall that most men barely came up to his shoulder. Another piece of detective work involved digging up ancient stacks of my family's letters and stories to piece together the book *Escaping to America,* the tale of my father's hair-raising escape from Poland in 1921.

"And the other jobs happened how? Well, I've become an adventurer by traveling to gold fields, roaring rivers, and many other incredible places to dig up material for my books. I get to be an actress and a comedian in costume when I present my books (especially *Davy Crockett Saves the World* and *The Old Chisholm Trail*). And right now, I'm trying to become a star-maker for someone who should have always been considered one of America's greatest heroes. When the truth is told, everything

"History books can be fun and full of adventure, but they must also be correct in every detail. However, so much research material is corrupted by mistakes and propaganda that it often takes a real detective to ferret out the truth."

you've heard about this guy will be turned on its head. Not only did he jump-start the Great American Dream of a better life on these shores, but my newest book, *John Smith Escapes Again!*, tells all about the great escapes of one of the very greatest escape artists of all time. How did this happen?"

ଔ   ଔ   ଔ

Born in Knoxville, Tennessee, the author/illustrator Rosalyn Good Schanzer grew up listening to colorful tales about her uncle's pink goat back in Poland, her father's route to school (which involved crawling under moving trains), her aunt's comic superheroes, Handsome Sam and Yashik, and her maternal grandfather's testimony at the Scopes Monkey Trial. Her early literary influences were as wide-ranging as the comic strip *L'il Abner*, the parodies featured in *Mad* magazine, Dr. Seuss's *Bartholomew and the Oobleck*, and Eastern European folk tales about foolish wise men of the mythical village of Chelm.

Schanzer received both a bachelor's degree in fine arts and a bachelor's of science in education from the University of Cincinnati in 1964. She married Steven Terry Schanzer in 1966 and worked as a designer for Hallmark Cards in Kansas City, Missouri, from 1964 to 1971. With more ideas than any one job could contain, Schanzer soon found work as a freelance illustrator for books, magazines, posters, and filmstrips. She had an award-winning filmstrip in the 1980 International Film Festival. From 1982 to 1988 she lectured in art classes at George Washington University. A nationally ranked competitive swimmer, she is also a world traveler and avid photographer. Some of her more exciting travels have included kayaking in Alaska, swimming with sharks in Belize, hiking the Andes Mountains in South America, rafting in Costa Rican rainforests, and sailing a boat with five men from Bermuda to Boston.

Today, as an author who enjoys discovering original source material and conducting accurate research for her books, Schanzer indulges her love of travel by visiting many of the sites where her stories took place and taking hundreds of pictures to use for reference. After illustrating a number of socially and religiously themed books for young children written by other people, she came up with her own concept and text for *Ezra in Pursuit*, an IRA/CBC Children's Choice Award winner that fosters a sense of history and place by taking the reader through a maze. *How Ben Franklin Stole Lightning* was also an IRA/CBC Childrens' Choice, as well as an IRA/CBC Teacher's Choice, indicating the attention that educators were beginning to give to her work. Both *How Ben Franklin Stole Lightning* and *How We Crossed the West*, her exciting story of the Lewis and Clark expedition, were named Notable Social Studies Trade Books. *Davy Crockett Saves the World*, a tall tale of Tennessee written and illustrated with rollicking humor, was named a *Booklist* Editor's Choice, an IRA/CBC Children's Choice, and an Oppenheim Toy Portfolio Platinum Award winner.

Mining her own family's history for *Escaping to America: A True Story*, Schanzer presented a realistic account of the hardships her father faced on his arduous journey to the United States after fleeing from Poland in 1921. Named a Sydney Taylor Notable Book by the Association of Jewish Libraries, it was also included in the CCBC Choices list.

Courtesy of the National Geographic Society

Schanzer's heartfelt approach to history, paired with her wry humor and insistence on accuracy of detail, makes for an unbeatable combination that draws young readers into the life and times of historical figures. This is especially true of one of her most praised book to date, *George vs. George: The American Revolution As Seen from Both Sides*. Covering the years leading up to the Revolution and the war itself, she focuses on George Washington and King George III of England, bringing them to life as fully rounded personalities rather than the stiff cardboard characters that they so often appear to be in books for children. Showing the ties that each had to family and home, their hobbies and skills, she truly indicates through words and pictures that there are always "two sides to every story." *George vs. George*, an ALA Notable Children's Book, was named a Best Book of the Year by *School Library Journal* and *Capitol Choices* and cited as a Recommended Book by the Orbis Pictus Award.

Rosalyn Schanzer lives with her husband in Fairfax Station, Virginia, where they often enjoy visits from their two grown children.

SELECTED WORKS WRITTEN AND ILLUSTRATED: *The Beggar's Treasure*, 1973; *My First Jewish Word Book*, 1992; *Ezra in Pursuit: The Great Maze Chase*, 1993; *Ezra's Quest: Follow That Dog*,

1994; *How We Crossed the West: The Adventures of Lewis and Clark*, 1997; *Gold Fever!: Tales from the California Gold Rush*, 1999; *Escaping to America: A True Story*, 2000; *The Old Chisholm Trail: A Cowboy Song*, 2001; *Davy Crockett Saves the World*, 2001; *How Ben Franklin Stole the Lightning*, 2003; *George vs. George: The American Revolution As Seen from Both Sides*, 2004; *John Smith Escapes Again!*, 2006.

SELECTED WORKS ILLUSTRATED: *Puck's Peculiar Pet Shop: A Tongue-Twister Story*, by Dean Walley, 1970; *The Pop-Goes-the-Joke Book*, selected by Peter S. Seymour, 1971; *The Golden Happy Birthday Book*, by Barbara Shook Hazen, 1976; *When an Elephant Goes Shopping*, by Wendy Cheyette Lewison, 1988; *What's the Matter With A. J.?: Understanding Jealousy*, by Lawrence Balter, 1989; *Linda Saves the Day: Understanding Fear*, by Lawrence Balter, 1989; *Where Is the Afikomen?*, by Judyth Groner and Madeline Wikler, 1989; *The Wedding: Adjusting to a Parent's Remarriage*, by Lawrence Balter, 1989; *In the Synagogue*, by Judyth Groner and Madeline Wikler, 1991; *Ten Good Rules*, by Susan Remick Topek, 1992; *Bunny's Hungry*, by Muff Singer, 1994; *Look Around with Little Fish*, by Muff Singer and Sarah Tuttle Singer, 1995; *All Year Round With Little Frog*, by Muff Singer, 1995; *Maccabee Jamboree: A Hanukkah Countdown*, by Cheri Holland, 1998; *The True-or-False Book of Horses*, by Patricia Lauber, 2000; *The True-or-False Book of Cats*, by Patricia Lauber, 2001; *The True-or-False Book of Dogs*, by Patricia Lauber, 2003.

SUGGESTED READING: *Something About the Author*, vol. 138, 2003.

WEB SITE: www.childrensbookguild.org/schanzer.htm

Gary D. Schmidt

April 14, 1957–

"I grew up in the small town of Hicksville—it really and truly was named Hicksville—on Long Island, in the days when we were crouching under our desks for atomic bomb drills and gathering together in the cafeteria to watch a single black-and-white television set project images of the Apollo astronauts splashing with their space capsules into the Pacific Ocean. Grumman Industries, where some of those capsules were made, was not far from my elementary school, and we would sometimes visit Brookhaven laboratories, where atomic research was being carried out. We had to wear tags on our jackets that would turn red if we became radioactive. The war in Vietnam was escalating, and one Sunday I was shocked to hear that a boy in our church had been killed. How could that be, when the whole war seemed just to be a television show? Early on I had the sense that the world was a large and looming presence, and though my suburban world seemed secure, that safety might be quite false. It was unsettling.

"But in the midst of these uncertainties there was story, with all the pleasures of its certainties: that good was stronger than evil, that characters went through hard times but came out all right in the end, that words meant something, that there was beauty and justice and nobility in the world, and that those things were worth fighting for. This was heady stuff in the days of Vietnam. I read *My Book House*, a set of half a dozen volumes that collected the best of Victorian and Edwardian children's poems and stories. These included the Norse myths—which had a lot to say about fighting for the right side despite the odds—and Tennyson and Wordsworth and Bryant and the Fireside Poets that seem so far away from us now. Later, when I read the great fantasy writers, they seemed to me to be old friends even though I was reading them for the first time. That was because the same writers who inspired them had filled my early years.

Photo by Gary Schmidt

"I read these books alone, or with my grandmother, but never in school. In my early years I was known to be a spectacularly bad reader. I was in the Pumpkin Reading Group, a euphemism for Kids Who Can't Read Their Way Out of a Paper Bag, which is itself a euphemism for Stupid Kids. We knew who we were, and our classmates knew who we were. We were always three or four books behind the top groups, and our teacher always looked at us rather sadly. I filled my desk with books. I read Benjamin Elkin and Dr. Seuss and then E. B. White and Hugh Lofting (every one of the Doctor Dolittle books) and Walter Farley and Robert Lawson. Then I moved on to Robert Louis Stevenson, Jack London, *The Swiss Family Robinson*, Howard Pyle's *The Adventures of Robin Hood*, and *Bambi*, one of the most beautiful books in the world.

"I never, ever went to the school library; I went instead to the public library. There I found the Bobbs-Merrill Childhood of Famous Americans series and the Freddy the Pig books, and then, one startling day, *The Old Man and the Sea*. After that, I convinced my grandmother that I needed an adult library card, and she got me one, over the objections of the librarian. Now I had no restrictions on the collections. On top was the word 'permanent.' I still have it.

"It did not occur to me then that I would ever become a writer myself. In fact, once high school began, I vacillated between studying to be a veterinarian and studying to be a lawyer—finally choosing law. I went on to study pre-law in college. But even then, I took literature courses and kept running into 'old friends' from *My Book House*: Shelley, Tennyson, Byron, Kipling. They were pesky—they wouldn't let me go, and so in my senior year I gave up all thought of law and became an English teacher, which I still am today. I went to graduate school to study medieval literature because I loved the language and the stories, and then I began to imagine writing—but only writing critical, academic books. My first foray into this was a dissertation which took two years to write.

"While typing out hundreds of footnotes one night I sat down and wrote: 'It was, as far as the weather goes, a most unusual day.' I have no idea where that came from, but it was the first line I had ever written for a story. In the middle of dissertating about medieval imagery, I crafted my first novel and sent it off to editor Jean Karl. She didn't publish it because it was awful, but it gave me the sense that I enjoyed crafting a story, developing characters, asking questions without knowing the answers. Still, it was four or five years later before I tackled another novel, *The Sin Eater*, which I sent to Virginia Buckley, forgetting to include a cover letter with the manuscript. Somehow she tracked me down, and we still work together.

"I am blessed to have a wonderful teaching job that allows me to integrate my writing and my classroom work—since I teach and write children's books—and I am blessed to have a wonderful old house with an outbuilding for my study (though it is unheated and gets mightily cold in a Michigan winter). I am blessed to have a creative wife who is also a writer, and six amazing children who sometimes give me material for my books. It is my hope that somehow my novels will address that sense I had as a child that the world loomed large and somewhat malevolent, and that they will speak to the power of our commonalities as human beings in a darkly beautiful world."

> *"Early on I had the sense that the world was a large and looming presence, and though my suburban world seemed secure, that safety might be quite false. It was unsettling."*

ॐ ॐ ॐ

Growing up in Hicksville, a suburb of New York City, Gary Schmidt was surrounded by friends of different ethnic and religious backgrounds. Summers during his adolescence were spent at a camp in the Catskill Mountains, where he worked his way up from counselor to program director. He received his B.A. in English literature and political science at Gordon College in Wenham, Massachusetts, and met his future wife, Anne, a fellow Gordon student, at the top of the John Hancock building in Boston. They were married in 1979, the same year they graduated. Together the newlyweds attended the University of Illinois at Urbana-Champaign where Gary earned a master's degree in English language and literature in 1981 and a Ph.D. in medieval language and literature in 1985. In search of a teaching position that would not involve large-university politics, Schmidt found his home at Calvin College, a small liberal arts college in Grand Rapids, Michigan. Since that time, he has successfully combined his academic career with writing for young people of all ages.

As a professor of children's literature, Schmidt has contributed to critical writing about the field in his biographies of Robert McCloskey, Robert Lawson, Hugh Lofting, and Katherine Paterson in the Twayne Authors Series. His scholarly work also includes a book on one of America's first financially successful writers, who happened to be a woman—*A Passionate Usefulness: The Life and Literary Labors of Hannah Adams*. He has co-authored and edited works on retelling folktales, the voice of the narrator, and a textbook on the children's literature field.

His first published children's books were a retelling of one of his childhood favorites, *Pilgrim's Progress*, and an edition of poems by Robert Frost. His first original work, *The Sin Eater*, is the haunting story of a boy recovering from his mother's death through the loving care of his grandparents and through following his own interest in the history of their town. This novel was named an ALA Best Book for Young Adults and established Schmidt as an author of note. He has continued to tackle difficult subjects, such as the historic brutality of the English toward the Irish in *Anson's Way*, which was named a *Booklist* Editors' Choice, and stories of the Holocaust in *Mara's Stories*, a *Horn Book* Fanfare title. In picture book tales he has retold the Irish legends of Saint Ciaran and Donal O'Donnell.

Wider acclamation came with the publication of *Lizzie Bright and the Buckminster Boy*, which was named both a Newbery Honor book and a Printz Honor book by the American Library Association in 2005. Based on a shameful incident that occurred

"It is my hope that somehow my novels will address that sense I had as a child that the world loomed large and somewhat malevolent. . . ."

on the coast of Maine in the early years of the 20th century, the story centers on the friendship between an African American girl from Malaga Island, settled by former slaves, and the son of the mainland town's new preacher, who is white. The two young people find themselves caught in a web of prejudice and intrigue as powerful forces from the town conspire to destroy the island community and displace its impoverished inhabitants. Named to many of the best-of-the-year lists, this novel also won state awards in Vermont, Maine, and Michigan.

A second Newbery Honor award was presented to Schmidt in 2008 for his book *The Wednesday Wars*, which is set during

Courtesy of Clarion Books

the turbulent years of the late 1960s, and involves conflicts that can develop within a family, school, and community, set against the backdrop of societal change. A theme that runs through Gary Schmidt's books is that conflict can develop at any time between people who are different from one another but that their underlying humanity can transcend those differences. The young people in his stories all find growth in looking beyond themselves and appreciating the "other" in their midst.

Gary Schmidt lives in a rambling farmhouse in Alto, Michigan, with his wife, the author Anne Elizabeth Stickney, and their six children.

SELECTED WORKS: *Pilgrim's Progress*, by John Bunyan, as reteller, illus. by Barry Moser, 1994; *Robert Frost*, as editor, illus. by Henri Sørensen, 1994; *The Sin Eater*, 1996; *The Blessing of the Lord: Stories from the Old and New Testaments*, as reteller, illus. by Dennis Nolan, 1997; *Anson's Way*, 1999; *William Bradford: Plymouth's Faithful Pilgrim*, 1999; *Saint Ciaran: The Tale of a Saint of Ireland*, illus. by Todd Doney, 2000; *Mara's Stories: Glimmers in the Darkness*, 2001; *Straw into Gold*, 2001; *The Great Stone Face: A Tale by Nathaniel Hawthorne*, as reteller, illus. by Bill Farnsworth, 2002; *The Wonders of Donal O'Donnell: A Folktale of Ireland*, illus. by Loren Long, 2002; *Lizzie Bright and the Buckminster Boy*, 2004; *In God's Hands*, with Lawrence Kushner, illus. by Matthew J. Baek, 2005; *First Boy*, 2005; *The Wednesday Wars*, 2007; *Trouble*, 2008.

SELECTED WORKS FOR ADULTS: *The Voice of the Narrator in Children's Literature*, with co-editor Charlotte F. Otten, 1989; *Robert McCloskey*, 1990; *Hugh Lofting*, 1992; *Sitting at the Feet of the Past: Retelling the North American Folktale for Children*, with co-editor Donald R. Hettinga, 1992; *Katherine Paterson*, 1994; *Robert Lawson*, 1997; *A Passionate Usefulness: The Life and Literary Labors of Hannah Adams*, 2004.

SUGGESTED READING: *Something about the Author*, vol. 135, 2003. Periodicals—Schmidt, Gary D., "Who Can Tell the Story?" *The Horn Book*, March/April 2005.

WEBSITE:
www.calvin.edu/publicationsspark/2006/spring/schmidt.htm

"**I** never knew I'd grow up to become a children's book writer. I only knew that I loved using my senses to notice all the marvelous things in the world. I was sensitive and shy, so I spent a lot of time observing—people, trees, sky, buildings, animals, quiet, noise. Like a squirrel, I gathered up images, impressions, feelings and thoughts, and stored them away for the future. These became the ingredients for some of my writing.

"I was born in New York City in the French Hospital. For the first four years of my life, I lived with my parents in an apartment building called 'The House of Joyful Living.' On the roof was a garden with potted grass and trees, a goldfish pond, an outdoor shower, a handball court and a hawk's-eye view of the tall buildings around us—even the Empire State Building! The people who gathered on the roof of the House of Joyful Living were friendly and warm. With two parents all to myself, I felt like I lived in paradise. *Then* . . . my two sisters, Iris and Wendy, were born and we had to move to a larger apartment in Brooklyn. There was no roof garden and my sisters and I slept in one bedroom, but from the sixth-story roof I could see the Statue of Liberty. It seemed that it was lifting its torch to only one person—me!

Photo by Wendy Goldberg

Roni Schotter

May 9, 1946–

"When I was nine, my parents bought a wooden puzzle map of the United States to try to show my sisters and me where we would be moving. They couldn't, because the tiniest piece of the puzzle had dropped out and was missing—Rhode Island. In Rhode Island, we had our own house and a small backyard where we planted, it seemed, one of everything—peas, tomatoes, cucumbers, peppers, eggplants, and a flurry of flowers. There, it *truly* seemed that I lived in paradise, and, lucky me—I had a room of my own!

"As I grew older, I grew shyer. It was hard for me to talk to people, especially the ones I most wanted to talk to! I couldn't even go to the library, because if I did, I'd have to talk to the librarian. Fortunately, my mother occasionally took me there, and, from time to time, people gave me books as presents; a neighbor gave me one of my favorites, *Charlotte's Web*. Once, someone give me a huge carton of used books. I read every one of them, and particularly remember a book of short biographies of then-famous women—Madame Chiang Kai-shek, Louisa May Alcott, Florence Nightingale, and others.

"I don't remember doing much writing. We hardly did any in school, but I do remember creating a newspaper, just for myself, at home. It had stories about some of the children I knew and advertisements for products I made up, like 'Gushy Hair Lotion,' which could be used as a hair straightener, or as an icing for cakes! My newspaper even included an advice column for which I wrote both the questions and answers.

"Around that same time, I wrote my first 'book,' a story I painstakingly typed on my mother's old typewriter so that it would look like a real 'chapter book.' I put it in a special paper cover and added gold, paste-on letters for the title, 'New Friends for Jody.' It was *my* story—a story about a shy girl who moved from New York to Rhode Island and had to make new friends. In it, I did what I do to this day—used my imagination to improve upon reality. I made things happen in my story that I couldn't make happen in real life. *That*, I discovered, is a large part of the pleasure and power of fiction.

"As time went on, I found friends, and was lucky enough to go to a summer camp where I met people much like me—children who grew quiet when they noticed the stars or the way a blade of grass bent in the wind.

"By the time I went to college (as, of course, an English major), I had become less shy. Busy with work and friends, I still found solitary moments to observe the world. That's when I began to write poetry. I loved sitting high up in the college library looking

> *"I made things happen in my story that I couldn't make happen in real life. That, I discovered, is a large part of the pleasure and power of fiction."*

out a window at the branches of a nearby tree and writing about how it looked, and made me feel. I had always loved to draw (another way of looking and seeing), so I took art classes along with my literature classes, and minored in art. Eventually, one of my poems was published in a college literary magazine. I loved seeing my words and my name in print!

"Right after I graduated, I married my husband who was studying then to become a Professor of English. For a year, we lived in England where he did research for his dissertation. When we returned to America, I got a job as assistant publicity director at a publishing house. I wrote press releases for the adult books—books that were written by extraordinary writers like Isaac Bashevis Singer, Joan Didion, Derek Walcott, and John McPhee. I also booked authors onto radio and television interview shows so that people could hear them talk about their books. In truth, I was still a bit shy, especially around such great writers, but I'm proud to say I managed!

"The office next to the publicity department where I worked was the children's book department. I loved everything in it— the colorful illustrations on the walls, the enticing books on the shelves. I became friends with the assistant editor and she began to sneak me the 'slush pile'—a huge pile of manuscripts that had to be read to see if any were good enough to publish. I learned a lot about children's books from reading that slush pile. In a short time, I knew that I wanted to work in children's books, so I left publicity to go to a different publishing house to begin a career in children's literature. Soon, I became an associate editor of children's books. I loved helping authors 'give birth' to their books for children. I loved every part—reading and editing the words, 'reading' and checking the art, writing the flap copy, discussing the stories with the authors. After a few years, I left to work at home, where I did freelance editing for various children's book companies.

"Then, something sad happened. My mother died of cancer. I wrote a description of the last ten days of her life, in a journal, just for myself, to help me feel better. My professor husband, who is also a writer (a playwright and lyricist), read what I'd written and suggested I try to get it published. I couldn't imagine such a thing, but eventually I sent what I'd written to a literary magazine. To my surprise and delight they decided to publish it! Then, a friend suggested I turn what I'd written into a novel for children. I couldn't imagine such a thing, but eventually I did just that. The little journal I had written to help heal some of the sadness I felt at my mother's death became my first book for children, a young-adult novel called *A Matter of Time*. Then one day a man named Martin Tahse called to say that he wanted to turn my novel into an ABC After School Special for children on television. I could never have imagined such a thing!

"I decided that if I could write a second book, I could then truly call myself that magical thing—a 'writer.' With such foolishness in my head, I had a good deal of trouble writing. Finally, *Northern Fried Chicken* was finished, my second young adult novel. After that, I felt more confident. I realized that many of the feelings and observations I'd had as a child were deep inside me and were like seeds, ripe and ready now to burst out of me in the form of books for children of all ages, in particular picture books—my favorite genre.

"I love to write, but also enjoy helping other people write, so I've taught adults in college and graduate school what I know about writing for children. I also visit elementary schools where I speak about my books, and encourage children to write their own stories. I'm often asked where my ideas come from, and what inspires me to write. I guess it all comes from being open and curious, from using my five senses to notice, well, *everything* about the world. Whatever makes me feel deeply, whatever resonates with the child that still lives inside me—that's what makes me want and need to write. For me, writing fiction is a bit like cooking. I mix real things with my imagination, and then stir in my feelings to create what I call 'Story Stew.' I feel lucky to be able to share my stews with readers who, hopefully, want to gobble them up!"

> *"I realized that many of the feelings and observations I'd had as a child were deep inside me and were like seeds, ripe and ready now to burst out of me in the form of books for children of all ages. . . ."*

ဆ ဆ ဆ

Roni Schotter had the unique experience of having her first novel win an Emmy Award for Outstanding Children's Entertainment Special when it was adapted for television. A graduate of New York University, she took a job after college as an assistant publicity director at Farrar, Straus & Giroux. She later moved to Lothrop, Lee & Shepard, at that time a division of William Morrow, to work in the children's department and eventually became an associate editor of children's books. After a few year she decided to work independently for various publishers, but always within the field of children's books. As she started writing books herself, she continued to do freelance editing, write sections of textbooks, and create fund-raising letters for nonprofit organizations.

One of Schotter's early picture books, *Captain Snap and the Children of Vinegar Lane*, illustrated by Marcia Sewall, is a classic story of a kindly curmudgeon who is befriended by neighborhood children when he falls ill. Text and art are perfectly matched in portraying the seaside village and its many characters. Named a Pick of the Lists by *American Bookseller* as well as a best book of the year by *School Library Journal* and *Booklist*, this gentle story of kindness rewarded also received a Parents' Choice award in the picture book category.

Several of Schotter's books, created in collaboration with artist Marylin Hafner, illuminate the traditions and customs of various Jewish holidays. *Hanukkah!* received a National Jewish Book Award and was followed by *Passover Magic* and *Purim Play*. In 2008 *Hanukkah!* was adapted for reissue in a board book edition for babies. *Dreamland*, a story of the power of imagination and belief in one's dreams, with evocative paintings by Kevin Hawkes, received the Irma S. Black Honor Book Award from Bank Street College of Education and was a Washington Irving Children's Choice Honor Book. Schotter has twice won the Washington Irving Children's Choice award, for *F is for Freedom* and for *Nothing Ever Happens on 90th Street*, which also became a Notable Book in the Language Arts and a *Booklist* Editors' Choice. *F is for Freedom*, a middle-grade novel about the days of the Underground Railroad, has been used widely in schools as a story about friendship and the power of literacy.

Courtesy of Farrar, Straus, and Giroux

In *The Boy Who Loved Words*, Schotter celebrates the excitement and beauty of language and its power to work wonders. Giselle Potter's illustrations evoke the story with unique folk-like paintings and collage cutouts for the words. This title won a Parents' Choice Gold Award. The warm-hearted relationship of a girl and her hard-working mother is captured in Schotter's finely tuned text and S. Saelig Gallagher's well-rounded illustrations in *Mama, I'll Give You the World*, which won an Oppenheim Toy Portfolio Platinum Award. A significant part of Roni Schotter's own past is the subject of her latest picture book, *The House of Joyful Living*, a semi-autobiographical look at the building where she first lived as a child.

Roni Schotter lives in Hastings-on-Hudson, New York, with her husband, Richard, a professor of Dramatic Literature and Playwriting at Queens College, City University of New York, and a visiting professor at Boston University. In 1994 they collaborated on *There's a Dragon About: A Winter's Revel*, a book about present-day children performing a medieval mummer's play in a neighborhood living room. The Schotters' son, Jesse, is attending graduate school to pursue a Ph.D. in literature and also writes fiction and poetry. They call their home the House of Words, and literature, the family business.

SELECTED WORKS: *A Matter of Time*, 1979; *Northern Fried Chicken*, 1983; *Rhoda, Straight and True*, 1986; *Efan the Great*, illus. by Rodney Pate, 1986; *Bunny's Night Out*, illus. by Margot Apple, 1989; *Captain Snap and the Children of Vinegar Lane*, illus. by Marcia Sewall, 1989; *Hanukkah!*, illus. by Marylin Hafner, 1990; *Warm at Home*, illus. by Dara Goldman, 1993; *When Crocodiles Clean Up*, illus. by Thor Wickstrom, 1993; *A Fruit and Vegetable Man*, illus. by Jeannette Winter, 1993; *There's a Dragon About: A Winter's Revel*, with Richard Schotter, illus. by R. W. Alley, 1994; *That Extraordinary Pig of Paris*, illus. by Dominic Catalono, 1994; *Passover Magic*, illus. by Marylin Hafner, 1995; *Dreamland*, illus. by Kevin Hawkes, 1996; *Nothing Ever Happens on 90th Street*, illus. by Krysten Brooker, 1997; *Purim Play*, illus. by Marylin Hafner, 1998; *Captain Bob Sets Sail*, illus. by Joe Cepeda, 2000; *F is for Freedom*, 2000; *Missing Rabbit*, illus. by Cyd Moore, 2002; *Room for Rabbit*, illus. by Cyd Moore, 2003; *Captain Bob Takes Flight*, illus. by Joe Cepeda, 2003; *In the Piney Woods*, illus. by Kimberly Bulcken Root, 2003; *Passover*, illus. by Erin Eitter Kono, 2006; *The Boy Who Loved Words*, illus. by Giselle Potter, 2006; *Mama, I'll Give You the World*, illus. by S. Saelig Gallagher, 2006; *When the Wizzy Foot Goes Walking*, illus. by Mike Wohnoutka, 2007; *Hanukkah!* (board book ed.), illus. by Marylin Hafner, 2008; *The House of Joyful Living*, illus. by Terry Widener, 2008; *Doo-Wop Pop*, illus. by Bryan Collier, 2008.

SUGGESTED READING: *Something About the Author*, vol. 149, 2004.

"I have been an artist since before I was born (at least!), and I have always wanted to make picture books for children. In fact, I recently came across an essay that I had written when I was in the fifth grade. I stated with absolute certainty that I was born to make picture books. By that time, I had already created my own little library, and over the years of my childhood I continued to make picture books of all shapes and sizes.

"Finally, with thousands of children's book ideas tucked inconspicuously inside each and every journal on a shelf full of journals, I set off to the School of Fine Art and Design at Purchase, New York. I studied fine art and graphic design and a week after graduation I was offered a summer position as an artist at ABC-TV in New York City. Soon after, I was hired by NBC-TV. Television was an exciting field because technology was growing rapidly, and I quickly became enthralled with animation. I spent the next ten years at NBC, creating most of the network's animated show openings and segments. I would often think and even say out loud that I couldn't believe that it was actually my job to play all day! The hours were long, the work was creative and challenging, but still, almost daily, I would continue to enter ideas for children's books into my journals, not even conscious of the fact that my art career had led me down a different path.

"When my first son, Drew, was due in May of 1991, I knew that I could not continue the ninety-hour weeks that my job required. I left NBC, had a baby, and moved out of Manhattan into a house in the suburbs, all in the same month. I felt as though someone had thrown me on Mars with a little alien to care for! For the first year or so, I concentrated on being a mom, only occasionally freelancing at NBC when they needed help. I found it fascinating to watch Drew grow and learn and laugh and develop. Now the children's book ideas were coming faster than I could write them down. My husband, Chris, is part of an incredibly talented family of musicians including his father, Mike Seeger, and his uncle, Pete Seeger. One day, I called Mike and asked him what he thought about my making children's books out of some of the folk songs that the Seeger family had made

Photo by Dylan Seeger

Laura Vaccaro Seeger

June 11, 1958–

famous. He told me about a little pamphlet that his mother, Ruth Crawford Seeger, had made some forty-five years earlier. She was not an artist, so the drawings were crude, but the idea was solid. She had wanted to make a children's book of the cumulative song, *Bought Me a Cat*, with stepped pages formatted to be read from back to front. I loved the idea, not only because I wanted to make a picture book, but also because there was such rich family history involved. I began work on the book, substituting the similar and well-known song, *I Had a Rooster*. Ruth was an incredible woman, a classical composer whose music is regularly performed at Lincoln Center. She died long before I met Chris, but I always found her legacy astounding.

"One thing led to another, and the book idea somehow turned into an entire children's video called *Pete Seeger's Family Sing-Along*. I teamed up with Chris, who is a talented sound editor at NBC, and a director from NBC with whom I had worked for many years. We produced a forty-minute video starring Pete, Mike, and their sister, Peggy Seeger. We shot live footage at five different locations. I created animations and Chris did all of the video and sound editing from the studio that he had built in our home. By this time my second son, Dylan, was born, and I was able to include both boys in this wonderful family project.

"One day, I met with a woman from Showtime about a project that she was producing. She needed some animation, but had not yet secured her budget, so she wasn't sure if the job would become a reality. We spoke for a couple of hours and found that we had quite a bit in common. We were both at the same stage in life, relatively new moms and interested in changing careers. She had just spent fifteen years in the children's publishing business and was switching to television; I had just spent fifteen years in television and wanted to switch to children's publishing. She suggested that I organize some of my ideas and when I had something to show a publisher, to check back with her to see if she might recommend someone for me to call. So I did just that. This woman, whose name I cannot remember for the life of me, never did get the budget for her animation project, but she changed my life forever.

"Of the three names that she had given me, the first was someone at Random House who by that time had moved to another publisher. The second was Margaret Ferguson at Farrar, Straus, & Giroux. Margaret was so nice and took time to meet with me. She almost accepted one of my submissions, but ultimately felt that her list was too small and she couldn't find a place for my books. The third name was Dick Jackson,

> "I spent the next ten years at NBC, creating most of the network's animated show openings and segments. I would often think and even say out loud that I couldn't believe that it was actually my job to play all day!"

president of DK Ink at the time. The woman who answered the phone at DK told me that Dick didn't work out of the New York office because he lived California. She gave me his California number and the next day, first thing in the morning, I woke up and called. I dialed the number, listened for the rings, and just as he picked up the phone and said "Hello," I realized what I had done and exclaimed, 'Oh my goodness! It's 6:00 in the morning in California! I am *so* sorry!' He laughed and said, 'It's okay, who *is* this?' I told him a little bit about myself, described my books, and he told me to send them to him and to call back in a couple of weeks. So I diligently sent him five or six book dummies and wrote on my calendar to call him in two weeks. When that day came, first thing in the morning, I woke up and made the call. I dialed the number, listened for the rings, and just as he picked up the phone and said 'Hello,' I exclaimed, 'Oh my goodness, I've done it again! I've woken you up! I am *so* sorry!' Again he laughed and told me that he liked my work and wanted me to meet with Neal Porter, Vice President of DK Ink, in New York. 'And give me a call to let me know how it goes,' he said, 'but not at 6 a.m!'

"I walked into Neal's office with a heavy box of book dummies and he offered to publish *I Had a Rooster*, finally making Ruth's vision a reality. Before the book was released, however, DK was purchased by the Pearson Group and DK Ink was shut down. Neal moved to Roaring Brook Press, and *I Had a Rooster* was ultimately published by Viking/Penguin Putnam. By this time, I had grown quite attached to Neal and had developed a profound and deep respect for him and his editing talent. We continued to meet to discuss book ideas and soon began work on *The Hidden Alphabet*. As I write this, I am beginning work on my ninth book with Neal.

"I consider myself incredibly lucky that I met Neal so early in my publishing career and that Dick Jackson did not hang up on me after I so rudely woke him at six o'clock in the morning! And now, more than ever, I am ecstatic to say out loud that it is actually my job to play all day!"

"I found it fascinating to watch Drew grow and learn and laugh and develop. Now the children's book ideas were coming faster than I could write them down."

0ʒ   0ʒ   0ʒ

Laura Vaccaro Seeger's picture books have been widely recognized for their innovative design and engaging concepts. A native of Long Island and an Emmy-award-winning creator of many network animations, she brings a cinematic concept to each of her books, making them interactive delights for young children and critical successes with reviewers. In her first book, an illustrated version of the folk song *I Had a Rooster*, the stepped pages create a unique way to follow the cumulative story through to its end. An accompanying CD features the musical version sung by the legendary folksinger, Pete Seeger, who is the uncle of Laura's husband.

For *The Hidden Alphabet*, which was named an ALA Notable Children's Book, the artist created a fresh new look for an alphabet book. A simple black die-cut frame around each illustration is lifted to reveal the pictured object cleverly transformed into the letter it represents. An arrowhead becomes the letter A, balloons turn into a letter B, and so on to the zippered Z. The simplicity of design and ingenuity of the concept make this book a graphic joy for children and adults alike. It was listed in Capitol Choices, CCBC Choices, and the New York Public Library's 100 Titles for Reading and Sharing as well as being named a *Kirkus* Editor's Choice and a *Child* Magazine Best Book of the Year.

Seeger next designed a book to convey the concept of color as imaginatively as she had presented the alphabet. *Lemons Are Not Red* again uses die-cut pages and rich, saturated colors to great advantage in an interactive format. The cut-out shape of a lemon appears with a red background showing through, but when the page is turned, the cut-out is over a yellow background, verifying the text: "Lemons are not red, Lemons are yellow." The game continues through many colors and paired objects, always related in some way, until the last page where the contrast of silver moon and black night ends the book as a bedtime story. Named for all the honors that her alphabet book received, *Lemons Are Not Red* was also cited as a Blue Ribbon title by the *Bulletin of the Center for Children's Books*.

After exploring letters and colors, Seeger next set her hand to expressing familiar emotions in a very special way. In *Walter Was Worried*, the letters for the word are used to form facial features for the character expressing the emotion. Title character Walter's mouth, for example, is a capital D, flat side down, while his eyes are a lower case o and e and his eyebrows are made of r's. Once the child catches on to the concept, it becomes a game to discover the letters in the features of Hopeful Henry, Frightened Frederick, and Puzzled Priscilla, among others, as the ongoing story of a storm links the characters together. *Walter Was Worried* was named an ALA Notable Children's Book, a *Child* Magazine Best Book of the Year, an IRA/CBC Children's Choice, and was listed in CCBC Choices.

Black? White! Day? Night!—A Book of Opposites followed the same format as *The Hidden Alphabet*, and was named an ALA Notable Book, a *Child* Magazine Best Book of the Year, a *Nick Jr./Family* magazine Best Book of the Year, a *Booklist* Editors' Choice, and a *Kirkus* Editors' Choice. It was also included in Capitol Choices and CCBC Choices. Another brilliant concept book for young children, *First the Egg*, was named a *New York Times* Best Illustrated Book in 2007. In 2008 it won both a Caldecott Honor Book award for illustration and a Theodor Seuss Geisel Honor award for most distinguished writing in a book for beginning readers.

Laura Seeger lives on Long Island, close to the beach and New York City, with her husband, Chris, and their two sons, Drew and Dylan. Their dog, Copper, plays a major role in one of the author/illustrator's 2007 titles, *Dog and Bear—Two Friends, Three Stories*, which won the *Boston Globe–Horn Book* picture book award and was named an ALA Notable Children's Book. Featuring an irrepressible dachshund and a multi-colored stuffed bear, three short stories in the book show the two characters engaging in child-like play. With an empathetic humor reminiscent of Arnold Lobel's Frog and Toad books, each of these vignettes has a childlike sensibility and a satisfying conclusion. A film version of one of the stories, produced by the author's son, Dylan, may be viewed on her web site.

Courtesy of Roaring Brook Press

SELECTED WORKS: *I Had a Rooster*, 2001; *The Hidden Alphabet*, 2003; *Lemons Are Not Red*, 2004; *Walter Was Worried*, 2005; *Black? White! Day? Night!—A Book of Opposites*, 2006; *Dog and Bear—Two Friends, Three Stories*, 2007; *First the Egg*, 2007; *Dog and Bear: Two's Company*, 2008; *One Boy*, 2008.

SUGGESTED READING: Seeger, Laura Vaccaro, "*Boston Globe–Horn Book* Acceptance Speech, *The Horn Book*, Jan/Feb 2008; Bean, Joy, "Black and White and Read All Over," *Publishers Weekly*, September 21, 2006.

WEB SITE: www.studiolvs.com

Courtesy of Random House, Inc.

"Dr. Seuss"

March 2, 1904–
September 24, 1991

The man known to the world as "Dr. Seuss" took his pen name from his mother's maiden name, which was also his own middle name. Henrietta Seuss Geisel had a gift for rhymes, and she would soothe the daily cares of her young son and daughter by chanting the German nursery rhymes she remembered from her own childhood. Dr. Seuss later credited his mother for both his talent and his creative zeal.

The Geisel family lived in Springfield, Massachusetts, a small, bustling city when Theodor Seuss Geisel was born in 1904. As the only son of prosperous German-American parents, Theodor was destined to take over the family brewery, which had been founded by his grandfather in the 1870s. However, before he was out of his teen years, the Kalmbach and Geisel brewery was forced to close shortly after the start of Prohibition in 1920.

By then, however, daily uncertainty was something the family had become used to. Throughout World War I, the Geisels, who spoke only German at home, knew they must prove their loyalty to America or risk ruin. Theodor—known as Ted outside of his family—sold war bonds and was one of ten Boy Scouts in Springfield to be rewarded for his high sales. It helped his effort, no doubt, that his grandfather bought $1,000 worth.

After the collapse of the family business, Ted's father (also named Theodor) took a job as the Springfield Superintendent of Parks, including the city zoo. Under Superintendent Geisel's leadership, the zoo expanded, and young Ted was a frequent visitor. He was even allowed to get into the cages with young tigers and lions. It comes as no surprise that when Ted began drawing cartoons in high school, his notebooks were filled with pictures of fantastical-looking animals.

As a student at Dartmouth College in New Hampshire, he contributed to the school's humor magazine. It was as an undergraduate cartoonist that he began signing his work with only his middle name, Seuss. After graduation in 1925, Ted enrolled as a graduate student at the University of Oxford in England, hoping to complete a doctoral degree in English literature. Within a year at Oxford, however, Ted had decided academic life was not for him. He left the university and toured Europe, living for a time in Paris. Before returning to the United States in February 1927, he became engaged to a former Oxford classmate, an American woman named Helen Palmer. Ted returned to Springfield, but after he sold a cartoon to the *Saturday Evening Post*, he decided to move to New York City where he could make the rounds of magazines that might buy his art. Helen was teaching high school in New Jersey when they married in the fall of 1927.

It was at this time that Ted Geisel began signing his work "*Dr. Seuss*"—perhaps poking a little fun at pretension and as a kind of joke on himself since he had never finished his doctoral studies. His work appeared mostly in obscure humor magazines but also occasionally in large-circulation periodicals like the *Saturday Evening Post* and *Vanity Fair*. One of the cartoons that appeared in the *Post* showed a knight trying to kill dragons with a well-known bug spray called Flit. An advertising executive for Flit, which was manufactured by Standard Oil of New Jersey, noticed the cartoon. Esso, as the company was then known, hired Geisel to draw cartoons to advertise Flit and other products made by the company. During the 1930s he created one of the most famous advertising slogans of the decade: "Quick, Henry, the Flit!" Ted took advantage of the flexible terms of his employment with Esso to experiment with other kinds of drawings and also to travel. Once, on an ocean liner returning from Europe, he became inspired by the rhythm of the ship's engines and found himself chanting two lines:

Courtesy of Random House, Inc.

And that is a story that no one can beat;
And to think that I saw it on Mulberry Street!

He wrote and illustrated his first book, *And To Think That I Saw It on Mulberry Street*, based on this simple rhyme. Rejected by 27 publishers the manuscript was eventually acquired by Vanguard Press through the help of a college friend and published in 1937. The next year Vanguard also published *The 500 Hats of Bartholomew Cubbins*, about a boy who cannot take his hat off for the king. In 1938 Bennett Cerf, the young co-owner of Random House, approached Ted about publishing exclusively with his company. With the next two books, *The King's Stilts* in 1939 and *Horton Hatches the Egg* in 1940, Geisel and Cerf developed a solid working relationship, and Ted remained with Random House for the rest of his career. Not long before he died, Random House bought Vanguard Press, making it possible for his first two books to join all the others under one imprint.

Throughout 1941 Ted Geisel used his comic gifts in political cartoons that appeared in a liberal New York City daily newspaper.

Courtesy of Random House, Inc.

He poked fun at Americans who believed the United States should not enter World War II. After the attack on Pearl Harbor, the targets of his cartoons became the leaders of the Axis powers, Hitler, Mussolini, and Tojo. He was commissioned a captain in the U.S. Army in 1943 and wrote documentary films for the army in Hollywood. He worked with the renowned film director Frank Capra on two Academy Award–winning documentaries, *Hitler Lives* in 1946 and *Design for Death* in 1947. He also wrote *Gerald McBoing-Boing*, which went on to win an Oscar in 1951 for the best animated cartoon.

After the war Ted continued writing and illustrating children's books at the rate of about one per year. Many of his best loved picture books were created in the late 1940s and early 1950s: *Bartholomew and the Oobleck*, *Horton Hears a Who!*, and *How the Grinch Stole Christmas*. During these years he was considered less a creative genius than a consummate professional and perfectionist. He once stayed in the Random House offices for four hours reworking a single line. He repeated the words over and over until he was able to remove the extra beat that bothered his ear. His work had a loyal following, but it was not until 1957 that "Dr. Seuss" became a household name with the publication of his first book for beginning readers.

The Cat in the Hat was created after *Life* magazine published an article written by John Hersey about illiteracy among American schoolchildren. The magazine suggested that children would read more if their reading books weren't so boring. Ted Geisel took on the challenge of creating a limited-vocabulary book that would be fun to read, and after spending an entire year working on it he gave the world *The Cat in the Hat*, launching the groundbreaking Beginner Books series at Random House. He later said it was the hardest job he'd ever had, creating a vibrant story using only 225 words. From then on, children did not have to learn to read by repeating stiff phrases from the Dick and Jane primers. Now they had memorable and wacky characters, playful—even outrageous—illustrations, and clever rhyme schemes delivered at breakneck speed. Ted Geisel wrote and illustrated many of the books in the Beginner Books series as Dr. Seuss. Those that he wrote but had illustrated by others, he published under the pseudonym Theo. LeSieg (Geisel spelled backwards).

Three of Dr. Seuss's books—*The Cat in the Hat*, *Green Eggs and Ham* (created on a $50 bet from Bennett Cerf that he couldn't write a book using only 50 words), and *One Fish, Two Fish, Red Fish, Blue Fish*—have been among the top-selling children's books of all time. Three of his picture books were presented with Caldecott Honor Book awards: *McElligot's Pool* in 1948, *Bartholomew and the Oobleck* in 1950, and *If I Ran the Zoo* in 1951. Whether the books received popular or critical acclaim, however, all Dr. Seuss stories featured a playful exploration of the sound of language. Nonsense, he believed, is the language children understand best; it confirms their own experience of life.

Some Dr. Seuss stories also contain moral messages, which can be read at many different levels. *Yertle the Turtle*, about a tyrannical leader and the rise of totalitarianism, and *The Sneetches*, about racial discrimination, offer direct messages. Others are somewhat subtler. In *The Lorax*, an allegory about the environment, the greedy owner of a lumber company destroys all the trees and puts himself out of business. (In 1989 a California logging town tried to have *The Lorax* banned from library and classroom shelves, arguing it was unfair to the lumber industry.) *The Butter Battle Book*, which found an audience among adults as well as children, appeared on the *New York Times* bestseller list. It was written at the time of a nuclear arms race and pictures two cultures that go to war over the proper way to butter bread, delivering a distinct anti-war message.

Throughout his career Geisel's work was recognized for excellence. In 1974 the Children's Literature Council of Southern California presented him with their award for "special contribution to children's literature." The American Library Association awarded him the Laura Ingalls Wilder medal for lifetime achievement in 1980, and in 1984 he received a special Pulitzer Prize citation for his lifetime contribution "to

Ted Geisel took on the challenge of creating a limited-vocabulary book that would be fun to read, and after spending an entire year working on it he gave the world The Cat in the Hat. . . .

the education and enjoyment of America's children and their parents." Though he had poked fun at himself by taking the title of "Dr." Seuss, he eventually was awarded honorary doctoral degrees from seven different universities for his contributions to literature and reading skills.

Toward the end of Ted Geisel's life, he wrote two books aimed at older readers. In *You're Only Old Once!*, he playfully points out to adults the hazards of aging. And in *Oh the Places You'll Go!*—a favorite gift for graduating students—he illuminates the difficulties and joys of finding one's way in the world. Both of these have been perennial bestsellers for their candid look at the stages of life.

Ted Geisel was a private man, full of fun and humor with his friends and family, but reluctant to be in the limelight. His first wife, Helen Palmer Geisel, had worked with him and had written four books for the Beginner Books series herself. After her death in 1967, Ted married Audrey Stone Dimond, in 1968. They lived at their home in La Jolla, California until his death in 1991 at the age of 87. In 2004, the 100th anniversary of Ted Geisel's birth was celebrated with the unveiling of the Dr. Seuss National Memorial, a sculpture garden in his hometown of Springfield, Massachusetts, created by Ted's stepdaughter Lark Grey Dimond-Cates. That same year his longtime publisher Random House launched a yearlong "Seussentennial" with publications and events celebrating his life and work. Every year on Ted Geisel's birthday, March 2, the National Education Association sponsors Read Across America Day, when adults and children engage in read-aloud activities—an exciting literacy event inspired by the man the world knew as "Dr. Seuss."

> *Nonsense, he believed, is the language children understand best; it confirms their own experience of life.*

SELECTED WORKS WRITTEN AND ILLUSTRATED: *And to Think That I Saw It on Mulberry Street*, 1937; *The 500 Hats of Bartholomew Cubbins*, 1938; *The King's Stilts*, 1939; *Horton Hatches the Egg*, 1940; *McElligot's Pool*, 1947; *Thidwick, the Bighearted Moose*, 1948; *Bartholomew and the Oobleck*, 1949; *If I Ran the Zoo*, 1950; *Scrambled Eggs Super!*, 1953; *Horton Hears a Who!*, 1954; *On Beyond Zebra*, 1955; *If I Ran the Circus*, 1956; *How the Grinch Stole Christmas*, 1957; *The Cat in the Hat*, 1957; *The Cat in the Hat Comes Back!*, 1958; *Yertle the Turtle, and Other Stories*, 1958; *Happy Birthday to You!*, 1959; *Green Eggs and Ham*, 1960; *One Fish, Two Fish, Red Fish, Blue Fish*, 1960; *The Sneetches, and Other Stories*, 1961; *Dr. Seuss's Sleep Book*, 1962; *Hop on Pop*, 1962; *Dr. Seuss's ABC*, 1963; *The Cat in the Hat Dictionary*, with P. D. Eastman, 1964; *Fox in Socks*, 1965; *I Had*

Trouble in Getting to Solla Sollew, 1965; *The Foot Book*, 1968; *I Can Lick Thirty Tigers Today! And Other* Stories, 1969; *Mr. Brown Can Moo! Can You?*, 1970; *The Lorax*, 1971; *Marvin K. Mooney, Will You Please Go Now!*, 1972; *The Shape of Me and Other Stuff*, 1973; *Did I Ever Tell You How Lucky You Are?*, 1973; *There's a Wocket in My Pocket!*, 1974; *Oh the Thinks You Can Think!*, 1975; *I Can Read with My Eyes Shut!*, 1978; *Oh Say Can You Say?*, 1979; *Hunches in Bunches*, 1982; *The Butter Battle Book*, 1984; *You're Only Old Once!: A Book for Obsolete Children*, 1986; *Oh, the Places You'll Go!*, 1990.

SELECTED WORKS WRITTEN: *Great Day for Up!*, illus. by Quentin Blake, 1974; *I Am Not Going to Get Up Today!*, illus. by James Stevenson, 1987; *My Many Colored Days*, illus. by Steve Johnson and Lou Fancher, 1996; *Hooray for Diffendoofer Day!*, with Jack Prelutsky, illus. by Lane Smith, 1998. As Theo. Le Sieg— *Ten Apples Up on Top!*, illus. by Roy McKie, 1961; *I Wish that I Had Duck Feet*, illus. by B. Tobey, 1965; *Come Over to My House*, illus. by Richard Erdoes, 1966; *The Eye Book*, illus. by Roy McKie, 1968 (illus. by Joe Mathieu, 1999); *In a People House*, illus. by Roy McKie, 1972; *Wacky Wednesday*, illus. by George Booth, 1974; *Would You Rather Be a Bullfrog?*, illus. by Roy McKie, 1975; *Hooper Humperdink?. . . Not Him!*, illus. by Charles E. Martin, 1976 (illus. by Scott Nash, 2006); *Please Try to Remember the First of Octember!*, illus. by Arthur Cumings, 1977; *The Tooth Book*, illus. by Roy McKie, 1981 (illus. by Joe Mathieu, 2000).

SUGGESTED READING: Cohen, Charles, *The Seuss, the Whole Seuss and Nothing but the Seuss: A Visual Biography of Theodor Seuss Geisel*, 2004; Krull, Kathleen, *The Boy on Fairfield Street: How Ted Geisel Grew Up to Become Dr. Seuss*, illus. by Steve Johnson and Lou Fancher, 2004; *Your Favorite Seuss: 13 Stories Written and Illustrated by Dr. Seuss with 13 Introductory Essays*, comp. by Janet Schulman and Cathy Goldsmith, 2004; Minnear, Richard H., *Dr. Seuss Goes to War: The World War II Editorial Cartoons of Theodor Seuss Geisel*, a selection with commentary, 2001; Fensch, Thomas, *The Man Who Was Dr. Seuss: The Life and Work of Theodor Geisel*, 2000; Morgan, Judith and Neil Morgan, *Dr. Seuss & Mr. Geisel*, 1995; Geisel, Audrey, ed., *The Secret Art of Dr. Seuss*, with an introduction by Maurice Sendak, 1995; Weidt, Maryann N., *Oh, the Places He Went: A Story About Dr. Seuss*, illus. by Kerry Maguire, 1994; MacDonald, Ruth K., *Dr. Seuss* (Twayne's United States Authors Series), 1988.

WEB SITES: www.seussville.com
www.catinthehat.org

An earlier profile of Dr. Seuss appeared in *More Junior Authors* (1963).

Photo by Jim Sidman

Joyce Sidman

June 4, 1956–

"As a child, I was always outside. I roamed through woods, fields, neighborhoods, taking snapshots with my eyes and my heart of all I experienced. The world was so large, tumultuous, and exciting that I didn't want to miss a thing. Being the middle one of three sisters helped—there was always something going on, day or night. We spent summers at a camp in Maine, where we crunched along pine-needled paths, dove off rafts, or paddled canoes most of the day. Our grandparents' farm was one big playground, complete with climbing trees, frog pond, and tractor. Outside: that's where I wanted to be.

"If nature framed my outer world, books and writing fed my inner world. Thanks to parents and teachers who fostered an early love of words, I turned toward literature as a flower seeks sun. By sixth grade, I had dreams of being an author. My best friend and I created what might now be called a graphic novel (but was then just a comic book) about four international friends who solved mysteries. My favorite book at the time was *The Diamond in the Window* by Jane Langton, as well as Joan Aiken's works about feisty girls who battled mysterious criminals and saved kingdoms.

"The emotional seesaws of adolescence plunged me into poetry, a love affair that has lasted until this day. During college, I absorbed the gamut of poetry, from T. S. Eliot to Scottish ballads; and learned sonnets, pantoums, and tercets with former poet laureate Richard Wilbur. Graduating with a degree in German literature, I later got licensed to teach English, but my heart was still in creative writing. I wandered through many kinds of jobs—bakery assistant, copy editor, journalist, substitute teacher—until I had children of my own and rediscovered the world of children's literature. What a rich world! My dormant yearning to write flared up even more strongly, and I began to steal time from parenthood to experiment with picture books and fantasy.

"Still, I didn't find my voice until I turned once again to poetry—children's poetry. I loved its sense of wonder, and the way it made the world seem fluid—everything connected to everything else. Walking on the beach one day with my four-year-old nephew, I watched him pounce on shells with delight, crying, 'This looks like a nose! This looks like a pencil! This looks like a rainbow!' And I thought: that is poetry: discovery, delight, metaphor. I also love the way poetry allows you to try on different realities, and to this day I gravitate toward 'mask' poetry—that is, taking the voice of something else. How liberating—and downright fun—to become a frog, or a dragonfly, or a tree for a morning, and look at the world through their eyes!

"One day in the library, I happened upon Alice Schertle's *Advice for a Frog*. Here was a poetry book that delved into science! It illuminated each creature's place in the natural world, and provided not just insight but information. I pored over Schertle's work and hunted for others like it: poetry that was both lyrical and learned. Deep inside me, something clicked. And I began to write my first poetry book, *Just Us Two: Poems About Animal Dads*. Miraculously, it was accepted for publication.

"I am still a roamer and a watcher. I still tramp over hill and dale, taking 'snapshots' with my eyes and heart. I try to drink in the world through all five senses, ponder it, and pour it out again in words. This is how I make sense of things. This is how, every day, I find joy in each new shell on the beach."

> *"The emotional seesaws of adolescence plunged me into poetry, a love affair that has lasted until this day."*

C03   C03   C03

Born in Hartford, Connecticut, Joyce Sidman received a B.A. from Wesleyan University, in Middletown, Connnecticut, in 1978, and a Teacher Licensure from Macalester College, in St. Paul, Minnesota, in 1983. She was a columnist for the St. Paul *Pioneer Press* from 1993 to 2000, and after that became a freelance columnist. Since 1997, Sidman has also served as a teacher in Minnesota's COMPAS program, which places writers and artists in the schools. She edited the 2002 COMPAS Anthology *Good Morning Tulip* and has also written book reviews for *Riverbank Review*.

Rediscovering the joy of childhood poetry after she had children of her own, Sidman published her first book in 2000 and received immediate recognition for her creative use of language.

Just Us Two: Poems About Animal Dads, with vibrant cut-paper illustrations by Susan Swan, was named to the Children's Literature Choice List, among other honors, and identified Sidman as a powerful new voice in children's poetry. Each of her books has had a particular focus. *Eureka!* her second title, highlighted inventors throughout history and was cited as one of the Bank Street College Best Books of the Year. *The World According to Dog* was named a Blue Ribbon title by the *Bulletin of the Center for Children's Books* and also won the Henry Bergh Children's Book Award from the ASPCA.

Sidman's most acclaimed work to date is *Song of the Water Boatman and Other Pond Poems*, in which she combined various forms of poetry with scientific explanations of the creatures, plants, and seasons of pond life. Included on the best of the year list of every major review journal, *Song of the Water Boatman and Other Pond Poems* was named an Outstanding Science Trade Book, an ALA Notable Children's Book, and an NCTE Notable Book in the Language Arts. It won the Lee Bennett Hopkins Poetry Award, and the expressive hand-colored woodcuts that accompany each poem earned a Caldecott Honor Award for illustrator Beckie Prange.

Courtesy of the Houghton Mifflin Company

Butterfly Eyes and Other Secrets of the Meadow is a companion volume to *Song of the Water Boatman*, employing the same blend of poetry, illustration, and scientific commentary, but this time the ecosystem explored is the meadow rather than the pond. *Butterfly Eyes* earned Sidman her second ALA Notable citation, a second ASPCA Henry Bergh Children's Book Award, and was also named an Outstanding Science Trade Book. It captured the top honors in the poetry category of a new online award, The Cybil, presented by the Children's and Young Adult Bloggers' Literary Awards Committee.

Meow Ruff is an introduction to concrete poetry for young children. In this volume, Sidman demonstrates the concept of concrete poetry through an ongoing story of two natural enemies who become friends, creating a unique and innovative book that became a *Booklist* Editors' Choice, a CCBC Choice, and an NCTE Notable Book in the Language Arts.

In her latest book, Sidman chronicles human emotion rather than natural phenomena. In *This Is Just to Say: Poems of Apology*, sixth-grade students write poems to apologize for real or imagined misdeeds, with response poems from those whom they are asking for forgiveness. The mixed-media illustrations connect each selection to objects found in real life, grounding the poetry in the world the students inhabit.

In addition to her own books, Sidman has contributed to several anthologies, among them *Line Drives: 100 Contemporary Baseball Poems*, *Stories from Where We Live: Great North American Prairie*, and *Gifts from Our Grandmothers*. Her stories, essays, and poetry have been published in a variety of journals and newspapers, including *Cricket*, *Cicada*, the *Minnesota Poetry Calendar*, and the *Christian Science Monitor*.

When she is not creating award-winning poetry, Sidman enjoys volunteer work. She runs a weekly book wagon at Children's Hospital in Minneapolis and helps with a variety of tasks for the Friends of the Wayzata Library in her hometown. She served as a judge for the Lee Bennett Hopkins Poetry Award in 2006, the year after she won the award herself. She also enjoys nature phenology (the study of the relation of biologic phenomena to natural weather patterns), dogs, gardening, and anything to do with ecology. She lives in Wayzata, Minnesota, with her husband Jim, their nearly grown sons, Eli and Gabriel, and their dog Watson.

SELECTED WORKS: *Just Us Two: Poems About Animal Dads*, illus. by Susan Swan, 2000; *Eureka! Poems About Inventors*, illus. by K. Bennett Chavez, 2002; *The World According to Dog: Poems and Teen Voices*, photographs by Doug Mindell, 2003; *Song of the Water Boatman and Other Pond Poems*, illus. by Beckie Prange, 2005; *Meow Ruff: A Story in Concrete Poetry*, illus. by Michelle Berg, 2006; *Butterfly Eyes and Other Secrets of the Meadow*, illus. by Beth Krommes, 2006; *This Is Just to Say: Poems of Apology*, illus. by Pamela Zagarenski, 2007.

SUGGESTED READING: Online—Black, Bruce, "One Poet's Process: Joyce Sidman," at http://wordswimmer.blogspot.com/2007/02/one-poets-process-joyce-sidman.html, February 2007.

WEB SITE: www.joycesidman.com

Photo by Eve Sciandra

Cat Bowman Smith

1939–

" As a kid in the 1940s, I had a friend whose Dad raised horses, and I had my own to ride for a few years. We would go off in the spring with the little foals following and be gone for an entire day eating wild strawberries for lunch. We were chased by cows, we were terrified by the ice breaking up as we crossed Lake Delta, and once my horse was nearly lost to quicksand. Every adventure I eventually carried over into my work.

"I have one older sister, Jeannine Lushbaugh, who now lives in California. My mother, who was ill during much of my childhood and given the Last Rites of the Catholic Church when I was six, lived long enough to see me educated, as she had wished, and died the day my final paper was due.

"As I remember now, my very first figure drawing class was shocking to me. Our model didn't show up so the teacher, Norm Bate, sat in a chair on a raised platform, and we drew him. At the age of 17 that was the first time I had drawn a figure from life. (Yes, he remained fully clothed.) I was so excited I wanted to run up and show him the end result of the drawing, but hey, this was college and I had to stay cool. As a senior, I was thrilled to attend Sylvia Davis's seminar and accompany her on trips to the Dryden Theater at the George Eastman house. Another senior reward was going to Harold Brennan's art history class, where I spent many hours wishing for a double major. Another memory that comes to mind is the day I acquired some paints recommended by a painter and sculptor teaching at R.I.T. His name was Fred Meyer. He directed me and my friend Mary Hendrickson to a shop on a long-gone street walled with tiny brick shops near the Genesee River. The dark little shop was nearly empty. When we told the man there what we had come for, he led us to a creaky elevator and then down to a room level with the river. A small dusty window at the top of the wall and a low-watt light bulb were the only light sources. He proceeded to open several bins of dry pigment, and the color in each bin was so intense it glowed as if lit from within. We each left with small brown bags of colors. They remained my mystical pigments.

"I work with watercolor and gouache on Arches 140-weight paper. I never trace even my own work except to roughly place objects in a complex layout. With every final illustration, I start a new drawing so my finals never exactly match my sketches. I have concluded that my brain argues with me whenever I redraw anything, letting me know full well that I have already done that! Tracing just dulls a work and I would rather look at a poorly drawn fresh piece than one that is boring. Because of burnout, I always need a couple weeks of 'down time' before starting another book. I also let family get in the way of my work at times. I'm probably something of an incurable enabler with my immediate family. Growing up with a sickly parent may have contributed to my doing that. Because of my family obligations, I even backed out of completing my last picture book project after working up sketches for it. I was really sorry about that because I missed the chance of working with John Grandits, who gave me my start at *Cricket* magazine.

"I don't maintain a sketchbook, although I probably should. I love to paint people or figures with gouache paint on a half piece of Arches. The few I have done are among my best work, and I hope to do more. After illustrating books, doing a single painting can be great fun.

"At age 97, my father is now living with me and the door revolves with four grandchildren. My Jack Russell terrier, Daisy, also lives with us. I currently have no book projects, so I'm busy rearranging my workspace to give me more room, and then I'm going to work on my art. It's what I love to do. Art is, after all, what life is."

> *"We were chased by cows, we were terrified by the ice breaking up as we crossed Lake Delta, and once my horse was nearly lost to quicksand. Every adventure I eventually carried over into my work."*

CﬗꙘ CﬗꙘ CﬗꙘ

Catharine Bowman Smith, nicknamed Cat, grew up in the village of Canastota, New York, and received a Bachelor of Fine Arts degree from Rochester Institute of Technology in 1961. In addition to spending a decade as an editorial illustrator for the local Rochester Gannett newspaper, she taught illustration at her alma mater. Not long after she started doing illustrations with *Cricket* magazine in 1985, she came to the attention of major U.S. publishers and has been illustrating books ever since. The winner of an SCBWI Don Freeman Memorial Grant, Smith has produced critically acclaimed artwork for over 50 books to date.

One of her early books, Constance Hiser's *Ghosts in the Fourth Grade*, a story about some feisty characters getting even with a class bully one memorable Halloween, won Hawaii's Nene

Award. In Sonia Levitin's *Nine for California*, a mother and her children, including the narrator, Amanda, plus other passengers, all squeeze into a stagecoach for a long trip to California during the Gold Rush era. Smith's illustrations in this title, which won the California Young Reader Medal, are sweet, rowdy, humorous, and offer many frontier facts, including details on how a stagecoach is made. *Nine for California* also won Missouri's Show Me Readers Award, as did its sequel, *Boom Town*, where Amanda's pie-making ambitions spark the growth of an actual California town, offering readers a look at how the West was settled. The artist's detailed watercolor illustrations perfectly capture the humor, warmth, and adventurous spirit of the settlers.

Smith's black-and-white illustrations add to the humor of Amy MacDonald's *No More Nice*, a Parents' Choice Silver Award winner about an overly polite boy who learns from his kind-hearted great-aunt how to think for himself. A sequel, *No More Nasty*, was winner of the West Virginia Children's Book Award and nominated for Children's Choice Awards in eleven states. In this story the great-aunt becomes the new substitute teacher for Parker's unruly fifth-grade class. Witty line drawings highlight the humor of Great-Aunt Mattie's unorthodox teaching methods. In Tynia Thomassie's *Feliciana Meets D'Loup Garou*, a Louisiana Young Readers Choice Honor Book, a spirited but cranky heroine who has been grounded for cutting off her pigtail, meets a swamp creature that supposedly preys on naughty children. Having much in common with Feliciana, however, the creature teaches her how to cope with a bad day instead. Smith's illustrations flawlessly capture the authentic Cajun atmosphere in this original tall tale.

Winner of an Oppenheim Toy Portfolio Platinum Award and cited as a Notable Children's Trade Book in the Field of Social Studies, Ruth Freeman Swain's *Bedtime!* is a quirky, informative look at sleeping habits throughout the ages. Smith's cheery watercolors cover the full range of sleep furniture from ancient Egyptian wooden beds to 16th century European communal beds to astronauts' zero gravity quarters. A second collaboration between Smith and Swain won an Oppenheim Toy Portfolio Gold Award. *Hairdo: What We Do and Did to Our Hair* playfully explores the history of hairstyles across many cultures and includes the reasons for changes in style and adornment. Smith's watercolor-and-ink illustrations fit seamlessly with the lighthearted text, accurately depicting hairstyles that reflect everything from religious views to idiosyncratic royal vanities.

"He proceeded to open several bins of dry pigment, and the color in each bin was so intense it glowed as if lit from within. We each left with small brown bags of colors. They remained my mystical pigments."

Cynthia DeFelice

Old Granny and the Bean Thief

Pictures by Cat Bowman Smith

In Cynthia DeFelice's *Old Granny and the Bean Thief*, which won the New York State Reading Association's Charlotte Award for Primary Grades, a thief keeps stealing Granny's beans, forcing her to go to town to report the theft. On the way, she meets an assortment of odd characters, and all of them return home with her to help drive the culprit away. Smith brings her own special talents to the folksy country fable by using a Southwestern palette of earth tones and dusky blue shades for her spirited gouache spreads. The artist's line-and-wash illustrations highlight important moments and add personality to the characters in Stephanie Greene's *Owen Foote, Mighty Scientist*, nominated for state awards in South Carolina, Indiana, and Oregon. This fast-paced story features two third-grade friends at odds over how to handle a science experiment that nearly turns into a failure. In her latest book, *Too Much Flapdoodle!*, Smith again teams up with Amy MacDonald for a Parker and Great-Aunt Mattie story, this one about life without modern electronics like laptops and cell phones.

Having lived in New York City and Santa Fe, New Mexico, Cat Bowman Smith now resides in Pittsford, New York, near Rochester.

SELECTED WORKS ILLUSTRATED: *General Butterfingers*, by John Reynolds Gardiner, 1986; *Monsters of Marble Avenue*, by Linda Gondosch, 1988; *Grab That Dog*, by Tomie dePaola, 1989; *Princess Bee and the Royal Good-Night Story*, by Sandy Asher, 1989; *Matthew the Cowboy*, by Ruth Hooker, 1990; *Max Malone and the Great Cereal Rip-Off*, by Charlotte Herman, 1990; *Max Malone Makes a Million*, by Charlotte Herman, 1991; *Ghosts in Fourth Grade*, by Constance Hiser, 1991; *Good Night, Feet*, by Constance Morgenstern, 1991; *Closet Gorilla*, by Frances Ward Weller, 1991; *Angel and Me and the Bayside Bombers*, by Mary Jane Auch, 1991; *The Stinky Sneakers Contest*, by Julie Anne Peters, 1992; *Max Malone, Superstar*, by Charlotte Herman, 1992; *Critter Sitters*, by Constance Hiser, 1992; *Angel and Me*, by Mary Jane Auch, 1992; *Chester the Out-of-Work Dog*, by Marilyn Singer, 1992; *Monkey Soup*, by Louis Sachar, 1992; *Peter's Trucks*, by Sallie Wolf, 1992; *Max Malone the Magnificent*, by Charlotte Herman, 1993; *Scoop Snoops*, by Constance Hiser, 1993; *Great Rabbit and the Long-Tailed Wildcat*, by Andy Gregg, 1993; *Grandfather's Wheelything*, by Duncan Ball, 1994; *Latchkey Dog*, by Mary Jane Auch, 1994; *Not-So-Normal Norman*, by Cynthia Stowe, 1994; *Scaredy Dog*, by Stephen H. Lemberg, 1994; *The Story of Zaccheus*, by Marty Rhodes Figley, 1995; *Mary and Martha*, by Marty Rhodes Figley, 1995; *Partners*, by Karen Waggoner, 1995; *Feliciana Feydra LeRoux: A Cajun Tall Tale*, by Tynia Thomassie, 1995; *Project Seasons: Hands-On Activities for Discovering the Wonders of the World*, by Deborah Parrella, 1995; *On Sally Perry's Farm*, by Leah Komaiko, 1996; *Nine for California*, by Sonia Levitin, 1996; *No More Nice*, by Amy MacDonald, 1996; *A Year on My Street*, by Mary Quattlebaum, 1996; *Underground Train*, by Mary Quattlebaum, 1997; *Boom Town*, by Sonia Levitin, 1997; *Feliciana Meets D'Loup Garou: A Cajun Tall Tale*, by Tynia Thomassie, 1998; *Taking Charge*, by Sonia Levitin, 1999; *Bedtime!* by Ruth Freeman Swain, 1999; *The Loudest, Fastest, Best Drummer in Kansas*, by Marguerite W. Davol, 2000; *Dave's Down-to-Earth Rock Shop*, by Stuart J. Murphy, 2000; *The Trouble with Cats*, by Martha Freeman, 2000; *No More Nasty*, by Amy MacDonald, 2001; *The Trouble with Babies*, by Martha Freeman, 2002; *Hairdo: What We Do and Did to Our Hair*, by Ruth Freeman Swain, 2002; *Just One More Story*, by Jennifer Brutschy, 2002;

Old Granny and the Bean Thief, by Cynthia DeFelice, 2003; *The Rosie Stories*, by Cynthia Voigt, 2003; *Owen Foote, Mighty Scientist*, by Stephanie Greene, 2004; *No More Nice/No More Nasty: 2-in-1 Flip Book*, by Amy MacDonald, 2005; *Auction*, by Tres Seymour, 2005; *Joshua, The Giant Frog*, by Peggy Thomas, 2005; *The Trouble with Twins*, by Martha Freeman, 2007; *Too Much Flapdoodle!*, by Amy MacDonald, 2008.

"What I remember most from my childhood is my extended family. I remember fishing with my great-grandpa, his pack of dogs, and my barefoot cousins on a pontoon boat in Oklahoma. I remember listening to my great-aunt Anne talk about her years at an Indian boarding school. I remember the way Grandma Dorothy fed crowds too big to fit into her shoebox of a house. I'd haunt the kitchen table, listening to the elder folks talk.

Photo by Frances Hill

"Daddy was the reader. Every Sunday, I'd go with him to the local convenience store, and we'd bring home his gun magazines and my superhero comics. Mama took me every Saturday morning to our local public library. It was entertainment that fit into our macaroni-and-cheese and garage sale budget.

"At school, I was the tallest girl in the class, shy, and bullied. One boy called me 'Queen Kong.' Books became a refuge, and later, a retreat.

Cynthia Leitich Smith

(LYE-tick) December 31, 1967–

"Reading led to writing poetry. My first published work, though, was as 'Dear Gabby,' writing a column for the sixth grade newsletter. I served as editor of my junior high and high school newspapers and then went on to journalism school at the University of Kansas, in Lawrence. I majored in news/editorial and public relations and gained professional experience while paying for my education. I worked as a reporting intern for small-town newspapers and in public relations for the Muscular Dystrophy Association, as well as in the corporate offices of Hallmark Cards and Phillips Petroleum.

"It's funny, though, looking back on my college years. For electives, I chose every available fiction writing class—Children's

Literature, Child Development, Children and Television. It was like my heart knew what I wanted to do before my brain did.

"I went on to The University of Michigan Law School in Ann Arbor, where I co-founded a feminist law journal and served as president of the Native law students' organization. I enjoyed law school, and it was there that I met my husband, Greg Leitich Smith, who is now a writer. I also studied law abroad in Paris and interned for a women's rights firm, a federal appellate judge, a legal aid office in Hawaii, and, again reporting, for the *Dallas Morning News*.

"After graduation, I got married and took a clerkship at the Department of Health and Human Services in Chicago. It wasn't my dream job, but the big-city newspapers weren't hiring. In April 1995, an email arrived at my federal office referencing 'events in Oklahoma City.' I remember rushing into the hallway, asking what had happened. Domestic terrorists had bombed the Murrah Federal Building, killing 168 people and injuring more than 800.

"Back then, it didn't seem like an ongoing threat. The men responsible were caught. But for me, with my strong ties to Oklahoma, it was a wake-up call, a reminder that life was short.

"Not long afterward, I took a long walk home, through the Loop, along Lake Michigan, and had a long talk with some ducks. Ducks are great listeners. That night, I told Greg that I wanted to quit my job and write children's books.

"He paused a moment and asked, 'Are you any good at it?'

"'I don't know,' I said.

"'Let's find out,' he replied.

"We relocated to Austin, Texas, which had a lower cost of living, and I took a part-time job tutoring English Composition to freshmen in a migrant students' program at St. Edward's University. Authors Kathi Appelt and Jane Kurtz became my early mentors and teachers as I reacquainted myself with the field.

"Taking the classic advice, 'write what you know,' I began by crafting authentic stories of contemporary Native kids like the one I had been."

> *"It was like my heart knew what I wanted to do before my brain did."*

ʚ ʚ ʚ

Cynthia Leitich Smith was born Cynthia Smith, a mixed-blood member of the Muscogee (Creek) Nation, in Kansas City, Missouri. The first person in her family to graduate from college, she received her bachelor of science in 1990 and her law degree in 1994. On September 4, 1994 she married patent lawyer Greg H. Leitich and the couple decided to combine their names in a non-traditional manner, thus becoming Mr. and Mrs. Leitich Smith.

At various times in her life, Cynthia has been a popcorn popper in a movie theater, a waitress, a gas station attendant, a telephone operator in a bank, an English tutor for children of migrant farm workers, a reporter, a law clerk, and a teacher of both legal writing and children's book writing. Along the way, she wrote stories on her lunch hours and after work, and eventually started writing full time.

Cynthia has written stories for a broad age range. *Jingle Dancer*, a picture book that nearly didn't get published due to various mergers in the publishing world, gives readers a new view of contemporary Native Americans by featuring a modern young girl who becomes a traditional jingle dancer at a powwow. Included on the Texas 2x2 Reading List, this title was a *Library Talk* Editors' Choice, a Read Across Texas Bibliography title, and a runner-up for the Storyteller Award of the Western Writers of America. *Jingle Dancer* and *Indian Shoes* were both chosen as Notable Social Studies Trade Books for Young People. *Indian Shoes*, a collection of six humorous interconnected stories for elementary age readers about the daily lives of a Seminole-Cherokee boy and his grandfather in urban Chicago and rural Oklahoma, was named to the CCBC Choices list and the Bank Street College's Best Children's Books of the Year.

A girl's deep personal loss and reconnection to her Native American roots are themes of Cynthia's middle-grade novel, *Rain Is Not My Indian Name*. The author was named Writer of the Year by the Wordcraft Circle of Native Writers and Storytellers for this story that was inspired, in part, by the death of a young athlete she knew, as well as several people in her life who were struggling with cancer. The audiobook version of *Rain Is Not My Indian Name* was aired on Red Tales, Aboriginal Voices Radio as the November 2005 Book of the Month. *Rain Is Not My Indian Name* and *Jingle Dancer* were both named to the National Education Association's Native American Book List and were also Oklahoma Book Award finalists.

Cynthia's first young adult novel, *Tantalize*, is a gothic fantasy that features a vampire-themed restaurant, a brutal murder, and a 17-year-old heroine whose first love interest is a werewolf in training. This dark but intoxicating romantic thriller is set in Austin, Texas where the author now lives.

Courtesy of Candlewick Press

Cynthia and her husband Greg became a writing team with *Santa Knows*, a humorous picture book that features a big brother's skepticism about the Christmas holiday. A pint-sized Scrooge, Alfie Snorklepuss tries to convince his younger sister there is no Santa until he is taught a lesson on Christmas Eve. Cynthia has also published short stories for anthologies such as *Period Pieces* and *In My Grandmother's House*, both of which were among the New York Public Library's Books for the Teen Age. She maintains an extensive web site about children's literature on which she writes articles, compiles bibliographies, interviews authors and illustrators, and provides links to many related sources. Named one of the top 10 sites for writers by *Writer's Digest* and included by the American Library Association in its list of Great Sites for Kids, www.cynthialeitichsmith.com is considered one of the best Internet resources for children's and young adult literature.

A featured speaker at numerous national conferences, Cynthia Leitich Smith is on the faculty of the Vermont College M.F.A. program on Writing for Children and Young Adults. She and her husband share their Texas home with four cats.

SELECTED WORKS: *Jingle Dancer*, illus. by Cornelius Van Wright and Ying-Hwa Hu, 2000; *Rain Is Not My Indian Name*, 2001; *Indian Shoes*, illus. by Jim Madsen, 2002; "The Gentleman Cowboy," in *Period Pieces*, ed. by Erzsi Deak and Kristin Litchman, 2003; "The Naked Truth," in *In My Grandmother's House*, ed. and illus. by Bonnie Christensen, 2003; "A Real-Live Blond Cherokee and His Equally Annoyed Soul Mate," in *Moccasin Thunder: American Indian Stories for Today*, ed. by Lori Marie Carlson, 2005; *Santa Knows*, with Greg Leitich Smith, illus. by Steve Björkman, 2006; *Tantalize*, 2007.

SUGGESTED READING: *Something About the Author*, vol.152, 2005; *Authors and Artists for Young Adults*, vol. 51, 2003. Periodicals—Lesesne, Teri S., "Cheering for Books: An Interview with Cynthia Leitich Smith," *Teacher Librarian*, October 2001; McElmeel,

Sharron, "Author Profile: Cynthia Leitich Smith," *Library Talk*, March/April 2002.

WEB SITE: www.cynthialeitichsmith.com

Photo by John Solano

Sonya Sones

"I'm sitting at my desk in my fourth grade classroom, writing a story. It's a rip-roaring comical tale about the adventures of a raindrop—the brief but ever so eventful life it has before it finally evaporates. This raindrop has a voice. This raindrop has personality plus. This raindrop needs its story told. So when my teacher, Mrs. Sables, tells us it's time to move on to our math lesson, my muse starts hollering in my ear, 'But you can't stop writing! Not yet! We're not finished!' And that's when something wonderful happens. Mrs. Sables sees the look on my face, sees the anguish of my frustrated creative urge, and says, 'You may continue working on your story until you are finished, Sonya.'

"Was it the respect Mrs. Sables chose to give me at that moment—her recognition of how important it was for me to tell my tale, her honoring of the inspired state I'd suddenly found myself in—that eventually turned me into a writer? I'll never know. But of all the years I spent in elementary school, that's the moment that made the most lasting and indelible impression on me.

"Maybe I would have become a writer anyway, because I've always loved words. I've always been awed by their incredible power, both to hurt and to heal. When I was a skinny little girl growing up just outside of Boston in the suburb of Newton, though, I thought I'd be an artist someday. I loved sneaking upstairs to the tiny room in our attic, where I'd while away the hours drawing pictures of dinosaurs.

"Every summer, my friends went off to their country homes or to camp, but *my* family couldn't afford such luxuries. So I traveled to the library down the street from my house and let books take me all the places I wished I could go. When I hit my teens, I began reading the diaries of Anaïs Nin and became an avid journal writer—sometimes scribbling as many as three or four entries a day. My journal was a selfless best friend who never tired of listening to me complaining about my life. But I had no idea that I'd become a writer. Not even when I turned sixteen and discovered the poetry of Richard Brautigan. Brautigan made poetry look so easy that I sat down and began writing reams of it myself. Of course, it was all deeply personal stuff, intended for my eyes only, but it sure felt great when it was gushing out of me onto those clean white pages.

"Who knows? Maybe if I hadn't enrolled in an animation class the summer I turned seventeen, I'd have become a writer sooner. But the minute I learned how to make animated films, I was off and running. I loved telling stories with pictures—loved being able to make all my wildest dreams come true on the silver screen. *That's* what I'd do with my life: I'd become a filmmaker!

"So, how did I end up living in Hollywood? What did Robin Williams have to do with how I met my husband? How did I get Woody Allen to perform magic tricks for me? What was it like to be kissed by John Travolta? Why did I quit show business to write books for teens? I love revealing the answers to these questions when I speak at schools and libraries all across the country. In fact, the only thing that I enjoy as much as writing is speaking about writing and teaching people how to write poetry.

"The woman who taught *me* how to write poetry was the great Myra Cohn Livingston. It was Myra who set me on the path to writing *Stop Pretending*, my first novel-in-verse. When I was writing those poems about my sister, I didn't even realize I was writing a novel. I just thought it was a themed collection of poems. It wasn't until my editor wrote me a letter full of poem-provoking questions that the collection morphed into a novel-in-verse. And once I began using poetry to tell my stories, I was hooked.

"I hadn't set out to write books for teens, but that turned out to be the voice that came most naturally to me. Lots of people talk about having an inner child, but *I've* got an inner teen. And she's right there with me, whispering in my ear whenever I sit down to write.

"When I'm not slaving away at a hot keyboard, I spend my time reading, taking photographs, dancing up a storm, and answering fan e-mail. I live with my family in California, where I long for snow in winter and fireflies in summer."

> *"Lots of people talk about having an inner child, but I've got an inner teen. And she's right there with me, whispering in my ear when-ever I sit down to write."*

CB   CB   CB

Born in Boston, Sonya Sones attended Hampshire College in western Massachusetts, where she received a B.A. in filmmaking and photography. During her college years, she taught animation to children while earning credit towards her degree. With grants from the National Endowment for the Arts, she taught in Omaha, San Francisco, Cambridge, and on the island of St. Croix. After graduation she worked on public television projects, making films for WGBH's *Zoom* program and PBS's *The Electric Company*. She also taught film classes at Harvard University.

Moving to California to be the personal assistant to a Hollywood movie director, Sones later found work as an animator, as a production assistant on a Woody Allen film, and as a still photographer and script supervisor on a Ron Howard film. Eventually, she began working as a film editor. At a taping of the *Mork & Mindy* television show, she met the man who was to become her husband.

When Sones had her first child, she stopped editing to spend time with her daughter and started designing hand-painted baby clothes for stores like Neiman Marcus and Macy's. After her second child was born, she took poetry classes at UCLA and studied under the well-known children's poet and anthologist Myra Cohn Livingston.

Sones' first book, *Stop Pretending*, is an autobiographical story in verse. With language and images that bring even mundane subjects to life, *Stop Pretending* tells the story of what happened when Sonya was 13 and her older sister was hospitalized for mental illness. This book won several awards, including the Christopher Award, the Myra Cohn Livingston Poetry Award, the Claudia Lewis Award for Poetry, and the Gradiva Award for Poetry from the National Association for the Advancement of Psychoanalysis. It was chosen as an ALA Popular Paperback for Young Adults, named a Notable Children's Trade Book in the Field of Social Studies, and included in the CCBC Choices list—an auspicious beginning for a first-time novelist.

What My Mother Doesn't Know is the story of a 14½-year-old girl who's trying to figure out the difference between love

Courtesy of Simon Pulse, Simon & Schuster

and lust. Winner of the Iowa Teen Book Award, it was also named a *Booklist* Editors' Choice, a Top Ten Editor's Choice on Teenreads.com, and a *VOYA* Top Shelf book for Middle School Readers.

Written in verse and letters, *One of Those Hideous Books Where the Mother Dies* is about a teen who is forced to move from Boston to Hollywood to live with her movie star father, a man she has never even met. The book explores some of the culture shock that Sones herself experienced when she moved from the East Coast to the West. Named a Society of School Librarians International Honor Book, it won the Rhode Island Teen Book Award and the New Hampshire Isinglass Teen Read Award. ALA named all three titles as both Quick Picks for Reluctant Young Adult Readers and Best Books for Young Adults. They were also named International Reading Association Young Adult Choices and cited among the New York Public Library's Books for the Teen Age.

Sonya Sones and her husband, Bennett, recently wrote a picture book together, which will be published at a future date. They have two teenage children, Ava and Jeremy, and live near the beach in California.

SELECTED WORKS: *Stop Pretending: What Happened When My Big Sister Went Crazy*, 1999; *What My Mother Doesn't Know*, 2001; *One of Those Hideous Books Where the Mother Dies*, 2004; "Cat Got Your Tongue?" in *Sixteen: Stories about That Sweet and Bitter Birthday*, ed. by Megan McCafferty, 2004; *What My Girlfriend Doesn't Know*, 2007.

SUGGESTED READING: *Something About the Author*, vol. 131, 2002; Sones, Sonya, "When Madness is in the Eye of the Beholder," *Times Educational Supplement*, July 27, 2001.

WEB SITE: www.sonyasones.com

Art Spiegelman

February 15, 1948–

Art Spiegelman's groundbreaking graphic novel, *Maus*, had its genesis in his family's history. Before World War II Spiegelman's father had been a well-to-do salesman and businessman in Poland. After serving in the Polish army at the start of the war, Vladek Spiegelman was detained in a German POW camp. By the time he returned to his family, the Nazi regime had started persecuting the Jews in Poland. Both Vladek and his wife, Anja, were sent to Auschwitz, the worst of the concentration camps, and were liberated when Germany lost the war. Their son, Richieu, and most of their relatives, however, did not survive the war years. After their release the Spiegelmans moved to Stockholm, Sweden, where Art was born in 1948.

When Art was three years old, the family immigrated to the United States and settled in the Rego Park neighborhood of Queens, New York. Spiegelman's father wanted him to become a dentist; after experiencing Auschwitz, he believed a medical person had a better chance of survival than an artist. But young Spiegelman, fascinated by *Mad* magazine and various superhero adventures, developed a passionate interest in comics and cartooning. By age 13 he was illustrating for his school newspaper; at 14, he sold his first piece of art to the Long Island *Post* for $15. While he attended the High School of Art and Design in New York City, his work appeared in alternative and underground publications, which, unlike traditional comics of the era, dealt with social issues, dark humor, and taboo subjects. He also wrote, printed, and distributed his own comic magazine called 'Blasé,' and turned down an offer to create a syndicated comic strip for the United Features Syndicate because he felt creating conventional comics would be too constricting.

Courtesy of Pantheon Books

He attended Harpur College (which later became the State University of New York at Binghamton), and his work appeared in the college newspaper; but he dropped out of school when his summer job at Topps Chewing Gum became full-time employment. At Topps he developed offbeat novelty toys like the Garbage Pail Kids series of trading cards and stickers that parodied the then-popular line of Cabbage Patch dolls. Although his successful business relationship with Topps lasted more than 20 years, Spiegelman never lost touch with the comic book world.

In 1968 Spiegelman suffered a breakdown and spent time in a mental hospital where some of his behavior, he later realized, mirrored that of his parents' during the Holocaust. Shortly after his release, his mother, who had periodically suffered from depression, committed suicide. Despite these personal calamities, the 1970s were a creative time for Spiegelman. Becoming a major figure in the "comix" movement—a term developed to set underground comics apart from traditional comic books—he drew a strip for *Short Order Comix*, created various books, and co-edited the alternative comix anthology *Arcade*. For a while, he taught at the San Francisco Academy of Art and later at the New York School of Visual Arts. In 1977 he married Françoise Mouly, an editor and graphic designer, and in 1980 the couple founded *RAW*, the acclaimed avant-garde comics magazine that gradually changed the public's perception of the genre. *RAW* featured the work of American and European artists as well as reprinting the work of historic cartoonists and illustrators of the past.

It was in *RAW* that *Maus* was first serialized. Born from a 1972 three-page strip featuring animals with human characteristics

Courtesy of Pantheon Books, Random House, Inc.

that Spiegelman initially thought would turn into a strip about slavery, the final version became, *Maus: A Survivor's Tale. I: My Father Bleeds History*, published in book form in 1986. Until then Spiegelman was largely unknown outside the underground comix world, but everything changed with the publication of this unique approach to the Holocaust.

In *Maus*, Spiegelman combined the comic book form with autobiography, including the story of his parents' ordeal during World War II. He then added an element of fantasy through the use of animal characters: the Nazis are depicted as cats, the Jews as mice, the Poles as pigs, the British as fish, the French as frogs, and the Americans as dogs. While the book explores several themes, including generational differences and the difficulty of dealing with traumatic events, the unifying factor is Spiegelman's effort to faithfully preserve his father's experiences while struggling to come to terms with their relationship. The plot moves back and forth in time, and the stark black-and-white drawings emphasize the factual aspects of the story.

Though at first people were outraged to see an artist portray the Holocaust in a comic-book format, Spiegelman was soon praised for his scrupulously researched and accurate description of life in the concentration camps. In the follow-up book, *Maus: A Survivor's Tale. II: And Here My Troubles Began*, Spiegelman continues the story, including the end of the war, his parents' eventual release from Auschwitz, his own birth, and his father's death in 1982. While the press could not agree on how to categorize these remarkable books, the two volumes helped to bring comic books into the mainstream and legitimize them as a serious art form, an impetus that led directly to the growth of the modern graphic novel.

In 1992 Spiegelman won a Special Pulitzer Prize for the two *Maus* books. They were cited as ALA Best Books for Young Adults, ALA Popular Paperbacks for Young Adults, and the New York Public Library's Books for the Teen Age. The volumes have received the Joel M. Cavior Award for Jewish Writing, a National Book Critics Circle nomination, a 1992 Eisner Award for Best Graphic Album, and awards abroad in such countries as Sweden, France, Germany, and Norway. In 1992 the second *Maus* title won the National Book Critics Circle Award, the *Los Angeles Times* book prize, and the Before Columbus Foundation Award. Writing these books was also a cathartic experience for Spiegelman, providing him a chance to confront his personal demons as well as offering him a better understanding of his relationship with his father, his mother's chronic depression, his deceased brother, and the very nature of survival.

Spiegelman's many awards include a Guggenheim fellowship, Italy's Yellow Kid Award, several Harvey Awards, the Inkpot Award, a Firecracker Alternative Book Award, and the Netherlands' Stripschappenning Award. In 1995 he received an Honorary Doctorate from his alma mater, SUNY Binghamton, and the following year the Jewish Culture Award. His artwork has appeared in numerous newspapers, magazines, and journals, among them the *New Yorker* where, from 1992 to 2003, he was a contributing editor and cover artist.

Spiegelman's first picture book for children, *Open Me . . . I'm a Dog!*, appeared in 1997. About a dog's many transformations until a curse finally turns him into a book, the puppy-sized book (which includes a leash) was an IRA/CBC Children's Choice. Wanting to put a new spin on children's literature, the artist, along with his wife, launched the large format Little Lit series in the year 2000. *Little Lit: Folklore and Fairy Tale Funnies*, is a provocative anthology of retold traditional fairytales spiced with an underground comics flavor by innovative cartoonists and artists such as Jules Feiffer, Ian Falconer, William Joyce, David Macaulay, and Barbara McClintock. With endpapers that are a stylized board game called "Fairy Tale Road Rage" created by Jimmy Corrigan and Chris Ware, this title was a 2000 National Parenting Publications (NAPPA) Award winner and a 2001 Eisner Award nominee in three categories. The second

Though at first people were outraged to see an artist portray the Holocaust in a comic-book format, Spiegelman was soon praised for his scrupulously researched and accurate description of life in the concentration camps.

book in the series, *Strange Stories for Strange Kids*, featured such disparate authors as Maurice Sendak, who wrote about a ravenous baby eating his parents; Paul Auster, whose Kafkaesque story concerns a disappearing man; and Crockett Johnson, who brought back the beginning of his classic Barnaby strip from the 1940s. In *It Was a Dark and Silly Night*, fifteen authors and artists from the picture book and comic book worlds start their stories with the sentence "It was a dark and silly night," with funny and creepy results. This book includes many of the authors and artists who created stories for the previous two books, as well as such notable additions as Lemony Snicket, Neil Gaiman, and Gahan Wilson. The endpapers are designed by *Where's Waldo?* creator Martin Handford. Finally, to cap off the series, choice stories from the three previous Little Lit books were collected for *Big Fat Little Lit*.

Art Spiegelman, along with his wife, created the cover for the *New Yorker* immediately following the terrorist attacks on September 11, 2001. The cover appears all black until, on closer inspection, the slightly darker image of the World Trade Center towers becomes visible. *In the Shadow of No Towers* chronicles the experience of Spiegelman and his family as they witnessed the attack on the World Trade Center from their lower Manhattan neighborhood; he further discusses his keenly felt political views using a variety of graphic techniques. This book was named a New York Public Library Book for the Teen Age and a Quill Award nominee, and cited as one of the *New York Times Book Review*'s 100 Notable Books of 2004.

The graphic novel genre is now thriving, thanks in large part to Spiegelman's critically acclaimed work and the interest he has shown in the work of other artists. His art has appeared in gallery shows and museums throughout the United States and abroad, including a 1991 show at New York City's Museum of Modern Art. Inducted into the Hall of Fame of the Will Eisner Comic Industry Awards as well as the Art Directors Club, Spiegelman was named one of the Top 100 Most Influential People by the editors of *Time* in 2005.

> *The graphic novel genre is now thriving, thanks in large part to Spiegelman's critically acclaimed work and the interest he has shown in the work of other artists.*

SELECTED WORKS FOR YOUNG READERS: *Open Me . . . I'm a Dog!* 1997; *Little Lit: Folklore and Fairy Tale Funnies*, ed. with Françoise Mouly, 2000; *Little Lit 2: Strange Stories for Strange Kids*, ed. with Françoise Mouly, 2001; *It Was a Dark and Silly Night . . .*, ed. with Françoise Mouly, 2003; *Big Fat Little Lit*, ed. with Françoise Mouly, 2006.

SELECTED WORKS FOR ADULTS: *The Complete Mr. Infinity*, 1970; *The Viper Vicar of Vice, Villainy, and Vickedness*, (privately printed), 1972; *Zip-a-Tune and More Melodies*, 1972; *Whole Grains: A Book of Quotations*, ed. with Bob Schneider, 1973; *Ace Hole, Midget Detective*, 1974; *Language of Comics*, 1974; *Breakdowns: From Maus to Now: An Anthology of Strips*, 1977; *Work and Turn*, 1979; *Every Day Has Its Dog*, 1979; *Two-Fisted Painters: Action Adventure*, 1980; *Jack Survives*, by Jerry Moriarty, ed. with Françoise Mouly, 1984; *How to Commit Suicide in South Africa*, by Holly Metz and Sue Coe, ed. with Françoise Mouly, 1985; *RAW: The Graphic Aspirin for War Fever*, ed. with Françoise Mouly, 1986; *Maus: A Survivor's Tale. I: My Father Bleeds History*, 1986; *Read Yourself RAW: Comix Anthology for Damned Intellectuals*, ed. with Françoise Mouly, 1987; *Agony*, ed. with Françoise Mouly and Mark Beyer, 1987; *Jimbo: Adventures in Paradise*, ed. with Françoise Mouly and Gary Panter, 1988; *RAW: Open Wounds from the Cutting Edge of Commix*, 1989; *RAW, No. 2*, ed. with Françoise Mouly, 1990; *RAW, No. 3: High Culture for Lowbrows*, 1991; *Maus: A Survivor's Tale. II: And Here My Troubles Began*, 1991; *Argonaut: Rediscovering American Resources*, by Warren Hinckle, illus. with Dan O'Neill and R. Crumb, 1992; *Skin Deep: Tales of Doomed Romance*, ed. with R. Sikoryak, 1992; *Love Is Strange: Stories of Postmodern Romance*, ed. by Joel Rose, 1993; *The Wild Party: The Lost Classic*, by Joseph Moncure March, 1994; *The History of Comix*, 1996; *The Narrative Corpse: A Chain Story by 69 Artists!* ed. with R. Sikoryak, 1998; *Comix, Essays, Graphics and Scraps: From Maustonow to Maus to Now*, 1998; *Jack Cole and Plastic Man: Forms Stretched to Their Limits*, with Chip Kidd, 2001; *In the Shadow of No Towers*, 2004.

SUGGESTED READING: Witek, Joseph, *Art Spiegelman: Conversations*, 2007; *Encyclopedia of World Biography*, vol. 25, 2005; Forget, Thomas, *Art Spiegelman*, 2005; *St. James Guide to Young Adult Writers*, 2nd ed., 2004; *Authors and Artists for Young Adults*, vol. 46, 2002; *Current Biography*, 1994; *World Authors 1990–1995*; Witek, Joseph, *Comic Books as History: The Narrative Art of Jack Jackson*, Art Spiegelman and Harvey Pekar, 1989.

WEB SITE: www.lambiek.net/artists/s/spiegelman.htm

Photo by Gina Stroud

**Jonathan
Stroud**

October 27, 1970–

"The impulse to write has always been with me. In class, age seven, I composed stirring tales about intrepid children, secret passages and robbers' treasure: one of these was so long that the teacher ran out of paper. I recorded improvised comic stories onto cassette, complete with funny accents. These are fortunately now lost. Around the same time I produced a multiple-choice adventure, 'Diamond Theft,' in which Lady Moneybags' diamond necklace is stolen by the wicked Steve Jones and the reader pursues him along varying routes. I still have this, complete with the tattered green paper binding that my dad glued round it—it is a prized possession: my first proper 'book'.

"Between the ages of eight and ten I was frequently ill with lung problems: pneumonia, bronchitis, asthma . . . the conditions were serious, but the words were fascinating. The months I spent in hospital, or at home in bed, were filled with imaginative escape—piles of cheap paperbacks bought by my mother and devoured with a terrible hunger. Picked clean, they littered the floor of my lair like bones.

"Later, my health improved and my energies returned. At age eleven, I was inspired by my finest teacher, Mr Bill Bowen, a soft-spoken Welshman with a beautiful singing voice. He played Mozart and Rossini in assemblies, and mimed pilgrims fighting foul fiends during Methodist hymns. He encouraged me to read out my stories—new tales of Mowgli and Sherlock Holmes— before the school; his passionate enthusiasm gave me confidence and strength. Twenty years later, he came to my wedding.

"In my early teens I fell heavily under the influence of Tolkien and read innumerable fantasy series, a few of which were not derivative. I was interested in role-playing games, with the minor problem that I could never understand the rules, so with my best friend I spent a number of years inventing games of our own. We did this separately, appearing triumphantly at intervals like mad scientists from our labs, waving our latest invention. This would be played once, maybe twice, and then the other inventor, spurred by envy, would hurry off to work on a rival game. The true excitement lay, not in playing, but in the act of creation, devising rules and patterns that become self-sufficient, separate from oneself. This is the same thrill that propels a writer too.

"Exams, and other pressures of growing up, squeezed such activity, but I maintained a continuous diary. Each day, without fail, I wrote a page about my adventures; if nothing else, it taught me how to weave words around even the most unpromising material. At university I read English Literature, so most of my time was spent studying other people's words, but I experimented with other kinds of writing: plays (bad), poems (worse), and dubious occasional pieces in the student newspapers.

"I graduated in traditional fashion—with a good degree and no clue what to do with it—and, lacking a vocation, joined the staff of a children's publisher in London. Here, finally, pieces of the jigsaw began to fall into place. Employing my old game-making skills, I worked as an editor of puzzle-books, while devising and writing new ones of my own. With these in print, I grew in confidence, and started on a novel—*Buried Fire*—a fantasy harking back to the books that had nourished me as a boy. The sprawling manuscript eventually came to the attention of a remarkable editor, Delia Huddy of Random House. With infinite tact and grace, she encouraged me to cut it down, and her calm presence sustained me through five subsequent novels.

"For years I wrote only at weekends and on days off, and fretted ceaselessly at the restrictions this imposed. At last I made a decisive move. I handed in my notice and in January 2002 became a full-time writer. My wife Gina supported me financially; we reckoned I had a year to make good before quitting the experiment. At this point, the djinni Bartimaeus took a hand. Within six months the rights were sold to his trilogy, and it has been my great good luck to have been happily following my impulse ever since."

"In class, age seven, I composed stirring tales about intrepid children, secret passages and robbers' treasure: one of these was so long that the teacher ran out of paper."

ᘓ ᘓ ᘓ

Born in Bedford, England and raised in St. Albans, near London, Jonathan Stroud had an early fascination with telling stories. At York University, as an English literature major, he developed a deep appreciation for the writing of famous authors. When he finished his degree in 1992, Stroud took a position in the editorial department at Walker Books in London. As an editor for children's books, he not only developed an understanding of the writing process but also gained insight into the visual aspects of children's books by working with illustrators and designers.

During this time Stroud was fortunate to work on a wide variety of books, including a children's version of the Bible, encyclopaedias, and game and puzzle books. In his spare time he created some puzzle books of his own. Three of his notable early entries in this genre were *Justin Credible's Worldplay World*, *The Lost Treasure of Captain Blood*, and *The Viking Saga of Harri Bristlebeard*, all published by Walker Books.

Now confident that his adult skills and sensibilities could fulfil his childhood dreams, Stroud turned to writing a novel of his own. *Buried Fire*, published in the United Kingdom in 1999 and the United States in 2004, displays the author's interest in the conflict between reality and fantasy. Three siblings named Michael, Stephen, and Sarah Macintyre help their local vicar unearth a secret buried near their village—a fire-breathing dragon.

Stroud published two more children's novels: *The Leap*, about a brother and sister who have different takes on whether or not their friend Max drowned in the mill pool, and *The Last Siege*, about a trio of friends who discover a ruined, deserted castle in the midwinter snow and let their imaginations run away with them. All three of these early novels, while very different in subject matter, use various points of view to suggest that truth is really a matter of perspective. Stroud, having mastered this blurring of the distinction between reality and fantasy, employed it with considerable skill in his next project—an ambitious fantasy trilogy.

The Bartimaeus Trilogy began in 2003 with the publication of *The Amulet of Samarkand*, which won a *Boston Globe–Horn Book* Honor Award in the U.S. and the Lancashire Children's Book Award in England. The story tells of a young magician's apprentice named Nathaniel who lives in an alternative universe, a London populated by magical people and creatures. He summons a smart-alecky 5,000-year-old djinni named Bartimaeus to help him steal a precious and powerful amulet from the evil magician, Simon Lovelace.

The trilogy continues with *The Golem's Eye*, in which Nathaniel's budding career in government is threatened by a number of crises, culminating in a series of attacks made by a

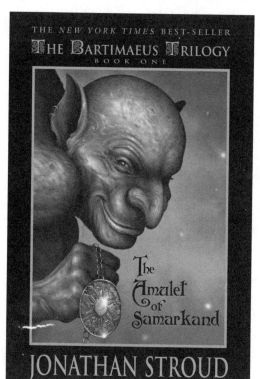

THE *NEW YORK TIMES* BEST-SELLER

THE BARTIMAEUS TRILOGY
BOOK ONE

The Amulet of Samarkand

JONATHAN STROUD

Courtesy of Hyperion Books for Children

seemingly indestructible clay golem. While struggling to combat the golem, Nathaniel and Bartimaeus also encounter Kitty, the leader of the mysterious Resistance, an organization seeking to overthrow the corrupt rule of the magicians. In the final novel, *Ptolemy's Gate*, Nathaniel, Bartimaeus, and Kitty again find their paths crossing as they uncover a conspiracy that proves to be the greatest threat ever faced by the magical world. Bartimaeus's energies, after years of being trapped on Earth, are rapidly being depleted, and Kitty discovers secrets from his past that could forever reshape the world. *Ptolemy's Gate* received the Corine International Book Award from the Bavarian section of the German Publishers and Booksellers Association.

In 2006 the Bartimaeus Trilogy won the Grand Prix de l'Imaginaire, a prize for fantasy and science fiction writing in France, and it also captured the Mythopoeic Fantasy Award for Children's Literature, awarded by the Mythopoeic Society in the U.S. Now translated into 35 languages, the series has achieved bestseller status worldwide. Movie rights have been sold to Miramax and the author is happily assured of being able to continue to write for a living. Jonathan Stroud lives in England with his wife Gina, their daughter Isabelle, and their son Arthur.

SELECTED WORKS (Dates are for British publication; U.S. dates, if different, are in parentheses): *Justin Credible's Worldplay World*, 1994; *The Lost Treasure of Captain Blood*, 1996; *The Viking Saga of Harri Bristlebeard*, 1997; *Buried Fire*, 1999 (2004); *Sightseers: Ancient Rome: A Guide to the Glory of Imperial Rome*, 2000; *The Leap*, 2001 (2004); *The Last Siege*, 2003 (2006); *The Amulet of Samarkand*, 2003; *The Golem's Eye*, 2004; *Ptolemy's Gate*, 2005 (2006).

SUGGESTED READING: *Something About the Author*, vol. 159, 2005. Periodicals—Margolis, Rick, "I Dream of Djinni," *School Library Journal*, January 2006.

WEB SITE: www.jonathanstroud.com

" Growing up on a dairy farm in rural Wisconsin, I loved books. The only public library was in a small town nearby and we'd go every Saturday. With little money for new books, their collection was old, so I spent hours with classic series like the Five Little Peppers, the Wizard of Oz, and Nancy Drew. About once every six weeks we'd take a trip to the largest nearby

Stephanie Stuve-Bodeen

August 6, 1965–

city, Eau Claire. My parents let me choose one book to buy, which is how I managed to build up my own library that included all of Laura Ingalls Wilder's Little House books and eventually, everything written by Judy Blume.

"All that reading made me want to be a writer, and I loved writing stories in elementary school. In eighth grade, I won a regional creative writing contest with a science fiction story. In college, I majored in journalism, but that wasn't the creative writing I wanted to do. When I was a junior, I nearly quit school. I went to tell my advisor, a dear professor nearing retirement, and he asked me, 'What do you really want to be?'

"I replied, 'I want to be a writer.'

"The conversation continued and he finally said, 'I believe that one day, all those people out there will be reading you.' He believed in me a whole decade before I did.

"I stayed in school, graduated, and went to be a Peace Corps volunteer in Tanzania, a life-changing experience. The week that sticks out for me is the one I spent with a Tanzanian family—a family of nine living in a tiny mud hut. They gave a face to poverty. At the time, it was the worst week of my life.

Photo by Norm Garon

"After returning to the U.S., my husband and I started a family and I became a stay-at-home mom. We spent hours at the library, bringing home stacks of picture books. We read so many, and I began to notice that some just weren't that great. I thought to myself, 'I could write a better book than that.' When I finally said it out loud to my husband, he replied, 'Then do it.'

"One weekend, some Peace Corps friends came for dinner and we talked about the week we each spent with our Tanzanian families. My friend Bobbi said, 'A little girl in my village had a rock for a doll.' Instantly, I remembered seeing the same thing when I was in Tanzania. That night I went to sleep and woke up about 3 A.M., ideas whirling, unable to sleep. I got up and found a notebook, then jotted down the first draft of *Elizabeti's Doll*. It happened to be my 30th birthday.

"Over the next few months, I revised my story until I thought it was finished. I believed it was good enough to be published and told my husband, 'Someone out there has got to love it.' I checked out every book I could find that dealt with how to write a picture book, where to send them, etc., and I got very lucky. The second publisher that saw my story called about two months later and said they wanted to publish it. Amazingly, they did not change one word of the original manuscript. So, the worst week of my life turned out to be the one of the best, and much of it was because I finally chose to believe in myself."

※　※　※

Stephanie Stuve-Bodeen graduated from the University of Wisconsin in River Falls with a B.S. in secondary education/ social studies and a minor in coaching. She and her husband, Tim Bodeen, joined the Peace Corps and went to Tanzania in 1989–90. Tim had aquaculture training, and Stephanie organized a library and helped with teacher training at a junior college. She also fell in love with the Tanzanian people. Upon her return to the United States, Stephanie began teaching. For a number of years she was a substitute teacher, but also held jobs as an eighth-grade geography teacher in Evansville, Minnesota and an eleventh- and twelfth-grade psychology and economics teacher in Battle Lake, Minnesota. Because her husband works for the U.S. Fish and Wildlife Service, their family has moved often, with stints in Wisconsin, Indiana, and Minnesota. For three years they lived on Midway Atoll National Wildlife Refuge, the northernmost island in the Hawaiian archipelago. In 2003 Stephanie earned an M.F.A. degree from Spalding University in Louisville, Kentucky.

Stephanie's first book, *Elizabeti's Doll*, won the Ezra Jack Keats New Writer Award and the Minnesota Book Award. Sensitive to the Tanzanian culture, *Elizabeti's Doll* is about a young girl who, while adjusting to the birth of her baby brother, finds a rock and makes it her baby. Elizabeth bathes the rock and feeds it, and learns the power of love when she must save it from burning in a fire. This title was also named an ALA Notable Children's Book, a Charlotte Zolotow Award Highly Commended Title, and a Best Book of the Year by *School Library Journal*, *Child* magazine, the Cooperative Children's Book Center, and the Bank Street College of Education.

In the sequel, *Mama Elizabeti*, the same Tanzanian girl learns the difference between caring for a real baby brother and

"The week that sticks out for me is the one I spent with a Tanzanian family—a family of nine living in a tiny mud hut. They gave a face to poverty. "

by STEPHANIE STUVE-BODEEN • illustrated by CHRISTY HALE

Courtesy of Lee & Low Books

caring for her beloved rock doll. This book received the Paterson Prize for Books for Young People and was cited as a Parents' Choice Fiction Award winner, a Society of School Librarians International Honor Book, and a Bank Street College Best Books of the Year title. It also received the very first Award for Best Children's Book by a Peace Corps writer in 2001. The third book in the series, *Elizabeti's School*, was named to Bank Street College Best Books of the Year and cited as an Outstanding Achievement in Children's Literature by the Wisconsin State Library Association. In this picture-book story, the young heroine comes to appreciate the knowledge she has gained in school when she discovers she can use her new math skills to count her new kittens.

Babu's Song, another story of Tanzania, features a boy who receives the gift of a handmade music box from his grandfather, which he soon sells. Feeling guilty, he gives the money to his grandfather, who pays his school tuition with the music box money and makes the soccer ball the boy wanted to buy. Told with economical language rich in emotion, *Babu's Song* won a *Storytelling World* Award and a Children's Africana Book Award. It was also named a Bank Street College Children's Book of the Year, a Parents' Choice Recommended title, and a CCBC Choice.

Stephanie contributed a short story, 'What I Did on My Summer Safari,' to *Memories of Sun*, a book edited by Jane Kurtz about the experiences of Americans in Africa and Africans in America. The story is based on a safari she took with an American diplomat and his family during her years in the Peace Corps. She has also written with great sensitivity about a young girl's experiences with a special-needs brother in *We'll Paint the Octopus Red* and *The Best Worst Brother*.

Stephanie Stuve-Bodeen and her family reside in Washington State near Mount St. Helen's; she teaches in the Whidbey Writers M.F.A. program on Whidbey Island. She has two teenage daughters, Bailey and Tanzie. Her first young-adult novel, *The Compound*, was published under the pen name S. A. Bodeen in 2008.

SELECTED WORKS: *Elizabeti's Doll*, illus. by Christy Hale, 1998; *We'll Paint the Octopus Red*, illus. by Pam DeVito, 1998; *Mama Elizabeti*, illus. by Christy Hale, 2000; *Elizabeti's School*, illus. by Christy Hale, 2002; *Babu's Song*, illus. by Aaron Boyd, 2003; "What I Did on My Summer Safari," in *Memories of Sun: Stories of Africa and America*, ed. by Jane Kurtz, 2003; *The Best Worst Brother*, illus. by Charlotte M. Fremaux, 2005. As S.A. Bodeen—*The Compound*, 2008.

SUGGESTED READING: *Something About the Author*, vol. 114, 2000. Periodicals—"Flying Starts," *Publishers Weekly*, June 23, 2008.

WEB SITE: www.rockforadoll.com

" A biography is incredibly difficult to write. On the one hand, I can discuss the facts of my life—where I grew up, where I went to school. But those statistics don't even dent the true things that have influenced and shaped my life: the middle-of-the-night conversations, the spontaneous road trips, watching my son climb a tree . . . it's like getting to know a character in a novel. Would you rather know where he graduated from college or watch him eat an artichoke at a dinner party?

"That being said, I grew up in East Providence, Rhode Island. My father was a sales engineer and my mother a homemaker. I'm the oldest of four, with two sisters and a brother. I always liked to keep busy, working on several projects at once. I wrote a little, but never thought of becoming a writer.

"I've always been an avid reader, and I still read several books a week. When I was young, it was mostly mysteries: Nancy Drew, Encyclopedia Brown. As I got older, my tastes became more eclectic: Carlos Castaneda, Kurt Vonnegut, Hermann Hesse, Anthony Burgess. I still love where your mind goes with a good book; it's the cheapest form of travel there is.

"I attended the University of Rhode Island and majored in journalism. When I graduated, I opted for the money and went into a career in sales and marketing. I worked in high-tech, made

Photo by Mark Morelli

Janet Tashjian

June 29, 1956–

a lot of great friends, but my heart wasn't in it. I quit one job and traveled around the world with my soon-to-be husband, Doug.

"Many people talk about the book that changed their lives. One that truly changed mine was *The Things They Carried* by Tim O'Brien. It was written with such simplicity and grace that when I finished it, I told my husband I was quitting my job to become a writer. I bought myself a box of pens, a stack of notebooks, and started writing. I enrolled in the M.F.A. program at Emerson College where I was lucky enough to train with some amazing writers: National Book Award Winner James Carroll was my thesis chair. Jack Gantos (of the *Joey Pigza* and *Rotten Ralph* books) was teaching a course entitled Writing Novels for Children. He seemed like a pretty cool guy, so I signed up. I think it's life's coincidences and accidents that often shape who we are. I'd never planned to write books for kids, but it turns out it's something I love to do.

"For me, being a novelist is it. I am humbled and grateful every day that this is how I make my living.

"What else to tell? I love the beach, love nature, hate people who talk on cell phones in public places. Hate pulling ticks off dogs, couldn't live a day without music, love to brainstorm ideas with my writer friends. Love to go to concerts, love to chase my son around the house and kiss him, love to refinish and paint old furniture. I hate it when people waste water or aren't passionate about life (especially at the same time).

"And no, you'll never catch me trying to eat an artichoke at a dinner party . . . I'm way too uncoordinated for that."

> "Many people talk about the book that changed their lives. One that truly changed mine was The Things They Carried *by Tim O'Brien.*"

ෆ   ෆ   ෆ

In 1978 Janet Souza Tashjian completed her B.A. at the University of Rhode Island, where she received the Academic Excellence Award in Journalism. In 1985 she married Douglas Tashjian, who works as a medical consultant. Janet spent fifteen years selling software and computers, managing sales forces, and running training classes before deciding to concentrate on becoming a writer. At Emerson College, where she earned her M.F.A. in 1994, she received the DuPrey Fiction Award.

Tashjian's first novel, *Tru Confessions*, was published in 1997. The story tells of twelve-year-old Trudy Walker, who dreams of a career in television and of finding a cure for her developmentally delayed twin brother, Eddie. Creating a documentary film for a video competition, she begins to understand the depth of her relationship with her brother and to accept his condition. *Tru*

Confessions received an Honor Book award from the Women's National Book Association and was named to the Books for the Teen Age list by the New York Public Library. For her sensitive portrayal of Eddie in the book, Tashjian received the Dolly Gray Children's Literature Award, sponsored by the Council for Exceptional Children.

In *Multiple Choice*—which was chosen as a Junior Library Guild selection and received the Pennsylvania Young Reader's Choice Award—teenager Monica Devon is becoming frightened by her own compulsive behaviors. Her love of wordplay and anagrams has led her to create a game called Multiple Choice in which a letter drawn from a Scrabble game set will dictate her actions. Eventually she confides her concerns to a guidance counselor and her parents. In *Fault Line*, another teenager, Becky Martin, has to learn to draw the line in her first serious relationship when her boyfriend's controlling behavior becomes abusive. These novels tackle tough contemporary issues in an honest, straightforward manner.

In *The Gospel According to Larry*, intelligent and idealistic Josh Swensen attempts to channel his thoughts through a Web site persona. He poses as "Larry," posting sermons against consumerism and celebrity worship. Soon he has a large following of adults and teens, but the tables are turned when his identity is discovered, forcing him into the kind of spotlight he ranted against. This title was cited as a Notable Social Studies Trade Book and an ALA Best Book for Young Adults.

Courtesy of Henry Holt and Company

In a sequel, *Vote for Larry*, Josh is attending Colorado University and directs his idealism toward young voters, resulting in a constitutional amendment lowering the age for the presidency and his own run for the White House.

Equally adept at writing for younger readers, Tashjian created a seven-year-old poet detective in *Marty Frye, Private Eye*, who rhymes his way through each of three mysteries. This title was named an IRA/CBC Children's Choice and cited by Bank Street College on its best books of the year list.

Janet Tashjian lives with her husband and their son, Jake, in Massachusetts.

SELECTED WORKS: *Tru Confessions*, 1997; *Marty Frye, Private Eye*, 1998; *Multiple Choice*, 1999; *The Gospel According to Larry*, 2001; *Fault Line*, 2003; *Vote for Larry*, 2004; *Larry and the Meaning of Life*, 2008.

SUGGESTED READING: *Something About the Author*, vol. 151, 2004.

WEB SITE: www.janettashjian.com
www.thegospelaccordingtolarry.com

Photo by Tom Foley

Catherine Thimmesh

(TIM-mesh)
September 20, 1966–

"Somewhere around the fourth or fifth grade, I returned to start a new school year and was greeted with a variation on the traditional (and much over-used) writing assignment: How did you spend your summer vacation? This year, the twist was: Describe your first day back at school after summer vacation. Well, out of the blue I had a 'light-bulb' moment and decided I would write my story (paragraph, really) from the perspective of the garbage can in the classroom. Now to me, at that time, I thought that was the single most clever concept in the entire world! From the perspective of the garbage can! Where did that come from? I didn't know but was so excited that I had hit upon the idea.

"To the best of my recollection, I had never read, heard, or heard of, a story being told from the perspective of an inanimate object—I thought it was my very own invention and I was darn proud to have come up with it. Cut to the chase. I wrote the story and waited with pumped-up anxiety to get it back with a beautiful red E-for-Excellent. When the paper was returned, there was no red E. In fact, there wasn't any letter whatsoever. There were scribbled words, though, and they said ominously: 'Please see me.' Fighting the knot in my throat, and the beginnings of tears in my eyes, I approached the teacher. 'Catherine, you didn't follow the directions; you'll have to do this over,' were the words that pierced my ears. As the teacher pointed out, the assignment was to tell about *my* first day back, and she was pretty sure that the garbage can and I were not the same. No mention of creativity, no mention of ingenuity. Not: 'You didn't follow the directions, but it was a fun idea.' I was completely crushed.

"That early experience was so negative it could have turned me against writing forever—stifled my creativity, my penchant for taking some risks. But oddly, and thankfully, it had the opposite effect. I was so determined to prove that I was indeed clever and creative and ingenious and that the teacher was just so wrong, that I think from that moment forward I put everything I had into all my stories. And of course, I would come to learn that not every idea I had was the most clever, creative, or ingenious. But through the years I did get plenty of positive feedback and encouragement from a number of truly superb teachers, both in elementary and in high school (though college was less formative.) My writing skills became better honed, and my enjoyment of writing, more entrenched.

"Despite a life-long love of writing, I never thought of becoming an author. Not once. It simply didn't occur to me— I'm not sure why. Like most authors, I've been an avid reader and lover of books. I never had my face glued to a book (like many authors, and like my older sister did). If the weather was nice, playing hide-and-seek tag outside was always just as good an option. I do remember that in most of the books of my youth, the boys got to have all the fun. Sure, I loved the Laura Ingalls Wilder books, but Laura's spunkiness couldn't hold a candle to the irrepressible Tom Fitzgerald in The Great Brain books. I remember being bugged by this (not to mention once being told by a librarian that the stories in my favorite series (The Great Brain) were 'boy' books). It all seemed so unfair. Perhaps that's why my first three books as an author concentrated on showing how smart, clever, and creative women and girls are and can be.

"Since I'm currently writing creative nonfiction, it's important to me to make my books accessible and fun to read. It's my goal to write in such a way that, should a teacher 'assign' students to read any of my books, I'm crossing my fingers that there won't be a loud, collective groan emanating from the classroom. When I'm not writing (or reading or playing with my two kids, Jaimie and Simon), I like to try new things, new experiences. Currently, I go to a Circus School where I am learning the flying trapeze. I've never been athletic, so it's been a real challenge—but, boy-oh-boy, is it fun! I can swing without safety lines now (there is a net), and do a few tricks. I've even hung upside down from my knees, flown through the air, and been caught on the other side

> *"That early experience was so negative it could have turned me against writing forever—stifled my creativity, my penchant for taking some risks. But oddly, and thankfully, it had the opposite effect."*

by the catcher! I like looking at the world upside down. It helps my writing too. After all, writing is all about a new outlook, a fresh perspective on a variety of common themes.

"And it is this new perspective that I search for in my life . . . and in my writing."

❀ ❀ ❀

Born and raised in Minneapolis, Minnesota, Catherine Thimmesh has two siblings, an older sister named Elizabeth and a younger brother, Joseph. In 1990 she graduated from the University of Minnesota with a B.A. in Art History. A few years later, in 1993, she married Paul Rachie, and they now have two children, Jaimie and Simon.

Thimmesh claims she hated nonfiction when she was young because she thought it was boring. Determined to change that perception in her first book, *Girls Think of Everything*, she brought together a fascinating and unexpected group of females who changed our lives with their remarkable practical inventions: Toll House cookies, Liquid Paper (commonly known as white-out), the Snugli for babies, a space bumper for astronauts, Scotchgard, and more. Showing how many obstacles women often had to overcome to be given credit for their work, the book also serves as a chronicle of the growth of women's rights and feminism. Winner of an IRA Children's Book Award, *Girls Think of Everything* was also named a Smithsonian Notable Book and an Outstanding Science Trade Book. From female inventors, Thimmesh moved to biographies of women who made discoveries in a variety of different fields. *The Sky's the Limit* profiles many resourceful women, including Beatrix Potter who, in addition to being a children's book author, discovered that lichen is both fungus and alga, and Jane Goodall who has spent a lifetime studying the behavior of chimpanzees. *The Sky's the Limit*, which covers the contributions of female scientists through present-day space exploration, was named a Smithsonian Notable Book and an Outstanding Science Trade Book for Children as well as a Notable Social Studies Trade Book. It also won the Minnesota Book Award for Children's Nonfiction.

For her third book, *Madam President: The Extraordinary, True (and Evolving) Story of Women in Politics*, which was designated a *New York Times* Notable Book of the Year, Thimmesh explored role models for a girl contemplating the possibility of becoming the President of the United States. The book profiles 23 women of power, both past and present, among them Abigail

Adams, Eleanor Roosevelt, Benazir Bhutto, Margaret Thatcher, and Condoleeza Rice. With wit and humor, Thimmesh indicates that women are definitely ready to occupy the Oval Office. In *Team Moon*, she chronicled the immense behind-the-scene efforts of some of the 400,000 people who put the Apollo 11 spacecraft on the Moon. A wide spectrum of individuals, many of whom are quoted directly in the book, worked to make that first Moon landing possible, and Thimmesh brings their collective effort into sharp focus. For this remarkable contribution to children's nonfiction, she was awarded the 2007 Robert F. Sibert award by the American Library Association. *Team Moon* was also awarded an Honorable Mention for the NCTE Orbis Pictus Award.

Courtesy of the Houghton Mifflin Company

Catherine Thimmesh lives in Eden Prairie, Minnesota, with her husband and two children. Along with writing, she loves reading, traveling, and practicing her skills on the flying trapeze, proving she is as adventurous as the subjects of her books.

SELECTED WORKS: *Girls Think of Everything: Stories of Ingenious Inventions by Women*, illus. by Melissa Sweet, 2000; *The Sky's the Limit: Stories of Discovery by Women and Girls*, illus. by Melissa Sweet, 2002; *Madam President: The Extraordinary, True (and Evolving) Story of Women in Politics*, illus. by Douglas B. Jones, 2004; *Team Moon: How 400,000 People Landed Apollo 11 on the Moon*, 2006.

SUGGESTED READING: *Contemporary Authors* Online, 2005.

WEB SITE: www.catherinethimmesh.com

"Looking back, it's easy to see how I have ended up as a children's book writer, but along the way it wasn't always quite that clear. True, as soon as I learned how to read, I was a voracious reader. And I did try my hand at writing stories even when quite young. I wrote my first 'novel' when I was seven, in pencil on the long yellow sheets of a legal pad. A few years later, after reading *The Witch of Blackbird Pond*, I wrote a melodramatic story that bore an uncanny similarity to *The Witch of Blackbird Pond*. Like most kids, what I loved, I copied. Thus books and

Lauren Thompson

November 7, 1962–

writing were always key. But I had many other interests as well. From an early age I loved to figure out how things were put together, and my parents were sure I was destined for a career in engineering. Math and science were always strong subjects for me, and in college my major was mathematics. I performed in plays with other kids from the neighborhood. I took piano, dance, and art lessons. My most common answer to the question, 'What do you want to be when you grow up?' was, 'A teacher.' This was probably because a love of learning was common among all my interests. I wanted to know everything and then tell others.

"Twice in my childhood, my family spent a year living in the Netherlands, and I became fluent in Dutch. In retrospect, it seems that fluency in two languages might have sharpened my appreciation for the magic of communication—but at the time, I only wanted to make friends. Alas, I now remember very little Dutch beyond numbers and a not-very-shocking curse word that must have thrilled us to repeat.

"During college, I loved the beauty of mathematical thought and language, in which spare, elegant proofs are most prized. But at the same time, I took as many creative writing classes as I could. When it was time to decide about graduate school, I knew that I had gone far enough with my math studies. I told my advisor that instead I wanted to do something in which the answers weren't in the back of the book. Eventually, I earned a Master's degree in English, and took creative writing classes all along the way. As is typical, the writing class instructors all assumed that we all wanted to write for adults. I dreamed of writing short stories and novels that expressed everything that I both understood and didn't understand about people and life. But writing was a terrible struggle for me. It seemed that 'frustrated would-be-writer' was as close to 'writer' as I was going to get.

"But then, after graduate school, I started working in children's book publishing, and while honing my skills as an editor, I discovered that I had finally found my voice as a writer, in writing for children. In the end, perhaps all my potential career paths have come together in this vocation. Like an engineer, I study

Photo by JuAnne Ng

Lauren Thompson

how to put words and texts together in order to have long-lasting integrity. Like a mathematician, I search for the most spare, elegant expression of an idea that I can formulate. Like an actor, I aim to present characters convincingly to my audience. Like a pianist, dancer, or any other artist, I try to tap a source deep within, balancing inspiration with plain old hard work. And like a teacher, I get to play a direct role in children's learning and growth. Through my books, I hope to kindle in at least a few young hearts the kind of passion I feel about language, and to affirm for children their emotional lives. Like a teacher, I bear the formidable responsibility of giving children their first taste of literacy. Unless children come to see books as their friends when they are young, it will be difficult to persuade them when they are older that books are not their foes. So, through a rather circuitous route, I have ended up as a children's book writer. Really, things couldn't have turned out any better."

ဢ ဢ ဢ

The daughter of a psychology professor and a nurse, Lauren Thompson received her B.A. from Mount Holyoke College and her M.A. in English from Clark University. After graduate school she began looking for a job in publishing. She found that her interviews with adult publishers went rather badly, but she thoroughly enjoyed her interviews with children's book publishers, with whom she could openly share how much she enjoyed picture books like *Blueberries for Sal*. Until then she hadn't thought of children's books as a form of writing, even though such books had been important to her as a child. Using her work experience in a children's editorial department as a crash course, she decided to try writing children's books herself and quickly realized that she had found her niche. She discovered that writing for children was, in one sense, easier than writing for adults, because she had at last discovered the audience that mattered most to her. But she learned that in another sense it was much harder—because writing children's books demanded concise and focused work.

Now a full-time author, Thompson believes that her eighteen years working in publishing taught her much about structure and pacing and about the importance of leaving something of the tale for the illustrations in picture books. Her Mouse books, which take off from very simple ideas, began with holiday themes— *Mouse's First Christmas* and *Mouse's First Halloween*—and have continued to explore the seasons, providing fine contributions to seasonal story times. In *One Riddle, One Answer*, Thompson

> *"In the end, perhaps all my potential career paths have come together in this vocation."*

a true story

Ballerina Dreams

by Lauren Thompson • Photographs by James Estrin

Courtesy of Feiwel & Friends

combined her two favorite interests—mathematics and creative writing—to create a riddle story about numbers within a folktale-like structure.

Thompson's awards include two Oppenheim Toy Portfolio awards—a Gold Award for *Little Quack's Bedtime*, and a Platinum Award for *A Christmas Gift for Mama*. *Polar Bear Night* received a Charlotte Zolotow Honor Award for picture book writing and was named an ALA Notable Children's Book. Several of Thompson's titles have been on the *New York Times* bestseller list, including *Mouse's First Halloween*, *Mouse's First Valentine*, *Mouse's First Day of School*, *Little Quack*, and *Polar Bear Night*, which was also named a *New York Times* Best Illustrated Book.

In 2007 Thompson was involved in a very special project that resulted in *Ballerina Dreams: A True Story*. The book recounts a story that editor Jean Feiwel spotted in the *New York Times* about a group of little girls who dreamed of dancing ballet. All of these girls were handicapped by cerebral palsy and other muscular disorders, but a gifted physical therapist, Joann Ferrara, found a way for them to perform with teenage helpers, and Thomspon wrote a story of their recital that captured the excitement of a dream come true. Illustrated with stunning photographs by James Estrin, *Ballet Dreams* was named an ALA Notable Children's Book. That honor was bestowed the same year to a very different book, *The Apple Pie That Papa Baked*, in which Thompson's lyrical rhythmic text is perfectly complemented by the folk art of illustrator Jonathan Bean.

The author lives with her husband, Robert E. Thompson, a college English teacher, and her son, Owen, in Brooklyn, New York.

SELECTED WORKS: *Mouse's First Christmas*, illus. by Buket Erdogan, 1999; *Love One Another: The Last Days of Jesus*, illus. by Elizabeth Uyehara, 2000; *Mouse's First Halloween*, illus. by Buket Erdogan, 2000; *One Riddle, One Answer*, illus. by Linda S. Wingerter, 2001; *Mouse's First Valentine*, illus. by Buket Erdogan, 2002; *Mouse's First Day of School*, illus. by Buket Erdogan, 2003; *A Christmas Gift for Mama*, illus. by Jim Burke, 2003; *Mouse's First Summer*, illus. by Buket Erdogan, 2004; *Little Quack's Hide and Seek*, illus. by Derek Anderson, 2004; *Polar Bear Night*, illus. by Stephen Savage, 2004; *Mouse's First Spring*, illus. by Buket Erdogan, 2005; *Little Quack*, illus. by Derek Anderson, 2005; *Little Quack's Bedtime*, illus. by Derek Anderson, 2005; *Mouse's First Snow*, illus. by Buket Erdogan, 2005; *Little Quack's New Friend*, illus. by Derek Anderson, 2006; *Mouse's First Fall*, illus. by Buket Erdogan, 2006; *The Apple Pie that Papa Baked*, illus by Jonathan Bean, 2007; *Ballerina Dreams: A True Story*, photos by James Estrin, 2007; *Wee Little Chick*, illus. by John Butler, 2008; *Hope Is an Open Heart*, 2008.

SUGGESTED READING: *Something About the Author*, vol. 132, 2002.

WEB SITE: www.laurenthompson.net

Terry Trueman

December 15, 1947–

"I was always fascinated by books. I liked the idea of them even before I could read very well. I discovered comics and *Mad* magazine and my dad's *Playboy* collection at a pretty early age. In fifth grade, my best friend was a neighbor kid named Brad Sather. His dad had a bookshelf in their house. I grew fascinated by the idea that a person, just a regular person, could have their very own library right in their own home. It seemed miraculous to me. As I got older, writers seemed pretty remarkable too. I was introduced to Hemingway and Fitzgerald in high school. And then, early in my college years, I found Vonnegut, John Barth, Jerzy Kosinski, William Kotzwinkle and Richard Brautigan. All these guys seemed very smart and cool. They seemed to know things that average people didn't know. I wanted in on those secrets too. Accepting an 'average' life became unfathomable to me, particularly the normal, average life as represented in my family. I was ready to be anything but normal!

"I thought seriously about becoming a writer when I was in high school and received my first positive feedback. I had a creative writing teacher named Kay Keyes, who thought I had talent. By the end of high school, I knew I wanted to be a writer. Mind you, I didn't have anything of any importance to say, but I knew that I wanted to write and be read. All I needed was material.

Courtesy of Terry Trueman

"Recently, I've been finishing work on a re-publication of my narrative poem *Sheehan*, along with a long interview about the poem and all it led to after being published. *Sheehan* is the story of my real-life son's birth and brain injury, and it was used in my best-known novel, *Stuck in Neutral*, with excerpts from the poem opening each chapter from Chapter Five on. *Stuck in Neutral* was my first novel, and my career as a novelist started with a bang, because the book was the winner of a Printz Honor. It was published when I was fifty-two years old.

"*Stuck in Neutral* was based on what I imagine my son Henry Sheehan's life could be like. Because it's a fictional work I didn't feel a great deal of research was necessary. Really this was a work from the heart. The story is about a father-and-son relationship more than it is about the medical dimensions of the condition. Any research I did involved looking into my own heart and spirit to be able to define the full range of what I felt about my son's situation. I had a clear idea of where I wanted the novel to start and a less clear idea of where I wanted it to end and I think the ending of the book reflects this. In fact I had only one rule when I went into the process of finding a publisher. I would not allow Shawn, the protagonist in the novel, to develop communication abilities at the end of the book. That would have been a cheat to everyone who deals with the realities of this kind of situation, and thank God no one ever came close to asking me to do that.

"There is so much to say about being a writer, about the luck or talent or hard work or whatever it is that allows some of us to labor successfully at this craft we love so much. And it's nothing short of miraculous to actually earn a livelihood doing the one thing that we'd happily do for free! I consider my life to be incredibly blessed. I can't think of anything better to say about myself than that."

ⓒ ⓒ ⓒ

Born in Birmingham, Alabama, Terry Trueman grew up in Seattle, Washington. In 1971 he received a B.A. in creative writing from the University of Washington. He received an M.S. in developmental psychology in 1975 and an M.F.A. in creative writing in 1985, both from Eastern Washington University.

Prior to writing novels, Trueman wrote poems, stories, and reviews. He taught in Australia, Honduras, and the United States. He also worked as a therapist at the Spokane Community Health Center in the late 1970s and as a substance abuse intervention specialist for the Spokane Public Schools in the early 1990s. He was a commentator, critic, and film reviewer on Spokane's KPBX-FM radio station from 1992 to 1995.

In his first novel, *Stuck in Neutral*, which was named a Michael L. Printz Award Honor Book, Trueman raises ethical issues about euthanasia through the story of a teenager who suffers from cerebral palsy and his father who, in his compassion, wants to end his son's life. The fact that a fully conscious and intelligent being is hidden within a broken body is a compelling factor in the book's success. Though it generated some controversy upon its publication, *Stuck in Neutral* was included among the New York Public Library's Books for the Teen Age, cited as a *Booklist* Editors' Choice, and named one of *Booklist's* 10 Best First Novels. In the United Kingdom it was a Publishers Association's NASEN Highly Commended title and a Sheffield Commended Book. It also won the Isinglass Teen Book Award and the Kentucky Bluegrass Award. It was nominated for state awards in twelve other states and included in the Great Stories Club, a program organized by ALA, with a grant from Oprah's Angel Network, to provide young adults with the opportunity to discuss books relevant to the challenges in their lives.

"Accepting an 'average' life became unfathomable to me, particularly the normal, average life as represented in my family. I was ready to be anything but normal!"

Courtesy of HarperCollins Publishers

Trueman takes readers inside the mind of a schizophrenic teenager in *Inside Out*, his second novel, which was an IRA Teacher's Choice, a New York Public Library Book for the Teen Age, and a *VOYA* Top Shelf Fiction for Middle School Readers. Caught up in a burglary gone wrong, the teenager must deal with the terror and confusion he feels when he can't distinguish the real from the imagined. This book was nominated for state awards in Florida, Iowa, Kentucky, Maryland, Rhode Island, and Washington.

Cruise Control, a companion book to *Stuck in Neutral*, tells the story of a family torn apart by disability and divorce, and was an IRA Young Adult Choice and an ALA Selected Audiobook for Young Adults. Two of Trueman's books—*Stuck in Neutral* and *Inside Out*—were named ALA Best Books for Young Adults and ALA Quick Picks for Reluctant Young Adult Readers; *Inside Out* appeared among the Top Ten Quick Picks for Reluctant Readers

Available in the U.K. only, *Swallowing the Sun* is set in Honduras, a location with which Trueman is familiar, and is about a teenager's efforts to save his friends and family after his village is destroyed by a mudslide. *No Right Turn* features a car that Trueman, like the main character, loves. It is, in fact, this Corvette that draws the teenage protagonist out of his shell, following the trauma of his father's suicide.

The father of two sons, Henry and Jesse, Terry Trueman lives in Spokane, Washington with his wife, Patti, and drives a 1976 Corvette Stingray.

SELECTED WORKS: *Black Lipstick: The Big Dipper Performances*, 1991; *Sheehan*, 1992; *Stuck in Neutral*, 2000; *What Stories Does My Son Need?: A Guide to Books and Movies That Build Character in Boys*, with Michael Gurian, 2000; *Boys and Girls Learn Differently! A Guide for Teachers and Parents*, with Michael Gurian and Patricia Henley, 2001; *Inside Out*, 2003; *Swallowing the Sun*, 2003; *Cruise Control*, 2004; "Honestly, Truthfully," in *Make Me Over: 11 Original Stories about Transforming Ourselves*, ed. by Marilyn Singer, 2005; "Fear," in *Every Man for Himself: Ten Short Stories about Being a Guy*, ed. by Nancy Mercado, 2005;

"Finishing Blocks and Deadly Hook Shots," in *Sports Shorts: Eight Short Stories*, 2005; "Apple Blossoms," in *Tripping over the Lunch Lady: and Other School Stories*, ed. by Nancy E. Mercado, 2006; *No Right Turn*, 2006; *7 Days at the Hot Corner*, 2007; *Hurricane: A Novel*, 2008.

SUGGESTED READING: *Something About the Author*, vol. 132, 2002.

WEB SITE: www.terrytrueman.com

The youngest of four children, Megan Whalen was born in Fort Sill, Oklahoma, and lived in several states in her youth. As a child she enjoyed reading; Joan Aiken and Roald Dahl were among her favorite authors.

In 1987 she received her B.A. degree with honors in English language and literature from the University of Chicago. While there, she studied Greek history, a required course; as her senior project she chose to study children's literature and write some of her own stories. After graduating, she spent seven years as a children's book buyer, and worked at Harper Court Bookstore in Chicago and Bick's Books in Washington, DC. Having married Mark Bernard Turner, an English professor at the University of Maryland, on June 20, 1987, Turner accompanied her husband on research trips to such places as New Jersey and California. In 1992, while her husband was serving a yearlong Guggenheim fellowship in Del Mar, California, Turner found herself with time on her hands and decided to try her hand at writing again. After her first son was born, Turner's husband often helped with the childcare while Turner worked on her stories.

Her first book, *Instead of Three Wishes*, is a book of seven short stories that involve magic in the lives of ordinary people. Included on the *Booklist* Editors' Choice List and the 1996–1997 Dorothy Canfield Fisher Children's Book Award Master List, this title is suffused with wit and humor and encompasses a variety of fairy tale motifs.

Photo copyright © Dudley Carlson

Megan Whalen Turner

November 21, 1965–

"A tantalizing, suspenseful, exceptionally clever novel."—*The Horn Book*

THE THIEF

MEGAN WHALEN TURNER

Courtesy of Greenwillow Books

Turner's first full-length novel, *The Thief*, won a 1997 Newbery Honor Book citation and was named an ALA Notable Children's Book, an ALA Best Book for Young Adults, a *Horn Book* Fanfare title, and a *Bulletin of the Center for Children's Books* Blue Ribbon title, as well as being named one of the New York Public Library's Books for the Teen Age. A complex fantasy full of wit, action, and suspense and populated with well-drawn, believable characters, *The Thief* is the tale of a convicted robber released from prison by a king's scholar who needs his help on a dangerous quest to find an ancient and powerful gemstone. More than just a fast-moving adventure, Turner's story is also a remarkable tale of redemption, philosophy, and the growth that is attained through knowledge.

This book led to two others in which Turner used her knowledge of Greek history, mythology, and geography to create a rich fictional world for her series. Some of her settings actually resemble modern-day landscapes around the Mediterranean Sea. A worthy sequel to *The Thief* is *The Queen of Attolia*, which won the Parents' Choice Fiction Gold Award and was named a Parents' Guide Honor book. It was also a CCBC Choice, a *Bulletin* Blue Ribbon title, a New York Public Library Book for the Teen Age, and one of *Booklist*'s Top Ten Fantasy Books for Youth in its year of publication. A complicated and multi-layered tale of love and war, *The Queen of Attolia* includes military actions and strategies reminiscent of Greek battles, politics, and intrigue, as well as a developing but complicated romance between the thief, Eugenides, and the Attolian queen. Like its predecessor, this is a fast-paced tale of drama and action.

In *The King of Attolia*, the third book in the series, Eugenides reluctantly becomes king. Surrounded by people who resent him for having "stolen" their queen via marriage and who underestimate his leadership abilities, he is often the target of sabotage. Full of political intrigue and espionage rather than actual fighting, *The King of Attolia* gives the characters added depth and dimension by more fully exploring their relationships, especially the interaction between the king and queen. Much of the story is seen from the interesting perspective of a guard named Costis who despises the king but, as his personal assistant, eventually comes to sympathize with him. *The King of Attolia* was named a *Horn Book* Fanfare title and a *School Library Journal* Best Book; it was also a finalist for the newly created Andre Norton Award for young adult science fiction and fantasy.

Turner's hobbies include cooking and traveling. She and her husband and their three children often relocate due to her husband's research.

SELECTED WORKS: *Instead of Three Wishes: Magical Short Stories*, 1995; *The Thief*, 1996; *The Queen of Attolia*, 2000; "The Baby in the Night Deposit Box," in *Firebirds: An Anthology of Original Fantasy and Science Fiction*, ed. by Sharyn November 2003; *The King of Attolia*, 2006.

SUGGESTED READING: *Something About the Author*, vol. 174, 2007.

WEB SITE: http://home.att.net/~mwturner/

Eleanor Updale

April 13, 1953–

"I live in London, England. I was born here, as were my three children, who are now in their teens. I'm new to writing, although there is evidence that I enjoyed it when I was very young. I have a copy of an old news film from 1959 showing me reading out a story I had written at school. But it is only recently that I found the courage to offer something to a publisher.

"I have done all sorts of jobs, mainly in broadcasting, where I was a producer for the BBC, working in News and Current Affairs through most of my twenties and thirties. I stopped doing that after my second child was born. My husband is also a journalist, and we found it difficult to manage with two of us working strange hours and likely to be sent away at a moment's notice.

"Like many other women, I found the break from paid work a wonderful opportunity to become involved in all sorts of new activities. I was invited to join the Clinical Ethics Committee at the biggest children's hospital in London, and to help a charity called Listening Books, which lends audio books to people who can't handle ordinary print (not just blind people, but the physically disabled, and people with dyslexia, too). I'm also a trustee of the biggest Arts prize in Britain, the Gulbenkian Museum Prize, that offers a cash reward to a British museum or gallery, large or small, which best demonstrates a track record of imagination, innovation and excellence through its work of the previous year. In different ways, all those interests have thrown up ideas and issues that have found their way into my books. Sitting on the Clinical Ethics Committee at Great Ormond Street Hospital in London, for example, I found lots of ideas for the character of Dr. Farcett, the doctor who takes care of Montmorency after his accident in the first book.

"While I was writing the first Montmorency book, a friend asked me to help her with some historical research. She was writing about Robert Hooke, a 17th century scientist whose work

Courtesy of Scholastic, Inc.

I had focused on years ago, when I was an undergraduate at Oxford University. I loved being back in the academic world, and so when it was suggested that I should enroll for a PhD course, I took the chance. I love dealing with old manuscripts, even when they take days to decipher.

"But just as I committed myself to the doctorate, a publisher offered to publish *Montmorency* and wanted more books to follow. I didn't want to give up writing *or* studying, and so for the past few years I have been doing two jobs. In some ways, they are complementary. Both require a lot of research (the Montmorency books are historical novels), and just as it can be fun to put the meticulous footnoting aside and dive into my invented world, the formal history keeps me on my toes when I'm writing fiction. I suppose if I had planned things properly, I wouldn't have chosen two different periods (my PhD is set in the late 17th and early 18th centuries, Montmorency in the late 19th and early 20th), but I am very lucky to have access to some of the greatest libraries and archives in the world.

"The basic idea for the Montmorency books grew out of stories I made up for my children when they were very young. In those days, the plots were more straightforward, and even more grounded in the sewers than the finished books; but Montmorency, who in some ways I think of as my fourth child, is fundamentally the same man born in my children's bedroom all those years ago.

"I write at all sorts of funny times, when I can get a break from my other commitments. Quite often I work through the night, when the phones don't ring, and the family is asleep. Because of the success of the books, I find myself traveling more and more to meet readers in schools, libraries and at festivals in Britain and abroad. I've also been appointed to some arts organizations, including the Prince of Wales Arts and Kids Foundation, of which I am now a patron. This foundation's aim is to give every child in Britain first-hand experience of the arts.

"So life is busy, and very different from what I ever expected it to be. My first book was published when I was fifty, and it's funny to be the new girl on the block at such an advanced age. One review even described me as a 'new young talent'. What a joy!"

ෆ ෆ ෆ

Eleanor Updale grew up in the Camberwell section of South London. When she left home to study history at St. Anne's College at the University of Oxford, she had hardly ever been outside London. Following her graduation, she worked for the British Broadcasting Corporation (BBC) on both radio and television programs.

Updale originally conceived the Montmorency tales— about a robber who sneaks around Victorian London through its foul-smelling sewers—as bedtime stories for her children. The children's fascination with the stories prompted Updale to research how the sewers worked and she gathered a great many notes, which were, unfortunately, misplaced when she and her family moved to a new home. When she finally decided to write the stories as books, she had to start over again to recreate the background.

Updale does extensive research, and not just the formal kind in libraries. Her search for authenticity has taken her, literally, down into the London sewers so she can see what they look like, right down to the brickwork laid centuries ago. Such trips are only allowed once a year with official guides who provide protective clothing. Updale has found that the filth, the odors and the inconvenience are well worth the wealth of information she brings back from these excursions and they certainly add to the authenticity of her 19th century settings.

Although Updale's novels contain no adolescent characters, the transitions that Montmorency goes through in his growing sense of himself do resemble those of many teen protagonists in

"The basic idea for the Montmorency books grew out of stories I made up for my children when they were very young. In those days, the plots were more straightforward, and even more grounded in the sewers than the finished books. . . ."

young adult novels. Montmorency's consciously split personality makes him a compelling character. Starting out as a nameless convict, identified only by a number and seemingly injured beyond repair, he becomes a medical guinea pig for the ambitious Dr. Farcett, who puts his broken body back together. Hearing about London's new sewer system during a medical meeting while he is on exhibit by the doctor, the prisoner formulates a plan to turn himself into a gentleman. After serving his time, and through the aid of his alter ego, Scarper, a seedy thief who uses

Courtesy Orchard Books, Scholastic

the sewer system for escape routes after his robberies, the newly named Montmorency slowly establishes himself as an aristocrat. He begins divorcing himself from the unseemly Scarper side of his character and struggles to transform emotionally and ethically into a real gentleman. With excellent characterization and a strongly realized sense of place, Updale brings Montmorency to life as his adventures continue in later volumes.

Montmorency: Thief, Liar, Gentleman? received a Nestlé Smarties Prize Silver award in the Ages 9–11 category when it was first published in Great Britain, and the British Children's Laureate, Michael Morpurgo, chose it as one of his all-time top ten books to get children interested in reading. It also won the Blue Peter Prize for "The book I couldn't put down," awarded by the British BBC's flagship children's television program. BBC Radio 7 serialized an abridged version of *Montmorency* on the Big Toe Radio Show. In America *Montmorency* was unanimously voted an ALA Best Book for Young Adults and was a *School Library Journal* Best Book of the Year, and a 2006 NPR Recommended Summer Read.

The first sequel, *Montmorency on the Rocks: Doctor, Aristocrat, Murderer?*, continues the story several years later; Montmorency is recovering from a drug addiction he picked up during his days as a spy and trying to solve two mysteries: the inexplicable deaths of babies in a remote area of Scotland and bomb explosions in London. This title was also named an ALA Best Book for Young Adults as well as an IRA/CBC 2006 Outstanding International Book. One of the settings in the book, the Chinese Pagoda in Kew

Gardens was reopened after the book was published, and Updale was invited to the ceremony with the Chinese Ambassador. In *Montmorency and the Assassins* the intrepid former thief makes his first visit to the United States, and in Updale's latest book, *Montmorency's Revenge*, the now middle-aged Montmorency's criminal alter ego has all but disappeared. A cliffhanger ending promises another book in store.

Eleanor Updale lives with her husband, James Naughtie, and their children—Andrew, Catherine and Flora—in London. She was awarded her Ph.D. in 2007, at the Centre for Editing Lives and Letters, Queen Mary, University of London.

SELECTED WORKS: *Montmorency: Thief, Liar, Gentleman?*, 2004; *Montmorency on the Rocks: Doctor, Aristocrat, Murderer?*, 2004; *Montmorency and the Assassins: Master, Criminal, Spy?*, 2006; *Montmorency's Revenge: Madman, Actor, Arsonist?*, 2007; *Saved*, 2008.

WEB SITE: www.eleanorupdale.com

Cornelius Van Wright and Ying-Hwa Hu

Ying-Hwa Hu writes: "Ever since I can remember, art came naturally to me. My parents were very supportive of what I enjoyed doing, and I decided early on to become an artist. Of course life does not always go in a straight line from point A to point B. I studied art in Taiwan and worked in advertising for a while before coming to the States. I became a teacher after graduating from St. Cloud University in Minnesota with a degree in art education, not trusting if I can make a living being a fine artist. I taught in the New York City public school system for a few years before I met my husband, an aspiring artist dormant in a corporate world and waiting to be free. Our dream to do art jelled us together and that was the beginning of our journey."

Cornelius Van Wright writes: "My dad was a carpenter (I still love working with wood) and my mom loved to doodle small pictures and make patterns with crayons. My older brother drew neat superheroes. So I copied them all. I was prone to get sick a lot as a child and didn't have to go to gym. I was given extra periods of art instead and enjoyed it. My middle school art teacher really encouraged me and sometimes gave me beautiful gifts of art materials (one was from France. I still have it!). I went to a specialized art high school and continued on to graduate from the School of Visual Arts College. I worked in advertising for a number of years, but pursued illustration on my lunch hours and weekends. Then I met Ying-Hwa. In the meantime, my job left New York City. Together we tapped into those lunch and weekend jobs and began our career in illustration work.

"We get a lot of assignments covering many different cultures in the world today. This often means we have a lot of homework to do. Our mission is to break up stereotypes, yet still try to keep all accuracy. What are typical stoves like in mainland China? How do you experience a Sabbath dinner? What would be worn at a Korean child's first birthday? Our own children are often our life models (though not without grumbling sometimes). And the families of their friends are most helpful to us. The parents we meet in the schoolyards seldom refuse to tell us about their cultures and the unique traits that are part of their lives. We love exploring facts about different parts of the world and learning about the history behind the people. This helps us to broaden our vision as artists as well. There is inside every artist the desire to explore the next phase of his/her creativity. We are right now in the transition of discovering more images from our own imaginations. This is very different from our familiar territory. It's like tapping into a new well, exciting but sort of scary because we don't know where it's going. It's like answering destiny's call when we first began our journey."

Photo by En-Szu Hu-Van Wright

Cઠ Cઠ Cઠ

Cornelius Van Wright 1960–

Ying-Hwa Hu (ing-hwa-hoo)

Ying-Hwa Hu and Cornelius Van Wright have been working together on children's book illustration since their marriage in 1988. Ying-Hwa grew up in Taiwan, where she took private art lessons during her last year of high school. She studied advertising and interior design in college and came to the United States to further her education and become an art teacher. Cornelius Van Wright was born and raised in New York City. He was drawn to illustrating books for children because of the free range of possibilities the field offered him. While working for an advertising company he would visit publishing houses on his lunch hour to show samples of his work. In this way he started illustrating books during evenings, weekends, and vacation time. Ying-Hwa's first job in book illustration came about from a chance encounter her husband had at a publishing house that was looking for an artist to do interior art for the Sweet Valley Kids series.

Once the two artists combined their talents, they found they made an award-winning combination. In an interview with Cynthia Leitich Smith, the author of one of their collaborations, the pair explained that they came from very different backgrounds. Cornelius was trained as a commercial artist, while Ying-Hwa came from a fine art education—two perspectives that can be far apart. They decided to learn from each other—he tried to be less controlling in his work and have more freedom and flow, while she started to pull back and paint in a more controlled way. Cornelius had been using oils, but found that Ying-Hwa's watercolors allowed more freedom of expression. Today they work on different aspects of each assignment. He may start off with the layouts and beginning sketches. Then they will discuss what works and what needs to be changed, and she will add some fine-tuning of characterization and proportion. Depending on their individual strengths, one of them may do more or less on a particular book, but they always discuss each project and consult each other about the work.

"Our dream to do art jelled us together and that was the beginning of our journey."

Coming from distinctly different cultures themselves, Van Wright and Hu have a special interest in illustrating books from a variety of ethnic backgrounds. The expressiveness and depth of their art creates a subtle message that although people come from many backgrounds, they all have the same joys and fears, longings and triumphs that stem from their common humanity.

Collaborations of Van Wright and Hu include books about historical figures and events as well as stories about contemporary children. *Zora Hurston and the Chinaberry Tree*, written by William Miller, depicts an episode in the early years of the acclaimed African American writer. The strong watercolor illustrations convey the changing emotions in Hurston's face as well as important details of the setting and time period. This title was a *Reading Rainbow* selection, an American Booksellers Pick of the Lists, and a CCBC Choice selection. That success was followed by a contemporary story of a Chinese-American boy, *Sam and the Lucky Money*, in which the illustrators captured evocative details of Chinatown along with the universal message of charity that develops through Sam's growing understanding. This book was also named an ABA Pick of the Lists and a CCBC Choice, as well as an IRA Notable Book for a Global Society and a Children's Book of the Year by the Bank Street College of Education. Bank Street College also honored *The Legend of Freedom Hill*, a story from the 1850s about two friends who are both "outsiders," one Jewish and one African American. With the combination of a strong text by Linda Jacobs Altman and vibrant illustrations by Van Wright and Hu, *The Legend of Freedom Hill* won a *Storytelling World* award and a Notable citation from the Association of Jewish Libraries.

For *Jingle Dancer*, their art complements Cynthia Leitich Smith's powerful story about the blending of old and new traditions in a Native American community. Every detail of costume and furniture (as well as the affection between generations) is rendered through the carefully researched illustrations. Delving further into the cultures of American Indians, the couple illustrated *We Are the Many*, a collection of biographical sketches of notable Native Americans from Squanto to Sherman Alexie, written by Doreen Rappaport. Both of these books were named Notable Social Studies Trade Books, reflecting the careful research and attention to historic and cultural detail in their art. *Zora Hurston and the Chinaberry Tree, Jewels, Mei-Mei Loves the Morning,* and *The Legend of Freedom Hill* have received this honor as well.

> "We get a lot of assignments covering many different cultures in the world today. This often means we have a lot of homework to do. Our mission is to break up stereotypes, yet still try to keep all accuracy."

For another book about an historical figure—*Coming Home: A Story of Josh Gibson, Baseball's Greatest Home Run Hitter*, by Nanette Mellage—Van Wright and Hu's flowing watercolor illustrations capture the excitement of the sport, both for fans and for players, with Gibson's astounding achievements reflected on each page. This book won a Carter G. Woodson Book Award for its evocative portrayal of an African American hero. Other prominent African Americans that the couple has depicted in books include Martin Luther King, Jr. and York, the only black man in the Lewis and Clark expedition. The artists have also created powerful images for books about Jewish culture in *In the Promised Land* and the importance of understanding between cultures in *Snow in Jerusalem*, the story of a Jewish boy and a Muslim boy who both are attached to the same stray cat.

Cornelius Van Wright and Ying-Hwa Hu live in New York City with their daughter and son.

SELECTED WORKS ILLUSTRATED BY CORNELIUS VAN WRIGHT AND YING-HWA HU: *Make a Joyful Sound: Poems for Children by African-American Poets*, ed. by Deborah Slier, 1994; *Zora Hurston and the Chinaberry Tree*, by William Miller, 1994; *Sam and The Lucky Money*, by Karen Chinn, 1995; *Daughter's Day Blues*, by

Linda Pegram, 1996; *Vanished!: The Mysterious Disappearance of Amelia Earhart*, by Monica Kulling, 1996; *An Angel Just Like Me*, by Mary Hoffman, 1997; *Best Older Sister*, by Sook Nyul Choi, 1997; *Building Friends*, by Ronald Kidd, 1997; *A House by the River*, by William Miller, 1997; *Jewels*, by Belinda Rochelle, 1998; *The Case of the Shrunken Allowance*, by Joanne Rocklin, 1999; *Mei-Mei Loves the Morning*, by Margaret Holloway Tsubakiyama, 1999; *George Washington: Our First President*, by Garnet Jackson, 2000; *Jingle Dancer*, by Cynthia Leitich Smith, 2000; *Let's Read about Martin Luther King, Jr.*, by Courtney Baker, 2001; *Snow in Jerusalem*, by Deborah De Costa, 2001; *Coming Home: A Story of Josh Gibson, Baseball's Greatest Home Run Hitter*, by Nanette Mellage, 2001; *We Are the Many: A Picture Book of American Indians*, by Doreen Rappaport, 2002; *Alicia's Happy Day*, by Meg Starr, 2002; *The Legend of Freedom Hill*, by Linda Jacobs Altman, 2003; *Willy Covan Loved to Dance*, by Sherry Shahan, 2004; *Jumping the Broom*, by Sonia Black, 2004; *In the Promised Land: Lives of Jewish Americans*, by Doreen Rappaport, 2005; *I Told You I Can Play*, by Brian Jordan, 2006; *American Slave, American Hero: York of the Lewis and Clark Expedition*, by Laurence Pringle, 2006; *Princess Grace*, by Mary Hoffman, 2008.

Courtesy of Lee & Low Books

SELECTED WORKS ILLUSTRATED BY CORNELIUS VAN WRIGHT: *If You Were an Ant*, by S. J. Calder, 1989; *Poems to Share*, by Leroy F. Jackson, 1990; *What I Want to Be*, by P. Mignon Hinds, 1995; *My Best Friend*, by P. Mignon Hinds, 1996; *Elizabeth's Song*, by Michael Wenberg, 2003.

SUGGESTED READING: *Something About the Author*, vol. 173, 2007. Online—Interview with Cynthia Leitich Smith (December 2001), at www.cynthialeitichsmith.com/lit_resources/authors/interviews/Hu_VanWright.html

DigiQuick Portrait Studio

Vivian Vande Velde

Vivian Vande Velde

June 18, 1951–

"**I** can't remember a time before I wanted to be an author. As someone who loved stories, I enjoyed experiencing them so much that I also wanted to create them. When I say I loved stories, that means *all* kinds of stories, not just the wonderful books in libraries, but also comic books, TV, movies, stories my friends and I would make up (which generally made little—if any—sense), and real stories people told about places they'd been and things they'd done.

"Still, my favorite stories have always been those *not* set here and now—those with historical settings or taking place in a different land or even on a different planet, and my absolute favorites are fantasies. I always loved the idea of wishes coming true, of magical creatures, and of people with special powers. Ghosts, curses, witches: that's my idea of fun, despite the fact that I have to admit I don't actually believe in them.

"Growing up, I loved fairy tales, both the ones I read and the Disney movies. At the same time, I also wondered why the princesses were always perfect: girls with perfect hair, girls who were never unsure of themselves, girls who never didn't know what to say or do. Why weren't any of them shy and self-conscious, like me? Weren't you allowed to be a princess if you were near-sighted and needed glasses? And what about the guys? Were there no clumsy princes? Were they never afraid? I wanted fairy tales about people who were more like me and the people I knew.

"Despite the fact that many of my stories are about vampires, werewolves, and trolls, many of them got their start from some tiny bit of reality. So, *Now You See It . . .* is about a girl who wears glasses. Like I do. (Of course, *I* never found a pair of glasses that let me see tiny blue creatures and doorways into others worlds and times.) *Smart Dog* is about a dog smart enough to talk because I had a dog who was so smart I was convinced she could understand everything I said and wished that she could answer back. *Troll Teacher* came about because, at the end of summer vacation, I used to worry about what the next year's teacher would be like.

"Some of my books start from the setting—the time and place—of a story. My mother grew up in France and lived there during World War II. She never was sent to live in the country and she never met a ghost, but the background for *A Coming Evil* comes from her. *There's a Dead Person Following My Sister Around* combines our yard (which includes a ditch that was part of the old Erie Canal) and a friend's old house (in which the family discovered a hidden room that may have been part of the Underground Railroad, the system of safe houses for slaves escaping from the pre–Civil War South). The idea for *Ghost of a Hanged Man* came from hearing a New Orleans tour guide talk about the city's above-ground crypts, and how dead bodies could not be buried below ground. Because of the danger of flooding, the bodies were too likely to rise up to the surface.

"So although it's hard to tell exactly where story ideas come from, many of my books come from something real, followed by asking myself, 'What if?' and then going off in a totally different direction.

"Now about that name of mine: Yes, Vivian Vande Velde is my real name. 'Vivian' is what my parents named me; 'Vande Velde' (two words, but one name) is my husband's last name. In Dutch, 'van' means 'from,' 'de' means 'the,' and 'velde' means 'plains.' 'Vivian,' by the way, means 'lively one.' So all in all that makes me The Lively One from the Plains. Uh-huh. Just don't call me that first thing in the morning."

CR   CR   CR

"Despite the fact that many of my stories are about vampires, werewolves, and trolls, many of them got their start from some tiny bit of reality."

Born in New York City, Vivian Vande Velde moved upstate with her parents, Pasquale and Marcelle Brucata, while she was still young. She has spent most of her life in Rochester, New York. Always a voracious reader, in eighth grade she found T. H. White's *The Once and Future King* and determined that *that* was the kind of story she wanted to write. After high school, she attended the State University of New York at Brockport for a year, 1969–1970, taking every literature course that interested her and then went to the Rochester Business Institute for secretarial training. Vivian married Jim Vande Velde, a computer analyst, in 1974. The birth of her daughter, Elizabeth, gave her a good reason to give up secretarial work—which she hated— and a chance to look for work she could do at home. Enrolling in a writing class, she began working on the story that would eventually become *A Hidden Magic*, enjoying the chance to make her princess plain, her prince vain, and the 'happily ever after' totally unexpected. It took two years to finish the book, and she sent it to 33 publishers before it was accepted. Illustrated by Trina Schart Hyman, *A Hidden Magic* hit just the right note with reviewers, who approved of its charming reversal of fairy tale patterns and its light-hearted humor. It was an American Booksellers Pick of the Lists and was named a Child Study Association Book of the Year, a NCTE Notable Trade Book in the Language Arts and one of the New York Public Library's 100 Titles for Reading and Sharing.

Courtesy of Harcourt Children's Books, Houghton Mifflin Harcourt.

In *A Well-Timed Enchantment*, the heroine goes back in time to balance the trouble she has caused by dropping a digital watch into a wishing well. A Junior Book Guild Selection, this book too became popular with reviewers and readers alike, and Vivian Vande Velde has been steadily producing new titles ever since. Her work mixes fantasy, Westerns, science fiction, and the occult with mystery, humor and continual surprises. She writes for several different age groups. In *User Unfriendly*, a group of young people is trapped in a frightening landscape created in a pirated computer game. *Dragon's Bait*, an ALA Quick Pick for Reluctant Young Adult Readers, a Junior Library Guild Selection, and a New York Public Library Book for the Teen Age, involves a falsely accused heroine who is condemned to death by dragon—and then rescued by the dragon.

Vande Velde's vampire novel, *Companions of the Night*, raises multi-layered questions about trust and love, and was an ALA Best Book for Young Adults, as well as an ALA Quick Pick for Reluctant Young Adult Readers. Two collections of her short stories were selected as ALA Quick Picks for Reluctant Young Readers: *Tales from the Brothers Grimm and the Sisters Weird* was also an ALA Best Book for Young Adults, and *Curses, Inc.* was one of New York Public Library's Books for the Teen Age.

Vande Velde's shivery *Ghost of a Hanged Man* blends mystery and a Western theme in a tale of revenge and survival in the 1870s, while the engaging *Never Trust a Dead Man*, which received the Edgar Allan Poe Award for best young adult mystery, is set in medieval times. *Heir Apparent*'s heroine, Gianinne, is caught in a total immersion virtual reality game damaged by anti-fantasy fanatics and must win a throne in order to return unscathed to her own time. Winner of the Anne Spencer Lindbergh Prize in Children's Literature, *Heir Apparent* underscores the dangers of censorship, especially censorship of the author's favorite genre—fantasy.

Ever versatile, Vande Velde continues to write for different age groups, mix humor with more serious themes and delve into the questions that interest her. In *Three Good Deeds*, written for third or fourth graders, a mischievous boy is turned into a goose until he can do the requisite good deeds, and he discovers that it is hard to know how to really help others. *Now You See It*, for slightly older readers, involves magical sunglasses that allow the heroine to see and enter another world. *The Book of Mordred*, set in Arthurian times, takes a more serious, thoughtful tone for older readers, and *Witch Dreams* returns to a fast-moving mystery-fantasy in which the heroine can literally enter the dreams of other characters.

Of her writing habits, Vivian Vande Velde says she writes every day if possible, and she recommends the same to new writers on her friendly web site. She belongs to two writing groups in Rochester and appreciates their ongoing support. She continues to be a voracious reader, enjoying fantasy and science fiction books the most.

SELECTED WORKS: *Once Upon a Test: Three Light Tales of Love*, illus. by Diane Dawson Hearn, 1984; *A Hidden Magic*, illus. by Trina Schart Hyman, 1985; *A Well-Timed Enchantment*, 1990; *User Unfriendly*, 1991; *Dragon's Bait*, 1992; *Tales from the Brothers Grimm and the Sisters Weird*, 1995; *Companions of the Night*, 1995; *Curses, Inc.*, 1997; *The Conjurer Princess*, 1997; *The Changeling Prince*, 1998; *Ghost of a Hanged Man*, 1998; *Smart Dog*, 1998; *A Coming Evil*, 1998; *Never Trust a Dead Man*, 1999; *There's a Dead Person Following My Sister Around*, 1999; *Troll Teacher*, illus. by Mary Jane Auch, 2000; *The Rumplestiltskin Problem*, 2000; *Magic Can Be Murder*, 2000; *Alison, Who Went Away*, 2001; *Being Dead*, 2001; *Heir Apparent*, 2002; *Witch's Wishes*, 2003; *The Book of Mordred*, 2005; *Now You See It*, 2005; *Three Good Deeds*, 2005; *Witch Dreams*, 2005; *All Hallow's Eve: 13 Stories*, 2006; *Remembering Raquel*, 2007; *Stolen*, 2008.

SUGGESTED READING: *Authors and Artists for Young Adults*, vol. 32, 2000; Zipes, Jack, ed., *Oxford Companion to Fairy Tales*, 2000; Reginald, Robert, *Science Fiction and Fantasy Literature, 1975–1991*,

1992. Periodicals—Goodson, Lori Atkins, "Finish that Chapter, Then Lights Out: A Reader Becomes a Writer, A Visit with Vivian Vande Velde," *Alan Review*, Fall 2004. Online—*Contemporary Authors Online*, 2003; Florence, Debbi Michiko, "Interview with Vivian Vande Velde," at www.debbimichikoflorence.com.

WEB SITE: www.vivianvandevelde.com

Photo by Roger Bunch

Patrice Vecchione

July 28, 1957–

"Before I could really talk, I was reciting poems, or that's how it seems in memory. From the time I was brand new, my mother read poetry to me. Her voice was magic. We loved A. A. Milne: 'I met a man as I went walking/We got talking, man and I. . . .' and Robert Louis Stevenson: 'I have a little shadow that goes in and out with me/ And what can be the use of him is more than I can see. . . .' I knew that shadow!

"Poetry taught me a lot about the world. We lived in a Manhattan apartment. My experiences were those of a city kid—subways and snow-turned-to-slush, museums and the ballet. I knew how night's darkness crept over the buildings. When I heard poems, my life got bigger. I traveled to distant places. I saw the changing of the guard at Buckingham Palace. I became the captain of a sailing ship. I had friends who were foxes.

"But it wasn't only the world at a distance that poetry gave me a window into; my very own inside world came into focus too. Poetry is a language itself. In a poem, contradictory things can sit side by side and share a sandwich. A poem shines light on small things that sometimes seem insignificant. Poems know tenderness as a good friend. They're the truth of not one right answer but many. When mad or lonely, I had poetry. It could make me brave. When lightning struck and thunder rumbled, I said poems in a small, jittery voice inside my head. This calmed me enough to crawl out from under the bed.

"The first book I bought with my own money was an anthology of poetry, *A Puffin Quartet of Poets*. It cost 60 cents. That's where I met Eleanor Farjeon. She showed me the natural world for the first time: 'I saw a shiver/ Pass over the river/ As the tide turned in its sleep,' wrote Farjeon. Oh, I thought, the tide is so very like us.

"Not until later did poetry wholly become my own. In high school, I began writing. On the outside, my life might have looked easy, but it didn't feel that way. Rather, happiness was a shifty, down-sliding thing. Life at home was difficult. My English teacher said, 'Write!' So I'd find hidden corners on campus where I could be alone and, with a pad of paper smaller than my palm and an equally small and very chewed-up pencil, I wrote myself into being. Then the world held still, if only briefly. When writing I couldn't be wrong or not smart enough.

"By this time, my family had moved to California. The local bookstore had a waterbed in the middle of it! There I discovered *Reflections on the Gift of a Watermelon Pickle*, an anthology of poetry that led me to want to make anthologies myself. I couldn't afford to buy it right away so—dare I admit this?—I hid it in the Economics section behind what looked like some very boring books. Each time I returned, my book was still hidden behind them. Its poems held my own crazy, whirligig, sometimes suffocating self. There I found my first Ferlinghetti: 'Fortune has its cookies to give out.' He wrote about a New York I knew. And even though we lived in California by then, I could still have that home, not just in memory but in poetry. I tasted William Carlos Williams' plums: 'so sweet and so cold.' Swift things were never swifter than in Elizabeth Coatsworth's poetry. The poems were like friends, friends whose hair color and favorite foods I would never know, but who knew me better than I knew myself. They seemed to listen as much as they spoke. Eventually, having earned enough from housecleaning and babysitting, I bought the book and brought it home.

"Now I make anthologies of poetry for children and teens. I write nonfiction and am the author of *Writing and the Spiritual Life: Finding Your Voice Within*. A book of my poems, *Territory of Wind*, was published a few years ago, and a new one will be coming out shortly. Who knew that way back then, my mother and those childhood poems were sprinkling me with fairy dust, sending me on my way! My wish is that young people will open my books and be inspired to think about the world in new ways, greet themselves on the pages, be introduced to writers who will help them find the answers to their very own necessary questions, the ones pressing inside."

> *"The poems were like friends, friends whose hair color and favorite foods I would never know, but who knew me better than I knew myself."*

CȜ CȜ CȜ

The daughter of Nicholas and Peggy Vecchione, Patrice Vecchione lived in Queens, New York, as a young child before moving to Manhattan. Her mother was a secretary who didn't really enjoy her job, and Patrice decided early on that she would choose a career that she could love. Her father, with a Ph.D. in psychology, worked at writing I.Q. tests in New York City, then later served as a counselor at the University of Chicago. Still later, he became a proctor at the University of California at Santa Cruz, the position he liked best. Patrice has one sister, Elizabeth, who is now a mother with two sons.

When she was eight, Vecchione and her family moved to Chicago, and when she was eleven, they settled in Santa Cruz, California, where she graduated from high school in 1975. While attending Cabrillo Junior College, she became inspired by her experiences in an early childhood education program to teach poetry to children, so she took a break from college to focus on that. During this transitional period, she also tried a variety of jobs, becoming a clown, a baker, and then a midwife's assistant. But at her father's prodding, she eventually went back to college. This time she attended Antioch University in San Francisco and in 1981 received a B.A. with a double major in creative writing and education.

For over 25 years Vecchione has taught poetry and creative writing to children and adults through her program "The Heart of the Word: Poetry and the Imagination." An eloquent speaker on the writing process and on writing as a spiritual practice, she has presented her work throughout the United States. She has also been a radio host for a children's program and a poetry show on Santa Cruz's KUSP, the National Public Radio affiliate for the Central Coast. Her poems have appeared in such magazines as *Quarry West* and *Puerto Del Sol* as well as anthologies such as *Women of the 14th Moon* and *Lovers*.

Her poetry anthologies have received numerous accolades. *The Body Eclectic* was a *Booklist* Editors' Choice and appeared on the Children's Literature Choice List. Celebrating the human body, it features more than 70 poems by such diverse writers as Walt Whitman, William Shakespeare, Lord Byron, Thomas Hardy, Virginia Woolf, Gary Soto, Shel Silverstein, Alice Walker, Pablo Neruda, Diane Ackerman, May Swenson, and Sherman Alexie.

Two of Vecchione's titles, *Truth and Lies* and *Revenge and Forgiveness*, were among *School Library Journal's* Best Books of the Year. *Truth and Lies* is an anthology of poems that seek to explore the difficulties of finding and adhering to the truth, and *Revenge and Forgiveness* was inspired by the events of September 11, 2001, asking readers to explore hard questions about how people deal with anger and grief. *Whisper and Shout* encourages students to memorize poetry, offering a collection of over 50 poems in a wide range of styles and moods. *Faith and Doubt* includes one of Vecchione's own poems as well as her own artwork in acrylic and collage on the cover.

Vecchione is grateful to have been recognized by the community in which she lives, writes, and teaches. In 1999 she was named Pacific Grove Artist of the Year; in 2000 she received the Gail Rich Award, a Santa Cruz award recognizing artistic contributions to the community. She lives in Monterey, California, with her husband, Michael Stark, a cabinetmaker, and two cats, Sophie and Nora.

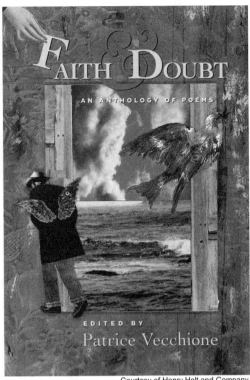

Courtesy of Henry Holt and Company

SELECTED WORKS FOR YOUNG READERS: *Truth and Lies: An Anthology of Poems*, as ed., 2001; *Whisper and Shout: Poems to Memorize*, as ed., 2002; *The Body Eclectic: An Anthology of Poems*, as ed., 2002; *Revenge and Forgiveness: An Anthology of Poems*, as ed., 2004; *Faith and Doubt: An Anthology of Poems*, as ed., 2007.

SELECTED WORKS FOR ADULTS: *Lighthouse Point: An Anthology of Santa Cruz Writing*, ed. with Steve Wiesinger, 1987; *In Celebration of the Muse: Writings by Santa Cruz Women*, ed. with Amber Coverdale Sumrall, 1987; *Catholic Girls: Stories, Poems, and Memoirs by Louise Erdrich, Mary Gordon, Audre Lorde, Mary McCarthy, Francine Prose, and 47 Others*, ed. with Amber Coverdale Sumrall, 1992; *Bless Me, Father: Stories of Catholic Childhood*, ed. with Amber Coverdale Sumrall, 1994; *Storming Heaven's Gate: An Anthology of Spiritual Writings by Woman*, ed. with Amber Coverdale Sumrall, 1997; *Territory of Wind*, 1998; *Writing and the Spiritual Life: Finding Your Voice by Looking Within*, 2001.

WEB SITE: www.patricevecchione.com

Photo by Kathleen Clark Moses

Neil Waldman

October 22, 1947–

"My earliest memories are of finger painting.

"I remember opening the brightly colored bottles for the first time, smelling their rich fragrance wafting into the air . . . and I remember the exquisite squishiness, rubbing finger paints onto my hands and face, and squeezing them between my fingers.

"I've included one of those memories in my memoir, *Out of the Shadows: An Artist's Journey*, and I wanted to share it here. It takes place early one morning in our apartment in the Bronx. I'd just returned from a trip to the live chicken market, and I was alone and soaking . . .

" . . . the next thing I knew, I was slipping through the door, creeping into the apartment. I pulled off my soggy shoes, hung my coat in the hall closet, and tiptoed into the kitchen. Lifting a set of finger paints, a tray of cupcake tins, and a stack of paper from the art shelf, I sat at the table and poured paint into the tins, spreading the paper across the tabletop.

"Within seconds, my hands were wet with color. First, I smeared the page with crimson. Then, I pushed a streak of orange across the red. Next came yellow, brown, and then purple. My fingers bolted back and forth across fiery oceans of color. Dipping my left hand into the darkest pan, I scraped it across the page. Black paint sprayed from my fingertips, splattering against the kitchen wall.

"'We'll have none of that!' My mother's voice sounded from behind me . . . and I froze.

"Squeezing a rag in the sink, she quickly wiped the wall clean. Then it was my turn. She led me back to the sink and soaped my face, my neck, my wrists, and my fingers, and rinsed them in warm water. Then she patted me dry and led me down the hall. Reaching into a closet, she pulled out one of her old white shirts.

"'This will be yours from now on,' she said.

"Slipping the huge garment over my shoulders, she began buttoning it down. And as she knelt there before me, I glanced into the mirror and grimaced. My hands, legs, and feet had disappeared beneath sleeves and waist that reached to the floor. Now she began rolling up the sleeves . . . until my fingers reappeared.

"'There,' she said, turning toward the mirror. 'That looks perfect. You see, Neilly, real artists have special pieces of clothing that they wear to protect their shirts and pants from the paint. They're called *smocks*. From now on, this will be *your* smock.'

"Taking my hand, she led me back into the kitchen and sat me down on a chair. Carefully covering a corner of the floor with unfolded newspapers and taping sheets of newspaper to the walls above them, she placed a little table in the corner.

"'And real artists,' she continued, 'have special places where they paint. They're called *studios*. From now on, this is going to be *your* studio. Now you won't have to worry about messing the walls, the floor, or yourself, and you can paint to your heart's delight.'

"She placed a box of crayons and a coloring book on the table, along with a stack of oak tag, three cupcake tins, and a set of finger paints.

"*"Can I keep painting right now?"*

"'Of course you can,' she answered. 'You can paint here whenever you like. . . .'

"It was decades later that it began to dawn on me that my mother had been a master teacher. Not only did she suggest to me that I was in fact, an artist, but she later began plastering the walls, doors, and windows of our apartment with her children's masterpieces. It is no coincidence that, as adults, three of her four children grew up to become artists."

೦಺ ೦಺ ೦಺

Neil Waldman spent his childhood in the Bronx borough of New York City. His family, recently emigrated from Russia, nurtured his early interest in art. Excursions with his grandfather to the Metropolitan Museum of Art and the Bronx Zoo created a lasting influence that can be seen in his later books. He received a bachelor's degree in fine arts from the Rochester Institute of Technology in 1969 and a master's degree from the same school in 1970. A freelance painter since 1971, Waldman has had paintings and prints included in prestigious collections around the world, in capitol buildings as well as museums and major corporations. He has also designed postage stamps for thirteen nations. Since 1994 he has taught in the Westchester Art Workshop of the State University of New York.

> *"It was decades later that it began to dawn on me that my mother had been a master teacher. Not only did she suggest to me that I was in fact, an artist, but she later began plastering the walls, doors, and windows of our apartment with her children's masterpieces."*

Beginning his career in publishing as a designer and illustrator of book jackets, Waldman created cover designs for more than 200 books during the 1970s and 1980s. His work appeared on a number of well-known and well-loved novels, including Gary Paulsen's *Dogsong* and *Hatchet*. Those two books and five others that feature his cover art have been designated Newbery Honor Books. Later in his career he contributed interior illustrations and picture-book art for both fiction and nonfiction; eventually he started to write as well as illustrate books for young readers.

Travel and the natural world have played a major role in Waldman's continuing education. Numerous trips to wilderness areas of the United States are apparent in his illustrated edition of Katharine Lee Bates's well-known poem *America the Beautiful*. The rich acrylic paintings in that volume depict the "purple mountain's majesty" of the Grand Tetons, the "fruited plains" of California's Napa Valley, and the natural beauty of other American sites that the artist had visited. In another book that celebrates the natural world, Kathi Appelt's *Bayou Lullaby*, Waldman's deep colored images of animals and plants of the swamp are set against the velvety dark background of the night. *Bayou Lullaby* was named a *School Library Journal* Best Book in 1995.

Many of Waldman's books reflect his Jewish heritage with themes from observing the Sabbath and the holiday traditions of Hanukkah and Passover to creation stories from Genesis and the 3,000 year history of Jerusalum (*The Golden City*). His book *Masada* was a *Smithsonian* Notable Book. A collection of Howard Schwartz's stories of the ancient city, *Jerusalem of Gold*, was illustrated by Waldman and won both the National Jewish Book award and the Aesop Prize in folklore. For Barbara Diamond Goldin's *The Passover Journey*, named an ALA Notable Children's Book and a Children's Book of the Month Club selection, Waldman used watercolor to great effect, highlighting various parts of the story with changing colors to reflect the many moods of that holiday's observance. Waldman's own daughter Sarah provided the text for *Light: The First Seven Days*, written in 1993 when she was a teenager. In this volume the artist used bright acrylic tones sparkling against a dark background to express the impact of the creation story, while his Adam and Eve figures show deeply colored skin tones to represent the multiethnic beginnings of human life.

A long fascination with the art of Vincent Van Gogh, whose work Waldman first encountered as a young child, inspired his book *The Starry Night*. The story began as a childhood fantasy of what it would be like if Van Gogh were to visit New

York City. While developing the story of a boy who comes across the great painter in Central Park and shows him the sights of Manhattan, Waldman connected with a director of the Children's Aid Society, an organization that helps inner-city children in New York develop their potential and involves, in part, introducing them to the arts. Waldman and his publisher, Boyds Mills Press, donated part of the proceeds of the sale of *The Starry Night*—which was named a Pick of the Lists by the American Bookseller's Association—to the work of the Children's Aid Society. A later book, *Dream Makers*, brings together the words of over 40 children from across the country, each offering his or her unique hopes, dreams, and wishes. Waldman conceived and illustrated the book in celebration of the Children's Aid Society's 150th anniversary in 2003.

Courtesy of Boyds Mills Press

Neil Waldman's art and writing have had a far-reaching effect on both children and adults. Notable among his many awards is the gold medal he received from the United Nations when his entry was selected as the official poster for the International Year of Peace. Today, it hangs in the halls of the General Assembly. Waldman lives with his wife Kathy in Westchester County, New York. He has three grown children and three grandchildren.

SELECTED WORKS WRITTEN AND ILLUSTRATED: *The Golden City: Jerusalem's 3,000 Years*, 1995; *The Two Brothers: A Legend of Jerusalem*, 1997; *Masada*, 1998; *The Starry Night*, 1999; *Wounded Knee*, 2001; *They Came from the Bronx: How the Buffalo Were Saved from Extinction*, 2001; *The Promised Land: The Birth of the Jewish People*, 2002; *The Snowflake: A Water Cycle Story*, 2003; *The Never-Ending Greenness: We Made Israel Bloom*, 2003; *Dream Makers: Young People Share Their Hopes and Aspirations*, 2003; *Say-Hey and the Babe: Two Mostly True Baseball Stories*, 2006; *Letter on the Wind*, by Sarah Marwil Lamstein, 2007.

SELECTED WORKS ILLUSTRATED: *Osceola's Head and Other American Ghost Stories*, by Walter Harter, 1974; *The Moving Coffins:*

Ghosts and Hauntings Around the World, by David C. Knight, 1983; *Toba*, by Michael Mark, 1984; *Tales of Terror: Ten Short Stories*, by Edgar Allan Poe, 1985; *Bring Back the Deer*, by Jeffrey John Prusski, 1988; *The Highwayman*, by Alfred Noyes, 1990; *Nessa's Fish*, by Nancy Luenn, 1990; *The Sea Lion*, by Ken Kesey, 1991; *The Gold Coin*, by Alma Flor Ada, 1991; *Gates of Shabbat: A Guide for Observing Shabbat*, by Mark Dov Shapiro, 1991; *Mother Earth*, by Nancy Luenn, 1992; *America the Beautiful*, by Katharine Lee Bates, 1993; *The Tyger*, by William Blake, 1993; *Light: The First Seven Days*, retold by Sarah Waldman, 1993; *The Passover Journey: A Seder Companion*, by Barbara Diamond Goldin, 1994; *Bayou Lullaby*, by Kathi Appelt, 1995; *Quetzal: Sacred Bird of the Cloud Forest*, by Dorothy Hinshaw Patent, 1996; *And the Earth Trembled: The Creation of Adam and Eve*, by Shulamith Levey Oppenheim, 1996; *By the Hanukkah Light*, by Sheldon Oberman, 1997; *A Horse Called Starfire*, by Betty Virginia Doyle Boegehold, 1998; *The Family Haggadah*, by Ellen Schecter, 1999; *The Wisdom Bird: A Tale of Solomon and Sheba*, by Sheldon Oberman, 2000; *Gates of Wonder: A Prayerbook for Very Young Children*, by Robert Orkand, et. al., 2000; *Too Young for Yiddish*, by Richard Michelson, 2002; *Jerusalem of Gold: Jewish Stories of the Enchanted City*, by Howard Schwartz, 2003; *Subways: The Story of Tunnels, Tubes, and Tracks*, by Larry Dane Brimner, 2004.

SUGGESTED READING: Waldman, Neil, *Out of the Shadows: An Artist's Journey*, 2006; *Something About the Author*, vol. 142, 2004.

WEB SITES: www.neilwaldman.com
www.thestarrynight.com

Sally M. Walker

October 16, 1954–

"When I was in fifth grade, my report card contained a note of concern from my teacher: 'Sally is a daydreamer. She doesn't seem to pay attention in class.' My most frequent daydream? That someday I'd write children's books. After closely questioning me, to make sure that I did indeed know what was going on in class, my parents (and eventually, my teacher) let me daydream in peace.

"Books have always occupied a central place in my life, occasionally in unexpected ways. There are few things I dislike more than clothes shopping. When I was a child, 'outfitting' me for a new school year—dresses (no pants for girls in those days!), shoes, socks—would have tried the patience of a saint. My mother stoically endured my shopping temper tantrums. However, once I became a reader, she had the perfect 'carrot' to keep me in line: If I behaved while we shopped for clothes, she would buy me the latest Nancy Drew or Walter Farley Black Stallion book. Worked like a charm; in fact, I still have and treasure all of them!

"Although I never kept a journal, I did write stories for pleasure. I gave them to my family as birthday, Christmas, and Mother's/Father's Day presents. During our childhood summers, my sister, a friend, and I wrote a weekly neighborhood newspaper that we sold to everyone who lived nearby. It contained the neighborhood gossip, jokes, and short stories that we wrote. The income from our literary venture was just enough to keep us supplied with the latest issues of *Superman*, *Archie*, and *Richie Rich* comics.

"I was born and raised in East Orange, New Jersey. The main branch of the East Orange Public Library was one of my regular haunts. My sister and I went at least once a week during the school year. In the summer we went even more often, usually several times a week. While horse, dog, mystery, and Robin Hood books were my fiction of choice, I did poke around in the nonfiction section—specifically horse, dog, and Robin Hood books—plus the library's local history collection.

"My father was an amazing nonfiction storyteller. On summer evenings, all the neighborhood children would gather in our backyard and listen to his true tales of the Indians and colonial settlers who had lived in our town long ago. I often sought out additional information about the people and

Photo by J. Womack

Sally M Walker

events in my father's stories in the library's newspaper archives and its microfilm collection. Both my parents valued learning and exploring; perhaps that's where my love of nonfiction began. They taught me to ask questions and seek answers. And most importantly, to recognize the 'story' in everything I discovered. I love doing research because research is all about 'story.'

"As a nonfiction writer, my quests for knowledge frequently come with a publisher's deadline. At those times, researching is like heating water for cooking pasta: I need a quick boil to get dinner on the table. At other times, research means allowing time for a long, slow simmer, like the type of cooking you need to make a savory stew. In fact, the simmering research process is a lot like . . . daydreaming. Oddly enough, I discovered that the daydream I spent my childhood cultivating is an important part of my creative process. When I wrote *Secrets of a Civil War Submarine*, for example, daydreaming let me join the crew inside a cold, wet submarine. Daydreams allowed me to jubilate with them when they successfully completed their mission, and to cry when they died in the dark, airless submarine almost immediately afterward.

"Parents often ask me what they can give a child who wants to be a writer. One thing is a library card. Another is plenty of paper and pens. But the *best* gift anyone can give a budding writer is time. Time to wander, time to learn, time to read, and above all, time to daydream."

Ȣ   Ȣ   Ȣ

> "They taught me to ask questions and seek answers. And most importantly, to recognize the 'story' in everything I discovered."

The daughter of an insurance agent and an accounting clerk, Sally MacArt became Sally M. Walker when she married the geologist James Walker in August 1974. The following year, she received her B.A. in physical science from Upsala College, a now-defunct institution located in her hometown of East Orange, New Jersey. For several years Walker lived in Nova Scotia, Canada, where her husband did postgraduate work. They eventually settled in the DeKalb, Illinois, area.

Walker's career path has always involved children's books. In addition to her writing, she has worked as a literature consultant, a children's book buyer, a children's book specialist, and a speaker at children's book conferences. From 1988 to 1994, she worked at the Junction Book Store in DeKalb, and from 1994 to the present, she has been associated with Anderson's Bookshops in Naperville, Illinois.

The author of nearly 50 books, Walker received the 2006 Robert F. Sibert Informational Book Award for *Secrets of a Civil War Submarine: Solving the Mysteries of the H. L. Hunley*. "Next to the birth of my two children," Walker says, "this is the most thrilling thing that's ever happened to me." In 1864, the *H. L. Hunley* became the first submarine to sink an enemy ship, but then promptly vanished. Combining the drama of a wartime shipwreck with compelling scientific writing, Walker reveals the secrets of the *Hunley*, from its construction to its disappearance in Charleston Harbor, with all its crew aboard. Walker's description of the submarine's recovery in 1995 and the use of forensic science to decipher the cause of its demise and the identities of its crew add a present-day element to the tale. Walker spent two years researching the book, with visits to the Warren Lasch Conservation Center in South Carolina, the Naval Historical Center and the Smithsonian Institution in Washington, D.C., and finally to the funeral procession for the recovered bodies of the *Hunley's* crew. As a parallel to *Secrets of a Civil War Submarine* but for a younger audience, Walker recently wrote *Shipwreck Search: Discovery of the H. L. Hunley* as part of the On My Own Science easy-reader series.

Many of Walker's books delve into the wonders of the natural world, exploring concepts in physics, geology, and biology. *Fossil Fish Found Alive: Discovering the Coelacanth* describes the surprise discovery of a fish that most experts thought extinct. Walker's fascinating study of this remarkable sea creature was cited as an ALA Notable Children's Book, a *School Library Journal* Best Book, and a Blue Ribbon title by the *Bulletin of the Center for Children's Books*. It was also named an Outstanding Science Trade Book for Children. Another title, *Mystery Fish*, tells the story of the coelacanth for beginning readers.

Three more of Walker's books have been listed as Outstanding Science Trade Books for Children: *Earthquakes*, *Sea Horses*, and *Fireflies*. Part of the Earth Watch series, *Earthquakes* presents clear explanations of how earthquakes occur and what safety measures can be taken in the event of one. Part of the Early Bird Nature series, *Fireflies* describes the physical characteristics, behavior, and life cycle of these insects. *Sea Horses*, also intended for primary-grade readers, was cited as an Honor Book by the Society of School Librarians International.

Walker has written books on physical science and simple machines for young readers as well as several biographies. Her best-known biography tells the singular story of a 19th century British paleontologist. *Mary Anning, Fossil Hunter* was cited as an IRA/CBC Children's Choice book and a Best of the Year by *Science Books and Films*. Based on primary source material but written for grade-schoolers, this informative book describes Anning's life and accomplishments, particularly her groundbreaking research into the study of fossils, in a way that young children can understand.

Sally M. Walker has two adult children: a daughter named Erine and a son named David. She lives in Dekalb, Illinois, where her husband is a geology professor at Northern Illinois University. She has taught children's literature courses at Northern Illinois

> "*. . . the* best *gift anyone can give a budding writer is time. Time to wander, time to learn, time to read, and above all, time to daydream.*"

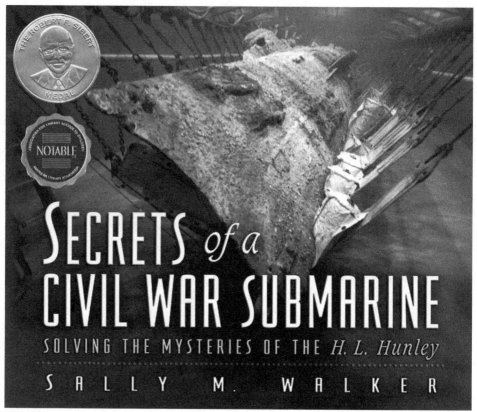

Courtesy of the Lerner Publishing Group

University and often visits classrooms to present programs about children's books.

SELECTED WORKS: *Glaciers: Ice on the Move*, 1990; *Born Near the Earth's Surface: Sedimentary Rocks*, 1991; *Water Up, Water Down: The Hydrologic Cycle*, 1992; *Volcanoes: Earth's Inner Fire*, 1994; *Earthquakes*, 1996; *Rhinos*, 1996; *Seahorse Reef: A Story of the South Pacific*, 1997; *Hippos*, 1997; *Opossum at Sycamore Road*, illus. by Joel Snyder, 1997; *The 18 Penny Goose*, illus. by Ellen Beier, 1998; *Manatees*, 1999; *Dolphins*, 1999; *Sea Horses*, 1999; *Mary Anning: Fossil Hunter*, illus. by Phyllis V. Saroff, 2000; *Fireflies*, 2001; *Inclined Planes and Wedges*, with Roseann Feldmann, 2001; *Levers*, with Roseann Feldmann, 2001; *Pulleys*, with Roseann Feldmann, 2001; *Screws*, with Roseann Feldmann, 2001; *Wheels and Axles*, with Roseann Feldmann, 2001; *Work*, with Roseann Feldmann, 2001; *Fossil Fish Found Alive: Discovering the Coelacanth*, 2002; *Jackie Robinson*, illus. by Rodney S. Pate, 2002; *Life in an Estuary*, 2003; *Rays*, 2003; *Bessie Coleman: Daring to Fly*, illus. by Janice Lee Porter, 2003; *Crocodiles*, 2004; *Secrets of a Civil War Submarine: Solving the*

Mysteries of the H. L. Hunley, 2005; *Supercroc Found*, illus. by Philip Hood, 2005; *Mystery Fish: Secrets of the Coelacanth*, illus. by Shawn Gould, 2005; *Electricity*, 2005; *Light*, 2005; *Magnetism*, 2005; *Matter*, 2005; *Sound*, 2005; *Heat*, 2005, *Early Bird Energy*, 2006; *Fossils*, 2006; *Minerals*, 2006; *Rocks*, 2006; *Soil*, 2006; *Shipwreck Search: Discovery of the H. L. Hunley*, illus. by Elaine Verstraete, 2006; *Caves*, 2007; *Volcanoes*, 2007; *Reefs*, 2007; *Glaciers*, 2007; *Mosquitoes*, 2008; *Jaguars*, 2008.

SUGGESTED READING: *Something About the Author*, vol. 135, 2003. Periodicals—Walker, Sally, "A Story Hidden Under the Sea," *Booklist*, Dec. 1, 2005.

"I wish someone had taken me in hand when I was young and had told me that I should be a writer. No one ever did that. I loved to write, but it never occurred to me that I could write books and magazine articles. I grew up in a tiny town in northeast Nebraska, and to my knowledge, no one there had ever written for a national magazine or published a book. However, I knew about newspaper writing, and that's the direction in which I headed. We had a weekly newspaper in tiny Newman Grove. It wasn't very good—mostly local news and ads, with lots of typos and grammatical glitches. I started working there as a sophomore in high school. I was sort of a 'girl Friday,' running errands, answering the phone, sweeping up, and helping to deliver the paper each Wednesday afternoon. I would leave school as soon as the last bell rang and zip the two blocks to the newspaper office, where I worked until 6 P.M. or so, helping to get the paper out. I learned immediately to love the smell of printer's ink and the excitement of being part of something so important to our community.

"Starting my junior year, I wrote a column about school events that appeared in the paper each week. Everyone knew what was going on, so this was more a formality, but seeing my byline on the front page and knowing I was helping to report the

Courtesy of Andrea Warren

Andrea Warren

October 30, 1946–

news sealed the deal that I would be a nonfiction writer. I didn't take a direct route. In college I worked on the school newspaper, but I majored in English and education and became an English teacher. That I would be a teacher was my family's expectation of me and I did not disappoint them. It was considered a safe career for a woman. (Did I mention that my mother was a teacher and my father was the local superintendent of schools?)

"Once I was a teacher, I finally began writing on the side and started publishing a few articles. I also got my master's degree in literature, but I knew journalism was what I really wanted. After eleven years of teaching, I went back to graduate school and got a master's degree in magazine journalism. I briefly edited a magazine, but then I finally started to write for a living. By then I was 35 years old.

"Since then, I have written hundreds of magazine articles, and contributed stories and articles to countless publications, from newsletters to professional journals. I have also begun creating a lasting body of work in the form of nonfiction books for young readers. I've combined my interests in history, story, nonfiction, and children, and I write about children, for children. But not just any children—brave, resourceful children who must overcome daunting odds of one kind or another. True stories of children who get caught up in extraordinary circumstances (of historical interest) and must use their wits and self-reliance to get along. I can't resist these stories, and I hope I can continue to write them for many decades."

> "I've combined my interests in history, story, nonfiction, and children, and I write about children, for children."

ભ ભ ભ

Andrea Warren was born in Norfolk, Nebraska, and grew up in nearby Newman Grove, the second of the five children of Ruth and J. V. Warren. She graduated from the University of Nebraska and received master's degrees from the University of Nebraska and the University of Kansas. She taught high school English and history for over a decade, then became a journalist and freelance writer.

Warren's nonfiction books for young readers have covered a variety of topics, beginning with the orphan trains of the late 19th and early 20th centuries. These trains transported orphaned and abandoned children from northeastern cities to small towns and farming communities in the Midwest and West to be adopted and/or put to work by new families. What Warren began as a magazine article morphed into an informative book for young readers. *Orphan Train Rider: One Boy's True Story* chronicles the real-life experiences of Lee Nailling, whose account alternates with chapters detailing the origins and evolution of this little-known chapter in American social history. The book won the *Boston Globe–Horn Book* Award for Nonfiction and was named an ALA Notable Children's Book. Later Warren published *We Rode the Orphan Trains*, in which she collected the varied stories of many different riders, some of whom were overworked while others were treated kindly. "I felt compelled to help record this history," Warren has said. "The riders still living were elderly, and we would soon lose their stories."

Inspired by her pioneer ancestors, Warren next wrote about one of the first generations of homestead children in her home state of Nebraska. This book, *Pioneer Girl: Growing Up on the Prairie*, received the Orbis Pictus Award for Outstanding Nonfiction for Children.

Warren then turned her attention to children exposed to the horrors of war. Troubled that some people thought only adults were sent to the concentration camps of World War II, she decided to examine what it was like for the young people who were subjected to the ordeal. In *Surviving Hitler: A Boy in the Nazi Death Camps*, Warren tells the story of Jack Mandelbaum, who as a child endured the horrors of this experience. A resident of Kansas City, Mandelbaum lived near Warren's home, so she was able to spend many hours with him, learning his story and finding the best way to tell it. *Surviving Hitler* won a Robert F. Sibert Honor Book citation and was named

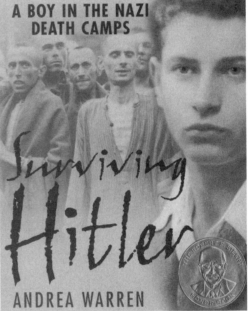

A BOY IN THE NAZI DEATH CAMPS

Surviving Hitler

ANDREA WARREN

Courtesy of HarperCollins Publishers

an ALA Notable Children's Book. It was also recognized as a Notable Children's Book of Jewish Content by the Association of Jewish Libraries.

Since the mid-1970s, Warren had wanted to write about Operation Babylift, in which nearly 3,000 orphaned Vietnamese children, many of them the mixed-race offspring of American soldiers, were airlifted out of Saigon, South Vietnam, in the final month of the Vietnam War. Warren is the adoptive parent of one of these Babylift children. Her daughter was only six months old when she was evacuated and had no memories of the event, so Warren searched for an older child who could remember the experience. She found Matt Steiner, who was almost nine when he boarded a plane for life with a new family in the United States. His story is told in *Escape from Saigon*.

Among Warren's many other laurels are a Jane Addams Honor Book Award, a Pennsylvania Young Reader's Award, a Dorothy Canfield Fisher Children's Book Award, and a Young Hoosier Book Award for *Orphan Train Rider*. Five of her titles— *Orphan Train Rider*, *We Rode the Orphan Trains*, *Surviving Hitler*, and *Pioneer Girl* and *Escape from Saigon*—have been named Notable Social Studies Trade Books for Young People. Warren lives in Prairie Village, Kansas, a suburb of Kansas City.

SELECTED WORKS: *Orphan Train Rider: One Boy's True Story*, 1996; *Pioneer Girl: Growing Up on the Prairie*, 1998; *We Rode the Orphan Trains*, 2001; *Surviving Hitler: A Boy in the Nazi Death Camps*, 2001; *Escape from Saigon: How a Vietnam War Orphan Became an American Boy*, 2004.

SUGGESTED READING: *Something About the Author*, vol. 98, 1998. Periodicals—Warren, Andrea, "Orphan Train Rider," *The Horn Book*, Jan/Feb 1997.

WEB SITE: www.andreawarren.com

Yoko Kawashima Watkins

October 5, 1933–

"**I** am the youngest of the three children of the Kawashima family. Although I was born in Japan, I grew up in northern Korea while my father was stationed in Manchuria and China as a diplomat. I received traditional Japanese training in dance, calligraphy, the way of tea, and flower arrangement. Mother, sister Ko, and I were forced to flee from Korea for our native Japan in 1945, separated from Father and brother Hideyo.

"Arriving by cargo ship at Fukuoka refugee center in southern Japan, we tried to wait for Father and brother to catch up with us, but we were forced to leave and set up makeshift living arrangements in Kyoto, where I enrolled in a girls' school and Ko entered Seian University. Mother journeyed on to where she was born—Aomori, in northern Japan—to see our grandparents on both sides of the family, while Ko and I scavenged for food. On learning of the death of her parents and my father's parents, our mother returned to Kyoto by train and collapsed and died of fatigue and malnutrition. Our brother joined Ko and me in the spring of 1948 at our makeshift quarters in a clog factory. In 1951 Father was released from a prison camp in Siberia and found us safe in Kyoto.

"Receiving a scholarship to Kyoto University, I studied English and later worked as a translator at Misawa Air Force Base, where I met my husband, Donald Watkins. We lived in Minnesota, Wisconsin, and Oregon before settling in Cape Cod, Massachusetts. We are the parents of four grown children. My sister Ko, who was injured in 1948 when the clog factory warehouse burned, now lives in nearby Boston.

"When neighbors complain about barking dogs or loud parties and circulate petitions to protest such annoyances, I refuse to sign. If they had walked with bombshells, they would be glad to hear dogs barking or young people enjoying themselves at a party. People who waste their time complaining about petty problems have never experienced the 'bottom of the bottom.' Also, material possessions or their lack mean very little to me. Even people who live in shacks can be grateful for a roof over their heads, no one to abuse them, and no bombs falling from the skies.

"This philosophy of life was born of my personal experience as a refugee when, at the age of eleven and a half, I had to flee from a comfortable home in North Korea. I left behind my favorite toys and Mama and Papa canaries with four tiny eggs in their nest. The memories of those times hold sorrow that will always remain sharp for me. I do not take any of life's gifts for granted. I enjoy the simplest things. I like the little wildflowers that grow along the roadsides. If tramped on, they always spring back, showing their beauty to all who pass. If I don't have a curtain on my window, it is because the tree out there is my curtain. I enjoy living in nature."

Photo by Ron Schloerb, *Cape Cod Times*

ख ख ख

Yoko Kawashima Watkins was born in her parents' hometown of Aomori, Japan. Her mother, Saki Kawashima, was an only child and prohibited by Japanese law from giving up her family name, so Yoko's father—Yoshio Kamada, a fifth son—took his wife's name when they married. Yoko was two months old when she moved with her family to Harbin, Manchuria, where her father was stationed as a diplomat. Manchuria, which Japan had recently annexed, was a dangerous environment, where Japanese officials and their families were often in fear of their lives, so her father moved the family across the border to Nanam, North Korea in 1934. Yoko enjoyed writing as a child and had her first story published in a Korean newspaper when she was only seven years old. Life became more precarious for the Kawashima family after Japan entered World War II and especially toward the end of the war.

In 1945, as it became clear that the Japanese were losing the war and the Koreans began to resist Japanese rule in earnest, Yoko was forced to flee Korea with her mother and her sister. Many years later, settled in the United States with her American husband, Yoko wrote the autobiographical novels that chronicle that harrowing escape from Korea and her survival in post–World War II Japan. They are stories of resilience and courage and have provided inspiring reading for many students and adults alike.

So Far from the Bamboo Grove, published in 1986, received many accolades. It was named one of *School Library Journal*'s Best Books of the Year and was designated an ALA Notable Children's Book. Cited as a Parents' Choice book, it also received the Judy Lopez Memorial Award, presented by the Los Angeles chapter of the Women's National Book Association. Many schools have adopted *So Far from the Bamboo Grove* in their reading programs.

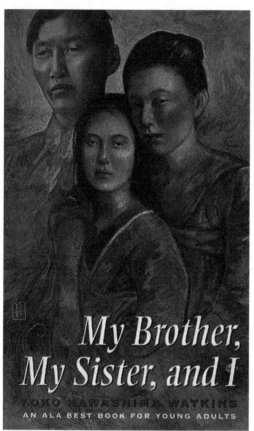

Courtesy of Simon & Schuster Children's Publishing

Watkins's next book, *Tales from the Bamboo Grove*, was a collection of Japanese folk tales that she remembered hearing during her childhood. Then, eight years after her first autobiographical novel was published, she continued the story of her own family's struggles in postwar Japan in *My Brother, My Sister, and I.* Chronicling how she and her sister lived in extreme poverty in Kyoto after the war ended, she tells a poignant story of suffering from taunting at school and of the joy she felt at the reunion with her brother in 1948. This book was also a recipient of the Judy Lopez Memorial Award and named a best book of the year by *Publishers Weekly*, the *New York Times*, and *Parenting* magazine. It was cited as a Notable Trade Book in the Field of Social Studies and a Best Book for the Teen Age by the New York Public Library.

Yoko Kawashima Watkins lives with her husband in Brewster, Massachusetts. She has received the Courage of Conscience Award from the Peace Abbey and has been named one of the Literary Lights for Children by the Associates of the Boston Public Library.

SELECTED WORKS: *So Far from the Bamboo Grove*, 1986; *Tales from the Bamboo Grove*, illus. by Jean and Mou-Sien Tseng, 1992; *My Brother, My Sister, and I*, 1994.

SUGGESTED READING: *Something About the Author*, vol. 93, 1997; *Contemporary Authors*, vol. 158, 1998.

"It's always hard to know what to say when people ask me to tell them a little bit about myself. Of course there's the regular stuff to talk about, like where I was born and where I live now. Then there are the harder, more interesting things to get into, like how I write my books and what I like best about being an author. Oh, and of course there's the question every kid seems to want answered—do I have any pets?

"So, starting with the easy stuff—I was born in Ann Arbor, Michigan, back in the days when there was no color TV, milk came in glass bottles and was delivered by a milkman, Barbie dolls came in only two varieties—blonde and brunette —and girls had to wear dresses to school every day, even in the cold, harsh Michigan winters when the temperature often dipped below zero. From the time I was about five, I was writing stories. I was a terrible speller, and still am, as a matter of fact, but writing stories and poems and songs was always my favorite thing to do.

"My dad was an English professor at the University of Michigan, who loved words, and books, and telling funny stories. My mother stayed home with my brother and sister and me until

Photo by Tobin Townsend

Sarah Weeks

March 18, 1955–

we'd all three gone off to college, at which point she went back to work as a bookkeeper in a law office. After going to college in Massachusetts, at Hampshire College where I studied music composition and poetry, I moved to New York City where I still live today.

"My original plan was to be a singer-songwriter. I did the cabaret scene in New York for a few years, ended up in an off-Broadway show for a year and eventually drifted into writing songs for kids. I wrote for Disney and *Sesame Street*, and after playing some of my songs for a friend, Laura Geringer, who also happened to be a children's book editor, I suddenly found myself writing books for kids. My first picture books were based on songs I'd written, which was great fun because I got to combine my love of writing with my love of performing.

"My sons, Gabe and Nat, are grown now, but when they were small they were a big influence on my writing. I wanted to write about the things they were interested in, and in language they would relate to. As they got older, my interest shifted from picture books and songs to middle grade fiction. I wrote the Guy series, which is humorous, boy-friendly fiction, and then I took the big leap into serious Young Adult literature, writing *So B. It* and *Jumping the Scratch*.

"The best thing about being an author is that I get to spend time doing what I like best—writing. I'm one of those writers who believes in the idea that it's best to write what you know. I love animals, and I know a fair amount about them, so a lot of my picture books are about animals and the environment. I love kids—the way they talk to each other and the things they think are funny—so my novels are realistic fiction about kids. Describing *how* I write is not easy. In fact, it's easier to describe how I *don't* write. I don't outline, I don't do any research if I can help it, and I don't write unless I feel like it.

"Besides writing I like to bake, talk on the phone, and watch Little League games. It's nice being able to write both picture books and novels because it means that I'm always shifting around, doing different things. One day I might be working on a rhyming book about a clothesline, the next day a song about a penguin, and the day after that a serious book about a girl who goes on a long journey in search of herself. Variety. That's what keeps life interesting.

"And finally, I know what you really want to know is whether I have any pets, so let me say now that no, I have no pets. But eventually I would like to have a dog."

> *"I love kids—the way they talk to each other and the things they think are funny—so my novels are realistic fiction about kids."*

☙ ☙ ☙

Sarah Weeks grew up wanting to be a teacher, a nurse, or a Dairy Queen employee. Instead she became the author of more than forty picture books and novels for children and young adults. Her sister Jane is a doctor and her brother Tom is a lawyer. A graduate of Hampshire College and New York University, Weeks continues to reside in New York City, where both her sons were born and raised.

When writing Weeks often works at her computer but edits with a pencil. She also sometimes uses a tape recorder, recording a section that she's composed and then editing as she listens to the playback. She has written for television, stage, and screen. A number of her picture books, such as *Crocodile Smile* and *Follow the Moon*, include songs that she performs on accompanying CDs. She writes many age levels, from preschoolers and early readers to middle-grade students and teenagers.

Courtesy of HarperCollins Publishers

Hurricane City, an alphabet book that follows a series of hurricanes as they blow through an imaginary city, was the winner of both the Georgia and the Maryland Children's Book Awards in 1995. *Oh My Gosh, Mrs. McNosh*, an IRA/CBC Children's Choice selection, features slapstick humor as Mrs. McNosh chases her runaway dog through a lake, a baseball field, and a wedding reception. Another Mrs. McNosh book, *Mrs. McNosh Hangs Up Her Wash*, was featured on the PBS reading readiness show *Between the Lions*. A rambunctious child banished to time-out imagines the misdeeds of truly wild animals in the humorous and inventive *If I Were a Lion*, which was cited as a Parents' Choice Approved Award winner and was nominated for state awards in Pennsylvania and Missouri. *Drip, Drop*, a spirited story about a nighttime rainstorm for early readers, was a *Parenting* magazine Best Book of the Year.

Titles in the Guy series, which seeks to entice middle-grade boys to read, have also received accolades, and *My Guy*, the third in the series, is being developed into a feature film by the Walt Disney Company.

Writing for a slightly older audience, Weeks found success as well. *So B. It*, a quirky and thought-provoking mystery about the search for identity, was among the Top Ten ALA Best Books for Young Adults in 2005, as well as being an ALA Notable Children's Book, a *Booklist* Editors' Choice, an IRA/CBC Young Adult Choice, an NCTE Notable Children's Book in the Language Arts, a Parents' Choice Gold Medal Award winner, and one of the New York Public Library's One Hundred Titles for Reading and Sharing. Featuring a 12-year old girl named Heidi It, who embarks on an unusual journey, this title also received the Virginia Young Readers Award, the Kentucky Book Award, and the Louisiana Young Reader's Choice Award.

Weeks has combined her interest in performing with her love of writing. She helped found the Authors Readers Theatre, a group of traveling authors that includes, along with Weeks, Avi, Sharon Creech, Walter Dean Myers, Pam Muñoz Ryan, Richard Peck, and Rachel Vail. A.R.T. performs dramatic staged readings and debuted in the fall of 2006, appearing at festivals and conferences around the United States. Weeks also visits schools throughout the country speaking to children, teachers, and librarians about her work. She is currently an adjunct faculty member in the Writing Program at the New School for Social Research in New York City.

SELECTED WORKS: *Hurricane City*, illus. by James Warhola, 1993; *Follow the Moon*, illus. by Suzanne Duranceau, 1995, reissued, 2003; *Red Ribbon*, illus. by Jeffrey Greene, 1995; *Noodles*, illus. by David A. Carter, 1996; *Little Factory*, illus. by Byron Barton, 1998; *Mrs. McNosh Hangs Up Her Wash*, illus. by Nadine Bernard Westcott, 1998; *Piece of Jungle*, illus. by Suzanne Duranceau, 1999; *Splish, Splash*, illus. by Ashley Wolff, 1999; *Happy Birthday, Frankie*, illus. by Warren Linn, 1999; *Regular Guy*, 1999; *Mrs. McNosh and the Great Big Squash*, illus. by Nadine Bernard Westcott, 2000; *Guy Time*, 2000; *Drip Drop*, illus. by Jane Manning, 2000; *My Guy*, 2001; *Bite Me, I'm a Book*, illus. by Jef Kaminsky, 2002; *Bite Me, I'm a Shape*, illus. by Jef Kaminsky, 2002; *Oh My Gosh, Mrs. McNosh*, illus. by Nadine Bernard Westcott, 2002; *My Somebody Special*, illus. by Ashley Wolff, 2002; *Guy Wire*, 2002; *Angel Face*, illus. by David Diaz, 2002; *Without You*, illus. by Suzanne Duranceau, 2003; *Two Eggs, Please*, illus. by Betsy Lewin, 2003; *Crocodile Smile: Ten Songs of the Earth As the Animals See It*, illus. by Lois Ehlert, 2003; *Paper Parade*, illus. by Ed Briant, 2004; *If I Were a Lion*, illus. by Heather M. Solomon, 2004; *So B. It*, 2004; *Beware of Mad Dog!*

(Boyds Will Be Boyds) 2004; *Get Well Soon, Or Else!* (Boyds Will Be Boyds) 2004; *Baa-Choo!*, illus. by Jane Manning, 2004; *I'm a Pig*, illus. by Holly Berry, 2005; *Who's Under That Hat?*, illus. by David A. Carter, 2005; *Overboard!*, illus. by Sam Williams, 2006; *Jumping the Scratch*, 2006; *Be Mine, Be Mine, Sweet Valentine*, illus. by Fumi Kosaka, 2006; *Ruff! Ruff! Where's Scruff?*, illus. by David A. Carter, 2006; *Counting Ovejahs*, illus. by David Diaz, 2006; *Danger! Boys Dancing!* (Boyds Will Be Boyds) 2006; *Fink's Funk!*, (Boyds Will Be Boyds), 2006; *Ella, Of Course*, illus. by Doug Cushman, 2007; *Pip Squeak*, illus. by Jane Manning, 2007; *Peek in My Pocket*, illus. by David A. Carter, 2007; *Bunny Fun*, illus. by Sam Williams, 2008; *Oggie Cooder*, 2008.

WEB SITES: www.sarahweeks.com
www.authorsreaderstheatre.com

"In Naugatuck, Connecticut, a mill town surrounded by countryside but a-bustle with the earnestness and fervor of World War II, I spent my childhood climbing trees and stone walls, playing Tarzan and Robin Hood, singing, drawing, and devouring books—history and mystery, mythology and *Winnie the Pooh*. I especially loved the hush of the library on hot summer days. Walking there was a pilgrimage, opening a new book as exciting as a curtain going up in theater. So striving to kindle that excitement in children far more beset by distractions has seemed both an honorable and an instinctive calling.

"I was lucky to be born into a big extended family in my mother's hometown, to grow up with parents, grandparents, and two generations of aunts and uncles. Even luckier, I see now, that they were a tribe of storytellers. The best entertainment on a summer evening was catching fireflies in the back yard amid reminiscences of colorful family characters and misadventures. My favorite, oft-related, was the wondrous tale of 'Uncle Ambrose and the big black dog,' remembered many years later in my picture book called *The Angel of Mill Street*. I especially loved my grandfather, a fellow bookworm, and my Uncle Fred,

Photo by Robert Tucker, Focalpoint Studio

Francis Ward Weller

October 5, 1935–

the family's prime chronicler and spell-weaver. Both informed the character of Rob Loud, the piper, in my first published book, the novel *Boat Song*.

"Just as I reached my teens, we moved to Pelham, New York, a town half an hour from Broadway, where I discovered what would become a lifelong love of theater. In high school I led cheers, sang with the dance band, wrote for the newspaper, and graduated first among equals in a bright and close-knit class, which included my future husband (another avid storyteller). At Mount Holyoke College, I gorged on English and French literature (especially loving drama and poetry), sang with a triple quartet, worked on the newspaper board, and spent my honors hours wrestling with James Joyce's *Ulysses*. For a year and a half before marrying Frank Weller in 1958, I did research in New York City for the *Reader's Digest*, and was fortunately assigned to help Cornelius Ryan with *The Longest Day*: a remarkable chance to experience the synthesis of inspiration, art, and grit involved in creating a book.

> "I especially loved the hush of the library on hot summer days. Walking there was a pilgrimage, opening a new book as exciting as a curtain going up in theater."

"Marriage took me to Newport, Rhode Island (confirming a permanent passion for the sea that started with teenage outings at Jones Beach), to Long Island, and to Jacksonville, Florida, a mind-altering experience amid the civil rights strife of the early 1960s. Then we spent twenty-five rich years in Madison, New Jersey, a good and happy place to raise our son and daughters. But increasingly drawn to Cape Cod, our family's perennial love and inspiration for several of my books—including *Riptide*, the most enduring—we moved to Orleans, just above the Cape's elbow, in 1989. Here, in our 'spare time,' my husband and I sing in a challenging chorale (which took us to the Saint Francis Day celebration described in *The Day the Animals Came*) and work hard for Cape Rep Theatre, a performing arts complex in buildings leased from the Commonwealth of Massachusetts, near Cape Cod Bay.

"Writing has run through all these years, and all endeavors. But surely my most purposeful writing I owe to Patricia Lee Gauch and her Rutgers writing-for-children workshop, which I was privileged to join nearly thirty years ago. Patricia—a fine writer, inspiring speaker, and generous teacher—has freely shared these skills with me and all the writers she's fostered during her subsequent years as editor at Philomel; and I've been (again!) lucky to have 'known her when.' I'll always be grateful also to my first editor, Judith Whipple of dear-departed Macmillan, who remembered from Mount Holyoke that I had a brain and read my manuscripts accordingly.

"As to the rest of 'where the books come from,' I can only say I seem to be set off by stories where reality intersects with wonder—and recall a favorite quotation from Robert Frost: '. . . like giants we are always hurling experience ahead of us to pave the future with, against the day when we may want to strike a line of purpose across it for somewhere.' I've found this to be true, mysterious, wonderful, and fortunate."

ᏣᏣ   ᏣᏣ   ᏣᏣ

The storytelling skills that Frances Ward Weller absorbed in her childhood—both by reading and listening to family tales—are evident in the books she has written over the last twenty years. Weller graduated summa cum laude in 1957 from Mount Holyoke College where she received an award for the best prose writing. After graduation she headed to New York City for a brief time to work as an editorial researcher for *Reader's Digest*. During this time she had an illustrious apprenticeship, working as research assistant to the journalist Cornelius Ryan, who was creating a book that would become a classic of military history, *The Longest Day: June 6, 1944*. Ryan's detailed study of the D-Day invasion of Normandy during World War II combined many eyewitness accounts that were skillfully interwoven into the narrative. For Weller this proved to be yet another example of the power of storytelling.

Weller's first book, *Boat Song*, is a compelling coming-of-age story in a seashore community on Cape Cod, a common setting for many of her books. Jonno, an 11-year-old boy who feels beset by his critical father, makes friends with an elderly bagpipe-playing Scot who took part in the D-Day invasion. Through his friendship with Rob Loud, Jonno learns to be more comfortable with himself. Hailed by critics, this debut novel effectively launched Weller's career in children's books.

Riptide, a picture book based on a true-life story, tells of an irrepressible golden retriever, the title character, who is a nuisance on the beach. In constant motion and full of energy, Riptide annoys everyone except his young owner, until the day he saves a girl from drowning in a true riptide. The dog's courage and personality shine throughout the story, while the full color illustrations by Robert J. Blake recreate the atmosphere of the beach and Riptide's boisterous behavior. An animal story with great appeal for children, *Riptide* was named a *School Library Journal* Best of the Year in 1990. It also won the Nebraska Golden

Courtesy of Philomel Books, Penguin USA

Sower Award in 1993 and the M. Jerry Weiss award of the New Jersey Reading Association in 1994.

Kinship between humans and animals is at the heart of Weller's *I Wonder If I'll See a Whale*, which features illustrations by Ted Lewin. The awe-inspiring experience of a successful whale-watching expedition is recreated in Weller's charming poetic text and Lewin's evocative art. Lewin also illustrated Weller's book on the heritage of a Yankee farmer, *Matthew Wheelock's Wall*, in which a New Englander builds an intricate fieldstone wall that becomes a sturdy monument to a disappearing way of life. Another enduring character of Weller's appears in a picture book illustrated by Marcia Sewall. *Madaket Millie* tells the fictionalized story of a Nantucket woman who lived by her own strength and wit, eventually being honored by the Coast Guard for her service to her island community.

A family story that Weller remembered hearing as a child found its way into her writing, first as a contribution to *Yankee* magazine in 1990 as "Uncle Ambrose and the Angel," and then, in 1998, as a picture book with atmospheric illustrations by Robert J. Blake, *The Angel of Mill Street*. In the text Uncle Ambrose, whose leg was hurt in an accident, struggles to get home on Christmas Eve during a blizzard. A mysterious black dog that no one ever saw before appears out of the shadows and leads him to safety, then disappears again into the snow.

In *The Day the Animals Came* many of the themes of Weller's books—the healing grace of animals, intergenerational friendships, and the clarity of children's experiences—come together. Ria misses her Caribbean home when she moves to New York City. Her babysitter, Mrs. Blum, takes her to the mammoth Cathedral of St. John the Divine for the blessing of the animals at the Feast of St. Francis, and Ria finds a way to finally feel at home in her new environment. Loren Long's sweeping acrylic paintings view the event from many different angles, helping young readers to imagine the joy and chaos of so many species coming together for the annual event.

Frances Ward Weller has visited schools throughout the country and appeared in Massachusetts libraries as a visiting author. She has served as President of the Board of Trustees of the Cape Cod Repertory Theatre in Brewster. She and her husband Frank have four grown children and now enjoy living year-round in South Orleans on Cape Cod.

SELECTED WORKS: *Boat Song*, 1987; *Riptide*, illus. by Robert J. Blake, 1990; *I Wonder If I'll See a Whale*, illus. by Ted Lewin, 1991; *The Closet Gorilla*, illus. by Cat Bowman Smith, 1991; *Matthew Wheelock's Wall*, illus. by Ted Lewin, 1992; *Madaket Millie*, illus. by Marcia Sewall, 1997; *The Angel of Mill Street*, illus. by Robert J. Blake, 1998; *The Day the Animals Came: A Story of Saint Francis Day*, illus. by Loren Long, 2003.

Rosemary Wells

January 29, 1943–

"I was born during the war, 1943. It is a long time ago now. In my opinion the postwar years—the 1940s and 1950s—were a kind of Athenian America. We were sandwiched between an earlier Spartan America that ended with the Depression and the Second World War. Spartan America still informed my generation. Its heroes were the Blitzed Londoners. Its great-grandfathers were yet around. We saw them occasionally on Armistice Day . . . the last soldiers of the Civil War with their white hair blowing in the wind, their knobby knees at rest in wheelchairs. The sandwich part on the other side of my childhood years is present-day, Late Rome America that followed abruptly the assassination of President Kennedy (which represented the assassination of American innocence) and continues beyond 9/11/01; the world in which my grandchildren are growing up.

"I was very much loved as a child. This is always the key thing. Anything else—rich or poor, exposure to the arts or not—matters only marginally compared to love. I was fortunate to have parents in the arts: my mother a dancer in the Russian ballet, my father a playwright and an actor.

"I was a lucky child. I grew up outdoors with a great love for the woods, for animals, for making tree houses, and for riding my bike everywhere for miles around. It was an unthreatened time and an age where innocence still prevailed in childhood.

Photo by Tim Cofeey

"I was not good in school unless I liked a subject. I lacked the personal discipline to get through things I was not good at. My mother was the most charming and brilliant person but she was not good at personal discipline of a practical or puritanical kind, so I learned personal discipline of another kind. That was the discipline to work very hard at what I loved. My father, who was a very agreeable man, agreed. What I loved was baseball, drawing, theatre, writing, magic, mysteries, and police stories. I drew very, very well as a young child and this carried me through adolescence.

"My very dicey high school transcript was further diced by a nearly year-long trip to England in junior year with my parents. A competitive college was not in my future. I went to a small and now defunct school and lasted only a year. Oddly enough, two of my lifelong best friends and meeting my dearest husband came of attending this indifferent academy. Consequently all my life's connections and family have resulted from it. A year out I went to the Boston Museum School; this was at the height of abstract expressionism and the nadir of respect for illustration.

"I married at 20 and took a job as an art assistant at a Boston textbook publisher. This was a very good thing for me to do. I learned professional dedication, ambition and application very quickly. I went on to New York publishing when my husband entered the Columbia school of architecture. I began illustrating in the year 1968 with a little Gilbert and Sullivan song for the Macmillan Company. I never looked back and since then have published over 120 books, mostly illustrated by me, some not, some young adult or middle grade, and many picture books. I have had the privilege of working with the great editors of the field and of my time, Susan Hirschman, Dick Jackson, Phyllis Fogelman, Amy Ehrlich, Regina Hayes, Michael DiCapua, David Lloyd, Barbara Marcus, Brenda Bowen, and Lisa Holton among them. Also, a great privilege has been working with Iona Opie on the Mother Goose books. Iona is a national treasure.

"Children's book publishing, in my view, is an imperfect field like any other. Nonetheless I have come to believe it is a unique one. Its existence represents the only corner of our young people's culture that is unpolluted for the most part with materialistic or inappropriate values. Enormously distinguished and bright people work in this field. They are all different in their approach but they all believe passionately in the lasting value of the finished work.

"I have two daughters, now in their late twenties and early thirties. I have two dear granddaughters, twins who will live long into this century. I am a widow, devoted to my family and my work.

"My work speaks for itself. There is nothing much to say about it or to explain it or where it comes from or how. It is usually funny because that what makes people come back to books. It is usually idiosyncratic. I dislike all mission statements or adult agendas in young people's literature. I write for the individual brightest child, believing that child can come from a trailer park in east Kentucky as easily as he or she can come from an upscale suburb of New York. I never write for groups of children, only for individuals. If my books have any single purpose it would probably be to say to children: 'You are not alone.'"

> *"I was very much loved as a child. This is always the key thing. Anything else—rich or poor, exposure to the arts or not—matters only marginally compared to love."*

ଓ ଓ ଓ

A multi-faceted talent, Rosemary Wells is as adept at writing contemporary and historical novels as she is at creating and illustrating some of the best-loved picture books of the last forty years. Her reading and appreciation of illustrations in books during her early years proved to be excellent preparation for her chosen career. In a speech delivered at the 2001 Rabbit Hill Festival in Westport, Connecticut, and later published in *School Library Journal*, Wells described her childhood reading experience and especially noted her debt to a favorite author and illustrator, Robert Lawson:

What I can never decide is whether it was his hilarious and exquisite drawings that influenced me most as a professional, or his intimate and equally hilarious writing. . . . I was continually amazed at the depth and liveliness of Mr. Lawson's drawings. That meant that one never tired of looking at them, any more than one tires of looking at the ocean or mountains. . . . This staring and never tiring is the single and simplest test of a great work of art.

When she began creating her own books for children, Wells alternated between picture books and novels. Her first few picture books included those illustrating songs from Gilbert and Sullivan operettas and poems by Robert Service. Her first young adult novel, *The Fog Comes on Little Pig Feet*, about a 13-year-old girl rebelling against the boarding school where she has been sent, received an Honor Book citation at the *Book World* Spring Children's Book Festival in 1972. Two later novels, *When No One Was Looking* and *Through the Hidden Door*, were nominated for the Edgar Allan Poe Award for young readers in 1981 and 1988 respectively. *Through the Hidden Door* was cited as a Best Book for Young Adults and *When No One Was Looking* received the Western Australian Young Readers' Book Award. Another compelling mystery, *The Man in the Woods*, won the Virginia Young Readers Award and was cited as one of the New York Public Library's Books for the Teen Age as well as a Parents' Choice title.

> "My work speaks for itself. There is nothing much to say about it or to explain it or where it comes from or how."

Always fascinated by history, Wells wrote an absorbing account of Mary Breckinridge, whose post-World War I journeys into Appalachia brought skilled nursing service for the first time to many remote mountain dwellers. *Mary on Horseback*, with softly atmospheric illustrations by Peter McCarty, was named a best book of 1999 by *Booklist*, *School Library Journal*, *The Horn Book*, the National Council of Teachers of English, and the National Council of Social Studies Teachers. Delving further back into American history and the art of healing, in 2007 Wells published *Red Moon at Sharpsburg*, the story of an adolescent girl struggling with loyalties, friendships, and hardships in the Shenandoah Valley of Virginia during the Civil War. After spending twelve years researching and writing the book, Wells created a story that illuminated the lives of ordinary people in wartime, especially the determination of one intelligent and courageous young woman. *Red Moon at Sharpsburg* was named a *Booklist* Editors' Choice and an ALA Notable Children's Book.

While her novels have received much recognition, it is through her picture books that Rosemary Wells has achieved her most widespread fame. Her books for preschoolers feature animal characters and highlight the real-life daily traumas of young children—starting school, dealing with bullies, sibling rivalry, and other concerns that loom large in a child's world. *Noisy Nora*, one of her early picture books, about a mouse girl who, as a middle child, craves more attention from her parents, was part of the Children's Book Showcase of the Children's Book Council when it was first published in 1974. That early recognition was followed by many other accolades: *Benjamin and Tulip* received a citation of merit from the Society of Illustrators, *Morris's Disappearing Bag* was presented the Irma Simonton Black Award in 1975, and in 1985 *Hazel's Amazing Mother* was named one of the *New York Times* Best Illustrated Books of the Year.

Wells introduced two of the most endearing and true-to-life characters in modern children's books in 1979 when she published the first of her Max and Ruby books. *Max's First Word*, *Max's New Suit*, *Max's Ride*, and *Max's Toys* were immediately taken to heart by children and parents alike who found the bunny siblings perfectly reflected family situations, always with a large dose of humor. Max is the younger brother, irrepressible and undaunted by his older sister Ruby, who is always trying to improve and instruct him. The characters were inspired by Wells's own children, Victoria and Marguerite, and reflected many of their interactions as five-year-old Victoria tried to influence the development of her baby sister, who remained oblivious to her efforts. Published in a sturdy format for toddlers, the Max and Ruby books were among the first board books of fine quality published for toddlers. The original four books were followed by another four in 1985 and many more Max and Ruby stories appeared in subsequent years. *Max's Christmas* was the first full-length picture book in this series and later entries, such as *Max's Chocolate Chicken* and *Max's Dragon Shirt*, were named to best of the year lists by *School Library Journal* and *The Horn Book*. In two of the titles the bunny characters appear in parallel stories inspired by the Greek myths of Pandora and King Midas. Max and Ruby have also inspired adaptations in both an animated show on the Nick, Jr. television channel and a live musical theater production.

Many more of Rosemary Wells's characters have channeled the experiences of preschoolers and primary-grade children. In *Shy Charles*, winner of the 1989 *Boston Globe–Horn Book* Award, Wells explored a common trait of small children through a mouse who resists all attempts of his parents to help him overcome his shyness. Faced with an emergency situation, Charles finally

"I never write for groups of children, only for individuals. If my books have any single purpose it would probably be to say to children: 'You are not alone.'"

Courtesy of Viking, Penguin Group (USA)

proves he can rise to the occasion. In books such as *My Kindergarten, Timothy Goes to School*, and *Emily's First 100 Days of School*, Wells helps children cope with the nearly universal anxiety about starting school. *Yoko*, published in 1998, introduced a kitten who is teased by her schoolmates for bringing sushi in her lunchbox, providing a subtle lesson about accepting cultural differences. Yoko has since starred in more stories about her Japanese heritage, such as *Yoko's Paper Cranes*. A compilation of six stories that illustrate the need for gentleness and understanding in school were combined in *Yoko's World of Kindness: Golden Rules for a Happy Classroom*.

For *My Very First Mother Goose*, Wells teamed up with the noted folklorist Iona Opie to create a rollicking collection of nursery rhymes for the very young. Vibrantly illustrated in bright primary colors, this volume received a *New York Times* Best Illustrated award and was cited by many journals as a best book of the year. Wells's delightfully humorous animal characters and exquisite attention to detail highlight each of the well-chosen rhymes in this volume and its companion book, *Here Comes Mother Goose*. Both were named ALA Notable Children's Books.

In collaboration with her longtime friend and fellow illustrator Susan Jeffers, Wells has provided young readers with another unforgettable character, McDuff the West Highland terrier. Both have enjoyed the companionship of "Westies" over the years, and their books about McDuff, written by Wells and illustrated by Jeffers, have proven to be great favorites ever since the first story—*McDuff Moves In*—appeared in 1997. In subsequent titles the child-like dog deals with getting lost, feeling jealous of a new baby, and many other situations that children often encounter. Wells and Jeffers have also collaborated on new adaptations and illustrated editions of enduring childhood classics such as Eric Knight's *Lassie Come-Home* and Rachel Fields's *Hitty: Her First Hundred Years*. In both volumes, Wells adapted the text and Jeffers provided the illustrations to make the stories more accessible for today's children.

Rosemary Wells has received some of the most prestigious lifetime achievement awards in the field. In 1991, she was presented the David McCord Children's Literature Citation, and in 2001 she received the Jo Osborne Award for Humor in Children's Literature from Ohio State University. The University of Southern Mississippi awarded Wells its Medallion in 2002 for outstanding contributions in the field of children's literature, and in 2006 she received the inaugural Carle Honor Illustrator Award from the Eric Carle Museum of Picture Book Art.

A tireless advocate for literacy and the importance of reading aloud to children, Rosemary Wells is a frequent presenter at conferences and book festivals with her message for parents to read to their children at least twenty minutes a day. Her books *Read to Your Bunny* and *My Shining Star: Raising a Child Who Is Ready to Learn* reiterate this message with her familiar animal characters in their bright colors and humorous poses. For many years Rosemary Wells made her home with her husband Tom in Scarborough, New York. After his death in 2001, Wells moved to Connecticut where she continues to write, illustrate, and speak out for literacy issues.

SELECTED WORKS ILLUSTRATED: *A Song to Sing, O!*, by W. S. Gilbert, 1968; *Hungry Fred*, by Paula Fox, 1969; *The Duke of Plaza Toro*, by W. S. Gilbert, 1969; *The Shooting of Dan McGrew and The Cremation of Sam McGee*, by Robert W. Service, 1969; *Marion's Manhole*, by Winifred Rosen, 1970; *The Cat That Walked by Himself*, by Rudyard Kipling, 1970; *Impossible Possum*, by Ellen Conford, 1971; *With a Deep Sea Smile*, by Virginia A. Tashjian, 1974; *Tell Me a Trudy*, by Lore Segal, 1977; *My Very First Mother Goose*, ed. by Iona Opie, 1996; *The Christmas Mystery*, by Jostein Gaardner, 1996; *Here Comes Mother Goose*, ed. by Iona Opie, 1999; *Getting to Know You! Rodgers and Hammerstein Favorites*, 2002; *Twinkle, Twinkle, Little Star*, by Jane Taylor, 2006; *Mother Goose's Little Treasures*, by Iona Opie, 2007.

SELECTED WORKS WRITTEN AND ILLUSTRATED: *John and the Rarey*, 1969; *Michael and the Mitten Test*, 1969; *The First Child*, 1970; *Martha's Birthday*, 1970; *Miranda's Pilgrims*, 1970; *Unfortunately Harriet*, 1972; *Noisy Nora*, 1973 (reissued with new illustrations 1997); *Benjamin and Tulip*, 1973; *Abdul*, 1975; *Morris's Disappearing Bag*, 1975 (reissued 1990); *Don't Spill It Again, James*, 1977 (reissued 1997); *Stanley and Rhoda*, 1978; *Max's First Word*, 1979 (reissued 1998); *Max's New Suit*, 1979 (reissued 1998); *Max's Ride*, 1979 (reissued 1998); *Max's Toys*, 1979

Courtesy of Dial Books for Young Readers

(reissued 1998); *Timothy Goes to School*, 1981 (reissued 2000); *Goodnight Fred*, 1981; *A Lion for Lewis*, 1982; *Peabody*, 1983; *Hazel's Amazing Mother*, 1985; *Max's Bedtime*, 1985 (reissued 1998); *Max's Bath*, 1985 (reissued 1998); *Max's Birthday*, 1985 (reissued 1998); *Max's Breakfast*, 1985 (reissued 1998); *Max's Christmas*, (reissued 2000), 1986; *Shy Charles*, 1988 (reissued 2001); *Max's Chocolate Chicken*, 1989 (reissued 1999); *The Little Lame Prince*, based on a story by Dinah Maria Mulock Craik, 1990; *Fritz and the Mess Fairy*, 1991; *Max's Dragon Shirt*, 1991; *Island Light* (Voyage to the Bunny Planet), 1992; *First Tomato* (Voyage to the Bunny Planet), 1992; *Moss Pillows* (Voyage to the Bunny Planet), 1992; *Max and Ruby's First Greek Myth: Pandora's Box*, 1993; *Max and Ruby's Midas: Another Greek Myth*, 1995; *Edward Unready for School*, 1995; *Edward's Overwhelming Overnight*, 1995; *Edward in Deep Water*, 1995; *Bunny Cakes*,

1997; *Bunny Money*, 1997; *Don't Spill It Again, James*, 1997; *Yoko*, 1998; *Read to Your Bunny*, 1998; *Old MacDonald* (Bunny Reads Back), 1998; *The Bear Went Over the Mountain* (Bunny Reads Back), 1998; *The Itsy-Bitsy Spider* (Bunny Reads Back), 1998; *Bingo* (Bunny Reads Back), 1999; *Max Cleans Up*, 2000; *Goodnight Max*, 2000; *Emily's First 100 Days of School*, 2000; *Bunny Party*, 2001; *Felix Feels Better*, 2001; *Letters and Sounds* (Get Set for Kindergarten), 2001; *How Many, How Much?* (Get Set for Kindergarten), 2001; *Discover and Explore* (Get Set for Kindergarten), 2001; *Adding It Up* (Get Set for Kindergarten), 2001; *Ready to Read* (Get Set for Kindergarten), 2001; *The World Around Us* (Get Set for Kindergarten), 2001; *Mama, Don't Go* (Yoko and Friends), 2001; *Yoko's Paper Cranes*, 2001; *Doris's Dinosaur* (Yoko and Friends), 2001; *Bubble-Gum Radar* (Yoko and Friends), 2002; *Play with Max and Ruby*, 2002; *Ruby's Beauty Shop*, 2002; *Emily's World of Wonders*, 2003; *Max's Christmas Stocking*, 2003; *Only You*, 2003; *Felix and the Worrier*, 2003; *Max Drives Away*, 2003; *Bunny Mail*, 2004; *Max's Halloween*, 2004; *Max's Valentine*, 2003; *My Kindergarten*, 2004; *Ruby's Rainy Day*, 2004; *Yoko's World of Kindness: Golden Rules for a Happy Classroom*, 2005; *Carry Me!*, 2006; *Max's ABC*, 2006; *My Shining Star: Raising a Child Who Is Ready to Learn*, 2006; *Max and Ruby's Show-and-Tell*, 2006; *Ruby's Falling Leaves*, 2007; *Max Counts His Chickens*, 2007; *Max's Bunny Business*, 2008; *Otto Runs for President*, 2008.

SELECTED WORKS WRITTEN: *The Fog Comes on Little Pig Feet*, 1972; *None of the Above*, 1974; *Leave Well Enough Alone*, 1977 (reissued, 2002); *When No One Was Looking*, 1984; *The Man in the Woods*, 1985 (reissued 2000); *Through the Hidden Door*, 1987 (reissued 2002); *Forest of Dreams*, illus. by Susan Jeffers, 1988; *Waiting for the Evening Star*, illus. by Susan Jeffers, 1993; *Lucy Comes to Stay*, illus. by Mark Graham, 1994; *Night Sounds, Morning Colors*, illus. by David McPhail, 1994; *Eric Knight's Lassie Come-Home*, as adapter, illus. by Susan Jeffers, 1995; *The Language of Doves*, illus. by Greg Shed, 1996; *McDuff Moves In*, illus. by Susan Jeffers, 1997; *McDuff Comes Home*, illus. by Susan Jeffers, 1997; *McDuff and the Baby*, illus. by Susan Jeffers, 1997; *McDuff's New Friend*, illus. by Susan Jeffers, 1998; *The Fisherman and His Wife: A Brand New Version*, illus. by Eleanor Hubbard, 1998; *Mary on Horseback: Three Mountain Stories*, illus. by Peter McCarty, 1998; *Tallchief: America's Prima Ballerina*, with Maria Tallchief, illus. by Gary Kelley, 1999; *Streets of Gold*, illus. by Dan Andreasen, 1999; *Rachel Field's Hitty, Her*

First Hundred Years, adapted and rewritten, illus. by Susan Jeffers, 1999; *McDuff Goes to School*, illus. by Susan Jeffers, 2001; *McDuff Saves the Day*, illus. by Susan Jeffers, 2002; *The House in the Mail*, with Tom Wells, illus. by Dan Andreasen, 2002; *Wingwalker*, illus. by Brian Selznick, 2002; *The Small World of Binky Braverman*, illus. by Richard Egielski, 2003; *McDuff Steps Out*, illus. by Susan Jeffers, 2004; *McDuff's Favorite Things*, illus. by Susan Jeffers, 2004; *McDuff's Hide and Seek*, illus. by Susan Jeffers, 2004; *McDuff's Wild Romp*, illus. by Susan Jeffers, 2005; *The Miraculous Tale of the Two Maries*, illus. by Petra Mathers, 2006; *The Gulps*, illus. by Marc Brown, 2007; *Red Moon at Sharpsburg*, 2007.

SUGGESTED READING: *Something About the Author*, vol. 156, 2005; Pendergast, Tom and Sara, eds., *St. James Guide to Children's Writers*, 1999; Pendergast, Tom and Sara, eds., *St. James Guide to Young Adult Writers*, 1999; Silvey, Anita, ed., *Children's Books and Their Creators*, 1995; *Something About the Author Autobiography Series*, vol. 1, 1986. Periodicals—Wells, Rosemary, "Rabbit Redux," *School Library Journal*, July, 2001; Wells, Rosemary, "Creating Yoko," *Book Links*, September 1998; Sutton, Roger, "A Second Look: *None of the Above*," *The Horn Book*, June/July, 1987.

WEB SITE: www.rosemarywells.com

An earlier profile of Rosemary Wells appeared in *Fourth Book of Junior Authors and Illustrators* (1978).

Bruce Whatley

February 13, 1954–

"Though I was born in Wales, I immigrated to Australia with my parents when I was five. Most of my childhood was spent in Australia, my early teens in a rough industrial town where the desert meets the sea. It was a great place to grow up in the late 1960s.

"I couldn't read until I was ten or so, but I've been drawing for as long as I can remember.

"At fifteen I moved back to Wales. I went to a traditional British Grammar School where the kids wore uniforms and the teachers black cloaks. My first day I arrived in brown flared pants and moccasins and was told to go and get a hair cut! What a rebel! As soon as I was old enough, I escaped to art college. I completed my Bachelor of Arts Degree (Mum was very proud!) specializing in advertising and illustration.

"I then worked in London for several years, in advertising agencies as an art director and at the same time working as a freelance illustrator. While in the London agencies I met Rosie Smith, now wife, mother, and co-author of many of my books.

"Rosie and I moved to Australia in 1980—originally for a year—and it's been our home ever since. Right through the 1980s and early 1990s I worked in the advertising industry in Sydney: art directing, writing TV commercials, illustrating, animating and occasionally having an exhibition of oils and water colours.

"It wasn't until I had children that I started to think about children's books. I had always bought picture books because I love illustrations, but I had never thought of doing one myself. My first attempt was a story called *Paroo and the Boing Boing Races*. I took it along with my illustration portfolio and a large plaster model I had made of the main character to see an editor at HarperCollins Sydney. She loved the illustrations and model but wasn't too sure about my writing. Not wanting to lose that contact, I said 'Oh, I've got an idea about my dog. I'll send it to you.'

"Trouble was I didn't have an idea about my dog!

"That night I went home and wrote the story. It wrote itself really. We had a white boxer at the time. She was a fantastic dog, but boy, was she ugly! I produced a dummy book, text and sketches, and sent it to the publisher two days later. They liked it.

Photo by Rosie Smith

"So in 1992 my first book was published: *The Ugliest Dog in the World*. This was followed quickly by another six books, the largest and most elaborate being my first major collaboration with Rosie, *Whatley's Quest*, a journey through the alphabet to find a hidden treasure, which turned out to be the ability to read.

"It was the success of *Whatley's Quest* that took us to the United States in 1995. We rented out our house in Australia, packed up the kids and moved to a small town on a lake in New Hampshire—and had a great time. Again it was only going to be for a year . . . but it ended up being four. During this time Rosie and I wrote *Detective Donut and the Wild Goose Chase* and

Captain Pajamas. I also illustrated *The Night Before Christmas* and *The Teddy Bears' Picnic*, among others.

"In late 1999 we moved back to Australia.

"I love to experiment with illustration styles. Lots of things can influence my approach to illustrating a picture book: the text itself, the age group the book is aimed at, or maybe an illustration style I've seen somewhere else that I find inspiring. *Dragons of Galapagos*, for instance, was drawn with my left hand. But that's a whole other story!

"I also tend to be my own worst critic. I very rarely look at a book once I've finished it. I think it's because by the time I finish it, I have thought of a better way of doing it. I find it's a constant learning process, that I'm illustrating things now I couldn't do a couple of years ago.

"As for my stories, Rosie and my children Ben and Ellyn are my main inspiration. Many of my books are a result of something they have said or done, usually really silly things. I continue to write and illustrate children's books full time—sometimes with Rosie, sometimes with other authors, as in *Diary of a Wombat*. To me a picture book is like a low-budget movie. Instead of a camera, I use a pencil or a brush. But I get to cast it, build the sets, design the costumes and makeup, produce and direct! I am sure I have way more fun doing my books than anybody could possibly have reading them. It is a magical place to be."

> "Lots of things can influence my approach to illustrating a picture book: the text itself, the age group the book is aimed at, or maybe an illustration style I've seen some-where else that I find inspiring."

CB CB CB

A versatile illustrator with a flair for humor, Bruce Whatley was born in Wales but immigrated to Australia with his parents when he was five. He lived first in Adelaide, then in Whyalla, South Australia. He returned to Britain in 1969 and studied Visual Communications at Manchester Polytechnic, specializing in illustration. One of his tutors was Tony Ross, a well-known illustrator of children's picture books. Whatley received his Bachelor of Arts Degree in 1975.

Much of his early career was spent in advertising as an art director and freelance illustrator. He worked in London from 1975 to 1980. After moving to Sydney, Australia with his wife, Rosie Smith, he spent two years doing freelance work. He then became a senior art director with McCann Erickson for two years, working on such diverse accounts as Coca-Cola, Levis, and Nescafé. When he returned to freelance illustration, he continued to illustrate for Levis, as well as State Rail, Stuart Membery, Johnson & Johnson, and *Good Weekend* Magazine.

He also animated TV commercials for Krondorf Wines and *Australia Post*.

During those years, Whatley exhibited his fine art—oils and watercolors—with the Australian Outback being his main theme. Rosie Smith provided some of the photographic references from which he worked. In 1992, Whatley's first picture book about the family dog, Skitty, *The Ugliest Dog in the World*, was published and named a Children's Book Council of Australia (CBCA) Notable Picture Book. He often collaborates on the concept and text of his books with his wife, Rosie Smith, and they give credit to their children, Ben and Ellyn, for many of their best ideas. Bruce and Rosie came out with their second book, *Looking for Crabs*, later in the same year. It was short-listed by the CBCA and was soon followed by another book about Skitty, called *That Magnetic Dog*. The 48-page adventure and alphabet book called *Whatley's Quest* appeared in 1994.

Courtesy of HarperCollins Publishers

Tales from Grandad's Attic became another CBCA Notable Picture Book. *Detective Donut and the Wild Goose Chase*, a spoof on *The Maltese Falcon* and other films from the 1930s, was an Honor Book for the CBCA Award and was selected by the Society of Illustrators in New York for their 40th Annual Award Exhibition. Their first book published in the United States, *Detective Donut* appeared while the Whatley family was living in New Hampshire. During that time Bruce turned two American classic stories about Mrs. Piggle-Wiggle—*The Won't-Take-a-Bath Cure* and *The Won't-Pick-Up-Toys Cure*—into illustrated picture books. He created swirling acrylic illustrations for a new edition of *The Night Before Christmas* and lush oil paintings for *The First Noel*, which was published with an accompanying CD of Elvis Presley's recording of the carol. A trilogy of song books— *The Teddy Bears' Picnic*, *Ain't No Bugs on Me*, and *What Will You Wear, Jenny Jenkins?*—presented illustrated songs arranged and performed by Jerry Garcia and David Grisman, packaged with an audio tape.

Returning to Australia in 1999, Bruce Whatley wrote and illustrated *Wait! No Paint!*, a twist on the traditional folk story "The Three Little Pigs" in which the illustrator inserts himself into the story. It won the South Dakota Prairie Bud Award, a children's choice competition for grades K–3. *Little White Dogs Can't Jump*, co-authored with Rosie Smith, harks back to their earliest work; it is a story of a family's ugly dog and how to get it into the back of the car. *Diary of a Wombat*, written by Jackie French, was named an ALA Notable Children's Book, a CBCA Honour Book, an Australian Bookseller's Association Book of the Year and a Koala Book Award Book of the Year. A nonfiction tale, *Quetta*, written by Gary Crew, involves the sinking of a passenger liner in 1890 and an unidentified baby girl who is saved. Another true story, *Dragons of Galapagos*, was both written and illustrated by Whatley and has the distinction of being the first book he illustrated with his left hand.

Bruce Whatley now lives on the coast in New South Wales, Australia, with his wife Rosie and their two children.

SELECTED WORKS WRITTEN AND ILLUSTRATED: *The Ugliest Dog in the World*, 1992; *Looking for Crabs*, with Rosie Smith, 1992; *I Wanna Be Famous*, 1993; *The Magic Dictionary*, 1993; *The Magnetic Dog*, with Rosie Smith, 1994; *Whatley's Quest*, with Rosie Smith, 1994; *Tales from Grandad's Attic*, with Rosie Smith, 1996; *Detective Donut and the Wild Goose Chase*, with Rosie Smith, 1997; *The Flying Emu*, 1999; *The First Noel*, 1999; *Captain Pajamas: Defender of the Universe*, with Rosie Smith, 2000; *Little White Dogs Can't Jump*, with Rosie Smith, 2001; *Cowboy Pirate*, 2001; *Wait! No Paint!*, 2001; *Dragons of Galapagos*, 2003; *Clinton Gregory's Secret*, 2008.

SELECTED WORKS ILLUSTRATED: *The Teddy Bears' Picnic*, arr. by Jerry Garcia and David Grisman, 1996; *The Won't-Take-a-Bath Cure*, adapt. from the text by Betty McDonald, 1997; *The Won't-Pick-Up-Toys Cure*, adapt. from the text by Betty MacDonald, 1997; *There Ain't No Bugs on Me*, arr. by Jerry Garcia and David Grisman, 1999; *The Night Before Christmas*, by Clement C. Moore, 1999; *What Will You Wear, Jenny Jenkins?*, arr. by Jerry Garcia and David Grisman, 2000; *All Things Bright and Beautiful*, by Cecil Frances Alexander, 2001; *Quetta*, by Gary Crew, 2002; *Diary of a Wombat*, by Jackie French, 2002; *Here Comes Santa Claus*, by Gene Autry and Oakley Haldeman, 2002; *The Perfect Pet*, by Margie Palatini, 2003; *Too Many Pears!*, by Jackie French, 2003; *On the First Day of Grade School*, by Emily Brenner, 2004; *I Want a Hippopotamus for Christmas*, by John Rox, 2005; *Pete the Sheep-Sheep*, by Jackie French, 2005; *Pig on the Titanic: a True Story*, by Gary Crew, 2005; *Ruthie Bon Bair:*

Do Not Go to Bed with Wringing Wet Hair, by Susan Lubner, 2006.

SUGGESTED READING: Watson, Victor, *The Cambridge Guide to Children's Books in English*, 2001; Scobie, Susan, comp., *The Dromkeen Book of Australian Children's Illustrators*, 1997.

"I have forever been on a search for meaning. From the time I can remember, I was fascinated with people and stories. I wanted to know where people came from; I watched how they cared for one another.

"I was born in Mobile, Alabama and spent almost all my childhood summers growing up in Louin, Mississippi, where I watched the socks spin at the washerteria and had picnics in the cemetery by myself. I wandered the cemetery and found all my kinfolks and wondered where they had gone, and what their lives had meant to them, to others. I missed them. I wanted my life to mean something, but I didn't know how to articulate that—I just felt it.

"My father was an Air Force pilot, so we moved a lot when I was young. When I was nine, I lived outside of Washington, D.C. during the height of the Cuban Missile Crisis. I wanted to know what it meant that we had to duck under our desks during air raid drills and be afraid of Cuba and Russia. Why? We were all just people! I spent many a night lying awake in my pink bedroom under a pink canopy, thinking about ways to get President Kennedy and Nikita Krushchev into a room and talk to them! 'If they'd just let me explain, I could convince the Russians not to bomb us. . . .' That was my prayer. I didn't talk with Krushchev and he didn't bomb the United States, and I wondered what it all meant, especially the next year, 1963, when President Kennedy was assassinated.

"In 1964 I was eleven. I went to Mississippi for the summer to find that the Pine View Pool had closed. So had the roller-skating rink and the Cool Dip ice cream parlor in Bay Springs. The Civil Rights Act had been passed, giving all Americans of all colors the right to eat in public restaurants, drink at the same

Courtesy of Deborah Wiles

Deborah Wiles

May 7, 1953–

drinking fountains, and swim in the same public pools. Many white-owned businesses in Mississippi shut their doors. Was this how we cared for one another?

"Four years later I was fifteen. Martin Luther King was assassinated in Memphis, and then Robert Kennedy was assassinated in Los Angeles. Both these events shot me through the heart and galvanized my thinking. I began to pay close attention to the news. There was a war going on in Vietnam. My father was going to have to fly in it. So my family moved to Charleston, S.C., where I went to high school with long-haired, angry boys who picketed the school with signs that said, 'Jesus had long hair!' There were fights in the lunchroom between black and white students. The school closed on Jewish high holy days—I hadn't even known there *were* Jewish high holy days. I was learning so much, and I searched for meaning in what I was learning. Why did people fight one another, why did they kill each other? These felt like such important questions, and no one could answer them.

"The books I have published are fiction, but they are emotionally true and come out of the experiences and feelings of my life."

"I found a lot of meaning and comfort in music and stories. I loved rock and roll, especially the Beatles and all protest music. I became the rebel—the black sheep—in my family. I read a lot, but I loved family stories even more. I still sat on the front porch in Mississippi and listened to aunts and uncles tell story after story about the old people who now rested in the Louin, Mississippi cemetery and I wondered about myself, now. Who was I becoming? What would I do with my life before it was my turn to rest in the Louin, Mississippi cemetery?

"I married young, at eighteen. I had children young and I was alone at a young age with my children. This also defined me as a human being and a writer. I know what it feels like to be scared, to have my heart broken, to be lonely, and to want to belong. I so wanted to belong. I wanted to be safe. I wanted to matter.

"I found my way by keeping a notebook of my thoughts and feelings and, finally, I wrote my own stories. The books I have published are fiction, but they are emotionally true and come out of the experiences and feelings of my life. I hope they connect with readers whose lives are surely different from my own, but whose hearts are the same color no matter who they are, and who want to belong, want to matter, want to find meaning. Writing stories is my way of making meaning."

ଔ   ଔ   ଔ

"I come from a family with a lot of dead people," pronounced Deborah Wiles as she began a speech at Vermont College in 2004. That provocative—and humorous—statement is an insightful clue to her core sensibility, her writing, and her characters, who are far from lifeless but are actually filled with warmth, vitality, and an appreciation for life and living.

Born Debbie Edwards, the author was the oldest of three children in a family that moved many times during her childhood as her father's Air Force career took them to Hawaii, Maryland, Washington, D.C, and Charleston, South Carolina. She graduated from Wagner High School on Clark Air Force Base in the Philippines. She learned that a base could be a temporary home but it was the summers she spent with family in Mississippi that became her taproot of place and belonging. The foundation of her writing is shaped by 3 Ms: moments, memory, and meaning. These are the keys that unlock her stories. Indeed, those Mississippi memories of katydids calling from the pines, listening to family stories on the porch, and having picnics in the cemetery have provided a fertile background for her books.

After high school graduation, Wiles attended Jones County Junior College in Mississippi, but her formal education was interrupted when she married after one semester. She wrote essays as a freelance writer for a long time while her children were growing up, and she held many jobs to support them. She worked as a journalist, oral history gatherer, teacher, school bus driver, burger queen, and underwear salesperson. Through all these endeavors Wiles observed and absorbed her experiences, eventually weaving them into the fabric of her stories.

Courtesy of Harcourt Children's Books, Houghton Mifflin Harcourt,

In her first novel, *Love, Ruby Lavender*, Wiles tapped into her beloved summer memories with a cast of very real characters. The book was named an ALA Notable Children's Books, an NCTE Notable Book in the Language Arts, and nominated for 26 state book awards.

In the same year she also published a picture book, *Freedom Summer*. The story grew out of her frustration during the summer of 1964 and expressed the injustice she had felt when the color of people's skin denied them access to the town swimming pool. Besides being named a Notable Social Studies Trade Book, *Freedom Summer* won the Coretta Scott King/John Steptoe Award for the illustrator, Jerome Lagarrigue, and the Ezra Jack Keats Award for both author and illustrator. Wiles's second picture book, *One Wide Sky*, evoked the natural world in rhyming counting couplets and included lullaby music.

With just three books to her credit, Wiles became the first children's book author to be named Writer-in-Residence at Thurber House, the boyhood home of James Thurber, in Columbus, Ohio, as well as the 2004 recipient of the PEN/Phyllis Reynolds Naylor Working Writer Fellowship. Then with the publication of *Each Little Bird That Sings* Wiles gained widespread recognition. The poignant story of ten-year-old Comfort Snowberger, who has attended 247 funerals because her family runs the town funeral home in Snapfinger, Mississippi, is a quintessential Southern coming-of-age novel. It won the E.B. White Read Aloud Award from the Association of Booksellers for Children and the Josette Frank Award from the Bank Street College; it was also named a Golden Kite Honor book and a finalist for the 2005 National Book Award for young people, among many other honors.

In 2004, after living for 25 years in Frederick, Maryland, Wiles returned to the Deep South. She lives in a little house in Atlanta, Georgia. Her four children are grown and she has three grandchildren. Her motto in life is stated by one of her most memorable characters, Uncle Edisto in *Each Little Bird That Sings*: "Open your arms to life! Let it strut into your heart with all its messy glory." In each of her books, Wiles helps her readers do just that.

SELECTED WORKS WRITTEN: *Love, Ruby Lavender*, 2001; *Freedom Summer*, illus. by Jerome Lagarrigue, 2001; *One Wide Sky*, illus. by Tim Bowers, 2003; *Each Little Bird That Sings*, 2005; *The Aurora County All-Stars*, 2007.

SUGGESTED READINGS: *Something About the Author*, vol. 171, 2007; Wiles, Deborah, Speech: "I Come from a Family with a Lot of Dead People," Vermont College, July 23, 2004.

WEB SITE: www.deborahwiles.com

"**H**ow to Become Rich and Famous in One Easy Step (and other stuff that has nothing to do with making kids' books) by your pal, Mo Willems

Photo by Cher Willems

"Okay, okay, I know you all want to get to the 'Rich and Famous' part right off, but I'm not gonna give that away without making you read some of my earnest pontificating about kids' books first, all right? So, settle in (and no reading ahead).

"Now where was I? Ah, yes . . . Why make kids' books (or as University students say, Childrens' Literature)? Well, let's go back to my childhood in New Orleans. Ever since I was quite young I dreamed of growing up and becoming, well, a Gas Station Attendant. Unfortunately, children can't really be Gas Station Attendants, just like they can't be Astronauts, or Lawyers, or Dental Hygienists. Sure, they can pretend to be those things, but that's just pretending.

"One thing children can be (for real) is author/illustrators. All they need is paper, pencil, and a bit of hard work and presto! they've created drawings and words that others can see and read! And (even cooler) this is true for anyone. Just make up a story or comic strip and show it to a friend and you've communicated with an audience, you've met a deadline, you're an author/illustrator!

Mo Willems

February 11, 1968–

"So, partly to sooth my bitterness about the whole Gas Station Attendant thing, I became a child author/illustrator at the age of three or four and I transformed. I was filled with stories for others to hear. I wrote, I drew, I shared. It was wonderful. Until I encountered that most insidious evil, Adult Politeness.

"Even if I knew my story was second-rate, invariably, patronizing Adults praised it to the skies. 'How good for someone your age!' 'Did you do that all by yourself?' 'My, my, my . . .' My, my, *what*? Soon, I couldn't tell if my stories were good or bad because these stupid adults pretended to like whatever I wrote.

"That's when I hit upon my clever scheme.

"I made my stories funny. Even foolish, patronizing Adults can't fake a laugh. So, now it was easy to tell if my doodles and silly stories worked. Laughs = good. Polite comments = it stinks.

"Look, there's nothing special about this; I was like all those other children who take great pleasure in making up funny stories for others. I just forgot to stop. While my peers foolishly gave up storytelling for Gas Station Attending or Lawyering or Hygienistizing, I drew comix for newspapers, told jokes in comedy clubs, made cartoon films, recalled stories on radio programmes (this was for the BBC so I'm allowed to spell 'programs' that way), wrote and drew for television, and finally made kids' books.

"And, yes, these books are a return to those quiet childhood days when writing and drawing and making stuff up was the most fun thing imaginable. Even now, my drawings remain as simply constructed as possible, so that kids can copy my characters to create their own adventures (much as I did with Charlie Brown and Snoopy years ago). And I still try to make my stories funny, so I know when they work. My life is no different than it was in the early 1970s; I'm a working author/illustrator.

"Pretty touching, eh? Oh. You're still waiting for the 'Rich and Famous' part. Okay, here we go . . . How to Become Rich and Famous in One Easy Step (by Mo Willems, who's neither, so I don't know why you're listening to him):

"Step One: Go into Crime (robbery is most effective). You'll get lots of money from the stuff you steal (particularly if you're stealing money) and one day (when you get caught) you'll get in the newspaper (maybe with a picture of your face and a profile, so make sure they get your best side) and you'll be famous (or infamous, which is close enough)!

"Or do you want to know how to be happy? Make a story for someone else and watch 'em read it. If they laugh, you'll be happy. Guaranteed."

> *"I was like all those other children who take great pleasure in making up funny stories for others. I just forgot to stop."*

ᘓ   ᘓ   ᘓ

The son of Dutch immigrants to America, Mo Willems was born in Illinois but grew up in New Orleans. In 1990 he graduated from New York University's Tisch School of the Arts, with a B.F.A. in Film, Television, and Animation, and immediately set off with a backpack and a sketchpad to see the world. The cartoon chronicle of that journey—*You Can Never Find a Rickshaw When It Monsoons*—was published in 2006. Between his return from world travels in 1991 and his highly successful start in publishing picture books in 2003, Willems worked variously as an animator, stand-up comic, radio commentator, ceramicist, and bubble gum card painter. From 1994 to 2002, Willems collected six Emmy awards for his work as a scriptwriter and animator for

Courtesy of Hyperion Books, Disney Press

Sesame Street. He created and directed *The Off Beats* for the Nickelodeon cable network and *Sheep in the Big City* for the Cartoon network, and served as a head writer for the animated series *Codename: Kids Next Door.* Early influences on his drawing were the work of Charles Schulz and Saul Steinberg. It was the spare and simple style of these now classic cartoonists and the honest emotion of their work, a combination of humor and melancholy, that Willems found highly appealing and eventually incorporated into his illustrations.

Mo Willems' first picture book made use of humor, economy of line, and childlike emotion, and also had an interactive quality. *Don't Let the Pigeon Drive the Bus!* became a critical success and an instant bestseller. It was named a *Booklist* Editors' Choice, a *Bulletin of the Center for Children's Books* Blue Ribbon title, and an ALA Notable Children's Book. Awarded a Caldecott Honor Book citation, *Don't Let the Pigeon Drive the Bus!* catapulted its creator to overnight stardom. His second book, *Time to Pee!*, published the same year, tackled the age-old problem of toilet training with characteristic humor and received a National Parenting Publications Award for a book for infants and toddlers.

Knuffle Bunny: A Cautionary Tale presented yet another large issue for small children—the temporary disappearance of a beloved stuffed animal. Willems has an uncanny knack for expressing childhood's true emotions, in both words and pictures. The inspiration for this title came from his young daughter Trixie, whose favorite stuffed toy was left behind at the neighborhood Laundromat. This traumatic drama for the preschool set became another bestseller, was cited on many best-of-the-year lists, and earned a second Caldecott Honor Book Award. It also received an Honor Book citation for the Charlotte Zolotow Award, presented for excellence in picture book writing, and won the Irma S. and James H. Black Award from Bank Street College.

Leonardo, the Terrible Monster, a delightful twist on children's fears of monsters, was named an ALA Notable Children's Book. The avian star of Willems's original success, that determined and sly con artist Pigeon, has appeared in several sequels and board book editions that continue to delve into thorny issues for young children, such as staying up past bedtime.

In *Knuffle Bunny Too: A Case of Mistaken Identity*, Willems presents another familiar situation when Trixie goes to school with her beloved stuffed animal only to discover that another girl in the class has an identical bunny. This leads to a nighttime crisis, and ultimately to a new best friend. As in the first Knuffle Bunny book, Willems's unique blend of cartoon-style art set against the photographic background of a city neighborhood produces a cinematic effect that is very appealing. This title won him a third Caldecott Honor Book Award.

In 2007 Willems introduced two new characters into his pantheon, Elephant and Piggie. In the classic tradition of easy-reader friendship stories, this series of books employs a limited vocabulary but is still attuned to the nuances of personality development. Accompanied, as always, by the artist's minimalist drawings and comic-book style action, one of the first Elephant and Piggie titles, *There Is a Bird on Your Head!*, received ALA's Theodor Seuss Geisel Award for the most distinguished book for beginning readers.

Mo Willems has embraced his new career as author/illustrator wholeheartedly. He has contributed to anthologies as diverse as *Guys Write for Guys Read*, compiled by Jon Scieszka; *Every Man for Himself*, a collection of growing-up stories for teenage boys; and *9-11: September 11th 2001*, in which comic book writers and artists tell memorable stories about that cataclysmic date. Willems has exhibited his work in galleries and museums across the nation and curated a show in 2006 for the Eric Carle Museum of Picture Book Art. After many years of living in Brooklyn, he moved to Massachusetts in 2008 with his wife and daughter.

SELECTED WORKS: *Don't Let the Pigeon Drive the Bus*, 2003; *Time to Pee!*, 2003; *Knuffle Bunny: A Cautionary Tale*, 2004; *The Pigeon Finds a Hot Dog!*, 2004; *Leonardo, the Terrible Monster*, 2005; *The Pigeon Has Feelings, Too!: A Smidgeon of a Pigeon*, 2005; *The Pigeon Loves Things That Go!: A Smidgeon of a Pigeon*, 2005; *Time to Say Please!*, 2005; *Don't Let the Pigeon Stay Up Late!*, 2006; *Edwina, The Dinosaur Who Didn't Know She Was Extinct*, 2006; *You Can Never Find a Rickshaw When It Monsoons: The World on One Cartoon a Day*, 2006; *Knuffle Bunny Too: A Case of Mistaken Identity*, 2007; *My Friend Is Sad* (Elephant and Piggie), 2007; *Today I Will Fly!* (Elephant and Piggie), 2007; *There Is a Bird on Your Head!* (Elephant and Piggie), 2007; *I Am Invited to a Party!* (Elephant and Piggie), 2007; *The Pigeon Wants a Puppy!*, 2008; *I Will Surprise My Friend!* (Elephant and Piggie), 2008; *I Love My New Toy* (Elephant and Piggie), 2008.

SELECTED WORKS AS CONTRIBUTOR: *9-11: September 11th 2001: The World's Finest Comic Book Writers and Artists Tell Stories to Remember*, 2002; *Thanks and Giving: All Year Long*, comp. by Marlo Thomas, 2004; *Guys Write for Guys Read: Boys' Favorite Authors Write about Being Boys*, ed. by Jon Scieszka, 2005; *Every Man for Himself: Ten Original Stories about Being a Guy*, ed. by Nancy Mercado, 2005; *Bizarro World*, 2006.

SUGGESTED READING: *Something About the Author*, vol. 154, 2005. Periodicals—Larson, Susan, "New Orleans Native Mo Willems Scores Again with *The Pigeon Wants a Puppy!*" *The Times-Picayune*, April 16, 2008; Minzesheimer, Bob, "Mo Willems Draws on the Funny Side of Failure," *USA Today*, May 8, 2006; Cramer, Susan Spencer, "Mo Willems: Making Failure Funny," *Publishers Weekly*, Feb. 21, 2005; Goodman, Martin, "Talking in His Sheep: A Conversation with Mo Willems," *Animation World Magazine*, June 25, 2001.

WEB SITE: www.mowillems.com

Photo by Jeff Bart

Jonah Winter

August 19, 1962–

"**I** guess you'd just have to say that I went into the family business: children's books. My mother is Jeanette Winter, the celebrated illustrator and author, a person who knew from an early age that she wanted to be a children's book illustrator. Me? I had no idea, when I was a kid, that I would someday go into this line of work.

"I wanted to be a professional clarinetist. And then when I went to college and lost the key to my clarinet case, I decided I wanted to be something even more practical than a clarinetist: a *poet*. Pulling the curtains closed on my dark dorm room, I wrote depressing poems about winter and graveyards. They weren't bad poems, but it was clear to me by the time I graduated from college that I would have to find a 'real job.' I mean, for a while I sat by the phone and waited for someone to call me, saying, 'Mr. Winter? We'd like to pay you millions of dollars to write short, obscure poems about basement apartments . . . how does *that* sound?!?'

"But alas, the call never came, and so I got a job as an editorial assistant at Alfred A. Knopf, in the children's book department. I worked for my mother's editor, Frances Foster. It paid a whopping $12,000 a year. The people were nice, though, and I enjoyed reading children's book manuscripts, especially picture book manuscripts, since I could usually read them from beginning to end without falling asleep or getting distracted. But after a year of the workaday world, I decided to go back to school, graduate school, in order to pursue my passion for writing poetry.

"I got a Master's of Fine Arts in Creative Writing which, along with 25 cents, might still get you a pack of gum. Originally, I had thought this degree would help me get a college teaching job, but then after graduating I learned the grim reality: In order to get a teaching job, I would need to have a book of my poems published by a reputable publisher. And this was easier said than done. I had used my time in graduate school to write poems, whereas apparently, had I been more practical-minded, I might have used this time making connections in the poetry world. But: I imagine it might be clear by this point in my story that practicality has never been my strong suit.

"So I got another publishing job at Alfred A. Knopf, and climbed the corporate ladder to the position of Associate Editor. At the end of my third year back in publishing, I did not earn enough money to take myself out for lunch on my birthday. So for my birthday lunch, I accepted the charity of an office-mate who gave me the dried wonton noodles that had come with her take-out hot & sour soup. I put them on a paper plate and dipped them in some spare mustard and duck sauce that I had saved for just such an emergency. As my tears fell onto the wonton noodles, making them saltier and soggier, I made what was to become a very important decision: I would move to San Francisco and pursue the life of a freelance children's book writer. Now there's a practical plan! My mother, upon hearing this plan, openly wept. She had always hoped I would become something respectable, like an editor.

"And yet . . . she had only just recently asked me to write the text for a picture book biography on Diego Rivera—she asked this of me because she was apparently quite fond of a series of adult poems I'd written in the form of book reports from the point of view of a misinformed, illiterate, adolescent narrator. The book, *Diego*, not only got published, but it turned out to be quite successful. The royalties from it helped to pay for my first couple of years being a renegade freelancer.

"During those years, I joined a band, 'Ed's Redeeming Qualities,' which toured around the country in dubious vehicles—a '73 Ford LTD named Mel and a Toyota minivan named The Ford. I played the clarinet, the accordion, the tin whistle, the mandolin, and a cardboard drum with a dog painted on it. And with the help of my literary agent, Liza Voges, I started getting more books published, including books that I illustrated myself.

"One morning I woke up and decided I wanted to illustrate my own books on baseball. I had collected baseball cards as a kid, and I was still obsessed with baseball cards as an adult, so I decided to create baseball cards for Negro League players who had never had baseball cards made of them during their careers in the Negro Leagues. This turned out to be the most fulfilling thing I had ever done, combining my interests in writing, painting, baseball and civil rights in one small picture book. A few years after this, a couple of books of my adult poems were published, as well as several more children's books. And there you have it. I'm still not a particularly practical person, but I do my best to do the things that bring me satisfaction and fulfillment. One of those things is writing and illustrating picture book biographies

> "I'm still not a particularly practical person, but I do my best to do the things that bring me satisfaction and fulfillment."

about people and subjects that matter to me. And I am grateful for this life."

cx cx cx

The son of Rodgers Lee and Jeanette Margot Winter, Jonah Winter has always enjoyed a challenge. Growing up in Fort Worth, Texas, he had very little interest in reading and preferred to be outside playing baseball or working on his baseball card collection. In interviews he has admitted that his early difficulty with reading ultimately prompted his desire to become a writer. He believed that if he worked hard enough at something, he could succeed at it. Similarly, while in grade school, he had little appreciation of music, yet through hard work and determination, he became known in high school as a proficient musician with the ability to play a wide variety of instruments, most notably his favorite, the clarinet.

Courtesy of Alfred A. Knopf, Random House, Inc.

After receiving his B. A. degree from Oberlin College in 1984, Winter worked as an editorial assistant at the publisher Alfred A. Knopf from 1984 to 1985. He left Knopf to work on his Master of Fine Arts at the University of Virginia, completing his degree in 1987. He returned to Knopf in 1989, this time as an associate editor, but left that position in 1991 to embark on a freelance writing career, drawing on all the things he had loved since childhood—art, baseball, and music—to write biographies for young readers.

His first book, a collaborative effort with his mother, the noted author/illustrator Jeanette Winter, was about the Mexican mural artist Diego Rivera. Illustrated by Jeanette and written by Jonah, *Diego* earned a Blue Ribbon citation from the *Bulletin of the Center for Children's Books* and was chosen by the *Hungry Mind Review* as one of the 100 Best Children's Books of the 20th Century. The success of *Diego* gave Winter the opportunity to pursue his writing career. Having written about Diego Rivera, he next turned his attention to Rivera's wife, the Mexican artist Frida Kahlo. His book *Frida*, published ten years after *Diego*, with illustrations by Ana Juan, was named an ALA Notable Children's Book.

Winter's broad interests prompt him to read extensively about his subjects before writing about them. With his poet's gift for language, he is able to take complicated life stories and make them accessible to young readers. His passion for baseball is apparent in *Fair Ball!*, a collection of fourteen biographies of players from baseball's Negro Leagues. A companion volume was published soon after—*¡Beisbol!*, a biographical volume focusing on Latino players. One of the Latino players led Winter to devote an entire book to him, and *Roberto Clemente: Pride of the Pittsburgh Pirates*, illustrated by Raúl Colón, was also named an ALA Notable Children's Book.

With his love of music and his own experience as a clarinet player, Winter enjoys writing about famous musicians to help young readers discover their work. *Once Upon a Time in Chicago*, another collaboration with his artist mother, is a biography of the swing-era big-band musician Benny Goodman, and *The 39 Apartments of Ludwig van Beethoven* is a humorous look at the legendary classical composer. *Dizzy*, a biography of jazz giant Dizzy Gillespie, with vibrant illustrations by Sean Qualls, explores the creative force behind Gillespie's style. *Dizzy* was named a *School Library Journal* Best Book, a BCCB Blue Ribbon title, and an ALA Notable Children's Book.

Married to Sally Ann Denmead since October 27, 2000, Winter presently lives in Pittsburgh, Pennsylvania after making his home for 25 years in New York City. In 1997 he was awarded a fellowship residency at the MacDowell Arts Colony; he also received the Cohen Award for best poem in the literary magazine *Plowshares* in 2000. His poetry was included in the 2001 edition of *The Pushcart Prize*, a collection of the best work from small presses. His has published two volumes of poetry for adults, entitled *Maine* and *Amnesia*.

SELECTED WORKS FOR CHILDREN: *Diego*, illus. by Jeanette Winter, 1991; *Once Upon a Time in Chicago: The Story of Benny Goodman*, illus. by Jeanette Winter, 2000; *Frida*, illus. by Ana Juan, 2002; *Paul Revere and the Bell Ringers*, illus. by Bert Dodson, 2003; *Roberto Clemente: Pride of the Pittsburgh Pirates*, illus. by Raúl Colón, 2005; *Dizzy*, illus. by Sean Qualls, 2006; *The 39 Apartments of Ludwig van Beethoven*, illus. by Barry Blitt, 2006; *The Secret World of Hildegard von Bingen*, illus. by Jeanette Winter, 2007; *Muhammad Ali: Champion of the World*, illus. by François Roca, 2008; *Steel Town*, illus. by Terry Widener, 2008.

SELECTED WORKS WRITTEN AND ILLUSTRATED: *Fair Ball!: 14 Great Stars from Baseball's Negro Leagues*, 1999; *¡Béisbol! Latino Baseball Pioneers and Legends*, 2001.

SELECTED WORKS FOR ADULTS: *Maine*, 2002; *Amnesia*, 2004.

SUGGESTED READING: Guidry, Nate, "Author Trumpets Dizzy's Career," *Pittsburgh Post-Gazette*, Sep. 13, 2006.

A biography of Jonah Winter's mother, Jeanette Winter, can be found in *Seventh Book of Junior Authors and Illustrators*, 1996.

Photo by Jason Stemple

Jane Yolen

February 11, 1939–

"**I** come from a line of storytellers. My great-grandfather was the Reb, the storyteller in a small village in the Ukraine, my father an author, my mother a mostly unpublished writer. From early childhood I have written. In fact, in first grade I was the heralded author of the class musical about talking vegetables. I played the chief carrot and our grand finale was a singing salad. When I was in eighth grade, I wrote a social studies essay about New York State's manufacturing, all in rhyme. I also wrote my first two books: a nonfiction book on pirates and an epic novel in seventeen pages. This was reflected later in my appreciation for the short story form.

"But if I had to point to my primary source of inspiration, it would be to the folk culture. My earliest readings were the folk tales and fairy stories I took home from the library by the dozens. Even when I was old enough to make the trip across Central Park by myself, I was still not too old for those folk fantasies. I still read fantasy stories and science fiction and folk literature for pleasure. And all those fey creatures, merfolk, tree maidens, and dragons of the old world find their way into many of my own tales.

"My father, who played the guitar and sang, first introduced me to folk songs, but I went him some better in learning every old English, Scottish, Irish, and Appalachian love song and ballad I ever heard. Years later, at Smith College, I made a relatively unhappy college career bearable by singing with a guitar-playing boyfriend at fraternity parties and mixers. We made a little money, a lot of friends, and imprinted hundreds of folk tunes on our hungry minds. Today, in addition to books and stories, I write songs and song lyrics for folksingers, rock groups, and composers, some of which have been recorded.

"I got into children's books basically because of a lie I told an editor. She was looking for writers and had found me by asking at Smith College if there were any recent graduates who might be working on book manuscripts. When she contacted me to ask if I had a manuscript, I lied and said I did. When she asked me to produce it, I had no choice but to sit down and write something quickly. I thought children's books would be the easiest and quickest. I was to discover painfully and thoroughly over the next 45 years that, in fact, children's books are among the most difficult manuscripts to write. But back then, I didn't know any better and wrote some picture books that an artist friend of mine illustrated. Needless to say, the editor rejected them, as did all the other editors to whom we submitted them.

"Then my father introduced me to a publishing friend who was vice-president of David McKay Co., who in turn, introduced me to her children's book editor, Rose Dobbs, an intimidating dragon of a woman. At that time I was working as a first reader, manuscript clerk, and assistant editor at Gold Medal Books, and it was my 22nd birthday. A light snow was falling as I walked to get to her office on my lunch hour. She greeted me with, 'I never buy from unknown writers.' But she looked over my work and found a one-page synopsis of *Pirates in Petticoats* of some interest.

"I vividly remember the hair net she wore. It had little colored beads that seemed to wink and blink at me. 'I never buy from unknowns,' she repeated. 'But. . . .' She had my synopsis, slightly wrinkled and coffee-stained, on her desk. 'But this interests me and I know you have written magazine articles and worked on your father's book.' (I had helped with the research and writing on *The Young Sportsman's Guide to Kite Flying*, a book my father had been asked to do.) 'So,' she went on, 'you are not entirely unknown. Do you think you could write a full-length manuscript?'

"Not trusting my voice, I nodded.

" 'Then I shall give you a contract,' she said. 'But I won't give you any money in advance,' she added. 'Because you are an unknown and I don't take such chances.'

> "I thought children's books would be the easiest and quickest. I was to discover painfully and thoroughly over the next 45 years that, in fact, children's books are among the most difficult manuscripts to write."

"Amazed at my boldness, I said, in a very small voice, 'If you give me a little bit of money, then I couldn't back out of it. I'd have to finish.'

" 'Well . . . all right,' she said. 'But remember, you mustn't tell anyone about this. It would get around. And I would be flooded with unknowns.'

"We shook hands and I went back out to the street, where suddenly a different kind of light was in the air. Everything was changed. After all, I had sold my first book!

"Not every author's story of a first book goes like that. It is, indeed, rare for an editor to buy a synopsis from an unknown writer. But Rose Dobbs took a chance, and although the book is no longer available, it was her willingness to sit down with a young writer a year later and go over the completed manuscript, word by word, that started me on the path of publication and a long and happy career in children's books."

ი ი ი

> "Amazed at my boldness, I said, in a very small voice, 'If you give me a little bit of money, then I couldn't back out of it. I'd have to finish.'"

Jane Yolen is a versatile writer who works in a number of different genres for readers from a variety of age groups. A fine stylist and wordsmith, she has written poetry, novels, picture books, biographies, songbooks, a cookbook, and collections of short stories, but is perhaps best known for her fantasy works and retellings of folktales. The daughter of Isabel and Will Yolen, Jane Yolen was born in New York City. As an infant, she lived for a few years in California, where her father worked in publicity for the movie industry, and later in Newport News, Virginia, with her maternal grandparents, while her father served in the army during World War II. Back in New York after the war, Jane's brother Steven was born. As Jane began her high school years, the family moved to Westport, Connecticut, where she received her first writing prize—the Scholastic Writing Award—for a poem called "Death, You Do Not Frighten Me." While attending Smith College, she won poetry and journalism awards and began publishing in small magazines. After receiving her B.A. degree in 1960, she moved to New York City, where she worked on a number of freelance writing assignments and met David Stemple, whom she married in 1962.

Yolen worked for Gold Medal Books and then for a book packager called Rutledge Press, where she wrote several uncredited works as an in-house editor. While at Rutledge, she met an editor who later published several of her books. But in the meantime, looking for a more literary job, Yolen became an assistant editor at Alfred A. Knopf, where she worked for nearly three years. Throughout the 1960s, she published a number of picture books.

When she and her husband took some time for an extended trip to Europe in 1966, she gathered material for future stories. An olive grove they visited in Greece, for example, formed the setting for the title story in *The Girl Who Cried Flowers*, published in 1974. That volume of poignant fantasy tales became a Golden Kite Award winner, a National Book Award finalist, and an ALA Notable Children's Book. The next year *The Transfigured Hart*, about a boy and girl who form an unlikely friendship to capture and protect a creature that might be a unicorn, was named a Golden Kite Honor Book. *The Moon Ribbon*, Yolen's second collection of fairytales, was also a Golden Kite Honor Book.

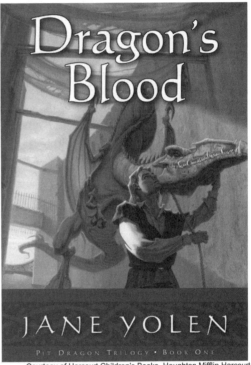

Courtesy of Harcourt Children's Books, Houghton Mifflin Harcourt

Upon returning home from Europe in 1966, the couple moved to Massachusetts, where Yolen's husband took a job at the University of Massachusetts Computer Center in Amherst. That same year, in July, their daughter, Heidi Elisabet, was born. Heidi became the prototype for the child in *Owl Moon*, the 1988 Caldecott Medal-winner; for Sarah in *The Gift of Sarah Barker*, a *School Library Journal* Best Book; and for Akki in the Pit Dragon trilogy. The first book in that series, *Dragon's Blood*, won a Parents' Choice Award and was named an IRA/CBC Children's Choice. *Heart's Blood*, the second book, was an ALA Best Book for Young Adults and an *SLJ* Best Book. A *Sending of Dragons* completed the trilogy, which established Yolen as one of the foremost writers of fantasy for young readers. After Heidi grew up and became a mother herself, she collaborated with her mother on several books, including four titles in the Unsolved Mysteries from History series, a collection of stories from ballets, *Meet the Monsters*, *Dear Mother/Dear Daughter*, and *Fairy Tale Feasts: A Literary Cookbook*.

Yolen's second child, Adam, born in 1968, became the prototype for Commander Toad and Jakkin in the Pit Dragon books. Adam's musical talents contributed to his mother's books as well, and when he was 15, he created the arrangements for

The Lullaby Songbook, which his mother edited. They went on to work on a several other books together—more music books and two novels, *Pay the Piper* and *Troll Bridge*. Yolen's third child, Jason, was born in 1970 while they were living in the Boston area, where Yolen's husband had started a computer company. The male counterpart of the little sister in *The Stone Silenus*, the boy Jeremy in *No Bath Tonight*, and the boy in *The Boy Who Spoke Chimp*, Jason grew up to become a professional photographer, and has illustrated a number of his mother's books, including her autobiographical *A Letter from Phoenix Farm* and *Wild Wings*, which won the National Outdoor Book Award.

Yolen has also tried her hand at writing humor and satire. Her Commander Toad series for beginning readers, a take-off on the numerous science fiction shows and movies of the 1960s and 70s, abounds in word play and action as the animal characters hurtle through space in their ship, *Star Warts*. Illustrated with great energy and abandon by Bruce Degen, the series has been an established favorite of early readers and their parents for many years. Yolen's retelling of the classic fairy tale "Sleeping Beauty," a beginning reader story called *Sleeping Ugly*, focuses on the theme of personality being more important than physical beauty. Told with humor and a light touch, the story carries a vital message for young readers. Her most recent contributions to humor for the youngest children include a series about silly dinosaurs. *How Do Dinosaurs Say Goodnight?* won a Christopher Award, and other entries in this picture-book series—all illustrated by Mark Teague—have been received with great delight by preschoolers and their caregivers.

Adept at writing picture-book texts, Yolen created the story for the 1988 Caldecott Medal winner, *Owl Moon*, which was inspired by her husband taking their daughter Heidi out to look for owls in the woods at night. The poetic text is a perfect complement to John Schoenherr's atmospheric watercolor paintings, which capture the wonder and delight of the experience. An earlier picture book, *The Emperor and the Kite*—based on Yolen's relationship with her late father, an international kite-flying champion—won a Caldecott Honor award for the illustrator Ed Young. The editor of this book, Ann K. Beneduce, would go on to edit nearly 30 more of Yolen's books over the course of 15 years.

One of Yolen's most enduring novels, *The Devil's Arithmetic*, won both the Sydney Taylor Award and the Jewish Book Council Award for its touching depiction of life in a concentration camp during the Holocaust. Also named a Nebula Award finalist, the story involves time travel when a teenage girl from the present day, disinterested in her Jewish heritage and family traditions, is magically transported to the village of her forebears, just before the family is rounded up to be taken to a camp. There she learns firsthand how enduring her heritage is and how important it is to honor its traditions. *The Devil's Arithmetic* was later made into a television movie starring Kirsten Dunst.

In 1988 Yolen received the Mythopoeic Fantasy Award for all three titles in the Young Merlin trilogy, which traces the childhood adventures of the legendary enchanter from age 7 to 12. For these books, Yolen researched the art of falconry and used falconry terms (Passager, Hobby, Merlin) as the titles for the books. Also in 1988, she received the World Fantasy Award for *Favorite Folktales from Around the World*. Containing 160 tales from over 40 cultures and traditions, this book has become a core resource for storytellers and established Yolen as a distinguished collector of traditional folklore.

Jane Yolen has garnered a number of awards for her body of work. She has received the 1988 Kerlan Award from the University of Minnesota, the 1985 Daedelus Award for fantasy short fiction, the 1990 Regina Medal from the Catholic Library Association, the National Storytelling Network 2003 ORACLE Award, the Roots Award for Science Fiction and Fantasy Female Writers, and the New England Science Fiction Association's Skylark Award for her work in science fiction. Having achieved a master's degree in education from the University of Massachusetts in 1976, she later received honorary doctorates from five colleges. A past president of the Science Fiction Writers of America and founding member of the Bay State Writers Guild and the Western Massachusetts Illustrators Guild, Yolen has served on the Society of Children's Book Writers and Illustrators' board of directors since its inception. Always looking for new challenges, she has recently turned her hand to writing graphic novels.

Since her husband's death, Yolen continues to split her time between her homes in Hatfield, Massachusetts and Scotland. In addition to her extensive writing, she is a storyteller, a teacher, and a songwriter. She also enjoys the role of grandmother to her six grandchildren. Hailed by the editors of *Newsweek* as America's Hans Christian Andersen and by the *New York Times* as a modern-day Aesop, Jane Yolen has made a significant mark on the imagination of today's young readers.

SELECTED WORKS WRITTEN: *Pirates in Petticoats*, illus. by Leonard Vosburgh; 1963; *See This Little Line?* illus. by Kathleen Elgin, 1963; *The Witch Who Wasn't*, illus. by Arnold Roth, 1964;

Gwinellen, The Princess Who Could Not Sleep, illus. by Ed Renfro, 1965; *Trust a City Kid* (written with Anne Huston), illus. by J.C. Kocsis, 1966; *The Minstrel and the Mountain: A Tale of Peace*, illus. by Anne Rockwell, 1967; *Isabel's Noel*, illus. by Arnold Roth, 1967; *The Emperor and the Kite*, illus. by Ed Young, 1968; *World on a String: The Story of Kites*, 1968; *Greyling: A Picture Story from the Islands of Shetland*, illus. by William Stobbs, 1968 (reillus. by David Ray, 1991); *The Longest Name on the Block*, illus. by Peter Madden, 1968; *The Wizard of Washington Square*, illus. by Ray Cruz, 1969; *The Inway Investigators; or, The Mystery at McCracken's Place*, illus. by Allan Eitzen, 1969; *It All Depends*, illus. by Don Bolognese, 1969; *Hobo Toad and the Motorcycle Gang*, illus. by Emily McCully, 1970; *The Seventh Mandarin*, illus. by Ed Young, 1970; *The Bird of Time*, illus. by Mercer Mayer, 1971; *The Girl Who Loved the Wind*, illus. by Ed Young, 1972; *Friend: The Story of George Fox and the Quakers*, 1972; *The Wizard Islands*, illus. by Robert Quackenbush, 1973; *The Magic Three of Solatia*, illus. by Julia Noonan, 1974; *Ring Out! A Book of Bells*, illus. by Richard Cuffari, 1974; *The Girl Who Cried Flowers and Other Tales*, illus. by David Palladini, 1974; *The Boy Who Had Wings*, illus. by Helga Aichinger, 1974; *The Adventures of Eeka Mouse*, illus. by Myra McKee, 1974; *The Rainbow Rider*, illus. by Michael Foreman, 1974; *The Little Spotted Fish*, illus. by Friso Henstra, 1974; *The Transfigured Hart*, illus. by Donna Diamond, 1975; *Hands*, illus. by Chi Chung, 1976; *Milkweed Days*, illus. with photos by Gabriel Amadeus Cooney, 1976; *The Moon Ribbon and Other Tales*, illus. by David Palladini, 1976; *Simple Gifts: The Story of the Shakers*, illus. by Betty Fraser, 1976; *An Invitation to the Butterfly Ball: A Counting Rhyme*, illus. by Jane Breskin Zalben, 1976; *The Seeing Stick*, illus. by Remy Charlip and Demetra Maraslis, 1977; *The Sultan's Perfect Tree*, illus. by Barbara Garrison, 1977; *The Hundredth Dove and Other Tales*, illus. by David Palladini, 1977; *Hannah Dreaming*, illus. with photos by Alan R. Epstein, 1977; *The Lady and the Merman*, illus. by Barry Moser, 1977; *The Giants' Farm*, illus. by Tomie de Paola, 1977; *Spider Jane*, illus. by Stefan Bernath, 1978; *The Simple Prince*, illus. by Jack Kent, 1978; *No Bath Tonight*, illus. by Nancy Winslow Parker, 1978; *The Mermaid's Three Wisdoms*, illus. by Laura Rader, 1978; *All in the Woodland Early: An ABC Book*, illus. by Jane Breskin Zalben, 1979; *The Giants Go Camping*, illus. by Tomie de Paola, 1979; *Dream Weaver and Other Tales*, illus. by Michael Hague, 1979; *How Beastly!: A Menagerie of Nonsense Poems*, illus. by James Marshall, 1980; *Spider Jane on the Move*, illus. by Stefan

Bernath, 1980; *Mice on Ice*, illus. by Lawrence DiFiori, 1980; *The Robot and Rebecca: The Mystery of the Code-Carrying Kids*, illus. by Jurg Obrist, 1980; *Commander Toad in Space*, illus. by Bruce Degen, 1980; *The Robot and Rebecca and the Missing Owser*, illus. by Lady McCrady, 1981; *Shirlick Holmes and the Case of the Wandering Wardrobe*, illus. by Anthony Rao, 1981; *The Acorn Quest*, illus. by Susanna Natti, 1981; *Brothers of the Wind*, illus. by Barbara Berger, 1981; *Sleeping Ugly*, illus. by Diane Stanley, 1981; *The Boy Who Spoke Chimp*, illus. by David Wiesner, 1981; *Uncle Lemon's Spring*, illus. by Glen Rounds, 1981; *The Gift of Sarah Barker*, 1981; *Dragon's Blood: A Fantasy*, 1982; *Neptune Rising: Songs and Tales of the Undersea Folk*, illus. by David Wiesner, 1982; *Commander Toad and the Planet of Grapes*, illus. by Bruce Degen, 1982; *Commander Toad and the Big Black Hole*, illus. by Bruce Degen, 1983; *The Stone Silenus*, 1984; *Children of the Wolf*, 1984; *Heart's Blood*, 1984; *Commander Toad and the Dis-Asteroid*, illus. by Bruce Degen, 1985; *Commander Toad and the Intergalactic Spy*, illus. by Bruce Degen, 1986; *Ring of Earth: A Child's Book of Season*, illus. by John Wallner, 1986; *Commander Toad and the Space Pirates*, illus. by Bruce Degen, 1987; *Owl Moon*, illus. by John Schoenherr, 1987; *Piggins*, illus. by Jane Dyer, 1987; *The Three Bears Rhyme Book*, illus. by Jane Dyer, 1987; *Too Old for Naps*, illus. by Alexi Natchev, 1987; *A Sending of Dragons*, 1987; *Commander Toad and the Voyage Home*, illus. by Bruce Degen, 1988; *The Devil's Arithmetic*, 1988; *Picnic with Piggins*, illus. by Jane Dyer, 1988; *Piggins and the Royal Wedding*, illus. by Jane Dyer, 1988; *The Faery Flag: Stories and Poems of Fantasy and the Supernatural*, 1989; *Dove Isabeau*, illus. by Dennis Nolan, 1989; *Best Witches: Poems for Halloween*, illus. by Elise Primavera, 1989; *Baby Bear's Bedtime Book*, illus. by Jane Dyer, 1990; *Dragon Night and Other Lullabies*, illus. by Demi, 1990; *Sky Dogs*, illus. by Barry Moser, 1990; *Elfabet: An ABC of Elves*, illus. by Lauren Mills, 1990; *The Dragon's Boy*, 1990; *Bird Watch*, illus. by Ted Lewin, 1990; *Dinosaur*

Courtesy of Philomel Books, Penguin USA

Dances, illus. by Bruce Degen; 1990; *Wizard's Hall*, 1991; *Hark! A Christmas Sampler*, illus. by Tomie de Paola, music by Adam Stemple, 1991; *All Those Secrets of the World*, illus. by Leslie Baker, 1991; *Encounter*, illus. by David Shannon, 1992; *Eeny, Meeny, Miney, Mole*, illus. by Kathryn Brown, 1992; *Letting Swift River Go*, illus. by Barbara Cooney, 1992; *A Letter from Phoenix Farm*, illus. with photos by Jason Stemple, 1992; *Hobby*, 1992; *Mouse's Birthday*, illus. by Bruce Degen, 1993; *Honkers*, illus. by Leslie Baker, 1993; *The Traveler's Rose*, 1993; *Welcome to the Green House*, illus. by Laura Regan, 1993; *Raining Cats and Dogs*, illus. by Janet Street, 1993; *What Rhymes with Moon?* illus. by Ruth Tietjen Councell, 1993; *Here There Be Dragons*, illus. by David Wilgus, 1993; *Here There Be Unicorns*, illus. by David Wilgus, 1994; *Beneath the Ghost Moon*, illus. by Laurel Molk, 1994; *Grandad Bill's Song*, illus. by Melissa Bay Mathis, 1994; *Good Griselle*, illus. by David Christiana, 1994; *The Girl in the Golden Bower*, illus. by Jane Dyer, 1994; *Old Dame Counterpane*, illus. by Ruth Tietjen Councell, 1994; *Animal Fare: Zoological Nonsense Poems*, illus. by Janet Street, 1994; *And Twelve Chinese Acrobats*, illus. by Jean Gralley, 1995; *Before the Storm*, illus. by Georgia Pugh, 1995; *Here There Be Witches*, illus. by David Wilgus, 1995; *The Ballad of the Pirate Queens*, illus. by David Shannon, 1995; *Merlin and the Dragons*, illus. by Ming Li, 1995; *The Wild Hunt*, illus. by Francisco Mora, 1995; *The Three Bears Holiday Rhyme Book*, illus. by Jane Dyer, 1995; *Water Music: Poems for Children*, illus. with photos by Jason Stemple, 1995; *Here There Be Angels*, illus. by David Wilgus, 1996; *Sacred Places*, illus. by David Shannon, 1996; *O Jerusalem*, illus. by John Thompson, 1996; *Sea Watch: A Book of Poetry*, illus. by Ted Lewin, 1996; *Meet the Monsters*, written with Heidi E. Y. Stemple, illus. by Patricia Ludlow, 1996; *Milk and Honey: A Year of Jewish Holidays*, illus. by Louise August, music by Adam Stemple, 1996; *Welcome to the Sea of Sand*, illus. by Laura Regan, 1996; *Passager*, 1996; *Hobby*, 1996; *Merlin*, 1997; *Nocturne*, illus. by Anne Hunter, 1997; *Child of Faerie, Child of Earth*, illus. by Jane Dyer, 1997; *Miz Berlin Walks*, illus. by Floyd Cooper, 1997; *Twelve Impossible Things Before Breakfast*, 1997; *The Sea Man*, illus. by Christopher Denise, 1997; *Here There Be Ghosts*, illus. by David Wilgus, 1998; *House, House*, illus. with photos by the Howes Brothers and Jason Stemple, 1998; *King Long Shanks*, illus. by Victoria Chess, 1998; *Raising Yoder's Barn*, illus. by Bernice Fuchs, 1998; *Welcome to the Ice House*, illus. by Laura Regan, 1998; *Tea with an Old Dragon: A Story of Sophia Smith, Founder of Smith College*, illus. by Monica Vachula, 1998; *Snow,*

Snow: Winter Poems for Children, illus. with photos by Jason Stemple, 1998; *The Originals: Animals That Time Forgot*, illus. by Ted Lewin, 1998; *Armageddon Summer* (with Bruce Coville), 1998; *The Book of Fairy Holidays*, illus. by David Christiana, 1998; *Moonball*, illus. by Greg Couch, 1998; *The Wizard's Map*, 1999; *The Pictish Child*, 1999; *The Mary Celeste: An Unsolved Mystery from History*, written with Heidi E. Y. Stemple, illus. by Roger Roth, 1999; *Boots and the Seven Leaguers*, 2000; *How Do Dinosaurs Say Goodnight*, illus. by Mark Teague, 2000; *Color Me a Rhyme: Nature Poems for Young People*, illus. with photos by Jason Stemple, 2000; *Off We Go!* illus. by Laurel Molk, 2000; *Queen's Own Fool*, written with Robert J. Harris, 2000; *Dear Mother, Dear Daughter: Poems for Young People*, with Heidi E. Y. Stemple, 2001; *The Wolf Girls: An Unsolved Mystery from History*, with Heidi E. Y. Stemple, illus. by Roger Roth, 2001; *Welcome to the River of Grass*, illus. by Laura Regan, 2001; *Odysseus in the Serpent Maze*, written with Robert J. Harris, 2001; *Harvest Home*, illus. by Greg Shed, 2002; *The Bagpiper's Ghost*, 2002; *Time for Naps*, illus. by Hiroe Nakata, 2002; *The Firebird*, illus. by Vladimir Vagin, 2002; *Animal Train*, illus. by Doug Cushman, 2002; *Bedtime for Bunny*, illus. by Lynn Norton Parker, 2002; *Hippolyta and the Curse of the Amazons*, written with Robert J. Harris, 2002; *Girl in a Cage*, written with Robert J. Harris, 2002; *Wild Wings: Poems for Young People*, illus. with photos by Jason Stemple, 2002; *Horizons: Poems as Far as the Eye Can See*, illus. with photos by Jason Stemple, 2002; *How Do Dinosaurs Get Well Soon?* illus. by Mark Teague, 2003; *The Sea King*, with Shulamith L. Oppenheim, illus. by Stefan Czernecki, 2003; *Where Have the Unicorns Gone?* illus. by Ruth Sanderson, 2003; *The Flying Witch*, illus. by Vladimir Vagin, 2003; *Hoptoad*, illus. by Karen Lee Schmidt, 2003; *Least Things: Poems about Small Natures*, illus. with photos by Jason Stemple, 2003; *Atalanta and the Arcadian Beast*, with Robert J. Harris, 2003; *My Brothers' Flying Machine*, illus. by Jim Burke, 2003; *Roanoke: The Lost Colony: An Unsolved Mystery from History*, with Heidi E. Y. Stemple, illus. by Roger Roth, 2003; *Sword of the Rightful King: A Novel of King Arthur*, 2003; *Eeny Up Above*, illus. by Kathryn Brown, 2003; *The Salem Witch Trials: An Unsolved Mystery from History*, with Heidi E. Y. Stemple, illus. by Roger Roth, 2004; *How Do Dinosaurs Clean Their Rooms?* illus. by Mark Teague, 2004; *How Do Dinosaurs Count to Ten?* illus. by Mark Teague, 2004; *The Barefoot Book of Ballet Stories*, with Heidi E. Y. Stemple, illus. by Rebecca Guay, 2004; *Fine Feathered Friends: Poems for Young People to Perform*, illus. with photos by Jason Stemple, 2004; *Jason and the Gorgon's Blood*, with Robert J. Harris, 2004; *Prince Across the Water*, with Robert J. Harris, 2004; *How Do Dinosaurs Eat Their Food?* illus. by Mark Teague, 2004; *The Perfect Wizard: Hans Christian Andersen*, illus. by Dennis Nolan, 2004; *Once upon a Time (She Said)*, 2005; *How Do Dinosaurs Learn to Read*, illus. by Mark Teague, 2005; *Grandma's Hurrying Child*, illus. by Kay Chorao, 2005; *Baby Bear's Chairs*, illus. by Melissa Sweet, 2005; *Pay the Piper*, with Adam Stemple, 2005; *Soft House*, illus. by Wendy Anderson Halperin, 2005; *How Do Dinosaurs Learn Their Colors?* illus. by Mark Teague, 2006; *How Do Dinosaurs Play with Their Friends?* illus. by Mark Teague, 2006; *Dimity Duck*, illus. by Sebastien Braun, 2006; *Troll Bridge*, with Adam Stemple, 2006; *Baby Bear's Books*, illus. by Melissa Sweet, 2006; *Count Me a Rhyme: Animal Poems by the Numbers*, illus. with photos by Jason Stemple, 2006; *Here's a Little Poem: A Very First Book of Poetry*, with Andrew Fusek Peters, illus. by Polly Dunbar, 2007; *Sleep, Black Bear, Sleep*, with Heidi E. Y. Stemple, illus. by Brooke Dyer, 2007; *Johnny Appleseed*, illus. by Jim Burke, 2008; *Sea Queens: Women Pirates Around the World*, illus. by Christine Joy Pratt, 2008.

SELECTED WORKS RETOLD: *The Sleeping Beauty*, illus. by Ruth Sanderson, 1986; *Tam Lin: An Old Ballad*, illus. by Charles Mikolaycak, 1990; *Wings*, illus. by Dennis Nolan, 1991; *A Sip of Aesop*, illus. by Karen Barbour, 1995; *The Musicians of Bremen: A Tale from Germany*, illus. by John Segal, 1996; *Once Upon a Bedtime Story: Classic Tales*, illus. by Ruth Tietjen Councell, 1997; *Pegasus, The Flying Horse*, illus. by Ming Li, 1998; *Prince of Egypt*, 1998; *Not One Damsel in Distress: World Folktales for Strong Girls*, ed. with Paula Wiseman, illus. by Susan Guevara, 2000; *Mightier Than the Sword: World Folktales for Strong Boys*, illus. by Raúl Colón, 2003; *Meow: Cat Stories From Around the World*, illus. by Hala Wittwer, 2005; *Fairy Tale Feasts: A Literary Cookbook for Young Readers and Eaters*, recipes by Heidi E.Y. Stemple, illus. by Philippe Béha, 2006.

SELECTED WORKS COMPILED OR EDITED: *The Fireside Song Book of Birds and Beasts*, with Barbara Green, illus. by Peter Parnall, 1972; *Zoo 2000: Twelve Stories of Science Fiction and Fantasy Beasts*, 1973; *Rounds and Rounds*, illus. by Gail Gibbons, music by Barbara Green, 1977; *Shape Shifters: Fantasy and Science Fiction Tales about Humans Who Can Change Their Shape*, 1978; *Favorite Folktales From Around the World*, 1986; *The Lullaby*

Songbook, illus. by Charles Mikolaycak, music by Adam Stemple, 1986; *Dragons and Dreams* (editor and contributor, with Martin H. Greenberg and Charles G. Waugh), 1986; *Spaceships and Spells* (editor and contributor, with Martin H. Greenberg and Charles G. Waugh), 1987; *Werewolves: A Collection of Original Stories* (editor and contributor, with Martin H. Greenberg and Charles G. Waugh), 1988; *Things That Go Bump in the Night* (editor and contributor, with Martin H. Greenberg), 1989; *The Lap-Time Song and Play Book*, illus. by Margot Tomes, music by Adam Stemple, 1989; *2041 AD: Twelve Stories About the Future by Top Science Fiction Writers*, 1991; *Vampires* (editor and contributor, with Martin H. Greenberg), 1991; *Street Rhymes Around the World*, illus. by 17 artists, 1992; *Jane Yolen's Mother Goose Songbook*, illus. by Rosekrans Hoffman, music by Adam Stemple, 1992; *Weather Report*, illus. by Annie Gusman, 1993; *Jane Yolen's Songs of Summer*, illus. by Cyd Moore, music by Adam Stemple, 1993; *Sleep Rhymes Around the World*, illus. by 17 artists, 1994; *Jane Yolen's Old MacDonald Songbook*, illus. by Rosekrans Hoffman, 1994; *Alphabestiary: Animal Poems from A to Z*, illus. by Allan Eitzen, 1995; *The Haunted House: A Collection of Original Stories* (editor and contributor, with Martin H. Greenberg), illus. by Doron Ben-Ami, 1995; *Camelot: A Collection of Original Arthurian Tales*, illus. by Winslow Pels, 1995; *Mother Earth, Father Sky: Poems of Our Planet* (compiler), illus. by Jennifer Hewitson, 1996; *Sky Scrape/City Scape: Poems of City Life*, illus. by Ken Condon, 1996; *Sing Noel*, illus. by Nancy Carpenter, music by Adam Stemple, 1996; *Once Upon Ice and Other Frozen Poems*, illus. with photos by Jason Stemple, 1997; *The Fairies' Ring: A Book of Fairy Stories and Poems*, illus. by Stephen Mackey, 1999; *The Liars' Book*, ed. with Linda Mannheim, illus. by Kevin Hawkes, 1999; *Mirror, Mirror*, with Heidi E. Y. Stemple, 2000; *Sherwood: A Collection of Original Robin Hood Stories*, 2000; *Fish Prince and Other Stories: Merman Folk Tales*, with Shulamith Oppenheim, 2001; *Apple for the Teacher: Thirty Songs for Singing While You Work*, music by Adam Stemple, 2005; *The Year's Best Science Fiction and Fantasy for Teens*, with Patrick Nielsen Hayden, 2005; *This Little Piggy: And Other Rhymes to Sing and Play*, illus. by Will Hillenbrand, music by Adam Stemple, 2006.

SELECTED WORKS FOR ADULTS: *Touch Magic: Fantasy, Faerie and Folklore in the Literature of Childhood*, 1981; *Tales of Wonder*, 1983; *Writing Books for Children*, 1983; *Cards of Grief*, 1984; *The Whitethorn Wood & Other Magicks*, 1984; *Dragonfield and*

Other Stories, 1985; *Merlin's Booke*, 1986; *Sister Light, Sister Dark*, 1988; *White Jenna*, 1989; *Guide to Writing for Children*, 1989; *Briar Rose*, 1992; *Storyteller*, 1992; *Xanadu* (editor and contributor, with Martin H. Greenberg), 1993; *Xanadu Two* (editor and contributor, with Martin H. Greenberg), 1994; *Xanadu Three* (editor and contributor, with Martin H. Greenberg), 1995; *Among Angels*, with Nancy Willard, 1995; *The Books of Great Alta*, 1997; *The One-Armed Queen*, 1998; *Gray Heroes: Elder Tales from Around the World*, ed., 1999; *Sister Emily's Lightship and Other Stories*, 2000; *The Radiation Sonnets*, 2003; *Take Joy: A Book for Writers*, 2003 (reissued as: *Take Joy: A Writer's Guide to Loving the Craft*, 2006).

SUGGESTED READING: Marcus, Leonard, *The Wand in the Word: Conversations with Writers of Fantasy*, 2006; *St. James Guide to Fantasy Writers*, 2006; Carpan, Carolyn, *Jane Yolen*, 2005; *Something About the Author*, vol. 158, 2005; Silvey, Anita, ed., *The Essential Guide to Children's Books & Their Creators*, 2003; Daniel, Susanna, *Jane Yolen*, 2003; McGinty, Alice B., *Meet Jane Yolen*, 2003; McElmeel, Sharron L., *100 Most Popular Picture Book Authors and Illustrators*, 2000; *St. James Guide to Young Adult Writers*, 1998; *Children's Literature Review*, vol. 44, 1997; *Dictionary of Literary Biography*, vol. 52, 1986; *Behind the Covers*, Jim Roginski, ed., 1985.

WEB SITE: www.janeyolen.com

An earlier profile of Jane Yolen appeared in *Fourth Book of Junior Authors and Illustrators*, 1978.

Bo Zaunders

June 5, 1938–

"I grew up on a small farm in a tiny village of five families, in southern Sweden. My first seven years of schooling took place in a one-room schoolhouse. In winter I went there on skis; for the rest of the year I either walked or bicycled. In first grade I received an A+ in art. From then on, my father saved all my drawings. Supportive of my creative efforts, he also instilled in me an interest in reading. Apart from children's literature—I particularly recall the 'William' books by the English writer Richmal Crompton (in Swedish translation)—I basically devoured anything I could lay my hands on. I also did a lot of walking in the woods daydreaming, which my parents, not without reason, interpreted as avoiding farm work.

"At age ten I spent one entire evening composing what I intended to be a novel. It's titled 'Vikingaliv' (Viking Life) and

I wrote it in pencil on a huge piece of paper while my parents were out to dinner. My inspiration: *The Long Ships* by Frans G. Bengtsson, which I had just read, and which had made a powerful impression. The hero of my story is Toke, a quick-witted Viking boy who, six years old, already is wielding a sword, valiantly defending his family during an enemy attack. I remember being totally absorbed in this endeavor, and that my parents, on their return, thought it amazing that I had managed to fill both sides of the paper to the last inch.

"I always had a knack for drawing cartoons, and—thanks to my father—still have caricatures of all my schoolmates. A cartoon caused me to get fired from the first job I ever had. I was sixteen, and, during the summer break, was employed by a company building a dam. When a cartoon I'd made of my boss, a rather disliked, comical-looking man in charge of the supply store, was put on the bulletin board, everyone was amused . . . except him.

"As a teenager I subscribed to *All Världens Berättare*, a pint-sized periodical with illustrated short stories by writers from all over the world. This was my introduction to any number of distinguished authors, such as Anatole France, Gogol, Dostoevsky, Gorky, Guy de Maupassant, Camus, Dickens, Proust, Edgar Allan Poe, and Mark Twain.

"Regarding Dickens, I vividly recall an evening when a friend and I read *The Pickwick Papers*. Taking turns, we read aloud, convulsing with laughter as we delighted in the company of the preposterous Mr. Pickwick and his circle of eccentric friends. Not until sunlight flooded the room did we realize it was morning and that we hadn't slept a wink all night.

Photo by Roxie Munro

"At twenty, I moved to Stockholm, and found a job, first at SAS, making diagrams, then as a layout man for Bonniers, one of Sweden's better-known publishing companies. Five years later, I took off for the United States, mostly on a whim. I landed a job as a technical illustrator for *Popular Mechanics* in New York City, where I stayed for nine months.

"By then New York had worked its magic. Soon I was back, employed by a small advertising agency. Starting out as a paste-up man, I rose to the rank of art director, and eventually became the agency's creative director. This was the beginning of a twenty-year career in advertising, a good portion of which was spent with Young & Rubicam at their various European offices—Stockholm, Madrid, with stops in Paris and London.

"In the mid-1980s, I became a freelance travel photographer, working for various newsletters and magazines. Soon, I also began writing travel and food articles. I illustrated a couple of children's books and, in 1998, wrote my first children's book.

"The books I have written so far have all been nonfiction, requiring a fair amount of research, which I enjoy. Writing is very hard work—much more demanding than, say, putting together ads, photographing or making cartoons. At the same time, few things could be more satisfying than seeing a paragraph come together exactly the way you want it.

"Even more gratifying is having a child with shining eyes come up to you, asking questions about some character whose story you labored over for months."

"I always had a knack for drawing cartoons, and—thanks to my father—still have caricatures of all my schoolmates. A cartoon caused me to get fired from the first job I ever had."

ଔ   ଔ   ଔ

From Sweden to New York City, from art director for advertising firms to children's book author and illustrator, Bo Zaunders has brought a keen curiosity, a love of books, and a creative perspective to his life and work. As a child growing up in Sweden, he was a voracious reader, a clever cartoonist, and a word maven. He has always been fascinated by the magic of words.

Creative opportunities in advertising lured him to New York City when he was 25. His initial stint as a technical illustrator for *Popular Mechanics* led to a career in advertising as an art director, then creative director, and a 20-year career with Young & Rubicam's international ad agency.

Not only was "Madison Avenue" the center of his professional life, it serendipitously led to his love life. Zaunders first met his future wife, the artist and children's book illustrator Roxie Munro, at P. J. Clarke's pub in New York City. He was there with other advertising people and Munro had stopped in to celebrate her sale of a cover to the *New Yorker* magazine. Zaunders gave her his business card expecting her to call. She promptly threw the card away, thinking it inappropriate that *she* should call *him*. A few weeks later Zaunders and Munro found themselves looking in the same store window—on Madison Avenue. "Don't we know each other?" They were married in 1986.

Like other second-career children's book creators, Zaunders came into the field from a seasoned creative background, one enhanced by his experiences as a freelance photographer and travel writer in the 1980s. He illustrated his first children's book in 1986. *Max, the Bad-Talking Parrot*, by Patricia Demuth, received an IRA/CBC Children's Choice Award and *Family Circle* magazine named it to their Best Book for Kids list. His second book as a children's illustrator, *One Gift Deserves Another*, by Joanne Oppenheim, was published in 1992.

Six years later, Zaunders switched roles and wrote his first children's book with his wife Roxie Munro illustrating the text. Their talents complement one another and their partnership has produced four remarkable nonfiction books to date. *Crocodiles, Camels & Dugout Canoes: Eight Adventurous Episodes* introduces readers to amateur explorers and their quest for fame and fortune. It was cited as a Notable Social Studies Trade Book for Young People.

Their next collaboration—*Feathers, Flaps & Flops: Fabulous Early Fliers*—focused on eight aviation pioneers. The short, lively biographical snapshots convey the time period, the daring, and the disasters of the early years of flight, and the book was selected for *School Library Journal's* Best Books of the Year. In *Gargoyles, Girders & Glass Houses: Magnificent Master Builders*, Zaunders and Munro pursue their mutual interest in architecture, delving into the lives and legacies of seven architectural wonders and the builders who created them. It was recognized as a Notable Social Studies Trade Book for Young People.

The Great Bridge-Building Contest is about a furniture-maker named Lemuel Chenoweth who demonstrated in 1850 that he could build a covered bridge across the Tygart River, one that later played a role in the Civil War. This story is a personal one for Munro as she is a descendant of Chenoweth and grew up hearing the account of his feat.

Zaunders and Munro live in New York City. After many years in this country, in 2005, Bo Zaunders became a United States citizen.

SELECTED WORKS ILLUSTRATED: *Max, the Bad-Talking Parrot*, written by Patricia Brennan Demuth, 1986; *One Gift Deserves Another*, written by Joanne Oppenheimer, 1992.

SELECTED WORKS WRITTEN: *Crocodiles, Camels & Dugout Canoes: Eight Adventurous Episodes*, illus. by Roxie Munro, 1998; *Feathers, Flaps & Flops: Fabulous Early Fliers*, illus. by Roxie Munro,

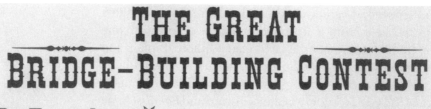

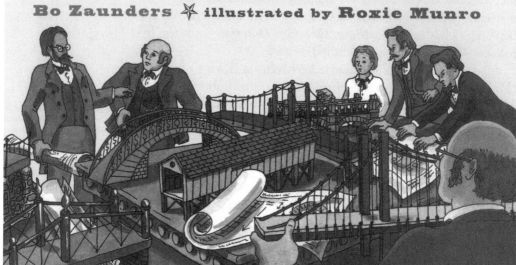

2001; *Gargoyles, Girders & Glass Houses: Magnificent Master Builders*, illus. by Roxie Munro, 2004; *The Great Bridge-Building Contest*, illus. by Roxie Munro, 2004.

SUGGESTED READING: *Contemporary Authors* Database Online, 2003; *Something about the Author*, vol. 137, 2003.

WEB SITE: www.bozaunders.com

Markus Zusak

January 1, 1975–

Markus Zusak, best known for his internationally acclaimed novels, *The Book Thief* and *I Am The Messenger*, was born in Sydney, Australia. He is the son of working-class immigrants, Lisa and Helmut Zusak, and the youngest of four children. His Austrian father is a commercial housepainter; his German mother, a maid. Originally, Markus planned on painting like his father but felt he had no talent for it. Instead he turned to books, studied teaching in college, and worked as a janitor and a high school English teacher. Much later, as an established writer, he would honor his father's profession by giving it to one of his most memorable characters in *The Book Thief*, Hans Hubermann.

Zusak began writing at age sixteen, finishing his first unpublished manuscript at eighteen. For the next few years, he struggled with various ideas, and finally wrote the somewhat autobiographical *The Underdog*, which introduces the character of Cameron Wolfe. It became his first published novel. Zusak acknowledges that his working-class upbringing has had an influence on his writing. In *Fighting Ruben Wolfe*, two boys from a blue-collar family get involved in amateur boxing to earn money. The relationship between the fictional brothers Cameron and Ruben is similar to Zusak's relationship with his own older brother; they even engaged in some backyard boxing when they were boys. In the book, the circumstances are more serious, and the brothers eventually must confront their feelings about their relationship when they end up facing one another in the ring. Dramatic and effective with its combination of humor and struggle, *Fighting Ruben Wolfe* was shortlisted for the Children's Book Council of Australia (CBCA) Older Readers Book of the Year, the Australian Booksellers Book of the Year, and the New South Wales Premier's Literary Awards Ethel Turner Prize for Young People's Literature. In the United States, *Fighting Ruben Wolfe* was named an ALA Best Book for Young Adults.

Courtesy of Random House, Inc.

In the third book about the Wolfe brothers, the two boys explore other aspects of their relationship when Cameron, who wants to get out of Ruben's shadow and become a writer, starts dating his older brother's cast-off girlfriend. Entitled *Getting the Girl* in the U.S. and *When Dogs Cry* in Australia, this book explores the juncture between romance and family loyalty with inventive images and complex interpersonal dynamics. In Australia, it was named a Young Adult Book of the Year by the Queensland Premier's Literary Awards and shortlisted for the CBCA Older Readers Book of the Year.

Zusak's 2006 Michael L. Printz Award Honor Book, *I Am the Messenger*, was initially inspired by his musings while he sat in a 15-minute parking zone outside his local bank. Named a *BCCB* Blue Ribbon title, a *Publishers Weekly* Best Book of the Year, and included in ALA's Top Ten Best Books for Young Adults, it's the story of a 19-year-old underachiever who, by inadvertently preventing a bank robbery, transforms his life. After the robbery, he receives by mail a series of mysterious coded messages inscribed on playing cards, messages that lead him to help other people and, by doing so, to help himself. Published as *The Messenger* in Australia, this dark, atmospheric tale was a CBCA Older Readers Book of the Year and won the New South Wales Premier's Literary Award's Ethel Turner Prize.

The Book Thief, an absorbing World War II–era story about a young girl and her foster family, a Jewish fighter they hide in their basement, and the neighbors in their small town near München who try to stand up to the Nazis in their own small ways, was inspired by stories Zusak heard as a child from his parents. One tale his mother told involved München being bombed when she was a young girl and how everything, including the sky, turned red. This visual image stayed with him, as did her story about a teenage boy who, out of pity, tried to give bread to an emaciated Jew being marched with other prisoners through the streets; both the teenager and the Jew were beaten by a Nazi soldier. This scene, expressing the human capacity for both great kindness and great cruelty, was included in *The Book Thief*. Zusak was also inspired by his father, who told him how he had avoided the Hitler Youth meetings he was supposed to attend as a boy.

Initially intended to be a 100-page novelette, *The Book Thief* took three years to complete. Perhaps the most innovative technique in the book was having the narrator of the story be Death, lending a surreal atmosphere that permeates the novel. When Zusak was up to about 250 pages, he made a major change in the personality of the narrator, who went from being simply macabre to an entity haunted by what humans can do to each other. In doing research for the book, Zusak visited Germany for the first time, and incidentally carved the initials of his characters Liesel and Rudy on the trunk of a German tree.

This mesmerizing and poetic novel was published as Zusak's adult fiction debut in his native Australia. It won the 2006 Kathleen Mitchell Award, given to writers of age 30 or under, and was shortlisted for the Australian Book Industry Awards. It was also shortlisted for the Best Book of the South East Asia and South Pacific Region Award. Because of *The Book Thief*, which the author himself cites as his best book to date, Zusak was chosen as one of the *Sydney Morning Herald's* Young Writers of the Year.

In America, where *The Book Thief* was published as a young adult novel, it was named a 2007 Michael L. Printz Honor Book and one of ALA's Top Ten Best Books for Young Adults as well as being included on the Best of the Year list for every major

> "The Book Thief offers a unique reading experience of the human capacities for great compassion and tremendous evil, as well as a demonstration of the power of language. It is about ordinary people finding ways to keep their lives steady in the midst of the chaos of war."

reviewing journal. It was nominated for a Quill Award and won the Jewish National Book Award and the Association of Jewish Libraries inaugural Teen Book Award. *The Book Thief* offers a unique reading experience of the human capacities for great compassion and tremendous evil, as well as a demonstration of the power of language. It is about ordinary people finding ways to keep their lives steady in the midst of the chaos of war.

Markus Zusak lives with his wife and daughter in New South Wales, Australia, where he teaches part-time and surfs in his spare time.

Courtesy of Alfred A. Knopf, Random House, Inc.

SELECTED WORKS (Dates are for Australian publication; U.S. dates, if different, are in parentheses): *The Underdog*, 1999; *Fighting Ruben Wolfe*, 2000 (2001); *When Dogs Cry*, 2001 (U.S. title: *Getting the Girl*, 2003); *The Messenger*, 2002 (U.S. title: *I Am the Messenger*, 2005); *The Book Thief*, 2005 (2006); "The First Six Killers," in *This Is Push: New Stories from the Edge*, ed. by David Levithan, 2007.

SUGGESTED READING: *Something About the Author*, vol. 149, 2004. Periodicals—Maslin, Janet, "Stealing to Settle a Score with Life," *New York Times*, March 27, 2007. Online—*Contemporary Authors Online*, September 13, 2007; Castellitto, Linda M., "Markus Zusak's Compelling Appointment with Death," *The Book Page*, at www.bookpage.com/0603bp/markus_zusak.html

WEB SITE: www.markuszusak.com

Awards and Honor Lists
(cited in this volume)

Aesop Prize and Aesop Accolades
The Children's Folklore Section of the American Folklore Society presents these awards to books for children and young adults in which folklore is central to the book's content. English language books published in the year of the award or the previous year are eligible.
See: www.afsnet.org/sections/children/

ALA Best Books for Young Adults
Chosen by a committee of the Young Adult Library Services Association, a division of the American Library Association, this list is compiled annually to present the books deemed most worthy for readers of ages 12–18 from those published in the previous year.
See: www.ala.org/ala/yalsa/booklistsawards/bestbooksya/bestbooksyoung.cfm

ALA Notable Children's Books
An annual list of distinguished books for children of ages birth through 14, compiled by a committee of the Association for Library Service to Children, a division of the American Library Association.
See: www.ala.org/ala/alsc/awardsscholarships/childrensnotable/default.cfm

American Booksellers Association Pick of the Lists
Chosen for spring and fall publishing seasons, these are the books that booksellers feel will be most popular with their patrons; published in spring and fall issues of *Bookselling This Week*.

Américas Award
Given in recognition of U.S. works of fiction, poetry, folklore, or selected nonfiction (from picture books to works for young adults) published in the previous year in English or Spanish that authentically and engagingly portray Latin America, the Caribbean, or Latinos in the United States. Sponsored by the national Consortium of Latin American Studies Programs (CLASP)
See: www.uwm.edu/Dept/CLACS/aa/index.html

Bank Street College of Education
The Bank Street College of Education in New York City publishes an annual list of the Best Children's Books of the Year, chosen by a committee that includes educators, librarians, authors, parents and psychologists, with input from young reviewers across the country. Books are chosen for literary quality, excellence of presentation and potential emotional impact on young readers. In addition, the committee gives three annual awards—The Josette Frank Award for fiction, the Flora Stieglitz Straus Award for nonfiction, and the Claudia Lewis Award for poetry.

See: www.bankstreet.edu/bookcom

Booklist Editors' Choice

Published each January in ALA *Booklist*, a reviewing journal of the American Library Association, this list cites approximately 40–60 titles chosen by the journal's editors as the most outstanding books of the year.
See: www.ala.org/booklist/

Boston Globe-Horn Book Awards

Given annually since 1967 for fiction/poetry, nonfiction, and picture books, these awards are chosen by a committee of three experts and administered by *The Horn Book* magazine and *The Boston Globe* newspaper. The awards are presented at a special award ceremony in the fall.
See: www.hbook.com/bghb/

Bulletin of the Center for Children's Books Blue Ribbon

The reviewing journal of the Center for Children's Books, an extensive reference collection of contemporary children's literature at the Graduate School of Library and Information Science at the University of Illinois, Urbana-Champaign, the *Bulletin* publishes an annual list of top titles of the year chosen by the editors and reviewers of the journal.
See: http://bccb.lis.uiuc.edu/blueindex.html

Caldecott Medal and Honor Awards

Announced annually at the Midwinter Conference of the American Library Association, the Randolph Caldecott Medal is presented by the Association for Library Service to Children to the illustrator of "the most distinguished picture book for children (from birth through age 14) published in the United States in the preceding year." Other books worthy of notice may also be cited. In 1971 the term "runners-up" was officially changed to "honor books" for these additional titles. The award is presented during the annual conference of the Association in early summer.
See: www.ala.org/ala/alsc/awardsscholarships/literaryawds/caldecottmedal/

Canadian Library Association Book of the Year for Children Award

Established in 1947 and administered by the Canadian Association of Children's Librarians, this award is sponsored by the National Book Service and presented annually to an author who is a Canadian citizen or permanent resident in Canada. Any work of creative writing is eligible. The Association also presents the Amelia Frances Howard-Gibbon Illustrator's Award and the Young Adult Canadian Book Award.
See: www.cla.ca

Carnegie Medal

This medal has been awarded annually since 1936 to the writer of an outstanding book for young people that was first published in the United Kingdom (or co-published elsewhere within a three-month time lapse). All categories of books for young people are eligible.

The award is administered by a committee of the Youth Libraries Group, a division of the Chartered Institute of Library and Information Professionals (CILIP) in the United Kingdom.
See: www.carnegiegreenaway.org.uk

CCBC Choices

The Cooperative Children's Book Center (CCBC) at the University of Wisconsin-Madison, a children's and young adult literature reference library, publishes an annual list of about 250 outstanding books, annotated and arranged by subject area and genre.
See: www.education.wisc.edu/ccbc/books/choices.asp

Charlotte Zolotow Award

Established in 1998 and administered by the Cooperative Children's Book Center, a children's literature library at the School of Education, University of Wisconsin-Madison, this award honors the author of a picture book text published in the United States in the preceding year.
See: www.education.wisc.edu/ccbc/books/zolotow.asp

Children's Book Council (CBC)

The Children's Book Council, Inc. is a not-for-profit organization of publishers and packagers of trade books for children and young adults, located in New York City. Its goals include enhancing public perception of the importance of children's reading and working with other professional groups to increase awareness of children's books.
See: www.cbcbooks.org

Christopher Awards

The Christopher Awards are presented to producers, directors and writers of books, motion pictures and television specials that affirm the highest values of the human spirit. Presented by The Christophers, an organization in New York City.
See: www.christophers.org.

Coretta Scott King Award

Since 1970 this annual award has recognized the creative work of African American authors whose books are deemed outstanding, educational, and inspiring. In 1974 a second award for illustrators was added, and honor books are also designated. Today the awards are administered by the Coretta Scott King Task Force of the American Library Association's Ethnic Multicultural Information Exchange Round Table and presented at a breakfast during the annual conference of the association.
See: www.ala.org/ala/emiert/corettascottkingbookawards/corettascott.htm

Costa Book Awards

These British prizes, formerly known as the Whitbread Awards, have been awarded since 1971 and were renamed when Costa Coffee took over sponsorship in 2006. Eligible authors must have been residents of the United Kingdom or Ireland for at least six

months of the previous three years. Awards are given in five categories: First Novel, Novel, Biography, Poetry and Children's Book. One of these five books has been selected since 1985 as the overall Book of the Year, making this the only prize that places children's books alongside adult books in competition.
See: www.costabookawards.com

Ezra Jack Keats Book Award

Established in 1985 to recognize and encourage authors new to the field of children's books, this award is given annually to an outstanding new writer of picture books for children (age 9 and under). In 2001 an illustrator award was added. The presentations are made jointly by the New York Public Library and the Ezra Jack Keats Foundation.
See: www.ezra-jack-keats.org/bookawards/index.html

Golden Kite Awards

Presented annually by the Society of Children's Book Writers and Illustrators, these four awards—for fiction, nonfiction, picture book text, and picture book illustration—are given to creators of children's books by their fellow authors and artists. The awards are announced in April of every year.
See: www.scbwi.org.

Horn Book Fanfare

This annual compilation of 20–30 titles recognizes outstanding books of the previous year. Titles are chosen by the review staff of *The Horn Book* magazine, and the list appears in the January issue each year.
See: www.hbook.com

International Reading Association (IRA) Teachers' Choices

This is an annual list of trade books that teachers have found to be exceptional for classroom use. Titles are selected by teams of teachers throughout the country and published in the November issue of *The Reading Teacher*, with annotations and suggestions for use in the curriculum.
See: www.reading.org/resources/tools/choices_teachers.html

International Reading Association (IRA) Young Adults' Choices

Begun in 1987, this compilation of approximately thirty titles of new books chosen by students in grades 7 to 12 from different areas of the country is published in the November issue of the IRA's *Journal of Adolescent & Adult Literacy*.
See: www.reading.org/resources/tools/choices_young_adults.html

IRA/CBC Children's Choices

A joint project of the International Reading Association and the Children's Book Council, these books are chosen by children polled in schools around the country. Available in the October issue of *The Reading Teacher*, a publication of the International Reading Association, at the CBC web site, and at the IRA web site.

See: www.reading.org/resources/tools/choices_childrens.html

Irma Simonton Black and James H. Black Award

Administered since 1973 by Bank Street College of Education, this award goes to an outstanding book in which text and illustrations are inseparable. Presented solely in Irma's name until 1992, when James Black's name was added, the award is chosen by children, who pick the winning book from a list compiled by librarians, writers, and educators.
See: http://streetcat.bnkst.edu/html/isb.html

Jane Addams Children's Book Award

Presented annually since 1953 by the Women's International League for Peace and Freedom and the Jane Addams Peace Association, this award is given to the children's book of the preceding year that most effectively promotes the cause of peace, social justice and world community.
See: www.janeaddamspeace.org

Junior Library Guild

The Junior Library Guild is a service that reviews books in manuscript form and selects twelve books a year for each of nine reading levels. Subscribers receive the books at a reduced price. The JLG editorial staff consistently chooses books that later win awards and appear on "Best" lists. Headquarters are in Worthington, Ohio.
See: www.juniorlibraryguild.com

Kate Greenaway Medal

This medal is awarded annually to an artist for excellence in illustrating a children's book published in the United Kingdom. The award was established in 1955 and is administered by a committee of the Youth Libraries Group, a division of the Chartered Institute of Library and Information Professionals (CILIP) in the UK. A short list of candidates is announced in April or early May of books published in the previous year; the winner is announced at an awards ceremony in July.
See: www.carnegiegreenaway.org.uk

Michael L. Printz Award

Conferred annually since 2000 by a committee of the Young Adult Library Services Association, a division of the American Library Association, this award honors a book that exemplifies literary excellence in young adult literature published for ages 12–18. The winning book can be fiction, nonfiction, poetry, or an anthology.
See: www.ala.org/ala/yalsa/booklistsawards/printzaward/Printz.cfm

Mildred L. Batchelder Award

Established in 1966 and presented by the Association for Library Service to Children, a division of the American Library Association, this award is named for a former executive

director of the association. It is presented to an American publisher for the most outstanding book of the preceding year originally published in a foreign language and subsequently translated into English and published in the United States. Beginning in 1994, honor books were named as well.
See: www.ala.org/ala/alsc/awardsscholarships/literaryawds/batchelderaward/batchelderaward.cfm

National Book Awards

Sponsored by the National Book Foundation, a consortium of publishers, and presented each year in November, these awards honor four full-length original works of fiction, nonfiction, poetry, and young people's literature by American authors. A panel of judges chooses the winner from a shortlist of five titles for each award. Awards for young people's books were given annually from 1969-1983 and then reinstated in 1996.
See: www.nationalbook.org

Nestlé Smarties Book Prize

Administered by Booktrust, an independent charity that promotes books and reading, this British award was presented for a work of fiction or poetry written by a citizen or resident of the United Kingdom. Gold, Silver, and Bronze awards were given in each of three age categories (0–5, 6–8, and 9–11). A panel of adult judges chose a shortlist and school classes competed to become Young Judges who determine the winners. The award was discontinued in 2008.
See: www.booktrusted.co.uk/nestle/

Newbery Medal and Honor Awards

Announced annually at the Midwinter Conference of the American Library Association, the Newbery Medal is presented by the Association for Library Service to Children to the author of "the most distinguished contribution to literature for children (from birth through age 14) published in the United States in the preceding year." Other books worthy of notice may also be cited; in 1971 the term "runners-up" was officially changed to "honor books" for these additional titles. The award is presented at a banquet during the annual conference of the association in early summer.
See: www.ala.org/ala/alsc/awardsscholarships/literaryawds/newberymedal/newberymedal.cfm

New York Public Library: 100 Titles for Reading and Sharing

An annual list of distinguished books of the year, published in an attractive booklet by the Office of Children's Services of The New York Public Library each November. Copies are available for a small fee from the Office of Branch Services, New York Public Library, 455 Fifth Ave, New York, NY 10016.
See: http://kids.nypl.org/reading/recommended.cfm

New York Public Library: Books for the Teenage

This is a comprehensive and retrospective list of titles for teens, published each year by the Office of Young Adult Services of the New York Public Library. Copies are available for a small fee from the Office of Branch Services, The New York Public Library, 455 Fifth Avenue, New York, NY 10016.

See: www.teensreadtoo.com/NYPL07.html

Notable Social Studies Trade Books for Young People

This fully annotated list of books intended for grades K-8, published in the previous calendar year, is compiled by a committee of the National Council for the Social Studies in cooperation with the Children's Book Council. To be listed, books must emphasize human relations, represent a diversity of groups, and be sensitive to a broad range of cultural experiences. The list is published in the April/May issue of *Social Education*, and is available as a brochure from the CBC: www.cbcbooks.org. (Before 1999, known as Notable Children's Trade Books in the Field of Social Studies.)

See: www.ncss.org/resources/notable

NSK Neustadt Prize for Children's Literature

This new award to promote writing that contributes to the quality of children's lives is administered by The University of Oklahoma and its quarterly publication, *World Literature Today*. It is presented every other year, beginning in 2003, to a living writer for significant achievement, either over a lifetime or in a particular publication. All nominations come from jury members.

See: www.ou.edu/worldlit/NSK/NSK.htm

Oppenheim Toy Portfolio

Founded in 1989 as the only independent consumer review of children's media, this group publishes a quarterly newsletter and field-tests products with families from all walks of life. It is administered by Joanne Oppenheim, an author and authority on child development and education, and Stephanie Oppenheim, a former attorney and leading consumer authority on children's media.

See: www.toyportfolio.com

Orbis Pictus Award for Outstanding Nonfiction

Given annually since 1990 by the National Council of Teachers of English to an informational children's book published in the preceding year, this award is named for the book *Orbis Pictus* published by Johan Amos Comenius in 1659 and generally considered to be the first book created exclusively for children. See: www.ncte.org/elem/awards/orbispictus

Outstanding Science Trade Books for Students

This annotated list of books, published in the previous calendar year, is compiled by a committee of the National Science Teachers Association in cooperation with the Children's Book Council. The committee uses rigorous guidelines for content and presentation, accuracy and appropriateness for age level. The list is published in *Science and Children* in the spring and available as a brochure from the CBC. From 1973 to 2001 this list was

known as Outstanding Science Trade Books for Children and covered grades K–8. Since 2002 books for grades 9–12 have been included.
See: www.nsta.org/publications/ostb/

Parents' Choice Awards

Established in 1978, The Parents' Choice Foundation is a not-for-profit evaluator of books and other media created to help parents make informed choices. The awards are given to books, toys, videos, computer programs, etc. that are judged to be the best and most appealing products in their genre and to have a unique, individual quality.
See: www.parents-choice.org.

Pura Belpré Awards

Co-sponsored by the Association for Library Service to Children and the National Association to Promote Library Services to the Spanish Speaking (REFORMA), these awards were first presented in 1996 and are given biennially to a Latino/Latina writer and an illustrator whose works affirm and celebrate the Latino experience. They are named for the first Latina librarian in the New York Public Library, and starting in 2009, will be presented annually.
See: www.ala.org/ala/alsc/awardsscholarships/literaryawds/belpremedal/belprmedal.cfm

Robert F. Sibert Informational Book Award

This award, established by the Association for Library Service to Children in 2001 with support from Bound to Stay Bound Books, Inc., is presented annually to the author(s) and illustrator(s) of the most distinguished informational book published during the preceding year. The award is named in honor of Robert F. Sibert, the long-time President of Bound to Stay Bound Books, Inc. of Jacksonville, Illinois.
See: www.ala.org/ala/alsc/awardsscholarships/literaryawds/sibertmedal/sibert_medal.cfm

School Library Journal Best Books of the Year

Published annually in their December issue, this list of 50-60 outstanding titles is compiled by the editors of *School Library Journal* from over 4,000 books reviewed throughout that year.
See: www.schoollibraryjournal.com

Scott O'Dell Award for Historical Fiction

Established by author Scott O'Dell and awarded annually since 1984, this prize is given to a book of historical fiction that is set in the "New World" (North America, Central America, South America) and published in the previous year by an American author.
www.scottodell.com/odellaward.html

State Awards

Most of the 50 states now sponsor children's choice awards through a state library association or educational media association. These awards are typically chosen from

lists of 10–20 titles prepared by adults and then voted on by children.
See: www.cynthialeitichsmith.com/lit_resources/awards/stateawards.html

Whitbread Book Awards
(See: Costa Book Awards)

Note: This is a sampling of the awards and lists that are cited most frequently in this volume. Other awards are explained in the context of profiles in this book. There are many ways in which children's book authors and illustrators are honored today, an indication of the growth of the field and recognition of the excellence found in a wide variety of children's books today. An extensive and continually updated compilation of children's literature awards and honors is available by subscription from the Children's Book Council: www.cbcbooks.org

Geographical Index

Authors and illustrators are listed for places where they were born, where they now reside, and where they spent significant years of their lives.

Alabama
McWhorter, Diane
Trueman, Terry
Wiles, Deborah

Alaska
Lavallee, Barbara

Arizona
Christiana, David
Collard, Sneed B. III
Crowe, Chris
Helquist, Brett

Arkansas
Kadohata, Cynthia

California
Bechard, Margaret
Blake, Robert J.
Bornstein, Ruth Lercher
Chodos-Irvine, Margaret
Choldenko, Gennifer
Collard, Sneed B., III
Cooper, Elisha
Crowe, Chris
Dillon, Diane
Downing, Julie
DuPrau, Jeanne
Edwards, Julie Andrews
Ering, Timothy Basil
Fancher, Lou
Ferris, Jean
Funke, Cornelia
Gelman, Rita Golden
Gonzalez, Maya Christina
Hautman, Pete
Herrera, Juan Felipe
Hobbs, Valerie
Johnson, Steve
Kadohata, Cynthia
Kerley, Barbara
Klass, David
Koss, Amy Goldman
Morales, Yuyi

O'Connor, Barbara
O'Dell, Scott
Otani, June
Paolini, Christopher
Patron, Susan
Pattou, Edith
Remkiewicz, Frank
Riordan, Rick
Rubin, Susan Goldman
"Seuss, Dr."
Sones, Sonya
Vecchione, Patrice

Colorado
Avi
Bell, Hilari
Colman, Penny
Downing, Julie
McCarty, Peter
Pattou, Edith
Peters, Julie Anne

Connecticut
Bernier-Grand, Carmen T.
Casilla, Robert
Collins, Suzanne
Cooper, Elisha
Gelman, Rita Golden
Giff, Patricia Reilly
Hobbie, Holly
McCarty, Peter
McClintock, Barbara
Meisel, Paul
Remkiewicz, Frank
Sanderson, Ruth
Sidman, Joyce
Weller, Frances Ward
Wells, Rosemary
Yolen, Jane

District of Columbia
Danziger, Paula
Karr, Kathleen
Kerley, Barbara
Reef, Catherine

Turner, Megan Whalen

Florida
GrandPré, Mary
Hiaasen, Carl
Krisher, Trudy
Qualls, Sean
Remkiewicz, Frank
Sanchez, Alex

Georgia
Cofer, Judith Ortiz
Kadohata, Cynthia
Krisher, Trudy B.
Wiles, Deborah

Illinois
Balliett, Blue
Codell, Esmé Raji
Cooper, Elisha
Crowe, Chris
Dessen, Sarah
Fleming, Candace
Kadohata, Cynthia
Lehman, Barbara
Nikola-Lisa, W.
Osa, Nancy
Pattou, Edith
Smith, Cynthia Leitich
Turner, Megan Whalen
Vecchione, Patrice
Walker, Sally M.
Willems, Mo

Indiana
Dotlich, Rebecca Kai

Iowa
Lavallee, Barbara

Kansas
Ferris, Jean
Warren, Andrea

Kentucky
Denslow, Sharon Phillips
Long, Loren

Louisiana

Willems, Mo

Maryland

Brashares, Ann
Collier, Bryan
Freymann-Weyr, Garret
Wiles, Deborah

Massachusetts

Atwater-Rhodes, Amelia
Balliett, Blue
Ering, Timothy Basil
Frederick, Heather Vogel
Hobbie, Holly
Hurst, Carol Otis
Jenkins, Emily
Lin, Grace
Mack, Tracy
O'Connor, Barbara
Pinkney, Myles C.
Rosoff, Meg
Sanderson, Ruth
"Seuss, Dr."
Sones, Sonya
Tashjian, Janet
Watkins, Yoko Kawashima
Weller, Frances Ward
Wells, Rosemary
Willems, Mo
Yolen, Jane

Michigan

Ering, Timothy Basil
Fancher, Lou
Koss, Amy Goldman
Perkins, Lynne Rae
Pohrt, Tom
Schmidt, Gary D.
Weeks, Sarah

Minnesota

Casanova, Mary
Crossley-Holland, Kevin
Erdrich, Louise
Gaiman, Neil
GrandPré, Mary
Hautman, Pete
Hu, Ying-Hwa
Johnson, Steve
Sidman, Joyce

Stuve-Bodeen, Stephanie
Thimmesh, Catherine

Missouri

Blackwood, Gary L.
Long, Loren
McMullan, Kate
Schaefer, Carole Lexa
Schanzer, Rosalyn
Smith, Cynthia Leitich
Wiles, Deborah

Montana

Collard, Sneed B. III
Nikola-Lisa, W.
Paolini, Christopher

Nebraska

Warren, Andrea

New Hampshire

Erdrich, Louise
Frederick, Heather Vogel
Montgomery, Sy
Whatley, Bruce

New Jersey

Aliki
Avi
Blake, Robert J.
Casilla, Robert
Cofer, Judith Ortiz
Colman, Penny
George, Lindsay Barrett
Gutman, Dan
Hobbs, Valerie
Howard, Arthur
Jeffers, Susan
Karr, Kathleen
Klass, David
Lehman, Barbara
Levithan, David
McClintock, Barbara
Montgomery, Sy
Osa, Nancy
Qualls, Sean
Robbins, Ken
Walker, Sally M.
Weller, Frances Ward
Wells, Rosemary

New Mexico

Smith, Cat Bowman
Nelson, Vaunda Micheaux

New York

Aiken, Joan
Aliki
Anderson, Laurie Halse
Avi
Balliett, Blue
Bolden, Tonya
Bootman, Colin
Brashares, Ann
Carlson, Lori Marie
Carpenter, Nancy
Christensen, Bonnie
Christiana, David
Collier, Bryan
Collins, Suzanne
Cooper, Elisha
Dahl, Roald
Danziger, Paula
Dillon, Diane
Dillon, Leo
Donnelly, Jennifer
Freymann, Saxton
Freymann-Weyr, Garret
Gaber, Susan
Gelman, Rita Golden
Giff, Patricia Reilly
Going, K. L.
Gutman, Dan
Hamilton, Emma Walton
Helquist, Brett
Howard, Arthur
Hu, Ying-Hwa
Jeffers, Susan
Jenkins, Emily
"Kerr, M.E."
Klass, David
Kuskin, Karla
Lehman, Barbara
Lin, Grace
Lionni, Leo
Mack, Tracy
McCarty, Peter
McClintock, Barbara
McWhorter, Diane
McMullan, Jim

COUNTRY

Australia
Hartnett, Sonya
Nix, Garth
"Rodda, Emily"
Whatley, Bruce
Zusak, Markus

Canada
Bechard, Margaret
Blackwood, Gary L.
Ellis, Deborah
McMullan, Jim
Oppel, Kenneth

China
McMullan, Jim

Dominican Republic
George, Lindsay Barrett

England
Aiken, Joan
Aliki
Almond, David
Bishop, Nic
Brooks, Kevin
Child, Lauren
Crossley-Holland, Kevin
Dahl, Roald
Edwards, Julie Andrews
Firth, Barbara
Gaiman, Neil
Hamilton, Emma Walton
Inkpen, Mick
Lawrence, John
Mason, Simon
Nicholson, William
Pearce, Philippa

Pratchett, Terry
Rosen, Michael
Rosoff, Meg
Sage, Angie
Stroud, Jonathan
Updale, Eleanor
Whatley, Bruce

France
Hallensleben, Georg
Murdocca, Sal

Germany
Funke, Cornelia
Hallensleben, Georg
Montgomery, Sy

Guam
Kerley, Barbara

Holland
Lionni, Leo

Ireland
Colfer, Eoin

Israel
Carmi, Daniella

Italy
Hallensleben, Georg
Lionni, Leo
O'Dell, Scott

Japan
Klass, David
Watkins, Yoko Kawashima

Korea
Watkins, Yoko Kawashima

Mali
Diakité, Baba Wagué

Mexico
Morales, Yuyi
Sanchez, Alex

Nepal
Kerley, Barbara

New Zealand
Bishop, Nic

Nigeria
Nicholson, William

Puerto Rico
Bernier-Grand, Carmen T.
Casilla, Robert
Cofer, Judith Ortiz

Scotland
Hedderwick, Mairi
Yolen, Jane

Sweden
Lindgren, Astrid
Spiegelman, Art
Zaunders, Bo

Switzerland
Aliki

Taiwan
Hu, Ying-Hwa

Tanzania
Stuve-Bodeen, Stephanie

Trinidad
Bootman, Colin

Wales
Dahl, Roald
Fisher, Catherine
Whatley, Bruce

Authors and Illustrators Included in This Series

The following list indicates the volume in which each person may be found:

J—*The Junior Book of Authors,* second edition (1951)
M—*More Junior Authors* (1963)
3—*Third Book of Junior Authors* (1972)
4—*Fourth Book of Junior Authors and Illustrators* (1978)
5—*Fifth Book of Junior Authors and Illustrators* (1983)
6—*Sixth Book of Junior Authors and Illustrators* (1989)
7—*Seventh Book of Junior Authors and Illustrators* (1996)
8—*Eighth Book of Junior Authors and Illustrators* (2000)
9—*Ninth Book of Junior Authors and Illustrators* (2004)
10—*Tenth Book of Junior Authors and Illustrators* (2008)

Archer, Jules—5
"Arden, Barbie"
   See Stoutenburg, Adrien
Ardizzone, Edward—M
Armer, Laura Adams—J
Armour, Richard—5
Armstrong, Jennifer—8
Armstrong, Richard—3
Armstrong, William H.—3
Arno, Enrico—4
Arnold, Caroline—7
Arnold, Tedd—8
Arnosky, Jim—5
Aronson, Marc—9
Arthur, Ruth—5
Artzybasheff, Boris—J
Aruego, Ariane
   See Dewey, Ariane
Aruego, José—4
Arundel, Honor—4
Asch, Frank—4
Ashabranner, Brent—6
Asher, Sandy—7
Ashmun, Margaret—J
Asimov, Isaac—3
Atwater, Florence—M
Atwater, Montgomery
   Meigs—M
Atwater, Richard—M
Atwater-Rhodes,
   Amelia—10
Atwood, Ann—4
Auch, Mary Jane—8
Aulaire, Edgar Parin d'—J
Aulaire, Ingri Parin d'—J
Austin, Margot—M
"Austin, R. G."
   See Gelman, Rita Golden
Averill, Esther—J
Avery, Gillian—4
Avi—5, 10
Ayer, Jacqueline—3
Ayer, Margaret—M
Aylesworth, Jim—7
Azarian, Mary—8

"Babbis, Eleanor"
   See Friis-Baastad,

Babbis—3
Babbitt, Natalie—4
Bach, Alice—5
Bagnold, Enid—4
Bailey, Carolyn Sherwin—J
Baity, Elizabeth Chesley—M
Baker, Alan—8
Baker, Betty—3
Baker, Jeannie—7
Baker, Keith—7
Baker, Leslie—7
Baker, Margaret J.—M
Baker, Margaret—J
Baker, Mary—J
Baker, Nina Brown—J
Baker, Olaf—J
Baker, Rachel—M
Balch, Glenn—M
Balderson, Margaret—4
Baldwin, James—J
Balet, Jan—3
Balian, Lorna—5
Ball, Zachary—4
Balliett, Blue—10
"Bancroft, Laura"
   See Baum, L. Frank—3
Bang, Betsy Garrett—5
Bang, Molly Garrett—5
Banks, Kate—9
Banks, Lynne Reid—6
Bannerman, Helen—J
Bannon, Laura—M
Barbour, Ralph Henry—J
Barne, Kitty—J
Barracca, Debra—7
Barracca, Sal—7
Barrett, Judi—6
Barrett, Ron—6
Barron, T.A.—8
Bartoletti, Susan
   Campbell—9
Barton, Byron—5
Bartos-Höppner, Barbara—4
Base, Graeme Rowland—7
Bash, Barbara—7
Baskin, Leonard—5
Baudouy, Michel-Aimé—3
Bauer, Joan—8

Bauer, Marion Dane—5
Baum, L. Frank—3
Baumann, Hans—3
Bausum, Ann—10
Bawden, Nina—4
Bayley, Nicola—6
Baylor, Byrd—4
Baynes, Ernest Harold—J
Baynes, Pauline—3
"BB"—3
"Beach, Webb"
   See Butterworth, W. E.—5
Beatty, Hetty
   Burlingame—M
Beatty, John—3
Beatty, Patricia—3
Becerra de Jenkins, Lyll
   See Jenkins, Lyll Becerra
de—7
Bechard, Margaret—10
Beckman, Gunnel—4
Bedard, Michael—7
"Beddows, Eric"—7
Beeler, Nelson F.—M
Begay, Shonto—7
Behn, Harry—M
Behrens, June—8
Beim, Jerrold—J
Beim, Lorraine—J
Beisner, Monika—6
Bell, Anthea—7
Bell, Corydon—3
Bell, Hilari—10
Bell, Margaret E.—M
Bell, Thelma—3
Bellairs, John—5
Belpré, Pura—4
Belting, Natalia Maree—3
Bemelmans, Ludwig—M
Benary-Isbert, Margot—M
Benchley, Nathaniel—4
Bendick, Jeanne—M
Bendick, Robert—M
Bennett, Jay—6
Bennett, John—J
Bennett, Rainey—4
Bennett, Richard—J
Benét, Laura—J

Brooke, William J.—8
Brooks, Bruce—6
Brooks, Gwendolyn—4
Brooks, Kevin—10
Brooks, Martha—7
Brooks, Polly Schoyer—7
Brooks, Walter R.—J
Broster, D. K.—J
Brown, Marc—5
Brown, Don—8
Brown, Edna A.—J
Brown, Jeff—9
Brown, Marcia—M, 9
Brown, Margaret Wise—J
Brown, Palmer—5
Brown, Paul—J
Brown, Roy—4
Browne, Anthony—6
Bruchac, Joseph—8
Bruckner, Karl—4
Bruna, Dick—5
Brunhoff, Jean de—J
Brunhoff, Laurent de—M
Bryan, Ashley—5
Bryson, Bernarda—3
"Buck, Nola"
    See Godwin, Laura—9
Buehner, Caralyn—8
Buehner, Mark—8
Buehr, Walter—3
Buff, Conrad—J
Buff, Mary Marsh—J
Bulla, Clyde Robert—M, 8
Bunting, A. E.
    See Bunting, Eve
Bunting, Eve—5
"Burbank, Addison"
    See Newcomb, Covelle—J
Burch, Robert—3
Burchard, Peter—3
Burgess, Melvin—9
Burgess, Thornton W.—J
Burglon, Nora—J
Burkert, Nancy Ekholm—3
Burleigh, Robert—7
Burnford, S. D.
    See Burnford, Sheila
Burnford, Sheila—4

Burningham, John—3
Burton, Hester—3
Burton, Virginia Lee—J
Busoni, Rafaello—J
Butler, Beverly—6
Butterworth, Oliver—4
Butterworth, W. E.—5
"Buxton, Ralph."
    See Silverstein, Virginia
B.—5
Byard, Carole—7
Byars, Betsy—3, 9

Cabot, Meg—9
Cabot, Meggin
    See Cabot, Meg
"Cabot, Patricia"
    See Cabot, Meg
Cadnum, Michael—9
Caduto, Michael—8
Cain, Errol Le
    See Le Cain, Errol
Caldecott, Randolph—J
"Calder, Lyn"
    See Calmenson,
Stephanie—8
Calhoun, Mary—3
Callen, Larry—5
Calmenson, Stephanie—8
Calvert, Patricia—6
Cameron, Ann—7
Cameron, Eleanor—3
Cameron, Polly—4
Camp, Walter—J
"Campbell, Bruce"
    See Epstein, Samuel
Cannon, Janell—8
Carbone, Elisa Lynn—9
Card, Orson Scott—10
Carigiet, Alois—3
Carle, Eric—4, 8
Carlson, Lori—10
Carlson, Nancy—8
Carlson, Natalie Savage—M
Carlstrom, Nancy White—6
Carmi, Daniella—10
Carpenter, Frances—M
Carpenter, Nancy—10

Carr, Harriett H.—M
Carr, Mary Jane—J
Carrick, Carol—4
Carrick, Donald—4
Carrick, Valery—J
Carris, Joan—7
"Carroll, Jenny"
    See Cabot, Meg—9
Carroll, Latrobe—M
Carroll, Ruth—M
Carter, Alden—7
Carter, Helene—M
Casanova, Mary—10
Caseley, Judith—7
Casilla, Robert—10
Cassedy, Sylvia—6
Casserley, Anne—J
Catalanotto, Peter—7
Caudill, Rebecca—M
Cauley, Lorinda Bryan—6
Cavanah, Frances—M
Cavanna, Betty—M
Cazet, Denys—7
Cepeda, Joe—9
Chaikin, Miriam—6
Chalmers, Mary—3
Chambers, Aidan—6
"Chambers, Catherine E."
    See Johnston, Norma—5
"Chance, Stephen"
    See Turner, Philip—4
"Chapman, Walker"
    See Silverberg, Robert—3
Chappell, Warren—3
"Charles, Nicholas"
    See Kuskin, Karla
Charlip, Remy—3
Charlot, Jean—M
"Chase, Alice Elizabeth"
    See McHargue, Georgess
Chase, Mary Ellen—4
Chase, Richard—M
Chastain, Madye Lee—M
Chauncy, Nan—3
Chen, Tony—5
Cherry, Lynne—7
Chess, Victoria—6
Chetwin, Grace—7

Chew, Ruth—6
Child, Lauren—10
Childress, Alice—5
Chipperfield, Joseph E.—M
Chocolate, Debbi—8
Chodos-Irvine, Margaret—10
Choi, Sook Nyul—8
Choi, Yangsook—9
Choldenko, Gennifer—10
Chorao, Kay—4
Chrisman, Arthur Bowie—J
Christelow, Eileen—7
Christensen, Bonnie—10
Christiana, David—10
Christie, R. Gregory—9
"Christopher, John"—4
Christopher, Matt—5
Church, Alfred J.—J
Church, Richard—M
Chute, B. J.—M
Chute, Marchette—M
Chwast, Jacqueline—4
Chwast, Seymour—4
Chönz, Selina—4
Ciardi, John—3
Clapp, Patricia—5
"Clare, Helen"
    See Clarke, Pauline
Clark, Ann Nolan—J
Clark, Emma Chichester—7
Clark, Mavis Thorpe—4
Clarke, Arthur C.—4
Clarke, Pauline—3
Cleary, Beverly—M, 8
Cleaver, Bill—4
Cleaver, Elizabeth—4
Cleaver, Vera—4
Clements, Andrew—8
Clements, Bruce—5
Clifford, Eth—6
Clifton, Lucille—5
Climo, Shirley—7
Cline-Ransome, Lesa—9
Clymer, Eleanor—4
Coatsworth, Elizabeth—J
Cobb, Vicki—5
Cober, Alan E.—4
Coblentz, Catherine Cate—J

Codell, Esmé Raji—10
Coerr, Eleanor—6
Cofer, Judith Ortiz—10
Coggins, Jack—M
Cohen, Barbara—5
Cohen, Daniel—6
Cohen, Miriam—5
Colby, Carroll B.—M
Cole, Babette—7
Cole, Brock—6
Cole, Joanna—5
Cole, William—4
Coleman, Evelyn—9
Colfer, Eoin—10
"Colin, Ann"
    See Ure, Jean—6
Collard, Sneed B., III.—10
Collier, Bryan—10
Collier, Christopher—5
Collier, James Lincoln—5
Collington, Peter—7
Collins, Suzanne—10
"Collodi, C."—J
Colman, Hila—3
Colman, Penny—10
Colón, Raúl—9
Colum, Padraic—J
Coman, Carolyn—8
Cone, Molly—3
Conford, Ellen—5
Conklin, Gladys—4
Conly, Jane Leslie—7
Conover, Chris—6
Conrad, Pam—6
Conroy, Robert
    See Goldston, Robert
    Conroy
"Cook, John Estes"
    See Baum, L. Frank
Coolidge, Olivia E.—M
Coombs, Patricia—5
Cooney, Barbara—M, 9
Cooney, Caroline B.—8
Cooper, Elisha—10
Cooper, Elizabeth K.—4
Cooper, Floyd—7
Cooper, Helen—9
Cooper, Ilene—8

"Cooper, Melrose"
    See Kroll, Virginia
Cooper, Susan—4, 8
Corbett, Scott—4
Corbin, William—M
Corcoran, Barbara—5
Cormack, Maribelle—J
Cormier, Robert—5
Cosgrave, John O'Hara,
II—M
Cosgrove, Margaret—4
Cottrell, Leonard—4
Couloumbis, Audrey—9
Courlander, Harold—M
Cousins, Lucy—8
Coville, Bruce—7
Cowcher, Helen—7
Cowley, Joy—9
Craft, Kinuko—9
Craft, Ruth—5
Craig, Helen—8
Craig, M. Jean—4
Craig, Margaret Maze—M
Crane, Walter—J
Crawford, Phyllis—J
"Crayder, Teresa"
    See Colman, Hila
Credle, Ellis—J
Creech, Sharon—7
Cresswell, Helen—4
"Crew, Fleming H."
    See Gall, Alice Crew
Crew, Helén Coale—J
Crew, Linda—7
Crews, Donald—5
Crews, Nina—9
Crichlow, Ernest—4
Cronin, Doreen—9
Cross, Gillian—6
Crossley-Holland, Kevin—4,
10
Crowe, Chris—10
Crowell, Pers—M
Crownfield, Gertrude—J
Crowther, Robert—9
Crump, Irving—J
Crutcher, Chris—7
Ctvrtek, Václav—4

Cuffari, Richard—5
Cullen, Countée—4
Culter, Jane—8
Cummings, Betty Sue—5
Cummings, Pat—6
Cummins, Julie—9
Cunningham, Julia—3
Curlee, Lynn—9
Curry, Jane Louise—4
Curtis, Christopher Paul—8
Cushman, Doug—8
Cushman, Karen—7
Cuyler, Margery—7

d'Aulaire, Edgar & Ingri Parin
  See Aulaire, Edgar & Ingri
Dabcovich, Lydia—6
Dadey, Debbie—8
Dahl, Borghild—3
Dahl, Roald—3, 10
Dalgliesh, Alice—J
Daly, Maureen—M
Daly, Niki—6
Dana, Barbara—7
Daniel, Hawthorne—J
Danziger, Paula—5, 10
Daringer, Helen Fern—M
Darling, Louis—M
Dash, Joan—9
Daugherty, James—J
"David, Jonathan"
  See Ames, Lee J.
Davies, Andrew—5
Davis, Jenny—7
Davis, Julia—J
Davis, Lavinia R.—J
Davis, Mary Gould—J
Davis, Robert—J
Davol, Marguerite—8
Day, Alexandra—7
de Angeli, Marguerite—J
de Brunhoff, Jean
  See Brunhoff, Jean de
de Brunhoff, Laurent
  See Brunhoff, Laurent de
de Groat, Diane—5
de Jenkins, Lyll Becerra

See Jenkins, Lyll Becerra de—7
de Jong, Dola—M
De La Mare, Walter—J
de Leeuw, Adèle—J
de Leeuw, Cateau
  See de Leeuw, Adèle
de Regniers, Beatrice Schenk—M
de Saint-Exupéry, Antoine
  See Saint-Exupéry, Antoine de
de Treviño, Elizabeth Borton
  See Treviño, Elizabeth Borton de
De Veaux, Alexis—7
DeClements, Barthe—6
Deedy, Carmen Agra—9
DeFelice, Cynthia—7
Degen, Bruce—6
Degens, T.—5
DeJong, Meindert—M
del Rey, Lester—3
Delacre, Lulu—8
Delessert, Etienne—6
"Delmar, Roy"
  See Wexler, Jerome
Delton, Judy—5
"Delving, Michael"
  See Williams, Jay
Demarest, Chris L.—9
Demi—6
Denslow, Sharon Phillips—10
Dennis, Morgan—M
Dennis, Wesley—M
Denslow, W. W.—4
dePaola, Tomie—5
Desimini, Lisa—7
Dessen, Sarah—10
Deucher, Sybil—M
Deuker, Carl—9
Deutsch, Babette—M
Dewey, Ariane—4
Dewey, Jennifer Owings—9
Diakité, Baba Wagué—10
Diamond, Donna—5
Diaz, David—7

DiCamillo, Kate—9
Dickinson, Peter—4
Dickson, Marguerite—M
Dillon, Eilís—3
Dillon, Leo & Diane—5, 10
Ditmars, Raymond L.—J
Dix, Beulah Marie—J
"Dixon, Paige"
  See Corcoran, Barbara
Doane, Pelagie—M
Doherty, Berlie—7
Dolan, Edward—8
Dolbier, Maurice—M
Domanska, Janina—3
Donnelly, Jennifer—10
Donovan, John—5
Dorris, Michael—7
Dorros, Arthur—7
Dotlich, Rebecca Kai—10
Doty, Roy—8
"Douglas, James McM."
  See Butterworth, W. E.
Dowden, Anne Ophelia—5
Downing, Julie—10
Doyle, Brian—9
Dragonwagon, Crescent—6
Draper, Sharon M.—8
Drescher, Henrik—6
Drummond, V. H.—3
"Drummond, Walter"
  See Silverberg, Robert
"Dryden, Pamela"
  See Johnston, Norma
du Bois, William Pène—J
du Jardin, Rosamond—M
Du Soe, Robert C.—M
Duder, Tessa—7
Duff, Maggie—6
Duffey, Betsy—8
Duggan, Alfred—4
Duke, Kate—8
Dulac, Edmund—J
"Duncan, Lois"—5
Duncan, Norman—J
Dunlop, Eileen—6
Dunrea, Olivier—7
DuPrau, Jeanne—10
Duvoisin, Roger—J

Dyer, Jane—7
Dygard, Thomas J.—6

Eager, Edward—M
Earle, Olive L.—M
Eastman, Charles A.—J
Eaton, Jeanette—J
Eberle, Irmengarde—J
Eckert, Allan W.—4
Edmonds, Walter D.—M
Edwards, Julie Andrews—10
Egan, Tim—9
Egielski, Richard—6
Ehlert, Lois—7
Ehrlich, Amy—7
Eichenberg, Fritz—M
Eipper, Paul—J
Eitan, Ora—9
Elkin, Benjamin—4
Ellis, Deborah—10
Ellis, Ella—5
Ellis, Sarah—7
Ellsberg, Commander
   Edward—J
Els, Betty Vander
   See Vander Els, Betty
Elting, Mary—M
Emberley, Barbara—3
Emberley, Ed—3
Emberley, Michael—9
Emberley, Rebecca—8
Emery, Ann—M
Engdahl, Sylvia Louise—4
English, Karen—9
Enright, Elizabeth—J
Epstein, Beryl Williams—M
Epstein, Samuel—M
Erdman, Loula Grace—M
Erdrich, Louise—10
Ering, Timothy Basil—10
Ernst, Lisa Campbell—7
Esbensen, Barbara Juster—8
Estes, Eleanor—J
"Estoril, Jean"
   See Allan, Mabel Esther—6
Ets, Marie Hall—J
Evans, Eva Knox—M
Evans, Shane—9

"Every, Philip Cochrane"
   See Burnford, Sheila—4
Eyerly, Jeannette—5
Eyre, Katherine
Wigmore—M

Fabre, Jean-Henri—J
Facklam, Margery—8
Falconer, Ian—9
Fall, Thomas—4
Falls, C. B.—J
Falwell, Cathryn—9
Fancher, Lou—10
Farber, Norma—5
Farjeon, Eleanor—J
Farley, Carol—5
Farley, Walter—J
Farmer, Nancy—7
Farmer, Penelope—4
Fatio, Louise—M
Faulkner, Anne Irvin
   See Faulkner, Nancy
Faulkner, Nancy—4
Feagles, Anita MacRae—4
Feelings, Muriel—4
Feelings, Tom—3, 8
Feiffer, Jules—9
Felsen, Gregor—J
Felton, Harold W.—M
Fenner, Carol—8
Fenton, Carroll Lane—M
Fenton, Edward—3
Fenton, Mildred Adams—M
Ferris, Helen—J
Ferris, Jean—10
Feydy, Anne Lindbergh
   See Lindbergh, Anne
Field, Rachel—J
Fife, Dale—4
Fillmore, Parker—J
Fine, Anne—7
Fine, Howard—9
Firth, Barbara—10
Fischer, Hans Erich—M
Fisher, Aileen—M
Fisher, Catherine—10
Fisher, Leonard Everett—3,
8

Fitch, Florence Mary—M
"Fitzgerald, Captain Hugh"
   See Baum, L. Frank
Fitzgerald, John D.—5
Fitzhugh, Louise—3
Flack, Marjorie—J
Flake, Sharon—9
Fleischman, Paul—5
Fleischman, Sid—3, 9
Fleming, Candace—10
Fleming, Denise—7
Fleming, Ian—5
Fletcher, Ralph—8
Fletcher, Susan—9
Flinn, Alex—9
Floca, Brian—9
Floethe, Richard—M
Floherty, John J.—J
Flora, James—3
Florian, Douglas—6
Forberg, Ati—4
Forbes, Esther—M
Foreman, Michael—6
Forman, James—3
Fortnum, Peggy—4
Foster, Genevieve—J
Foster, Marian Curtis
   See "Mariana"
Fox, Mem—6
Fox, Paula—4
Fradin, Dennis Brindell—8
Frampton, David—9
Franchere, Ruth—4
"Francis, Dee"
   See Haas, Dorothy
Franklin, George Cory—M
François, André—3
Françoise—M
Frascino, Edward—5
Frasconi, Antonio—3
Fraser, Claud Lovat—J
Frazee, Marla—9
Frederick, Heather
Vogel—10
"Freedman, Peter J."
   See Calvert, Patricia—6
Freedman, Russell—6
Freeman, Don—M

Freeman, Ira Maximilian—M
Freeman, Lydia—M
Freeman, Mae Blacker—M
Freeman, Suzanne—8
French, Allen—J
French, Fiona—7
"French, Paul"
   See Asimov, Isaac—3
Freschet, Berniece—4
Freymann, Saxton—10
Freymann-Weyr, Garrett—10
Friedman, Frieda—M
Friermood, Elisabeth
   Hamilton —M
Friis, Babbis
   See Friis-Baastad, Babbis
Friis-Baastad, Babbis—3
Fritz, Jean—3, 8
Froman, Robert—4
Frost, Frances—M
Fry, Rosalie K.—3
Fuchs, Erich—4
Fujikawa, Gyo—4
Funke, Cornelia—10
Fyleman, Rose—J

Gaber, Susan—10
Gackenbach, Dick—5
Gaer, Joseph—M
Gág, Flavia—M
Gág, Wanda—J
"Gage, Wilson"—3
Gaiman, Neil—10
Galdone, Paul—3
Gall, Alice Crew—J
Gallant, Roy A.—5
Galt, Tom—M
Gammell, Stephen—5
Gannett, Ruth Chrisman— M
Gannett, Ruth Stiles—4
Gans, Roma—5
Gantos, Jack—5
Garcia, Rita Williams
   See Williams-Garcia, Rita
Gardam, Jane—5
Garden, Nancy—5
Gardiner, John Reynolds—6
Gardner, Beau—6

Gardner, John—5
Garfield, Leon—4
Garland, Sherry—7
Garner, Alan—3
Garnett, Eve—5
"Garrett, Randall"
   See Silverberg, Robert
Garrigue, Sheila—6
Garst, Shannon—J
Garza, Carmen Lomas—8
Gates, Doris—J
Gatti, Attilio—J
Gauch, Patricia Lee—5
Gay, Kathlyn—8
Gay, Zhenya—M
Geisel, Theodor Seuss
   See "Seuss, Dr."
Geisert, Arthur—7
Gekiere, Madeleine—3
Gelman, Rita Golden—10
George, Jean Craighead—M,
8
George, Kristine
O'Connell—9
George, Lindsay Barrett—10
Geras, Adèle—8
Gerrard, Roy—7
Gerstein, Mordicai—6
Gibbons, Gail—6
Giblin, James Cross—6
"Gibson, Josephine"
   See Hine, Al & Joslin,
   Sesyle
Gibson, Katharine—J
Giff, Patricia Reilly—5, 10
Gilchrist, Jan Spivey—7
Gill, Margery—4
Gilson, Jamie—6
Ginsburg, Mirra—6
Giovanni, Nikki—5
Giovanopoulos, Paul—4
Gipson, Fred—3
Girion, Barbara—6
Girvan, Helen—M
Glaser, Milton—4
Glass, Andrew—6
Glenn, Mel—7
Glubok, Shirley—3

Goble, Dorothy
   See Goble, Paul
Goble, Paul—4
Godden, Rumer—M
Godwin, Laura—9
Goffstein, M. B.—4
Going, K. L.—10
Goldsmith, Diane Hoyt
   See Hoyt-Goldsmith,
   Diane
Goldston, Robert Conroy—4
Gollomb, Joseph—J
González, Lucía M.—8
Gonzalez, Maya
Christina—10
Goodall, John S.—4
Goode, Diane—5
Goor, Nancy—7
Goor, Ron—7
Gordon, Sheila—7
Gorey, Edward—4
Gorog, Judith—7
Goudey, Alice E.—3
Goudge, Elizabeth—3
Grabianski, Janusz—3
Graham, Bob—9
Graham, Lorenz—3
Graham, Margaret Bloy—M
Graham, Shirley—M
Gramatky, Hardie—J
GrandPré, Mary—10
Gray, Elizabeth Janet—J
Gray, Libba Moore—8
Green, Roger Lancelyn—3
Greenaway, Kate—J
Greenberg, Jan—6, 9
Greene, Bette—5
Greene, Constance C.—4
Greene, Stephanie—9
Greenfeld, Howard—7
Greenfield, Eloise—5
Greenwald, Sheila—5
Greenwood, Ted—4
"Gregory, Jean"
   See Ure, Jean
Grierson, Elizabeth W.—J
Grifalconi, Ann—3
Griffin, Adele—8

Griffith, Helen V.—7
"Griffith, Jeannette"
  See Eyerly, Jeannette
Griffiths, Helen—4
Grimes, Nikki—8
Grinnell, George Bird—J
Gripe, Harald
  See Gripe, Maria
Gripe, Maria—3
"Groat, Diane de"
  See de Groat, Diane
Grossman, Bill—9
Grove, Vicki—9
Guevara, Susan—8
Guiberson, Brenda—9
Guillot, René—M
Guin, Ursula K. Le
  See Le Guin, Ursula K.
Gundersheimer, Karen—6
Gurko, Leo—3
Gurko, Miriam—3
Gutman, Dan—10
Guy, Rosa—5

Haar, Jaap ter—4
Haas, Dorothy—6
Haas, Irene—3
Haas, Jessie—8
Haddix, Margaret Peterson—8
Hader, Berta—J
Hader, Elmer—J
Hadith, Mwenye—7
Hadley, Lee
  See "Irwin, Hadley"
Hafner, Marylin—6
"Hagon, Priscilla"
  See Allan, Mabel Esther
Hague, Michael—5
Hahn, Mary Downing—6
Halacy, D. S., Jr.—5
Haley, Gail E.—3
Hall, Donald, Jr.—5
Hall, Lynn—5
Hall, Rosalyn Haskell—M
Hallensleben, Georg—10
Halperin, Wendy Anderson—8

Hamanaka, Sheila—9
Hamilton, Emma Walton—10
"Hamilton, Gail"
  See Corcoran, Barbara
Hamilton, Virginia—4, 9
Hamre, Leif—4
Handford, Martin—7
Handforth, Thomas—J
Handler, Daniel
  See "Snicket, Lemony"—9
Hanlon, Emily—6
Hansen, Joyce—8
Harkins, Philip—M
Harness, Cheryl—8
Harnett, Cynthia—3
Harris, Christie—4
"Harris, Lavinia"
  See Johnston, Norma
Harris, Robie H.—9
Harris, Rosemary—4
Harrison, Ted—8
Harshman, Marc—9
Hartman, Gertrude—J
Hartnett, Sonya—10
Harvey, Brett—6
Haseley, Dennis—7
Haskell, Helen Eggleston—J
Haskins, James
  See Haskins, Jim
Haskins, Jim—6
Hastings, Selina—8
Haugaard, Erik Christian—3
Hautman, Pete—10
Hautzig, Deborah—5
Hautzig, Esther—3
Havighurst, Marion—M
Havighurst, Walter—M
Haviland, Virginia—4
Havill, Juanita—7
Hawkes, Kevin—7
Hawkinson, John—4
Hawthorne, Hildegarde—J
Hays, Michael—8
Hays, Wilma Pitchford—3
Haywood, Carolyn—J
Hazen, Barbara Shook—6
Headley, Elizabeth
  See Cavanna, Betty

"Hearn, Lian"
  See Rubinstein, Gillian
Hearne, Betsy—6
Hedderwick, Mairi—10
Heide, Florence Parry—4
Heine, Helme—6
Heinlein, Robert A.—M
Heller, Ruth—7
Helquist, Brett—10
Hendershot, Judith—6
Henderson, Le Grand
  See Le Grand
Henkes, Kevin—6
Hennessy, B. G.—7
Henry, Marguerite—J
Henstra, Friso—4
Hentoff, Nat—3
Heo, Yumi—9
Herald, Kathleen
  See Peyton, K. M.
Herman, Charlotte—7
Hermes, Patricia—6
Herrera, Juan Felipe—10
Hess, Fjeril—J
Hess, Lilo—5
Hesse, Karen—8
Hest, Amy—7
Hewes, Agnes Danforth—J
Heyliger, William—J
Hiaasen, Carl—10
High, Linda Oatman—10
Hightower, Florence—3
Highwater, Jamake—5
Hildick, E. W.—4
Hill, Douglas—6
Hill, Eric—6
Hillenbrand, Will—8
"Hillman, Martin"
  See Hill, Douglas
Hillyer, V. M.—J
Himler, Ronald—6
Hine, Al—3
Hines, Anna Grossnickle—6
Hinton, S. E.—4
"Hippopotamus, Eugene H."
  See Kraus, Robert
Hirsch, S. Carl—3
Hirschi, Ron—8

Hirsh, Marilyn—5
Hitz, Demi
    See Demi
Ho, Minfong—7
Hoban, Lillian—3
Hoban, Russell—3
Hoban, Tana—4
Hobbie, Holly—10
Hobbs, Valerie—10
Hobbs, Will—7
Hoberman, Mary Ann—6
Hodges, C. Walter—3
Hodges, Margaret—4
Hoff, Syd—3
Hoffman, Mary—7
Hoffman, Rosekrans—7
Hoffmann, Felix—3
Hofsinde, Robert—3
Hogan, Inez—M
Hogner, Dorothy—J
Hogner, Nils—J
Hogrogian, Nonny—3
Holabird, Katharine—8
Holberg, Richard A.—J
Holberg, Ruth—J
Holbrook, Stewart—3
Holland, Isabelle—5
Holland, Kevin Crossley
    See Crossley-Holland,
    Kevin
Holland, Rupert Sargent—J
Holling, H. C.—J
Holling, Lucille W.
    See Holling, H. C.
Holm, Anne—4
Holm, Jennifer—9
Holman, Felice—4
Holt, Kimberly Willis—9
Hoobler, Thomas &
Dorothy—8
Hooks, William H.—6
Hoover, Helen M.—5
Hopkins, Lee Bennett—5
Hopkinson, Deborah—9
Höppner, Barbara Bartos
    See Bartos-Höppner,
    Barbara
Horvath, Polly—9

Hosford, Dorothy—M
Hotze, Sollace—7
Houston, Gloria—7
Houston, James A.—4
Howard, Arthur—10
Howard, Elizabeth
    Fitzgerald—7
Howard, Elizabeth—M
Howard, Ellen—7
Howe, Deborah—6
Howe, James—6
Howker, Janni—6
Hoyt-Goldsmith, Diane—7
Hu, Ying-Hwa
    See Van Wright,
    Cornelius—10
Hudson, Cheryl Willis—8
Hudson, Jan—7
Hudson, Wade—8
Hughes, Dean—6
"Hughes, Eden"
    See Butterworth, W. E.—5
Hughes, Langston—4
Hughes, Monica—6
Hughes, Shirley—5
Hunt, Clara Whitehill—J
Hunt, Irene—3
Hunt, Mabel Leigh—J
Hunter, Kristin—4
Hunter, Mollie—3
Huntington, Harriet E.—M
Hurd, Clement—M
Hurd, Edith Thacher—M
Hurd, Thacher—6
Hürlimann, Bettina—3
Hurmence, Belinda—6
Hurst, Carol Otis—10
Hurwitz, Johanna—6
Hutchins, Pat—4
Hutchins, Ross E.—3
Hutton, Warwick—6
Hyde, Margaret O.—3
Hyman, Trina Schart—4, 8

Ibbotson, Eva—9
Ichikawa, Satomi—7
"Ilin, M."—J
Ingpen, Robert—7

Inkpen, Mick—10
Ipcar, Dahlov—3
"Irving, Robert"
    See Adler, Irving—3
Irwin, Annabelle Bowen
    See "Irwin, Hadley"
"Irwin, Hadley"—6
Isaacs, Anne—8
Isadora, Rachel—5
Isbert, Margot Benary
    See Benary-Isbert,
    Margot
Ish-Kishor, Sulamith—5
Iterson, S. R., van—4

"J Marks"
    See Highwater, Jamake
Jackson, Jacqueline—4
Jacques, Brian—7
Jacques, Robin—3
Jaffe, Nina—8
Jagendorf, Moritz A.—M
Jakobsen, Kathy—9
"James, Dynely"
    See Mayne, William—3
"James, Mary"
    See "Kerr, M. E."
James, Synthia Saint
    See Saint James, Synthia
James, Will—J
Janeczko, Paul B.—6
Janosch—4
Jansson, Tove—3
Jardin, Rosamond du
    See du Jardin, Rosamond
Jarrell, Randall—3
Jasperson, Willliam—7
Jauss, Anne Marie—4
Jeffers, Susan—4, 10
Jenkins, Emily—10
Jenkins, Lyll Becerra de—7
Jenkins, Steve—8
Jeschke, Susan—5
Jewett, Eleanore M.—M
Jiménez, Francisco—9
Johnson, Angela—7
Johnson, Annabel—3
Johnson, Crockett—3

Johnson, D. B.—9
Johnson, Dolores—8
Johnson, Edgar—3
Johnson, Gerald W.—3
Johnson, J. Rosamond
   See Johnson, James
   Weldon
Johnson, James Weldon—4
Johnson, Margaret Sweet—J
Johnson, Paul Brett—9
Johnson, Siddie Joe—J
Johnson, Steve—10
Johnson, Steven T.—8
Johnston, Johanna—4
Johnston, Norma—5
Johnston, Tony—6
Jonas, Ann—7
Jones, Adrienne—5
Jones, Diana Wynne—5
Jones, Elizabeth Orton—J
Jones, Harold—3
Jones, Jessie Orton—5
Jones, Marcia Thornton—8
Jones, Mary Alice—M
Jones, Rebecca C.—7
Jones, Tim Wynne
   See Wynne-Jones, Tim
Jones, Weyman B.—4
Jong, Dola de
   See de Jong, Dola
Joose, Barbara M.—7
Jordan, June—4
Jordan, Sandra—9
"Jorgenson, Ivar"
   See Silverberg, Robert
Joslin, Sesyle—3
Joyce, William—6
Judson, Clara Ingram—J
Jukes, Mavis—6
Juster, Norton—4
Justus, May—J

Kadohata, Cynthia—10
Kahl, Virginia—M
Kalashnikoff, Nicholas—M
Kalman, Maira—7
Karas, G. Brian—8
Karl, Jean E—5

Karr, Kathleen—10
Kästner, Erich—3
Kasza, Keiko—7
Kaye, Marilyn—7
Keats, Ezra Jack—M
Keeping, Charles—3
Kehret, Peg—8
Keith, Eros—4
Keith, Harold—M
Keller, Beverly—7
Keller, Holly—9
Kelley, True—8
Kellogg, Steven—4, 9
Kelly, Eric P.—J
Kelsey, Alice Geer—M
Kendall, Carol—3
"Kendall, Lace"
   See Stoutenburg, Adrien
Kennaway, Adrienne—7
Kennedy, Richard—5
Kennedy, X. J.—6
Kent, Jack—5
Kent, Louise Andrews—J
Kepes, Juliet—3
Ker Wilson, Barbara—4
Kerley, Barbara—10
Kerr, Judith—5
"Kerr, M. E."—4, 10
"Kerry, Lois"
   See "Duncan, Lois"
Kessler, Ethel—5
Kessler, Leonard—5
Kettelkamp, Larry—3
Khalsa, Dayal Kaur—7
Kherdian, David—5
Kimmel, Elizabeth Cody—9
Kimmel, Eric A.—7
"Kincaid, Beth"
   See Applegate, Katherine
Kindl, Patrice—8
King-Smith, Dick—6
Kingman, Lee—M
"Kinsey, Elizabeth"
   See Clymer, Eleanor
Kinsey-Warnock, Natalie—8
"Kirtland, G. B."
   See Hine, Al & Joslin,
   Sesyle

Kitamura, Satoshi—8
Kitchen, Bert—7
Kjelgaard, Jim—J
Klass, David—10
Klass, Sheila Solomon—8
Klause, Annette Curtis—7
Klein, Norma—5
Kleven, Elisa—7
Kline, Suzy—7
Knight, Eric—4
Knight, Hilary—4
Knight, Kathryn Lasky
   See Lasky, Kathryn
Knight, Ruth Adams—M
Knipe, Alden Arthur—J
Knipe, Emilie Benson—J
"Knox, Calvin M."
   See Silverberg, Robert
Knox, Rose B.—J
Knudson, R. R.—6
Koehn, Ilse—5
Koering, Ursula—M
Koertge, Ron—7
Koller, Jackie French—9
Komaiko, Leah—8
Konigsburg, E. L.—3, 8
Korman, Gordon—7
Koss, Amy Goldman—10
Krahn, Fernando—4
Krasilovsky, Phyllis—M
Kraus, Robert—3
Krauss, Ruth—M
Kredel, Fritz—M
Krementz, Jill—5
Krensky, Stephen—6
Krisher, Trudy—10
Kroeger, Mary Kay—9
Kroll, Steven—5
Kroll, Virginia—8
Krull, Kathleen—7
Krumgold, Joseph—M
Krush, Beth—M
Krush, Joe—M
Krüss, James—3
Kudlinski, Kathleen—9
Kuklin, Susan—7
Kullman, Harry—5
Kurelek, William—5

Kurtz, Jane—8
Kuskin, Karla—3, 10
Kvasnosky, Laura McGee— 9
Kyle, Anne D.—J
Kyle, Elisabeth—M

L'Engle, Madeleine—M, 9
La Mare, Walter De
  See De La Mare, Walter
Laan, Nancy Van
  See Van Laan, Nancy
Laboulaye, Édouard—J
LaMarche, Jim—9
Lamb, Harold—J
Lambert, Janet—3
Lamorisse, Albert—4
Lampman, Evelyn Sibley—M
Lamprey, Louise—J
Landau, Elaine—8
Langstaff, John—3
Langton, Jane—5
Lansing, Marion Florence—J
Larrick, Nancy—8
Lasker, Joe—5
Laskowski, Jerzy—3
Lasky, Kathryn—6
Latham, Jean Lee—M
Lathrop, Dorothy P.—J
Lattimore, Deborah
  Nourse—7
Lattimore, Eleanor
  Frances—J
Lauber, Patricia—3
Laut, Agnes C.—J
Lavallee, Barbara—10
Lavies, Bianca—7
Lawlor, Laurie—9
Lawrence, Iain—9
Lawrence, Jacob—4
Lawrence, John—10
Lawrence, Louise—6
Lawrence, Mildred—M
Lawson, Don—6
Lawson, Marie Abrams
  See Lawson, Robert
Lawson, Robert—J
Le Cain, Errol—6
Le Grand—J

Le Guin, Ursula K.—4, 9
Le Sueur, Meridel—M
Le Tord, Bijou—6
Leach, Maria—4
Leaf, Munro—J
Lee, Dennis—7
Lee, Dom—8
Lee, Jeanne M.—8
Lee, Manning de V.—M
Lee, Marie G.—8
Lee, Mildred—3
Lee, Tina—M
Leedy, Loreen—7
Leeming, Joseph—J
Leeuw, Adèle de
  See de Leeuw, Adèle
"Leeuwen, Jean Van
  See Van Leeuwen, Jean
Lehman, Barbara—10
Leighton, Margaret—M
Lenski, Lois—J
Lent, Blair—3
Lent, Henry B.—J
"Leodhas, Sorche Nic"
  See "Nic Leodhas,
  Sorche"
Lerner, Carol—6
Leroe, Ellen W.—7
"LeSieg, Theo."
  See "Seuss, Dr."
Lessac, Frané—8
Lester, Alison—8
Lester, Helen—8
Lester, Julius—4, 8
Levin, Betty—6
Levine, Ellen—7
Levine, Gail Carson—8
Levinson, Riki—6
Levithan, David—10
Levitin, Sonia—5
Levoy, Myron—5
Levy, Elizabeth—5
Lewellen, John—M
Lewin, Betsy—8
Lewin, Ted—7
Lewis, C. S.—M
Lewis, E. B.—8
Lewis, Elizabeth Foreman—J

Lewis, J. Patrick—7
Lewis, Richard—7
Lewiton, Mina—M
Lexau, Joan M.—4
Ley, Willy—3
Lifton, Betty Jean—3
Lin, Grace—10
Lindbergh, Anne—6
Lindbergh, Reeve—7
Linde, Gunnel—4
Lindenbaum, Pija—7
Linderman, Frank B.—J
Lindgren, Astrid—M, 10
Lindgren, Barbro—6
Lindman, Maj—J
Lindquist, Jennie D.—M
Lindquist, Willis—M
Lingard, Joan—5
Lionni, Leo—3, 10
Lipkind, William—M
Lippincott, Joseph
  Wharton—M
Lipsyte, Robert—5
Lisle, Janet Taylor—6
Little, Jean—4
Lively, Penelope—4
Livingston, Myra Cohn—4
Lloyd, Megan—8
Lobel, Anita—3
Lobel, Arnold—3, 9
"Lockhart, E."
  See Jenkins, Emily
"Locke, Robert"
  See Bess, Clayton
Locker, Thomas—6
Löfgren, Ulf—4
Lofting, Hugh—J
London, Jonathan—8
Long, Loren—10
Long, Sylvia—9
Longstreth, T. Morris—M
Look, Lenore—9
Lord, Beman—4
Lord, Bette Bao—6
"Lord, Nancy"
  See Titus, Eve
Lorraine, Walter—4
Lottridge, Celia Barker—9

Lovelace, Maud Hart—J
Low, Alice—6
Low, Joseph—3
Lownsbery, Eloise—J
Lowry, Lois—5
Lubell, Cecil—4
Lubell, Winifred—4
Lucas, Jannette May—J
Luenn, Nancy—8
Lunn, Janet—6
Lynch, Chris—7
Lynch, P. J.—8
Lyon, George Ella—7
Lyons, Mary E.—7

Macaulay, David—5
MacBride, Roger Lea—8
MacDonald, Amy—8
"MacDonald, Golden"
  See Brown, Margaret
  Wise
MacDonald, Suse—6
MacGregor, Ellen—M
Machotka, Hana—7
Mack, Stan—4
Mack, Tracy—10
Mackay, Constance
  D'Arcy—J
MacKinstry, Elizabeth—M
MacLachlan, Patricia—6
MacPherson, Margaret—4
Macy, Sue—9
Maestro, Betsy—6
Maestro, Giulio—6
Magorian, Michelle—6
Maguire, Gregory—8
Mahy, Margaret—4, 9
Maitland, Antony—4
Malcolmson, Anne—M
Malkus, Alida Sims—J
Malvern, Corinne
  See Malvern, Gladys
Malvern, Gladys—J
Manes, Stephen—7
Manning-Sanders, Ruth—3
Manushkin, Fran—8
Marcellino, Fred—7
Mare, Walter De La

  See De La Mare, Walter
"Mariana"—3
Marino, Jan—7
Maris, Ron—8
Mark, Jan—5
Markle, Sandra—9
Marrin, Albert—7
Mars, W. T.—4
Marsden, John—9
Marshall, James—4
Martin, Ann M.—7
Martin, Bill, Jr.—6
"Martin, Fredric"
  See Christopher, Matt
Martin, Jacqueline Briggs— 9
Martin, Patricia Miles
  See "Miles, Miska"
Martin, Rafe—7
Maruki, Toshi—6
Marzollo, Jean—6
Mason, Miriam E.—M
Mason, Simon—10
Matas, Carol—7
Mathers, Petra—7
Mathis, Sharon Bell—4
Matsuno, Masako—4
Mayer, Marianna—4
Mayer, Mercer—4
Mayne, William—3
Mays, Victor—4
Mazer, Harry—5
Mazer, Norma Fox—5
McCaffrey, Anne—5
McCarty, Peter—10
McCaughrean, Geraldine—8
McClintock, Barbara—10
McCloskey, Robert—J, 9
"McClune, Dan"
  See Haas, Dorothy
McClung, Robert M.—M
McCord, David—3
McCracken, Harold—J
"McCulloch, Sarah"
  See Ure, Jean
McCully, Emily Arnold—4
McCurdy, Michael—7
McDermott, Beverly
  Brodsky

  See Brodsky, Beverly
McDermott, Gerald—5
"McDole, Carol"
  See Farley, Carol—5
"McDonald, Jamie"
  See Heide, Florence
  Parry—4
McDonald, Megan—7
McDonnell, Christine—6
McGinley, Phyllis—J
McGovern, Ann—4
McGowen, Tom—9
McGraw, Eloise Jarvis—M, 9
McHargue, Georgess—5
McKay, Hilary—8
McKenna, Colleen—10
McKillip, Patricia A.—5
McKinley, Robin—5
McKissack, Fredrick L.—7
McKissack, Patricia—7
McKown, Robin—3
McLean, Allan Campbell—4
"McLennan, Will"
  See Wisler, G. Clifton—7
McMahon, Patricia—8
McMeekin, Isabel
McLennan—M
McMillan, Bruce—6
McMullan, Jim—10
McMullan, Kate—10
McNaughton, Colin—8
McNeely, Marian Hurd—J
McNeer, May—J
McNeill, Janet—4
McPhail, David—5
McSwigan, Marie—M
McWhorter, Diane—10
Mead, Alice—9
Meade, Holly—8
Meader, Stephen W.—J
Meadowcroft, Enid—J
Meaker, Marijane
  See "Kerr, M. E."
Means, Florence Crannell—J
Medary, Marjorie—J
Meddaugh, Susan—7
Mehdevi, Anne Sinclair—4
Meigs, Cornelia—J

Pringle, Laurence—4
Proudfit, Isabel—M
Provensen, Alice—3, 9
Provensen, Martin—3, 9
Pryor, Bonnie—8
Pullman, Philip—6
Pyle, Katharine—J

Quackenbush, Robert—4
Qualls, Sean—10
Quennell, Charles Henry
   Bourne—M
Quennell, Marjorie—M

Rabe, Berniece—5
Rackham, Arthur—J
Radunsky, Vladimir—9
Raffi—6
Rahn, Joan Elma—6
Rand, Anne (or Ann)—3
Rand, Gloria—8
Rand, Paul—3
Rand, Ted—6
Randall, Florence Engel—6
"Randall, Robert"
   See Silverberg, Robert
Rankin, Louise S.—M
Ransome, Arthur—J
Ransome, James E.—7
Ransome, Lesa Cline
   See Cline-Ransome, Lesa
Raphael, Elaine
   See Bolognese, Don &
   Elaine Raphael—4
Rapp, Adam—9
Rappaport, Doreen—7
Raschka, Chris—7
Raskin, Ellen—3
Rathmann, Peggy—8
Ravielli, Anthony—3
Rawlings, Marjorie
Kinnan—3
Rawls, Wilson—6
Ray, Deborah Kogan—6
Ray, Jane—7
Raynor, Mary—5
Reed, Philip—3
Reed, W. Maxwell—J

Reeder, Carolyn—7
Reef, Catherine—10
Rees, David—5
Reeves, James—3
Regniers, Beatrice Schenk de
   See de Regniers, Beatrice
Schenk
Reiser, Lynn—8
Reiss, Johanna—5
Remkiewicz, Frank—10
Rendina, Laura Cooper—M
Renick, Marion—M
Rey, H. A.—J
Rey, Lester del
   See del Rey, Lester
"Rhine, Richard"
   See Silverstein, Virginia
B.—5
"Rhue, Morton"
   See Strasser, Todd
Ribbons, Ian—4
Rice, Eve—5
Richard, Adrienne—5
Richter, Hans Peter—4
Rigg, Sharon
   See Creech, Sharon
Ringgold, Faith—7
Ringi, Kjell—4
Riordan, Rick—10
Robbins, Ken—10
Robbins, Ruth—3
Roberts, Willo Davis—5
Robertson, Keith—M
Robinet, Harriette Gillem—9
Robinson, Barbara—5
Robinson, Charles—6
Robinson, Irene B.—J
Robinson, Mabel Louise—J
Robinson, Tom—J
Robinson, W. W.—J
Rochman, Hazel—7
Rockwell, Anne F.—5
Rockwell, Harlow—5
Rockwell, Thomas—5
"Rodda, Emily"—10
Rodgers, Mary—5
Rodowsky, Colby—6
Rogers, Fred McFreeley

See "Rogers, Mister"
Rogers, Jacqueline—9
"Rogers, Mister"—7
Rohmann, Eric—8
Rojankovsky, Feodor—J
Rolt-Wheeler, Francis—J
Roop, Peter & Connie—8
Roos, Ann—M
Roos, Stephen—6
Root, Barry—8
Root, Kimberly Bulcken—8
Root, Phyllis—8
Rose, Elizabeth—3
Rose, Gerald—3
Rosen, Michael—10
Rosen, Michael J.—8
"Rosenberg, Ethel"
   See Clifford, Eth—6
Rosenberg, Liz—10
Rosoff, Meg—10
Ross, Gayle—8
Ross, Pat—7
Ross, Tony—6
Rostkowski, Margaret—6
Roth, Susan L.—7
Rounds, Glen—J
Rourke, Constance—M
Rowe, Dorothy—J
Rowe, Jennifer
   See "Rodda, Emily"—10
Rowling, J. K.—8
Rubel, Nicole—5
Rubin, Susan Goldman—10
Rubinstein, Gillian—9
Ruby, Lois—6
Ruckman, Ivy—6
Ruffins, Reynold
   See Sarnoff, Jane & Reynold
Ruffins
Rugh, Belle Dorman—3
Rumford, James—9
Russo, Marisabina—7
Ryan, Cheli Durán—5
Ryan, Pam Muñoz—9
Ryden, Hope—9
Ryder, Joanne—6
Rylant, Cynthia—6

S., Svend Otto—6
Sabin, Edwin L.—J
Sabuda, Robert—8
Sachar, Louis—7
Sachs, Marilyn—4
Sadler, Marilyn—8
Sage, Angie—10
Saint James, Synthia—9
Saint-Exupéry, Antoine de—4
Salassi, Otto R.—6
Salisbury, Graham—8
Samuels, Barbara—7
San Souci, Daniel—7
San Souci, Robert D.—7
Sanchez, Alex—10
Sánchez, Enrique O.—9
Sánchez-Silva, José—3
Sandberg, Inger—3
Sandberg, Lasse—3
Sandburg, Helga—3
Sanders, Scott Russell—7
Sanderson, Ruth—10
Sandin, Joan—6
Sandoz, Mari—3
Sanfield, Steve—8
Santore, Charles—10
Sarg, Tony—J
Sargent, Pamela—6
Sargent, Sarah—6
Sarnoff, Jane—5
Sasek, Miroslav—3
Sattler, Helen Roney—6
Sauer, Julia L.—M
Savage, Deborah—7
Savage, Katharine—4
Savery, Constance—J
Savitz, Harriet May—5
Sawyer, Ruth—J
Say, Allen—6
Sayers, Frances Clarke—J
Sayre, April Pulley—9
Scarry, Richard—3
Schaefer, Carole Lexa—10
Schaefer, Jack—3
Schami, Rafik—7
Schanzer, Rosalyn—10
Schechter, Betty—4
Scheele, William E.—3

Schertle, Alice—8
Schick, Eleanor—5
Schindelman, Joseph—3
Schindler, S. D.—7
Schlee, Ann—5
Schlein, Miriam—M
Schmid, Eleonore—4
Schmidt, Gary D.—10
Schneider, Elisa
   See Kleven, Elisa
Schneider, Herman—M
Schneider, Nina—M
Schnur, Steven—8
Schoenherr, John—4
"Scholefield, Edmund O."
   See Butterworth, W. E.
Scholz, Jackson V.—M
Schoonover, Frank—M
Schotter, Roni—10
Schroeder, Alan—8
Schultz, James Willard—J
Schulz, Charles—3
Schwartz, Alvin—5
Schwartz, Amy—6
Schwartz, David M.—6
Schweninger, Ann—7
Scieszka, Jon—7
Scoppettone, Sandra—5
Scott, Ann Herbert—4
Scott, Jack Denton—6
Scoville, Samuel, Jr.—J
Seabrooke, Brenda—7
Seaman, Augusta Huiell—J
"Sebastian, Lee"
   See Silverberg, Robert
Sebestyen, Ouida—5
*See*ger, Laura Vaccaro—10
"Sefton, Catherine"
   See Waddell, Martin
Segal, Lore—4
Segawa, Yasuo—4
Seidler, Tor—6
Seignobosc, Françoise
   See Françoise
Selden, George—4
Selsam, Millicent E.—M
Selznick, Brian—9
Sendak, Maurice—M

Seredy, Kate—J
Serraillier, Ian—3
Service, Pamela F.—7
Seuling, Barbara—9
"Seuss, Dr."—M, 10
Sewell, Helen—J
Sewell, Marcia—5
Seymour, Tres—8
Shannon, David—8
Shannon, George—6
Shannon, Monica—J
Shapiro, Irwin—J
Sharmat, Marjorie
   Weinman—5
Sharmat, Mitchell—6
Sharp, Margery—3
Shaw, Nancy—7
Shecter, Ben—3
Shelby, Anne—8
Shepard, Ernest—M
Sherburne, Zoa Morin—4
Shimin, Symeon—3
Shippen, Katherine B.—M
Shotwell, Louisa R.—3
Showers, Paul C.—4
Shreve, Susan—6
Shub, Elizabeth—5
Shulevitz, Uri—3, 9
Shura, Mary Francis—3
Shusterman, Neal—7
Shuttlesworth, Dorothy E.—5
Sidjakov, Nicolas—M
Sidman, Joyce—10
Siebert, Diane—7
Siegal, Aranka—5
Sierra, Judy—8
Silva, José Sánchez
   See Sánchez-Silva, José
Silverberg, Robert—3
Silverman, Erica—8
Silverstein, Alvin—5
Silverstein, Shel—5
Silverstein, Virginia B.—5
Simon, Charlie May—J
Simon, Hilda—4
Simon, Howard—M
Simon, Seymour—5
Simont, Marc—M, 9

Singer, Isaac Bashevis—3
Singer, Marilyn—6
Sis, Peter—6
Skinner, Constance
  Lindsay—M
Skurzynski, Gloria—5
Sleator, William—5
Slepian, Jan—5
Slobodkin, Louis—J
Slobodkina, Esphyr—3
Slote, Alfred—5
Small, David—6
"Small, Ernest"
  See Lent, Blair
Smith, Cat Bowman—10
Smith, Cynthia Leitich—10
Smith, Dick King
  See King-Smith, Dick
Smith, Doris Buchanan—5
Smith, Janice Lee—7
Smith, Jessie Willcox—J
Smith, Lane—7
Smith, Robert Kimmel—6
Smith, William Jay—5
Snedeker, Caroline Dale—J
Sneve, Virginia Driving
  Hawk—7
"Snicket, Lemony"—9
Snyder, Zilpha Keatley—3
So, Meilo—9
Sobol, Donald J.—4
Soe, Robert C. Du
  See Du Soe, Robert C.—M
Soentpiet, Chris K.—8
Sommerfelt, Aimée—3
Sones, Sonya—10
Sørensen, Henri—9
Sorensen, Virginia—M
Soto, Gary—7
Souci, Daniel San
  See San Souci, Daniel
Souci, Robert D. San
  See San Souci, Robert D.
Southall, Ivan—3
Spanfeller, Jim—4
Speare, Elizabeth
George—M
Spencer, Cornelia—J

Sperry, Armstrong—J
Spiegelman, Art—10
Spier, Peter—3
Spilka, Arnold—3
Spinelli, Eileen—9
Spinelli, Jerry—6
Spirin, Gennady—7
Springer, Nancy—9
Springstubb, Tricia—6
Spykman, Elizabeth C.—M
Spyri, Johanna—J
St. George, Judith—6
"St. John, Nicole"
  See Johnston, Norma
Stanley, Diane—6
Stanley, Jerry—7
"Stanton, Schuyler"
  See Baum, L. Frank
Staples, Suzanne Fisher—7
Stapp, Arthur D.—M
"Stark, James"
  See Goldston, Robert
  Conroy
Steele, Mary Q."
  See "Gage, Wilson"—3
Steele, William O.—M
Steig, William—3, 9
Stein, Evaleen—J
Steptoe, Javaka—8
Steptoe, John—4
Sterling, Dorothy—3
Sterne, Emma Gelders—M
Stevens, Janet—6
Stevenson, Augusta—M
Stevenson, James—5
Stewart, Sarah—8
Stine, R. L.—7
Stobbs, William—3
Stock, Catherine—7
Stockum, Hilda van
  See van Stockum, Hilda
Stoddard, Sandol—4
Stoeke, Janet Morgan—8
Stolz, Mary—M
Stone, Helen—M
Stong, Phil—M
Stoutenburg, Adrien—3
Strasser, Todd—6

Streatfeild, Noel—J
Stroud, Jonathan—10
Stuve-Bodeen, Stephanie—10
Suba, Susanne—M
Sublette, C. M.—J
Sueur, Meridel Le
  See Le Sueur, Meridel—M
Sullivan, George—8
Summers, James L.—M
Sutcliff, Rosemary—M
Swarthout, Glendon—4
Swarthout, Kathryn—4
Sweat, Lynn—7
Sweet, Melissa—9
Sweet, Ozzie—6
Swift, Hildegarde Hoyt—J
Syme, Ronald—M

Taback, Simms—8
Tafuri, Nancy—6
Talbert, Marc—7
Tamarin, Alfred H.—5
Tanaka, Shelley—9
Tashjian, Janet—10
Tashjian, Virginia A.—5
Tate, Eleanora E.—7
"Tatham, Campbell"
  See Elting, Mary
Taylor, Mildred D.—5
Taylor, Sydney—M
Taylor, Theodore—4
Taylor, William—7
Teague, Mark—8
Teale, Edwin Way—3
Tejima, Keizaburo—7
Temple, Frances—7
Tenggren, Gustaf—M
Tenniel, Sir John—J
ter Haar, Jaap
  See Haar, Jaap ter
Terris, Susan—5
Testa, Fulvio—7
Tharp, Louise Hall—M
"Thayer, Jane"
  See Woolley, Catherine
"Thayer, Peter"
  See Ames, Rose Wyler
Thesman, Jean—7

Thiele, Colin—5
Thimmesh, Catherine—10
Thomas, Jane Resh—8
Thomas, Joyce Carol—8
Thomas, Rob—8
Thompson, Kay—4
Thompson, Lauren—10
Thomsen, Gudrun Thorne
   See Thorne-Thomsen,
Gudrun
Thomson, Peggy—6
Thorne-Thomsen, Gudrun—J
Thrasher, Crystal—6
Thurber, James—M
Thurman, Judith—6
Tiegreen, Alan—5
Titherington, Jeanne—6
Titus, Eve—3
Todd, Ruthven—M
Tolan, Stephanie S.—6
Tolkien, J. R. R.—M
Tomes, Margot—5
Tompert, Ann—6
Tord, Bijou Le
   See Le Tord, Bijou
Torrey, Marjorie—M
Tousey, Sanford—J
Townsend, John Rowe—4
Travers, Pamela—J
Trease, Geoffrey—M
Treece, Henry—M
Tresselt, Alvin—M
Treviño, Elizabeth Borton
de—3
Trez, Alain—3
Trez, Denise—3
Tripp, Valerie—8
Tripp, Wallace—5
Trivizas, Eugene—8
Trnka, Jirí—3
Trueman, Terry—10
Tudor, Tasha—J
Tunis, Edwin—M
Tunis, John R.—M
Tunnell, Michael O.—8
Turkle, Brinton—3
Turner, Ann—6
Turner, Megan Whalen—10

Turner, Philip—4
Turngren, Annette—M
Tusa, Tricia—9

Uchida, Yoshiko—M
Uden, Grant—4
Udry, Janice—3
Ullman, James Ramsey—4
"Uncle Shelby"
   See Silverstein, Shel
Ungerer, Tomi—3
Unnerstad, Edith—3
Unwin, Nora S.—M
Updale, Eleanor—10
Ure, Jean—6
Urmston, Mary—M
"Usher, Margo Scegge"
   See McHargue, Geor-
   gess—5

Vagin, Vladimir —9
Vail, Rachel—7
Van Allsburg, Chris—5
"Van Dyne, Edith"
   See Baum, L. Frank
van Iterson, S. R.
   See Iterson, S. R., van
Van Laan, Nancy—8
Van Leeuwen, Jean—5
van Stockum, Hilda—J
Van Woerkom, Dorothy—5
Van Wright, Cornelius—10
Vance, Marguerite—M
VanCleave, Janice—8
Vande Velde, Vivian—10
Vander Els, Betty—6
Veaux, Alexis De
   See De Veaux, Alexis
Vecchione, Patrice—10
Ventura, Piero—7
Verne, Jules—J
"Victor, Kathleen"
   See Butler, Beverly
Vigna, Judith—7
Vincent, Gabrielle—6
Vining, Elizabeth Gray
   See Gray, Elizabeth
Janet

Viorst, Judith—4
Vivas, Julie—7
Vivier, Colette—4
Voake, Charlotte—7
Voight, Virginia Frances—M
Voigt, Cynthia—5

Waber, Bernard—3
Waddell, Martin—7
Wahl, Jan—3
Waldeck, Jo Besse McEl-
   veen—J
Waldeck, Theodore, J.—J
Walden, Amelia
   Elizabeth—M
Waldman, Neil—10
Walker, Sally M.—10
Wallace, Barbara Brooks—6
Wallace, Bill—7
"Wallace, Daisy"
   See Cuyler, Margery
Wallace, Dillon—J
Wallace, Ian—6
Wallner, John C.—5
Walsh, Ellen Stoll—8
Walsh, Jill Paton
   See Paton Walsh, Jill
Walter, Mildred Pitts—6
Ward, Lynd—4
Warnock, Natalie Kinsey
   See Kinsey-Warnock,
   Natalie
Warren, Andrea—10
Watanabe, Shigeo—6
Waters, Kate—8
Watkins, Yoko
   Kawashima—10
Watson, Clyde—4
Watson, Sally Lou—4
Watson, Wendy—4
Watts, Bernadette—7
Weaver, Will—9
Weber, Lenora Mattingly—M
Weeks, Sarah—10
Weil, Lisl—4
Weisgard, Leonard—J
Weiss, Ann E.—6
Weiss, Harvey—3

Weiss, Nicki—6
Weller, Frances—10
Wellman, Manly Wade—M
Wells, Rhea—J
Wells, Rosemary—4, 10
Werlin, Nancy—9
Wersba, Barbara—3
Werstein, Irving—4
Werth, Kurt—M
Westall, Robert—5
Westcott, Nadine
Bernard—6
Weston, Martha—9
Wexler, Jerome—7
Whatley, Bruce—10
Wheeler, Francis Rolt
See Rolt-Wheeler,
Francis
Wheeler, Opal—M
Whelan, Gloria—8
White, Anne Hitchcock—4
White, Anne Terry—M
White, E. B.—M
White, Eliza Orne—J
White, Robb—J
White, Ruth—7
Whitney, Elinor—J
Whitney, Phyllis A.—J
Wibberley, Leonard—M
Wick, Walter—8
Widener, Terry—9
Wier, Ester—3
Wiese, Kurt—J
Wiesner, David—7
Wijngaard, Juan—8
Wikland, Ilon—4
Wilder, Laura Ingalls—J
Wildsmith, Brian—3
Wiles, Deborah—10
Wilkinson, Barry—4
Wilkinson, Brenda—5
Willard, Barbara—4
Willard, Nancy—5
Willems, Mo—10
Willey, Margaret—7
"William, Kate"
See Armstrong, Jennifer
Williams, Barbara—6

"Williams, Charles"
See Collier, James Lin-
coln
Williams, Garth—M
Williams, Jay—4
Williams, Karen Lynn—8
"Williams, Patrick J."
See Butterworth, W. E.
Williams, Sherley Anne—7
Williams, Ursula Moray
See Moray Williams,
Ursula
Williams, Vera B.—5
Williams-Garcia, Rita—8
Williamson, Joanne S.—3
Wilson, Barbara Ker
See Ker Wilson, Barbara
Wilson, Budge—7
Wimmer, Mike—9
Windsor, Patricia—5
"Winfield, Julia"
See Armstrong, Jennifer
Winter, Jeannette—7
Winter, Jonah—10
Winter, Paula—6
Winterfeld, Henry—3
Winthrop, Elizabeth—5
Wiseman, David—5
Wisler, G. Clifton—7
Wisniewski, David—7
Wittlinger, Ellen—9
Woerkom, Dorothy Van
See Van Woerkom,
Dorothy
Wojciechowska, Maia—3
Wolf, Bernard—5
Wolff, Ashley—6
"Wolff, Sonia"
See Levitin, Sonia
Wolff, Virginia Euwer—7
Wolitzer, Hilma—5
Wolkstein, Diane—5
"Wolny, P."
See Janeczko, Paul B.
Wondriska, William—3
Wong, Janet S.—9
Wood, Audrey—6
Wood, Don—6

Wood, Esther—J
Wood, James Playsted—4
Woodruff, Elvira—8
Woodson, Jacqueline—8
Woody, Regina J.—M
Woolley, Catherine—M
Worth, Kathryn—J
Worth, Valerie—5
Wrede, Patricia C.—7
Wright, Betty Ren—6
Wrightson, Patricia—4
Wuorio, Eva-Lis—3
Wyeth, N. C.—J
Wyler, Rose
See Ames, Rose Wyler
Wyndham, Lee—M
Wynne-Jones, Tim—8

Yaccarino, Dan—9
Yamaguchi, Marianne—3
Yamaguchi, Tohr—3
Yarbrough, Camille—7
Yashima, Taro—M
Yates, Elizabeth—J
Yates, Raymond F.—M
Yee, Paul Richard—7
Yep, Laurence—5
Ying-Hwa, Hu
See Van Wright, Cornelius
Ylla—M
Yolen, Jane—4, 10
Yorinks, Arthur—6
York, Carol Beach—5
Youd, Samuel
See "Christopher, John"
Young, Ed—3, 9
Young, Ella—J
Yumoto, Kazumi—9

Zalben, Jane Breskin—5
Zarchy, Harry—M
Zaunders, Bo—10
Zei, Alki—4
Zelinsky, Paul O.—6
Zemach, Harve & Margot—3
Ziefert, Harriet—7
Zim, Herbert S.—J
Zimmer, Dirk—6

Zimnik, Reiner—3
Zindel, Paul—5
Zion, Gene—M

Zollinger, Gulielma—J
Zolotow, Charlotte—M, 8
Zusak, Markus—10

Zwerger, Lisbeth—6
Zwilgmeyer, Dikken—J